ITALIAN WINES 1998

Gambero Rosso Editore   Slow Food Editore

italianwines

1998

VINI D'ITALIA 1998

IS THE ENGLISH LANGUAGE EDITION OF THE ITALIAN JOINT PUBLICATION BY
GAMBERO ROSSO EDITORE AND SLOW FOOD EDITORE

GAMBERO ROSSO EDITORE
VIA ARENULA, 53 - 00186 ROMA
TEL. 39-6-68300741 - FAX 39-6-6877217

SLOW FOOD ARCIGOLA EDITORE
VIA MENDICITÀ ISTRUITA, 45 - 12042 BRA (CN)
TEL. 39-172-412519 - FAX 39-172-411218

EDITORIAL STAFF FOR THE ORIGINAL EDITION

CHIEF EDITORS
DANIELE CERNILLI AND CARLO PETRINI

SENIOR EDITORS
GIGI PIUMATTI AND MARCO SABELLICO

PRINCIPAL CONTRIBUTORS
ERNESTO GENTILI, VITTORIO MANGANELLI
FABIO RIZZARI AND SANDRO SANGIORGI

OTHER MEMBERS OF THE TASTING PANELS
GIULIO COLOMBA, GIANNI FABRIZIO, MARCO OREGGIA,
NEREO PEDERZOLLI, PIERO SARDO

CONTRIBUTORS
GILBERTO ARRU, ANTONIO ATTORRE, PAOLO BATTIMELLI, ALBERTO BETTINI, WALTER BORDO,
PIERLUIGI CALABRETTA, ANTONIO CIMINELLI, VALERIO CHIARINI, DARIO COLETTI,
MASSIMO DI CINTIO, EGIDIO FEDELE DELL'OSTE, MARCO LISI, GIACOMO MOJOLI, FRANCO MORI,
DAVIDE PANZIERI, STEFANO PASTOR, MARIO PAPANI, GUIDO PIRAZZOLI, MICHELE PIZZILLO,
VITO PUGLIA, GIOVANNI RUFFA, DIEGO SORACCO, HERBERT TASCHLER, PAOLO TRIMANI,
ANDREA VANNELLI, MASSIMO VOLPARI, RICCARDO VISCARDI, ALBERTO ZACCONE

WITH SPECIAL THANKS TO
NINO AIELLO, ENRICO BATTISTELLA,
BRUNO BEVILACQUA, ROBERTO CASULLO, SERGIO CECCARELLI, REMO CAMURANI,
MARCO CASOLANETTI, STEFANO FERRARI, ROSANNA FERRARO, NICOLA FRASSON,
FABIO GIAVEDONI, LORENZO L'ECRIVAIN, VITO LACERENZA, GIANCARLO LO SICCO,
PASQUINO MALENOTTI, ROBERTO MINNETTI, ENZO MERZ, STEFANO MAURO, DANNY MURARO,
FILIPPO PARODI, NICOLA PERULLO, VALENTINO RAMELLI, CARLO RAVANELLO,
GABRIELE RICCI ALUNNI, LEONARDO ROMANELLI, MAURIZIO ROSSI, MASSIMO TOFFOLO,
PAOLO VALDASTRI, VALERIO ZORZI

EDITORIAL ASSISTANTS
MARCO OREGGIA AND UMBERTO TAMBURINI

EDITORIAL COORDINATOR
GIORGIO ACCASCINA

LAYOUT
FABIO CREMONESI

TRANSLATIONS EDITED BY
RICHARD BAUDAINS

TRANSLATORS
PATRICIA GUY, STEPHEN HOBLEY, GILES WATSON

PUBLISHER
GAMBERO ROSSO, INC.

USA OFFICE
225, LAFAYETTE STREET - NEW YORK, NY 10012
TEL. 212- 3348499 FAX 212 3349173

ITALY OFFICE
VIA ARENULA, 53 - 00186 ROMA
TEL. 39-6-68300741 - FAX 39-6-6877217

COMMERCIAL MANAGER
FRANCESCO DAMMICCO

ASSISTANT COMMERCIAL MANAGER
FABIO PARASECOLI

THE GUIDE WAS CLOSED SEPTEMBER 30, 1997

PRINTED IN ITALY BY CONTI TIPOCOLOR SRL - VIA G. GUINIZZELLI, 20 - CALENZANO (FI)

5

CONTENTS

INTRODUCTION

Italian Wines 1998 is the first English-language version of "Vini d'Italia", a guide that is being published this year for the eleventh time in Italian and for the fifth in German. The aim of the book is to  illustrate the current state of premium wine production in Italy through profiles of 1392 wineries and tasting notes on 8501 different wines. This makes Italian Wines 1998 the largest and most comprehensive overview of top quality Italian winemaking available anywhere in the world. It is a project to which hundreds of tasters have contributed, assessing the wines presented at blind comparative tastings in panels made up of at least five members and convened in the areas where the wines were produced. As a result, no Guide taster - not even the two editors - had the opportunity to pass judgement in isolation. In this way excessively personal views are avoided and maximum objectivity assured. Ratings are expressed not in point scores but in broader bands which are indicated by the wine glass symbol which has become one of the trademarks of the Guide. There are four categories, on a scale from a simple listing up to the top Three Glasses award. In the 1998 edition of the Guide, only 117 wines won this coveted accolade. In evaluating wines obviously intensity, finesse, balance, concentration and length, the classic benchmark qualities assessed by tasters the world over, are taken into consideration, but it is an important principle of the Guide that wines are also assessed according to their category, vintage and place of origin, and ratings should be interpreted in this way. We feel it is pointless to compare radically different wines on the same scale: the criteria for assessing a Chianti Classico must be different to those for a Barolo, for example, and must above all take into account the wine's ability to reflect its "terroir" and the character of its grape varieties. In all these respects the approach adopted by our Guide is very different to that of a solitary taster who might sample hundreds of wines every day, assigning scores out of a hundred to each. Behind a façade of apparently painstaking precision, qualitative differences will tend to become blurred by numbers which in any case are unlikely to be duplicated at subsequent tastings. Although such detailed marking may be theoretically valid when evaluating wines from a single type and vintage - for example a comprehensive vertical tasting of '93 Barolo - it is utterly inappropriate as the basis for a universal, objective system for classifying wine. Leaving these issues and returning to the description of the Guide, readers will notice that in addition to the current awards indicated by black Glasses, wines are also listed with white symbols next to them. These refer to scores given in previous editions of the Guide, and which are confirmed where the wines in question are still drinking at the level for which the original award was made. Finally, a word or two about how we procure wines for tastings: we prefer to obtain bottles directly from the producer in order to ensure that we taste all samples in the same, optimal condition. Poor storage can sometimes ruin an excellent wine. We would also like to add that the fact that almost all the producers we approach agree to present their wines is a demonstration of faith in the Guide that gives us very special satisfaction. Without presuming to to be definitive arbiters in an area of subjective judgement, we believe that the respect of those whose wines we judge, together with the esteem of our readers, is a legitimate endorsement of our efforts.

Daniele Cernilli and Carlo Petrini

THE INTERNATIONAL
SLOW FOOD MOVEMENT

Slow Food is an international movement which was founded in Italy in 1986. Today there are 25,000 members in the organization's home country and as many again in 35 others around the world. Each "Convivium" - as the local Slow Food branches are called - promotes the knowledge and enjoyment of food and wine, organizing meetings, tastings, courses and visits. Slow Food's aims are to provide instruction in the art of tasting, to protect oenological and gastronomic heritage, and to inform consumers. Events organized by Slow Food include: the Salone del Gusto at Turin, a major exhibition of wines and food from all over the world (the second Salone del Gusto will be held at the Lingotto on 5-9 November 1998); Cheese, an international trade fair dedicated to cheeses of all kinds held at Bra, where the Slow Food movement was founded and where its headquarters are still located; regional Wine Conventions held in Piedmont, Tuscany and Friuli-Venezia Giulia; and the Laboratori del Gusto which consist of workshops on food and wine tasting lead by experts and producers. The most recent Slow Food project is called the "Arca del Gusto" and it aims to identify and to provide a symbolic Ark for the salvation of high quality regional foods, crops, handicrafts, recipes, and animal or vegetable species threatened with extinction by the "Flood" of standardization that is overwhelming the food and wine trade. Slow Food Editore, the movement's publishing house, prints guides (including the "Osterie d'Italia" restaurant guide and "Vini d'Italia", published jointly with Gambero Rosso and now also available in English as "Italian Wines 1998"), tourist itineraries, cookbooks, studies on a range of subjects and three magazines: "Slowfood" covers the movement's activities and is distributed to members; "Slowine" reports on the world of wine and wine-related topics; and "Slow, messaggero di gusto e cultura" is a 160-page quarterly journal published in Italian, English and German. "Slow" deals with food, consumer trends and tendencies in taste, art and travel in the spirit of the "savoir-vivre" philosophy the movement has espoused, incorporating contributions from prestigious international writers and presented in an elegant graphic format. "Slow" is available from good bookshops and is distributed to all members of the Slow Food movement.

GAMBERO ROSSO
The international publisher for wine lovers

GAMBERO ROSSO is an Italian publishing house specialized in the field of leisure time passions—wine, food and travel. Since its first appearance in 1986 as a weekly supplement in a popular national newspaper, GAMBERO ROSSO has grown from an eight-page insert into a well-known and trusted authority, producing thirty books a year for a world-wide audience of expert professionals, enthusiastic travelers and discriminating wine and food lovers. GAMBERO ROSSO's guides played an important role in promoting and explaining the dramatic changes in Italian winemaking during the last decade to a new, younger generation of consumers. Its lively, comprehensible writing and even-handed evaluation of value for money in the sector has won GAMBERO ROSSO publications ranks of loyal readers. Since 1996, GAMBERO ROSSO has organized the most important tastings of Italian wine in the United States.
Among its Italian publications are
• the monthly magazine, GAMBERO ROSSO dedicated to food, wine, and tourism;
• a wide range of handbooks on wine, spirits, and food, including the popular ALMANACCO DEL BEREBENE, a guide to less expensive Italian wines and ALMANACCO DEI GOLOSI, a guide to the best specialty food shops and food products of Italy;
• a best-selling annual wine guide, VINI D'ITALIA, produced in collaboration with Slow Food;
• a best-selling annual restaurant guide, RISTORANTI D'ITALIA;
• a best-selling annual hotel guide, ALBERGHI D'ITALIA.

English language publications (by the American subsidiary, GAMBERO ROSSO INC. in New York) include
• GAMBERO ROSSO WINE TRAVEL FOOD, a quarterly magazine distributed on news stands and in bookshops in the United States and Canada and sent to subscribers all over the world;
• WINE GAMES, an interactive CD-ROM;
• the guide to ITALIAN WINES 1998, a comprehensive description of the year's best, as rated by Gambero Rosso and Slow Food experts.

• The GAMBERO ROSSO website in Italian and English has become the most important Internet source of information about Italian wine:
http://www.gamberorosso.it

THREE GLASS AWARDS 1998

PIEDMONT

BARBARESCO '94	GAJA	26
BARBERA D'ALBA BRICCO MARUN '95	MATTEO CORREGGIA	40
BAROLO '93	ERALDO VIBERTI	79
BAROLO '93	F.LLI REVELLO	77
BAROLO '93	GIANFRANCO ALESSANDRIA	85
BAROLO BOSCARETO '93	FERDINANDO PRINCIPIANO	91
BAROLO BRIC DEL FIASC '93	PAOLO SCAVINO	51
BAROLO BRICCO FIASCO '93	AZELIA	49
BAROLO BRUNATE '93	ROBERTO VOERZIO	80
BAROLO CEREQUIO '93	MICHELE CHIARLO	38
BAROLO GINESTRA VIGNA CASA MATÉ '93	ELIO GRASSO	89
BAROLO MONFORTINO RISERVA '90	GIACOMO CONTERNO	87
BAROLO PAJANA '93	DOMENICO CLERICO	86
BAROLO SPERSS '93	GAJA	26
DOLCETTO D'ALBA BARTUROT '96	CA' VIOLA	94
DOLCETTO D'ALBA BOSCHI DI BERRI '96	MARCARINI	74
DOLCETTO DI DOGLIANI SIRI D'JERMU '96	F.LLI PECCHENINO	61
LA VIGNA DI SONVICO '95	CASCINA LA BARBATELLA	100
LANGHE LARIGI '95	ELIO ALTARE	70
LANGHE DARMAGI '94	GAJA	26
LANGHE ROSSO BRIC DU LUV '95	CA' VIOLA	94
LANGHE ROSSO MONPRÀ '95	CONTERNO FANTINO	87
LOAZZOLO PIASA RISCHEI '94	FORTETO DELLA LUJA	81
MONFERRATO ROSSO PIN '95	LA SPINETTA	46
SUL BRIC '95	FRANCO M. MARTINETTI	117
VALENTINO BRUT ZERO RISERVA '93	PODERI ROCCHE DEI MANZONI	90

LOMBARDY

FRANCIACORTA MAGNIFICENTIA	UBERTI	154
FRANCIACORTA CUVÉE ANNAMARIA CLEMENTI '90	CA' DEL BOSCO	151
FRANCIACORTA GRAN CUVÉE BRUT '93	BELLAVISTA	150
VALTELLINA SFURSAT 5 STELLE '95	NINO NEGRI	145

TRENTINO

SPUMANTE GIULIO FERRARI RISERVA DEL FONDATORE '89	FERRARI	184
ROSSO FAYE '94	POJER & SANDRI	172

THE STARS

This year we introduce a new symbol alongside that of the wine glass. In recognition of consistency at the very highest level, we give a star to all those producers who have won the Three Glass award at least ten times. The ten producers who have achieved this feat to date are listed below together with the number of Three Glass wines they have presented since the first edition of the Guide in 1988. At the top of the table is Angelo Gaja with no fewer that 18 successes, already only two short of a second star. He is followed by Elio Altare, the guru of the new wave in Barolo and Maurzio Zanella's Ca' del Bosco estate, undisputed leader in Franciacorta now allied to the Marzotto Group. The superb Barolo producer, Aldo Conterno, and Tuscany's Fattoria di Felsina, have both scored 11 successes. The producers with ten awards so far are: Castello di Ama, the famous Tuscan estate; the Giacomo Conterno winery, producer of the great traditional Barolo Monfortino; the innovative Silvio Jermann and great Josko Gravner from Friuli Venezia Giulia; and another of the new generation of Barolo producers, Paolo Scavino. Currently waiting for a star, with 9 wins up to now, we find: the outstanding Barolo producer Domenico Clerico; the Castello di Fonterutoli and Tenuta Fontodi, leading figures in the Tuscan renaissance with their Chianti and Super Tuscan Concerto and Flaccianello; and finally Gianfranco Gallo from Vie di Romans, the wizard of Sauvignon Blanc from Isonzo.

18
ANGELO GAJA (Piedmont)

13
ELIO ALTARE (Piedmont)
CA' DEL BOSCO (Lombardy)

11
ALDO CONTERNO (Piedmont)
FATTORIA DI FELSINA (Tuscany)

10
CASTELLO DI AMA (Tuscany)
GIACOMO CONTERNO (Piedmont)
IOSKO GRAVNER (Friuli Venezia Giulia)
VINNAIOLI JERMANN (Friuli Venezia Giulia)
PAOLO SCAVINO (Piedmont)

A GUIDE TO VINTAGES, 1970-1995

	BARBARESCO	BRUNELLO DI MONTALCINO	BAROLO	CHIANTI CLASSICO	VINO NOBILE DI MONTEPULCIANO	AMARONE
1970	●●●●	●●●●	●●●●	●●●●●	●●●●	●●●●
1971	●●●●	●●●	●●●●●	●●●●●	●●●●	●●●●
1972	●	●	●	●●	●	●
1973	●●	●●●	●●	●●	●●●	●●
1974	●●●●	●●	●●●●	●●●	●●●	●●●●
1975	●●	●●●●●	●●	●●●●	●●●●	●●●
1976	●●	●	●●	●●	●●	●●●●
1977	●●	●●●●	●●	●●●●	●●●●	●●●
1978	●●●●●	●●●●	●●●●●	●●●●●	●●●●●	●●●
1979	●●●●	●●●●	●●●●	●●●●	●●●●	●●●●
1980	●●●●	●●●●	●●●●	●●●●	●●	●●●
1981	●●●	●●●	●●●	●●●	●●●	●●●
1982	●●●●●	●●●●●	●●●●●	●●●●	●●●●	●
1983	●●●●	●●●●	●●●●	●●●●	●●●●	●●●●●
1984	●	●●	●●	●	●	●●
1985	●●●●●	●●●●●	●●●●●	●●●●●	●●●●●	●●●●
1986	●●●	●●●	●●●	●●●●	●●●●	●●●
1987	●●	●●	●●	●●	●●	●●
1988	●●●●●	●●●●●	●●●●●	●●●●●	●●●●●	●●●●●
1989	●●●●●	●●	●●●●●	●	●	●●
1990	●●●●●	●●●●●	●●●●●	●●●●●	●●●●●	●●●●●
1991	●●●	●●●	●●●	●●●	●●●	●●
1992	●●	●●	●●	●	●	●
1993	●●●	●●●●	●●●	●●●●	●●●●●	●●●●
1994	●●	●●●	●●	●●	●●	●●
1995	●●●●●	●●●●●	●●●●●	●●●●●	●●●●●	●●●●●

HOW TO USE THE GUIDE

KEY

○ WHITE WINES
◉ RED WINES
● ROSÉ WINES

RATINGS

LISTING WITHOUT A GLASS SYMBOL:
A WELL MADE WINE
REPRESENTATIVE OF ITS CATEGORY

▼
ABOVE AVERAGE TO GOOD IN ITS CATEGORY, EQUIVALENT TO 70-79/100

▼▼
VERY GOOD TO EXCELLENT IN ITS CATEGORY, EQUIVALENT TO 80-89/100

▼▼▼
OUTSTANDING WINE IN ITS CATEGORY, EQUIVALENT TO 90-99/100

(♀, ♀♀, ♀♀♀) THE WHITE GLASSES REFER TO RATINGS GIVEN IN PREVIOUS EDITIONS OF THE GUIDE, AND WHICH ARE CONFIRMED WHERE THE WINES IN QUESTION ARE STILL DRINKING AT THE LEVEL FOR WHICH THE ORIGINAL AWARD WAS MADE

STAR ★

IS GIVEN TO ALL THOSE ESTATES WHICH HAVE WON AT LEAST TEN THREE GLASS AWARDS

GUIDE TO PRICES (1)

1 UP TO $ 8 AND UP TO £6
2 FROM $ 8 TO $ 12 AND FROM £ 6 TO £ 8
3 FROM $ 12 TO $ 18 AND FROM £ 8 TO £ 11
4 FROM $ 18 TO $ 27 AND FROM £ 11 TO £ 15
5 FROM $ 27 TO $ 40 AND FROM £ 15 TO £ 20
6 MORE THAN $ 40 AND MORE THAN £ 20

(1)Approx. retail prices in USA and UK

ASTERISK *
INDICATES ESPECIALLY GOOD VALUE FOR MONEY

NOTE
PRICES REFER TO RETAIL AVERAGES. INDICATIONS OF PRICES FOR OLDER VINTAGES INCLUDE APPRECIATION WHERE APPROPRIATE

ABBREVIATIONS

A.A.	Alto Adige
Cl.	Classico
C.S.	Cantina Sociale
Cant.	Cantina
Cast.	Castello
C. Am.	Colli Amerini
COF	Colli Orientali del Friuli
Cons.	Consorzio
Coop.Agr.	Cooperativa Agricola
M.	Metodo
M.to	Monferrato
P.R.	Peduncolo Rosso
Pav.	Pavese
Prosecco di V.	Prosecco di Valdobbiadene
Rif. Agr.	Riforma Agraria
Spumante M.Cl.	Spumante Metodo Classico
Sup.	Superiore
T.	Terre
Ten.	Tenute
Tenim.	Tenimenti
V.	Vigna
Vign.	Vigneto

VALLE D'AOSTA

Wine grapes are to be found throughout the Valle d'Aosta, and are grown in vineyards which stretch for some 80 kilometres along the Dora Baltea river. Starting right from the border with Piedmont, one comes across various different vine varieties - both indigenous and international - which contribute to the production of wines with the single denomination, Vallée d'Aoste. This appellation includes some 20 sub-denominations. Nebbiolo - the most widely planted variety at the mouth of the valley - gives us Donnas, a richly-structured wine with characteristics similar to its neighbour Carema. Heading on towards Aosta itself, viticulture is practised almost exclusively on the right bank of the Dora Baltea. As we continue along the region's Wine Road, which leads eventually to the foothills of Mont Blanc, we encounter, one after another, the best-known sub-denominations of the valley. After Donnas and its red, the wine type changes completely at Chambave which is famous for its Muscat, found in both dry and dessert versions. As well as this classic, which has gained a certain reputation amongst wine lovers, the zone also produces excellent red wines, such as Petit Rouge and Fumin. Going up river we reach the provincial capital Aosta where, on the first of the foothills which lead up to the Gran San Bernardo, we encounter vineyards planted with other white and red varieties, ranging from chardonnay to petit arvine, and from pinot nero to gamay. At this point the valley widens and in the zone around Aymavilles, homeland of Torrette, vineyards stretch out both on the right and the left bank of the river. A few kilometres further on,

we reach Morgex, where grapes are grown at incredibly high altitude for the production of the famous Blanc de Morgex. This year we include in the Guide, as has we have done in the past couple of years, the six estates which represent the best of the region's production. At the top of our chart is the Les Crêtes estate, with three wines worthy of the Two Glass designation and the rest of its products scoring only slightly lower. After a settling-in period of a few years - the winery was founded at the end of the 1980s - today production has established itself at a very high quality level. In the next few years, when the experimental ageing of certain wines in barriques has also been completed, the number of bottles produced will rise to more than 100,000. The other private estate which represents a touchstone in the Valle d'Aosta is that of Costantino Charrère (also active partner in, and moving spirit behind, Les Crêtes); this winery confirms, with a Two Glass wine, its ability to produce quality reds. Amongst the cooperatives - of which there are six in the valley - the one which has achieved the highest standard of quality is La Crotta di Vegneron in Chambave. As in every year's tastings, this winery had at least one wine which received a Two Glass rating, but the entire range has improved, confirming this cooperative's desire to grow and to compete with top wines from all over Italy. The series of wines from the Institut Agricole Régional also scored quite well, even if the experimental wines aged in barrique showed slightly less well this year. However, the new Vin du Prévôt (cabernet and merlot) deservedly obtained Two Glasses.

AOSTA

AYMAVILLES (AO)

INSTITUT AGRICOLE RÉGIONAL
REG. LA ROCHERE, 1/A
11100 AOSTA
TEL. 0165/553304

COSTANTINO CHARRÈRE
FRAZ. DU MOULIN, 28
11010 AYMAVILLES (AO)
TEL. 0165/902135

The Institut Agricole was founded in 1982 by the Casa Ospitaliera del Gran San Bernardo in conjunction with the Regione Autonoma Valle d'Aosta. With its research, this school contributes to improving agriculture in general in the Valle d'Aosta, and especially the region's viticulture. Its practical experimentation is then translated, thanks to the care and diligence of those responsible for the various sectors - Luciano Rigazio for agriculture and Grato Praz for winemaking - into producing wines of quality. The research is centred on two product lines: one being white and red wines vinified in stainless steel, designed for drinking in the year after production; the other, much more experimental line (a mere few hundred bottles), is based on the study of ageing in barrique. This year we witnessed a good general display by the products in the first category, that is, of wines which are for immediate drinking. The whites made from pinot grigio, chardonnay, petite arvine and müller thurgau were especially successful. The Chardonnay, in particular, demonstrates the potential of this variety when very densely planted in vineyards at around 700 metres above sea level. The decision to pick the grapes when very ripe leads to the wine having a high level of alcohol and more than satisfactory structure, but detracts a little from its finesse. The Petit Rouge - characterized by unusual aromas, with an almost aromatic background mingling with red berry fruit scents, and a very pleasing flavour - scored better than the correct but unexceptional Gamay and Pinot Noir. The range of wines in barrique from the '95 vintage is less impressive than these wines have been in previous years. The best wine of all is the excellent cabernet sauvignon and merlot Vin du Prévot with its complex nose and rich, deep fruit on the palate. The Chardonnay scored highest amongst the whites.

Costantino Charrère's own small estate produces 15,000 bottles annually of good quality wine. It is a rather unusual winery, whose efforts are concentrated exclusively on the production of red wines: its success is reflected in the high scores its wines have earned. Vin de La Sabia - one of the standard-bearers of the estate - fully deserves its Two Glass rating. This is a red made from fumin and petit rouge grapes from old vines, grown on sandy soil, with high-density planting. Its colour is a deep garnet red; it has a very positive aroma, with hints of ripe red berry fruits, spices and black pepper; on the palate it offers soft, rich, concentrated fruit, and good length of flavour. Charrère's Prëmetta - a unique wine produced as it is in the valley exclusively by Costantino - is always an interesting product. It is a red with a character that reminds one of a Grignolino from Piedmont, even down to its pale colour; the same resemblance is to be found on the nose, with its aromatic background and light vegetal tones, as well as on the palate; no great concentration and a finish characterised by acidulous/tannic notes. The estate's Torrette, which this year is once again the most interesting of the wines of this type tasted, is a deep garnet colour, with intense aromas of red berry fruits; on the palate, it is full and mouth-filling. The '96 Les Fourches, a red made from grenache grapes, was still in cask and therefore not available for tasting.

● Vin du Prévôt '95	♥♥	4
○ Vallée d'Aoste Chardonnay '96	♥	3
○ Vallée d'Aoste Chardonnay Barrique '95	♥	4
○ Vallée d'Aoste Müller Thurgau '96	♥	3
○ Vallée d'Aoste Petite Arvine '96	♥	4
○ Vallée d'Aoste Pinot Gris '96	♥	3
● Trésor du Caveau '95	♥♥	4

● Vin de La Sabla '96	♥♥	4
● Vallée d'Aoste Prëmetta '96	♥	4
● Vallée d'Aoste Torrette '96	♥	3
● Vin Les Fourches '95	♀	4

AYMAVILLES (AO)

LES CRÊTES
LOC. VILLETOS, 50
11010 AYMAVILLES (AO)
TEL. 0165/902274

CHAMBAVE (AO)

LA CROTTA DI VEGNERON
P.ZZA RONCAS, 2
11023 CHAMBAVE (AO)
TEL. 0166/46670

Leaving the Turin to Mont Blanc motorway at Aosta Ovest, you may note and admire to your left one of the most picturesque vineyards of the entire valley. This is the Coteau La Tour, owned by the Les Crêtes winery. It is a small hillside, entirely planted with vines, which stands apart from the rest of the estate. On top of this site with its magnificent exposure stands a little building that, in the next few years, will be renovated and turned into a tasting room. This zone represents the heart of the Les Crêtes estate's vineyards and consists of a single five-hectare parcel of land: a real rarity in the Valle d'Aosta, where property is normally very fragmented. The rest of the vineyards are spread around the neighbouring communes and give this estate a total area of over ten hectares under vine. The great potential of the vineyards is then transformed into excellent wines by the skills of Costantino Charrère, who is one of the partners in the estate. The Chardonnay - which has always proved extremely reliable - is in 1996 again the region's outstanding white wine.The Petite Arvine, the estate's other white, and the Torrette, the typical red of Aymavilles, are very pleasant indeed, while the Pinot Noir is somewhat less interesting. This year, we had a chance to taste the estate's first experiments in barrique - for the moment, just a thousand bottles of each type of wine - and the results are very positive. The '95 Chardonnay, whose explanatory neck-label sets it apart from the standard version, confirms all of its potential, with added complexity provided by the toasty notes of the oak. The Coteau La Tour, a monovarietal Syrah, has rich aromas reminiscent of red berry fruits, liquorice, spices and pepper; on the palate, it is full-bodied and round, with a good long finish. An excellent Fumin concludes the range.

The Moscato Passito di Chambave, the star wine of the denomination and of the commune which gives it its name, is this year once again the best wine of the Crotta. It is an intensely rich wine made from semi-dried grapes: it has a brilliant colour with golden highlights and a bouquet which displays notes of dried figs, roasted hazelnuts and honey, without losing the aromatic aroma typical of the grape variety from which it is made. On the palate, it is dense, almost honey-like, with a long finish enlivened by subtle acidity. The other dessert wine of the winery, the Nus Malvoisie Flétri, is also very interesting: it differs from the Moscato in that it spends a short time in barrique. The Fumin, the important red of the estate, is also aged in wood. The current vintage has a very dense colour; its aromas are not particularly intense, but combine toasty notes with those of ripe fruit. On the palate, it is well-balanced and has good structure, with a slightly astringent medium-length finish. The winery of Chambave distinguishes itself by producing - apart from these thoroughbreds, of which only a few thousand bottles are made - a series of very attractive wines at competitive prices. Amongst the whites we should especially like to point out the Chambave Muscat which, even in the dry version, demonstrates the skill of the cellar's winemakers in handling moscato grapes. The other wines all achieved respectable scores and deserve at the very least a mention: Müller Thurgau and the dry Nus Malvoisie amongst the whites, Chambave Rouge and Nus Rouge amongst the reds.

● Coteau La Tour '95	♟♟	5
○ Vallée d'Aoste Chardonnay Cuvée Frissonière-Les Crêtes '95	♟♟	5
○ Vallée d'Aoste Chardonnay Cuvée Frissonière-Les Crêtes '96	♟♟	5
○ Vallée d'Aoste Petite Arvine Vigne Champorette '96	♟	4
● Vallée d'Aoste Fumin La Tour des Crêtes '95	♟	5
● Vallée d'Aoste Pinot Noir La Tour des Crêtes '96	♟	3
● Vallée d'Aoste Torrette Vigne Les Toules '96	♟	3

○ Vallée d'Aoste Chambave Moscato Passito '95	♟♟	4
○ Vallée d'Aoste Chambave Muscat '96	♟	3
○ Vallée d'Aoste Nus Malvoisie '96	♟	3
○ Vallée d'Aoste Nus Malvoisie Flétri '95	♟	4
● Vallée d'Aoste Fumin '95	♟	3
● Vallée d'Aoste Nus Rouge '96	♟	2
● Vallée d'Aoste Chambave Rouge '96		2
○ Vallée d'Aoste Müller Thurgau '96		3
● Vallée d'Aoste Fumin '94	♟♟	3

CHAMBAVE (AO)

EZIO VOYAT
VIA ARBERAZ, 13
11023 CHAMBAVE (AO)
TEL. 0166/46139

MORGEX (AO)

CAVE DU VIN BLANC DE MORGEX
ET DE LA SALLE
CHEMIN DES ILES, 1
FRAZ. LA RUINE
11017 MORGEX (AO)
TEL. 0165/800331

For years now, this winery has concentrated on the three wines which have made it famous around the world. Already at the end of the 19th century, Ezio Voyat's grandfather, Leonardo, was studying viticulture and became, during the Phylloxera epidemic, a specialist in the art of re-grafting; the present owner inherited the company from his father in the 1950s and has since dedicated himself to the upkeep of the family's own vineyards in Chambave. There are two hectares under vine, from which, on average 12,000 bottles are produced annually of the classic Moscato Passito, of Moscato Secco and of Rosso Le Muraglie. The dry white is called La Gazzella and is a vino da tavola , like all of Voyat's wines. This year, too, it is of above-average quality: a very attractive dry muscat, with intense scents of musk and apples, and with the typical aromatic note of the grape variety. On the palate, it has good structure and refreshing acidity, again with aromatic fruit and a slight bitter-almondy note on the finish. The '94 Passito Le Muraglie - less interesting than on other occasions - promises aristocratic style in its deep amber colour, but does not carry through on the palate which is a little too syrupy. The Rosso Le Muraglie - made from a blend of petit rouge, dolcetto and gros vien - is characterized by a pronounced acidulous note.

The vineyards which cover the northernmost part of the Valle d'Aosta, where the majestic Valdigne begins, are those which produce Blanc de Morgex et de La Salle. This is a white obtained from the blanc de Morgex grape variety, grown on the mountainous left bank of the Dora Baltea on terraces reaching up to 1300 metres above sea level - unbelievably high altitudes for viticulture. This wine is commonly known as "the white of the glaciers". In 1983 the vine-growers of the two communes united, creating the Cave du vin Blanc de Morgex et de La Salle: originally, there were 65 members who represented 70 percent of the growers of the entire zone; today, there are 95 members - almost all the producers the communes of Morgex and La Salle. The winery, owned by the region, is beside the road which leads up to Monte Blanc, and is equipped not only for production, but also for sales, and has a restaurant attached. Four wines are produced, all from the same blanc de Morgex variety: two are DOC and two are vini da tavola. The most important wine, of which more than 50,000 bottles are released annually, is the Blanc de Morgex et de la Salle: the '96 once again easily earns its One Glass rating. It is a very pale-coloured white, with a bouquet of medium intensity in which grassy notes combine with hints of wild flowers. It does not have great structure on the palate, but has an appealing, citrusy finish which is savoury and refreshing. The 1995 Spumante Metodo Classico and the Blanc des Glaciers, a white vino da tavola , are of slightly less interest. The range is completed by a simpler sparkling wine, the Blanc Fripon and by the Grappa di blanc de Morgex. As from this year the Cave has equipped itself, thanks to voluntary contributions from its members, with facilities for welcoming visitors and providing tastings and guided tours.

O La Gazzella Moscato '95	♥	4
O Vino Passito Le Muraglie '94	♥	6
● Rosso Le Muraglie '94		4
O Vino Passito Le Muraglie '92	♀	5

O Vallée d'Aoste Blanc de Morgex et de La Salle '96	♥	2
O Blanc des Glaciers '96		2
O Vallée d'Aoste Blanc de Morgex et de La Salle Metodo Classico '95		4

PIEDMONT

There have been two exciting developments in Piedmont this year. The first is the definitive entry of Dolcetto into the catalogue of the great wines of the region. The second is, although this hardly seemed possible, a further improvement in the general quality of Piedmontese wines, across the board. As far as Dolcetto is concerned, the '96 vintage at last produced top quality grapes almost everywhere and, consequently, excellent wines that can be happily cellared for a year or two. Wineries which have been known for years for their Dolcetto are now finally obtaining the recognition they deserve: specialists such as Marcarini from La Morra, Ca' Viola from Montelupo d'Alba, and Pecchenino from Dogliani, for example. There are almost certainly other producers who deserve to be in the Three Glasses class for their Dolcetto, but at the time of our tastings these were the most obvious winners; we hope to be able to report on others in future editions of the Guide. The other significant achievement of Piedmontese winemaking is the consistently high quality of wines released in 1997, beginning with the '93 Barolo. This was a good vintage, but not a great one. The wines may not have great structure, but nevertheless many have been brought up to Three Glass level by skillful work both in the vineyard and the cellar. Prominent among the producers are several new names, a fact which provides evidence of the continuing growth of the Langhe. Ferdinando Principiano makes high quality, limited production wines, and is surely destined for fame in the next few years. Then there is the able Gianfranco Alessandria, another native of Monforte and from La Morra the young Rovello brothers and Eraldo Viberti. Elio Grasso returns to the top echelons of the Guide with an extraordinary Barolo Casa Maté. Almost all the acknowledged great names of Barolo have proved their worth, including Clerico, Scavino, Azelia, Michele Chiarlo and Roberto Voerzio, while Giovanni Conterno gets top marks for a superlative Barolo Monfortino '90. In the southern part of the region the success of Barbera continues, both as a varietal and in cuvées, with the '95 vintage which yielded more powerful and more complex wines than have been seen for several years. The Three Glass producers in this category : La Barbatella (La Vigna di Sonvico), Ca' Viola (Bric du Luv), Elio Altare (Larigi), La Spinetta (Pin), Franco Martinetti (Sul Bric), Conterno Fantino (Monpré), and, from the Roero, Matteo Correggia with his Barbera Bricco Marun. Two wines which repeat the success of last year, confirming their recent entries into the list of Italy's finest, are the Loazzolo "passito" from Giancarlo and Silvia Scaglione and the Brut Zero from Valentino and Jolanda Migliorini. Last but not least, the inimitable Angelo Gaja, who even in poor vintages succeeds in making excellent Barolo Sperss, Darmagi and Barbaresco, gains the triple distinction that has become customary for his winery.

AGLIANO TERME (AT)

Agostino Pavia e Figli

Fraz. Bologna, 33
14041 Agliano Terme (AT)
tel. 0141/954125

The recent construction of new vinification premises is tangible evidence of a constant striving for growth in this winery. Turning their backs on the days of bulk wine (notwithstanding the few demijohns that continue to leave the winery for die-hard customers of the old school), Agostino Pavia and his two sons, Giuseppe and Marco, have now set out to make wines of quality. New premises, some barriques, a bit of cabernet sauvignon, plans to buy a few hectares of well-sited vineyards, all these are the palpable signs of a desire for improvement. The results are evident in the wines presented for tasting. This year there were three types of Barbera, the most important varietal in the area, and one Grignolino. The cru La Mareschialla, coming from the vineyard of the same name and aged for about a year in barrique, is without doubt a successful wine: deep ruby red colour, subtle on the nose, toasty with obvious, well-married berry fruit, good follow through on the palate, clean, medium weight and reasonably full bodied. The Bricco Blina is more typical: clear aroma of cherries on the nose, well balanced on the palate with typical green youthfulness in the finish; very drinkable and easy to like. The Moliss is a little disappointing: thin, unbalanced by the alcohol, and lacking in grip. The Grignolino is honest enough, an up-front wine with attractive hints of geraniums and pepper, good body, tannic, well balanced, with a characteristic bitter twist to the finish.

● Barbera d'Asti Bricco Blina '95	▼	2*
● Barbera d'Asti Sup. La Marescialla '95	▼	4
● Grignolino d'Asti '96	▼	2*
● Barbera d'Asti Moliss '95		2
● Barbera d'Asti Bricco Blina '94	▽	2
● Barbera d'Asti Sup. La Marescialla '93	▽	4
● Barbera d'Asti Sup. La Marescialla '94	▽	4

AGLIANO TERME (AT)

Renato Trinchero

Via Noce, 56
14041 Agliano Terme (AT)
tel. 0141/954016

Agliano is an authentic cru site for barbera, producing excellent wines, full of perfume, body and personality. The Trinchero family built its small winery on the hills here as long ago as 1928. Their 12 hectares of vineyards are all well-sited for vine growing on the predominantly clayey soil. Like many others, they use the Guyot training system, the best for hillside vineyards producing small quantities of grapes for wines of quality, such as the two flagship Trinchero wines, La Vigna del Noce and La Barslina. These are both cru Barbera productions from two old vineyards, dating back, respectively, to 1929 and 1936. The first is smooth and full bodied; retasted in the '93 version since the current vintage is not yet bottled, the wine is soft and very drinkable with clear aromas of fruit at a peak of ripeness, even if it lacks a little of that freshness that would have given it better balance in the end. The Barslina, on the other hand, is definitely well balanced and has gone through short ageing in small oak barrels to give it a welcome tannicity and a freshness that is a good foil on the nose to the alcohol; attractive hints of cherry, plums and blackberries prepare the palate for the excellent drinkability of this Barbera, full of the varietal character of the grape. The Trabic, made from merlot, is perfectly sound with the typical vegetal nose of the variety; full bodied and smooth. Lastly, the Barbera d'Asti '96, is very up-front and easy to drink.

● Barbera d'Asti La Barslina '94	▼▼	4
● Barbera d'Asti '96	▼	2*
● Trabic '94	▼	4
● Barbera d'Asti La Barslina '93	▽▽	4
● Barbera d'Asti Vigna del Noce '93	▽▽	4
● Barbera d'Asti La Barslina '90	▽	4
● Barbera d'Asti Vigna del Noce '90	▽	4
● Le Taragne '93	▽	4

AGLIÈ (TO)

CIECK
STRADA BARDESONO
FRAZ. S. GRATO
10011 AGLIÈ (TO)
TEL. 0124/32225-330522

Since they decided to combine forces in 1985, and to concentrate on quality wines, Remo Falconieri and Lodovico Bardesono have not put a foot wrong. This year too, they have come out with one wine well above average, the Erbaluce from Vigneto Misobolo, which, with their two sparkling wines, confirms their current high ranking. The Erbaluce is a very delicate wine with good tipicity, both on the nose and the palate. This is a white wine without a pronounced bouquet, but it succeeds because of its good definition and fresh hints of straw and meadow flowers. On the palate it is well balanced and full bodied with a rich and balanced finish, refreshed by a youthful greenness and a bitter twist at the end. The two sparkling wines are very good; both called San Giorgio, they come from different vintages and are vinified in different ways. San Giorgio Brut '90 is fermented in wood and hence has the classic toastiness that goes so well with the yeast on the nose; very complex bouquet, attractive and well balanced on the palate, even if not quite as full bodied as the previous vintage. The standard San Giorgio Brut is very good, if a little less elegant. Passito Alladium '92 is attractive and full bodied, with a bright bouquet, and sharp hints of citrus fruit blending well with the toastiness from the wood; on the palate, delicate, very drinkable, medium weight. The delightful Rosso Cieck '95, made from local grape varieties neiretto, barbera, nebbiolo, and mustera, deserves a mention.

ALBA (CN)

CERETTO
LOC. S. CASSIANO, 34
12051 ALBA (CN)
TEL. 0173/282582

Notwithstanding its distinctive style, the Ceretto production as a whole seems to be going through an evolutionary phase, as the company develops strategies for further enhancement of quality. Given that we are not talking about a family-run business, the results will not necessarily be quick in coming. Meanwhile, one positive note is that the Barbaresco Bricco Asili '94 has overcome the difficulties of the vintage to become an example of the perfect marriage of tradition and innovation. Deep and bright garnet red in colour, berry fruit up front on the nose combined with hints of vanilla and coffee, full bodied on the palate and amply supported by lively tannins with a long finish. A naturally lighter wine, Barbaresco Asij is a less dense garnet red, well advanced in its maturation, attractive, with hints of figs and almonds, many-layered and balanced on the palate. In other words, a well made wine, even if a little feminine. Barolo Zonchera has made the most of the raw material provided by the '93 vintage and is showing better than the previous two years; a full bodied and well defined wine, but a good example of oenological expertise rather than an intrinsically great wine. Arneis Blangé, another carefully thought out wine, is a bit short on the palate, but is bright enough with a good bouquet. Dolcetto d'Alba Rossana is better than last year's version and comes out with a bright ruby red colour, a full bouquet with attractive vinosity, rich aromas of strawberries and raspberries, well balanced on the palate and buoyed up with fresh fruit.

	Wine		
O	Erbaluce di Caluso Spumante Brut San Giorgio '90	♉♉	4
O	Erbaluce di Calus Vigna Misobolo '96	♉♉	3
O	Caluso Passito Alladium Vigneto Runc '92	♉	4
●	Cieck Rosso '95	♉	3
O	Erbaluce di Caluso Spumante Brut San Giorgio	♉	4

	Wine		
●	Barbaresco Bricco Asili '94	♉♉	6
O	Langhe Arneis Blangé '96	♉	4
●	Barbaresco Asij '94	♉	5
●	Barolo Zonchera '93	♉	5
●	Dolcetto d'Alba Rossana '96	♉	4
●	Barbaresco Bricco Asili '85	♉♉♉	6
●	Barbaresco Bricco Asili '86	♉♉♉	6
●	Barbaresco Bricco Asili '89	♉♉♉	6
●	Barbaresco Bricco Asili '88	♉♉♉	6
●	Barolo Bricco Rocche '89	♉♉♉	6
●	Barolo Brunate '90	♉♉♉	6
●	Barolo Prapò '83	♉♉♉	6
●	Barbaresco Bricco Asili '93	♉♉	6
●	Monsordo Rosso '93	♉♉	6
O	La Bernardina Brut '93	♉	5

ALBA (CN)

PIO CESARE
VIA CESARE BALBO, 6
12051 ALBA (CN)
TEL. 0173/440386

Pio Cesare is back with its best wines to the fore after a string of difficult vintages in which they had not been made. The wines in question are Barolo Ornato and Barbaresco Bricco, two established classics of the Langhe in which Pio Boffa tries to balance the elements of tradition and innovation, international taste and local "terroir". The '93 vintage has produced in both cases wines more elegant than structured. Ornato is an already mature garnet red; the bouquet has hints of coffee and mature fruit; smooth on the palate and many-layered; definite notes of wood on a finish that is however not of the longest. Hints of chocolate and vanilla characterise the complex aromas of the Bricco; on the palate the wine develops well and correctly, but without excitement. The Barbaresco '93 is surprisingly full of rich flavours and begins with an overwhelming floral bouquet; full bodied and at its peak. The standard Barolo is just as well developed, but it lacks a little in structure and is a little short on the palate. The standard Barbaresco '94, showing good balance despite the poor year, passed its tasting test comfortably. The wines for more immediate drinking seem to favour simplicity over complexity. Thus the Dolcetto, Arneis, Barbera, and Chardonnay L'Altro are correct, bright and fresh, but lacking in character. Chardonnay Piodilei, aged in barrique, shows the quality of the grapes that went into it, but is a little overpowered by the oak.

ALBA (CN)

PODERI COLLA
LOC. S. ROCCO SENO D'ELVIO, 82
12051 ALBA (CN)
TEL. 0173/290148

The annual production capacity of this young winery is more than 100,000 bottles, all the wines coming from company-owned vineyards in some of the best sites of the Langhe, particularly Bussia for Barolo and Roncaglia for Barbaresco. Barolo Bussia Dardi Le Rose gives its best, thanks to its complexity, above all on the nose, with attractive aromas of ripe fruit and undergrowth; on the palate the wine is full bodied, well balanced, and long finishing with a pleasing bitter twist. Barbaresco Tenuta Roncaglia, deliberately made as an elegant wine rather than a powerful one, has a bouquet of ripe fruit with barely perceptible hints of wood; smooth, easy to drink, attractive, and only very slightly tannic. Barbera d'Alba '95, fresh fruity and up-front, has good body on the palate. The Nebbiolo is made in a similar style but is slightly more austere due to its deliberately higher tannin levels. Bricco del Drago '93 (made from dolcetto and nebbiolo) is slightly dumb, while the '94 version is better balanced, if a little lacking in weight. The Dolcetto '96 is a correct wine, but lacking the lush fruit of this felicitous vintage; it is somewhat dumb on the nose and spare on the palate. The Sanrocco of the same vintage is bright and simple, while the Freisa '96 has a slightly bitter finish. The pinot noir-based Langhe Campo Romano is correct and attractive, but bright and one dimensional rather than full bodied.

● Barbaresco '93	♛♛	5
● Barbaresco Bricco '93	♛♛	6
● Barolo Ornato '93	♛♛	6
● Barbera d'Alba '95	♛	3
● Barolo '93	♛	5
● Dolcetto d'Alba '96	♛	3
○ Langhe Arneis '96	♛	4
○ Langhe Chardonnay Piodilei '95	♛	5
○ Piemonte Chardonnay L'Altro '96		3
● Barolo Ornato '85	♛♛♛	6
● Barolo Ornato '89	♛♛♛	6
● Barbaresco Bricco '90	♛♛	6
● Barolo '92	♛♛	5
● Barolo Ornato '90	♛♛	6

● Barbaresco Tenuta Roncaglia '94	♛♛	5
● Barolo Bussia Dardi Le Rose '93	♛♛	5
● Barbera d'Alba '95	♛	3
● Bricco del Drago '93	♛	4
● Bricco del Drago '94	♛	4
● Dolcetto d'Alba '96	♛	3
● Langhe Campo Romano '96	♛	4
● Nebbiolo d'Alba '95	♛	3
○ Langhe Bianco Sanrocco '96		3
● Langhe Freisa '96		3
● Barbaresco Tenuta Roncaglia '93	♛♛	5
○ Bonmé	♛♛	4

ALBA (CN)

ALBA (CN)

PRUNOTTO
REG. S. CASSIANO, 4/G
12051 ALBA (CN)
TEL. 0173/280017

MAURO SEBASTE
VIA GARIBALDI, 222/BIS
FRAZ. GALLO
12051 ALBA (CN)
TEL. 0173/262148

Patience is paying off for the Antinori family, who have allowed the Alba-based Prunotto winery that they wanted so much, the time to develop a new identity, without undue haste and without any sudden break with the past. Indeed, links with the past have been stressed in order to build a solidly based production of quality wines. This year the wines tasted have been truly superb. We begin with a long awaited return to form on the part of Barbera Pian Romualdo: a dense, tightly knitted wine, deep ruby red in colour, a nose of cherries and raspberries mixed with new oak; no giant in structure, this is a wine based on smooth elegance backed up with fresh acidity. Dolcetto Mosesco is a rich wine in all senses, starting with the colour. Almost austere in its uncompromising focus it has sharp almond and bilberry flavours, and packs a punch on the palate, finishing very long. Before going on to the reds for longer ageing, we recommend the Barbera d'Asti Fiulot, once again one of the best wines for immediate drinking of the vintage. The Barolo '93 is subtle but surprisingly long; this is no monster of a wine, but it did attract our attention with its well defined character. Barolo Cannubi is a wine of future complexity: sweet richness of extract on the nose, excellent in its well balanced smoothness. The Barolo from Bussia is more incisive; mature and full bodied, the development of the tannins here is all-important. Tasting the Barbaresco '93 again shows how well this wine has developed, while the Montestefano is elegant rather than complex. Nebbiolo Occhetti falls below its usual standard.

Mauro Sebaste is still waiting to being work on the modernisation and extension of his cellars which will enable him to produce his numerous wines better and more efficiently. He makes two lines. The first and more commercial one, is the Alti Bricchi label, while the other comprises traditional wines from Alba made with great artistry and technical ability. The Roero Arneis, straw yellow in colour with greenish reflections, is both fruity and floral on the nose, while on the palate it has average weight and length. The Dolcetto d'Alba has a rich violet colour and is fruity and vinous enough on the nose to make it attractive for drinking now. Centobricchi, a cuvée of 90 percent barbera and 10 percent nebbiolo aged for one year in barriques of different ages (new, first year and second year), is one step up in quality: the wine is at its best on the nose with aromas of ripe fruit married with spices and vanilla from the wood. Barolo Monvigliero is very elegant and well developed: its ruby red colour has tinges of orange and its bouquet is of mature berry fruit and flowers, the palate is pleasantly well evolved. Barolo Le Coste, only slightly inferior in quality, has less body and elegance, is slightly further down the track of maturation, and has characteristic hints of liquorice and vegetal undergrowth on the palate. Next year will see the arrival of a new Barolo cru, Prapò.

● Barbera d'Alba Pian Romualdo '95	♟♟	4
● Barolo '93	♟♟	5
● Barolo Bussia '93	♟♟	6
● Barolo Cannubi '93	♟♟	5
● Dolcetto d'Alba Mosesco '96	♟♟	4
● Barbaresco Montestefano '94	♟	5
● Barbera d'Asti Fiulot '96	♟	2
● Nebbiolo d'Alba Occhetti '95	♟	4
○ Roero Arneis '96	♟	3
● Barbaresco Montestefano '85	♟♟♟	6
● Barolo Bussia '85	♟♟♟	6
● Barolo Cannubi '85	♟♟♟	6
● Nebbiolo d'Alba Occhetti '89	♟♟♟	5
● Barbaresco Montestefano '93	♟♟	5

● Barolo Monvigliero '93	♟♟	5
● Centobricchi '95	♟♟	4
● Barolo Le Coste '93	♟	4
● Dolcetto d'Alba La Serra '96	♟	3
○ Roero Arneis '96	♟	3
● Centobricchi '94	♟♟	4
● Barolo Le Coste '92	♟	4
● Barolo Monvigliero '92	♟	5

ALFIANO NATTA (AL)

ASTI

FATTORIE AUGUSTUS
FRAZ. CASARELLO, 2
15021 ALFIANO NATTA (AL)
TEL. 0141/922124

IL MILIN
FRAZ. S. MARZANOTTO, 216
14050 ASTI
TEL. 0141/592460

On the way to the winery headquarters, located in the eighteenth century castle of Razzano, we took a side road with owner Augusto Olearo to the Castelletto Merli district and the fourteenth century monastery that is being restored there. "This will be our new cellars", announces Olearo. Work could continue for a long time yet, but in the end there will be room for an exhibitions or concert room and a series of apartments for "agriturismo" holidays on the estate. His three passions are art, restoration, and, above all, wine - which means Barbera. Barbera d'Asti Campasso Vigna di Ca' Farotto '95 will be examined next year, when it has been bottled. Barbera d'Asti Superiore Vigna del Beneficio, the flagship wine, shows itself once again to be a high quality bottle, even if the nature of the '94 vintage means that it is not as big as the previous vintage. The bouquet is very intense and long, with a marked jammyness on the nose and notes of bitter cocoa; full bodied on the palate, but not over-powerful; the tannins softened by barrique ageing blend well with the bitter cherry finish. Barbera Del Monferrato Vivace Vigna Monte Ubaldo '96 has a fruity enough bouquet, slightly marred by harsh vegetal tones; a typical semi-sparkling wine on the palate, well balanced with refreshing flavours and light tannins. Lastly, Grignolino Del Monferrato Casalese Vigna di Ca' Delù '96 is worthy of note: good tipicity and structure, but a little tired on the nose.

Milin, in local dialect, was a name given to someone who could make a thousand bricks a day; an unusual name for a winery, but explained by the presence of an old brick-kiln nearby. Claudio Rovero is also an unusual character, a type of Hemingway of the Asti region who sees working on the land as a source of life energy as Hemigway saw literature. He certainly keeps himself busy; a winery, a distillery, and "agriturismo" holiday apartments on the estate, are all time-consuming activities, even if the work is shared with his brothers and sister, Franco, Michelino and Rosanna. The grapes come from 16 hectares of vineyards on three estates: Milin, Villa Drago and Serra Valdonata. The red wine varieties are grignolino, barbera, pinot noir, cabernet sauvignon and, from this year, merlot and nebbiolo; the whites are sauvignon and riesling. None of the wines are really astounding, but they are worth looking at. Barbera Rouvé which undergoes a minimum of one year in wood before bottle ageing, and the Pinot Nero - six months in cask for this one - give a good account of themselves. The first has good fruit on the nose, not yet completely harmonised with the wine, and then surprises with its structure, soft tannins, and full bodied finish. The other wine has a delicate and well defined bouquet; red currants are predominant, while the palate has good fruit and is very uncomplicated. The Grignolino is also worthy of note, with an attractive nose of geraniums, dried roses and a slight touch of pepper on the nose. The acidity and tannins are well balanced on the palate, making this a very drinkable wine. Barbera Giustin can also be recommended. The Sauvignons are good, both the one aged in barrique and the other aged in stainless steel.

● Barbera d'Asti Sup. Vigna del Beneficio '94	♟	4
● Barbera del M.to Vivace Vigna Monte Ubaldo '96	♟	2*
● Grignolino del M.to Casalese Vigna di Ca' Delù '96		2
● Barbera d'Asti Sup. Vigna del Beneficio '93	♟♟	3
● Barbera d'Asti Campasso Vigna di Ca' Farotto '94	♟	2

● Barbera d'Asti Rouvé '95	♟	4
● Grignolino d'Asti Vigneto La Casalina '96	♟	2
○ Monferrato Bianco Sauvignon '96	♟	3
○ Monferrato Bianco Sauvignon Vinificato in Legno '95	♟	3
● Monferrato Rosso Pinot Nero '95	♟	3
● Barbera d'Asti Vigneto Gustin '96		3
● Rouvé '90	♟♟	4
● Barbera d'Asti Rouvé '94	♟	4
● Monferrato Rosso Cabernet '94	♟	3

BARBARESCO (CN)

BARBARESCO (CN)

CA' ROMÉ
VIA RABAJÀ, 36
12050 BARBARESCO (CN)
TEL. 0173/635175-635126

TENUTE CISA ASINARI
VIA RABAJÀ, 43
12050 BARBARESCO (CN)
TEL. 0173/635222

Some may doubt it, but it is undeniably true that things are changing at Ca' Romé. Let us be clear about it, a strong belief in the value of tradition means that this is nothing earth-shattering, but little by little the company is reacting to the changing environment it operates in: suppliers of good quality grapes are rarer and rarer, so more effort goes into growing the company's own grapes; the market, especially abroad, has dictated a separation of the commercial activities from the wine-producing side; and Giuseppe's ideas are gaining ground in comparison to the traditional ways of his father. The wines are a logical consequence of the structure of the company, rather like a well established branded product where only the packaging is up for modification. The Barbaresco cuvée is as good as usual: concentrated and austere with a soft, fruity beginning and then finishing attractively long, tannic and dry. The Barolo is only slightly less good; with definite berry fruit on the nose and a full bodied structure, it needs further ageing. The Barbera is powerful and concentrated with good balance between softness and tannins, but it needs a little tweaking to give it more elegance. Less interesting than previous versions, the Da Pruvé assemblage of nebbiolo and barbera aged in barrique is a little unbalanced on the nose and sharp on the palate, but it is full bodied and long-finishing all the same.

With considerable problems of rain during the harvest, the '94 vintage did not allow Alberto Di Gresy to make a Barbaresco to his usual high standard. Apart from anything else, a vineyard like La Martinenga benefits from good weather in good years, but suffers particularly badly in difficult years. That said, the Barbaresco '94 does not have any defects, quite the opposite, it is well made, but it does seem to be a little dilute and lacks the body and grip of happier vintages. The colour is a light garnet red, there are soft hints of macerated flowers and clear suggestions of fruit-in-alcohol on the nose, easy to drink on the palate, and despite not being very long it is well balanced. The Villa Martis selection is from the '94 vintage, too, but stands out for its full bodied nature: deep ruby red colour, nose combining the lively fruitiness of barbera and complex floral nature of nebbiolo, long, easily likeable, and well balanced on the palate. Dolcetto Monte Aribaldo '96 has the usual aromatic bouquet, but lacks a bit in body; in fact, this vineyard in the commune of Treiso has obviously suffered from a poor vintage. Moscato La Serra is more reliable, and, as usual, impeccably made: well defined aromatic bouquet with hints of sage and grapefruit on the nose, together with firm sweetness; the right amount of acidity and sparkle make the wine both balanced and refreshing. The Sauvignon is slightly one dimensional: dominated on the nose by raw peppers, but full flavoured and attractive on the palate.

● Barbaresco Maria di Brun '93	♥♥	5
● Barbera d'Alba La Gamberaja '95	♥	4
● Barolo Rapet '93	♥	5
● Da Pruvé '93	♥	4
● Barbaresco Maria di Brun '89	♀♀	5
● Barolo Rapet '89	♀♀	5
● Barbaresco '93	♀	5
● Barbaresco Maria di Brun '90	♀	5
● Barolo Rapet Ris. '90	♀	6
● Barolo Vigneto Carpegna '89	♀	5

● Barbaresco Martinenga '94	♥	5
● Dolcetto d'Alba Monte Aribaldo '96	♥	3
● Villa Martis '94	♥	3
○ Langhe Sauvignon '96	♥	4
○ Moscato d'Asti La Serra '96	♥	3
● Barbaresco Gaiun '85	♀♀♀	6
● Barbaresco Camp Gros '90	♀♀	6
● Barbaresco Gaiun '90	♀♀	6
● Barbaresco Camp Gros '93	♀	6
● Barbaresco Martinenga '93	♀	5

BARBARESCO (CN)

GIUSEPPE CORTESE
LOC. RABAJÀ, 35
12050 BARBARESCO (CN)
TEL. 0173/635131

All credit to Giuseppe and his son Piercarlo; hail storms and other problems made '94 a vintage best forgotten, and the decision was made not to come out with the Barbaresco. For a winery producing 35,000 bottles this is no small sacrifice, especially considering the amount of money that has recently been invested in the building of a bigger and more modern winery. Holding the fort for the Cortese name have been the more ordinary foot soldier wines, which, as often happens even in metaphors, have done very well, with the sole exception of the white wine, which we were not much impressed with this year. First of all, Barbera Morassina: coming from a thirty-year old vineyard in the Trifolera locality, and after a year in large Allier and Slavonian oak barrels, the wine emerges full bodied and elegant, with a well developed palate and an attractive finish of dried roses. The standard Barbera is noteworthy, too: vinified and aged purely in stainless steel, the wine has good fruit, is well defined, long-finishing, and, above all, has a excellent follow through, from nose to finish. The Dolcetto is just as good: one month in barrel has rounded out any harsh tannins, it displays typical vinosity on the nose, first soft and bitter, then attractively tannic on the palate, leaving, at the end, tastes of rose petals steeped in alcohol. The Nebbiolo is correct enough, but not very exciting.

BARBARESCO (CN)

★ GAJA
VIA TORINO, 36
12050 BARBARESCO (CN)
TEL. 0173/635158

The word that best describes Angelo Gaja in his work is "intense". Feeding all this intensity is, first of all, a constant tension, but then he also has the ability to demand, and to get, the best from himself and from everyone who works for him. This is very clear when he tastes one of his own wines that he is not entirely happy with: he is not content to accept the excuse of a poor vintage, but searches for other explanations with the almost frantic energy of a young man who will not let go until he finds them. This intensity of character has produced a succession of great wines, a sequence of oenological experiences that succeed in marrying stylistic perfection with the demands of a "terroir". Barolo Sperss unites both traditionalists and innovators in one sigh of profound appreciation. Right from the impenetrable colour it is obvious that this has the power of a memorable Barolo: attractive for its unmistakable bouquet of flowers, vibrant on the palate, solid and richly concentrated in structure. Barbaresco '94 shows how such demanding standards overcome the difficulties of poor vintages. Bright intensity of colour is combined with rare subtlety on the nose, the bouquet is many-layered, all-embracing, full of sensations that go from spices to mature fruit and leave an aromatic herbiness to lighten it all; balance, achieved without excessive power, is the first sensation on the palate. Darmagi '94 is not as big a wine as previous vintages, but its severe full bodied charms are a measure of its undeniable class. Chardonnay Rossj-Bass is richly-extracted and a real pleasure; a foretaste of the Gaia & Rey to come.

● Barbera d'Alba '95	♀	3
● Barbera d'Alba Morassina '95	♀	4
● Dolcetto d'Alba Trifolera '96	♀	3
● Langhe Nebbiolo '95		3
● Barbera d'Alba Morassina '93	♀♀	3
● Barbaresco Rabajà '90	♀	4
● Barbaresco Rabajà '92	♀	4
● Barbaresco Rabajà '93	♀	4

● Barbaresco '94	♀♀♀	6
● Barolo Sperss '93	♀♀♀	6
● Langhe Darmagi '94	♀♀♀	6
● Sito Moresco '94	♀♀	5
○ Langhe Chardonnay Rossj-Bass '96	♀♀	6
○ Langhe Sauvignon Alteni di Brassica '96	♀♀	5
● Langhe Rosso Sitorey '95	♀	5
● Barbaresco '91	♀♀♀	6
● Barbaresco San Lorenzo '90	♀♀♀	6
● Barbaresco Sorì Tildin '90	♀♀♀	6
● Barolo Sperss '91	♀♀♀	6
○ Chardonnay Gaia & Rey '94	♀♀♀	6
● Darmagi '90	♀♀♀	6

BARBARESCO (CN)

I PAGLIERI
VIA RABAJÀ, 8
12050 BARBARESCO (CN)
TEL. 0173/635109

BARBARESCO (CN)

CASCINA LUISIN - LUIGI MINUTO
LOC. RABAJÀ, 23
12050 BARBARESCO (CN)
TEL. 0173/635154

The best wine from the Roagna family this year is a splendid Barbaresco '89: deep garnet red, charged with all the deeply felt traditionalism of its maker and the sensual richness that this vintage conferred on its wines. The ample bouquet is multi-faceted: plum jam, cherries, cocoa, and cinnamon, amongst other things, form an intriguing kaleidoscope of aromas. The palate is simpler: a rich extract, and fine, lively, ripe tannins lead to a long and pregnant finish. Patience has paid off in the end for this meticulous producer who has waited for exactly the right moment before releasing a top quality wine onto the market. Unfortunately, nothing in the rest of his production bears the same hallmark. And yet Alfredo Roagna's vineyards are obviously set up for quality organic winemaking, and his winery has a traditional, almost fundamentalist, approach. Of course, recent vintages have not been kind enough to provide the quality of grapes needed for such an approach, but the full value of the vineyards and of his experience has yet to emerge.

The new cellar is almost finished and Roberto has officially joined his father Luigi in running the winery. This is all quite logical, but finding a son who can follow in the footsteps of his father with dedication and competence, and finding a father who is so enthusiastic about what his son has done that he has taken on new heart himself, is not such an everyday event. It is however, a good reason to have confidence in the future of this winery, confidence also borne out by the wines produced for tasting, which, without overstating the case, certainly justify Luigi's enthusiasm. Proof of their reliability lies in the two off vintage Barbarescos. We preferred the standard version. In this wine grapes grown in the Basarin area (the cru version will come next year) give bouquet and simpler fruit, while the power comes from fruit grown at Rabajà: well defined, alcoholic, with hints of plums, tobacco and cocoa on the nose, good follow through on the palate with the right amount of tannin and alcohol, good length. The single cru Rabajà is less fruity and more austere, with good body and length, just slightly unbalanced by a hint of bitterness. The Dolcetto has good, medium weight varietal character: coming from vineyards at Trifolera, it has three months in wood and emerges floral and fruity with ripe tannins and soft acidity - very drinkable. The Barbera is similarly rich and fruity, with ripe cherries on the nose, but an underlying note of reduction spoils its elegance.

● Barbaresco Ris. '89	♥♥	6
● Barbaresco '93	♥	5
● Barolo La Rocca e La Pira '92	♥	4
● Barbaresco Ris. '90	♀♀	6
● Barolo La Rocca e La Pira '91	♀♀	4
● Crichet Pajé '88	♀♀	6
● Crichet Pajé '89	♀♀	6
● Opera Prima X	♀	5

● Barbaresco '94	♥♥	4
● Barbaresco Rabajà '94	♥♥	4
● Barbera d'Alba Asili '96	♥	3
● Dolcetto d'Alba Bric Trifula '96	♥	3
● Barbaresco Rabajà '92	♀♀	4
● Barbaresco Rabajà '91	♀	4
● Barbaresco Rabajà '93	♀	4

BARBARESCO (CN)

BARBARESCO (CN)

MOCCAGATTA
VIA RABAJÀ, 24
12050 BARBARESCO (CN)
TEL. 0173/635152-635228

CASCINA MORASSINO
VIA OVELLO, 32
12050 BARBARESCO (CN)
TEL. 0173/635149

First of all, we would like to congratulate Franco and Sergio Minuto for creating three top quality wines in the very difficult '94 vintage; who knows what wonders will emerge when the '96 versions of these same wines come out in two years' time! Three fundamental qualities lie behind the estate philosophy: lack of pretension, patience, and experience. Going on to the wines themselves (and there are many of them), we begin with the Barbera Basarin '94, which is made from 40 year-old vines and one third aged for 15 months in new barriques. 4,500 bottles of this wine were produced from the Basarin vineyard in Neive. Healthy, opaque colour with no edges, sweet vanilla and ripe fruit nose, rich and concentrated on the palate, smooth, broad and full bodied, already well balanced. The two Barbarescos, Bric Balin and Vigneto Cole, also from the '94 vintage, are just as good. The rivalry between the two crus has been famous for years, and the producer is proud of the fact that each possesses characteristics which appeal to different clients. Bric Balin is a blend of selected grapes from different vineyards in Barbaresco and is aged in French oak barriques; Vigneto Cole, a great cru from a tiny, forgotten site, is aged for two years in large Slavonian oak. Chardonnay Buschet '95 is always one of the best made in the Langhe. It has an almost golden colour with hints of butter and hazelnuts on the nose; fresh, full bodied and long on the palate. The other wines are from the '96 vintage; they are all good value for money and are all well made, if less exciting.

The Bianco family's Cascina Morassino comprises five hectares of vineyards, some surrounding the house and others a short distance away. Among these is the Ovello vineyard, in the foothills north of Barbaresco. Some news, first of all, that can be gleaned from the wording on the '96 vintage labels: "Cascina Morassino di Roberto Bianco" is the official wording that confirms the reins of responsibility have now passed from father to son. In reality, nothing has changed and nothing will change, because in this small family-run estate everyone has their own job role and they have all worked together in complete harmony for years. In the difficult '94 vintage a rigorous selection was made, both in the vineyards and in the cellars, to make 3,000 bottles of Barbaresco which fully deserve the Two Glass award for the second year running. Somewhere between ruby red and garnet, the ample bouquet is full of spices and dried roses; the palate is intense, broad, tannic and full of long-finishing flavour. The Barbera d'Alba '95, aged partly in French oak barriques and partly in tank, is a pleasant surprise with its elegance and varietal tipicity: delicate nose with the vanilla of the wood well amalgamated with the cherry fruit, soft and velvety on the palate despite the tannins and the characteristic acidity of this grape variety. The Dolcetto d'Alba '96 completes the range: opaque colour with violet reflections, fresh and fruity with hints of raspberries and roses, austere and hard on the palate, this should improve with further bottle age given the excellence of the vintage. The Langhe Nebbiolo '96 was not yet ready at the time of our tasting and is late on the market; we will comment on this wine next year.

● Barbaresco Bric Balin '94	♥♥	5
● Barbaresco Vigneto Cole '94	♥♥	5
● Barbera d'Alba Vigneto Basarin '94	♥♥	4
○ Langhe Chardonnay Buschet '95	♥♥	4
● Barbaresco Vigneto Basarin '94	♥	5
● Barbera d'Alba Vigneto Buschet '96	♥	3
● Dolcetto d'Alba Vigneto Buschet '96	♥	3
○ Langhe Chardonnay '96	♥	3
● Langhe Freisa '96		3
● Barbaresco Bric Balin '90	♥♥♥	5
● Barbaresco Bric Balin '93	♥♥	5
● Barbaresco Vigneto Cole '93	♥♥	5

● Barbaresco '94	♥♥	4
● Barbera d'Alba '95	♥♥	4
● Dolcetto d'Alba '96	♥	3
● Barbaresco '93	♥♥	5
● Barbera d'Alba '94	♥	4

BARBARESCO (CN)

WALTER MUSSO
VIA D. CAVAZZA, 5
12050 BARBARESCO (CN)
TEL. 0173/635129

Walter Musso is certainly not lacking in imagination and enthusiasm: in addition to the classic red wines of the Barbaresco area, he has also thrown himself into the production, limited for the moment, of a Brut Metodo Classico sparkling wine and a "passito" Chardonnay, almost entirely for family consumption. There are also two other Chardonnays, one of which is aged in barrique (which Walter is not keen on doing), and is made almost exclusively for the export market. Going on to the more important wines, Barbaresco Pora '93 is a soft wine, a little short of attack on the nose and the palate: ruby-cum-garnet red colour with orange-tinged borders, quite delicate bouquet of fruit and flowers coming through on the palate with the beginnings of a characteristic note of tarriness. The Dolcetto d'Alba is medium weight, aromatic and vinous on the nose, a classic "all through the meal" wine, not big in structure, but very happily drinkable. The Freisa is worth mentioning and has been made in the traditional manner, that is to say, slightly sparkling and slightly acidic on the palate. The Chardonnay Langhe is a simpler and less opulent wine than many produced in the area, but shows the local potential of the variety nevertheless.

●	Barbaresco Pora '93	▼	4
●	Dolcetto d'Alba '96	▼	2
○	Langhe Chardonnay '96	▼	3
●	Langhe Freisa '96		2
●	Barbaresco '89	YY	4
●	Barbaresco Bricco Rio Sordo '93	YY	4
●	Barbaresco Pora '90	Y	4
●	Barbaresco Rio Sordo '90	Y	4

BARBARESCO (CN)

PRODUTTORI DEL BARBARESCO
VIA TORINO, 52
12050 BARBARESCO (CN)
TEL. 0173/635139-635119

This important and historic winery, run by Celestino Vacca and his son Duccio, with the help of oenologist Giovanni Testa, vinifies the grapes from about 60 member growers. The Riserva Barbarescos come from the best crus in the region, such as Rabajà, Asili, Ovello and Rio Sordo, but are not yet on the market, so we have to content ourselves with commenting on the Barbaresco '93 and the Nebbiolo Langhe '95. These wines are both well made and both on sale at very reasonable prices - they could, therefore, be very useful in winning new converts to the world of the great red wines of the Langhe. The Nebbiolo has medium weight and length; ruby red in colour with orange tinges, it has a bouquet of roses and berry fruit. The Barbaresco has the same characteristics, but is more austere and slightly further on in its cycle of maturation with more pronounced notes of liquorice and tar. Even without being able to comment on the "family jewels", these wines show the Produttori del Barbaresco as one of the most serious producers engaged in the quest for quality, both in the vineyards and in the cellars.

●	Barbaresco '93	▼	4
●	Langhe Nebbiolo '96	▼	3*
●	Barbaresco Montestefano Ris. '89	YY	5
●	Barbaresco Montestefano Ris. '90	YY	5
●	Barbaresco Ovello Ris. '89	YY	5
●	Barbaresco Paje Ris. '90	YY	5
●	Barbaresco Rabajà Ris. '90	YY	5
●	Barbaresco Rio Sordo Ris. '90	YY	5
●	Barbaresco Moccagatta Ris. '90	YY	5
●	Barbaresco '90	Y	4
●	Barbaresco Asili Ris. '90	Y	5

BARBARESCO (CN)

ALBINO ROCCA
VIA RABAJÀ, 15
12050 BARBARESCO (CN)
TEL. 0173/635145

BARBARESCO (CN)

BRUNO ROCCA
VIA RABAJÀ, 29
12050 BARBARESCO (CN)
TEL. 0173/635112

The Albino Rocca estate lives up to expectations again this year, confirming the reputation it has gained in recent years as one of the leading producers at Barbaresco. The irrepressible enthusiasm of the son, Angelo, the happy working partnership with the technician Beppe Caviola, and the farsighted decision to concentrate on modern, high quality production have all contributed to the successes of recent years. Currently, the nine hectares of family-owned vineyards are sited in various parcels in the commune of Barbaresco and produce about 45,000 bottles - a decidedly low yield, even considering the poor vintages and a deliberate decision to harvest at below officially permitted levels. Langhe La Rocca '96, a barrique aged white wine made from cortese and bottled at the beginning of July, has, amazingly, more than 13 degrees of alcohol. Dolcetto d'Alba Vignalunga '96 is also high in alcohol and has a dark ruby red colour and an intense berry fruit bouquet; rich, concentrated, soft and attractively long on the palate. Barbera d'Alba Gepin '95 deserves its Two Glasses. This is a well balanced and highly drinkable wine although the effect of new wood ageing has yet to harmonise completely with its ample proportions. There are two '94 Barbarescos: the Vigneto Loreto version (a limited production of only 1,300 bottles) matures in traditional Slavonian oak, while the Vigneto Brich Ronchi is aged in barriques. Despite the dominance of the new oak it is one of the most attractive Barbarescos of the vintage.

Bruno Rocca is modest enough to consider his wines just "normal" or at most "good enough", and he does not like being complimented to his face. We are very glad therefore to have the opportunity to praise him in writing. This likeable vigneron, (and incidentally fearless cross-country motorcycle racer), pretends to be too busy, or too cynical, or just too wily, to care what we think about his wines when we taste his Chardonnay or his Barbera, not to mention his Dolcetto. But when it comes to his Rabajà his attitude quickly changes, the tasting becomes more serious and he pays more attention to our comments. It is impossible not to like this wine. For a long time the skill and expertise Rocca puts into his Rabajà have made it one of our favourites. The '94 version is one of the darkest in colour and has a nose dominated by the spicy bouquet of oak that grows less intense as the wine is exposed to air; on the palate it is full bodied, soft and broad; the abundant tannins are as soft as the finish. On the Cadet di Neive property there are a few rows of chardonnay and a good barbera vineyard with vines that are over 40 years old. The Barbera d'Alba '95 is up-front and concentrated, very elegant both on the nose and the palate. Langhe Chardonnay Cadet '96 is aged for about six months in barrique and is an ever-more convincing example of its type: deep straw yellow colour, ample bouquet of ripe bananas, honey and vanilla; remarkable for the balance of its concentrated fruit and fresh acidity on the palate. Lastly, the Dolcetto d'Alba Vigna Trifolé, coming from the vineyard of the same name in Barbaresco, is simple, but correctly made.

●	Barbaresco Vigneto Brich Ronchi '94	🍷🍷	5	● Barbaresco Rabajà '94	🍷🍷	5
●	Barbaresco Vigneto Loreto '94	🍷🍷	4	○ Langhe Chardonnay Cadet '96	🍷🍷	4
●	Barbera d'Alba Gepin '95	🍷🍷	4	● Barbera d'Alba '95	🍷	4
●	Dolcetto d'Alba Vignalunga '96	🍷🍷	3	● Dolcetto d'Alba Vigna Trifolé '96	🍷	3
○	Langhe Bianco La Rocca '96	🍷	4	● Barbaresco Rabajà '88	🍷🍷🍷	5
●	Barbaresco Vigneto Brich Ronchi '93	🍷🍷🍷	5	● Barbaresco Rabajà '89	🍷🍷🍷	5
●	Barbaresco Vigneto Brich Ronchi '91	🍷🍷	5	● Barbaresco Rabajà '93	🍷🍷🍷	5
●	Barbaresco Vigneto Loreto '93	🍷🍷	4	● Barbaresco Rabajà '90	🍷🍷	5
●	Dolcetto d'Alba Vignalunga '95	🍷🍷	3	● Barbaresco Rabajà '92	🍷🍷	5
●	Barbaresco Vigneto Brich Ronchi '92	🍷	5	○ Langhe Chardonnay Cadet '95	🍷🍷	4
●	Barbera d'Alba Gepin '94	🍷	4	● Barbaresco Rabajà '91	🍷	5

BAROLO (CN)

CANTINA F.LLI BARALE
VIA ROMA, 6
12060 BAROLO (CN)
TEL. 0173/56127

Not everyone is aware that the cru Bussia, one of the best vineyards in the entire Langhe and a source of great nebbiolo-based wines, is also capable of producing excellent Dolcettos. Those who have taken up the cause include the Barale family, famous producers of Barolo, whose best wine this year was, in fact, a Dolcetto. Their vineyard selection Dolcetto d'Alba Bussia '96 is a classic ruby red with violet reflections; rich, brambly fruit nose with attractive vinosity behind it; up-front on the palate, firm tannins right through to the finish. This wine could age well and do much to revive the tradition of cellaring Dolcetto wines for a while, a habit that has been lost in the Langhe. On the subject of wines to lay down, the impressive Barolo Castellero is at its usual level of excellence. Medium garnet red in colour; already attractively mature on the nose with hints of bitter cherries steeped in alcohol and macerated flowers; firm on the palate, well balanced with rounded tannins. The Barbera '95 is less rich and a little thinner than usual, which puzzled us: it is probably the result of a vintage in which continuous rain penalised the quality of the first two thirds of the harvest. The Chardonnay is not meant to be a big wine and is true to type: light and easy to drink.

BAROLO (CN)

GIACOMO BORGOGNO & FIGLI
VIA GIOBERTI, 1
12060 BAROLO (CN)
TEL. 0173/56108

The wines presented for tasting this year by Borgogno reflect an important and positive change in the production. The Boschis family does not intend to forget its glorious past, but at the same time they cannot ignore the innovations that are increasingly apparent in the area. This is the inspiration for their Barolo Classico '93, a tight, youthful and attractive wine; rich and concentrated starting with the colour, full and stylish with a most attractive nose and above all, firm and powerful on the palate. This is where the new development lies: a new sense of vitality and a multi-layered balance full of nuance on the palate. The standard Barolo has the same energy. It is deeply coloured and richly perfumed on the nose although nevertheless a little thin on the palate to balance out the hefty dose of tannins it possesses. The Barbera d'Alba is a good, full bodied wine that has a modern liveliness and very pronounced, uplifted fruit on the nose. The palate is naturally fresh without being too heavyweight, and the acidity is moderated by the richness of extract. Only the Dolcetto seems a bit impersonal, even if the colour and the bouquet would seem to promise something more. The wines put forward this year are an encouraging selection overall and bring to mind the tasting of a memorable Barolo '58, still alive and kicking today, that was considered revolutionary in its day; history may be repeating itself for this estate.

● Barolo Castellero '93	♼♼	5
● Dolcetto d'Alba Bussia '96	♼♼	3
● Barbera d'Alba Preda '95	♼	4
○ Langhe Chardonnay '96		3
● Barolo Castellero '91	♼♼	5
● Barbaresco Rabajà '90	♼	5
● Barbaresco Rabajà '91	♼	5
● Barbaresco Rabajà Ris. '93	♼	5
● Barolo Castellero '90	♼	6
● Barolo Castellero '92	♼	5

● Barolo Classico '93	♼♼	5
● Barbera d'Alba '96	♼	2
● Barolo '93	♼	4
● Dolcetto d'Alba '96		3
● Barolo '89	♼	5
● Barolo '91	♼	4
● Barolo Classico '88	♼	5
● Barolo Classico '89	♼	5
● Barolo Classico Ris. '90	♼	5
● Barolo Liste '88	♼	6
● Barolo Liste '89	♼	6

BAROLO (CN)

GIACOMO BREZZA & FIGLI
VIA LOMONDO, 4
12060 BAROLO (CN)
TEL. 0173/56354-56191

BAROLO (CN)

MARCHESI DI BAROLO
VIA ALBA, 12
12060 BAROLO (CN)
TEL. 0173/56101

The Brezza family's activities have a certain importance for the economy of Barolo; they possess about 20 hectares of vineyards in the best cru zones (Cannubi, Sarmassa, Castellero, Cannubi Muscatel, San Lorenzo and Fossati, for example) and in addition have always managed the Brezza Hotel-Restaurant, soon to be improved with a swimming pool. The winery dates back to 1885 and was recently extended to provide more storage space for bottled wine-Brezza wines in fact need particularly long cellaring before they are ready to be released. On our last visit we were welcomed by young Enzo, who has been in charge of the winery for years and aims to maintain the best winemaking traditions of the Langhe as his trademark: clean, well defined wines with no woodiness, good structure and good ageing potential. We tasted an excellent Cannubi '93 with a bouquet of tobacco, fennel and cherries; full bodied and austere on the palate it should have a good future in front of it. Of the two Sarmassa '93 wines, the Bricco version, made with the grapes from the best sites, has more character (delicious spicy hints of liquorice and chocolate), while the other wine is more mature and a simpler wine. The Barbera Cannubi Muscatel '95 has only been bottled recently but the one characteristic that stands out is its elegance, while the Dolcetto San Lorenzo '96 is impressive for the deep colour and ample bouquet that is typical of the "terroir". Langhe Chardonnay '96, a beguilingly simple wine, finished complete malolactic fermentation and hence has aromas of ripe fruit and honey on the nose and is full bodied, smooth and well balanced on the palate.

It is to this winery's credit that it succeeds in giving all its most important wines the same unmistakable character. It is a subtle hallmark and it lies in a complex of nuances that emerges through repeated tasting, both in horizontal and vertical comparisons of different vintages and different crus. We always like the Barolos, which are particular good this year but can be relied on whatever the vintage. The Riserva '91 is full bodied and lively, starting with its garnet red colour; fully mature on the nose with hints of fruit distillate and liquorice; full and well balanced with a good firm follow through from nose to finish on the palate. Barolo '93 Coste di Rose is brighter but just as fully mature; plums and bitter cherries on the nose, multi-layered on the palate, long-finishing. The exemplary Cannubi Riserva '90, a symphony of elegance, character, liveliness and balance, has a dark garnet colour; hints of cloves, juniper and tobacco overlay a sweet jammyness on the nose; the power of the palate is impressive and very long. Barolo Le Lune is good value-for-money and good quality too; it shows how attractive the great wines of the Langhe can be when they are young. The long-awaited Cabernet Sauvignon Regret will not let the admirers of this grape variety down. Its concentration, fruit and firmness on the palate are representative of the variety at its best, but quite frankly, and fortunately in our opinion, the Barolos are much more exciting.

● Barbera d'Alba Cannubi Muscatel '95	♀♀	4
● Barolo Cannubi '93	♀♀	5
● Barolo Bricco Sarmassa '93	♀	5
● Barolo Sarmassa '93	♀	5
● Dolcetto d'Alba San Lorenzo '96	♀	3
○ Langhe Chardonnay '96	♀	3
● Barbera d'Alba Cannubi '93	♀♀	4
● Barolo Cannubi '90	♀♀	6
● Barolo Cannubi '91	♀♀	5
● Barolo Castellero Ris. '90	♀♀	6
● Barolo Sarmassa '91	♀♀	5
● Barolo Sarmassa Ris. '90	♀♀	6

● Barolo Cannubi Ris. '90	♀♀	6
● Barolo Coste di Rose '93	♀♀	5
● Barolo Ris. '90	♀♀	5
● Cabernet Sauvignon Regret '93	♀♀	5
● Barbaresco Creja '93	♀	5
● Barolo Le Lune '93	♀	4
● Dolcetto d'Alba Boschetti '96	♀	3
● Dolcetto d'Alba Madonna di Como '96	♀	3
○ Gavi di Gavi '96	♀	4
○ Moscato d'Asti '96	♀	3
● Dolcetto d'Alba Le Lune '96		3
● Barolo Estate Vineyard '90	♀♀♀	6
● Barolo di Barolo Estate Vineyard '91	♀♀	6

BAROLO (CN)

BARTOLO MASCARELLO
VIA ROMA, 15
12060 BAROLO (CN)
TEL. 0173/56125

Last year we described how traditional methods are staunchly upheld by this producer, so in line with the views of Bartolo Mascarello and his partner Alessandro Fantino we prefer not to pass judgement on their Barolo '93, which is being bottled as we go to press with this Guide. We will describe it next year. Meanwhile, we have noticed how the Barolo '92 has matured positively, showing once again that the fruit quality of Mascarello's wines can be good even in poor vintages. The wine is now much more together on the nose and the imbalance on the palate caused by harsh tannins has smoothed out; both flavour and follow through are now as they should be. San Lorenzo, lying partly in La Morra and partly in Barolo, is one of the best vineyards of the entire Langhe and is where Bartolo and Alessandro get the nebbiolo grapes for their Barolo and also where their rich and lively Barbera comes from. The Barbera is a deep garnet red colour, slightly dumb on the nose, but firm and full bodied on the palate with good acidity to back it up. The Dolcetto is made to be a lighter and more modern wine: pale ruby red colour, the bouquet of ripe berry fruit stands up to the vinosity well; not intended to be a big wine, but certainly well balanced.

BAROLO (CN)

PIRA
VIA VITTORIO VENETO, 1
12060 BAROLO (CN)
TEL. 0173/56247

Chiara Boschis does not conform to the popular image of a female winemaker. First of all, despite belonging to a family who have been involved in winemaking for ever, her origins are not on the land and she has not specifically studied winemaking. She has a degree in business studies, and up to a few years ago she had no idea of the radical change of life style that was in store for her. It was tasting great Barolos from vintages ancient and modern that converted her to a career in winemaking. Her family (they own Borgogno) enabled her to do something practical to realise her dream. With their help she revived the tiny Pira winery, taking over the cultivation of the two and a half hectares of vineyards in the heart of the cru Cannubi that belong to this historic estate. Chiara has a disarming willingness to learn; you soon understand that this is definitely not a hobby for her, but hard work spiced with trials and tribulations. If it was always likely that the Barolo Riserva '90 would turn out well, given the nature of the vintage and its long ageing before release, the '93 shows Chiara's real skill as a winemaker. It is not quite Three Glass standard, but it comes very close: dark garnet red colour; complex, soft and wild at the same time with hints of mint, earthiness and blackberry jam; on the palate the tannins are enveloped by firm fruit.

● Barbera d'Alba		
Vigna San Lorenzo '95	♟	4
● Dolcetto d'Alba '95	♟	4
● Barolo '83	♟♟♟	6
● Barolo '84	♟♟♟	6
● Barolo '85	♟♟♟	6
● Barolo '89	♟♟♟	6
● Barolo '88	♟♟	6
● Barolo '90	♟♟	6
● Barolo '91	♟	6
● Barolo '92	♟	5

● Barolo '93	♟♟	5
● Barolo Ris. '90	♟♟♟	6
● Barolo '90	♟	5

BAROLO (CN)

GIUSEPPE RINALDI
VIA MONFORTE, 3
12060 BAROLO (CN)
TEL. 0173/56156

BAROLO (CN)

LUCIANO SANDRONE
VIA ALBA, 57
12060 BAROLO (CN)
TEL. 0173/56239

"All the places were taken so we sat down on the wrong side". A line from Brecht may seem to have little to do with winemaking in the Langhe, but in fact it says something important about the need for critical awareness in making fundamental choices. Giuseppe Rinaldi's attitude to innovation is not one of unthinking rejection (in reality, there are two or three 225 litre barrels in his cellar) but is based rather on a stubborn search for whys-and-wherefores. His wines are the logical consequence of this outlook; they all spend a long time in wood, even the Dolcetto and the Freisa, which have nothing in common with run-of-the-mill semi-sparkling versions of these wines, and are all full of uncompromising big barrel bouquets ; dried flowers and spices for the Dolcetto; violets, dog roses and tarriness for the Barbera; an ethereal raspberry essence for the Freisa; juniper, hazelnuts, plums, bitter cherries in alcohol, cocoa and tarriness again for the Barolos. They are all difficult wines, dense, full of tannin and alcohol. Some labels carry the slightly polemical phrase " from our own vineyards" or the names of several crus together to underline the origins of the assemblage. We particularly liked the Freisa (long, dry, good follow through from nose to palate), the Barbera (concentrated fruit, touches of freshness and softness), and above all, the Barolo Brunate Le Coste (soft and velvety at first, then more robust and austere on the finish, for long ageing). The Dolcetto is lighter and thinner with violet tinges to its ruby red colour and characteristic vinosity. Rinaldi's other Barolo appears a little rough and aggressive.

This is a period of emancipation of winemaking methods for the top producers of the Langhe. Like many others, Luciano Sandrone is changing his perception of Barolo. Once known for making dense concentrated wines with the last drop of extract wrung out of them, he is now aiming to produce more youthful wines which are easier to like and suppler on the palate. These might have been natural characteristics of the '91 and '92 vintages, but now with the release of the '93 we are sure that the typology of the wine itself has changed. Sandrone's Barolo '93 has a bright garnet red colour, if a little lacking in depth, it is graceful and pleasingly complex on the nose with well defined notes of berry fruit; firm on the palate with good acidity, sweet tannins and good nose-to-finish follow through. The wine lacks that little extra complexity, which would otherwise give it more interest and better harmony. The Dolcetto, on the other hand, is a sound and vigorous wine: straight ruby red in colour, firm and broad on the palate, good strong balance between tannins and fruit. The Nebbiolo d'Alba Valmaggiore is one of the best in its category: deep colour, well defined nose with inviting floral bouquet, some surprises on the palate, attractive almond twist on the finish. All in all, these are good wines and they do fit into the new modernisation philosophy, even if it seems to us that Barolos should, by definition, be bigger wines than they are here.

● Barolo Brunate Le Coste '93	♟♟	5
● Langhe Freisa '95	♟♟	3
● Barbera d'Alba '95	♟	3
● Barolo Ravera San Lorenzo '93	♟	5
● Dolcetto d'Alba '95	♟	3
● Barolo '90	♟♟	6
● Barolo '91	♟♟	5
● Barolo Brunate '90	♟♟	5
● Barolo Brunate '91	♟♟	5
● Barolo Brunate '92	♟♟	5

● Dolcetto d'Alba '96	♟♟	3
● Nebbiolo d'Alba		
Valmaggiore '95	♟♟	4
● Barolo '93	♟	5
● Barolo '83	♟♟♟	6
● Barolo '84	♟♟♟	6
● Barolo Cannubi Boschis '85	♟♟♟	6
● Barolo Cannubi Boschis '86	♟♟♟	6
● Barolo Cannubi Boschis '87	♟♟♟	6
● Barolo Cannubi Boschis '89	♟♟♟	6
● Barolo Cannubi Boschis '90	♟♟♟	6
● Barolo Cannubi Boschis '88	♟♟	6
● Dolcetto d'Alba '95	♟♟	3
● Barolo Cannubi Boschis '91	♟	6

BAROLO (CN)

BAROLO (CN)

GIORGIO SCARZELLO & FIGLI
VIA ALBA, 29
12060 BAROLO (CN)
TEL. 0173/56170

SEBASTE
LOC. S. PIETRO DELLE VIOLE
12060 BAROLO (CN)
TEL. 0173/56266

"There is a little valley kissed by the first rays of sunlight in the morning...fertile slopes surround it, decorated with centuries-old rows of vines... and there, perched on the hill....the village of Barolo." If you are in the Langhe and, above all if you like wine, Barolo is one place you have to see. And if while you are there you visit Giorgio Scarzello you will see a small estate with vines on a grand cru site, Ciabot Merenda at Sarmassa. A charming family where Gemma, Giorgio's wife, would like to produce a Barbera in barrique like the wines that are making the reputations of their neighbours; and where Giorgio keeps quiet because he remembers the time when Barolo was criticised for tasting too much of wood. Three generations of vigneron winemakers, with the latest scion of the family at oenological school and already working in the winery, have built up a store of experience and know-how. They make a range of highly traditional wines, without their being in any way inferior, such as the Dolcetto, which is aromatic and vinous at the same time, violet-tinged, rich in extract, tannic and pleasantly bitter on the finish; or the Barbera, aged for a short time in wood, a bit lean but well balanced, fresh, long-finishing and richly fruity; or the Barolo, well defined, rich in alcohol, broad in flavour, medium weight, austerely tannic and with a long finish tasting of fruit preserved in spirit.

Donato Lanati, the consultant oenologist who has advised this winery for some time now , has perfected the Barolo Bussia '93, aiming to enhance the finesse that this celebrated vineyard site can confer without taking away any of the full bodied nature of true Barolo. The result is a top class wine: beginning with its lively colour and bouquet of ripe and attractive fruit, the youthfulness of the wine suggests that the nose will become even more complex and interesting with time; the palate is not as yet very mature, but it is extremely well balanced. The standard Barolo is a pleasing, well made wine. Naturally it reflects the character of the cru wine in a minor key but nevertheless, all the elements of a quality wine are there. The Bricco Viole is a barrique aged blend of nebbiolo and barbera typical of the Langhe which somehow misses the point; there are no particular defects, but it is not assertive enough for this type of wine and it seems only right to expect more from it. The Freisa is as attractive and well made as ever and is an example of easy-drinking vinosity that comes out best on the palate. The Arneis del Roero is a worthy follow up to last year's successful wine and is a better-than-average, unpretentious white wine; the floral nose is particularly attractive and it is well balanced on the palate.

● Barolo '93	♟♟	5
● Dolcetto d'Alba '96	♟♟	3
● Barbera d'Alba '96	♟	3
● Barolo Vigna Merenda '90	♟♟	5
● Barolo '91	♟	5
● Dolcetto d'Alba '95	♟	3

● Barolo Bussia '93	♟♟	5
● Barolo '93	♟	5
● Bricco Viole '93	♟	4
● Langhe Freisa '96	♟	2
○ Roero Arneis '96	♟	3
● Barolo Bussia '85	♟♟♟	6
● Barolo Bussia Ris. '84	♟♟♟	6
● Barolo Bussia '90	♟♟	6
● Barolo '90	♟	5
● Barolo Ris. '89	♟	5
● Bricco Viole '90	♟	4

BAROLO (CN)

TENUTA LA VOLTA
LOC. LA VOLTA, 13
12060 BAROLO (CN)
TEL. 0173/56168

BAROLO (CN)

ALDO VAJRA
VIA DELLE VIOLE, 25
LOC. VERGNE
12060 BAROLO (CN)
TEL. 0173/56257

The Riserva del Fondatore Barolo is a great wine. Work to ensure its success began in the vineyards with the selection of grapes from the least productive vines, maceration took place on the skins without regulation of the temperature but with frequent intervention to punch down the cap on the surface of the fermenting must. Finally the wine was left to mature in barrel for five years. The result is a garnet red Barolo, unrelentingly traditional in style, vigorous, almost over rich; hazelnuts, coffee, chocolate and prunes on the nose; concentrated, well balanced, long-finishing, austere, richly extracted, buoyed up with a high enough alcohol content to soften any polyphenolic astringencies. The rest of the range is at its usual high standard - very reliable, and above all, good value for money. The Barolo '93 shows the advantages of its vineyard altitude and soil composition on the nose; the Barbera is a serious wine without concession to modern tastes, containing good fruit and lively acidity; the Dolcetto begins smoothly, becomes tannic, then fresh and long-finishing; in our eyes, the Vendemmiaio (80 percent nebbiolo, 20 percent barbera) continues to be marred by a certain rusticity and is the least successful of all the range; the version presented this year has certainly not aged well. All in all, the future of this winery seems to be with its cru wines: the Riserva del Fondatore is an outstanding example and some of the Dolcettos still ageing in the cellars also confirm the point.

Aldo Vajra confirms his status as one of the best producers of Dolcetto in the region with an excellent Coste & Fossati: healthy ruby red, bright in colour and impenetrably opaque at the same time; full and complex bouquet with aromas ranging from berry fruit to almonds. Without being either too aggressive or too one dimensional and vinous on the palate, it is full bodied, not over tannic, long finishing, richly extracted and very enjoyable to drink. A good standard Dolcetto recently released will give pleasure for a few years to come. The Langhe Chardonnay '96 is fresh and attractive, clean and with a slight spritz on the tongue; this is deliberately made for early drinking, without too many complications from yeasts or woodiness. The Langhe Bianco is more complex; this is made of riesling, which has not yet developed the distinctive aromas of the variety, but is destined to improve over the next two or three years in a similar fashion to the first vintages of this successful and innovative white wine from the Langhe. The surprise, at least as far as packaging is concerned, is Vajra's Freisa, which with the '96 vintage has a new name, Kyè and a new artistically designed label. This is a powerful wine, structured and rich in extract, with a pleasant and typical bitter twist to the finish; it is one of the very finest dry, non-sparkling Freisas there is. The timetable for the release of the '93 Barolos means that we have only been able to taste the standard version which is elegant rather than powerful with a well defined but slightly woody nose: soft and easy to drink.

● Barolo Riserva del Fondatore '90	ΨΨ	6
● Barbera d'Alba Sup. Bricco delle Viole '95	Ψ	3
● Barolo '93	Ψ	5
● Dolcetto d'Alba Vigna La Volta '96		3
● Vendemmiaio '94		5
● Barbera d'Alba Sup. Bricco delle Viole '93	Ψ	3
● Barbera d'Alba Sup. Bricco delle Viole '94	Ψ	3
● Barolo Vigna La Volta '91	Ψ	4

● Barolo '93	ΨΨ	5
● Dolcetto d'Alba Coste & Fossati '96	ΨΨ	4
● Langhe Freisa Kyè '96	ΨΨ	5
○ Langhe Bianco '96	Ψ	4
○ Langhe Chardonnay '96	Ψ	3
● Barbera d'Alba Bricco delle Viole '93	ΨΨ	5
● Barolo Bricco delle Viole '91	ΨΨ	4
● Dolcetto d'Alba Coste & Fossati '95	ΨΨ	4
● Freisa delle Langhe '93	ΨΨ	4

BOCA (NO)

BRA (CN)

PODERE AI VALLONI
VIA TRAVERSAGNA
28010 BOCA (NO)
TEL. 0322/87332

CANTINE GIACOMO ASCHERI
VIA PIUMATI, 23
12042 BRA (CN)
TEL. 0172/412394

The Podere Ai Valloni from Boca is back in the Guide after an absence of a few years. It is a small, three-hectare estate owned by the Torinese lawyer Guido Sartorio and situated in the heart of the Monte Fenera Park just above the Boca Sanctuary itself. In this superb site looking out over the Sesia Valley viticulture has largely been given up in favour of forestry, but there are still some nebbiolo, croatina and vespolina vineyards for the production of Boca. The tiny quantities of wine, dedicated to Guido's wife Cristina, come in vintages of no more than 5,000 bottles and are made with scrupulous attention to detail and the explicit aim of creating a Great Red. The vineyards are run by Salvatore Follesa, a Sardinian immigrant to the hills of Novara who hands over only the best bunches of grapes from the harvest to the oenologist Armando Cordero. Cordero, one of Piedmont's finest winemakers, has at his disposal a tiny but well equipped cellar that is ideal for the production of serious red wines. The Boca we tasted was the '90, one of the best vintages this century. The result is a triumph, well-flagged by an opaque colour, already hinting strongly at this wine's potential. The bouquet may lack a little in elegance, but it is nonetheless austere and complex with marked aromas of ripe fruit and spices; good structure, very drinkable, full of extract and broad on the palate. The slightly tough final tannins are well balanced by the power of the wine and its long liquorice finish.

Matteo Ascheri, who is constantly engaged in refining his wines through vineyard experimentation, runs this family-owned winery with the valuable help of his mother Cristina and his sister Maria Teresa. The wide range of wines he makes comes from more than 25 hectares of vineyards spread over various communes in the Langhe and Roero. The Barolo Vigna Farina has a ruby red colour with just discernible orange-tinged edges, has faint hints of berry fruits and spices on the nose, good balance and medium weight palate, and an attractively dry finish. Both the Dolcettos, Vigna Sant'Anna and Vigna Nirane, have come out well. The first has a ruby red colour with purple edges, an easily likable nose of violets and pepper, and is well balanced and easy to drink. The second has violet edges to a ruby red colour, a more complex nose with hints of cherries, raspberries and cinnamon, and a firm grip on the palate with a bitter twist on the finish. The Rocca d'Auçabech is made from freisa grapes picked in the commune of Serralunga d'Alba: ruby red tending to garnet in colour, fruity nose enhanced by a spell in Allier oak barriques, full bodied with slightly evident acidity and tannins. Meanwhile, the experimental vineyard at Montelupa di Bra has provided its first vintage and, judging by first preliminary tastings, the results are very encouraging. The range finishes with two very correct wines: Arneis Cristina and Nebbiolo d'Alba Vigna San Giacomo.

● Boca '90	♟♟	5

● Barolo Vigna Farina '93	♟	5
● Dolcetto d'Alba Vigna Nirane '96	♟	3
● Dolcetto d'Alba Vigna S. Anna '96	♟	3
● Rocca d'Auçabech '93	♟	4
● Nebbiolo d'Alba S. Giacomo '95		3
○ Roero Arneis Cristina Ascheri '96		3
● Barolo '92	♀	4
● Barolo Vigna Farina '90	♀	5
● Barolo Vigna Farina '91	♀	5
● Bric Mileui '93	♀	4
● Verduno Pelaverga Costa dei Faggi '95	♀	3

CALAMANDRANA (AT)   CALOSSO (AT)

MICHELE CHIARLO
S.S. NIZZA-CANELLI
14042 CALAMANDRANA (AT)
TEL. 0141/75231

SCAGLIOLA
FRAZ. S. SIRO, 42
14052 CALOSSO (AT)
TEL. 0141/853183

Architecturally, from the outside, the building looks uninspiringly modern. Go inside the winery at Calamandrana however (there are two other wineries at Barolo and at Gavi), and the impression is completely different. The technologically-advanced equipment, the order, cleanliness, and the spaciousness of the entire complex are very impressive. Running through the wines in front of us we begin with the Barberas: the '95 combines finesse and completeness on the nose with full bodied balance on the palate; the '94 Valle del Sole cru has a fascinating and more complex nose and a firm grip on the palate. The red line-up includes the effortlessly elegant Barilot cuvée of nebbiolo and barbera with its bouquet of wood, liquorice and peppery spices, and very successful, full bodied follow through from nose to palate. The Countacc (barbera, nebbiolo and cabernet sauvignon) is as successful as usual, concentrated on the nose and displaying excellent structure. Picking wines from the classic range, and beginning with the Barolos, there is the standard version, which is attractive, long-finishing and reasonably full bodied. The Vigna Rionda displays a nice balance of elegance and power with concentrated and well-rounded fruit. The Cannubi is full bodied and elegant, well developed and intense in the finish. Finally, we get to the fascinating Cerequio, with its open, broad and ample bouquet and its rich, velvety, well balanced palate. The feature of this wine is the concentration and intensity of the fruit. Of the Gavis we tasted, the Fornaci di Tassarolo single vineyard selection proved to be the best. The Plenilunio (chardonnay, sauvignon and cortese) is very respectable. Equally correct are the Nivole Moscato and the excellent Extra Brut with its good nose and well developed bouquet, refreshing acidity and good structure.

"Vines are like women who know their worth and need to be wooed gently; perhaps this is the reason why a vigneron will love them more than any other type of crop he can make grow on his stubborn soil". This quotation from N. Guild sums up the philosophy of the Scagliola brothers who, not without some flight of fancy, have named their most important Moscato Volo di Farfalle ('Flight of the Butterfly') and introduced a pretty butterfly on the label to put tastes into pictures. Made from selected grapes, slightly late-picked, the wine is filtered just before bottling but not clarified: good depth of colour, broad and rich on the nose, fruity with a delicate muskiness, well defined and well balanced, full bodied and successful, long on the palate. The other Moscato is delicately fruity on the nose, but a little short and cloying. From 13 hectares of vineyards on the San Siro hillside come, amongst other things, a Barbera named SanSi, half of which is aged in new oak barriques after completing its malolactic fermentation: very typical nose, hints of ripe bitter cherries beneath attractive oak; full bodied, but with a nervy acidity that it is not yet balanced. Total production is 3,000 bottles. The Dolcetto Monferrato is not as good, but does have a certain tipicity: fresh and vinous bouquet, up-front and dry on the palate. The Chardonnay Casot dan Vian is a balanced wine, soft, fresh-tasting and full in the finish. The Cortese and the Barbera del Monferrato can best be described as correct, but they do not inspire.

● Barolo Cerequio '93	♆♆♆	6
● Barilot '94	♆♆	5
● Barolo Cannubi '93	♆♆	6
● Barolo Vigna Rionda '93	♆♆	5
● Countacc! '94	♆♆	5
○ Michele Chiarlo Extra Brut '93	♆♆	4
● Barbera d'Asti Sup. '95	♆	3
● Barbera d'Asti Sup. Valle del Sole '94	♆	4
● Barolo '93	♆	4
○ Gavi Fornaci di Tassarolo '94	♆	4
○ Monferrato Bianco Plenilunio '95	♆	4
○ Gavi Fornaci di Tassarolo '90	♉♉♉	5
● Barolo Cerequio '88	♉♉♉	6
● Barolo Cannubi '90	♉♉♉	6

○ Moscato d'Asti Volo di Farfalle '96	♆♆	3
● Barbera d'Asti SanSì '95	♆	4
○ Moscato d'Asti '96	♆	2*
○ Piemonte Chardonnay Casot dan Vian '96	♆	2
● Monferrato Dolcetto '96		2
● Barbera d'Asti SanSì '94	♉	3

CALOSSO (AT)

CANALE (CN)

TENUTA DEI FIORI
VIA VALCALOSSO, 3
REG. RODOTIGLIA
14052 CALOSSO (AT)
TEL. 0141/826938-966500

CASCINA CA' ROSSA
LOC. CASE SPARSE, 56
12043 CANALE (CN)
TEL. 0173/98348-98201

There is a lot going on at Tenuta dei Fiori; the house and the reception rooms are being renovated and the cellars are being extended too. Walter Bosticardo is preparing for the time when he will finally cease his activities selling agricultural products and turn all his energies to his vineyards and his wines. Behind the mask of the ready smile and the vigneron's cordiality there lies a firm determination not to be diverted from his goals. The magic whereby Walter made his Moscato, first refermenting it by the champagne method then enriching it with a drop of moscato "passito", speaks for itself. Just as wonderful is the unusual Gamba di Pernice, made from a rare and difficult variety rescued from oblivion with the planting of 4,000 rootstocks. The wine has good ageing potential and is already showing interesting maturation features: deep ruby red in colour, a spicy peppery bouquet with a grassy background, good structure and good definition. Barbera d'Asti Vigneto del Tulipano Nero is successful on the nose with hints of tarriness and plums and has an attractive vein of acidity and woodiness supported by the alcohol content. The Barbera d'Asti '94 with the unusual name of "is" has everything going for it: enhanced by maturation in oak, decorated with labels by the artist Erik Keller, it is very smooth on the nose where the oak gives way to hints of blackberries and bitter cherries; soft, well balanced, fresh and full bodied without being over-the-top. Chardonnay Vento is a well-behaved combination of fruit, acidity and alcohol with hints of apple and banana on the nose. Chardonnay Al Sole is pale gold in colour, elegantly floral on the nose with vanilla and spices in the background, soft and attractively full bodied this is a wine of distinct charm.

Angelo Ferrio came to our attention last year with a most attractive Arneis; now he is busily engaged in making a Roero that justifies the recently-acquired reputation of this DOC. This is where the Valmaggiore vineyard at Vezza comes in, purchased recently and planted with nebbiolo. Another hectare and a half just acquired on the superb hillside site of Santo Stefano, is again dedicated to the production of Piedmont's noble grape variety. These two vineyards account for little more than three and a half hectares of the estate's twelve hectare total and, since it is physically impossible to use machinery, they are entirely cultivated by hand by our agile vigneron - such is his determination to make a top quality red wine. The Arneis '96 is a good wine, but not as good as the previous vintage; in fact, it has provided the incentive for Angelo to consider making a cru wine in the future as well as a standard Arneis to guarantee a uniform level of quality. We will report on his final decision in the next Guide. The present Arneis has a pale straw yellow colour with greenish reflections and a bouquet of apples and camomile; medium weight, well balanced, good depth of flavour. A One Glass award also goes to the Birbét made from brachetto, which has an attractive bouquet of strawberries and roses, is medium-sweet on the palate and leaves the mouth refreshed with a delicate spritz.

● Barbera d'Asti is '94	♥♥	4
● Barbera d'Asti		
Vigneto del Tulipano Nero '95	♥	3
○ Chardonnay Al Sole '95	♥	4
○ Chardonnay Il Vento '96	♥	2*
● Gamba di Pernice '95	♥	4
● Barbera d'Asti		
Vigneto del Tulipano Nero '94	♀	3
○ Chardonnay Al Sole '94	♀	3
○ Pensiero '91	♀	5

● Birbét Dolce '96	♥	3
○ Roero Arneis '96	♥	3

CANALE (CN)

CANALE (CN)

CASCINA CHICCO
VIA VALENTINO, 144
12043 CANALE (CN)
TEL. 0173/979069

MATTEO CORREGGIA
VIA S. STEFANO ROERO, 124
12043 CANALE (CN)
TEL. 0173/978009

Enrico and Marco Faccenda's winery shows tangible signs of consistently high standards, even if the quality curve is flat. Production has already reached 80,000 bottles per year, half of which is white wine. This year the whites have proved equally successful as the '95s. The real news is the production of the Barbera d'Alba Loira , thanks to the acquisition of three hectares of new vineyards in the Castellinaldo area. On the nose this is an up-front and generous wine, full of the aromas of raspberries, redcurrants and ripe cherries combined with delicate hints of barrique wood; full bodied and well balanced on the palate, good structure with a pleasant bitter twist to the tannins. Roero Valmaggiore '95, aged in barrique for the first time, is generous with its intense and long-lasting bouquet of violets, liquorice and roasted coffee; the tannins are still a little harsh on the palate, but good structure and full body give it length. Going on to the whites, the Favorita '96 has a delicate bouquet of ripe citrus fruit and bananas, on the palate it is markedly full flavoured and dry; an attractive wine with a bitter twist to its finish. The elegant and entirely typical Arneis '96 is just as good, with its well defined bouquet of hazelnuts and peaches, sound structure and firm and fresh palate and attractive almondy aftertaste. Lastly, the brachetto-based Birbét Dolce has a soft and aromatic bouquet with characteristic hints of roses and raspberries; sweet and light on the palate without a trace of sharpness.

Matteo Correggia's two finest wines are, as usual, quite superb in their power and elegance and it is no surprise that this year again the Barbera Bricco Marun and Nebbiolo La Val dei Preti have come out at the highest level in our tastings. The first wine has an opaque garnet/ruby red colour with firm youthful edges. On the nose it has a multi-layered sumptuous complexity of its own, constantly evolving in the glass; aromas of black cherries and violets are interwoven with hints of menthol, coffee and sweet spices in a masterly composition. On the palate the broad, full bodied structure is stiffened with such an extract of fruit brightened with hints of coffee and liquorice that the finish goes on for ever. The second wine has a deep ruby red colour, a full bouquet with tinges of berry fruit and plums, coffee essence and spices, with a faint touch of woodiness from the barrel. Firm and rich on the palate, broad and well structured with a rich finish adorned by noble tannins. The standard Roero and Barbera wines are very good. The first has a sweet bouquet of raspberries, freshly-picked mint and vanilla; it is full bodied, rounded and well balanced. The second is graced with a deep colour, full flavoured and firm with a good nose of fruit, vanilla and spices. The dry Anthos made from brachetto, is always good. Last on the list is a charming and easily-drinkable Arneis. A piece of news to finish with: Matteo and his wife Ornella (otherwise known as the indispensable office administrator) have bought three and a half hectares of splendidly- sited vineyards in the Rocche di Canale area planted with nebbiolo.

● Barbera d'Alba Bric Loira '95	▼	4
● Birbét Dolce '96	▼	3
○ Langhe Favorita '96	▼	3
○ Roero Arneis '96	▼	3
● Roero Valmaggiore '95	▼	4
● Birbét Secco '96		3

● Barbera d'Alba		
Bricco Marun '95	▼▼▼	4
● Nebbiolo d'Alba		
La Val dei Preti '95	▼▼	4
● Anthos '96	▼	3
● Barbera d'Alba '96	▼	3
● Roero '96	▼	3
○ Roero Arneis '96		3
● Barbera d'Alba		
Bricco Marun '94	♀♀♀	4
● Nebbiolo d'Alba		
La Val dei Preti '93	♀♀♀	4
● Barbera d'Alba '95	♀	3
● Roero '95	♀	3

CANALE (CN)

CARLO DELTETTO
C.SO ALBA, 43
12043 CANALE (CN)
TEL. 0173/979383

A greater area of vineyards producing the same amount of wine as last year indicates low yields are the order of the day and reflect Antonio Deltetto's desire to improve the quality of his wines even further. In fact, four new hectares of vineyards have been acquired at Vezza and at Castellinaldo to add to the 14 that are already estate-owned or rented. More equipment in the cellars has allowed Antonio to spend more time in the vineyards, thanks to an increased rapidity in the vinification and bottling processes. We begin our survey of the wines with the Roero Arneis San Michele, which is as excellent this year as it was last. Pale straw yellow with greenish reflections, fresh citrus fruit aromas combined with hints of banana and boiled sweets with tinges of vanilla in the background. Full bodied and well supported with a good dose of acidity; a long finish combines smoothness with a faint bitter twist. The Roero Madonna dei Boschi '95 gets a One Glass award with its ruby red tending-to-garnet colour and its delicate berry fruit, coffee and spices nose; long and attractive on the palate. The Favorita San Michele is always a pleasure: pale in colour, up-front and fruity on the nose with hints of aniseed; easy to drink and with good grip on the palate. The standard Arneis has tones of citrus fruit and fennel on a fruity bouquet and is well balanced and easy to like, a charming and fresh-tasting wine. To finish the list of wines, there is the correct Barbera Bramé.

CANALE (CN)

FUNTANIN SPERONE
VIA TORINO, 191
12043 CANALE (CN)
TEL. 0173/979488

Bruno and Piercarlo Sperone are two young, enthusiastic vignerons whose pleasure in their work comes out when they talk about their winery, their passion for winemaking, and how they taste wines from all over the world and, when they can, visit these areas abroad to compare notes. The range of their wines reflects their enthusiasm; these are quality products, technically well made and with real personality. The pick of the bunch is the Roero Arneis Pierin di Soc '96, which showed commendably: pale straw yellow, full and elegant on the nose with aromas of peaches, apricots, wild flowers and cedar wood; full bodied and firm on the palate with a tautness that refreshes the long, smooth finish. The Roero has a ruby red colour with clear edges and a fruity nose with hints of blackberries and ripe raspberries, violets and vanilla. Good structure and firm on the palate; long finish with lively tannins at the end. The Favorita is also a success: pale straw yellow with greenish reflections; attractive boiled sweet and banana bouquet and hint of woodiness; full flavoured and well balanced on the palate. The standard Arneis has good varietal character but lacks that final touch of finesse on the nose; it is redeemed by its balance and easy drinkability.

○ Roero Arneis S. Michele '96	♈♈	3
● Barbera d'Alba Bramè '95	♈	3
○ Langhe Favorita S. Michele '96	♈	3
○ Roero Arneis '96	♈	3
● Roero Madonna dei Boschi '95	♈	3

○ Langhe Favorita '96	♈	3
● Roero '95	♈	4
○ Roero Arneis Pierin di Soc '96	♈	3
○ Roero Arneis '96		2

CANALE (CN)

CANALE (CN)

FILIPPO GALLINO
FRAZ. VALLE DEL POZZO, 63
12043 CANALE (CN)
TEL. 0173/98112

MALVIRÀ
VIA S. STEFANO ROERO, 144
12043 CANALE (CN)
TEL. 0173/978057-978145

Filippo Gallino's estate finds its place into the Guide thanks to the constant improvements of recent years. The Gallino family have been vignerons for several generations and began to bottle their own Arneis back in 1972. Currently their bottled wine production stands at about 30,000 units per year, of which 10,000 are Arneis, and the remainder are made from barbera, nebbiolo and brachetto. Filippo, his wife Maria, and son Gianni, personally look after the seven hectares of vineyards and the technologically well equipped winery. The Roero Superiore '95 is, without doubt, the most successful of their wines: standard ruby red in colour, full and up front aromas of violets, vanilla, sweet spices and jam on the nose; firm, full bodied and broad on the palate with soft tannins. The next wine is the Barbera d'Alba Superiore '95 with its beautiful, deep, ruby red colour, and powerful bouquet which combines a slight toastiness with predominant aromas of bitter cherries, blackberries and ripe plums; on the palate it is particularly full bodied and smooth, with good extract, soft tannins, and a long finish. The Arneis '96 is clean and well defined on the nose with slight notes of pineapple and toasted bread; good structure is marred by a touch of bitter astringency, due perhaps to the day-long criomaceration. Lastly, a Birbét Dolce worth a mention: good varietal character and easy to drink with a palate which follows up well on the aromatic brachetto bouquet.

Roberto and Massimo Damonte are tireless in their efforts to make the most balanced wines possible. Experimentation in the cellars, for example, is not merely technological support, it is a challenge to be met with passion. Roberto's enthusiasm as he leads us around the barriques armed with tasting glasses is contagious, and all the more so because the results this year are better than ever. We have no hesitation in giving the Roero Superiore '95 a Two Glass award. It is a wine of distinction with a ruby red colour, full blown bouquet of raspberries, redcurrants, vanilla and coffee; full bodied but never blowsy, with a good tannic backbone to the structure and a rich and attractively dry finish. Its little brother, the Renesio, is soft and velvety on the palate, while the bouquet has delicate hints of raspberries and ripe berry fruit. The Saglietto is the top Arneis: hints of apricot, vanilla and nutmeg on the nose; soft and full bodied on the palate; long, rich in flavour and broad on the finish. The other two cru Arneis, Trinità and Renesio, are not quite as good. The white wine selection finishes with a pleasant Favorita and an interesting vino da tavola aged in barrique called Tre Uve. The latter is an excellent example of a Piedmontese assemblage of arneis, sauvignon, and chardonnay and constitutes a serious white wine, both for its bouquet and for its palate: almost golden straw yellow, rich and smooth to taste, with hints of toasted wood on the finish that will blend in with time. In contrast, the San Gugliemo is an assemblage of barbera, nebbiolo and bonarda which still needs time to round out completely, while the Birbét is a sweet wine made from brachetto with attractive flavours of fruit and roses.

● Roero Sup. '95	♚♚	4
● Barbera d'Alba Sup. '95	♚	3*
● Birbét Dolce '96		3
○ Roero Arneis '96		3

○ Langhe Tre Uve '95	♚♚	4
○ Roero Arneis Saglietto '96	♚♚	3
● Roero Renesio '95	♚♚	4
● Roero Superiore '95	♚♚	4
● Birbét Dolce '96	♚	3
○ Langhe Favorita '96	♚	3
● Langhe S. Guglielmo '95	♚	4
○ Roero Arneis Renesio '96	♚	3
○ Roero Arneis Trinità '96	♚	3
● Roero Superiore '90	♚♚♚	5
● Roero Superiore '93	♚♚♚	4
○ Roero Arneis Saglietto '95	♚♚	3
● Roero Renesio '94	♚♚	4
● Roero Superiore '94	♚♚	4

CANALE (CN)

CANALE (CN)

MONCHIERO CARBONE
VIA S. STEFANO ROERO, 2
12043 CANALE (CN)
TEL. 0173/95568

MARCO E ETTORE PORELLO
C.SO ALBA, 71
12043 CANALE (CN)
TEL. 0173/978080

Marco Monchiero is an experienced oenologist whose style can best be described as traditional with useful bits of modernity thrown in. His production technique has the aim of making balanced wines, starting with a technologically well equipped cellar, but not forgetting the essential element of great winemaking: vineyards managed to produce the best quality raw material. Our guide in the winery visit is Marco and Lucia Carbone's son, Francesco, who has just graduated as an oenologist from the school at Alba. In the tiny winery there is a line-up of barriques made by different coopers from variously-sourced woods which are used for the ageing of the most important wines. Sometimes different woods are used for the wines from the same vineyards in order to find the combinations best suited to the wine's character and the wood's potential before the final assemblage. This research project requires great determination, but provides valuable information on how things can be done better, both in the cellars and the vineyards. One result so far is the very successful Roero Superiore '95, which gains the Two Glass award: beautiful, ruby red colour, fascinating hints of raspberries, coffee essence and menthol on the nose; well structured on the palate, full bodied without being blowsy; rich and fruity on the finish. The Barbera MonBirone is also a success: deep ruby red colour; hints of blackberries, violets and liquorice on the nose with underlying barrel woodiness; not excessively powerful on the palate, but remarkable for its excellent balance. The first vintage of a white wine called Tamardi and made from a blend of chardonnay with 25 percent arneis shows a bouquet somewhat dominated by wood and a palate of average power. In conclusion, the Roero Arneis is very decent everyday drinking.

In the last edition of the Guide, Ettore and Marco's estate came to prominence above all thanks to an excellent Arneis. This year's successes inevitably include some red wines too, particularly the Roero and the Barbera. To confirm the good impressions made by the wines in bottle we went to the cellars, where we found ourselves in the midst of work being carried out to build new premises for red wine production. Marco told us about other investments, in vineyards planted with barbera and nebbiolo vines that formerly had been rented, and in barriques that were used in the cellars for the first time with the '95 vintage. Their effect was immediately obvious with the Barbera d'Alba Bric Torretta, where a sweet spiciness and hints of toasted nuts enrich the fruity bouquet; the tannins are soft and well supported by big structure; the finish has a faint undertow of black liquorice to it. The bouquet of the Roero Bric Torretta '95 shows the effect of small oak too, but not so much that the other aromas of flowers and fern-like undergrowth are overwhelmed; full bodied and full of flavour on the palate with a smooth vanilla aftertaste. We thought the Arneis Vigneto Camestri '96 was not quite as good; it lacked the excellent bouquet of the previous vintage's wine, and was a bit harsh in acidity on the palate. Lastly, the dry Birbét is a soft and well built wine, but the bouquet is a little tired.

●	Barbera d'Alba MonBirone '95	♟♟	3
●	Roero Superiore '95	♟♟	4
○	Langhe Tamardì '95	♟	4
○	Roero Arneis '96		3
●	Roero '94	♟♟	4
●	Barbera d'Alba MonBirone '94	♟	3

●	Barbera d'Alba Bric Torretta '95	♟	3
●	Roero Bric Torretta '95	♟	3
●	Birbét Secco '96		2
○	Roero Arneis		
	Vigneto Camestrì '96		3

CANDIA CANAVESE (TO)

MASSIMO PACHIÉ
VIA ROMA, 1
10010 CANDIA CANAVESE (TO)
TEL. 0125/641176 - 011/9834549

The Colombaio di Candia e Castiglione vineyard belongs to the antique dealer Massimo Pachié and has been developed over the years by Luigi Ferrando, who uses it to supply the grapes for a very singular, full bodied version of Erbaluce di Caluso. Luigi has always known where to find the best grapes in this part of Piedmont and has been a proponent of this particular Erbaluce del Colombaio di Candia since the early 1980s; in fact, he continues to be involved both in its production and in its marketing. The three hectare vineyard is in an excellent position at the foot of the castle of San Giorgio Canavese, facing Lake Candia. In a normal year - not '96, when hail swept away almost all the crop - production reaches about 20,000 bottles. The new vintage has a deep straw yellow colour; the bouquet is typical for the grape; not so much fruity and intense as yeasty and full of the aromas of nuts and bread crusts; on the palate it still suffers from an aggressive acidity, but is also full bodied and decidedly long; all in all, this is a white wine made to last.

○	Erbaluce di Caluso Colombaio di Candia '96	🍷	3
○	Erbaluce di Caluso Colombaio di Candia '95	🍸	3

CANELLI (AT)

GIUSEPPE CONTRATTO
VIA G. B. GIULIANI, 56
14053 CANELLI (AT)
TEL. 0141/823349

"New shot, new number" is the croupier's cry at the dice table for the beginning of a new game. The Contratto company changed hands two years ago, and the new dice-throwers are the new owners, Antonella and Carlo Bocchino; so far it looks as if they are doing well. Metaphors apart, the new management is working hard on the winery. On the one hand they are renovating the old buildings intelligently with one eye on function and the other on aesthetics, and rationalising the structure of the winery with its underground sparkling wine cellars excavated for some way into the hillside. On the other hand, they are making wines with more personality. This year's news is the Asti De Miranda, one of the very few moscatos in the region to be vinified in the Metodo Classico. This is an Asti of great character, full of flavour and elegant, with the sweetness counterbalanced by healthy acidity. Still in the sparkling wine sector, the vintage Riserva Giuseppe Contratto is a textbook success. Full and elegant on the nose, with aromas of honey and dry biscuits, combined with a delicious, lively yeastiness; broad, charming and long on the palate. The red wines include one called Solus Ad (named after D'Annunzio's "Solus ad Solam"), made from barbera grapes from old vines on high hillside sites, and aged in new oak barriques : deep garnet red colour; mature, broad, and well developed bouquet; the palate reflects the nose and shows a wine with a good fruit and wood balance and full body. Barolo Tenuta Secolo comes from the prestigious Cerequio vineyard and, in the '93 version, has a nose barely tinged with vanilla and rich fruit: tannic without being austere on the palate, broad and deeply flavoured; long and intense on the finish.

○	Asti De Miranda Metodo Classico '95	🍷🍷	4
●	Barbera d'Asti Solus Ad '95	🍷🍷	5
●	Barolo Cerequio Tenuta Secolo '93	🍷🍷	6
○	Spumante Metodo Classico Brut Ris. Giuseppe Contratto '90	🍷🍷	5
●	Barbera d'Asti Solus Ad '90	🍸🍸	5
●	Barolo Cerequio Tenuta Secolo '90	🍸🍸	6
○	Spumante Metodo Classico Brut Ris. '89	🍸🍸	5
●	Barbera d'Asti Solus Ad '93	🍸	4
●	Barolo Cerequio Tenuta Secolo '92	🍸	6

CANELLI (AT)

CANELLI (AT)

LUIGI COPPO & FIGLI
VIA ALBA, 66
14053 CANELLI (AT)
TEL. 0141/823146

GANCIA
C.SO LIBERTÀ, 66
14053 CANELLI (AT)
TEL. 0141/8301

The Asti area must not be forgotten: there are producers in Asti who are less famous but just as exciting as their brethren in the celebrated Langhe on the other side of the river Tanaro. True, everyone is familiar with Moscato, but the respect given to a great wine like Barbera d'Asti is still not enthusiastic enough. The Coppo brothers have always believed in it and make a range of Barbera with different characteristics to suit different tastes. Results have already been very positive, but experimentation, above all with the use of oak, is one of the features of the qualitative development of this estate. Continual research is being made into cellar techniques to make wines with more fruit and to complement the fruit with the oak rather than overwhelm it, which seems to be what making barrique-aged Barbera has been all about in recent years. The Pomorosso is typical: the toastiness of the nose is restrained, the wine is full-bodied and complex with aromas of cherries and blackberries; intriguing and stylish on the palate, well knit together and long finishing. The Barbera Camp du Rouss is a big, up-front wine; but well-balanced and soft on the palate despite the freshness of the fruit. The Mondaccione is a Freisa of great character, harmony and depth; while the Chardonnay Monteriolo is a sure-fire winner: deep and rich on the nose, full-bodied on the palate, all-enveloping, a wine with many facets. The Coste Bianche is a simpler wine, but full-bodied and elegant at the same time. We finish with a rarity that is produced only in the best years, the Piero Coppo Brut: delicate and continuous perlage; broad, well-developed and fruity bouquet with hints of oak and hazelnuts; full-bodied and well-rounded on the palate with an excellent balance of fruit and acidity.

Gancia, with its 15 million bottles of still and sparkling wine produced every year, is one of the most famous Italian wine producers in the world. The wines we sampled for this edition of the Guide show the importance of Italian sparkling wines, and particularly sparkling wines from Canelli. For the first time we tasted the Mon Grande Cuvée Riserva '92. This is a Cuvée Speciale made from chardonnay grown on the Canelli hills and elaborated according to the Metodo Tradizionale Classico first adopted by the Gancia family in 1865. Barrel fermentation and long contact with the lees gives this sparkling wine a finesse and a multi-faceted richness. The colour is a deep straw yellow and the bouquet is very clean, with a balanced toastiness and well-defined aromas of hazelnuts and spices; powerful and full-bodied on the palate with good acidity balanced by weight. The finish is broad and well-balanced, the aftertaste clean and dry with a final pleasant bitter almond twist. The standard Mon Grande Cuvée is a comfortable One Glass award winner and is less aristocratic, but very fresh and drinkable all the same. Excellent as usual, the Asti Atto Primo which has a good aromatic nose, very typical of the moscato grape, and is broad, sweet and well-balanced on the palate. Barolo Cannubi Ca' dei Gancia '93, another one of the company's flagship wines, was still in the process of ageing when the Guide went to press; so it will be evaluated next year.

● Barbera d'Asti Pomorosso '94	♀♀	5
○ Piemonte Chardonnay Monteriolo '95	♀♀	5
○ Piero Coppo Brut Ris. del Fondatore '86	♀♀	6
● Barbera d'Asti Camp du Rouss '95	♀	4
● Mondaccione '94	♀	4
○ Piemonte Chardonnay Costebianche '96	♀	3
● Barbera d'Asti Pomorosso '90	♀♀♀	5
○ Metodo Classico Ris. Coppo '91	♀♀	5
● Barbera d'Asti Camp du Rouss '94	♀	4
● Barbera d'Asti Pomorosso '93	♀	5
○ Chardonnay Monteriolo '94	♀	5

○ Mon Grande Cuvée Ris. '92	♀♀	6
○ Asti Atto Primo	♀	3
○ Mon Grande Cuvée	♀	4
● Barolo Cannubi Ca' dei Gancia '92	♀♀	6
○ Vintage dei Gancia '91	♀♀	5

CAREMA (TO)

CANTINA DEI PRODUTTORI NEBBIOLO DI CAREMA
VIA NAZIONALE, 28
10010 CAREMA (TO)
TEL. 0125/811160

In places such as Carema it is no exaggeration to talk about heroic viticulture. Certainly climatic conditions can make it difficult to produce great wines. After the fabled vintages of the 1980s: '88, '89 and '90 when the Cantina Produttori consistently scored top marks in tastings, in recent years the north-east part of Piedmont, and the Canavese area in particular, has had to contend with some tough years. In '91 and '92 the top white label Carema Carema cuvée was not even produced, and even the standard Carema was made in reduced quantities of only a few thousand bottles. The '92 tasted this year shows how hard this historic cooperative had to work to overcome the difficulties of the vintage. The wine has a bright red colour with faint brick-red edges; quite closed on the nose, but with clean aromas of ripe fruit in the background; medium weight and attractive, very drinkable and enhanced by a good, firm tannic backbone. The wine is a good result for a cooperative with the important social function of making viticulture possible in the area.

●	Carema '92	🍷	2
●	Carema Carema '90	YY	3
●	Carema '91	Y	3

CASTAGNOLE LANZE (AT)

LA SPINETTA
VIA ANNUNZIATA, 17
14054 CASTAGNOLE LANZE (AT)
TEL. 0141/877396

Giorgio Rivetti's wines always do well in blind tastings, and yet again this year he presents us with a series of top class wines, particularly the Pin, which gains Three Glasses once more. Dolcetto San Rumu comes out for its last vintage with the '96, now that the vineyard has been replanted with nebbiolo: attractive, aromatic and vinous, full bodied and easy to drink. By contrast, the production of Barbera d'Asti Ca' di Pian will actually increase in the future. This wine currently shows a very balanced use of barrique. Ten months' ageing succeeds in smoothing out any harsh acidity with the vanilla sweetness of new wood without compromising the fruit. The character of the Chardonnay Lidia is becoming better defined every year; Rivetti aims to enhance the aromatic qualities of the variety without making it too big and fat a wine, unlike many of its counterparts in the Langhe. The '96 seems very successful. It has an intense nose of deliciously ripe fruit and comes across very elegant on the palate at the same time. Moscatos of various types account for the bulk of La Spinetta's production, and the Moscato Bricco Quaglia emerges as one of the best of its type: clean, aromatic typicity on the nose; rich and full flavoured on the palate. The Pin is made of 50 percent nebbiolo and 25 percent each of cabernet and barbera; here it gets Three Glasses in one of its best ever versions: very impressive, deep, dark ruby red colour; broad, spicy, berry fruit nose; full bodied with good structure and balance which guarantees long ageing, not that it is not a pleasure to drink now.

●	Monferrato Rosso Pin '95	🍷🍷🍷	5
●	Barbera d'Asti Ca' di Pian '96	🍷🍷	3
○	Moscato d'Asti Bricco Quaglia '96	🍷🍷	3
○	Piemonte Chardonnay Lidia '96	🍷🍷	5
●	Dolcetto d'Alba S. Rumu '96	🍷	3
●	Monferrato Rosso Pin '94	YYY	5
○	Moscato d'Asti Bricco Quaglia '88	YYY	4
●	Pin '90	YYY	6
●	Pin '93	YYY	5
○	Piemonte Chardonnay Lidia '95	YY	4
●	Pin '92	YY	5

CASTAGNOLE MONFERRATO (AT)

MARCO MARIA CRIVELLI
VIA VITTORIO EMANUELE, 16
14030 CASTAGNOLE MONFERRATO (AT)
TEL. 0141/292533-292357

Viticulture has ancient origins in this part of the Monferrato and the vineyard-decorated hills are very pretty, but despite the obvious potential provided by sites, micro-climate and vine varieties alike, improvements have been slow in coming. One of the few interesting producers of the area, Marco Maria Crivelli's small winery owns about four hectares planted with barbera, grignolino and ruché making about 20,000 bottles per year. He has been active in Castagnole Monferrato for some years, displaying undeniable skill and enthusiasm in the management of his vineyards and traditional grape varieties. Beginning with the Grignolino '96, this has quite a pale colour, a clean and sound nose typical of the grape variety, but it is somewhat thin and aggressive on the palate and dominated by harsh acidity. We did not have the opportunity to taste the Barbera d'Asti Superiore this year, so we had to make do with the Monferrato Vivace '96; full of froth and colour, fresh on the nose and very drinkable, excellent for rustic picnics based on salami and Spanish omelettes. The Ruché di Castagnole Monferrato '96 comes right from this zone (the DOC is named after it) and is at the height of fame and fashion; good clear ruby red tending to garnet red colour, firm spices and pepper nose, very long and lively, good palate supported by acidity and a bitter twist on an aromatic finish. Food pairing is not easy with this wine, but try a drop with a good Gorgonzola for an intriguing and unusual combination.

●	Ruché di Castagnole Monferrato '96	▼▼	4
●	Barbera del M.to Agiuiusa Vivace '96		2
●	Grignolino d'Asti '96		3
●	Ruché di Castagnole Monferrato '95	▽▽	4
●	Barbera d'Asti Sup. '93	▽	3
●	Barbera d'Asti Sup. '94	▽	3

CASTELLINALDO (CN)

TEO COSTA
VIA S. SERVASIO, 1
12050 CASTELLINALDO (CN)
TEL. 0173/213066

Teo Costa's winery comes back to the Guide after a one year interlude. This is a family winery ably run by Roberto, who aims to get the best from the winery's own grapes. Together with ten or so other vignerons from Castellinaldo, Roberto Costa has founded the Associazione dei Vinaioli di Castellinaldo and started a group project for the improvement of quality. This enthusiastic little group works not only to sell its own wine, but also to spread the word about the quality of food and wine from the whole Castellinaldo district. One of their strategies for success has been to adopt a common bottle for the entire group, with the words "Vinaioli di Castellinaldo" on the neck. Then they opened the Cantina Comunale where you can taste wines from the zone, and they are also amongst the first to have gained official recognition for a new sub-denomination in the Barbera d'Alba DOC. And in fact it is exactly this, the Barbera d'Alba Castellinaldo from the '95 vintage, that is the best wine from Teo Costa this year. This is a very good red wine that has had well judged wood ageing: garnet red, not the deepest but very bright, fresh aromas of ripe fruit well integrated with the toastiness of the wood; not as big in structure as a Barbera from the Langhe on the palate, but a fine elegant wine with ripe, almost sweet fruit, lifted by strong acidity and firm body. The other wines are just as good: the Roero Arneis Vigneto Serramiana is attractive, fresh and fruity with a slightly sweet touch to the finish, and Roero Superiore Vigneto Batajot is not a huge wine, but well balanced on the palate.

●	Castellinaldo Barbera d'Alba '95	▼▼	4
○	Roero Arneis Vigneto Serramiana '96	▼	3
●	Roero Sup. Vigneto Batajot '94		4

CASTELLINALDO (CN)

CASTELLO DI ANNONE (AT)

EMILIO MARSAGLIA
VIA MUSSONE, 2
12050 CASTELLINALDO (CN)
TEL. 0173/213048

VIARENGO & FIGLIO
VIA ROMA, 88
14034 CASTELLO DI ANNONE (AT)
TEL. 0141/401131

Marina and Emilio Marsaglia continue to work on their vinification techniques year after year in the search for perfection. The results are commendable and some of their wines have distinguished themselves again in our tastings this year. In our opinion the least successful wine was the Roero Arneis Serramiana which this year, unlike other vintages, has had a spell in wood. In our view this unbalances it; the wood is too invasive for a wine that appears a little short of fruit in the first place. The Roero Arneis '96, however, is very attractive; this is a wine that is not based on power but on freshness and intense fruitiness. Straw yellow in colour, with a bouquet of wild flowers, aniseed and cedar wood; clean, up-front and full flavoured on the palate, with just the right touch of green youthfulness to lift the finish. Barbera di Castellinaldo '95 is a bigger wine than the previous vintage, but it still lacks the power to compete with the best Barberas of the Langhe; it scores on finesse and elegance rather than weight or structure. The same can be said for the Roero Superiore '96; again this wine is fuller and more attractive than the '95 : intense bouquet, well balanced on the palate, good grip and taut structure.

The disappearance of Paolo Dania from the scene does not seem to have changed this company's production philosophy. It is true that the wines we tasted this year still bear the mark of Dania's expert touch, but the Viarengo family do not intend any break with existing strategies. The cellars of the castle of Annone have built up a solid reputation in recent years for wines of character that are above all reliable. In fact, even when vintages have been difficult, such as in '94 and '95, selective harvesting and good cellar techniques have resulted in wines of an encouraging standard. One such is the Barbera d'Asti Il Falé, which gains a deserved Two Glass rating: a slighter wine than normal, it is still complex, broad on the palate and elegant. Ruby red tending to garnet red of average intensity; oak well integrated in a delicate bouquet of fruit and flowers; almondy overtones and a healthy vinosity to complete the picture; well balanced on the palate, attractive finish. Certainly, the '90 had a bit more fruit, but even in off vintages Il Falé keeps its charm intact. Grignolino Della Tagliata '96 is well made, piquant and lively, the best vintage ever: typical orangey pink colour with a bouquet of berry fruit and spices, up-front and easy to like; good acidity on the palate supporting a good length of finish. Barbera Mora '96 is a simple, rustic wine, fulfilling the potential of a promising vintage. Gavi Alvise is light and enjoyable, better than last year's version, as is the Dolcetto d'Alba.

● Roero Sup. '96	♥♥	3
● Castellinaldo Barbera d'Alba '95	♥	4
○ Roero Arneis '96	♥	3
● Roero Sup. '95		3
● Castellinaldo Barbera d'Alba '94	♀	4

● Barbera d'Asti Sup. Il Falé '95	♥♥	4
● Barbera d'Asti Bricco Morra '96	♥	3
● Grignolino d'Asti Della Tagliata '96	♥	3
● Dolcetto d'Alba '96	♥	3
○ Gavi Alvise '96	♥	3
● Barbera d'Asti Sup. Il Falé '94	♀♀	4
● Barbera d'Asti Sup. Il Falé '93	♀♀	4
● Barbera d'Asti Sup. Il Falé Ris.'90	♀♀	4
● Barbera d'Asti Bricco Morra '95	♀	2

CASTELNUOVO DON BOSCO (AT)   CASTIGLIONE FALLETTO (CN)

GILLI
VIA NEVISSANO, 36
14022 CASTELNUOVO
DON BOSCO (AT)
TEL. 011/9876984

AZELIA
VIA ALBA-BAROLO, 27
12060 CASTIGLIONE FALLETTO (CN)
TEL. 0173/62859

Gianni Vergnano's well equipped and very functional winery turns out about 100,000 bottles of good quality wine every year. The estate-owned vineyards lie next to the beautiful farmhouse winery and are planted with the classic varieties for the area: freisa, malvasia and bonarda, together with some supplementary chardonnay, a variety that is doing very well in this part of Piedmont. The estate is run by Gianni's partners, Carlo Feyles and Gianni Matteis, and the wines that give it prominence on both the regional and national markets remain the Malvasia di Castelnuovo Don Bosco and the Freisa. Vergagno's Malvasia di Castelnuovo Don Bosco has nothing to fear any longer from comparison with the more traditional and more famous sweet wines of the area, Brachetto d'Acqui and Moscato d'Asti, since it is now one of the best in this category. The colour is a bright palish red; the bouquet has an intense aromatic quality with marked hints of roses and strawberries; the palate is clean and attractive, medium weight; long-finishing with a reminder of the floral qualities first encountered on the nose. The Freisa d'Asti '95 from the Forno vineyard is a good bottle and which even after a year's ageing has lost none of its original freshness. A wine that is simpler, but attractive for its fresh youthfulness and its bubbliness is the Freisa d'Asti Vivace '96. The series of wines tasted finishes with a correctly made Chardonnay and an enjoyable Bonarda.

This season's excitement began with a stupendous Barolo Fiasco Riserva '90 and a superb standard Barolo '91, but then things got even better with the excellent nebbiolo-based wines of the '93 vintage. First there was the Barolo Bricco Fiasco with its particularly smooth bouquet, where the integration of fruit and French oak is confidently handled and magnificently rich; the attractive aromas of freshly-cut hay, camomile flowers and leather are sweet and strong at the same time. The palate is a perfect follow through from the bouquet and already very soft, with acids and tannins there only to add weight to a firm, fruity structure. The Three Glass award is fully justified by the exceptional finesse and perfect balance that Luigi Scavino has succeeded in giving this wine. The standard Barolo from the same vintage is only slightly less rich; clean and fresh on the nose it is still a little harsh on the palate due to tannins that have not yet softened. Dolcetto Oriolo di Montelupo Albese is always excellent, one of the best of its category in the Langhe thanks to outstanding fruit quality and rich body, full of extract. The estate is always more than reliable for its Barbera d'Alba Vigna Punta, the '95 version of which was unfortunately not yet ready for tasting at the time of our visit. Barrel tastings from the barriques promised great things for vintages yet to be bottled. Which brings us to the news of the recent acquisition of a beautiful new vineyard in Serralunga, which will provide its first wines in just two years' time.

● Malvasia di Castelnuovo		
Don Bosco '96	♟♟	3
● Freisa d'Asti Vigna del Forno '95	♟	2*
● Freisa d'Asti Vivace '96	♟	2
● Piemonte Bonarda '96		2
○ Piemonte Chardonnay '96		2

● Barolo Bricco Fiasco '93	♟♟♟	5
● Barolo '93	♟♟	5
● Dolcetto d'Alba		
Bricco Oriolo '96	♟♟	3
● Barolo '91	♟♟♟	5
● Barbera d'Alba		
Vigneto Punta '93	♟♟	4
● Barolo '92	♟♟	5
● Barolo Bricco Fiasco Ris. '90	♟♟	6
● Barbera d'Alba		
Vigneto Punta '94	♟	4
● Barolo Bricco Fiasco '90	♟	5

CASTIGLIONE FALLETTO (CN)   CASTIGLIONE FALLETTO (CN)

CASCINA BONGIOVANNI
VIA ALBA-BAROLO, 4
12060 CASTIGLIONE FALLETTO (CN)
TEL. 0173/262184

F.LLI BROVIA
VIA ALBA-BAROLO, 28
12060 CASTIGLIONE FALLETTO (CN)
TEL. 0173/62852

This winery was already vinifying its own grapes back in 1963. Production stopped for a period but now, after a gap of several years, the management of the cellars has been taken up again by the young Davide Mozzone who, with the help of his father and his aunt, presents his first wines for tasting this year, the Dolcetto d'Alba '96 and Barolo '93. These wines bring him into our Guide at the right level. The two and a half hectares of estate-owned vineyards, south-east facing and about 40 years old, are located in the vicinity of Castiglione Falletto. Annual production is about 3,000 bottles of Dolcetto and 10,000 of Barolo, most of which are destined for the export market. The Dolcetto was particularly enjoyable this year and rewards Davide's efforts to give it structure and personality. The wine undergoes a four-day maceration and is neither clarified nor filtered; it has an extremely deep ruby red and violet colour and a well delineated fruity, floral bouquet. It displays good structure on the palate with rich extract that blends in well with the sweet tannins and a vein of fresh acidity. The Barolo '93 is truly a great wine interpreted in the modern style which combines great body, elegance and drinkability. Ageing is carried out partially in barrique; the wine has a bright, deep ruby red colour with faint orange tinges to the edges. The attractive and intense aromas of berry fruit, spices and vanilla are to be plainly found again on the palate, with an intriguing hint of liquorice on the finish. The Barolo '93 fully deserves its Two Glass award; we congratulate this promising producer on its present achievements and look forward to those to come.

One of the things to be particularly prized in a winery is a consistent level of quality right across the range, in contrast to the questionable policy of some producers who turn out limited quantities of one or two top end wines in order to promote a range of other inferior ones. The Brovias have an exemplary record on this score; you can choose any one of their wines, from the Arneis to the Barolo, and be sure of never being disappointed. Of the wines recently put on the market the Barolo Rocche dei Brovia '93 is one of the best examples of a what was certainly a good, but also quite difficult, vintage. The nose is unusually fresh and fruity, broad and very sharply defined; the palate is long and broad with a finish that goes on and on with leather and tarriness in lovely counterpoint. The acidity and the tannins give rare pleasure by being used only to enrich a soft and velvety texture. The Villero from the same vintage is slightly more closed on the nose, while the expert touch of a great winemaker comes through on a confidently elegant palate whose structure is never overblown, but serves instead to guarantee long ageing potential. The fact that the two capable Brovia daughters have begun to work full time in the cellars does not seem to have changed the long ageing requirements of the winery, so, at the moment of going to press, we cannot comment on the wines from the '96 vintage. These wines apart, we are left on tenterhooks to wait for new products from the Serralunga vineyards that the estate has recently acquired; Elena and Cristina have excellent material to work with.

● Barolo '93	ΨΨ	4
● Dolcetto d'Alba '96	Ψ	3

● Barolo Rocche dei Brovia '93	ΨΨ	5
● Barolo Villero '93	ΨΨ	5
● Barolo Monprivato '90	ΨΨΨ	6
● Barolo Garblèt Sué '91	ΨΨ	5
● Barolo Monprivato '88	ΨΨ	6
● Barolo Monprivato '89	ΨΨ	6
● Barolo Rocche dei Brovia '89	ΨΨ	6
● Barolo Rocche dei Brovia '90	ΨΨ	6
● Barolo Rocche dei Brovia '91	ΨΨ	6
● Barolo Villero '92	ΨΨ	6

51

CASTIGLIONE FALLETTO (CN)

CASTIGLIONE FALLETTO (CN)

CAVALLOTTO
LOC. BRICCO BOSCHIS, 40
12060 CASTIGLIONE FALLETTO (CN)
TEL. 0173/62814

★ PAOLO SCAVINO
VIA ALBA-BAROLO, 59
12060 CASTIGLIONE FALLETTO (CN)
TEL. 0173/62850

Cavallotto's Barolos have always had something special about them, thanks to longer maturation and an unusually late release date compared to other producers, designed to allow the wines to develop their typically complex characteristics of elegance, style and longevity. This year's release includes the Cru Bricco Boschis Vigna Colle Sud Ovest '90, which has aged for six years in large barrels (on average 50 hectolitres) and one year in bottle. Fine garnet red colour, deep and intense on the nose, where hints of vanilla and smoky undertones integrate with aromas of black cherry, plums and tar; rich on the palate, long-finishing, a wine that combines mature fruit, good alcohol and balanced tannins. Slightly lighter in body due to the more difficult vintage, the '91 version is nevertheless extremely satisfactory: sound colour, broad and intense bouquet, attractively drinkable, but quite tannic on the finish at the same time. Gildo and Olivio Cavallotto have been involved in making wine exclusively from their own grapes for the last fifty years, and they are now helped by Olivio's children, Giuseppe, Alfio and Laura. Their 23 hectares of splendidly sited vineyards are mostly at Bricco Boschis, although there is a small site at Vignolo, too. Dolcetto Vigna Scot is a classic wine of its type with a well defined bouquet, a dry and full flavoured palate, excellent for fruit, length and alcoholic balance. The charming Freisa has a fresh and fruity nose, a structured and alcoholically balanced palate, and an attractive bitter twist to the finish. The Nebbiolo is a classic.

Scavino's great achievement has been to endow his wines with the depth that comes from intimate knowledge of a "terroir" and skill in using his grapes to their maximum potential. Enrico's discrete knack of absorbing the technical winemaking tips that he has picked up on his travels in Italy and abroad, without slavishly following winemaking fashions, has helped as well. Barolo Bric del Fiasc '93 is the first wine to come out of the latest modernised production cycle and is convincing proof that the nebbiolo grape can produce wines of extreme elegance. Although not a big wine it has an unusually complex nose: deep garnet red colour, richly-extracted fruit enhanced by a pervasive series of aromas ranging from liquorice to tobacco, from vanilla to hazelnut, from roses in alcohol to cloves; the palate is extremely supple and the wine most enjoyable. Despite the fact that the '93 vintage did not produce good enough grapes in the Cannubi district to bring the wine up to the level of other vintages, this Barolo is a fascinating example of the cru all the same. Bright in colour; berry fruit on the nose with hints of mint and violets; very satisfying on the palate, well balanced with a clean and attractive finish. The Barbera aged in cask is, as usual, rich and elegant.

● Barolo Colle Sud-Ovest Ris. '90	♀♀	6
● Barolo Colle Sud-Ovest Ris. '91	♀♀	5
● Dolcetto d'Alba Vigna Scot '96	♀	3
● Langhe Freisa Bricco Boschis '96	♀	3
● Langhe Nebbiolo '94	♀	4
● Barolo Vigna S. Giuseppe Ris. '89	♀♀♀	6
● Barolo Colle Sud-Ovest Ris. '88	♀♀	6
● Barolo Vigna S. Giuseppe Ris. '85	♀♀	6
● Barolo Vigna S. Giuseppe Ris. '88	♀♀	6
● Barolo Vigna S. Giuseppe Ris. '90	♀♀	6
● Barolo Vigna Sud-Ovest Ris. '89	♀♀	6
● Barolo Vignolo Ris. '89	♀♀	6
● Barolo Vignolo Ris. '90	♀♀	6
● Barolo Vigna S. Giuseppe Ris. '91	♀	5

● Barolo Bric dël Fiasc '93	♀♀♀	6
● Barbera d'Alba		
Affinato in Carati '94	♀♀	5
● Barolo Cannubi '93	♀♀	6
● Dolcetto d'Alba		
Vigneto dël Fiasc '96	♀	3
● Barbera d'Alba		
Affinato in Carati '89	♀♀♀	5
● Barolo Cannubi '85	♀♀♀	6
● Barolo Bric dël Fiasc '89	♀♀♀	6
● Barolo Bric dël Fiasc '90	♀♀♀	6
● Barolo Rocche		
dell'Annunziata Ris. '90	♀♀♀	6
● Barolo Cannubi '91	♀♀♀	6
● Barolo Cannubi '92	♀♀♀	5

CASTIGLIONE FALLETTO (CN)

TERRE DEL BAROLO
VIA ALBA-BAROLO, 5
12060 CASTIGLIONE FALLETTO (CN)
TEL. 0173/262053

There are two ways of getting to taste all the different red wines of the Langhe; either you go from one producer to another selecting their specialities in a "do-it-yourself" tasting tour, or you visit a winery like this, perhaps without real high points, but with genuinely reliable wines. Sheer numbers and wide geographical spread mean that Terre del Barolo can provide an extensive range of different wines. Among those that we picked out this year is a Dolcetto, the Bricco del Ciabot, that stands out for its text book cherry bouquet; soft on the palate and ever expanding until it fills the mouth with long-finishing fruitiness. If you prefer a simpler, easy-to-drink Dolcetto, you can choose between the shy Cascinotto and the incisive Montagrillo. Or perhaps you would like a classic Dolcetto? Take the Castello then, it lacks some of the up-front characteristics of its cousins from Diano but, by way of compensation, has greater depth. Two Barberas? Choose between the standard version, which has a good colour, but a certain vegetal quality on the nose, and a short finish; and, on the other hand, the Vigneti Roere, which is fruitier, more vinous on the nose and more alcoholic on the palate. As for the Barolos, the Castiglione Falletto boasts an uncharacteristic sweet bouquet, logically enough reflected on the palate with soft and immediate flavours, which redeem the wine in the end. By contrast, the somewhat tired nature of the standard Barolo suggests a lack of attention paid to this wine in comparison with the cru versions. A "bonne bouche" to finish with? You can find this in the delicate and attractive bouquet of the Pinot Nero; a deep coloured wine, attractive without being too overwhelming on the palate.

CASTIGLIONE FALLETTO (CN)

VIETTI
P.ZZA VITTORIO VENETO, 5
12060 CASTIGLIONE FALLETTO (CN)
TEL. 0173/62825

This year's range of wines from Vietti clearly demonstrates that they are steadily absorbing all the advances in winemaking current in the Langhe, which applies equally to the Currado family's endeavours to endow their young easy-to-drink wines with better defined character and their efforts to make their more structured wines more accessible. Dolcetto d'Alba Tre Vigne is a very successful example of how to combine freshness with intensity: lively ruby red colour; on the nose, plum and berry fruit aromas dominate this wine's typical vinosity; on the palate the same concentration of fruit makes for a sound and confident wine. Dolcetto della Vigna Lazzarito has been deliberately made a touch more austere however it suffers from the difficulties of the '95 vintage which mean both nose and palate are a little below their usual standard . The three Barolos tasted are all from the '93 vintage and all show the same interesting stylistic development. The most fascinating is the Castiglione, which combines the power of a well built red wine with the whole gamut of olfactory possibilities typical of the nebbiolo grape: deep garnet red colour, delicate but ample floral bouquet, up-front tannins on the palate and evident, vigorous structure. The Barolo Brunate has good depth and although incapable of the same spontaneity as the Castiglione, it is full of character and certainly capable of ageing. At the time of tasting, Barolo Lazzarito di Serralunga is the most closed and mysterious of the three, but wines from this particular strip of red marl vineyard are rarely early developers and this is quite normal.

● Diano d'Alba Bricco del Ciabot '96	♈♈	3*
● Barbera d'Alba Vigneti Roere '95	♈	3
● Barolo Castiglione Falletto '93	♈	4
● Diano d'Alba Cascinotto '96	♈	3
● Langhe Rosso '95	♈	3
● Barolo '93		4
● Barbera d'Alba La Morra '96		2
● Diano d'Alba Montagrillo '96		3
● Dolcetto d'Alba Castello '96		3
● Diano d'Alba Cascinotto '95	♉♉	2
● Barbera d'Alba Sorì della Roncaglia '95	♉	3
● Barolo Baudana Ris. '90	♉	5
● Barolo Castello Ris. '90	♉	5
● Barolo Codana Ris. '90	♉	5

● Barolo Lazzarito '93	♈♈	6
● Barolo Brunate '93	♈♈	6
● Barolo Castiglione '93	♈♈	6
● Dolcetto d'Alba Tre Vigne '96	♈♈	3
● Dolcetto d'Alba Lazzarito '95	♈	4
● Barbera d'Alba Scarrone '95	♈	4
○ Roero Arneis '96	♈	4
● Barolo Rocche di Castiglione '88	♉♉♉	6
● Barolo Rocche di Castiglione '85	♉♉♉	6
● Barolo Villero '82	♉♉♉	6
● Barbera d'Alba Scarrone '94	♉♉	4
● Barolo Castiglione '91	♉♉	6
● Barolo Villero Ris. 90	♉♉	6

CASTIGLIONE TINELLA (CN)

CAUDRINA
STRADA CAUDRINA, 20
12053 CASTIGLIONE TINELLA (CN)
TEL. 0141/855126

CASTIGLIONE TINELLA (CN)

LA MORANDINA
VIA MORANDINI, 11
12053 CASTIGLIONE TINELLA (CN)
TEL. 0141/855261

Romano Dogliotti fits in his duties as President of the Consorzio di Tutela del Moscato d'Asti (the Moscato d'Asti growers' association) with his other, highly appropriate, occupation as a producer of excellent wines typical of the Castiglione Tinella area, Moscato d'Asti and Asti Spumante. 20 hectares of estate-owned vineyards produce about 150,000 bottles per year, mostly of Moscato d'Asti, but 15 percent Asti as well, all of which are finding an increasing number of admirers, both on the export market and at home. A well equipped winery enables him to make some of the best wines of their type, in both categories, with supreme skill as well as experience. This year the Asti La Selvatica is a little below par, due to a pronounced bitterness on the finish that spoils the palate of a wine that initially promises well. However, as usual, the two versions of Moscato d'Asti, La Galeisa and La Caudrina, are convincing successes. La Galeisa has typical sage and citrus fruit expressed with elegance on the nose. The palate opens sweet but finishes with an attractive bitter twist. La Caudrina has notable intensity and length and very attractive appearance in the glass with its good sparkle and straw yellow colour. In previous vintages both these Moscatos have already been proved to age well in the short term, but we recommend that they are drunk at the height of their freshness to appreciate them at their best.

This estate is located at Castiglione Tinella, the commune with the most vines in all Italy. The view from the winery is one of uninterrupted vineyards stretching into the distance - vineyards which grow the grapes for some of the very best Moscato d'Asti. Ever since its foundation in 1988, La Morandina has been one of the most interesting producers in the area; today, as well as an excellent Moscato, it makes two versions of Barbera d'Asti and a Chardonnay that are all fresh and clean, and capable of showing good varietal character. The brothers Giulio and Paolo Morando live up to habitually high expectations with a sparkling Moscato d'Asti '96: fresh aromas of sage and flowers, good bubble on the palate and light acidity on the finish provide an invitation to keep on drinking glass after glass of this wine. The Chardonnay is straw yellow with green reflections; not a big wine and quite short on the finish, but well balanced and enjoyable to drink. Of the two Barberas we prefer - just - the Zucchetto, which has had a brief passage in oak and has excellent balance, entirely without the dominance of high acidity typical of many Barberas. The barrique aged Barbera Varmat is an interesting wine: deep, opaque ruby red; long and broad bouquet with marked effects of oak; full bodied and satisfying on the palate.

O Moscato d'Asti La Caudrina '96	🍷🍷	3
O Moscato d'Asti La Galeisa '96	🍷🍷	4
O Asti La Selvatica '96		4

● Barbera d'Asti Zucchetto '95	🍷🍷	3
O Moscato d'Asti '96	🍷🍷	3*
● Barbera d'Asti Varmat '95	🍷	4
O Langhe Chardonnay Pian Bellino '96	🍷	3

CASTIGLIONE TINELLA (CN) CASTIGLIONE TINELLA (CN)

ELIÓ PERRONE
STRADA S. MARTINO, 2
12053 CASTIGLIONE TINELLA (CN)
TEL. 0141/855132

PAOLO SARACCO
VIA CIRCONVALLAZIONE, 6
12053 CASTIGLIONE TINELLA (CN)
TEL. 0141/855113

This is a privileged area for Moscato d'Asti and this winery is one of its best exponents, raising the image of a wine that deserves to be better known, particularly in Italy. The estate is run by the young Stefano Perrone, helped by his parents in the vineyards, and now has a bigger and more modern winery where the almost 60,000 bottles produced per year can be made in the best conditions possible. Apart from Moscato, Stefano Perrone is very keen on the barrique vinification of Chardonnay and Barbera d'Asti, both of which have come out well in this year's tastings. The Chardonnay has a bright golden straw yellow colour; the bouquet of ripe fruit and flowers is very intense, with clear hints of honey and vanilla; broad and supported with fresh acidity on the palate. The Barbera from rented vineyards in Agliano Asti is a successful wine too: very good on the nose, fruity, spicy and sweet; slightly lean on the palate. The two Moscatos are both good: the Sourgal is fresher and more up-front with an attractive green youthfulness to the finish; the Clarté is less ready in coming forward, but quite complex on the nose.

Paolo Saracco concentrates on Moscato, rightly enough, but he is also keen to get to grips with other varieties, such as chardonnay (two versions are already in production), Rhine riesling, sauvignon and pinot noir (on the market in the next few years). His decision to give most attention to the most important grape in the zone, which he transforms into a fascinating and unique wine of its type, seem to be a logical step in raising the image of the area. The purchase of another five hectares of vineyards to add to the estate's large existing holding will lead to a total annual production of about 140,000 bottles of Moscato d'Asti. The two versions of Moscato di Saracco '96 came out at the top of their class in our tastings: the Moscato d'Autunno has greater complexity and body, while the standard version shines for its freshness, up-front nature on the nose and easy drinkability. Both wines show the results of expert vinification and the cleanest possible cellars, so the nose shows the whole spectrum of aromas typical of the grape variety. This year we were only able to taste the Chardonnay Prasuè, which is fruity and floral on the nose with good concentration and length, has a corresponding palate, and sufficient acidity to support a well structured body.

O	Char-de S. Ris. '95	♟♟ 4	O	Langhe Chardonnay Prasuè '95	♟♟	3
●	Barbera d'Asti Grivò '95	♟ 3	O	Moscato d'Asti '96	♟♟	3
O	Moscato d'Asti Clarté '96	♟ 3	O	Moscato d'Asti		
O	Moscato d'Asti Sourgal '96	♟ 3		Moscato d'Autunno '96	♟♟	3
			O	Moscato d'Asti		
				Moscato d'Autunno '95	♟♟	3

CHIERI (TO)

COCCONATO D'ASTI (AT)

MARTINI & ROSSI
FRAZ. PESSIONE
10020 CHIERI (TO)
TEL. 011/94191

BAVA
STRADA MONFERRATO, 2
14023 COCCONATO D'ASTI (AT)
TEL. 0141/907083

Despite the change of ownership (it has been part of the Bacardi drinks colossus now for several years), Martini & Rossi has done little to revamp its basic lines. It is difficult to find experiments with new cru selections and, with the exception of the launch of the vintage Montelera sparkling wine in 1993, the range of sparkling wines remains the same as it has always been for years. Well respected products such as the Montelera Brut and the Montelera Riserva Brut are the quality base for a company that is more famous for its Vermouths, one of which is the principal ingredient for the world's most popular cocktail, the Martini. Montelera Brut is made from 60 percent pinot noir and 40 percent pinot bianco and aged for about 24 months before disgorgement: delicate, clean and full of yeastiness on the nose; well balanced with a good bitter twist on the palate, the excellent acidity guarantees notable freshness. The Riserva Brut is a sparkling wine too, and uses roughly the same cuvée but with slightly more pinot noir in it and aged for 48 months; it is more complex on the nose with a greater concentration of flavour on the palate than the simple Brut. But Martini & Rossi's real warhorse in the sparkling wine sector is the Asti, a sweet wine made from moscato grapes grown on the hills of Santo Stefano Belbo and produced in quantities of millions of bottles. As usual, it is one of the best on the market and stands out for the aromatic qualities of the grape variety, for its attractive depth of flavour and for its freshness supported by good acidity. Lastly, look out for the Oltrepó Riesling Italico, a widely distributed Charmat method sparkling wine which is enjoyable drinking and good value for money.

Every year the Bava winery is awarded prizes for the quality of its wines in competitions throughout the world, and they invariably perform well in our tastings too. Credit for this is due in equal parts to the three Bava brothers - Roberto, Giulio and Paolo - who share the sales and production duties between them. All the wines we tasted this year did well, but the two top range, full bodied Barbera d'Astis are especially worthy of note. Barbera d'Asti Superiore Stradivario and Barbera d'Asti Superiore Arbest are good examples of the potential of the grape variety, despite the fact that the '94 vintage was not particularly favourable. The first is the better of the two, thanks to its greater complexity, its finer and more rounded bouquet, and its great structure. Its strong finish is amply supported by the wood. Made to the same criteria, with the same search for concentration, the Monferrato Bianco Alteserre has a deep golden colour which is the obvious sign of body. The Moscato d'Asti Bass Tuba is as good as ever: hints of musk on the nose with the intense aromatic quality typical of the grape variety; fresh and easy to drink but with good weight on the palate and well balanced acidity. The Malvasia di Castelnuovo Don Bosco is an enjoyable drink with a perfumed bouquet. The sparkling wine we tasted this year is the Giulio Cocchi Brut Millesimo 1990, a Metodo Classico made from the pinot grape with a delicate yeast and biscuit bouquet: full and complex on the front palate, dry and long on the finish.

O	Asti	♀	3
O	Montelera Brut	♀	4
O	Montelera Brut Ris.	♀	5
O	Oltrepò Pavese Riesling Italico		3
O	Montelera Brut Ris. '90	♀♀	5

●	Barbera d'Asti Sup.		
	Stradivario '94	♀♀	5
●	Barbera d'Asti Sup. Arbest '94	♀	3
O	Giulio Cocchi Brut '90	♀	4
O	Monferrato Bianco Alteserre '95	♀	4
O	Moscato d'Asti Bas Tuba '96	♀	3
●	Malvasia di Castelnuovo		
	Don Bosco '96		3
●	Barbera d'Asti Sup.		
	Stradivario '93	♀♀	4
⊙	Giulio Cocchi		
	Metodo Classico Rosé '93	♀♀	4

COSSOMBRATO (AT)

COSTIGLIOLE D'ASTI (AT)

CARLO QUARELLO
VIA MARCONI, 3
14020 COSSOMBRATO (AT)
TEL. 0141/905204

BERTELLI
FRAZ. S. CARLO, 38
14055 COSTIGLIOLE D'ASTI (AT)
TEL. 0141/966137

A vigneron of the old school, a small winery, a proudly unfashionable grape variety, a strictly hand crafted style of winemaking: these are the essential elements of Carlo Quarello's Grignolino del Monferrato Casalese Cré, which is produced at Alfiano Natta just outside of the province of Asti on a three and a half hectare vineyard managed by the grower in person. We have already highlighted this producer and his wines in several past editions of the Guide and every year we enjoy rediscovering the slightly atypical nose of his red wine, almost like some relic of times gone by, in this world where the language of wine is the international-speak of cabernet and chardonnay and grignolino is strictly a local dialect. . Like the successful '95 the most recent vintage has been a good one for Carlo, who can therefore give us his Cré in two versions, the standard label and the cru Marcaleone which is only produced in the best years. The first is a fresh and attractive Grignolino with an elegant floral nose; dry and up-front on the palate, manifestly easy to drink. The second is more serious and has got to be worked at more; as usual for the Marcaleone, it is incredibly deep in colour, full on the nose and big on the palate, not typical at all for the grape variety. The finish is characteristically high in tannin, but well balanced by the acidity. The other wine that Quarello makes, the Crebarné, is based on barbera and well worth a look: vinified from super ripe grapes, the colour and bouquet are both rich, it has good structure and length, and certainly deserves its rating.

The most outstanding creation of this laboratory winery in 1996 is without doubt the Plissé, a vino da tavola based on the traminer grape that is fuller and richer this year than in previous vintages: it has subtle, delicate aromatic qualities on the nose, and a long, well defined and not at all cloying palate made in the Alsace style. The two new Sauvignons, the vino da tavola I Fossaretti '95 and the Monferrato Montetusa '96, are also very interesting wines. The first is simple and correct, with uncomplicated aromatic qualities and moderate alcohol; the second is a bigger wine with more alcohol, surprisingly soft and clean with fresh hints of sage on the nose; it is a pity that it turns out rather sweet on the palate, making it difficult to use as a food wine, despite its undeniable charm and elegance. Bertelli's Chardonnays are inconsistent: a sumptuous '93 was followed by a difficult '94. The '95, on the other hand, is definitely a good wine, but it lacks the aromatic quality and the richness of extract that made the Giarone '93 one of the best Chardonnays ever produced in Piedmont. Cabernet Sauvignon I Fossaretti '94 is more reliable: good fruity nose, fresh palate, slightly harsh tannins not yet integrated. From the '94 vintage, the Barbera Montetusa '94 is a bit dumb on the nose and its lean body is overwhelmed by the wood; while the Barbera Giarone is softer and better balanced on the palate; its slender structure, however, does not make for length on the finish. Given the power of the '95 vintage Barberas, traditionally the strongest varietal in this excellent winery's portfolio, it has been decided to put back the release of these wines until the Spring of 1998.

● Grignolino del M.to Casalese Cré Marcaleone '96	♥♥	3*
● Grignolino del M.to Casalese Cré '96	♥	2*
● Crebarné '96	♥	4

○ Monferrato Sauvignon Blanc Montetusa '96	♥♥	5
○ Piemonte Chardonnay Giarone '95	♥♥	5
○ Plissé Traminer '96	♥♥	4
● Barbera d'Asti Giarone '94	♥	5
● Barbera d'Asti Montetusa '94	♥	5
● Cabernet Sauvignon I Fossaretti '94	♥	5
○ Sauvignon I Fossaretti '95	♥	5
● Barbera d'Asti Giarone '90	♥♥	5
● Cabernet Sauvignon I Fossaretti '93	♥♥	5
○ Chardonnay Giarone '93	♥♥	5
● Barbera d'Asti Giarone '93	♥	5

COSTIGLIOLE D'ASTI (AT)

Cascina Castlèt

Strada Castelletto, 6
14055 Costigliole d'Asti (AT)
tel. 0141/966651

Here Barbera is King; which is unsurprising considering that Costigliole is the heartland of this Piedmontese red wine. After dividing her time for many years between a wine shop in Turin and the vineyards near Asti, for some time now Mariuccia Borio has been in control of the family winery that has been handed on from generation to generation. As well as working on the revitalisation and image rebuilding of barbera, Mariuccia is also President of a dynamic association called Le Donne del Vino, clear evidence of this likeable woman's boundless enthusiasm that becomes a torrent of loquacity when the talk turns to winemaking. All the recent releases did well in our blind tastings: Barbera Superiore Litina is the most successful with its bright ruby red colour cloaked with delicate garnet reflections and hints of woody spiciness overlaying the fruit, well balanced, rounded and long-finishing on the palate. The Passum '92 is more complex and further advanced in maturation: garnet red with definite shades of orange, a nose tending firmly towards spiciness (cinnamon and tarry wood) and ripe fruit (plums); the palate contains all these flavours but is not perfectly balanced, the alcohol is there, but the structure and freshness which would bring harmony, are lacking. The Policalpo is less well developed; the nose is a little closed and dumb, the palate lacks backbone. Among the other releases we found perfectly honest and correct wines such as the standard Barbera d'Asti, the Barbera called Goi ('joy' - in Piedmontese dialect), and the Moscato. The oenological consultant is the well known Armando Cordero, aided by the promising young winemaker, Giorgio Gozzelino.

● Barbera d'Asti '96	🍷	3
● Barbera d'Asti Passum '92	🍷	4
● Barbera d'Asti Policalpo '94	🍷	4
● Barbera d'Asti Sup. Litina '94	🍷	3
● Barbera del Monferrato Goi '96	🍷	2*
○ Moscato d'Asti '96		3
● Passum '91	YY	4
○ Avié '93	Y	4
● Passum '90	Y	4
● Policalpo '89	Y	4
● Policalpo '90	Y	4

CUCCARO MONFERRATO (AL)

Liedholm

Villa Boemia
15040 Cuccaro Monferrato (AL)
tel. 0131/771916

A solitary dirt track along the crest of the hills leads to Villa Boemia at Cuccaro, a tiny outpost of the Monferrato Casalese overlooking Alessandria down in the valley. There is a sharp contrast in the landscape between the hills, their green woods interspersed with geometric vineyards, and the sudden immensity of the Po Valley down below. Carlo Liedholm's modern winery is in an oasis of calm and in his well equipped up-to-date cellars he and his oenological consultant, Donato Lanati, make classic Monferrato wines and two internationally inspired cuvées. The Bianco della Boemia, an assemblage of equal parts of pinot bianco and cortese, has been partly aged in new wood barriques for the first time this year. This process has given it delicate cinnamon aromas together with a fine bouquet of meadow flowers; on the palate it is fresh and well balanced, but lacks a little in body. Its red wine brother, Rosso della Boemia, is made form an assemblage of several different grape varieties, including cabernet and barbera; the '94 version is not as good as previous years, but considering the difficulties of the vintage, it is a good wine and shows how effectively Carlo Liedholm has worked in both the vineyard and the cellars. Grignolino del Monferrato Casalese '96 has a fine colour; a clean bouquet of roses, wet walnuts and white pepper; smooth and easy to drink, well managed tannins and an attractive bitter twist on the aftertaste. Barbera d'Asti '95 has a light ruby red colour, faint but well defined hints of bitter cherries and vegetal undergrowth on the nose, and is well balanced on the palate, if a little lacking in body.

● Barbera d'Asti '95	🍷	2
○ Bianco della Boemia '96	🍷	3
● Grignolino del M.to Casalese '96	🍷	2
● Rosso della Boemia '94	🍷	5
● Rosso della Boemia '90	YY	5
● Rosso della Boemia '91	YY	5

DIANO D'ALBA (CN)

DIANO D'ALBA (CN)

MATTEO E CLAUDIO ALARIO
VIA S. CROCE, 23
12055 DIANO D'ALBA (CN)
TEL. 0173/231808

BRICCO MAIOLICA
VIA BOLANGINO-RICCA, 7
FRAZ. RICCA D'ALBA
12055 DIANO D'ALBA (CN)
TEL. 0173/612049

We find Matteo Alario's wines increasingly interesting, particularly the two Dolcetto di Diano wines, which have in this winery a worthy champion for their denomination; their style combines elegance and balance with a quite exceptional concentration and structure. In short, these are wines that can be drunk with pleasure now, but which would also benefit from cellar ageing. The grapes for Matteo's up-coming Barolos from the '95 and '96 vintages come from a scant hectare of vineyards in the commune of Verduno and, after vinification, are left to mature in barrique in his newly equipped cellars, which are now being extended even further. The range opens with the Dolcetto Montagrillo: the impenetrably dark colour of this wine is a sign of how big it will be; both nose and palate have an array of tastes and aromas from the fruity to the floral, while sweet and supple tannins envelope the palate. This great Dolcetto however is pipped at the post by a hair's breadth by the Costa Fiore, which draws greater depth and complexity from a particularly favourable vineyard site. Barbera Valletta and Nebbiolo Cascinotto come from lesser vintages compared to '96 and are less structured than the two Dolcettos; they are both, however, skilfully made wines with an accurate dose of new oak and they came over well in tastings.

Visitors to Bricco Maiolica come to taste the excellent wines, particularly a wonderful Dolcetto di Diano d'Alba, and also to admire the pedigree Piedmontese beef cattle, which are no less important for the business. Annual production reaches a very respectable 100,000 bottles made from 17 hectares of vineyards sited around the farmhouse and the new modern winery. We begin with the two white wines from the range, the Rolando and the Moscato d'Asti. The first, made of chardonnay, arneis and favorita, is a classically fruity and attractive white wine without any grand pretensions and very easy to drink; the second is redeemed by good typicity, although Moscato in this area is not normally at its best. The two Dolcettos are at quite another level of quality: the standard version is a complex and well balanced wine with a good bouquet of roses and berry fruit; the cru Bricco Maiolica is an even bigger smoother wine with rich extract and good length. Barbera Vigna Vigia has typical vinosity and freshness thanks to the characteristic acidity of the variety and decent enough weight. It is ready for drinking now. Nebbiolo Cumot is better on the nose (alcohol-led and floral) than on the palate, where the tannins are a bit harsh and intrusive.

● Dolcetto di Diano d'Alba Costa Fiore '96	♟♟	3*
● Dolcetto di Diano d'Alba Montagrillo '96	♟♟	3*
● Barbera d'Alba Valletta '95	♟	4
● Nebbiolo d'Alba Cascinotto '95	♟	4
● Barbera d'Alba Valletta '93	♟♟	4
● Dolcetto di Diano d'Alba Costa Fiore '95	♟♟	3
● Nebbiolo d'Alba Cascinotto '93	♟♟	4
● Dolcetto di Diano d'Alba Montagrillo '95	♟	3

● Dolcetto di Diano d'Alba Sörì Bricco Maiolica '96	♟♟	3
● Barbera d'Alba Vigna Vigia '95	♟	3
● Dolcetto di Diano d'Alba '96	♟	2*
● Nebbiolo d'Alba Il Cumot '95	♟	3
○ Langhe Rolando '96		3
○ Moscato d'Asti Sörì Valdavì '96		3
● Dolcetto di Diano d'Alba Sörì Bricco Maiolica '95	♟♟	3
● Barbera d'Alba Vigna Vigia '94	♟	4
● Nebbiolo d'Alba Il Cumot '94	♟	4

DIANO D'ALBA (CN)

PRODUTTORI DIANESI
VIA VITTORIO EMANUELE, 17/A
12055 DIANO D'ALBA (CN)
TEL. 0173/69219

These four vignerons from Diano, who first got together in the early 1970s, continue to produce the typical Dolcetto of their area, with the aim of combining good quality with value for money. Diano d'Alba was the first area in Italy to classify its entire vineyard territory into sub-zones, thus allowing producers in this part of the Langhe to vinify grapes from each cru site separately to bring out their best potential. The Produttori di Diano make three types of Dolcetto, one standard version and two crus. This year the Sorì La Rocca and the Sorì Santa Lucia have both come out well. The first is the classic Dolcetto from this winery: a red wine with good structure, deep colour, up-front on the palate, easy to drink, with a satisfying almondy twist to the finish. The Santa Lucia is good, too, but a little less full in body; full flavoured and very drinkable. The standard Dolcetto is a decent wine suitable for drinking throughout the meal.

● Dolcetto di Diano d'Alba Sorì La Rocca '96	🍷	3*
● Dolcetto di Diano d'Alba Sorì Santa Lucia '96	🍷	3*
● Dolcetto di Diano d'Alba '96		2

DOGLIANI (CN)

CELSO ABBONA
REG. S. LUCIA, 36
12063 DOGLIANI (CN)
TEL. 0173/70668

Sergio Abbona has many plans in the pipeline for the production of new wines from Cà Neuva in the next few years. This young vigneron has not, however, underestimated the potential of his Dolcettos, which deserve their reputation for quality. A good vintage in '96 helped Sergio and his father Celso to make 34,000 bottles of standard Dolcetto, 9,000 bottles of Dolcetto 'L Sambù (which have more bottle age) and, lastly, 5,000 bottles of Nebbiolo Il Bric. The standard Dolcetto is mostly vinous on the nose, broad on the tongue, and fresh-tasting with an unexpected lingering aroma of cherries. 'L Sambù is more intriguing on the nose because of a hint of quinine that enhances the ample fruitiness of the bouquet; good acidity on the palate and slight almond twist to the finish. The Bric has all the freshness that has become the hallmark of Abbona winemaking; bright ruby red colour, intense aromatic nose beginning with well evolved honey and chestnuts and finishing with mature berry fruit; medium weight on the palate which is dominated by a well balanced acidity.

● Dolcetto di Dogliani 'L Sambù '96	🍷	3
● Dolcetto di Dogliani Cà Neuva '96	🍷	2*
● Il Bric '96	🍷	2

DOGLIANI (CN)

FRANCESCO BOSCHIS
FRAZ. S. MARTINO DI PIANEZZO, 57
12063 DOGLIANI (CN)
TEL. 0173/70574

Francesco and Simona already have the help of their sons Marco and Paolo in the production of an ever-wider and more interesting range of wines. In fact, despite being principally Dolcetto producers (30,000 bottles), the Boschis family always present small parcels of interesting wines from other denominations every year. This year we were particularly impressed with a Freisa. Against all the odds, Francesco succeeds in giving it an unusually rich colour, bouquet and body, without losing any of its freshness. The Grignolino was just as good; without ever being overblown, it boasts the classic fruity bouquet of its type with hints of tomato-vine leaves on the nose; simple but long on the palate. The Barbera has an uncomplicated nose of thyme and strawberries, is light with good acidity on the palate, and a consistent follow through. The winery's classic range includes a correctly made, but uninspiring, standard Dolcetto, and two cru versions, each with its own style and hence different market positioning. The Vigna dei Prey is more robust and austere, just right for the Italian market: the '96 is violet in colour and very opaque, the nose has hints of apples and fermenting fruit; smooth, because the alcohol dominates the acidity, and lacking only marginally in length of bouquet on the finish. The more delicate Sorì San Martino is destined mostly for the export market; of all the Boschis wines it was the one that we have liked the most this year: the colour is not of the deepest but it is nicely tinged with violet; the ripe fruit on the nose is not overwhelmed by the marked vinosity; there is good, well-balanced acidity on the palate which finishes with a twist of bitter fruit.

DOGLIANI (CN)

QUINTO CHIONETTI & FIGLIO
B.TA VALDIBERTI, 44
12063 DOGLIANI (CN)
TEL. 0173/71179

For many winemakers in Dogliani, Quinto Chionetti, who has probably seen more vintages than anyone in the area, is the un-elected but indisputable maestro of the vine. Other producers ask him the secret behind his winemaking and he always replies with disarming simplicity that the answer is not important, it is the soil that makes the wines for him. Then, later on in the conversation, you find that Quinto does not think that owning old vineyards with low-yielding vines in excellent sites, or being able to mature the grapes in stainless steel to maintain the maximum freshness, is at all important. Whatever the merits of this way of thinking, the two cru wines of the estates are excellent exponents of both the "terroir" and the varietal character of the grape. Unfortunately, this year we cannot comment on the two '96 Dolcettos; neither were on the market at the time of tasting. Since Quinto Chionetti's aim is to only release his wines after due bottle ageing, we will come back to his wines in the next edition. Retasting the '95 vintage proves the point; Chionetti wines do improve with age. The Briccolero is the most structured of them, and is made from grapes which grow on clay-rich, sun-baked slopes; it is still broad and youthful on the nose; the taste is rich and full of alcohol, almost caressable. The San Luigi comes from tufa-rich soil with an east-facing exposure and has attained excellent balance whilst retaining its youthfulness a year after release.

● Barbera d'Alba Vigna Le Masserie '95	♏	3
● Dolcetto di Dogliani Sorì S. Martino '96	♏	3
● Dolcetto di Dogliani Vigna dei Prey '96	♏	3
● Langhe Freisa Bosco delle Cicale '96	♏	3
● Piemonte Grignolino '96	♏	3
● Dolcetto di Dogliani '96		2
● Dolcetto di Dogliani Vigna dei Prey '95	♀	3

● Dolcetto di Dogliani Briccolero '95	♀♀	3
● Dolcetto di Dogliani San Luigi '95	♀	3

DOGLIANI (CN)

DOGLIANI (CN)

PODERI LUIGI EINAUDI
B.TA GOMBE, 31/32
CASCINA TECC
12063 DOGLIANI (CN)
TEL. 0173/70191

F.LLI PECCHENINO
B.TA VALDIBÀ, 41
12063 DOGLIANI (CN)
TEL. 0173/70686

Paola and Roberta Einaudi have celebrated the centenary of their winery with the creation of a new cuvée dedicated to its founder, Luigi Einaudi. The wine is made from barbera, cabernet and merlot, separately vinified and then assembled to undergo 18 months' ageing in barriques. Tasting notes show the wine succeeds in marrying together character, structure and drinkability. The colour is a beautiful ruby red with garnet tinges; there is a sweet fruitiness on the nose enhanced with subtle grassiness; soft on the palate without the least hint of flabbiness, easy to drink, clean and fruity on the finish. In fact, all the Einaudi wines we tasted this year are more than reliable, thanks to the work of the able oenologist Lorenzo Raimondi. The two Dolcetto cru wines are impressive: the Filari '95 has benefited from a spell in barrique: ruby red colour, well-composed nose, bright and lively on the palate; fresh tasting to start with, then rich in extract and high in alcohol, all well-balanced with the toastiness of the wood. The Tecc has a slightly more mature colour, and a ripe fruit nose with a rich and complex bouquet; well-rounded on the palate, fresh, full-flavoured, fruity and good bitter twist on the finish. The Barolo has good structure, but is not yet fully balanced, the tannins being still too dominant. The Barbera is excellent, a classic of its type, with a bouquet of bitter cherries and an attractive alcohol component. Finally, the Vigna Meira is a white wine made from the tocai and pinot grigio that the estate has always grown : barrique fermentation has given it lovely golden reflections and softened the palate.

The Pecchenino brothers aim higher every year, making a range of spot-on wines including some examples of Dolcetto di Dogliani that are clear indications of its potential. Attilio and Orlando resolve the vexed question of whether to use wood or not in the production of Dolcetto by making three outstanding wines in three completely different ways - so outstanding in the case of the Sirì d'Jermu that this wine wins, for the first time, a Three Glass award. This superb Dolcetto di Dogliani, which for years has been one of the most reliable wines in the Langhe, stays on the skins for a couple of days and then matures in partly-used small oak: complex and well developed nose with good breadth and spiciness; strong tannins on the palate supported by rich extract, making the wine well-balanced and long finishing. The Pizabò, however, has a shorter maceration and matures in stainless steel: the result is an overwhelming bouquet of plums and a firm, alcoholic palate only slightly less complex than the Sirì d'Jermu, on a musky background. This year sees the launch of a Dolcetto that has been in barrique for a good 18 months, the Bricco Botti. The barriques have left their mark on the wine's opaque violet hue, and on the bouquet; a fresh-tasting front palate is swiftly succeeded by sensations of powerful alcohol and rich extract. The wine as a whole is still a little dominated by the toastiness of the oak. New oak has also been used for La Castella, an assemblage of nebbiolo and barbera, this year with a small addition of cabernet, which has blended in magnificently and given the wine extra smoothness and colour. The Freisa is a clean and up-front wine; the Chardonnay, on its first showing, is still unbalanced.

● Dolcetto di Dogliani I Filari '95	¶¶	4
● Dolcetto di Dogliani Vigna Tecc '95	¶¶	3
● Luigi Einaudi Rosso '95	¶¶	5
● Barolo Costa Grimaldi '93	¶	5
● Piemonte Barbera '95	¶	3
○ Vigna Meira Bianco '96	¶	3
● Barolo Costa Grimaldi '89	¶	5

● Dolcetto di Dogliani Sirì d'Jermu '96	¶¶¶	3
● Dolcetto di Dogliani Bricco Botti '95	¶¶	4
● Dolcetto di Dogliani Pizabò '96	¶¶	3
● Langhe La Castella '95	¶¶	4
● Langhe Freisa Valdibacco '96	¶	3
○ Langhe Chardonnay Vigna Maestro '96		3
● Dolcetto di Dogliani Pizabò '95	¶¶	3
● Dolcetto di Dogliani Sirì d'Jermu '95	¶¶	3
● Vigna La Castella '93	¶¶	4
● Vigna La Castella '94	¶	4

DOGLIANI (CN)

DOGLIANI (CN)

PIRA
B.TA VALDIBERTI, 69
12063 DOGLIANI (CN)
TEL. 0173/78538

SAN FEREOLO
B.TA VALDIBÀ, 59
12063 DOGLIANI (CN)
TEL. 0173/742075

The vineyards of this estate straddle two distinct denominations, Dolcetto and Barbera d'Alba on one side, Dolcetto di Dogliani on the other. Pira is particularly good at the Alba wines. The Barbera Vendemmia Tardiva has attained a good balance between the soft and alcoholic over-ripe fruit and the bright freshness that is a characteristic of the variety: deeply coloured, the rich extract is evident from the nose and there is an clean and inviting aroma of ripe fruit; elegant in structure, easy to drink and firm on the finish. What is immediately striking about the Dolcetto Vigna Fornaci is its vinosity, but also its aroma and broad, if not particularly long palate. The Barbera Vigna Fornaci is not as big a wine as the late harvest version but it is not without an attractive drinkability, a fine bouquet, a clean palate and good character. The Dolcetto di Dogliani Bricco Botti is a little dumb and inarticulate; it does not have any particular faults, but it does not fully live up to the vineyard's potential. The Dolcetto di Dogliani Vigna Landes is more up front and one dimensional, a classic red to be drunk relatively quickly. This reappearance in the Guide is particularly well deserved for a producer who has succeeded in creating its own individual style and is keen to have it compared with the best that the wine world can offer at the moment.

It is well worth the steep climb up to Nicoletta Bocca's house; "house", we call it, rather than "winery", because to reach the vinification facility you have to go through some of the rooms of the home; it is so small and neat that it looks more like a wine collector's hideaway than a winery easily capable of producing 15,000 bottles per year. It is worth the climb, as we were saying, to see the panoramic view and to visit what Nicoletta calls "a nature park of vines". You see vines with knotted rootstocks planted in tight rows on slopes too steep for any other type of crop, and canes tied onto wooden stakes with raffia; ancient methods of cultivation that are part of our heritage, but which are still useful and functional, as well. In the cellars experiments are carried out with a sense of empirical curiosity, and Nicoletta is fascinated by how unpredictable the results can be. One of the best results is a blend based on barbera with small amounts of dolcetto and nebbiolo, first presented for tasting in the autumn of 1997: deep, youthful ruby red; pervasive and encouragingly broad bouquet of bilberries and liquorice; firm start on the palate, good structure, no surprises in its development on the palate. Such rich potential suggests that freshness is not the be-all and end-all of this wine and it could stand being made in a more demanding style than at present. The Dolcetto San Fereolo has a deep colour and intense blackberry aromas; it is rich in extract and in alcohol, even though some greater complexity on the palate would not come amiss. Some of the dolcetto grapes are also used for a standard non-cru version.

● Barbera d'Alba Vendemmia Tardiva '95	￥￥	4
● Barbera d'Alba Vigna Fornaci '95	￥	3
● Dolcetto di Dogliani Vigna Fornaci '96	￥	3
● Dolcetto di Dogliani Bricco dei Botti '96		3
● Dolcetto di Dogliani Vigna Landes '96		3

● Dolcetto di Dogliani San Fereolo '96	￥￥	3
● Il Brumaio '95	￥￥	3
● Dolcetto di Dogliani '96		3
● Dolcetto di Dogliani San Fereolo '95	￥	3

DOGLIANI (CN)

SAN ROMANO
B.TA GIACHELLI, 8
12063 DOGLIANI (CN)
TEL. 0173/76289

FARIGLIANO (CN)

GIOVANNI BATTISTA GILLARDI
CASCINA CORSALETTO, 69
12060 FARIGLIANO (CN)
TEL. 0173/76306-76813

At only his second vintage ever, Bruno Chionetti is a worthy and exciting new entrant in the Guide with some very promising wines. Bruno used to be in advertising, but his family background on the land was too strong a pull. When he was asked if he wanted to put an old estate in Dogliani back on its feet again he did not think twice, and now he produces 16,000 bottles of Dolcetto per year in a well equipped and up-to-date winery. He was the first to use the newly approved DOC sub-zone on his labels, which he does with pride in a vineyard that is difficult to work, but which, by way of compensation, gives him quite exceptional aromatic potential. With such a site and with a 40- year old vineyard Bruno does not take any chances in the cellars when it comes to the potential extract and aromas from these grapes. Thus, he has decided to use temperature-controlled vinification, with only brief maceration and then ageing in stainless steel only. The Dolcetto Vigna del Pilone (sub-zone Còrnole) has an intense bouquet of plums and spirit and is extremely elegant; the richness of this wine unfolds on the palate, creating a sensation of balance between the firm tannins, the alcohol and the fruit. All in all, a superb specimen of the Dolcetto di Dogliani denomination. The Vigna del Romano (sub-zone Madonna delle Grazie) is quick to display its intense aroma of cherries, mingled with sage and vine leaves; it is, however, more acidic and less full-bodied on the palate, despite a very respectable length of finish.

The Gillardi name on a bottle of Dolcetto is a guarantee of the perfect composition of the two elements that intrigue every fan of this wine, bouquet and complexity on the palate. The Dolcetto Cursalet has a very deep ruby red colour, clear evidence of its rich concentration, and displays broad, intoxicating aromas of ripe grapes and more mature macerated fruit, with an aromatic hint of plum stones. On the front palate, warm alcohol is balanced by firm acidity and the lingering finish has an intense, aromatic fruitiness. Dolcetto Vigneto Maestra is a little below par compared to its excellent previous vintages and displays less youthful vigour; both colour and bouquet are more evolved than with the Cursalet, and the nose is enriched with intriguing hints of wood ageing; the alcohol is more powerful than the fruit on the palate; clean, fruit finish, but no more than average length. Giovanni and Pinuccia's other wine is improving; made as a result of a suggestion by their son Giacolino and enigmatically called Harys, a reference to the syrah grape it is based on together with a small amount of cabernet sauvignon. It is a bright ruby red with promising violet tinges and well defined aromas of berry fruit and green pepper on the nose. Although the bouquet is not yet showing much development, it is clearly a wine with good ageing potential. The palate is the most complex feature: rich and grainy with abundant wood tannins which are steadily being assimilated.

● Dolcetto di Dogliani		
Vigna del Pilone '96	♀♀	3
● Dolcetto di Dogliani		
Vigna del Romano '96	♀	2*

● Dolcetto di Dogliani		
Cursalet '96	♀♀	3
● Harys '95	♀♀	5
● Dolcetto di Dogliani		
Vigneto Maestra '96	♀	3
● Dolcetto di Dogliani		
Cursalet '95	♀♀	3
● Dolcetto di Dogliani		
Vigneto Maestra '95	♀♀	3
● Harys '93	♀	5

GATTINARA (VC)

ANTONIOLO
C.SO VALSESIA, 277
13045 GATTINARA (VC)
TEL. 0163/833612

The Antoniolo family name has been firmly linked to the concept of quality in wine for a long time. Their consistent production of modern wines rooted in ancient traditions sets a fine example in a difficult area where nebbiolo can be used to great effect, but can also be a great disappointment. Rosanna is primarily involved with the commercial side of the business and is assisted by her two children, Lorella in the accounts department, and Alberto, who works tirelessly in the vineyards and the cellars. Invaluable technical assistance comes from consultant oenologist Giancarlo Scaglione. Among the wines presented for tasting, as far as power is concerned, Gattinara San Francesco '90 is a clear winner: ruby red with faint orange edges; hints of flowers and pollen on the nose, with ripe blackberries and raspberries, and a touch of cinnamon; soft and firm on the palate with a long finish attractively tinged with velvety tannins. The Osso San Grato '91 comes from a difficult vintage, but has a fresh delicacy of touch. It is slightly pale ruby red with attractive aromas of raspberries and fresh-picked flowers; full-bodied, well-balanced, good finish. The standard Gattinara '93 is a pleasant and uncomplicated wine: ruby red with orange tinges to the edges; flowers and spices on the nose with mineral overtones; rounded and easy to drink with a delightful liquorice twist to the finish. Lastly, two wines that are more than just correct: Erbaluce di Caluso and the Coste della Sesia Nebbiolo Juvenia.

GATTINARA (VC)

GIANCARLO TRAVAGLINI
STRADA DELLE VIGNE, 36
13045 GATTINARA (VC)
TEL. 0163/833588

Considering the output of more than 300,000 bottles a year, and above all the consistently high quality of his wines, Giancarlo Travaglini must be one of the leading producers of northern Italy. The 32 hectares of estate-owned vineyards are cultivated with great care in a rocky zone that makes viticulture difficult. There are two Travaglini Gattinaras; the standard one and the Riserva Numerata, which is only made in the best years. Giancarlo does not bottle single cru selections because he believes in the assemblage of wines from separate vineyards, each with its own character, to give a more complete and harmonious final result, much in the same way as many traditional Barolo producers blend their grapes. This year there was no Riserva Numerata, and to taste again such splendours as the '90 vintage provided again, we shall have to wait for the '93 to be ready. The standard Gattinara '93, which scored very well, is ruby red with faintly orange edges; soft and attractive on the nose with hints of violets, raspberries, sweet almonds and nutmeg; full bodied, good structure with well-integrated tannins that make the liquorice-tinged finish attractively dry. The Proposta Bianco is good; based on chardonnay, sauvignon, pinot noir and pinot grigio the colour is a deep straw yellow and there are precise aromas of apples, peaches and tomato-plant flowers on the nose; well-developed, but youthful enough for easy drinkability. At the same level, the Proposta Rossa is ruby red tending to garnet and has an intense bouquet of plums, spices and straw; easy to drink without lacking in character; finishing well.

● Gattinara S. Francesco '90	▼▼	5
● Gattinara '93	▼	4
● Gattinara Vigneto Osso S. Grato '91	▼	5
● Coste della Sesia Nebbiolo Juvenia '96		3
O Erbaluce di Caluso '96		3
● Gattinara Vigneto Castelle '89	▼▼	5
● Gattinara Vigneto Castelle '90	▼▼	5
● Gattinara Vigneto Osso S. Grato '89	▼▼	5
● Gattinara Vigneto S. Francesco '89	▼▼	5
● Gattinara Vigneto Osso S. Grato '90	▼	5

● Gattinara '93	▼▼	4
O Proposta Bianco	▼	2
● Proposta Rosso	▼	2
● Gattinara Ris. Numerata '88	▼▼	5
● Gattinara Ris. Numerata '89	▼▼	5
● Gattinara Ris. Numerata '90	▼▼	5
● Gattinara '90	▼	4

GAVI (AL)

GAVI (AL)

NICOLA BERGAGLIO
LOC. PEDAGGERI, 59
FRAZ. ROVERETO
15066 GAVI (AL)
TEL. 0143/682195

GIAN PIERO BROGLIA
TENUTA LA MEIRANA
LOC. LOMELLINA, 14
15066 GAVI (AL)
TEL. 0143/642998

Construction work on the big new semi-underground vinification plant has slowed down and is still a long way from completion, but when in a year's time it is finished, it will offer the possibility of unloading grapes at harvest time for gravity-fed processing, an important step forward for the winery. The estate is completely family-run; Gianluigi, who is helped by his ever-more enthusiastic son Diego, believes firmly in the potential of the family's own ten hectares of red, iron-rich, clay soil, an important asset in the production of white wines with structure. But if the new winery is visible only in the form of a hand-made model at the moment, the existing cellars are obviously still quite capable of producing quality wines. The standard Gavi '96 is excellent value for money: fine, pale straw yellow colour enhanced with faint greenish reflections; subtle bouquet of flowers and fresh hay; fresh acidity on the palate balanced by a good structure; slight aftertaste of Golden Delicious apples on the finish. The Gavi '96 from the Minaia vineyard is more concentrated as is clear immediately from the deeper straw yellow colour and the more intense bouquet, enriched with hints of minerals and fresh hazelnuts; bigger structure also means this wine is longer on the palate. The finishes is clean, with a hint of bitter almond.

You can see most of the estate's vineyards in a beautiful view over the hills from the big windows round Gian Piero Broglia's office. Even the briefest chat to Dr Broglia reveals his entirely justified pride in producing one of Italy's most famous and most popular wines. Tangible proof of Broglia's competence lies in the consistently high level of quality of the wines produced by this historic estate in the last few years. The Gavi Bruno Broglia '96 is the flagship wine, and is made from vines dating back to the 1950s: excellent colour; up front, broad aromas of cherry, pear and lime blossom; fresh, smooth, and well structured. The Gavi Villa Broglia '96 is the product of careful grape selection in the cellars. It has a clean bouquet of apricots and mint which reappears on the palate over a full-flavoured body; rich in extract and long finishing. The Gavi '96 La Meirana has a more subtle bouquet with faint hints of broom overlaying soft summer fruit; good structure, well balanced, with an attractive, youthfully green finish. The semi-sparkling Roverello '96 lacks a little in finesse, despite its bouquet of sweet lemons and ferny undergrowth; fresh and easy on the palate, with hints of carbonic acid from the bubbles and a bitter twist on the finish. This year we are pleased to recommend the sparkling wine, Gavi Extra Brut '92, a Metodo Classico wine produced only in the best vintages: clear, golden straw yellow; aristocratic bouquet of honey, white blossom and super-ripe fruit; clean and full-flavoured on the palate, but not particularly long or completely balanced in its maturation.

○ Gavi '96	♟	2*
○ Gavi Minaia '96	♟	3

○ Gavi di Gavi Bruno Broglia '96	♟	4
○ Gavi di Gavi La Meirana '96	♟	3
○ Gavi di Gavi Villa Broglia '96	♟	3
○ Gavi Spumante Extra Brut '92	♟	4
○ Gavi di Gavi Roverello '96		3
● Vigna delle Pernici '95		3
○ Gavi di Gavi Bruno Broglia '95	♟	4

GAVI (AL)

CASTELLARI BERGAGLIO
FRAZ. ROVERETO, 136
15066 GAVI (AL)
TEL. 0143/644000

GAVI (AL)

LA SCOLCA
FRAZ. ROVERETO
15066 GAVI (AL)
TEL. 0143/682176

Wanda Castellari and Mario Bergaglio's affable son, Marco, greet us in their beautiful villa garden and give us an update on the wine production. At the villa door itself an old woman enjoying the sun on this early summer morning bids us good day; this is Marco's grandmother. It was her husband who founded the winery some years ago, and now the most important wine in the range bears his name, Pilin. This is a barrique-aged Gavi di Rovereto that gets a fully deserved Two Glass award in its début vintage. Bright, golden straw yellow colour; harmonious and elegant with aromas of tropical fruit, mint and vanilla. Full-bodied and full-flavoured on the front palate, it broadens out in the mouth with a refreshing acidity that carries it through to a long finish with delicate hints of fresh butter and bananas. The Gavi Barric is a good wine: fruit, vanilla and acacia flowers on the nose; full-bodied, soft and balanced on the palate; the finish is slightly dominated by the wood. The Gavi di Rovereto is also worth a mention: straw yellow with an apple, apricot and white blossom bouquet, fully balanced on the palate. The standard Gavi is floral and fruity on the nose, fresh and attractive on the palate. Lastly, the Brisé scored commendably: a semi-sparkling Gavi which is very clean and well balanced with sharply-defined fruit and a welcome sparkle that endows the wine with freshness and texture on the palate.

The '97 vintage saw the completion of major extension work at Giorgio Soldati's historic winery. State-of-the-art equipment now allows the winery to deal with grapes coming from different vineyards in a gravity-fed system that guarantees maximum quality for each separate batch and, of course, extreme rapidity of processing. Such advanced technology is fully in keeping with the international prestige of this 30-hectare five-million-bottle-per-year estate with vineyards located entirely in Rovereto di Gavi. This year we were given the Brut Nature version of the Millesimato '86 sparkling wine for tasting, although the simple Brut continues to be made. This latter, is an ever-more convincing wine which is particularly interesting for its well developed and ample bouquet: golden yellow colour with a tight fine-bubbled perlage; soft hints of russet apple compôte, fresh butter, white blossom and brioche on the nose; dry on the front palate, with a pronounced sparkle that enlivens a broad, full-flavoured palate to finish rich and long. The Gavi Etichetta Nera is made from the oldest and most favourably sited vines: deep, straw yellow colour, hints of apples, peaches, and meadow flowers on the nose; subtle and fresh-tasting on the palate, well balanced as a whole. Lastly, the Gavi Valentino has a straw yellow colour with faint green reflections; hints of flowers and toasted bread on the nose; up front on the palate with slightly intrusive acidity.

O Gavi di Rovereto Pilin '95	❦❦	4
O Gavi '96	❦	3
O Gavi Barric '94	❦	4
O Gavi Brise '96	❦	3
O Gavi di Rovereto '96	❦	4

O Soldati La Scolca Spumante Brut '86	❦❦	5
O Gavi dei Gavi Etichetta Nera '96	❦	5
O Gavi Valentino '96		3
O Soldati La Scolca Spumante Brut	❦❦	4
O Soldati La Scolca Spumante Brut '84	❦❦	5
O Soldati La Scolca Spumante Extra Brut	❦❦	4

GAVI (AL)

MORGASSI SUPERIORE
LOC. CASE SPARSE FERMORIA, 7
15066 GAVI (AL)
TEL. 0143/642007

We were so sure of the potential of this young producer that we have followed its fortunes for some time; this year, at last, it gains a place in the Guide thanks to an excellent selection of wines. In 1990, the Piacitelli family was brave enough to buy 30 hectares of land that had not been cultivated for 20 years and to build a modern, well-equipped winery there. The rest of the story can best be summarised by the evidence in the tasting glass. The winery is run by Mario Piacitelli and his daughter Cecilia, whose husband Christian Roger works in a different field, but lends his services as an expert sommelier. Technical consultancy comes from Giancarlo Scaglione, while the able cellar-master, Alessandro Rastero, deserves credit for much of the work as well. Two wines have won a well-deserved "One Glass" award, the Gavi '96 and the chardonnay-based Fiordiligi '95. The first has a pale straw yellow colour and a deep bouquet of apples, grapefruit, fresh hay and pollen; full-flavoured and easy to drink on the palate with a satisfying almondy finish. The second has a deeper colour and elegant hints of hazelnuts, cream, tropical fruit and flowers on the nose enlivened with a touch of lemon; good structure, refreshing acidity, rich and long on the finish. The Timorasso has too much of a mineral aroma to its bouquet, but has a sound structure on the palate. The vineyards are all named after characters from Mozart's operas; some of them are experimental and the tiny productions we have tasted so far have all been most encouraging.

GAVI (AL)

VILLA SPARINA
FRAZ. MONTEROTONDO, 56
15066 GAVI (AL)
TEL. 0143/634880-634958

Villa Sparina has the reputation of being one of Gavi's most prestigious quality producers, and indeed recent vintages have confirmed its place among the top estates in the area. There is enthusiastic modernisation going on in this beautiful eighteenth century villa. The Moccagatta family's desire to improve is untiring and is certainly among the reasons for their success. Mario is the dynamo of the vineyards and a convinced proponent drastic pruning. He is also currently President of the Consorzio di Tutela of Gavi, and is assisted at the winery by his son Stefano, who looks after the commercial side of the business. The other son, Massimo, is completing his studies and helping in the vineyards at the same time. Bruna, Mario's very able wife, is mistress of the house and in charge of hospitality at Villa Sparina. The Gavi La Villa '96 is one of the best vintages ever: straw yellow in colour with faint green reflections, broad bouquet of tropical fruit, flowers and apples; full and satisfying on the palate; long and intensely fruity finish. The Gavi Cremant '90 Metodo Classico is to be recommended. The standard Gavi and the Müller-Thurgau are both good. The real stars of the current vintage, however, are the reds from the Ovada district. Scrupulous care in the vineyards and new vinification techniques have given us two great Dolcettos. The d'Giusepp, an authentic Villa Sparina cru, is so full-bodied it is almost over-the-top, but is elegant and velvety nonetheless. The Bric Maioli is a second wine in name only and is extremely attractive. The Barbera should be good, but unfortunately it is still confined to barrique.

O Fiordiligi '96	♥	4
O Gavi '96	♥	3
O Timorasso '95		4
● Leporello '96		3

● Dolcetto d'Acqui Bric Maioli '96	♥♥	3
● Dolcetto d'Acqui d'Giusep '96	♥♥	4
O Gavi Cremant Pas Dosé '90	♥♥	5
O Gavi di Gavi La Villa '96	♥♥	4
O Gavi di Gavi '96	♥	3
O Monferrato Müller Thurgau '96	♥	3
O Gavi di Gavi La Villa '95	♀♀	4

GHEMME (NO)

ANTICHI VIGNETI DI CANTALUPO
VIA MICHELANGELO BUONARROTI, 5
28074 GHEMME (NO)
TEL. 0163/840041

We have seen a long and consistent series of successful Ghemme wines from the Arlunno family, but it did not seem fair to expect too much from a difficult vintage such as '91. In fact, the Collis Breclemae '91 did so well in our tasting that we were sorry for ever having doubted it. The wine has a medium ruby red colour with orange-tinged edges. Age has not compromised its fresh fruit nose and the bouquet is enjoyably complex: strawberries, raspberries and rosemary are the first sensations; broad aromas of tar and dried flowers follow. The front palate is typical of a big wine and firm, noble tannins make the long, fruit-and-liquorice finish austere. The Collis Carellae '90 is even marginally better: deep ruby to garnet red with extraordinarily firm and undiluted edges; soft and ample bouquet unfolding into aromas of plums, cinnamon, berry fruits and violets; complex palate with a long and concentrated finish. The Ghemme '90 has an opaque ruby to garnet red colour and a bouquet of flowers, fruit, and sweet spices with a faint mineral undertone; balanced and full-bodied, rich finish brushed with sweet tannins. The Collis Carellae '91 is ruby red colour with orange tinges to the edges and has a complex bouquet of dried flowers, dried figs, tar and toasted almonds; rich and well-judged balance on the palate; dry finish. Villa Horta is an attractive, fruity, easy drinking wine made of vespolina. Both the Mimo, a rosé made from nebbiolo, and the white Carolus are enjoyable, light wines.

● Ghemme Collis Breclemae '91	🍷🍷	4
● Ghemme Collis Carellae '90	🍷🍷	5
● Ghemme '90	🍷	4
● Ghemme Collis Carellae '91	🍷	4
● Villa Horta '96	🍷	2
○ Carolus '96		2
⊙ Mimo '96		2
● Ghemme Collis Breclemae '88	🍸🍸	5
● Ghemme Collis Breclemae '89	🍸🍸	5
● Ghemme Collis Carellae '89	🍸🍸	5
● Ghemme Collis Carellae '88	🍸	5
● Ghemme Signore di Bayard '90	🍸	5

INCISA SCAPACCINO (AT)

ERMANNO E ALESSANDRO BREMA
VIA POZZOMAGNA, 9
14045 INCISA SCAPACCINO (AT)
TEL. 0141/74019-74617

Ermanno Brema deserves a vote of thanks for continuing to produce Dolcetto d'Asti, a red that could be easily claim a place on Slow Food's Ark for food and wine products threatened with extinction. Once again this year, we have given Two Glasses to Brema's Dolcetto d'Asti Vigna Impagnato '95. This is a big-structured wine with a deep colour: the bouquet is clean, spicy and full of aromas, some more concentrated, such as the note of toastiness, others sweeter like the ripe fruit; full-bodied on the palate and still maturing into balance, but a confident red buoyed up by rich fruit which softens the tannins on a long finish. The Barbera d'Asti Le Cascine '95 is the other Brema wine that undergoes barrique ageing and is only slightly less convincing. It is not yet balanced and it lacks the body of previous vintages. Of the wines tasted this year, all made from grapes from Brema-owned vineyards, the Grignolino d'Asti Le Rocche stands out: pale but bright ruby red; typical, delicate, spicy varietal nose of black pepper and faintly aromatic fruit; easy to drink with classic finish of tannins combined with acidity. This very quaffable series of red wines concludes with the semi-sparkling Dolcetto d'Asti Vigna Montera '96, the full-bodied Barbera Del Monferrato Vigna Castagnei from the same vintage, and the classic Brachetto Carlotta.

● Dolcetto d'Asti Vigna Impagnato '95	🍷🍷	3
● Barbera d'Asti Sup. Le Cascine '95	🍷	4
● Grignolino d'Asti Bric Le Rocche '96	🍷	2
● Piemonte Brachetto Carlotta '96	🍷	4
● Barbera del M.to Vigna Castagnei '96		2
● Dolcetto d'Asti Vigna Montera '96		2
● Barbera d'Asti Sup. Le Cascine '94	🍸🍸	4
● Dolcetto d'Asti Vigna Impagnato '94	🍸🍸	3

IVREA (TO)

LUIGI FERRANDO & FIGLIO
C.SO CAVOUR, 9
10015 IVREA (TO)
TEL. 0125/641176

LA MORRA (CN)

LORENZO ACCOMASSO
VIA ANNUNZIATA, 34
12064 LA MORRA (CN)
TEL. 0173/50843

Luigi Ferrando has presented us with a range of good quality wines once again this year. Although the top Carema Etichetta Nera is missing from the line up (1990 was the last vintage made of this prestige selection), Luigi has succeeded in finding some interesting wines amongst the traditional whites of the Canavese area. The highest scores go to the Solativo '96, the flagship cru Erbaluce di Caluso Cariola, another Erbaluce called Campore from the vineyards of the Gabriele and Fiamenghi family, the Caluso Passito Boratto '91, and the white table wine, Montodo. The Solativo is made from semi-dried or "passito" grapes: golden yellow colour, intense bouquet of citrus fruit and acacia flowers; full-bodied and broad with an attractively long, sweet finish. The Erbaluce Cariola has a deep, almost golden colour; the subtle bouquet happily contrasts almonds with oak; full-bodied on the palate, broad structure, well balanced, good full flavour on the finish. The Campore scored marginally lower. It has a style based more on weight than elegance. The Montodo table wine is something completely different: made from pinot grigio grapes from vineyards belonging to the Biglia family, it has an intense bouquet with hints of aromatic fruit, is well-rounded on the front palate but perhaps a little short in the finish. The Caluso Passito '91 is a successful wine which combines a diffuse bouquet with a notably broad and rich palate. The standard Erbaluce, the Canavese Bianco (a new DOC) Castello di Loranzè and the Montodo Rosso are worth a brief look.

Congratulations! Lorenzo Accomasso has now been bottling his Barolo for a full 40 years now, not that a few brief decades is very long for a grand old man like him who has always been a vigneron. On such an important anniversary we had to include his entry in the Guide, even if we cannot comment on his latest Barolos until the next edition. The '92 has not yet been bottled, while the '93 versions are still undergoing bottle maturation as we go to press. From our barrel tastings, the Rocche appears very lively, clean and soft and it should develop well in bottle. Right from the outset it has shown berry fruit and white chocolate aromas. The Rochette '93 has six months' more ageing than the Rocche and should be more severe overall. The Dolcetto '95 has a ruby red colour enlivened with purple tinges; the cherry bouquet is firm and subtle at the same time and is balanced by an uncomplicated vinosity; rich in alcohol on the palate with attractive fruity length. We suggest you go and taste the wines in person; Lorenzo's sister, Elena, will welcome you like a true public relations professional.

O Solativo '96	▽▽	5
O Caluso Passito Boratto '91	▽	5
O Erbaluce di Caluso Cariola '96	▽	3
O Erbaluce di Caluso Campore '96	▽	3
O Montodo Bianco '96	▽	3
O Canavese Bianco Castello di Loranzè '96		3
● Montodo Rosso '96		1
O Erbaluce di Caluso Ferrando '96		3
O Caluso Passito '90	▽▽	6
● Carema Etichetta Nera '88	▽▽	6
● Carema Etichetta Nera '90	▽▽	6
● Carema Etichetta Bianca '90	▽	5
● Carema Etichetta Bianca '91	▽	4

● Dolcetto d'Alba Rocchettevino La Pria '95	▽	3
● Barolo Rocche '91	▽▽	5
● Barolo Vigneto Rocchette '90	▽▽	6
● Barolo Rocche Ris. '90	▽	6

LA MORRA (CN)

LA MORRA (CN)

★ ELIO ALTARE
B.TA POZZO, 51
FRAZ. ANNUNZIATA
12064 LA MORRA (CN)
TEL. 0173/50835

RENATO RATTI ANTICHE CANTINE
DELL'ABBAZIA DELL'ANNUNZIATA
FRAZ. ANNUNZIATA, 7
12064 LA MORRA (CN)
TEL. 0173/50185

With the wines presented for tasting this year Elio Altare can say that he has realised one of his most secret and ardent desires; he has succeeded in giving all his wines the unique and unmistakable personality of their vineyards of origin. Altare is not only a revolutionary producer and a great innovator, he also possesses the magical ability to endow his wine with his own personal style, thereby enhancing the qualities given by the soil, climate and position of his vineyards in Annunziata di La Morra. From the Larigi to the Dolcetto the house style embodies softness, judgement and opulence that is breathtaking. The Vigna Larigi has a ruby red colour without being of the deepest hue; the nose is immediately remarkable with a bouquet that keeps on developing; a magisterial grip on the palate is sustained by a richness of extract that melts away leaving the heavily-laden aromas the task of defining an impressive finish. The depth of sensation coming from the La Villa is exciting: this cuvée of Nebbiolo and Barbera has a certain severe austerity but it never makes the wine harsh and unapproachable; quite the contrary, it enriches the bouquet, giving it breadth; the palate might be defined as muscular, but there is a multi-layered softness behind it to control the firmness. The Villa Arborina is lively, spare and floral at the same time; a lovely example of nebbiolo with rare definition. The two Barolos are paragons: the standard version is incisive and vigorous, one for the traditionalists; while the Vigna Arborina fulfils the dreams of the innovators with its elegance. Lastly, the Barbera and the Dolcetto are most attractive, text-book varietals.

This historic producer now operates from two winery sites, one at Annunziata della Morra and the other at Costigliole d'Asti, producing a wide range of wines. Massimo Martinelli, together with Pietro and Giovanni Ratti are anxious not to rest on the laurels of their undoubtedly glorious past and are enthusiastically experimenting with various types of wine and different cellar techniques. This year their most interesting wines have been the Barolos and the Villa Pattono wines from the Asti region. The Marcenasco '93 is a typical Barolo of the old school, with orange edges and a bouquet already on its way to maturity; it shows well. The two cru Marcenasco wines, Conca and Rocche, are, however, noticeably better, and they both score higher thanks to superior complexity and elegance. We must admit to a slight preference for the Rocche, which is rich in alcohol, fruit and body, and at the same time, thanks to its noble tannins, soft and satisfying on the palate. The Villa Pattono '95, made from barbera, freisa, uvalino and merlot, is especially good, with its finely-judged balance between fruit and oak on the nose. The Cabernet Sauvignon I Cedri is of similarly high quality and is made with elegance rather than power in mind. The Merlot scores at the same level as the other prestige crus, while slightly lower ratings go to the barrique-aged Barbera Torriglione, the Dolcetto Colombè from the vineyards at Mango, and the Nebbiolo Ochetti. The standard Dolcetto d'Alba is to be recommended.

●	Langhe Larigi '95	♟♟♟	6
●	Barolo '93	♟♟	5
●	Barolo Vigneto Arborina '93	♟♟	6
●	Dolcetto d'Alba '96	♟♟	3
●	Langhe Arborina '95	♟♟	6
●	Langhe La Villa '95	♟♟	6
●	Barbera d'Alba '95	♟	4
●	Barolo Vigneto Arborina '89	♟♟♟	6
●	Barolo Vigneto Arborina '90	♟♟♟	6
●	Barolo Vigneto Arborina '93	♟♟♟	6
●	Langhe Larigi '94	♟♟♟	6
●	Vigna Arborina '89	♟♟♟	6
●	Vigna Arborina '90	♟♟♟	6
●	Vigna Arborina '93	♟♟♟	6
●	Vigna Larigi '90	♟♟♟	6

●	Barolo Conca Marcenasco '93	♟♟	6
●	Barolo Rocche Marcenasco '93	♟♟	6
●	Cabernet Sauvignon I Cedri '95	♟♟	4
●	Merlot '95	♟♟	4
●	Villa Pattono '95	♟♟	4
●	Barbera d'Alba Torriglione '95	♟	4
●	Barolo Marcenasco '93	♟	5
●	Dolcetto d'Alba Colombè '96	♟	3
●	Nebbiolo d'Alba Ochetti '95	♟	4
●	Dolcetto d'Alba '96		3
●	Barolo Rocche Marcenasco '83	♟♟♟	6
●	Barolo Rocche Marcenasco '84	♟♟♟	6
●	Barolo Conca Marcenasco '90	♟♟	5
●	Barolo Rocche Marcenasco '90	♟♟	5
●	Cabernet Sauvignon I Cedri '94	♟♟	4

LA MORRA (CN)

LA MORRA (CN)

BATASIOLO
FRAZ. ANNUNZIATA, 87
12064 LA MORRA (CN)
TEL. 0173/50130-50131

ENZO BOGLIETTI
VIA ROMA, 37
12064 LA MORRA (CN)
TEL. 0173/50330

Batasiolo is back on form after the disastrous '92 vintage for Barolo and the equally disastrous '95 for the early-drinking wines. The samples we have tasted this time are a return to the glories of the past and a most reassuring quality. Of course, we were expecting the whites to be good, given the involvement of specialist consultant Giorgio Graj, but the reds do not let the side down either. The Barolo Corda della Bricolina '93 does not reach the heights of the vintages we have given top awards to in the past, but it is clearly an outstanding wine: bright, limpid garnet red; complex bouquet dominated by macerated violets, hazelnuts and spices; expansive on the palate, full-bodied, almost over-rich, long finishing. Barolo Bofani does not have such a strong character, but it is clean and well made. The Dolcetto del Bricco di Vergne is much improved: a red for drinking now, vinous and enjoyably full-flavoured. The two Chardonnays are made in different styles but are both very enjoyable. The barrique-aged Morino '94 shows how the oak helps the development of the nose: bright golden colour with a bouquet of peaches and bananas sweetened by hints of cinnamon; full-bodied, lively and long on the palate. The Moscato Bosc dla Rei is very good and designed to be broad on the palate rather than rich on the nose; it stands out for its slight sparkle and long well-evolved palate. The splendid Moscato Passito is full-bodied, well-balanced and altogether fascinating, a graceful wine for sipping slowly.

It would take a Bruce Springsteen ballad to describe the scene in this corner of the Langhe: father and son washing the barriques in the courtyard, the door bell ringing, dogs barking, the sound of footsteps, the burning July sun. A man in his early thirties comes out to meet us wearing boots, jeans and a black shirt. It is him, Enzo Boglietti, the rock star of Barolo. He welcomes us into the kitchen and begins to talk. He has been married for two weeks and has been making wine for five or six years. Two godfathers keep watch over him, just like Jerry Lee Lewis and Roy Orbison; the one looks after his modern side (the barrique), the other looks after his traditional, melodic lyricism (in other words, balance). And this is what his wines are like. He makes two Barolos, the Case Nere in barrique and the Brunate in big barrels. We preferred the second for its fine interpretation of the vintage. But the best wine of all from this winery is undoubtedly the Barbera Vigna dei Romani, which is made from old vines in the Fossati vineyard; here the use of barriques is not over-the-top and does not create any of the usual complications. This is a great wine, vinified with an expert touch, where the varietal aromas blend perfectly with the sweetness of the wood; easy to drink and velvety on the palate with real thoroughbred style. Going on to the Dolcettos, the standard one has good varietal character, while the Tigli Neri, punningly named after its four vineyards of origin, is more structured and generally a more serious wine. Lastly, the Buio is a blend of Nebbiolo and Barbera which has already picked up a good reputation for itself at home and abroad.

●	Barolo Corda della Briccolina '93	♟♟	6
○	Moscato d'Asti Bosc dla Rei '96	♟♟	4
○	Piemonte Moscato Passito		
	Muscatel Tardì '96	♟♟	5
○	Langhe Chardonnay Morino '94	♟	5
○	Langhe Chardonnay Serbato '96	♟	3
●	Barolo Bofani '93	♟	5
●	Dolcetto d'Alba		
	Bricco di Vergne '96	♟	4
●	Barolo Corda della Briccolina '88	♟♟♟	6
●	Barolo Corda della Briccolina '89	♟♟♟	6
●	Barolo Corda della Briccolina '90	♟♟♟	6
●	Barolo Bofani '90	♟♟	6
●	Barolo Boscareto '90	♟♟	6
●	Barolo Corda della Briccolina '91	♟♟	6

●	Barbera d'Alba		
	Vigna dei Romani '95	♟♟	4
●	Barolo Vigna Case Nere '93	♟♟	5
●	Barolo Vigna delle Brunate '93	♟♟	5
●	Buio '94	♟♟	4
●	Dolcetto d'Alba Tigli Neri '96	♟♟	3
●	Dolcetto d'Alba '96	♟	3
●	Barbera d'Alba		
	Vigna dei Romani '94	♟♟♟	4
●	Barolo Vigna delle Brunate '91	♟♟	5
●	Barolo Vigna delle Brunate '92	♟♟	5
●	Buio '93	♟♟	4
●	Dolcetto d'Alba		
	Vigna dei Fossati '94	♟♟	3

LA MORRA (CN)

GIANFRANCO BOVIO
B.TA CIOTTO, 63
FRAZ. ANNUNZIATA
12064 LA MORRA (CN)
TEL. 0173/50190

Walter and Carla Porasso have been the heart and soul of the Bovio winery ever since they took it on when they were young and turned it into the idyllic corner of the Langhe that it is now. The people and the wines have grown up together; in the best years they have been garlanded with honours, in the worst there have been unending difficulties, but nothing has been allowed to upset the mutual regard between Gian Bovio and the Porassos. The transparency of the wines reflects the transparency of this relationship. Barolo Arborina is garnet red, but bright garnet red; it has the unmistakable varietal aroma of plums and something that is almost menthol, and quite typical for this cru; medium weight, not too alcoholic, soft tannins stimulating the palate without being at all aggressive and bringing out the minty qualities of the long finish. The Gattera is only marginally inferior. It has a superb fruity bouquet, is greener and more youthful on the palate, but without any harshness. The Dolcetto is up front and easy to drink with the vinous bouquet of a lively, simple and refreshing wine. The Il Ciotto has more to it than just its sparkle; lively acidity makes it refreshing and easy to drink. The Regiaveja has greater pretensions but needs further work to bring it up to scratch; the problem is an over-mature bouquet, although admittedly some people do like that style. Fortunately, Walter seems to be about to put things right with new wood ageing techniques. The winery also produces a Chardonnay: bananas on the nose, rich in alcohol, but a little unbalanced by lack of aroma.

LA MORRA (CN)

CORINO
FRAZ. ANNUNZIATA, 24
12064 LA MORRA (CN)
TEL. 0173/50219-509452

Renato Corino might call himself a keep-fit fanatic, but for him keeping in shape is more a consequence of hard work in the vineyards than in the gym. What could be called his "training programme" gives him good results in 13 hectares of vineyards planted with dolcetto, nebbiolo and barbera (half of which are estate-owned) in one of the best spots in the Langhe, at Annunziata della Morra. Plaudits and work-load alike are shared with his brother Giuliano, and in just one decade the winery has gained a solid reputation for quality in the Italian wine world. House style is based on getting the best from each vineyard site, particularly for the Barolo. A good example is the Vigneto Rocche, a real delight with its colour somewhere between deep ruby red and garnet red and its complex, elegant bouquet of interwoven aromas of ripe fruit, spices and vanilla; the palate is rich and full with dense, soft tannins. The Vigna Giachini version is more masculine in character: weight, finely-judged balance and strength on the finish come after a deep, strong colour; the wine has an uncompromising bouquet of fruit, tar and alcohol; and there are tannins and fruit to be found again on the palate. As usual the Barbera Vigna Pozzo has a full bouquet with aromas of fruit well integrated with the toastiness of the wood; on the palate the structure is supported by characteristic varietal acidity and the alcohol buoys up the fruit. The uncomplicated non-cru version has an attractive nose and an easy drinkability. The Dolcetto is a soft and easy wine that will not disappoint: fresh, dry and with a winning, lively vinosity.

Wine	Rating	Score
● Barolo Vigneto Arborina dell'Annunziata '93	ΨΨ	5
● Barolo Vigneto Gattera dell'Annunziata '93	ΨΨ	5
● Barbera d'Alba Il Ciotto '96	Ψ	3
● Barbera d'Alba Regiaveja '94	Ψ	4
● Dolcetto d'Alba Vigneto Dabbene dell'Annunziata '96	Ψ	3
○ Langhe Chardonnay Vigna La Villa '96		3
● Barolo Vigneto Arborina dell'Annunziata '90	ΨΨΨ	6
● Barolo Vigneto Arborina dell'Annunziata '92	ΨΨ	6

Wine	Rating	Score
● Barolo Vigna Giachini '93	ΨΨ	5
● Barolo Vigneto Rocche '93	ΨΨ	5
● Barbera d'Alba '96	Ψ	3
● Barbera d'Alba Vigna Pozzo '95	Ψ	4
● Dolcetto d'Alba '96	Ψ	3
● Barolo Vigna Giachini '89	ΨΨΨ	5
● Barolo Vigneto Rocche '90	ΨΨΨ	5
● Barbera d'Alba Vigna Pozzo '91	ΨΨ	4
● Barbera d'Alba Vigna Pozzo '94	ΨΨ	4
● Barolo Vigna Giachini '90	ΨΨ	5
● Barolo Vigna Giachini '92	ΨΨ	5
● Barolo Vigneto Rocche '92	Ψ	5

LA MORRA (CN)

LA MORRA (CN)

DOSIO
REG. SERRADENARI, 16
12064 LA MORRA (CN)
TEL. 0173/50677

ERBALUNA
B.TA POZZO, 43
12064 LA MORRA (CN)
TEL. 0173/50800

Beppe Dosio thinks holidays are now an unattainable luxury. The ever-wider range of wines he makes in his 60,000 bottle production run means that he has no time to relax any more. Fortunately, he can rely on the help of his faithful cellar master, Giorgio Vaira. If you are confused by the range of wine he produces, this is how they are classified: the traditional wines of the Langhe range has a complementary range of special non-DOC blends which seem to be acquiring their own identity as the years go on; then, inside these two major ranges there will often be two versions of the same wine, one made as a lighter or heavier version of the other. This year the Barolo was somewhat lean and over-mature with a porty nose, firm tannins, and a brief but attractive hazelnut aroma. The Barbera is soft and pleasant enough, but there is not much to it. Of the two Dolcettos, we prefer the Nassone, which is usually more rustic in style: it has a pronounced cherry nose, and is tight on the palate with all the taste elements well blended together. The Serradenari is softer and, though it does not have any defects, it has less character. The Freisa can be recommended for its freshness and good definition. As for the barrique wines, the Momenti, made from barbera and nebbiolo, is on the up and up and shows more skilful handling of wood than usual; over-oaking, however, is definitely the problem with the chardonnay-based Barilà . Still in the barrique category and on its first release, the Eventi is a stunning success. This assemblage of equal parts of Barbera, Dolcetto and Nebbiolo has delicately balanced fruit and vanilla on the nose, while the elements of freshness and body are nicely judged on the palate.

Making wines organically is not easy. Apart from the limitations this imposes on the fermentation and the ageing process, the length of time needed to make a vineyard completely organic means that results are slow to emerge. But patience has paid off for the Oberto family, who, 13 years after going organic, seem to have found the right balance in their wines between the constraints of organic cultivation and the production of quality wine. Severino Oberto, helped by his brother Andrea and father Sisto, has put together a selection of wines this year that are distinguished for their definition and their stability. The Dolcetto is made in the winning La Morra mould with a bright colour and a heady bouquet of bitter cherries and fresh almonds; the palate is elegant and long without being over-complex. The Barbera Selezione is more concentrated than the standard version and, aged in oak, displays a deeper colour; the bouquet succeeds in balancing vinosity with an intriguing hint of berry fruits; the structure is supported by acidity, and helped by rich extract. The Obertos own seven hectares of vineyards and produce about 30,000 bottles per year. The principal grape is nebbiolo, which is used to make a standard Barolo and the Rocche cru selection. The former is elegant, not over rich and floral on the nose; it comes over as soft on the palate and ready to drink now. The Barolo Rocche is a more ambitious wine: deep garnet red in colour; liquorice and tobacco mixed with cherries and plums on the nose; firm on the palate with some lively tannins on the tongue; well knit together and long finishing. Apart from the wine, this hard working family also manages a very decent "agriturismo" business next to the cellars.

● Barbera d'Alba Sant'Anna '95	▼	2*
● Barolo Fossati '93	▼	5
● Dolcetto d'Alba Nassone '96	▼	3
● Eventi '95	▼	4
● Momenti '94	▼	4
○ Barilà '94		4
● Dolcetto d'Alba Serradenari '96		3
● Langhe Freisa Serradenari '96		3
● Barolo Fossati '90	▼▼	5
● Barolo Fossati '92	▼▼	5
● Barolo Fossati '91	▼	5

● Barolo Rocche '93	▼	4
● Barbera d'Alba Selezione '96	▼	3
● Barolo '93	▼	4
● Dolcetto d'Alba '96	▼	3
● Barbera d'Alba '96		2

LA MORRA (CN)

SILVIO GRASSO
CASCINA LUCIANI, 112
FRAZ. ANNUNZIATA
12064 LA MORRA (CN)
TEL. 0173/50322

The oenological traditions of the Grasso family have missed out a generation, and it is the grandson Federico who has inherited the passion for top class winemaking from his grandfather. This good-natured vigneron has the enthusiasm and the undoubted skill of a true cellar master, even if brief maceration and total commitment to ageing in French oak are not ideas that have been handed down through the generations. But the ends justify the means, and all credit must go to Federico and his wife Marilena for the excellent work that they are doing. The two Barolo crus are very good: the Bricco Luciani has a garnet red colour, a bouquet of flowers, berry fruit and sweet spices, and a firm, well-balanced, and smooth palate that follows through well from the nose. The Ciabot Manzoni has a nose that is more elegant than powerful, softly enveloping the senses with well-defined wood aromas; it is soft, full-bodied, rich in alcohol, with tannins that still clearly need softening out. The Barolo '93 is a less complex wine with a colour tinged with orange reflections; the nose is less striking than in the cru version (flowers and fruit) and the palate shows an extract that is on the lean side. The Nebbiolo is very good and it is only at the palate stage that the poor vintage makes itself felt: firm bouquet with complex aromas of coffee, plums and violets; good on the front palate and well-balanced, but lacking in the final burst of energy that comes only with the better vintages. The same is true for the barrique-aged Barbera Fontanile: the nose is somewhat closed and the toastiness of the oak masks what fruit there is; the finish is firm and correct, but short and not very smooth. Lastly, the Dolcetto has a deep cardinal-red colour; the nose displays aromas of fruit and fermentation; it has a good palate and is very drinkable.

LA MORRA (CN)

MARCARINI
P.ZZA MARTIRI, 2
12064 LA MORRA (CN)
TEL. 0173/50222

The Marcarini family get their grapes from some of the best cru sites in La Morra, most particularly the slopes towards Barolo, and make extremely reliable, good quality wines. All the products tasted this year were exceptionally good, with one wine standing head and shoulders above the rest, the Dolcetto Boschi di Berri. This is an extraordinary Dolcetto that always comes out at the top of its class; this year, because it has made the most of an excellent vintage, it fully deserves its Three Glass award. The wine is made from very old vines, some of them even pre-phylloxera, and is velvety and well-balanced. Compared to other Dolcettos from this area, which tend to be made more like Barolos, the Boschi di Berri is silky, elegant and delicate. The bouquet is clean and intense with hints of bitter cherries and fresh fruit; the colour is a limpidly clear garnet red. Concentrated and well-balanced on the palate with prominent but unobtrusive tannins and a finish with a delicate almond twist. The two Barolos are excellent; if the Brunate is slightly superior to the La Serra it is because of the greatness of the cru site. The experimental Barbera d'Alba Ciabot Camerano is a definite success, but the richness of the fruit and the toastiness of the wood have yet to balance out completely. Lastly, the Dolcetto Fonatanazza, the Boschi di Berri's younger brother, is less structured but fruity and easy to drink nonetheless. This year the Marcarinis have begun to make a few thousand bottles of Barolo Chinato, in the tradition of some of the oldest wine producers of the Langhe. It only remains for us to congratulate the new generation, Luisa Bava and her husband Manuel, who have made such a good job of running the family estate since they took over the reins a few years ago.

● Barolo Bricco Luciani '93	♟♟	5
● Barolo Ciabot Manzoni '93	♟♟	5
● Nebbiolo Langhe '94	♟♟	4
● Barbera d'Alba Fontanile '94	♟	4
● Barolo '93	♟	4
● Dolcetto d'Alba '96	♟	3
● Barolo Bricco Luciani '90	♟♟♟	5
● Barbera d'Alba Fontanile '93	♟♟	4
● Barolo Bricco Luciani '91	♟♟	5
● Barolo Bricco Luciani '92	♟♟	5
● Barolo Ciabot Manzoni '90	♟♟	5
● Barolo Ciabot Manzoni '92	♟	5

● Dolcetto d'Alba		
Boschi di Berri '96	♟♟♟	3
● Barolo Brunate '93	♟♟	5
● Barolo La Serra '93	♟♟	5
● Barbera d'Alba		
Ciabot Camerano '95	♟	4
● Dolcetto d'Alba Fontanazza '96	♟	3
● Barolo Brunate Ris. '85	♟♟♟	6
● Barolo Brunate '90	♟♟	6
● Barolo Brunate '91	♟♟	5
● Barolo Brunate '92	♟♟	5
● Barolo La Serra '90	♟♟	6
● Dolcetto d'Alba		
Boschi di Berri '95	♟♟	4
● Barolo La Serra '92	♟	5

LA MORRA (CN)

LA MORRA (CN)

MAURO MOLINO
B.TA GANCIA, 111
FRAZ. ANNUNZIATA
12064 LA MORRA (CN)
TEL. 0173/50814

MONFALLETTO
CORDERO DI MONTEZEMOLO
FRAZ. ANNUNZIATA, 67/BIS
12064 LA MORRA (CN)
TEL. 0173/50344

This family-run estate is still not as well known as it should be considering the style, attractiveness and consistent quality of the wines it produces. The Acanzio is an outstanding Nebbiolo/ Barbera blend that comes right back on form this year. It is assembled following a system of cuvée selection similar to that used in Champagne: just before bottling, the best barriques are picked out and the proportions of the blend decided on the basis of the characteristics of the two separately aged varietals. The result is a seductive mix of power and elegance: deep, opaque ruby red; a rich bouquet of plums and almonds, musk and cinnamon; soft on the front palate, well-balanced, steadily unfolding to a clean, nutty finish. The cru wine of the estate, the Barolo Conca, is excellent: limpid, deep colour with a delicate, fruity nose of some finesse with hints of flowers; on the palate, freshness and the finely-judged softness of the tannins make up for the absence of aromatic complexity on the finish. The standard Barolo is made in a completely different mould and is intended for those who like traditional-style Nebbiolos: garnet red colour, baked plums on a moderate nose, good alcohol on the palate and not too big a wine. The Dolcetto is very traditional, with delicate hints of strawberries on the nose that go beyond simple vinosity; fresh acidity gives the impression of early picked fruit. The Chardonnay '96 is another big, characterful wine where oak has successfully enhanced rather than dominated: as well as vanilla on the nose, the bouquet also contains sage, white peaches and apricots; the notable acidity is balanced by good structure; broad nutmeg finish.

To find this winery, aim for the magnificent cedar of Lebanon on the top of Monfalletto hill. It was planted by Costanzo Falletti di Rodello in 1856 on the occasion of his marriage to Eulalia Della Chiesa di Cervignasco, as a sign of their love for the spot. Monfalletto owns 26 hectares of vineyards in one parcel surrounding the estate buildings, on a site which also goes under the name Gattera, and roughly another three hectares in the Villero vineyard at Castiglione Falletto, which produces the grapes for Barolo Enrico VI. The recently renovated winery is stupendous, fully equipped with stainless steel tanks, traditional barrels and, most the recent additions, a large number of barriques. We will not mention the view except to say that it is one of the most beautiful in the Langhe. In the tasting we were particular impressed with the '93 Barolos. The differences between the two crus, both vinified in the same way, remain and will grow more accentuated as time goes on. The colours are very similar: a good, deep, ruby red with garnet reflections. The nose is splendid in both cases: the Monfalletto is more open, with aromas of ripe berry fruit overlaying spices; the Enrico VI may be more closed, but it is just as attractive. On the palate, the Monfalletto is more enjoyable at the moment because it is better balanced; the other wine has bigger tannins, but also more extract and a longer finish. The three '96 reds are well made and all have good cru character. They are: a Nebbiolo aged in barriques for some months; a generous and very floral Dolcetto; and an extremely fruity and full-flavoured Barbera. We finish with the Langhe Rosso (1,500 bottles of pinot nero), the Chardonnay Elioro, and the Langhe Bianco which is made from arneis grown at La Morra.

● Acanzio '95	♈♈	4
● Barolo Vigna Conca '93	♈♈	5
○ Langhe Chardonnay Livrot '96	♈♈	4
● Barolo '93	♈	4
● Dolcetto d'Alba '96	♈	3
● Acanzio '90	♉♉	4
● Barolo Vigna Conca '90	♉♉	5
● Barolo Vigna Conca '92	♉♉	5
○ Langhe Chardonnay Livrot '95	♉♉	4
● Acanzio '93	♉	4
● Acanzio '94	♉	4

● Barolo Enrico VI '93	♈♈	5
● Barolo Monfalletto '93	♈♈	5
● Barbera d'Alba '96	♈	4
● Dolcetto d'Alba '96	♈	3
○ Langhe Chardonnay Elioro '96	♈	4
● Langhe Nebbiolo '96	♈	3
● Langhe Rosso '95	♈	4
○ Langhe Bianco '96		4
● Barbera d'Alba '95	♉♉	4
● Barolo Enrico VI '90	♉♉	6
● Barolo Enrico VI '92	♉♉	5
● Barolo Monfalletto '90	♉♉	6
● Barolo Monfalletto '92	♉	5

LA MORRA (CN)

LA MORRA (CN)

ANDREA OBERTO
VIA G. MARCONI, 25
12064 LA MORRA (CN)
TEL. 0173/509262

F.LLI ODDERO
VIA S. MARIA, 28
12064 LA MORRA (CN)
TEL. 0173/50618

This year, Fabio Oberto starts what must be an exciting career in one of the most reliable wineries of the area with the affectionate and expert guidance of his father Andrea. Our best wishes to him. Going on to the wines, they are now gaining in complexity and merit detailed description. The Barolo immediately looks rich in the glass; on the nose, the fruit is a little hidden at the moment because the wine is still in its dumb phase but on the palate the fullness of body and balance typical of the Rocche vineyard is clearly shown, even if the wood tannins still make the wine astringent and have not been completely tamed by the fruit. The Barbera d'Alba Boiolo '96 has been vinified in the traditional manner and is an impressive wine: intense aromas of cherries, berry fruit and cedar wood; soft on the front palate followed by full body and a long consistent finish. The Barbera Giada '95 was aged in barrique and bottled only a few days before this Guide went to press; we will comment on it next year when it has had sufficient bottle age. The two Dolcettos are both elegant wines. The Vantrino Albarella has the bigger structure of the two and takes its name from its two vineyards of origin, one at La Morra and the other at Barolo, which endow it with an aroma of fresh peach skins; the palate is firm but finely-balanced. The San Francesco is more vegetal and has a higher acidity with a clear vine-leaf bouquet and an attractive and well-managed spritz .

This estate is so old that its exact date of foundation cannot be traced! The winery has, however, always belonged to the Oddero family who, generation after generation, have extended both buildings and vineyards so that today they own a total of 45 hectares. The vineyards are for the most part planted with nebbiolo and are located in some of the best south-facing slopes of the Langhe - Vigna Rionda, Mondoca di Bussia Soprana, Rocche di Bussia, and Brunate, not forgetting Rive di Parà, three hectares of vineyards with a traditional brick-built tower or "specula " that dominates the site and provides magnificent views over the vineyards of the Langhe. Experience and tradition are the two cornerstones of this winery. The best wine of the '93 vintage is the Barolo Vigna Rionda: garnet red with orange reflections and a full bouquet, rich in alcohol, with hints of spices, fruit and dried roses; dry on the palate, quite well balanced, with tannins as yet not fully blended in. The Rocche dei Rivera comes from the cru vineyard site in Castiglione Falletto. It scores lower than the Vigna Rionda because of a weakness in the bouquet, where the fruit and spice aromas do not come through with sufficient power or immediacy; nevertheless, it is an attractive wine to drink thanks to its balance and already well-developed maturity. The Dolcetto is a good wine with a ruby red colour enlivened with bright violet reflections; fresh, vinous and fruity nose; good follow-through on the palate, adequately tannic with an enjoyable almond twist on the finish. The Chardonnay is floral and fruity and very easy to drink. It is worth visiting the winery to see the small but interesting collection of old agricultural implements displayed at the cellar entrance.

● Barbera d'Alba		
Vigneto Boiolo '96	🍷🍷	3*
● Barolo Vigneto Rocche '93	🍷🍷	5
● Dolcetto d'Alba		
S. Francesco '96	🍷🍷	3*
● Dolcetto d'Alba		
Vantrino Albarella '96	🍷🍷	3*
● Barbera d'Alba Giada '93	🍷🍷	4
● Barolo Vigneto Rocche '90	🍷🍷	5
● Barolo Vigneto Rocche '91	🍷🍷	5
● Dolcetto d'Alba		
S. Francesco '95	🍷🍷	3
● Dolcetto d'Alba		
Vantrino Albarella '95	🍷🍷	3
● Barolo '92	🍷	5

● Barolo Vigna Rionda '93	🍷🍷	5
● Barolo Mondoca di Bussia		
Soprana '93	🍷	5
● Barolo Rocche dei Rivera '93	🍷	5
O Chardonnay Collareto '96	🍷	3
● Dolcetto d'Alba '96	🍷	3
● Barolo Vigna Rionda '89	🍷🍷🍷	6
● Barolo '92	🍷🍷	5
● Barolo Mondoca di Bussia		
Soprana '89	🍷🍷	5
● Barolo Vigna Rionda '90	🍷🍷	6

LA MORRA (CN)

F.LLI REVELLO
FRAZ. ANNUNZIATA
12064 LA MORRA (CN)
TEL. 0173/50276-50139

Enzo and Carlo began their wine producing careers by taking over from their father in 1990. Their first Barolo was a rushed job in the '92 vintage; last year they got into the Guide and surprised everyone with a splendid Dolcetto, which made us predict, even then, that great things would follow. This year, they presented us with a very respectable series of wines and shot to the top of the ratings with one Three Glass wine. Where will it end? We shall see; the barrel samples are all very promising, but for the moment let us enjoy a great Barolo from the Rocche, Gattera and Giachini vineyards (future vintages will also be made in single vineyard versions), macerated briefly on the skins and aged in 600 litre barrels (again, in future vintages, contact with the skins will be reduced even more with the introduction of a horizontal rotary fermenter and classic barriques will be brought into use). The wine is rich, velvety and aristocratic with aromas of vanilla, mint, plums and quinine; full-bodied, well-rounded and long finishing. The Barbera Ciabot du Re displays the same finely-judged use of new wood (Elio Altare's influence, here) on a powerful body to produce an elegant, fruity, richly-extracted wine that is still bright and youthful. The standard Barbera is also smooth, with firm structure, good body and rich extract. The Dolcetto is concentrated in the Barolo style. Both wines have had a short spell in barrique, both are fragrant, floral and seductive. We cannot wait for next year's surprises.

LA MORRA (CN)

ROCCHE COSTAMAGNA
VIA VITTORIO EMANUELE, 12
12064 LA MORRA (CN)
TEL. 0173/50230-509225

What is the secret to the marriage of wine and wood? This is the question that Alessandro Locatelli has asked himself for years - his preference for barriques is no passing fad, but a conviction that has grown though long reflection. In the end he too has come to the inevitable answer: in winemaking, wood is only a means and not an end. Barolo Rocche, aged in large barrels, has a good colour and a clean and broad bouquet of sweet fruit. The seduction begun by the nose continues on the palate with a structure that is characteristically a little raw, but made with great skill. Barolo Vigna Francesco, on the other hand, is a smoother wine which comes from a more prolific vineyard; in this case the sweetness of the nose has the vanilla character that comes from new oak barrels, and the fruit is not lacking either. The Vigna Francesco is not as broad on the tongue as the Rocche and is less obviously varietal in character. The Barbera is particularly good and, fruitier than usual, it succeeds in marrying vinosity with a youthful nose of strawberries which follows right through to the finish; quite a short wine, but as enjoyable as all the other major wines from this producer for its full flavour on the palate. The Dolcetto is deliberately made in a simpler style and can be recommended to anyone who is looking for refreshing acidity and lightweight drinkability.

● Barolo '93	♟♟♟	5
● Barbera d'Alba Ciabot du Re '95	♟♟	4
● Dolcetto d'Alba '96	♟♟	3
● Barbera d'Alba '96	♟	3
● Dolcetto d'Alba '95	♟♟	3

● Barbera d'Alba Annunziata '95	♟♟	4
● Barolo Rocche dell'Annunziata '93	♟♟	5
● Barolo Vigna Francesco '93	♟	5
● Dolcetto d'Alba '96		3
● Barolo Rocche di La Morra '91	♟♟	5
● Barolo Vigna Francesco '90	♟♟	5
● Barbera d'Alba Rocche di La Morra '94	♟	3

LA MORRA (CN)

AURELIO SETTIMO
FRAZ. ANNUNZIATA, 30
12064 LA MORRA (CN)
TEL. 0173/50803

In uncertain vintages such as '93, Aurelio Settimo's Barolos are generally interesting and enjoyable. The non-cru Barolo in particular has improved enormously in recent years and in our latest tastings it actually outperformed the cru selection. The differences between the two wines are mostly the result of coming from different vineyards; the first is from San Martino while the cru originates at the prestigious Rocche site. Both are vinified traditionally and particular care is taken with long bottle ageing, which Tiziana thinks is so important that she has had a building adapted for the purpose with the instalment of air-conditioning. The standard Barolo is produced in quantities of about 20,000 bottles; it has a bright, even, garnet red colour; the fascinating and delicate bouquet has aromas ranging from just hints of musk to rich mixtures of dried fruit, chestnuts and almonds; on the palate the wine is broad and, as usual, rich in tannin, but without any bitter harshness and the finish is clean. 7,000 bottles of Barolo Rocche were produced in '93; it is largely identical in style and quality. The bouquet is well-developed with a porty nose of plums in spirit; the palate is classically broad and alcoholic. There was no Nebbiolo produced this year, but the Dolcetto (4,000 bottles) is worth a look: it has a violet-red colour with a certain sign of maturity around the edges; slightly closed on the nose which tends towards the vegetal, powerful for a Dolcetto, richly alcoholic, a little short in the finish.

LA MORRA (CN)

MAURO VEGLIO
LOC. CASCINA NUOVA, 50
12064 LA MORRA (CN)
TEL. 0173/509212

The faith placed in this young emerging producer over the years has been repaid with a steady improvement in quality which is not merely calculated on tasting scores but emerges rather in the sure-footed confidence of his management of the estate and the control of his winemaking. Veglio has at its disposal nine hectares of vines in the communes of La Morra (Rocche, Arborina, and Gattera) and Monforte (Castelletto) owned by father-in-law Enrico Saffirio, a famous Barolo producer of some years back. Currently, hailstones permitting, production is at around 40,000 bottles per year. With the '93 vintage, Mauro launches the Rocche dell'Annunziata cru, which immediately wins a Two Glasses award. This is a deep ruby red wine, with a nose dominated by the spiciness that comes from barriques; austere in the mouth with good extract and noble tannins. The Barolo '93, sourced partly from the Castelletto vineyard and partly from other sites in La Morra, scored only marginally lower: the colour is slightly lacking, however the nose has the classic leather and raspberries and the palate is already quite balanced, although leaner than the cru version. Going on to the Barberas, the Cascina Nuova '95 is aged in new barriques for about 18 months and still has the toastiness of the oak; a big wine with a soft finish which will benefit from a couple of years' bottle-ageing. The standard Barbera from the '96 vintage has an up-front, concentrated nose, with fruity, cherry aromas and clear hints of violets; the palate is simple but well-balanced, undisturbed by any sharpness of acidity. The Dolcetto '96 is also a good wine, with classic varietal character and finely-judged tannins.

● Barolo '93	♙♙	5
● Barolo Rocche '93	♙♙	5
● Dolcetto d'Alba '96	♙	3
● Barolo Rocche '89	♟♟	6
● Barolo '92	♟	4
● Barolo Rocche '90	♟	6
● Barolo Rocche Ris. '90	♟	6

● Barbera d'Alba		
Cascina Nuova '95	♙♙	4
● Barolo '93	♙♙	5
● Barolo Rocche '93	♙♙	5
● Barbera d'Alba '96	♙	3
● Dolcetto d'Alba '96	♙	3
● Barbera d'Alba		
Cascina Nuova '94	♟♟	4
● Barolo '92	♟	4

LA MORRA (CN)

LA MORRA (CN)

ERALDO VIBERTI
B.TA TETTI, 53
12064 LA MORRA (CN)
TEL. 0173/50308

GIANNI VOERZIO
REG. LORETO, 1/BIS
12064 LA MORRA (CN)
TEL. 0173/509194

There are producers who are almost obsessive in the attention to detail they give to their wines. They are they type who believe as much in personal satisfaction is in financial returns. Then there are those who are concerned above all with margins, who study things like market trends, exchange rates, and consumer demand. It often happens that the former do not have the financial resources to expand, while the latter can always find the cash to invest in a facelift operation when the occasion demands. This is not the place to discuss these issues at length, but it is nice to be able to report that sometimes a producer of the first type can claim his moment of glory; this is the case of Eraldo Viberti and his Barolo '93: garnet red with bright, youthful reflections; concentrated nose of plums and spices; excellent follow-through on the palate; full-bodied, long-finishing, with attractive hints of coffee and liquorice to enrich the fruit. This is not all; despite problems at harvest time, the Dolcetto is also very good: it has a clean nose with an intense bouquet of roses and cherries; very easy to drink, well-balanced, chewy and well-proportioned. The same goes for the Barbera: deep ruby red with violet tinges; spicy, good balance of residual sugar and alcohol on the one hand and tannins and acidity on the other. And to think there are those who say that it was impossible to make wines of quality on this side of La Morra !

The cellars may be extremely well equipped, the view towards Roddi and the Roero may be stunning, the conversation may be intriguing, but rule number one is that, if a producer insists on taking you to see the vineyards, he is among the ones who count. Gianni Voerzio is one of these, and a tasting of his current range confirms the quality, and the consistency of his wines. Taking them in alphabetical order, the Arneis is one of the best of its type: clean, floral, delicate, soft on the front palate, with a fresh and elegant finish. The Barbera is rich with a fruity bouquet, displaying an attractive mixture of liveliness and seduction. The Barolo is a full-bodied classic, an aristocratic wine that begins with a certain reserve, grows to a crescendo, and finishes very firmly. The Dolcetto seems better than in previous vintages: classic, clean and well-balanced; one of those wines that are always welcome. The Freisa, with its attractive sparkle, is always good; it avoids any bitterness and is classically fresh, fruity, and slightly astringent on the finish. Then we come to the nebbiolo and barbera blend aged in new oak: ruby red with violet tinges, blackcurrant jam on the nose, vanilla and tobacco both in the bouquet and the palate; soft and fresh-tasting, marred only by a somewhat heavy-handed use of wood.

● Barolo '93	♟♟♟	5
● Dolcetto d'Alba '96	♟♟	3
● Barbera d'Alba Vigna Clara '94	♟	4
● Barbera d'Alba Vigna Clara '91	♟♟	4
● Barbera d'Alba Vigna Clara '93	♟♟	4
● Barolo '90	♟♟	5
● Barolo '91	♟♟	5
● Barolo '92	♟♟	5
● Barbera d'Alba Vigna Clara '92	♟	4

● Barbera d'Alba		
Ciabot della Luna '95	♟♟	4
● Barolo La Serra '93	♟♟	5
● Dolcetto d'Alba		
Rocchettevino '96	♟♟	3
● Serrapiù '95	♟♟	4
● Langhe Freisa		
Sotto I Bastioni '96	♟	4
○ Roero Arneis Bricco Cappellina '96	♟	4
● Barolo La Serra '90	♟♟	5
● Barolo La Serra '91	♟♟	5
● Barolo La Serra '92	♟♟	5
● Serrapiù '90	♟♟	4
● Serrapiù '92	♟♟	4
● Serrapiù '94	♟♟	4

LA MORRA (CN)

ROBERTO VOERZIO
LOC. CERRETO, 1
12064 LA MORRA (CN)
TEL. 0173/509196-50123

Roberto's abiding passions are Pinuccia, wine, and rock music. We have mentioned the first two in previous years but we only discovered the third this year. It is rock music that accompanies Voerzio's work in the cellars with a vibrant repetitive rhythm that is not unlike the impetuous, visceral, and spontaneous nature of his Barolos. These wines are currently one of the most marvellous meeting points in the Langhe between the waves of innovation that are sweeping the area and an affectionate link with tradition. The energy of the wine matches the energy of its maker, who continues to look for the answers to problems of quality in the vineyard, much like any congenitally dissatisfied small farmer. The Barolo Brunate is an impressive wine not so much for its tightly-knit depth of body as for its succulent drinkability, its sensual nature, lively and at the same time rich, complex and well-defined: the colour is a deep garnet red; on the nose the most obvious aromas in a complex and substantial whole are aromatic herbs, hazelnuts, cherries preserved in spirit, and cocoa; the palate is taut and nervy and yet also exuberantly giving. The tarriness which has traditionally been a characteristic of Cerequio Barolos has never been part of such an attractive, rounded, full-blown bouquet; of course, the rich fruit of better vintages is lacking, but the Cerequio vineyard itself confers class and style on its wines. Barolo La Serra comes out with the usual multi-layered bouquet and palate that are its best features. As for the future, the cognoscenti have their eyes on the new wine that Voerzio will be making from the recently acquired Santa Maria di La Morra vineyard.

LERMA (AL)

ABBAZIA DI VALLECHIARA
LOC. CASCINA ALBAROLA, 16/B
15070 LERMA (AL)
TEL. 0143/877618

After a promising start, this winery seemed to take a wrong turning on the road to success. Uncertainty in the company's economic future lead to uneven quality and delays in bottling. We are particularly happy, therefore, to be able to reinstate this producer from the Ovada region in the Guide after two years' absence, and hope that the problems of the past will remain just a bad memory. Good results have not been slow in emerging this year. The Abbazia di Vallechiara is managed by a true factotum, Elisabetta Currado, who also happens to be a very able and tenacious oenologist. The property consists of 28 hectares of land of which 12 hectares are currently under vine (some splendid sites have yet to be replanted). The pride of the estate are a number of extremely old and steep plots of dolcetto, not to mention the well equipped winery in a splendid location that was once the site of an ancient abbey. The Dolcetto di Ovada '95 is a success once again: bright ruby red still displaying flashes of violet; more complex on the nose than usual for the variety, successfully blending the characteristic vinosity and fruit of this grape with the rarer aromas of leather and quinine; as might be expected from its appearance and bouquet, the wine is rich and full-bodied on the palate and has a long and harmonious finish. The Torre Albarola '93 is an unusual blend of dolcetto, barbera and lancillotta that still bears the mark of barrique ageing on the nose; it is vigorous and austere and still raw from the interaction of tannins and acidity. The Due Donne from the poor '94 vintage lacks structure and is a little weak.

● Barolo Brunate '93	▼▼▼	6
● Barolo La Serra '93	▼▼	6
● Barolo Cerequio '93	▼▼	6
● Dolcetto d'Alba '96	▼▼	3
○ Langhe Chardonnay Fossati e Roscaleto	▼▼	4
● Barolo Brunate '90	♈♈♈	6
● Barolo Brunate '89	♈♈♈	6
● Barolo Cerequio '91	♈♈♈	6
● Barolo Cerequio '90	♈♈♈	6
● Barolo Cerequio '88	♈♈♈	6
● Barolo Brunate '92	♈♈	6
● Barolo Brunate '91	♈♈	6
● Barolo La Serra '92	♈♈	6
● Barolo Cerequio '92	♈	6

● Dolcetto di Ovada '95	▼▼	3
● Due Donne '94	▼	4
● Torre Albarola '93	▼	5

LOAZZOLO (AT)

FORTETO DELLA LUJA
CASA ROSSO, 4
REG. BRICCO
14050 LOAZZOLO (AT)
TEL. 0141/831596

Forteto della Luja is becoming one of the great classic producers of Italian "after dinner" sipping wines. Last year we were amazed by the broad and well-evolved elegance of the Loazzolo, this year it is the freshness that has impressed us. In fact, with this late-picked moscato wine Scaglione has managed to balance sweetness and youth without losing any of the subtle richness of the bouquet. The colour of the Loazzolo '94 is mid-gold; the nose contains all the most noble aromas of the variety, roses, violets and mint made even smoother by hints of cedar wood, melon and white peaches; on the palate a delicious sweetness suffuses the mouth delicately and with style; the finish is long and marked by a return of the bouquet. This Piasa Rischei is a great wine in miniature and proof of the value of the old-fashioned, almost heroic viticulture of Loazzolo. The Brachetto Pian dei Sogni is an attractive wine as well: unmistakable orange-tinged ruby red colour, impressive for the breadth and depth of its complex bouquet; much simpler on the palate and finishing with the usual bitter twist. On the other hand, the Moscato d'Asti could be better: the aromatic bouquet is fine, the structure on the palate is fine, what it lacks is definition and balance. The Monferrato Rosso Le Grive, made from pinot noir and barbera, is reliable but a bit lean.

MANGO (CN)

CASCINA FONDA
LOC. CASCINA FONDA, 45
12056 MANGO (CN)
TEL. 0173/677156

Secondino Barbero would have liked to celebrate ten years of winemaking with his sons Massimo and Marco in the new winery, but it is not ready and he must still run all the risks of making a technologically demanding wine in a place that is practically a garage. And yet, even with this handicap, he returns to the Guide with an excellent Asti Spumante by making the best of an excellent vintage. The finesse of the perlage is impressive in a beautiful, golden straw yellow colour; the bouquet is outstanding for its breadth and length rather than for its intensity and includes aromas of lavender, figs and citrus fruit; the soft bubbles give the wine length on the tongue and the finish has a typical bitter-sweet twist. The Moscato is reliable as well: it has a deep colour with green reflections and a generous bouquet of fresh grapes softened by a hint of almonds, and it does not seem as sweet as most Moscatos thanks to its sparkle and lively acidity. The Dolcetto is an honest, vinous wine and worth a look, despite accounting for only a tiny fraction of the 80,000 bottles a year produced by this winery. This disparity between red wines and white will be remedied next year when the Barbero family intend to diversify by reviving the old practice of producing barbera, as well as moscato, in the Mango area.

○ Loazzolo Piasa Rischei '94	🍷🍷🍷	6
● Piemonte Brachetto		
Pian dei Sogni '94	🍷🍷	5
● Monferrato Rosso Le Grive '95	🍷	4
○ Moscato d'Asti San Maurizio '96	🍷	3
○ Loazzolo Piasa Rischei '93	🍷🍷🍷	6
● Piemonte Brachetto		
Pian dei Sogni '93	🍷🍷	5
● Le Grive '94	🍷	4

○ Asti '96	🍷🍷	3
○ Moscato d'Asti '96	🍷	3
● Dolcetto d'Alba '96		1

MANGO (CN)

CASCINA PIAN D'OR
FRAZ. BOSI, 15/BIS
12056 MANGO (CN)
TEL. 0141/89440

This year Walter Barbero has taken over the management of Cascina Pian d'Or from his father, Giuseppe, who founded it ten years ago. And it is this year that the winery has been completed with the addition of the only facility it lacked, a temperature-controlled store for bottled wines. In this connection, Walter underlines his concern to deliver a wine as delicate as a Moscato in perfect condition, and indeed freshness is one of the principal problems he has with this wine. The Bricco Riella, for example, has always been for people who do not want immediacy in their Moscato but look instead for a fatter and more mature wine, which can, however, have some quite unusual aromas. This year it has a nose of hazelnuts and coffee creams, while there is a sweet smoothness that dominates the palate, finishing with a hint of over-ripe apples. The same style and the same mature aromas can be found on the Asti Spumante, but here leading to a greater complexity in the wine. The nose is typical Asti , but it also includes sweet aromas of apricots and coconut, while the abundant carbon dioxide, despite being a bit too quick to escape, refreshes the palate and leaves space for a sweet aromatic finish.

MOASCA (AT)

PIETRO BARBERO
V.LE SAN GIUSEPPE, 19
14050 MOASCA (AT)
TEL. 0141/856484

Barbera d'Asti La Vignassa is becoming a classic wine that can be relied on, in good and bad vintages alike. Massimo Barbero will be extremely pleased with this situation, as this is the wine that he has concentrated most of his efforts for quality on. The Vignassa '94 has a different character to the richer '93: bright mid-ruby red; deliciously fresh bouquet with hints of strawberries and aromatic herbs; very promising on the front palate, easy and fragrant follow-through to the finish. The positive start in the tasting for this Moasca-based company continues with another Barbera, the Camparò: deep colour; up-front with a bouquet full of grace and liveliness; broad on the palate and only lacking a touch of complexity on the finish. The third Barbera, the Bricco Verlenga, is the only one to lack that extra touch of personality which would make it stand out; it has good varietal character, nonetheless, and there is certainly nothing unpleasant about it. Within its own modest limits, the Chardonnay Sivoy DOC Langhe is a good wine, too, with well-defined aromatic qualities and good length on the palate. The same applies to the Gavi di Rovereto from the Poggio vineyard: it is very representative of the DOC, but would benefit from more character on the nose and a bigger palate. The one wine that puzzled us is the Moscato Moncravello, which is too lean and, for such an aromatic varietal, unexpectedly closed on the nose. To sum up, the overall results of this year's tasting are a step in the right direction, especially considering the very fair value for money the wines offer.

○ Asti Acini '96	▼	3
○ Moscato d'Asti Bricco Riella '96	▼	3

● Barbera d'Asti Sup. Camparò '95	▼▼	3
● Barbera d'Asti Sup. La Vignassa '94	▼▼	4
● Barbera d'Asti Sup. Bricco Verlenga '95	▼	3
○ Gavi di Rovereto Vigna Il Poggio '96	▼	3
○ Langhe Chardonnay Sivoy '96	▼	3
○ Moscato d'Asti Moncravello '96		3
● Barbera d'Asti Sup. La Vignassa '93	♀♀	4

MOMBELLO MONFERRATO (AL)   MOMBERCELLI (AT)

FELICE COPPO
CASCINE COSTE, 15
15020 MOMBELLO MONFERRATO (AL)
TEL. 0142/944503

LUIGI SPERTINO
STRADA LEA, 505
14047 MOMBERCELLI (AT)
TEL. 0141/959098

Annamaria Bovio is generous with her hospitality and, between a slice of "salame" and a slice of "lardo", her son Felice Coppo tells us about his Bastiàn Cuntrari. This is what he jokingly describes as "the wine that is not" (the '95 vintage is only 3,000 bottles) and is a Barbera sourced from four hectares of vineyards, two of which have very old vines. Partly for this reason, but mostly because of severe pruning, yields are extremely low (about 25-30 quintals per hectare). In the vineyards Felice is helped by his mother and Valerio Scarrone, a young agronomist from Coldiretti, who provides valuable technical advice and has a say in all the viticultural decisions. Another interesting point to note is that Luca Maroni has been a consultant on the wines since 1996. The first results of this collaboration were to take the '95 out of barrique early and the decision not to mature the '96 in small oak at all, in order to enhance the qualities of the grape to the maximum. The Bastiàn Cuntrari Tipe III (the '95 vintage) has a deep, dark ruby red colour; intense, long and full on the nose, with marked aromas of tar and violets which complement the fruit and sweet spiciness. Full-bodied, pervasive and soft on the palate with an attractive hint of liquorice on a long-lasting finish. The '96 was unready for tasting and will be examined next year.

Last year was not the most fortunate for Luigi and Mario Spertino's winery. Their two flagship wines, the Grignolino and the Barbera, lacked personality and although the wines were certainly correct, we were expecting something more from a producer that has had such good results in the past. The Grignolino d'Asti '96 has a pale cherry colour; on the nose there is an attractive hint of sharp fruit, but it is a bit one dimensional; the palate is lively enough and certainly typical for the variety, but it is short nonetheless. The Grignolino Vendemmia Tardiva has a limpid appearance and is a bigger wine: delicate hints of ripe fruit and pepper emerge on the nose and although it is light in structure it is longer-finishing than the first wine. Rosso No. 2 is a youthful Barbera d'Asti and is best served cool; this is a refreshing, easy-to-drink wine without any pretensions to complexity. This year's version of the Spertino's most serious wine, Rosso No. 1, was not yet ready for tasting, and neither was the Vindipaglia, another wine that we have been impressed with in previous years.

● Bastiàn Cuntrari Tipe III '95	▾▾	4
● Bastiàn Cuntrari '93	♈♈	4

● Grignolino d'Asti		
Vendemmia Tardiva '96	▾	3
● Barbera d'Asti Rosso N° 2 '96		3
● Grignolino d'Asti '96		3
○ Vindipaglia '92	♈♈	5
● Rosso N° 1 '91	♈	4

MONCHIERO (CN)

GIUSEPPE MASCARELLO & FIGLIO
VIA BORGONUOVO, 108
12060 MONCHIERO (CN)
TEL. 0173/792126

MONDOVÌ (CN)

IL COLOMBO
VIA DEI SENT, 2
12084 MONDOVÌ (CN)
TEL. 0174/41607-43022

We are extremely happy to say that the latest release of the Barolo Monprivato, one of the glories of the Langhe, has turned out to be a full-bodied and fascinating wine, despite the difficulties of the '92 vintage. Mauro Mascarello has triumphed over all the vicissitudes of nature to make a full blown wine that is a perfect example of the best traditions of the area. The colour is a limpid and mature garnet red; the bouquet is intense and full of mature fruit with hints of liquorice and medicinal herbs; the palate is lively, and the tannins are firm without ever being harsh, leading on to a perfect harmony of aromas on the finish. The other Barolo, from the Bricco di Castiglione Falletto vineyard, is less fully formed: indeed, it is not fair to expect such weight from this wine, but there is a fully developed bouquet and a soft well-balanced palate. After the unfortunate '94 vintage the Dolcetto, from the Castiglione vineyard, comes back on form: mid-ruby red colour; vinosity slowly revealing berry fruit on the nose; firm on the palate with good acidity, but lacking a little power on the finish. Better results should come with the '96 vintage, but not before; the '95 was not easy for the young-wines-to-drink-early category either. The Codana has all the firmness of Barbera from the Langhe and, even if it does not reach the same levels as in previous editions of the Guide, it is a reliable wine.

Did you know that there was such a denomination as Dolcetto Langhe Monregalesi? Do not worry if the answer is no; the usual standard in this DOC has not been very encouraging, up until now. This year however an excellent example of this denomination enters the Guide, and we are sure we will hear more of it. Adriana and Carlo Riccati's winery stands on a high hill along the road from Bastia to Vicoforte. They are helped in the vineyards surrounding the winery by Giuseppe Giusta, who decided he wanted to become a vigneron only eight years ago. All three of them work in a winery that still needs modernisation, but they do have some promising raw material to work with. Their particular creations are two Dolcettos that are very different, but complementary in style. The Colombo comes from an authentic cru site, a 50-year old vineyard on a south-facing slope of tufa-rich soil. After a '95 that was really too overblown, the '96 has an intense violet-tinged colour and a full and up-front bouquet of ripe fruit spiced with vegetal nuances; rich in extract on the palate, sweet fruit combined with good depth of flavour on the finish. The other Dolcetto comes from the Chiesetta site, a younger vineyard facing north-west on the brow of a hill, which also benefits from the aromatic qualities conferred by its sub-soil. This second wine is naturally leaner and more up front than the first, but it retains the ready drinkability that is the house style of this winery. Its violet-tinged colour is as youthful as its lively, vinous aroma of strawberries and bilberries. The two wines are made in quantities of, respectively, 8,000 and 2,500 bottles and are, for the moment, on sale only in Piedmont.

● Barolo Monprivato '92	♈♈	5
● Barbera d'Alba Codana '94	♈	4
● Barolo Bricco di Castiglione Falletto '92	♈	5
● Dolcetto d'Alba Bricco di Castiglione Falletto '95	♈	4
● Barolo Monprivato '85	♈♈♈	6
● Barbaresco Marcarini '88	♈♈	5
● Barbera d'Alba Codana '93	♈♈	4
● Barolo Monprivato '89	♈♈	6
● Barolo Monprivato '90	♈♈	6
● Barolo Monprivato '91	♈	6
● Barolo Santo Stefano di Perno '91	♈	5

● Dolcetto delle Langhe Monregalesi Il Colombo '95	♈♈	3
● Dolcetto delle Langhe Monregalesi Il Colombo '96	♈♈	3
● Dolcetto delle Langhe Monregalesi Vigna Chiesetta '96	♈	2*

MONFORTE D'ALBA (CN)

GIANFRANCO ALESSANDRIA
LOC. MANZONI, 13
12065 MONFORTE D'ALBA (CN)
TEL. 0173/78576-787222

The estate possesses four hectares of vineyards; two are dedicated to the production of Barolo, one and a half for Barbera, and a scant half for Dolcetto. These are small numbers indeed for an able producer who loves all aspects of his work, from the vineyard to the bottle. The score we gave to the Barbera '95 last year was not particularly generous; having said that, let us pass on to this year's excellent results. The Dolcetto '96 is clothed in a deep ruby red colour, has an intense and extremely well defined vinous nose, and a full-bodied palate with excellent fruit and a long finish; this is a benchmark wine for the denomination. Only 3,300 bottles of Barbera d'Alba were made in the '96 vintage: deep garnet red; full of fruit on the nose, very concentrated on the palate with finely judged acidity and good structure; all in all, an excellent result for a wine that comes from vines of between 25 - 30 years old. The Barbera d'Alba Vittoria '95 was aged in new barriques for 17 months and produced in quantities of 2,500 bottles; in the event we liked it less than the standard '96 version, precisely because of the dominance of the oak; final judgement will have to wait until the wine matures further. Lastly, the Barolo '93 from the San Giovanni zone near Bussia can easily be counted as one of the best of its vintage and gains the Three Glass award without any hesitation. For the 3,200 bottles produced, ageing took place 70 percent in 500 litre casks and 30 percent in large Slavonian oak. The result is an opaque, garnet red coloured Barolo with hints of flowers on the nose; firm and full-bodied on the palate with ripe noble tannins and a very long finish; an excellent wine now that will be even better in a few years' time.

MONFORTE D'ALBA (CN)

BUSSIA SOPRANA
LOC. BUSSIA SOPRANA, 87
12065 MONFORTE D'ALBA (CN)
TEL. 039/305182

Silvano Casiraghi is from Monza and was a wine dealer for 22 years before he decided in 1992 to make wine on his own account. As a site, he chose the Bussia and Mosconi crus, both top locations in the commune of Monforte. In 1995 Guido Rossi joined him as a business partner and with this added help they now vinify the grapes from 12 hectares of estate-owned vineyards and another six rented hectares. They produce the traditional wines of the area: Dolcetto and Barbera d'Alba, and two cru Barolos (Bussia and Vigna Colonello), joined from the '95 vintage with another cru Barolo (Mosconi). Casiraghi's début in the Guide comes with two exceptionally characterful Barolos, both with an excellent structure and aged in barrique to give spiciness, softness and balance. The Bussia is ruby red with orange edges; the bouquet of berry fruit and flowers is not particularly intense but is well defined; it is full-bodied and well supported by ripe and unobtrusive tannins. The Vigna Colonello is just fractionally better: it is similar to the Bussia, but with a greater concentration and length and with the softness in the mouth that is a sign of quality and of balance. We tasted the '93 vintage Barbera Vin del Ross, another barrique aged wine which is produced only in the best years, and found it correct and well made without having much to say for itself.

● Barolo '93	▼▼▼	5
● Barbera d'Alba '96	▼▼	3
● Dolcetto d'Alba '96	▼▼	3
● Barbera d'Alba Vittoria '95	▼	4

● Barolo Vigna Colonello '93	▼▼	6
● Barolo Bussia '93	▼	5
● Barbera d'Alba Vin del Ross '93		4

DOMENICO CLERICO
LOC. MANZONI CUCCHI, 67
12065 MONFORTE D'ALBA (CN)
TEL. 0173/78171

Clerico likes to affect a certain nonchalance about his success and says that he is just lucky. When you get to know him and how he works and get to taste his wines, you realise that, in fact, he leaves nothing to chance. Attention to detail and dogged determination are some of the characteristics that have brought him to the position he is in, although credit must also go to his wife Giuliana for her unstinting assistance. The Pajana '93 is the result of his desire to make a universal Barolo, reflecting its "terroir", but a fundamental archetype at the same time. The depth of this wine starts with the colour: the bouquet is full of intense aromas of mature nebbiolo and the breadth that comes with perfect aromatic development; the palate is firmly authoritative, while the tannins blend into the imposing structure of the wine allowing it to finish with length and consistency. The length of flavours and aromas is what the Pajana and Clerico's other cru, the Mentin Ginestra, have in common. This second Barolo is just as good as the Pajana but completely different: the colour is a mature garnet red, the nose has mineral notes and, at the same time, aromas of plums and coffee; the palate is dry and full-bodied, lively and exciting on the finish. The Arte '95 is less powerful and more elegant than normal and increasingly seems to be the experimental proving ground for Clerico's new ideas. The excellent Dolcetto '96 and the simply correct Barbera '95 are both worth a mention.

●	Barolo Pajana '93	TTT	5
●	Barolo Ciabot Mentin Ginestra '93	TT	5
●	Dolcetto d'Alba '96	TT	3
●	Langhe Arte '95	TT	5
●	Barbera d'Alba '95	T	4
●	Arte '93	YYY	5
●	Arte '90	YYY	5
●	Barolo Ciabot Mentin Ginestra '85	YYY	6
●	Barolo Ciabot Mentin Ginestra '86	YYY	6
●	Barolo Ciabot Mentin Ginestra '89	YYY	6
●	Barolo Ciabot Mentin Ginestra '92	YYY	5
●	Barolo Pajana '90	YYY	6
●	Barolo Pajana '91	YYY	6
●	Arte '94	YY	5
●	Barolo Pajana '92	YY	6

MONFORTE D'ALBA (CN)

★ ALDO CONTERNO
LOC. BUSSIA, 48
12065 MONFORTE D'ALBA (CN)
TEL. 0173/78150

Aldo Conterno was not able to produce the usual spectacular results (his magnificent career up to now has been adorned with an unbroken string of Three Glass awards) from the difficult '93 vintage. The Barolo Cicala is already proving to be a big wine with sweet hints of tobacco on the nose and a noticeable oakiness; the palate is less well-developed but firmer, thanks mainly to the acidity; this excellent wine will only be at its best in a few more years. The Barolo Colonello has a slightly more open and more developed bouquet with attractive and delicate aromas, while the palate is medium weight with a finish which is reminiscent of the wet earth that some tasters say is the true characteristic of Barolo; soft, dried grape tastes appear in the finish. The Favot reminds us of the stupendous '90 vintage, although the '95 has greater finesse and an aromatic complexity which shows Conterno's great skill in his choice of wood ageing; the structure is very decent and there are elegant hints of fresh herbs and liquorice on the finish. Experiments in the fermentation and ageing of chardonnay produce better results, year after year; we tasted the Bussiador '95, in which has the complex bouquet of sweet fruit leaves generous space for the toastiness of the barrique. The Chardonnay Printanié is simpler and more up front, as tradition dictates, and has nothing in common with the yeasty, barrique fermentation style of the elegant Bussiador. Lastly, do not forget the Dolcetto d'Alba, which is still a little unbalanced on the nose, but has a very respectable structure.

●	Barolo Cicala '93	TT	6
●	Barolo Colonnello '93	TT	6
●	Dolcetto d'Alba Bussia '96	TT	3
●	Langhe Favot '95	TT	5
○	Langhe Chardonnay Bussiador '95	TT	5
○	Langhe Chardonnay Printanié '96	T	4
●	Barolo Bussia Soprana '93	T	6
●	Barolo Bussia Soprana '85	YYY	6
●	Barolo Gran Bussia Ris. '82	YYY	6
●	Barolo Gran Bussia Ris. '88	YYY	6
●	Barolo Gran Bussia Ris. '89	YYY	6
●	Barolo Gran Bussia Ris. '90	YYY	6
●	Barolo Vigna Colonnello '88	YYY	6
●	Barolo Vigna Colonnello '89	YYY	6
●	Barolo Vigna Colonnello '90	YYY	6

MONFORTE D'ALBA (CN)

MONFORTE D'ALBA (CN)

★ GIACOMO CONTERNO
LOC. ORNATI, 2
12065 MONFORTE D'ALBA (CN)
TEL. 0173/78221

CONTERNO FANTINO
VIA GINESTRA, 1
LOC. BRICCO BASTIA
12065 MONFORTE D'ALBA (CN)
TEL. 0173/78204

It was quite predictable that Giovanni Conterno would have produced a great wine with his Monfortino '90, but not just how overwhelming it would turn out to be on tasting. This is a Three Glass wine that is already magnificent, but which the fortunate few will be able to taste at its best in 10 years' time. The definition and finesse of the nose is textbook sharp, with hints of liquorice and berry fruit that are already blending into a bouquet of rare fascination; the palate has power and length, with an expansive, enveloping richness on the tongue and unbelievably soft tannins. The Barolo '93 reveals its origins with the typically fresh, elegant and slightly tarry nose of the cru Francia where Giovanni Conterno gets all his grapes; a faint touch of wood can also be noticed in the bouquet. The palate is austere with good extract and a finish with attractive hints of resin; the acidity is perfectly in balance in this Barolo which is destined for long ageing. The Freisa is magnificent; made as a still wine for moderate ageing, it has good structure and although not elegant, is rich in extract, nervy and full of flavour. The combination of serious concentration and inviting suppleness shows Giovanni Conterno's skill in getting the best out of this often-undervalued, but unique varietal. The Dolcetto is good, too; the bouquet is not huge, but it is rich on the palate and benefits from a brief spell in wood, like all wines produced by the great Giovanni Conterno. The last recommendation is a Barbera '96 which is fresh and fruity and well-rounded, if lacking a bit in body.

An organization that works to perfection, this is Conterno Fantino, an estate where the ideal distribution of labour is the secret of faultless quality. Guido Fantino is the oenological brain, Claudio and Diego Conterno are the viticultural heart, and between them things work like clockwork. Guido works at the vinification with the experience of a veteran and the passion of youth; the others are the toilers in the vineyard whose aim in life is to produce the best grapes possible from one of the most noble and impressive vineyards in the entire Langhe, the cru Ginestra in Monforte. This is the origin of that excellent red wine, the Monprà, where nebbiolo grapes find a sublime and unforgettable marriage with cabernet sauvignon. Deep ruby red, almost opaque, in colour; the nose reveals the fusion of the mineral character of Bordeaux's favourite grape with the mature and voluptuous floral aromas of the nebbiolo; in short, an irresistible, delicate and complex mixture of berry fruit and spice aromas; the front palate is predictably firm, authoritative and full-bodied, well-supported by the strength of the tannins and with the softness of the rich extract making for an exciting finish. The Barolo Sorì has depth of colour and a bouquet with an intriguing hint of meatiness mixed with aromas of crushed petals; the palate has good follow-through, full structure and subtle astringency. The Barolo Vigna del Gris is rich in alcohol and has a broad, rich palate with ripe and abundant tannins. The Dolcetto stands out for its easy drinking qualities and its good structure, it has good breadth on the palate, but lacks length. Lastly, the Chardonnay is attractive enough, but not particularly special.

● Barolo Monfortino Ris. '90	♟♟♟	6
● Barolo Cascina Francia '93	♟♟	6
● Dolcetto d'Alba '96	♟♟	4
● Langhe Freisa '96	♟♟	4
● Barbera d'Alba '96	♟	4
● Barolo Cascina Francia '85	♟♟♟	6
● Barolo Cascina Francia '87	♟♟♟	6
● Barolo Cascina Francia '89	♟♟♟	6
● Barolo Cascina Francia '90	♟♟♟	6
● Barolo Monfortino Ris. '85	♟♟♟	6
● Barolo Monfortino Ris. '87	♟♟♟	6
● Barolo Monfortino Ris. '88	♟♟♟	6
● Barolo Monfortino Ris. '82	♟♟♟	6
● Barolo Monfortino Ris. '74	♟♟♟	6

● Langhe Rosso Monprà '95	♟♟♟	5
● Barolo Sorì Ginestra '93	♟♟	5
● Barolo Vigna del Gris '93	♟♟	5
● Dolcetto d'Alba Bricco Bastia '96	♟	3
○ Langhe Chardonnay Bastia '96	♟	5
● Barolo Sorì Ginestra '86	♟♟♟	6
● Barolo Sorì Ginestra '90	♟♟♟	6
● Barolo Sorì Ginestra '91	♟♟♟	5
● Monprà '94	♟♟♟	5
● Barolo Sorì Ginestra '92	♟♟	5
● Barolo Vigna del Gris '89	♟♟	6
● Barolo Vigna del Gris '90	♟♟	6
● Monprà '93	♟♟	5

MONFORTE D'ALBA (CN)

MONFORTE D'ALBA (CN)

ALESSANDRO E GIAN NATALE FANTINO
VIA G. SILVANO, 18
12065 MONFORTE D'ALBA (CN)
TEL. 0173/78253

ATTILIO GHISOLFI
REG. BUSSIA
CASCINA VISETTE
12065 MONFORTE D'ALBA (CN)
TEL. 0173/78345

The Fantino brothers' cellars are situated in a beautiful eighteenth-century family home about two hundred metres from the centre of the village. The seven hectares of vineyards, however, which are mostly planted to nebbiolo and barbera, are situated in one parcel at Dardi, near the famous Bussia slopes. The idea of taking up a career as wine growers came to the brothers in the late1980s and their first vintage was in1989. One of the two, Alessandro, has worked for years with Bartolo Mascarello in Barolo, where one would expect he has acquired invaluable experience and intimacy with the secrets of winemaking in the Langhe. Currently the wines (15,000 bottles per year) fail to reveal the full potential of the estate, in part because of a series of poor vintages and in part because the vineyards are being replanted. The Nebbiolo Passito - an unusual if not unique wine - is certainly the Fantino's jewel in the crown: picked a couple of weeks before the nebbiolo for Barolo in order to preserve higher acidity, the grapes are put on cane racks to dry in ventilated store rooms for three months. After scrupulous selection, bunch by bunch, the grapes are pressed, left to ferment slowly and aged in big barrels. The '90, on sale this year, has a deep, lively ruby red colour; it is concentrated and full on the nose with hints of citrus peel, pine resin, eucalyptus, liquorice and chocolate; soft on the front palate, almost chewy, then dry from the tannins, leaving the finish clean with lasting hints of liquorice and violets. The Barolo Vigna dei Dardi '93 has hints of cherry brandy on the nose and a dry palate, but lacks softness. The Barbera d'Alba 96 had only just been bottled when we tasted it; it created a positive impression, without being over serious.

The Visette vineyard needed an enthusiastic young man like Gianmarco Ghisolfi to bring this noble but little known cru to public attention. Situated at about 340 metres above sea level between Arnulfo and Pianpolvere, this authentic "grand cru" site faces south to south west. The soil is typical of this slope in Monforte, light brown marl that gives its wines a delicious aromatic quality, balance on the palate and a solid structure. The only drawback is that the Visette site is particularly subject to the vagaries of climatic conditions at harvest time. The '91 and '92 vintages were difficult but with the '93, Ghisolfi shows a Barolo that is full of character, a deep, lively garnet red colour, subtle and complex on the nose. There is softness on the front palate, followed by increasing intensity of flavours and balance. The Dolcetto d'Alba offers a chance to appreciate the wonders of the '96 vintage, from the deep colour it shows on cursory visual examination to the rich bouquet that unfolds in layers. It has a sharply-defined palate which is firm without excess. Ghisolfi has not, however, found the same rich resources of the '93 vintage in the '95 for the Barbera Vigna Lisi; as a result the wine is less complete; it is, however, well made, bright and well defined.

● Barolo Vigna dei Dardi '93	🍷🍷	5
● Nebbiolo Passito Vigna dei Dardi '90	🍷🍷	5
● Barbera d'Alba Vigna dei Dardi '96	🍷	3*
● Barolo Vigna dei Dardi '92	🍷🍷	5
● Barbera d'Alba Vigna dei Dardi '95	🍷	3
● Nebbiolo Passito Vigna dei Dardi '93	🍷	4

● Barolo Bricco Visette '93	🍷🍷	5
● Barbera d'Alba Vigna Lisi '95	🍷	4
● Dolcetto d'Alba '96	🍷	3
● Barbera d'Alba Vigna Lisi '93	🍷🍷	3
● Barolo Bricco Visette '90	🍷🍷	5
● Barbera d'Alba Vigna Lisi '94	🍷	4
● Barolo Bricco Visette '91	🍷	4
● Barolo Bricco Visette '92	🍷	4

MONFORTE D'ALBA (CN)

ELIO GRASSO
LOC. GINESTRA, 40
12065 MONFORTE D'ALBA (CN)
TEL. 0173/78491

The appeal of the role of the "contadino" and the call of the land are aspects of the collective consciousness that can be suppressed, but never completely disappear. Elio Grasso worked as a banker for most of his life, but his origins and his family history never left him. When he decided to be a vigneron he was going back to his roots. Elio approaches his work with a nervous energy that is his biggest asset; whether he working in the vineyards, maintaining the cellars or creating his wines, he works with the passion of total involvement. What bigger reward could he have than the Barolo Casa Maté? This is a wonderfully articulated wine that succeeds in being at the same time spontaneous, full-bodied and deep: promisingly opaque in colour, it displays a full bouquet of liquorice and plums with hints of nutmeg and white pepper on the nose; firm on the palate, and proudly firm, with tannins which are balanced and softened by the body of the wine. The other Barolo, the Vigna Chiniera is only half a step below, an indication of how hard Grasso worked in a vintage that was not always easy: bright garnet red with a bouquet of berry fruit on the nose following through to an easy richness of alcohol; full on the palate without ever being blowsy. The taste of oak stands out in the Barbera Vigna Martina, but the real feature of this wine is the excellent quality of the grapes, which can be seen in the depth of colour, the bouquet of bitter cherries, the structure and the long finish. The Chardonnay Educato is another good example of a well-managed barrique-aged wine and is at the same level of excellence as the Barbera. Only the Nebbiolo Gavarini lacks some of its usual fascination.

MONFORTE D'ALBA (CN)

GIOVANNI MANZONE
VIA CASTELLETTO, 9
12065 MONFORTE D'ALBA (CN)
TEL. 0173/78114

Giovanni Manzone's tiny winery can be found at Serra di Castelletto, once an independent commune, now part of Monforte. Extension work has now been completed on the cellars; the idea was not so much to increase production capacity as to make working conditions less cramped than they were. The estate possesses seven hectares of vines, comprising the La Serra vineyard surrounding the house, which is planted to rossese bianco, dolcetto and barbera, and the Gramolere vineyard planted to nebbiolo for Barolo. This cru site probably derives its name from the dialect word "gramon" ("gramigna" in Italian, meaning "weeds") and there is a curious local saying, "vineyards full of weed, the wine is good indeed". Weeds or not, the Barolo Gramolere is always a good wine; the '93 we tasted reached Two Glass level and the only doubts were over a dominant grassiness on the nose and an undeveloped bouquet; it was, however, much more successful on the palate, which has fullness of body and a good dose of tannins. This is a Barolo for laying down. Still on the subject of the Gramolere, we learn from Giovanni Manzone that he has put aside a good part of the '93 vintage for further ageing and that, when it emerges in 1999, it will be officially classed as "Riserva". This year the Dolcetto La Serra '96 shows very well, better even than the '95. It has an impressively deep colour and a palate rich in extract. The Bricco Serra '94 will not disappoint; made of the rare rossesse bianco grape variety, it has a bouquet with hints of citrus fruit peel, peach stones and tropical fruit.

● Barolo Ginestra		
Vigna Casa Maté '93	▼▼▼	5
● Barbera d'Alba Vigna Martina '94	▼▼	5
● Barolo Gavarini Vigna Chiniera '93	▼▼	5
○ Langhe Chardonnay Educato '95	▼▼	4
● Langhe Nebbiolo Gavarini '96	▼	3
● Barolo Gavarini Vigna Chiniera '89	♀♀♀	6
● Barolo Ginestra		
Vigna Casa Maté '90	♀♀♀	6
● Barbera d'Alba Vigna Martina '93	♀♀	5
● Barolo Gavarini Vigna Chiniera '90	♀♀	6
● Barolo Ginestra		
Vigna Casa Maté '89	♀♀	6
● Dolcetto d'Alba Gavarini		
Vigna dei Grassi '95	♀♀	3

● Barolo Gramolere '93	▼▼	5
● Dolcetto d'Alba La Serra '96	▼▼	2*
○ Bricco Serra '94	▼	4
● Dolcetto d'Alba La Serra '95	▼	2*
● Barolo Gramolere '90	♀♀	5
● Barolo Gramolere '91	♀♀	5
● Barolo Gramolere Ris. '90	♀♀	6
● Barbera d'Alba La Serra '93	♀	3
● Barolo Gramolere '92	♀	5

MONFORTE D'ALBA (CN)

ARMANDO PARUSSO
TIZIANA E MARCO PARUSSO
LOC. BUSSIA, 55
12065 MONFORTE D'ALBA (CN)
TEL. 0173/78257

Seven years ago, when Armando Parusso died leaving a truly promising winery to Marco and Tiziana, we thought that it was all too early for these two youngsters from Bussia. But sheer determination and an ability to work together as a team has ensured that Armando's children have been able to bring their father's efforts to fruition. Difficult vintages have not helped in the process of finding a personal style in a zone where change has been happening so quickly anyway, but this year's wines have proved that at least some of their objectives have been realised. Marco and Tiziana can now be proud of their Barolos. The Rocche vineyard gives a deeply coloured, youthful red wine; the bouquet opens out gently giving out hints of herbs and spices, gradually followed by more definite aromas of raspberries, plums and liquorice; this subtlety is apparent on the palate too, where, typically, the wine's depth of structure is revealed by the presence of the requisite tannins. Barolo Munie is full-bodied and traditional in style, with a deep garnet colour and an intense bouquet of cherries and roses; rich on the palate, leading to a firm, dry and only slightly bitter finish. The non-cru Barolo is no blockbuster, but it is certainly well made. The Bricco Rovella Bianco has improved; the sauvignon gets the better of the chardonnay more and more, not only in actual percentage terms in the cépage, but also because of its aromatic character and its dominance on the palate. The Bricco Rovella Rosso opens gradually, and offers a good example of the balanced use of wood.

MONFORTE D'ALBA (CN)

PODERI ROCCHE DEI MANZONI
LOC. MANZONI SOPRANI, 3
12065 MONFORTE D'ALBA (CN)
TEL. 0173/78421

In the world of great Italian sparkling wines one star has shone brighter and brighter over the last two years: the Brut Zero from Valentino and Jolanda Migliorini. Made of barrique-aged chardonnay, this is a unique sparkling wine that is difficult to describe alongside the best examples from Trentino and Lombardy, but we do know that the '93 version survives the comparison well. Golden yellow in colour, endowed with a delicate perlage, the touch of vanilla coming from the wood is clear enough, but wrapped up in subtle hints of pears and peaches, flowers, nuts and citrus-fruit peel on the nose. The '93 vintage also provides the first Barolos of the new production cycle; put to the test, they survive well enough, even if they are not exceptional. The Cappella di Santo Stefano vineyard gives us an elegant red wine: well-developed with its bouquet of crushed violets and plums, long and complex in its flavours, endowed with soft tannins and well-balanced, if medium-weight, structure. Barolo Vigna Big is a big wine in all senses, starting with the depth of colour; on the nose there are noticeable hints of jam and liquorice, which return on the palate, with its underlying tannins and long finish. Barolo Vigna d'la Roul is mature and well-balanced, while the standard Barolo is surprisingly rich. The barrique aged Chardonnay Angelica shows excellent fruit, but is not yet ready. The Bricco Manzoni is its usual elegant self, while the Dolcetto from the Vigna Martinera has a quite irresistible bouquet.

Wine	Rating	Score
● Barolo '93	▼▼	5
● Barolo Bussia Vigna Munie '93	▼▼	5
● Barolo Bussia Vigna Rocche '93	▼▼	5
● Langhe Rosso Bricco Rovella '95	▼▼	5
○ Langhe Bianco Bricco Rovella '96	▼▼	4
● Dolcetto d'Alba '96	▼	3
● Barbera d'Alba Bricco Pugnane '90	♀♀	4
● Barolo Bussia '90	♀♀	5
● Barolo Bussia Vigna Munie '92	♀♀	4
● Barolo Bussia Vigna Rocche '92	♀♀	5
● Barolo Mariondino '90	♀♀	5
● Bricco Rovella Rosso '94	♀♀	4
○ Langhe Bianco Bricco Rovella '95	♀♀	4

Wine	Rating	Score
○ Valentino Brut Zero Ris. '93	▼▼▼	5
○ Riserva Elena Spumante '90	▼▼	4
● Barolo Cappella di Santo Stefano '93	▼▼	6
● Barolo Rocche '93	▼▼	5
● Barolo Vigna Big '93	▼▼	6
● Barolo Vigna d'la Roul '93	▼▼	6
● Bricco Manzoni '94	▼▼	5
● Dolcetto d'Alba Vigna Matinera '96	▼▼	3
○ Langhe Chardonnay l'Angelica '95	▼	5
○ Valentino Brut Zero Ris. '92	♀♀♀	5
● Barolo Vigna Big Ris. '89	♀♀♀	6
● Barolo Vigna Big Ris. '90	♀♀♀	6
● Barolo Vigna d'la Roul Ris. '90	♀♀♀	6
● Bricco Manzoni '93	♀♀	5

MONFORTE D'ALBA (CN)

FERDINANDO PRINCIPIANO
VIA ALBA, 19
12065 MONFORTE D'ALBA (CN)
TEL. 0173/787158

This Three Glass award goes to a winery that appears in the Guide for the first time this year, for a Barolo that repeated tasting has shown to be easily one of the best wines of the '93 vintage. This new winery has a long history. The parents have always produced grapes from the nine hectares of family-owned vineyards. Their son, Ferdinando, fresh from oenological school and guided by the advice of some of the best producers in the area, decided to embark on making his own wine a few years ago. His first wine was the Barbera Pian Romualdo '93: well-structured and with the requisite amount of new oak on the nose, a success repeated by the 3,000 bottles produced in the '94 vintage. Young Ferdinando's expert touch can also be seen in the 6,000 bottles of the aromatic Dolcetto S. Anna '96. Only 1,300 bottles were produced of the Barolo Boscareto '93 (production will increase in the future): firm and concentrated with excellent ripe fruit on the nose and a well-judged amount of new French oak to keep the wine youthful; smooth vanilla and hints of tar on the palate, the overall impression being exceptionally well-defined and enviably smooth. Ferdinando Principiano has succeeded in imbuing his wine with the singular power of this fine vineyard in the commune of Serralunga, and it will certainly improve over a long period of time, as the sweetness of the wood blends with the ripeness of the nebbiolo.

● Barolo Boscareto '93	ΨΨΨ	5
● Barbera d'Alba		
Pian Romualdo '93	ΨΨ	4
● Barbera d'Alba		
Pian Romualdo '94	ΨΨ	4
● Dolcetto d'Alba S. Anna '96	Ψ	3

MONFORTE D'ALBA (CN)

FLAVIO RODDOLO
BRICCO APPIANI
12065 MONFORTE D'ALBA (CN)
TEL. 0173/78535

The latest news from this producer, the début of Flavio Roddolo's first Barolo, should not be allowed to obscure the quality and consistency of the rest of the range, whether Dolcetto, Barbera, Nebbiolo, but obviously it is the new wine which attracts the limelight. Source of this Barolo is a small estate-owned vineyard called Ravera or Bricco Ravera, located on the edge of the Monforte zone going towards Serralunga, on a slope defined as "excellent" in the Atlas of vineyards of the Langhe. Flavio Roddolo's wine (only 1,800 bottles, for the moment) has a bouquet with clear undertones of wood beneath the fruit and a slight tarriness: quite closed on the palate with good tannins and acidity; medium weight, it will take at least another couple of years for this to come to its peak. 1996 was one of the best harvests for dolcetto in recent years and since Flavio Roddolo is one of the experts in this field it is not surprising that his wine is superlative: fresh and very fruity, not too high in alcohol, well-structured and well-balanced, highly aromatic and very drinkable. As a bonus, this particular Dolcetto d'Alba is made to last, and will be at its best only after many months of bottle age. The worthy Barbera '95, tasted when just bottled, still had the primary aromas of crushed grape and is full-bodied and well-rounded at the edges by its time in wood.

● Barbera d'Alba '95	ΨΨ	3*
● Barolo '93	ΨΨ	5
● Dolcetto d'Alba '96	ΨΨ	3*
● Dolcetto d'Alba '95	ΨΨ	3
● Nebbiolo d'Alba '94	ΨΨ	3
● Barbera d'Alba '94	Ψ	3

MONFORTE D'ALBA (CN) MONLEALE (AL)

F.LLI SEGHESIO
FRAZ. CASTELLETTO, 20
12065 MONFORTE D'ALBA (CN)
TEL. 0173/78108

VIGNETI MASSA
P.ZZA G. CAPSONI, 8
15059 MONLEALE (AL)
TEL. 0131/80302

This promising winery must think of last year as a temporary hiatus. Recent successes have encouraged the Seghesios to expand the output of their winery - one glance at how much work has gone on in the vineyards and the cellars is sufficient to understand their commitment - but the quality of the grapes produced has not always been what it should. Hence, the wines on tasting are good, but they do not cause the usual enthusiasm. The Barbera Vigneto della Chiesa '95 stands out for its vivacity; deeply coloured, attractive with a fruity nose, but lacking in the complexity of aroma and depth of flavour that the '94 had. The standard Barbera is a bright, up-front wine and is significant because, coming from the '96 vintage, it gives an idea of how good the Vigneto della Chiesa '96 will be when it finishes its time in barrique. The Dolcetto d'Alba just missed a Two Glass award; despite never having been one of this producer's mainstream wines, it has an ample and distinctive bouquet and long-finishing balance on the palate. The Barolo La Villa '93 has a pale garnet red colour, delicate aromas of fruit and flowers and distinct toastiness from the wood, but it is quite closed on the palate. Possibly the various elements of this wine have not yet come together, and it may be that a Barolo which such a lot of body needs further ageing.

A graduate of the Oenological School of Alba, Walter Massa looks after the family estate with dedication. The basic ingredients of the "recipe" for this top wines are simple and infallible: low yields per hectare, the minimum crop from each vine, cellar technology focused on extracting the best from the best quality grapes. The barrique-aged Bigolla '95 has the unmistakable varietal bouquet of barbera. Ruby to garnet red colour, it has a concentrated and creamy nose of cherry, liquorice and coffee, is up-front on the palate, full-bodied and well-structured with a long fruity finish. The Vecchia Carreta, made of barbera with added croatina, cabernet and nebbiolo, comes a close second. Ruby red with the beginnings of orange reflections, the particular cépage results in broad aromas of ripe raspberries and blackberries, spices and cocoa, with overtones of slight grassiness; full-bodied, good acidity, rounded tannins, a little dumb on the finish. The Barbera Monleale has a mature, ruby red colour with hints of bitter cherries, vanilla and cinnamon on the nose; full-bodied and slightly tight on the palate. Cortese Cerreta d'Orois is pale straw yellow in colour, and has hints of apples and wild flowers on the nose; attractive and easy to drink, even if lacking a bit in backbone. The Timorasso is made from the grape of the same name, the conservation of which Walter regards as a personal challenge. It has a mineral and vegetal nose and if it lacks a little in freshness, this is compensated for by the smoothness and fullness of body. The two Barberas, Campolungo and Cerreta Soprana, the Cortese Casareggio and the Muscaté are well made and correct.

● Barolo Vigneto La Villa '93	▼▼	5
● Barbera d'Alba '96	▼	3
● Barbera d'Alba Vigneto della Chiesa '95	▼	4
● Dolcetto d'Alba Vigneto della Chiesa '96	▼	3
● Barolo Vigneto La Villa '91	▼▼▼	5
● Barbera d'Alba Vigneto della Chiesa '93	▼▼	4
● Barbera d'Alba Vigneto della Chiesa '94	▼▼	4
● Barolo Vigneto La Villa '89	▼▼	5
● Barolo Vigneto La Villa '90	▼▼	5
● Barolo Vigneto La Villa '92	▼▼	5

● Bigolla '95	▼▼	4
● Vecchia Cerreta '95	▼▼	4
● Colli Tortonesi Monleale '95	▼	4
O Piemonte Cortese Cerreta d'Oro '95	▼	3
O Timorasso '95	▼	4
O Muscaté '96		3
● Piemonte Barbera Campolungo '96		2
● Piemonte Barbera Cerreta Soprana '96		3
O Piemonte Cortese Casareggio '96		2
● Bigolla '93	▼▼	4

MONTÀ D'ALBA (CN)

GIOVANNI ALMONDO
VIA S. ROCCO, 26
12052 MONTÀ D'ALBA (CN)
TEL. 0173/975256

The hills of Santo Stefano, Canale and Montà (one of the Roero's best vineyard areas) finish in the north at Bric Valdiana, less than a kilometre from Montà as the crow flies. Here Domenico Almondo owns two and a half hectares (another half a hectare will come on stream in 1999) of vineyards planted to nebbiolo which produce the 4,000 bottles of his Roero cru called, naturally, Bric Valdiana. The limestone soil of these hills ensures bouquets of remarkable finesse, as the Bric Valdiana demonstrates: hints of violets, coffee, jam, liquorice and rosemary blend together to make ample and attractive bouquets; a deep colour reveals the wine to be full-bodied; layer by layer, it develops an austere harmony on the palate, before finishing with soft tannins and the return of violets and liquorice. The Bricco delle Ciliegie is also very good: bright, straw yellow colour, precise aromas of apricot, apple and toasted bread with undertones of vanilla; full-bodied and attractively full-flavoured. Vigne Sparse is straw yellow with greenish reflections and has a bouquet of tropical fruit, yeasty bread and grapefruit peel. On the palate it is smooth and fresh with a slight bitter twist to the finish. Lastly, the Fosso della Rosa is always good; made from brachetto, it has an elegant bouquet of roses and is well-balanced on the palate.

MONTEGROSSO D'ASTI (AT)

TENUTA LA MERIDIANA
FRAZ. TANA, 5
14048 MONTEGROSSO D'ASTI (AT)
TEL. 0141/956172

As usual, the Tenuta La Meridiana showed us a wide range of well made wines. Giampiero Bianco has a mission to show how good the winemaking potential of this corner of the Monferrato is. He also believes that specialisation in barbera is not the only way forward, but in fact it is the Barbera d'Asti that showed best in this year's tastings, despite indifferent vintages. The Vigna Le Gagie '95 has its usual light and delicate character: mature, limpid ruby red; ripe fruit and spiciness on the nose; a simple palate with characteristic acidity emerging on the finish. If you want greater depth of flavour and a more intriguing and complex nose, go for the Barbera made from the old vines of Bricco Sereno: opaque in colour with a bouquet of macerated blackberries, bitter cherries and almonds blending with delicate overtones of vanilla and pepper; full-bodied and well-balanced on the palate by firm acidity. The Bianco Vigneti Delizia e Collina is more interesting and more expressive than in the past; the unusual cépage of chardonnay, cortese and favorita gives it softness on one hand and vivacity on the other. The Grignolino is more neutral, and despite the winery's best efforts it still does not live up to expectations. The Vigneti del Papa Malaga is an aromatic and enjoyable sparkling red wine.

○ Roero Arneis		
Bricco delle Ciliegie '96	▼▼	3
● Roero Bric Valdiana '95	▼▼	4
● Fosso della Rosa '96	▼	3
○ Roero Arneis Vigne Sparse '96	▼	3

● Barbera d'Asti Sup.		
Bricco Sereno '94	▼	3
● Barbera d'Asti Le Gagie '95	▼	2*
○ Vigneti Delizia e Collina '96	▼	3
● Grignolino d'Asti		
Vigna Maestra '96		3
● Vigneti del Papa Malaga '96		3
● Barbera d'Asti		
Bricco Sereno '93	▽	3

MONTELUPO ALBESE (CN) MONTEU ROERO (CN)

CA' VIOLA
VIA LANGA, 17
12050 MONTELUPO ALBESE (CN)
TEL. 0173/617570-617119

ANGELO NEGRO & FIGLI
FRAZ. S. ANNA, 1
CASCINA RIVERI
12040 MONTEU ROERO (CN)
TEL. 0173/90252

Beppe Caviola is always running from one producer to another with sound advice and remedies for their problems, even today when he is at the height of his reputation. We hope that he has at least left himself some time to enjoy the triumphs of his Bric du Luv '95 and his Dolcetto d'Alba Barturot '96, two great wines he has made together with his partner and untiring grower, Maurizio Anselma. The first wine deserves the Three Glass award for the density and almost tangible texture of its colour, not to mention the rich and complex bouquet. The scent of ripe plums stands out, but the elegance of the nose emerges with the hints of white chocolate and spices in the background. On the palate the promise of the bouquet is well borne out; the wine is polished, faultless, and develops to a rich and long lasting finish. This was not the only wine to reach these heights in this year's tastings: the Barturot was also awarded Three Glasses. This is a deeply coloured Dolcetto with a dusky Mediterranean bouquet and good fruit in the rich and broad flavours on the palate; the soft tannins are particularly impressive and the wine is full-bodied and long finishing. The standard Dolcetto should not be ignored and would stand up well to any other in the premium category: ruby red in colour with velvety violet reflections; the whole bouquet is very well knit together, while the palate starts with richness and ends with elegance. The latest wine in the range, Rangone, is made from pinot noir and seems at the moment to be more powerful than stylish.

When Angelo Negro started his career as a winemaker, all he had was one hectare of land at Perdaudin and some debts inherited from his father. Now, Angelo could leave his four children a estate with more than 30 hectares of vineyards and a production capacity of almost 200,000 bottles per year. Furthermore, he has now bought and restored the San Vittore estate at Canale which will come into production in the year 2000 with new barbera and nebbiolo vineyards. Angelo told us this as we walked over a great cement square (about 3,000 square metres), the foundations of the new cellars. This year, his best wine is the Barbera Bric Bertu '95: opaque in colour and with a complex bouquet of raspberries, coffee, cocoa and finely ground cinnamon; good follow through on the palate with body and length over a background of liquorice and toffee. The Nicolon '95 acquits itself well, even if it is less powerful on the nose (cherries and bilberries), and not such a powerful wine; nevertheless it is well-balanced in its tannins and acidity. The Roero Prachiosso '95 has a noticeable bouquet of strawberries and bitter cherries, together with hints of flowers and tar. On the palate it is soft, without harshness, but not over long in finishing. The Arneis Perdaudin '96 remains the best known wine from this winery, but the current vintage has difficulty in reaching the level of previous years: it has hints of hay, butter and flowers but overall it lacks aroma on the nose; on the palate it is smooth and rounded, but slightly flabby. Peraudin Passito is an interesting wine produced with the best grapes of the estate; sweet and sharply-defined nose of honey and mint, dried grapes and jam; rich and concentrated on the palate, with an aftertaste of sweet citrus fruit.

● Dolcetto d'Alba Barturot '96	♥♥♥	3
● Langhe Rosso Bric du Luv '95	♥♥♥	5
● Dolcetto d'Alba '96	♥♥	3
● Langhe Rosso Rangone '95	♥	5
● Bric du Luv '93	♀♀	4
● Bric du Luv '94	♀♀	4
● Dolcetto d'Alba Barturot '94	♀♀	3
● Dolcetto d'Alba Barturot '95	♀♀	3

● Barbera d'Alba Bric Bertu '95	♥♥	4
● Barbera d'Alba Nicolon '95	♥	3
○ Perdaudin Passito	♥	5
○ Roero Arneis Perdaudin '96	♥	4
● Roero Prachiosso '95	♥	3
○ Langhe Favorita '96		3
○ Roero Arneis '96		3
● Barbera d'Alba Bric Bertu '94	♀	4

MORIONDO (TO)

TERRE DA VINO
VIA ROMA, 50
10020 MORIONDO (TO)
TEL. 011/9927070

MORSASCO (AL)

LA GUARDIA
REG. LA GUARDIA
15010 MORSASCO (AL)
TEL. 0144/73076

The vast range of wines from Terre da Vino, a company that comprises no fewer than 17 wineries, always has something new to offer on the quality front. The faith that was put into the enterprise some years ago is being justified. It is not only individual wines that are coming to the fore now, but the entire production which all benefits from consistently good winemaking. We begin with the top scoring wines. The Barbera La Luna e i Falò maintains consistent quality from vintage to vintage and the '95 clearly brings out the character of the DOC with its attractively direct flavours. Although perhaps the new oak is a little too dominant on the nose, the presence of such good fruit in such a difficult year is an achievement in itself. The Barbaresco La Casa in Collina '93 is a great success: traditional in style with an attractive liquorice, tobacco and plum jam nose, this is a generous wine on the palate, full bodied and well balanced. The Barolo Paesi Tuoi of the same vintage is similarly full bodied, but perhaps too lean on the nose and it does not have quite the same finish. The good news continues with the Gavi wines, both fascinating and both very different. The Ca' da Bosio is very up-front without being overblown, while the Cascine dell'Aureliana is much better defined on the palate and simpler on the nose. The Favorita Brichet surprised us with its completeness, quite belying the simplicity of the bouquet. The Arneis Langhe and Erbaluce di Caluso have less character, while the Chardonnay della Tenuta Magnona is dominated by wood to such an extent that the fruit is completely masked.

The Priarone family have been the owners of this beautiful estate since 1969 and can well claim the title of ambassadors of Dolcetto d'Ovada for the world, especially since more than half of their estimable production goes abroad. Four out of Franco's five children help in the winery: Bruna looks after the administration, Graziella works both in the cellars and on the promotional side, Ottavio looks after sales, and Giorgio is responsible for the vineyards. This year the Bricco Riccardo was not as good as in previous years, though it did not lack in structure. On the other hand, the Villa Delfini cru was definitely very good: youthful violet and ruby red colour; ripe fruit on the nose with hints of figs and prunes, vanilla and spices; good backbone and well rounded off with a subtle layer of tannins. The Gamondino scored well; it has good body, even if the bouquet is not quite up to its usual standard. The Gavi is interesting: hints of cinnamon, flowers and tamarind on the nose; attractive and easy to drink. Both Chardonnays are worthy of mention: the Butas has a bouquet of bananas and acacia flowers and is fresh and well balanced on the palate; the Chardonnay di Morsasco has subtle hints of flowers, hazelnuts, honey and vanilla on the nose and has a soft wood-influenced palate. Lastly, the standard brachetto-based wine, named with sardonic humour Figlio di un Bacco Minore ("Offspring of a Minor Grape"), gets its pass marks with a bouquet of roses and plums and a fresh, full flavoured palate.

● Barbaresco La Casa in Collina '93	♥♥	4
● Barbera d'Asti La Luna e i Falò '94	♥♥	3*
● Barbera d'Asti La Luna e i Falò '95	♥♥	4
● Barolo Paesi Tuoi '93	♥	4
○ Gavi Cascine dell'Aureliana '96	♥	2*
○ Gavi di Gavi Ca' da Bosio '96	♥	3
○ Langhe Arneis '96	♥	3
○ Langhe Favorita '96	♥	2*
● Malvasia di Castelnuovo Don		
Bosco Abbazia Vezzolano '96	♥	2*
○ Erbaluce di Caluso La Baiarda '96		3
○ Gavi di Gavi Masseria		
dei Carmelitani '96		3
● Barbera d'Asti La Luna e i Falò '93	♀♀	4
● Barbera d'Asti La Luna e i Falò '90	♀♀	4

● Dolcetto di Ovada		
Villa Delfini '94	♥♥	4
○ Chardonnay di Morsasco '94	♥	4
● Dolcetto di Ovada		
Gamondino '95	♥	3
● Dolcetto di Ovada Sup.		
Vigneto Bricco Riccardo '95	♥	3
● Figlio di un Bacco Minore '96	♥	4
○ Gavi di Gavi '96	♥	4
○ Piemonte Chardonnay Butas '96	♥	4
● Dolcetto di Ovada Sup.		
Vigneto Bricco Riccardo '94	♀♀	3
● Dolcetto di Ovada		
Villa Delfini '93	♀♀	4
● Dolcetto di Ovada Gamondino '93	♀	3

NEIVE (CN)

PIERO BUSSO
B.TA ALBESANI, 8
12057 NEIVE (CN)
TEL. 0173/67156

Piero Busso's wines are always interesting and well made, and they never lack character or personality. Proof of his skills comes with the wines released for 1997, beginning with the Langhe Bianco '95, a successful, value-for-money cuvée of chardonnay and sauvignon which will benefit from further bottle ageing as the French oak takes the edge off its greenness. The Barbaresco '94 is a good wine: not particularly complex, but endowed with a rich bouquet of ripe berry fruit and solid structure; it stood out during our blind tasting and can be counted a definite success, especially considering the poor vintage. The Dolcetto '96 has good extract and fine palate and is, perhaps, the best this winery has ever made; the violet-tinged, ruby red colour is immediately attractive; the bouquet is intense, clearly defined and very fruity, although perhaps as yet a little undeveloped; full bodied and long-finishing on the palate, this is a wine which will clearly continue to improve over the next couple of years at least. The Barbera '95 is a little dumb and the oak does not succeed in counteracting the rampant acidity. The Nebbiolo, newly classified as DOC Langhe, is an interesting red: fresh and fruity on the nose, but austere and tannic on the palate. Inspired by his success, Piero Busso has already began extension work on his winery, which will have new underground cask and bottle ageing cellars completed this year.

NEIVE (CN)

F.LLI CIGLIUTI
LOC. SERRA BOELLA, 17
12057 NEIVE (CN)
TEL. 0173/677185

Renato Cigliutti and his family constitute the very model of a self sufficient wine estate, capable of carrying out all phases of production for about 25,000 bottles per year, beginning in the vineyards and finishing with sales. The Barbaresco '94 is more influenced by wood than is normal for this producer's house style and is very attractive on the nose; it is not a huge wine and not long finishing, perhaps, but this shows how difficult the '94 vintage was. The fresh, up-front Barbera d'Alba '96 is clean, well defined and easy to like, excellent with the traditional "antipasti" and first courses of the cuisine of the Langhe. The Bricco Serra '95 is a more serious wine, both for the tannins of the nebbiolo and for the effects of wood ageing; at the moment it is at its best on the nose, with a good sweetness and depth of aroma. The Dolcetto d'Alba Serraboella '96 is fruity and very drinkable. Bad news, however, for lovers of Freisa, the Cigliutti family have decided to cease production of this lively summer drinking wine from the '96 vintage and have replanted the vineyard with vines destined to make bigger wines, in line with the policy of concentrating on serious wines for long ageing.

● Barbaresco Vigna Borgese '94	🍷🍷	4
● Dolcetto d'Alba		
Vigna Majano '96	🍷🍷	3*
○ Langhe Bianco '95	🍷🍷	3*
● Langhe Nebbiolo '95	🍷	4
● Barbera d'Alba		
Vigna Majano '95		3
● Barbaresco Vigna Borgese '93	🍷🍷	4
● Barbaresco Vigna Borgese '91	🍷	4
● Barbaresco Vigna Borgese '92	🍷	4
● Barbera d'Alba		
Vigna Majano '94	🍷	3

● Barbaresco Serraboella '94	🍷	5
● Barbera d'Alba '96	🍷	4
● Bricco Serra '95	🍷	5
● Dolcetto d'Alba Serraboella '96	🍷	3
● Barbaresco '83	🍷🍷🍷	5
● Barbaresco Serraboella '90	🍷🍷🍷	5
● Barbaresco Serraboella '92	🍷🍷	5
● Barbaresco Serraboella '93	🍷🍷	5
● Bricco Serra '94	🍷	5

NEIVE (CN)

NEIVE (CN)

GASTALDI
VIA SERRA BOELLA, 2
12057 NEIVE (CN)
TEL. 0173/677400

BRUNO GIACOSA
VIA XX SETTEMBRE, 52
12057 NEIVE (CN)
TEL. 0173/67027

The hot news is that the Gastaldi winery has come out with its first Barbaresco, which has emerged in tastings as one of the most elegant of the '94 vintage: the attractive tones of wood on the nose are still unblended, but the full bodied nature of this wine ensures good bottle ageing potential, although being a '94, it is based more on finesse than power. As far as the famous and much heralded Rosso is concerned, Bernardino Gastaldi has surprised everyone slightly by coming out with the '92 vintage, keeping back the '90 for further ageing and skipping the '91 altogether. The Rosso suffered from being tasted only a few days after bottling and was therefore somewhat unbalanced, but it has bigger structure than the vintage might suggest and an attractive fruitiness to the nose; the colour was, as usual, a deep and fascinating, almost impenetrable, ruby red. The wine will need several months' bottle ageing before beginning to show at its best. The Bianco '95 is very drinkable, full flavoured and up-front; vinified without the use of wood, it displays the natural fruitiness of its chardonnay and sauvignon cépage to the maximum. At the time of printing, the Dolcetto '96 was not yet bottled, so the first comments on this wine must come from the fans of Gastaldi wines themselves, who will find it in specialist wine shops from Christmas 1997.

Bruno Giacosa is internationally famous as one of the top winemakers in Italy, and has made some of the country's best wines ever, such as Barolo Collina Rionda '82 and Barbaresco S. Stefano '78. So why is it that our Guide does not give him Three Glass awards any more? Bruno Giacosa makes wines to last, that in the first phases of bottle ageing do not emanate those well defined and smooth flavours and aromas that seduce tasters, especially on the nose. For this reason, in tastings of recent vintages the Barolos and Barbarescos of this great winemaker have not shone as brightly as they might, and this is reflected in our tastings notes. We can only add the hope that Giacosa's latest wines will evolve with bottle age. The Roero Arneis is fresh and floral, well defined and immediately pleasing on the nose, textbook clean and full bodied; this is one of the best wines of the vintage. The Nebbiolo d'Alba Valmaggiore, also from Roero, shows clear varietal character (fruity on the nose and quite tannic on the palate), in a similar fashion to the famous Dolcetto Basarin from Neive. The Spumante is full bodied and broad on the palate, as usual, but has a bouquet obscured by sulphur. The colour of the Barolo Collina Rionda '93 is not the deepest, while the nose is lean and shows the beginnings of a faint tarriness; full bodied on the palate with marked acidity and tannins, the finish suggests that this wine is already well advanced in its maturation. The Barolo Falletto, also from the magical vineyards of Serralunga, is better structured and more full bodied, with good attack on the palate.

● Barbaresco '94	♛♛	5
○ Langhe Bianco '95	♛♛	5
● Rosso Gastaldi '92	♛♛	6
● Dolcetto d'Alba Sup.		
Moriolo '90	♛♛♛	5
● Rosso Gastaldi '88	♛♛♛	6
● Rosso Gastaldi '89	♛♛♛	6
○ Bianco Gastaldi '92	♛♛	5
○ Bianco Gastaldi '94	♛♛	5
○ Chardonnay '92	♛♛	5

● Barolo Collina Rionda '93	♛♛	6
● Barolo Falletto '93	♛♛	6
○ Roero Arneis '96	♛♛	4
○ Bruno Giacosa Extra Brut '94	♛	4
● Dolcetto d'Alba Basarin '96	♛	3
● Nebbiolo d'Alba		
Valmaggiore '95	♛	4
● Barolo Collina Rionda Ris. '82	♛♛♛	6
● Barolo Rocche di Castiglione		
Falletto '85	♛♛♛	6
● Barbaresco S. Stefano '90	♛♛	6
● Barbaresco S. Stefano '93	♛♛	6
● Barolo Collina Rionda Ris. '90	♛♛	6
● Barolo Falletto '90	♛♛	6
● Barolo Villero '90	♛♛	6

NEIVE (CN)

NEIVE (CN)

GIACOSA FRATELLI
VIA XX SETTEMBRE, 64
12057 NEIVE (CN)
TEL. 0173/67013

PAITIN
PASQUERO ELIA
VIA SERRA BOELLA, 20
12057 NEIVE (CN)
TEL. 0173/67343

Fratelli Giacosa's re-entry in the Guide represents the reappearance of one of the biggest wine firms in the Langhe, with a production of 600,000 bottles per year and 15 hectares of company-owned vineyards, some of which lie in the prestigious Monforte and Castiglione zones. Credit for the company's good showing goes largely to a special cuvée of Barbera, fermented for 12 days on the skins and then aged for one year in small French oak barrels before ageing in bottle for another eight months. The '95 vintage is attractive and well balanced on both the nose (well defined aromas of blackberries and hints of vanilla), and the palate, where it stands out for drinkability. We also tasted the '93 vintage and got the impression that, despite being made for elegance rather than power, this wine would also age well. The Barbaresco and the Barolo are more than decent: the former is perhaps a little raw and rustic in style, but redeems itself with its splendid extract; the latter has a long, concentrated finish with a bouquet that develops aromas of plums, tar and roses. The white wines are made in a collaboration with another historic Piedmontese company and will do much to raise the reputation of some of the lesser wine growing areas of the lower Langhe. We tasted a Chardonnay made from grapes produced at Benevello, barrel fermented with selected yeasts and aged for a long time both in large oak and in bottle; we thought it was deliciously elegant, delicate, floral and fresh.

This estate has used its excellent vineyard sites and well equipped winery as the starting points for the production of what are becoming increasingly consistent, premium quality wines. Attractively fresh with hints of mint and basil on a good ground of berry fruit, the nose of the Barbaresco '94 is particularly striking; the palate is bright and very drinkable and has considerable finesse, despite the presence of tannins in abundance. The Langhe Paitin '95 is made of nebbiolo and barbera with small amounts of cabernet sauvignon and syrah; it is a great success: seductive on the nose thanks to a finely judged period in oak; the palate is particularly well balanced and rounded and the tannins of the nebbiolo and the acidity of the barbera are softened by rich, fleshy fruit. The Dolcetto '96 is an interesting wine with an especially successful nose, which is fresh and elegant and quite without the overblown character that is so common with this grape variety; rounded and very drinkable on the palate without much tannin and of average weight; in short, this is a wine that may not destroy all the opposition in a blind tasting, but it is guaranteed to be delicious at table, served with the food of the Langhe. The Barbera Campolive is the one disappointment in this year's tasting; the wood completely obscures the fruit without contributing the classic, elegant spiciness of the barrique.

● Barolo Bussia '93	♟	5
● Barbaresco '94	♟	4
● Barbera d'Alba Mariagioana '93	♟	3
● Barbera d'Alba Mariagioana '95	♟	3
○ Langhe Chardonnay '96		2

● Barbaresco Sorì Paitin '94	♟♟	5
● Dolcetto d'Alba Sorì Paitin '96	♟♟	3
● Langhe Paitin '95	♟♟	5
● Barbera d'Alba Campolive '95		4
● Barbaresco Ris. '90	♟♟	6
● Barbaresco Sorì Paitin '93	♟♟	5
● Paitin '90	♟♟	5
● Barbaresco Sorì Paitin '90	♟	5
● Paitin '91	♟	4

NEIVE (CN)

SOTTIMANO
LOC. COTTÀ, 21
12057 NEIVE (CN)
TEL. 0173/635186

The promise that this winery showed last year has been fulfilled - in part. Rino Sottimano is reorganising the production side of things, and in 1997 he made the decision to use the help of the young and capable consultant, Beppe Caviola. We will have to wait for at least another couple of years before we see the results of this partnership in practical terms, but in any case nothing could have been done about the poor quality raw material that went into the Barbaresco '94. The wine has a subtle bouquet and an attractive smoothness to the palate but it is thin and already well advanced in its evolution. It is left to two young wines, the Dolcetto and the Maté to provide the good news. The latter is made from 100 percent brachetto and has a nice, subtle colour; the precise aromatic character of the varietal stands out clearly with hints of flowers and citrus fruit peel; not very firm on the front palate, but gradually and successfully unfolding in flavour; the aroma in the finish could be better. The Dolcetto d'Alba Bric del Salto '96 has the typical richness of its vintage starting with the colour; on the nose vinosity is balanced by aromas of fruit and flowers; the full bodied palate derives from rich extract combined with soft tannins. The other Dolcetto, the Cottà, looks good on first examination, but turns out to have less character in the end; we were disappointed with the way its bouquet and palate unfolded.

NEVIGLIE (CN)

F.LLI BERA
CASCINA PALAZZO, 12
12050 NEVIGLIE (CN)
TEL. 0173/630194

The wines that do well naturally in this area are the Moscatos, but the Beras are very enthusiastic about red wines, too and this makes for increased work for the family, who already produce about 96,000 bottles per year. Fortunately, Sisto and Maria have the help of young Attilio and Walter, Alida and Flavia. Moscato is at home here, as we were saying, and this year too the estate's most successful wine is the Moscato cru Su Reimond. The colour is a limpid, pale straw yellow; the bouquet is delicate and ethereal, elegantly spanning the range from floral to resinous; the front palate is multi layered and the sparkle is light, accompanying a full flavoured body to a long finish. By contrast, the standard Moscato seems one dimensional, but it is still definitely a wine of quality. The Asti is up front and lively with a youthful hint of mint on the nose and a good prickle on the palate, which is definitely not sweet but is typically aromatic. The Spumante Brut just missed a Two Glass award; the bouquet is sharply defined but simply composed with only a few element (pears, hazelnuts and toasted bread), while the palate is remarkable for its balance, but lacks length. The '95 Barbera does not come up to the standard of the '94 (which proved to be excellent on re-tasting this year) due to a lack of complexity and richness of fruit. It is, however, clear that this is a potential flagship wine for the estate. Lastly, the Dolcetto is decent enough, fruity on the nose and firm on the palate.

● Dolcetto d'Alba Bric del Salto '96	♟♟	2*
● Barbaresco Pajoré Vigna Lunetta '94	♟	4
● Dolcetto d'Alba Cottà '96	♟	3
● Langhe Rosso Maté '96	♟	2
● Barbaresco Brichet '89	♟♟	5
● Barbaresco Brichet '90	♟	5
● Barbaresco Brichet '93	♟	4
● Barbaresco Seiranera '93	♟	4

○ Moscato d'Asti Su Reimond '96	♟♟	3
○ Asti Cascina Palazzo '96	♟	3
○ Bera Brut	♟	4
● Barbera d'Alba '95	♟	2
● Dolcetto d'Alba '96	♟	2
○ Moscato d'Asti '96	♟	3
● Barbera d'Alba Sassisto '94	♟♟	4

NIZZA MONFERRATO (AT)   NIZZA MONFERRATO (AT)

BERSANO ANTICHE CANTINE
CONTI DELLA CREMOSINA
P.ZZA DANTE, 21
14049 NIZZA MONFERRATO (AT)
TEL. 0141/721273

CASCINA LA BARBATELLA
STRADA ANNUNZIATA, 55
14049 NIZZA MONFERRATO (AT)
TEL. 0141/701434

Bersano is one of the great names in the history of Piedmontese winemaking, and continues to be so. The company's founder, Arturo Bersano, was one of the legendary figures of winemaking in the Monferrato area. He was a staunch upholder of tradition (do not miss the museum of country life and the exhibition of historic labels at the company headquarters) who also knew how to turn himself into a modern entrepreneur with a concern for oenology. Back in the 1970s Bersano had already started buying up vineyards, and the company now has possessions in some of the best sites of the Langhe as well as the property at Nizza Monferrato based on the Cremosina estate. More recently, the new owners have bought the La Generala estate di Agliano in the Monferrato, a magnificent parcel of land in the heart of Barbera country. The wines produced for tasting this year give a glimpse of the company's potential under its able and energetic director, Domenico Conta. The Gavi from one of the best estates of the area, Tenuta Marchese Raggio, which has been rented by Bersano for the last 10 years, has great finesse and definition. This is a white that shows the cortese grape at its best: delicate but immediate on the nose; satisfactorily full in flavour with well balanced youthfulness and a long finish. The Barbera Vigna della Cremosina is an excellent wine made more for elegance than for power. There are two attractive sweet wines: the Brachetto d'Acqui Vigna Castelgaro with its unmistakable bouquet of roses and the Moscato d'Asti Vigna San Michele, with its elegant aromatic qualities. The Spumante Metodo Classico Arturo Bersano is a good, very drinkable wine with a toasted bread nose.

It is absolutely essential in winemaking to know what your aims are, something that the likeable and affable Angelo Sonvico is well aware of. In 1982, following his own preference for barbera and cabernet and the advice of his friend, the oenologist Giuliano Noé, he bought a beautiful property with vineyards attached on a slope in Nizza Monferrato. Every year since he has turned out prize winning wines, including a string of products which have won Gambero Rosso Three Glass awards with almost derisory ease. In this year's tastings the best wine was the barbera/cabernet sauvignon blend La Vigna di Sonvico. The two varietals ripen together in the same vineyard, and provide the grapes for a wine that explodes in the glass; deep ruby red colour enlivened with bright purple reflections, a nose full of fruity redcurrant, blackcurrant and bitter cherry; aromas elegantly combined with the hints of toasted coffee beans and cocoa of superbly judged oak; both elegant and powerful on the palate, full bodied, rich and long with a perfect follow through from nose to finish. The La Vigna dell'Angelo also shows very well: a deep ruby red colour precedes an intense and sophisticated nose with attractive fruity hints of berry fruit, plums and cherries, all sharply defined under a cloak of vanilla from the wood; the palate is broad and rich in alcohol, with good length and concentration. The standard Barbera is well made, fresh and fruity (raspberries and bitter cherries), if a little lacking on the palate. The white wine made from sauvignon and cortese needs working on; it is good on the palate, but dumb on the nose.

O Gavi di Gavi Tenuta Marchese Raggio '96	ΨΨ	4
● Barbera d'Asti Vigna Cremosina '95	Ψ	4
● Brachetto d'Acqui Vigna Castelgaro '96	Ψ	4
O Moscato d'Asti Vigna S. Michele '96	Ψ	4
O Spumante Arturo Bersano Ris. '92	Ψ	4

● La Vigna di Sonvico '95	ΨΨΨ	5
● Barbera d'Asti Sup. La Vigna dell'Angelo '95	ΨΨ	5
● Barbera d'Asti La Barbatella '96	Ψ	4
O Monferrato Bianco Noè '96	Ψ	4
● Barbera d'Asti Sup. Vigna dell'Angelo '89	ΨΨΨ	5
● La Vigna di Sonvico '90	ΨΨΨ	5
● La Vigna di Sonvico '91	ΨΨΨ	5
● La Vigna di Sonvico '93	ΨΨΨ	5
● La Vigna di Sonvico '94	ΨΨΨ	5
● Barbera d'Asti Sup. Vigna dell'Angelo '93	ΨΨ	5
● Barbera d'Asti Sup. Vigna dell'Angelo '94	ΨΨ	5

NIZZA MONFERRATO (AT)

SCARPA
VIA MONTEGRAPPA, 6
14049 NIZZA MONFERRATO (AT)
TEL. 0141/721331

NIZZA MONFERRATO (AT)

FRANCO E MARIO SCRIMAGLIO
VIA ALESSANDRIA, 67
14049 NIZZA MONFERRATO (AT)
TEL. 0141/721385-727052

Mario Pesce's guiding principles are a rigid respect for tradition, an exclusive dedication to making wines that reflect the characteristics of their vineyards of origin, and a decision to concentrate exclusively on quality. Mario, the current owner of the estate, is assisted by his nephews, Carlo (the oenologist) and Mario Castino, who together ensure the rigorous selection in the vineyard. The company owns 25 hectares and rents or has available for use another10. Production never exceeds 100,000 bottles and includes most of the principal wines of the Monferrato and the Langhe, plus some magnificent rediscoveries, such as the Rouchet. Owing to the long periods of ageing involved, only a few of the Scarpa wines were ready for tasting this year. Of those we did taste, we were particularly impressed with the Rouchet Bricco Rosa, with its limpid cardinal-red colour and violet reflections; the wine has a fresh and intriguing nose of attractive and well defined aromas of roses mingled with fruit and woodiness; long and well made on the palate, strong and velvety at the same time, balanced but not yet completely rounded out, clean finishing with an attractive almond twist. The Dolcetto La Selva di Moirano has a fresh, vinous nose with good cherry fruit, a classic purple colour and an enjoyable palate with marked tannin in evidence. The Barbera d'Asti Castelrocchero '95 is still evolving and will be examined next year.

Winemaking in the Monferrato area is going through an interesting phase. After the revitalisation that was helped by vintages such as '85, '88 and '90, few producers have had the necessary tenacity to continue the process of improvement. However, Mario Scrimaglio is one of the small group of producers who have gone on to greater things and he continues to produce good wines, even in poor vintages. His secret is the naturally acquired countryman's skill in selecting and buying grapes, an easy task in good vintages, but extremely difficult in bad ones. The Barbera d'Asti Superiore '95 is made in a reliable traditional style and has a bright ruby red colour; the bouquet is creditably broad with aromas of vanilla, bitter cherries and plums; the front palate is not the biggest, but it is lively and the taste develops on the palate with unexpected length on the finish. The Croutin version of this wine is firmer on the palate and reflects the natural vitality of the grape variety: the colour is a dusky ruby red that shows how mature the wine is; the nose has hints of berry fruit and spices and the alcohol on the front palate contrasts well with the dryness of the tannins and acidity on the finish. The Barbera d'Asti Bricco Sant'Ippolito did not impress us, as neither nose nor palate were balanced. On the other hand, the Cortese dell'Alto Monferrato (the still version) is a genuinely exciting white wine with a bouquet of flowers and green apples; rich and lively on the palate with a very clean finish. The Vivace semi-sparkling version is attractive but a bit one dimensional.

● Rouchet Bricco Rosa '96	♥♥	5
● Dolcetto La Selva di Moirano '95	♥	4
● Freisa La Selva di Moirano '95	♥	4
● Rouchet Bricco Rosa '90	♥♥♥	5
● Barbera d'Asti La Bogliona '89	♥♥	5
● Barolo Tettimora '88	♥♥	6
● Rouchet Bricco Rosa '93	♥♥	5
● Rouchet Bricco Rosa '94	♥♥	5
● Barolo Tettimora '90	♥	6

● Barbera d'Asti Sup. '95	♥♥	3
● Barbera d'Asti Sup. Croutin '95	♥	4
○ Alto M.to Cortese '96	♥	2*
○ Alto M.to Cortese Vivace '96		2
● Barbera d'Asti Sup. Croutin '90	♥♥	5
● Barbera d'Asti Sup. '93	♥	3

NOVELLO (CN)

ELVIO COGNO
LOC. RAVERA, 2
12060 NOVELLO (CN)
TEL. 0173/731405-50759

Elvio Cogno is Novello's greatest champion and therefore has both the duty and the honour of representing his village in contests with other communes. It is a responsibility which motivates Elvio and his partner Walter Fissore and keeps them on their toes, especially in poor vintages. In fact there are no sudden lapses in quality, and all the estate's wines are made with the same pride and generosity. At the top of the range is the Barolo Ravera, of course, with its deep garnet red colour and characteristic and intense bouquet of plums; the abundant tannins on the palate are well integrated into the body of the wine without leaving any bitterness. The Barbera is not lacking either in colour - which is very concentrated - nor in rich fruit, broad flavours or freshness; this wine fails to come up to the level of the Barolo only because of the over enthusiastic use of wood. The Dolcetto is a big wine, too: the colour is a well defined ruby red announcing a good concentration of fruit and a frank, vinous nose, followed by a palate rich in extract where the slight clumsiness of the tannins only becomes obvious after the extract has faded. The white wine called Nas-Cetta is made from local varieties and is rustic and tasty.

●	Barbera d'Alba Bricco del Merlo '95	🍷🍷	4
●	Barolo Ravera '93	🍷🍷	5
●	Dolcetto d'Alba Vigna del Mandorlo '96	🍷🍷	3
○	Nas-Cetta '96		4
●	Barolo Ravera '92	♀♀	5
●	Dolcetto d'Alba Vigna del Mandorlo '95	♀♀	3
●	Barbera d'Alba Bricco del Merlo '94	♀	4

NOVI LIGURE (AL)

CASCINA DEGLI ULIVI
STRADA MAZZOLA, 12
15067 NOVI LIGURE (AL)
TEL. 0143/744598

Regulations stipulate Gavi must be made from cortese grapes grown and vinified within the DOC zone. Unfortunately, the Cascina degli Ulivi lies just 600 metres on the wrong side of the boundary and, despite the fact that the Cascina's grapes come from some of the best sites in Tassarolo, and that Stefano Bellotti has labelled his wine Gavi for the last 20 years, the entire1996 production was confiscated by the authorities and the wine subsequently declassified to Monferrato Bianco. The wines, however, remain the same; the standard selection and the cru I Filagnotti. The former is very drinkable and has a good fruity bouquet; the palate is not the huge, but it is frank and has good flavour and moderate acidity. By contrast, the cru has better structure. It is still dumb on the nose, but already well balanced on the palate; it needs another one or two years' bottle age to come to its peak. One positive piece of news for consumers is that the prices of Gavi this year are much lower than they have been in the past. The other wines from this estate consist of interesting reds. We picked out the Nibiô, a dolcetto which has benefited from the excellent '96 vintage, and is full bodied and well balanced. We also enjoyed the Monbè '95, made from barbera, and the Amoroso, a sweet wine made from moscato rosso and malvasia. Lastly, it is worth pointing out that the Cascina degli Ulivi's wines bear the Demeter logo, the symbol of the association of organic producers.

○	Monferrato Bianco '96	🍷	2*
○	Monferrato Bianco I Filagnotti '96	🍷	3
●	Monferrato Dolcetto Nibiô '96	🍷	3
●	Mounbè '95		3
●	L'Amoroso		3

NOVI LIGURE (AL)

OTTIGLIO (AL)

LAURA VALDITERRA
STRADA MONTEROTONDO, 75
15067 NOVI LIGURE (AL)
TEL. 0143/321451

CAVE DI MOLETO
REG. MOLETO
15038 OTTIGLIO (AL)
TEL. 0142/921455

Laura Valditerra looks after her own seven hectares of vineyards personally, with passionate dedication and enthusiasm. Production has gone up to 30,000 bottles this year, well on the way to Laura's projected ideal for the size of the estate, which she puts at about 40,000 bottles. Two wines were put forward for this edition of the Guide: the standard Gavi '96, and the 25 percent barrique aged Gavi Selezione '95, which can be recognised on the label by the "di" of Valditerra picked out in black. The standard Gavi is attractively fresh and full bodied, as can be seen from the straw yellow colour with strong greenish reflections; the nose has apples, unripe bananas and lemon liqueur mixed in with an attractive hint of hay; full bodied on the front palate, firm and well balanced, with a refreshing vein of acidity which leads into an enjoyable and satisfying finish. The second wine is produced in tiny quantities (and will not be released at all for the '96 vintage): pale straw yellow with green reflections; a subtle nose with hints of peaches and aromatic herbs enriched with a very delicate note of vanilla; easy to drink and well balanced, pleasantly fresh.

In 1992, the Swiss group Merone-Holderbank, the biggest cement producers in the world and the owners of the Cuvaison winery in the Napa Valley, turned its attention to this tiny corner of the Monferrato and bought the long abandoned hamlet of Moleto, together with the 120 hectares of land that surround its famous cellars. Obviously, the first task was to save what was possible in the existing vineyards (only eight out of the original 60 hectares), to replant where necessary, and to renovate the cellars. Given the amount of work and time involved in this process, the first years have been used for experimentation in the vineyards and the production of only a few thousand bottles, but output is planned to go up to roughly 100,000 bottles in the future, thanks to the potential of about 22 hectares of vineyards. The company has decided to concentrate mainly on traditional local wines, but with one or two internationally inspired additions. Consequently, the vineyards are mainly planted to barbera and grignolino, with small parcels of cabernet sauvignon, merlot, chardonnay and cortese. On its début in the Guide, the Cave di Moleto presented us with three well made wines. We particularly like the Barbera Mülej, which comes from the difficult '94 vintage and has an impressively deep colour; the nose has plum jam aromas with hints of vanilla and toasted bread; it is full bodied and attractively soft on the palate. Both the Grignolino, with its intense pepper nose and big tannic structure, and the soft and sweet-wooded Chardonnay, are very creditable wines.

O Gavi '96	♟	3
O Gavi Selezione '95	♟	4

● Barbera del M.to Mülej '94	♟♟	4
● Grignolino del M.to Casalese '96	♟	3
O Piemonte Chardonnay '96	♟	3

PIOBESI D'ALBA (CN)

TENUTA CARRETTA
LOC. CARRETTA, 2
12040 PIOBESI D'ALBA (CN)
TEL. 0173/619119

PRASCO (AL)

VERRINA - CASCINA TORNATI
VIA S. ROCCO, 14
15010 PRASCO (AL)
TEL. 0144/375745

For some time now, the Miroglio family have been working to upgrade the quality of the wines from Tenuta Carretta. Evidence of this comes in the form of the massive investment made in building a large winery and replanting the vineyards with selected clones, but the big news, and what really comes out in our tastings, is that the vineyard yields have begun to be cut. The property comprises 52 hectares of vineyards located in Piobesi, Barolo (almost three hectares in the Cannubi cru), Treiso (eight hectares in the Bordino cru) and San Rocco Seno d'Elvio. Technical matters are supervised by the oenologist Sergio Carniccio, who also looks after the vineyards, and current production stands at about 400,000 bottles per year. Of the many wines presented for tasting, we liked the Barolo and the Barbaresco, both from the '93 vintage. The former has a mid-ruby red colour with slightly orange edges; a bouquet of flowers, plums, peppers and cloves; good structure on the palate, and soft and pleasantly dry on the finish. The latter has an already quite mature ruby red colour, a nose of dried flowers with minerally overtones, is medium weight on the palate and has reasonably good balance despite slightly harsh tannins. The Arneis Vigna Canorei has hints of meadow flowers and apples on the nose, is soft on the palate and very drinkable. The fresh, easy drinking Favorita has a nose dominated by mature aromas, while the Nebbiolo Bric Tavoleto has spicy pepper and cinnamon overlaying a bouquet of violets; on the palate it is an up-front and well balanced wine with a firm, dry finish. Lastly, the Bric Quercia is a good wine with some elegance, and the standard Dolcetto is well made and enjoyable.

According to Nicolò Verrina, of all the Dolcettos of Piemonte, that grown at Ovada has the best traditions : certainly the wines have a distinctive, slightly rustic character all of their own. The Vigna Oriali '96 is an excellent example of this compact and well structured, richly satisfying style of Dolcetto. Located on a fine site in the Prasco Alto area, the Oriali vineyard is planted with vines that are, on average, 35 years old. The low yields that Nicolò insists on have a beneficial effect on the wine which has a deep ruby red colour with broad, youthful purple edges; the nose is particularly powerful with aromas that range from cherries to violets to white pepper; the full bodied nature of the wine is immediately apparent on the palate as it opens out, soft and broad, to finish with a slight bitter almond twist and intense fruitiness. The Podere Semonina is not as good, but it is a very creditable wine all the same, and is very drinkable: ruby red with violet edges; the nose is up front with hints of ripe cherries and pepper with grassy overtones; full bodied with marked acidity and a fruity finish with a bitter twist. The Barbera is not quite such good news; the bouquet is slightly dirty and the palate slightly unbalanced. This, however, is an untypical blind spot for a small producer that has impressed us favourably with its best wine, the Dolcetto di Ovada.

● Barolo Poderi Cannubi '93	♥♥	4
● Barbaresco Poderi Bordino '93	♥	4
● Langhe Bric Quercia '95	♥	4
○ Langhe Favorita '96	♥	3
● Nebbiolo d'Alba Bric Tavoleto '94	♥	3
○ Roero Arneis Vigna Canorei '96	♥	3
● Dolcetto d'Alba '96		3

● Dolcetto di Ovada Vigna Oriali '96	♥♥	2*
● Dolcetto di Ovada Podere Semonina '96	♥	2
● Barbera del Monferrato '96		1
● Dolcetto di Ovada Podere Semonina '95	♀	2
● Dolcetto di Ovada Vigna Oriali '95	♀	2

QUARGNENTO (AL)

ROCCHETTA TANARO (AT)

COLLE MANORA
STRADA BOZZOLE, 4
15044 QUARGNENTO (AL)
TEL. 0131/219252

BRAIDA
VIA ROMA, 94
14030 ROCCHETTA TANARO (AT)
TEL. 0141/644113

We begin with the sad news of the death of Eleonora Limonci, who founded this estate and quickly made it into a model for viticulture in the Alessandria area. She was assisted in this task by consultant oenologist Donato Lanati, whose expert advice is still the inspiration behind the development of the wines. Two elegant white wines based on sauvignon are this year's stars. The Mimosa is a monovarietal with attractive depth of colour, ripe peaches and pears on the nose, a fresh fullness of flavour on the palate and an encouragingly long finish. The Mimosa Diane, by contrast, is part sauvignon and part other white grape varieties authorised for the Monferrato region: the colour is richer than the first wine and the nose has aromas of spices, flowers and jam on it, while the palate unfolds delicately and very attractively. The Barbera Del Monferrato Pais conforms to what might be expected from its easy, youthful appearance: limpid ruby red colour, light aromas of bitter cherries on the nose, very drinkable with moderate acidity. The other Barbera, the Collezione '95, has more definition; we noted too much wood on the nose and the structure was not very big, but the palate had good balance and length to it. The Palo Alto is a much bigger wine; made from a blend of pinot noir, cabernet sauvignon, merlot and barbera, the berry fruit aromas and clear hints of vanilla on the nose are well integrated; on the palate the alcohol is counterbalanced by a good dose of tannins.

This year Braida has begun to market the wines of the small Serra dei Fiori winery, which they manage in collaboration with two other partners. The Serra dei Fiori comes out with two enjoyable white wines, a Chardonnay and a Langhe, as well as a Dolcetto d'Alba. This latter has a mid-ruby red colour; a pleasant, sweet alcoholic nose, and a palate with well integrated tannins and attractive length. Returning to the Braida label, the Barbera Bricco della Bigotta '94 has overcome the difficulties of the vintage in the generosity it manages on the palate, but has problems on the nose which appears over mature. The Barbera Ai Suma is more successful, deeper in flavour and altogether more enjoyable; this has a much more generous palate. The Bricco dell'Uccellone is a rich wine full of personality, starting with its mature ruby red colour; the nose is full of complex nuances of aroma rather than one single note; the palate is well balanced, and if there is a fault, it is the slight lack of length. The Brachetto has up-front aromatic character and a good follow through from nose to palate; sweet flavours caress the tongue refreshed by sparkling bubbles. The other wine with bubbles from the Bolognas is the Barbera La Monella: it has an attractive nose and its usual, reliable, easy drinkability. Bacialé is a blend of pinot noir and barbera which has not yet come up to the levels it reached a couple of vintages ago; this vintage is well made, but has not got a lot to say for itself.

O Monferrato Bianco Mimosa '96	ΨΨ	4
● Monferrato Rosso Palo Alto '95	ΨΨ	5
● Barbera del M.to Collezione '95	Ψ	4
● Barbera del M.to Pais '96	Ψ	3
O Monferrato Bianco		
Mimosa Diane '95	Ψ	4
● Manora Collezione '93	ΨΨ	5
● Palo Alto '93	ΨΨ	5
● Barbera del M.to Pais '95	Ψ	3
● Manora Collezione '94	Ψ	5
● Palo Alto '94	Ψ	5

● Barbera d'Asti Ai Suma '95	ΨΨ	6
● Bricco dell'Uccellone '94	ΨΨ	5
● Dolcetto d'Alba Serra dei Fiori '96	ΨΨ	3
● Barbera d'Asti Sup.		
Bricco della Bigotta '94	Ψ	5
● Barbera del M.to La Monella '96	Ψ	3
● Brachetto d'Acqui '96	Ψ	4
● Monferrato Rosso Il Bacialé '96	Ψ	4
O Langhe Bianco Il Fiore '96	Ψ	3
O Langhe Chardonnay		
Asso dei Fiori '96	Ψ	4
● Barbera d'Asti Ai Suma '89	ΨΨΨ	6
● Bricco dell'Uccellone '91	ΨΨΨ	6

RODELLO (CN)

VITICOLTORI ASSOCIATI DI RODELLO
VIA MONTÀ, 15
12050 RODELLO (CN)
TEL. 0173/617159-617318

ROSIGNANO MONFERRATO (AL)

VICARA
CASCINA MADONNA DELLE GRAZIE, 5
15030 ROSIGNANO MONFERRATO (AL)
TEL. 0142/488054

The '96 vintage was a busy and successful one for the Viticoltori di Rodello; in fact, they have had their best ever results and show significant peaks of achievement both with the wines made for ageing and those for more immediate drinking. The Viticoltori produce three cru wines, each with their own markedly different character, each designed for the requirements of different consumers. This year the best of them is the Vigna Buschin, which is usually their lightest and freshest-tasting wine: the '96 vintage has a particularly good, bright colour of average; the bouquet runs through the whole gamut of dolcetto aromas, from the fruity to the vegetal with a reassuring freshness; the palate is just as good and begins softly, unfolds sweetly, and finishes relatively long. The Vigna Deserto is drawn from vineyards sited lower down from the Buschin vineyards, on soil that is richer in clay; it scored only marginally lower: deep, mature colour, well composed bouquet; firm, full bodied and alcoholic on the palate. The Bricco San Lorenzo is named after the vineyard on top of a hill in the winery estate and earns a respectable score in the tasting: the bouquet is dominated by hints of grassiness and the palate is subtle and well composed, but it does not have the charm of the other two wines. The non-cru Dolcetto accounts for two thirds of the 50,000 bottles produced and is a good quality product, despite not having the character of the cru wines: mid-red colour, vinous and up-front on the nose, a little dilute on the palate, but with a good, clean cherry finish.

Vicara is the product of a joint venture that began in 1992 when three small estates reorganised themselves into one medium-to-large size one comprising 40 hectares of vineyards. The three partners are Diego Visconti, the company president; Carlo Cassinis, the managing director; and Domenico Ravizza, who looks after the winery and who is helped by his father Giuseppe in taking care of the vineyards. The sales function is taken care of by the able commercial director, Sandro Chiriotti. The range of wines they make is very broad. We begin with one of the best value-for-money wines, the Rubello. Created in the 1970s by Carlo Cassinis and given an official classification as DOC Monferrato this year, it has a ruby red colour with orange tinges at the edges; the nose is very individual and contains hints of blackcurrants, blackberries, and vanilla together with overtones of grassiness; it is full bodied and well supported by acidity on the palate; and has a good, fruity finish brushed with noble tannins. The Barbera Cantico della Crosia scored only slightly lower: jam, cocoa and brioche on the nose; full bodied on the palate and enlivened with attractive acidity. The standard Grignolino has a very pale and limpid ruby red colour; the bouquet is floral and spicy; fresh and easy-drinking on the palate. The Barbera Vivace is well defined and refreshing, while the Barbera Superiore is enjoyably rustic in style. Lastly, two excellent white wines: the Monferrato Chardonnay has a bouquet of hazelnuts and vanilla and some weight to it, while the Airales is a fresh, delicate wine made of chardonnay, cortese and sauvignon.

● Dolcetto d'Alba		
Vigna Buschin '96	♈♈	2*
● Dolcetto d'Alba		
Bricco S. Lorenzo '96	♈	2*
● Dolcetto d'Alba		
Vigna Deserto '96	♈	3
● Dolcetto d'Alba '96		2

● Monferrato Rubello '95	♈♈	3
● Barbera del M.to Sup. '95	♈	3
● Barbera del M.to Sup.		
Cantico della Crosia '95	♈	3
● Barbera del M.to Vivace '96	♈	2*
● Grignolino del M.to Casalese '96	♈	3
○ Monferrato Airales '96	♈	3
○ Monferrato Chardonnay '96	♈	3
● Rubello di Salabue '93	♈♈	3
● Barbera del M.to Sup.		
Cantico della Crosia '94	♈	3

S. GIORGIO CANAVESE (TO)   S. MARTINO ALFIERI (AT)

ORSOLANI
C.SO REPUBBLICA, 5
10090 S. GIORGIO CANAVESE (TO)
TEL. 0124/32386

MARCHESI ALFIERI
CASTELLO ALFIERI
14010 S. MARTINO ALFIERI (AT)
TEL. 0141/976288

We have had to wait years for the right conditions to make a new vintage of Orsolani's Caluso Passito La Rustìa. The wait has been well worth it; the new Caluso is an extremely high quality product that will easily stand up to comparison with the best Italian "passito" wines. Young Gianluigi Orsolani, who created it, is convinced of the potential for Erbaluce Passito; he should be more than happy with this result. The vineyards for this wine are located on the highest and sunniest slopes of the morainic hills of the Canavese district. The grapes selected are the most sunbaked ("arrostita" in Italian, "rustìa" in Piedmontese dialect) that can be found. After harvesting, they are left to dry on reed matting until March, when they are pressed at exactly the right point of sugar concentration. Following fermentation, the wine is left to age in small barrels for more than five years, and then in bottle for another three or four years. Today, nine years after the harvest, the wine has an almost coppery golden colour, the nose is very delicate, and the toastiness of the wood has blended in perfectly with the fruit. The palate is full bodied, composed and well balanced, with hints of fruitiness that range from orange peel to hazelnuts; this is a truly aristocratic and satisfying "passito" wine. The same hillside vineyards give us the Erbaluce di Caluso La Rustìa, and here again we have one of the best examples of the denomination. The '96 vintage may lack a little finesse on the nose, but it is full bodied, well balanced and enjoyably full flavoured on the palate.

Marchesi Alfieri is successfully carving out a place for itself among the top producers of the Asti region by specialising both in the traditional classics such as Barbera, and in innovative wines for the area. And in fact, it is one of new red, the Pinot Nero San Germano, that shows best this year: not designed to be a big wine, it has an extremely elegant character; bright ruby red in colour with a clear varietal bouquet of ripe cherries and hints of vanilla and cinnamon; multi layered on the palate, easy to drink and very broad in the mouth. For something more demanding we must go to the Barbera Alfiera: this is an elegant wine, too, and its varietal character comes out both on the fruity intensity of the nose and the bright flavours on the palate; the barrique ageing has been well managed, in a way that it enhances the complexity of the wine rather than covers it up. The Barbera La Tota is usually more rustic in style; this year it is softer, and brought into balance by the fruit and vinosity of the bouquet before being given a lift by the strength of the alcoholic. Only the riesling-based Bianco dei Marchesi left us disappointed: the nose is faint and the palate unbalanced. The Grignolino Sansoero is worth recommending.

O Caluso Passito La Rustìa '88	ΨΨ	5
O Erbaluce di Caluso La Rustìa '96	Ψ	3
O Brut Nature Cuvée '91	Ψ	4

● Barbera d'Asti Alfiera '93	ΨΨ	5
● Monferrato Rosso San Germano '94	ΨΨ	5
● Barbera d'Asti La Tota '95	Ψ	4
O Monferrato Bianco dei Marchesi '96		3
● Piemonte Grignolino Sansoero '96		3
● Barbera d'Asti Alfiera '92	ΨΨ	5
● Barbera d'Asti La Tota '94	Ψ	5
● San Germano Pinot Nero '93	Ψ	5

S. MARZANO OLIVETO (AT)   S. STEFANO BELBO (CN)

ALFIERO BOFFA
VIA LEISO, 50
14050 S. MARZANO OLIVETO (AT)
TEL. 0141/856115

CA' D'GAL
STRADA VECCHIA, 108
FRAZ. VALDIVILLA
12058 S. STEFANO BELBO (CN)
TEL. 0141/847103

This company's major asset is the reliability of its wines across the board. Obviously when nature does her worst, poor harvests result in poor quality grapes and the average standard of wines will fall; but with this selection Alfiero Boffa shows us once again that he can defend his corner in adversity. His best wine from the difficult '95 vintage is the Barbera Cua Longa: a bright, impeccably made, straightforward wine with a lively colour; reasonably rich on the nose with hints of raspberries and mint; well defined on the palate with a bracing acidity that also gives a kick to the flavour. We were looking forward to the Barbera Collina della Vedova after the success of the '93 vintage, but, although the current wine is clearly elegant, it does not come up to the same standard. The more traditional and more powerful Barbera Muntrivé displays its usual vigour on the palate, but is not always fully balanced. If it is the refreshing simplicity of a Barbera Del Monferrato Vivace that you are looking for, the '96 Vigoroso is a good choice; if, however, you prefer something a bit smoother, softer and with more body, then you will not go wrong with the Vigna More '95. The Moscato Vigna Lupa is alcoholic and on the sweet side; it seems to be Boffa's attempt to make a traditional style wine, but just a touch of extra freshness would not have gone amiss.

Riccardo Boido and his children Alessandro and Laura have shown us their skill in making consistently good Moscatos, as well as other still red and white wines. Their winery is in the heart of Moscato country, where the high hills with their steep breezy terraces provide the top sites for the cultivation of this aromatic grape. The Boidos use their best vineyards on one particular "sorì" (a south-facing slope) to make 5,000 bottles of the Vigna Vecchia. The wine has a pale straw yellow colour, the apple bouquet has a firm aromatic quality of its own, and the palate unfolds well, without any cloying and with a fine follow through from nose to finish. The non-cru Moscato is produced in quantities of 20,000 bottles and is just as good. The '96 is particularly well endowed with a varietal bouquet that is sweet, intense and plumped out with aromas of bananas and Golden Delicious apples; this makes for a very tactile palate which finishes with a definite touch of honey. The Chardonnay, which is almost all drunk on warm summer evenings by guests at the family's "agriturismo" complex, is to be recommended. The red wines comprise a sharp Dolcetto and the well reputed Pian del Gaje, made of freisa, dolcetto and barbera and designed to combine freshness and length at the same time; unfortunately, delayed bottling meant that we were unable to taste it for inclusion in the Guide this year.

●	Barbera d'Asti Vigna Cua Longa '95	♥♥ 3	○	Moscato d'Asti Ca' d'Gal '96	♥	3
●	Barbera d'Asti Vigna Muntrivé '95	♥ 3	○	Moscato d'Asti Vigna Vecchia '96	♥	3
●	Barbera d'Asti Vigne Uniche Collina della Vedova '94	♥ 4	○	Langhe Chardonnay '96		3
●	Barbera d'Asti Vigna More '95	♥ 3				
●	Barbera del M.to Vigoroso '96	♥ 3				
○	Moscato d'Asti Vigna Lupa '96	3				
●	Barbera d'Asti Vigna Cua Longa '93	♥♥ 4				
●	Barbera d'Asti Vigne Uniche Collina della Vedova '93	♥♥ 4				

S. STEFANO BELBO (CN)   S. STEFANO BELBO (CN)

PIERO GATTI
LOC. MONCUCCO, 28
12058 S. STEFANO BELBO (CN)
TEL. 0141/840918

SERGIO GRIMALDI
LOC. SAN GRATO, 15
12058 S. STEFANO BELBO (CN)
TEL. 0141/840341

The denomination "Moscato Piemonte" on the label is not a trick; Piero Gatti's wine is really a top quality Moscato d'Asti and the reason the label does not describe it as such deserves spelling out. Piero's splendid vineyards look down on the town of Santo Stefano and his grapes always ripen early, before the public weighing station is open and ready to register grapes produced for DOCG production. So, once again, in the average good conditions of the '96 harvest, Piero Gatti decided to pick his grapes early rather than risk them over ripening and losing essential aromas and acidity. Once again, of course, he forfeited the right to the DOCG Moscato denomination. In fact, his Moscatos are amongst the freshest that are made: typical varietal aromas are enriched with bananas and apples, and the sweetness that lies on the mid-palate is refreshed by healthy acidity. The other wines in the range must not be forgotten; they allow the estate to avoid the dangers of concentrating only on Moscato and to benefit from vineyard sites that are well suited to the production of aromatic grapes. Both the semi-sparkling Freisa and the sparkling Brachetto are decent wines, but they do have their ups and downs. The former is lighter and less successful than in the past, while the latter is more intense in both colour and fruit, shows great character, and has a reasonably long finish.

After the depredations of the miserable '95, the conditions of the '96 vintage certainly helped in the production of a more characterful Moscato, which only just missed out on a Two Glass award. But the contribution of the new cellars that the Grimaldis have recently constructed and, above all, the effort that has gone into making this Moscato the winery's principal product must not be underestimated. The wine has a bright but pale colour; the bouquet amply spans the range from flowers to fruit, even if there are still some signs of fermentation; on the palate a refreshing sparkle is followed by finely judged and well defined sweetness. Sergio and Angela can be very happy with the quality of the 30,000 bottles they made. The rest of the production includes 4,000 bottles of Chardonnay and 6,000 bottles respectively of Brachetto and an uncomplicated Barbera "vivace". The Chardonnay is mature: the dominant perception on the nose is of yeast, and there is also a sweet aroma of ripe apricots which blends in well with the softness on the palate. The Brachetto has the best sensations of freshness and acidity of all the wines; the colour is pale, the bouquet vinous, and it is bright and enjoyable to drink. The soils of the family's own vineyards endow all the wines with a maturity that seems to be the hallmark of the estate, and which will interest anyone who prefers their wines - especially aromatic ones - not too aggressive on the palate.

○ Piemonte Moscato '96	♇	3
● Piemonte Brachetto '96	♇	3
● Langhe Freisa La Violetta '96		3

○ Moscato d'Asti Ca' du Sindic '96	♇	3
○ Langhe Chardonnay Zamblino '96		3
● Piemonte Brachetto Ca' du Sindic '96		3

S. STEFANO BELBO (CN)

IL FALCHETTO
VIA VALLE TINELLA, 16
12058 S. STEFANO BELBO (CN)
TEL. 0141/840344

S. STEFANO BELBO (CN)

VIGNAIOLI DI S. STEFANO BELBO
FRAZ. MARINI, 12
12058 S. STEFANO BELBO (CN)
TEL. 0141/840419

There are so many members of the Forno family involved in running Il Falchetto that this one family has no difficulty in running such a big company. Mother Raffaella marshals an entire army of sons and daughters - Adriano, Chiara, Cinzia, Fabrizio, Giorgio and Roberto - and it can easily be imagined that some kind of almost military discipline is needed to manage the production of their vast range of wines. The wines all reach a good standard, even if this year no single product has emerged as the company's flag-bearer. We begin with the area's most famous wine, the Moscato. This year the Ciombi is better balanced than most; the bouquet has delicate hints of grapes and the palate is clean and sweet. The Fant is much more interesting: deep colour and typical varietal bouquet with additional hints of pineapple and elderflower; the palate is consequently firm, fresh and long. The Cortese is the most intriguing of the white wines, with a grassiness on the nose that reemerges in the mouth to enliven a full bodied, well-rounded wine. The Arneis displays good aromatic quality and green youthfulness, while the Chardonnay lacks varietal definition. As for the reds, apart from recommending the Freisa for its clean bouquet and palate, the Grignolino must be tasted to appreciate its concentration, its deep colour and grassy bouquet, its weight on the palate and tannic astringency on the finish. The Dolcetto starts simply vinous and then reveals its fruit as the palate unfolds. The best red from this estate is still the Barbera: the barrel ageing of this wine would be more successful if it resulted in a greater complexity of aroma and extract, but overall it cannot be faulted for fruit and balance.

The Vignaioli of Santo Stefano are a mixed group of moscato growers who have acquired the reputation over the years for making consistently good quality wines that are also good value for money. Little by little they have channelled their initial enthusiasm and entrepreneurial spirit into the acquisition of new vineyards and a replanting programme that accords with modern practices and tradition at the same time. The latest purchase is in the San Martino district and consists of a vineyard that is not only one of the best sited the area, but also part of the fabric of local history; it used to belong to the Incisa family, who were the first to cultivate moscato in that region five hundred years ago. Bringing things up to date, both of last year's Moscatos from the Vignaioli show liveliness, and modern, enjoyable drinkability. We prefer the Asti version for its deep colour and delicate bouquet. As the bubbles end, the sweetness of flavour continues to develop, and finishes elegantly with a slight twist of citrus peel. The Moscato is very elegant on the nose, too; its delicacy on the palate is a result of leanness and delivering the right intensity of sparkle on the tongue. In the next edition of the Guide we will probably be able to comment on another Vignaioli product, the Moscato "passito", which is always an eagerly-awaited wine, since it is only made in the best years and regularly does well in tastings.

O Cortese dell'Alto Monferrato		
Vigna Piena Grassa '96	Y	3
O Langhe Arneis '96	Y	3
O Moscato d'Asti		
Tenuta dei Ciombi '96	Y	3
O Moscato d'Asti		
Tenuta del Fant '96	Y	4
● Barbera d'Asti		
Vigna Zio Rico '95	Y	4
● Dolcetto d'Alba Soulì Braida '96	Y	3
● Freisa d'Asti '96		3
● Grignolino d'Asti Furnet '96		3
O Langhe Chardonnay '96		3

O Asti '96	Y	4
O Moscato d'Asti '96	Y	3

S. VITTORIA D'ALBA (CN)   SERRALUNGA D'ALBA (CN)

CINZANO
VIA STATALE CINZANO, 63
12069 S. VITTORIA D'ALBA (CN)
TEL. 0172/477111

GIUSEPPE CAPPELLANO
VIA ALBA, 13
FRAZ. BRUNI
12050 SERRALUNGA D'ALBA (CN)
TEL. 0173/613103

The Metodo Classico Cinzano Pasdosé is the sparkling wine that gives the best idea of Italian expertise in "bubble making". Retasting the Riserva '89 shows how essential finesse of bouquet, delicacy of perlage, and consistency and subtlety of flavour are to a great sparkling wine. If you want a fatter more all-enveloping flavour, or immense complexity on the nose, perhaps with some toastiness thrown in, then the Pasdosé is not for you - it is made to win you over with sheer elegance alone. This historic Alba-based producer also makes an aromatic and well balanced "Metodo Martinotti" (Charmat Method) sparkling wine, the Pinot Chardonnay: straw yellow with green reflections; fresh, clean, yeasty aromas; lively, refreshing perlage. The Asti has a full, rich bouquet and is, perhaps, the best we have ever tasted at Cinzano: golden reflections in the colour; tropical fruit on the nose mingling with sage, citrus fruit and peaches; softness on the front palate combined with a dense and ample structure balanced out finally by the effect of the bubbles. If the high standard of the wines in this selection were to translate into levels of consistent achievement Cinzano would have nothing to fear from comparison with any of the top sparkling wine producers of Italy.

Perseverance implies a consistency in behaviour, motivated by worthy ideals and deeply rooted convictions. This is Teobaldo Cappellano's driving force, and he has persevered steadily in the development of his wines since his arrival at Serralunga in 1970. The starting point was the creation, step by step, of a winery that understood the ancient traditions of the area while being able to absorb all the innovations that came from outside, little by little. The project is still evolving and is, of course, subject to the variations that nature imposes. Thus great advances were made with the '90 and '92 Barolos; and things stood still in '89 and for the latest vintage presented for tasting, the '93. This wine comes from the Gabutti cru, as normal, and has a limpid garnet red colour; an alcohol-rich bouquet shows how far advanced it is on the nose and there is lots of body on the palate, too, but that is all; the overall sensation is flat and lacking in excitement. The Dolcetto d'Alba is back to the levels of concentration of a few years ago and stands out once more: deep ruby red in colour; ample vinosity is no hindrance to the fruity bouquet, while the structure of the wine is well supported by vibrant, youthful tannins. The Barbera is tighter and more unyielding; it has a weak but typically varietal nose and is somewhat one-dimensional on the palate. The Arneis is another one of Cappellano's wines we are happy to recommend, but there are no great depths to it, despite its easy drinkability.

O Asti	☐ 3	● Barolo Chinato	☐☐ 5
O Pinot Chardonnay Brut	☐ 3	● Barbera d'Alba Gabutti '95	☐ 4
O Cinzano Padosé Spumante		● Barolo Otin Fiorin	
Extra Brut '89	☐☐ 5	Collina Gabutti '93	☐ 5
		● Dolcetto d'Alba '96	☐ 3
		O Roero Arneis '96	☐ 3
		● Barolo Otin Fiorin	
		Collina Gabutti '90	☐☐☐ 6
		● Barolo '91	☐☐ 5
		● Barolo '92	☐☐ 5
		● Barolo Otin Fiorin	
		Collina Gabutti '91	☐☐ 5

SERRALUNGA D'ALBA (CN)

TENIMENTI FONTANAFREDDA
VIA ALBA, 15
12050 SERRALUNGA D'ALBA (CN)
TEL. 0173/613161

This year's range from Fontanafredda gets the best results yet; many wines have come up to the heights of Two Glass level and it seems that, at last, this winery is really beginning to realise its enviable potential. Two Dolcettos were put forward for tasting; the one from Treiso has a deep ruby red colour, clean vinosity, and an attractive drinkability that should be taken advantage of quickly. Just the colour of the other Dolcetto, the Diano d' Alba Vigna La Lepre, is enough to show how much more character it has; the nose is more complex and the palate shows rich extract combined with a firm, long finish. Of the still whites, we liked the Chardonnay, which has a superb, uncomplicated, nose and is very easy to drink; the Gavi is less successful and seems rather flabby. The Moscato is a pleasant surprise, fresh, modern and balanced, while the Asti is a reliable and well established classic. A well made, traditional-style Barbaresco '93 heads the range of reds for ageing: bright garnet red colour, all-enveloping and complex on the nose, firm on the palate with a big structure that develops well. The Barolo Galarey is also well made, but is not as firm on the palate. Of the Metodo Classico sparkling wines, there are good results for both the Contessa Rosa and the Gatinera, which reach their usual levels of excellence with good finesse and depth; the Blanc de Blancs is a lively, elegant wine; and the Gran Riserva '85, made from 100 percent pinot noir, is perfect for those who like their sparkling wine to display the evolution that comes with age.

●	Barbaresco Coste Rubin '93	🍷🍷	4
●	Barolo di Serralunga '93	🍷🍷	4
●	Diano d'Alba Vigna La Lepre '96	🍷🍷	3
○	Contessa Rosa Brut '92	🍷🍷	4
○	Gatinera Gran Riserva '85	🍷🍷	6
○	Gatinera Brut '89	🍷🍷	5
○	Asti '96	🍷	3
○	Langhe Chardonnay Ampelio '96	🍷	3
○	Moscato d'Asti Le Fronde '96	🍷	3
○	Spumante Blanc de Blancs '91	🍷	4
●	Barolo Galarey '93	🍷	5
●	Dolcetto d'Alba di Treiso '96	🍷	3
●	Barolo Vigna La Rosa '90	YY	5
●	Barolo Vigna Lazzarito Ris. '90	YY	6

SERRALUNGA D'ALBA (CN)

GABUTTI - FRANCO BOASSO
B.TA GABUTTI, 3/A
12050 SERRALUNGA D'ALBA (CN)
TEL. 0173/613165

Take the road to Serralunga and follow the directions for the Parafada and Gabutti districts; at the bottom of the slope you will find the Boasso family's winery. Before going inside, stop a while and admire the countryside spread out before you; from here you can see the manor of Castiglione Falletto and the magnificent hilltops as far as the castle at Perno. Franco Boasso owns four hectares in the Gabutti and Parafada vineyards; these are entirely south-facing and lie side by side at altitudes between 280 and 350 metres above sea level on the same hillside. Understanding these details is crucial to understanding these vineyards' enormous potential. We tasted two great '93 Barolos. The non-cru version has a colour somewhere between ruby red and garnet; the bouquet of raspberries and sweet tobacco is clean and intense; on the palate the wine already seems well balanced, thanks to the softness of the alcohol and the well integrated soft tannins. The Gabutti '93 is deeper in colour and fuller on the nose, with a sweet and spicy element suggesting cinnamon, vanilla and talcum powder; the palate is richer, more tannic and much longer finishing. The Dolcetto Vigna Parafada '96 is very successful, thanks to its well defined and typical bouquet of ripe cherries and bitter almonds, which comes back on the aftertaste; nevertheless it still seems rather hard and aggressive on the palate and, like all Dolcettos from the area, would benefit from more bottle age. The Barbera '96 is late in its release and we will therefore reserve judgement until next year.

●	Barolo '93	🍷🍷	4
●	Barolo Gabutti '93	🍷🍷	5
●	Dolcetto d'Alba Vigna Parafada '96	🍷	3
●	Dolcetto d'Alba '96		2
●	Barolo Gabutti '90	YY	5
●	Barolo Gabutti '92	Y	5

SERRALUNGA D'ALBA (CN) SERRALUNGA D'ALBA (CN)

ETTORE GERMANO
B.TA CERRETTA, 1
12050 SERRALUNGA D'ALBA (CN)
TEL. 0173/613528-613112

VIGNA RIÖNDA - MASSOLINO
P.ZZA CAPPELLANO, 6
12050 SERRALUNGA D'ALBA (CN)
TEL. 0173/613138

Sergio Germano is President of the Bottega del Vino at Serralunga and is determined to set a good example in a wine-producing zone that is becoming progressively less sleepy. In fact, he has all but finished building spacious new premises for the bottling plant and for the barrique and traditional, large barrels in the ageing cellars. The company owns five and a half hectares of vineyards planted to nebbiolo, barbera and dolcetto, as well as a small amount of chardonnay, and currently makes a total of 22,000 bottles per year, soon to be 30,000 when all the vines have come into production. This year we tasted a Chardonnay '96 (3,200 bottles) which has a good, bright straw yellow colour, a nose of apples, and is fresh, fruity, and very drinkable, with an attractive youthful twist on the finish. There are two '96 Dolcettos (6,500 bottles total): the Lorenzino is vinous on the nose and is moderately full bodied and fruity on the palate; the Pra di Po, by contrast, is a thoroughbred wine that we particularly liked for its deep colour, its long and subtle bouquet, its softness, ripe extract, and long, satisfying finish. The Balàu '95, a blend of dolcetto and barbera, is a drinkable, medium-weight wine. The Barbera Vigna della Madre (a scant 1,500 bottles) is not too big in structure and a little unbalanced on the finish, but nonetheless enjoyable. The Barolo '93 (4,000 bottles) has been matured in both large barrels and four to five year-old barriques: garnet red in colour; complex and well defined on the nose; full bodied on the palate with a long, clean finish. The Barolo Cerretta '93 (4,200 bottles) was aged in new barriques for 22 months and is still clearly dominated by the new oak, both on the nose and the palate; its excellent structure should, however, guarantee correction of the imbalance with bottle age

The Massolino family estate owns 16 hectares of vineyards and makes a total of about 100,000 bottles per year, making it one of the most important producers in the Langhe. Their success is based on young Franco's enthusiasm, father Giovanni's perseverance, and uncle Renato's valuable experience. This year they have had three aces up their sleeves. The Trump Card is without doubt the Barolo Riserva Vigna Margheria '90 (2,500 bottles); but who would have ever thought that we would be tasting yet another superb wine from the legendary '90 vintage this year? The Margheria site is located just in the lee of the Rivette and Marenca vineyards and over the years has consistently produced wines with particularly rich bouquets. Indeed, this '90 vintage has a wonderfully clean and complex nose of ripe raspberries laid over a spicy background of cloves, fennel seeds and tea; an ample body and abundant tannins fill the palate, and the wine ends with a long, sweet liquorice finish. The Vigna Riönda '92 (17,000 bottles) is almost miraculously free of the usual faults of the vintage: attractively spicy (cinnamon and pepper), good structure, but lacking in the smoothness of previous years. The Vigna Parafada '93 (8,000 bottles) is very enjoyable and the only one of the three Barolos to have been aged in barrique: deep ruby red; vanilla on the nose; long and concentrated on the palate. The Nebbiolo '94, with its delicate bouquet of roses and strawberries and the Dolcetto Barilot '95, which displays good character and balance after a year's bottle ageing, are both very attractive wines. The Barbera Margheria is less of a success this year. Readers of last year's Guide please note, the Dolcetto Barilot described then was the '94, not the '95.

● Barolo '93	♟♟	4
● Barolo Cerretta '93	♟♟	5
● Dolcetto d'Alba Pra di Po '96	♟♟	3
● Barbera d'Alba		
Vigna della Madre '95	♟	3
● Dolcetto d'Alba Lorenzino '96	♟	3
● Langhe Rosso Balàu '95	♟	4
○ Langhe Chardonnay '96	♟	3
● Barolo '91	♟♟	4
● Barolo '92	♟	4
● Dolcetto d'Alba Pra di Po '95	♟	3

● Barolo Vigna Parafada '93	♟♟	5
● Barolo Vigna Riönda '92	♟♟	4
● Barolo		
Vigneto Margheria Ris. '90	♟♟	5
● Dolcetto d'Alba Vigneto Barilot '95	♟♟	3
● Langhe Nebbiolo '94	♟	3
● Barbera d'Alba		
Vigneto Margheria '95		3
● Barolo Parafada Ris. '90	♟♟♟	5
● Barolo Vigna Riönda Ris. '90	♟♟♟	5
● Barolo '90	♟♟	5
● Barolo Parafada '90	♟♟	5
● Barolo Parafada '91	♟♟	5
● Barolo Vigna Riönda '90	♟♟	5
● Barolo Vigneto Margheria '90	♟♟	5

SERRALUNGA DI CREA (AL)   SPIGNO MONFERRATO (AL)

TENUTA LA TENAGLIA
STRADA SANTUARIO DI CREA, 6
15020 SERRALUNGA DI CREA (AL)
TEL. 0142/940252

CASCINA BERTOLOTTO
VIA PIETRO PORRO, 70
15018 SPIGNO MONFERRATO (AL)
TEL. 0144/91551

Delfina Quattrocolo's winery is in one of the mostly magical corners of the Monferrato region, where woods and vineyards recede into the distance in a regular pattern on the hills. Cultural activities are an integral part of the life of this winery; you are just as likely to be welcomed to a concert or an exhibition combined with a wine tasting as to enjoy just the simple hospitality that comes naturally to the estate's owner. Delfina's daughter, Erika, is a graduate of the Oenological School of Alba and helps her mother in the vineyards and the cellars, while invaluable technical assistance comes from consultant winemaker Donato Lanati. The Barbera d' Asti Emozioni and the Syrah Paradiso achieve consistently good results. The former has a deep ruby red colour, and a soft, broad bouquet with aromas of cherries, toasted coffee and wood ageing; the palate is rich and well balanced by the acidity with a fruit and spice finish cloaked by noble tannins. The latter has a slightly insipid ruby red colour and has a delicate nose of berry fruit, pepper, tobacco and citrus fruit peel; solid on the front palate, with a good fruity follow-through and hints of liquorice on the finish. The Barbera Giorgio Tenaglia displays a bouquet of cherries and ripe blackcurrants, with hints of coffee and menthol; not badly balanced on the palate with a long, dry finish. Two good wines follow: the Grignolino, with its nose of pepper and roses and its full body; and the Chardonnay, with its excellent varietal character. The Barbera Bricco Crea is slightly disappointing, due to signs of over-maturity on the nose. The wine called L'Oltre is worth recommending; it is is made from a small parcel of chardonnay, with grapes that are picked slightly over-ripe and fermented in barrique.

On the way up from Spigno Monferrato towards Serole there are few vines to be seen. The steep slopes are largely covered with patches of chestnut and oak trees and the idea that this typically Apennine countryside could also be a good site for vineyards seems more and more unlikely as the altitude increases. And yet this was once an area where viticulture did flourish right up until the beginning of this century. Then suddenly, in a splendid site 400 metres above sea level, we arrive at the Cascina Bertolotto vineyards, and the Guide's report begins. Giuseppe Traversa and his children, Marida and Fabio, cultivate 15 hectares of vineyards and produce about 45,000 bottles. The Dolcetto La Muïëtte is excellent: fermented traditionally in open top wooden vats the colour is ruby red-to-garnet and the bouquet is spicy with hints of thyme, raspberries and cocoa; ample and full bodied on the palate with a liquorice finish and well integrated tannins. The Barbera I Cheini is only marginally less successful: ruby red tending to garnet in colour; slightly clumsy bouquet of jam, tobacco and cocoa, while the palate has good body and a touch too much acidity. The Dolcetto La Cresta displays a blackcurrant and pepper nose; easy to drink but just a little short on the finish. The Cortese Il Barigi is well made and has a youthful bouquet of apples and grass from the fields; good balance on a palate characterised by softness and lightness of touch. Lastly, the Brachetto Il Virginio has fresh hints of roses and pears on the nose, is sweet and clean on the palate and has a decent refreshing sparkle.

● Barbera d'Asti Emozioni '95	▼▼	5
● Paradiso '95	▼▼	5
● Barbera d'Asti		
Giorgio Tenaglia '96	▼	4
● Grignolino del M.to		
Casalese '96	▼	3
○ Piemonte Chardonnay '96	▼	3
● Barbera d'Asti Bricco Crea '96		3
● Emozioni '92	▼▼	5
● Emozioni '94	▼▼	5
● Paradiso '93	▼▼	5
● Paradiso '94	▼▼	5
● Barbera d'Asti		
Giorgio Tenaglia '95	▼	5

● Dolcetto d'Acqui La Muïëtte '95	▼▼	3*
● Barbera del Monferrato		
I Cheini '96	▼	4
● Dolcetto d'Acqui La Cresta '96	▼	3
● Piemonte Brachetto		
Il Virginio '96	▼	3
○ Cortese dell'Alto Monferrato		
Il Barigi '96	▼	3
● Dolcetto d'Acqui La Muïëtte '94	▼▼	3

STREVI (AL)

STREVI (AL)

BANFI VINI
VIA VITTORIO VENETO, 22
15019 STREVI (AL)
TEL. 0144/363485

MARENCO
P.ZZA VITTORIO EMANUELE, 10
15019 STREVI (AL)
TEL. 0144/363133

The 1997 vintage has seen the completion of rebuilding work at the old winery in Strevi and extension work on the Gavi vinification plant at Novi; Giuseppina Viglierchio, the energetic president of this important winery, has been busy. Of the wines presented for tasting this time, the Strevi Moscato d'Asti stands out: pale straw yellow colour streaked with bright greenish reflections; hints of peach, aniseed, sage and lemon on the nose in an admirably harmonic composition; firm and sweet on the palate, tempered by a refreshing vein of acidity and softened by a attractive sparkle that enlivens an intensely long and fruity finish. The Brachetto Vigneto La Rosa is almost as good: limpid cherry red colour with a well defined bouquet of roses, geraniums and citrus fruit peel; good body on the palate, invigorated by a pleasing hint of acidity. The Dolcetto Argusto has a mid-ruby red colour enhanced by the wine's time in barrique, a bouquet of plums, vanilla and rosemary, and a medium-weight palate with good balance. The Gavi Vigna Regale displays fragrant fruity aromas with hints of apples, apricots and lemon liqueur, while the palate is soft and well fleshed out at the same time. The sparkling versions of Brachetto and Moscato are to be recommended; they are both clean, fresh and obviously likeable. The non-cru Gavi (white label) has a correct pale straw yellow colour, but the floral bouquet and light body are both simple and undemanding, and it is a bit short on the finish.

The Marenco family have been making the local wines of the Strevi area for three generations. Now, Giuseppe Marenco heads the enterprise with his three daughters, Doretta, Michela and Patrizia, and two of the sons-in-law, Giovanni Costa and Armando Giraudi. There is a lot to do; 60 hectares of vineyards on the lovely hills north west of Strevi and a production of 300,000 bottles per year make it essential that everyone pulls their weight and the winery functions efficiently. Extension work has just been completed on the cellars and new technology has been installed. As for the wines, we begin with the excellent Dolcetto d'Acqui Marchesa, which has a deep ruby red colour with violet edges and a soft nose with hints of bitter cherries, almonds and cream; full bodied on the palate, all-enveloping on the finish with an attractive bitter twist. The traditional dessert wines all reach a good standard: the Brachetto Pineto is ruby red with purple edges, has a nose of pears and roses that follows right through to the finish, and is sweet on the palate with a good, refreshing sparkle; the Moscato Scrapona has a golden straw yellow colour and displays hints of peaches and lemon liqueur on a sweet, up-front and well composed palate. The Barbera Bassina has violet edges to its ruby red colour and ripe fruit on the nose; it is easy to drink and enlivened by noticeable acidity. Last on the list are two well made wines: the fresh, easy-drinking Cortese Valtignosa and the semi-sparkling Barbera Masino.

O	Strevi Moscato d'Asti '96	🍷🍷	3
O	Gavi Principessa Gavia '96	🍷	3
O	Gavi Vigna Regale '95	🍷	4
O	Asti '96	🍷	3
●	Acqui Brachetto d'Acqui Vigneto La Rosa '96	🍷	4
●	Brachetto d'Acqui Spumante '96	🍷	4
●	Dolcetto d'Acqui Argusto '95	🍷	4
●	Dolcetto d'Acqui Argusto '93	🍷	4
O	Banfi Brut Metodo Classico '91	🍷	4

●	Barbera d'Asti Bassina '95	🍷	2*
●	Brachetto d'Acqui Pineto '96	🍷	4
●	Dolcetto d'Acqui Marchesa '96	🍷	2*
O	Moscato d'Asti Scrapona '96	🍷	3
O	Cortese dell'Alto M.to Valtignosa '96		2
●	Barbera del M.to Masino '96		2

TASSAROLO (AL)

CASTELLO DI TASSAROLO
CASCINA ALBORINA
15060 TASSAROLO (AL)
TEL. 0143/342248

The products of the Castello di Tassarolo are faithful expressions of the owner's concept of wine in general. Even the briefest of chats with Marchese Paolo Spinola reveals the clarity and good sense of his thoughts on the subject, and it is no accident that his wines consistently reflect this. Angelo Berruti, the oenologist, has shown his expertise in applying the Marchese's philosophy to the wines, while it is the Marchese's father, Massimiliano Spinola, who markets the wines, 80 percent of which are exported. Of those tasted, we particularly liked the Ambrogio Spinola, a limited production wine (4,000 bottles only) based on sémillon, sauvignon and cortese that is only made in the best years: pale, limpid straw yellow; delicate, fragrant nose with hints of apples, bananas and toasted bread stiffened by notable freshness; subtle but firm on the palate and progressively more and more satisfying as the flavours unfold; long and well balanced on the finish. The Vigneto Arborina also does well in the tasting: greenish reflections on a straw yellow colour with a subtle bouquet of apples, apricots and vanilla; soft and fresh-tasting on the palate with a good finish of fruit and boiled sweets. The Gavi Castello di Tassarolo is always good: straw yellow with clear green reflections; bananas, fennel seeds and vanilla on the nose leading to a soft and subtle finish.

O Ambrogio Spinola '95	🍷	4
O Gavi Castello di Tassarolo '96	🍷	3
O Gavi Vigneto Alborina '95	🍷	4
O Gavi Vigneto Alborina '93	🍷🍷	4
● Rosso '94	🍷	4

TASSAROLO (AL)

LA ZERBA
VIA FRANCAVILLA, 1
15060 TASSAROLO (AL)
TEL. 0143/342259

The Lorenzi family winery offers the consumer the valuable guarantee of a consistently high quality standard Gavi which never fails to score well in our annual tastings. The '96 is no exception: straw yellow with sharp greenish reflections leading to a subtle nose of apples, unripe bananas and a faint grassiness; slightly tight on the front palate, good structure, and fresh, satisfying finish. The Terrarossa has a full straw yellow colour with green reflections and displays an attractive bouquet of apples, grapefruit peel and fresh aromatic herbs; good structure right from the front palate with an all-enveloping follow-through to the finish, where the parting impression is marred by a hint of astringency and lack of final balance. It is rigorous grape selection from the best vineyard that produces such excellent quality grapes for the Terrarossa, and perhaps the wine itself deserves more bottle age before release. The aim of making a long-lived, serious wine using 20 percent on-skin maceration is an admirable one; it remains to be established, however, in our opinion, what the right maturation period is for this wine, that has already clearly demonstrated its thoroughbred status.

O Gavi La Zerba '96	🍷	2
O Gavi Terrarossa '96	🍷	3

TORINO

Franco M. Martinetti
Via S. Francesco da Paola, 18
10123 Torino
tel. 011/8395937

The story behind Franco Martinetti's wines is linked to the career of Giuliano Noè, the expert oenologist. Their relationship can be compared to that of an expert tailor with his best client; Franco, the client, knows what he wants from his wine down to the last detail; Giuliano, the tailor, has the sensitivity and skill to interpret his client's desires in a real, living product. Martinetti puts the best grapes at Noè's disposal (the material, to continue with our simile) and after sketching the outline of the final product (the suit) he wants, gives his tailor the responsibility of making it. Martinetti then looks after the production phase, leaving any tricky problems to his technical expert. The Sul Bric is the latest result of this fruitful relationship. Made from barbera and cabernet sauvignon in more or less equal quantities, the Sul Bric was vinified at the Vinchio Co-operative winery in vats that allowed a brief but intense maceration, before the barrique ageing, which took place under Martinetti's supervision. And it is the the way in which the wine interacts with the wood which is the measure of its greatness. The colour is deep ruby red; the very well composed bouquet of great complexity manages to be fresh and youthful at the same time; the ripe exuberance of the barbera is counter balanced by the dry authority of the cabernet in a highly successful and long-finishing partnership on the palate. As well as the Sul Bric, Martinetti's production of 50,000 bottles includes a barrique-aged 100 percent Barbera called Montruc, an elegant and attractive Gavi, and a youthful Barbera called Il Bric dei Banditi. But Franco's real dream is to make a Barolo, and the Langhe will rejoice when he does.

●	Sul Bric '95	🍷🍷🍷	5
●	Barbera d'Asti Sup. Montruc '95	🍷🍷	5
●	Barbera d'Asti Bric dei Banditi '96	🍷	3
○	Gavi Minaia '95	🍷	4
●	Sul Bric '94	YYY	5
●	Barbera d'Asti Sup. Montruc '94	YY	5
●	Barbera d'Asti Sup. Montruc '93	YY	5
●	Sul Bric '93	YY	5

TREISO (CN)

Orlando Abrigo
Fraz. Cappelletto
12050 Treiso (CN)
tel. 0173/630232

No fewer than five hillside ridges meet at Treiso, a topography which alone increases the possibilities for the diversified winemaking which is reflected in Abrigo's wide range. The Barbaresco Pajoré is always good: the ruby red reflections of youth can still be found in the colour, elegant aromas of vanilla and berry fruit on the nose. It is velvety on the front palate before abundant tannins render it more severe but at the same time giving it excellent ageing potential. A new vintage of Barbera Mervisano appears for the first time in several years. Made from 40-year-old vines with yields of less than 50 hectolitres per hectare and bottled unfiltered after 15 months in barrique, the Mervisano is spicy and elegant on the nose and has an attractive palate where the sugars and the alcohol balance the abundant tannins and refreshing acidity; the finish is very long. The other Barbera is lighter in structure. It is aged for one year in used barrels and six months in bottle, which makes it fruitier, livelier and easier to drink, but also deprives it of elegance, which is not helped by the slight hint of over-maturity on the finish. The Dolcetto has such great character on the nose (cherries and cloves) and on the palate (still spicy, vinous and full bodied) that it deserves a few more months of bottle age to soften the tannins. The Chardonnay is good on the nose, too (apples and pears with a good floral component), but it has too much acidity on the palate and, above all, is excessively dominated by the wood. The Freisa is correctly made and very drinkable.

●	Barbaresco Vigna Pajoré '94	🍷🍷	5
●	Barbera d'Alba Mervisano '94	🍷	4
●	Barbera d'Alba Vigna Roreto '94	🍷	2
●	Dolcetto d'Alba Vigna dell'Erto '96	🍷	2
○	Langhe Chardonnay Rocca del Borneto '94	🍷	4
●	Langhe Freisa '96		2
●	Barbaresco Vigna Pajoré '93	YY	5
●	Barbera d'Alba Vigna del Campo della Fontana '94	Y	3

TREISO (CN)

TREISO (CN)

FIORENZO NADA
LOC. ROMBONE
12050 TREISO (CN)
TEL. 0173/638254

PELISSERO
VIA FERRERE, 19
12050 TREISO (CN)
TEL. 0173/638136-638430

The Seifile has been recognised as a masterpiece for some time, with the one drawback that its current production level stands at only just over 2,000 bottles. On the nose it has berry fruit aromas with hints of liquorice, combined with the sweetness and spiciness that comes from the use of oak. Bruno Nada prepares this wine by using old vines to make a powerful barbera to which he then adds some nebbiolo to give extra complexity. Even in a really difficult year like this one, the Seifile has a touch more elegance than the norm and a textbook rotundity to the palate that pushes it very close to the top-ranking Three Glasses class. Bruno's search for old barbera vineyards is now probably at the point where in the next few years the production of the much sought after Seifile will increase significantly. The Barbaresco '94 is one of the best of its vintage and it stood out in the tasting for its youthful nose, enhanced with hints of sweet tobacco and smoke, and a more than respectable structure with an abundance of lively tannins. The Dolcetto comes out extremely well, both thanks to the excellent vintage and because of Bruno's decision to prune drastically and keep yields down: bright ruby red colour, up-front on the nose, fresh and fruity; rich, enveloping and full of flavour on the palate, with an uncomplicated length of finish.

The assets of this estate lie in the 15 hectares of vineyards sited in the hillside bowl facing Neive and Barbaresco, in a good cellar equipped with all sorts of barrels and barriques, and in the energy of the young and enthusiastic Giorgio Pelissero. Some of his experiments may not turn out as expected, and some wines, such as the Favorita, have more local curiosity value than intrinsic quality, but when it comes to wines like the Vanotu, the Augenta and the Barbera, their real class emerges. The first of these wines has big structure and is very long and broad on the nose with aromas or bilberries, pepper and quinine; the second has good extract, is firm on the palate and has a particularly long finish; the third is fresher, brighter and very easy to drink while retaining at the same time what seems to be the house style depth of flavour and complete consistency from nose to finish. The other Dolcetto is very respectable and, not having been aged in wood, is softer, more perfumed and readier to drink than the Augenta, with an emphasis on the seductive powers of a fresh and floral nose. This is the first vintage of the standard Barbera, which comes from a recently acquired vineyard, and has been aged successively in large Slavonian oak barrels, in 600 litre casks, and in new barriques; in this instance it has been let down by the quality of the grapes, but great things are expected in future vintages (as they are with some of the other experiments we have tasted here; of which more later). One more wine to finish the list, the Grignolino: good enough to bear comparison with the best of its type, but not particularly exciting all the same.

● Barbaresco '94	⟡⟡	5
● Dolcetto d'Alba '96	⟡⟡	4
● Seifile '94	⟡⟡	5
● Seifile '93	⟡⟡⟡	5
● Barbaresco '90	⟡⟡	6
● Barbaresco '91	⟡⟡	5
● Barbaresco '92	⟡⟡	5
● Barbaresco '93	⟡⟡	5
● Dolcetto d'Alba '95	⟡⟡	3
● Seifile '92	⟡⟡	5

● Barbaresco Vanotu '94	⟡⟡	5
● Barbera d'Alba I Piani '96	⟡⟡	3
● Dolcetto d'Alba Augenta '96	⟡⟡	3
● Barbaresco '94	⟡	5
● Dolcetto d'Alba Munfrina '96	⟡	3
● Piemonte Grignolino '96		3
● Barbaresco Vanotu '90	⟡⟡	5
● Barbaresco Vanotu '92	⟡⟡	5
● Barbaresco Vanotu '93	⟡⟡	5
● Dolcetto d'Alba Augenta '95	⟡⟡	3
● Barbaresco Vanotu '91	⟡	5
● Barbera d'Alba I Piani '95	⟡	3

VERDUNO (CN)

VERDUNO (CN)

F.LLI ALESSANDRIA
VIA BEATO VALFRÉ, 59
12060 VERDUNO (CN)
TEL. 0172/470113

BEL COLLE
FRAZ. CASTAGNI, 56
12060 VERDUNO (CN)
TEL. 0172/470196

The figure of Giovan Battista Alessandria, with his enigmatic expression and forbidding moustache, looks down from his place above the mantelpiece and follows his grandson as he rushes around the winery. If the picture could speak it would be to express surprise at the preponderance of technological equipment in the cellars and astonishment at the waste involved in such heavy pruning in the vineyards. But young Gian, named after his grandfather in the picture, knows that progress in the family business will not come by following tradition to the letter, but by questioning it all the time. One of the concrete results of this philosophy is the Barolo Monvigliero, back on form again with the '93 vintage: good fruit on the nose, even if qualified by somewhat intrusive signs of wood ageing; soft underlying tannins with dominant acidity and alcohol not yet in complete harmony. The Nebbiolo has good colour and, despite naturally not being as big a wine as the Barolo, shows good, clean fruit and has a satisfactory balance between softness and acidity. The Barbera has a nose of bitter cherries, but is then broad, full bodied and firm on the palate. The Pelaverga has real rarity value - in fact it is almost completely unknown outside the area: deep cherry red, mostly vegetal on the nose, firm on the palate with a lively and refreshing acidity on the tongue; on the finish the bouquet is extremely clean and there is good berry fruit length. Lastly, the delicate white wine based on favorita can be recommended.

Bel Colle produce an innovative range of wines under the Le Masche label which are all matured in barrique but released only in the best years. So we had to wait until the '95 vintage for a chance to taste the Pelaverga Le Masche again. According to its maker Paolo Torchio, this is one of the company's flagship wines. It stands out for its lively, deep ruby red colour, makes one wonder about the balance between the fruit and the wood in the mid-palate but finishes dry and enjoyable. The Chardonnay Le Masche tries harder to bring out its varietal character: pale in colour, good development from nose to palate with a hint of brioche on the nose and apple on the finish. The traditional Langhe and Roero wines come out well, too, from the correctly made Arneis to the more positive Favorita which displays lightness and delicacy without being in any way a throw-away wine. The Dolcetto is a bit one dimensional: clean and fruity; up-front and refreshing, but not especially exciting. The standard Pelaverga has an intriguing white pepper nose and is much lighter than its wood-aged cousin. Bel Colle's best wine this time is the Barolo: it is quite far forward both in colour and bouquet, but well composed on the palate; unfolds well on the tongue, has soft, firm, stylish tannins and finishes with a clean aftertaste of fresh fruit.

● Barolo Monvigliero '93	♀♀	5
● Barbera d'Alba '95	♀	3
● Dolcetto d'Alba '96	♀	3
● Langhe Nebbiolo '95	♀	3
● Verduno Pelaverga '96	♀	3
○ Langhe Favorita '96		3
● Barolo Monvigliero '90	♀♀	5
● Barbera d'Alba '94	♀	3
● Barolo '91	♀	4

● Barolo Vigna Monvigliero '93	♀♀	5
● Verduno Pelaverga Le Masche '95	♀♀	4
● Dolcetto d'Alba '96	♀	3
● Verduno Pelaverga '96	♀	3
○ Langhe Chardonnay Le Masche '96	♀	3
○ Langhe Favorita '96	♀	3
○ Roero Arneis '96	♀	3
● Barolo Vigna Monvigliero '90	♀♀	5
● Verduno Pelaverga Le Masche '94	♀♀	3
● Barbera d'Alba Le Masche '93	♀	4

VERDUNO (CN)

COMMENDATOR G. B. BURLOTTO
VIA VITTORIO EMANUELE, 28
12060 VERDUNO (CN)
TEL. 0172/470122

Staunch family tradition provides the strength and motivation for their work, it also sets the limits for what Giuseppe, Marina and their enthusiastic son Fabio can achieve. They were probably the first to make a 100 percent varietal Pelaverga, at a time when this variety was not regarded as raw material for a rare DOC wine, but was mixed in the vat with all the rest. Today this is still one of the producer's most successful wines: bright cherry colour, subtle and attractive bouquet, fresh and well composed on the palate. The problem with the Barbera, Fabio explains, is that they are still experimenting with the use of the new wood barrels that have recently been adopted for the making of red wines (in fact, all the '95 vintage was aged in barrique). But the problems of new wood will only disappear with the use of fresher wine; the current vintage seems decidedly tired. The Mores, a barrique-aged blend made predominantly from nebbiolo, is a moderate success: immediately fresh and vinous on the nose with later hints of camomile; the palate is based on a balance between the firm acidity which comes from barbera and the structure of the nebbiolo. Lastly, the Dives is a Sauvignon that suffers from over-oaking in years when the fruit is less rich and power-packed than it might be, like this one.

○	Langhe Sauvignon Dives '95	▼	4
●	Barbera d'Alba Boscato '95	▼	3
●	Mores '94	▼	4
●	Verduno Pelaverga '96	▼	3
●	Barolo Monvigliero '88	▽▽	5
●	Barbera d'Alba Boscato '94	▽	3
●	Barolo '90	▽	5
●	Barolo Monvigliero '89	▽	5
●	Barolo Neirane '88	▽	5
●	Barolo Neirane '90	▽	5
●	Barolo Neirane '89	▽	5

VERDUNO (CN)

CASTELLO DI VERDUNO
VIA UMBERTO I, 9
12060 VERDUNO (CN)
TEL. 0172/470125-470284

Gabriella Bianco is the one who welcomes you graciously to the splendid eighteenth-century villa that used to belong to King Carlo Alberto, and the one who gives you a guided tour of the little wine museum. In fact, the winery is not to be found here, but at Barbaresco, where Franco Bianco looks after the production of the Castello di Verduno wines. It is difficult to make much comment on the Barbaresco because of the vintage; this is only its first, and only 1,800 bottles were produced altogether. Barolo, however, accounts for 35,000 bottles, and it has come out well. The Monvigliero is the most prestigious cru: deep colour; traditional, broad, vegetal bouquet with aromas of rich, ripe plums; the rich, fleshy palate is composed of a solid amalgam of alcohol, extract, and soft tannins. The Massara is dominated by the wood, which makes it less successful than the other Barolo, despite its similarity in style. The Barbera has just as deep a garnet red colour as the Barolo, and a nose that is basically vegetal in style, followed by a juicy palate with typical varietal acidity. As this Guide was going to press, we tasted the Pelaverga, an extremely rare varietal with a characteristic spiciness, drawn almost exclusively from vineyards in the commune of Verduno: it was a very attractive, medium bodied wine, enlivened by tannin and fresh acidity.

●	Barolo Monvigliero '93	▼▼	5
●	Verduno Pelaverga '96	▼▼	4
●	Barbaresco '94	▼	4
●	Barbera d'Alba Bricco del Cuculo '95	▼	3
●	Barolo Massara '93	▼	5
●	Barbaresco Rabajà '93	▽▽	5
●	Barolo Monvigliero '90	▽▽	5
●	Verduno Pelaverga '95	▽▽	4
●	Barbaresco Vigna Faset '93	▽	5

VIGNALE MONFERRATO (AL) VIGNALE MONFERRATO (AL)

BRICCO MONDALINO
REG. MONDALINO, 5
15049 VIGNALE MONFERRATO (AL)
TEL. 0142/933204

COLONNA
CA' ACCATINO, 1
FRAZ. S. LORENZO
15049 VIGNALE MONFERRATO (AL)
TEL. 0142/933241-933239

A natural sparsity of fruit and abundance of tannins makes Grignolino a much misunderstood wine with an almost exclusively local consumption. This is a shame, since the unique character of this wine, with its ample bouquet of flowers, spices and farmyard smells, makes it the perfect partner for some of the more rustic foods in the Italian repertoire; the richness of a fragrant plate of salami, for example, is cut very well by Grignolino tannins. If anyone wants to try this combination for themselves they will not go wrong choosing one of Mario Gaudio's two Grignolinos, the non-cru version with its excellent varietal character, or the cru Bricco Mondalino with its satisfying depth of flavour. The former has a pale cherry red colour, delicate aromas of almonds, pepper and roses, and good grip on the palate, which has an attractively spicy finish. The latter is made from slightly late-harvested grapes from the Bricco Mondalino site: ruby red colour, full bouquet of ripe cherries, dried roses, pepper and coffee; broad and full bodied on the palate with a long, dry finish dominated by the fruit. The Barbera Il Bergantino is an enjoyable wine with fascinating hints of cocoa, vanilla and cherries on the nose; elegant and full bodied. The Barbera Vivace is good, too: clean bouquet of fruit and spice; refreshing sparkle on the tongue. The Malvasia is sweet without being cloying, has a well defined bouquet of roses, and provides fresh easy drinking.

Alessandra Colonna is a very self-confident and determined young woman who has run the family estate since 1993. A law graduate by training, she has the sharpest of ideas, and delights in telling us about her work promoting the Monferrato region as vice president of the Enoteca at Vignale. She has a forward looking approach which is reflected in the character of her wines. The range includes the local Grignolino and Barbera, both made in a new, personal style, as well as two wines for more international tastes, the Chardonnay and the Mondone. Advice from consultant oenologist Donato Lanati and practical help in the cellars and vineyards from Ezio Boccalatte, are crucial to Alessandra's success. We will taste the '95 vintage of the estate's most famous wine, Mondone, next year when it has completed its period of ageing. The Grignolino '96 has a pale ruby red colour, the nose has strong hints of peanuts and white pepper on a fruity background; dry and deliciously full flavoured; well managed tannins and equally attractive bitter twist on the finish. The Chardonnay '96 is a bright straw yellow colour; the bouquet is subtle and broad with hints of bread crusts and meadow flowers; clean and fresh on the palate; firm and well structured, while at the same time maintaining easy drinkablity.

● Barbera d'Asti Il Bergantino '95	♟♟	3
● Grignolino del M.to Casalese		
Bricco Mondalino '96	♟♟	3
● Barbera del M.to Vivace '96	♟	2*
● Grignolino del M.to Casalese '96	♟	3
● Malvasia di Casorzo		
Molignano '96	♟	3
● Barbera d'Asti Il Bergantino '94	♟♟	3
● Grignolino del M.to Casalese		
Bricco Mondalino '95	♟♟	3
● Barbera d'Asti Il Bergantino '93	♟	3

● Grignolino del M.to		
Casalese '96	♟	2
○ Piemonte Chardonnay '96	♟	3
● Mondone '94	♟	4

VINCHIO (AT)

CANTINA SOCIALE DI VINCHIO
E VAGLIO SERRA
REG. S. PANCRAZIO, 1
14040 VINCHIO (AT)
TEL. 0141/950138

Thanks to a policy of rigorous grape selection and to the use of sophisticated vinification technology, this winery has proved itself in recent years to be among the best cooperatives in Italy. Nevertheless the '95 vintage, which was particularly difficult for Barbera, tested their ambitions severely. The Vigne Vecchie, the top of the range Barbera d'Asti, shows what little room there was for manoeuvre. It has only average depth of the colour and a very up-front bouquet with little complexity; the acidity is well managed, but it is a pity that the palate lacks body and length. The Barbera d'Asti Superiore is correct but unexciting: the bouquet is so slow in coming out that it could almost be described as timid; the traditional vinosity and weight of alcohol is better on the palate however, and the finish has satisfactory length. We are not convinced that anything better could have been done with the '95 vintage, so better results must wait for '96, which already looks more promising. We like the non-cru Barbera '96, which charms with its delightfully direct nose, easy drinkability and freshness. We do not expect anything much in terms of structure from the Barbera Del Monferrato Vivace, but it would help if it were better balanced.

● Barbera d'Asti Sup. Vigne Vecchie '95	▼	4
● Barbera d'Asti '96	▼	2*
● Barbera d'Asti Sup. '95	▼	2*
● Barbera del M.to Vivace '96		2
● Barbera d'Asti Sup. Vigne Vecchie '90	YY	5
● Barbera d'Asti Sup. Vigne Vecchie '91	YY	5
● Barbera d'Asti Sup. Vigne Vecchie '94	YY	5
● Barbera d'Asti Sup. '94	Y	2
● Barbera d'Asti Sup. Vigne Vecchie '93	Y	5

VIVERONE (BI)

LA CELLA DI S. MICHELE - ENRIETTI
VIA CASCINE DI PONENTE, 21
13040 VIVERONE (BI)
TEL. 0161/98245

After their success in previous years with the Erbaluce di Caluso Cella Grande the Enriettis have now added other new wines to the range. First comes a Charmat method sparkling wine called Cella Grande di San Michele, which is already on the market; a limited production Metodo Classico sparkling wine will follow in the future together with an even tinier production of Passito. All these wines are to be made with erbaluce di Caluso grapes from the eight hectares of estate vineyards on the slopes of the Serra d'Ivrea, facing Lake Viverone. The two wines we tasted this year show the high level of quality attained by this small winery, especially with the straight Erbaluce di Caluso, which is one of the best in the area. This is a very singular white wine: straw yellow colour with greenish reflections; good aromas of lemon liqueur and scents of meadow flowers on the nose; not a big wine, but delicate and full flavoured with a long, concentrated finish. The Brut Cella Grande di San Michele is an enjoyable wine, even if the perlage is not the most subtle, and is made from erbaluce grapes by the so-called "Metodo Italiano Lungo": lemon liqueur on the nose like the Erbaluce, dry on the palate, with a good dose of refreshing acidity. This is a good start for a winery that began only a few years ago, more as a hobby than a business, and which the Enrietti family have steadily got more and more enthusiastic about, to the extent that a production of as many as 60,000 bottles per year is forecast for the near future.

○ Brut Cella di San Michele	▼	3
○ Erbaluce di Caluso Cella Grande '96	▼	3

OTHER WINERIES

The following producers obtained good scores in our tastings with one or more of their wines:

PROVINCE OF ALESSANDRIA

La Slina,
Castelletto d'Orba, tel. 0143/830542,
Dolcetto di Ovada Vigneto Pianterasso '96

Cantina Produttori del Gavi,
Gavi, tel. 0143/642786,
Gavi Etichetta Nera '96

La Chiara,
Gavi, tel. 0143/642293,
Gavi di Gavi Vigneto Groppella '96

Tenuta S. Sebastiano,
Lu Monferrato, tel. 0131/741353,
Barbera del M.to Risà '93

Cantina Tre Castelli,
Montaldo Bormida, tel. 0143/85136,
Dolcetto di Ovada Sup. Colli di Carpeneto '95

Isabella,
Murisengo, tel. 0141/693000,
Barbera d'Asti '94

Il Vignale,
Novi Ligure, tel.0143/72715
Gavi '96

Vigna del Pareto,
Novi Ligure, tel. 010/8398776
Gavi Vigna del Pareto '96

Annalisa Rossi Contini,
Ovada, tel. 0143/833696,
Dolcetto di Ovada Vigneto Ninan '95

Cantine Valpane,
Ozzano Monferrato, tel. 0142/486713,
Barbera del M.to Valpane '93

Livio Pavese,
Treville, tel. 0142/487215,
Barbera d'Asti Sup. '95

Giulio Accornero,
Vignale Monferrato, tel. 0142/933317,
Barbera del M.to Sup. Giulin '95

Cascina Alberta,
Vignale Monferrato, tel. 0142/933313,
Barbera del M.to Vigneto Vecchio '95

PROVINCE OF ASTI

La Giribaldina,
Calamandrana, tel. 0141/718043,
Barbera d'Asti Cala delle Mandrie '95

Vittorio Bera, Canelli, tel. 0141/831157,
Moscato d'Asti '96

Cascina Barisel,
Canelli, tel. 0141/824849,
Barbera d'Asti La Cappelletta '93

Cascina Garitina,
Castelboglione, tel. 0141/762162,
Barbera d'Asti Bricco Garitta '95

Villa Fiorita,
Castello di Annone, tel. 0141/401852,
Maniero '95,
Il Giorgione '94

Cantina di Castelnuovo Calcea,
Castelnuovo Calcea, tel. 0141/957137,
Barbera d'Asti Sup. Bricco Vignole '95

Renaldo Graglia,
Castelnuovo Don Bosco, tel. 011/9874708,
Malvasia di Castelnuovo Don Bosco '96

Corte del Cavaliere,
Fontanile, tel. 0141/739355,
Barbera d'Asti Sup. '95

Cantina di Mombaruzzo,
Mombaruzzo, tel. 0141/77019,
Barbera d'Asti Vigneti Storici '95

Clemente Guasti,
Nizza Monferrato, tel. 0141/721350,
Barbera d'Asti Fonda S. Nicolao '93

Castello del Poggio,
Portacomaro, tel. 0141/202543,
Barbera d'Asti Val del Temp '94

Cascina l'Arbiola,
S. Marzano Oliveto, tel. 0141/856194,
Barbera d'Asti La Romilda I '95

Franco Mondo,
S. Marzano Oliveto, tel. 0141/834096,
Barbera d'Asti Vigna delle Rose '95

Cantine Sant'Agata,
Scurzolengo, tel. 0141/203186,
Ruché di Castagnole M.to Na' Vota '96

PROVINCE OF BIELLA

Sella, Lessona, tel. 015/99455,
Bramaterra '93,
Lessona '93

PROVINCE OF CUNEO

Luigi Penna,
Alba, tel. 0173/286948,
Dolcetto d'Alba Bricco Galante '96

La Cornarea,
Canale, tel. 0173/979091,
Roero Arneis '96

Ca' du Russ,
Castellinaldo, tel. 0173/213069,
Roero Arneis Costa delle Rose '96

Stefanino Morra,
Castellinaldo, tel. 0173/213489,
Roero Arneis Vigneto San Pietro '96

Cantina del Dolcetto,
Clavesana, tel. 0173/790451,
Dolcetto di Dogliani '96

Casavecchia,
Diano d'Alba, tel. 0173/69205,
Diano d'Alba Sorì Bruni '96

Il Palazzotto,
Diano d'Alba, tel. 0173/69187,
Diano d'Alba Sorì Cristina '96

Paolo Monte,
Diano d'Alba, tel. 0173/69231,
Diano d'Alba Vigna Vecchia '95

Mario Cozzo,
Dogliani tel. 0173/70571,
Dolcetto di Dogliani Vigna Pregliasco '96

Del Tufo,
Dogliani, tel. 0173/70692,
Dolcetto di Dogliani Vigna Spina '95

Aldo Marenco,
Dogliani, tel. 0173/721090,
Dolcetto di Dogliani Bric Bosc d'Agnel '96

Carlo Romana,
Dogliani, tel. 0173/76315,
Dolcetto di Dogliani Bric dij Nor '96

Anna Maria Abbona,
Farigliano, tel. 0173/797228,
Dolcetto di Dogliani Sorì dij But '96

Mario Marengo,
La Morra, tel. 0173/50127
Barolo Brunate '93

Sergio Degiorgis,
Mango, tel. 0141/89107,
Moscato d'Asti Sorì del Re '96

Destefanis,
Montelupo Albese, tel. 0173/617189,
Dolcetto d'Alba '96

Cantina del Castello,
Neive, tel. 0173/67171,
Barbaresco Santo Stefano '93

Cantina del Glicine,
Neive, tel. 0173/67215,
Barbaresco Marcorino '93

Parroco di Neive,
Neive, tel. 0173/67008,
Barbaresco Vigneto Gallina '94

Pasquale Pelissero,
Neive, tel. 0173/67376,
Barbaresco Cascina Crosa '93

Punset,
Neive tel. 0173/67072,
Barbaresco Campo Quadro '94

Giovanni Stra e Figlio,
Novello, tel. 0173/731214,
Dolcetto d'Alba '96

Mossio F.lli,
Rodello, tel. 0173/617149,
Dolcetto d'Alba Bricco Caramelli '96

PROVINCE OF TORINO

Cooperativa della Serra,
Piverone, tel. 0125/72166,
Erbaluce di Caluso '96

PROVINCE OF VERCELLI

Mauro Fanchino,
Gattinara, tel. 0163/834461,
Gattinara '93

Nervi, Gattinara, tel. 0163/833228,
Gattinara Molsino '93

Luigi Perazzi,
Villa del Bosco, tel. 0163/860034,
Bramaterra '91,
La Sassaia '91

LIGURIA

The growers of Pigato celebrated after a good vintage, the producers of Vermentino had a satisfied smile too, and those of Rossese di Dolceacqua also had every good reason to be happy: in short, everyone - or almost everyone - is happy. There is now a demand for the wines of Liguria and producers are not complaining about slack sales. The concept of quality, now that producers have a clearer idea of what the term means, is becoming an increasingly concrete reality and is forcing winemakers to be ever more rigorous in their approach: a silent, compelling revolution is sweeping through the region's wineries. Regional grape varieties continue to play the leading roles on the Ligurian stage, with some producers bravely seeking to resurrect long-lost indigenous cultivars. Others on the other hand are talking discreetly about plans to make more internationally-styled wines by adopting French grape varieties. There is considerable debate about whether to age in barrique, and if so, for how long. Meanwhile, the cru concept is increasingly gaining ground. All this curiosity and excitement can only have a positive effect in stimulating the producers. There is, however, insufficient attention paid - if any is at all - by official government bodies to the wine sector; nor are local producers particularly skilled in liaising with the mass media in order to create a quality image for Liguria's top wines. Turning to the producers reviewed in this edition of the Guide, Riccardo Bruna deserves particularly high marks for his ability to produce individualistic, modern wines which are nevertheless typical of their denomination: his Russeghine, undoubtedly the best of the Pigatos, is a good case in point. Excellent results were also achieved in the small enclave devoted to pigato around Albenga, both by Claudio Vio and by a new and

significant entry to the Guide, Umberto Calleri's Vecchia Cantina. He is a committed traditionalist who makes excellent, appealingly aromatic wines with flavours all their own. Emanuele Trevia's wines all scored well. The wines of Vladimiro Galluzzo - particularly worthy of praise for keeping alive a rare, delicious and exciting wine like his passito - are very good indeed. This is also the right year for the Vermentino Vigna U Munte, the pride of the Tenuta Colle dei Bardellini, and for the impressive Pigato Le Petraie, star of the Lupi winery range. Also, how could we fail to praise the skill of the Rondelli brothers in making their delicious Vermentino Vigna Campetto and splendid Bricco Arcagna? Mandino Cane plays a starring role in the Riviera Ligure di Ponente with an elegantly quaffable Rossese di Dolceacqua Superiore. We take this opportunity to make a somewhat bitter reflection on an indisputable fact: this wine, for centuries the pride of the west of the Ponente, is under serious threat of extinction for a number of reasons , including the rising age of the growers and the scarce interest shown by the younger generation, problems of mechanization, and the splitting-up of properties. The effect of all this can be summed up in a single statistic : production has fallen from 8,000 hectolitres in 1972 to 1,300 in 1995. In the Levante - which on the whole has not yet seen a noticeable improvement in quality - one particular estate in the Cinque Terre is taking on a high profile, that of Walter De Battè, producer of an excellent Sciacchetra and a Cinque Terre worthy of interest. Most, though not all, of the historic wineries of this area continue to perform satisfactorily, if unexceptionally. A new talent whom we are delighted to welcome to this year's edition of the Guide is the young and promising Ivan Giuliani of Podere Terenzuola.

ALBENGA (SV)

ANFOSSI
VIA PACCINI, 39
FRAZ. BASTIA
17030 ALBENGA (SV)
TEL. 0182/20024

This estate has a very wide and attractive assortment of products: extra virgin olive oil and additive-free food specialities which include pesto, olive and vegetable pastes, artichoke cream (a must!) and products preserved in oil. All are prepared with great skill and expertise in the suitably equipped rooms of the handsome castle which is part of the property. The many and diverse crops are looked after by Mario Anfossi, aided and abetted by Paolo Grossi. The estate policy is to use as few chemical substances as possible in order to safeguard the quality and original flavours of the foodstuffs. In the similarly well-equipped winery, Anfossi vinifies the pigato, vermentino and rossese grapes from the ten hectares or so of vineyards which constitute his holdings. Both the Pigato cru Le Caminate and the basic version from the '96 vintage are of good quality. The former comes from the Campochiesa vineyard and benefits from a brief maceration on the skins, as is evidenced by its rich colour; it has elegant aromas of herbs and meadow flowers, with gentle hints of honey and aniseed; on the palate, it is well-balanced and has good fruit, enlivened by a delicate savoury vein, and an appealingly herbaceous finish. The standard version displays a bright straw colour and an attractively fresh nose with thyme, sage, peach and lily of the valley notes. On the palate, it shows reasonable depth, fullness and sapidity. The forward and immediately appealing Vermentino offers typical Ligurian scents of basil and broom, coupled with fruity sensations of peaches and apples; its colour is brilliant and the palate echoes the sensations of the nose, with an attractive almondy aftertaste. The Rossese is also worthy of note: it offers delicate red berry fruit tones and a light, well-balanced structure.

ALBENGA (SV)

CASCINA FEIPU DEI MASSARETTI
LOC. MASSARETTI, 8
FRAZ. BASTIA
17030 ALBENGA (SV)
TEL. 0182/20131

The historic estate of Bice and Pippo Parodi lies in a zone known as I Massaretti which has always been considered ideal for grape-growing. The suitability of the land was enough to convince this delightful couple, who were already keen viticulturalists, to plant their own vineyards in 1965. Today, their daughter Ivana and son-in-law Gianni Enrico also work full-time on the estate, which produces 50,000 bottles of wine - 80 percent of which is Pigato - as well as a small quantity of extra virgin olive oil and of olives preserved in brine. The '96 Pigato has a brilliant straw-colour with light greenish reflections; on the nose, estery banana and pear drop notes combine with hints of aromatic herbs and citron peel. On the palate, it displays reasonably good balance and a typically almondy finish. Bice and Pippo celebrated their golden wedding anniversary by producing, from the '96 vintage, a special selection of Pigato aged in barrique called Due Anelli ('Two Rings') - which will be released in December 1998. The producers themselves have certain doubts about the use of small, new oak casks. We too would like to stress that wood-ageing is not a cure for all ills. However - and this was confirmed by a tasting of the above wine, which revealed pretty good structure - the idea of selecting the grapes more rigorously is undoubtedly a good one: wise old veteran that he is, Parodi has clearly made yet another good decision in his endeavour to further raise quality at the winery.

○ Riviera Ligure di Ponente Pigato '96	♀	3
○ Riviera Ligure di Ponente Pigato Le Caminate '96	♀	3
○ Riviera Ligure di Ponente Vermentino '96	♀	3
● Riviera Ligure di Ponente Rossese '96		2

○ Riviera Ligure di Ponente Pigato '96	♀	3

ALBENGA (SV)

LA VECCHIA CANTINA
VIA CORTA, 3
FRAZ. SALEA
17030 ALBENGA (SV)
TEL. 0182/559881

Liguria is indeed the quintessence of sun, sea and sand, but it has also a splendid hinterland cloaked in olive groves and Mediterranean scrub land. In this environment, in the heart of the Albenga zone, one finds the pretty little village of Salea, home of the Calleri family's winery. It is a clean and tidy cellar which is always a pleasure to visit. The owner, Umberto, thanks to the single-mindedness which is typical of people from this region, has also successfully tended the family's vineyards with a combination of passion and skill; following well-established tradition, he vinifies the two typical grape varieties of the area, vermentino and pigato. The four hectares of vines, all with excellent exposure, are cultivated on a predominantly red, clayey soil; the yield is around 42 hectolitres per hectare, giving a total of about 19,000 bottles. After a brief period in the "Other Wineries" section of our Guide, this estate has, with the '96 vintage, launched itself towards what we hope will be a permanent listing in the Guide proper. The '96 Pigato fully deserves its Two Glass rating: it has a bright, clear, straw-yellow colour; its nose displays finesse and balance and is aromatic rather than fruity, with vegetal scents of Mediterranean flora and more delicate aromas of peach-skins. It is soft and mouth-filling rather than crisp and lively on the palate, with flavours that perpetuate the sensations of the bouquet, and has a long, pleasant finish. The Vermentino, by nature a less serious wine, did not score quite so highly. Although it has attractive, rounded honey and fruit aromas and its crisp acidity gives it an appealing freshness, it is still a little unbalanced.

CAMPOROSSO (IM)

TENUTA GIUNCHEO
LOC. GIUNCHEO
18033 CAMPOROSSO (IM)
TEL. 0184/288639

The area under vine of this estate amounts to three hectares planted with vermentino at the Giuncheo vineyard and four hectares of rossese vines at the Pian del Vescovo cru. The two sites, ably tended by Marco Romagnoli, enjoy splendid hillside locations and are both planted using cordon spur training systems. The winery - a converted former Second World War bunker - has been completely transformed this year by the installation of computer-controlled tanks and new winemaking equipment in general. The estate's owner, Arnold Schweizer, offers two versions of his wines: a standard range and a more up-market selection which bears the name of the vineyard on the label. However, there is no difference in the source of the fruit, merely in the way the wines themselves are made: more rigorous selection of the grapes, a short period "sur lie" for the white and barrique-ageing for the red. The two Vermentinos had no trouble in scoring over 70 points. The standard version has a brilliant straw colour and a delicate nose with floral hints which are still a little masked by a slight touch of sulphur. Nevertheless, the wine is well-balanced, fresh and eminently drinkable. The Vermentino Le Palme, richer both in colour and on the nose, displays complex aromas reminiscent of Mediterranean scrub land. It is balanced and mellow on the palate, with fruit flavours which echo the sensations of the bouquet perfectly. The Rossese Vigneto Pian del Vescovo is definitely a premium wine and narrowly missed out on a Two Glass rating; it has a tempting oaky-aromatic bouquet, good depth of fruit and a typical bitter-cherry finish; the slight lack of balance apparent at the moment will disappear with just a little bottle-age. The basic Rossese gets a mention for its correct, straightforward style.

○ Riviera Ligure di Ponente		
Pigato '96	♟♟	3*
○ Riviera Ligure di Ponente		
Vermentino '96	♟	3

○ Riviera Ligure di Ponente		
Vermentino '96	♟	3
○ Riviera Ligure di Ponente		
Vermentino Le Palme '96	♟	4
● Rossese di Dolceacqua		
Vigneto Pian del Vescovo '96	♟	4
● Rossese di Dolceacqua '96		3

CASTELNUOVO MAGRA (SP)   CHIAVARI (GE)

OTTAVIANO LAMBRUSCHI
VIA OLMARELLO, 28
19030 CASTELNUOVO MAGRA (SP)
TEL. 0187/674261

ENOTECA BISSON
C.SO GIANELLI, 28
16043 CHIAVARI (GE)
TEL. 0185/314462

When Ottaviano Lambruschi decided, at the beginning of the 1970s, to start up this estate and thereby dedicate himself to his life's great passion, he could have just bought some existing vineyards and started to make wine from the grapes he grew. But that would have been much too simple for him! He bought some woodland, razed it to the ground, and then planted vermentino in its place: the result was the creation of one of the best crus of the Colli di Luni, the Costa Marina vineyard. This tells us a great deal about the tenacity of this perfectionist producer, whose diligence guarantees a uniform high level of quality in his wines and gives them, above all, notable personality. He now shares the merit with his son Fabio, an agronomist whose enthusiasm is no less than his father's. We begin our survey of the wines with the Costa Marina itself. A deep straw-yellow in colour, it has a complex, well-knit nose, with scents of apples, unripe bananas, hazelnuts and hints of resin and broom: on the palate, it has soft, silky fruit, with a fresh, crisp underlying acidity. The other cru, the Sarticola, is not quite up to par: it offers a good bouquet with suggestions of aromatic herbs, ferns and flowers, but is a little lacking in body. The wine named after the estate's founder, released for the first time this year, is made from a selection of grape varieties all grown in the same vineyard, and benefits from a brief sojourn in barrique. It has a glossy golden colour and a nose which offers vanilla, apple and floral notes. The fruit on the palate echoes the sensations on the nose, but the finish shows a little too much oak. The basic Vermentino is also decent.

If some of Liguria's historic wines still survive today, and are indeed commercially viable, undoubtedly much of the merit is due to the patient and single-minded efforts of Piero Lugano. His wine shop in the centre of Chiavari has, since the end of the '70s, been the site of enthusiastic experiments in microvinification. Nowadays his estate produces as much as 65,000 bottles a year, but Piero has no intention of resting on his laurels as the new wine called Marea, the latest in a long string of creations, bears witness. It is made from the typical grape mix of the Cinque Terre - albarola, bosco, and vermentino - grown in the ideally-situated Volastra vineyard at Riomaggiore. Lugano maintains the typical peasant tradition of that zone by macerating on the skins, but with the use of modern oenological techniques. The wine has a rich straw colour and aromas with strong peach, sage and iodine notes; it makes up for a slight scarcity of structure with appealing, characteristic saltiness on the palate. The Caratello - a wine made from semi-dried albarola grapes is good and comes very close to rating Two Glasses . Among the Vermentinos, the Vigna Erta is not quite as good as usual: its nose lacks freshness. On the other hand, we did like the Monte Bernardo, with its fine scents of aromatic herbs and peaches. Its refreshingly citrusy note makes it a very pleasant drink indeed. The basic Vermentino is also worthy of mention: it combines aromas of wild flowers and aniseed with fresh, well-balanced, easy fruit on the palate. At the time of our tasting, the Acinirari was anything but ready, but this wine gives the impression that it will live up to its usual form: our evaluation of it will appear in the next Guide.

○ Colli di Luni Vermentino		
Costa Marina '96	♀	3
○ Ottaviano Lambruschi	♀	3
○ Colli di Luni Vermentino '96		2
○ Colli di Luni Vermentino		
Sarticola '96		2

○ Caratello '95	♀	4
○ Golfo del Tigullio Vermentino		
Monte Bernardo '96	♀	3
○ Marea '96	♀	3
○ Golfo del Tigullio Bianchetta		
Genovese '96		1
○ Golfo del Tigulio Bianchetta		
Genovese u Pastine '96		2
○ Golfo del Tigullio Vermentino '96		2
○ Golfo del Tigullio Vermentino		
Vigna Erta '96		3
⊙ Golfo del Tigullio Ciliegiolo '96		1
● Golfo del Tigullio Rosso		
Mosaico '95		3
○ Acinirari '94	♀	5

DIANO CASTELLO (IM)

DOLCEACQUA (IM)

Maria Donata Bianchi
Via delle Torri, 16
18010 Diano Castello (IM)
Tel. 0183/498233

Giobatta Mandino Cane
Via Roma, 21
18035 Dolceacqua (IM)
Tel. 0184/206120

The wines of this producer are exemplary. They have character, personality and the quality - which is on a steady upward curve - to satisfy even the most demanding palates. Emanuele Trevia however is not resting on his laurels. Alert and restless as a ferret, he dedicates himself heart and soul to his work both in the vineyard and in the winery, with a mixture of stubborn determination and constant apprehension. His style is becoming increasingly refined, his winery increasingly functional and beautiful, adorned as it is with frescoes on wine-related themes and with a number of Allier barriques which are giving him excellent results. He also shares with his friend Vladimiro Galluzzo (Cascina delle Terre Rosse) the desire to compare experiences with his winemaking peers in order to learn something from them that will make his wines (perhaps) even better: this, in a region where individualism would appear to be the watchword of most producers, is a rare quality indeed. His best wine in our tastings was the Pigato, stunningly intense on the nose as well as on the palate. It is a thoroughly satisfying wine, with a complex palette of aromas - peaches, acacia honey, aromatic herbs, balsamic notes - and a palate which combines balance, good fruit and substance, as well as a fresh, savoury tone. The Vermentino is also very persuasive, with its broad, lively aromas which remind one of apples, broom and sage; it is full and rich on the palate, with firm structure and real character. We should like to stress that both wines can be kept and will in fact improve in bottle, as will the Rossese della Riviera Ligure di Ponente. The barrique-aged Vermentino and Pigato were not yet available when we carried out our tastings.

Dolceacqua is not only the most beautiful spot in the valley; it is also the nerve centre of Rossese production, the wine named after this ancient village. A mixture of history and legend links the rossese grape to the oenological skills (real or apocryphal) of the Marquises of Doria, who did, however, give real impetus to its cultivation. Recently, we have seen a marked improvement in quality, underpinned by greater care in tending and exploiting the vineyards, resulting in greater finesse and personality in the wines. In some of the leading growers in the zone one finds an innovative approach which, unfortunately however, is not yet very widespread; this new creativity manifests itself in wines - made only from carefully selected grapes - which are no longer merely bland and commercial. Mandino Cane was one of the first to understand this open secret: drastic thinning in the vineyard, strict selection of the clusters and vinification using appropriate, modern equipment. These methods may seem obvious, but in these parts certain prejudices regarding modern winemaking techniques die hard. The Dolceacqua Superiore Vigneto Arcagna remains a benchmark and deservedly rates Two Glasses . It is a brilliant ruby red; its bouquet displays a delicate hint of wood as well as wild strawberry, blackberry and red currant notes; on the palate, it is firmly structured, with an attractive vein of acidity, but it also shows broad, fleshy fruit and a fine, long bitter-cherry finish. This year we include for the first time another Dolceacqua Superiore, the Vigneto Morghe, which is notable for a nose in which one finds suggestions of wood resin and aromatic herbs. In the mouth, it has medium-structured fruit supported by good acidity, but it is not yet very well-knit.

O Riviera Ligure di Ponente Pigato '96	🍷🍷	4
O Riviera Ligure di Ponente Vermentino '96	🍷🍷	4
● Riviera Ligure di Ponente Rossese '96		3

● Rossese di Dolceacqua Superiore Vigneto Arcagna '96	🍷🍷	4
● Rossese di Dolceacqua Superiore Vigneto Morghe '96	🍷	4

DOLCEACQUA (IM)

TERRE BIANCHE
LOC. ARCAGNA
18035 DOLCEACQUA (IM)
TEL. 0184/31426

FINALE LIGURE (SV)

CASCINA DELLE TERRE ROSSE
VIA MANIE, 3
17024 FINALE LIGURE (SV)
TEL. 019/698782

The Rondelli brothers have come a long way since 1980 when they founded their winery, inspired by a long-held dream: that of making hand-crafted wines. The property is named "Terre Bianche" after the impressively large and fissured morphological mass, resulting from erosion, which surrounds their vineyards at a place called Brunetti. The estate has gradually become larger as new parcels of vineyard have been bought or rented in the hillsides around Arcagna. It is a family-run business, with Claudio very much in charge. Mario Ronco joins as consultant oenologist this year while Paolo, who manages the family's holiday accommodation, lends a hand when necessary. The Bricco Arcagna, a Rossese di Dolceacqua given just the right amount of ageing in new oak casks, is excellent. It has a deep ruby colour and a broad, complex nose, with vanilla and tarry notes which lead into scents reminiscent of wild black berry fruits; it also displays similar fruit character on the palate, along with fullness, length and a pleasant vein of acidity. The traditionally-made Rossese is praiseworthy, with its balsamic, fruity nose, its satisfying body and balance, and its subtle almondy aftertaste. The Vermentino is also good: it is fragrant and floral, and on the palate is appealingly soft, yet lively. The Pigato combines aromatic style with fresh, incisive fruit on the palate. The special selection of Vermentino, Vigna Campetto, deserves high marks, with its fine, distinctive bouquet of flowers, wild herbs and citrus fruits and its personality and length on the palate. The Pigato Vigna Arcagna is a bit below par, as is the Aurin, a wine made from semi-dried vermentino, pigato and rossese grapes which has been aged in new barriques for two years; it is over-alcoholic and lacking in balance.

This year, once again, the wines of Vladimiro Galluzzo are consonant with his fine reputation, confirming the estate's excellent state of health. He owns around four hectares of hillside vineyards divided between the Manie plateau and Borgio Verezzi which, were it not for the rows of vines, are so manicured as to look like tennis courts - right down to the colour of the clay. Here he grows the typical indigenous varieties: lumassina, rossese, vermentino and pigato. From the latter two cultivars, as a result of careful grape selection during the harvest and appropriate vinification and ageing techniques, four different wines are obtained. These are two traditional varietals, suitably reinterpreted to give them real personality; a blend fermented and aged in barrique; and an unfortified dessert wine. The wines we tasted were all good and well-made. The Vermentino earns Two Glasses this year: it is complex on the nose with hints of peach blossom, almonds and strong floral scents and rich and intense on the palate; broad, soft and very slightly alcoholic, it also has a touch of bitterness which gives it elegance. The Pigato follows close behind, with its frank, aromatic nose . It is savoury and well-balanced on the palate, with a good alcohol level and a certain depth of character. Le Banche, the barrique-conditioned wine, needs some bottle-age to show at its best: there is a little too much oak on the nose, whereas the good fruit and texture on the palate are evidence of its quality. The Passito is a wine that demands attention: hints of honey, apricots and sultanas on the nose, it is fat and rich, but rendered harmonious - and deliciously drinkable - by its refreshing acidity. The fragrant and youthful Rossese and the skilfully vinified Acerbina from lumassina grapes, though quite different from one another, are both eminently quaffable.

● Rossese di Dolceacqua Bricco Arcagna '95	🍷🍷	5
○ Riviera Ligure di Ponente Vermentino Vigna Campetto '96	🍷🍷	4
○ Riviera Ligure di Ponente Pigato '96	🍷	4
○ Riviera Ligure di Ponente Pigato Vigna Arcagna '96	🍷	4
○ Riviera Ligure di Ponente Vermentino '96	🍷	4
● Rossese di Dolceacqua '96	🍷	4
○ Passito '93	🍷🍷	6
○ Riviera Ligure di Ponente Pigato '96	🍷🍷	4
○ Riviera Ligure di Ponente Vermentino '96	🍷🍷	4
○ L'Acerbina '96	🍷	3
○ Le Banche '96	🍷	5
● Riviera Ligure di Ponente Rossese '96		4

FOSDINOVO (MS)

PODERE TERENZUOLA
VIA VERCALDA, 14
54035 FOSDINOVO (MS)
TEL. 0187/68951

IMPERIA

TENUTA COLLE DEI BARDELLINI
VIA FONTANAROSA, 12
LOC. S. AGATA
18100 IMPERIA
TEL. 0183/291370

Twenty-four year old Ivan Giuliani is the moving force behind his family's estate, and he has shown himself to be full of bright and constructive ideas. This young man, in charge here since 1993 - previously they sold wine in bulk - is a keen sommelier, and is constantly striving to improve his knowledge and skills. He is also not afraid to compare his methods and approach with those of other producers, and regularly travels around the country to taste their wines. This small winery, with production amounting to a mere few thousand bottles, lies on a hillside behind Fosdinovo. Here, amidst the olive groves planted with the indigenous razzuolo, cipresso and leccino varieties - source of a very respectable extra virgin oil - are located about two and a half hectares of vineyards growing the typical cultivars of the Colli di Luni: vermentino and sangiovese. The density of planting is around 5,000 guyot trained vines per hectare. Average age of the vines is around 13 years and yields are pegged at 63 quintals per hectare. The vineyards are situated in two different zones: Terenzuola for the vermentino and Belvedere for the red grapes, which for now remain that most Italian of all varieties, sangiovese, although plans for the future are based on merlot. Ivan, working with great zeal both in the vineyard and in the winery - where he employs brief maceration on the skins at controlled temperatures and careful maturation of the wine "sur lie" - has obtained from the '96 vintage, a wine of considerable character. It has a handsome straw-yellow colour; on the nose it is rich and full, with active herbaceous notes and scents of Mediterranean flora. Its typical almondy finish is already attractive, but the wine needs a little more time for the palate to come together: there is every reason to believe that it will do so.

The property managed by Pino Sola consists of around three and a half hectares of vineyards, from which he obtains just over 20,000 bottles of his two single-vineyard wines: Vermentino Vigna u Munte and Pigato La Torretta. The rest of his production - between 60,000 and 70,000 bottles in total - comes from grapes purchased from local growers. Pino's wines are always well-made, thanks also to the technical help provided by Giuliano Noè. This year we were particularly impressed by the Vigna u Munte's finesse and its frank expression of typical varietal style. It has a brilliant straw colour with greenish reflections and a rich nose, with hints of fruit, citron and broom; on the palate, it displays broad, silky fruit, underscored by a pleasing savoury quality which serves to enliven the rich, concentrated finish. The La Torretta is only marginally inferior: it has a medium-deep straw hue and lively nose of aromatic herbs and conifer, with an intriguing underlying hint of saltiness. It still has to knit together on the palate, but it already shows good weight and a harmonious and long finish. The basic Vermentino and Pigato are well worthy of their listings: the former has aromas of herbs and dried seeds as well as delicate fruity notes, and is light and quaffable on the palate. The latter - richer in colour and flavour - is faintly aromatic, with balsamic and salty hints. Finally, we should like to mention two other excellent products of the estate: an extra-virgin olive oil and a Vermentino Grappa made from the pomace of the Vigna u Munte.

○ Colli di Luni Vermentino '96	♀	3

○ Riviera Ligure di Ponente Vermentino Vigna u Munte '96	♀♀	4
○ Riviera Ligure di Ponente Pigato '96	♀	4
○ Riviera Ligure di Ponente Pigato La Torretta '96	♀	4
○ Riviera Ligure di Ponente Vermentino '96		3

PIEVE DI TECO (IM)

Tommaso e Angelo Lupi
Via Mazzini, 9
18026 Pieve di Teco (IM)
tel. 0183/36161-21610

For some forty years now, brothers Tommaso and Angelo Lupi have been involved in the heterogeneous world of wine. Besides from their family winery, they also run a wine shop in Imperia and are passionate and enthusiastic ambassadors for Bacchus' favourite beverage. A vast range of wines is produced each year by this old winery housed in what, in 1350, used to be a monastery. The '96 wines are good, beginning with the standard Vermentino: bright straw in colour, it offers a light floral bouquet. The fruit on the palate is set off by just the right amount of acidity to give the wine length of flavour. The basic Pigato is also appealing, with its good balance of acidity and soft fruit. It is deliciously quaffable and displays fresh aromas of flowers and Mediterranean broom. The single-vineyard Le Petraie is more complex: it is a straw-coloured wine with a broad, though not particularly intense, fruity bouquet. The palate echoes the sensations on the nose, but is not yet totally harmonious. The Vignamare, a blend of vermentino and pigato which has spent some time in small barrels, displays fine aromas of peaches and apricots enveloped in a gentle mantle of oakiness. On the palate, it is dry but delicate and well-balanced. The Ormeasco was only presented in the basic and Sciac-tra versions. The former is a well-made product: ruby in colour, it has a vinous nose which conjures up scents of cherries and blackberries; it is lightly tannic and has an attractive bitter-cherry flavour. The latter wine has a beautiful cherry-red colour and offers berry fruit (wild strawberry and raspberry) aromas which lead into an enticing flavour which is dry, savoury and light, yet complex and satisfying. The Rossese di Dolceacqua is simple and straightforward.

○	Riviera Ligure di Ponente Pigato Le Petraie '96	🍷🍷	4
○	Riviera Ligure di Ponente Pigato '96	🍷	3
○	Riviera Ligure di Ponente Vermentino '96	🍷	3
○	Vignamare '96	🍷	4
⊙	Riviera Ligure di Ponente Ormeasco Sciac-tra '96	🍷	3
○	Riviera Ligure di Ponente Vermentino Le Serre '96		4
●	Riviera Ligure di Ponente Ormeasco '96		3
●	Ormeasco Superiore Le Braje '94	🍷 (outline)	4
○	Vignamare '95	🍷 (outline)	4

RANZO (IM)

A Maccia
Via Umberto I, 56
Fraz. Borgo
18028 Ranzo (IM)
tel. 0183/318003

The Val d'Arroscia zone around Ranzo, situated between the Provinces of Imperia and Savona, is considered to be the birthplace of pigato, which is by far the most commonly planted grape variety in the area. Fernanda Fiorito and her daughter Loredana Faraldi boast, with well-justified pride, about the historic importance of their vineyards. These were wrested from the maquis and from the steep slopes of a landscape of rare beauty, in which dry-stone walls are not merely a characteristic decorative feature but also, and above all, an arduous necessity. If we consider that it is only the distaff side of the family which has set about taming this hostile terrain, we cannot hide the admiration and sympathy we feel for these tenacious ladies. There are plans for an estate shop, on the site of the old warehouse, which will serve to improve the - already delightful - level of hospitality offered to visitors to the winery. Apart from the Pigato, here one can purchase a fragrant olive paste, excellent olives in brine, and an extra virgin oil with scents of aromatic herbs and almonds and a delicate, rounded, fruity flavour that is typically Ligurian - all available in pretty gift baskets. Technical consultant to the winery is oenologist Piertro Trevia. The '96 Pigato has a brilliant, rich straw-yellow colour; its bouquet is intense and characteristic, with typical aromas of camomile, pine resin and wild herbs and a faint suggestion of sea air. On the palate, it is soft and substantial, with an appealing salty savouriness which underpins its long finish, in which one also finds an enticing - and typical - touch of bitterness.

○	Riviera Ligure di Ponente Pigato '96	🍷	3

RANZO (IM)

BRUNA
VIA UMBERTO I, 81
FRAZ. BORGO
18028 RANZO (IM)
TEL. 0183/318082

RIOMAGGIORE (SP)

WALTER DE BATTÈ
VIA PECUNIA, 168
19017 RIOMAGGIORE (SP)
TEL. 0187/920127

It is our opinion that Riccardo Bruna cannot - and this vintage confirms it - but be satisfied with his efforts. The right winemaking approach combined with good soil and excellent fruit (a splendid microclimate has always favoured grape-growing in this area, which is the birthplace of pigato) have been the key elements in his success. The winery's two whites, both Pigatos but from different vineyards, represent a successful synthesis of modernity and tradition: essentially they are fresh, clean wines, which do not however foresake flavour, personality and typicity. The Rossese also preserves fully its varietal character; it is fruity and easy to drink. The property consists of about four hectares and has been making wine since the '70s, wines that are as genuine, natural and environment-friendly as humanly possible. This activity was originally little more than a hobby for the owner, but it has now taken on sufficient importance for it to have become his full-time job. The star wine of the small range is Le Russeghine, a stylish white which easily earns Two Glasses and which again confirms itself as the estate's standard-bearer. It has a fine golden straw colour and a broad, fruity and aromatic bouquet, with intense wood resin and wild flower notes; it is pleasantly savoury and generous on the palate, with rich, balanced, well-textured and long-lasting fruit. The Villa Torrachetta - a Pigato from a vineyard at Ortovero capable of producing notable wines - also showed well: it has an elegant, fruity nose, with scents of peaches and hints of aromatic herbs. These sensations are echoed on the palate, where the fruit is rounded and long, with a typical bitter-almondy undertone.

Albarola, bosco and just a little vermentino are the varieties cultivated on Walter De Battè's estate but in the near future a few vines of ruzzese, an ancient indigenous grape type and - this is an especially intriguing prospect - a red cultivar may well also put in an appearance. From the grapes grown at the moment, De Battè obtains a Cinque Terre that always improves with at least a year's bottle-age. With this in mind he is seriously considering the possibility of releasing it a bit later. After having spent a brief time on the skins, part of the wine goes into wood and part into stainless steel, and a final blend of these two lots is made before bottling. Then, by letting the wine settle in tank and filtering as little as possible, the wine clarifies itself quite naturally. The '96 vintage is a deep straw colour which gives an indication of the wine's rich bouquet: here one finds predominantly aromatic and salty notes, combined with hints of grass and wild flowers and an attractive overlay of oak. The wine is still a little unknit on the palate, with the oak not yet perfectly integrated with the abundant alcohol, softness and savoury flavours; nevertheless, this is undoubtedly a vintage that will age well. The Sciacchetra, a famous wine of great tradition, appeals to us immediately with its rich amber colour; it has a deep, long-lasting and inviting nose, with resinous tones which combine with appealing apricot and honey notes and delicate nutty hints. On the palate, though still not fully ready for drinking, it is well-balanced, with a tannic vein which balances the wine's notable, but not cloying, sweetness.

○ Riviera Ligure di Ponente		
Pigato Le Russeghine '96	🍷🍷	3*
○ Riviera Ligure di Ponente		
Pigato Villa Torrachetta '96	🍷	3
● Riviera Ligure di Ponente		
Rossese '96		3

○ Cinque Terre Sciacchetrà '96	🍷🍷	6
○ Cinque Terre '96	🍷	4

RIOMAGGIORE (SP)

FORLINI E CAPPELLINI
P.ZZA DUOMO, 6
FRAZ. MANAROLA
19010 RIOMAGGIORE (SP)
TEL. 0187/920496

The Cinque Terre, rightly considered one of the most beautiful areas of the whole of Liguria, is dotted with numerous villages, hidden among the cliffs of the Riviera di Levante. They form a stunning landscape of terraced vines, olive groves, citrus orchards and fishermen's houses standing sheer above the sea. Here one begins to comprehend the Ligurians' character: reserved, independent-minded, ready to welcome the benefits of tourism, but never to give up their identity. To really understand this difficult environment you have to live and breathe it, tramping along rugged paths or up steep steps set into the rock face. Sweat and solitude: that is life for the Cinque Terre's farmers. This is a land made workable through tremendous toil, moving tons of rock by hand in order to obtain cultivable soil. Fully conscious of these conditions, Germana and Alberto continue undaunted to go up and down, tending their rows of vines. These are of the typical local varieties albarolla, bosco and vermentino, planted on stony, clayey soil. With the '96 vintage, barriques made their first appearance in this winery: a small amount of wine spent about six months in these small oak casks prior to being blended with the wine vinified and stored in stainless steel. The'96 vintage produced just over 7,000 bottles. In the glass, the wine is a bright straw-yellow; its aromas are reminiscent of grass, of Mediterranean broom, and of the sea; the fruit on the palate is elegant with a fairly good balance between softness and acidity, and an oakiness that is not dominant but which still needs to integrate fully.

○ Cinque Terre '96	🍷	4

SARZANA (SP)

IL MONTICELLO
VIA GROPPOLO, 7
19038 SARZANA (SP)
TEL. 0187/621432

This estate is included once again in the Guide proper this year, after being consigned to the "Other Wineries" page last year because of the poor quality of the '95 vintage. Maria Antonietta Bacciarelli and Pier Luigi Neri have virtually totally handed over the running of the company to their two sons: Davide, who looks after the vineyards and sales and Alessandro, in charge of the handsome winery built in 1992. A great deal has changed since, some years ago, the family started making 2,000 bottles of wine, almost for fun - but winning compliments from friends who tried it. What was a hobby has become a full-time job and annual production has reached 15,000 bottles; the family would now like to increase production still further in order to give the company more stability. The estate (nine hectares are either owned or rented by the Neris) is divided between olive groves and vineyards which are almost exclusively planted with vermentino. The Colli di Luni Vermentino is the flagship wine of the range. It has a straw colour with pale green highlights and an elegant nose with a delicately fruity nose of apples, peaches, herbs and wild flowers. On the palate, it is well-balanced and again gently fruity, with subtle savoury notes which render the finish fresh and appealing. The Groppolo and the Rupestro are both decent and well-made. The former is a white blend which is light and crisp on the palate; the latter - a red made from sangiovese, with the addition of merlot, ciliegiolo and canaiolo - has a pleasantly rustic character.

○ Colli di Luni Vermentino '96	🍷	3
○ Groppolo '96		2
● Rupestro '95		2

SOLDANO (IM)

Enzo Guglielmi
C.so Verbone, 143
18030 Soldano (IM)
Tel. 0184/289042

VENDONE (SV)

Claudio Vio
Fraz. Crosa, 16
17030 Vendone (SV)
Tel. 0182/76338-76297

Enzo Guglielmi is a true son of the soil, outwardly informal but with a lively, practical and forward-thinking mind. He cares little about his external appearance, but likes to get down to the nitty gritty. As the descendant and successor of a long line of wine growers, he has improved his vineyard stock by replanting, changing training systems and thereby reducing yields. Here, as is the case throughout the Ligurian hinterland, producers also have to struggle with the problems caused by the rocky nature of the terrain, which calls for hard, continuous labour and the burning up of both physical and nervous energy in order to obtain results. We must not forget that some time ago many producers decided to give up the risks and strenuous toil of viticulture for the easier and more remunerative activity of growing flowers. The property consists of a couple of hectares at I Pini, considered the best area of the commune of Soldano, which is entirely planted with bush-trained rossese vines. The small but well-equipped winery contains stainless steel tanks which are used both for fermentation and for maturation, operations carried out under the guidance of oenologist Giampaolo Ramo. His experience as a winemaker has each year an increasing benefit on the wines, and he is to thank for the constant quality and notable longevity of the estate's products. The '96 vintage is a little lacking in its bouquet, which gives mere hints of red berry fruits and faded roses; the fruit on the palate is attractively rounded, with excellent balance and length.

This year, after the previous two in which the Vermentino obtained higher marks in our tastings, the Pigato has come to the fore, regaining its position as the estate's top wine and deservedly earning Two Glasses . The grapes for this wine come from around Albenga, an area which has become the home of pigato "par excellence". The wine has a deep straw-yellow colour and a nose of considerable character, with aromas which highlight the typical aromatic tones reminiscent of the Ligurian brush land, combined with fruity notes of peaches and apricots. The flavours echo the sensations of the bouquet and the entry on the palate is good. The wine's rich, mellow fruit is counterpointed by a fresh, citrusy vein, and the finish is attractively long and clean. As for the Vermentino, which from this winery at any rate is always similar in style to the Pigato, the '96 is straw in colour, with bright greenish reflections which herald a fresh, youthful nose with hints of sage and wood resin notes. On the palate, it is very easy to drink but has reasonable structure; it is well balanced and long, with an attractive and typical bitter-almond finish. A small quantity of red grapes are also grown here, used for the limited production of Ronco Brujau, a fresh and charming red. For some years now, young Claudio Vio has taken over the reins of this family-run estate, making wines exclusively from grapes from his own vineyards. He owns five hectares from which he produces around 12,000 bottles of wine as well as a good extra virgin olive oil.

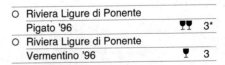

● Rossese di Dolceacqua Sup. '96	♟	3

| ○ Riviera Ligure di Ponente Pigato '96 | ♟♟ | 3* |
| ○ Riviera Ligure di Ponente Vermentino '96 | ♟ | 3 |

OTHER WINERIES

The following producers obtained good scores in our tastings with one or more of their wines:

PROVINCE OF GENOVA

Domenico Barisone,
Genova, tel. 010/6516534,
Bianco di Coronata '96

Bruzzone,
Genova, tel. 010/7455157,
Bianchetta Genovese '96

F.lli Parma,
Ne, tel. 0185/337073,
Golfo del Tigullio Vermentino I Cansellé '96

PROVINCE OF IMPERIA

Adriano Maccario,
Dolceacqua, tel. 0184/206013,
Rossese di Dolceaqua '96

Antonio Perrino,
Dolceacqua, tel. 0184/206267,
Rossese di Dolceacqua '96

Laura Aschero,
Pontedassio, tel. 0183/293515,
Riviera Ligure di Ponente Pigato '96,
Riviera Ligure di Ponente Vermentino '96

Lorenzo Ramò,
Pornassio,
tel. 0183/33097,
Riviera Ligure di Ponente Ormeasco '96,
Riviera Ligure di Ponente Ormeasco
Sciac-trà '96

PROVINCE OF LA SPEZIA

Fattoria Il Chioso,
Arcola, tel. 0187/986620,
Colli di Luni Vermentino '96,
Colli di Luni Rosso '96

'r Mesueto,
Arcola, tel. 0187/986190,
Colli di Luni Vermentino '96

Andrea Spagnoli,
Arcola, tel. 0187/987160,
Colli di Luni Vermentino '96

Luciana Giacomelli,
Castelnuovo Magra, tel. 0187/674155,
Colli di Luni Vermentino '96

Il Torchio,
Castelnuovo Magra, tel. 0187/674075,
Colli di Luni Vermentino '96,
Colli di Luni Rosso '96

La Colombiera,
Castelnuovo Magra, tel. 0187/674265,
Colli di Luni Vermentino '96,
Colli di Luni Rosso Terrizzo '95

Cascina dei Peri,
Castelnuovo Magra, tel. 0187/674085,
Colli di Luni Vermentino '96

Podere Lavandaro,
Fosdinovo, tel. 0187/68202,
Colli di Luni Vermentino '96

**Cooperativa Agricola di Riomaggiore,
Manarola, Corniglia, Vernazza
e Monterosso**,
Riomaggiore, tel. 0187/920435,
Cinque Terre Costa de Posa di Volastra '96,
Cinque Terre Costa de Sèra
di Riomaggiore '96,
Cinque Terre '96,
Cinque Terre Sciacchetrà '95

PROVINCE OF SAVONA

Filippo Ruffino,
Varigotti, tel. 019/698522,
Mataossu,
Riviera Ligure di Ponente Pigato '96

LOMBARDY

Lombardy's rise to prominence alongside the other great wine producing regions of Italy is inexorable. For years, we have accused its producers of stagnation, but for some time now a new wind has been blowing in the region. Undoubtedly, the classic wine producing areas remain the most important, meaning, above all, Franciacorta, Valtellina, and Oltrepò Pavese. For some years now, Franciacorta has had successful producers operating at an international level: Ca' del Bosco gains yet another accolade with its superlative Franciacorta Cuvée Annamaria Clementi '90. Bellavista rivals that with an exceptionally fine vintage Franciacorta Gran Cuvée Brut '93, while Uberti gives us a superb Franciacorta Magnificentia. Often the term "standardization" actually means a levelling down, but in Franciacorta, for a couple of years now, it has meant levelling up. There is healthy competition between wine producers, or perhaps it would be better to call it collective effort, that has led to a visible improvement in the quality of all their wines and in particular of their Franciacorta (do not ever call it "spumante"!). Developments of recent years are propelling this corner of Lombardy into the category of the great wine producing zones of the world. From other parts of the region, there were excellent results with both reds and white wines. Valtellina has an undoubted leader in the Nino Negri company from Chiuro, whose Sfursat 5 Stelle this year is on a par with the best vintages. But the other wineries of the region have also produced equally good reds, just as modern and well made, with due attention to yields and the use of oak in the cellars, two aspects of winemaking that not every producer in the area used to get right. We gave no Three Glass award in the province of Pavia, but we are sure it will not be long in coming. The time when the Oltrepò Pavese was the mass producer of bulk wines for the bottlers in other regions has now passed. For some time, the watchword in these gentle hills has been quality. Under the microscope come considerations such as vineyard sites, clonal selections of native varieties, and vinification and ageing methods. Leaders in this modernisation are Monsupello, certainly, but also Vercesi from Castellazzo and Ca' di Frara, all destined to join Italy's élite. This year in the Oltrepò we tasted impeccable examples of Metodo Classico sparkling wines, and whites made from riesling, sauvignon and chardonnay, as well as Pinot Nero and Cabernet wines that are just as good as their counterparts in more prestigious regions. On the shores and hinterland of Lake Garda, too, in the south eastern part of the region, there is an air of change. We have not found any wines at the very highest level yet, but there are a number of producers who are gearing up to the creation of top quality wines, following the example of Ca' dei Frati and Cascina La Pertica, to name just two. Here and there, one or two of the many Lombard DOCs are marking time, not participating in the general modernisation of vineyards, cellars, and wine styles. But these are increasingly in the minority and we are sure they will not resist the contemporary trends for much longer.

ADRO (BS)

COLA
VIA SANT'ANNA, 22
25030 ADRO (BS)
TEL. 030/7356195

Battista Cola and his son Stefano continue the good work at their winery in Adro, where they have already reached a production level of 80,000 bottles, of which more than 30,000 are Franciacorta. At the time of our tastings the Extra Brut was not yet available, but in fact the simple Brut was quite enough to ensure Cola a place in the Guide: bright straw yellow, subtle greenish reflections, attractive ripe fruit bouquet (apples particularly) yeasty with a hint of new wood on the nose; fresh tasting, well balanced, good structure, lightly aromatic. Two red wines are worth noting: Terre di Franciacorta Rosso '95: rich vinosity, bouquet of berry fruits and cherries, very drinkable; and the latest wine to come from this producer: the red DOC cru Tamino, coming from the vineyard of the same name on the slopes of Monte Alto near Adro. Made from a cépage of cabernet sauvignon (50 percent), merlot (30 percent) and equal measures of barbera and nebbiolo, it is aged for one year in oak barriques. This first vintage has rich extract, and good fruit on the nose and the palate, but despite being well balanced and full bodied with an attractive spiciness, it suffers from harsh tannins. The Terre di Franciacorta Bianco '95 is fresh, correct and easy to drink.

ADRO (BS)

CONTADI CASTALDI
VIA COLZANO, 32
25030 ADRO (BS)
TEL. 030/7450126

Contadi Castaldi makes a high profile debut in the Guide this year. The winery is an offshoot of the Bellavista estate created at the express desire of the group managing director, Martino de Rosa, who has ambitious plans for its future. Current production stands at about 200,000 bottles per year, but this will soon rise to over a million. The winery has found itself a most unusual location in the old brickworks at Adro, which have now been perfectly restored and adapted for the purpose. Head of the production team is Mario Falchetti, a graduate of agricultural studies, who directed the zonal research projects at the Agricultural Institute of San Michele All'Adige for years. Of the Franciacortas we tasted this year, we particularly liked the Brut, with its soft and fruity nose and full bodied and balanced palate, full of vanilla. The Satèn is one of the best of its type - fruity and well rounded; what makes it really attractive is the addition of an unusual hint of musk. In a region where pink wines have little standing, this Rosé is much better than average and it completely seduced us with its full bodied palate and fresh, soft fruit aromas. The Zero is an Extra Brut which stands out for the excellent way it has aged and its full bodied nature, even if it seems a little softer than its name would suggest. Lastly, we recommend an excellent Terre di Franciacorta Bianco '96, and a correctly made Rosso '94. The Pinodisé is a successful "liquoroso" wine, and one of the very few to be made in this area.

O Franciacorta Brut	ΨΨ	4
● Terre di Franciacorta Rosso '95	Ψ	2
● Terre di Franciacorta Rosso Tamino '95	Ψ	3
O Terre di Franciacorta Bianco '96		2
O Franciacorta Bianco Selezione '94	ΨΨ	3
O Franciacorta Extra Brut '92	ΨΨ	4
O Terre di Franciacorta Bianco Vigneto Tignazzi '95	ΨΨ	3
O Franciacorta Brut	Ψ	4
O Terre di Franciacorta Bianco '95	Ψ	3

O Franciacorta Brut	ΨΨ	4*
⊙ Franciacorta Rosé	ΨΨ	5
O Franciacorta Satèn	ΨΨ	5
O Pinodisé	ΨΨ	5
O Terre di Franciacorta Bianco '96	ΨΨ	3*
O Franciacorta Zero	Ψ	5
● Terre di Franciacorta Rosso '94		3

CAMIGNONE (BS)

CATTURICH-DUCCO
VIA DEGLI EROI, 5
25040 CAMIGNONE (BS)
TEL. 030/6850566

CANNETO PAVESE (PV)

FIAMBERTI
VIA CHIESA, 17
27044 CANNETO PAVESE (PV)
TEL. 0385/88019

Count Piero Catturich-Ducco is one of the most important producers in Franciacorta with a good 75 hectares of vineyards spread over five communes in the DOC zone. Catturich-Ducco came to prominence in the 1970s, and even then was ahead of its time in the application of barrique ageing to red wines. Piero Catturich-Ducco was also something of a pioneer when, at the beginning of the next decade, he decided to reconvert the vineyards back onto the Guyot system with a planting density of about 5,000 vines per hectare. This year in the tastings we were shown two excellent Franciacortas and one Terre di Franciacorta Bianco that was correct enough, but can surely be improved. Franciacorta Torre Ducco has an attractive, pale straw yellow colour, a fine perlage and a fresh, fruity, delicately floral bouquet. Soft and fruity on the palate with just the right amount of bubble, this is a well balanced and sophisticated wine that deserves its Two Glass award. The Pas Dosé '92 has a slightly vegetal and reticent bouquet with hints of toastiness; correct and fresh on the palate, this is a pleasant enough wine, but somewhat lacking in body.

The Fiamberti family have been winemakers for two centuries. Their winery can be found just below the seventeenth-century church at Canneto, a district in the foothills of the Oltrepò Pavese that apparently gets its name from the harvesting of canes in the area, once used as supports for the vines. This is ideal red wine country (the whites are not bad, either) and the Fiambertis cultivate some fifteen hectares of vines in the communes of Canneto, Castana, Montescano and Stradella. The bread-and-butter wines are the classic reds, beginning with the Buttafuoco '96, made of barbera, croatina, uva rara and vespolina grapes from the Podere Solenga vineyard, which the family have owned since 1814. This is a real old timer's wine: deep purple in colour, huge vinous bouquet with hints of wild blackberries, violets and carnations; dry, full bodied and satisfying. The Sangue di Giuda '96, from the Costa Paradiso vineyard on a south-east facing slope of the Canneto hills, is a good example of its type. Made predominantly (80 percent) from croatina, with equal measures of barbera and uva rara, it has a dark, ruby red colour, a creamy foaming spritz, and an intense bouquet of raspberries, blackberries and bitter almonds; on the palate, it is sweet, sparkling, full bodied and fruity, with a substantial bitter twist to the finish (what the local inhabitants call "almondy"). Lastly, the Charmat method Brut Fiamberti is made entirely of pinot noir and left on the lees for six months: intense bouquet of toasted bread and berry fruit, dry on the palate, medium weight and quite long finishing.

O Franciacorta Brut Torre Ducco	🍷🍷	4
O Franciacorta Pas Dosé '92	🍷	4
O Terre di Franciacorta '96		2

● Oltrepò Pavese Buttafuoco '96	🍷	3
O Oltrepò Pavese Pinot Nero Brut	🍷	4
● Oltrepò Pavese Sangue di Giuda Costa Paradiso '96	🍷	3

CANNETO PAVESE (PV)

Bruno Verdi

Via Vergomberra, 5
27044 Canneto Pavese (PV)
tel. 0385/88023

Paolo Verdi, Bruno's son, comes from a family that has been involved in vineyard husbandry and wine making in Oltrepò Pavese for seven generations. Results are now very encouraging from the quality point of view. His vineyards lie in the first range of hills in Oltrepò between the communes of Canneto and Castana, and he make good reds and whites alike, vinified with one eye on tradition but in a thoroughly modern manner. The cellars are equipped with the latest technology and have a bottling line with sterile micro filtration capabilities. This year's top-of-the-class is the Riesling Renano '96 from the Costa vineyard: golden straw yellow with green reflections, intense varietal bouquet, fresh, full bodied, elegant and long finishing. Only very slightly inferior to the '95 vintage version, the Moscato '96 is sweet and rich with a well defined bouquet of orange blossom, sage and apricots. We liked the Vergomberra Brut Classico '94, made from 100 percent pinot noir, with its sharp aromas of redcurrants and biscuits. The Riserva Cavariola '91 is a lively, up-front Oltrepò Pavese Rosso from the company's cru vineyard: 0.83 hectare planted with croatina, barbera, uva rara and vespolina at a density of 4,000 vines per hectare. Bonarda '96 is an uncomplicated and attractive wine, semi-sparkling, with a full bouquet of wild blackberries and a definite bitter almond finish. The Buttafuoco '93 is just as good and, aged in Slavonian oak, it has developed well and justifies its One Glass award from last year.

○	Oltrepò Pavese Riesling Renano Vigneto Costa '96	▼▼	3
●	Oltrepò Pavese Bonarda Vivace '96	▼	3
○	Oltrepò Pavese Brut Classico Vergomberra '95	▼	4
○	Oltrepò Pavese Moscato '96	▼	2
●	Oltrepò Pavese Rosso Cavariola Ris. '91	▼	4
●	Oltrepò Pavese Barbera '90	▽▽	3
●	Oltrepò Pavese Bonarda '93	▽▽	3
●	Oltrepò Pavese Rosso Cavariola Ris. '90	▽▽	4
●	Oltrepò Pavese Bonarda '95	▽	3
●	Oltrepò Pavese Buttafuoco '93	▽	3

CAPRIOLO (BS)

Ricci Curbastro

Via Adro, 37
25031 Capriolo (BS)
tel. 030/736094

Despite his other commitments as President of the Consorzio Vini (Growers' Association) of Franciacorta, Riccardo Ricci Curbastro works incredibly hard on his family-owned winery, which proves itself to be one of the most interesting in the area year after year. Some of the vineyards have been replanted and the cellars have been modernised under the direction of two expert oenologists, Alberto Musatti and the New Zealander, Owen J. Bird. The Terre di Franciacorta Bianco '96 has a floral nose with hints of mint and sage; spicy and fresh tasting on the palate. Vigna Bosco Alto '95 has a bright deep straw colour, an intense nose of honey, meadow flowers, peaches and vanilla, and is rich and full bodied on the palate; perhaps it is a little over mature on the finish and slightly past its peak, but it remains good all the same. Made only in magnums, the Franciacorta Brut '91 has a delicate perlage and an attractive nose of peaches, flowers and freshly picked herbs; long and full of flavour on the palate. Satèn '92 is pleasingly well knit and delicate with underlying hints of wood and vanilla on the nose, fresh and well balanced on the palate. The Extra Brut '93 has a lively, intense nose with hints of lime and subtle yeastiness; full bodied on the palate, creamy bubble, good nose and length. The two reds are good, particularly the Santella del Gröm '94.

○	Franciacorta Brut Magnum '91	▼▼	5
○	Franciacorta Extra Brut '93	▼▼	4*
○	Franciacorta Satèn '92	▼▼	4*
○	Terre di Franciacorta Bianco '96	▼	2
○	Terre di Franciacorta Bianco Vigna Bosco Alto '95	▼	3
●	Terre di Franciacorta Rosso '95	▼	2
●	Terre di Franciacorta Rosso Santella del Gröm '94	▼	3
○	Franciacorta Satèn	▽▽	4*
○	Brolo dei Passoni '94	▽	5
○	Franciacorta Brut	▽	4
○	Franciacorta Extra Brut '90	▽	4
○	Franciacorta Extra Brut '91	▽	4
●	Pinot Nero '94	▽	3

CASTEGGIO (PV)

FRECCIAROSSA
VIA VIGORELLI, 141
27045 CASTEGGIO (PV)
TEL. 0383/804465

CASTEGGIO (PV)

LE FRACCE
VIA CASTEL DEL LUPO, 5
27045 CASTEGGIO (PV)
TEL. 0383/804151

The Odero family's famous winery is back in the Guide this year: an estate of 22.65 hectares, 16 of which are vineyard, replanted between 1990 and 1995 with grafts selected from old vines on the property. This is also about the time the family began to use the services of Franco Bernabei, who is bringing the rather limited number of wines in the range up to scratch. They comprise: one Riesling Renano, one Pinot Nero, two Oltrepò reds, the Villa Odero "normale" and the Riserva. It would not be a bad idea to add at least one Bonarda to the range and in fact, the managing director, Pietro Calvi di Bergolo, is already planning this. Probably there will be other developments in the future, too. For the moment, we must limit ourselves to Frecciarossa's traditional wines. The Riesling Renano '96 has an elegant varietal bouquet, but is still green and somewhat sour, needing further bottle ageing. The Pinot Nero '93, vinified with the skins and aged partly in Slavonian oak and partly in barriques, has a good bouquet of red currants, tobacco and spices, a well defined palate, perhaps a little astringent, but attractive all the same. Despite the poor vintage, the Villa Odero Rosso '92 has an interesting nose of cinnamon, blackberries and cherries and well balanced structure. The Riserva '91 is spicier and more complex; better developed on the nose than the palate, this will improve with age, acquiring completeness and balance.

Belonging to the Bussolera Foundation and managed by oenologist Francesco Cervetti, this winery continues to practice scrupulous vineyard husbandry: low yields, no herbicides, no insecticides, no antibiotics . This is admirable, environmentally friendly vineyard management which produces healthy grapes capable of making great wines, both reds and whites. So far so good; but there are some red Riservas that should have been put forward for tasting sooner. This is the case with the Bohemi '91, made from barbera (55 percent), croatina (25 percent), and pinot noir (20 percent) from vineyards in San Biagio. This is an extremely strong Oltrepò Pavese Rosso (14.35 percent alcohol), aged 12 months in small oak barrels, bottled in July '94, and put on the market on1st December 1996. Despite its ample structure, the wine appears to have passed its peak and, consequently, does not get the Two Glass award it would have deserved before. Wine must be given the time to mature, but not too long. By contrast, the Riesling Renano '96 is faultless: fresh-tasting, full bodied, full on the palate, clear varietal character (sour apple, fresh peach, flintiness). This is coming up to its peak for drinking but it will last some time because of its solid structure. A One Glass award for the Pinot Grigio '96 from the Mairano vineyard with its bouquet of acacia flowers, and also for the Extra Brut '95 Cuvée Bussolera, a 100 percent pinot noir sparkling wine made by the Charmat method. (By the by, this could be better described as the Martinotti method, after the real inventor of tank fermentation for sparkling wines, the Italian Francesco Martinotti, Director of the Royal Oenological Station at Asti).

● Oltrepò Pavese Pinot Nero '93	♀	4
● Oltrepò Pavese Rosso Villa Odero '92	♀	3
● Oltrepò Pavese Rosso Villa Odero Ris. '91	♀	4
○ Oltrepò Pavese Riesling Renano '96		3

○ Oltrepò Pavese Riesling Renano '96	♀♀	4
○ Oltrepò Pavese Extra Brut Cuvée Bussolera '95	♀	4
○ Oltrepò Pavese Pinot Grigio '96	♀	4
● Oltrepò Pavese Rosso Bohemi '91	♀	5
● Oltrepò Pavese Bonarda '94	♀♀	4
● Oltrepò Pavese Bonarda '95	♀♀	4
● Oltrepò Pavese Cirgà '90	♀♀	5
● Oltrepò Pavese Cirgà '91	♀♀	5

CASTEGGIO (PV)

RUIZ DE CARDENAS
STRADA ALLE MOLLIE, 35
27047 CASTEGGIO (PV)
TEL. 0383/82301

CAZZAGO S. MARTINO (BS)

CONTI BETTONI CAZZAGO
VIA MARCONI, 6
25046 CAZZAGO S. MARTINO (BS)
TEL. 030/7750875

The problem for all very small wineries (total production 10-15,000 bottles) is to maintain a consistent level of quality over the years. It is not easy making great wines and there are many variables affecting quality in both the vineyard and the cellars. It is even more difficult when dealing with such a difficult grape variety as pinot noir, which can be highly successful or, equally easily, distinctly disappointing. This is the case with Brumano '93, Oltrepò Pavese Pinot Nero, which is only worth mentioning in passing, despite all the efforts of Ruiz de Cardenas and Giancarlo Scaglione, his consultant. The same goes for the Baloss Pinot Nero '96, a lighter wine (pale garnet red, fruity bouquet, soft on the palate) which, when tasted, was still out of balance due to its recent bottling (June '97). The Birbo, a Pinot Nero from Casteggiano re-fermented in the bottle, was fruity, fizzy, and easy-to-drink. The most successful wine was the Metodo Classico non-vintage Extra Brut, made from chardonnay (73 percent - one third fermented in new oak) and pinot noir; matured for 36 months on the lees and disgorged in March 1997. The perlage is lively, delicate and long lasting; the colour is a clear straw yellow; brioche, berry fruit and bay leaf on the bouquet; dry, fresh, attractive and refreshing on the palate.

The Bettoni Cazzago family have ancient links with the land. Both Count Carlo in the eighteenth century and Count Lodovico in the nineteenth were known to favour viticulture on their vast possessions. Their wines were drunk by Napoleon Bonaparte, Joseph II of Austria, Napoleon III and Giacomo Puccini, just to name a few. Today, Vincenzo Bettoni Cazzago has taken a degree in agricultural studies and is continuing the family tradition by making a range of interesting wines, including Franciacorta, at his eighteenth century villa at Cazzago San Martino. This year we tasted an excellent Brut: deep straw yellow with green reflections, full bouquet of ripe peaches and pears, vanilla, yeast and toastiness; well balanced with a good body, and long-finishing on the palate. The Franciacorta Tetellus '91 has a pale straw yellow colour, delicate perlage and a subtle bouquet of freshly baked bread, with hints of bay leaves and attractive vegetal touches. On the palate, despite the creaminess of the perlage the wine is a little thin and lacking in length. The Terre di Franciacorta Bianco Tetellus '96 was very satisfactory, with a sweet, buttery, tropical fruit bouquet, fruity palate and good depth of flavour.

O Oltrepò Pavese Extra Brut M. Classico	♟	4
● Oltrepò Pavese Pinot Nero Baloss '96		3
● Oltrepò Pavese Pinot Nero Brumano '93		4
O Oltrepò Pavese Pinot Nero in bianco Birbo '96		3
● Oltrepò Pavese Pinot Nero Brumano '92	♟♟	4
● Oltrepò Pavese Pinot Nero '94	♟	3

O Franciacorta Brut	♟♟	4
O Franciacorta Spumante Brut Tetellus '91	♟	4
O Terre di Franciacorta Bianco Tetellus '96	♟	3

CAZZAGO S. MARTINO (BS)   CAZZAGO S. MARTINO (BS)

CASTELFAGLIA
LOC. BOSCHI, 3
FRAZ. CALINO
25040 CAZZAGO S. MARTINO (BS)
TEL. 059/908828

GUARISCHI
VIA PAOLO VI, 62
FRAZ. CALINO
25040 CAZZAGO S. MARTINO (BS)
TEL. 030/7250838-775005

The name Cavicchioli has been synonymous with some of the best bubbles from Emilia for generations, but their CastelFaglia winery in the Franciacorta area of Lombardy has been worthy of note for several years now as well. With14 hectares of vineyards and a winery excavated out of the rock beneath the castle of Faglia at Calino, this winery produces carefully made, value for money, sparkling and still wines. This year, we particularly liked the Franciacorta Brut, an easy Two Glass award winner: bright pale straw yellow, delicate perlage, fine and full bouquet with hints of peaches and pears, vegetal and floral overtones; on the palate, elegant, well balanced, fruity and smooth, leaving the mouth refreshed and with an slight aftertaste of vanilla on the finish. Terre di Franciacorta Bianco Vigna del Castelletto '96 has a bright straw yellow colour and fruity bouquet with recognisable hints of peaches, apricots and vanilla; fresh and full on the palate, with a hint of vanilla on the finish. The Rosso Castelletto di Calino '95 is a medium weight red, well balanced and full of youthful berry fruit; soft and attractive, only slightly tannic; in other words, one of those reds that could also be served slightly chilled.

The Guarischi family make prestigious still wines and Franciacorta in the eighteenth century cellars of the aristocratic Maggi family, with grapes drawn from 43 hectares of vineyards. Gian Carlo Guarischi has successfully delegated the technical side of the business to oenologist Massimo Azzolini, who has assembled a wide range of well made wines. This year, we tasted an excellent Franciacorta Brut: bright pale straw yellow, lively and delicate perlage, creamy bubble; yeasty, toasted bread on the nose, hints of brioche; fruity, soft, and quite long on the palate. The Terre di Franciacorta Bianco '96 is a good, standard, fresh and fruity wine, while the barrique aged Chardonnay Le Solcaie succeeds thanks to its clear definition, softness and elegant complexity. The beautiful labels are the responsibility of Monica Guarischi, who looks after the commercial side of the company. Among the reds special mention should be made of Solcaie '94, still a bit hard and closed, but rich in extract, fruity on the nose, and full of notably fine grained tannins. Lastly, the Terre di Franciacorta Rosso '95 boasts an excellent ruby red colour, has a fresh and fruity bouquet, good weight and a successful dose of tannins, indicating good ageing potential.

O Franciacorta Brut	▼▼	4*
O Terre di Franciacorta Bianco Vigneti del Castelletto '96	▼	3
● Terre di Franciacorta Rosso Castello di Calino '95	▼	3
O Terre di Franciacorta Bianco Vigneti del Castelletto '94	♀♀	3*
O Franciacorta Brut	♀	4
O Terre di Franciacorta Bianco '95	♀	2
● Terre di Franciacorta Rosso '93	♀	2*
● Terre di Franciacorta Rosso Vigneti del Castelletto '93	♀	3*

O Franciacorta Brut	▼▼	4*
O Terre di Franciacorta Bianco Le Solcaie '95	▼▼	4
● Terre di Franciacorta Rosso Le Solcaie '94	▼▼	4
O Terre di Franciacorta Bianco '96	▼	3
● Terre di Franciacorta Rosso '95	▼	2*
O Franciacorta Bianco Le Solcaie '93	♀♀	3
O Franciacorta Brut Selezione '91	♀♀	5
● Franciacorta Rosso Le Solcaie '92	♀♀	3
● Franciacorta Rosso Le Solcaie '93	♀♀	3
O Franciacorta Brut	♀	4

CAZZAGO S. MARTINO (BS)   CELLATICA (BS)

MONTE ROSSA
VIA MARENZIO, 14
FRAZ. BORNATO
25040 CAZZAGO S. MARTINO (BS)
TEL. 030/725066

COOPERATIVA VITIVINICOLA
DI CELLATICA GUSSAGO
VIA CAPORALINO, 23/A - 25
25060 CELLATICA (BS)
TEL. 030/2522418

Paolo Rabotti and his wife Paola Rovetta have created one of the best wineries in Franciacorta. Their son, Emanuele, helps them on the production side in the winery and they have the assistance of consultant oenologist Cesare Ferrari. Franciacorta Cabochon '92, the prestige Riserva of the House, is one of the best ever tasted and misses the Three Glass award by a whisker. It is complex and multi-layered on the nose, with hints of honey and beeswax, vanilla and a delicate toastiness. The base wine has been wood aged and, typically enough, is soft, broad and smooth on the palate; all in all, an extremely elegant wine, but a little lean; just a touch more body and structure would have brought this into the very top class. Alongside this wine, one of the best Franciacorta Brut wines ever produced by Monte Rossa: complex, full bodied and fresh on the nose, followed by an elegant palate where the bubbles literally caress the taste buds before vanishing and leaving an attractive fruitiness on the finish. One of the best of its type, the Sec has a bouquet of ripe fruit and meadow flowers and has a clean softness to it. Once again, the Satèn is excellent, full of softness and attractively mature. Among the still wines, the Cèp '95 can be recommended: complex bouquet (pastry shop, bilberry, plums, mint, and toasted bread) and unusually rich extract for a Franciacorta red. Lastly, we tasted an excellent Terre di Franciacorta Bianco '96 and a Franciacorta Rosé that has some very good points, even if its colour is a bit anaemic.

In the tastings this year one of the highest marks of all, if not the very highest, for a non-vintage Brut went to a Franciacorta produced by this cooperative. Founded in the 1950s, the cooperative of Cellatica currently groups together about 115 members, representing a combined total vineyard area of more than 120 hectares, 40 of which are managed directly by the cooperative's staff. What is the secret of their success? Probably the same that lies behind the success of numerous other cooperatives in recent years: a new outlook on the part of the members and good technical management at the top. Local oenologist Corrado Cugnasco masterminds the wines: DOC Cellatica, DOC Terre di Franciacorta, DOCG Franciacorta, and the table wines. It is he who made the Brut, with its classic bright straw yellow colour and greenish reflections, its intense and delicate bouquet full of fruitiness, a twist of candied lemon peel, and hints of vanilla. Full bodied on the palate with fresh acidity; elegant with good extract; well balanced and notably long-finishing. In other words, this Brut is a marvel, and even more so considering its reasonable price. Alongside this wine, there is also a good Terre di Franciacorta Rosso '95 and a decent Bianco '96 from the same denomination. Not bad as an opening entry in the Guide!

○ Franciacorta Brut		🍷🍷	4*
○ Franciacorta Brut Cabochon '92		🍷🍷	5
○ Franciacorta Brut Satèn		🍷🍷	5
○ Franciacorta Sec		🍷🍷	4
● Terre di Franciacorta Rosso Cèp '95		🍷🍷	3*
⊙ Franciacorta Rosé		🍷	4
○ Terre di Franciacorta Bianco Ravellino '96		🍷	2
○ Franciacorta Brut Cabochon '90		🍷🍷	5
○ Franciacorta Brut Satèn		🍷🍷	5
○ Franciacorta Extra Brut '92		🍷🍷	5
○ Franciacorta Brut		🍷	4
⊙ Franciacorta Rosé Brut Cabochon '92		🍷	5

○ Franciacorta Brut		🍷🍷	4*
● Terre di Franciacorta Rosso '95		🍷	2*
○ Terre di Franciacorta Bianco '96			2

CENATE SOTTO (BG)

Monzio Compagnoni
Via degli Alpini, 3
24069 Cenate Sotto (BG)
tel. 030/9884157

CHIURO (SO)

Nino Negri
Via Ghibellini, 3
23030 Chiuro (SO)
tel. 0342/482521

As planned, Monzio Compagnoni have opened a new vinification and bottling plant at Nigoline di Corte Franca, in the Franciacorta area, whilst at the same time keeping the original premises at Cenate Sotto, near Bergamo, and the ageing cellars at Scanzorosciate in the Valcalepio. Scanzorosciate is also home to the moscato rosso that, after 40 days' "appassimento" on cane racks, goes into a rare and precious dessert wine called Don Quijote which is sold in specially made slender 0.375 litre bottles. While the '94 vintage produced a good bouquet and not much body, the '95 was a great success: brick red with shades of amber, intense and complex bouquet of roses, nutmeg, wild strawberries and dried grapes; sweet without being cloying on the palate; full flavoured and appealing with elegant undertones of chestnut flower honey, sage, plum jam and vanilla. Wines excused for their absence at the tasting were the new Rosso di Nero (100 percent pinot noir), the Rosso (cabernet sauvignon), and the Bianco di Luna (chardonnay), none of which are yet on the market. Two Colle della Luna wines are worth noting: the Bianco '96, made of chardonnay and pinot bianco, partially aged in barriques, aromas of tropical fruits, musk and lemon liqueur, with a faintly spicy undertone; the Rosso '95, made from cabernet sauvignon and merlot, once again partially aged in oak, has a bouquet of bitter cherry jam and is full bodied, correctly tannic, and finishes with a twist of liquorice and vegetal undergrowth. The Metodo Classico Brut is excellent, made from 100 percent chardonnay aged for 24 months on the lees during fermentation, it is soft, fresh, and fruity, with biscuits and Golden Delicious apples on the nose.

Oenologically speaking, the Valtellina has incredible potential, and if today it is gearing up to a general leap forward in quality it is partly thanks to the hundred-year old Nino Negri winery. Of course, behind the success of this winery there are the long term projects of one of the major players in Italian wine, Gruppo Italiano Vini, who in recent years have put their faith not only in the Valtellina as a zone, but also in the capabilities of Nino Negri's managing director, the oenologist Casimiro Maule. The result? Yet again, a richly deserved Three Glass award for the Sforzato 5 Stelle '95, a magnificent example of the marriage of hard work in the vineyards and wizardry in the cellars. On the nose, it is elegant and balsamic, with its high alcoholic content well integrated, and with new oak giving it hints of bay leaf and juniper berry. On the palate it is full bodied, lively, richly fruity, welcoming and long. Even the standard Sforzato '95 shows all the merits of an excellent vintage and its Two Glass rating seems a little mean. A welcome newcomer to the range, made to celebrate the centenary of the Nino Negri company, is the Valtellina 1897, a thoroughly modern wine based on the chiavennasca grape from the '95 vintage: partly barrel fermented this is a spicy wine with touches of sweetness and aromatic qualities, full bodied on the palate and smooth finishing. Never disappointing, Nino Negri Riserva '90 is perhaps a little thinner than the '89. True to type and stylistically faultless, the Sassella and the Inferno Botti d'Oro '94 are both very drinkable. The Fracia '94 is intriguing and delicate in its bouquet, fruity and full bodied on the palate, while the Ca' Brione '96, vinified off the skins, is a well knit wine with a good depth of flavour and original style.

● Moscato di Scanzo Passito Don Quijote '95	¶¶	6
○ Brut Classico Monzio Compagnoni '96	¶	5
○ Colle della Luna Bianco '96	¶	4
● Colle della Luna Rosso '95	¶	4
○ Bianco di Luna '90	¶¶	4
○ Bianco di Luna '93	¶¶	3
○ Colle della Luna Bianco '93	¶¶	4
● Rosso di Nero '93	¶¶	4
○ Colle della Luna Bianco '95	¶	4
● Rosso della Luna '93	¶	4

● Valtellina Sfursat 5 Stelle '95	¶¶¶	5
● Valtellina 1897 Centenario '95	¶¶	5
● Valtellina Sfursat '95	¶¶	4
● Valtellina Sup. Nino Negri Oro Ris. '90	¶¶	4
● Valtellina Sup. Fracia Nino Negri Oro '94	¶	3
● Valtellina Sup. Inferno Botti d'Oro '94	¶	3
● Valtellina Sup. Sassella Botti d'Oro '94	¶	3
○ Vigneto Ca' Brione Bianco '96	¶	4
● Valtellina Sfursat 5 Stelle '89	¶¶¶	5
● Valtellina Sfursat 5 Stelle '94	¶¶¶	5
● Valtellina Sfursat '94	¶¶	4

CHIURO (SO)

CASA VINICOLA NERA
VIA IV NOVEMBRE, 43
23030 CHIURO (SO)
TEL. 0342/482631

The general level of winemaking in the Valtellina is improving. This means that every year when we go to press with our Guide worthy winemakers we have not yet discovered batter on the doors of the editorial department to be included, despite the limited space permitted by the iron laws of page layouts. This year, logic and common sense told us to keep a column available for the Nera winery, who continue to make, let us be clear about it, a range of Riserva wines in a style and of a quality much in demand by the market. Ably directed by Piero Nera, one of the "doyens" of winemaking in the Valtellina, as he likes to describe himself, his company has played a leading role in the winemaking history of the valley. With about 35 hectares of company-owned vineyards, Nera makes a range of wines for all sectors of the market, from the wines tasted here to more commercial ones of decent quality. This year's tasting had to cope with difficult vintages. We found a perfectly correct Sforzato '93: old style, rich on the palate, hints of tar on the nose, a whisker away from Two Glass level. The Grumello Riserva '89 has typical nebbiolo style: delicate bouquet, full bodied, slight acidity on the finish. The two Riserva '90s, the Sassella and the Inferno, are well made and typical of local traditional style; both are fruity and well defined on the nose, smooth and broad on the palate.

●	Valtellina Sforzato '93	▼	5
●	Valtellina Sup. Grumello Ris. '89	▼	4
●	Valtellina Sup. Inferno Ris. '90	▼	4
●	Valtellina Sup. Sassella Ris. '90	▼	4
●	Valtellina Sup. Sassella Ris. '89	▽▽	4
●	Valtellina Sforzato '91	▽	4

CHIURO (SO)

ALDO RAINOLDI
VIA STELVIO, 128
23030 CHIURO (SO)
TEL. 0342/482225

The extension work on the Rainoldi winery has now been completed and, at least as far as the ageing cellars are concerned, has proved to be far sighted in concept as well as notable in the size of the investment involved. The size and number of the new French barriques lends prestige to the winery, and a well ventilated and cleverly designed area for the drying of Sforzato grapes is a significant addition. These improvements, together with the assured quality of fruit from regular, trusted suppliers, have helped to ensure the success of Rainoldi wines presented for tasting. This is true for the Ghibellino '95, a particularly perfumed and delicate barrel fermented white wine made from the chiavennasca grape: full bodied on the palate with good fruit and length of bouquet on the finish. Rainoldi has provided us with one of the best Sforzatos tasted this year: the '94 has hints of toastiness on the nose over a background of cocoa and spiciness; elegant with good structure on the palate combined with finely judged hints of sweetness; ready to drink now, but with obvious ageing potential as well. The Sassella '94 is well made with attractive spiciness and good balance; very fresh and drinkable on the palate. The Grumello '94 has a good cherry nose and is ready to drink now, but it is a little thin as a whole.

●	Valtellina Sforzato '94	▼▼	4
○	Chiavennasca Bianco Ghibellino '95	▼	4
●	Valtellina Superiore Sassella '94	▼	3
●	Valtellina Superiore Grumello '94		3
●	Valtellina Superiore Inferno Barrique Ris. '89	▽▽	5
●	Valtellina Superiore Inferno Barrique Ris. '90	▽▽	4
●	Valtellina Superiore Sassella '90	▽▽	4
●	Valtellina Sforzato '90	▽	4

COCCAGLIO (BS)

COCCAGLIO (BS)

TENUTA CASTELLINO
VIA S. PIETRO, 46
25030 COCCAGLIO (BS)
TEL. 030/7721015-7701240

LORENZO FACCOLI & FIGLI
VIA CAVA, 7
25030 COCCAGLIO (BS)
TEL. 030/7722761

The Bonomi family own about 14 hectares of beautiful vineyards sited in a natural bowl on the slopes of Mount Orfano. For years, Tenuta Castellino has been regarded as one of the best producers in the area, thanks to careful attention to detail at all stages in the production process. Moreover, the Bonomi family have a perfectly equipped winery and a very able technical team to ensure success. The staff includes an oenologist in charge of day-to-day production, Luigi Bersini; the agronomist Pierluigi Donna; and the guru of Franciacorta, technical consultant Cesare Ferrari. We anticipated good results in our tastings, and were particularly impressed with the style and drinkability of the two '93 Franciacortas. The Satèn version has a limpid, deep straw yellow colour and a complex and elegant nose based on ripe fruit and floral aromas ranging from yeasts to meadow flower honey; full bodied on the palate, well balanced, and successfully aged with a truly unusual smoky overtone to the nose. The Brut '93 is even better and ran dangerously close to getting our highest award: straw yellow with greenish reflections; intense bouquet that is fresh, clean and fruity, while being soft and complex at the same time; full bodied, well balanced, good structure with a long, aromatic finish. The Capineto '94 is a full bodied and fruity Bordeaux blend, with fine grained tannins, while the Terre di Franciacorta Rosso '95 is an easy-to-drink wine. Lastly, we found the Bianco '96 to be fresh, fruity and well balanced.

The Faccoli family have made a good Franciacorta and an interesting DOC white wine for years. The estate was founded in 1963 by Lorenzo Faccoli, but only began selling bottled wine in 1970. Their vineyards amount to little more than four hectares on moraine soil on the slopes of Mount Orfano, but they do guarantee a high level of quality in the production of about 40,000 bottles per year. The Faccoli family in the winery consists of Lorenzo, who looks after all stages of production, and his sons, Claudio and Gianmario. Claudio is also vice president of the Consorzio di Tutela del Franciacorta growers' association. The two Franciacortas put forward for tasting here were most encouraging and justify this tiny company's reputation for reliability. The Brut was particularly good: limpid, pale straw yellow with greenish reflections; creamy effervescence and fine perlage; soft, well developed bouquet, complex, slightly reticent but very attractive; full bodied, soft, very toasty on the palate with great elegance and good length. The Extra Brut is in the same mould, even if it seemed less full bodied to us: hints of musk, ferny undergrowth and truffles on the nose and attractively rounded on the palate. The Terre di Franciacorta '96 is correctly made and a pleasure to drink, but we think it could be improved on.

O Franciacorta Brut '93	YY	5
O Franciacorta Satèn '93	YY	5
● Capineto '94	Y	4
O Terre di Franciacorta Bianco '96	Y	3
● Terre di Franciacorta Rosso '95	Y	3
O Franciacorta Bianco '94	YY	3
O Franciacorta Bianco Solicano '93	YY	4
O Franciacorta Satèn '92	YY	4*
O Terre di Franciacorta Bianco Solicano '95	YY	3*
O Franciacorta Brut	Y	4
O Franciacorta Brut '90	Y	4
O Terre di Franciacorta Bianco '95	Y	2*
● Terre di Franciacorta Rosso '94		2

O Franciacorta Brut	YY	4*
O Franciacorta Extra Brut	YY	4
O Terre di Franciacorta Bianco '96	Y	2

CORTEFRANCA (BS)

CORTEFRANCA (BS)

BARONE PIZZINI PIOMARTA
VIA BRESCIA, 5
LOC. TIMOLINE
25050 CORTEFRANCA (BS)
TEL. 030/984136

F.LLI BERLUCCHI
VIA BROLETTO, 2
LOC. BORGONATO
25040 CORTEFRANCA (BS)
TEL. 030/984451-9828209

Giulio Pizzini Piomarta's winery was founded in 1870 and is one of the oldest in the area. Today, the estate boasts 15 hectares of vineyards on a sheltered slope in the Torbiere di Provaglio Nature Park. The vineyards have an average age of 15 years and the most recent are planted with a density of 4,500 vines per hectare. The winery has state of the art equipment and the recent modernisations in both the vineyards and the cellars have paid off with good results. In fact, the company makes a range of excellent wines, including the outstanding Franciacorta Extra Brut Bagnadore V. This '92 vintage wine has a limpid, pale straw yellow colour, an excellent perlage and an intense bouquet of yeast, toasted bread, ripe fruit, butter and hazelnuts; soft and elegant on the palate with well evolved flavours and full bodied, balanced structure. The Franciacorta Brut also deserves its high score for a clean, fresh nose, full of fruit and flowers, and for its depth of flavour. The two Terre di Franciacorta Bianco wines also stand out: the '96 for rich floral aromas and softness, depth and length on the palate; and the Pulcina '95 for the way in which hints of vanilla have blended into a full bodied palate with excellent length. The rest of the range consists of a good Franciacorta Extra Brut, which is perhaps past its best but drinkable enough and an interesting Terre di Franciacorta Rosso, which is full of vegetal aromas and rich extract.

Wines made by the Berlucchi brothers and sisters have done well in our tastings this year as well. Francesco, Gabriella, Marcello, Roberto and Pia Berlucchi follow the family tradition of winemaking, taking great care in the production of sparkling wines from 50 hectares of company-owned vineyards located in the moraine hills that shelter Borgonato. If not quite as inspired as last year's vintage, the Franciacorta '93 still stands out for its particularly fine perlage, and its soft bouquet of yeastiness and delicate nuances of toasted bread; full bodied on the palate, rich in fruit and acidity, a very enjoyable wine. The Terre di Franciacorta Bianco '96 has a limpid, pale straw yellow colour, a fresh and subtle bouquet and good acidity on the palate; unfortunately, it is a little thin, but the fruitiness comes round on the nose at the end and the finish is clean. The Terre di Franciacorta Bianco Dossi delle Querce '95 is satisfactory enough, but is dominated by the wood and seems too old for its real age. Of the reds we liked the correct and enjoyable Terre di Franciacorta '95, with its good fruit and slim structure, but found the cru Dossi delle Querce '93 less interesting.

○ Franciacorta Brut	♉♉	4
○ Franciacorta Extra Brut Bagnadore V '92	♉♉	5
○ Terre di Franciacorta Bianco '96	♉♉	3*
○ Terre di Franciacorta Bianco Pulcina '95	♉♉	3*
○ Franciacorta Extra Brut	♉	4
● Terre di Franciacorta Rosso '95	♉	3

○ Franciacorta Brut '93	♉♉	4
○ Terre di Franciacorta Bianco '96	♉	3
○ Terre di Franciacorta Bianco Dossi delle Querce '95	♉	4
● Terre di Franciacorta Rosso '95	♉	2
● Terre di Franciacorta Rosso Dossi delle Querce '93		4
○ Franciacorta Brut '92	♉♉	4*
◉ Franciacorta Rosé '92	♉♉	4

CORTEFRANCA (BS)

GUIDO BERLUCCHI & C.
P.ZZA DURANTI,4
LOC. BORGONATO
25040 CORTEFRANCA (BS)
TEL. 030/984381-984293

Berlucchi is one of the famous names in winemaking and was the founder of the Metodo Classico sparkling wine industry in Italy. Before Guido Berlucchi, Franco Ziliani and Giorgio Lanciani decided to make sparkling wines in the castle of Borgonato in 1961, Franciacorta was more famous for the beauty of its villas and its countryside than for its wine, let alone a prestigious sparkling wine. Today the company produces millions of bottles which are sold all over the world. Berlucchi does not, however, make DOC or DOCG wines, since the base wines are bought in from appropriate areas outside the Franciacorta denomination zone. For some years, though, a subsidiary winery called Antica Cantina Fratta has made sparkling wines exclusively from grapes from its own vineyards, situated at Monticelli Brusate, including an excellent Terre di Franciacorta Bianco and a good Franciacorta Brut. We re-tasted the '92 this year and found it to be extremely elegant and obviously capable of acquiring greater complexity with further ageing. The Terre '96 is fresh, fruity, well balanced and full bodied, with attractive hints of vanilla on the palate. Of the Berlucchi wines, our favourite was an excellent cuvée special, the Cellarius, which has a soft yeastiness on the nose, and is fresh, delicate and fruity on the palate. The other Berlucchi wines are all good quality, particularly the soft, fruity Max Rosé.

CORTEFRANCA (BS)

MONZIO COMPAGNONI
C.DA MONTI DELLA CORTE
FRAZ. NIGOLINE
25040 CORTEFRANCA (BS)
TEL. 030/9884157

Marcello Monzio Compagnoni has made excellent wines in the Valcalepio part of the province of Bergamo for years. In addition, since the '95 vintage, he has rented a beautiful Franciacorta property from Baron Monti della Corte at Nigoline di Cortefranca. Having modernised the estate he now makes something like 100,000 bottles a year of excellent DOC and DOCG Franciacorta wines with the technical assistance of oenologist Alberto Musatti and agronomist Fabrizio Zardini. The Brut has a bright straw yellow colour and a fine perlage; fresh on the nose with hints of mint and sage and elegant touches of toasted bread; soft, creamy vanilla on the palate with good length. The Terre di Franciacorta Bianco Ronco della Seta is one of the best of its type from this vintage: deep straw yellow with elegant greenish reflections; intense bouquet, full and fruity with hints of apples; fresh and full bodied on the palate, which has been enriched by a brief spell in new oak barrels. The Rosso DOC '95 and the Ronco della Seta from the same vintage are both correctly made and drinking well.

○ Cellarius Brut Ris.	♈♈	5
○ Terre di Franciacorta Bianco		
Antiche Cantine Fratta '96	♈♈	3*
○ Cuvée Imperiale Brut '93	♈	5
○ Cuvée Imperiale Brut Extreme	♈	4
⊙ Cuvée Imperiale Max Rosé	♈	4
○ Bianco Imperiale		3
○ Cuvée Imperiale Brut		4
○ Franciacorta Brut		
Antiche Cantine Fratta '92	♉♉	4*
○ Terre di Franciacorta Bianco		
Antiche Cantine Fratta '95	♈	3

○ Franciacorta Brut	♈♈	4
○ Terre di Franciacorta Bianco		
Ronco della Seta '95	♈♈	3*
● Terre di Franciacorta Rosso		
Ronco della Seta '95	♈	3

CORVINO S. QUIRICO (PV)   DESENZANO DEL GARDA (BS)

TENUTA MAZZOLINO
VIA MAZZOLINO, 26
27050 CORVINO S. QUIRICO (PV)
TEL. 0383/876122

VISCONTI
VIA C. BATTISTI, 139
25015 DESENZANO DEL GARDA (BS)
TEL. 030/9120681

As we said in the 1997 edition of this Guide, the elements for making good wine are all in place: 14 hectares of well-run vineyards cultivated without the use of chemical fertilizers and with pest sprays kept to the minimum, and a well-equipped winery as well. The potential is there but, as we said then, it has only partially been realised. Take as an example the Noir Pinot Nero '93: this has been made from ripe grapes picked at a low yield per hectare; maturation was in French oak barriques (Allier, Tronçais, and Nevers) for one year followed by a year in the bottle before release. This should be a wine with a high quality to match its high price. Instead it is only "satisfactory": the colour is garnet red, but a shade too pale; the bouquet has the typical redcurrants, raspberries and spice of the variety; enjoyable, full-flavoured, and well balanced on the palate with a vegetal background and liquorice and almonds to finish; clean, but not as long finishing as one of Mazzolino's top wines should be. We awarded it One Glass and hope for better in years to come, or at least a return to the level of the Noir '90 again. Of the other wines we tasted, we liked the Camarà Riesling Italico '96 with its lime tree, camomile and apple bouquet. The Brut Classico '90 can be recommended: made from pinot noir, it has matured nicely and has a well defined nose of toasted hazelnuts.

This winery began operations in the area at the beginning of the century and still today selects and buys grapes from local growers which it then vinifies in its own cellars. The resulting wines are quality-orientated products which are sold at extremely reasonable prices. Once again this year we particularly liked the good structure and fresh fruit flavours of the Lugana S.Onorata, made from grapes from the vineyard of the same name. The wine has a fresh, fruity bouquet with ripe grape aromas; good weight on the palate, but not as impressive for intensity of flavour or as aromatic as last year's vintage. The Black Label Lugana Ramoso '96 is also good: clean and fruity on the nose, soft and full bodied, almost unctuous in its fruitiness, satisfactory length. The standard Lugana, the Colle Lungo cuvée, is well made, clean, fresh and attractively drinkable. The Lugana Brut Metodo Classico has been well made and is a wine of some distinction: yeast and toasted bread aromas on the nose, fruity on the palate with a fine perlage. It is also worth mentioning that all these products are good value for money.

● Oltrepò Pavese Pinot Nero Noir '93	♥	6
○ Oltrepò Pavese Brut Classico Mazzolino '90		4
○ Oltrepò Pavese Riesling Italico Camarà '96		3
● Oltrepò Pavese Pinot Nero Noir '90	♥♥	6
● Corvino '94	♥	4
● Oltrepò Pavese Barbera '95	♥	3
● Oltrepò Pavese Bonarda '95	♥	3
● Oltrepò Pavese Pinot Nero '91	♥	4
● Oltrepò Pavese Rosso Terrazze '95	♥	3

○ Lugana Brut M. Cl.	♥	3*
○ Lugana Ramoso '96	♥	2*
○ Lugana S. Onorata '96	♥	3*
○ Lugana Collo Lungo '96		2
○ Lugana S. Onorata '95	♥♥	3
○ Lugana Brut M. Cl.	♥	3
○ Lugana Ramoso '95	♥	2

ERBUSCO (BS)

ERBUSCO (BS)

BELLAVISTA
VIA BELLAVISTA, 5
25030 ERBUSCO (BS)
TEL. 030/7760276

★ CA' DEL BOSCO
VIA CASE SPARSE, 20
25030 ERBUSCO (BS)
TEL. 030/7760600

Vittorio Moretti and Mattia Vezzola have created one of the most reputable wineries in Italy, let alone Franciacorta. Year after year Bellavista produces wines of the highest quality, not just at prestige level, but throughout their wide range of Franciacorta and other wines. Not one of the wines we tasted this year was awarded less than Two Glasses, which is something that very few other companies can claim. First in line is the Franciacorta Gran Cuvée Brut '93: limpid, pale straw yellow with green reflections, a most delicate perlage; cedar wood, grapefruit and meadow flowers on the nose; creamy sparkle on the tongue; good depth of flavour with hints of vanilla and ripe fruit; good length. The Gran Cuvée Satèn is a lighter wine in structure and much softer: fruity, complex, richly flavoured and well balanced; attractive hints of vanilla and boiled sweets on the finish. The Franciacorta Brut has a bouquet of ripe fruit and yeast and is attractively fresh and long. The rest of the range comprises very successful wines such as: the Bianco del Convento dell'Annunziata '94, one of the most interesting whites made in Franciacorta; the exemplary chardonnay-based Uccellanda; Terre di Franciacorta Bianco, one of the best white DOCs of the year; and, lastly, one of the best vintages ever made of the red Solesine, a spicy Bordeaux blend with fine grained tannins, named after its vineyard of origin.

Maurizio Zanella created Ca' del Bosco to make a dream come true, and in doing so he created a legend in the wine world. Incredibly enough, it all started with the little vineyard behind the villa where his family came for their weekends in the country. Enormous effort and enthusiasm has gone into this enterprise; that much is clear just from tasting the Cuvée Annamaria Clementi '90, a Three Glass award winner this year and the thirteenth such award in Maurizio's career. The colour is a limpid, deep straw yellow; the bouquet opens out in a wide spread of aromas that are fresh and complex at the same time; full bodied and fruity on the palate with a magical balance of acidity, velvety structure, creaminess on the tongue, and hints of vanilla; very long finishing. A quite exceptional wine. None of the rest of the range will disappoint, either. We are still waiting for the Franciacorta Dosage Zéro and the Brut '93 to finish ageing, but we did manage to taste a fragrant Franciacorta Brut, a soft and complex Franciacorta Satèn '92 that got one of our top scores, and the deeply coloured Rosé '93, full of cassis and raspberries, which is probably the best in its category in the zone. Going on to the still wines, we found the world class Terre di Franciacorta Chardonnay '95 to be just that fraction less successful than the superb '93, but the '94 vintage Pinèro is one of the best ever. The attractive sauvignon-based Elfo 6 has good varietal character, and both the Terre di Franciacorta Bianco '96 and the Rosso '95 are amongst the best we have tasted this year.

Wine	Glasses	Score
○ Franciacorta Gran Cuvée Brut '93	▼▼▼	5
○ Bianco del Convento dell'Annunciata '94	▼▼	4
○ Franciacorta Brut	▼▼	5
○ Franciacorta Gran Cuvée Satèn	▼▼	5
● Solesine '94	▼▼	5
○ Terre di Franciacorta Bianco '96	▼▼	5
○ Uccellanda '94	▼▼	5
○ Franciacorta Extra Brut Vittorio Moretti Ris. '88	▽▽▽	6
○ Franciacorta Gran Cuvée Pas Operé '91	▽▽▽	5
● Casotte '93	▽▽	5
☉ Franciacorta Gran Cuvée Rosé '92	▽▽	5
● Solesine '93	▽▽	5

Wine	Glasses	Score
○ Franciacorta Cuvée Annamaria Clementi '90	▼▼▼	6
○ Elfo 6 '96	▼▼	4
○ Franciacorta Brut	▼▼	4*
☉ Franciacorta Brut Rosé '93	▼▼	5
○ Franciacorta Satèn '92	▼▼	6
● Pinèro '94	▼▼	6
○ Terre di Franciacorta Bianco '96	▼▼	4
○ Terre di Franciacorta Chardonnay '95	▼▼	6
● Terre di Franciacorta Rosso '95	▼▼	4
○ Franciacorta Chardonnay '93	▽▽▽	6
○ Franciacorta Cuvée Annamaria Clementi '89	▽▽▽	6
○ Franciacorta Dosage Zéro '92	▽▽▽	5

ERBUSCO (BS)

ERBUSCO (BS)

CAVALLERI
VIA PROVINCIALE, 96
25030 ERBUSCO (BS)
TEL. 030/7760217

FERGHETTINA
VIA CASE SPARSE, 4
25030 ERBUSCO (BS)
TEL. 030/7268308

Cavalleri is one of the best known and most important companies in Franciacorta and in the last decade it has won much acclaim for some outstanding wines. We are of the opinion, however, that quality has been somewhat variable in the last two or three vintages, especially with the still wines. The red Tajardino, for example, has not regained the memorable elegance and intensity of the '88 vintage. We tasted the '94 this year and found a confused nose on a light wine with raw tannins. The Merlot Corniole makes its debut on the market this year and great things are expected from it. The Terre di Franciacorta Rosso '95 is correctly made and a pleasure to drink. Overall the whites showed better. The Chardonnay Rampaneto '96 is an elegant wine with good structure, fruit, and varietal character. The sparkling wines include an excellent Pas Dosé '92: a fine perlage, elegant and well evolved mineral aromas on the nose, creamy on the tongue, soft and fresh on the palate. The Franciacorta Satèn is soft and well rounded, but the nose is not the cleanest and the vanilla is a bit over dominant; the palate is well balanced and the body slim and moderately elegant. The Brut Blanc de Blancs is a good wine and almost gets Two Glasses: lactic aromas with vanilla on the nose; light, fresh with an subtle, attractively bitter twist to the finish.

Roberto Gatti manages one of the best wineries in Franciacorta with great skill. We say that not only because of the encouraging results of this year's tastings, but also because our visit to the Ferghettina cellars gave us a good idea of how much effort this amiable vigneron puts into his work. For two or three years now Roberto has been making extremely interesting experimental wines, using a mixture of indigenous and international grapes from his vineyards in Adro, Erbusco and Cortefranca. The results of this work will become apparent in the next few years; barrel tastings conducted so far suggest great things to come. In the meantime, Ferghettina makes an excellent Franciacorta Brut: straw yellow with bright greenish reflections; inviting vanilla and spice bouquet with hints of fresh fruit and flowers; fresh and well balanced palate although we thought previous vintages of this wine had more substantial body. The Terre di Franciacorta Rosso '95 just misses a Two Glass award: deep ruby red colour, full bouquet of raspberries and blackcurrants; subtly tannic on the palate and very drinkable. The Terre di Franciacorta Bianco '96 is good, but not as full bodied and sharply defined as in the previous vintage. The Chardonnay-based Favento makes its debut with the '96 vintage: good fruit and structure, but lacking in freshness on this first attempt.

○ Franciacorta Nondosato '92	♀♀	5
○ Terre di Franciacorta Bianco Rampaneto '96	♀♀	3*
● Corniole '94	♀	4
○ Franciacorta Brut Blanc de Blancs	♀	4
○ Franciacorta Satèn	♀	4
○ Terre di Franciacorta Bianco '96	♀	3
● Terre di Franciacorta Rosso '95	♀	3
● Tajardino '94		4
○ Franciacorta Collezione '91	♀♀	5
○ Franciacorta Satèn	♀♀	5
○ Franciacorta Brut	♀	4
⊙ Franciacorta Collezione Rosé '92	♀	5
○ Franciacorta Pas Dosé	♀	4

○ Franciacorta Brut	♀♀	4*
○ Terre di Franciacorta Bianco '96	♀	2
○ Terre di Franciacorta Chardonnay Favento '96	♀	3
● Terre di Franciacorta Rosso '95	♀	2*
○ Franciacorta Brut	♀♀	4*
○ Terre di Franciacorta Bianco '95	♀♀	2*

ERBUSCO (BS)

ERBUSCO (BS)

ENRICO GATTI
VIA METELLI, 9
25030 ERBUSCO (BS)
TEL. 030/7267999

PRINCIPE BANFI
VIA ISEO, 20
25030 ERBUSCO (BS)
TEL. 030/7750387

Four out of the four Gatti wines we tasted were awarded well deserved Two Glasses, and one of these, the Gatti Rosso '95, very nearly got three. These are better results than many of the prestigious, historic estates of the Franciacorta obtained and prove that enthusiasm, dedication and skill are just as important as size and tradition, if not more so. Lorenzo Gatti and his brother-in-law, Enzo Balzarini, produce about 60,000 bottles per year. As we were saying, the Gatti Rosso is currently the most outstanding of their wines. Made from cabernet sauvignon and merlot and aged in French oak barriques, the wine has an opaque ruby red colour with violet reflections and has an intense, complex nose with aromas of raspberries and blackcurrants, vanilla and subtle suggestions of brioche. It is ample on the palate, rich in fruit, and full of fine grained tannins. Similar character can be found in the Terre di Franciacorta Rosso, also from the '95 vintage, which has a marked cabernet presence on the nose, together with blackberries, vanilla, printer's ink, mint and quinine; full bodied, well balanced, rich in fruit and depth of flavour. The Terre Bianco '96 has an elegant, well balanced nose with hints of apples, pears and grapefruit peel and is full flavoured and long on the palate. Last but not least, we tasted an excellent Franciacorta which was soft and fruity both on the nose and on the palate, where hints of vanilla and flowers come back in the finish after a creamy sparkle on the tongue that is really "comme il faut".

The Principe Banfi family bought Pope Pius IX's former hunting lodge and its beautiful estate in 1970. Surrounded by vineyards at the top of a hill on the estate proper, the old vinification facilities have been put back in order and the ageing cellars for sparkling Franciacorta and the still wines have been dug out below. Proof of Alfredo and Roberto Principe's dedication comes with the Two Glass award for no fewer than three of the wines presented for tasting this year. The Franciacorta Brut has a deep straw yellow colour, a fine perlage and a most attractive nose of apples and pears with hints of sage, talcum powder, and freshly mown grass; fresh, soft and fruity on the palate with an elegant hint of vanilla on the finish. We particularly liked the Chardonnay Vigna Pio IX '96 for its floral, fruity bouquet, and for its well rounded balance on the palate. The Terre Bianco from the same vintage showed much the same characteristics, but is slightly more delicate in structure, although attractively fresh and aromatic. The DOC Rosso '95 is very good, but we were not impressed with the Franciacorta Extra Brut which seemed a bit too lean and should have been fresher; however, coming from a former papal estate, we can consider this transgression merely venial.

○ Franciacorta Brut	♟♟	4*
● Gatti Rosso '95	♟♟	4
○ Terre di Franciacorta Bianco '96	♟♟	2*
● Terre di Franciacorta Rosso '95	♟♟	2*
○ Franciacorta Bianco '94	♟♟	2*
● Gatti Rosso '91	♟♟	4
○ Terre di Franciacorta Bianco '95	♟♟	2*
○ Franciacorta Brut	♟	4
● Gatti Rosso '93	♟	4
● Terre di Franciacorta Rosso '94	♟	2

○ Franciacorta Brut	♟♟	5
○ Terre di Franciacorta Bianco '96	♟♟	3*
○ Terre di Franciacorta Chardonnay Pio IX '96	♟♟	4
● Terre di Franciacorta Rosso '95	♟	3
○ Franciacorta Extra Brut	♟♟	4
○ Franciacorta Bianco '94	♟	2
● Franciacorta Rosso '92	♟	2
● Franciacorta Rosso '93	♟	2*

ERBUSCO (BS)

UBERTI
VIA E. FERMI, 2
25030 ERBUSCO (BS)
TEL. 030/7267476

This winery is on a sharp upward curve. Yet again, Agostino and Eleonora Uberti, with technical assistance from Cesare Ferrari, have presented us with an excellent range of wines. The Uberti family have made wine for generations and the secret of their success lies in their meticulous attention to detail, which means amongst other things, vineyards that look more like a garden and scrupulously run cellars. This explains how little masterpieces like the latest cuvée of Magnificentia come about. This Blanc de Blancs Franciacorta filled even the most sceptical tasters with enthusiasm when we tried it: limpid, deep straw yellow with green reflections and a very fine perlage; complex and intriguing bouquet (typical Uberti style) of russet apples, pears and peaches with hints of yeast, vanilla and sage; fresh and fruity with rich extract on the palate; soft, elegant and very long finishing. The Franciacorta Comarì del Salem has big structure with both yeast and wood toastiness on the nose; very youthful on the palate. Balance and freshness, fruit and softness are the order of the day for the other cuvées and for the still wines. We particularly liked the Maria dei Medici and Frati Priori white wines, both from the '95 vintage, the cuvée Francesco I Extra Brut (the fruit is excellent), the Terre di Franciacorta Rosso '94 and the Frati Priori '94.

GAVARDO (BS)

TREVISANI
VIA GALUZZO, 2
LOC. SOPRAZOCCO
25085 GAVARDO (BS)
TEL. 0365/32825

The brothers Giampietro and Mauro Trevisani are back in the Guide with wines from their beautiful estate near Lake Garda. Their vineyards benefit from an excellent microclimate and lie at an altitude of 370 metres above sea level. Thanks to the influence of the lake close by, daytime temperatures are always moderate and never too cold even in winter, while at night cold air currents from the Sabbia valley mean that temperatures drop considerably; such variations help the grapes to keep their crisp, aromatic qualities. This year we tasted a good barrique aged Cabernet, the Due Querce '94, which impressed us with its intensity, the quality of its berry fruit nose, and the hints of vanilla and spices on the bouquet; soft, full bodied and ample on the palate; as good as the best examples from previous vintages. The other Cabernet from this estate, the Suèr '95, is less of a show wine, but just as well made and enjoyable. The Rosso del Benaco '94 is made from traditional local grapes and has a certain rustic charm on the nose, which gives it an attractive easy drinking quality, especially with food - either poultry or steak would be a good match. The Chardonnay Balì (the name for a local wind) '96 gets our approval: attractively soft with an intense bouquet of fresh fruit and meadow flowers; the softness of the extract is balanced by juicy acidity, fruit and good length.

○ Franciacorta Magnificentia	▼▼▼	5*
○ Franciacorta Brut Comarì del Salem '91	▼▼	5
○ Franciacorta Francesco I Extra Brut	▼▼	4
○ Terre di Franciacorta Bianco dei Frati Priori '95	▼▼	4
○ Terre di Franciacorta Bianco Maria dei Medici '95	▼▼	4
● Terre di Franciacorta Rosso '94	▼▼	2*
● Terre di Franciacorta Rosso dei Frati Priori '94	▼▼	4
○ Franciacorta Francesco I Brut	▼	4
○ Terre di Franciacorta Bianco '96	▼	2
○ Franciacorta Magnificentia	♈♈♈	5

● Due Querce '94	▼▼	4
○ Chardonnay Balì '96	▼	3
● Rosso del Benaco '94	▼	4
● Suèr '95		3
● Due Querce '93	♈♈	4
● Suèr '93	♈♈	3
○ Chardonnay Balì '95	♈	3

GODIASCO (PV)

CABANON
LOC. CABANON
27052 GODIASCO (PV)
TEL. 0383/940912

The Mercandelli family's Godiasco estate breaks the 80-point barrier with the Cabanon Blanc '96 Opera Prima, made from100 percent sauvignon grown on sparse limestone soil at 300 metres above sea level. The wine has a limpid golden colour with a sharply defined nose of lychees combined with hints of fig leaves; full flavoured, soft, fresh and lively at the same time, it has a long aromatic finish. As far as the Riesling Renano '96 is concerned, only its youthful, slightly bitter flavours (they will pass with time) keep it from reaching the same level as the Sauvignon. Nonetheless, this is an important wine: golden colour with intense greenish reflections; wood, roses and flint on the nose; dry, full flavoured and fruity on the palate. The Chardonnay '96 gets One Glass for its varietal character and comes in one of those modish cobalt blue bottles. Primula '96 is a sparkling white wine made from chardonnay and riesling that has some natural sediment left from the action of the yeasts in a continuing bottle fermentation; after our initial surprise at finding this residue we judged the wine to be satisfactory enough, with good character. The Bonarda '96 also has a slight re-fermentation in bottle and is full bodied and fragrant.

○	Opera Prima Cabanon Blanc '96	▼▼	4
○	Oltrepò Chardonnay '96	▼	4
○	Oltrepò Pavese Riesling Renano '96	▼	4
●	Oltrepò Pavese Bonarda vivace '96		3
○	Oltrepò Pavese Pinot Grigio '96		3
●	Oltrepò Pavese Bonarda Ris. '91	▽▽	4
●	Oltrepò Pavese Rosso Infernot Ris. '91	▽▽	5
●	Oltrepò Pavese Bonarda Vigna Vecchia '93	▽	4
●	Oltrepò Pavese Bonarda vivace '95	▽	3

GRUMELLO DEL MONTE (BG)

CARLOZADRA
VIA GANDOSSI, 13
24064 GRUMELLO DEL MONTE (BG)
TEL. 035/832066-830244

With forty years' experience in making sparkling wines, oenologist Carlo Zadra moved from the Trentino to the hills of Bergamo to create this outstanding Gran Riserva '87. Made from pinot noir drawn from an old gravel soil vineyard at Rovere della Luna, the base wine was aged for 16 months in barriques before Metodo Classico bottle fermentation began in March 1989; disgorgement was on 9th October 1996 and topping-up was completed without a "liqueur d'expedition". The result is a particularly complex wine on the nose (vanilla, biscuits, incense, butter, and blackcurrants) with a rich, mature palate that still retains its freshness. The strain of yeasts that was used for the '86 vintage has been changed for this well deserved Two Glass wine. The Brut Millesimato '93 (disgorged January 1997) is also very good and combines the fruitiness of pinot noir with the floral aromas of chardonnay and pinot bianco. More controversial is the Extra Dry Tradizionale '90, which is pleasant enough, but could be fruitier and softer, as might be expected from something less dry than a Brut. The Donna Nunzia '96 is a highly perfumed dry moscato giallo wine made in tiny quantities of just 2,500 bottles; it is a great success. Lastly, the Don Lodovico is an attractive, 100 percent pinot noir with good varietal character, from vineyards lying between Trento and Bolzano.

○	Carlozadra Classico Brut '93	▼▼	5
○	Carlozadra Classico Gran Riserva '87	▼▼	6
○	Carlozadra Classico Extra Dry Tradizione '90	▼	5
●	Don Ludovico Pinot Nero '95	▼	4
○	Donna Nunzia Moscato Giallo '96	▼	3
○	Carlozadra Classico Brut '92	▽▽	4
○	Carlozadra Classico Brut Nondosato '91	▽▽	4
○	Carlozadra Classico Extra Dry Tradizione '89	▽▽	4
○	Carlozadra Classico Gran Riserva '86	▽▽	5
●	Don Ludovico Pinot Nero '93	▽▽	4

GRUMELLO DEL MONTE (BG)

TENUTA CASTELLO
VIA CASTELLO, 15
24064 GRUMELLO DEL MONTE (BG)
TEL. 035/830244-4420817

The big news from the Tenuta Castello, the 37-hectare estate owned by the Reschigna-Kettliz, with 20 hectares of vineyards, is the '94 vintage of a rare red dessert wine. The Valcalepio Moscato Passito DOC from Grumello del Monte is made from the moscato di Scanzo grape and has a garnet colour with mahogany tinges; the bouquet is rich and all-enveloping with burnt apple and dried fruit aromas (raisins and figs) mingled with hints of chocolate. Sweet and tangy on the palate, it has evident tannin and acidity and firm underlying flavours of jam and cinnamon. Presented in half litre bottles, this is an excellent wine that has already reached its peak on the nose, but needs to acquire greater balance on the palate. The Colle del Calvario Rosso '93 is a Bordeaux blend that has been partly aged in barrique. It is a good wine with better structure than the '92 vintage we tasted last year: deep garnet colour with a full bouquet of vanilla, straw and blackberries; austere on the palate with good concentration of flavours (liquorice and ferny undergrowth); attractively full bodied but lacking a little in elegance. Of the whites, the Aurito '95, a barrique aged Chardonnay della Bergamasca, stands out: intensely spicy with good varietal character and a youthful bitter twist. The two Valcalepio wines are worth a mention; the Bianco '96 is floral and slightly fruity; the Rosso '95 is fragrant and vinous with an attractive underlay of freshly cut grass and bitter cherries.

○ Chardonnay della Bergamasca Aurito '95	🍷	4
● Valcalepio Moscato Passito '94	🍷	6
● Valcalepio Rosso Colle del Calvario '93	🍷	4
○ Valcalepio Bianco '96		3
● Valcalepio Rosso '95		3
○ Aurito '92	🍷🍷 (outline)	4
● Valcalepio Rosso Colle del Calvario '90	🍷🍷 (outline)	4
○ Chardonnay della Bergamasca Aurito '94	🍷 (outline)	4

MONTALTO PAVESE (PV)

DORIA
CASA TACCONI, 3
27040 MONTALTO PAVESE (PV)
TEL. 0383/870143

There is very little wrong with this year's Doria wines, despite the fact that they do not score as highly as in the '97 Guide. It is not always possible to do better than last time; the important thing is to concentrate on putting quality first. The Doria family's commitment is not in doubt; viticulture is carried out in collaboration with the University of Milan, and winemaking is overseen by the oenologist Beppe Bassi. This year the best Doria wine is the Pinot Nero Querciolo '95: aged for one year in Allier and Nevers barriques, the colour is a limpid garnet red and the bouquet is an intense mixture of blackcurrant and raspberry jam with hints of vanilla and dried violets; full bodied on the palate, ample, soft and elegant with a clear underlay of fruit liqueur and game; very long finishing. The other Querciolo '95 is a pinot noir vinified off the skins. This white wine, that has also been aged in oak, is awarded the same One Glass rating as last year. One Glass also for Le Briglie '96, another "blanc de noir", but this time without the oak ageing; it has a subtle but fragrant bouquet of ripe apples and bananas. The Ronco Bianco Vigna Tesi '95 is a Rhine riesling half vinified with cold maceration, half in small oak barrels; it does not have the richness of the '94, but it is an enjoyable wine all the same and has good varietal character, body and length. The Ronco Rosso Vigna Siura '94 (barbera, croatina and uva rara) has a good jammy nose of plums and blackberries and a dry, elegant taste; the '93 was, however, richer and more complex.

● Oltrepò Pavese Pinot Nero Querciolo '95	🍷🍷	5
○ Oltrepò Pavese Pinot Nero in bianco Le Briglie '96	🍷	4
○ Oltrepò Pavese Riesling Renano Roncobianco Vigna Tesi '95	🍷	4
● Oltrepò Pavese Rosso Roncorosso Vigna Siura '94	🍷	4
● Oltrepò Pavese Pinot Nero Querciolo '91	🍷🍷 (outline)	5
● Oltrepò Pavese Pinot Nero Querciolo '93	🍷🍷 (outline)	5
○ Oltrepò Pavese Riesling Renano Roncobianco Vigna Tesi '94	🍷🍷 (outline)	4

MONTECALVO VERSIGGIA (PV)

CASA RE

FRAZ. CASA RE
27047 MONTECALVO VERSIGGIA (PV)
TEL. 0383/99986

The Casa Re estate is new as a full column entry in the Guide. Owned by the Casati family from Monza since 1981, the property includes 20 hectares of vineyards in the heart of the Versa Valley cultivated according to EC Regulation 2078, which imposes amongst other things, the use of natural fertiliser and the reduction of pest control treatment to the minimum. Density of planting is 4,000 vines per hectare and yields are low. The vines are trained on the Guyot and cordone speronato (a spur pruned cordon) systems on limestone and marl soil in well-sited vineyards. The cellars are modern and technical assistance comes from the oenologist Donato Lanati. The whites did well this year. We start with the Riesling '96 from the Il Fossone vineyard, made of riesling italico with small amounts of Rhine riesling: fresh, zingy and fruity with the attractive benzine aromas so often found in riesling. The Chardonnay della Valle Versa '94 is still very young: bright golden colour, distinct muskiness on the nose mixed with sage and bay leaf and mingled with hints of honey and honeysuckle which emerge in the finish; full bodied, soft and broad with a long ripe apple finish. Lastly, the Pinot Nero Brut made according to the "metodo italiano lungo", a slow vat fermentation system, is worth a look. This is a wine with a lively sparkle, delicate, tight perlage and good bouquet of yeast and berry fruit. It is dry on the palate and clean finishing with underlying hints of biscuits and ripe fruit.

O	Oltrepò Pavese Riesling Italico Podere Fossone '96	🍷	3
O	Valle Versa Chardonnay '94	🍷	4
O	Oltrepò Pavese Brut '95		4

MONTICELLI BRUSATI (BS)

CASTELVEDER

VIA BELVEDERE, 4
25040 MONTICELLI BRUSATI (BS)
TEL. 030/652308

Renato Alberti runs a wonderful estate with the resources of more than 11 hectares of vineyards at his disposal. The vineyards, half of which are actually owned by Castelveder, are planted on limestone soil and favourably sited on Monte Madonna della Rosa at Monticelli Brusati, next to the remains of a mediaeval castle. The cool cellars where the still wines and the Franciacorta are made are dug out of the white limestone of the mountain. While waiting for a vintage Brut as good as the '92 we tasted last year, we had to "make do with" the standard, non-vintage cuvée, which in fact turned out to be one of the best we tasted this year. Renato and his consultant oenologist, Teresio Schiavi, have made a Brut with a pale, limpid straw yellow colour and a nose of freshly baked bread, yeast and flowers. The palate is very clean and has a sparkle with good creamy consistency, an easy-drinking freshness, and good fruit. We did not think the Extra Brut was as interesting; it is so lean that it lacks the fruit which makes this style such a pleasure to drink. The Terre di Franciacorta Bianco '96 is fresh, fruity and well made, as usual; like all the Castelveder wines it is also good value for money.

O	Franciacorta Brut	🍷🍷	4*
O	Franciacorta Extra Brut	🍷	4
O	Terre di Franciacorta Bianco '96	🍷	2*
O	Franciacorta Brut '91	🍸🍸	4
O	Franciacorta Brut '92	🍸🍸	4
O	Franciacorta Brut	🍸	4

MONTICELLI BRUSATI (BS) MONTICELLI BRUSATI (BS)

LA MONTINA
VIA BAIANA, 17
25040 MONTICELLI BRUSATI (BS)
TEL. 030/653278

LO SPARVIERE
VIA COSTA, 2
25040 MONTICELLI BRUSATI (BS)
TEL. 030/652382

With a battery of no fewer than five Franciacortas, three of which scored over 80 points in our tastings and two that only just fell below that level, Giancarlo and Osvaldo Bozza can rightly be regarded as amongst the leading producers in the area. This year, we were particularly impressed with the Franciacorta Extra Brut: bright, deep colour, fresh bouquet full of ripe fruit with delicate vegetal notes; full bodied and dry on the palate, ample and elegant. The Satèn has a bouquet dominated by floral aromas and a most attractive hint of lemon grass; slim, creamy and light on the palate with good aromatic touches and a subtle almondy twist to the finish. The Brut is exemplary for its style and definition: yeast and freshly baked bread on the nose, crisp and long finishing. The Millesimato is not quite as good as the '91, despite having attractive hints of brioche and vanilla on both the nose and the palate. Not many producers have yet got to grips with Franciacorta Rosé as a style, but the Bozza is one of the best of them all, and is full of fruity aromas if a little lean. Both the '95 reds are well made and attractive, above all the Dei Dossi cru, which displays good depth and balance together with soft tannins. The Terre di Franciacorta Bianco from the Palanca vineyard is its usual reliable self.

The Gussalli Beretta family's beautiful estate is a welcome newcomer to the Guide. Situated in a perfectly restored sixteenth century villa near Monticelli Brusati, it owes its name to the sparrow hawk depicted on the coat of arms above the great fireplace. Oenologist Francesco Polastri makes the wide range of wines in the well equipped villa cellars. The two Franciacortas are the most important wines. The Brut has a bright straw yellow colour and a fine creamy sparkle; the fruity bouquet has vegetal nuances and floral aromas which follow through perfectly in a finish with good length. The Extra Brut is more complex and has a greater spiciness and elegance on the nose; the palate is also extremely well defined with a perfect sparkle, rich fruit, and excellent length. The Terre di Franciacorta Bianco Riserva '95 is one of the best of its vintage: bright straw yellow colour; soft and broad bouquet with hints of brioche; dry, well rounded, balanced and well formed on the palate with a vanilla finish. Of the other wines we tasted, the Terre di Franciacorta Bianco '96 is an honest, fruity, drinkable wine, but we do have a few reservations about the reds, which have yet to find their best form.

○	Franciacorta Brut	ΥΥ	4
○	Franciacorta Extra Brut	ΥΥ	4*
○	Franciacorta Satèn	ΥΥ	4*
○	Franciacorta Brut '93	Υ	5
⊙	Franciacorta Rosé	Υ	4
○	Terre di Franciacorta Bianco Vigneto Palanca '96	Υ	2
●	Terre di Franciacorta Rosso '95	Υ	2
●	Terre di Franciacorta Rosso Vigneto dei Dossi '95	Υ	3
○	Franciacorta Brut	ΥΥ	4*
○	Franciacorta Brut '91	ΥΥ	4*
○	Franciacorta Crémant	ΥΥ	4
○	Franciacorta Extra Brut	ΥΥ	4
●	Franciacorta Rosso '93	Υ	2

○	Franciacorta Brut	ΥΥ	4
○	Franciacorta Extra Brut	ΥΥ	4
○	Terre di Franciacorta Bianco Ris. '95	ΥΥ	3
○	Terre di Franciacorta Bianco '96	Υ	2
●	Terre di Franciacorta Rosso '95		2
●	Terre di Franciacorta Rosso Vino del Cacciatore '94		3

MONTICELLI BRUSATI (BS)

VILLA

FRAZ. VILLA
25040 MONTICELLI BRUSATI (BS)
TEL. 030/652329-6852305

With an excellent Rosso '94 from the Gradoni vineyard and four great Franciacortas, Alessandro Bianchi's Villa winery confirms its status as one of the best in the region. Oenologist Corrado Cugnasco uses 25 hectares of vineyards to produce a range of quality wines, like the Gradoni. The '94 is made from the classic cépage stipulated by the DOC regulations plus a small percentage of a native variety called villa. The wine is a deep, dark ruby red with a nose that would not disgrace a New World wine for intensity; pencil lead, berry fruit, pepper, tobacco and juniper berries are all there. The palate displays rich fruit and depth with fine grained tannins and delicious hints of mint and spices. Just think what this wine could be like in a 5-star vintage! The Franciacortas are excellent, beginning with the Brut '91: ripe fruit on both the nose and palate with delicate hints of nutmeg. Re-tasting shows how excellent the '93 Franciacortas are: the Extra Brut has an intense yeastiness and is soft and long; the Brut is elegant and well balanced with attractive hints of citrus peel; the Extra Dry Cuvette stands out for its full bodied rotundity and the fresh elegance of its bouquet. All the other wines are more than decent.

○	Franciacorta Brut Ris. '91	🍷🍷	5
●	Terre di Franciacorta Rosso Gradoni '94	🍷🍷	4
○	Terre di Franciacorta Bianco '96	🍷	2
○	Terre di Franciacorta Bianco Marengo '95	🍷	4
○	Terre di Franciacorta Chardonnay '96	🍷	3
●	Terre di Franciacorta Rosso '95	🍷	2
○	Franciacorta Brut '88	🍷🍷 (white)	4
○	Franciacorta Brut '93	🍷🍷 (white)	4
○	Franciacorta Cuvette '93	🍷🍷 (white)	5
●	Franciacorta Rosso Gradoni '93	🍷🍷 (white)	4
○	Franciacorta Extra Brut '93	🍷 (white)	4
○	Terre di Franciacorta Bianco '95	🍷 (white)	3

MONTÙ BECCARIA (PV)

VERCESI DEL CASTELLAZZO

VIA AURELIANO, 36
27040 MONTÙ BECCARIA (PV)
TEL. 0385/60067

The Vercesi brothers, from Castellazzo di Montù Beccaria, have made a good Pinot Nero '94 from French clones in the Luogo di Monti vineyard. The wine was aged in barriques and has a garnet red colour and a bouquet of vanilla and macerated berry fruit with the classic game and vegetal undergrowth aromas that come with ageing; soft and ample on the palate, but enriched with ripe tannins and a characteristic undertow of redcurrants and liquorice. Two other Pinot Neros are vinified off the skins to produce white wines: the delightful Gugiarolo '95 is fresh and fruity with hints of apples and peaches, while the semi-sparkling Le Marghe '96 has a sharp fruit and yeast bouquet. The Vespolina '96 is a red wine made from the grape of the same name, known locally as ughetta, and has a bouquet of cloves, ginger and green pepper to accompany its unusual flavours; this is a wine that is very good drunk cellar-cool with well matured salami. The Orto di San Giacomo '93 is a sound wine that has aged well; made from a carefully studied blend of local and international grapes (35 percent barbera, 30 percent pinot noir and 35 percent bonarda), the wine has acquired an elegant spiciness from its barrique ageing. The Pezzalunga is an Oltrepò Pavese Rosso '96 made of barbera and bonarda together with the maximum amounts of ughetta and uva rara permitted by DOC regulations; it stands out for its rustic charm and approachability.

●	Oltrepò Pavese Pinot Nero Luogo dei Monti '94	🍷🍷	4
●	Oltrepò Pavese Rosso Orto di S. Giacomo '93	🍷	4
○	Oltrepò Pavese Pinot Nero in bianco Gugiarolo '95	🍷	3
●	Oltrepò Pavese Rosso Pezzalunga '96	🍷	3*
●	Vespolino '96	🍷	3
○	Oltrepò Pavese Pinot Nero in bianco Le Marghe '96		3
●	Oltrepò Pavese Bonarda Fàtila '89	🍷🍷 (white)	4
●	Oltrepò Pavese Bonarda Fàtila '90	🍷🍷 (white)	4
●	Oltrepò Pavese Bonarda Fàtila '91	🍷🍷 (white)	4

MORNICO LOSANA (PV)

CA' DI FRARA
FRAZ. CASA FERRARI
27040 MORNICO LOSANA (PV)
TEL. 0383/892299

PASSIRANO FRANCIACORTA (BS)

IL MOSNEL
VIA BARBOGLIO, 14
FRAZ. CAMIGNONE
25040 PASSIRANO
FRANCIACORTA (BS)
TEL. 030/653117-654236

Owned by the Bellani family since 1905, Ca' di Frara makes a spectacular entry to the Guide for the first time this year. The vineyards lie in the communes of Mornico Losana and Oliva Gessi (the name derives from chalk and limestone soils; "gesso" is Italian for chalk) and are now cultivated with the minimum chemical treatment possible to provide a series of estimable wines; we hope that things will continue in this way in the years to come. We begin with the Riesling Renano '95, made from slightly late picked grapes. Only the first 50 litres of free run must are drawn off from every quintal of grapes to make this wine which has a green gold colour and intense bouquet of limes, russet apples, and lemon liqueur. On the palate it is full flavoured and well developed with a good backbone of acidity. The late harvest Pinot Grigio '95 Raccolta Tardiva is the next success. It comes from grapes grown on sandy soil and is a golden straw yellow: ample and well composed on the nose (honey, roses, pineapple, fresh hay); full bodied, intense and powerful on the palate with a long, elegant finish. Thanks to its sound structure this wine has good ageing potential. The '96 Chardonnay is already looking very mature, but it is a sound wine made from a vineyard where yields are kept to 30 or 40 quintals per hectare. Among the reds, the Pinot Nero I Rari '94 stands out; the name ("the rare ones") refers to the extremely limited yields, which amount to about one bottle per vine. The wine is aged for 18 months in barriques: subtle nose with hints of vanilla and redcurrants; full bodied and velvety on the palate. The Bonarda '96 is worth looking at: blackberries and bitter cherries on the nose, semi-sparkling with a clean bitter almond background.

It has taken 30 years of hard work for Emanuela Barboglio to bring this estate up to the top rank in Franciacorta. The 40 hectares of vineyards have just about finally been put in order and provide the grapes for a wide range of top quality red, white and sparkling wines. Credit for this success must also go to Emanuela's children, Lucia and Giulio Barzanò, who work in the winery full time. Four Franciacortas were presented for tasting; we particularly liked the Brut '91 with its fresh, yeast and toasted bread aromas, and its winning creaminess on the tongue. The non-vintage Brut is also full bodied, aromatic on the nose and the palate, and has good structure and length. As usual, the Nouvelle Cuvée seduced us with its softness, the just-out-of-the-oven brioche and pastry shop bouquet, and its attractive fruitiness on the palate. The Extra Brut was less attractive; it suffers from lack of fruit and signs of age. As far as the still wines are concerned, the red Fontecolo '93, made from cabernet sauvignon, cabernet franc, merlot and barbera, can be counted a success. It is deep ruby red and on the nose is full of elegant berry fruit with nuances of vanilla and printers' ink. The oak is finely judged and the palate full bodied and richly fruity. The Chardonnay Campolarga '96 also gets Two Glasses for its elegant intensity. Finally, the Pinot Nero Pienne '95, the Terre di Franciacorta Rosso '94 and the Bianco Sulif '96 are all good wines.

O Oltrepò Pavese Pinot Grigio Raccolta Tardiva '95	♥♥	4
O Oltrepò Pavese Riesling Renano '95	♥♥	3
● Oltrepò Pavese Bonarda '96	♥	3
O Oltrepò Pavese Chardonnay '96	♥	3
● Oltrepò Pavese Pinot Nero I Rari '94	♥	4

O Franciacorta Brut	♥♥	4*
O Franciacorta Brut '91	♥♥	5
O Franciacorta Brut Nouvelle Cuvée	♥♥	4*
● Terre di Franciacorta Rosso Fontecolo '93	♥♥	4
O Franciacorta Extra Brut	♥	4
● Pienne '95	♥	4
O Terre di Franciacorta Bianco '96	♥	3
O Terre di Franciacorta Bianco Sulif '96	♥	4
O Terre di Franciacorta Chardonnay Campolarga '96	♥	3
● Terre di Franciacorta Rosso '94	♥	3
O Franciacorta Brut '90	♥♥	5
O Franciacorta Brut Nouvelle Cuvée	♥♥	4

POLPENAZZE DEL GARDA (BS)

CASCINA LA PERTICA
FRAZ. PISCEDO
25040 POLPENAZZE DEL GARDA (BS)
TEL. 0365/651471

Ruggero Brunori is doing his bit to revive the good name of wines from Lake Garda. With advice from consultant oenologist Franco Bernabei, Ruggero is a perfectionist in both the vineyards, where international varieties and local grapes are planted side by side, and in the cellars, where modern equipment and new oak barriques have been installed. The red wine Le Zalte '94 is made of cabernet sauvignon and is soft and broad with fine grained tannins and an attractive berry fruit palate. The Garda Rosso Le Sincette has a more complex cépage of groppello, barbera, marzemino, sangiovese and cabernet: the '94 vintage has a deep ruby red colour and a berry fruit and vanilla nose with some vinosity; tannic with notable freshness on the palate, good fruit and decent length. The Groppello is a good wine and one of the best in its class: well balanced with lots of body and easy drinkability. The Brut Le Sincette is made from chardonnay and erbamatta grapes; fresh and fruity with good acidity, very drinkable,. The Chiaretto has quite a dark colour and a clean berry fruit nose with notable raspberry aromas; well balanced and medium bodied. Last in this interesting range of wines is the Le Sincette, made from sauvignon and chardonnay picked in the vineyard of the same name: dry and a bit lean, but well made and enjoyable to drink.

●	Le Zalte Rosso '94	🍷🍷	4
⊙	Garda Bresciano Chiaretto Le Sincette '96	🍷	3
●	Garda Bresciano Groppello '96	🍷	3
●	Garda Bresciano Rosso Le Sincette '94	🍷	3
○	Le Sincette Brut	🍷	4
○	Le Sincette Bianco '96		3
●	Garda Bresciano Rosso Le Sincette '93	🍸	3
○	Le Sincette Bianco '95	🍸	3
●	Le Zalte Rosso '93	🍸	4

PROVAGLIO D'ISEO (BS)

BERSI SERLINI
VIA CERRETO, 7
25050 PROVAGLIO D'ISEO (BS)
TEL. 030/9823338

The winery and its 35 hectares of vineyards are situated in the beautiful countryside of the Cerreto district, between Provaglio d'Iseo and Timoline di Cortefranca. The winery, located in the original fifteenth century estate complex that is the Bersi Serlini family's home, has been extended and re-equipped with the most modern technology available. Cellar equipment and "terroir" however are not the only explanations for the consistently good results obtained in our tastings. There is also Arturo Bersi Serlini's dedication and the expertise of the oenologist Corrado Cugnasco to consider. This year, once again, we liked the finesse and the elegance of the Franciacorta Extra Brut '92, a vintage wine with a bright straw yellow colour and green reflections together with a soft, intense bouquet of ripe fruit, vanilla and butter; fresh on the palate with a creamy sparkle and good structure; elegant with vegetal and spicy nuances. Re-tasting the Brut '91 confirms last year's positive impression. The Franciacorta Brut is equally good, with intense floral and yeast aromas on the nose and soft fruit on the palate combined with freshness and an attractive closing hint of vanilla. The Demi-Sec Nuvola seems slightly inferior to previous versions, perhaps because of an excess of sweetness that compromises the balance of the finish. Lastly, the Terre di Franciacorta Rosso '95 is up to the mark, as normal.

○	Franciacorta Brut	🍷🍷	4*
○	Franciacorta Extra Brut '92	🍷🍷	5
○	Nuvola Démi Sec	🍷	5
●	Terre di Franciacorta Rosso '95	🍷	5
○	Franciacorta Brut '91	🍸🍸	5*
○	Franciacorta Extra Brut	🍸🍸	5
○	Nuvola Démi Sec	🍸🍸	5
○	Franciacorta Brut	🍸	4
○	Terre di Franciacorta Bianco	🍸	3
●	Terre di Franciacorta Rosso	🍸	3

PUEGNAGO DEL GARDA (BS)

ROCCA DE' GIORGI (PV)

COMINCIOLI
VIA ROMA, 10
25080 PUEGNAGO DEL GARDA (BS)
TEL. 0365/651141

ANTEO
LOC. CHIESA
27043 ROCCA DE' GIORGI (PV)
TEL. 0385/48583-99073

Giovanni Battista and Gianfranco Comincioli make an interesting range of wines on the Brescia side of Lake Garda. For years, their most reliable product has been the Chiaretto, one of the best of its type. This year's version is no exception; the wine stands out for its good, limpid, pale cherry red colour and for its extremely attractive fresh and fruity nose; as usual, on the palate it is fresh, flavoursome, fruity and full bodied. The Garda Rosso from the Pedemùt vineyard seems less satisfactory than in previous vintages: it has good structure, but a fuzzy nose and slightly unbalanced palate. What is good, however, is the Groppello. This original wine is made from slightly late harvested grapes which are then left to dry partially on cane racks before crushing. It has a deep colour, an imposing bouquet and a structure that appears more elegant every year. We are quite sure that the Cominciolis are on the right route to win considerable acclaim with this wine. The Perlì, a white made from trebbiano and erbamatta, a rare local grape variety used to give acidity to the blend gets Two Glasses. The '96 vintage has a deep straw yellow colour and an intense, almost aromatic bouquet of ripe fruit, flowers and slightly vegetal gooseberry. The palate confirms our judgement of the nose and displays good structure with rich extract balanced by lively acidity.

Rocca de'Giorgi is universally regarded as one of the best sites for pinot noir in Oltrepò Pavese. Anteo have vineyards in the right place (30 hectares in the Chiesa district) and well equipped cellars, together with a competent technical staff. The question therefore arises, why is all this potential not being fully realised? Let us be clear about this, the wines are correct; it is just that they could be (and should be) better. We sincerely hope that Antonella and Piero Cribellati, the owners of Anteo, can break the 80-point barrier in the future. Meanwhile, as we have said for the past few years, they'll have to "make do" (if that is the right expression) with just One Glass awards. The Brut Classico Oltrepò Pavese Selezione del Gourmet has a berry fruit and biscuit nose, is full bodied and fundamentally well balanced, but it would benefit from a little extra freshness. The Nature (Extra Brut) Metodo Classico '91 is slightly more successful: the fruit of the pinot noir combines well with the floral nature of the chardonnay; there is a lively sparkle, good perlage and a well defined nose of redcurrants and almond blossom, together with a hint of bay leaf; the palate is dry without astringency and there is an attractive, if not over-long, aromatic finish. Of the reds, the Bonarda vivace '96 stands out for its clean vinosity and for its lively balance on the palate.

○	Perlì '96	♥♥	4	○	Oltrepò Pavese Nature		
⊙	Garda Bresciano Chiaretto '96	♥	4		Extra Brut '91	♥	5
●	Garda Bresciano Groppello '95	♥	4	○	Oltrepò Pavese Pinot Nero Brut		
●	Garda Bresciano Rosso				Classico Sel. Gourmet	♥	5
	Vigna Pedemùt '95		4	●	Oltrepò Pavese		
⊙	Garda Bresciano Chiaretto '95	♥♥	3		Bonarda vivace '96		3
●	Barbera di Lombardia			○	Oltrepò Pavese Pinot Nero Brut	♥	4
	Il Roccolo '94	♥	4	○	Oltrepò Pavese Pinot Nero		
●	Garda Bresciano Rosso				Brut Classico	♥	5
	Vigna Pedemùt '94	♥	3	○	Oltrepò Pavese Pinot Nero		
					Extra Brut Classico	♥	5

RODENGO SAIANO (BS)

S. GIULETTA (PV)

MIRABELLA
VIA CANTARANE, 2
25050 RODENGO SAIANO (BS)
TEL. 030/611197

ISIMBARDA
FRAZ. CASTELLO
27046 S. GIULETTA (PV)
TEL. 0383/899256

Mirabella makes its first entry in our Guide this year. The estate is based at Rodengo Saiano and, founded 18 years ago, has 40 hectares of vineyards, a modern winery, and an annual production of about 350,000 bottles of still wine and Franciacorta. Teresio Schiavi is the oenologist, but the company is actually owned by a group of businessmen and professionals from Brescia, including the famous film director Lina Wertmüller. The Mirabella Brut '90 impressed us with the elegance of its ample bouquet of fruit and yeast with hints of flowers. It is clean and delicate on the palate with a fine, regular perlage and leaves a fresh finish with a delicate vegetal nuance. The Brut also has a remarkably elegant nose with fresh citrus peel aromas perfectly blended with the peaches, pears, and yeastiness of the nose; subtly aromatic, well balanced and long on the palate. The Terre di Franciacorta Barrique '95 has a bright, straw yellow colour with green reflections; fresh bouquet of ripe fruit and vanilla with elegant toasty aromas; good structure, freshness and notable richness of flavour on the palate. Lastly, we liked the Terre Bianco '96, which is simpler in style but easy to drink, and the Rosso Barrique '95, full of berry fruit and vanilla, soft and attractive on the palate, but slightly leaner than it might be.

The Isimbarda estate is owned by Luigi Meroni and takes its name from the Marchesi Isimbarda family, who lived in the area in the seventeenth century. The vineyards cover 33 hectares at altitudes of between 200 and 350 metres above sea level, and are managed according to modern criteria; high density planting and severe pruning give a production of between 1.5 and a maximum 3 kilograms of grapes per vine. The winery is modern and well equipped: soft pressing, temperature controlled fermentation in stainless steel tanks, large barrels, barriques, and cold sterile bottling are the order of the day. This is the first year that we have tasted the wines for the Guide, and we were particularly impressed with the whites. The clear leader is the Riesling Oltrepò Pavese '96, made from mainly riesling italico with the addition of a little Rhine riesling: golden straw yellow colour with bright greenish reflections; lemon grass and roses on the nose with mineral touches; dry, fresh, full flavoured, clean and long finishing. The "blanc de noir" Pinot Nero '96, is also good: pale straw yellow with green reflections; light but well defined bouquet with slightly sour berry fruit aromas; dry with young, green flavours and a finish of wet almonds with good enough length. The reds are all extremely young, but what stands out at the moment is the Barbera '96. It is still closed and dominated by raw acidity, but it has good ageing potential. It will be interesting to see how this estate develops in the future since so much serious work has already been done, especially in the vineyards.

○	Franciacorta Brut	▼▼	4
○	Franciacorta Brut '90	▼▼	5
○	Terre di Franciacorta Bianco Barrique '95	▼▼	4
○	Terre di Franciacorta Bianco '96	▼	3
●	Terre di Franciacorta Rosso Barrique '95	▼	4

○	Oltrepò Pavese Pinot Nero in bianco '96	▼	3
○	Oltrepò Pavese Riesling Italico '96	▼	3
●	Oltrepò Pavese Barbera '96		3

SIRMIONE (BS)

CA' DEI FRATI
VIA FRATI, 22
FRAZ. LUGANA
25010 SIRMIONE (BS)
TEL. 030/919468

Ca' dei Frari, owned by the Dal Cero brothers, is one of the best known and most reputable wineries of the Lombard side of Lake Garda. Certainly, it is one of the most active producers of Lugana, a white wine with fresh, fruity, easy drinking qualities that has gained considerable popularity in the last 20 years. The '94 Lugana from Dal Cero is straw yellow colour with green reflections. It has an intense bouquet of peaches and pears with attractive vegetal nuances, and particularly good, full bodied, fresh fruit on the palate. The '95 is very similar, but more floral on the nose and with a touch of extra softness. The best Lugana from this estate is the one aged in wood from grapes picked in the Brolettino vineyard. The '95 has a golden straw yellow colour, an intense pastry shop bouquet and a fresh fruity rotundity on the palate, with a hint of vanilla on the finish. The '96 is a little greener, in all senses, both in colour and on the nose (apricots, peaches, gooseberries and spring blossom); the palate is soft and well built and shot through with an elegant vein of acidity. The sweet wine Tre Filer is also very good; we tasted the '94 and the '95 vintages and found them both to be balanced and long finishing - both worthy Two Glass award winners. The Pratto, another white, this time made from wood aged chardonnay and sauvignon, gets the same award: very fresh and full bodied, lots of flavour with hints of vanilla and a long finish. We close this entry by reminding you of the good Cuvée dei Frati Brut and the '94 Ronchedone, a red wine made from merlot and malbec that slips down very well.

○	Lugana Il Brolettino '95	▼▼	4
○	Lugana Il Brolettino '96	▼▼	4
○	Pratto '95	▼▼	4
○	Tre Filer '94	▼▼	5
○	Tre Filer '95	▼▼	5
○	Cuvée dei Frati Brut	▼	4
○	Lugana '95	▼	3
○	Lugana '96	▼	3
●	Ronchedone '95	▼	4
○	Lugana Il Brolettino '94	▽▽	4
○	Lugana il Brolettino '93	▽▽	3
○	Pratto '94	▽▽	4
○	Tre Filer '89	▽▽	5

TEGLIO (SO)

FAY
VIA PILA CASELLI, 1
LOC. S. GIACOMO
23030 TEGLIO (SO)
TEL. 0342/786071

Despite the incursions of some poor vintages in recent years and his other commitments as mayor of the town of Teglio, Sandro Fay has not given up his original passion for vine and wine and has lost none of his skill as an accomplished oenologist. In this year's tastings, he put forward an excellent and highly individual Sforzato '94, showing us that his clear thinking applies not only to his public role, but also to vinification techniques, with particular reference to the process of drying grapes for this wine. The Sforzato is in fact extremely well made, and succeeds in the difficult task of striking a balance between ripeness of fruit and freshness on the palate: concentrated, fruity and well composed on the nose; rich in fruit and long finishing. The Inferno '94 has an unmistakeable style influenced by the use of late harvested fruit and good structure with hints of bitterness on the palate. By comparison, the Sassella '94 is a more straightforward wine with a good backbone and mineral hints on the palate. Like almost all the other Valgella wines we tasted this year, the Vigna Cima '92 was a disappointment; it lacks freshness on the palate and is a little too old on the nose.

●	Valtellina Sforzato '94	▼▼	4
●	Valtellina Superiore Inferno '94	▼	3
●	Valtellina Superiore Sassella '94	▼	3
●	Valtellina Superiore Valgella Cima '92		4
●	Valtellina Superiore Valgella Ca' Morei '90	▽▽	5
●	Valtellina Superiore Valgella Ca' Morei '92	▽▽	4
●	Valtellina Sforzato '92	▽	4
●	Valtellina Superiore Sassella '91	▽	3
●	Valtellina Superiore Valgella '91	▽	2
●	Valtellina Superiore Valgella Ris. '90	▽	4

TIRANO (SO)

TORRICELLA VERZATE (PV)

CONTI SERTOLI SALIS
P.ZZA SALIS, 3
23037 TIRANO (SO)
TEL. 0342/704533

MONSUPELLO
VIA SAN LAZZARO, 5
27050 TORRICELLA VERZATE (PV)
TEL. 0383/896043

For too long Sforzato was thought to be a wine that could only be made in a bombshell style, a sort of super-charged drink with an extremely high level of alcohol, to be contemplated only at the end of a meal. And there was no discussion about it. Fortunately, things have changed and now in many cases Sforzato has become a wine that retains its stature but is made in a more elegant, better balanced, and more easily drinkable style. Credit for this change in style goes to oenologists like Claudio Introini, who has re-invented this wine in the beautiful Sertoli Salis cellars in the space of only a few years. The Sforzato Canua '94 has repeated the success of previous years, amply proving its consistency by yet again scoring well over 80 points. Spicy on the nose, with a typical, intoxicating jammy bouquet; the raisined fruit flavours come through perfectly and leave a slightly bitter twist on the palate to balance the natural sweetness. Further ageing will make this wine even more enjoyable. The Corte della Meridiana '94 is showing well at the moment and has good structure and a promising future with liquorice and fruit flavours which need time to blend fully. The Saloncello '95 is slightly disappointing, considering it comes from such a good vintage. The Sassella '94, however, is well made with an attractive bouquet of plums and a smooth, well rounded palate. Just missing a One Glass award, the Valtellina '94 is clean, easy to drink and very straightforward, while the Torre della Sirena has a subtle, floral bouquet and an extremely enjoyable, fragrant and curiously honeyed flavour on the palate.

Carlo Boatti and his enthusiastic son Pierangelo have dedicated themselves to the search for quality, and it is now paying off. The high standard of Monsupello wines begins in the vineyards, where agronomist Paolo Fiocchi uses selected clones of traditional and experimental vines (from sauvignon to Rhine riesling) and variations in soil and microclimate to enhance the individual aromatic character of each variety. The formidable range of high quality wines begins with the Nature Classico. Made from 90 percent pinot noir and 10 percent partially barrique aged chardonnay, it undergoes 42 months' bottle fermentation: extremely fine perlage, very complex bouquet of blackcurrants, bitter almonds, toasted hazelnuts and incense; decidedly elegant, full bodied and quite long on the palate. The Brut Classico '92 is excellent and well balanced with a firm, full body. The two Chardonnays are equally good: the '96 has a hawthorn blossom and Golden Delicious apple bouquet and is soft but fresh on the palate. The barrel fermented Senso '95 has very pleasurable honey and vanilla aromas. The Sauvignon '96 (30 percent barrique aged) has a bouquet of flowers, aniseed and tropical fruit with a smoky, spicy, mineral undertow. Named after its rootstock code, the Pinot Nero 3309 from the '96 vintage is a successful wine displaying cassis, vegetal undergrowth aromas and sweet tannins. The Great Ruby '96 is a lightly sparkling red with attractive vinosity and bitter cherry and almond flavours. Most unusually, the La Cuenta '95 is made from no fewer than seven white grape varieties (mostly aromatic in style) left to dry until Christmas; pressing produces a mere 25 litres of juice per quintal which is fermented and then aged for 24 months in heavily toasted French barriques; excellent with foie gras and blue cheeses.

● Valtellina Sforzato Canua '94	ΨΨ	5
● Valtellina Sup. Corte della Meridiana '94	ΨΨ	4
○ Terrazze Retiche di Sondrio Torre della Sirena '96	Ψ	3
● Valtellina Sup. Sassella '94	Ψ	3
● Terrazze Retiche di Sondrio Il Saloncello '95		4
● Valtellina '95		2
● Valtellina Sforzato Canua '90	ΨΨ	5
● Valtellina Sforzato Canua '92	ΨΨ	5
● Valtellina Sforzato Canua '93	ΨΨ	5
● Valtellina Sup. Corte della Meridiana '90	ΨΨ	5
● Valtellina Sup. Sassella '93	Ψ	3

○ La Cuenta Passito '93	ΨΨ	6
○ Oltrepò Pavese Brut Classico '92	ΨΨ	4
○ Oltrepò Pavese Chardonnay '96	ΨΨ	3
○ Oltrepò Pavese Pinot Nero Classico Nature	ΨΨ	4
○ Oltrepò Pavese Chardonnay Senso '95	ΨΨ	4
● Oltrepò Pavese Pinot Nero 3309 '96	Ψ	4
● Oltrepò Pavese Rosso Great Ruby '96	Ψ	3
○ Oltrepò Pavese Sauvignon '96	Ψ	3
○ Oltrepò Pavese Pinot Nero Classico Monsupello Brut '91	ΨΨ	4
○ Senso Chardonnay '93	ΨΨ	4

VILLA DI TIRANO (SO)

TRIACCA
VIA NAZIONALE, 121
23030 VILLA DI TIRANO (SO)
TEL. 0342/701352

ZENEVREDO (PV)

TENUTA IL BOSCO
LOC. IL BOSCO
27049 ZENEVREDO (PV)
TEL. 0385/245326

It is undeniably true that the clonal selection of the nebbiolo grape begun many years ago by Domenico Triacca is now producing concrete, high quality results. The selections obtained have had a high cost in terms of both time and money, but Triacca's work has far reaching implications for the quality of the viticulture of the entire Valtellina. It is a pleasure to say that already tangible evidence of improvement is not lacking; a number of Triacca wines we tasted this year scored easily over 80 points. The first of these is a real surprise, the Prestigio '94: spicy and elegant on the nose with signs of new oak used in an expert fashion, remarkably smooth on the palate, broad and soft on the finish. The Riserva Triacca '91 is its usual reliable self, a complex wine with hints of tobacco on the nose and superb concentration of fruit on the palate. The Tradizione '94 has a clean bouquet with peppery vegetal aromas and is smooth on the palate with good fruit, but is still developing in the bottle. Triacca has recently acquired the historic Tona winery and two wines from this stable showed well in our tastings: the Perlavilla '94 is a correctly made local wine that is both fresh and very drinkable, and the Sforzato Il Corvo '94 is an intense, well made red with a personality all of its own.

The very modern and extremely well equipped Tenuta Il Bosco winery (6,000 square metres of floor space and 20,000 hectolitres storage capacity) is part of the Zonin empire. A total of 118 hectares of vineyards supply the grapes for very competent vinification. The Bonarda '96 is made in a semi-sparkling style through tank fermentation and is always good quality: fragrant, full flavoured, and very drinkable thanks to a good dose of residual sugar. Given its reasonable price, it is not surprising to see that it is also commercially successful. The Riesling Renano vivace '96 gets One Glass for its light sparkle, its pale straw yellow colour, and its intense bouquet of roses and fresh fruit; it is dry and fruity on the palate with an attractive touch of green youthfulness. The Cortese vivace '96 is clean, simple, floral and worth a look. Of the sparkling wines, the non-vintage Il Bosco Extra Dry comes out well: lively sparkle, subtle and well defined perlage, intense bouquet of biscuits, redcurrants and ripe apples; firm, fresh and fruity on the palate with toasted hazelnuts on the finish. The Oltrepò Classico Il Bosco '92 repeats its success in last year's Guide with a Two Glass rating, and shows the benefits of long ageing on both the nose and the palate.

● Valtellina Prestigio '94	♟♟	4
● Valtellina Sforzato Il Corvo '94	♟♟	4
● Valtellina Superiore Ris.		
Triacca '91	♟♟	4
● Valtellina Perlavilla '94		3
● Valtellina Tradizione '94		3
● Valtellina Superiore Ris.		
Triacca '90	♟♟	4
● Valtellina Tradizione '91	♟♟	3
● Valtellina Monastero		
La Gatta '91	♟	3
● Valtellina Prestigio '91	♟	3
● Valtellina Sforzato '94	♟	4

○ Oltrepò Pavese		
Bonarda vivace '96	♟	2
○ Oltrepò Pavese Extra Dry		
Il Bosco	♟	4
○ Oltrepò Pavese Riesling		
Renano vivace '96	♟	2
○ Oltrepò Pavese		
Cortese vivace '96		2
○ Oltrepò Pavese		
Brut Classico '92	♟♟	2
● Oltrepò Pavese Bonarda '95	♟	2*
○ Oltrepò Pavese Pinot		
Spumante Phileo	♟	3
● Oltrepò Pavese Pinot Nero '95		2

OTHER WINERIES

The following producers obtained good scores in our tastings with one or more of their wines:

PROVINCE OF BERGAMO

Tenuta degli Angeli,
Carobbio degli Angeli, tel. 035/951489,
Valcalepio Moscato Passito di Carobbio '92

Cantina Sociale Bergamasca,
S. Paolo d'Argon, tel. 035/951098,
Valcalepio Bianco '96,
Valcalepio Rosso '95,
Merlot '96

Pecis, S. Paolo d'Argon, tel. 035/959104,
Valcalepio Rosso '95,
Valcalepio Bianco '96

Bonaldi-Cascina del Bosco,
Sorisole, tel. 035/571701,
Cantoalto '90,
Valcalepio Rosso '95

PROVINCE OF BRESCIA

Lantieri de Paratico,
Capriolo, tel. 030/736151 - 7460111,
Terre di Franciacorta Bianco Colzano '96,
Franciacorta Brut,
Franciacorta Extra Brut

Tenuta Priore,
Cazzago S. Martino, tel. 030/7254710,
Terre di Franciacorta Bianco '96,
Franciacorta Brut

Cascina Ronco Basso,
Coccaglio, tel. 030/7721689,
Terre di Franciacorta Rosso '95,
Franciacorta Brut

Barboglio, Cortefranca, tel. 030/9826831,
Terre di Franciacorta Rosso S. Michele '95,
Franciacorta Brut

Provenza, Desenzano, tel. 030/9910006,
Lugana Vigne Molin '96

Zambiasi Paolo,
Desenzano, tel. 030/9120216,
Montecorno '93

Boschi, Erbusco, tel. 030/7703096,
Terre di Franciacorta Rosso '95,
Franciacorta Brut

San Cristoforo, Erbusco, tel. 030/7760268,
Terre di Franciacorta Rosso '95,
Terre di Franciacorta Bianco '96

Costaripa,
Moniga del Garda, tel. 0365/502010,
Chiaretto del Garda Rosamara '96,
Chiaretto del Garda '96

F.lli Maiolini, Ome, tel. 030/652161,
Terre di Franciacorta Rosso
Ruc di Gnoc '95,
Terre Bianco Ronchello '96,
Franciacorta Brut

Bredasole, Paratico, tel. 030/910407,
Terre di Franciacorta Rosso '95,
Franciacorta Brut

Le Marchesine, Passirano, tel. 030/657005,
Franciacorta Nondosato '93

Marchesi Fassati di Balzola,
Passirano,
tel. 02/8692132,
Terre di Franciacorta Rosso '95,
Franciacorta Brut

Tenuta Roveglia,
Pozzolengo, tel. 030/918663,
Lugana Vigne di Catullo '96

Leali di Monteacuto,
Puegnago, tel. 0365/651291,
Groppello '96

La Meridiana, Puegnago, tel. 0365/651265,
Livina '96

Capoferri, Rovato, tel. 030/7721470,
Franciacorta Brut,
Franciacorta Brut '90

Le Chiusure,
San Felice, tel. 0365/626243,
Campei '96

PROVINCE OF MANTOVA

Stefano Spezia, Mariana, tel. 0376/735012,
Ancellotta '95,
Lambrusco '96

Cantina Sociale di Quistello,
Quistello, tel. 0376/618118,
Lambrusco Mantovano Banda Rossa '96,
Lambrusco Mantovano Banda Blu '96

PROVINCE OF PAVIA

Cantina Soc. Intercomunale,
Broni, tel. 0385/51505,
Pinot Nero in bianco '96,
Oltrepò Pavese Pinot Spumante

Angelo Ballabio, Casteggio,
tel. 0383/82724,
Oltrepò Pavese Bonarda '96

Cantina Soc. Casteggio,
Casteggio, tel. 0383/890696,
Oltrepò Pavese Pinot Nero '95,
Spumante Chardonnay '96

Travaglino, Casteggio, tel. 0383/872222,
Oltrepò Pavese Cabernet Sauvignon '95,
Oltrepò Pavese Rosso Le Fracchie '95,
Oltrepò Pavese Pinot Nero Brut Classico

Cà Montebello, Cigognola, tel. 0385/85182,
Oltrepò Pavese Pinot Nero '96,
Oltrepò Pavese Pinot Nero in bianco '96,
Oltrepò Pavese Buttafuoco '96,
Oltrepò Pavese Rosso Custirò '96

Monteruco, Cigognola, tel. 0385/85151,
Oltrepò Pavese Rosso Ris. Metellianum '93,
Oltrepò Pavese Bonarda '95

Montelio, Codevilla, tel. 0383/373090,
Comprino Rosso '94,
Oltrepò Pavese Pinot Nero '94,
Oltrepò Pavese Cortese '96

La Costaiola,
Montebello, tel. 0383/83169,
Oltrepò Pavese Barbera I Due Draghi '96,
Oltrepò Pavese Pinot Nero in bianco
Trasparenza di Pinot '96

Pietro Torti,
Montecalvo Versiggia, tel. 0385/99763,
Oltrepò Pavese Rosso Verzello '93,
Oltrepò Pavese Bonarda '96

Cascina Gnocco,
Mornico Losana, tel. 0383/873226,
Oltrepò Pavese Rosso Il Nibbio '94,
Oltrepò Pavese Riesling Italico
Ambrogina '96,
Oltrepò Pavese Moscato Adagetto '96

Cantine Scuropasso,
Pietra De' Giorgi, tel. 0385/85143,
Oltrepò Pavese Sangue di Giuda '96

Martilde,
Rovescala, tel. 0385/756280,
Oltrepò Pavese Rosso Ris. Pindaro '93,
Oltrepò Pavese Bonarda Ghiro '93,
Oltrepò Pavese Barbera La Strega '94

San Giorgio,
San Giuletta, tel. 0383/899168,
Castelsangiorgio '94

La Versa,
Santa Maria Della Versa,
tel. 0385/278229,
Oltrepò Pavese Pinot Nero Vigna del Ferraio '93,
Oltrepò Pavese Rosso
Roccolo del Casale '90

PROVINCE OF SONDRIO

Balgera,
Chiuro, tel. 0342/482203,
Valtellina Sup. Balgera '90

Vinicola Mamete Prevostini,
Mese, tel. 0343/41003,
Valtellina Sup. Sassella '94,
Valtellina Sup. Grumello '94,
Valtellina Sup. Corte di Cama '90

F.lli Bettini,
S. Giacomo di Teglio, tel. 0342/786068,
Valtellina Sfursat '90,
Valtellina Sup. Vigna la Cornella '94

AR.PE.PE.,
Sondrio, tel. 0342/214120,
Valtellina Sup. Sassella Ris.
Rocce Rosse '89,
Valtellina Sup. Sassella Stella Retica '94,
Valtellina Sup. Grumello '90 Buon Consiglio

Alberto Marsetti,
Sondrio, tel. 0342/216329,
Valtellina Sup. Grumello '94

Cantina Sociale Villa di Tirano,
Villa di Tirano,
tel. 0342/795107,
Valtellina Sforzato '94

TRENTINO

We were perhaps expecting better from the Trentino. At our tastings for this edition of the Guide the region performed below its real potential, and for once this is cannot be put down to a difficult vintage. Responsibility lies with the producers, who perhaps have not had the courage to fully commit themselves to quality and to modernisation. In a province whose 8,700 hectares of vineyard represent over 40 percent of the total farming land, this is rather disappointing. Neither should it be forgotten that the well-known Agricultural Institute of San Michele all'Adige every year turns out a large number of highly qualified graduates in oenology. Over a million quintals of grapes are harvested every autumn, and are mostly transformed into DOC wines, which are technically correct but often just sink into anonymity. A part of the blame, in our opinion, lies also with the provincial administration which by virtue of its autonomy provides various forms of backing, making life a lot easier both for private producers and the cooperative cellars - altogether more than twelve thousand wine-making estates - but in many cases depriving both of the incentive of healthy competition. Thanks to this situation several of the region's big cooperative wineries have become leaders on the international winemaking scene, producing millions of bottles a year. But by their side we would like to see a more forceful presence of wines of super-premium quality, a category which in this region is restricted to a small body of first-rate producers. Once again we award a prize to the Lunelli brothers with their Giulio Ferrari Riserva del Fondatore, a classic of Italian sparkling wines.

Alongside this winner, for the first time our highest award has been received by another Metodo Classico, the Graal Brut from Cavit with its best vintage ever, the '93. This is an important result for winemaking in the Trentino, proving once again that even the biggest organizations - and here we are talking about a real giant - can reach the top. Lastly two international quality reds have passed the tasting test with the crucial ninety out of a hundred: they are both Bordeaux-style blends which show that the province of Trento is in no way inferior to the most famous wine regions of the world. Pojer & Sandri with their Faye '94 repeat the previous year's success, while the Marchese Guerrieri Gonzaga adds his fourth Three Glasses to the award-winning vintages of San Leonardo. There were also other wines on the verge of claiming top awards, from excellent, established producers such as Elisabetta Foradori and the cooperative La Vis, to other small estates which equally distinguished themselves in tastings: for example Castel Noarna, Longariva, Maso Cantanghel, Pravis and Balter, to mention just a few. These are estates which, with the vineyards and human resources at their disposal, have a real chance of achieving excellence, if only they are willing to accept a challenge, as all the winegrowers of the Trentino should be.

AVIO (TN)

TENUTA SAN LEONARDO
LOC. BORGHETTO ALL'ADIGE
38060 AVIO (TN)
TEL. 0464/689004

AVIO (TN)

VALLAROM
LOC. MASI DI VO' SINISTRO, 21
38063 AVIO (TN)
TEL. 0464/684297

To repeat it is almost superfluous: the wines of the Marchesi Guerrieri Gonzaga represent for the Trentino the fusion of tradition and capacity for innovation. Past and future mingle on this highly attractive estate, admirably managed by the marquess Carlo, who has a thorough knowledge of oenology and has brought his young son Anselmo into the family wine-growing business. Only red varieties are grown at San Leonardo, cabernet and merlot. In spite of the size of the estate, Carlo Guerrieri Gonzaga has decided to vinify only grapes destined for the wine bearing the estate's name, of which nearly 50,000 bottles are produced. With rare exceptions, both the Cabernet and the Bordeaux blend Villa Cresti will disappear, while the Merlot will be produced in quantities of no more than a few thousand bottles a year. San Leonardo, a red whose quality improves from year to year, will be the focal point of production. This is a wine which can compete confidently at international level, thanks to the skilfully calculated combination of vigorous tannic structure and soft fruit. The '94 is an exceptional wine for its vintage. We expect it to peak in 5-6 years, by which time it should have mellowed and developed complexity, and be ready to be appreciated in all its stylish elegance.

The results of this vintage were a source of amazement for the entire tasting commission; the professor's wines are not really up to it. They are technically correct, but do not display that character and verve which we have so often encountered. The wines are probably handicapped by unsatisfactory harvests, which no natural winemaking methods are able to rectify, not even when carried out by Attilio Scienza, one of the leading Italian authorities in the field. It is a shame, because all the essentials for great wine were there; expectations were high for the Cabernet Sauvignon, vinified in '93 and meticulously aged in wood of various dimensions. Alas, tasting these hopes were dashed. The same goes for the Pinot Nero Riserva '94 and the Chardonnay Riserva '95. They are clearly wines of quality with appeal and personality, but they are only good, not outstanding. Knowing Professor Scienza, we reckon this verdict will spur him on to startling us in the near future with wines from the experimental varieties grown on the estate. Vallarom goes back to medieval times, and even then was synonymous with quality, a bastion of the defence of local winegrowing in the lower Vallagarina. These lands are the birthplace of the "vinum bonum" of the Trentino and a challenge for Attilio Scienza: even if the battle over one harvest has been partly lost, he can still win the war.

● San Leonardo '94	♥♥♥	5
● Trentino Merlot '95	♥♥	3*
● San Leonardo '88	♥♥♥	5
● San Leonardo '90	♥♥♥	5
● San Leonardo '93	♥♥♥	5
● San Leonardo '91	♥♥	5
● Trentino Cabernet '93	♥♥	3*
● Trentino Cabernet '94	♥♥	3*
● Trentino Merlot '92	♥♥	3*
● Villa Gresti '93	♥♥	3*

○ Trentino Chardonnay Ris. '95	♥	4
● Trentino Marzemino '96	♥	3
● Trentino Pinot Nero Ris. '94	♥	4
● Trentino Cabernet Sauvignon Ris. '93		4
● Trentino Cabernet '90	♥♥	5
● Trentino Cabernet Sauvignon Ris. '94	♥♥	4
○ Trentino Chardonnay '92	♥♥	5
○ Trentino Chardonnay '95	♥♥	4
○ Trentino Chardonnay Ris. '90	♥♥	5
○ Trentino Chardonnay Ris. '93	♥♥	4
○ Trentino Chardonnay Vendemmia Tardiva '92	♥♥	5
○ Trentino Pinot Bianco '95	♥♥	3*

CIVEZZANO (TN)

FAEDO (TN)

MASO CANTANGHEL
LOC. FORTE
VIA MADONNINA, 33
38045 CIVEZZANO (TN)
TEL. 0461/859050

GRAZIANO FONTANA
VIA CASE SPARSE, 9
38010 FAEDO (TN)
TEL. 0461/650400

For two years Piero Zabini was more concerned with the renovation of his cellar in the Austro-Hungarian fortress overlooking the Valsugana than with wine. The results of the 1996 harvest at once made up for this lapse, proving this melodramatic grower's mastery of production strategy, based on the care for his few, prized hectares of vineyard. Almost all the new wines scored Two Glass ratings. The Chardonnay Vigna Piccola has balance and a subtle hint of wood, while the unoaked white blend of chardonnay, sauvignon and pinot bianco named Forte di Mezzo (after the fortress), is very fruity and enjoyable. The reds are even more balanced and impressive. The most recent, a 100 percent merlot called Tajapreda, is a highly concentrated, exuberant, wine: enjoyable and undemanding, it nevertheless maintains all the vigour of the grape variety. It is also very good value for money. The skilful vinification is the work of rising Trentino winemaker Enrico Paternoster. The Rosso di Pila, a powerful Cabernet Sauvignon already considered a classic of it type in the Trentino, is lush and impressively soft with some vanilla. The autographed Pinot Nero '95 Riserva is rather closed and sharp, this last fault due to youth. Possibly because it was made when the fortress-cum-cellar was still at sixes and sevens from the alterations.

Graziano Fontana, an untalkative grower and staunch producer of whites, is a skilful vinifier of small batches of grapes. In spite of the modern, well-equipped cellar the concept of quantity does not interest him. This year for the first time small batches of pinot nero and lagrein were made. The latter variety, a red whose character is still rustic but clearly defined, is the confirmation of the level of quality achieved by this tiny estate up in the hills. The wines, especially the whites and the Pinot Nero, are genuine and individual, with the marked character of the wines of Faedo, character which emerges especially in the traditional Müller Thurgau, Sauvignon and Chardonnay, even though they do not have the concentration and aroma of previous vintages. The Sauvignon stands out in particular for its tropical fruit aromas and good substance on the nose and the palate. The Pinot Nero is fairly light and simple, vinified with great precision but without allowing the grapes to give of their best. Pinot Nero is probably a variety which needs to be reviewed in the Trentino. The Lagrein is very successful, pleasing both in aroma and on the palate. It does not have the power and energy displayed by this varietal in the Alto Adige but it is definitely one of the most enjoyable tasted, with a good ruby colour, elegant fruity aromas, and a full and long-lasting flavour, slightly tannic.

● Cabernet Sauvignon Rosso di Pila '95	🍷🍷	5
○ Trentino Bianco Forte di Mezzo '96	🍷🍷	3*
○ Trentino Chardonnay Vigna Piccola '96	🍷🍷	4
● Trentino Merlot Tajapreda '96	🍷🍷	3*
● Trentino Pinot Nero Piero Zabini '95	🍷	5
● Cabernet Sauvignon Rosso di Pila '93	🍷🍷	4
● Cabernet Sauvignon Rosso di Pila '94	🍷🍷	5
● Rosso di Pila '91	🍷🍷	6
● Rosso di Pila '92	🍷🍷	5

● Trentino Lagrein di Faedo '95	🍷🍷	3*
○ Trentino Müller Thurgau '96	🍷🍷	3*
○ Trentino Sauvignon di Faedo '96	🍷🍷	3*
○ Trentino Chardonnay '96	🍷	3
● Trentino Pinot Nero di Faedo '95	🍷	4
○ Sauvignon di Faedo '94	🍷🍷	3*
○ Sauvignon di Faedo '95	🍷🍷	3*
○ Trentino Müller Thurgau '94	🍷🍷	3*
● Trentino Pinot Nero '94	🍷🍷	4*
○ Trentino Chardonnay '95	🍷	3*
○ Trentino Müller Thurgau '95	🍷	3

FAEDO (TN)

POJER & SANDRI
LOC. MOLINI, 6
38010 FAEDO (TN)
TEL. 0461/650342

ISERA (TN)

CANTINA D'ISERA
VIA AL PONTE, 1
38060 ISERA (TN)
TEL. 0464/433795

Mario and Fiorentino have succeeded again, once more winning the Three Glasses with their superb red Faye '94, and strengthening a reputation built up over twenty years. In the case of Faye, white wine specialists Pojer and Sandri work with cabernet, merlot and lagrein: in a few years' time their new Valbona estate in the Val di Cembra will be in production, giving them the chance to try their hand with traditional local varieties. These two growers certainly love a challenge. Faye, although from young vineyards, is a real force of nature, a complex and densely-textured red with great concentration, capable of maturing with elegance. In short, it is the result of an approach which has positive effects on all their other wines, beginning with the chardonnay-based Faye Bianco. This wine is strongly characterized by wood flavours but at the same time is elegant and technically very correct. The richly perfumed, stylish Essenzia is a very appealing late harvest wine based on white varieties, which has set an example for winemakers both in the Trentino and beyond. The range also includes classic whites, Chardonnay, Müller Thurgau, Nosiola, Sauvignon and a wonderful aromatic Traminer, perhaps the best in the province. No Metodo Classico Spumante this year, but to be going on with we recommend the excellent Schiava, a fresh, enjoyable and distinctly "Pojer-and-Sandrian" wine, as is the Vin dei Molini. Although we were slightly disappointed by the Pinot Nero, especially the Riserva, the overall picture is very positive.

Cooperative winegrowing organizations in the Trentino are seeking to diversify and consolidate their collective oenological know-how. In this sense Isera is one of the region's most representative cellars. Growers and technicians are united in their commitment to their land, the Vallagarina, and the marzemino grape. It is our pleasure to report the great improvement in the wines of this well-established cooperative, founded ninety years ago, thanks to an Austrian law issued in 1873, when the Trentino and Alto Adige still formed the southern part of the Austro-Hungarian empire. The current figures are: 200 member growers,170 hectares of vineyard and an annual production of 20,000 quintals of grapes. Almost all the varieties covered by the Trentino DOC are harvested here, with one dominating all the others: Marzemino, of which Isera is unanimously considered the capital. The Cantina d'Isera is obviously among the market leaders with this local speciality, and now produces a special green label selection of the varietal, sourced from five different vineyards. The result is a model Marzemino: full, intense, soft and highly perfumed. The other reds, Cabernet and Merlot plus a blend called Novecentosette in honour of the year of foundation, have good structure, in common with the ample selection of whites: Chardonnay, Pinot Grigio, Sauvignon, Müller Thurgau and a delicate Moscato Giallo. Each is the result of accurate and modern vinification, and is good value for money.

● Rosso Faye '94	♟♟♟	5
○ Essenzia Vendemmia Tardiva '96	♟♟	4
○ Trentino Chardonnay '96	♟♟	3*
○ Trentino Müller Thurgau '96	♟♟	4
○ Trentino Traminer '96	♟♟	4
● Trentino Pinot Nero Ris. '94	♟	4
● Rosso Faye '93	♟♟♟	5
○ Essenzia Vendemmia Tardiva	♟♟	4
○ Spumante Cuveé Brut '91	♟♟	4
● Trentino Pinot Nero Ris. '93	♟♟	5

● Trentino Marzemino Etichetta Verde '96	♟♟	3*
● Trentino Merlot '95	♟♟	2*
● Trentino Cabernet '95	♟	2*
● Trentino Marzemino '96	♟	2
○ Trentino Pinot Grigio '96	♟	2
● Trentino Rosso Novecentosette '94	♟	3
○ Trentino Chardonnay '96		2
○ Trentino Moscato Giallo '96		2

ISERA (TN)

DE TARCZAL
LOC. MARANO
38060 ISERA (TN)
TEL. 0464/409134-409086

LASINO (TN)

PRAVIS
VIA LAGOLO, 28
38076 LASINO (TN)
TEL. 0461/564305

This aristocratic grower is a staunch upholder of oenological tradition in the Vallagarina and an indefatigable promoter of the cause of good wine. In keeping with his personality, Ruggero de Tarczal has made a discreet return to our Guide, but the selection of wines he presented is decidedly well-made, and a big improvement on previous vintages. This is due both to a new attention to cellar practices and to generally renewed commitment; in fact he has regained his past status and is now looking with confidence to the future. The cellar and all the vineyards used to belong to the Contessa Alberti and Gezà Dell'Adami de Tarczal, Admiral of the Royal Imperial Austro-Hungarian fleet, ancestor of the present owner. The best wine we tasted is the Marzemino, the pride of the neighbourhood and the result of the ability of this grower, both in the vineyard and among his ancient casks. It is purple-red in colour, with an aroma of violets both on the nose and the palate, and is attractive, elegant and distinctive. The Merlot and Cabernet have all the requisites for a return among the top wines of the Trentino, especially when the new Pragiara is ready, the Bordeaux blend bottled only in very good years which is de Tarczal's prestige label. Among the whites there is a traditional Chardonnay and a most interesting, tangy, mature - and moreover very good value - Pinot Bianco '96.

The Pravis estate has a precise objective: the re-establishment of old local varieties in order to give character and simple authenticity to their wines, in a style which combines tradition with new prospects for the future. Nosiola, groppello, franconia, moscato giallo, rebo and müller thurgau, this last by now acclimatised, are the emblems of the estate whose vineyards are often tiny, situated in widely differing positions. The return to traditional local approaches has resulted in a new gem: Arèle 1983, a Vino Santo from nosiola grapes aged patiently in small barrels. A real mediterranean wine, vigorous and warm with an enticing finish. The young Nosiola we found typical and enjoyable, with its delicate aroma of fresh hazel-nuts and distinct character. Equally good were the aromatic Müller Thurgau and the Polin, a100 per cent pinot grigio bottled without clarification, which gives it a slight coppery hue. The Schiava Gentile is an attractive peachy pink, and is cheerful easy drinking. The Chardonnay was less appealing, an inexpensive white whose only reason for existing is to make up the range. Moving on to the reds, while awaiting the Fratagrande '95, we have two other valid examples: Syrae, from syrah grapes, and Rebo Rigotti, named after the Trentino researcher who perfected the cross between marzemino and merlot. A last mention for El Filò, a groppello partly from new vineyards and partly from ones nearly 100 years old. A rustic wine from the past, but also an example of traditional winemaking which Pravis means to defend against the standardization of tastes and production. We wish them good luck.

●	Trentino Marzemino di Isera '96	🍷🍷	3*
●	Trentino Cabernet Sauvignon '95	🍷	3
●	Trentino Merlot d'Isera '95	🍷	3
O	Trentino Pinot Bianco '96	🍷	2*
O	Trentino Chardonnay '96		2

●	Syrae '95	🍷🍷	4
O	Trentino Müller Thurgau St. Thomà '96	🍷🍷	3*
O	Trentino Nosiola Le Frate '96	🍷🍷	3*
O	Vino Santo Le Arele '83	🍷🍷	5
O	Trentino Pinot Grigio Polin '96	🍷	3
●	Valdadige Schiava Sort'Magre '96	🍷	2*
O	Trentino Chardonnay '96		1
O	Kerner '95	🍷🍷	3
●	Trentino Cabernet Fratagranda '92	🍷🍷	4
O	Trentino Müller Thurgau St. Thomà '95	🍷🍷	3
O	Trentino Nosiola Le Frate '95	🍷🍷	3
O	Vino Santo Le Arele	🍷🍷	4

LAVIS (TN)

NILO BOLOGNANI
VIA STAZIONE, 19
38015 LAVIS (TN)
TEL. 0461/246354

Diego Bolognani and his brothers, cellarmen by family tradition, can now extend the range of their wines with their own red grapes, from vineyards recently bought in the Trento hills. Up till now only white wines had been marketed with the family label, although the winery vinifies thousands of quintals of red grapes, to be sold exclusively in bulk. We have followed this producer's development for several years. Bolognani's wines today offer good quality, made in a style which gives them immediate drinkability, but which perhaps deprives them of some personality. This is evident in their collection of whites, which are pleasant, well-made, but lacking the charm which we think Bolognani could impart to their wines. However a satisfactory standard has been maintained by the 1996 Pinot Grigio, a vigorous wine of seductive flowery aromas, with some apple and excellent structure on the palate, and also by the Moscato Giallo, a wine which few producers tackle, because of the hazards involved. This one however is flawless, ripe and alluring. Also good are the Müller Thurgau, fruity with a vague hint of riesling, the Nosiola, slightly bitter, full-flavoured, enjoyable, and the Sauvignon, with nettles and tomatoes on the nose and peppery in the mouth. The Chardonnay on the other hand is light, closed and unaccountably sharp and citrusy. We await the reds with confidence.

LAVIS (TN)

CANTINA SOCIALE LA VIS
VIA CARMINE, 12
38015 LAVIS (TN)
TEL. 0461/246325

La Vis is the best cooperative winery in the Trentino and easily among the first five in Italy. Its status is undeniable. It is of little importance that La Vis does not win a Three Glass award in the 1998 edition of our Guide. It has presented a range of products of unqualified merit. All the wines, despite the volumes produced, have marked personality and represent exceptional value for money and clear-cut, reliable quality. Ritratto, a blend of teroldego and lagrein, is a rich, mature red with great impact on the nose and palate. Similar structure is displayed by another of the Ritratti series, a broad, powerful Cabernet Sauvignon, partially penalised by its youth. The serious whites are also excellent, in particular a superbly satisfying Chardonnay. The other reds are also very good, not only the superior Pinot Nero Riserva but the basic range from the Teroldego Rotaliano to the Cabernet. The Müller Thurgau and Pinot Grigio, both the basic version and the selection, again prove very agreeable drinking with unfailing style. The Nosiola is tasty and highly drinkable and the Trento Talento Arcade an appealing sparkler which is improving rapidly. The two Sorni DOCs, the white from nosiola, chardonnay and pinot bianco and the red from teroldego and lagrein, are worth special mention for their simply delightful quality - and at such a reasonable price! Lastly, the Moscato Rosa, a jewel which we will certainly hear more about in the future.

O	Müller Thurgau della Val di Cembra '96	♟♟	3*
O	Trentino Moscato Giallo '96	♟♟	3*
O	Trentino Pinot Grigio '96	♟♟	3*
O	Trentino Nosiola '95	♟	3
O	Trentino Sauvignon '96	♟	3
O	Trentino Chardonnay '96		3
O	Müller Thurgau della Val di Cembra '95	♟♟	3
O	Trentino Moscato Giallo '94	♟♟	3
O	Trentino Moscato Giallo '95	♟♟	3
O	Trentino Pinot Grigio '95	♟♟	3
O	Sauvignon Atesino '95	♟	3
O	Trentino Chardonnay '95	♟	3
O	Trentino Nosiola '95	♟	3

●	Ritratto '95	♟♟	5
●	Trentino Cabernet Sauvignon Ritratti '95	♟♟	4*
O	Trentino Chardonnay Ritratti '96	♟♟	4
O	Trentino Müller Thurgau '96	♟♟	3*
O	Trentino Nosiola '96	♟♟	2*
O	Trentino Pinot Grigio Ritratti '96	♟♟	4
●	Trentino Pinot Nero Ritratti '95	♟♟	4*
O	Trentino Sorni Bianco '96	♟	2*
●	Ritratto '91	♟♟♟	4
O	Trentino Pinot Grigio Ritratti '95	♟♟♟	4*
O	Trentino Chardonnay '95	♟♟	2*

LAVIS (TN)

CESCONI
VIA MARCONI, 39
LOC. PRESSANO
38015 LAVIS (TN)
TEL. 0461/240355

This estate's wines immediately conquered the field, outstripping at numerous tastings the habitual leaders of Trentino winemaking. The Cesconi family, Paolo and his four sons Franco, Roberto, Lorenzo and Alessandro are growers, in whom the energy of the countryman and the will to learn constitute a winning combination. After only two vintages of their own, made in the small cellar situated in the hills among vineyards kept like gardens, their white wines- there will be no reds until recently planted vineyards at another of their properties at Ceniga di Drò comes into production- made everybody sit up. The Traminer Aromatico is broad on the nose and smooth in the mouth, with a long finish, the Pinot Bianco rivals its exclusive counterparts in the Alto Adige with its delicate aromas, attractive development of flavour and long, well-defined finish. The Sauvignon has varietal character, good texture, freshness and elegance, with flavours reminiscent of nectarines. The Chardonnay is very fruity and enjoyable, but it is still too young to expect balance and complexity, while the Pinot Grigio is sturdy and intense with hints of pear, fresh, and very drinkable. Five wines, four hits and the only lacuna the small quantities produced to date; a total of less than 30,000 bottles a year, which makes Cesconi a collector's item.

MEZZOCORONA (TN)

MARCO DONATI
VIA CESARE BATTISTI, 41
38016 MEZZOCORONA (TN)
TEL. 0461/604141

Marco Donati confirms his place among the most intelligent growers of the Trentino. He is a keen producer of classic wines of the Piana Rotaliana, and although he does not neglect experimentation with new varieties, or the production of spumante and small lots of a few specific wines, he definitely concentrates on Teroldego. This is his wine, from the vineyards surrounding his small estate on the Noce, where the ideal soils for viticulture, formed by the watercourse through the centuries, are situated. A firm believer in reds, Donati makes Teroldego with a pronounced "Rotaliano" character, but he also produces a traditional Lagrein, a subtly fragrant Pinot Nero which is slender and drinkable, and an appealing, fresh and elegant Merlot. Marco also experiments with unusual grape mixes such as the Vino del Maso, teroldego vinified with lagrein and merlot, and his range also includes some whites. Besides the varietals, there is a cuvée of Sauvignon, Chardonnay and Moscato Giallo. From this blend he makes the Terre del Noce, a white with good structure and immediate freshness, aromatic and delightful. His Sauvignon is interesting, although it could have been more concentrated, and the technically correct Pinot Grigio has flavour and fragrance to match another of his whites, the Müller Thurgau. Not to be left out is the Moscato Rosa, always one of the Trentino's most enjoyable wines. Marco Donati is a first-rate grower, from a family which has been tending vineyards for five generations, but he has the ability and wholehearted ambition to go much further.

○ Sauvignon Atesino '96	￥￥	3*
○ Trentino Pinot Bianco '96	￥￥	3*
○ Trentino Pinot Grigio '96	￥￥	3*
○ Trentino Traminer Aromatico '96	￥￥	3*
○ Trentino Chardonnay '96	￥	3

○ Bianco Terre del Noce '96	￥￥	3*
● Moscato Rosa Atesino '95	￥	4
● Rosso Vino del Maso '96	￥	4
○ Sauvignon Atesino '96	￥	3
● Teroldego Rotaliano '96	￥	3
○ Trentino Müller Thurgau '96		3
○ Trentino Pinot Grigio '96		3
○ Bianco Terre del Noce '95	￥￥	3*
● Moscato Rosa Atesino '94	￥	4
⊙ Trentino Lagrein Rosato '95	￥	2

MEZZOCORONA (TN)

F.LLI DORIGATI
VIA DANTE, 5
38016 MEZZOCORONA (TN)
TEL. 0461/605313

Franco and Carlo Dorigati are cellarmen. They do not enjoy talking and avoid being drawn into local arguments about theories of winemaking, but they are alert and ready to take on a challenge. With the help of Enrico Paternoster, one of the most competent oenologists currently working in the Trentino, it has taken them only a few years to gain a leading place among the region's small producers. Although gratified, they let their wines speak for themselves, starting, naturally, with the Teroldego. The standard selection is well made, clean and balanced; it is ready and should be drunk young. The Riserva Teroldego, the '94 Diedri, is very different, with a good deep colour and a profusion of aromas and flavours. It is a most attractive red with a depth worthy of far more widely recognised wines, and deserves applause. The other wines are also sound and flawless, the red Rebo from the merlot/marzemino crossing, the rosé Lagrein, and the two full-flavoured whites Chardonnay and Pinot Grigio. The Trento Talento spumante, the Methius Riserva '91, is again highly commended. Every year we have the pleasure of noting its distinctive aroma of resin with hints of tropical fruit, and delicate, very fine and long-lasting perlage. On the palate it is impressive, full, with a long, satisfying flavour which is rarely found in other sparklers of the Trentino.

●	Teroldego Rotaliano Diedri Ris. '94	▼▼	5
○	Trento Methius Ris. '91	▼▼	5
●	Rebo '95	▼	3
●	Teroldego Rotaliano '96	▼	3
○	Trentino Chardonnay '96	▼	2
⊙	Trentino Lagrein Kretzer '96	▼	2
○	Trentino Pinot Grigio '96	▼	2
○	Rebo Atesino '94	▽▽	3*
●	Teroldego Rotaliano Diedri '90	▽▽	5
●	Teroldego Rotaliano Diedri Ris. '92	▽▽	4
○	Trentino Chardonnay Le Alte '94	▽▽	4
○	Trento Methius '90	▽▽	5

MEZZOCORONA (TN)

MEZZACORONA
VIA IV NOVEMBRE
38016 MEZZOCORONA (TN)
TEL. 0461/605163

1998 is the year of the new winery, an enormous modern building erected in record time, and an award-winning example of modern architecture. A new building, but the same approach to production, under the dedicated management of Fabio Rizzoli: quality combined with substantial output. And in fact the standard of the wines produced by this cooperative with its one thousand member growers, is consistently good. Their top red, Teroldego, maintains all its unmistakeable vigour and grapey character in thousands and thousands of bottles. The Riserva '94 is a particularly interesting wine. Further confirmation of quality comes from the Lagrein, a wine from a twin variety of Teroldego: it is a deep ruby colour, seemingly aggressive on the nose, immediately attractive on the palate. We tasted a threesome of highly aromatic whites: Traminer, Müller Thurgau and Chardonnay, all attractive wines with good acidity, offering agreeable drinking. The two examples of spumante classico were of unquestionably high quality. Both the Rotari Arte Italiana and the Rotari Riserva '93 have the MezzaCorona hallmark, fruit reminiscent of mountain apples and well-developed flavour, elegance and length. These first class sparklers are the products with which the winery intends to challenge the entire Italian spumante sector by attacking the international market: the aim, to increase the market share of Trentino DOC abroad and consolidate the MezzaCorona brand through volume of production and competitive pricing. Prosit!

○	Trento Rotari Ris. '93	▼▼	4*
●	Teroldego Rotaliano Riserva '94	▼▼	3*
○	Trentino Traminer Aromatico '96	▼▼	3*
○	Trento Rotari Brut Arte Italiana	▼▼	3*
○	Trentino Chardonnay '96	▼	2
●	Trentino Lagrein '95	▼	3
○	Trentino Müller Thurgau '96	▼	2
○	Spumante Metodo Classico Rotari Ris. '88	▽▽	4
●	Trentino Cabernet Sauvignon Oltresarca '94	▽▽	3*
○	Trento Rotari Brut Ris.	▽▽	4

MEZZOLOMBARDO (TN)　　MEZZOLOMBARDO (TN)

COOPERATIVA ROTALIANA
C.SO DEL POPOLO, 6
38017 MEZZOLOMBARDO (TN)
TEL. 0461/601010

BARONE DE CLES
VIA MAZZINI, 18
38017 MEZZOLOMBARDO (TN)
TEL. 0461/601081

Discretion is the trademark of this large cooperative: a quiet and steady devotion to the improvement of the wines of the Campo Rotaliano, the vineyards on the plain between the river Adige and the smaller Noce , a little north of Trento, almost on the border of the Alto Adige. Behind it lie seventy years of commitment, over 260 member growers, and 35,000 quintals of grapes. These come from widely differing vineyards, not only on the plain where the main variety, Teroldego, is grown but also higher up, in the hills which overlook the Rotaliano. Evidence of improving quality is immediate in the whites, from the Chardonnay to the Müller Thurgau, wines with fruit and good structure. An example is the Pinot Bianco, one of the best in the Trentino. It has firm character, but at the same time is fragrant and delightfully drinkable with an inviting, complex softness. The leader among the reds is Teroldego, of which the Riserva '94, bottled with a new white label, is definitely the best. For some years the top of its class, it is medium bodied, with distinctive fruit, and a highly individual bite of acidity. Equally successful is the standard Teroldego vintage '96: a very fresh and drinkable wine. The Merlot and Lagrein are selections - their labels the work of artist Paolo Tait, a rising young painter of the Trentino - which display character and definite potential for development. The whole winery, under the management of good-humoured Luciano Lunelli, is due for modernisation. Plans for the building of new premises are ready, but the main objective will be above all to develop quality.

To describe this estate is to tell the history of the Trentino. As long ago as the14th century the ancient family of de Cles owned vineyards on the terraces round Castel Cles, their fief from time immemorial. The land still belongs to the family, although the vineyards surrounding the castle have given way to thriving orchards. This was the birthplace in 1485 of Bernardo de Cles, the best-known member of the dynasty, who became Bishop of Trento and Bressanone, then Cardinal, and finally High Chancellor to King Ferdinand of Austria. The de Cles family are therefore historically the most ancient growers in the Trentino. The tradition is carried on today by the barons Michele, Guido and Leonardo. The estate vineyards are devoted mainly to teroldego, the grape producing the red wine of the same name, the most representative product of the Piana Rotaliana. Here the de Cles family have always had the best vineyards. Over the last few vintages, with the aid of renewed efforts on the part of Baron Leonardo, who is in charge of vinification, the estate has taken a definite turn for the better. The wines have regained their form, and once again display unquestionable class. The Maso Scari '96 is a concentrated Teroldego, with room for improvement but decidedly enjoyable. The Lagrein has appeal, even if it is less interesting than wines from the same variety made in the Alto Adige. The same goes for the Merlot. We also tasted a fragrant Moscato Giallo and a spicy Traminer. We will have to wait for the new wave wines, but we are certain that when they arrive we will not be disappointed.

O	Trentino Pinot Bianco '96	YY	2*
●	Teroldego Rotaliano '96	Y	2
●	Teroldego Rotaliano Ris. '94	Y	3
O	Trentino Chardonnay '96	Y	2
●	Trentino Lagrein Tait '95	Y	3
O	Trentino Müller Thurgau '96	Y	2
●	Teroldego Rotaliano Ris. '93	♈♈	3
●	Teroldego Rotaliano '94	♈	2*
O	Trentino Chardonnay '95	♈	2
●	Trentino Lagrein '94	♈	2*
O	Trentino Pinot Bianco '95	♈	2*
O	Trentino Pinot Grigio '95		2

●	Teroldego Rotaliano		
	Maso Scari '96	YY	3*
●	Trentino Lagrein '96	Y	3
O	Trentino Moscato Giallo '96	Y	3
O	Trentino Traminer '96	Y	3
●	Rosso del Cardinale '89		4
●	Trentino Merlot '92		3

MEZZOLOMBARDO (TN) NOGAREDO (TN)

FORADORI
VIA D. CHIESA, 1
38017 MEZZOLOMBARDO (TN)
TEL. 0461/601046

CASTEL NOARNA
VIA CASTELNUOVO, 1
38060 NOGAREDO (TN)
TEL. 0464/435222-413295

In order to bring out the vital personality of her wines, Elisabetta Foradori has decided to use a freer hand. The meticulous but slightly academic winemaking which characterised some of her wines in the past has given way to simplicity and a certain amount of improvisation. Her instinct for winemaking, which she was born to and has become her life, is her guide, and perhaps it is only nature which has let her down this year. For the first time after a string of unquestionable successes, the wines of this historic estate cannot be included among those receiving our highest award. However this is almost a minor detail in the context of the wines we tasted. The reds are all first class and taking the strict average of the scores achieved in tasting, are the best in the Trentino. Three Teroldegos, including one Riserva, and two blends, the Karanar and the Ailanpa easily achieved Two Glass ratings. The Granato is a unique example of power and complexity, a drinking experience which only a Foradori Teroldego can provide. The vintage has held back the other Teroldegos, especially the Vigneto Sgarzon, but they are still wonderfully drinkable reds of great structure. Elisabetta has already planned her comeback and will continue to concentrate on Teroldego, carrying out an even more rigorous selection. If the vintage is favourable, the results should be outstanding.

It is difficult to convey the vitality of Marco Zani in a few words, he is so full of proposals, ideas, notions, enthusiastic plans in constant evolution. These highly individual wines derive from vineyards surrounding his ancient castle on the hills of Rovereto. Wines which are the result of a specific production philosophy aimed at achieving quality of the highest level. All the requisites are there, even if the vineyards are still young and the vintages have been a bit up and down. This year we very much liked the Cabernet Romeo '93, an intense, textured ruby in colour, soft and velvety; it will improve in the bottle. The same can be said for the Bianco di Castelnuovo, from a cépage which produces a complex wine on the nose and on the palate. The Sauvignon is good, among the best in the Trentino. The Nosiola is again a top example of this variety, but we are reserving judgement on the Chardonnay which is still too young. The Mercuria is likeable and unusual, a pleasant and fragrant red blend, and the Schiava of above average quality. It comes from an ancient vineyard on the hill dominated by this castle which is part of the Vallagarina's history. The future, in terms of winemaking, is all in the expert hands of the young Zani.

● Ailanpa '95	▼▼	4
● Granato '95	▼▼	5
● Karanar '95	▼▼	4
● Teroldego Rotaliano '96	▼▼	3*
● Teroldego Rotaliano Morei '96	▼▼	3*
● Teroldego Rotaliano Sgarzon '95	▼▼	4
● Granato '91	▼▼▼	5
● Granato '93	▼▼▼	5
● Teroldego Rotaliano Sgarzon '93	▼▼▼	4*
● Teroldego Rotaliano Sgarzon '94	▼▼▼	4*

○ Bianco di Castelnuovo '95	▼▼	4
● Trentino Cabernet Romeo '93	▼▼	4
○ Trentino Nosiola '96	▼▼	3*
○ Trentino Sauvignon '96	▼▼	3*
● Trentino Cabernet Sauvignon Mercuria '96	▼	3
● Valdadige Schiava Scalzavacca '96	▼	2
○ Trentino Nosiola '95	▼▼	3
● Valdadige Schiava Scalzavacca '95	▼▼	2
● Mercuria Rosso '95	▼	3
○ Trentino Chardonnay Campo Grande '95	▼	4
○ Trentino Chardonnay Reno '95	▼	3

NOGAREDO (TN)

NOMI (TN)

LETRARI
VIA LODRON, 4
38060 NOGAREDO (TN)
TEL. 0464/411093-414147

LUCIANO BATTISTOTTI
VIA III NOVEMBRE, 21
38060 NOMI (TN)
TEL. 0464/834145

The Letari are a wine producing family; Lionello, the father, with almost fifty years of oenological experience behind him is in charge, flanked by his daughter Lucia, a keen winemaker. Lucia is wholeheartedly committed to Cabernet Sauvignon, and with the '94 vintage she scored her first, unqualified success: an impressive wine, dark red with tints of garnet, evolved, with good tertiary aroma, full and long-lasting in the mouth. It is a wine capable of improving and achieving superlative quality. The Letraris are also building a new, modern cellar in the midst of the vineyards near Rovereto. However, staying with the wines still produced in Palazzo Lodron, the Marzemino is always first choice among the reds. Two versions, two selections, the same scores, even if we expected to find a touch of greater complexity in the more important Selezione '96. This we did find in the Sauvignon, which is very concentrated, with good intensity of colour and herbaceous nose - most noticeably elderberry - good structure and a long finish. The other whites, the Müller Thurgau, the Chardonnay and the Pinot Bianco were also interesting. We would have liked more grip both in the Spumante Metodo Classico (Lionello Letrari is a pioneer producer of spumante in the Trentino) and in the Moscato Rosa, which was unaccountably flat in the bottle, lacking the character which has made it a classic of the region.

Battistotti is a family-run winery which has been operating in the Vallagarina for almost fifty years. It has always offered undemanding wines which are good value for money. Management now is in the hands of three young brothers, Elio, Enzo and Luciano, who has a diploma in oenology from the school of San Michele all'Adige. He is in charge of all the stages of vinification and a taster on various commissions controlling the DOC wines of the Trentino. Cellar techniques are irreproachable and all the wines are absolutely flawless, with agreeably spontaneous character. The Marzemino can be considered a model of its type: ruby-red in colour, it has a delicate aroma of violets and soft red fruit; on the palate it is dry, flavoursome, full and balanced and is one of the best tasted in the preparation of this Guide. Also good were the Chardonnay, which is fresh and direct, and the Merlot. The latter is still young and made in a simple style perhaps intended to encourage the consumer to get to know this wonderful variety. The Schiava, is a delightful, mouth-watering rosé. The Battistotti also produce Müller Thurgau, Nosiola, Moscato Giallo and Cabernet; they make a spumante classico, Le Bastie, named after the vineyard of origin, and - although it did not appear this year - a Moscato Rosa. Only a few thousand bottles of these last two wines are produced, almost as a whim, but they demonstrate the enthusiasm and abilities of this rapidly expanding winery.

●	Trentino Cabernet Sauvignon Ris. '94	♟♟	3*
●	Trentino Marzemino '96	♟♟	2*
●	Trentino Marzemino Selezione '96	♟♟	3*
O	Trentino Sauvignon '96	♟♟	3*
O	Trentino Chardonnay '96	♟	3
●	Trentino Moscato Rosa '95	♟	5
O	Trentino Pinot Bianco '96	♟	3
O	Trento Brut Letrari '93	♟	4
O	Spumante Metodo Classico Ris. '91	♟♟	5
●	Trentino Moscato Rosa '93	♟♟	5
●	Trentino Moscato Rosa '94	♟♟	5
O	Trentino Pinot Bianco '94	♟♟	3

●	Trentino Marzemino '96	♟♟	3*
●	Trentino Cabernet '96	♟	3
O	Trentino Chardonnay '96	♟	3
●	Trentino Merlot '96	♟	3
⊙	Schiava Atesina '96		2
O	Trentino Müller Thurgau '96		3

ROVERETO (TN)

BALTER
VIA VALLUNGA, 26
38068 ROVERETO (TN)
TEL. 0464/430101

ROVERETO (TN)

LONGARIVA
LOC. BORGO SACCO
VIA ZANDONAI, 6
38068 ROVERETO (TN)
TEL. 0464/437200

Nicola Balter is a dedicated grower and the quality displayed by his wines places them among the protagonists of the oenological revival in the Trentino. But because he is among those who initiated the changes, Nicola is paying the price along with numerous other small, talented producers, of an evolution which has suddenly become uncertain, in spite of their far-reaching projects. This is mainly due to difficult vintages, but Trentino winegrowers also find themselves in a dilemma in the face of the strong competition of the cooperatives, and often tempted by expediency. And so the estates - and this one is perhaps not only the best managed in the province but also the one with the greatest natural assets - are feeling the consequences. The Cabernet Sauvignon, of outstanding potential for two vintages, now displays only its frankness and unyielding vigour, but lacks that exclusive touch of finesse. The most recent release of the spumante classico Trento DOC, symbol of the estate, does not have that "bearable lightness" which is essential for top quality sparklers. Nicola Balter makes up for this with two highly satisfactory whites: the Sauvignon which is full-flavoured with a very direct appeal, and the new Clarae, an aromatic blend characterised by delicate, stimulating harmony of expression. The Traminer is sound and the Rossinot, a cuvée based on pinot nero, lagrein and schiava gentile, is pleasant and highly drinkable.

Marco Manica produces a line up of wines as interesting as they are numerous: thirteen first class samples as proof of the established merit of this modern estate of the Vallagarina. The wines, especially the reds, have personality and consistency. The Marognon, a Cabernet Sauvignon Riserva '94, is intense, complex and tannic with a potential which immediately earned it a place among the best of the Trentino. Excellent performances also from the Zinzele, a promising Pinot Nero - the vines are still very young - and from the Tovi, an outstanding Merlot which we will hear more of in the future. The traditional Marzemino is technically flawless with an unusually attractive purplish colour. Satisfactory among the whites is the Cascari, a flowery Sauvignon, well-structured and straightforward, while the Perer, one of the region's historic Chardonnays, was slightly disappointing, probably due to an unfavourable year for this variety in the Vallagarina. The Graminè, a coppery hued Pinot Grigio, is pleasant and unusual, and the Pergole, a delicate Pinot Bianco, is very easy drinking. Marco Manica is becoming increasingly reliable, and with some favourable harvests, and just a little patience, his already excellent wines will become very impressive.

○ Clarae '95	🍷🍷	4
○ Trentino Sauvignon '96	🍷🍷	3*
○ Trento Balter Brut	🍷	4
● Trentino Cabernet Sauvignon '93	🍷	4
○ Trentino Traminer Aromatico '96	🍷	3
☉ Rossinot '96		2
○ Sauvignon Atesino '94	🍷🍷	3
○ Trento Balter Brut	🍷🍷	4*
● Trentino Cabernet Sauvignon '91	🍷🍷	3*
○ Sauvignon Atesino '95	🍷	3
● Trentino Cabernet Sauvignon '95	🍷	4
○ Trentino Traminer Aromatico '95	🍷	3

● Trentino Cabernet Sauvignon Marognon Ris. '94	🍷🍷	4
● Trentino Pinot Nero Zinzele Ris. '93	🍷🍷	4
○ Trentino Sauvignon Cascari '96	🍷🍷	3*
● Trentino Cabernet Quartella '94	🍷	3
● Trentino Marzemino '96	🍷	3
● Trentino Merlot Tovi Ris. '94	🍷	4
○ Trentino Pinot Grigio Graminè '96	🍷	3
● Trentino Rosso Tre Cesure '94	🍷	3
○ Trentino Chardonnay Perer '96		3
○ Trentino Chardonnay Perer '95	🍷🍷	3*
● Trentino Merlot Tovi '92	🍷🍷	3*
● Trentino Merlot Tovi '93	🍷🍷	3*

ROVERETO (TN)

ARMANDO SIMONCELLI
LOC. NAVESÈL, 7
38068 ROVERETO (TN)
TEL. 0464/432373

Armando Simoncelli, an untalkative winegrower with a gruff manner who is always busy in his vineyard, seems almost old-fashioned. A transformation takes place as soon as he opens the doors of his cellar, establishing the friendly atmosphere which good wine evokes. He is a full-time grower who concentrates on making good wine and does not enjoy publicity events and gatherings. He has always been well-known for his Marzemino, the red wine which is the pride of the Vallagarina, in his hands a skilled creation at the top of its category. For some time he has also been trying his hand at whites and two years ago succeeded in producing a Chardonnay and a Pinot Bianco of incredible complexity and fullness, with an entirely Trentino-style finesse. Due to the inconstancies of the weather this success was not repeated the following vintage, but his whites, including a spumante which is a perfect example of Metodo Classico although of artisan production - remain among the most interesting of the area. The same goes for the equally satisfying reds, foremost being the Marzemino, followed by the Merlot and the Cabernet, although both were perhaps bottled too young. The Bordeaux blend, Navesèl, named after the family holding of this friendly grower, is a wine which in a good vintage can line up with the best in the country.

S. MICHELE ALL'ADIGE (TN)

AZIENDA VITIVINICOLA
DELL'ISTITUTO AGRARIO PROVINCIALE
VIA E. MACH, 2
38010 S. MICHELE ALL'ADIGE (TN)
TEL. 0461/615252

This cellar, experimental from the year of its foundation, 1874, hardly ever gets a wine wrong, thanks to a sort of progressive conservatism which has benefits for the whole winemaking sector of the region. Conservative because the results are a faithful copy of the provincial standard, wines which are very good but rarely outstanding. The best wine in this edition of the Guide is the Merlot, of an impressive cardinal red, intense, spicy and peppery on the nose, with plum and wild berries in the mouth. The Castel San Michele, the first Bordeaux blend produced in the Trentino, did not seem as complex, and had slightly faulty wood influence, and flavours which still have to unfold. The other reds are more or less on a par. The Pinot Nero has orange tints, is closed, but is reasonably drinkable. The Lagrein is agreeable but seems a weaker version than its counterparts of the Alto Adige. Moving on to the whites, we found the late harvest Riesling Renano very appealing; the Trento DOC spumante was good and the Müller Thurgau attractively fragrant. The Moscato Rosa is very well made and pleasantly perfumed, although the finish lacks persistence. The wines are respectable, but the overall quality of production is probably conditioned by the political context - the Agricultural Institute is run by the autonomous Province of Trento - and as a consequence it risks becoming entrenched rather than looking towards the future.

● Trentino Marzemino '96	▼▼	3*
○ Trentino Chardonnay '96	▼	3
● Trentino Merlot '96	▼	3
● Trentino Rosso Navesel '94	▼	3
● Trentino Cabernet '96		3
○ Trentino Pinot Bianco '96		3
○ Trentino Chardonnay '94	♈♈	3
○ Trentino Chardonnay '95	♈♈	3*
○ Trentino Pinot Bianco '95	♈♈	3

● Trentino Merlot '95	▼▼	4
○ Trentino Riesling Renano '94	▼▼	4
● Trentino Castel San Michele '94	▼	4
● Trentino Lagrein '95	▼	3
● Trentino Moscato Rosa '93	▼	5
○ Trentino Müller Thurgau '96	▼	3
○ Trento Talento San Michele	▼	4
○ Trentino Pinot Bianco '96		3
● Castel San Michele '93	♈♈	4
○ Prepositura Atesino '93	♈♈	4*
○ Spumante Riserva del Fondatore '89	♈♈	5
○ Trentino Pinot Bianco '94	♈♈	3
○ Trentino Pinot Bianco '95	♈♈	3*

S. MICHELE ALL'ADIGE (TN) S. MICHELE ALL'ADIGE (TN)

ENDRIZZI
LOC. MASETTO
38010 S. MICHELE ALL'ADIGE (TN)
TEL. 0461/650129

ZENI
FRAZ. GRUMO
VIA MARCONI, 31
38010 SAN MICHELE ALL'ADIGE (TN)
TEL. 0461/650456

There is art in every corner of this estate. It is even on the bottles, with the designs of Giuseppe Debiasi, one of the best known artists of the Trentino. The owners, Christine and Paolo Endrici, want to wed their passion for wine with their interest in the new artistic trends in Europe. German-born Christine has discovered a firm believer in experimentation in her husband Paolo. The estate's technical consultants are in fact the nearby Agricultural Institute, and with their help it aims at further diversifying production. The '96 vintage has confirmed the merits of the wines produced by the Endricis (the similarity of the names is mere coincidence; Endrizzi was the name of the first owners of the winery). The more traditional Teroldego, Pinot Nero, Chardonnay and Pinot Grigio maintain the standard described in previous editions of the Guide: they are correct, honestly priced, agreeable, but not impressive. (This verdict however is common to almost all the producers of the Trentino). Their Collezione wines are of more interest. The Chardonnay is full, robust and balanced, penalized only by the freakish behaviour of the '94 harvest. The Cabernet Sauvignon '93 although strongly characterized by its time in barriques has an explosive quantity of ripe fruit. The wine which had the most success with our commission was the Masetto spumante, a Trento DOC Brut with lots of character, complex fruit and satisfying yeasty overtones. Finally the dessert wine Dulcis in Fundo, is an intriguing blend of chardonnay, traminer aromatico, moscato giallo and sauvignon, which really does have, as the name suggests, a sweet finish.

For more than twenty years the Zeni brothers Andrea and Roberto have been in the top rank of production of Trentino DOC wines. They began almost for fun, but with great enthusiasm, as soon as they got their diplomas from the nearby Agricultural Institute of San Michele all'Adige. It only took them a few years to earn a reputation which travelled well beyond the confines of the region. Their wines have perhaps not always displayed marked personality, but the Zenis have not been discouraged and are back in the Guide this year, thanks to a general improvement over the whole range, and in particular in their Teroldego Rotaliano. This is a wine which immediately reveals personality with its lively aroma and strong grapey character. The Riesling Renano, a wine to come back to in a few years' time, is one of the best tasted this year, light and fresh. Their range of whites comprises practically every varietal covered by the Trentino DOC, including Nosiola and Müller Thurgau. The Sauvignon '96, with elderberry and pepper on the nose and in the mouth, is commendable; it is an inviting wine with remarkable length and freshness. Another credit to this estate is the Moscato Rosa. The first vintages suffered from over-high yields but now with production reduced and different clones, the wine has acquired fullness, with strong scents of wild roses and a pleasantly spicy note of juniper.

○ Trento Masetto	🍷🍷	4
○ Dulcis in Fundo '95	🍷	4
● Teroldego Rotaliano '96	🍷	3
● Trentino Cabernet Collezione '93	🍷	4
○ Trentino Chardonnay Collezione '94	🍷	4
○ Trentino Pinot Grigio '96		3
○ Trentino Chardonnay Tradizione '95	🍷🍷	3
● Trentino Moscato Rosa Collezione '94	🍷🍷	5

● Teroldego Rotaliano Pini '93	🍷🍷	4
● Teroldego Rotaliano '96	🍷	3
● Trentino Moscato Rosa '96	🍷	4
○ Trentino Riesling Renano Reré '96	🍷	3
○ Trentino Sauvignon '96	🍷	3
○ Trentino Nosiola '96		3

TRENTO

TRENTO

CAVIT CONSORZIO DI CANTINE SOCIALI
VIA DEL PONTE, 31
LOC. RAVINA
38100 TRENTO
TEL. 0461/381711

CESARINI SFORZA
VIA STELLA, 9
LOC. RAVINA
38100 TRENTO
TEL. 0461/923360

Cavit is a colossus on an international scale, with almost six thousand member growers, and a production which has even reached the markets of the Far East. It is pointless to talk of figures: they are all huge and pay tribute to the energy of a top company which has also made its bid for quality, with undeniable success. The wine in question is the superb Graal '93 Riserva spumante. A sparkler with outstanding elegance, sophisticated, developed fruit and a wonderfully complex finish. A Trento Talento DOC which once again proves the ability of this region to produce classic style sparkling wines. Further confirmation is provided by the other Cavit Brut, the Firmato (annual production almost one million bottles) whose delightful flavours have a touch of refined seductiveness. These two sparklers are a triumph, but the other whites this year are also well up in the top range, starting with the very complete Chardonnay Collezione di Maso Toresella '95, with its rich golden hue, good structure and fruit and vanilla aromas. The Vino Santo and the Vendemmia Tardiva are also highly commended, as is the Quattro Vicariati, a red blend in the Bordeaux style. The other wines from the Bottega de' Vinai and Terrazze della Luna ranges are very well made.

Trento is a focal point for top level spumante production. Three distinguished producers of DOC bubbles are concentrated in the space of a few hundred metres, at Ravina along the Brennero motorway. This is one of them. Completely restructured by the father and son owners, Lamberto and Filippo Cesarini Sforza, this winery has for years been committed to the development of spumante made both by the "classico" and tank re-fermentation methods. In fact the Cesarini have evolved their own spumante technique, based on the so-called "cuve close" system. And it is from the Metodo Cesarini Sforza Lungo that the first, excellent results arrive. The Riserva dei Conti is a spumante with very fine perlage, characteristic intensity on the nose and a well-balanced flavour of mature yeasts; a mouth-filling, satisfying wine. The same can be said for the white label Riserva, another captivating sparkler. The silver label Blanc de Blancs is a slender Chardonnay wine with an unusual youthful zest which makes an ideal aperitif. Finally, the Metodo Classico Brut Millesimato (black label with the golden eagle, the symbol of Trento) has a delicacy of aroma and fullness of flavour perfectly in line with the standards of the Trento DOC.

○	Trento Graal Brut Ris. '93	♟♟♟	4*
○	Trentino Chardonnay		
	Maso Toresella '95	♟♟	4
○	Trentino Vino Santo '89	♟♟	5
○	Trento Brut Firmato	♟♟	4*
○	Vendemmia Tardiva		
	Collezione '95	♟♟	4
○	Bianco Maso Toresella '94	♟♟	3
●	Trentino Marzemino		
	Terrazze della Luna '95	♟♟	3
○	Vendemmia Tardiva		
	Collezione '94	♟♟	4

○	Brut Riserva	♟♟	4*
○	Brut Riserva dei Conti	♟♟	4*
○	Blanc de Blancs	♟	4
○	Trento Classico		
	Riserva Aquila Reale '92	♟	5
○	Brut Riserva	♟♟	4*
○	Brut Riserva dei Conti	♟♟	4*
○	Trento Classico Brut	♟♟	5
○	Blanc de Blancs	♟	4
●	Trentino Lagrein		
	Villa Graziadei '94	♟	3
○	Trento Classico		
	Riserva Aquila Reale	♟	6

TRENTO

FERRARI
VIA DEL PONTE, 15
LOC. RAVINA
38040 TRENTO
TEL. 0461/972311

The Lunelli brothers always aim for the top, firmly convinced in the undeniable attraction of their own spumante, the sparklers which are perhaps the most imitated in Italy. Once again they have outstripped their rivals, despite the competition of excellent wines from the Trentino and elsewhere. For the present they remain unequalled, thanks to the consistent quality of a production which in terms of quantity, is momentous. The Riserva '89 Giulio Ferrari, which has always been a benchmark for Italian spumante, deserves particular praise. It is elegant, well-defined, flawless, full and long-finishing. The rest of the range, by now extensive, is excellent, from the Demi-Sec to the Maximum, from the Brut to the Perlè, from the Rosé to the Brut Incontri, the latest wine from Ferrari. Features common to all are finesse and abundance of fruit, with floral undertones, a hint of spices and just the right body, which makes these sparklers ideal for drinking with a wide range of dishes. For some years, under a different label, the Lunelli brothers have also produced their own estate wines. For the moment only whites are involved, but a Pinot Nero and a Bordeaux blend from vineyards owned by them in the lower Vallagarina are on the way. Meanwhile the whites are increasingly successful, thanks to a combination of elegance, definition and structure. This is especially true of the new Sauvignon Villa San Nicolò, which flanks the Villa Margon and the Villa Gentilotti, whites whose merits are beyond question but which are still evolving, and will be best tasted with a few years of bottle age.

TRENTO

LE MERIDIANE
LOC. CASTELLER, 6
38100 TRENTO
TEL. 0461/920811

This estate is one of the most attractive new arrivals on the Trentino winemaking scene. It is in a wonderful position - the old cellar, completely restored, is situated on the most charming of the vine-clad hills of Trento, a little south of the city - and operates rigorous grape selection. The fruit is produced by five long-established families of growers, and from them originate the same number of wines, scrupulously vinified by a team under the supervision of Giorgio Flessati. Production comes to less than 60,000 bottles a year, with red wines slightly outnumbering the whites. The reds scored an immediate success. First is a splendid Merlot, the Vigneto San Raimondo, which comes from a vineyard almost 40 years old at Novaline di Trento, a zone which has always been ideal for this variety. The '94 vintage is impressive to say the least: it is a rich, refined wine with hints of tobacco and a long, smooth finish, which at the tasting scored very high marks. The same results were obtained by the '94 Cabernet Vigneto San Bartolomeo, a wine of vanilla overtones, with good concentration and finesse. Although the Chardonnay was our preference among the whites, the other two, a Sauvignon and a Müller Thurgau, show that this estate has achieved its quality objectives right from the start.

○ Spumante Giulio Ferrari		
Riserva del Fondatore '89	♟♟♟	6
○ Trento Brut Perlé '93	♟♟	5
○ Trento Ferrari Incontri	♟♟	3*
○ Trento Maximum Brut	♟♟	4
○ Villa Gentilotti '95	♟♟	4
○ Villa Margon '95	♟♟	4
○ Trento Ferrari Brut	♟	4
○ Spumante Giulio Ferrari		
Riserva del Fondatore '88	♟♟♟	6
○ Spumante Metodo Classico		
Giulio Ferrari		
Riserva del Fondatore '86	♟♟♟	6
○ Spumante Giulio Ferrari		
Riserva del Fondatore '87	♟♟	5

● Trentino Cabernet Sauvignon		
Vigneto San Bartolomeo Ris. '94	♟♟	3*
○ Trentino Chardonnay '95	♟♟	3*
● Trentino Merlot		
Vigneto San Raimondo Ris. '94	♟♟	3*
○ Sauvignon Atesino '95	♟	3
○ Trentino Müller Thurgau '95	♟	3

TRENTO

VOLANO (TN)

MASO MARTIS
VIA DELL'ALBERA, 52
LOC. MARTIGNANO
38040 TRENTO
TEL. 0461/821057

CONCILIO VINI
VIA NAZIONALE, 24
38060 VOLANO (TN)
TEL. 0464/411000

Maso Martis is an estate whose potential is not yet fully expressed. The wines are technically correct, they are presented attractively with charming attention to detail, from the label to their triangular boxes, but they are definitely capable of improvement. Perhaps after three years of praise in the pages of this Guide, we were looking for the very best this year. Antonio Stelzer has not disappointed us, but he has probably concentrated too much on experimentation in the cellar, trying to develop a new and very special "passito" wine and neglecting the Chardonnay and his prized Spumante Classico. The winery was set up for the production of sparkling wines and possesses about a dozen hectares of vineyard in a single plot, located on the sunniest hill of the city. The Chardonnay is a superior wine with positive attack and all the potential of the '95 vintage, but it fizzles out slightly and the aromas, in particular the buttery notes, fade. In the two sparklers the character of the Trento DOC are strongly evident; the '93 Riserva is an especially full, almost over-powerful spumante. A bright future almost certainly awaits the interesting "passito" Sole d'Autunno, from chardonnay grapes dried out on racks, crushed in the spring and aged in small oak barrels. It has well-defined aroma, pleasant flavours of dried fruit, a good balance between sweet and acid and is not cloying. It is a wine which one should be in no hurry to open, since it will continue to improve with time

Tradition and innovation are the watchwords for the management of this company which year after year consolidates both sales and the quality of its products - a difficult result to achieve, but up till now director Giorgio Flessati has managed it. He is not only an expert oenologist, he has also learned the arduous task of combining quantity and quality in the management of the firm, following commercial strategies worked out in conjunction with the other local wineries which make up this dynamic partnership. In this way the Concilio Vini, one of the highest profile producers on the Italian domestic market, has succeeded in introducing lines which are decidedly superior quality. All six of the wines entered in the various tastings for the Guide passed the test with good marks and the Merlot Riserva Novaline comfortably won a Two Glass award, displaying both finesse and backbone in a wonderful round palate. Precise vinification and a very careful use of wood, which reveals the expert hand of winemaker Enrico Paternoster, lies behind this result. Almost a thousand barriques are lined up on the premises of this estate, a battery which no other cellar in the Trentino can boast. Good performances from the other reds too - an intensely flavoured Pinot Nero Riserva, and a Cabernet perhaps still too grassy - and from the three top line whites. These are all slender wines, with good fruit which are attractively presented. The label of the Traminer Aromatico stands out in particular for its spirited and intelligent design - exactly the qualities the Concilio would like to be known for.

O	Sole d'Autunno	♟	5
●	Trentino Moscato Rosa '95	♟	5
O	Trento Talento Riserva Brut '93	♟	5
O	Trentino Chardonnay '96		3
O	Trentino Chardonnay '94	♟♟	3
O	Trentino Chardonnay '95	♟♟	3*
O	Trento Brut Ris.	♟♟	4
O	Trento Talento Riserva Brut '92	♟♟	5
O	Chardonnay Sole d'Autunno	♟	5
O	Trento Talento Brut '92	♟	4

●	Trentino Merlot Novaline Ris. '94	♟♟	3*
●	Trentino Cabernet Sauvignon Ris. '93	♟	3
O	Trentino Chardonnay '96	♟	2
O	Trentino Gewürztraminer '96	♟	2
●	Trentino Pinot Nero Ris. '94	♟	3
O	Trentino Sauvignon '96	♟	2
●	Trentino Marzemino Monografie '95	♟♟	3
●	Trentino Merlot Novaline Ris. '91	♟♟	5
O	Trento Angelo Grigolli Ris.	♟♟	5
O	Trentino Chardonnay Monografie '95	♟	2
●	Trentino Merlot Novaline Ris. '93	♟	3

OTHER WINERIES

The following producers in the province of Trento obtained good scores in our tastings with one or more of their wines:

Spagnolli,
Aldeno, tel. 0461/842578,
Trento Brut

Madonna delle Vittorie,
Arco, tel. 0464/505542,
Trentino Riesling Renano '96

Maso Roveri, Avio, tel. 0464/684395,
Trentino Pinot Grigio '96

Cantina Soc. di Toblino,
Calavino, tel. 0461/564168,
Trentino Nosiola '96,
Trentino Cabernet '95,
Trentino Merlot '95

Vallis Agri, Calliano, tel. 0464/84113,
Trentino Marzemino '96

Nicolodi, Cembra, tel. 0461/683020,
Trentino Müller Thurgau '96,
Cimbrus '96

Maso ai Dossi, Cimone, tel. 0461/842781,
Donet Brut,
Trentino Marzemino '96

Arcangelo Sandri, Faedo, tel. 0461/650935,
Trentino Schiava '96

Villa Piccola, Faedo, tel. 0464/650560,
Trentino Pinot Nero '95,
Trentino Traminer '96

Renzo Gorga, Folgaria, tel. 0464/721161,
Pradaia '95

Abate Nero, Gardolo, tel. 0461/246566,
Trento Brut,
Trento Extra Brut

Castel Warth, Giovo, tel. 0461/684140,
Rubro '95,
Trento Brut

La Vigne, Isera, tel. 0464/434600,
Trentino Cabernet '95

Enrico Spagnolli,
Isera, tel. 0464/409054,
Trentino Marzemino '96,
Trentino Moscato Giallo '96

Pisoni,
Lasino, tel. 0461/564106,
Trento Brut,
Trento Brut Ris.

Cantina Sebastiani,
Lavis, tel. 0461/246315,
Trentino Chardonnay '96

Casata Monfort, Lavis, tel. 0461/241484,
TrentinoTraminer '96

Vignaioli Fanti,
Lavis, tel. 0461/241000,
Incrocio Manzoni 6.0.13 '95,
Trentino Nosiola '96

Conti Martini,
Mezzocorona, tel. 0461/603932,
Teroldego Rotaliano '96,
Trentino Moscato Giallo '96

Grigoletti, Nomi, tel. 0464/834215,
Trentino Chardonnay '96,
Retiko '96

Maso Lock,
Povo, tel. 0461/810071,
Trentino Merlot '96

Gaierhof,
Roverè della Luna, tel. 0461/658514,
Teroldego Rotaliano '96,
Trentino Pinot Nero '96

Bossi Fedrigotti,
Rovereto, tel. 0464/439250,
Trentino Traminer '96

Cadalora,
Santa Margherita di Ala, tel. 0464/696540,
Trentino Pinot Nero Vignalet '93

Giovanni Poli,
Santa Massenza, tel. 0461/864119,
Trentino Cabernet '96

Baroni a Prato,
Segonzano, tel. 0461/686241,
Trentino Pinot Nero '95,
Trentino Chardonnay '95,
Trentino Cabernet '95

Maso Bergamini,
Trento, tel. 0461/983079,
Trentino Lagrein '96,
Trentino Moscato Rosa '95

ALTO ADIGE

No fewer than nine wines with Three Glasses and an increase in winery entries from 36 to 44, despite the handicaps that might be expected from poor vintages like '96 for white wines and '94 for reds: this is the Alto Adige profile in this year's Guide. It is the sort of triumph which could perhaps have been predicted, but is nevertheless symptomatic of the huge strides forward that this region is making. The Alto Adige is fortunate in having an excellent cross-section of producers that includes what must be some of the world's best cooperatives, a number of high class private wineries and many fine young oenologists and growers who will ensure a sound future for winemaking in this part of north-east Italy. Turning to this year's tastings, the top prize winners were two cooperatives, the Cantina Produttori Santa Maddalena of Bolzano and the Cantina Produttori San Michele Appiano of Appiano sulla Strada del Vino. Both, for the first time ever, win Three Glass awards for two wines, an extremely satisfying result for these leading producers' associations. Witnessing the Cabernet Mumelterhof '95 from Santa Maddalena, compete shoulder to shoulder in a blind tasting with two such established stars as Gaja's Darmagi '93 and the Solaia '94 from Antinori is a great pleasure. And what about the splendid Sanct Valentin Sauvignon '96 and Pinot Grigio '95 from San Michele Appiano, two whites right at the top of their respective categories? Among the other producers, many wines got higher ratings than would have been possible even

a couple of years ago, for example, and to mention only two, the Merlot Brenntal '95 from the Cantina Produttori of Cortaccia and the classic Cabernet Sauvignon Lafoa '94 from Colterenzio. Then there is the white Contest '94 from Hirschprunn Casòn, an estate owned by one of the great figures of winemaking in Alto Adige, Alois Lageder. This is a revolutionary wine made with a totally non-standard cépage for the region. The traditional varieties meanwhile are represented by the Gewürztraminer Campaner '96 from the Cantina Produttori of Caldaro and the Lagrein Taberhof, from Santa Maddalena again. Last in the list of top award winners is an extraordinary sweet white wine, the Aureus '95 from Josef Niedermayr, which was only made in quantities of a few thousand bottles and which will be so difficult to find that we fear our readers will not thank us for recommending it. Of the great names in Alto Adige, only Paolo and Martin Foradori's Hofstätter is absent from the Three Glass award list, but this is due to poor vintages for their best wines; they will be back again when the '95 vintage is released, if our barrel tastings are anything to go on. Of the emerging producers, we recommend first of all Reinhold Messner's Castel Juval, then Josephus Mayr's Unterganzner, Franz Pfeil's Kränzel, Peter Dipoli's Voglar, and Hans and Andreas Burger's Turnhof. Franz Haas and Ignaz Niedrist should not be forgotten, but then they can no longer be considered newcomers to the top rank of producers.

ANDRIANO/ANDRIAN (BZ) APPIANO/EPPAN (BZ)

CANTINA PRODUTTORI ANDRIANO
VIA DELLA CHIESA, 2
39010 ANDRIANO/ANDRIAN (BZ)
TEL. 0471/510137

CANTINA PRODUTTORI SAN MICHELE
APPIANO/ST. MICHAEL EPPAN
CIRCONVALLAZIONE, 17/19
39057 APPIANO/EPPAN (BZ)
TEL. 0471/664466

The Cantina Andriano, founded in 1893, is not only the oldest cooperative in Alto Adige, but also the most surprising source of good wines. The white wines in general and the excellent Tor di Lupo range (named after a local landmark and symbol of this wine growing village) are consistently outstanding, year after year. Once again, the Chardonnay Tor di Lupo excelled; the '94 has a complex and fruity bouquet which is nicely integrated with elegant wood nuances and superb structure, making for a well balanced and most attractive ensemble. Another success is the Sauvignon di Terlano '96 with its characteristic grassy aromas, big structure and freshness. The Müller Thurgau di Terlano does not quite come up to its previous high standard and the Traminer Aromatico '96 seems tired and over-the-hill. Of the red wines, the Lagrein Tor di Lupo '94 stands out for its weighty concentration and power on the nose where aromas of ink and oak blend well. The palate is rich and full bodied. Lastly, the Schiava S. Giustina '96 is worth mentioning as a fresh and elegant example of the Cantina's excellent range.

We cannot add much to our annual assertion that, in our opinion, this is the best producer in the Alto Adige, especially for white wines. This year, however, we feel obliged to add a codicil. Hans Terzer, the "kellermeister", also showed us two red wines that are at the top of their respective categories: the Pinot Nero '95 and the Cabernet Sauvignon '94, both part of the up-market Sanct Valentin range. Returning to the main business, Terzer again produced the usual collection of great white wines; in fact, the whites have never been better than this year and no fewer than six of them got to our final tasting for the Three Glass awards. Two whites passed the test. The first is the splendid Sauvignon Sanct Valentin, this time the '96 vintage, with its broad and exotic bouquet. The other is the outstanding barrique aged Pinot Grigio Sanct Valentin '95 (the wrong vintage was quoted in last year's Guide; we tasted the '94 then, not the '95, which was tasted for the first time this year). These two wines are both displays of virtuoso skill on the part of Hans Terzer, who proves himself to be one of the best white winemakers in the whole of Italy. Other good wines include the Pinot Bianco Schulthauser '96 (perhaps the best vintage yet), the barrique aged Chardonnay Sanct Valentin '95, and a magisterial version of the Sauvignon Lahn '96, the Sanct Valentin's younger sister and for the first time nearly as good as the senior wine. Lastly, the Gewürztraminer Sanct Valentin '96 is a good wine, but not quite as good as the '95 in our opinion.

○ A. A. Chardonnay Tor di Lupo '94	♟♟	4
● A. A. Lagrein Scuro Tor di Lupo '94	♟♟	4
○ A. A. Terlano Sauvignon Classico '96	♟♟	3
● A. A. Schiava S. Giustina '96	♟	2
○ A. A. Terlano Müller Thurgau '96	♟	2
○ A. A. Chardonnay Tor di Lupo '93	♟♟	4
● A. A. Lagrein Scuro Tor di Lupo '91	♟♟	4
○ A. A. Terlano Sauvignon Classico '94	♟♟	3
○ A. A. Terlano Sauvignon Classico '95	♟♟	3*

○ A. A. Pinot Grigio St. Valentin '95	♟♟♟	4
○ A. A. Sauvignon St. Valentin '96	♟♟♟	5
● A. A. Cabernet Sauvignon St. Valentin '94	♟♟	5
○ A. A. Chardonnay St. Valentin '95	♟♟	5
○ A. A. Gewürztraminer St. Valentin '96	♟♟	5
○ A. A. Pinot Bianco Schulthauser '96	♟♟	3*
● A. A. Pinot Nero St. Valentin '95	♟♟	5
○ A. A. Sauvignon Lahn '96	♟♟	3*
○ A. A. Riesling Montiggl '96	♟	3
○ A. A. Sauvignon St. Valentin '94	♟♟♟	4
○ A. A. Sauvignon St. Valentin '95	♟♟♟	4
○ A. A. Chardonnay St. Valentin '93	♟♟	4

APPIANO/EPPAN (BZ)

KÖSSLER - PRAECLARUS
SAN PAOLO/ST. PAULS
39057 APPIANO/EPPAN (BZ)
TEL. 0471/660256

APPIANO/EPPAN (BZ)

VITICOLTORI ALTO ADIGE/
SÜDTIROLER WEINBAUERNVERBAND
VIA CIRCONVALLAZIONE, 17
39057 APPIANO/EPPAN (BZ)
TEL. 0471/660060

This is one of the few Alto Adige producers to make both top class sparkling wines and serious reds. The best example of a pair might be the sparkling Praeclarus Noblesse '89, re-tasted this year and up to its usual excellent standard, and the spectacular Lagrein Scuro '95, sold under the Kössler & Ebner label. This is an intensely fruity red on the nose with blackberry and raspberry aromas and a palate that combines richness and drinkability at the same time. Such a combination is the winemaker's equivalent of squaring the circle, or rather avoiding the situation where complexity has to be sacrificed in favour of immediate aroma in the bouquet and drinkability on the palate. This kind of result is possible - even desirable - with a grape such as lagrein, which is extremely high in polyphenols and anthocyans and relatively low in tannins. The range finishes with a good Cabernet-Merlot St. Pauls '95 and the usual, reliable, non-vintage Praeclarus Brut, one of the region's classic sparkling wines. The Merlot Tschidererhof '94 is less successful, however; it was not helped by the poor vintage.

Founded almost 20 years ago as a secondary cooperative, with the role of blending and selling under its own label wines that had been produced by other cooperative wineries in the area, the Viticoltori Alto Adige performs its task with mixed fortunes. This year, for example it presented some of its best varietals ever, and wines from the prestige golden torch label literally shone with quality at our tastings. Indeed, two of them reached Two Glass level: the excellent Pinot Bianco Eggerhof Plattenriegel '96, one of the best of its vintage, and the very aromatic and full bodied Lagrein Pischlhof Riserva '95. Then followed a series of reds and whites that are correctly made, but do not have enormous character. Wines worth picking out in this group are the Pinot Grigio Unterebnerhof '96, the Valle Isarco Müller Thurgau '96, the Terlano Sauvignon Classico '96 and the Chardonnay Zobelhof '96. Two special cuvée wines need to be assessed outside this group, the Schlosshof Baron Felix Longo Cabernet Riserva '92 and Pinot Nero Riserva '94. In theory these are the cooperative's best red wines, but, perhaps because of the vintage, they are no more than satisfactory; they may be technically well made, as usual, but they have a certain leanness of structure.

● A. A. Lagrein Scuro '95	▼▼	4
● A. A. Cabernet-Merlot St. Pauls '95	▼	5
○ A. A. Spumante Praeclarus Brut	▼	5
● A. A. Merlot Tschidererhof '94		5
● A. A. Cabernet-Merlot '93	▼▼	4
● A. A. Cabernet-Merlot '92	▼	4
● A. A. Lagrein Scuro '92	▼	3
● A. A. Pinot Nero '92	▼	4
○ A. A. Spumante Praeclarus Noblesse '89	▼	5

● A. A. Lagrein Scuro Pischlhof Ris. '95	▼▼	4
○ A. A. Pinot Bianco Eggerhof Plattenriegl '96	▼▼	3*
● A. A. Cabernet Schlosshof Felix Longo Ris. '92	▼	5
○ A. A. Chardonnay Zobelhof '96	▼	3
○ A. A. Pinot Grigio Unterebnerhof '96	▼	3
● A. A. Pinot Nero Schlosshof Felix Longo '94	▼	5
○ A. A. Terlano Sauvignon Cl. '96	▼	3
○ A. A. Valle Isarco Müller Thurgau '96	▼	3
○ A. A. Chardonnay Zobelhof '95	▼▼	3*

BOLZANO/BOZEN

BOLZANO/BOZEN

CANTINA CONVENTO MURI-GRIES
P.ZZA GRIES, 21
39100 BOLZANO/BOZEN
TEL. 0471/282287

CANTINA DI GRIES
P.ZZA GRIES, 2
39100 BOLZANO/BOZEN
TEL. 0471/270909

Located in the heart of the city of Bolzano, the Monastery of Muri-Gries traces its origins back to the eleventh century. The monks have always made wine here, so tradition and continuity are the watchwords in the monastery's cellars, which are gaining more and more of a reputation for themselves. The Lagrein is the wine that has attracted particular attention recently. The variety itself is indigenous to the alluvial soil at Gries and finds ideal growing conditions there. Furthermore, Christian Werth, the cellarmaster, is one of the most dedicated and skilled interpreters of this characterful and ever more popular wine. Even the normal Lagrein Scuro '95 from Muri-Gries stands out from the crowd thanks to its intense violet-tinged colour, its fruity bouquet and soft body. Yet it takes the Lagrein Abtei Riserva '95 to show the full potential of the grape: intense and concentrated on the nose with a complex play of aromas; firm and velvety at the same time, this is one of the best wines to come out of the entire Alto Adige region. The Lagrein Kretzer, the popular rosé version of the varietal, is a fresh, fruity wine with a thirst quenching liveliness. Unfortunately, one of the monastery's rarest wines, the Moscato Rosa of Muri-Gries, was not ready in time for the Guide, but previous tastings have shown it be one of the best dessert wines of the region.

Overall, the wines were not up to last year's standard, but the Cantina di Gries did well enough with at least some of them to confirm its reputation. The '94 versions of the Lagrein Grieser Prestige Line Riserva and the Lagrein Grieser Baron Eyrl Riserva are not as good as they were in '93 and both are only just better than satisfactory. The Merlot Siebeneich Prestige Line Riserva '95 is, however, an excellent substitute. This is a red with a rich, intense bouquet in which varietal aromas are supported by tobacco and a light oak background. The wine is well made and constructed out of excellent raw material, which gives some idea of how good the other reds of the '95 vintage should be once they are ready for tasting. Surprisingly, the best red from the '94 vintage is the Mauritius, a wine made from a blend of various grapes which shows all the depth and concentration that the Lagreins lack. The range is completed by a satisfactory Santa Maddalena, the Troglerhof '96, which is as simple and attractive as it should be, and a no-more-than-decent Merlot Graf Huyn Riserva '94, which underlines yet again the disappointing quality of this vintage in Alto Adige.

● A. A. Lagrein Abtei Ris. '95	♟♟	5
⊙ A. A. Lagrein Kretzer '96	♟♟	3
● A. A. Lagrein Scuro Gries '95	♟♟	4
○ A. A. Pinot Grigio '96	♟	3

● A. A. Merlot Siebeneich Prestige Line Ris. '95	♟♟	5
● Mauritius '94	♟♟	5
● A. A. Lagrein Scuro Grieser Baron Eyrl Ris. '94	♟	5
● A. A. Lagrein Scuro Grieser Prestige Line Ris. '94	♟	5
● A. A. Merlot Graf Huyn Ris. '94	♟	5
● A. A. Santa Maddalena Tröglerhof '96	♟	3
● A. A. Lagrein Grieser Prestige Line Ris. '93	♟♟♟	5
● A. A. Lagrein Grieser Baron Carl Eyrl Ris. '93	♟♟	4

BOLZANO/BOZEN

BOLZANO/BOZEN

CANTINA PRODUTTORI
SANTA MADDALENA
VIA BRENNERO, 15
39100 BOLZANO/BOZEN
TEL. 0471/972944

FRANZ GOJER GLÖGGLHOF
VIA RIVELLONE, 1
FRAZ. S. MADDALENA
39100 BOLZANO/BOZEN
TEL. 0471/978775

The cooperative of Santa Maddalena is one of the most outstanding examples of its type in Alto Adige. Located in the centre of the city of Bolzano, it stands at the edge of the DOC Santa Maddalena Classico zone. Last year, the cooperative won acclaim for its superb Cabernet Mumelterhof '94, and this year the news is that the '95 is just as good: complex and elegant on the nose, full of spice and berry fruit; ample, concentrated body; rich, well balanced and long on the palate. Three Glasses. And this time the cellarmaster, Stephan Filippi, has also come up with a second success, using the local lagrein grape. His Taberhof '95 shares the honours with the Lagrein from Cantina Muri-Gries at the top of its category (both wines show similar, extraordinary character and express the potential of the grape perfectly). On the one hand, the Taberhof is big and fully fleshed out; on the other, full of subtle aromas and fragrant notes of violets and vanilla; the texture is velvet smooth, attractively tannic and well balanced. All in all, a most exceptional wine. The Lagrein Perlhof '95 follows the same pattern, in miniature. The Cantina's principal wine is the famous Santa Maddalena, which it makes in three Classico versions: standard, Huck am Bach, and Steiler. Unfortunately, the climatic conditions of the '96 vintage were not good enough to bring out the best in these wines and they did not live up to our expectations; which is also true for the Cantina Santa Maddalena's white wines in this vintage. Only the Riesling '96 managed to redeem itself thanks to a mixture of varietal character, drinkability and structure.

Franz Gojer is famous, first of all, for his Santa Maddalena wines, and then for his Lagreins. This year the order has been reversed in the Guide. Gojer's Lagrein Riserva '95 has dominated the field and come out as one of the best of its type. This is a red of serious stature: full bodied, concentrated and very enjoyable to drink, in the best traditions of this expert winemaker. Once again the potential of the lagrein grape is unmistakeable, and this is surely a pointer to the future for high quality winemaking in Alto Adige. The Lagrein '96 is also very good; it may be simpler and more dilute than its elder brother, but it provides enjoyably easy drinking all the same. The house speciality is the Santa Maddalena, and here things begin to get more problematical. The Rondell '96 passes the test, even if previous vintages, such as the '95, have had greater depth of flavour. But then again, perhaps it was the '95 that was the exception to the rule, not the '96. The Santa Maddalena Classico '96 is a little below par and obviously suffers from the difficulties inherent in a vintage when rain struck often and heavily during the harvesting period. In this context, and despite the lack of high points overall in the range, Gojer remains one of the best private producers in Alto Adige.

● A. A. Cabernet Mumelterhof '95	ΨΨΨ	4
● A. A. Lagrein Scuro Taberhof Ris. '95	ΨΨΨ	4
● A. A. Lagrein Scuro Perlhof '95	ΨΨ	3
○ A. A. Riesling '96	ΨΨ	2
⊙ A. A. Lagrein Rosato '96	Ψ	1
● A. A. Santa Maddalena Cl. Huck am Bach '96	Ψ	3
● A. A. Santa Maddalena Cl. Stieler '96	Ψ	2
● A. A. Santa Maddalena Cl. '96	Ψ	2
● A. A. Cabernet Mumelterhof '94	ΨΨΨ	3*
○ A. A. Chardonnay Kleinstein '95	ΨΨ	3*
● A. A. Lagrein Scuro Taberhof Ris. '94	ΨΨ	5

● A. A. Lagrein Scuro Ris. '95	ΨΨ	4
● A. A. Lagrein Scuro '96	Ψ	3*
● A. A. Santa Maddalena Rondell '96	Ψ	3
● A. A. Santa Maddalena Classico '96		3
● A. A. Santa Maddalena Classico '95	ΨΨ	3*
● A. A. Santa Maddalena Rondell '95	ΨΨ	3*
● A. A. Lagrein Scuro Ris. '93	Ψ	4

BOLZANO/BOZEN

Thomas Mayr e Figlio
Via Mendola, 56
39100 Bolzano/Bozen
tel. 0471/281030

In addition to the traditional range from this winery, Mayr has shown us two interesting newcomers to the list. One is the Vernissage, a non-vintage red wine which stands out for its richness of character and a balance weighted in favour of drinkability. The second is the Creazione Rosa '95, a sweet wine made of moscato rosa that stands up well to comparison with the more traditional wines from this variety of comparable vintages, not ceding an inch in the search for aromatic intensity. This does not mean, however, that the traditional range of wines are any the worse. Quite the contrary. The Lagrein Scuro '95 is the standard non-cru version of this wine (the cru selection will come out in 1998) and it easily gets a Two Glass rating, just as it did two years ago: intense bouquet of blackcurrants and bilberries, full flavoured and rich on the palate; just like the best Lagrein ought to be. The '96, however, seemed more dilute and neutral to us, predictably enough in this extremely wet vintage. The same applies to the Santa Maddalena Rumpelhof '96, which just reaches One Glass level with its fruity bouquet and light body.

● A. A. Lagrein Scuro '95	▼▼	3*
● Creazione Rosa '95	▼▼	5
● A. A. Lagrein Scuro '96	▼	3
● A. A. Santa Maddalena Cl. Rumplerhof '96	▼	3
● Vernissage	▼	4
● A. A. Lagrein Scuro '93	▽▽	3
● A. A. Lagrein Scuro Ris. '94	▽▽	4
● A. A. Lagrein Scuro '94	▽	3
● A. A. Santa Maddalena Cl. Rumplerhof '94	▽	3
● A. A. Santa Maddalena Cl. Rumplerhof '95	▽	3

BOLZANO/BOZEN

Heinrich Plattner - Waldgrieshof
Santa Giustina, 2
39100 Bolzano/Bozen
tel. 0471/973245

This year, Heinrich Plattner has shown us what must be, perhaps, his best ever range of wines. One wine in particular aroused our enthusiasm: the formidable Cabernet Sauvignon '95. This is a big wine with an intense and all-enveloping bouquet, which still has a touch of youthful astringency on the palate, but which already shows the richness and tightly knit structure associated with the polyphenols present in a great red wine. The '94 vintage of the same wine is also very good, but a little more dilute, readier to drink and certainly less suitable for bottle ageing. As usual, the Lagrein Scuro, this time from the '95 vintage, is a good example of its type and a great success. It has a broad bouquet, dominated by sweet aromas of blackcurrants and oak and an easy drinkability, which is remarkable for a wine of this weight and concentration of fruit; both these qualities make it one of the best Lagreins of the vintage. The rest of the range leaves us less enthusiastic: the Moscato Rosa '96 is satisfactory, but a bit dilute on the nose; the Pinot Grigio '96 is successful enough (but the '95 was better); and the Pinot Nero '95 disappointed us, frankly we expected more from this one. The Santa Maddalena Classico '96 completes the range: satisfactory and easy to drink, not much more could legitimately be expected from this vintage.

● A. A. Cabernet Sauvignon '94	▼▼	5
● A. A. Cabernet Sauvignon '95	▼▼	5
● A. A. Lagrein Scuro '95	▼▼	4
● A. A. Moscato Rosa '96	▼	5
○ A. A. Pinot Grigio '96	▼	3
● A. A. Pinot Nero '95	▼	4
● A. A. Santa Maddalena Classico '96		3
● A. A. Lagrein Scuro '93	▽▽	4
● A. A. Lagrein Scuro '94	▽	4
○ A. A. Pinot Grigio '95	▽	3
● A. A. Santa Maddalena '95	▽	3
○ A. A. Terlano Pinot Bianco '95	▽	4

BOLZANO/BOZEN

BOLZANO/BOZEN

HANS ROTTENSTEINER
VIA SARENTINO, 1/A
39100 BOLZANO/BOZEN
TEL. 0471/282015

THURNHOF
VIA CASTEL FLAVON, 7
39100 BOLZANO/BOZEN
TEL. 0471/288460

We begin this entry dedicated to one of Bolzano's greatest winemakers by passing on our congratulations. This is the best range of wines he has ever shown us, and we would like to be the first to acknowledge the fact. Apart from anything else, Rottensteiner is not one of the fashionable producers of the moment, he is just happy to do the best he can and then let the wines speak for themselves. The best of the bunch is the Lagrein Grieser Riserva '94. The vintage was not great, but the fact that such a good wine can come out of it underlines the importance of grape selection in the vineyards. This Lagrein in particular succeeds in offsetting the natural modesty of fruit from a poor vintage with an easy drinkability and fragrance of bouquet that make it quite simply, delicious. The two special cuvée wines are both good: the Cabernet Select Riserva '93 and the Pinot Nero Select Mazon Riserva '93 are both well made, if not exceptionally powerful, wines. The Pinot Nero is, perhaps, the more interesting of the two as far as style and origins are concerned. The grapes come from one of the best sites in Alto Adige for the variety, the Mazon area, as the name would suggest, and Rottensteiner's version is on the lines of an old fashioned Burgundy, with the same mature bouquet and mature flavours, together with the rustic touch of slightly raw tannins and acidity. The Santa Maddalena Classico Premstallerhof '96 is the house speciality and can be recommended, together with two well made whites, the Pinot Bianco and the Gewürtzraminer, both '96 vintage.

Only two entries from Hans Berger and his son Andreas, but what wines! Both are real blockbusters which scored well over the Two Glass threshold, and both say volumes about the skill and dedication that Hans and his son put into their winemaking. It is worth underlining that these results come after the adoption of organic winemaking with its commitment to complete respect for the environment. But let us return to these two red wines. The Lagrein '95 is superb, one of the best of the vintage: rich and concentrated on the palate with tannins which seem to have softened already; well-rounded with good fruit, enormous bouquet on the nose with intense fruitiness, but also slightly one dimensional in the typical Lagrein fashion. The Cabernet Wienegg Riserva '94 is also very good: rich and concentrated despite the poor vintage, blackcurrants and ripe berry fruit on the nose, rich, soft and broad palate. Considering the vintage, this is a superb wine. At this point it only remains for us to look forward to tasting Hans and Andreas Berger's wines again, and since in the case of the Cabernet the next vintage will be the '95, it should be a very interesting experience indeed.

● A. A. Cabernet Select Ris. '93	🍷🍷	5
● A. A. Lagrein Scuro Grieser Select Ris '94	🍷🍷	4
● A. A. Pinot Nero Select Mazzon Ris. '93	🍷🍷	5
○ A. A. Gewürztraminer '96	🍷	3
○ A. A. Pinot Bianco '96	🍷	3
● A. A. Santa Maddalena Cl. Premstallerhof '96	🍷	3
● A. A. Cabernet Select Ris. '90	🍷🍷	5
● A. A. Cabernet Select Ris. '91	🍷🍷	4
● A. A. Lagrein Scuro Grieser Select Ris. '91	🍷🍷	3
● A. A. Lagrein Scuro Grieser Select Ris. '92	🍷	4

● A. A. Cabernet Wienegg Ris. '94	🍷🍷	4
● A. A. Lagrein Scuro '95	🍷🍷	5

CALDARO/KALTERN (BZ)

CANTINA VITICOLTORI DI CALDARO
VIA DELLE CANTINE, 12
39052 CALDARO/KALTERN (BZ)
TEL. 0471/963149

This Caldaro cooperative has assumed a role of primary importance on the winemaking scene in Alto Adige, a status it confirms with the passing of every vintage. The reds have been particularly impressive recently, particularly the Cabernet and the Schiava, but this year cellarmaster Helmuth Zozin has also brought out a high quality white wine. The Gewürztraminer Campaner '96 stands head and shoulders above the competition: full flavoured and well evolved, with hints of rose petals and dried grapes, full bodied and deeply concentrated on the palate, this is an excellent example of its type, if a little stretched in this vintage. Although the two '94 Cabernets, the Riserva and the Campaner, cannot fully compete with the '93 , thanks to their structure, fruit, body and elegance they still rank among the top Italian Cabernets. One more red wine deserves particular attention: the Pinot Nero Riserva '95 still has a slight woodiness to it, but it has good character on the nose and an attractively full body. The Cantina Viticoltori of Caldaro are one of the best producers of Schiava from the Lake Caldaro Classico zone, and not much more need be said apart from the fact that the Lago di Caldaro Pfarrhof '96 is one of the best of its DOC. Some of the other whites from the Cantina's huge range were a slight disappointment, the two Pinot Biancos (Vial and Pfarrhof), for example. But, considering all the positive things there are to say about the Cantina Viticoltori, we can close a blind eye to that.

CALDARO/KALTERN (BZ)

CASTEL SALLEGG - GRAF KUENBURG
VICOLO DI SOTTO, 15
39052 CALDARO/KALTERN (BZ)
TEL. 0471/963132

Just for once the best wine from this historic winery is not the Moscato Rosa. After a year's absence, the Castel Sallegg winery returns to the Guide, but this time principally thanks to a red wine, the Merlot '95. Merlot made in the "grand vin" style is becoming increasingly popular in Alto Adige. This one has a slightly vegetal bouquet with eucalyptus aromas accompanying more classic tobacco and plums on the nose, big structure, and tannins that are still a little raw, but well on the way to integration. The Cabernet, from the '95 vintage again, is almost as good: well made, perhaps lacking a little in richness of fruit, but possessing an elegant nose. Finally we arrive at the Moscato Rosa '93, and we feel obliged to remark that, although this should be the estate's best wine, it does not live up to the standard of previous vintages: very mature, heavy and marmaladey, this does not have the aromatic intensity that is so typical of the variety, and it does not have the power it had in the 1960s and 1970s. This is a wine that seems to fall between two stools; part modern, part old fashioned. Whatever the case, it does not live up to its reputation, at least in our opinion.

○ A. A. Gewürztraminer		
Campaner '96	♟♟♟	3
● A. A. Cabernet Sauvignon		
Campaner Ris. '94	♟♟	3
● A. A. Cabernet Sauvignon Ris. '94	♟♟	5
● A. A. Lago di Caldaro Pfarrhof '96	♟♟	3
● A. A. Pinot Nero Ris. '95	♟♟	4
● A. A. Cabernet Ris. '92	♟♟♟	5
● A. A. Cabernet Sauvignon Ris. '93	♟♟♟	5
● A. A. Cabernet Sauvignon		
Campaner Ris. '93	♟♟	4*
○ A. A. Gewürztraminer		
Campaner '95	♟♟	3*
○ A. A. Gewürztraminer		
Campaner '94	♟♟	3

● A. A. Merlot '95	♟♟	5
● A. A. Cabernet '95	♟	5
● A. A. Moscato Rosa '93	♟	6

CALDARO/KALTERN (BZ)

CALDARO/KALTERN (BZ)

KETTMEIR
VIA DELLE CANTINE, 4
39052 CALDARO/KALTERN (BZ)
TEL. 0471/963135

PRIMA & NUOVA/ERSTE & NEUE
VIA DELLE CANTINE, 5
39052 CALDARO/KALTERN (BZ)
TEL. 0471/963122

We have a great respect for the Kettmeir company of Caldaro, one of the great wineries of Alto Adige, and for this reason we always expect that little bit of extra something from the wines. Kettmeir is commercially extremely successful, but despite the fact that steps have been taken in the right direction in recent years, we would really have been much happier if we had found better wines than we did this year. Part of the trouble is to do with poor vintages: '96 for white wines and '92 for the company's prestige red wine. But this is an excuse that only goes so far. We begin with the best of this year's wines: the Cabernet Maso Castello '92. On the nose this is already far advanced, with the typical aromas of a fully evolved wine; soft on the palate with almost completely integrated tannins, but without the necessary richness of body or extract to keep the palate lively. This wine has been well made within the understandable limits imposed by a difficult vintage and, indeed, scores its highest mark ever in our Guide. Of the white wines, the Pinot Grigio Maso Rainer '96 is just satisfactory and less firm and concentrated than last year's version, while the Sauvignon '96 is correctly made, attractive, and shot through with a vein of acidity that gives it good drinkability. Lastly, the Spumante Brut is an honest and technically perfect wine made mostly from chardonnay; drinking well now.

This big, modern winery in Caldaro presents a wide range of correctly made wines every year. Every so often one of them stands out, but mostly they have a reputation for being reliable and good value for money. Certainly however, the Pinot Bianco Brunar '96 has more to it than just reliability, with its intensely fruity nose and full flavours and its firm body and excellent length. This is a first rate wine, the product of excellent grapes expertly managed in a technologically well equipped winery. The same goes for the Cabernet '94, one the of the best of its vintage. Perhaps it does not have the breadth and concentration of some of the '93s or of the first '95s we have tasted this year, but it is an excellent wine for such a poor vintage: the bouquet is, as it should be, without excessive vegetal character, the palate is full bodied, and the tannins soft and well-rounded. The range of good quality wines continues with four expertly made '96 vintage whites: the Pinot Bianco, the Gewürztraminer, the Chardonnay Puntay and the Sauvignon Stern. These all have good varietal bouquets and easy drinkability. We finish with a satisfactory Lago di Caldaro Leuchtenburg, from the '96 vintage, which is not up to the standard of previous vintages: in short, well made, but a bit dilute.

● A. A. Cabernet Sauvignon Maso Castello '92	♀♀	4*
○ A. A. Pinot Grigio Maso Reiner '96	♀	3*
○ A. A. Sauvignon '96	♀	3*
○ Spumante Brut	♀	4
○ A. A. Chardonnay Maso Reiner '95	♀♀	3*
● A. A. Cabernet Sauvignon Maso Castello '91	♀	3
○ A. A. Pinot Grigio Maso Reiner '95	♀	3
○ A. A. Riesling Renano Maso Reiner '95	♀	3

● A. A. Cabernet '94	♀♀	5
○ A. A. Pinot Bianco Brunar '96	♀♀	4
○ A. A. Chardonnay Puntay '96	♀	4
○ A. A. Gewürztraminer Puntay '96	♀	4
● A. A. Lago di Caldaro Scelto Leuchtenburg '96	♀	4
○ A. A. Pinot Bianco Puntay '96	♀	4
○ A. A. Sauvignon Stern '96	♀	4
○ A. A. Chardonnay Puntay '92	♀♀	5
○ A. A. Chardonnay Puntay '93	♀♀	4
○ A. A. Chardonnay Puntay '94	♀♀	4
● A. A. Lago di Caldaro Scelto Leuchtenburg '95	♀♀	4
● A. A. Lago di Caldaro Scelto Puntay '94	♀♀	3*

CARDANO/KARDAUN (BZ)

JOSEPHUS MAYR -
ERBHOF UNTERGANZNER
VIA CAMPIGLIO, 15
39053 CARDANO/KARDAUN (BZ)
TEL. 0471/365582

Take note of this tiny winery in Cardano. For several years now, Josephus Mayr has regularly presented us with such good wines that it will not be a surprise to see him come up with a Three Glass award in the future. For the moment, he gets close enough with a superb red wine, the Composition Reif '95, made of a blend of cabernet sauvignon (80 percent) and lagrein (20 percent). Only 700 bottles (yes, seven hundred) were made of a wine that is as good as it is almost unfindable: extremely intense bouquet with aromas of berry fruit and vanilla; fine grained soft tannins dominate the palate and melt into a structure full of fleshy fruit and soft, concentrated extract. The two Lagrein Riservas ('94 and '95) are both very good, and this time can be more readily found on the market. The '95 is slightly more rustic and cruder on the nose; it obviously needs a few more months' bottle age to be at its best. The '94, however, is very drinkable now: soft and smooth on the palate, full of ripe fruit on the nose. The Cabernet Sauvignon '95 is simply delicious: full bodied and firm on the palate with the great advantage of sweet, velvety tannins that make it surprisingly easy to drink. The Santa Maddalena '96 is attractive enough, but it suffers from the poor vintage and is in essence just a simple, light wine.

●	A. A. Cabernet Sauvignon '95	🍷🍷	5
●	A. A. Lagrein Scuro Ris. '94	🍷🍷	4
●	A. A. Lagrein Scuro Ris. '95	🍷🍷	4
●	Composition Reif '95	🍷🍷	5
●	A. A. Santa Maddalena '96	🍷	3
●	A. A. Lagrein Scuro Ris. '93	🍸🍸	4
●	A. A. Cabernet '94	🍸	4
●	A. A. Cabernet Sauvignon '94	🍸	4
●	A. A. Santa Maddalena '95	🍸	3

CERMES/TSCHERMS (BZ)

GRAF PFEIL WEINGUT KRÄNZEL
VIA PALADE, 1
39010 CERMES/TSCHERMS (BZ)
TEL. 0473/564549

Count Franz Pfeil is an individualist. His wines, which proved to be of excellent quality once again this year, are impeccably sourced from vineyards at the Kranzlhof estate, a few kilometres outside Merano on the high green terraces of the Burgraviato. Individuality and character is what this young landowner looks for in his wines, with some expression of the vintage and place of origin. Of the Kranzlhof whites, the Pinot Bianco '96 stands out for its subtle fruity flavour, its attractive freshness and elegant structure. The Pinot Bianco "passito" Dorado '94 also passes the test with a rich bouquet and well balanced finesse. This time, the Kränzel reds are a pleasant surprise, too. There may still be slightly too much barrique wood on the nose of the Pinot Nero '95, but it still has full body with rich extract and good fruit. The Sagittarius '95 is a cuvée of Cabernet, Merlot and Lemberger with an arresting bouquet of fruit tinged with grassiness; full bodied, straightforward and elegant.

○	A. A. Dorado '94	🍷🍷	5
○	A. A. Pinot Bianco '96	🍷🍷	4
●	A. A. Pinot Nero '95	🍷🍷	5
●	A. A. Sagittarius '95	🍷🍷	5
○	A. A. Pinot Bianco '95	🍸🍸	4
○	A. A. Sauvignon '95	🍸🍸	4
●	A. A. Meranese Hügel '95	🍸	3

CHIUSA/KLAUSEN (BZ)

CORNAIANO/GIRLAN (BZ)

CANTINA PRODUTTORI
VALLE ISARCO/EISACKTALER
S.S. DEL BRENNERO, 61
LOC. LE COSTE, 91
39043 CHIUSA/KLAUSEN (BZ)
TEL. 0472/847553

CANTINA PRODUTTORI
COLTERENZIO/SCHRECKBICHL
STRADA DEL VINO, 8
39050 CORNAIANO/GIRLAN (BZ)
TEL. 0471/664246

The Cooperative of the Valle Isarco makes clean and serious white wines that achieve particular character and individuality in this tiny DOC, but in recent years the winery has definitely kept a low profile. Now it is emerging and it seems that the new wind blowing across the viticultural scene in Alto Adige is also blowing through Chiusa. The two classic grape varieties of the area are veltliner and kerner, which make basic, good value wines. But the most common grape in the Isarco valley is sylvaner. And it is with the sylvaner-based Dominus '96 that the Cantina Produttori is breaking new ground with a successful technique that involves the very careful vinification of selected grapes, followed by eight months' barrique maturation. The Dominus '96 first won us over and then astonished us with its ripe fruit, its rich body and elegant freshness, accompanied by soft shades of vanilla. It would be worth trying similar experiments with other wines, given, of course, the availability of the essential element in the process: top quality grapes. The Cantina Produttori also make a Müller Thurgau in the Aristos range; we tried the '96 and liked it very much for its delicate hints of sage and fruit, for its sharp freshness and slim body. The Gewürztraminer, the Pinot Grigio and the standard Sylvaner from the '96 vintage are fresh, fruity white wines that are typical products of the Isarco valley, even if rather light and uncomplicated. It only remains to comment on the one DOC red wine from Isarco, the Klausner Laitacher '96, made from an interesting blend of schiava, lagrein and portugieser. We are sure that we will hear more about the Cantina Produttori in the future.

Luis Raifer, the guru of winemaking in Alto Adige, has been in charge of what must be its most important cooperative for many years. The winery is an integral part of local life and, besides being equipped with the most up-to-date technology, advises its grower-members on all aspects of viticulture. Add to that the fact that technical supervision comes from a top class oenologist, Donato Lanati, and the profile of one of Italy's leading producers is complete. Year after year, the wines Colterenzio put forward for our tastings prove to be of the highest quality. This year is no exception; the top Three Glass award goes to a magisterial example of the Cabernet Sauvignon Lafoa from the difficult '94 vintage. This is a great red wine with a nose of rare elegance, where aromas of pencil lead and vanilla from the wood blend in perfectly with the berry fruit from the grapes. The extremely soft and velvety tannins have the elegance of those of a great Bordeaux. The '94 is even better than the '93, which on paper at least was the better of the two vintages. Moving on, there are splendid wines throughout the entire range: from the Chardonnay Cornell '95 and Chardonnay Coret '96 to a real classic, the Gewürztraminer Cornell '96; not to mention the blend which is the most important new release of the year from Colterenzio, the Mittenburg Cornelius Bianco '95. In our opinion the Merlot Siebeneich, the Cornelius Rosso and Pinot Nero Schwarzhaus all suffered from the problems of the '94 vintage and unfortunately, the Pinot Bianco Weisshaus, which got Three Glasses for the '95 vintage, gets only One Glass for the '96.

○ A. A. Valle Isarco Gewürztraminer '96	🍷	2
○ A. A. Valle Isarco Müller Thurgau Aristos '96	🍷🍷	3
○ A. A. Valle Isarco Pinot Grigio '96	🍷🍷	2
○ A. A. Valle Isarco Sylvaner Aristos '96	🍷🍷	3
○ A. A. Valle Isarco Sylvaner Dominus '96	🍷🍷	3
○ A. A. Valle Isarco Kerner '96	🍷	2
● A. A. Valle Isarco Klausner Laitacher '96	🍷	2
○ A. A. Valle Isarco Veltliner '96	🍷	2

● A. A. Cabernet Sauvignon Lafoa '94	🍷🍷🍷	6
● A. A. Cabernet Sauvignon Lafoa '93	🍷🍷	6
○ A. A. Chardonnay Coret '96	🍷🍷	4
○ A. A. Chardonnay Cornell '95	🍷🍷	5
○ A. A. Gewürztraminer Cornell '96	🍷🍷	5
○ Mittenberg Cornelius Bianco '95	🍷🍷	5
● A. A. Cabernet Sauvignon Merlot Cornelius '94	🍷	6
● A. A. Merlot Siebeneich '94	🍷	5
○ A. A. Pinot Bianco '96	🍷	3
○ A. A. Pinot Bianco Weisshaus '96	🍷	4
● A. A. Pinot Nero Schwarzhaus '94	🍷	5

CORNAIANO/GIRLAN (BZ) CORNAIANO/GIRLAN (BZ)

CANTINA PRODUTTORI
CORNAIANO/GIRLAN
VIA S. MARTINO, 24
39050 CORNAIANO/GIRLAN (BZ)
TEL. 0471/662403

K. MARTINI & SOHN
VIA LAMM WEG, 28
39050 CORNAIANO/GIRLAN (BZ)
TEL. 0471/663156

This cooperative makes the legendary "Gschleier von alten Reben", the best Schiava in Alto Adige. With absolutely nothing in common with the pale, light wines that wash down slices of "speck" in the wine bars of Bolzano, this Schiava from Cornaiano is a serious red that actually grows into something surprisingly like a great Pinot Noir after a few years' ageing. This year it was the turn of the '95 vintage, which provided an excellent harvest locally, and we were tempted to give it Three Glasses, if only to be controversial and to underline that awards in the Guide are relative to specific categories. Of course, this wine does not have the opulence and the length of a Cabernet, but such an enticing bouquet, combined with such easy drinking are to die for, and enough to carry all before them. In the end, the decision was taken: Two Glasses... but it was so nearly Three. The famous cooperative of Cornaiano is expertly managed by one of the key figures in Alto Adige winemaking, Helmuth Spitaler, and it makes a whole range of wines. The Pinot Bianco Plattenriegel '96 has a good bouquet and a fine backbone to the palate. The Cabernet Sauvignon Optimum '95 may be a little incomplete on the nose, but only because of its youth. Lastly, we can recommend the Schiava Fass No. 9 from the '96 vintage for its bouquet and its drinkability.

This fine producer from Cornaiano has done well again this year, above all in the red wine category, where the two '95 Lagreins both easily pass the Two Glass mark. The best wine overall is the Lagrein Maturum '95, which is a house speciality: very fruity on the nose with typical berry fruit aromas and slight vegetal flavours on the finish; powerful, rich in extract and quite long. Much the same, but just a little more dilute, the Lagrein Ruelshof '95 still has impressive structure, but is softer and more easily drinkable. The Cabernet-Lagrein Caldirus '95 is an interesting wine, but perhaps not yet completely balanced: vegetal and well advanced in its evolution on the nose and a little dilute. In other words, this is a wine that does not quite live up to its own aspirations. The range is completed by two schiava-based red wines, the Lago di Caldaro Classico Feltron '96 and the Schiava Palladium '96. The first has the greater body of the two - marginally - but both are simple, medium weight wines for easy drinking.

● A. A. Cabernet Optimum '95		♥♥	5
○ A. A. Pinot Bianco			
Plattenriegl '96		♥♥	4
● A. A. Schiava "Gschleier			
von alten Reben" '95		♥♥	4
● A. A. Schiava Fass n°9 '96		♥	3
● A. A. Cabernet Optimum '90		♀♀	5
● A. A. Cabernet Optimum '92		♀♀	4
● A. A. Cabernet Optimum '93		♀♀	5
○ Strahler '95		♀♀	4

● A. A. Lagrein Scuro Maturum '95		♥♥	4
● A. A. Lagrein Scuro Rueslhof '95		♥♥	4
● A. A. Cabernet-Lagrein			
Coldirus '95		♥	4
● A. A. Lago di Caldaro Classico			
Felton '96			3
● A. A. Schiava Palladium '96			3
● A. A. Cabernet-Lagrein			
Coldirus '94		♀♀	3*
● A. A. Lago di Caldaro Classico			
Felton '95		♀	3
● A. A. Lagrein Scuro Maturum '93		♀	5
● A. A. Lagrein Scuro Rueslhof '94		♀	4
● A. A. Schiava Palladium '95		♀	3

CORNAIANO/GIRLAN (BZ)

CORNAIANO/GIRLAN (BZ)

JOSEF NIEDERMAYR
VIA CASA DI GESÙ, 15
39050 CORNAIANO/GIRLAN (BZ)
TEL. 0471/662451

IGNAZ NIEDRIST
VIA RONCO, 4
39050 CORNAIANO/GIRLAN (BZ)
TEL. 0471/664494

It is a great pleasure to welcome Josef Niedermayr into the club of Three Glass award winners. He deserves it for his undoubted entrepreneurial panache, but mainly because the skill of his young oenologist, Lorenz Martini, with the help of mother nature, have provided him with one of the best ranges of wines in the Alto Adige today. Niedermayr has given us the most exquisite pleasure with the Aureus '95, a sweet, wine made from partially dried and botrytis affected chardonnay, pinot bianco and sauvignon. Just a few thousand bottles of this authentic nectar were made, but in terms of intrinsic quality, intensity of flavour, and certain aspects of the palate profile this wine is similar to a top Austrian Beerenauslese. Amongst the reds, both the Pinot Nero Riserva '94 and the Lagrein Gries Riserva '94 are at the top of their respective categories. We are keen, however, to taste next year's versions of these two wines; the vintage is so much better that we are certain to be delighted. The Euforius '94 is a blend of various grape varieties and one of the rare non-DOC wines of the region; it is almost as good as the first two wines. The Cabernet Riserva '94 is not the most powerful of its class, but it is well made. The whites are less successful than the reds and only the Terlano Hof zu Pramol '96 scored comfortably in the Two Glass range. Unfortunately, the Sauvignon Lage Naun '96 did not live up to expectations (the '95 was a completely different matter) and the Gewürztraminer Lage Doss '96 was acceptable if unexciting. The Lago di Caldaro Scelto Classico Superiore Ascherhof '96 and the Santa Maddalena Classico Egger-Larcherhof '96 are both schiava-based reds, and both good wines in their own categories, with excellent aromatic bouquets and delicious, easy drinkability.

Riesling seems to be the wine closest to Ignaz Niedrist's heart. His Riesling Renano has swept all before it in comparative tastings with Rieslings from Alto Adige, Friuli, and other parts of Italy. It is, in fact, Italy's finest Riesling. The '96 is no exception to this rule and does not seem to have been affected by the generally poor quality of the vintage compared to previous years. Niedrist's Riesling Renano '96 has a complex fruit bouquet with mineral and grapefruit aromas, a taut, aristocratic and full bodied palate and a finish with a faint bitter twist. Just the lightest lack of final polish and the obvious comparisons with the best Rieslings of Alsace, the Mosel and the Rheingau prevent it from getting the very top award. But the distance between Niedrist's achievements and those of the acknowledged international masters, such as Robert Weil, Willi Schaefer or Fritz Haag, is minimal. Riesling is not the whole story, however, in this beautiful little winery. The Pinot Nero '95 is very good, too: complex varietal nose (be careful to open the bottle some minutes before serving to appreciate this at its best), very aristocratic varietal character on the palate, much better than last year's version from the '94 vintage. Finally, the Pinot Bianco '96 is a simple, attractive wine that does not have any pretensions to greatness, but performs well in the local context.

O Aureus '95	♟♟♟	5
● A. A. Cabernet Ris. '94	♟♟	5
● A. A. Lagrein Gries Ris. '94	♟♟	4
● A. A. Pinot Nero Ris. '94	♟♟	5
O A. A. Terlaner Hof zu Pramol '96	♟♟	4
● Euforius '94	♟♟	5
O A. A. Gewürztraminer Lage Doss '96	♟	4
● A. A. Lago di Caldaro Cl. Sup. Ascherhof '96	♟	3
● A. A. Santa Maddalena Cl. Egger-Larcherhof '96	♟	3
O A. A. Sauvignon Lage Naun '96	♟	4
● A. A. Lago di Caldaro Cl. Sup. Ascherhof '94	♟♟	3

● A. A. Pinot Nero '95	♟♟	4
O A. A. Riesling Renano '96	♟♟	4
O A. A. Pinot Bianco '96	♟	3
● A. A. Pinot Nero '91	♟♟	5
● A. A. Pinot Nero '92	♟♟	4
● A. A. Pinot Nero '93	♟♟	4
O A. A. Riesling Renano '93	♟♟	4
O A. A. Riesling Renano '95	♟♟	3*
● A. A. Pinot Nero '94	♟	4

CANTINA PRODUTTORI
CORTACCIA/KURTATSCH
STRADA DEL VINO, 23
39040 CORTACCIA/KURTATSCH (BZ)
TEL. 0471/880115

TIEFENBRUNNER
VIA CASTELLO, 4
LOC. NICLARA/ENTIKLAR
39040 CORTACCIA/KURTATSCH (BZ)
TEL. 0471/880122

The cooperatives in Alto Adige are probably, as we have said, the best in the world. Their managers are skilled and capable people who are key figures in the agricultural life of the region. At Cortaccia it is the urbane and capable Arnold Terzer who has made this well equipped cooperative famous, thanks to two top quality wines which are regular Three Glass prize winners. After several years of success the Cabernet Freienfeld was missing from our tastings (it was not produced in the '94 vintage) but its place was taken by the extraordinary Merlot Brenntal '95. This is an impeccably made red wine which displays a sophisticated berry fruit nose, well integrated with the vanilla and spices that come from barrique ageing. It is extremely elegant on the palate with soft, sweet tannins that complement the fleshy extract and the general balance. This is, perhaps, the best Merlot ever made in the Alto Adige. The Freienfeld '95 will come out later this year so we must make do, if that is the right expression, with the excellent Cabernet Kirchhügel '95 and the delicious Chardonnay Eberlehof '95, with its faintly perceptible vanilla overtones. To finish with a pair of wines deliberately made in a simpler style, we can recommend the Pinot Nero Vorhof '95 and the Lagrein Scuro Forhof '94.

Great festivities at Herbert Tiefenbrunner's winery. The estate's flagship wine, the müller thurgau-based Feldmarschall is 25 years old, which is quite something considering that there were very few prestigious wines at all in Alto Adige when it was first created. Herbert Tiefenbrunner's role in developing quality wine production in the area is well known, and today, helped by his son Christoph, he continues to make a reliable series of premium wines which includes one or two outstanding products. A good example this year is the Chardonnay Linticlarus '95, a barrique aged white wine that came out top of its category. The Feldmarschall '96 is good too, and manages to combine the typical aromatic qualities of the grape with a palate that is not over-dry. There are some well made reds with relatively modest structure, such as the Cabernet Sauvignon Linticlarus '94 and the Pinot Nero Linticlarus '94, which have both obviously suffered from the poor vintage, despite reaching Two Glass standard. After them, in terms of quality, come the Lagrein Scuro '95 and the Gewürztraminer '96, which is something of a Tiefenbrunner speciality but unfortunately a little dilute in this vintage. The Pinot Bianco Prendnerhof '96 is fruity and attractive, but just a bit simple. The '96 vintage, in fact, penalised both the standard Chardonnay and the Sauvignon Kirchenleiten; they are both well made, but they lack varietal character and depth.

● A. A. Merlot Brenntal '95	♍♍♍	5
● A. A. Cabernet Kirchhügel '95	♍♍	4
○ A. A. Chardonnay Eberlehof '95	♍♍	4
○ A. A. Chardonnay Felsenhof '96	♍	3
● A. A. Lagrein Scuro Forhof '94	♍	4
○ A. A. Müller Thurgau Hofstatt '96	♍	3
● A. A. Pinot Nero Vorhof '95	♍	5
○ A. A. Sauvignon '96	♍	3
● A. A. Schiava Grigia Sonnentaler '96	♍	2*
● A. A. Cabernet Freienfeld '92	♍♍♍	5
● A. A. Cabernet Freienfeld Ris. '90	♍♍♍	6
● A. A. Cabernet Freienfeld '91	♍♍	6
● A. A. Cabernet Freienfeld '93	♍♍	6
● A. A. Cabernet Kirchhügel '94	♍♍	5

● A. A. Cabernet Sauvignon Linticlarus '94	♍♍	5
○ A. A. Chardonnay Linticlarus '95	♍♍	5
● A. A. Pinot Nero Linticlarus '94	♍♍	5
○ Feldmarschall von Fenner zu Fennberg '96	♍♍	5
○ A. A. Gewürztraminer '96	♍	3
● A. A. Lagrein Scuro '95	♍	4
○ A. A. Pinot Bianco Prendnerhof '96	♍	3
○ A. A. Chardonnay '96		3
○ A. A. Sauvignon Kirchenleiten '96		4
● A. A. Cabernet '94	♍♍	4
● A. A. Cabernet Sauvignon Linticlarus '90	♍♍	5

CORTACCIA/KURTATSCH (BZ) CORTINA/KURTINIG (BZ)

BARON WIDMANN
VIA IM FELD, 1
39040 CORTACCIA/KURTATSCH (BZ)
TEL. 0471/880092

PETER ZEMMER
STRADA DEL VINO, 24
39040 CORTINA/KURTINIG (BZ)
TEL. 0471/660256

Cortaccia is one of the most southerly viticultural areas in Alto Adige and has the benefit of a slightly warmer climate, especially in the second half of the month of September and during the entire month of October - exactly the ripening period of the best red wine grapes, merlot and cabernet in particular. This is why the area is famous for its great reds, and for Schiava, which is not as imposing a wine, but benefits from all the same advantages. One of the best red wine makers in Cortaccia is Andreas Widmann, a young grower with a special knack for making fine Merlots. The '95 vintage does not reach the heights attained by the excellent '93, not so much because of any lack of structure, but because of the slightly dominant vegetal aromas alongside the classic berry fruit and vanilla. The Schiava '96 is as delicious as always; this is one of Italy's best light red wines and has such an intensely fragrant bouquet and simple attractive style that it never fails to charm. Drunk at cellar temperature (14 degrees) it can really be quite seductive. The whites are less interesting. None of them seemed to come up to previous standards: the Sauvignon '96 has modest body with some clumsy acidity; the Pinot Bianco '96 was satisfactory, but certainly not as big a wine as last year's vintage.

If you are looking for a less well known wine producer in Alto Adige who creates premium white wines at very reasonable prices, Peter Zemmer is your man. All five of his wines from the modest '96 vintage have passed the test for inclusion in this Guide. We thought the best was the Chardonnay '96: good fruit and varietal character on the nose, soft and relatively fleshy on the palate. This wine has no pretensions as a blockbuster with complicated vanilla and toasty bouquets, but relies on the fruit aromas of the grape. Both the Riesling and the Sauvignon are good; both have a well composed nose, not excessively aromatic but not too vegetal or bitter either, common features of '96 vintage where high levels of malic acid often resulted in unbalanced wines. The Pinot Grigio also passes the test; it has good varietal character, but is a bit dilute; fruity but slightly bland on the nose, big enough on the palate and well balanced overall, even if lacking a little in intensity and length. The only wine that falls below the generally high level seemed to us to be the Müller Thurgau '96, which was light and anonymous. Obviously, this is the grape variety that must have suffered most from the difficult weather conditions of the '96 vintage.

● A. A. Merlot '95	♀♀ 5
● A. A. Schiava '96	♀♀ 2*
○ A. A. Pinot Bianco '96	♀ 3
○ A. A. Sauvignon '96	3
● A. A. Cabernet '91	♀♀♀ 5
● A. A. Merlot '93	♀♀♀ 5
● A. A. Cabernet '90	♀♀ 4
● A. A. Cabernet Feld '93	♀♀ 5
● A. A. Cabernet Sauvignon '90	♀♀ 4
● A. A. Merlot '91	♀♀ 4
● A. A. Merlot '92	♀♀ 5
● A. A. Merlot '94	♀♀ 5
○ A. A. Pinot Bianco '95	♀♀ 3*
● A. A. Schiava '95	♀♀ 2*

○ A. A. Chardonnay '96	♀♀ 3*
○ A. A. Pinot Grigio '96	♀ 3
○ A. A. Riesling '96	♀ 3
○ A. A. Sauvignon '96	♀ 3
○ A. A. Müller Thurgau '96	3

LAIVES/LEIFERS (BZ)

PETER DIPOLI
VIA VADENA, 12
39055 LAIVES/LEIFERS (BZ)
TEL. 0471/954227

MAGRÈ/MARGREID (BZ)

HIRSCHPRUNN/CASÒN
P.ZZA S. GERTRUDE, 5
39040 MAGRÈ/MARGREID (BZ)
TEL. 0471/920164

Peter Dipoli has had an excellent education in the practices of winemaking. He was at the Agricultural Institute of San Michele all'Adige at the same time as some of the brightest stars in the rebirth of winemaking in northern Italy - from Silvio Jermann to Mario Pojer, but also Salvatore Maule, Roberto Zeni, Domenico Pedrini, and many other skilful winemakers from all over Italy. He has also travelled the world to winkle out the secrets of international winemaking. Now, finally, he has managed to realise the ambition of his youth to own his own vineyard and winery, an historic "maso" at Egna that is currently being restored and will begin to operate at the end of 1998. Meanwhile, he sources grapes from a single hectare of sauvignon vineyards at Penone, high above Cortaccia, at 550 metres above sea level, and from roughly two hectares at Magré planted to merlot and cabernet. The fruit is taken to Faedo for crushing at the winery of his friends Pojer & Sandri. The results so far are excellent. The Voglar '96 is a sauvignon-based wine named after its vineyard, literally "the fireplace", and has a typical varietal bouquet and a firm palate, perhaps a little unbalanced by excess acidity. But it was the red '95 Yugum that amazed everyone. The name comes from the Latin for "yoke", but is also the ancient word for a particular form of vine training. This is the first year the wine has been bottled and it performed exceptionally well in all our tastings, coming very close to the dizzy heights of a Three Glass award. Seventy percent merlot, 30 percent cabernet sauvignon; a density of 7,000 vines per hectare; Guyot-trained vines; yields at about 50 hectolitres per hectare; powerfully built, its only defect, a slight vegetal aroma on the nose.

The wine world needs successful managers like Alois Lageder, and not only in Italy. Only in its second year of production, and his second-string estate has already hit the target with a Three Glass wine. The winning entry is an innovative creation called Contest from the '94 vintage, made of 40 percent pinot grigio, 30 percent chardonnay, and another 30 percent made up of sauvignon, riesling, chenin blanc, sémillon, marsanne, rousanne and viognier. One year on the lees in barriques (half of which new) and here we are talking about a minor masterpiece. This is a wine which succeeds in blending a very respectable structure with a surprising elegance and ease of drinking. The nose is particularly fine and impressive with its tropical fruit aromas, vanilla and toastiness from the wood. In short, this is a great, world class white wine. The Casòn '94 is almost at the same level of achievement in its own category; a red made from merlot (60 percent), cabernet franc and cabernet sauvignon (25 percent) and then 15 percent made up from lagrein, petit verdot and syrah. As the cépage suggests, once again this is an innovative wine for the region, but looking further afield, it has certainly similarities with some of the more aristocratically elegant Saint Emilions. The nose is already complete, with tobacco and berry fruit aromas characteristic of the dominant merlot grape; full bodied and extremely well balanced; had it just had an extra touch of intensity to it, we would have been talking about a double success for the Hirschprunn winery. Lastly, two white wines, the Sauvignon and the Chardonnay, both '96: well made, simple, varietally correct on the nose, but nothing exceptionally exciting.

● A. A. Merlot-Cabernet Yugum '95	🍷🍷	5
○ A. A. Sauvignon Voglar '96	🍷🍷	4
○ A. A. Sauvignon Voglar '93	🍷🍷	4
○ A. A. Sauvignon Voglar '94	🍷🍷	4
○ A. A. Sauvignon Voglar '95	🍷🍷	4

○ Contest '94	🍷🍷🍷	5
● Casòn '94	🍷🍷	5
○ A. A. Chardonnay '96	🍷	3
○ A. A. Sauvignon '96	🍷	3
○ A. A. Sauvignon '95	🍷🍷	3*
● Corolle '93	🍷🍷	4
○ A. A. Chardonnay '95	🍷	3
○ A. A. Gewürztraminer '95	🍷	3
○ A. A. Pinot Grigio '95	🍷	3
○ Etelle '95	🍷	3

MAGRÈ/MARGREID (BZ)   MARLENGO/MARLING (BZ)

ALOIS LAGEDER
TENUTA LÖWENGANG
39040 MAGRÈ/MARGREID (BZ)
TEL. 0471/809500

CANTINA PRODUTTORI BURGGRÄFLER
VIA PALADE, 64
39020 MARLENGO/MARLING (BZ)
TEL. 0473/47137

There is lots of news this year from Alois Lageder, one of the key figures in Alto Adige winemaking: a brand new winery with state-of-the-art technology; the transfer of the company headquarters from Bolzano to Magré; commercial and critical success with few parallels in Italy. All of this is the result of an impeccable professionalism that has made Lageder one of the great ambassadors for Italian wine at home and abroad. He makes a vast range of wines; perhaps, if we may be so bold as to say it, too big. There are three principal lines. The first includes the two wines from Tenuta Löwengang, the Cabernet and the Chardonnay (this year '93 and '94 respectively), and the Cabernet Sauvignon Cor Römigberg '93. All three are impeccably made, however, the reds suffer from a slight lack of structure and intensity, much like good Bordeaux in an off year. The Chardonnay is more successful: rich and elegant, but already well developed. Just for once, the Chardonnay is beaten into second place by the Benefizio Porer '96, the best wine of Lageder's second line, a barrel aged Pinot Grigio that has an intense varietal bouquet and is surprisingly well balanced. The two white blends, the Dornach '95 and the Tannhammer Caius '95, are both good, while the two cru wines, Haberlehof Pinot Bianco and Lehenhof Sauvignon di Terlano (both '96), are fruity and fragrant. Only one wine has won through from the third line which consists of basic varietals: the Pinot Bianco '96 is outstanding in its class, almost as good as the Haberlehof in terms of profile, it scored almost as high in our tastings.

The undisputed signature wine of this winery is the splendid Pinot Nero Tiefenthalerhof '95. It misses a Three Glass award by a hair's breadth, but can we add, for the benefit of those readers who will go to the lengths of reading this text as well as just looking at the scores, that we believe this to be one of the best examples of Pinot Nero we have tasted this year. Full stop. The bouquet is complex although perhaps slightly vegetal which is why we eventually marked it down to Two Glasses, but it has good depth and classic pinot noir character. The flavours are broad, the tannins are soft, and the general impression is of a sophisticated, aristocratic wine that lacks only a little concentration. But would that there were more wines like this! Certainly the Pinot Nero Tiefenthalerhof is now firmly on the list of wines to watch closely next time round. The Lagrein-Cabernet Mervin '95 is not at the same level, but is a good wine nonetheless: almost opaque in colour, with an attractive bouquet of berry fruit and vanilla, but a little dried out on the palate where the tannins are not completely balanced by the extract. The light red wine, Meranese Schickenburg, is Merano's answer to Bolzano's Santa Maddalena in the sense that it, too, is made of schiava grapes cultivated very close to the city centre; the '96 is a bit off-form, clumsier and lighter than last year's version. Unfortunately, the Chardonnay Tiefenthalerhof '96 is no better, with its neutral nose and rather short finish.

●	A. A. Cabernet Cor Römigberg '93	🍷🍷	6
●	A. A. Cabernet Löwengang '93	🍷🍷	5
O	A. A. Chardonnay Löwengang '94	🍷🍷	5
O	A. A. Pinot Bianco '96	🍷🍷	3*
O	A. A. Pinot Bianco Haberlehof '96	🍷🍷	4
O	A. A. Pinot Grigio Benefizium Porer '96	🍷🍷	4
●	A. A. Pinot Nero Mazon Ris. '95	🍷🍷	5
O	A. A. Terlano Sauvignon Lehenhof '96	🍷🍷	4
O	Dornach '95	🍷🍷	4
O	Tannhammer Caius '95	🍷🍷	4
●	A. A. Cabernet Cor Römigberg '90	🍷🍷🍷	6
●	A. A. Cabernet Löwengang '92	🍷🍷🍷	5
●	A. A. Cabernet Cor Römigberg '91	🍷🍷	6

●	A. A. Pinot Nero Tiefenthalerhof '95	🍷🍷	4
●	A. A. Lagrein-Cabernet Mervin '95	🍷🍷	5
O	A. A. Chardonnay Tiefenthalerhof '96		3
O	A. A. Meranese Schickenburg '96		3
O	A. A. Pinot Bianco V. T. '93	🍷🍷	6
●	A. A. Pinot Nero Tiefenthalerhof '94	🍷🍷	3*

MELTINA/MÖLTEN (BZ)

VIVALDI - ARUNDA
CIVICO, 53
39010 MELTINA/MÖLTEN (BZ)
TEL. 0471/668033

The same sparkling wines sold with the brand name Vivaldi in Italy are distributed under the Arunda label in Alto Adige and the rest of Europe. We point this unusual arrangement out every year for the sake of our German-speaking readers. The owner, cellarmaster, and guiding light at the winery is Joseph Reiterer, who besides being a very charming man is also one of the best technical experts on sparkling wine in Italy. This year we particularly liked his Vivaldi Brut '93: aromatic and extremely easy to drink, perhaps a little one dimensional, but an excellent wine in its category, a moderately aged Metodo Classico, made in a style which aims at the maximum freshness and fragrance on the nose. (The result is that the bottle empties much faster than you might think!) The Extra Brut Vivaldi '93 and Vivaldi Riserva '90, are good, but a little clumsy in their acidity and, all in all, less easy to drink. The same goes for the Cuvée Marianna Extra Brut (non-vintage despite being the company's flagship wine): it is well made and full of flavour, but unbalanced by the slight bitterness of excess acidity combined with carbon dioxide. This is a sparkling wine stripped to the bare essentials; the bouquet is based on primary and yeast aromas but the wine is perhaps too hard on the finish. These are not serious defects, but features which do affect the drinkability.

MONTAGNA/MONTAN (BZ)

FRANZ HAAS
VIA VILLA, 6
39040 MONTAGNA/MONTAN (BZ)
TEL. 0471/812280

"Almost a goal!", as the legendary sports commentator Nicolò Carosio used to shout so energetically, an exclamation we could repeat with reference to the two Franz Haas wines that just missed Three Glass awards. The first, one of our old favourites, is the Pinot Nero Schweizer '95, the second is the Moscato Rosa, also from the Schweizer range and also a '95. These are excellent wines, two little gems that the simple Two Glass rating does not do justice to, at all. The Pinot Nero is the best that Haas has ever made: good complexity on the nose with the same mix of rustic and berry-fruit character that characterises some of the best Aloxe-Cortons from the Côte de Beaune; it is soft and easy to drink, perhaps held back from the heights of achievement in its category by being slightly one dimensional on the palate. The Moscato Rosa is delicious, and the best in its class for the second year running: characteristically aromatic bouquet with intense aromas of dog roses; very sweet on the palate with a finish that tends towards bitterness for a moment then returns to the intense aromas of the bouquet. A new wine this year that did well is the Manna '95, an IGT Mitterburg white, made with a blend of several varieties: intense vegetal aromas mixed with sage and cumin; full bodied and firm on the palate with relatively well balanced acidity. The other white wines, which are this estate's staple fare, are all correctly made. The best are the Gewürztraminer and the Pinot Bianco, both '96; while the '96 Pinot Grigio is a bit neutral and one dimensional.

○ A. A. Spumante Brut Vivaldi '93	🍷🍷	5
○ A. A. Spumante Cuvée Marianna Extra Brut	🍷	5
○ A. A. Spumante Extra Brut Vivaldi '93	🍷	5
○ A. A. Spumante Vivaldi Extra Brut Riserva '90	🍷	5
○ Vivaldi Cuvée Marianna Extra Brut	🍷🍷	5
○ Vivaldi Extra Brut Ris. '87	🍷🍷	6
○ Vivaldi Extra Brut Ris. '89	🍷🍷	5

● A. A. Moscato Rosa Schweizer '95	🍷🍷	5
● A. A. Pinot Nero Schweizer '95	🍷🍷	5
○ A. A. Mitterberg Manna '95	🍷🍷	5
○ A. A. Gewürztraminer '96	🍷	3
○ A. A. Pinot Bianco '96	🍷	3
○ A. A. Pinot Grigio '96	🍷	3
○ A. A. Gewürztraminer '95	🍷🍷	4
● A. A. Merlot Schweizer '93	🍷🍷	4
● A. A. Moscato Rosa '94	🍷🍷	5
● A. A. Pinot Nero Ris. '91	🍷🍷	5

NALLES/NALS (BZ)

ORA/AUER (BZ)

CASTELLO SCHWANBURG
VIA SCHWANBURG, 16
39010 NALLES/NALS (BZ)
TEL. 0471/678622

CLEMENS WALDTHALER
VIA DEL RIO, 4
39040 ORA/AUER (BZ)
TEL. 0471/810182

The splendid castle of Schwanburg lies half way between Bolzano and Merlano, near Terlano, and dominates the upper valley of the river Adige. The vineyards surrounding the castle are mostly Guyot-trained, in contrast to the Pergola Trentina system generally used in the rest of the valley. This is the policy of Dieter Rudolph Carli, one of the best growers in the Alto Adige, an able businessman and one of the region's top experts on red wine, and in particular Cabernet Sauvignon. This year his Castel Schwanburg Cabernet '94 suffered from the vintage; despite displaying its usual style and elegance on the nose it is predictably short of body. It is a good wine that just lacks an extra touch of depth and complexity. There were two wines, however, that we liked very much this year. The first is a splendid Riesling '96, one of the best in its class and, more importantly, one of the best whites ever to come out of this estate: good, varietal bouquet with mineral hints; very aristocratic in style, firm on the palate, shot through with an attractive vein of acidity. The second wine is the Schiava Schlosswein '96: a riot of fragrant fruit on the nose, easy to drink and very attractive. Possibly a minor wine, but very well made. The Cabernet Sauvignon Riserva '93 is a little over the hill and the Sauvignon '96 has slightly diluted varietal character but both are satisfactory wines. On the other hand, we have yet to find a completely convincing version of the Terlano Pinot Bianco Sonnenburg; this time we tried the '95 and, once again, found it too dominated by vanilla from the oak.

The Waldthaler family have run this little estate in Ora for generations. This year it had a real triumph in our tastings with six out of six wines presented winning awards. At this point the Waldthalers' debut in the Guide becomes a pleasure as well as an obligation on our part. We start with the best wine of the range, the Lagrein Raut '94: this is a powerful red with opulent extract, but at the same time it is soft, fruity and easy to drink. If the '94 is this good, who knows what will come from the superior '95 vintage? We shall have to wait until next year to find out. The Cabernet Raut '95 is also very good. Once again, we found an impressively rich wine with intense berry fruit aromas; very firm on the palate, perhaps a little too much so, and still with a few youthful rough edges to be smoothed out yet. The Cabernet '95 from the standard range has similar character to the Raut, without being such a rich, well built wine. The Merlot Raut '95 is good, but given the success of the other samples, we were expecting it to be even better: good varietal character, but closed on the nose due to its extreme youth. We finish with the Pinot Bianco '96, which is a very satisfactory white wine, if a bit simple and lacking in structure.

● A. A. Cabernet Castel Schwanburg '94	ΨΨ	5
O A. A. Riesling '96	ΨΨ	3*
● A. A. Schiava Schlosswein '96	ΨΨ	2'
● A. A. Cabernet Sauvignon Ris. '93	Ψ	4
O A. A. Sauvignon '96	Ψ	3
O A. A. Terlano Pinot Bianco Sonnenberg '95	Ψ	4
● A. A. Cabernet Castel Schwanburg '90	ΨΨ	6
● A. A. Cabernet Castel Schwanburg '93	ΨΨ	5
● A. A. Cabernet Ris. '90	ΨΨ	5
O A. A. Chardonnay '95	ΨΨ	3*
^ A. Pinot Grigio '95	ΨΨ	3*

● A. A. Cabernet Raut '95	ΨΨ	4
● A. A. Lagrein Scuro Raut '94	ΨΨ	4
● A. A. Cabernet '95	Ψ	3
● A. A. Merlot Raut '95	Ψ	4
O A. A. Pinot Bianco '96	Ψ	3

SALORNO/SALURN (BZ)

STAVA/STABEN (BZ)

HADERBURG
POCHI, 31
39040 SALORNO/SALURN (BZ)
TEL. 0471/889097

CASTEL JUVAL - UNTEROTL
JUVAL, 1B
39020 STAVA/STABEN (BZ)
TEL. 0473/667580

Luis Ochsenreiter, from the Haderburg estate above Salorno, has always been one of the pioneering free thinkers of Alto Adige winemaking. Back in 1976, he was the first to make a commercially viable Metodo Classico sparkling wine, and he remains one of the best producers in the category. As in previous years, his Haderburg Pas Dosé '91 is a successful wine with fresh, well developed character and an attractive weight to it. What Luis Ochsenreiter does not seem to have worked out yet, however, is what he is trying to achieve with his still wines. The Sauvignon Stainhauser '96 comes out well; it has good grassy varietal aroma on the nose and a round, full bodied palate but it is rather subtly flavoured. The Chardonnay and Traminer Aromatico need more time to develop their own characters to the maximum. Lastly, the Pinot Nero: the Haderburg estate lies at the heart of the best area in the region for this variety, but although its Pinot is a respectable wine, it does not quite live up to expectations.

We would like to bring this small estate in the Venosta valley to your attention. Located near the castle of Juval, about 20 kilometres from Merano it comprises about five hectares of vineyards. Martin Aurich, an oenologist from the staff at the Laimburg Experimental Institute, is the technical consultant. The most news worthy fact about the estate is the name of its owner. Reinhold Messner mean anything to you? The conqueror of the Himalayan peaks, one of the most famous mountaineers in the world? This is the man. Less well known is that Messner has always been a winelover and that now he has begun to produce wine himself. And, in contrast to some of his colleagues on the superstar circuit, he has decided to do it seriously. We were completely bowled over by his Riesling '96. It is a masterpiece: intensely fruity on the nose with grapefruit aromas and a smokiness in the background; rich and full bodied on the palate with excellent acidity. This is a great white wine. The Pinot Nero '95 is of similar quality, with the slight reservation that it lacks a little structure, but it could easily rival many legendary Santenay wines of the same vintage: blackberries and blackcurrants on the nose, extremely drinkable. The Pinot Bianco '96 is not as good as the other two wines. It is much lighter and blander, but you cannot have everything at this latitude with a vintage like the '96. Our congratulations to Messner and Aurich.

○ A. A. Sauvignon Stainhauser '96	🍷🍷	4
○ Spumante Pas Dosé '91	🍷🍷	5
● A. A. Pinot Nero Stainhauser '95	🍷	5

● A. A. Val Venosta Pinot Nero '95	🍷🍷	5
○ A. A. Val Venosta Riesling '96	🍷🍷	4
○ A. A. Val Venosta Pinot Bianco '96	🍷	4

TERLANO/TERLAN (BZ)

TERMENO/TRAMIN (BZ)

CANTINA TERLANO
VIA COLLINA D'ARGENTO, 7
39018 TERLANO/TERLAN (BZ)
TEL. 0471/257135

CANTINA PRODUTTORI DI TERMENO
STRADA DEL VINO, 122
39040 TERMENO/TRAMIN (BZ)
TEL. 0471/860126

The Terlano cooperative has not succeeded in bringing out any Three Glass wines in recent years. Considering the potential at their disposal, particularly in the white wine categories, this is a real shame. For our part, we have repeated our criticisms every year and, although the winery has not managed to produce anything at the highest level this year either, they have at least made considerable progress. The white wines, particularly, deserve our praise. The Terlano Classico '95, in the old style bottle, is a fine, elegant wine with attractive body and freshness of fruit that balances the new wood well. The Pinot Grigio Klaus '95 has good varietal character on the nose, and is firm and full bodied with good concentration of flavour on the palate. This is perhaps the way forward, as far as a style for the future is concerned. The Sauvignon, the Pinot Bianco and the Chardonnay are good, clean wines, but they lack that little extra something that would give them more personality. The same goes for the Merlot '94 and the Pinot Riserva '94: very pleasant to drink, but no real character. We sincerely hope that the cellarmaster, Hartmann Dona, will be able to deliver wines which obtain better results next year.

The cooperative at Termeno has shown us some exquisite wines in recent years. Even if it has not produced anything to create a sensation yet, and even if none of the wines have yet had that little extra touch necessary to break through to Three Glass level, the dedication shown by cellarmaster Wilhelm Sturz and his team is beginning to have an effect. Two wines particularly stood out in our tastings: the Gewürztraminer Maratsch '96 which, with its intense fruity nose, its elegant structure, full body and easy drinkability, is one of the best of its type in the Alto Adige, and its rival from the same vintage, the Gewürztraminer Nussbaumerhof, which is more famous, but this time not quite as good. The Chardonnay Glassien '96 lines up among the best Chardonnays in the region, thanks to its well defined, firm structure and its subtle nose. The Pinot Grigio Unterebnerhof '96 on the other hand cannot compete with its predecessor from the '95 vintage. The Pinot Bianco '96 is a well made white wine; fruity and with an attractive freshness. The Pinot Nero Schiesstandhof '95 is not quite ready yet, but is clearly a clean wine with marked personality and a faint hint of oak on the nose. Last but not least, the Schiava Huxenbichler '96 is one of the most typical examples of this delicious wine. We await future vintages of these wines with great confidence in the outcome.

○ A. A. Pinot Grigio Klaus '95	🍷🍷	4
○ A. A. Terlano Classico '95	🍷🍷	5
● A. A. Merlot '94	🍷	3
● A. A. Pinot Nero Ris. '94	🍷	5
○ A. A. Terlano Chardonnay Kreuth '95	🍷	4
○ A. A. Terlano Pinot Bianco Vorberg '95	🍷	4
○ A. A. Terlano Sauvignon '96	🍷	4
○ A. A. Terlano Sauvignon Cl. '95	🍷	5
○ A. A. Terlano Pinot Bianco '79	🍷🍷🍷	5
○ A. A. Terlano Sauvignon Cl. '93	🍷🍷	6
● A. A. Lagrein Scuro '94	🍷	4
● A. A. Santa Maddalena Hauserhof '94	🍷	3

○ A. A. Chardonnay Glassien Renomée '96	🍷🍷	3
○ A. A. Gewürztraminer Maratsch '96	🍷🍷	3
○ A. A. Gewürztraminer Nussbaumerhof '96	🍷	3
○ A. A. Pinot Bianco '96	🍷	2
○ A. A. Pinot Grigio Unterebnerhof '96	🍷	3
● A. A. Pinot Nero Schiesstandhof '95	🍷	4
● A. A. Schiava Hexenbichler '96	🍷	3
○ A. A. Gewürztraminer Nussbaumerhof '94	🍷🍷	4
○ A. A. Gewürztraminer Nussbaumerhof '95	🍷🍷	4

TERMENO/TRAMIN (BZ)

TERMENO/TRAMIN (BZ)

HOFSTÄTTER
P.ZZA MUNICIPIO, 5
39040 TERMENO/TRAMIN (BZ)
TEL. 0471/860161

PODERI CASTEL RINGBERG
E KASTELAZ ELENA WALCH
VIA A. HOFER, 1
39040 TERMENO/TRAMIN (BZ)
TEL. 0471/860172

This is a transitional year in the Guide for the important Hofstätter winery from Termeno. The major news is that control of the firm is now definitively in the hands of Martin Foradori, one of the young lions of Alto Adige winemaking and the son of Paolo Foradori, who ran the winery for many years and who stays on to give expert advice. Martin's assumption of control coincides with the completion of splendid new cellars, constructed on the site of the old winery in the centre of Termeno. Future events will include the release of the '95 vintage red wines, and barrel tastings already suggest they will be exceptionally fine. Of the wines we tasted this year, there was nothing at Three Glass level, although they were all at least correctly made. And there were, of course, some very good wines. As usual the Pinot Nero Vigneto S. Urbano stood out, and it remains the best of its type in the Alto Adige; but it did seem to us lighter and less successful than in previous vintages. The Pinot Nero Mazzon '95 gets much the same rating, which says a lot about what to expect from the forthcoming '95s. The classic Pinot Nero Riserva '94, the Crozzolhof '96 (simpler and more up-front), and the Lagrein Steinraffler '95, are all good. But the real surprise is that the wine that came closest to getting Three Glasses this year is a magisterial version of the Gewürztraminer Kolbenhof '96, the best the Foradori's have ever produced. It has extremely well defined varietal character, typical floral aromas, and good structure. The one tiny defect is an excessively bitter finish. The Kolbenhof's little sister, the standard Gewürztraminer '96 is less complex, but extremely drinkable. We finish with three orthodox, correctly made whites : the '96 Pinot Bianco Villa Barthenau, Chardonnay and Riesling.

The wines that Elena Walch shows us every year are always at the cutting edge of technical perfection. Perfectly vinified grapes, correct varietal bouquets, good drinkability and good balance are the order of the day. The only possible doubts are about the complexity and depth of some of these wines. And here, quite often, our tasting panel fail to agree. There are those who think the wines are perfect as they are and there are those who think they need a bit more power and concentration, especially the reds. However, everyone acknowledges the reliability of Signora Walch's wines and the fact that they are instantly recognisable. In other words what is potentially lacking is personality, although this is not the case for the two best wines, the Cabernet Sauvignon Riserva '93 and the Chardonnay '94, both from the Castel Ringberg property. The former has a very elegant and attractive nose with particularly subtle fruit, not at all compromised by the oak. Balance and subtlety are also the hallmarks of the palate; despite its relative lack of complexity. The latter, in its own way, has very similar features and here the new oak blends in very well with the fruit. Again, the Chardonnay Cardellino '96 has a fragrant and intensely fruity bouquet and satisfactory structure, while the Gewürztraminer Kastelatz '96 is correctly aromatic and well balanced. The only slightly disappointing wine this year was the Pinot Grigio Castel Ringberg '96, which did not have the cleanest of noses and was somewhat one dimensional.

○ A. A. Gewürztraminer		
Kolbenhof '96	♀♀	4
● A. A. Lagrein Steinraffler '95	♀♀	4
● A. A. Pinot Nero Ris. '94	♀♀	4
● A. A. Pinot Nero Mazzon '95	♀♀	4
● A. A. Pinot Nero		
Vigneto S. Urbano '94	♀♀	6
○ A. A. Chardonnay '96	♀	3*
○ A. A. Gewürztraminer '96	♀	3*
○ A. A. Pinot Bianco		
Villa Barthenau '96	♀	4
● A. A. Pinot Nero Crozzolhof '96	♀	4
○ A. A. Riesling '96	♀	3*
● A. A. Pinot Nero		
Vigneto S. Urbano '93	♀♀♀	6

● A. A. Cabernet Sauvignon		
Castel Ringberg Ris. '93	♀♀	5
○ A. A. Chardonnay		
Castel Ringberg '94	♀♀	4
○ A. A. Chardonnay Cardellino '96	♀	4
○ A. A. Gewürztraminer Kastelaz '96	♀	4
○ A. A. Pinot Grigio		
Castel Ringberg '96		4
● A. A. Cabernet Sauvignon		
Castel Ringberg Ris. '92	♀♀	5
○ A. A. Chardonnay Cardellino '95	♀♀	4
○ A. A. Pinot Grigio		
Castel Ringberg '94	♀♀	3
○ A. A. Pinot Grigio		
Castel Ringberg '95	♀♀	4

VADENA/PFATTEN (BZ)

VARNA/VAHRN (BZ)

ISTITUTO SPERIMENTALE LAIMBURG
LOC. LAIMBURG, 6
39051 VADENA/PFATTEN (BZ)
TEL. 0471/969210

CANTINA DELL' ABBAZIA DI NOVACELLA
VIA DELL'ABBAZIA, 1
39040 VARNA/VAHRN (BZ)
TEL. 0472/836189

The usual series of well made wines, some points of real interest, but nothing that really excited us. This is the summary of our impression of Laimburg this year. Apart from anything else, the fact that we were looking at '94 vintage reds and '96 vintage whites was enough to ensure that expectations could not be too high. There were two wines, however, the Riesling '96 and the Sauvignon '96, that came out towards the top of their respective categories. The Riesling is very successful and could stand many years' ageing: typical bouquet with minerals and smokiness already quite well developed; good structure still dominated by a strong vein of acidity. The Sauvignon has a good nose, marked by aromas of sage and fine concentration of flavour on the palate. Two of the winery's core products are next in ranking, the Cabernet Riserva '94, a bit more dilute than last year's version and the familiar Gewürztraminer, Laimburg's pride and joy, although this year with the '96 vintage it does not display the richness of flavour and extract that won it Three Glasses two years ago. Next down in the scale are the Pinot Bianco '96 (correctly made), the Merlot '95 (we expected better concentration of flavour), and the Lagrein Riserva (a good wine, but obviously not one of the top priorities of the winery). We are still not convinced by the Moscato Rosa; despite the fact that the '95 version seems good, it still lacks that extra touch of varietal character, especially on the nose. The Chardonnay '96 was quite a disappointment: neutral on the nose and lacking in weight.

Urban Von Klebersburg, guiding light at the cellars of the Abbey of Novacella, is keeping a lot of surprises up his sleeve for next year. There were already some changes in the vinification and ageing of the '97 vintage - nothing revolutionary, but rather the adoption of slightly more modern techniques than have hitherto been used. We are very pleased to see it; we know that the vineyards and the grapes from this estate have the potential to make great wines, above all with varieties such as sylvaner and müller thurgau. Here we are in a marginal area for the cultivation of vitis vinifera and therefore vineyard management is of paramount importance in the production of quality fruit. Particular problems arise however because market forces impose the bottling and sale of wines before they are ready. Novacella's Sylvaner needs to be aged for at least one year before it begins to show its best and clearly the practice of bottling in the winter months following the harvest was just not doing it justice. This year we tasted the '96, a white wine with enormous structure on the palate but a confused bouquet, not helped by premature bottling, before the wine had properly settled. It will not take much to put this right in the future and create a jewel of a Sylvaner. No problems with the Moscato Rosa, on the other hand, from the '94 and the '95 vintages. Both are splendid wines with typical dog rose aromas and intense bouquets that reappear in the finish. Both have structures worthy of the best of their category. Perhaps the '94 is the fuller bodied of the two, but in terms of aroma and flavour there is little to choose between them.

● A. A. Cabernet Ris. '94	♟♟	5
○ A. A. Gewürztraminer '96	♟♟	4
○ A. A. Riesling Renano '96	♟♟	4
○ A. A. Sauvignon '96	♟♟	4
○ A. A. Chardonnay '96	♟	4
● A. A. Lagrein Scuro Ris. '94	♟	4
○ A. A. Pinot Bianco '96	♟	4
● A. A. Merlot '95	♟	4
● A. A. Cabernet Ris. '93	♟♟	5
○ A. A. Chardonnay '95	♟♟	5
○ A. A. Gewürztraminer '95	♟♟	4
○ A. A. Riesling Renano '95	♟♟	4
○ A. A. Sauvignon '94	♟♟	4
○ A. A. Sauvignon '95	♟♟	4

● A. A. Moscato Rosa '94	♟♟	5
● A. A. Moscato Rosa '95	♟♟	5
○ A. A. Valle Isarco Sylvaner '96	♟	3
● A. A. Pinot Nero '95	♟♟	4
● A. A. Lago di Caldaro '95	♟	3
● A. A. Santa Maddalena '95	♟	3
○ A. A. Valle Isarco Kerner '95	♟	4

OTHER WINERIES

The following producers in the province of Bolzano obtained good scores in our tastings with one or more of their wines:

Cantina Produttori S. Paolo/ Kellereigenossenschaft St. Pauls,
Appiano/Eppan,
tel. 0471/662183,
A. A. Pinot Bianco '96,
A. A. Lagrein Scuro Exclusiv Gries Ris. '94

Stroblhof,
Appiano/Eppan,
tel. 0471/662250,
A. A. Chardonnay '96,
A. A. Gewürztraminer '96,
A. A. Müller Thurgau '96

Malojer Gummerhof,
Bolzano/Bozen, tel. 0471/972885,
A. A. Chardonnay Gummerhof '95,
A. A. Lagrein Scuro Gummerhof '94

Georg Mumelter,
Bolzano/Bozen,
tel. 0471/973090,
A. A. Pinot Grigio Griesbauerhof '96

Eduard Pfeifer,
Bolzano/Bozen, tel. 0471/972275,
A. A. Lagrein Scuro Pfannestielhof '96

Georg Ramoser,
Bolzano/Bozen, tel. 0471/975481,
A. A. Lagrein Scuro Untermoserhof '95

Stefan Ramoser,
Bolzano/Bozen,
tel. 0471/979048,
A. A. Lagrein Scuro Fliederhof '95

Heinrich Rottensteiner,
Bolzano/Bozen,
tel. 0471/973549,
A. A. Lagrein Scuro Obermoser Grafenleiten '95

Anton Schmid - Oberrautner,
Bolzano/Bozen, tel. 0471/281440,
A. A. Lagrein Scuro Ris. '94

Loacker Schwarhof,
Bolzano/Bozen, tel. 0471/365125.
A. A. Gewürztraminer '96,
A. A. Pinot Nero '96

Peter Sölva & Sohn - Paterbichl,
Caldaro/Kaltern,
tel. 0471/964650,
A. A. Lago di Caldaro Scelto Cl. Sup. Peterleiten '96,
A. A. Merlot Desilvas '95

Josef Brigl,
Cornaiano/Girlan, tel. 0471/662419,
A. A. Pinot Nero Kreuzbichler '94

Lorenz Martini,
Cornaiano/Girlan, tel. 0471/664136,
A. A. Spumante Comitissa Brut '88

Cantina Produttori Merano/ Meraner Kellerei,
Merano/Meran,
tel. 0473/235544,
A. A. Chardonnay Goldegg '96,
A. A. Gewürztraminer Graf Von Meran '96,
A. A. Cabernet-Merlot Graf Von Meran '94

Cantina Produttori Nalles, Niclara, Magré/Kellereigenossenschaft Nals, Margreid, Entiklar,
Nalles/Nals, tel. 0471/678626,
A. A. Terlano Sauvignon Cl. Mantele '96,
A. A. Cabernet Ansitz Von Menz Baron Salvadori '94,
A. A. Pinot Nero Ansitz Von Menz Baron Salvadori '94,
Anticus Ansitz Von Menz Baron Salvadori '93

Franz Pratzner - Tenuta Falkenstein,
Naturno/Naturns,
tel. 0473/666054,
A. A. Val Venosta Pinot Bianco '96,
A. A. Val Venosta Riesling '96,
A. A. Val Venosta Pinot Nero '95

Sebastian Stoker,
Terlano/Terlan, tel. 0471/256032,
Stoker Sekt.

VENETO

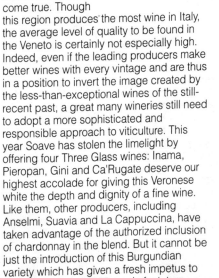

The Veneto is nursing the dream of becoming Italy's most important winemaking region and the thirteen Three Glass awards given this year demonstrate that this dream could come true. Though this region produces the most wine in Italy, the average level of quality to be found in the Veneto is certainly not especially high. Indeed, even if the leading producers make better wines with every vintage and are thus in a position to invert the image created by the less-than-exceptional wines of the still-recent past, a great many wineries still need to adopt a more sophisticated and responsible approach to viticulture. This year Soave has stolen the limelight by offering four Three Glass wines: Inama, Pieropan, Gini and Ca'Rugate deserve our highest accolade for giving this Veronese white the depth and dignity of a fine wine. Like them, other producers, including Anselmi, Suavia and La Cappuccina, have taken advantage of the authorized inclusion of chardonnay in the blend. But it cannot be just the introduction of this Burgundian variety which has given a fresh impetus to quality: 1996 and 1995 are, in fact, two excellent vintages, and producers have also begun to make efforts to cut down their yields. Valpolicella is passing through a delicate phase: producers are literally overwhelmed by the relentless demand for Amarone and therefore seem to be dedicating themselves entirely to this premium wine, while letting Valpolicella, which also actually has considerable commercial potential, fall by the wayside. The zone is in ferment: wineries are being renovated, as are production techniques, but what is really called for in order to give continuity to this favourable trend is a greater awareness of vine management. Allegrini and Dal Forno demonstrate enviable winemaking skills throughout their ranges. Accordini, Le Salette, Venturini and Begali concentrate their energies on some splendid Amarone; Speri gives us a taste of the great potential of Recioto, as do Viviani and Bussola. From the Custoza area, we find some superb dessert wines, and particularly an unusual Moscato produced by Vigne di San Pietro. Le Tende and Corte Gardoni are also making fine wines. La Cavalchina performed very well, both with its wines from Lake Garda and those from near Mantua. In the Province of Vicenza, Fausto Maculan continues to be the trailblazer, but we also draw your attention to the encouraging progress of Cavazza and to the well deserved re-entry into the Guide of La Biancara. Vignalta is a touchstone in the Colli Euganei, a zone which seems perpetually on the verge of a major breakthrough, but which to date has never expressed its full potential. The Valdobbiadene area is producing very reliable wines: the good impressions of last year were confirmed, and the conviction is growing among major producers (Bisol, Adami and Ruggeri, for example) that quality must be based primarily on grape selection; refined technology in the winery comes later. In the Marca Trevigiana, Serafini e Vidotto have again produced a great Rosso, and their quality-led example is beginning to be followed by other estates, such as Conti Collalto, which has great potential. On the plain of the Piave, Molon continues to excel with some very stylish whites.

ARQUÀ PETRARCA (PD) BARDOLINO (VR)

VIGNALTA
VIA MARLUNGHE, 7
35032 ARQUÀ PETRARCA (PD)
TEL. 0429/777225

GUERRIERI RIZZARDI
P.ZZA GUERRIERI, 1
37011 BARDOLINO (VR)
TEL. 045/7210028

What would the Colli Euganei be without Vignalta? This fundamental touchstone for quality serves as an example to large and small producers alike of the splendid potential of the Colli Euganei. Vignalta continues to improve, making its finer wines increasingly more interesting, but also including the less expensive selections in their Marlunghe range in this rising quality trend. From the Marlunghe line comes a lovely surprise: an elegant Colli Euganei Bianco, with intense aromas and well-structured fruit, an excellent example of how to combine immediacy and depth. The Merlot shows similar characteristics: it is an attractive and youthful red, with a spicy and herbaceous nose, broad yet delicate flavours and a versatile, balanced style. The Colli Euganei Rosso '95 has good depth, apparent even from its rich ruby colour. Black berry fruits are the central component of the bouquet, which also offers delicate hints of spices; the austere "goût de terroir" typical of the volcanic Colli Euganei is apparent on the palate, well balanced, however, by fleshy fruit. The '94 Gemola, a blend of merlot and cabernet franc in which Zanovello concentrates his efforts in order to make it the estate's premium red, is a paradigm of measure and elegance. The Sirio is excellent too. It is a dry Moscato with a very broad range of aromas, including luxuriant floral notes, and soft, long-flavoured fruit on the palate.

This is one of the most beautiful estates in the Province of Verona: its vineyards are spread amongst some of the best sites of the three major DOC zones (Bardolino, Valpolicella, Soave). Its winery is well equipped and the owner, Countess Guerrieri, does not skimp on either physical or financial resources in order to make it a model for all to imitate. During the last few years, however, we have had the feeling that the company's potential has not been exploited to the full. This year, at last, we believe that there are positive signs of revival. All three wines presented in our tastings - there are in fact many more actually produced - easily earned One Glass ratings and indeed came close to scoring even higher. The Bianco Castello Guerrieri - made from garganega, sauvignon, cortese and marco bona - is an interesting experiment which balances the freshness of the first three grapes with the richness of the last, an indigenous variety which is partially raisined. The wine's colour is deep; its nose is fairly closed, but reveals attractive concentration; the palate confirms this sensation, and the firm, rich flavour evolves into a clean finish. The more lively Soave from the Costeggiola vineyard, with its generous nose of apples and almonds, displays full, rather rustic fruit on the palate which echoes the aroma. From the Calcarole vineyard in Negrar comes an Amarone which appears to have stood up well to the uncertainties of the '91 vintage. Though it does not have the depth of previous years such as the '88 or the '90, it makes up for this with an extremely attractive bouquet and gentle, supple and complex fruit on the palate.

○ Colli Euganei Bianco Marlunghe '96	♀♀	2*
○ Sirio '96	♀♀	2*
● Colli Euganei Gemola '94	♀♀	4
● Colli Euganei Merlot Marlunghe '96	♀	3
○ Colli Euganei Pinot Bianco '96	♀	3
● Colli Euganei Rosso '95	♀	3
● Colli Euganei Cabernet Ris. '90	♀♀♀	5
○ Colli Euganei Pinot Bianco '95	♀♀	3
● Gemola '93	♀♀	4

○ Castello Guerrieri Bianco '96	♀	3
○ Soave Classico Costeggiola '96	♀	2*
● Amarone Calcarole '91	♀	5

BARDOLINO (VR)

F.LLI ZENI
VIA COSTABELLA, 9
37011 BARDOLINO (VR)
TEL. 045/7210022

The wines from Zeni which deserve mention are numerous and, even if this year there are no real stars, the range remains one of the most reliable from the zone. Let us begin with the two Bianco di Custozas, which were given identical scores but which are very different in style. The basic version - more youthful even in its colour - has fresh, simple aromas and a very lively flavour. The version from the Vigne Alte range offers broad aromas of peaches and apricots; the fruit on the palate shows reasonable fullness and good balance. The '95 Bardolino Superiore is everything a Bardolino should be: it has a brilliant colour and red berry fruit scents with slightly spicy notes; the fruit on the palate echoes that on the nose, and is fresh and immediate. The two very interesting Chiarettos demonstrate how a producer's deft touch can turn a minor wine into a charming and attractive product. The Vigne Alte version has a more herbaceous and spicy appeal, while the standard wine is more fruity: both are light and elegant on the palate. The difference between the standard Soave and the Vigne Alte is more distinct: indeed, we found the former really too dilute, but the latter displayed delightful, clean aroma and a rare tightness of flavour. As regards Valpolicella, the Marogne selection '95 Superiore is soft and adequately complex on the nose; the other Valpolicellas still need to improve. The '93 Amarone does not have the class of more successful vintages, but nevertheless shows an attractive sober style, as well as well-knit and reasonably long-flavoured fruit.

○ Bianco di Custoza '96	🍷	1*
○ Bianco di Custoza Vigne Alte '96	🍷	2
○ Soave Cl. Vigne Alte '96	🍷	3
⊙ Bardolino Chiaretto '96	🍷	1*
⊙ Bardolino Chiaretto Vigne Alte '96	🍷	2
● Amarone '93	🍷	4
● Valpolicella Superiore Marogne '95	🍷	3
● Recioto della Valpolicella '94		4
● Valpolicella Superiore Vigne Alte '95		3
● Amarone '88	🍸🍸🍸	5
● Amarone '90	🍸🍸	4
● Amarone Barrique '90	🍸🍸	5
● Amarone Vigne Alte '90	🍸🍸	5

BASSANO DEL GRAPPA (VI)

VIGNETO DUE SANTI
V.LE ASIAGO, 84
36061 BASSANO DEL GRAPPA (VI)
TEL. 0424/502074

Stefano Zonta is doing a good job and, even if his wines did not score amazingly highly, our feeling is that his estate will soon be considered one of the best in the Veneto: one only has to consider his quality-lead choices as regards vineyard management or the maturation of the wines, which reveal his intention not to skimp on expense or energy in keeping up with the times. We cannot expect immediate results from such an ambitious transformation, but our tasting of the '95 Cabernet Riserva demonstrates encouraging progress: the colour is a concentrated ruby red; on the nose one finds hints of blackberries and bilberries mingled with notes of vanilla and spices; its structure on the palate is firm, with rich fruit and tannins, but the finish does not fully live up to our expectations. Successive tastings of this wine showed a gradual improvement in the evolution and persistence of the flavour, and this suggests that a further period of ageing is necessary. The standard version of Cabernet has, on the other hand, a generous fragrance, attractive colour and easy, heady fruit on the palate. The Breganze Bianco also shows a marked improvement on previous years; it has a cleaner and richer nose, and good weight of fruit on the palate to counterbalance its characteristic acidity. The Prosecco remains a reliable product which does not change much from vintage to vintage: both Zonta and the winery that performs the prise de mousse are to thank for this. Below par, however, were the Malvasia, once the winery's speciality, and the Merlot, which was strangely unbalanced on the nose and lacking in definition on the palate.

● Breganze Cabernet Riserva '95	🍷🍷	4
○ Breganze Bianco '96	🍷	2
○ Prosecco Spumante Extra Dry	🍷	2
● Breganze Cabernet '95	🍷	3
● Breganze Rosso Merlot '95		2
○ Malvasia Campo dei Fiori '96		3
● Breganze Cabernet '94	🍸	3
● Breganze Cabernet Riserva '94	🍸	4
● Breganze Rosso '94	🍸	2

BREGANZE (VI)

CONEGLIANO (TV)

MACULAN
VIA CASTELLETTO, 3
36042 BREGANZE (VI)
TEL. 0445/873733

ZARDETTO
VIA MARCORÀ, 15/A
LOC. OGLIANO
31015 CONEGLIANO (TV)
TEL. 0438/208909

Fausto Maculan becomes more and more like a mature athlete - you choose the sport - who, after a long series of successes, becomes a more canny competitor, watching, waiting, studying his adversaries - and then seizes his moment to come up with a spectacular performance which immediately reminds everyone of his greatness. This year the Three Glass-winning sprint is provided by his Cabernet Ferrata, a red of exceptional poise and style. It is deeply coloured and supremely elegant in the evolution of its bouquet, which starts off gently and builds to a crescendo, becoming full and definite. We also like the Ferrata for its length - always a sign of a great wine -, a progression of aromas, but also of soft and sapid tannins. The Torcolato, with its Mediterranean aromas, remains a very reliable classic. This wine's forte is its complete flavour, a winning combination of sweetness and elegance. The Acininobili - the other sweet wine - is less precise than usual, but still shows rare depth and richness. The Cabernet Fratta - a paradigm of harmony between its various components - also received high marks. Less successful were the dry whites, including the more prestigious ones such as the Sauvignon and the Chardonnay from the Ferrata vineyard, or the old warhorse Prato di Canzio: none of them showed sufficient character to rise above anonymity. The Merlot Marchesante and the Brentino Rosso were quite good among the mid-range reds, if a little cold; the others suffered from the same problem as the whites.

The style of the Zardetto winery's products is easily recognizable: we might define it as "gentle", the result of combining high-quality grapes with very sophisticated production techniques. The wines of Pino and Fabio Zardetto may indeed not show great personality, but they are certainly clean and well-sculpted, and they do reveal a certain varietal character. The new wine from the winery this year is a Colli di Conegliano Bianco made from a blend of incrocio Manzoni and chardonnay: the wine has a pale straw colour; its bouquet is evocative rather than well-defined; on the palate, it shows good acidity and a smooth finish. Among the Proseccos, we highlight the Brioso (a Frizzante) and the Brut, for some time now a speciality of this Conegliano winery. The Brioso is one of the most pleasant of its type: it has well-integrated carbon dioxide, and on the nose, offers hints of pears and apples; its liveliness on the palate makes it particularly easy to drink, but also, surprisingly, gives it a long and fruity finish. The Prosecco Spumante Brut is more linear: the wine displays attractive yeasty hints alongside ripe fruit; it is dry and lively on the palate, with good freshness and balance. Among the wines which did not score particularly well we nevertheless mention the Extra Brut sparkling wine - correct but a little too straightforward - and the Dry version of Prosecco, called Zeroventi which refers to the residual sugar in the wine. The Cartizze is as reliable as ever, even if the '96 vintage was not particularly kind to this famous sub-zone of the commune of Valdobbiadene.

● Cabernet Sauvignon Ferrata '94	♀♀♀	5
● Breganze Cabernet Fratta '94	♀♀	5
○ Acininobili '95	♀♀	6
○ Breganze Torcolato '95	♀♀	5
● Breganze Rosso Brentino '95	♀	3
● Breganze Merlot Marchesante '95	♀	4
● Breganze Cabernet Palazzotto '95		4
○ Breganze di Breganze '96		3
○ Breganze Chardonnay Ferrata '95		5
○ Prato di Canzio '95		4
○ Breganze Sauvignon Ferrata '96		4
○ Acininobili '91	♀♀♀	6
● Cabernet Sauvignon Ferrata '90	♀♀♀	5
● Cabernet Fratta '93	♀♀	5

○ Cartizze	♀	4
○ Colli di Conegliano Bianco '96	♀	3
○ Prosecco Brut	♀	3
○ Prosecco di Conegliano Brioso	♀	2
○ Zardetto Extra Brut		3
○ Zeroventi		3

CUSTOZA (VR)

FAEDO DI CINTO EUGANEO (PD)

CAVALCHINA
LOC. CAVALCHINA
37060 CUSTOZA (VR)
TEL. 045/516002

CA' LUSTRA
VIA S. PIETRO, 50
35030 FAEDO DI CINTO EUGANEO (PD)
TEL. 0429/94128

The Piona family's two estates these days run neck and neck : if some years ago La Prendina made more ambitious and often better wines, today the Calvalchina property near Lake Garda is in no way inferior, and is also turning out some very interesting products, such as the Bianco di Custoza Amedeo. It is the first really successful experiment of ageing this style of wine in wood. The wine is a bright straw-yellow; the nose has good concentration of fruit alongside distinct and elegant oaky notes; on the palate, the fruit is broad, charming and balanced. The basic Custoza - more delicate even in appearance - does not however lack character. The bouquets displays a very attractive aromatic vein, while the flavour has become longer, without losing its proverbial gentleness. The carefully-made Chiaretto is a fine expression of young, spicy freshness. The two Bardolinos are both decent, without showing any particular élan. La Rosa - a dessert wine - does not, though, have the characterful flavour of last year: it has very pronounced aromas of flowers and red berry fruits, but is a little too thin to be satisfying. Le Pergole del Sole made from müller thurgau is the other dessert wine: elegant and reliable it is a model of delicacy and rounded fruit. Going on to the La Prendina wines, we note the repeated success of the Sauvignon: broad and richly endowed with supple hints on the nose, it shows good evolution on the palate and a very crisp, clean finish. The Riesling, with its scents of elderflower and its precise, lively and really delicious fruit, is of similar quality. The Cabernet Il Falcone, though expressing its obvious breed, performed a little less well than in the past.

Ca' Lustra may be considered a beacon for the Colli Euganei; not only for its geographic location, but mainly for the way it confirms the true potential of the zone. This series of bustling hills - for many just a Sunday tourist destination - can offer a whole variety of exposures and soils, just waiting for producers ready to believe in their worth. That is what Franco Zanovello has done, and he must be commended for continuing to broaden his knowledge of his "terroir" and about winemaking in general. The varied range of Ca'Lustra includes, among others, two wines peculiar to Zanovello: an Incrocio Manzoni and a Chardonnay aged in barrique that show good personality and are always reliable. The Vigne Linda has a marked floral bouquet, whose fruit is echoed in the well-balanced flavour. The Vigne Marco shows an appealing complexity of aroma, with vanilla notes combined with sweet apricot jam scents; on the palate, the fruit is rounded and has notable length . The Fior d'Arancio made from the moscato type of the same name is a fragrant dessert wine, with characteristic floral and citrusy aromas; though not as rich as the '95, it nevertheless has a mouth-watering savoury quality. The style of the Colli Euganei Rosso - an impeccably-made wine, which reveals unexpected force on the palate - is somewhat more complex. The Chardonnay and the Colli Euganei Bianco - two reasonably priced products which Zanovello should be able to improve on in future - are more linear. Apart from Ca'Lustra, Franco also looks after the Vignalta estate; the total vineyard area under his control is now some 50 hectares.

○ Bianco di Custoza Amedeo '96	🍷🍷	3
○ Garda Riesling Prendina '96	🍷🍷	3
○ Garda Sauvignon Prendina '96	🍷🍷	3*
○ Le Pergole del Sole '94	🍷🍷	6
○ Garda Pinot Bianco Prendina '96	🍷	1*
⊙ Bardolino Chiaretto '96	🍷	2
⊙ La Rosa Moscato Rosa '96	🍷	4
● Cabernet Vigneto Il Falcone Prendina '94	🍷	4
● Bardolino '96		2
● Bardolino Superiore Santa Lucia '95		2
● Cabernet Vigneto Il Falcone Prendina '93	🍷🍷	4
○ La Rosa Moscato Rosa '95	🍷🍷	4

○ Colli Euganei Bianco '96	🍷	2*
○ Colli Euganei Chardonnay Vigna Marco '96	🍷	4
○ Colli Euganei Fior d'Arancio Spumante '96	🍷	3
○ Incrocio Manzoni 6.0.13 Vigna Linda '96	🍷	4
● Colli Euganei Cabernet '95	🍷	3
● Colli Euganei Rosso '96	🍷	2*
● Colli Euganei Merlot '95	🍷	2
● Colli Euganei Rosso '95	🍷	2

FARRA DI SOLIGO (TV)

FUMANE (VR)

MEROTTO
VIA TREVISET, 68
FRAZ. COL S. MARTINO
31010 FARRA DI SOLIGO (TV)
TEL. 0438/898195

ALLEGRINI
CORTE GIARA, 7
37022 FUMANE (VR)
TEL. 045/7701138-7702306

The Cartizze is the best wine from Merotto this year. From the most famous hills of Valdobbiadene comes a delicate and easy-drinking sparkling wine which is characterized by its very attractive fruity bouquet, its well-integrated carbon dioxide, and particularly by its attractive flavour evolution, which is sweetish, fresh and long. It was not easy to produce a good Cartizze in '96, a year in which the irregular ripening of the bunches created many problems. Credit for the high level of quality goes to Graziano Merotto, who knows the zone well and is able to acquire the best parcels of grapes and vinify them without losing any of their flavours or aromas. When, on the other hand, the grapes do not come up to par, as in the case of the Prosecco Dry Colle Molina, there is not much Merotto can do: we did not find the fragrance and personality which have always been this wine's salient features. The other fullish Prosecco, the Dry Primavera di Barbara, is more incisive. It shows good concentration even in its colour, and the pear and apricot notes make the bouquet rich and heady; on the palate, the sugars are not cloying, and the carbon dioxide and the acidity contribute to its successfully balanced flavour. Another well-made product is the Prosecco Frizzante, from which we cannot expect great excitement, but which in fact rises above the mediocrity of most wines of its type by virtue of its appealing, clean quaffability. The Cabernet Sauvignon Grevo is again worthy of its rating: it has a good, lively ruby colour and well-defined aromas of grass, bell peppers and blackberries; it is supple on the palate, but not particularly long. Less interesting than usual are the Prosecco Tranquillo Olchera and the Prosecco Extra Dry.

Wine is love, spirituality and reason, history and innovation: whoever makes it nurses the desire to make others happy and at the same time to express himself fully, governing nature with a sort of primordial respect. To make Amarone means to accept a long period of waiting that does not end with the harvest, but extends into the winter. During this latter season the grapes fall into what could be called a state of active lethargy: they seem to be quite still, but within they are undergoing those transformations which make them richer, giving them new aromas and a rich, deep flavour. To handle the drying and the vinification well, one has to have in mind the wine that one wants to make. One has to know how to match the vigour of the alcohol and the almost boundless aromatic force with a firm structure which gives these components harmony and definition. That is the Amarone '91: a complex balance of vitality and warmth. We also like the Recioto '94, a wine in which aromas of black pepper, bilberries, roses and hazelnuts mingle as they swirl up from the glass. The graceful fruit on the palate is characterized by a sweetness which allies with the firm tannins to produce a flavour of remarkable balance. Fine red wines demonstrate a balance of forceful fruit and elegance, thus making them versatile partners for food; Allegrini's Valpolicellas are mouth-filling and can happily be matched with meat or cheese, but their verve may also allow them to be served with fish. The white Fiorgardane '95, made from semi-dried grapes, is a wine of great power and impact: it completes the series of Two Glass wines from this winery.

● Piave Cabernet Sauvignon Grevo '96	♀	2*
○ Cartizze	♀	4
○ Prosecco di Valdobbiadene Dry Primavera di Barbara	♀	4
○ Prosecco di Valdobbiadene Frizzante	♀	2*
○ Prosecco di Valdobbiadene Extra Dry		2
○ Prosecco di Valdobbiadene Tranquillo Olchera '96		2

● Amarone Classico Superiore '91	♀♀♀	5
● La Poja '92	♀♀	6
● Recioto Cl. della Valpolicella Giovanni Allegrini '94	♀♀	5
● Valpolicella Classico '96	♀♀	2*
● Valpolicella Superiore La Grola '94	♀♀	4
● Valpolicella Superiore Palazzo della Torre '94	♀♀	4
○ Passito Fiorgardane '95	♀♀	5
● Amarone Classico '88	♀♀♀	5
● Amarone Classico '90	♀♀♀	5
● La Poja '90	♀♀♀	5
● Recioto Cl. della Valpolicella Giovanni Allegrini '93	♀♀♀	-

FUMANE (VR)

LE SALETTE
VIA PIO BRUGNOLI, 11/C
37022 FUMANE (VR)
TEL. 045/7701027

The Valpolicella zone can be proud to number Le Salette among its top producers, especially in a year which has seen this denomination near Verona stand back and take something of a pause for thought. All of Franco Scamperle's wines are clean and well-made, and some, indeed, are excellent. His Amarone, for example, makes the most of the unexceptional potential of the '93 vintage: it has a deep ruby colour; the nose is not particularly intense, but rather opens up gradually to reveal suggestions of cherries, chocolate and faded roses. The rich, vigorous fruit evolves and fills the mouth, and the finish is clean and aromatic. The Recioto Le Traversagne, which has never been a heavyweight but rather a model of immediate freshness and well-balanced, sweet fruit once again displays very refined and attractive style. The young Valpolicella - one of the most interesting '96 wines around - has a good deep colour; on the nose we find floral hints and appealing tangy notes; the fruit on the palate is rounded and fleshy, but balanced by fresh acidity. Of the Valpolicella Superiores, Ca' Carnocchio and I Progni, we preferred the former, which shows measure and balance: a bright ruby colour and an attractively rich nose, with notes of spices and sour cherries. It is similarly harmonious on the palate, with an attractive, clean finish. The Valpolicella I Progni seems neutral and lacks definition on the finish. One wine which Scamperle still has to work on quite a bit is the Bianco Passito Cesare which, at the moment at least, is rather too simplistic.

● Amarone Marega '93	🍷🍷	4
● Recioto della Valpolicella Le Traversagne '94	🍷🍷	4
● Valpolicella Classico '96	🍷	1*
● Valpolicella Superiore Ca' Carnocchio '94	🍷	4
● Valpolicella Superiore I Progni '94		3
○ Bianco Passito Cesare '94	🍷	4
● Amarone Marega '92	🍷🍷	4
● Recioto della Valpolicella Le Pergole Vecie '93	🍷🍷	5
● Recioto della Valpolicella Le Traversagne '93	🍷🍷	4
● Valpolicella Superiore Ca' Carnocchio '93	🍷	4

GAMBELLARA (VI)

LA BIANCARA
C.DA BIANCARA, 8
36053 GAMBELLARA (VI)
TEL. 0444/444244

The Gambellara zone badly needs growers like Angiolino Maule who believe in the garganega grape variety - known here as "il garganega" and who take great pains, particularly from the viticultural point of view, to give it a quality image. The ground rules which are the basis for the quality of his wines are: vineyards with low yields per vine, strict selection during the harvest and picking at maximum ripeness. We should like to add that, over the years, Maule has become an increasingly skilled and self-confident winemaker; indeed, one gets the impression that he no longer aims for concentration at all costs, which may only serve to stifle a wine's finesse, but that he lets his products have a character and personality of their own. His Gambellara Sassaia, therefore, is one of the most elegant and attractive whites we tasted this year in the Veneto. It has a deep straw colour; its bouquet does not aim for varietal breadth but has an inviting, precise, unforced style, with a characteristic peach kernel note. In the mouth, the wine shows an appealing and typical tannic vein, and the evolving fruit is underpinned by good acidity, the excellent finish echoes the aromatic sensations present on the nose and front palate. The Gambellara I Masieri also stands out - if in a somewhat minor key - for its harmony and fragrance. The tasting of cask samples of the '96 Pico de Laorenti (practically speaking, a Gambellara aged in barrique) and of the '95 Recioto confirm Maule's attention to detail and his search for freshness and length of flavour in his wines. Finally, we draw your attention to the pleasingly well-made Rosso (a Bordeaux blend), of which the '95 is the first release. It is a wine with an attractive nose, and which is not especially rich but well-balanced on the palate.

○ Gambellara Sassaia '96	🍷🍷	2*
○ Gambellara I Masieri '96	🍷	1*
○ Pico de Laorenti '95	🍷	3
○ Recioto di Gambellara '94	🍷	5
● Rosso La Biancara '95	🍷	3

GAMBELLARA (VI)

ZONIN
VIA BORGOLECCO, 9
36053 GAMBELLARA (VI)
TEL. 0444/640111

ILLASI (VR)

DAL FORNO
VIA LODOLETTA, 4
FRAZ. CELLORE
37030 ILLASI (VR)
TEL. 045/7834923

Zonin is making great efforts to bring all of its wines - from the humblest to the most prestigious - up to a notable level of quality. In view of the size of the company, it is clear that this process of improvement will not be completed in the space of a couple of years, but Zonin's recent investments in the vineyard, in personnel and in the winery demonstrate that the right conditions exist for their goal to be attained. If certain products still require more adroit fine-tuning, such as those from Valpolicella, others, like the wines from Friuli, have shown a marked improvement. The company is primarily known as a producer of inexpensive wines, but there are also some high points in the range, represented by the wines from the Treviso area. The Prosecco Brut, for example, stands out not only for its expected clean, correct style, but also for its positive bouquet, in which yeasty notes combine with varietal aroma. The Prosecco Frizzante has also improved and no longer displays thin, banal flavours and aromas. The results from the Tenuta Ca'Bolani in Friuli are even more encouraging. The Tocai offers a refreshing, verdant nose, deliciously supple fruit on the palate, and good length. The Riesling, with its floral scents and typical liveliness on the palate, is more aromatic and delicate. Of the reds from the Aquileia DOC, the Refosco is the one in which the youthful fragrance of the bouquet is most in harmony with the gentleness of the flavour; the others lack that extra dash of aroma and flavour which would help them rise from anonymity. We expect greater things from the Gambellara Il Giangio and the red Berengario, two very different wines but with an equally important role to play in Zonin's potential quest for quality.

Sometimes a cask sample can conjure up in the taster's mind the promise of a wine of historic greatness, only to be followed by disappointment when the wine is released and fails to match one's expectations. In this case, however, the wine is all we hoped for and more. Dal Forno's '90 Amarone is the most eagerly awaited wine in the recent history of Valpolicella; it embodies the quality of a truly memorable vintage and the skill of a vigneron who is capable of producing results even when faced with the toughest conditions. The wine is even better than we remembered it - once again, Romano has waited for just the right moment, giving a monumental Amarone the time to become attractively approachable and for the massive level of alcohol the chance to knit with the fruit, thus allowing the wine's complex, refined aromas to emerge. It is a masterpiece of intensity, of power and length on the palate. Our enjoyment of it has been heightened by our anticipation: now its ripe nose really enchants us, with its aromas of black cherries, bay leaves, cocoa and cinnamon. Dal Forno's skill is not limited to the Amarone, he also gives us a'92 Valpolicella capable of doing justice to a type of wine which many producers in the Valpolicella zone tend to play down. It has a ripe, concentrated garnet colour; a nose of great richness and charm; on the palate, it is silky and deliciously balanced.

●	Aquileia Refosco Ca' Bolani '96	♀	2
○	Aquileia Riesling Ca' Bolani '96	♀	2
○	Aquileia Tocai Ca' Bolani '96	♀	2
○	Prosecco Frizzante	♀	1
○	Prosecco Spumante Brut	♀	1
○	Gambellara Podere Il Giangio '96		1
●	Amarone Podere Il Maso '92	♀	4
●	Berengario '93	♀	4

●	Amarone Vigneto di Monte Lodoletta '90	♟♟♟	6
●	Valpolicella Superiore '92	♟♟	4
●	Amarone Vigneto di Monte Lodoletta '86	♟♟♟	6
●	Amarone Vigneto di Monte Lodoletta '87	♟♟♟	6
●	Amarone Vigneto di Monte Lodoletta '88	♟♟♟	6
●	Amarone Vigneto di Monte Lodoletta '89	♟♟♟	6
●	Recioto della Valpolicella Vigneto di Monte Lodoletta '88	♟♟♟	6
●	Valpolicella Superiore '91	♟♟	4

ILLASI (VR)

ILLASI (VR)

SANTI
VIA UNGHERIA, 33
37031 ILLASI (VR)
TEL. 045/7834544

TRABUCCHI
VIA MONTE TENDA, 3
37031 ILLASI (VR)
TEL. 045/7833233 - 049/8755455

This year's tastings have seen the Santi wines show small signs of improvement. It is still too early for us to consider this a real turnaround compared to the recent unimpressive performances, but we get the impression that the Gruppo Italiano Vini wants to turn Santi into a model modern winery, capable of producing large volumes but still giving its wines a certain amount of character. The best of the current wines remains the Soave Sanfederici, which for the first time breaks the 80-point barrier. It has a bright, deep straw colour; the nose is inviting, with fresh, youthful aroma but also clear potential for keeping. It has good fruit on the palate, with well balanced alcohol and acidity. About twenty years ago the Valpolicella Castello d'Illasi was a paradigm of intensity, but it then started to show less character and it gradually fell into oblivion. The '95 vintage has rediscovered some of its traditional vigour and even if today we prize fresh fruitiness rather higher than the rusticity of the past, this wine seems nevertheless, on the whole, to have improved. Its colour is a fine, deep ruby; it displays delicate aromas of cherries macerated in alcohol; on the palate, we are well aware of the wine's appreciable alcohol content, which is however, well integrated with the fruit, this in turn, carries over into a really pleasing finish. Among the less happy notes; a chronic lack of zest in wines such as the Bianco di Custozas and the Bardolinos. The Valpolicella Le Solane continues, however, to be a decent, honest wine.

Giuseppe Trabucchi has such an irrepressible passion for wine that he has decided, in spite of his pressing duties as a lawyer, to up-grade the family estate which is sited in one of the most beautiful spots - and one of the best for viticulture - in the Illasi Valley. His energies are dedicated unreservedly to quality and the adoption, as far as possible, of organic viticulture. Unfortunately however, in winemaking the return on effort is not always equable, and if the estate's first releases provided exciting results, the more recent wines have struggled to show the same verve. The '93 Amarone, is the fruit of a rather difficult vintage, but from Trabucchi one expects, nevertheless, a substantial and interesting wine; this one lacks definition on both the nose and palate, and the alcohol typical of Amarone is rather spirity; among its positive aspects is reasonable evolution of fruit on the nose, enhanced by the floral aromas that are a hallmark of the estate's wines. The Valpolicella Superiore - though from an awkward year like '94 - has a more marked personality: its colour is fairly intense; on the nose it has a minerally note, as well as more precise scents of blackberries, vanilla and raspberries under spirit; it displays good, well-defined fruit on the palate and has an attractive, rich (and slightly alcoholic) finish. The Recioto was not submitted for tasting, so we hope to be able to give our comments on it in the next edition of the Guide, especially considering the excellent impression it has created in the past.

○ Soave Sanfederici '96	♟♟	2*
● Valpolicella Le Solane '94	♟	2
● Valpolicella Superiore Castello d'Illasi '95	♟	2
● Bardolino Ca' Bordenis '96		2
○ Bianco di Custoza Chiaro di Luna '96		2
○ Bianco di Custoza I Frari '96		2
● Amarone '90	♟♟	5
● Amarone '91	♟	5

● Amarone '93	♟	6
● Valpolicella Superiore Terre di San Colombano '94	♟	4
● Amarone '90	♟♟	5
● Recioto della Valpolicella '93	♟♟	5
● Amarone '91	♟	5

LAZISE (VR)

LAZISE (VR)

LAMBERTI
VIA CASARA DI SOTTO, 1
37010 LAZISE (VR)
TEL. 045/6770233

LE TENDE DI FORTUNA E LUCILLINI
LOC. LE TENDE
FRAZ. COLÀ
37010 LAZISE (VR)
TEL. 045/7590748

White wines are becoming the speciality of this large winery in Lazise: after the positive impression we gained last year, we can affirm that the quality level of the whites this year has continued to improve. Unfortunately, the same is not true of the reds, and even if a blandish style is fine for the simpler and cheaper wines, like the young Valpolicella, it seems a pity to us that the winery cannot come up with an Amarone worthy of the name. On the bright side, however: the Soave Santepietre, tasted several times and always with high marks, displays excellent balance and intensity, and has the quality to stand up to the best wines of its denomination. Its colour is a deep straw, its aromas are inviting and refined; the fruit on the palate is well-structured and reflects the skill of the winemaker. Close behind comes the equally exciting Bianco di Custoza Orchidea Platino which has a greenish tinge to its hue. It shows good evolution on the nose, and is delicate and refreshing in the mouth. The Lugana Oro, even though it did not repeat the fine performance of the '95, is still a dependable wine; clean-cut and simple on the nose, it reveals positive fruit on the palate, well supported by fresh acidity. The Bianco di Custoza and the Pinot Grigio, both from the Santepietre range, flatter on the nose, only to deceive somewhat on the palate. Overall, then, the range creates a positive impression ; when the reds reach the same level as the whites, Lamberti will really have a production to be proud of.

For the second year running, the Cicisbeo is the top wine of this estate from near Lake Garda. This is a red obtained from a blend of equal parts of cabernet franc and cabernet sauvignon, matured in partly new barriques and given around six months in bottle before release. It has good depth of colour and the attractive long aroma, with its hints of raspberries and almonds, shows nice evolution. It is elegant on the palate, with good balance and length in the finish, and with fine, lively fruit. The other red of Le Tende (again a Bordeaux-style blend) called Sorbo degli Uccellatori only scored average marks; in fact, it is rather too vinous on the nose and also lacks the requisite complexity on the palate. The standard Bianco di Custoza is an improvement on recent vintages; it has a bit more colour, and on the nose it displays some richness; on the palate, too, one finds attractive fruit and very pleasant development. Perhaps we expected more depth on the palate from the barrique-aged version, called Lucillini, but apart from the structure which does need to be richer, we still get a soft, elegant and admirably long-flavoured wine. The Bardolino has also improved: the winery is seeking to make it less bland than is the norm, by retaining the quaffability but at the same time giving it more defined personality.

O Soave Santepietre '96	YY	1*
O Bianco di Custoza Orchidea Platino '96	Y	3
O Bianco di Custoza Santepietre '96	Y	1
O Lugana Oro '96	Y	3
● Amarone Corte Rubini '93	Y	4
● Valpolicella Classico Santepietre '96		1
O Pinot Grigio Santepietre '96		1
● Amarone Corte Rubini '91	Y	4

● Cicisbeo '95	YY	3*
● Bardolino Classico '96	Y	1
O Bianco di Custoza Lucillini '96	Y	3
O Bianco di Custoza Oro '96	Y	2*
☉ Bardolino Chiaretto '96		1
● Sorbo degli Uccellatori '95		3
O Amoroso Passito '93	YY	4
● Cicisbeo '94	YY	3
● Sorbo degli Uccellatori '94	Y	3

MARANO DI VALPOLICELLA (VR) MARANO DI VALPOLICELLA (VR)

PAOLO BOSCAINI
VIA CADELOI
FRAZ. VALGATARA
37020 MARANO DI VALPOLICELLA (VR)
TEL. 045/6800840

GIUSEPPE CAMPAGNOLA
VIA AGNELLA, 9
FRAZ. VALGATARA
37020 MARANO DI VALPOLICELLA (VR)
TEL. 045/7703900

The results which emerge from our tastings of the Boscaini wines are rather contradictory. Recent vintages had convinced us that the wines were getting constantly better; this year, the influence of the last few difficult vintages has made itself felt, but this cannot be the only explanation for certain disappointing wines. We expected, for example, another good performance from the Valpolicella San Ciriaco, a youthful, innovatively-styled wine, which was the real revelation of last year's Guide. Instead, we sampled a correct, but thinnish wine, lacking the spicy, fleshy fruit which had earned it a Two Glass rating last year. Another wine we looked forward to was the '93 Amarone, certainly not the product of a great vintage, but nevertheless a wine of potential structure and quality: once again we were let down. Much more exciting was the Amarone Ca'de Loi '90, the real star of the company's range. It is rich in colour and has forceful, warm, round aromas; on the palate, the fruit evolves well, and the finish is aromatic, precise, and very attractive. Next, a well-balanced, if not very concentrated white, the Lugana Lunatio. Its nose is lively and well-defined and it is equally fresh and crisp on the palate. The Soave is somewhat softer, with a delicate floral bouquet, as well as an appealing persistence of flavour. The wines from Lake Garda however, the Custoza and the Bardolinos, are neutral and lacking in zest, as are the Valpolicella Superiore and the "ripasso" wine, all products from Boscaini's cheaper range.

This company's entry into the Guide bears witness to the fact that the revolution which has taken place in Valpolicella in recent years does not concern only independent-minded and ambitious small producers, but also some of the larger wineries who have decided to change direction. Giuseppe Campagnola is a young entrepreneur who is learning to produce quality wines, yet still with a keen eye to the market place. His range, therefore, though it displays reliable quality throughout as well as offering good value for money, does not contain any real stars. The company, which oversees about 110 hectares of vineyards, buys grapes from a great many growers throughout the Province of Verona and produces around three million bottles. Giuseppe is aided in his quest for better quality by his enthusiastic father, Luigi, who knew when it was the right time to hand over the reins to the younger generation. The first result is a well-balanced '93 Amarone; it is certainly not particularly complex, but demonstrates a fresh, supple style. Richer wines are in the process of ageing in the Campagnola cellars, but this wine is certainly clean, well-balanced and attractively long on the palate. The '96 Valpolicella is a classic red for drinking within the year and is fragrant and fruity. The Valpolicella Superiore has an appealing delicate bouquet, even fruit on the palate and an aromatic finish. On the palate, the Soave Classico combines a necessary touch of acidity with soft, evolving fruit.

Wine		
● Amarone Ca' de Loi '90	♟♟	5
● Amarone Vigneti di Marano '93	♟	4
○ Lugana Lunatio '96	♟	2*
○ Soave Classico Sup. Monteleone '96	♟	2
○ Bianco di Custoza Carmina '96		1
● Valpolicella San Ciriaco '96		2
● Valpolicella Superiore Marano '95		3
● Amarone Ca' de Loi '88	♟♟	5
● Valpolicella Classico San Ciriaco '95	♟♟	2

Wine		
○ Soave Classico Le Bine '96	♟	2*
● Amarone '93	♟	4
● Valpolicella '96	♟	1*
● Valpolicella Superiore Le Bine '95	♟	2*

MARANO DI VALPOLICELLA (VR)   MARANO DI VALPOLICELLA (VR)

CASTELLANI
VIA GRANDA, 1
FRAZ. VALGATARA
37020 MARANO DI VALPOLICELLA (VR)
TEL. 045/7701253

F.LLI DEGANI
VIA TOBELLE, 9
FRAZ. VALGATARA
37020 MARANO DI VALPOLICELLA (VR)
TEL. 045/7701850-7701163

The restructuring announced in last year's Guide has now been completed, but just as the winery was about to begin its new quest for quality, we witnessed the division of the property between the two Castellani brothers. This family matter however has been resolved without any rancour, and indeed it seems to have given a new impetus to the winery. The wines presented this year received excellent scores for both ranges: La Bionda, the cheaper line, and I Castei, which is intended to be the fruit of more careful selection. It is in the former range - as has also happened in the past - that we found the best wines. The '95 Recioto has all the requisites of a fine wine, and is a perfect example of the quality of the vintage. It has a deep, bright ruby colour; its fruity aromas are broad and complex and its flavour is sweet but also fresh and long: a real model of elegance. The Amarone displays firm fruit and an intense, rich fullness rendered attractive by aromatic notes of cherries, bilberries and black pepper. The Amarone I Castei is even more alcoholic and has even richer fruit, but they are not in such good balance as in the previous wine. The Recioto - perhaps the wine of those tasted, deserving longer ageing - is simple, and has a fresh, uncomplicated sweetness. We also liked the Valpolicella Superiore I Castei, a light wine but one which fully respects the style of its denomination. Less successful was the version from La Bionda, which seemed overly mature.

The Degani family estate continues to provide reliable wines, thereby demonstrating that, if one wants to, one can select the grapes in order to make good quality products even in difficult vintages. The proof is their '92 Amarone, whose strength lies in its measure and harmony. Its colour is an opaque garnet; the nose has sweet honey, juniper and sour cherry jam notes. The rich, charming fruit evolves well on the palate and the finish echoes the aromas. The Valpolicella Superiore '94, one of the most interesting of its category - though very inexpensive - is more hearty and naturally more youthful. This wine should certainly make those producers in the zone who devote little attention to their Valpolicella (with the excuse that it can anyway only be sold at a low price) and thus threaten the future of this DOC as a whole, think twice. The Valpolicella Superiore is fairly rich on the nose, exuberant and soft on the palate, clean and long in the finish. The deliciously attractive Recioto gives us an inkling in a sweet style of what the Amarone '95 will be. Designed to be enjoyed young, it has also shown that it has some ageing capacity, and the first releases are still on top form. Finally, we note the successful, youthful version of Valpolicella whose moderate ambitions in no way detract from its cleanness, delicious fruit and quaffability. Aldo and Angelo Degani's hard work in the vineyards and winery are paying off, as is Luca's technical expertise: we wish them happy and continued growth.

● Amarone I Castei '93	♀♀	4
● Amarone La Bionda '93	♀♀	4
● Recioto della Valpolicella La Bionda '95	♀♀	4
● Recioto della Valpolicella I Castei '95	♀	4
● Valpolicella Cl. Superiore I Castei '95	♀	3
● Recioto della Valpolicella I Castei '94	♀♀	4
● Recioto della Valpolicella La Bionda '94	♀♀	4

● Amarone '92	♀♀	4*
● Recioto della Valpolicella '95	♀♀	4*
● Valpolicella Superiore '94	♀♀	3*
● Valpolicella Classico '96	♀	1*
● Amarone '91	♀♀	4
● Recioto della Valpolicella '93	♀♀	4

MARANO DI VALPOLICELLA (VR)   MARANO DI VALPOLICELLA (VR)

GIUSEPPE LONARDI
VIA DELLE POSTE, 2
37020 MARANO DI VALPOLICELLA (VR)
TEL. 045/7755154

SAN RUSTICO
VIA POZZO, 2
FRAZ. VALGATARA
37020 MARANO DI VALPOLICELLA (VR)
TEL. 045/7703348

The results obtained this year by Giuseppe Lonardi demonstrate that, after the period of euphoric enthusiasm experienced in Valpolicella in the last four years, Nature has decided to withdraw, at least in part, its support of the zone's producers. A young company such as this is more likely to suffer than most in difficult years, not yet being in a position to fully overcome the obstacle of a poor vintage. Only the Recioto really stands out in a range which is barely satisfactory this year. This wine is in fact from the '95 harvest, but does not seem to have taken full advantage of a vintage which many describe as historic. It has a medium-deep colour and a very good bouquet, with scents of red berry fruits alongside the distinct vanilla tones from the wood; its fruit is sweet, but well-integrated in a structure of some intensity. The Valpolicella Superiore - which seeks to combine the traditional flavours and aromas deriving from the "ripasso" method with a more modern purity of fruit - seems a bit tired, perhaps because of a selection of the grapes which favours the Amarone, leaving the Valpolicella as very much a second-string wine. Similarly, the '96 Valpolicella does not show well, tasting rather thin and estery. We looked forward with a certain interest to the Privilegia, a red aged in barrique made from a blend of corvina and rondinella: the wine has a satisfyingly deep colour, a promising nose which evolves with breadth and length , but its flavour remains narrow and lacking in flesh. Lonardi's dedication to transforming his family winery into a more professional operation is beyond question and we shall continue to watch - and support - his efforts.

After a couple of years in which the quality of this winery had shown a few fluctuations, we have noted a partial improvement which also promises well for the future. The Campagnola brothers, like all the producers in Valpolicella, have had some difficult vintages to work with in the period between '91 and '94: this prevented them from bringing out the best in the Il Gaso vineyard, one of the viticultural gems of the zone. Retasting the '92 Amarone Il Gaso confirms the rating in the previous Guide; the '93 version is still maturing, though the first barrel tastings have impressed us considerably. The quality of the basic '93 Amarone is more evident in its harmony than in its power or concentration. However, it is a very attractive wine, both on the nose - where we find the typical scents of an Amarone - and on the palate, where the fruit is relatively closed but evolves well. As regards the Reciotos, we were a little disappointed by the basic '93 version, but the sparkling '95 is really interesting: it has a brilliant ruby colour; the bouquet shows red berry fruit accompanied by hints of rosemary; on the palate, the sweetness is held in check by the carbon dioxide, and the finish offers a pleasing spicy aftertaste. The early drinking style of Valpolicella is also improving and we appreciated the producer's efforts to make it not only quaffable, but also a wine of some character. The Valpolicella Superiore - which lacked vivacity and personality - needs, on the other hand, to be more reliable.

● Privilegia '94	♟	4
● Recioto della Valpolicella '95	♟	4
● Valpolicella Classico '96		1
● Valpolicella Superiore '94		2
● Recioto della Valpolicella '94	♟♟	4
● Amarone '91	♟	4

● Amarone '93	♟	4
● Valpolicella Classico '96	♟	2*
● Recioto della Valpolicella '95		4
● Recioto della Valpolicella Spumante '95		4
● Amarone Vigneti del Gaso '90	♟♟	5
● Amarone Vigneti del Gaso '91	♟♟	5
● Amarone Vigneti del Gaso '92	♟	5
● Valpolicella Superiore '93	♟	3

MEZZANE DI SOTTO (VR)

MEZZANE DI SOTTO (VR)

CORTE SANT'ALDA
VIA CAPOVILLA, 28
LOC. FIOI
37030 MEZZANE DI SOTTO (VR)
TEL. 045/8880006

VILLA ERBICE
VIA VILLA, 22
37030 MEZZANE DI SOTTO (VR)
TEL. 045/8880086

The range of wines shown by Corte Sant'Alda proves that last year's success was no accident. The Amarone presented this year, from the difficult '92 vintage, does not have the power of the '90, but shows admirable cleanness and finesse. It has a bright garnet colour; on the nose, the alcohol typical of Amarone is well-balanced by delicate fruit. On the palate, the flavour is quite restrained, while showing good evolution and underlying richness. There are really very few producers who released a '92 wine of this quality. We were not, on the other hand, able to taste the '95 Recioto, since its mighty flavour and structure still have to harmonise and it therefore needs to mature a little longer. We recognize the ever-greater care taken over the vinification of the Valpolicellas, but they obviously do not match the wines made from dried grapes in the quality of the fruit used. They do however also contribute to the good name of this estate. The '96 version has a handsome, lively colour, with simple but very pleasant aromas, and an estery vein which is not at all bothersome; on the palate, there is quite good fruit, but it is light and does not evolve much. The Valpolicella Superiore '94 is of similar quality, even if its character is different: this wine has a more mature nose and a richer, more alcoholic flavour. The Mithas, the other Superiore, offers a more complex style: its colour does not reveal much concentration, unlike the bouquet which appears compact and ready to open up with time; its flavour is clean, supported by fruit which evolves with imperturbable calm.

This winery is specializing more and more in wines made from semi-dried grapes. The Recioto and the Amarone, though they are the fruit of not particularly successful vintages, are among the most interesting wines in their respective categories. The Valpolicella and the Soave, on the other hand, do not display any particularly marked personality, they remain correct but of merely satisfactory quality. The Valpolicella, from the Monte Tombole vineyard, does not have an especially deep ruby colour; on the nose it offers pleasing, if a little unknit, scents of bottled cherries but we failed to find similar fruit on the palate; overall the wine does not leave much of an impression. The Soave Panvinio is a little edgy. The Recioto however is something else entirely: powerful and concentrated even in appearance, it displays fresh, youthful aromas of berry fruits and herbs and has very positive fruit on the palate, its roundness well-balanced by still-firm tannins. The '92 Amarone could not repeat the performance achieved by the '91, but nevertheless acquits itself more than honourably. The lightness caused by the diluted vintage is evident even in its transparent garnet colour; the surprisingly intense, if not very broad bouquet displays a hint of oak which is just starting to harmonize with the fruit. In the mouth, the fruit is intense on entry and soft and rounded on the middle palate, but falls away a little on the finish.

● Amarone '92	▼▼	5
● Valpolicella di Mezzane '96	▼	2
● Valpolicella Superiore '94	▼	3
● Valpolicella Superiore Mithas '94	▼	4
● Amarone '90	▼▼▼	5
● Amarone Mithas '88	▼▼	5
● Valpolicella Superiore Mithas '93	▼▼	4
● Recioto della Valpolicella '94	▼	4

● Recioto della Valpolicella '94	▼▼	4
● Amarone '92	▼	5
○ Soave Panvinio '96		2
● Valpolicella Superiore Monte Tombole '94		3
● Amarone '90	▼▼	5
● Amarone '91	▼▼	5
● Valpolicella Superiore Monte Tombole '93	▼	3

MIANE (TV)

GREGOLETTO
·VIA S. MARTINO, 1
FRAZ. PREMAOR
31050 MIANE (TV)
TEL. 0438/970463

Gregoletto is increasingly becoming a red wine producer. The well-established vocation of the Miane area for growing cabernet and merlot represents the basis for the constant improvement of the three products which every year compete for the title of best wine of the vintage from this estate. This year, all three showed very well, fully expressing the undoubted quality of the fruit, tried and tested vinification techniques and skilled use of wood for ageing. The '93 Rosso made from a blend of the two Bordeaux varieties along with marzemino, has certainly benefited from the maturation which the Gregolettos have given it, becoming inviting and complex with its aromas of herbs, spices and black berry fruits, as well as acquiring notable balance on the palate: if it only had greater depth, it would be able to stand up to even the very best of Italian reds. The Cabernet '95 - compact, firm and concentrated - displays a stimulating freshness on the nose, and also shows excellent evolution of fruit on the palate. The Merlot is softer and more restrained, with enticing aromas of red berry fruits and liquorice, but is fairly light in the mouth. The Colli di Conegliano is again the best of the whites: it has no ambitions to be a great wine, but is fragrant and enjoyable. The Incrocio Manzoni and the Verdiso both deserved One Glass, while the sparkling wines -the Brut and the Prosecco Extra Dry - and the other still whites were less convincing.

MONTEBELLO (VI)

DOMENICO CAVAZZA & F.LLI
SELVA, 42
36054 MONTEBELLO (VI)
TEL. 0444/649166

The last few years have seen the Cavazza winery continue to grow and become a real model for all the producers in the Province of Vicenza. It is, in fact, from the vineyards of the Colli Berici that the most important products of the company - this year, the two Cabernets - come. The Cicogna is one of the most interesting reds in the entire Veneto, showing not only the characteristic elegance of cabernet, but also the effect of the soil in the Colli Berici. It has a deep colour; on the nose, one finds sweet fruit and vanilla notes as well as drier hints of spices and roasted hazelnuts; the fruit evolves well on the palate and is long-lasting, without being really massive. The Cabernet Capital S. Libera stands out for its firmer tannins: it is again concentrated in colour, with minerally, mature aromas and dry fruit on the palate; it only lacks a little zest on the finish. However, the real surprise in out tastings was the Gambellara Capitel S. Libera which finally showed well on the nose, with its restrained, easy but very precise scents. The flavour offers a well-balanced combination of fruit and acidity. Among the new wines, we should like to mention the first, interesting vintage of a Sauvignon Colli Berici, which is not yet fully-defined on the nose but which is already pretty well-balanced on the palate. Unfortunately the Merlot Cicogna is missing from the range: after the splendid '92, it has never been presented again. The Recioto, from which we expected rather more in view of Cavazza's reputation, was again not entirely convincing. The Gambellara Monte Boccara is notable for its value for money.

● Cabernet '95	🍷🍷	3*
● Rosso Gregoletto '93	🍷🍷	4
● Merlot '95	🍷	3
○ Colli di Conegliano Bianco Albio '96	🍷	2
○ Incrocio Manzoni 6.0.13 '96	🍷	2
○ Verdiso '96	🍷	2
● Rosso Gregoletto '92	🍷🍷	4
● Merlot '94	🍷	2

● Colli Berici Cabernet Cicogna '94	🍷🍷	4
● Colli Berici Cabernet Capitel S. Libera '94	🍷	3
○ Colli Berici Sauvignon '96	🍷	2
○ Gambellara Cl. Capitel S. Libera '96	🍷	2
○ Recioto di Gambellara '94	🍷	4
○ Gambellara Cl. Monte Boccara '96		1
● Colli Berici Cabernet Capitel S. Libera '93	🍷🍷	3

MONTEFORTE D'ALPONE (VR)   MONTEFORTE D'ALPONE (VR)

ROBERTO ANSELMI
VIA S. CARLO, 46
37032 MONTEFORTE D'ALPONE (VR)
TEL. 045/7611488

CA' RUGATE
VIA MEZZAVILLA, 12
FRAZ. BROGNOLIGO
37032 MONTEFORTE D'ALPONE (VR)
TEL. 045/6175082

The estate plan which Roberto Anselmi has recently embarked upon is beginning to show results. Though he already owns some of the best vineyards in the commune of Monteforte, Anselmi has added to his property by purchasing another important slice of the Monte Foscarino. Again this year, it is from this vineyard that the company's most significant white comes: it is a wine which adds depth and roundness to the archetypal lively style of a Soave. The Capitel Foscarino has a deep straw colour, and aromas of apples, pineapples, and peaches made even more creamy by the ever-present almondy note. The fruit on the palate displays the characteristics of the '96 vintage: it is supple and very elegant, with good acidity and a clean finish. After the splendid performance by the '93 vintage, we were rather looking forward to the Recioto I Capitelli '95, especially in view of the quality of the harvest. Well, even if it did not rate Three Glasses this aristocratic dessert wine is certainly pretty exciting. Its golden colour is deep and evocative; the nose is strong and rich, but lacks, perhaps, its usual clarity. On the palate, the fruit is sweet and full and evolve very well, showing richness and concentration and a welcome touch of acidity. The Soave San Vicenzo is once again pleasant and easy-drinking: it does not have the body of last year's, but maintains an exemplary cleanness of style. This year we were not able to taste the barrique-aged Soave Capitel Croce or the Realda, the Cabernet made from a vineyard located right in front of the winery.

The Tessari brothers represent one of the best examples of the good things that have been happening in the Soave zone in recent years. For years, Amedeo and Giovanni sold their wine to bulk up the top Soaves of a number of well-known producers. Then a combination of courage and recklessness convinced them to go into debt and build a small winery with the objective of finally expressing the true value of their grapes. First results were promising and so, in spite of countless practical difficulties, they were persuaded to continue in their efforts - all the way to our top award. The single-vineyard Soave Monte Alto is an enticing modern white, remarkable for its aromatic breadth and finesse on the palate: its golden colour stimulates the imagination, and the lively and complex nose testifies to the quality of the maturation in barrique. The bouquet has clean, precise definition but at the same time an intriguing and mysterious quality. We also find the same subtle grassy hints and almondy, floral notes on the palate, sustained by rich, deep and very long fruit. If in this wine Ca'Rugate demonstrates all its desire for innovation, in the version from Monte Fiorentino we see - and enjoy - a Soave whose strong points are its fragrance and quaffability. It has a straw-yellow colour with appealing greenish highlights, and scents on the nose of apples, plums and medlars; the palate reveals a thirst-quenching acidity which gives persistence to the flavour. The Recioto di Soave is delicate and well-made, if a little too simplistic, while the basic Soave was not able to benefit in '96 from the same quality of fruit as in the previous year.

○ Recioto di Soave I Capitelli '95	🍷🍷	5
○ Soave Cl.		
Capitel Foscarino '96	🍷🍷	4
○ Soave Cl. San Vincenzo '96	🍷	3
○ Recioto di Soave I Capitelli '93	🍷🍷🍷	6
○ Recioto dei Capitelli '87	🍷🍷🍷	6
○ Recioto dei Capitelli '88	🍷🍷🍷	6
○ Recioto di Soave I Capitelli '94	🍷🍷	5
● Realda '90	🍷🍷	5
● Realda '91	🍷🍷	4
● Realda '92	🍷🍷	4

○ Soave Cl. Sup. Monte Alto '96	🍷🍷🍷	3
○ Soave Cl. Sup.		
Monte Fiorentine '96	🍷🍷	3
○ Recioto di Soave La Perlare '94	🍷	4
○ Soave Classico '96		2
○ Soave Cl. Sup. Monte Alto '95	🍷🍷	2
○ Soave Cl. Sup.		
Monte Fiorentine '95	🍷🍷	2
○ Recioto di Soave '94	🍷	4

GINI

Via G. Matteotti, 42
37032 Monteforte d'Alpone (VR)
tel. 045/7611908

Achieve greatness in Soave, tease out all its subtle finesse without renouncing on rounded structure, challenge the top winemakers in Italy armed with a notoriously difficult grape like garganega: this is Sandro and Claudio Gini's mission, and one in which moreover, they have succeeded. Certainly the inclusion of chardonnay in the blend has helped them, as it has all the producers in the zone, but these brothers from Monteforete have avoided the risk of homogeneity and their principal wines offer two different, but equally genuine and aristocratic examples of Soave. The Salvarenza, fermented and matured in barriques, has a brilliant greenish-gold colour. Its spectrum of aromas is broad and will inspire every taster to find new nuances: ripe pineapple, almonds and cinnamon notes emerge at first, giving way to voluptuous vanilla and peach jam. On the palate, the entry is clean and elegant , and the fruit evolves towards a very long finish. The Froscà , made in stainless steel, has irresistible freshness with a nose of citrus, green apples, plums and hazelnuts which is echoed in the palate, where the remarkably measured and long fruit is well supported by a fresh acidity. The basic Soave is also one of the best in its category. The two dessert wines , the Salvarenza Col Foscarin and Renobilis, are very exciting: two Recioto di Soaves which show concentrated sweetness and a rich yet measured array of aromas. Finally, a wine to keep an eye on is the Pinot Nero from the high Sorai vineyard.

○	Soave Cl. Sup. Contrada Salvarenza Vecchie Vigne '96	🍷🍷🍷	4
○	Recioto di Soave Col Foscarin '93	🍷🍷	4
○	Recioto di Soave Renobilis '93	🍷🍷	5
○	Soave Cl. La Froscà '96	🍷🍷	2*
●	Pinot Nero Sorai Campo alle More '94	🍷🍷	4
○	Chardonnay Sorai '95	🍷	4
○	Sauvignon Maciete Fumé '96	🍷	4
○	Soave Classico '96	🍷	2
○	Soave Cl. Sup. Contrada Salvarenza Vecchie Vigne '95	🍸🍸🍸	4
○	Chardonnay Sorai '94	🍸🍸	4
○	Recioto di Soave Renobilis '91	🍸🍸	5

MONTEFORTE D'ALPONE (VR)

LA CAPPUCCINA

Via San Brizio, 125
Fraz. Costalunga
37032 Monteforte d'Alpone (VR)
tel. 045/6175840-6175036

La Cappuccina, after the good performance offered last year, confirms its place as one of the most reliable estates in the zone. The '96 vintage cannot be compared with the better '95, but the Tessari brothers were able to handle the fruit available in such a way as to make wines that are still full-flavoured, well-defined and which reflect their soils of origin. In this context, the Soave Fontego is exemplary, with its bright, intense colour; its fresh, rich, slowly-elvolving nose and its elegant, savoury fruit, well-balanced by crisp acidity. Another eagerly awaited, and really satisfying wine is the first barrique-aged Soave from this Costalunga winery, the San Brizio '95. It has a glorious golden colour with greenish highlights; the complex nose, though it still shows marked oaky notes, also displays rich, elegant fruit; it has attractively evolving fruit on the palate, and the flavour is very long. The Recioto di Soave is improving; it is a sweet, fragrant, relatively easy but nonetheless long-finishing wine. The Sauvignon, made to highlight the characteristic herbaceous notes in the bouquet, does not display much breadth but rather shows lively and extremely delicious fruit. Only the basic Soave did not perform up to par, leaving the impression of a correct wine, but one lacking the satisfying aromas and flavours which this estate always strives for. The Cabernet Madégo '95 will be evaluated in the next Guide, as it was not yet ready at the time of our tastings.

○	Soave Fontego '96	🍷🍷	3
○	Soave San Brizio '95	🍷🍷	3*
○	Recioto di Soave Arzìmo '94	🍷	4
○	Sauvignon '96	🍷	3
○	Soave Classico '96	🍷	2
●	Madégo '94	🍸🍸	2
○	Sauvignon '95	🍸🍸	2
○	Recioto di Soave Arzìmo '93	🍸	4

MONTEFORTE D'ALPONE (VR)   MONTEFORTE D'ALPONE (VR)

UMBERTO PORTINARI
VIA S. STEFANO, 2
FRAZ. BROGNOLIGO
37030 MONTEFORTE D'ALPONE (VR)
TEL. 045/6175087

F.LLI PRA
VIA DELLA FONTANA, 31
37032 MONTEFORTE D'ALPONE (VR)
TEL. 045/7612125

This small estate, which entered the Guide for the first time last year, once again scored very highly in spite of the fact that the '96 vintage really is not comparable to '95. Umberto Portinari was able to overcome the difficulties of the harvest, giving his wines exemplary definition and cleanness. The system which has made him famous in the zone is that of "rationalized double ripening", with which Portinari seeks greater concentration of sugars and aroma. Using this method, the Albare vineyard yields a Soave that is deep in colour, has a rich, sweet nose and soft yet fresh fruit which evolves on the palate; one is very much aware of the particular texture given by the garganega grape and, even though it does not have the depth of the '95, this wine remains a classic of its type. The Soave - also from the Albare vineyard, but made from normally-ripened grapes - has a more modern style: it offers peachy and exotic fruit notes on the nose and the palate is very lively with good structure. Of a similar style, but if anything even more complete, is the Soave from the Ronchetto vineyard, a white which combines the qualities of lightness and length of flavour which are essential in a Soave. Portinari's style is easy to recognize: he never makes showy products, but rather wines that are subtle, very fresh and which are memorable for their elegance. Only the Soave Albare '94 did not convince us. It seemed a rather old-fashioned wine, very different from the '95, which we tasted again with great pleasure.

When the products of this estate are being tasted, there is always debate as to which will be the better of Graziano Pra's two Soaves - the basic one, or that made from grapes from the Monte Grande vineyard - seeing that, in recent years, they have taken turns in coming out on top in this gripping (if unofficial) competition. For the first time the result of our comparison is a tie, even if it is at a slightly lower level of quality than usual. The standard Soave reflects precisely the character of the '96 vintage, which has given us wines that are very lively, but which are a bit light and lacking the length of flavour that was one of the most attractive features of the '95s. Its colour is a bright straw-yellow; we find a broad range of aromas on the nose, made up of fruit underpinned by herbaceous scents; the entry and the evolution on the palate are satisfyingly well-integrated, but the fruit lacks the depth which has earned this wine higher marks in the past. The Monte Grande is more delicate, even in appearance. The nose offers fresh, light fruit which promises well but does not quite deliver, while on the palate the wine is lightweight, but shows clean, supple fruit: perhaps it is holding back and will develop with bottle age, but it was not very forthcoming at the time of our tastings. Unfortunately, for some years now, we have not been able to taste the Pra brothers' Recioto - which used to be really wonderful - nor the barrique-aged Soave from the Sant'Antonio vineyard the '92 vintage of which we so much enjoyed.

O	Soave Vigna Albare '96	🍷🍷	2*
O	Soave Vigneto Ronchetto '96	🍷🍷	2*
O	Soave Vigna Albare Doppia Maturazione Ragionata '96	🍷	2*
O	Soave Vigna Albare Doppia Maturazione Ragionata '95	🍷🍷	2

O	Soave Cl. Vigneto Monte Grande '96	🍷	3
O	Soave Classico '96	🍷	3
O	Soave Cl. Vigneto Monte Grande '95	🍷🍷	3

NEGRAR (VR)

NEGRAR (VR)

BERTANI
LOC. NOVARE
ARBIZZANO DI VALPOLICELLA
37024 NEGRAR (VR)
TEL. 045/6011211

TOMMASO BUSSOLA
VIA MOLINO TURRI, 30
FRAZ. S. PERETTO
37024 NEGRAR (VR)
TEL. 045/7501740

The innovative wines in the range continue to improve steadily, but the Veronese classics are sadly not keeping up - with the exception of the Amarone '88, interpreted as ever in the impeccable Bertani style, with its combination of cleanness, maturity and alcoholic richness. The fruit of an excellent vintage, this wine is deliciously ready to drink, but also has reassuringly good ageing potential. It has a good deep garnet colour; the broad nose is evocative rather than well-defined but the entry on the palate is full and positive, as is the evolution of the fruit, which is vigorous and shows unmistakable breed. The Valpolicellas, on the other hand, lack personality; on the whole, they seemed rather tired and short of bottle-ageing potential. The Soave, from which we certainly did not expect massive structure, is decidedly more interesting: it surprised us with its pleasing, well-defined aroma, and lively, nimble flavour. The white Le Lave, made from chardonnay and garganega, is also very good: it has a deep colour and broad aromas which show perfect balance between the sweet, fruity varietal notes and hints of vanilla. Its positive fruit on the palate, culminates in a fleshy and very crisp aftertaste. The Catullo Rosso is reliable. It is a blend of corvina and cabernet sauvignon which has dense colour and an incisive bouquet (although without the finesse of the '93) and supple, long fruit on the palate.

Tommaso Bussola represents the new wave of growers in Valpolicella, not so much in the sense that he embodies the features of the new generation of producers, but because of his particular charisma. We like the way he almost suffers in his intense relationship with the land, and we admire the healthy presumptuousness of someone who works hard and expects to be respected for doing so. We also appreciate the charm of someone who lays himself open to criticism and who takes risks and is not afraid of making mistakes. This year Bussola again offers us some wines of excellent quality, even if sooner or later he is going to have to do something about perfecting their stability. The '94 Recioto is majestic and overwhelming even in its dark, deep colour; the bouquet shows an initial deceptive lightness, then the richer notes begin to prevail and involve us totally. The fruit evolves splendidly on the palate, showing a bold sweetness and echoing the aromas note for note; the firm tannic backbone also ensures perfect balance. We found similar gustiness and depth in the '93 Amarone, which is naturally drier but equally concentrated, with rich, floral scents and aroma of fruit in alcohol; it also displays clean, long fruit on the palate. We award One Glass this year to the Peagnà, the white dessert wine, an experiment which we think Bussola should persevere with because we feel it can get even better. The two Valpolicellas both showed a notable level of quality.

● Amarone '88	ΨΨ	5
○ Le Lave '95	ΨΨ	3*
○ Catullo Bianco '95	Ψ	2*
○ Soave Classico '96	Ψ	3
● Catullo Rosso '94	Ψ	3
● Valpantena SeccoBertani '94	Ψ	3
● Valpolicella Superiore '94		3
● Valpolicella Sup. Ognissanti '93		3
● Amarone '85	ΨΨ	6
● Amarone '86	ΨΨ	5
● Catullo Rosso '93	ΨΨ	3

● Amarone '93	ΨΨ	6
● Recioto della Valpolicella '94	ΨΨ	5
● Valpolicella Cl. Superiore '93	Ψ	3
○ Peagnà Passito	Ψ	5
● Valpolicella Classico '96		2
● Amarone '90	ΨΨ	6
● Recioto della Valpolicella '93	ΨΨ	5

NEGRAR (VR)

Cantina Sociale Valpolicella

Via Ca' Salgari, 2
37024 Negrar (VR)
tel. 045/7500070

This year may be considered a pause for reflection for the Negrar Cooperative, or rather a period in which to prepare itself for the better results which will undoubtedly arrive in the very near future. The goal of the Director, Daniele Accordini, is to balance the economic demands of the growers - particularly regarding the quantities which everyone wants to go on producing regardless - with the more rigorous control of the quality and state of health of the grapes. One cannot expect all the members to fall immediately into line, but our tasting of cask samples of the more important wines showed that the majority are taking the right path. For now, the Valpolicellas are pleasant and, encouragingly, correctly-made. The Superiore Vigneti di Torbe '94 has a deep colour; its aroma conveys warmth and breadth, with scents of cherries in alcohol and almonds; it has sound structure and length of flavour on the palate. The Valpolicella Superiore '95 is lighter, but is nevertheless very typical of its denomination. The Amarone Jago '90 stands out for its supple, well-balanced fruit; even though it does not show much concentration, it is measured and long. It is probable, as is the case also of the standard Amarone from the same vintage, that these wines reflect the direction in which Accordini's skills as a winemaker are going to take the winery; certainly, however, they do not come from outstanding vintages and are not yet the fruit of thorough viticultural research. The Recioto shows itself to be the best of these wines, with a '95 which is impeccable both in its bright, deep colour as well as in its clean, fruity nose; it also shows an elegant sweetness on the palate and a good aromatic finish.

● Recioto della Valpolicella Vigneti di Moron '95	🍷🍷	4
● Amarone Dominii Veneti '93	🍷	4
● Amarone Vigneti di Jago '93	🍷	5
● Valpolicella Classico Superiore '95	🍷	2
● Valpolicella Superiore Vigneti di Torbe '94	🍷	2
● Recioto della Valpolicella Dominii Veneti '94	🍷🍷 (white)	4
● Amarone Vigneti di Jago '90	🍷 (white)	5

NEGRAR (VR)

Le Ragose

Via Ragose, 1
Fraz. Arbizzano
37024 Negrar (VR)
tel. 045/7513241

The quality of a producer anywhere in the world emerges in difficult vintages, when despite the multitude of problems which can affect a whole growing season (and not just the harvest), he succeeds in extracting the maximum possible from a wine. The Galli family of Le Ragose have in their cellar an excellent Amarone '91, which is certainly different from the massive '88 and '90, but still reveals that combination of fruit and balance which is the hallmark of this Negrar winery. It has a good, deep garnet colour; the nose opens up slowly, perhaps with less clarity than usual, but eventually conquers the taster's attention with hints of liquorice, macerated flowers, and fruit in alcohol. The fruit on the palate - certainly its best feature - is not at all affected by the lightness of the year, and reveals its usual power, well supported by the tannic backbone. We were not able to taste another of Le Ragose's specialities, the Recioto, but we can put this down to Arnaldo Galli's legendary patience: he believes, despite the commercial pressure to release new vintages early, in always giving his wines sufficient ageing. The Cabernet repeats its usual notable performance: it has abundant aromas and full, supple fruit on the palate. The Valpolicella Le Sassine is rather linear, with reasonable colour, an inviting freshness on the nose and a nimble, lightish and fairly long-lasting flavour. The fragrant and simple Valpolicella Classico '96 is well-made but we were a bit disappointed by the Valpolicella Superiore '93.

● Amarone '91	🍷🍷	5
● Cabernet Le Ragose '94	🍷	4
● Valpolicella Cl. Superiore Le Sassine '93	🍷	3
● Valpolicella Classico '96	🍷	2
● Valpolicella Superiore '93		3
● Amarone '86	🍷🍷🍷 (white)	5
● Amarone '88	🍷🍷🍷 (white)	5
● Amarone '90	🍷🍷 (white)	5
● Cabernet Le Ragose '92	🍷🍷 (white)	4
● Recioto della Valpolicella '93	🍷🍷 (white)	4
● Cabernet Le Ragose '93	🍷 (white)	4

NEGRAR (VR)

NEGRAR (VR)

GIUSEPPE QUINTARELLI
VIA CERÈ, 1
37024 NEGRAR (VR)
TEL. 045/7500016

VILLA SPINOSA
LOC. JAGO
37024 NEGRAR (VR)
TEL. 045/7500093

A few years ago we wrote that Quintarelli was preparing his son-in-law Celestino to take over the reins of his estate, and described the intense relationship between two powerful personalities, responsible over the course of the years for a long string of thrilling wines. We are now obliged to report that Celestino no longer works at the winery; he has decided to go his own way, and for Quintarelli there is no choice but to carry on alone and seek to repeat the glorious success his vineyards have given him in the past. The wines shown this year were still the fruit of their collaboration, in which Giuseppe played a creative, conceptual role, while Celestino was in charge of putting these ideas into practice. The '90 Amarone displays the unmistakable style of the estate, with great richness even in its mature garnet colour. The concentrated but exuberantly fruity bouquet contains scents of jam, oriental spices and almond toffee. The soft, warming fruit embraces the palate, and evolves into a long, satisfying finish. If we may criticize this wine, it is because it lacks just that touch of fleshiness which would have earned it our maximum accolade. The constantly surprising Alzero - made from semi-dried Cabernet grapes - shows the same impressive intensity: its colour is a lively, deep garnet; its spicy nose, with its notes of garden herbs and black berry fruits, is underpinned by a distinct but attractive minerally vein; the aromas are echoed on the palate, alongside an almost sweet flavour; the soft tannins give structure to the dense, long-lasting fruit. Finally, we were not really impressed by the overly-mature Valpolicella Superiore.

This estate, certainly one of the most promising in the fast-changing panorama of Veronese wines, belongs to Enrico Cascella, who has run it for just under ten years. He is in the middle of an impressive restructuring programme, which involves both vineyard renewal and the review of winemaking methods, aimed at bringing his winery into line with the new progressive standards being set in the region. Results are already evident in the form of some very good wines, but there are still significant logistical problems to resolve: for example, that of the very brief period of bottle-ageing which he is able to give his wines, which means showing them when they are still unbalanced, and before the fruit has a chance to express itself to the full. Certain of the benefit that a few months in the bottle will have for the Amarone, the Recioto and the Valpolicella Superiore, we shall hold back our comments on these wines until the next edition of the Guide. The Valpolicella Antanel was presented in two versions: an easier one from the '95 vintage which shows in abundance the immediate and pleasantly fruity features of this style of wine, and the more complex '93, from which we expected a little more weight, particularly in view of Cascella's aspirations. The Cabernet Sauvignon shows promising concentration which is immediately evident in the colour. Bilberries and blackcurrants characterize the nose while on the palate, the fruit is supple and harmonious and leads into a medium-long finish.

● Alzero '91	▼▼ 6
● Amarone '90	▼▼ 6
● Valpolicella Superiore '91	4
● Alzero '90	▼▼▼ 6
● Amarone '84	▼▼▼ 6
● Amarone '86	▼▼▼ 6
● Amarone Ris. '83	▼▼▼ 6
● Amarone Ris. '85	▼▼▼ 6
● Amarone '88	▼▼ 6
● Recioto della Valpolicella '88	▼▼ 6
● Valpolicella Superiore '90	▼ 5

● Cabernet Sauvignon '95	▼ 3
● Valpolicella Classico Antanel '95	▼ 3
● Valpolicella Classico Antanel '93	3
● Recioto della Valpolicella '95	▼▼ 4
● Cabernet Sauvignon '94	▼ 4

NEGRAR (VR)

NERVESA DELLA BATTAGLIA (TV)

VIVIANI
VIA MAZZANO, 8
37024 NEGRAR (VR)
TEL. 045/7500286

SERAFINI & VIDOTTO
VIA ARDITI, 1
31040 NERVESA DELLA BATTAGLIA (TV)
TEL. 0422/773281

Claudio Viviani knows that Nature does not follow precise rules, but secretly he would like to be able to keep total control, and his meticulous efforts in both the vineyards and the winery demonstrate the point. This young, ambitious grower succeeds in transferring into his bottles all his intensity and passion, and even when the wines are not 100 percent successful, one is still very much aware of the quality of the fruit. This is the case with the '94 standard Recioto, in which we appreciate good depth even in its colour. The nose - although not especially pronounced - shows good evolution, while on the palate, the lightly sweet fruit is balanced by the tannins, develops well and only lacks a touch of concentration. The '93 Recioto from the La Mandrela vineyard displays much greater richness and offers much more positive, vigorous sensations. Its dense colour leaves us in no doubt as to its concentration; the nose reveals the typical warmth of partially dried grapes; ripe blackberry and almond notes tumble over each other on the palate, where the soft, sweet fruit evolves to great effect, leaving an elegant and long finish. There is nothing wrong with either of the Valpolicellas, but both the early drinking version, which is the more fragrant of the two, and the Superiore could do with slightly more structure, enabling them to offer a little more complexity as they age.

The Marca Trevigiana is a fertile and romantic area which can reward those who are able to bring out its best qualities and express its secret energy. Antonello Vidotto and Francesco Serafini have not had it easy: this splendid and very beautiful zone appeared to remain indifferent to their efforts and seemed not to respond to their overtures. However, it was just a matter of adapting. Once they had understood this, the growers of the Abazia di Nervesa began to work in harmony with the land, recognizing its limits and making the most of its qualities, and today they turn out some very fine wines indeed. The Rossos which have been released in the last three years are show the diversity which it typical of any fine wine. If the '93 had a Bordeaux-like style and the '94 a more Mediterranean profile, the most recent vintage has a more distinctly Veneto imprint. Bordeaux blends have a long, well- documented history in North Eastern Italy; the Rosso dell'Abazia '95 is an excellent example, which sums up all the best qualities of the genre. Its colour is a bright, deep ruby. One is immediately aware of a verdant note in the complex nose, in which scents of thyme, rosemary and bay give way to a bouquet redolent of black berry fruits, honey, almonds and citrus. The vigorous fruit seems to well up directly from the soil; the firm tannins give the fruit real structure and amazing length on the palate. The range presented this year also includes the increasingly interesting Pinot Nero and a sort of second-label red called Phigaia, which shows supple elegance. The rich, refined Bianco is made from a blend of chardonnay and sauvignon.

● Recioto della Valpolicella La Mandrela '93	♟♟	5
● Recioto della Valpolicella '94	♟	4
● Valpolicella Classico '96	♟	2
● Valpolicella Superiore '94	♟	3
● Amarone '90	♟♟	5
● Amarone '91	♟♟	5
● Valpolicella Superiore '93	♟	3

● Il Rosso dell'Abazia '95	♟♟♟	5
● Phigaia After the Red '95	♟♟	4
● Pinot Nero '95	♟♟	5
○ Il Bianco dell'Abazia '96	♟♟	4
○ Prosecco del Montello	♟	3
● Il Rosso dell'Abazia '93	♟♟♟	5
● Il Rosso dell'Abazia '94	♟♟♟	5
● Il Rosso dell'Abazia '92	♟♟	5
● Pinot Nero '94	♟♟	5
● Cabernet del Montello '94	♟	3

OTTELLA
LOC. OTTELLA, 1
FRAZ. S. BENEDETTO DI LUGANA
37019 PESCHIERA DEL GARDA (VR)
TEL. 045/7551950

ZENATO
VIA S. BENEDETTO, 8
FRAZ. S. BENEDETTO DI LUGANA
37019 PESCHIERA DEL GARDA (VR)
TEL. 045/7550300

This small estate in the Province of Verona is beginning to reap the rewards it deserves. Francesco Montresor's efforts, which began at least eight years ago with the restructuring of the family vineyards, have not been limited to putting his Lugana on a quality footing, but have also been successfully turned towards red wines. His Campo Sireso - a blend of cabernet, merlot, croatina and barbera - gains high scores thanks to its complete, satisfying style. Its good, deep colour is matched by excellent breadth on the nose; on the palate, the fruit, well-balanced by the tannins, is fleshy and deep. The less ambitious Rosso Ottella, the second-label wine of the estate, also stands out for its frank, easy-drinking style. Going on to the whites, we note the happy success of the Incrocio Manzoni, which has never been as intense in its floral aroma as this year, nor as positive and long-lasting in its flavour. The basic Lugana, though a fairly simple wine, displays quaffable spicy fruit, highlighted by a bitter-almond aftertaste. The Le Creete selection naturally offers greater complexity: this is a Lugana of class which displays well the clean, forthright style of the grape variety. Its colour is a deep straw yellow and it has restrained, but well-defined nose of fruit and almonds; on the palate, it shows good, well-balanced, and long development. A tasting of previous vintages of this wine confirmed the ageing potential of Lugana, a white of rare suppleness which is unjustly underrated.

Sergio Zenato has, over the years, built a reputation for himself as a clear-sighted and shrewd selector, capable of immediately understanding the value of a parcel of grapes, or the ageing capacity of a cask of wine. His main skill lies in being able to bring out the best in the aromas and rich flavours of a product, without its losing any of its qualities during ageing. He is also very adept in striking a balance between a wine's various components, and timing its release to perfection. These are the secrets behind the best Amarone of his career, a wine which has been jealously guarded and cared for, and brought out only when it is ready to express itself to the full. Its style self-confidently reflects the two souls of Valpolicella - the more mature and traditional alongside the more youthful and innovative - and, very diplomatically, confirms the value of both with the simple naturalness of its quality. The wine displays warmth even in its colour, with its intense, mature garnet hints; the initial impression of surprising freshness on the nose gives way to sweet, rich and fleshy notes of glazed almonds and jam; on the palate, its vigour is tempered by the delicacy and balance which result from its long maturation. Zenato's flair, aided by his children Alberto and Nadia, also gives us a basic Amarone which easily overcomes the problems of a difficult year like '91, and demonstrates a well-made, linear style. We found no stars this year among the Luganas, usually the specialities of the house, but all were well-handled in order to bring out the frank quaffability of their fruit.

	Wine	Rating	Score
●	Campo Sireso '95	♟♟	3
○	Lugana Le Creete '96	♟♟	3*
○	Incrocio Manzoni 6.0.13 '96	♟	2*
○	Lugana '96	♟	2
●	Rosso Ottella '96	♟	2*
●	Campo Sireso '92	♟♟	3
○	Lugana Le Creete '95	♟♟	3
●	Campo Sireso '94	♟	3
●	Rosso Ottella '95	♟	2

	Wine	Rating	Score
●	Amarone Cl. Sergio Zenato '88	♟♟♟	6
●	Amarone '91	♟♟	4
●	Valpolicella Superiore Ripassa '94	♟	3
○	Lugana S. Cristina Vigneto Massoni '96	♟	3
○	Lugana San Benedetto '96	♟	3
○	Lugana Sergio Zenato '95	♟	4
○	Lugana Sergio Zenato '94	♟♟	4
●	Amarone '90	♟♟	4
●	Cabernet Sauvignon S. Cristina '90	♟♟	4
●	Cabernet Sauvignon S. Cristina '93	♟	4
●	Valpolicella Superiore Ripassa '93	♟	3

PRAMAGGIORE (VE)   S. AMBROGIO DI VALPOLICELLA (VR)

RUSSOLO
VIA LIBERTÀ, 36
30020 PRAMAGGIORE (VE)
TEL. 0421/799087

ALEARDO FERRARI
VIA GIARE, 15
FRAZ. GARGAGNAGO
37010 S. AMBROGIO DI VALPOLICELLA (VR)
TEL. 045/7701379

It was not easy to repeat the fine performance of last year, when the '95 vintage gave Russolo some very fine wines indeed. However, this year too, the Pramaggiore winery put on a good show, with a great number of better-than-average products. The best of the range is the Merlot I Legni, obtained (as are almost all their wines) from the Grave del Friuli: the colour shows good intensity and the nose is very elegant, with a vegetal nuance which complements the more precise scents of blackberries and sour cherries. The wine's entry on the palate is fairly restrained, but then it opens up and even though it does not offer great concentration it does display excellent balance and a flavour which echoes its aromas. The Müller Thurgau Mussignaz is an excellent example of harmony between nose and palate: it is very rich in it aroma - in which we can pick out lime leaves and elderflower - and similarly supple and lively on the palate. This wine does not earn a higher score only because the '96 vintage left it a little short of structure. The Chardonnay, which has never before reached this level of quality, is rich, fruity and long. It has a good, intense colour, an immediate and well-defined nose and elegance and length on the palate. The Tocai - which is fresher, more lively and well-perfumed - is certainly not lacking in fruit, and shows delicious varietal character. We found the Pinot Bianco and the Sauvignon, also from the Ronco Calaj range, very well made, while the Sauvignon I Legni seemed unbalanced and unexciting and was not up to par. Among the other reds, the Cabernet and the Refosco as satisfactory, unlike the more ambitious Borgo di Peuma, which appears still in search of a clearly defined style.

After a series of fortunate years, Aleardo Ferrari has not been able to maintain the standard of quality to which we had become accustomed, and his range of wines seems to have been all too unfavourably conditioned by the unpredictable nature of the most recent vintages. The Valpolicella Superiore '94, a not particularly concentrated red, but nevertheless one with supple, long-lasting fruit, is an exception. Its colour is a medium-deep ruby; on the nose, ripe fruit notes merge with scents of aromatic herbs; the fruit develops well on the palate, and shows good balance. Last year the Recioto scored very highly, and we expected it to do so again, particularly in view of the quality of the '95 vintage. Surprisingly it was rather neutral, and devoid of the breadth and richness which have always been its principal features. The '93 Amarone also left us somewhat perplexed: it did not demonstrate its normal tightness and clarity of flavour and aromas; rather, the fruit seemed thin and overwhelmed by the oak. We like the liveliness of the Pelara, an easy but well-made wine with a spicy bouquet and light but long fruit flavour on the palate.

○ Friuli Grave Chardonnay Ronco Calaj '96	♥♥	3
● Friuli Grave Merlot I Legni '95	♥♥	4
● Friuli Grave Cabernet I Legni '95	♥	4
○ Friuli Grave Pinot Bianco Ronco Calaj '96	♥	3
○ Friuli Grave Sauvignon Ronco Calaj '96	♥	3
○ Friuli Grave Tocai Ronco Calaj '96	♥	3
○ Müller Thurgau Mussignaz '96	♥	3
● Friuli Grave Refosco I Legni '95		4
● Cabernet I Legni '94	♥♥	4
○ Sauvignon I Legni '94	♥♥	4
● Friuli Grave Cabernet Franc Ronco Calaj '95	♥	3

● Amarone '93	♥	5
● Pelara '96	♥	2
● Valpolicella Superiore '94	♥	2
● Recioto della Valpolicella '95		4
● Amarone '92	♥♥	5
● Recioto della Valpolicella '94	♥♥	4
● Valpolicella Superiore '93	♥	2

S. AMBROGIO DI VALPOLICELLA (VR) S. BONIFACIO (VR)

MASI
VIA MONTELEONE
FRAZ. GARGAGNAGO
37010 S. AMBROGIO DI VALPOLICELLA (VR)
TEL. 045/6800588

INAMA
VIA IV NOVEMBRE, 1
37047 S. BONIFACIO (VR)
TEL. 045/6101411-7610517

Masi's best scores this year were obtained by the Serego Alighieri wines, a sort of premium range offered by the Gargagnago winery. We were very impressed with the Amarone Vajo Armaron '90, a very carefully made red which demonstrates all the magnificence of a traditional Amarone, yet which shows refined, clean fruit flavours. Its colour is an opaque garnet; its nose has good depth, initially yielding macerated sour cherries, and then hints of roses and cocoa; on the palate, there is similarly broad structure, and well-balanced, mature and generous fruit. The Bianco Serego Alighieri, a blend of garganega and sauvignon, is floral, fine and notably long: it cannot be considered a wine of great richness, but rather a brilliant "exercice de style". We also tasted an interesting Valpolicella Superiore from the Serego Alighieri line which is no heavyweight, but has an attractively ripe style and long finish. We were less convinced by the Recioto, especially in view of the splendid performances of recent years: the Serego Alighieri version lacks the measure which would balance its undoubtedly vigorous fruit. The Campofiorin - another wine that did not score its usual high marks - is made by the method of re-fermenting a Valpolicella on Recioto pomace. We found it to be strained rather than enriched by this practice, about which there is much debate in Valpolicella. Among the Lake Garda wines, we note the success of the Bardolino La Vegrona. The basic Amarone on the other hand is restrained almost to the point of anonymity, and does not come up to par.

Stefano Inama is a very talented producer who, in the space a few years, has succeeded in realizing the potential of his best vineyard sites and transforming his winery into a model of modern efficiency. This evolution has been marked by numerous experiments, not all of them successful in themselves, but which have helped him to establish a high and constant level of quality across the range. The Soave Du Lot is obtained from a garganega vineyard with little more than 1,000 vines per hectare and shows a balance between the character of the variety, the soil and the exposure which gives perfect concentration of aromas and flavours. The wine has a bright golden colour; in the rich, complex bouquet, we detect hints of liquorice, ripe bananas, hazelnuts, flowers and spices. What is really striking is the texture of the wine in the mouth, with its combination of vigour and silkiness. As in the case of the Du Lot, the Sauvignon Vulcaia Fume also shows how oak can help make a white wine great by accentuating its immediacy. A brilliant gold in colour, this monovarietal offers exotic dense, rich fruit on the nose, made even more complex by hints of vanilla and cinnamon, and a full, rounded flavour. The two Soaves from the Vigneti di Foscarino are explosively fruity, vigorous and long-lasting, the '95 being softer and more mature, and the '96 crisper, more zesty and vivacious.

● Amarone Vajo Armaron '90	▼▼	5
● Amarone '93	▼	4
● Bardolino La Vegrona '96	▼	3
● Recioto della Valpolicella Casal dei Ronchi Serego Alighieri '94	▼	5
● Valpolicella Superiore Serego Alighieri '94	▼	3
○ Bianco Serego Alighieri '96	▼	3
● Amarone Classico '88	▼▼▼	6
● Amarone '90	▼▼	5
● Recioto della Valpolicella Amabile degli Angeli '93	▼▼	4
● Recioto della Valpolicella Casal dei Ronchi '93	▼▼	5
● Amarone Campolongo Torbe '90	▼	5

○ Sauvignon Vulcaia Fumé '96	▼▼▼	4
○ Soave Cl. Sup. Vigneto Du Lot '96	▼▼▼	4
○ Soave Cl. Sup. Vigneti di Foscarino '95	▼▼	4
○ Soave Cl. Sup. Vigneti di Foscarino '96	▼▼	4
○ Sauvignon Vulcaia '95	▼▼	4
○ Soave Cl. Sup. Vin Soave '96	▼	3
○ Chardonnay Campo dei Tovi '94	▼▼	4
○ Sauvignon Vulcaia '94	▼▼	4

S. PIETRO DI FELETTO (TV)   S. PIETRO IN CARIANO (VR)

BEPIN DE ETO
VIA COLLE, 32/A
FRAZ. RUA
31020 S. PIETRO DI FELETTO (TV)
TEL. 0438/486877

ACCORDINI
VIA ALBERTO BOLLA, 9
FRAZ. PEDEMONTE
37029 S. PIETRO IN CARIANO (VR)
TEL. 045/7701733

The recently established Colli di Conegliano denomination has brought under its wing Prosecco and a number of new wines which, until a short time ago, were only entitled to "vino da tavola " status. The outstanding wine of the DOC is Il Greccio, which has for some years been the star wine of the Bepin de Eto range. The Two Glass award of last year was in fact for the '94 vintage, which we erroneously listed as '95. This in fact turned out to be an accurate, but not very difficult prediction, since the '95, released this year is indeed of the usual high standard. It is a white wine with a lively golden colour, whose nose displays attractive floral aromas, as well as clean fruit; on the palate the fruit returns full and rich, and on the finish it echoes perfectly the sensations on the nose. The Incrocio Manzoni scored marginally lower, but is still a well-made white, characterized by herbal nuances, medium-weight fruit on the palate and a lively, pleasing style. Similar fragrance is offered by the Prosecco Spumante, a model of stylishness and character on the nose; its fruit evolves in a well-defined manner on the palate, with a delicate mousse and clear varietal notes on the finish. We were not able to taste the Faé "passito" or the sparkling Incrocio Manzoni, two wines which were not yet ready when the Guide went to print, but which have always been highlights of the company's range: we shall describe them in the next edition. We were less impressed than usual with the Cabernet, from which we did not expect great intensity, but rather more stylishness than we found this year. The Prosecco Tranquillo, on the other hand, is a correct wine and bears witness to Ceschin's adroitness in handling raw material which is not necessarily premium quality.

This small and relatively new company has already established a position of note in the rapidly-changing panorama of Valpolicella. Tiziano Accordini enjoys the help of his father in managing the vineyards, while in the winery he can count on the advice of his brother Daniele, Director of the Cantina Sociale. Their collective efforts, particularly successful with "passito" styles, have created three excellent wines and one real superstar. This is the Amarone Il Fornetto, a fine example of the modern style of Amarone, which however does not renounce full-bodied intensity. It has a deep, opaque colour and a nose which is rich, full and concentrated. The powerful, explosive fruit on the palate is, however, never unbalanced and it shows fine texture, and a long finish. The basic Amarone, also from the '93 vintage, is elegant and agreeable and shows how this type of wine does not have to be a heavyweight, even though it displays the requisite richness and character. The Recioto shows attractive, fragrant aroma and well-modulated sweetness, lifted by fresh acidity. The white dessert wine, the Bricco delle Bessole, is more alcoholic, mature and almost old-fashioned in style. Its amber colour heralds aromas of ripe figs, almonds and spices; on the palate, the aromas of the full, sweet fruit echo those on the nose, and the finish is beautifully clean. The two Valpolicellas could do with being better-defined. If the '96 Classico displays an estery aspect on the nose and very light fruit, the '95 Superiore seems rather too mature in its bouquet and reveals alcohol that is not well balanced with its flavours.

○ Colli di Conegliano		
Il Greccio '95	♟♟	2*
○ Incrocio Manzoni 6.0.13 '96	♟	2*
○ Prosecco di Conegliano		
Spumante	♟	2*
○ Prosecco di Conegliano		
Tranquillo '96		1
○ Colli di Conegliano		
Il Greccio '94	♟♟	2
● Cabernet '95	♟	1

● Amarone della Valpolicella Cl.		
Vigneto Il Fornetto '93	♟♟♟	5
● Amarone della Valpolicella Cl.		
Acinatico '93	♟♟	5
● Recioto della Valpolicella		
Acinatico '95	♟♟	4
○ Passito Bricco delle Bessole '95	♟♟	4
● Valpolicella Classico '96		2
● Valpolicella Classico		
Superiore '95		4
● Amarone della Valpolicella Cl.		
Acinatico '91	♟♟	4
● Recioto della Valpolicella '94	♟	5
○ Passito Bricco delle Bessole '94	♟	4

S. PIETRO IN CARIANO (VR)   S. PIETRO IN CARIANO (VR)

LORENZO BEGALI
CENGIA DI NEGARINE, 10
37029 S. PIETRO IN CARIANO (VR)
TEL. 045/7725148

BRIGALDARA
VIA BRIGALDARA, 20
FRAZ. S. FLORIANO
37029 S. PIETRO IN CARIANO (VR)
TEL. 045/7701055

After having earned a full listing in last year's Guide, Lorenzo Begali deservedly retains his place, thanks to the passion and courage he shows as a grower who is prepared to forsake quick profits by only bottling the very best wine that he produces. The rest, which is not at all bad, usually makes some astute wholesale dealer very happy. For example, take the Valpolicella Classico '96. Most producers rely on refined technology to ensure success with basic level Valpolicella. Begali, even though he does not have particularly sophisticated cellar equipment, has made a very acceptable, pleasant light red which is certainly far superior to most of the mediocre versions of this DOC on the market. His real passion, however, is for wines made from semi-dried grapes, with which he scores high even when the vintages are not ideal. The '92 Amarone is a carbon copy of the '91. It has good concentration of colour and a nose - perhaps its best feature - which evolves richly, with ripe red berry fruit and hints of cocoa and spice; the palate combines high alcohol with satisfying depth of fruit; it still lacks a bit of finesse and balance, but this will come with a little bottle-age. The Recioto '95 is excellent, its real forte being the extraordinary freshness which in no way detracts from the exuberance of such an intense sweet wine. The colour is a deep ruby; on the nose we find scents of blackberry and rosemary, and just a hint of cinnamon while on the palate, its sweetness is full and well-balanced, underpinned by lively acidity and gentle tannins.

The long series of difficult vintages has again taken its toll on quality at this winery; Stefano Cesari has not succeeded in getting the better of years like '93 and '94 and for this reason, his wines seem to lack that verve which on other occasions had given them measure and balance. The estate's desire to make quality wines is undoubted, so we hope that we shall soon see the results: it is vital that Valpolicella's moment of glory be an ongoing phenomenon and not just a passing phase. Turning to the wines, the Recioto '94 reveals good basic style, but already seems a little tired and lacks overt sweetness, thus leaving it in limbo, neither a real dessert wine nor a completely dry one. Cesari was right, on the other hand, to wait for the Amarone '91: an extra year's ageing has given it a more definite and broader spectrum of aromas; the fruit on the palate is not that of great years, but the wine does display a forward, rich and alcoholic style. Heartened by the latter wine, we look forward with confidence to the '93 Amarone which, from our initial tastings, seems bigger and more concentrated than the '91, and therefore even more in need of ageing. The '96 Valpolicella is made in the modern style: it has a very pale colour, a nose of red berry fruit sustained by pleasant vinosity and a supple flavour which echoes the aromas. We might have expected greater intensity, however, from the Valpolicella Superiore. Despite coming from the very good '95 vintage this wine never really takes off.

● Amarone '92	ҮҮ	4*
● Recioto della Valpolicella '95	ҮҮ	4*
● Valpolicella Classico '96	Ү	1*
● Amarone '91	ҮҮ	4
● Recioto della Valpolicella '94	ҮҮ	4

● Amarone '91	Ү	5
● Recioto della Valpolicella '94	Ү	5
● Valpolicella Classico '96	Ү	2
● Valpolicella Superiore Il Vegro '95	Ү	3
● Amarone '90	ҮҮ	4
● Valpolicella Superiore Il Vegro '93	ҮҮ	3
● Recioto della Valpolicella '93	ҮҮ	5

S. PIETRO IN CARIANO (VR)   S. PIETRO IN CARIANO (VR)

GIUSEPPE BRUNELLI
VIA CARIANO, 10
37029 S. PIETRO IN CARIANO (VR)
TEL. 045/7701118

NICOLIS
VIA DI VILLA GIRARDI, 29
37029 S. PIETRO IN CARIANO (VR)
TEL. 045/7701261

In the past few years, Luigi Brunelli has spoilt his admirers with a range which has always contained two or three excellent wines, and even if he did show a certain haste in releasing products which deserved longer ageing, there has always been evidence of indisputable quality. His results this year are less striking: the '94 Amarone seems immature, well-made but unexciting and incapable of conveying the richness of its raw material: it does not rate above satisfactory. The colour is an appealingly light, ruby-garnet. It is fairly simple on the nose, with evident red berry aromas but the fruit on the palate is rather shy, and does not really evolve, thus giving an impression of slight lack of balance. The Recioto Corte Cariano from the great '95 vintage - another wine which promised much - is also somewhat lacking in character. The colour is not very concentrated and the nose displays essentially estery notes which dominate any varietal aromas; the fruit on the palate offers little more than a pleasant sweetness. The Passito Bianco Re Sol, which is very similar to the previous vintage, shows fairly monotonous fruit, though it does reveal some potential for improvement. The Valpolicellas are less successful than usual; if this was only to be expected for the early bottled version and for the basic Superiore, we thought that the Pariondo would show definite signs of quality; unfortunately, the wine we tasted was thin and rather feeble.

Nicolis is carving out an ever more well-defined place for itself among Valpolicella's top producers. The Recioto, which for a couple of years now has represented the company's real strength, once again shows a very graceful, clean style. Its colour is deep ruby; the nose of violets and red berry fruits is rendered even more elegant by hints of aromatic herbs; there is full, sweet fruit on the palate, which evolves well and is balanced by the wine's other components. If this is the Recioto from the excellent '95 vintage, one can imagine what the Amarone will be like! We enjoyed the '92 edition of this wine, which was not overly affected by the problems of the vintage: it does not display great intensity, but it has sufficient alcohol and good balance, even if the oak is a little too much in evidence. The Valpolicella Superiore shows good character; we should perhaps like it to be more balanced and a little less spirity, but it is nevertheless a hearty wine, though with a different style to the Amarone. We were very pleasantly surprised by the Chardonnay, rightly interpreted as a young wine for quaffing - and all the better for it. The only wines to leave us a little perplexed were the '96 Valpolicella and the Bardolino, the quality of whose fruit was all too clearly mediocre and which could not be saved even by skillful vinification. From the vineyards which the Nicolis family owns in Bardolino comes a Chiaretto which is of above-average quality for its DOC.

O Passito Bianco Re Sol '94	♀	4
● Amarone '94	♀	5
● Recioto della Valpolicella '95	♀	4
● Recioto della Valpolicella Corte Cariano '95	♀	4
● Valpolicella Cl. Superiore Pariondo '93		2
● Valpolicella Classico '96		1
● Valpolicella Superiore '95		2
● Amarone '93	♀♀	5
● Amarone Corte Cariano '90	♀♀	5

● Recioto della Valpolicella '95	♀♀	4
O Chardonnay '96	♀	2*
⊙ Bardolino Chiaretto '96	♀	2*
● Amarone Ambrosan '92	♀	5
● Valpolicella Superiore '95	♀	3
● Bardolino Classico '96		2
● Valpolicella Classico '96		2
● Amarone '91	♀♀	5
● Amarone Ambrosan '90	♀♀	5
● Recioto della Valpolicella '94	♀♀	4
● Valpolicella Classico '95	♀	1

S. PIETRO IN CARIANO (VR)   S. PIETRO IN CARIANO (VR)

SANTA SOFIA
VIA CA' DEDÉ, 61
FRAZ. PEDEMONTE
37029 S. PIETRO IN CARIANO (VR)
TEL. 045/7701074

F.LLI SPERI
VIA FONTANA, 14
FRAZ. PEDEMONTE
37029 S. PIETRO IN CARIANO (VR)
TEL. 045/7701154

This company is specializing more and more in the production of the white wines of Verona and, from one point of view this is a positive: certainly we have noticed a constant improvement in the whites from year to year. On the other hand, we must point out that Santa Sofia no longer makes reds (its more traditional specialities) of such high quality as in the past. However, beginning our reviews on a positive note, the Soave Monte Foscarino is a very satisfying wine. It has a deep straw-yellow colour and on the nose we find appealing scents of apples combined with more subtle floral and almond notes; the palate stands out for the its harmony. While this is not an especially complex wine, it is nevertheless an extremely enjoyable drink. The Soave Costalta, which also displays its clarity of style even in the colour, shows rather more complexity: it has a good, deep bouquet, with pear, hazelnut and apricot notes; these aromas are also echoed in the flavour, which is positive and long in the finish. Again from Soave comes a really well-made Recioto: it boasts an attractive freshness on the nose, and on the palate it displays supple, well-balanced fruit as well as well-modulated sweetness. The Chiaretto is not, and has no ambition to be, particularly intense, but should be enjoyed for its liveliness and delicacy. We expected rather more from the Amarone '90; though it is the fruit of an undoubtedly outstanding vintage, this red is not as exciting as it should be. Its transparent garnet colour and its fairly straightforward bouquet are not really redeemed by an alcoholic, but not very broad flavour. Both the Valpolicellas - the Monte Gradella and the basic '96 - demonstrate that this wine type is not exactly closest to this producer's heart.

The Recioto La Roggia - one of the finest wines we have ever tasted from Valpolicella - is an outstanding product which clearly exemplifies what a perfect dessert wine should be like. The La Roggia vineyard, located in the commune of Fumane, enjoys a warm, well-ventilated climate which allows the grapes to achieve a particularly high degree of ripeness, which in turn makes them better adapted to drying, virtually without any danger of rot. Pressing is carried out in February; maceration lasts for just over two weeks, and then the must - which is still very rich in sugars - begins its fermentation in barriques. A further year's ageing in large barrels is needed to tame all this concentration, followed by a period of bottle-ageing which helps develop this wine into the very quintessence of rich, sweet fruit. Its colour is a deep, opaque ruby. Its rich and singular nose displays scents of hazelnuts, cocoa, blackberries, liquorice and thyme. The extraordinarily long-lasting fruit on the palate displays all the sweetness of the large black cherries found in Valpolicella, a delicious flavour that just seems to go on and on. This wine is the brainchild of Paolo Speri, a young and impassioned producer, who has shown particular ability in convincing his uncles, brothers and cousins of the exceptional quality potential of the family estate. From the La Roggia vineyard also comes an exuberant and alcoholic Passito Bianco, with fresh but mouth-filling sweet fruit on the palate.

O Soave Costalta '96	▼▼	3
O Recioto di Soave '95	▼	4
O Soave Monte Foscarino '96	▼	2
⊙ Bardolino Chiaretto '96	▼	2
● Valpolicella Classico '96		2
● Amarone '90		5
● Valpolicella Superiore		
Monte Gradella '95		3

● Recioto della Valpolicella Cl.		
La Roggia '94	▼▼▼	4
O Passito Bianco La Roggia '94	▼▼	4
● Valpolicella Classico '96	▼	1
● Valpolicella Cl. Superiore		
La Roverina '95	▼	2
● Amarone		
Vigneto Sant'Urbano '90	♀♀♀	5
● Amarone		
Vigneto Sant'Urbano '91	♀♀	5
● Recioto della Valpolicella		
I Comunai '94	♀♀	5
● Valpolicella Cl. Superiore		
Vigneto Sant'Urbano '93	♀♀	4

S. PIETRO IN CARIANO (VR) S. PIETRO IN CARIANO (VR)

F.LLI TEDESCHI
VIA VERDI, 4/A
FRAZ. PEDEMONTE
37029 S. PIETRO IN CARIANO (VR)
TEL. 045/7701487

F.LLI TOMMASI
VIA RONCHETTO, 2
FRAZ. PEDEMONTE
37029 S. PIETRO IN CARIANO (VR)
TEL. 045/7701266-7701437

In last year's Guide we noted that this estate - as befits both its traditions and its potential - was starting to show some signs of revival. We hoped for confirmation in this year's tastings but, sadly, it was not forthcoming. Certainly, the vintages presented did not lead us to expect staggering results, but the Tedeschi winery really can do better. The most interesting product in the range, the vino da tavola Capitel San Rocco '93, does not have a particularly deep colour; on the nose one finds attractive ripe fruit notes alongside sweet, spice but there is no great structure on the palate, and the flavour is a little short. We had been looking forward to the '93 Amarones: the standard version still requires some bottle age, and we shall therefore postpone our judgment until next year's Guide. The Capitel Monte Olmi showed decently, without any particular faults, but by the same token it lacked the high points of aroma and flavour which such an important wine should display. The two Valpolicella Superiores, - both the standard version and the Capitel dei Nicalò - are simple and lacking in the body and depth which we should be able to find, at least in the single-vineyard selection. The sweet white Vin della Fabriseria, a pale gold-coloured "passito", confirms the standard it showed last year. It has interesting floral aromas, but is not entirely convincing on the palate. The Recioto Monte Fontana '91 was mistakenly listed in last year's Guide as the '93. The real '93, tasted this year, confirms the Tedeschis' skill with dessert wines, even if it did not show as well as the previous vintage.

We are pleased to hail the return to the pages of the Guide of one of Valpolicella's best-known names. The Tomassi brothers own three, increasingly autonomous companies; one keeps the original family name, while the other two are known as Villa Girardi and Il Sestante. There is no shortage of vineyards; Tomassi own a total of some 78 hectares, some of which are in very good sites. The ever-greater collaboration between the older and younger generations is producing a marked improvement in quality. In this year's tastings, the Villa Girardi line earned the highest marks, with particular plaudits going to an interesting '93 Amarone. This is a wine with well-defined macerated flowers and fruit on the nose, good evolution on the palate, and a long, rich finish. The Lugana, too, is more than just well-made: it has clean, though not especially broad aromas, which are perfectly echoed by the fragrant fruit on the palate. The '96 Valpolicella does not display much body, but has an enjoyable spicy, easy-drinking style. The best wine from Il Sestante is an attractive, youthful Lugana; though less full-bodied than the one above, it is perhaps more ready for drinking. The Amarone from the Ca' Florian vineyard, which amazed us in a couple of tastings with its rich, vigorous fruit, seemed anonymous and lacklustre on other occasions. From the Tommasi range (the one which offers the keenest value for money), we draw attention to a correct '93 Amarone.

○ Vin della Fabriseria San Rocco '93	♀	5
● Amarone Capitel Monte Olmi '93	♀	5
● Capitel San Rocco '93	♀	4
● Recioto della Valpolicella Capitel Monte Fontana '93	♀	5
● Valpolicella Superiore '94		2
● Valpolicella Superiore Capitel dei Nicalò '94		3
● Recioto della Valpolicella Capitel Monte Fontana '91	♀♀	4
● Amarone '91	♀	4
● Amarone Capitel Monte Olmi '91	♀	4

● Amarone Villa Girardi '93	♀♀	5
● Amarone Ca' Florian Tommasi '90	♀	5
● Amarone Il Sestante '93	♀	5
● Amarone Tommasi '93	♀	5
● Valpolicella Classico Villa Girardi '96	♀	2
○ Lugana Il Sestante '96	♀	3
○ Lugana Terre Lunghe Villa Girardi '96	♀	2
● Valpolicella Cl. Superiore Il Sestante '94		4
● Valpolicella Cl. Superiore Rafael Tommasi '95		3

S. PIETRO IN CARIANO (VR)   S. PIETRO IN CARIANO (VR)

MASSIMO VENTURINI
VIA SEMONTE, 20
FRAZ. S. FLORIANO
37029 S. PIETRO IN CARIANO (VR)
TEL. 045/7701331-770330

VILLA BELLINI
VIA DEI FRACCAROLI, 6
LOC. CASTELROTTO DI NEGARINE
37029 S. PIETRO IN CARIANO (VR)
TEL. 045/7725630

This estate owns some of the finest vineyards in the commune of San Pietro: the Monte Masua and the Semonte Alto have been known for many years as sites capable of producing suitable grapes to make great Amarone. The Venturini brothers' '93 Amarone, though not the best wine they have ever made, stands clearly above the average standard of its DOC and reassures us of its producers' quest for quality. It has an invitingly deep ruby-garnet colour and a good range of aromas, with scents of freshly crushed petals, red berry fruits, and a well-integrated hint of oak. The fruit on the palate is positive and generous, and evolves with good length on the finish: the alcohol still has to knit fully with the fruit, but we are certain that this Amarone will age well. We expected a bit more from the Recioto Le Brugnine, especially as the standard version had scored very high marks. Though it demonstrates, particularly on the nose, the undoubted quality of the raw material, it seems rather constricted on the palate and unable to display its fruit and structure to the full. The Valpolicella Superiore Semonte Alto is only satisfactory, but as we are dealing here with the '93 vintage - hardly the best of the last few years - we can conclude that the Venturinis did the best job possible. The Valpolicella from the '96 vintage, which really tested the patience of the zone's growers, is again well-made. It is a wine which should be drunk within a year of the harvest.

Marco Zamarchi and Cecilia Trucchi made a courageous choice when they bought the most beautiful property in Castelrotto: not only do they live there, but they have also revived the noble vine-growing tradition that the estate had enjoyed for centuries. It is too early to expect great results, and much still needs to be done, but the passion which these two thoroughbred Veronese invest in their work has already produced some fine bottles and made Villa Bellini into a really enchanting domain. The estate operates according to strictly organic principals, and for this reason the wines are more prone to suffer when vintages are difficult. Thus the '92 Amarone only just succeeds in earning a One Glass rating, because it simply lacks the well-defined aromas and the depth which are essential elements of a fine wine. On the other hand, we thoroughly enjoyed the Amarone Riserva '90, in which we found a fabric of great force and length. Its colour is still very youthful; the nose displays enticing sweet fruit, given added definition by a touch of vanilla; the plump fruit on the palate evolves beautifully and with admirable balance. We draw your also attention to a '92 Recioto and to a Valpolicella Superiore which are both correctly made. Marco and Cecilia's relaxed, laid-back approach to life is embodied in all of the estate's wine, and particularly in the rose' Il Brolo, a product of rare charm and freshness.

● Amarone '93	♈♈	4
● Recioto della Valpolicella Le Brugnine '94	♈	4
● Valpolicella Cl. Superiore Semonte Alto '93	♈	3
● Valpolicella Classico '96	♈	1*
● Recioto della Valpolicella Classico '94	♉♉	4
● Amarone '92	♉	4

● Amarone Ris. '90	♈♈	5
● Amarone '92	♈	4
● Recioto della Valpolicella '92	♈	4
⊙ Il Brolo '96	♈	1*
● Valpolicella Cl. Superiore '95		3
● Amarone '90	♉♉	5
● Recioto della Valpolicella Amandorlato '90	♉♉	4
● Amarone '91	♉	5

SALGAREDA (TV)

ORNELLA MOLON TRAVERSO
VIA RISORGIMENTO, 40
FRAZ. CAMPODIPIETRA
31040 SALGAREDA (TV)
TEL. 0422/804807

SOAVE (VR)

CANTINA DEL CASTELLO
CORTE PITTORA, 5
37038 SOAVE (VR)
TEL. 045/7680093

Giancarlo Traverso and Ornella Molon's career as wine producers has not always been accompanied by the fame which they now enjoy: years of working their way up through the industry has taught them respect for their customers and the value of having the right wine at the right price. The improvements shown by their estate are admirable and demonstrate an ambition for quality which is as strong as it is rare in the Piave. If initially it seemed to be the reds that represented the best of the estate, we can now also include two whites in the picture, a splendid and surprising Traminer and a refined and polished Sauvignon. The Traminer came to our notice last year with a display of notable richness: in the '96 version, it has taken on a refined elegance in its floral aromas, without losing any of the nuances which include rose, elderflower and hazelnut. On the palate, its characteristic plumpness is tempered by fresh acidity, the fruit has depth and evolves well, and the flavours bring back the initial sensations on the nose. The Sauvignon has a lively, minerally bouquet and appealing, supple, fleshy yet fresh fruit which lingers on the palate. Continuing with the whites, we note a considerable improvement in the Chardonnay matured in barrique, which now only lacks a certain frankness on the nose; the fruit on the palate is really impressive. The Cabernet performed well, in this vintage more forthcoming and complex on the nose, while retaining the force of flavour which has always set it apart. The Merlot shows an attractive rich style: even from a far-from-ideal vintage, it is scores a Two Glass rating.

Tasting Arturo Stocchetti's wines points up in exemplary manner the differences between the '95 and '96 vintages. The former produced grapes which were rich in aroma and extract, capable of giving broad, deeply-flavoured Soaves. On the other hand the fruit in '96 was more dilute and consequently the wines are somewhat lacking in concentration and depth. This vintage however constitutes only a temporary set back in the quest for quality which the Cantina del Castello has undertaken in the last few years. Turning to the tasting notes, the basic Soave Classico has a fairly pale colour; pleasantly yeasty on the nose; the fruit does not open up much on the palate, and the flavour remains on the middle palate without ever being very exciting. The more fully-flavoured Soave from the Monte Pressoni vineyard shows a well-defined and attractively deep straw colour; it offers white peach and plum on the nose and the markedly full fruit unravels stylishly on the palate, well supported by fresh acidity. We expected similar personality from the Soave Classico Monte Carniga, which is usually rich and mouth-filling, but this wine in fact only displayed correct but straightforward fruit. It has a clean bouquet, but is a bit short on the palate, even if the general impression it leaves is a pleasant one. Stocchetti still has to find the right definition in his Recioto di Soaves; these wines are either too simplistic or do not succeed in expressing their fruit to the full. The best of the three presented is the Selezione '93, well-balanced and with aromas which are then echoed in the mouth.

● Piave Cabernet Ornella '94	❢❢	4
● Piave Merlot Ornella '94	❢❢	4
○ Sauvignon di Campodipietra '96	❢❢	3
○ Traminer di Campodipietra '96	❢❢	3*
○ Piave Chardonnay Ornella '96	❢	3
● Piave Raboso '93	❢	4
● Piave Cabernet Ornella '93	❢❢	3
○ Sauvignon di Campodipietra '95	❢❢	3
○ Traminer di Campodipietra '95	❢❢	3

○ Recioto di Soave Selezione '93	❢	4
○ Soave Classico '96	❢	2
○ Soave Classico Monte Carniga '96	❢	3
○ Soave Classico Monte Pressoni '96	❢	3
○ Recioto di Soave Corte Pittora '95		4

SOAVE (VR)

SOAVE (VR)

LEONILDO PIEROPAN
VIA CAMUZZONI, 3
37038 SOAVE (VR)
TEL. 045/6190171

SUAVIA
VIA CENTRO, 14
FRAZ. FITTÀ
37038 SOAVE (VR)
TEL. 045/7675089

The Soave La Rocca '95 is masterly: it contains an almost indefinable force, substance and energy which nevertheless appeals immediately to one's sensibilities, satisfying the ultimate desire for a combination of rich, granitic structure on one hand and elegance on the other. It is only apparently delicate and yielding, but is in reality firm, deep and incredibly complex - and at the same time supple and velvety. Its golden colour suggests manifest intensity, but its nose evolves gradually, yielding a complex and inviting gamut of aromas, including, most notably, dry mineral tones, a light floral nuance, sweet honeyed scents and a typical almondy note. The flavour fully lives up to expectations, with its well-structured, concentrated fruit and its rounded, lively finish. The Calvarino, on the other hand, is a model of fruity elegance, striking a balance as it does between the typical delicacy of a Soave and the fleshy fruitiness of a modern white wine. The clean-cut basic version demonstrates the light and lively style of Soave, which is capable of improving with time, acquiring complexity on the nose and a majestic breadth on the palate. Though not particularly long, it is very skilfully made. Leonildo and Teresita Pieropan have enjoyed considerable success in recent years, but their recent investments in the vineyard show that they are prepared to continue to strive hard to maintain their position among the leading producers of this fast-evolving zone.

We are rediscovering the wines of Soave, and reassessing a DOC area which, up until just a few years ago, was thought of merely as a source of very ordinary whites. We owe this renewed interest to those producers who never gave up caring for their vineyards, even when the price of grapes did not allow them to maintain a winery as well. The rewards these people are reaping today are not only financial, but also include the realization of every grower's dream: to see the fruits of a year of toil expressed in wines made by their own hands. The Tessari family has worked with courage and self-sacrifice to gear its vineyards increasingly for quality production and to install the necessary equipment to bring their winery up-to-date. Giovanni and his daughters share the quality of perseverance combined with a will to learn, and their efforts have been repaid by the constant improvements in their wines. This is true even of their basic Soave, which is perhaps the best in its category: this intensely-coloured white has an appealing rustic quality in its aromas, with their notes of plums, apricot kernels and mint. On the palate, the fleshy fruit evolves in dynamic fashion, well sustained by clean acidity. From the Monte Carbonare vineyard, on the other hand, comes a more complex style of Soave: the notes of citrus fruit are more evident, enveloped in creamy, ripe peach aromas; the fruit is balanced by a more restrained acidity, which gives way to long, mouth-filling softness. The Recioto di Soave, which also mirrors the estate's sensitive approach to winemaking, offers rich, but fairly simple fruit.

O Soave Cl. Sup. Vigneto La Rocca '95	♟♟♟	3
O Soave Cl. Sup. '96	♟♟	2
O Soave Cl. Sup. Vigneto Calvarino '96	♟♟	3
O Passito della Rocca '88	♟♟♟	5
O Passito della Rocca '93	♟♟♟	5
O Recioto di Soave Le Colombare '93	♟♟	4
O Soave Cl. Sup. Vigneto Calvarino '95	♟♟	3
O Soave Cl. Sup. Vigneto La Rocca '94	♟♟	3

O Soave Classico '96	♟♟	2
O Soave Classico Monte Carbonare '96	♟♟	3
O Recioto di Soave La Boccara '95	♟	5
O Soave Classico Monte Carbonare '95	♟♟	3

SOMMACAMPAGNA (VR) SONA (VR)

LE VIGNE DI SAN PIETRO
VIA S. PIETRO, 23
37066 SOMMACAMPAGNA (VR)
TEL. 045/510016

DANIELE ZAMUNER
VIA VALECCHIA, 40
37060 SONA (VR)
TEL. 045/6081090

Sud is the name of an explosively-flavoured white dessert wine which stunned us with its exciting Mediterranean exuberance, full of rich aromas and flavours enveloped in a structure which is traditional in its intensity, yet extremely modern in its finesse. Made from moscato fior d'arancio, it is the fruit of impassioned research which Carlo Nerozzi began some five years ago. Until last year, the wine was known as Due Cuori, and it is the intention of the producer to change its name each year should the characteristics of the wine itself warrant it. Sud is golden in colour, with greenish highlights; it has aromas of honey, flowers, and fresh and candied citrus fruits. Its sweetness is immediately apparent on the front palate and evolves gently in the mouth, never becoming cloying thanks to the fresh acidity; the finish is long and aromatic. Le Vigne di San Pietro also presented another eagerly-awaited wine this year, the Refolà, made from lightly dried cabernet sauvignon grapes: it has a very warm and mature nose, is rich (even in appearance), and shows attractive texture on the palate. We believe that the Refolà may soon take its place in the very top flight of Italian wines: the '93 certainly displayed sufficient extract, but lacked just a touch of breadth and complexity in its aromas. The Balconi Bianco confirmed its quality as a Riesling of essential aromatic purity: it displays mineral notes, accompanied by scents of peaches and pears; the acidity is the dominant element on the palate, but it also has clean, fleshy fruit and sound length. The Bianco di Custoza is also better this year: it has assumed a more complete style and a degree of fibre that will allow it to age better.

The Zamuner estate, situated between Valpolicella and Lake Garda, was created essentially in order to produce sparkling wines, but over the years its output has become more wide ranging. Even if its original products do not sometimes shine, we can nevertheless find points of interest in the still wines. The Bianco Montespada, made from the Custoza blend, is a case in point. This is a wine with a character which goes beyond mere simple freshness: its colour is an intense straw-yellow and its beautiful, concentrated nose displays apricots and almonds; on the palate we find crisp acidity, well-balanced by the richness of the alcohol and extract. Lively flavour is also the main characteristic of the other white, the Valecchia made from 100 percent chardonnay: the colour is again bright and the attractive nose includes hints of peaches, hazelnuts and aromatic herbs. The fruit is impressive on the front palate, but does not follow through and evolve, a weakness which brought down its overall score. We did not expect anything more than a pleasant fruitiness from the vinous and quaffable Rosso Montespada. We shall wait for next year's Guide to review the other red, the Valecchia, which last year, with its '94 vintage, earned impressive marks. As we suggested, the sparkling wines were not on top form this year, especially as regards their clarity of fruit: both the Brut (made entirely with pinot nero) and the Extra Brut '91 rated between a mere mention and One Glass. The more vivacious Brut Rosé is floral and appealing on the nose, and well-balanced and elegant on the palate.

○ Sud '95	▼▼▼	5
○ I Balconi Bianco '95	▼▼	4
● Refolà Cabernet Sauvignon '93	▼▼	5
○ Bianco di Custoza '96	▼	2
● Bardolino '96		2
⊙ Bardolino Chiaretto '96		3
○ Moscato Due Cuori '94	♀♀	5
● Refolà Cabernet Sauvignon '92	♀♀	5
○ I Balconi Bianco '94	♀♀	4

○ Bianco Montespada '96	▼	2*
○ Bianco Valecchia '96	▼	4
⊙ Spumante Metodo Classico Brut Rosé '92	▼	4
○ Spumante Metodo Classico Extra Brut '91	▼	4
○ Spumante Metodo Classico Brut Pinot Nero		4
● Rosso Montespada '96		2
● Rosso Valecchia '94	♀♀	3
○ Spumante Metodo Classico '91	♀♀	4

SUSEGANA (TV)

Conte Collalto
Via XXIV Maggio, 1
31058 Susegana (TV)
tel. 0438/738241

The Collalto estate is well known in the Piave and is not a new discovery either for the Guide, but it is the real revelation in the Veneto this year. All last year's good intentions have been transformed into satisfying results, as the considerable viticultural resources of this estate at Susegana begin to bear fruit. The red wines are the speciality of the house and if in recent vintages the Cabernets held pride of place, this year the choice is wider. The common distinguishing characteristic of the entire range is a perfectly-balanced, soft fleshiness of fruit that is modern and fresh. The Incrocio Manzoni Rosso '96 stands out as the best of the assortment, with its intense ruby colour; on the nose it offers fresh, youthful blackberry and on the palate it reveals really satisfying and attractive rounded fruit. The '95 version is a little bit tougher and has higher acidity, but the overall impressions are equally positive. Another wine which has shown remarkable improvement is the '95 Wildbacher, which goes beyond its traditional simple, herbaceous varietal style to become more complex and challenging. Of the two Cabernets, it is the Riserva which earns the best score: it has concentrated colour and although its bouquet still has to open up fully, it already promises a great deal; the positive fruit on the palate is underpinned by firm tannins. The Cabernet Torrai scored only marginally lower: it has a nice supple style and only lacks a tiny bit of verve. Only the Conegliano Rosso was less than we expected. Among the whites, the elegant and balanced Colli di Conegliano and the floral and spicy Incrocio Manzoni Bianco were especially pleasing.

●	Incrocio Manzoni 2.15 '95	🍷🍷	2*
●	Incrocio Manzoni 2.15 '96	🍷🍷	2*
●	Piave Cabernet Riserva '93	🍷🍷	4
●	Wildbacher '95	🍷🍷	2*
●	Cabernet Torrai '93	🍷	4
○	Colli di Conegliano Bianco '96	🍷	2
○	Incrocio Manzoni 6.0.13 '96	🍷	2
●	Cabernet Torrai '92	🍸🍸	4
●	Incrocio Manzoni 2.15 '94	🍸	2
●	Piave Cabernet Riserva '92	🍸	4
●	Wildbacher '94	🍸	3

VALDOBBIADENE (TV)

Desiderio Bisol & Figli
Via Fol, 33
Fraz. S. Stefano
31049 Valdobbiadene (TV)
tel. 0423/900552-900138

The Prosecco Garnei embodies the very essence of the prettiness and spontaneity of the Marca Trevigiana; it conveys the sweep of its busy yet gently rolling hills; it is a distillation of the area's verdant freshness which gives the taster the impression of capturing the area in his glass. The Garnei's style is remarkably satisfying: it is an excellent example of that lightness of expression that is fundamental to Prosecco, while also demonstrating the balance and depth which are the characteristics of any fine wine. Its colour is a bright straw-yellow, and the mousse is perfect; ripe apple lies at the heart of its mouth-watering aromas. There is a suggestion of well-balanced sweetness on the palate, its long, soft fruit being underpinned by perfectly integrated acidity. Turning to the other wines, the entire Bisol range shows its usual high level of quality. The Prosecco Extra Dry Colmei reveals an appealing scent of citrus fruits, combined with excellent tightness of fruit on the palate. The incisive style of the Prosecco Brut Crede, with its green, youthful aromas, stands in marked contrast to the mellow gentleness of the Prosecco Dry Salis. The fruit of the Cartizze is precise yet mouth-filling, that of the extremely enjoyable Prosecco Extra Dry Vigneti del Fol is measured and clean. The Prosecco Tranquillo Molera again demonstrates its reliability, while the '90 Metodo Classico sparkling wine shows absolute high quality.

○	Cartizze	🍷🍷	4
○	Cuvée del Fondatore Eliseo Bisol '90	🍷🍷	5
○	Prosecco di Valdobbiadene Dry Garnei '96	🍷🍷	4
○	Prosecco di Valdobbiadene Dry Salis	🍷🍷	3
○	Prosecco di Valdobbiadene Extra Dry Colmei	🍷🍷	3
○	Prosecco di Valdobbiadene Spumante Brut Crede	🍷🍷	3
○	Prosecco di Valdobbiadene Extra Dry Vigneti del Fol	🍷	3
○	Prosecco di Valdobbiadene Tranquillo Molera '96	🍷	3

VALDOBBIADENE (TV)

VALDOBBIADENE (TV)

BORTOLIN SPUMANTI
VIA MENEGAZZI, 5
FRAZ. S. STEFANO
31049 VALDOBBIADENE (TV)
TEL. 0423/900135

BORTOLOMIOL
VIA GARIBALDI, 166
31049 VALDOBBIADENE (TV)
TEL. 0423/975494

After skilfully taking advantage of the excellent '95 harvest, Valeriano Bortolin's winery confirms its position as one of the best in the zone by also producing good quality wines in '96. The fine potential shown last year in some experimental vinifications of grapes from the new Rua di Feletto vineyard has now been realized in the Prosecco Extra Dry Rù, probably the best wine in its category. It reveals a subtle bead as well as good depth of colour; the aromas evolve well on the nose, combining sweetish nuances with drier notes. The refined fruit develops on the palate, showing just a hint of sweetness, and an almost sumptuous balance and length of flavour. The rounder Prosecco Dry is of similar quality, confirming its outstanding score in last year's Guide, with its typical floral aroma and harmony on the palate. The Prosecco Extra Dry, the wine of which Bortolin produces the biggest quantities, comes very close to breaking the 80-point barrier. It shows considerably more than its usual correct style: it in fact reveals very satisfying verve in its bouquet and dynamic, lively and long-lasting fruit in the mouth. The only wine to score less well than last year is the Cartizze whose aromas, though clean, seemed a little less positive than usual. The two Brut wines, however, are extremely reliable: the straightforward Prosecco maintains its stimulating clean style on both nose and palate while the Vigneto del Convento, a sparkling wine made from a 30/70 blend of chardonnay and prosecco, stands out for its vivid freshness of flavour and its rousing finish. Valeriano is certainly preparing a successful future for his children Claudia, Andrea and Diego, who have recently joined him in the business.

Giuliano Bortolomiol, one of the fathers of modern Prosecco, began making sparkling wines in 1948. Since the early days he has sought to bring out the best in the zone, and he still represents a model for many producers. Today, at the age of 75, he has assembled a staff which, under his expert guidance, is constantly improving the quality of the winery's production. The most important ideas come from his daughter Maria Elena, ideas then put into practice by the young winemaker Gianfranco Zanon who this year presented a very satisfactory range of wines. Bortolomiol produces around a million and a half bottles, purchasing mainly grapes, but also musts and wines; the quality control for the various bottlings has become extremely rigorous. The Prosecco Selezione Banda Rossa is the winery's most representative product, a soft and elegant Extra Dry, characterized by rich, fruity aromas; it is well-defined on the palate, and boasts a well-integrated and long-lasting mousse. The Prosecco Brut, which is better than in previous years, also displays a very subtle perlage; it is lively on the nose, and shows positive fruit on the palate and a fairly long finish. The basic Prosecco Extra Dry is also surprising. It has well-outlined aromas of apples and almonds, and there is an appealing harmony between the carbon dioxide and the fruit. The Cartizze, a Bortolomiol speciality, has a delicate straw-yellow colour and another long-lasting mousse; the aromas of peaches and pears are echoed on the palate, where the fruit has a definite sweet vein. Only the Prosecco Tranquillo left us somewhat unconvinced, due to a lack of character.

O Prosecco di Valdobbiadene Dry	♼♼	3*
O Prosecco di Valdobbiadene Extra Dry Rù	♼♼	3*
O Cartizze	♼	4
O Prosecco di Valdobbiadene Brut	♼	3
O Prosecco di Valdobbiadene Extra Dry	♼	3
O Spumante Brut Vigneto del Convento	♼	3

O Cartizze	♼	4
O Prosecco di Valdobbiadene Brut	♼	2
O Prosecco di Valdobbiadene Extra Dry	♼	2*
O Prosecco di Valdobbiadene Extra Dry Banda Rossa	♼	3*

VALDOBBIADENE (TV)

VALDOBBIADENE (TV)

CANEVEL SPUMANTI
VIA CALPIANDRE, 25
31049 VALDOBBIADENE (TV)
TEL. 0423/975940

CANTINA PRODUTTORI
DI VALDOBBIADENE
VIA PER S. GIOVANNI, 65
FRAZ. BIGOLINO
31049 VALDOBBIADENE (TV)
TEL. 0423/982070

One of the great qualities of this winery is its ability to come to terms with the characteristics of a vintage, and to bring out the best from it. If the hot '95 vintage gave us broad, soft Proseccos, the cooler '96 yielded more lively and fragrant sparklers; Roberto De Lucchi is always able to handle the variables and at the same time maintain the house style, with its particular maturity on the nose, a bouquet both appealing and satisfying. We enjoyed the Prosecco Brut, one of the best in its category. It has a straw-yellow colour and a rich mousse; on the nose, youthful green apple mingles with sweeter scents of pears and bananas, while in contrast to the softness of the aromas, the flavour is frank, crisp and dry. The Prosecco Tranquillo, another wine with a marked personality, is the best yet produced by Canevel: it combines a striking straw colour with refreshing aromas, in which one detects herbs and almonds as well as varietal peach and pear. The wine develops on the palate with balance, vitality and a surprisingly long finish. The sparkling Prosecco Extra Dry - light and with perfectly-integrated carbon dioxide - shows the elegance of which this wine from the Treviso area is capable when it is really true to type. The Millesimato is as delicate as ever, refined on the nose but slightly sweeter than on other occasions. Canevel's good all-round performance is evident also in a very pleasant Verdiso, and in the Cartizze which although perhaps less massively fruity than usual remains a model of reliability.

The Cantina Produttori di Valdobbiadene offers the clearest example of the growth which this zone has seen in the last few years. Last year we noted that the quality of this cooperative is not only to be found in the top of the range Val d'Oca wines: in fact the standard Prosecco Brut today ranks among the best of the kind. It is an impeccably made sparkling wine, given real definition by a subtle and long-lasting mousse; appealing nose, with a rich, sweetish vein, and a firmer style on the palate, where good fruit gives concentration and length. This year, the Val d'Oca range includes two notable products, the Prosecco Extra Dry and the Cartizze. The former is very intense and positive, with a winning aromatic bouquet reminiscent of peaches and pears. It also has full fruit on the palate and stands out for its splendid, warm, Mediterranean finish. The Cartizze has a well-balanced rather dry flavour, with a youthful bouquet and a very elegant overall style. The Prosecco Tranquillo, which is no longer merely an honest, straightforward wine but is becoming increasingly tasty, shows typical, gentle varietal flavour and aromas. The Prosecco Frizzante is in a similar vein: it is beautifully clean, and its carbon dioxide is very pleasantly integrated. Director Aldo Franchi's aim to combine modern technology with more rigorous grape selection is showing results: the winery will enjoy even greater success when this goal has been fully achieved.

O Prosecco di Valdobbiadene Brut	♟♟	2
O Prosecco di Valdobbiadene Extra Dry	♟♟	3
O Prosecco di Valdobbiadene Tranquillo '96	♟♟	2
O Cartizze	♟	4
O Prosecco di Valdobbiadene Millesimato '96	♟	4
O Verdiso '96	♟	2

O Cartizze Val d'Oca	♟♟	4
O Prosecco di Valdobbiadene Val d'Oca Extra Dry	♟♟	3*
O Prosecco di Valdobbiadene Brut	♟	2
O Prosecco di Valdobbiadene Val d'Oca Frizzante	♟	3
O Prosecco di Valdobbiadene Val d'Oca Tranquillo	♟	3

VALDOBBIADENE (TV)

COL VETORAZ
VIA TRESIESE, 1
FRAZ. S. STEFANO
31049 VALDOBBIADENE (TV)
TEL. 0423/975291

The '96 vintage was, once again, a very happy one for Col Vetoraz. Careful tasting of the wines of the estate headed up by Loris Dall'Acqua reveals both the indisputable quality of its vineyards and the sophisticated vinification techniques employed. The '96 Proseccos are all technically very clean - a quality which cannot be taken for granted in the area. However, their most pleasing feature is the varietal character to be found in every bottle, beginning with the Cartizze, one of the best wines of this year. It has a straw colour, with a bright golden tinge; on the nose, it offers complex aromas, with ripe apricot and attractive, fresh, floral scents; on the palate it has full, rich but not cloying fruit, and a delightful finish. The similarly well made Prosecco Brut scored only a few points less: its principal quality is its perfect balance; the colour, bouquet and flavour all reveal a combination of freshness and roundness which evolves with great richness into a long finish. Another exemplary bouquet - positive and broad, richly fruity, a real model of immediacy - is that of the Prosecco Extra Dry: these aromas give way to splendidly well-balanced fruit on the palate. The Prosecco Tranquillo Tresiese also offers marked varietal aroma with light but long-lasting fruit flavour and pleasant fresh acidity.

VALDOBBIADENE (TV)

LE COLTURE
VIA FOL, 5
FRAZ. S. STEFANO
31049 VALDOBBIADENE (TV)
TEL. 0423/900192

In order to gauge the quality of a company which produces sparkling Prosecco, it is best to examine the wine made in the greatest volume, the classic Extra Dry. Since this is the most widely produced style, it is common to find different bottlings released during the course of the year, a practice which aims to guarantee the constant availability of a fresh and fragrant wine. The Le Colture winery is in the spotlight precisely for its Prosecco Extra Dry, and we were able to verify the consistent quality of all the lots released. Its colour is straw-yellow, made even brighter by the carbon dioxide; the nose is fairly restrained to begin with, but evolves gently with increasingly evident peach, pear and floral tones; the fruit on the palate - its best feature - is full, well-balanced, and promptly echoes the bouquet. The Ruggeri brothers' best-known wine, the Prosecco Dry Funer, offers fruit which is less rich and less sweet than usual this year; its style is subtle and gentle, barely spicy on the nose, with a fine balance between the sugars and the carbon dioxide, and a fairly long finish. The Prosecco Tranquillo Masarè, with its characterful apple and pear on the nose, and its delicate, very pleasant flavour, has improved compared to previous vintages. The Incrocio Manzoni has a floral and quite complex bouquet: it is not a particularly concentrated white, but the fruit evolves well and its finish is highly enjoyable. The elegant and well-made Prosecco Brut also wins a One Glass rating. The Cartizze, a wine renowned generally for its inconsistency, failed to repeat the excellent performance of the '95 vintage.

O Cartizze	♈♈	4
O Prosecco di Valdobbiadene Brut	♈♈	3
O Prosecco di Valdobbiadene Extra Dry	♈♈	3
O Prosecco di Valdobbiadene Tranquillo Tresiese '96	♈	3

O Prosecco di Valdobbiadene Extra Dry	♈♈	3
O Incrocio Manzoni 6.0.13 '96	♈	3
O Prosecco di Valdobbiadene Brut	♈	3
O Prosecco di Valdobbiadene Dry Funer	♈	3
O Prosecco di Valdobbiadene Tranquillo Masarè '96	♈	3
O Cartizze		5

VALDOBBIADENE (TV)

ANGELO RUGGERI
VIA FOL, 18
FRAZ. S. STEFANO
31049 VALDOBBIADENE (TV)
TEL. 0423/900235

This small Valdobbiadene company has, for years, offered reliable quality and a rigorous respect for varietal style. The incontrovertible quality of the vineyards worked by Vittore and Remigio Ruggeri is matched by winemaking techniques which are constantly being brought up to date. The best wine of the range presented this year is a Spumante Brut made from prosecco and chardonnay, which is capable of combining the aromatic qualities of the two varieties with a spankingly clean flavour: a result due also to the perfect integration of the carbon dioxide, which gives added length to the fruit. The enjoyable, delicate Prosecco Extra Dry has elegant fruit and good length. The Cartizze, which has been a speciality of the firm for some years now, has richer, more intense aromas; it also has well-built fruit on the palate, where the sweetness is held in check by the mousse. The carbon dioxide is, on the other hand, a bit dominant in the Prosecco Dry made with grapes from the Funer vineyard, although the quality of the fruit is evident in the richness of the nose, with its typical scents of pears and almonds, and the length of the finish. The very well-made Prosecco Frizzante does not, however, display much character. All of the Ruggeris' wines still offer good value for money, even if the average cost of grapes and wines in the zone has risen considerably in the last two years.

VALDOBBIADENE (TV)

RUGGERI & C.
VIA PRÀ FONTANA
31049 VALDOBBIADENE (TV)
TEL. 0423/975716

The qualities which strike one most, reviewing one's tastings notes from this company, is the unrivalled consistency of the wines, and the winemaker's ability to give each one irreproachable balance and clarity of expression. The credit for this goes to Paolo Bisol, known to all and sundry as "the Ibex of the vineyards": the nickname, given to him by a colleague because of his thin, long-limbed appearance, refers also to his role in tirelessly hunting down skilled growers and persuading them to sell him their grapes. The fruits of this invaluable work, which involves a combination of human relations and viticultural expertise, are evident in every one of the million and a half bottles produced each year. The quality of the Prosecco Extra Dry Oro, of which around 600,000 bottles are made, no longer surprises us. One recognizes the skill with which this wine is made in its bright colour and in its well-integrated mousse, but also in its positive fruity aroma and its delicious length. The other Extra Dry, the Giustino B., is very different. Made from 100 percent prosecco grapes - an oddity, seeing that generally producers take advantage of the permitted addition of pinot bianco or chardonnay - it shows greater richness even in its colour; the inviting and essential bouquet is well-sculpted and the fruit on the palate unrolls to display surprising complexity. The Santo Stefano, the more rounded dry Prosecco, is again rich and mouth-filling: though it does not show the depth of the '95 vintage, it yields its creamy sweetness with sensuousness and balance. The similarly-styled Cartizze has extremely fresh lime-like scents on the nose and fruit which evolves beautifully on the palate. The Frizzante version is one to watch, but we were not totally convinced by the Tranquillo.

○	Angelo Ruggeri Spumante Brut	♟♟	2*
○	Cartizze	♟	3
○	Prosecco di Valdobbiadene Dry Funer	♟	2
○	Prosecco di Valdobbiadene Extra Dry	♟	2
○	Prosecco di Valdobbiadene Frizzante		1

○	Cartizze	♟♟	4
○	Prosecco di Valdobbiadene Dry Santo Stefano	♟♟	3*
○	Prosecco di Valdobbiadene Extra Dry Giustino B. '96	♟♟	4
○	Prosecco di Valdobbiadene Extra Dry Oro	♟♟	3*
○	Prosecco di Valdobbiadene Frizzante	♟	2

VALDOBBIADENE (TV)

S. Eurosia di Geronazzo
Via della Cima, 2
Fraz. S. Pietro di Barbozza
31049 Valdobbiadene (TV)
tel. 0423/973236

The pleasant surprise provided by the wines of S. Eurosia last year was repeated in the tasting of the latest vintage. Strong point of this winery at San Pietro is the meticulous quality of the vinification carried out by director Giuseppe Geronazzo (witness to this is the fact that certain major Alto Adige producers entrust Geronazzo with the second fermentation in bottle of their sparkling wines). The estate produces only a very small proportion of its grape requirements, the rest, as often happens in these parts, is purchased from a large number of trusted growers. With the '96 vintage, production reached 400,000 bottles, embracing all the typical major wine styles of the area. The most interesting wine in the range is the Prosecco S. Eurosia Brut, a real combination of power and elegance, with fragrant, clean scents of apples and measured fruit on the palate which is lifted by superbly-integrated carbon dioxide. The Prosecco Extra Dry is more exuberant and impetuous; its bouquet shows, besides the peach and pear notes typical of the variety, appealing citrus aromas. It has a delicacy and balance on the palate which bear witness to the quality of the fruit. Another well-made wine is the fresh and deliciously quaffable Prosecco Tranquillo. The Cartizze has a bright, deep colour and a rich aroma, as well as a well-modulated, unexaggerated sweetness, and a harmony which is the trump card of the entire S. Eurosia range.

VALDOBBIADENE (TV)

Tanorè
Via Mont
Fraz. S. Pietro di Barbozza
31049 Valdobbiadene (TV)
tel. 0423/975770

Located in the heart of the Cartizze appellation, in an enchanting spot which immediately reveals its viticultural heritage, Renato and Sergio Follador's estate is a small, but important, rising star in the zone. The estate, called Tanorè after the nickname of the Follador brothers' father, comprises around seven hectares and vinifies, almost exclusively, the family's own grapes: this allows the brothers to keep close control on quality from the vine to the bottle. Production is concentrated on sparkling wines, which are released only when the carbon dioxide has had a chance to integrate fully, and harmoniously, with the wine in question. The Prosecco Extra Dry was tasted a number of times, and always stood out as one of the best of its type. It has a straw colour, made even richer by the creaminess of the mousse, and intense scents of pears lie at the heart of its lively, yet broadly aromatic and rich nose. The fruit evolves nicely on the palate, lifted by the perlage, and the finish is clean and satisfying. The aromas of the Prosecco Brut are more piquant, and combine attractive green notes with flowers and scents of citrus fruit; these notes are also apparent on the palate, where the fruit is nimble and lively, and has good evolution, leaving a delicate, almondy finish. The Cartizze is also of the same excellent quality: everything about it is appealing, right down to its deep, bright colour, enlivened by the fine mousse. On the nose it offers soft, well-knit fruit and on the palate the crisp acidity ably cuts through the sweetness, leaving a long, harmonious finish.

○ Prosecco di Valdobbiadene S. Eurosia Brut	♙♙	2*
○ Prosecco di Valdobbiadene Extra Dry	♙♙	2*
○ Cartizze	♙	4
○ Prosecco di Valdobbiadene Tranquillo '96	♙	2

○ Cartizze	♙♙	4
○ Prosecco di Valdobbiadene Extra Dry	♙♙	2*
○ Prosecco di Valdobbiadene Brut	♙	2

VALEGGIO SUL MINCIO (VR)   VERONA

CORTE GARDONI
LOC. GARDONI
37063 VALEGGIO SUL MINCIO (VR)
TEL. 045/7950382

BALTIERI
VIA VILLA PIATTI, 5
LOC. MIZZOLE
37030 VERONA
TEL. 045/557616

The Corte Gardoni estate plays a leading role in the varied panorama of the wineries around Lake Garda for two important reasons. Firstly because it produces the classic wines of the area with rare dedication, turning out DOC products with real personality, but also because of its innovative "vini da tavola" . These are wines which Gianni Piccoli makes with the humility of someone who is always prepared to learn, and the support of his sons, Mattia and Stefano, who are now involved in every phase of production, from the cultivation of the many vineyards right through to bottling. Their care may be witnessed in all their wines, starting with the two Bardolinos, once again the best of their respective categories. The '95 Superiore has the structure and fruit of a good Valpolicella, seasoned with a spicy freshness that is typical of Garda wines. It has a lively ruby colour; on the nose, one finds scents of red berry fruits, and the fruit evolves elegantly on the palate. The single-vineyard Le Fontane has a more fragrant, youthful nose, with aromas which return in the nimbly-structured fruit on the palate. The only negative impression this year was created by the Bianco di Custoza, there being a certain unevenness between the samples we tasted. However the I Fenili '93 - the best dessert wine ever produced by the Piccoli family - fully made up for this. In recent years the Fenili has displayed the ripe, positive fruit you would expect in a wine made from semi-dried garganega grapes, but in the '93 vintage it has also acquired an absolutely irresistible finesse and Mediterranean charm, characterized by scents of citron and candied hazelnuts, and crisp, lively yet concentrated fruit on the palate.

After keeping a close eye on this winery - one of the most promising in Valpolicella - for a couple of years, we have this year decided to include it in the Guide. Baltieri is located at Mizzole, in the so-called "extended" Valpolicella zone in which we continue to find new, quality-conscious producers. Here we are to the east of Verona, where the soil is predominantly calcareous and stony and produces wines which combine good structure with rich aromas. Baltieri owns two farms: Il Bosco, of around 30 hectares, which yields Amarone and Recioto, and the ten hectares or so of I Ronchi, dedicated to the production of Valpolicella Superiore and to that of innovative red and white wines. The vinification and ageing techniques employed here reflect all the developments that have been made in Italy in the last ten years. One is aware right from the colour and the bouquet of Baltieri's wines that what is in the glass is a modern interpretation of the classic wines of Valpolicella, but on the palate the traditional richness obtained by drying the grapes is by no means lacking. The Amarone is an opaque ruby shade; on the nose, the sweet notes of cherries under alcohol combine with bay leaf and black pepper. On the palate, the wine shows vigorous, rich fruit, and good depth and evolution. Its slightly harsh finish, influenced perhaps by the wood, is the only feature which needs to be perfected; the body and structure of this Amarone are really exceptional. The Recioto is similarly impressive: it is again very densely coloured, with extremely lively aromas of black berry fruits; on the palate it is uncloyingly sweet, silky and long. The Valpolicella Superiore demonstrates its usual elegance, and though not particularly richly-structured displays delicate, long fruit aroma.

●	Bardolino Superiore '95	▼▼	2*
○	Passito Bianco I Fenili '93	▼▼	4
●	Bardolino Cl. Le Fontane '96	▼	2
○	Bianco di Custoza '96		2
☉	Bardolino Chiaretto '96		2
●	Bardolino Superiore '94	♆♆	2
●	Rosso di Corte '92	♆♆	4
●	Bardolino Cl. Le Fontane '95	♆	2
○	Passito Bianco I Fenili '92	♆	4

●	Amarone '93	▼▼	5
●	Recioto della Valpolicella '93	▼▼	4
●	Valpolicella Superiore '93	▼	3*

VERONA

BOLLA
P.zza CITTADELLA, 3
37122 VERONA
TEL. 045/8670911

The Amarone is again becoming Bolla's most representative wine. We had already noticed, even in the version from the difficult '89 vintage, a marked improvement on previous releases, and also a greater attention to detail. With the '90 presented this year, Bolla appears to be launching an salutary project aimed at improving the quality of the full range of wines, including the most simple ones, which still represent the weak link in their overall production. To deal with the Amarone first, it has a very concentrated, youthful colour; the refined and elegant nose displays the richness typical of grapes which have been dried, with scents of cherry brandy, cocoa and roasted hazelnuts; the palate mirrors this combination of intensity and finesse, with its good tannic backbone and dense, fleshy fruit which echoes that found in the bouquet. In short, this is an exciting modern Amarone. Another wine which has improved is the basic Soave, which was itself, once upon a time, the real standard bearer of the company. Though not a white of any great structure, it nevertheless displays more than mere clean, straightforward fruit, offering a fresh, positive bouquet and good liveliness on the palate. The Sauvignon and the Merlot were a little disappointing: they were certainly well-made, but could, in our opinion, show a bit more personality. The Cabernet Sauvignon Creso is as good as one could expect from the '91 vintage, with a clean but not very concentrated nose, and attractive, supple fruit on the palate. The Valpolicella Superiore Le Pojane is also appealing.

VERONA

CECILIA BERETTA
VIA S. EUROSIA
FRAZ. MIZZOLE
37030 VERONA
TEL. 045/8402021

The Cecilia Beretta estate was not able to repeat its fine performance of last year, when three out of its four wines earned Two Glass ratings. This can, however, be put down mainly to the fact that this year the wines came from a string of not particularly good vintages. The '94 Valpolicella Superiores suffered most: both are very well-made, but lacking the zip and concentration they have shown in previous vintages. The Roccolo di Mizzole has a medium-deep colour; its bouquet is positive, with hints of vanilla alongside red berry fruit scents; on the palate, the entry is good, but the fruit does not evolve in such a way as to make the wine really satisfying. The Terre di Cariano offers more neutral sensations: its undoubtedly well-structured fruit seems to be held in check by the wood. The Soave Terre di Brognoligo is evidently made from carefully selected grapes, but is rather closed and incapable of displaying its true colours. The highlight of the range is the Amarone Terre di Cariano '93, extremely elegant as usual on the nose, with fruit which evolves well on the palate and which is well balanced by the typical high alcohol and the rich, soft tannins. The Recioto di Soave released for the first time this year, though certainly not without merit, does not yet seen to have had the benefit of the care and attention that might transform it into a great dessert wine.

●	Amarone '90	♥♥	4
●	Creso Rosso '91	♥	5
●	Merlot Colforte '96	♥	3
●	Valpolicella Superiore Le Pojane Jago '94	♥	3
○	Sauvignon Lunaia '96	♥	3
○	Soave Classico '96	♥	1*
●	Amarone Riserva '89	♥♥	4
●	Creso Rosso '90	♥♥	5
●	Valpolicella Superiore Jago '93	♥	3

●	Amarone Terre di Cariano '93	♥♥	5
●	Valpolicella Superiore Roccolo di Mizzole '94	♥	3
●	Valpolicella Superiore Terre di Cariano '94	♥	3
○	Recioto di Soave Terre di Brognoligo '93	♥	4
○	Soave Terre di Brognoligo '96	♥	3
●	Amarone Terre di Cariano '90	♥♥	5
●	Valpolicella Terre di Cariano '93	♥♥	3

VERONA

VERONA

MONTRESOR
VIA CA' DEI COZZI, 16
37124 VERONA
TEL. 045/913399

F.LLI PASQUA
VIA BELVIGLIERI, 30
37131 VERONA
TEL. 045/8402111

The classic wines of Lake Garda (as was the case last year) are those which best express the potential of this winery. Both the basic Bianco di Custoza and the Montefiera are at the top of their category, offering different, but equally successful, interpretations of this DOC. The former is bright, clean and appealingly fresh and lively and long on the palate. The Montefiera has more depth of colour and more breadth on the nose, with hints of pineapple and flowers; it has surprisingly rich fruit on the palate, underpinned by fresh acidity. The Lugana, on the other hand, does not live up to the '95: it is rather neutral on the nose, the flavour is disappointing and it lacks its usual personality. Similarly unsatisfactory is the Cabernet Sauvignon Campo Madonna, but its faltering performance can be put down to the '96 vintage which, in the Verona area, was especially unkind to the reds. To be honest, neither were we really convinced by the Rustego '95, obtained exclusively from late-harvested Corvina grapes: we remembered it being more clean and intense, and this time found it a bit short. Good results were achieved by the Pinot Grigio and by the chardonnay-based sparkling wine, made by the "Charmat lungo" method. These are both made with a firm but gentle hand; two examples of delicious quaffing wines. The Valpolicella Superiore, the Amarone and the Recioto were, as usual, well-made but considering the ambitions which this winery has nursed for some years now, we would like to see a little more élan and richness from them.

A level of quality ranging from average-to-good is gradually spreading across the whole of Pasqua's ever-growing range: we did not find any real stars this year, but Giancarlo Zanel's winemaking - under the supervision of the Pasqua cousins - cannot be faulted. As an example, we cite a wine which scores well, year in year out, the Soave Montegrande. This is the ideal bottle for anyone who is seeking a fresh, young wine, but nevertheless wants a product with good fleshy fruit and a certain satisfying richness. Its colour is bright straw and its scents of peaches and pears mingle with herbal tones; on the palate the fruit is lively, becoming full and pleasantly long-lasting. The Lugana Ca' Nova - a white which very nearly earned a Two Glass rating - is crisper and drier than the Soave, yet with a charm that renders its aromas and flavours very attractive. To close the white wine section, we draw your attention to a surprising Trentino Müller Thurgau, the quintessence of charming, floral fruit. One might have expected more from the Amarone, but it cannot have been easy to deal with the fruit of the vintages presented. The Villa Borghetti '92 has all the basic requisites of a good, full-bodied red, but lacks a certain style on the nose and palate that would make it into a really fine wine. The '93 Casterna, designed to combine ease of drinking with Amarone's characteristic richness, revealed rather insufficient depth of fruit; it was not wholly convincing. From this outstanding vineyard site in the commune of Fumane also comes a pleasant, medium-bodied Valpolicella Superiore with elegant floral aromas. The Morago Cabernet seems to have suffered from the '94 vintage, and is thin and short: it did not live up to our expectations.

O	Bianco di Custoza '96	♟	2*
O	Bianco di Custoza Montefiera '96	♟	3
O	Chardonnay Spumante	♟	2
O	Lugana Lissara Vecchia '96	♟	2
O	Valdadige Pinot Grigio '96	♟	2*
●	Amarone Riserva del Fondatore '92	♟	5
●	Recioto della Valpolicella '95	♟	4
●	Valpolicella Superiore Capitel Crosara '95	♟	3
●	Cabernet Sauvignon Campo Madonna '96		3
●	Rustego '95		3
●	Amarone Capitel della Crosara '90	♟♟	5
●	Amarone della Cantina Privata '90	♟	5

O	Soave Vigneti di Montegrande '96	♟♟	3*
O	Lugana Vigneto Ca' Nova '96	♟	3
O	Trentino Müller Thurgau '96	♟	3
●	Amarone Vigneti di Casterna '93	♟	5
●	Amarone Villa Borghetti '92	♟	5
●	Valpolicella Superiore Vigneti di Casterna '94	♟	3
●	Valpolicella Superiore Villa Borghetti '94	♟	3
●	Morago Cabernet Sauvignon '94		5
●	Amarone Vigneti di Casterna '90	♟♟	5
●	Morago Cabernet Sauvignon '93	♟♟	5
●	Valpolicella Superiore Vigneti di Casterna '93	♟♟	3

VIDOR (TV)

ADAMI
VIA ROVEDE, 21
FRAZ. COLBERTALDO
31020 VIDOR (TV)
TEL. 0423/982110

The Adami brothers fully confirm their splendid performance of last year: all their wines come out at the top of their respective categories. For at least three years now, they have been following a quality plan aimed at up-grading their wines, based on increasingly more severe grape selection and this has certainly contributed to the fine results. The other major factor is Franco Adami's unquestionable skill as a winemaker. If the '95 vintage was characterised by the outstanding intrinsic quality of the grape, the more difficult '96 was handled with the patience and care of a winemaker who really understands both the virtues and the limits of prosecco. The grapes were rigorously selected and the wines allowed to express their natural potential, without forcing them to be something they are not. In this way, the Adamis have produced a Prosecco Brut of unmatchable finesse, with a subtle balance of freshness and softness, and with frank aroma which reveals a spicy vitality and a fleshy fruitiness. The more creamy and mouth-filling Prosecco Extra Dry has perfectly integrated carbon dioxide, which both highlights the aromatic qualities of the wine and acts as a vehicle for the evolution of the flavour. The most exciting wine in the range however is Adami's Cartizze, the best we tasted this year. This sumptuous, full-bodied wine not only displays the most refined of bouquets, graced with notes of hazelnut and melon, but it also reveals exquisitely tight texture on the palate. The Prosecco Dry Giardino, though not as rich as the '95, again shows its balance on the palate, and reveals those particular greenish notes on the nose which have made it famous. The still Prosecco Tranquillo from the same vineyard is more intensely flavoured this year, while the incrocio Manzoni is notable for its crisp, straightforward style.

O	Cartizze	🍷🍷	4
O	Prosecco di Valdobbiadene Brut	🍷🍷	3*
O	Prosecco di Valdobbiadene Extra Dry	🍷🍷	3
O	Prosecco di Valdobbiadene Dry Giardino	🍷	3
O	Prosecco di Valdobbiadene Tranquillo Giardino '96	🍷	3
O	Incrocio Manzoni 6.0.13 Le Portelle '96		3

VIDOR (TV)

BRONCA
VIA MARTIRI, 20
FRAZ. COLBERTALDO
31020 VIDOR (TV)
TEL. 0423/987201-987009

The Bronca sisters' winery, which made its first appearance in the Guide last year, confirms its status as one of the most interesting new producers in the area. To make a good Prosecco once is not all that difficult, but to ensure constant quality year in, year out, is much harder. This challenge has been taken up and won by this winery at Colbertaldo, by taking full advantage of good vineyards and a simple, straightforward approach to winemaking. This is based, as far as Piero Balcon is concerned, on healthy grapes, obtained from the estate's own vineyards, and also on the rigorous selection of cuvées for the "prise de mousse". When he is not wholly satisfied with the contents of a particular tank, he merely sells it off. The result is an excellent Prosecco Brut, fresh and crisp on the nose, with dry, long-lasting fruit on the palate, sustained by the elegant perlage, and a clean, aromatic finish. Ersiliana and Antonella Bronca's Prosecco Frizzante is, we believe, the best we tried this year. One can certainly taste the quality of the grapes, and the nose shows variety and complexity. On the palate, the subtle carbon dioxide firmly underpins the nimble fruit. The Prosecco Tranquillo, which is almost as good, has a broad, inviting fruity nose. It has good weight on the palate, and displays a depth of fruit often lacking in wines of this type. The Livio Bronca Brut, which the winery offers as an attractive alternative to Prosecco - it is made from pinot bianco - is light and floral. The Prosecco Extra Dry, lacking somewhat in vigour on the nose and palate, scored lower than it did last year.

O	Prosecco di Valdobbiadene Brut	🍷🍷	3*
O	Prosecco di Valdobbiadene Extra Dry	🍷	3
O	Prosecco di Valdobbiadene Frizzante	🍷	2
O	Prosecco di Valdobbiadene Tranquillo '96	🍷	3
O	Spumante Livio Bronca Brut	🍷	3

VIDOR (TV)

VIDOR (TV)

DAL DIN
VIA MONTEGRAPPA, 31
31020 VIDOR (TV)
TEL. 0423/987295

DE FAVERI
VIA G. SARTORI, 21
FRAZ. BOSCO
31020 VIDOR (TV)
TEL. 0423/987673

In the 1997 Guide we described Riccardo Piazza's winery as one of the most reliable and consistent in the area. This year, however, in spite of a number of interesting new products, the Dal Din wines were somewhat disappointingly uneven. This is particularly true of the prosecco-based sparkling wines: only the Cartizze, made with the habitual care, acquitted itself with honour. It has a brilliant straw colour and a rich mousse. The nose is crisp, with attractive pear and apple notes and on the palate it has well-regulated sweetness and a medium-length finish. The Prosecco Brut and the Prosecco Extra Dry alternated good showings with occasions on which they appeared very unbalanced. The Prosecco Tranquillo was on decidedly good form, with its fresh aromatic bouquet and clean palate; well-defined scents of ripe bananas and charming length of flavour are its main features. Of similar quality is the Incrocio Manzoni Bianco which has a very floral nose, fresh acidity sustaining the fruit on the palate, and just enough length to break into the 70-points bracket. The Cabernet - too thin and short - is a wine with evident problems. The white Coltorondo made from incrocio Manzoni aged in barrique, did not succeed in demonstrating its full potential.

The '96 vintage provided the producers of Prosecco with grapes which were close in quality to the superb '95 crop, but which yielded very different wines. If the '95s were broad, soft and rich, the more recent vintage gave us wines which were drier in style and underpinned by a green, almost cutting acidity. A perfect example of these characteristics is Lucio De Faveri's Prosecco Brut, one of the best of its type tasted this year. It has a straw colour, highlighted by a fine mousse; the bold, almost overpowering nose offers very direct, positive scents of green apples and we find the same attractive vigour on the palate, where its fruit combines suppleness with fragrance. The Prosecco Dry, naturally somewhat more rounded, but nevertheless firm, is an outstanding sparkling wine. Its deepish straw appearance is enlivened by the mousse and the rich floral tones combine with fresh, fruity aromas on the nose. The fruit evolves well on the palate, displaying a marked, but not cloying sweetness, and the wine shows perfect continuity of aroma and flavour. The Cartizze, too, though it does not reveal as much personality, is a very satisfying wine, with its distinct scents of citrus fruits and its very attractive flavour. The well-proportioned Prosecco Extra Dry is not particularly intensely flavoured, but is undoubtedly very elegant. The Prosecco Tranquillo, whose quaffability is enhanced by a very slight spritz, is also well-made. Only the Frizzante failed to live up to expectations.

O Cartizze	♟	4
O Incrocio Manzoni 6.0.13 '96	♟	3
O Prosecco di Valdobbiadene		
Tranquillo '96	♟	2
O Coltorondo Bianco '94		3

O Prosecco di Valdobbiadene		
Brut	♟♟	3
O Prosecco di Valdobbiadene		
Dry Bottiglia Nera	♟♟	4
O Cartizze	♟	4
O Prosecco di Valdobbiadene		
Extra Dry	♟	3
O Prosecco di Valdobbiadene		
Tranquillo '96	♟	3
O Prosecco di Valdobbiadene		
Frizzante		2

OTHER WINERIES

The following producers obtained good scores in our tastings with one or more of their wines:

PROVINCE OF PADOVA

Borin, Monselice,
tel. 0429/74384,
Colli Euganei Cabernet Sauvignon
Vigna Costa '95

La Montecchia,
Selvazzano Dentro, tel. 049/637294,
Colli Euganei Cabernet '96

PROVINCE OF TREVISO

Carpené Malvolti,
Conegliano, tel. 0438/410575,
Prosecco Tranquillo Bianco dei Carpené '96

Dall'Armellina,
Mareno di Piave, tel. 0438/308878,
Incrocio Manzoni 6.0.13 '96

Moletto,
Motta di Livenza, tel. 0422/860576,
Piave Tocai Italico '96, Riesling '96

Nardin,
Ormelle, tel. 0422/851002,
Lison Cabernet '95,
Prosecco Borgo Molino

Vincenzo Toffoli,
Refrontolo, tel. 0438/894240,
Prosecco Extra Dry,
Marzemino Passito '95

Bruno Agostinetto,
Valdobbiadene, tel. 0423/972884,
Prosecco di Valdobbiadene Extra Dry

Ciodet,
Valdobbiadene, tel. 0423/973131,
Prosecco di Valdobbiadene Extra Dry

Col de' Salici,
Valdobbiadene, tel. 055/291424,
Prosecco di Valdobbiadene Dry,
Prosecco di Valdobbiadene Extra Dry

Valdo Spumanti,
Valdobbiadene, tel. 0423/972403,
Prosecco di Valdobbiadene
Extra Dry Cuvée di Boj

PROVINCE OF VENEZIA

Santa Margherita,
Fossalta di Portogruaro, tel. 0421/246111,
Laudato di Malbech '93

Tenuta Teracrea,
Portogruaro, tel. 0421/287041,
Malvasia di Teracrea '96

PROVINCE OF VERONA

Lenotti,
Bardolino, tel. 045/7210484,
Amarone '90,
Soave Vigna Campo d'Oro '96

Corte S. Arcadio,
Bussolengo, tel. 045/7575331,
Bianco di Custoza La Boschetta '96,
Bianco di Custoza '96

Tenuta Sant'Antonio,
Colognola ai Colli, tel. 045/7650383,
Chardonnay Torre dei Melotti '96

Armani,
Dolcé, tel. 045/7290033,
Sauvignon Campo Napoleone '96

Tenuta Novaia,
Marano di Valpolicella, tel. 045/7755129,
Amarone '90

Marcato, Roncà, tel. 045/7460070,
Colli Berici Merlot dell'Asinara '95

Villa Monteleone,
S. Ambrogio di Valpolicella,
tel. 045/7704974,
Valpolicella Sup. Campo S. Lena '94

Giuseppe Fornaser,
S. Pietro in Cariano,
tel. 045/7701651,
Amarone Monte Faustino '91,
Passito Bianco Bure Alto '95

Luigi Vantini,
S. Pietro in Cariano,
tel. 045/7701374,
Amarone '90

Bisson,
Soave, tel. 045/7680775,
Recioto di Soave '95

Coffele,
Soave, tel. 045/7680007,
Soave Classico Ca' Visco '96

Arcadia,
Verona, tel. 045/8204466,
Soave Pagus di Montecchia '96

Cantina Sociale della Valpantena,
Verona, tel. 045/550032,
Bianco di Custoza '96,
Valpantena '96

PROVINCE OF VICENZA

Villa dal Ferro,
S. Germano dei Berici, tel. 0444/868025,
Colli Berici Merlot Campo del Lago '93,
Colli Berici Cabernet Le Rive Rosse '92

FRIULI VENEZIA GIULIA

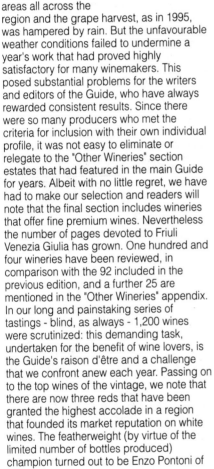

The rise in standards throughout Friuli Venezia Giulia continues, encouraged by a what can safely be regarded as a good vintage. Hail in spring and summer buffeted areas all across the region and the grape harvest, as in 1995, was hampered by rain. But the unfavourable weather conditions failed to undermine a year's work that had proved highly satisfactory for many winemakers. This posed substantial problems for the writers and editors of the Guide, who have always rewarded consistent results. Since there were so many producers who met the criteria for inclusion with their own individual profile, it was not easy to eliminate or relegate to the "Other Wineries" section estates that had featured in the main Guide for years. Albeit with no little regret, we have had to make our selection and readers will note that the final section includes wineries that offer fine premium wines. Nevertheless the number of pages devoted to Friuli Venezia Giulia has grown. One hundred and four wineries have been reviewed, in comparison with the 92 included in the previous edition, and a further 25 are mentioned in the "Other Wineries" appendix. In our long and painstaking series of tastings - blind, as always - 1,200 wines were scrutinized: this demanding task, undertaken for the benefit of wine lovers, is the Guide's raison d'être and a challenge that we confront anew each year. Passing on to the top wines of the vintage, we note that there are now three reds that have been granted the highest accolade in a region that founded its market reputation on white wines. The featherweight (by virtue of the limited number of bottles produced) champion turned out to be Enzo Pontoni of the Miani estate, who was awarded Three Glasses for no fewer than three wines: his COF Bianco, COF Sauvignon and the COF Tocai Friulano, all '96 vintage. Girolamo Dorigo was again a Three Glass winemaker with his Chardonnay Ronc di Juri; so too were Tonino and Valneo Livon with their Sauvignon Valbuins; Silvio Jermann of Vinnaioli Jermann with his ever-dependable Vintage Tunina; the La Castellada estate owned by Nicolò and Giorgio Bensa with their Bianco della Castellada; Gianfranco Gallo's Vie di Romans for the Vieris Sauvignon; Villa Russiz, owned by the Istituto A. Cerutti and run by Gianni Menotti, which produced a superb red, the Merlot Graf de La Tour; and the Abbazia di Rosazzo estate, part of the Zamò & Zamò portfolio, also reconfirmed its standing with its Ronco dei Roseti '92. Livio Felluga, with Terre Alte, and the Venica & Venica estate owned by Gianni and Giorgio Venica, with their Pinot Bianco, made a welcome return to the top flight. The year's newcomers were Paolo Rodaro, who conjured up an impressive Sauvignon, Marco Felluga's Russiz Superiore, where we tasted an excellent red in the '93 Riserva degli Orzoni, and Fabio Coser of Ronco dei Tassi, who has made a beautifully balanced Collio Bianco Fosarin. There were a number of wineries jostling for attention just below the top producers and their wines were the subject of keen debate among the tasters, a discussion that will certainly be continued by consumers. As always, our reviewers have toiled in good faith. Readers will bear in mind that the Guide is not Holy Writ. It is, we hope, a practical, non-denominational tool with which to assess and compare the country's wines.

BAGNÀRIA ARSA (UD)

TENUTA BELTRAME
LOC. ANTONINI, 6/8
FRAZ. PRIVANO
33050 BAGNÀRIA ARSA (UD)
TEL. 0432/923670

The vine-encircled farmhouse of the Beltrame estate has been superbly restored to create a large, attractive reception facility and, more significantly, to set up a capacious cellar with modern stainless steel equipment and oak barrels. This year the winery, which is situated in the northern part of the Friuli Aquileia DOC zone, has a fine range to offer. The 25 hectares under vine - out of a total of 40 on the estate - are on gravel and clay soils that can guarantee premium-quality wines if properly looked after. Cristian Beltrame and Giuseppe Collino, the estate's consultant, are the winemakers. Their very successful Sauvignon is a delicate, elegant wine with notes of elderflower and red peppers on the nose. The salty palate confirms this impression, adding nice acidity and pleasing length. The Chardonnay is equally elegant, offering hints of tropical fruit on the nose. The entry on the palate is vigorous, followed up with admirable harmony and length. Next we sampled their nicely balanced Pinot Bianco, which maintains on the palate the intense aroma of apples first hinted at in the nose. All in all a refreshingly consistent and very agreeable bottle. Elegance is also the hallmark of the Beltrame Pinot Grigio, which has an abundance of fruit both in the glass and on the palate, although the acidity undermines the overall balance to a certain extent. The Tocai Friulano has distinct notes of pear on the nose and splendidly chewy fruit on the palate but again the finish is a little compromised by marked acidity. Finally, the Beltrame estate's Merlot, Refosco dal Peduncolo Rosso '95, and their sweet, golden-hued Verduzzo Friulano are all well worth a mention in dispatches.

BAGNÀRIA ARSA (UD)

MULINO DELLE TOLLE
VIA ROMA, 29
LOC. SEVEGLIANO
33050 BAGNÀRIA ARSA (UD)
TEL. 0432/928113

Giorgio and Eliseo Bertossi are cousins as well as joint-owners of the Mulino delle Tolle estate, which extends over 15 hectares or so on the northern boundary of the Friuli Aquileia DOC zone. Giorgio is a winemaker and his cousin is a qualified agronomist. They produced their first wine together in 1988 and today they put over 30,000 bottles a year on the market. The cellar was restructured in the early 1990s and is now equipped with stainless steel and oak barrels of various sizes for the Mulino delle Tolle reds. The Malvasia, a very enjoyable wine, has attractive aromas of spring flowers and an elegant, refreshing palate that brings to mind beeswax. There are distinct notes of pear and apple in the Tocai Friulano. The palate is uncomplicated and direct, echoing the aromas of the nose with satisfying consistency while the finish has plenty of fruit and length. Moving on to the Chardonnay, here we note a varietal aroma of boiled sweets over a yeasty background. The promise of the nose is fully maintained on the palate, where the same subtle aromas gently emerge. The Cabernet Franc, too, brings out all the varietal character of the grape. Grassy aromas mingle with Morello cherry on the nose and the palate is equally distinctive, something that is not often achieved with this less-than-cooperative grape. The Riesling is an unassertive will-o'-the-wisp of a wine but nonetheless worthy of note and it should be emphasized that the variety is one that in Friuli Venezia Giulia rarely yields wines good enough to warrant a One Glass rating in the Guide.

○ Friuli Aquileia Sauvignon '96	♼♼	2*
○ Friuli Aquileia Chardonnay '96	♼	2
○ Friuli Aquileia Pinot Bianco '96	♼	2
○ Friuli Aquileia Pinot Grigio '96	♼	2
○ Friuli Aquileia Tocai Friulano '96	♼	2
○ Verduzzo Friulano '95		3
● Friuli Aquileia Merlot '95		2
● Friuli Aquileia Refosco P. R. '95		2

● Friuli Aquileia Cabernet Franc '96	♼	2
○ Friuli Aquileia Chardonnay '96	♼	2
○ Friuli Aquileia Tocai Friulano '96	♼	2
○ Malvasia '96	♼	2
○ Friuli Aquileia Riesling '96		2

BERTIOLO (UD)

CABERT
VIA MADONNA, 27
33032 BERTIOLO (UD)
TEL. 0432/917434

The Cantina del Friuli Centrale at Bertiolo was founded by a group of major growers who joined together to build a facility capable of handling the more than 30,000 quintals of grapes produced on the associates' collective holdings of 290 hectares. The winery produces two major lines. The Cabert brand is reserved for the catering industry while the Cavaliere di Bertiolo label is distributed through retail outlets. In 1996, production reached a total of 800,000 bottles. Credit for the high level of quality goes to the growers themselves who look after the estates and to Daniele Calzavara, the winemaker who is in charge of the cellar. Once again, the outstanding Cabert riserva is the '93 vintage Refosco dal Peduncolo Rosso, an oak-aged red from the Eccher Sequals vineyard. Bright ruby red in the glass, it suggests violets and stewed cherries on the nose, while apparent on the palate is nicely judged oak, consistency, fullness of flavour and mouth-filling length. The Cabernet Sauvignon Riserva '93 from the Stroili estate is another impressive wine. Aged in small barrels, it has nice balance both on the nose and on the palate where the intriguingly rich fruit mingles with spicy overtones and smoky oak flavours. Another well-merited mention goes to the Merlot Riserva '93, which has a touch of green that is unusual both for the variety and for the maturity of the wine. Then the '96 vintage Pinot Grigio, which confirms the solid quality of the Cabert range, proffers notes of pear and walnut skins backed up by good acidity. The '96 Refosco has an intense ruby red hue and a nose of spices with stewed red berries. The tannin and acidity on the palate are nicely balanced. The best of the other wines mentioned below is the Sauvignon.

BUTTRIO (UD)

CLAUDIO E LIVIO BUIATTI
VIA LIPPE, 25
33042 BUTTRIO (UD)
TEL. 0432/674317

Once again, Claudio Buiatti's cellar has earned a place in the Guide with a range of wines that is thoroughly workmanlike, if not truly outstanding. The seven hectares of hillside vineyards he farms at Buttrio get the benefit of the specialist training he received at agricultural college in Cividale to which he adds the dedication to quality that his father Livio instilled in him long ago. Claudio is a fourth-generation winemaker, turning out mainly white wines while reds account for around 35 percent of production, almost all of which is sold on the domestic market. The '96 Buiatti Pinot Grigio presents faint onion-skin highlights on examination in the glass and its aromas are elegant, balanced and rich in fruit, an impression confirmed on tasting. A hint of acidity in the finish adds zest. The nose of the Malvasia is redolent of yellow plums with vegetal notes while in the mouth it is refreshing, nicely structured and long - a perfect match for fish. Best of the Buiatti One Glass wines is the '95 Refosco dal Peduncolo Rosso. It makes an excellent impression on the nose, where cherry and wild berry aromas emerge. These are picked up again on the palate and the rounded, velvety tannins remain unruffled by the distinct note of acidity. The Cabernet immediately gives you the grassy aromas of cabernet franc (or probably in fact the related carmenère) mingled pleasantly with bilberry and raspberry. In the mouth, the grassy notes are muted by prunes and raspberry again in a surprisingly round and complex palate. The other Buiatti wines listed below are all very well made and offer excellent value for money.

● Friuli Grave		
Refosco P. R. Ris. '93	♟♟	3*
● Friuli Grave		
Cabernet Sauvignon Ris. '93	♟	3
● Friuli Grave Refosco P. R. '96	♟	2
○ Friuli Grave Pinot Grigio '96	♟	2
● Friuli Grave Merlot '96		2
● Friuli Grave Merlot Ris. '93		3
○ Friuli Grave Sauvignon '96		2
○ Friuli Grave		
Traminer Aromatico '96		2

● COF Cabernet '94	♟	3
● COF Refosco P. R. '95	♟	3
○ COF Malvasia '96	♟	3
○ COF Pinot Grigio '96	♟	3
○ COF Pinot Bianco '96		3
○ COF Riesling '96		3
○ COF Sauvignon '96		3
○ COF Tocai Friulano '96		3
○ COF Verduzzo Friulano '96		3

BUTTRIO (UD)

CONTE D'ATTIMIS - MANIAGO
VIA SOTTOMONTE, 21
33042 BUTTRIO (UD)
TEL. 0432/674027

The estate that Alberto d'Attimis-Maniago runs belongs to one of the most historically important families in the region. They have been involved in viticulture since the early 16th century and today cultivate 70 or so hectares of vineyards, and sell about 400,000 bottles each year. We were impressed by the elegance of the Chardonnay's fruit aromas, present both on the nose and in the mouth, and by the length of its finish, which has a nice tang of acidity in the aftertaste. The Pinot Bianco was clean-tasting and delicate, the nuances of green apples providing a beautifully sustained keynote from the aroma through to the finish. Next we sampled a '95 Picolit, which was straw yellow with green highlights in the glass where the aromas recall dried fruit, especially sultanas and figs. Medium-sweet and medium-bodied, it has an inviting finish. The Schioppettino '96, a red made entirely from this native Friulian variety, is well worth looking out for. The nose discloses Morello cherries, bramble and spices. A nicely concentrated wine not without elegance, it has plenty of fruit and good beefy tannins. We have also listed the Vignaricco '93, a blend mainly of cabernet sauvignon and merlot with a little schioppettino. The Sauvignon, Pinot Grigio, Merlot '95 and Verduzzo Friulano Tore delle Signore '95 all earned a mention for their distinctive varietal character.

BUTTRIO (UD)

GIROLAMO DORIGO
VIA DEL POZZO, 5
33042 BUTTRIO (UD)
TEL. 0432/674268

Problems at the estate unrelated to wine production have had one or two unavoidable knock-on effects. In some cases, two vintages of the same wine have been put on the market too close to each other. Others that we sampled - the flagship reds - proved too young to drink and may not be released yet. Yet others are already on sale but deserved a little more attention than they actually got - the Sauvignon for instance. Fortunately however the underlying quality is rock solid, as the Three Glass award demonstrates. Last year's Chardonnay, for example, certainly has nothing to be ashamed of. Awesomely rich in pineapple, mint and grapefruit flavours, its mouth-filling, mature elegance offers a finish that evokes all the above mentioned sensations, but this time enhanced by buttery, smoky grace notes. The same skill and substance is also apparent in the previous year's vintage, albeit with a little less freshness a more markedly lactic character and looser texture. The Dorigo spumante once again asserts its right to the title of the region's finest sparkling wine. Made in a tried and trusted - and very French - style, it is rich in extract with notes of yeast, ripe fruit and honey. The Ronc di Juri still needs time to mature but is already full of personality and has a thumping entry on the palate. The Pinot Grigio is redolent of flowers and fresh crusty bread, leading into a nice, dry palate of medium length. Then the Schioppettino, the only red that has definitely been released, has a nose of cherry and blackcurrant laced with vanilla; a sinewy wine, it lacks a little balance. The Verduzzo's elegant aromas of lime blossom and walnut win your heart immediately and, last but certainly not least, Girolamo's Picolit lives up to its reputation as a rare jewel. The nose conjures up figs, candied citrus fruits, hazelnut and almond paste, taking you into a palate that is velvet-smooth and glycerine-rich, but has a question mark against its finesse.

● COF Schioppettino '96	Ψ	4
○ COF Chardonnay '96	Ψ	3
○ COF Picolit '95	Ψ	6
○ COF Pinot Bianco '96	Ψ	3
○ COF Pinot Grigio '96		3
○ COF Sauvignon '96		3
○ COF Verduzzo Friulano Tore delle Signore '96		4
○ COF Verduzzo Friulano Tore delle Signore '95		4
● Vignaricco '93		4
● COF Merlot '95		3

○ COF Chardonnay Vigneto Ronc di Juri '96	ΨΨΨ	4
○ COF Chardonnay Vigneto Ronc di Juri '95	ΨΨ	4
○ COF Picolit '96	ΨΨ	6
○ COF Verduzzo Vigneto Ronc di Juri '94	ΨΨ	5
○ Dorigo Brut '89	ΨΨ	4
○ Ronc di Juri '96	ΨΨ	4
○ COF Pinot Grigio '96	Ψ	3
● Schioppettino '94	Ψ	5
● Montsclapade '92	ΨΨΨ	5
● Pignolo di Buttrio '89	ΨΨΨ	6
○ COF Verduzzo Vigneto Ronc di Juri '91	ΨΨΨ	5

BUTTRIO (UD)

BUTTRIO (UD)

DAVINO MEROI
VIA STRETTA DEL PARCO, 1
33042 BUTTRIO (UD)
TEL. 0432/674025

MIANI
VIA PERUZZI, 10
33042 BUTTRIO (UD)
TEL. 0432/674327

Paolo Meroi firmly believes in low yields, for white wines as well as reds, ageing in small oak barrels and malolactic fermentation. And it is no coincidence that he works with the legendary Enzo Pontoni, renowned for Miani wines. This hard-working team continues to produce superb bottles, much to the delight of wine-lovers everywhere. Paolo calls his blend of merlot, cabernet sauvignon and refosco del peduncolo rosso Dominin, after his grandfather. The '95 version of this premium quality wine has an intense ruby hue and a complex nose of wild berries, bramble, spices and prunes with overtones of citrus. The palate is soft and fruity with echoes of herbal teas and red berries. Ribolla Gialla '96 is tinged with gold in the glass. The nose is deep and rich with nuances of wood and banana and in the mouth, the vanilla and fruit nicely offset by the characteristic acidity of the variety that carries over into the finish. The mushroomy aromas of the Picolit, immediately obvious on the nose, are a sign that the grapes have been partially dried. The wine itself is dense and concentrated, rich in sugar and rich in alcohol, and its subtle, ever-changing flavours of fruit salad and dried figs are a delight. In contrast, there are shades of old gold in the Verduzzo Friulano, where an initial toastiness soon gives way to vanilla, confectioner's cream and hazelnut. The rich, concentrated flavour brings out all the verduzzo grape's tannins and there is also plenty of length. Finally, the well balanced bouquet of the Tocai Friulano '96 reveals nuances of ripe apple before the finely textured palate kicks in with chewy fruit and a consistently full flavour.

Where Enzo Pontoni is concerned, you can never award too many accolades. His Bianco is a stunning blend of chardonnay, pinot grigio, malvasia and riesling. Its bright, intense straw yellow introduces a bouquet of great generosity and complexity (wisteria, rennet, honey and vanilla) and a soft yet tangy palate whose alcohol is a beautifully measured, subtly wooded balance of power and elegance that delights the taste buds. It's the same story with the Tocai: bright and lustrous in the glass with a nose of confectioner's cream, acacia blossom, apple and milk of almonds; the palate is dry and concentrated, the finish soft and long. And it is to winemakers like Enzo Pontoni that we owe the resurgence of interest in Tocai, which so often tends to be rough and unpredictable. The Sauvignon is every bit as concentrated and long in the finish as the Tocai. Its elegant notes of toasty oak and white peach are lusciously rich, continuing in the mouth where they are agreeably complemented by the zesty acidity. The Ribolla and the Rosso have all the hallmarks of great wines. The Ribolla has a sweet toasty oak aroma nuanced with whitecurrant while the Rosso has notes of vanilla, Morello cherry and pencil lead. Both are big, concentrated wines that manage to remain stylish and eminently drinkable.

O COF Picolit '96	♥♥	5
O COF Ribolla Gialla '96	♥♥	4
O COF Tocai Friulano '96	♥♥	4
O COF Verduzzo Friulano '95	♥♥	4
● Dominin '95	♥♥	4
● COF Refosco P. R. '95	♥	4
O COF Picolit '95	♀♀	5
O COF Ribolla Gialla '94	♀♀	4

O COF Bianco '96	♥♥♥	4
O COF Sauvignon '96	♥♥♥	4
O COF Tocai Friulano '96	♥♥♥	4
O COF Ribolla Gialla '96	♥♥	4
● Rosso Miani '95	♥♥	5
● COF Merlot '94	♀♀♀	5
● COF Merlot '93	♀♀	5
O COF Sauvignon '94	♀♀	4

BUTTRIO (UD)

BUTTRIO (UD)

LINA E PAOLO PETRUCCO
VIA MORPURGO, 12
33042 BUTTRIO (UD)
TEL. 0432/674387

GIGI VALLE
VIA NAZIONALE, 3
33042 BUTTRIO (UD)
TEL. 0432/674289

The estate of Lina and Paolo Petrucco has made a storming comeback into the Guide, collecting a fine series of high scores. Their 20 hectares of vines are superbly located on the hills at Buttrio and production is supervised by Flavio Cabas, a winemaker who may be young but who has years of experience behind him. The cellar is very well equipped and turns out about 100,000 bottles a year, all of them of good quality. The one that our tasters liked best is the Cabernet Franc '95. Its nose is redolent of hay, grass, liquorice and autumn leaves following which the well judged oak allows the chewy fruit to come through on the palate. The satisfying, rich finish is accompanied by engagingly soft tannins. What won the Ribolla Gialla '96 its Two Glasses was the bouquet of yellow flowers, ripe fruit and citrus but it also has nice breadth of palate and the finish lingers. The Pinot Grigio is a refreshing drink with an abundance of fruit, which stands out for its elegance. Then in the Chardonnay we found vegetal notes over a background of yeast, good continuity from nose to palate and sound structure. Apple and tomato leaves were to the fore in the nose of the Sauvignon, a balanced, well rounded wine that nonetheless reveals tangy acidity. The Merlot Vigna del Balbo '95, obtained from very old vines, an outstandingly concentrated wine albeit rendered slightly thin by the acidity typical of the vintage. We also awarded a mention to the Tocai Friulano '96 and the Refosco dal Peduncolo Rosso '95.

Gigi Valle sources large quantities of grapes from various properties in some of the finest growing areas in the hills of Friuli, and this perhaps explains the diversification of labels. However, having tasted as many as nineteen wines from the various ranges - San Blâs; Collezione Gigi Valle; Selezione Araldica; Linea Valle - our tasters were not fully convinced of the personality of the wines and what we tended to note was a certain uniformity across the production as a whole. Two sweet whites, however, did fully deserve their higher scores. The San Blâs '96 and the Verduzzo Friulano '95 are both nicely balanced, well rounded wines that avoid excessive sugariness. L'Ambrosie San Blâs, a sweet malvasia-based white, is only a whisker below; it has baked apple and peach aromas and is a little mature. The Cabernet, one of the '89 Riserva wines from the Collezione Gigi Valle, is noteworthy for its grassy, minty aromas and well rounded tannins. Here at least the panel found proof of what Gigi Valle is can do. His stylish Pinot Bianco elegantly evokes pear on the nose and also has a fine fruity finish. The other wines we have listed below are less interesting but well made nonetheless: Bianco San Blâs '95 (obtained from tocai, pinot bianco and sauvignon grapes); Ribolla Gialla '96 from the Linea Valle range and from the San Blâs '95 collection, Riesling Araldo '96 and Rosso Florean '95 (from merlot, cabernet sauvignon and refosco dal peduncolo rosso grapes).

● COF Cabernet Franc '95	▼▼	3
○ COF Ribolla Gialla '96	▼▼	3
○ COF Chardonnay '96	▼	3
○ COF Pinot Grigio '96	▼	3
○ COF Sauvignon '96	▼	3
● COF Merlot Vigna del Balbo '95	▼	4
● COF Refosco P. R. '95		3
○ COF Tocai Friulano '96		3

● COF Cabernet Ris. Gigi Valle '89	▼	5
○ COF Picolit San Blâs '96	▼	5
○ COF Pinot Bianco '96	▼	4
○ COF Verduzzo Friulano '95	▼	4
○ COF Bianco San Blâs '95		5
○ COF Ribolla Gialla '96		4
○ COF Ribolla Gialla San Blâs '95		5
○ COF Riesling Araldo '96		5
● COF Rosso Florean '95		4
○ L'Ambrosie San Blâs		5
● COF Cabernet Ris. Gigi Valle '88	▼	5
● COF Merlot Ris. Gigi Valle '89	▼	5

CAPRIVA DEL FRIULI (GO) CAPRIVA DEL FRIULI (GO)

CASTELLO DI SPESSA
VIA SPESSA, 1
34070 CAPRIVA DEL FRIULI (GO)
TEL. 0481/639914

RONCÙS
VIA MAZZINI, 26
34070 CAPRIVA DEL FRIULI (GO)
TEL. 0481/809349

The castle in the village of Spessa is actually a manor house built in 1881 and situated in the middle of a 57-hectare estate, 25 of which are under vine. The current owner is Loretto Pali, a businessman with a wide range of interests who believes in - and therefore also invests in - the wine industry. The splendid grounds of the castle, including a thoroughbred racing stable, are a worthy setting for an original and very practical cellar complex: the vinification and barrel-fermentation facilities are on the ground floor while a long internal passageway leads down to the ageing cellar, which was created out of a air raid shelter dating from the 1930s. No daylight enters this room, which has a constant temperature all year round, and it is here that the Pinot Bianco di Santarosa '91 has matured. We have already reviewed this wine twice and although it is now very evolved, it fully deserves its Two Glasses. In contrast the Rosso Conte di Spessa '92 is still on the youngish side, as may be noted both from its bright ruby red colour and its tannins. It is a complex, full-bodied wine with wild berry and tar flavours that bode well for its future development. The Pinot Bianco '96 has an intense bouquet that hints at citrus and apples, both of which are also present on the elegant palate. The Sauvignon we tasted next presents well in the glass, offering distinctive notes of elderflower and tomato blossom over a red pepper background. Assertive acidity on the palate tends to overpower a fruity texture where apple and red pepper are again the key aromas. The tasting was rounded off by a Tocai Friulano '96 whose aromas proved to be disappointingly mature and which was not up to the standards of previous vintages.

As you chat to Marco Perco about his vineyards and his wines you realize at once that this is a young man with clear ideas and a mind of his own. We discussed the need to enhance the Friulian character of white wines and of the various attempts, which Perco thinks are essential, to instil into the product a "goût de terroir" and a personality that reflects the beliefs of the winemaker. Marco tries to put these ideas into practise with a rigorous field selection policy that involves low yields and late harvests and by adopting cellar techniques that will enhance the character of the variety. His wines are not DOC labelled by deliberate choice because the estate's ten hectares are distributed over a number of plots in both the Collio and Isonzo appellations, a fact which would create complications for labelling and potential confusion in the mind of the consumer. Results are beginning to justify Marco's decisions for all his wines are worth a closer look. The bright straw yellow Sauvignon is outstanding. It has the characteristic varietal aromas of elder flower over a nice oak background. The fat, full-flavoured palate is complemented by good acidity and length. The Tocai Friulano is low in acidity because the grapes were harvested only when fully mature. The vegetal aromas recall bitter herbs. A stylish nose of fresh fruit and tobacco introduces Perco's Pinot Bianco. The palate has good breadth and lots of warm, sweet fruit flavour. And finally the Roncùs Bianco '96, a blend of pinot, malvasia and ribolla in which the fruit and tobacco aromas are at the moment slightly masked by wood but which will certainly come through with time. The chewy palate confirms the nose, adding a hint of roast coffee, and the finish is gratifyingly long.

● Collio Rosso			
Conte di Spessa '92	♟	4	
○ Collio Pinot Bianco '96	♟	4	
○ Collio Sauvignon '96	♟	4	
○ Collio Pinot Grigio '96		4	
○ Collio Tocai Friulano '96		4	
○ Collio Pinot Bianco			
di Santarosa '91	♟♟	4	
○ Collio Tocai Friulano '95	♟♟	4	

○ Sauvignon '96	♟♟	4
○ Pinot Bianco '96	♟	4
○ Roncùs Bianco '96	♟	4
○ Tocai Friulano '96	♟	4

CAPRIVA DEL FRIULI (GO)

RUSSIZ SUPERIORE
VIA RUSSIZ, 7
34070 CAPRIVA DEL FRIULI (GO)
TEL. 0481/80328-92237

CAPRIVA DEL FRIULI (GO)

MARIO SCHIOPETTO
VIA PALAZZO ARCIVESCOVILE, 1
34070 CAPRIVA DEL FRIULI (GO)
TEL. 0481/80332

Patrizia Felluga used to tell our tasters that she was happy with her red wines but in future would pay more attention to the whites. Could it have been inspired foresight? Was it self-confidence or was it simply faith in the terroir, microclimates, vine stock and winemaking skills at her disposal? Whatever the reason, the goal of a great red wine has been achieved and all the makings of an equally awesome white are also to hand. This is what has gone into the Rosso degli Orzoni, named after the counts who had already discovered the viticultural potential of the area: Bordeaux blend, maceration for two weeks, 18 months in oak and a year's bottle ageing. Fruit, rose-water, spices and confectioner's cream on the nose and an aristocratically elegant palate that has great length and a thoroughly convincing style. The other Villa Russiz wines turned out to be worthy companions, starting with the Cabernet, which is still the best interpretation of cabernet franc in the region. Eye-catching Villa Russiz whites were the graceful, flowery Roncuz, blended from chardonnay, sauvignon, riesling and ribolla and then vinified and matured in stainless steel. We would have liked it to show a little more body, though. The Pinot Grigio was a complex wine with lots of personality while the Pinot Bianco impressed as a luscious and very civilized bottle. The Sauvignon's rue and mint aromas are as well defined as its textbook structure on the palate. In contrast, the Tocai offers apple and pear aromas and a tangy, well-rounded palate with a pleasantly smoky finish. And to round off this report, we should also mention the Verduzzo, albeit with reservations about the excessive sulphur that tends to cloak the wine's other considerable attractions.

The big news this year is that Mario Schiopetto has not been awarded his customary Three Glasses, but a glance at the tasting list below will reveal that the estate continues to produce top-drawer wines. Health problems have prevented the great Mario from following the maturation of his wines with his usual constant presence but he has been well supported by his sons Giorgio and Carlo in the vineyard and in the cellar while daughter Maria Angela continues to take care of the commercial side of the business. The highest-scoring Schiopetto wine was the Blanc des Rosis '96, a blend of tocai friulano, pinot bianco, sauvignon and malvasia. An exceptional wine, slightly penalized for its over-emphatic notes of sauvignon on the nose and particularly on the palate, its fresh-tasting, complex elegance - muted at first, then increasingly distinct - and long finish cannot fail to win admirers. There are faintly aromatic spicy notes in the Malvasia, a refreshing wine with great personality and rich fruit. The Merlot '95's oak is very nicely judged. Its ripe plum over red fruit flavour has good texture and constancy and is reflected in the nose, which is also nuanced with leather and tobacco. The Pinot Bianco is stylish, refreshing and seriously long, flaunting delicate creamy notes. The author of these notes is not a fan of Pinot Grigio but had to review his opinion of the variety after tasting Mario's extraordinary product. The palate is balanced, broad and fruity; exceptionally elegant for a Pinot Grigio, the warm, full flavours round off with a hint of fresh apple. Red pepper, mint and sage dominate the nose of the solid, refreshingly dry Sauvignon '96 and the Tocai Friulano '96 showed aromas of dried flowers and almonds; the palate is positive and satisfying, right through to the characteristic almond finish of the variety.

● Collio Rosso Riserva degli Orzoni '93	♟♟♟	5
● Collio Cabernet Franc '95	♟♟	4
○ Collio Pinot Bianco '96	♟♟	4
○ Collio Pinot Grigio '96	♟♟	4
○ Collio Sauvignon '96	♟♟	4
○ Collio Tocai Friulano '96	♟♟	4
○ Roncuz '96	♟	4
○ Verduzzo Friulano '95	♟	4
○ Collio Pinot Bianco '95	♟♟	4
● Collio Cabernet Franc '94	♟♟	4
● Collio Rosso Riserva degli Orzoni '90	♟♟	5
● Collio Rosso Riserva degli Orzoni '92	♟♟	5

○ Blanc des Rosis '96	♟♟	4
○ Collio Malvasia '96	♟♟	4
○ Collio Pinot Bianco '96	♟♟	4
○ Collio Pinot Grigio '96	♟♟	4
○ Collio Sauvignon '96	♟♟	4
○ Collio Tocai Friulano '96	♟♟	4
● Collio Merlot '95	♟♟	4
● Rivarossa '95	♟	4
○ Collio Riesling '96	♟	4
○ Collio Pinot Bianco '94	♟♟♟	4
○ Collio Sauvignon '89	♟♟♟	4
○ Collio Tocai Friulano '93	♟♟♟	4
○ Collio Tocai Friulano '94	♟♟♟	4
○ Collio Tocai Friulano '95	♟♟♟	4
● Collio Merlot '94	♟♟	4

A magazine
for intelligent travelers,
gourmets on a budget,
value-conscious buyers
of nothing but the best.

For people who know
what they want and what it's worth
- with a little help from us.

http://www.gamberorosso.it

In
English
and
Italian

**GAMBERO ROSSO'S
GUIDES AND MAGAZINES
AT YOUR FINGERTIPS**

CAPRIVA DEL FRIULI (GO)　　CAPRIVA DEL FRIULI (GO)

VIDUSSI GESTIONI AGRICOLE
VIA SPESSA, 18
34070 CAPRIVA DEL FRIULI (GO)
TEL. 0481/80072

VILLA RUSSIZ
VIA RUSSIZ, 6
34070 CAPRIVA DEL FRIULI (GO)
TEL. 0481/80047

The Vidussi company, owned by Signora Causero Vidussi, has 30 hectares of vines lying mainly in the Collio DOC zone, the other properties being in the Colli Orientali del Friuli appellation. The winemaker, Paolo Fornasiero, dedicates just as much attention to the vineyards as he does to the recently renovated cellars, which have been extended and equipped to meet the challenge of the future. His Chardonnay is a cuvée of which ten percent is fermented and matured for five months in new five-hectolitre barrels. The oak is discreet and the nose has a distinctly floral aroma with suggestions of elderflower and boiled sweets. The palate is firm and full-flavoured, yet soft, warm and elegant. Merlot, cabernet sauvignon and cabernet franc are the varieties that are blended, then matured in small oak barrels and bottle aged for at least four months, to make the Ronc dal Rol '95. The fruit comes from a vineyard of the same name near Capriva. The nose is redolent of plum tart, very ripe red berries and spices. Mouth-filling, complex and well structured in the mouth, the finish is genuinely delicious. Aromas of wild berries and autumn leaves emerge from the Refosco, weakening on the palate under the impact of roughish tannins and acidity that nevertheless fail to conceal the gutsy fruit underneath. In the glass, the Verduzzo is a vibrant old gold; the typical notes of apple and chamomile are present on both the nose and the palate. Flowery, rather than fruity, is the adjective that springs to mind to describe the bouquet of the Malvasia Istriana. It is every bit as elegant as the Pinot Bianco, where the accent is on fresh fruit salad and apple. Finally the fresh-tasting Tocai Friulano mingles warm fruit and vegetal aromas, signing off with a note of lemon.

In his Merlot Graf de la Tour '94, Gianni Menotti has presented us with an even better wine than his spectacular '93 vintage. And in doing so he has demonstrated that it is possible, without going to extremes in the cellar, to make a truly great red capable of seeing off challengers from all over the viticultural world. A superlative powerhouse of a wine that is quite awesomely rich, it reveals all its strength and complexity on the nose. Already mouth-filling on entry, the fruit takes on breadth in mid-palate and closes on a glorious top note. The structure is superb, the texture a delight. The Sauvignon de la Tour '96 is immediately impressive on the nose, where tomato leaf and apricot emerge. Entry on the palate is soft, becoming tangier and meatier before the fruit returns triumphantly in the finish. The nose of the Tocai Friulano '96 - awarded a well deserved Two Glasses - is bright and stylish. Almond, apple and plums come out strongly. On the palate, the initial softness soon shades into a refreshingly dry flavour that is rounded and muscular rather than refined, with good structure. Two Glasses also went to the flowery, fruity Pinot Bianco. Elegant on the nose, it seduces the palate with a stunning series of variations on the theme of fruit. Well balanced, it has admirable texture backed up by adequate acidity. Richness and complexity in which pear and apple come out strongly characterize the Pinot Grigio, whose quality is underlined by the long, long finish. There are delicate aromas of cedar and flowers in the nose of the Riesling, which is full flavoured and concentrated on the palate. Flowers are again present in the delightful finish. Without going into detail on the other wines sampled, they are all of sound, reliable quality.

○ Collio Chardonnay '96	♟♟	3*
● Ronc dal Rol '95	♟♟	3*
● COF Refosco P. R. '96	♟	3
○ COF Verduzzo Friulano '96	♟	3
○ Collio Pinot Bianco '96	♟	3
○ Collio Malvasia Istriana '96	♟	3
○ Collio Tocai Friulano '96	♟	2*
● COF Schioppettino '96		3

● Collio Merlot Graf de La Tour '94	♟♟♟	5
○ Collio Malvasia Istriana '96	♟♟	4
○ Collio Pinot Bianco '96	♟♟	4
○ Collio Pinot Grigio '96	♟♟	4
○ Collio Riesling '96	♟♟	4
○ Collio Sauvignon de La Tour '96	♟♟	4
○ Collio Tocai Friulano '96	♟♟	4
○ Collio Ribolla Gialla '96	♟	4
○ Collio Sauvignon '96	♟	4
● Collio Cabernet '95	♟	4
● Collio Merlot '95	♟	4
● Collio Merlot Graf de La Tour '93	♟♟♟	5
○ Collio Sauvignon de La Tour '91	♟♟♟	4
○ Collio Sauvignon de La Tour '94	♟♟♟	4
○ Collio Tocai Friulano '95	♟♟♟	4

CIVIDALE DEL FRIULI (UD)

DAL FARI
VIA DARNAZZACCO
33043 CIVIDALE DEL FRIULI (UD)
TEL. 0432/731219

Renzo Toffolutti is a qualified engineer and entrepreneur who also takes a passionate interest in the winery he has built in the middle of his 12 hectares of vineyard. His first vintage was 1988, an excellent year in Friuli and for the Dal Fari estate. Problems from these early days of the estate have been resolved by converting previously mono-clonal vineyards to mixed planting, increasing the density per hectare and reducing yields per vine. We are now beginning to see encouraging results, thanks also to the crucial contribution of consultant winemaker Fabio Coser. The superb Cabernet '95 has a crystal clear ruby colour and a nose in which liquorice and cherries dominate. The entry on the palate is uncompromising and the soft tannins merge seamlessly with the chewy fruit; a seriously powerful wine with structure and a long finish. The creamy nose of the Chardonnay '96 evokes distinct hints of vanilla and yeast, and the rich, tropical fruit palate has just enough acidity to brighten up the finish. Apple is one of the principal aromas revealed by the Dal Fari Pinot Grigio. The attractive palate is full bodied and broad as well as elegant. The stylish Tocai Friulano offers pear on the nose, and is fleshy and flavoursome on the palate. The Merlot '95 has a classy nose of cherry and bilberry tart as well as plenty of body but the tannins and acidity mean it lacks suppleness. Results obtained by the Sauvignon '96 in various tastings have been contradictory so our reviewers awarded no more than a mention. Finally the Schioppettino '95 is an attractively bright ruby tinged with purple in the glass and the nose has notes of spices and Morello cherry, although there is an intrusive acidity on the palate that brought down its overall score.

●	COF Cabernet '95	YY	4
●	COF Merlot '95	Y	4
○	COF Chardonnay '96	Y	4
○	COF Pinot Grigio '96	Y	4
○	COF Tocai Friulano '96	Y	4
○	COF Sauvignon '96		4
●	COF Schioppettino '95		4
○	COF Tocai Friulano '95	YY	3
●	Rosso d'Orsone '90	Y	4
●	Rosso d'Orsone '91	Y	4

CIVIDALE DEL FRIULI (UD)

DON GIOVANNI - LUCIA GALASSO
LOC. SPESSA
STRADA DI PLANEZ, 32
33040 CIVIDALE DEL FRIULI (UD)
TEL. 0432/730292

Lucia Galasso is the engagingly sociable owner of the estate and wife of Giovanni Crosato, a busy, dynamic winemaker and mayor of one of the towns in the Collio DOC zone. Last year, the winery could not be included in the Guide because its wines are bottled and released very late. The grapes come from a five -hectare plot with vines over 35 years old and they now go to make three wines, which are no longer limited to multi-varietals as was the original intention. The Don Giovanni Rosso and Don Giovanni Bianco cuvées have now been joined by the Tocai Friulano '96. This is an interesting white with a particularly enticing nose, in which flowery aromas mingle with mint, apple and toasty oak. The palate is not as meaty as you might expect but is nonetheless eminently drinkable, with a delicious vanilla note that re-emerges in the finish. Don Giovanni Rosso is obtained mainly from cabernet sauvignon, together with cabernet franc, merlot and schioppettino. The bramble and wild berry nose ushers in a fruity, well rounded palate underpinned by massive tannins. In our reviewers' opinion, the Don Giovanni Bianco is the best of the estate's wines. Obtained from tocai, sauvignon and pinot bianco grapes, it releases soft, intense aromas of apple, acacia blossom and pear that complement each other beautifully and are mirrored in the palate, where the glycerine adds notes of sweetness. The long, dry follow through has great texture and enough alcohol to ensure lots of warmth.

○	Don Giovanni Bianco	YY	4
○	COF Tocai Friulano '96	Y	4
●	Don Giovanni Rosso	Y	4

CIVIDALE DEL FRIULI (UD) CORMONS (GO)

PAOLO RODARO
VIA CORMONS, 8
LOC. SPESSA
33040 CIVIDALE DEL FRIULI (UD)
TEL. 0432/716066

TENUTA DI ANGORIS
LOC. ANGORIS, 7
34071 CORMONS (GO)
TEL. 0481/60923

We have been saying for some time now that sooner or later Paolo Rodaro would give us a very pleasant surprise. And here it is in the shape of his Sauvignon '96, one of those wines that make you sit up and take serious notice at the very first sip. Suave yet sustained, lingering notes of rue and peach lead into a wine that stands out above all for its splendid polish and balance. Rodaro also makes many other wines, all of them well made starting with the Riesling. A bit of a lightweight, it can still lay claim to attractive nuances of citrus, honey and flowers with faint, stylish hints of petrol. The Tocai is perhaps a little too reminiscent of sauvignon and the bitter notes are a touch assertive but the alcohol-focused structure eventually emerges against a background of pear, apple and aniseed. Rodaro's Verduzzo is bright old gold with a nose of sultanas and honey. The palate is full bodied with all the astringency you expect from the variety. In the mouth, the Chardonnay is broad and substantial, like the Pinot Bianco and the Ribolla, all of which follow through the fruity aromas of the nose nicely on the palate. This year's Pasît, however, was less convincing than the '95. The strong notes of traminer are upset by a vaguely acetic note and there is a less than satisfactory continuity on the palate. Finally, the Refosco redeems its boisterously excessive aromas with a fine, rich texture on the palate and is the best of Rodaro's reds (which, it should be said, are his weak spot).

For some years, Luciano Locatelli's policy has been to concentrate his efforts on the wines from his best vineyards. This has given rise to the Ronco Antico label (a Collio DOC wine from the 12-hectare vineyard at Ca' delle Vallate between Cormons and Dolegna) and the Podere ranges (partly in the Rocca Bernarda subzone in the Colli Orientali del Friuli DOC and partly near the cellars in the Isonzo DOC), which now complement the more traditional lines. With over 130 hectares under vine, annual output ranges from 700,000 to one million bottles, 100,000 of which are sold under the premium labels. Natale Favretto, the estate's highly skilled winemaker, keeps a watchful eye on both vineyards and cellar while Claudia Locatelli looks after sales and marketing. We particularly like the Pinot Grigio del Pecol dei Lupi. Its apple and pear aromas revealed an unexpected note of vanilla (it is vinified exclusively in stainless steel). The palate is broad, full bodied and agreeably complex. Spìule, a white fermented and matured in small oak barrels, is obtained from chardonnay and sauvignon grapes grown in the Rocca Bernarda vineyards. Stylish, refreshing, flowery and fruity at the same time, both the entry on the palate and finish are enlivened by perky acidity. The mid-palate boasts luscious fruit and the oak is measured with supreme delicacy. Part of the Sauvignon from the Podere Rocca Bernarda, too, was oaked but with moderation. It has a nice note of elderflower and very good texture. The grapes for the Picolit were dried on rush mats for over a month before pressing. The wine then matured slowly in wood. It has decidedly toasty aromas but they are amply compensated by the lingering, unstinting generosity of the sweet-yet-tangy palate and very ripe or sun-dried fruit. The distinguishing feature of the Merlot Ronco Antico '95, which is aged in five-hectolitre barrels, is the aroma of cherry and concentrated red berries.

O COF Sauvignon Bosc Romain '96	♀♀♀	3
O COF Riesling '96	♀♀	3
O COF Tocai Friulano Bosc Romain '96	♀♀	3*
O COF Verduzzo Friulano Pra Zenar '96	♀♀	4
O COF Chardonnay '96	♀	3
O COF Pinot Bianco '96	♀	3
O COF Ribolla Gialla '96	♀	3
O Pasît '96	♀	4
● COF Refosco P. R. '96	♀	3
O COF Pinot Bianco Bosc Romain '95	♀♀	3
O COF Tocai Friulano Bosc Romain '95	♀♀	3
O Pasît '95	♀♀	4

O COF Picolit '96	♀	5
O COF Sauvignon Podere Rocca Bernarda '96	♀	3
O Isonzo Friuli Pinot Grigio Podere Pecol dei Lupi '96	♀	3
O Spìule	♀	3
● Collio Merlot Ronco Antico '95	♀	3
● COF Refosco P. R. Podere Rocca Bernarda '95		3
O Collio Pinot Grigio Ronco Antico '96		3

CORMONS (GO)

BRUNO & MARIO BASTIANI
VIA SAVAIAN, 36
34071 CORMONS (GO)
TEL. 0481/60725

Mario and Marinella Bastiani run a tiny - just seven hectares - estate that is committed to the pursuit of quality. As so often is the case in this area, some of their plots are on the hillsides of the Collio DOC zone and the rest in the low-lying Isonzo appellation, both of which have demonstrated their enormous winemaking potential. Mario also has a modest livestock breeding business that provides him with organic fertilizers for his vineyards. Together with his rigorous policy of low yields per hectare and per vine, this has enabled him to produce a range of seriously good wines. In our opinion, the best bottle from the '96 vintage is the Ribolla Gialla, a thoroughly sound Two Glass wine. Obtained from a native grape variety, it mingles spring flowers and ripe white plums on the nose. The fruit returns on the elegant, glycerine-rich palate, which is soft and attractively textured. In contrast, the Tocai Friulano loses out due to a vaguely aromatic overtone that masks the directness of its bold, substantial fruit. Despite this reservation, it is almost on a par with the Ribolla Gialla. The varietal notes of the Isonzo Friuli DOC Sauvignon evoke red pepper and elderflower. The structure is good, the entry clean and the typical aromas return in the finish. Mario Bastiani's Riesling is refreshing, attractively flowery and sufficiently acid-rich to merit a One Glass rating. His Merlot is mouth-filling, albeit perhaps a shade too vegetal, and is well worth a mention.

○ Collio Ribolla Gialla '96	🍷🍷	3
○ Collio Tocai Friulano '96	🍷	2*
○ Isonzo Friuli Riesling '96	🍷	2*
○ Isonzo Friuli Sauvignon '96	🍷	3
● Isonzo Friuli Merlot '96		2

CORMONS (GO)

BORGO DEL TIGLIO
VIA S. GIORGIO, 71
FRAZ. BRAZZANO
34071 CORMONS (GO)
TEL. 0481/62166

Nicola Manferrari deserves recognition for two reasons: first of all for having understood long ago the importance of red wines in the Collio appellation and secondly for being the forerunner of the renaissance of Tocai Friulano. His varietal Tocai '95 is excellent. The aromas of almond, new-mown grass and caramel lead into a long, refreshing and excitingly potent palate. Unfortunately, after tasting ten or so bottles from different sources, we were forced to conclude that the wine was indeed somewhat evolved, a problem that may well be related to a problem with corks. Manferrari's hard-to-find Sauvignon continues to impress our reviewers, demonstrating its maker's predilection for wines of structure that appeal to the palate rather than the nose. Powerful, well balanced, long and stylish, its aromas evoke peach, pear, honey and sweet wood. The Rosso, as so often, is a well made wine with a soft, fruity richness and plenty of muscle. Delightful bramble aromas tell you that the blend is firmly cabernet sauvignon-based. The Chardonnay also performed well. Its intense, lactic aromas are nicely offset by elegant fruit and a firm texture on the palate. The Bianco on the other hand was less convincing.

○ Collio Chardonnay '95	🍷🍷	4
○ Collio Sauvignon '95	🍷🍷	4
○ Collio Tocai Friulano '95	🍷🍷	4
● Collio Rosso '93	🍷🍷	5
○ Bianco '95	🍷	4
○ Collio Tocai Ronco della Chiesa '90	🍷🍷🍷	4
○ Bianco '94	🍷🍷	4
○ Collio Chardonnay '94	🍷🍷	4
○ Collio Tocai Friulano Ronco della Chiesa '94	🍷🍷	4
● Collio Rosso '92	🍷🍷	5

CORMONS (GO)

CORMONS (GO)

BORGO SAN DANIELE
VIA S. DANIELE, 16
34071 CORMONS (GO)
TEL. 0481/60552

BORIS E DAVID BUZZINELLI
LOC. PRADIS, 22/BIS
34071 CORMONS (GO)
TEL. 0481/62272

Borgo San Daniele has this year again produced a top flight range of wines. The brother and sister team who own the winery, cellar master Mauro Mauri and estate manager Alessandra, are reaping the fruits of a decision made in 1994 to modify and renovate their vinification technology. Anyone who visits Borgo San Daniele will note their committed approach and the passionate dedication that inevitably produces premium wines. The estate's ten hectares are spread across the Collio and Isonzo DOC zones and yield about 35,000 bottles. This year pride of place must go to the Gortmarin '94, a blend of merlot, cabernet franc and sauvignon grapes from the vineyard of the same name. Ripe red berries beautifully balanced by toasty oak characterize the warm, broad palate. The structure and complexity are remarkable although the boisterous tannins still have a little way to go. The Arbis Rosso '95, also blended from cabernet franc and sauvignon grapes, is another very drinkable wine. Its tempting, well balanced nose is mirrored on a palate where the vegetal and ripe red berry aromas stand out. Next we sampled the very agreeable Isonzo Chardonnay '96 whose superbly harmonious finish is preceded by citrus and hedgerow perfumes and a rich, fat body that is balanced by apple and tangerine acidity. The prevailing aromas in the Isonzo Pinot Bianco '96 are banana and tobacco while the palate offers flavours of vanilla and tropical fruit as well as better than average length. The Arbis Bianco '96 blend reveals promising aromas of fruit and red pepper but the assertive acidity renders it thin on the palate. The Pinot Grigio and Tocai Friulano, both '96 vintages, are well made wines.

We have praised before the evident dedication brothers Boris and David Buzzinelli nurture for their winery, and the resulting wines, but there are now two further goals. The first is the completion of work on the cellar and the second is fine-tuning the quality of their two labels, Carlo Buzzinelli and BorDavi; two tasks which are neither easy nor able to be shared with anyone else. This year we particularly liked the Collio Sauvignon '96 sold under the Carlo Buzzinelli Vigneto di Pradis label, an intensely typical wine with a nose of sage and peppermint. It has great body and balance on the palate with a long, varietal finish. The rich, fruit salad nose of the Collio Pinot Grigio '96 is picked up nicely on the palate, which lingers attractively. Next the bright ruby red Collio Merlot '94 proved complex, with good fruit and spice notes on the nose, following through well on the palate in rich, full velvet soft flavours. Apple was to the fore in the nose of the Collio Pinot Bianco '96 and the long, pleasantly tangy palate had plenty of breadth. And finally, but not in order of merit, came the Collio Tocai Friulano '96, where buttery notes in no way compromise the elegance and intensity of the nose. The palate is refreshing, with moderate body and good acidity that contribute to more than satisfactory length in the finish.

O	Isonzo Friuli Chardonnay '96	♛♛	4
●	Gortmarin '94	♛♛	4
●	Arbis Rosso '95	♛	3
O	Isonzo Friuli Pinot Bianco '96	♛	4
O	Arbis Bianco '96		3
O	Collio Tocai Friulano '96		4
O	Isonzo Friuli Pinot Grigio '96		4

●	Collio Merlot Carlo Buzzinelli '94	♛♛	3*
O	Collio Pinot Grigio Carlo Buzzinelli '96	♛♛	3*
O	Collio Sauvignon Carlo Buzzinelli '96	♛♛	3*
O	Collio Pinot Bianco Carlo Buzzinelli '96	♛	3
O	Collio Tocai Friulano Carlo Buzzinelli '96	♛	3

CORMONS (GO)

Maurizio Buzzinelli
Loc. Pradis, 20
34071 Cormons (GO)
Tel. 0481/60902

Maurizio selects small amounts of the best grapes from his eight hectares at Pradis and vinifies them in part in wood to make the cru Faet. The remaining fruit is fermented in stainless steel and sold under the basic Collio DOC label. We had a foretaste of the Tocai Friulano Vigneto Faet '96. On the nose there were dominant aromas of banana and vanilla from the wood but the fruit emerged on the palate, together with slightly unbalanced acidity, although the wine was well balanced overall. The Malvasia Istriana '96 has a flowery and delicately fruity nose, firm acidity in the mouth and very nice finish. Next we tried the standard selection Tocai Friulano '96, which revealed intense pear and tomato leaves on the nose and medium structure on the palate. On the nose the Pinot Bianco '96 evoked golden delicious apples and honey, leading into an elegant and delicate palate whose full flavour was enhanced by tangy acidity. Finally the Müller Thurgau '96 revealed an elegant keynote of apple with aromatic nuances on the nose, followed through well on the palate but lost a little vigour in the finish.

CORMONS (GO)

Paolo Caccese
Loc. Pradis, 6
34071 Cormons (GO)
Tel. 0481/61062

After the difficult vintage of 1995, our tasters wondered how Paolo Caccese had been able to produce such a fine range of premium wines. Now that we have sampled the products from the much more favourable 1996 harvest, we can confirm that the answer lies in his passionate commitment to the land he cultivates. Paolo loves his work and constantly strives to improve the quality of his wines. It is the young reds that stand out, beginning with the Cabernet Franc '96, a bright purple-red wine with typical fruit and notes of capsicum and wood that mingle very successfully on the nose. The characteristically vegetal palate has lots of chewy fruit and a dry, compact, full bodied flavour. In contrast, the Collio Merlot '96 reveals unusual grassy notes over an astringent, tannin-rich palate. Caccese's Collio Müller Thurgau - a thoroughly reliable product over the years - is particularly good this year. Distinct notes of apple in the bouquet lead into an attractive palate that reflects the nose, promising plenty of length and a slightly expansive finish. One Glass has again been awarded to the Collio Malvasia Istriana '96. Elegant and refreshing, it is flowery rather than fruity (but with vegetal notes) and its beautifully balanced body alternates fruit with acidity. Fresh crusty bread and rennet emerge in the nose of the Collio Pinot Bianco, which is balanced on the palate and has a long, almondy finish. To round off, Paolo's Pinot Grigio, which has refreshing apple notes on the nose, goes on to tempt you with pear drop flavours on the palate, moderate acidity and remarkable structure.

O Collio Malvasia Istriana '96	♟	3
O Collio Müller Thurgau '96	♟	3
O Collio Pinot Bianco '96	♟	3
O Collio Tocai Friulano '96	♟	3
O Collio Tocai Friulano Vigneto Faet '96	♟	4

● Collio Cabernet Franc '96	♟♟	4
● Collio Merlot '96	♟	4
O Collio Malvasia Istriana '96	♟	3
O Collio Müller Thurgau '96	♟	4
O Collio Pinot Bianco '96	♟	4
O Collio Pinot Grigio '96	♟	4
O Collio Riesling '96		3
O Collio Tocai Friulano '96		3
O La Veronica '95		5

CORMONS (GO)

CORMONS (GO)

CANTINA PRODUTTORI DI CORMONS
VIA VINO DELLA PACE, 31
34071 CORMONS (GO)
TEL. 0481/60579

SERGIO E MAURO DRIUS
VIA FILANDA, 100
34071 CORMONS (GO)
TEL. 0481/60998

Generally speaking a new winery in the first years of production tends to be judged by local standards. Then as it develops, the terms of comparison becomes wider and more demanding. This year we tasted a total of 24 wines from this cooperative based at Cormons, eight of which failed to reach the threshold for entry to the Guide, seven earned a mention (Chardonnay, Tocai, Pinot Grigio and Madreterra from the Isonzo; Pinot Grigio, Chardonnay and Melograno from the Collio DOC) and the rest - and there are a considerable number of them - gained awards. The Pinot Bianco has fruit salad aromas, good texture and plenty of fruit and length. The Tocai reveals elegant notes of apple in the nose backed up by good acidity, grassy notes and moderate fruit. Green apple is the dominant note in the bouquet of the Ribolla, which is fresh-tasting and very drinkable though not without subtlety. Next, the Bianco Pietra Verde reveals a fresh, stylish nose of pear, confectioner's cream and walnut. The entry in the mouth is salty but the flavour softens in mid-palate; unfortunately the finish is a little flustered and lacks length. The Bianco Collio, with notes of broom and strawberry fruit gums, is a dry-tasting, serious wine with good balance but again lacking in length. Faint notes of geranium and firm red berries emerge in the Collio Merlot, which has a refreshing finish that echoes the entry. The Isonzo Merlot offers soft, rich fruit and medium body on the palate, moderate length and an attractively fruity aftertaste. The very typical, unsophisticated Cabernet Franc has forthright vegetal aromas over raspberry and a tight-knit texture. Finally, we recall in previous editions having written that the most important thing about the Cantina's Vino della Pace was the idea behind it; this year the wine lives up to the ideal. It is well worth trying.

Around Cormons it often happens that a part of an estate's vineyards lie on the hills of the Collio DOC zone while others are sited on the lower slopes of the neighbouring Isonzo del Friuli appellation. This is the case with the Drius winery, run by father Sergio and son Mauro who again this year have produced an admirable range of wines. Their Tocai Friulano Isonzo stands head and shoulders above the rest. Its clean aromas bring together distinct notes of apple and pear, the entry on the palate is powerful, steady, rich in fruit with good length and just the right degree of acidity. The Pinot Bianco, which has always been one of the estate's flagship products, came within a whisker of a Two Glass award. It boasts a splendid straw yellow hue and an apple and lavender nose. On the palate, a hint of acidity detracts from the broad, warm structure and its generous, chewy fresh fruit. The Sauvignon Collio is reminiscent of sage and rue on the nose. Its mouth-filling assertive palate has lots of fruit but is perhaps short on elegance. The Pinot Grigio Collio reveals creamy lactic notes over a complex and well balanced fruit salad background. It follows through nicely on the palate, where there is still a vigorous trace of acidity. Last of the One Glass wines was the Malvasia Isonzo, which has a typically clean, delicate nose and surprising character in the mouth, only slightly attenuated by varietal acidity. It is a dry, well rounded wine that makes a perfect accompaniment for fish dishes. Finally, the Riesling '96 and the Cabernet '95 were both well worth their mention.

O	Collio Pinot Bianco '96	ŶŶ	3
O	Vino della Pace '95	ŶŶ	6
O	COF Ribolla Gialla '96	Ŷ	3
O	Collio Collio '96	Ŷ	3
O	Collio Tocai Friulano '96	Ŷ	3
O	Friuli Isonzo Bianco Pietra Verde '96	Ŷ	2
●	Friuli Isonzo Cabernet Franc '96	Ŷ	2
●	Collio Merlot '95	Ŷ	3
●	Friuli Isonzo Merlot '96	Ŷ	2

O	Isonzo Friuli Tocai Friulano '96	ŶŶ	3
O	Collio Pinot Grigio '96	Ŷ	3
O	Collio Sauvignon '96	Ŷ	3
O	Isonzo Friuli Malvasia Istriana '96	Ŷ	3
O	Isonzo Friuli Pinot Bianco '96	Ŷ	3
O	Isonzo Friuli Riesling '96		3
●	Isonzo Cabernet '95		3
O	Collio Pinot Grigio '95	ŶŶ	3
O	Isonzo Friuli Pinot Bianco '95	ŶŶ	3
O	Isonzo Friuli Riesling '95	ŶŶ	3

CORMONS (GO)

LIVIO FELLUGA
VIA RISORGIMENTO, 1
FRAZ. BRAZZANO
34071 CORMONS (GO)
TEL. 0481/60203

At well over 80 years of age, Livio Felluga is one of the historic figures of modern Italian winemaking and continues to be an authority in the world of premium wines. It is certainly not easy to supervise 130 hectares of vineyards and an output of several hundred thousand units, especially when a top quality product is demanded for every single bottle. The '95 vintage Terre Alte, a blend dominated by tocai, pinot bianco and sauvignon, is well up to the usual superb standards. The gold-flecked hue is followed by a rich, powerful nose where apple and aromatic overtones prevail, echoed on the intense palate and the leisurely finish, which again offers aromas of apple. It is an eminently cellarable wine, as is the Merlot Sossò '94. Its triumphantly rich, velvety nose has ripe red berries mingled with nuances of liquorice and tar, and the muscular, full flavoured palate is backed up by abundant tannins. Once again, the Chardonnay Esperto has proved to be a marvellous wine and quite exceptional value for money. The nose is stylish and refreshing, the fruit tea aromas belying its spell of wood ageing. Soft on the palate, it also has plenty of texture and an elegance that is almost flowery as well as great balance and tempting length. On the nose, the Tocai Friulano presents aromas of sage and pear. The palate is long, ending on the characteristic varietal note of almonds. The Sauvignon, too, is a text book varietal with its red pepper and elderflower nose and vegetal notes in the finish. In the Pinot Grigio, pear vies with apple in the key note in the bouquet. Finally, a splendid "vino da meditazione" to round off with. When our tasters sampled the Picolit '93 again this year, it came very close indeed to being awarded a full Three Glasses.

CORMONS (GO)

EDI KEBER
LOC. ZEGLA, 17
34071 CORMONS (GO)
TEL. 0481/61184

If we were to concentrate our attention exclusively on Three Glass wines, we would have to say that the genial Edi Keber missed out - if only by a whisker - on a repetition of last year's success. But a broader assessment of the tasting results obtained leads to the conclusion that the entire Keber range is of premium quality. There were two wines in the running for Three Glasses and they only just failed to make the grade. The Pinot Bianco '96 gained excellent marks. Its nose is stylish but at the same time intensely fruity. Green apple emerges in the mouth in a complex, well balanced and consistent palate that has length and zest. The oak in which the outstanding Merlot '95 matured is immediately obvious on the nose, where it mingles attractively with rich red fruit. The full flavoured, balanced palate follows through to reveal good structure and considerable ageing potential. A comfortable Two Glasses also went to the Tocai Friulano '96 for its depth of vanilla and white plum aromas, mirrored on a palate underpinned by good alcohol that takes its leave slowly with a flavour of plums in the finish. "Stylish" is the adjective that springs to mind for the Collio Bianco, a blend of tocai friulano, malvasia istriana and ribolla gialla. The nose has apple and whitecurrant, and in the mouth it is soft, lingering and very drinkable. The Cabernet '96 obtained its One Glass with plenty to spare. The generous nose reveals red berries and grass, picked up by full flavours that lead into an end palate where the cabernet's distinctive vegetal notes are tempered by glycerine. In contrast, the varietal aromas of the Sauvignon are indistinct on the nose but emerge more clearly on the palate, which is fresh with the tang of grapefruit. The Pinot Grigio, another One Glass winner, has an aroma which brings back memories of russet apples.

○	COF Bianco Terre Alte '95	▼▼▼	5
●	COF Merlot Rosazzo Sossò Ris. '94	▼▼	5
○	Chardonnay Esperto '96	▼▼	3*
○	COF Pinot Grigio '96	▼	4
○	COF Sauvignon '96	▼	4
○	COF Tocai Friulano '96	▼	4
○	Terre Alte '89	▽▽▽	5
○	Terre Alte '90	▽▽▽	5
○	Terre Alte '92	▽▽▽	5
○	Terre Alte '93	▽▽▽	5
○	COF Picolit Rosazzo Ris. '93	▽▽	5
●	COF Merlot Sossò Ris. '90	▽▽	5

○	Collio Bianco '96	▼▼	3
○	Collio Pinot Bianco '96	▼▼	3
○	Collio Tocai Friulano '96	▼▼	3
●	Collio Merlot '95	▼▼	4
●	Collio Cabernet '96	▼	3
○	Collio Pinot Grigio '96	▼	3
○	Collio Sauvignon '96	▼	3
○	Collio Tocai Friulano '95	▽▽▽	3
●	Collio Cabernet '95	▽▽	3
●	Collio Merlot '94	▽	4

CORMONS (GO)

CORMONS (GO)

LA BOATINA
VIA CORONA, 62
34071 CORMONS (GO)
TEL. 0481/60445

MAGNÀS - ANDREA E LUCIANO VISINTIN
VIA CORONA, 47
34071 CORMONS (GO)
TEL. 0481/60991

The vineyards of La Boatina, owned by businessman Loretto Pali, occupy 20 hectares on the southernmost edge of the Collio DOC zone at Cormons. This year the winemaker, Flavio Berin, has come up with an extremely interesting range of products, as can be seen from the flurry of awards. The wine we like best was the Pinot Bianco '96, which revealed elegant banana and apple on the nose and a balanced zesty softness on the palate. Two Glasses also went to the Merlot '95 for its concentrated raspberry and bilberry aromas, soft tannins on the palate, full fruity body and long finish. Equally impressive was the Bordeaux blend Picol Maggiore '93, whose round, intense nose releases concentrated wild berries, following through with a mouth-filling palate to conclude with a fine fruit-rich aftertaste. The Cabernet Sauvignon '95 came close to earning Two Glasses for its intense, almost opaque ruby colour, and aromas of wild berries, cherries and baked plums that usher in a mellow palate let down slightly only by roughish tannins. The Ronco Boatina, blended from riesling and ribolla gialla, has a fresh, stylish nose of mild tobacco, lemon, apple, yellow plum and spring flowers. The entry on the palate is understated, picking up the aromas of the bouquet before burgeoning into a satisfying finish. We also awarded One Glass to the zesty Chardonnay, the Tocai Friulano, which nicely exemplifies the variety's typical pear and apples aromas, and the elegantly well balanced, lingering Pinot Grigio. Our congratulations, then, to La Boatina, a dependable producer of premium wines that again fully deserves its profile in the Guide.

The decision to admit Magnàs, a traditional small-scale producer, to the Guide last year was a good one. This diversified family business is now run by Luciano Visintin and his son Andrea, the former concentrating on the five hectares or so of vineyards and the latter busying himself in the cellar. About one hectare of the estate lies in the Collio appellation and the remainder in the Isonzo del Friuli DOC. The La Boatina Pinot Bianco impressed us for its elegance on the nose notwithstanding gutsy fruit aromas and the fine follow through on the palate, enhanced by tangy acidity that expanded in the finish. The Chardonnay Isonzo is obtained from very young vines but still came close to a Two Glasses rating. Its typical notes of yeast and apple emerge distinctly on the nose and on the palate and it also has fairly good structure. Initially, the Tocai Friulano is a little metallic but then the variety's characteristic almond notes triumph to herald a palate that is refreshing, soft, consistent and long. The Pinot Grigio puts the accent on pear. The Sauvignon is another wine which pays the price for being obtained from young vines, and it lacks something in balance. But given the serious professionalism of the Visintins, all we have to do is wait.

○	Collio Pinot Bianco '96	🍷🍷	3
●	Collio Merlot '95	🍷🍷	3
●	Collio Rosso Picol Maggiore '93	🍷🍷	3
●	Collio Cabernet Sauvignon '95	🍷	3
○	Collio Chardonnay '96	🍷	3
○	Collio Pinot Grigio '96	🍷	3
○	Collio Tocai Friulano '96	🍷	3
○	Ronco Boatina	🍷	3
○	Collio Sauvignon '96		3
●	Collio Cabernet Franc '95		3

○	Isonzo Friuli Pinot Bianco '96	🍷🍷	2*
○	Collio Tocai Friulano '96	🍷	2
○	Isonzo Friuli Chardonnay '96	🍷	2
○	Isonzo Friuli Pinot Grigio '96		2
○	Isonzo Friuli Sauvignon '96		2

CORMONS (GO)

CORMONS (GO)

ROBERTO PICECH
LOC. PRADIS, 11
34071 CORMONS (GO)
TEL. 0481/60347

ISIDORO POLENCIC
LOC. PLESSIVA, 12
34071 CORMONS (GO)
TEL. 0481/60655

The labels on Roberto Picech's wines bear the words "Le vigne del Ribèl" with an accompanying illustration of a prickly-backed hedgehog. This is a reference to Roberto's father Egidio; a somewhat blunt-mannered character but an admirable example of an enterprising generation of former tenant farmers who have transformed their small holdings into independent wine estates. Today the Picech family possesses five hectares of vines, which they have worked since 1920 and from which they obtain 25,000 bottles a year. It was Roberto - as different from his father as chalk is from cheese - who laid down the estate's current quality-driven strategy and he has no intention of resting on his laurels. In 1995, he decided not to harvest the red grapes ahead of time in September to avoid the heavy rainfall and his courage was rewarded by two weeks of brilliant sunshine in early October. The vintage produced two superb wines, the Merlot and the Cabernet Sauvignon '95. The first of these was slowly matured in oak and greets the nose with lingering aromas of Morello cherry and red berry preserve. It follows through nicely on the palate, which is full bodied despite the presence of young tannins that will mellow with the passage of time. The richly perfumed Cabernet Sauvignon was matured in Slavonian oak and reveals notes that range from Morello cherry to very ripe plums on the nose, with the same aromas nicely evoked in the mouth-filling palate. The Collio Tocai, a blend of tocai, malvasia and ribolla, lacks something in elegance. Notes of vanilla, milk, barley and honey emerge on the nose and the palate is soft and alcohol-rich with plenty of balance and length. The Picechs' Malvasia Istriana has a lively, tempting elegance and the Tocai Friulano and Sauvignon were both well worth a mention.

Last year, Doro Polencic's estate was included in the Guide for the first time and this year's vintage has also produced wines that made a very favourable impression on our tasters. The twenty hectares of vineyards lie almost exclusively (90 percent) in the Collio DOC, the remainder being in the Isonzo appellation. The generously proportioned Polencic cellars, completed in the early 1980s, are made to handle an annual production of around 1,500 quintals of wine. Doro's family, in the persons of daughter Elisabetta and son Michele, takes an active part in the running of the business. Their excellent Sauvignon '96 is intense on the nose, where typical vegetal and grapefruit aromas emerge discreetly. The well balanced palate is backed up by plenty of body and enviable texture. The Pinot Bianco is another text book varietal; the apple, berries and ripe yellow plums on the nose are also present on a palate that has the right degree of acidity to underpin its lingering finish. Pineapple and pear are the keynote aromas of the Pinot Grigio, and come back on a refreshing, broad palate. The Chardonnay, too, gained a score that took it within a hair's breadth of a Two Glass rating. The nose is reminiscent of honey, pineapple, spring flowers and hazelnut and the entry is soft, although the palate becomes slightly more assertive as the acidity emerges before signing off with a finish that highlights its freshness. Both the delicate, stylish Ribolla Gialla and the solidly made, attractively textured Tocai Friulano came close to One Glass ratings.

●	Collio Cabernet Sauvignon '95	▽▽	4	○ Collio Pinot Bianco '96	▽▽	3
●	Collio Merlot '95	▽▽	4	○ Collio Pinot Grigio '96	▽▽	3
○	Collio Bianco '96	▽	4	○ Collio Sauvignon '96	▽▽	3
○	Collio Malvasia Istriana '96	▽	3	○ Collio Chardonnay '96	▽	3
○	Collio Pinot Bianco '96	▽	3	○ Collio Ribolla Gialla '96		3
○	Collio Sauvignon '96		3	○ Collio Tocai Friulano '96		3
○	Collio Tocai Friulano '96		3	○ Collio Pinot Bianco '95	▽▽	3
○	Collio Sauvignon '95	▽▽	3	○ Collio Tocai Friulano '95	▽▽	3
○	Passito di Pradis '94	▽▽	5			

CORMONS (GO)

CORMONS (GO)

ISIDORO E ALESSANDRO PRINCIC
LOC. PRADIS, 5
34071 CORMONS (GO)
TEL. 0481/60723

DARIO RACCARO
VIA S. GIOVANNI, 87/B
34071 CORMONS (GO)
TEL. 0481/61425

Sandro Princic and his wife Grazia are paragons of the hospitality - as well as the oenological quality - to be found on the hillsides at Pradis. It is certainly an ideal spot in which to produce first rank wines but as always an expert hand is essential. And Sandro's winemaking skills were acquired under the severe eye of his father, Doro, a source of viticultural lore still consulted by a good many producers today. We were not able to award another Three Glasses to any of the Princic wines this time but Sandro is not one to take umbrage. His customers still fall over themselves in the rush to get their hands on his wine. But the estate came very close to another top award with the Pinot Bianco '96. The rich fruit on the nose is complex and elegant at the same time, following through well on the refreshing palate, where a note of tangy green apple emerges in the lingering finish. As always, the Tocai Friulano was a high scorer with its aromas of pear and apple. Weighty rather than elegant, it has an uncompromising palate that is full bodied, fresh-tasting and remarkably long. The apple-dominated nose of the Pinot Grigio is modulated by delicate spicy notes and its fullness on the palate is tinged with just enough acidity to balance its buttery texture before apple emerges again in the aftertaste. In the Sauvignon, an elegance reminiscent of peaches gives way to the opulent fullness of the palate. The limited-production Malvasia is unexpectedly dry, its vegetal, aromatic notes of pear pips inviting you to serve it with fish. If Sandro had a little more time for red wines then his Merlot would win more than just the One Glass it easily deserved for its enticing hints of Morello cherry emerging against a backdrop of luscious red berries. We can only hope that the imperturbable winemaker from Pradis will take up the challenge.

Dario Raccaro makes an immediate impression with his serious, professional attitude and commitment to winemaking; utterly reliable like his wines, which have a faithful following among the hundreds of private customers who make up at least 70 percent of his clientele. If further proof of his standing were needed, he has for many years been President of the group of producers at Cormons who run the prestigious municipal enoteca. Dario's small estate is run to strict professional standards with consistently low yields. Recently Raccaro has also rented an excellent plot between Brazzano and Cormons and we look forward to sampling the results of this new investment in the very near future. In the meantime, he has turned out a superb Malvasia Istriana with a complex, stunningly elegant nose that is delicate yet intense, evoking acacia blossom and faint overtones of apple. The Tocai Friulano gained its One Glass with points to spare for its clean fresh fruit aromas mingling with vegetal notes. The fullness of the entry on the palate is unexpected, and the mid-palate is well balanced, the glycerine being nicely offset by acidity and a satisfying finish. This is definitely a wine to come back to in the future. The '96 Sauvignon was only moderately typical but nonetheless fresh and clean tasting. And finally the Merlot '96 - still very young and relatively uncomplicated when we tasted it - revealed notes of green hazelnut on the nose and a core of Morello cherry in the finish.

O	Collio Pinot Bianco '96	♼♼	3
O	Collio Pinot Grigio '96	♼♼	3
O	Collio Tocai Friulano '96	♼♼	3
O	Collio Malvasia '96	♼	3
O	Collio Sauvignon '96	♼	3
●	Collio Merlot '95	♼	3
O	Collio Pinot Bianco '95	♼♼♼	3
O	Collio Tocai Friulano '93	♼♼♼	3
●	Collio Cabernet Franc '94	♼♼	3
O	Collio Pinot Grigio '95	♼♼	3
O	Collio Tocai Friulano '95	♼♼	3

O	Collio Malvasia Istriana '96	♼♼	3*
O	Collio Tocai Friulano '96	♼	3
O	Collio Sauvignon '96		3
●	Collio Merlot '96		3

CORMONS (GO)

RONCO DEI TASSI
LOC. MONTE, 38
34071 CORMONS (GO)
TEL. 0481/60155

CORMONS (GO)

RONCO DEL GELSO
VIA ISONZO, 117
34071 CORMONS (GO)
TEL. 0481/61310

Fabio Coser spares no effort to get the best from his raw material and this year, for the second time, he has succeeded in producing a Three Glass wine. The other occasion was ten years ago, when he hit the jackpot with a memorable Sauvignon (last year he also went very close with his Collio Rosso Cjarandon '94 and Tocai Friulano '95). His latest hit is the Collio Bianco Fosarin '96, a blend of tocai friulano, ribolla gialla, malvasia istriana and barrel-matured pinot bianco. Bright straw yellow, with a rich, complex nose of elegant flowers and fruit, it releases refreshing apple, pear and yellow plum fruit on entry, then warm alcohol emerges in mid-palate before a perfectly balanced finish with superb texture. The '96 Tocai Friulano is another outstanding wine where elegant pear notes stand out in the rich fruit aromas. The balance is remarkable and the rich flavour is underpinned by exactly the right acidity. The flavours in the mouth echo the nose in textbook fashion and the palate has lots of attractive chewy fruit. The Pinot Grigio also has plenty of fruit, as well as breadth and balance, and the palate is fresh-tasting yet rich in complex, balanced flavour. Coser's Collio Rosso Cjarandon '95 is a Bordeaux blend from a difficult vintage and is not as impressive as its predecessor. The wood could have been better judged; nonetheless it lets grassy notes come through over wild berries and Morello cherry. The entry on the palate is full flavoured but the tannins aren't as rounded as they might have been. It takes its leave with a rich abundance of fruit. All in all, though, Fabio and his wife Daniela have had wonderful success with their four-hectare estate, which produces 20,000 bottles a year. They deserve a special acknowledgement for their unfashionable decision to limit themselves to a select range of wines at a time when other producers are churning out more and more different labels, crus and varieties.

It's not easy to make an assessment of Giorgio Badin's wines because only familiarity over many years can give an insight into how they develop. His estate management has always aimed at low yields per vine and his highly individual use of hyperoxygenation in the cellar produces results that at first sight seem contradictory. Hard though it is to believe, his wines are ready - and in perfect condition - at the end of October. Then they mature and reduce in the bottle through to the following spring before the structure and ageing potential become obvious as the aromas finally find their feet. For this reason we have not reviewed the Merlot '95 or the Cabernet Franc '96, both of which were awesomely powerful on the palate but uncertain on the nose. The passage of time will show just how good the Tocai '96 is. At the moment, the nose is slightly blurred even though the palate is already outstanding. The Bianco Làtimis '96, obtained from old tocai vines blended with 20 percent chardonnay, is a thumping good wine and the Riesling - one of the few truly excellent examples of this varietal in Friuli - has impressive cellarability. Badin's lemony gold Chardonnay is 50 percent barrel-fermented and offers a balanced, agreeable nose of pear with herbal and peach tea aromas that are also present on the palate, which is dry, soft and blessed with substantial fruit. The barrel-matured Pinot Grigio Sot lis Rivis is muscular rather than elegant and finally the dry, concentrated Sauvignon also repays attention.

O	Collio Bianco Fosarin '96	♍♍♍	3
O	Collio Pinot Grigio '96	♍♍	3
O	Collio Tocai Friulano '96	♍♍	3
●	Collio Rosso Cjarandon '95	♍	4
●	Collio Rosso Cjarandon '94	♐♐	4
O	Collio Bianco '95	♐♐	3
O	Collio Tocai Friulano '95	♐♐	3

O	Isonzo Friuli Bianco Làtimis '96	♍♍	4
O	Isonzo Friuli Chardonnay '96	♍♍	4
O	Isonzo Friuli Riesling '96	♍♍	4
O	Isonzo Friuli Tocai Friulano '96	♍♍	3*
O	Isonzo Friuli Pinot Grigio Sot lis Rivis '96	♍	4
O	Isonzo Friuli Sauvignon '96	♍	4
●	Isonzo Merlot '91	♍♍♍	4
O	Isonzo Tocai Friulano '94	♍♍♍	4
O	Isonzo Friuli Tocai Friulano '95	♍♍♍	4
●	Isonzo Merlot '92	♐♐	4
O	Isonzo Friuli Chardonnay '95	♐♐	4
O	Isonzo Friuli Pinot Grigio Sot lis Rivis '95	♐♐	4

CORMONS (GO)

GIOVANNI SREDNIK
LOC. PRADIS, 1
34071 CORMONS (GO)
TEL. 0481/60873

Quality you can bank on is the reason behind the inclusion in the Guide for the second year running of the estate owned by Giovanni Srednik and his daughter Laura. It is thanks to the efforts of Giovanni in the vineyard and Laura, who has a diploma in agriculture, that we are now able to list the winery among the first rank in the region. Other news from the Sredniks, such as their anxiously awaited white blend, should come soon after the splendid vintage of 1997 on their eight-hectare property at Pradis. Watch this space. Meanwhile the '96 wines created a very good overall impression, beginning with the Ribolla Gialla. The bright gold-flecked colour here introduces distinct notes of intense fruit and heavyish vanilla which originate in the structure of the wine and from not wood maturation; the Sredniks employ barrel ageing exclusively for reds. The palate evokes banana and yellow plums over excellent acidity. The Müller Thurgau '96 is pale straw yellow, its fresh penetrating nose redolent of ripe plum-dominated fruit. It follows through nicely on the unpretentious palate, where apple fruit reappears. Peach tea, acacia blossom and hints of vanilla can all be noted in the bouquet of the Srednik Tocai Friulano '96, whose straightforward but beautifully balanced palate reveals the typical tocai notes of almond in the finish. The Chardonnay, like the Pinot Grigio and the Merlot well worth a mention, was impressive on entry but the bitterish note in the finish brought its overall score down.

○	Collio Ribolla Gialla '96	🍷🍷	3
○	Collio Müller Thurgau '96	🍷	3
○	Collio Tocai Friulano '96	🍷	3
○	Collio Chardonnay '96		3
○	Collio Pinot Grigio '96		3
●	Collio Merlot '96		3

CORMONS (GO)

OSCAR STURM
LOC. ZEGLA, 1
34071 CORMONS (GO)
TEL. 0481/60720

A winery as good as Oscar Sturm's could not stay tucked away in the "Other Wineries" section for long. Even an only moderately successful vintage such as the '96 was enough for him to make a comeback with a range of wines that are well made - Sturm's products are never anything else - and all scored commendably in our tastings. The Sturm family, which comes originally from the Stiria region of Austria, has been settled here for more than a century and today produces more than 40,000 bottles a year from slightly more than ten hectares of vineyards, mainly in the Collio DOC zone. In the cellars, which were completely restructured a few years ago, the Sturms can rely on the winemaking expertise of Giovanni Crosato. Their Tocai Friulano '96 is a Two wine with points to spare. The intense rennet and hazelnut nose is picked up in the aromas on the palate, fresh-tasting and nicely balanced between elegance and weight. The long finish is attractively fruity. Sturm's Bianco '95 is an expertly oaked blend of pinot grigio, chardonnay and sauvignon. The entry on the palate is warm yet fresh-tasting, then the relaxed acidity emerges to lead into a ravishingly attractive finish. Vanilla and cream aromas mingle with tropical fruit and yeast in the nose of the Chardonnay '96 to continue on the moderately rich palate. The Pinot Grigio '96 is elegant and hard to pin down on the nose but pear eventually comes forth from the complex fruit. There is pear again in the balanced, nicely textured refreshing palate. Then we sampled the Sauvignon, which had lovely varietal aromas, including peach and sage, moderate structure and tangy acidity. The Sturm reds were less exciting but nonetheless well worth listing.

○	Collio Tocai Friulano '96	🍷🍷	3
○	Bianco '95	🍷	3
○	Chardonnay '96	🍷	3
○	Collio Pinot Grigio '96	🍷	3
○	Collio Sauvignon '96	🍷	3
●	Collio Cabernet Franc '96		3
●	Merlot Andritz '95		3

CORMONS (GO)

SUBIDA DI MONTE
LOC. MONTE, 9
34071 CORMONS (GO)
TEL. 0481/61011

The '95 vintage might not have been particularly rewarding for Gigi Antonutti's estate but this year we are happy to report that there has been a significant improvement in quality, now that the restructuring programme has been completed. This major step forward is partly a result of the excellent '96 vintage but it is also due to the wider range of vinification techniques possible in the new cellar. The lovely Bianco Subida '96, officially a vino da tavola, is assembled from traminer, tocai friulano and riesling grapes which have a young, fresh nose nuanced with sulphur that time will tone down, leaving the fruit, where pear stands out. The aromas are mirrored on the refreshing, extract-rich and slightly bitter palate leading into a triumphantly long finish. This year the Collio Merlot Riserva '94 again proved to be a very fine wine indeed. Complex, attractively structured and full flavoured on the palate, it boasts vigorous tannins that will mellow in years to come. The Pinot Bianco '96 has a clear straw colour and classy apple fruit on the nose and is well made, uncomplicated and pleasantly long in the mouth. Subida's Pinot Grigio '96 is unexpectedly delicate, offering nuances of pear on the nose. Dry on the palate, it has moderate acidity and good length. Finally the Tocai Friulano '96 has an intense nose of almonds and fruit followed up by a fresh-tasting, fruity palate and a deliciously lingering finish.

○ Bianco Subida '96	🍷🍷	3
○ Collio Pinot Bianco '96	🍷	3
○ Collio Pinot Grigio '96	🍷	3
○ Collio Tocai Friulano '96	🍷	3
● Collio Merlot Ris. '94	YY	4

CORMONS (GO)

FRANCO TORÒS
VIA NOVALI, 12
34071 CORMONS (GO)
TEL. 0481/61327

Franco Toròs has yet to pull a Three Glass wine out of the hat, but the general quality of his production continues to improve steadily. His nine-hectare estate is worth a visit, if nothing else to see just how a top flight winery is run. Visitors' response to his renovated and extended cellars is invariably positive; the facility allows Toròs a wide range of technical options as well as ideal conditions for barrel-ageing and cellaring his wines prior to release. The excellent Tocai Friulano '96 is unassertive but elegant, offering notes of acacia blossom and freshly-picked hazelnuts. The palate follows through well with good structure, style and an opulent, lingering flavour. Franco's classy Pinot Grigio is redolent of spring flowers, pear and apple, all reflected in the rich, complex palate and its juicy, refreshing texture. What impressed us about the Merlot '95 was the breadth of the bouquet, which mingled kirsch, pink peppercorns and cassis. Alcohol-rich and tannic, the palate recalls a mixed fruit preserve rich in cherry, damson and raspberry. The very alcoholic Pinot Bianco has a stylish nose with overtones of apple, nice balance and good length. Next the wood-matured Chardonnay '95 revealed distinct golden highlights in the glass that introduced aromas of banana and vanilla. However, the toasty oak needs a little more time to blend with the fruit on the palate. In contrast the Chardonnay '96 - vinified exclusively in stainless steel - is a more straightforward wine; its varietal, yeasty flavours and pear drop aromas are balanced very attractively on the palate by the tangy acidity. The Cabernet Franc '95 produced similar tasting notes. The nose lacks a little balance but the splendidly mellow palate has just the right combination of tannins and acidity. Soft yet vegetal in flavour, it has a deliciously fruity finish.

○ Collio Pinot Grigio '96	🍷🍷	3*
○ Collio Tocai Friulano '96	🍷🍷	3*
● Collio Merlot '95	🍷🍷	3*
● Collio Cabernet Franc '95	🍷	3
○ Collio Chardonnay '96	🍷	3
○ Collio Chardonnay '95	🍷	4
○ Collio Pinot Bianco '96	🍷	3
○ Collio Chardonnay '94	YY	4
● Collio Merlot '94	Y	3

279

CORNO DI ROSAZZO (UD) CORNO DI ROSAZZO (UD)

CA' DI BON
VIA CASALI GALLO, 1
33040 CORNO DI ROSAZZO (UD)
TEL. 0432/759316

COLLAVINI
VIA DELLA RIBOLLA GIALLA, 2
33040 CORNO DI ROSAZZO (UD)
TEL. 0432/753222

The Ca' di Bon estate belongs to a husband and wife team, Ameris and Gianni Bon, with a characteristically Friulian winemaking philosophy. Their seven hectares at Corno di Rosazzo are scattered over three DOC zones; Friuli Grave, Colli Orientali del Friuli and Collio. Some of the estate's production is sold unbottled so the '96 vintage only rendered about 30,000 bottles, but these are divided between as many as twelve different labels, which means that very few bottles of any one wine are ever available. The pick of the bunch this year is the lovely Ribolla Gialla '96, a fresh, stylishly flowery wine on the nose that has typical acidity on a palate where green apple and not quite ripe white plum stand out. The glycerine-rich texture makes the long finish a very rewarding experience. The copper-flecked Pinot Grigio reveals somewhat unsophisticated fruit on the nose but there is superb balance on the palate between its acidity and the pear and apple flavours. The Bons' Merlot is a well rounded wine with delicately spicy aromas redolent of cherries and raspberry. It has plenty of tannins on the palate where good structure offsets the lively acidity. The Sauvignon, a more impressive wine on the palate than on the nose, only just failed to win a One Glass rating. The Tocai Friulano, Refosco dal Peduncolo Rosso and Verduzzo Friulano are all well made wines. The white Ronco del Nonno is a cuvée of pinot bianco, sauvignon and tocai friulano

Manlio Collavini is head of a winery that vinifies more than 30,000 hectolitres every year as well as being the leading producer of sparkling wines in Friuli (annual output is around 400,000 bottles, including both charmat-method and classic-method products). Only part of the grapes used come from vineyards on the estate and Collavini also vinifies and distributes the range of Count Douglas Attems, historic president of the Consorzio Collio producers' consortium, whose reds are outstanding premium wines. The Merlot '94 Riserva di Casa sold under the Collavini label is a good wine that fully deserves the One Glass it was awarded during our tasting. The nose is reminiscent of red berry, cherry and bilberry preserve, nicely mirrored in the temptingly rich fruity palate, and the wine will certainly improve after a little time in the cellar. Another convincing wine was the Pinot Grigio Villa di Canlungo '96. Classy fruit on the nose was followed up by distinct pear notes on the palate, underpinned by refreshing acidity - a bit of a surprise as the label describes the wine as a "late vintage". The Chardonnay dei Sassi Cavi is obtained from grapes grown in the Friuli Grave DOC zone and has characteristic varietal aromas of banana and boiled sweets. Apricot emerges on the fruit-rich palate. Next came Grigio, the sparkling wine with which Collavini has carved out a leading share of the spumante market and which rated One Glass in our tasting. The delicate perlage reveals notes of pear and apple, followed through nicely on the palate before a finish with an agreeably tangy note of acidity. Finally the Sauvignon Borgo Blanc di Casa suffered from excessive acidity but was nonetheless worthy of a mention.

O	COF Ribolla Gialla '96	🍷🍷	3*
O	COF Pinot Grigio '96	🍷	3
●	COF Merlot '96	🍷	3
●	COF Refosco P. R. '96		3
O	COF Tocai Friulano '96		3
O	COF Verduzzo Friulano '96		3
O	Ronco del Nonno '96		3
O	Sauvignon '96		3

●	Collio Merlot Riserva di Casa '94	🍷	3
O	Collio Pinot Grigio Villa del Canlungo '96	🍷	3
O	Friuli Grave Chardonnay dei Sassi Cavi '96	🍷	3
O	Grigio Spumante	🍷	3
O	Collio Sauvignon Blanc Borgo di Casa '96		2

CORNO DI ROSAZZO (UD)

CORNO DI ROSAZZO (UD)

ADRIANO GIGANTE
VIA ROCCA BERNARDA, 3
33040 CORNO DI ROSAZZO (UD)
TEL. 0432/755835

LEONARDO SPECOGNA
VIA ROCCA BERNARDA, 4
33040 CORNO DI ROSAZZO (UD)
TEL. 0432/755840

Adriano Gigante is a man who practises what he preaches. Just as he did last year, he has again postponed bottling until early September because he thinks it is the right thing for his wines. Unfortunately, the Guide's publishing deadlines do not always fit in with the praiseworthy bottling schedules of producers, but we could not exclude Adriano Gigante, given the quality of the '95 vintage wines that we tasted during the year. The best of these - out of a total of 50,000 bottles that Adriano obtains from his 11-hectare property - was without doubt the Tocai Friulano. Intense, broad and fruity on the nose, it is full flavoured and mouth-filling on the palate, with an attractive hint of aniseed. The Verduzzo Friulano '95 offers a complex bouquet of honey and dried flowers leading into an unaggressively sweet palate and a generously long, fruity finish. Gigante's Chardonnay '95 has good acidity and plenty of fruit, overlaid with complex aromas of yeast, crusty bread and pear on the nose. A slightly dilute palate detracted from the score of the Sauvignon '95, which nonetheless yielded nicely balanced varietal aromas of tomato leaf and elderflower. The Pinot Grigio '95 came close to a One Glass ranking with its faintly bitter, toasted barley sugar nose and the Cabernet Franc '95, despite a rather overstated note of the variety's typical grassy aroma, was adequately complex. To round off, the Merlot '95 was also worth its mention.

Graziano Specogna hopes in the future to increase his production of red wine, for which he believes his "terroir" has a particular vocation. He also wants to expand the use of wood in the cellar to broaden his product range. To these ends he has recently put in another two hectares of red varieties, bringing the total area up to that of the whites, a rather unusual choice for Friuli. For some time now, Valdino Diust, the estate's long-standing consultant analyst and winemaker, has been joined by Alexander Trolf, a young Austrian winemaker with great expertise in the use of small oak barrels. The results are there for all to see. The very successful Chardonnay '95 was almost entirely fermented in wood. The entry on the nose is exciting, offering herbal infusions, wood and bottled fruit that lead into a refreshing palate where milk and aromatic herb flavours - especially mint - are in evidence. The finish is rigorous and elegant. On the nose, the Cabernet '95 releases an intense aroma of red berries and Peruvian bark. Concentrated on the palate, it is potent and lingering with unobtrusive tannins. A hint of tannin-inspired astringency penalized the supple, fresh, fruity Merlot '95 which revealed green, almost vegetal, nuances on the nose. The gold flecks in the colour tell you that the '96 is one of Specogna's traditionally fatty Tocai Friulano whites. The fullness and warmth on the palate are delicious and the pear and apple seed aromas are sustained by good length.

O	COF Tocai Friulano '95	♙♙	3*
O	COF Chardonnay '95	♙	3
O	COF Sauvignon '95	♙	3
O	COF Verduzzo Friulano '95	♙	3
O	COF Pinot Grigio '95		3
●	COF Cabernet Franc '95		3
●	COF Merlot '95		3

O	COF Chardonnay '95	♙♙	3
●	COF Cabernet '95	♙♙	3
●	COF Merlot '95	♙	3
O	COF Tocai Friulano '96	♙	3
O	COF Chardonnay Barrique '94	♉♉	3
●	COF Merlot '93	♉♉	3
●	COF Merlot '94	♉	3

CORNO DI ROSAZZO (UD)   CORNO DI ROSAZZO (UD)

ANDREA VISINTINI
VIA GRAMOGLIANO, 27
33040 CORNO DI ROSAZZO (UD)
TEL. 0432/755813

ZOF
VIA GIOVANNI XXIII, 32/A
33040 CORNO DI ROSAZZO (UD)
TEL. 0432/759673

The results achieved by Andrea Visintini's winery, in the Guide for the second time, are very impressive indeed. The estate comprises 17 hectares, three of which are at Cormons in the Collio appellation. Only the best of the wine goes into the roughly 50,000 bottles that the winery sells each year at amazingly low prices. Once again, the Tocai Friulano earned Two Glasses. Its typical pear and apple seed nose is fresh and enticing. The round palate follows through well with loads of fruit and length. The Pinot Grigio is equally good. Onionskin reflections in the glass introduce a complex nose rich in fruit. Full flavoured and glycerine-rich on the palate, it is redolent of pear, above all in the long finish. The Merlot '96 is another fine wine whose cherry and plum aromas were even more intense on the palate than the nose. Salty in the mouth, it is full flavoured and boasts attractive tannins. Just below these three came the Cabernet. Tobacco and roasted coffee beans emerge on the nose while the remarkable structure of the finely textured palate evokes toasty notes, baked red fruit and new-mown grass. The Pinot Bianco comes from Plessiva at Cormons and offers elegant notes of apple. The palate is warm and soft, with fruit you can get your teeth into. Visintini's Ribolla Gialla is typical, the flowery notes dominating fruit aromas on the nose. Apple and whitecurrant fruit comes out again on the palate together with acidity. Finally, the Traminer Aromatico is as varietal a wine as you will find in Friuli, revealing candied fruit and lavender over a background of petrol.

In the world of winemaking, a handover from one generation to the next often means an unexpected improvement in quality. It was certainly the case with the Zof estate when Daniele, a qualified winemaker and member of the Zof family's younger generation, took over. There were no miracles involved, of course. Daniele simply began to let a cellar that vinifies grapes from a superb winemaking zone express itself to the full. He is ably assisted in this mission by the consultant Donato Lanati and his Enosis organization. The Zofs own eight hectares under vine and rent a further seven. A proportion of the wine they obtain goes to make about 55,000 bottles a year, the rest being sold through the family farm holiday business. We sampled six of the ten Zof wines, all of which earned at least a mention and two scored very well. The Pinot Grigio, vinified off the skins, has full, complex aromas redolent of flowers. The palate is full and well balanced, with apple and pear to the fore, while lively acidity sustains the finish. The Sauvignon has a nice bright colour and reveals crisp, intense aromas of peach and sage that are carried through well onto the palate. Balance, structure and length are impeccable and the finish is reminiscent of fruit. Notes of hedgerow, pear and fruit salad emerge on the nose of the Tocai Friulano. Nicely balanced in the mouth, it is soft-flavoured and very likeable. The Pinot Bianco and Merlot were both comparatively uncomplicated but dependable. The Va' Pensiero '93, obtained from schioppettino and cabernet sauvignon grapes, had notes of tar over bilberry and bramble but failed overall to excite the tasters. We look forward to subsequent experiments with this wine, some of which were assembled from different grapes.

○ COF Tocai Friulano '96	🍷🍷	2*
○ COF Pinot Grigio '96	🍷🍷	2*
● COF Merlot '96	🍷🍷	2*
● COF Cabernet '96	🍷	2
○ COF Ribolla Gialla '96	🍷	2
○ COF Traminer Aromatico '96	🍷	2
○ Collio Pinot Bianco '96	🍷	2
○ Collio Malvasia Istriana '96		2
○ COF Tocai Friulano '95	🍷🍷	2

○ COF Pinot Grigio '96	🍷🍷	2*
○ COF Sauvignon '96	🍷🍷	2*
○ COF Tocai Friulano '96	🍷	2*
○ COF Pinot Bianco '96		2
● COF Merlot '96		2
● Va' Pensiero '93		4

DOLEGNA DEL COLLIO (GO)

DOLEGNA DEL COLLIO (GO)

CA' RONESCA
LOC. LONZANO, 27
34070 DOLEGNA DEL COLLIO (GO)
TEL. 0481/60034

VENICA & VENICA
VIA MERNICO, 42
LOC. CERÒ
34070 DOLEGNA DEL COLLIO (GO)
TEL. 0481/61264

Ca' Ronesca continues to turn out the wines of outstanding quality we would expect from an estate with such a distinguished history, ideally located vineyards in the Collio and Colli Orientali DOC zones, and superbly equipped facilities. Further improvements are on the way too, thanks to replanting that will replace old vine stock and introduce new, low yielding pruning systems; we wish every good fortune to Sergio Comunello, the founder of the estate, to his nephew and winery manager Paolo Bianchi, and their winemaker Franco Della Rossa. In this year's tastings we particularly liked their Marnà '95, a blend of pinot bianco and malvasia istriana. It has perfumes of gooseberry, vanilla and banana and follows through well, offering plump fruit and good acidity. The well balanced Collio Pinot Bianco '96 was equally good, its classy typical golden delicious nuances hinting at excellent length. The estate's fine COF Picolit is well up to last year's high standard, catching the eye with its remarkable green and gold highlights and the nose with notes of honey, almonds and figs. The stylish sweet-yet-dry palate is rounded off by a finish of ripe fruit. The Collio Pinot Grigio '96 very nearly gained a full Two Glasses for its elegant, complex pear-dominated fruit and balanced acidity but was let down by a lack of structure. The COF Pinot Grigio Podere di Ipplis '96 obtained similar marks for its intense, stylish, ripe fruit aromas and lemony finish. The Sauvignon had lovely notes of red pepper and, together with the Malvasia Istriana and the Cabernet Franc del Collio, is well worth attention.

After years of top quality winemaking, the Venica brothers this year produced two nominations for Three Glasses. At the end of the day they picked up the top award for their Pinot Bianco '96, a wonderfully balanced wine with a nose redolent of rennet, spring flowers and faint, fresh grassy notes. The luscious palate mirrors these aromas beautifully, the fruit is nicely balanced by acidity and there is plenty of structure to take you through to the lingering finish. The Merlot Perilla '93 is the first of a long list of premuim quality wines. After alcoholic and malolactic fermentation, it went into wood for 18 months before maturing for another two years in the bottle. The intense colour introduces attractive toasty notes on the nose, evoking wild berries (bilberry and raspberry) and very ripe cherries. The wood is present again on the palate, this time in the company of tannins and balanced fruit. The Venicas' Sauvignons are legendary, beginning with their standard selection '96. Tomato leaf and peppermint stand out on the nose and the palate is well balanced, delicate, sustained and long. The Sauvignon Ronco delle Mele '96 is one of their crus. It regales the nose with intense aromas in which tomato leaf and lemon verbena dominate. The palate is mouth-filling, well structured and superbly balanced. The Cero '93, another vineyard selection, is fermented in stainless steel and aged for eight months in new oak without malolactic fermentation. The wood is immediately obvious both on the nose and in the mouth, masking to a certain extent the fruit and understated acidity. Rosso delle Cime '93, obtained from cabernet sauvignon with a little refosco and merlot, is soft and luscious on the palate. Finally the velvety Tocai Friulano with its extract-rich walnutskin aroma on the nose and zesty flavour also proved to be a wine of considerable substance.

O	COF Picolit '96	🍷🍷	5
O	COF Pinot Bianco '96	🍷🍷	3*
O	Marnà '95	🍷🍷	4
O	COF Pinot Grigio Podere di Ipplis '96	🍷	4
O	Collio Malvasia Istriana '96	🍷	3*
O	Collio Pinot Grigio '96	🍷	3
O	Collio Sauvignon '96	🍷	3
●	Collio Cabernet Franc '96	🍷	3*
O	COF Pinot Grigio Podere di Ipplis '95	🍷🍷	4
O	COF Picolit '95	🍷🍷	5
●	Sariz '93	🍷	4

O	Collio Pinot Bianco '96	🍷🍷🍷	4
●	Collio Merlot Perilla '93	🍷🍷	4
●	Rosso delle Cime '93	🍷🍷	5
O	Collio Sauvignon '96	🍷🍷	4
O	Collio Sauvignon Ronco delle Mele '96	🍷🍷	4
O	Collio Tocai Friulano '96	🍷🍷	3*
O	Collio Chardonnay '96	🍷	4
O	Collio Sauvignon Cerò '93	🍷	4
O	Collio Ribolla Gialla '96		4
O	Collio Sauvignon '88	🍷🍷🍷	4
O	Collio Sauvignon '90	🍷🍷🍷	4
O	Bianco dei Venica '95	🍷🍷	4
O	Collio Pinot Bianco '95	🍷🍷	4
●	Collio Merlot Perilla '91	🍷🍷	4

DUINO-AURISINA (TS)

FAEDIS (UD)

EDI KANTE
LOC. PREPOTTO, 3
FRAZ. S. PELAGIO
34011 DUINO-AURISINA (TS)
TEL. 040/200761

PAOLINO COMELLI
VIA DELLA CHIESA
LOC. COLLOREDO DI SOFFUMBERGO
33040 FAEDIS (UD)
TEL. 0432/711226-504973

Poor vintages take their toll even when the producer is as serious as Edi Kante. In past years, our tasting notes have bristled with adjectives like "powerful", "rich", "well structured", "balanced" and "broad". But if we look at this year's notes, we find "very high acidity", "a touch too lean", "rather uninteresting" and "fairly dilute" although expressions such as "elegance", "breeding", "clean-tasting" and "nicely judged wood" are still there. It is clear that while the raw material was unimpressive, the winemaking skill is as good as ever. It would be unrealistic to expect uniformly top-flight results every time, but when the winemaking gets tough, the experts know how to make the best of what they have. The Chardonnay, for example, reveals mint, papaya, confectioner's cream and delicate wood on the nose. The palate is stylish, tangy and lingers attractively over flowery aromas. It may not be up to some of Kante's previous Chardonnays but it is still a very satisfying wine. The nose of the Sauvignon has a keynote of butter and white plum, but there is an unexpected and inexplicable hiatus in the fresh, full flavoured palate. The Vitovska again has a nicely balanced nose of honey, lemon-balm and kiwi but is astringent and lacks structure on the palate. The Terrano, however, is a completely different story. Here we find a bright ruby hue from which emerges a very spicy nose and there is attractive chewy fruit to follow. It has more character than balance, but that is in the nature of the variety. Edi tells us that he may not make any more Terrano because so many people have criticised its eccentricity. Let's hope he has second thoughts.

For the past two years we have not been able to taste the wines of notary Pierluigi Comelli, universally known as Pigi. Now they are again available, they make a brilliant re-entry into the Guide. Comelli has invested substantial sums in hills which, although spectacularly beautiful, are not well known for the generosity of their climate. However, scrupulous attention to the vineyard, which is planted at a density of 5,000 vines per hectare, and the craft of winemaker Roberto Ottogalli and consultant Fabio Coser, mean that excellent wines can be obtained despite the location. The Merlot '96 came close to the 80-point threshold, thanks to a concentration on the nose that allowed all the complexity of the fruit to emerge. The palate has fruit again, mingling with the slightly austere tannins. There is an even more evident asperity in the Cabernet Sauvignon, which nevertheless fully deserved its mention. The whites from the Comelli cellars all scored well. The full flavoured Tocai Friulano has a fresh, fruit-rich finish that is truly captivating. The aromas of the Pinot Grigio disclose elegant, refreshing apple mingling on the palate with nearly ripe plum and marked acidity. The Sauvignon has notes of apple, faint red pepper and elderflowers on the nose. The elderflower also emerged on the palate, this time with sage and green notes. Finally the Chardonnay: elegant and interesting, the bouquet revealing vanilla and tropical fruit and the palate with good acidity and balance.

O	Chardonnay '95	🍷🍷	4
O	Sauvignon '95	🍷🍷	4
O	Vitovska '95	🍷	4
●	Carso Terrano '94	🍷	4
O	Chardonnay '90	🍷🍷🍷	4
O	Chardonnay '94	🍷🍷🍷	4
O	Sauvignon '91	🍷🍷🍷	4
O	Sauvignon '92	🍷🍷🍷	4

O	COF Chardonnay '96	🍷	3
O	COF Pinot Grigio '96	🍷	3
O	COF Sauvignon '96	🍷	3
O	COF Tocai Friulano '96	🍷	3
●	COF Merlot '96	🍷	3
●	COF Cabernet Sauvignon '96		3

FARRA D'ISONZO (GO)

FARRA D'ISONZO (GO)

BORGO CONVENTI
STRADA COLOMBARA, 13
34070 FARRA D'ISONZO (GO)
TEL. 0481/888004

CASA ZULIANI
VIA GRADISCA, 23
34070 FARRA D'ISONZO (GO)
TEL. 0481/888506

For his wines from the excellent '96 vintage, Gianni Vescovo has obtained a long and thoroughly deserved string of awards. Vescovo's wines are bottled under three labels: Borgo Conventi, I Fiori and La Colombara. Borgo Conventi includes a range of premium wines from 40 hectares of vineyards in the Collio DOC zone, among them the Colle Russian cru. The area lying between Farra and Mariano supplies grapes for the I Fiori label, and the La Colombara range is reserved for selected flag-bearer wines such as the Moscato Rosa. Our favourite this year was the Collio Chardonnay '95 Colle Russian whose golden colour is accompanied by rich, complex secondary aromas of fruit, citron, honey and oak. The refreshing acidity has plenty of grip and the palate has complexity and depth, with hints of candyfloss leading into a great finish. The outstanding characteristic of the Braida Nuova '93 is the complexity of its nose, where young fruit blends with the typical grassy nuances of the cabernet franc grape, and follows through well on the tannin-rich palate. The bright ruby Braida Nuova '94 offers liquorice, tar and cream on the nose while the rich fruit comes out on the nicely balanced palate before the leisurely finish rounds things off. The intense aromas of the Tocai Friulano Collio '96 are redolent of cloves, pepper, sage and celery. The Moscato Rosa from the Isonzo Friuli DOC zone is a bright cherry red with aromas of violets. Appealing rather than elegant, it offers a sweet palate with a faint hint of carbon dioxide. The I Fiori Chardonnay '96 and Refosco '96 from the Isonzo Friuli appellation are nicely made and good value for money.

This year Casa Zuliani has made a storming entry into the Guide. The owner, Bruna Zuliani, converted the entire production of the estate to winemaking in the early 1970s and the area planted to vine currently stands at 14 hectares, a part in the Collio DOC zone and the remainder in the Isonzo del Friuli appellation. Gianni Bignucolo is the highly skilled consultant winemaker and Claudio Tomadin looks after sales. The secret of their success lies in yields that range from 60 quintals per hectare in the Collio to 70 in the Isonzo zone. Their Pinot Bianco Collio '96, the best of the wines we tasted, has a classy, refreshing nose of golden delicious apple backed up by nice green notes. The palate echoes these aromas and has good breadth and continuity as well as just the right degree of acidity in the finish. In the Collio Chardonnay, an elegant wine that also follows through well in the mouth, a faint hint of reduction immediately gives way to broad fruit. In contrast, the Isonzo Chardonnay has more green notes and a lovely lingering finish. The Isonzo Sauvignon is stylish and refreshing, evoking elder and tomato leaves on the nose, while the Collio version puts the accent on sage and rue. The Collio Pinot Grigio is well-defined, nicely balanced and broad, following through well with the elegance that characterizes all the wines from Casa Zuliani. The reds performed well, too, during our tasting. The Cabernet Franc del Collio came within a whisper of winning Two Glasses and the Isonzo Friuli Cabernet Franc was only a notch or two below. Both are rich in red berry fruit, herbs and spices but the Collio version has, perhaps, the more compact structure. Finally the Collio Merlot had a nose of cherry, cassis and spices, following through nicely into a palate with good juicy fruit.

○ Collio Chardonnay Colle Russian '95	♀♀	4
○ Collio Tocai Friulano '96	♀♀	4
● Braida Nuova '93	♀♀	5
● Braida Nuova '94	♀♀	5
● Isonzo Friuli Moscato Rosa La Colombara '96	♀	4
○ Isonzo Friuli Chardonnay I Fiori '96		3
● Isonzo Friuli Refosco P. R. I Fiori '96		3
● Braida Nuova '91	♀♀♀	5
● Braida Nuova '90	♀♀	5

○ Collio Pinot Bianco '96	♀♀	3*
○ Collio Chardonnay '96	♀	3
○ Collio Pinot Grigio '96	♀	3
○ Collio Sauvignon '96	♀	3
○ Isonzo Friuli Chardonnay '96	♀	2*
○ Isonzo Friuli Sauvignon '96	♀	2*
● Collio Cabernet Franc '96	♀	3
● Collio Merlot '96	♀	3
● Isonzo Friuli Cabernet Franc '96	♀	2*

FARRA D'ISONZO (GO)

FARRA D'ISONZO (GO)

★ VINNAIOLI JERMANN
VIA MONTE FORTINO, 21
LOC. VILLANOVA
34070 FARRA D'ISONZO (GO)
TEL. 0481/888080

TENUTA VILLANOVA
VIA CONTESSA BERETTA, 29
LOC. VILLANOVA
34070 FARRA D'ISONZO (GO)
TEL. 0481/888013

This year, Silvio Jermann is celebrating both twenty-five years of winemaking and the twentieth anniversary of his Vintage Tunina, considered by many to be the finest white wine in Italy. The occasion was marked by an event of extraordinary interest - a tasting of many of the vintages of Silvio's magnificent flagship white and other Jermann wines - and Vintage Tunina was the star of the celebrations, winning its now traditional Three Glasses. A fabulous white wine blended from sauvignon and chardonnay grapes, Vintage Tunina '95 regales the nose with classically inviting, elegantly fruity, sweet aromas carried through onto a refreshing, complex palate that continuously discloses new secrets and offers spectacular length combined with a gentle yet solid structure. The Capo Martino is another excellent wine, its straw yellow hue flecked with green and gold and its delicate, generous nose a nicely balanced composition of wood, herbal infusions, grapefruit, pear and yellow plums. The velvety elegance of the palate is balanced, full flavoured and lingering, revealing notes of coffee, hazelnut, mixed berries and citrus fruits. The Vinnae, a blend of ribolla gialla with riesling and malvasia, made our panel sit up and take notice. Elegant as ever, the nose highlights delicate but distinct cream and fruit aromas while the complex fruit on the palate is dominated by tangy apple. Jermann's outstanding Chardonnay, Where Dreams... '95, has crisp golden highlights in the glass and notes of banana and vanilla on the nose. The palate is soft and refreshing, revealing tropical fruit and banana that is echoed in the long, long finish. And to conclude our review, we could not overlook the Riesling Afix '96, which Silvio has dedicated to his youngest son Alojz Felix. The aromas are unabashedly varietal, introduced by notes of citron. The palate is fascinatingly drinkable with nicely judged balance and plenty of freshness.

The winery that Paolo Cora runs with the assistance of Alberto Grossi and their loyal winemaker Graziano Ceccutto is getting ready to celebrate its fifth century of activity in 1999. It has consolidated its place in the Guide with a splendid range of wines that emerged not only from a good growing season and a favourable vintage but also from unremitting efforts in vineyard and cellar. We were particularly impressed by the Collio Ribolla Gialla selezione Montecucco '96 for the delicacy of its stylish aromas of intense fruit modulated by gentle oak-inspired vanilla. The palate mirrored the nose, evidencing good texture, style and plenty of length. The exemplary elderflower and fresh fruit on the nose of Collio Sauvignon Montecucco '96 is a revelation and the palate hovers enchantingly between acidity and fruit. The Villanova Collio DOC vineyards produced a lovely pale straw yellow Pinot Grigio '96 with attractive floral and pear aromas that are not quite up to the high standard of the palate, which is well balanced, long and elegant. The Tocai Friulano '96 has a crisp nose of apple and white plum. The palate is clean, unambivalent and nicely balanced with a hint of astringency. We then sampled a Merlot '96 from the vineyard in the Isonzo Friuli DOC zone which presented Morello cherry and wild berries, followed up by vegetal notes on the palate, very dry tannins and never-ending fruit. This year's novelty is a '96 vintage blend of chardonnay, tocai friulano and malvasia istriana called Meni. A very young wine recently bottled, it had slightly aggressive notes of sulphur on the nose and faint aromas over a background of fruit. The palate is fruity and floral, revealing mouth-filling flavour, moderate acidity and a finish that lacks a touch of balance. We look forward to the 1997.

O	Vintage Tunina '95	🍷🍷🍷	5
O	Capo Martino '95	🍷🍷	5
O	Pinot Grigio '96	🍷🍷	4
O	Riesling Afix '96	🍷🍷	4
O	Vinnae '96	🍷🍷	4
O	Where the Dreams		
	Have No End '95	🍷🍷	5
O	Chardonnay '96	🍷	4
O	Pinot Bianco '96	🍷	4
O	Capo Martino '91	🍷🍷🍷	5
O	Capo Martino '93	🍷🍷🍷	5
O	Vintage Tunina '89	🍷🍷🍷	5
O	Vintage Tunina '90	🍷🍷🍷	5
O	Vintage Tunina '93	🍷🍷🍷	5
O	Vintage Tunina '94	🍷🍷🍷	5

O	Collio Ribolla Gialla		
	Montecucco '96	🍷🍷	4
O	Collio Sauvignon		
	Montecucco '96	🍷🍷	4
O	Collio Pinot Grigio '96	🍷	3
O	Collio Tocai Friulano '96	🍷	3
O	Meni '96	🍷	3
●	Isonzo Friuli Merlot '96	🍷	3
●	Collio Cabernet Sauvignon		
	Montecucco '94		4
O	Collio Chardonnay Montecucco '95		4
O	Isonzo Friuli Malvasia '96		3
O	Collio Chardonnay Montecucco '94	🍷🍷	4
●	Collio Rosso '94	🍷	3

GONARS (UD)

GORIZIA

DI LENARDO
VIA BATTISTI, 1
FRAZ. ONTAGNANO
33050 GONARS (UD)
TEL. 0432/928633

FIEGL
LOC. LENZUOLO BIANCO, 1
FRAZ. OSLAVIA
34170 GORIZIA
TEL. 0481/31072

Although only a young man, Massimo Di Lenardo has run the family winery for several years, trying with some success to introduce a modern image to both the estate and the wines. The main policy dictums of the Di Lenardo estate, which is situated in the Friuli Grave DOC zone not far from Palmanova, can be summed up as follows: straightforward but well made, varietal wines; competitive pricing (the estate has won lots of value-for-money credits over the years); meticulous care for the vineyard and in the cellar (new plantings at 6,000 vines per hectare, low yields per vine, hyperoxygenation). The Tocai Friulano, traditionally a very good wine, excelled itself in the '96 vintage. There are elegant, attractive aromas of pear on the nose that follow through consistently on the palate. The aromas and flavours marry so well that we were happy to award Two Glasses. The red Ronco Nolè '95 blend of merlot, cabernet franc and cabernet sauvignon confirmed its status with aromas of red fruit, liquorice and dried flowers and a fine fruit-rich entry on the palate, leading into a broad, convincing finish. The Tiare d'Albe '96, a blend of tocai, chardonnay and sauvignon, starts off by disclosing notes of green apple and hedgerow, good fruit and moderate structure but slightly over-assertive acidity detracts from the finish. The Pinot Bianco '96 has an intense nose in which green apple is prominent. The entry on the palate is impressive and there is nice acidity to underpin the finish. The Pinot Grigio '96 is another good, honest wine with a keynote aroma of pear while the Sauvignon and Chardonnay scored highly enough to merit a mention.

Apart from the Traminer, all the Fiegl wines we sampled confirmed the reliability of an estate whose premium label products we review here. One of the wines - the Merlot - is on the starting blocks for a Three Glass award and the Leopold Cuvée Blanc is working its way through the qualifying rounds. To begin with the Merlot, it is clean, broad, rich and juicy on the nose, developing great power and balance on the palate where the aromas of tobacco and pencil lead are disturbed only by roughish tannins, a frequent - regrettable - characteristic of the red wines of Friuli. The Leopold white is obtained from tocai, pinot bianco, sauvignon and ribolla and is fresh on entry, becoming dry and more substantial in the mid-palate. Alcohol and extract are well balanced by acidity and residual bitter almond aroma. The Fiegl Pinot Grigio is another major wine, its up-front aromas of broom blossom introducing a dry, almost austere, palate. The Sauvignon scored almost as highly and revealed aromas of tomato leaf and white peach on the nose. It is a powerful, complex wine with lively, tangy acidity. The Chardonnay has lots of flavour and varietal character; its fruit is reminiscent of apple and citrus. The Tocai also proved an attractive wine - Tocai seems to be enjoying a revival of interest in Oslavia. This interpretation has good length and plenty of warmth thanks to its alcohol. There is enough acidity to give it liveliness and it is thoroughly convincing in the end after a hesitant start. The Ribolla, in contrast, can't seem to make up its mind. The acidity is a shade overplayed and the floral aromas lack clarity.

O Friuli Grave Tocai Friulano '96	YY	2*
O Friuli Grave Pinot Bianco '96	Y	2*
O Friuli Grave Pinot Grigio '96	Y	2*
O Tiare d'Albe '96	Y	2*
● Ronco Nolè '95	Y	3
O Friuli Grave Chardonnay '96		2
O Friuli Grave Sauvignon '96		2

● Collio Merlot '95	YY	4
O Collio Pinot Grigio '96	YY	3
O Leopold Cuvée Blanc '95	YY	4
O Collio Chardonnay '96	Y	3
O Collio Sauvignon '96	Y	3
O Collio Tocai Friulano '96	Y	3
O Collio Ribolla Gialla '96		3
O Collio Sauvignon '95	YY	3
O Leopold Cuvée Blanc '94	YY	4

GORIZIA

GORIZIA

★ Josko Gravner
Loc. Lenzuolo Bianco, 9
Fraz. Oslavia
34170 Gorizia
tel. 0481/30882

La Castellada
Fraz. Oslavia, 1
34170 Gorizia
tel. 0481/33670

Josko Gravner's name is a byword in Italian wine, and there is ample confirmation of his standing in the range of wines we tasted this year, all of the very highest quality and with impressive peaks of excellence. None however, managed to gain a Three Glass rating. Best of the bunch was the Sauvignon, which offers yeast, vanilla and fruit on the nose and elegant, persuasive fruit on the palate, where only a slight excess of astringency and wood mars the overall balance. The lovely Chardonnay has the usual highlights in the glass and a classy, delicate nose that reveals toasted hazelnut and tropical fruit. It lacks the complexity of previous vintages and above all is unexpectedly short on the palate. The Breg '94, assembled from a number of autochthonous varieties together with sauvignon, riesling italico and pinot grigio, was marked only a point or two lower than the Chardonnay. It presents milky aromas, reasonable depth and decent concentration. Although very frank, the '94 lacks the fascination of the very best vintages. The Ribolla turned out to be a little cloying on the palate with rather more alcohol than extract.

From the lofty superiority of its wind-swept, sun-drenched hill, Oslavia has always been the detached, oenological beacon of the far North-east of Italy. And this year, Oslavia has once again sent out a clear, courageous message. It is time to put an end to the proliferation of labels, often slapped onto wines that are fundamentally similar or mere marketing inventions with no basis in fact. Much better to restrict production to one or two monovarietals with genuine local credentials, flanked by one white and one red cuvée. Giorgio and Nicolò Bensa have been testing the market with this new philosophy and the results are very encouraging. In a difficult year like 1995, they have produced wines that come very close to the level of the 1990s. The Bianco, blended from wines that were previously bottled separately (tocai, pinot grigio, sauvignon and ribolla), was the biggest surprise of all. It is delicately balsamic, with notes of medicinal herbs, and caresses the palate first with a velvet touch, next becoming dry and refreshing, then soft again; sheer pleasure that lingers deliciously. The Rosso is also exciting. Blended from cabernet sauvignon and merlot, it is macerated slowly, fermented in open vats and aged unhurriedly in wood. The entry on the nose is an impressive concentration of bramble, raspberry and spice and the palate is tannic to the point of austerity. Then it opens out in gentler secondary aromas reminiscent of liquorice and milky coffee. The Ribolla is more delicate and fruity, contrasting fresh green notes with the creamier aromas of toasty oak.

○ Chardonnay '94	♟♟	5	
○ Sauvignon '94	♟♟	5	
○ Breg '94	♟	5	
○ Ribolla Gialla '94	♟	5	
○ Chardonnay '83	♟♟♟	5	
○ Chardonnay '87	♟♟♟	5	
○ Chardonnay '88	♟♟♟	5	
○ Chardonnay '92	♟♟♟	5	
○ Chardonnay '93	♟♟♟	5	
○ Collio Chardonnay '90	♟♟♟	5	
○ Collio Chardonnay '91	♟♟♟	5	
○ Collio Sauvignon '89	♟♟♟	5	
○ Sauvignon '93	♟♟♟	5	
○ Collio Ribolla Gialla '92	♟♟♟	5	

○ Bianco della Castellada '95	♟♟♟	5	
○ Collio Ribolla Gialla '95	♟♟	5	
● Rosso della Castellada '92	♟♟	5	
○ Bianco della Castellada '92	♟♟♟	5	
○ Bianco della Castellada '94	♟♟♟	5	
○ Collio Chardonnay '94	♟♟♟	5	
○ Collio Sauvignon '93	♟♟♟	5	
○ Bianco della Castellada '93	♟♟	5	
○ Collio Chardonnay '93	♟♟	5	
○ Collio Pinot Grigio '93	♟♟	5	
○ Collio Ribolla Gialla '93	♟♟	5	
● Rosso della Castellada '90	♟♟	5	
● Rosso della Castellada '91	♟♟	5	

GORIZIA

GRADISCA D'ISONZO (GO)

PRIMOSIC - MARKO PRIMOSIG
VIA MADONNINA DI OSLAVIA, 3
FRAZ. OSLAVIA
34170 GORIZIA
TEL. 0481/535153

MARCO FELLUGA
VIA GORIZIA, 121
34072 GRADISCA D'ISONZO (GO)
TEL. 0481/99164-92237

The Primosig winery has two ranges. Our review focuses on the premium label, around which the Primosiges have concentrated their efforts first to consolidate the position of their white blend and then to create a top red cuvée. 1996 was a decidedly good vintage, especially for Ribolla. Oak-matured only briefly so as not to mask its typical hedgerow aromas, it is attractive and unassertive yet far from insubstantial, as the characteristic lingering acidity amply demonstrates. The Sauvignon was vinified exclusively in stainless steel and is a wine that lives up to the expectations of its producer and the market. Its strong points are substantial extract and gutsy alcohol, together with crisp, primary aromas. The other wines we sampled were all eminently drinkable, beginning with the Pinot Grigio. One quarter fermented in oak, it offers lactic and ripe fruit notes on the nose, with a lingering follow-through and a moderate full body. Primosig also partially barrel-ferments the Chardonnay, which is more convincing on the nose, where nuances of tobacco and crusty bread emerge, than on the fairly one-dimensional palate. Finally, the estate blend of sauvignon, chardonnay and ribolla; this is fermented and matured in second year oak barrels and also has interesting, well-developed, tertiary aroma but will need better vintages to express sufficient structure to match its promise on the nose.

Marco Felluga is not only one of the cornerstones of Italian winemaking, he is also one of those charismatic figures who helped to write the history of wine in Friuli and he has no intention of retiring from the current oenological scene. If any confirmation were needed, we have only to look at the range of wines he produces. We enjoyed most of all two white table wines. The first is the Marco Felluga '96, obtained from chardonnay grapes fermented and matured in oak for six months. On the nose it was lactic and creamy while still letting plenty of tropical fruit and hazelnut come through and was soft, nicely balanced and pleasantly mouth-filling. The Molamatta is a blend of ribolla, tocai and pinot bianco vinified in stainless steel that has weight and elegance backed up by tangy fruit and a good follow-through. Marco Felluga's Pinot Bianco and Tocai, both lovely wines, are very similar in style. The Pinot Bianco has a nose of green apple in contrast to the Tocai's apple seeds but both have attractive acidity and interesting texture. The Pinot Bianco wins on style but the Tocai is more complex. The other whites we tasted had good entries on the palate. The flinty Pinot Grigio takes time to disclose everything it has to offer but falls short of convincing. The daisy aroma of the Chardonnay is a shade too penetrating but the alcohol-rich palate has plenty of length. Although dry, floral and elegant, the Ribolla lacks depth. The red wines included an agreeable Cabernet that has young aromas of red berries mirrored on a nicely balanced palate that invites you to reach for a second glass. The '95 vintage Merlot is a more serious wine than its predecessor. More time in the cellar will be required to mellow out its aristocratic austerity.

O	Collio Ribolla Gialla Gmajne '96	♟♟	4
O	Collio Sauvignon Gmajne '96	♟♟	4
O	Collio Chardonnay Gmajne '96	♟	4
O	Collio Pinot Grigio Gmajne '96	♟	4
O	Klin '94	♟	4
O	Collio Chardonnay Gmajne '95	♟♟	4
O	Collio Picolit '93	♟♟	5
O	Collio Sauvignon Gmajne '95	♟♟	4
O	Klin '93	♟♟	4

O	Collio Pinot Bianco '96	♟♟	3
O	Collio Tocai Friulano '96	♟♟	3
O	Marco Felluga '96	♟♟	4
O	Molamatta '96	♟♟	4
●	Collio Merlot '95	♟♟	3
O	Collio Chardonnay '96	♟	3
O	Collio Pinot Grigio '96	♟	3
O	Collio Ribolla Gialla '96	♟	3
●	Collio Cabernet '95	♟	3
●	Carantan '93	♟♟	4

The International Slow Food Movement

Slow Food is an international movement, which was founded in 1989 and is active in 35 countries worldwide, with 40,000 members and 305 **Convivia**.

Slow Food has a cultural agenda: it propounds a **philosophy of pleasure**, has a **taste education** programme, works towards **safeguarding** traditional food and wine heritage, and providing **consumer information**. Slow Food helps the younger generations establish a proper relationship with food; it promotes tourism that respects and cares for the environment; and it assists projects with the same interests.

Slow Food Events
important food and wine events for enthusiasts and professionals: the **Salone del Gusto, Sapori del mondo in Piemonte** (The Hall of Taste, Savors of the World in Piedmont, Turin, Italy, 5-9 November '98); **Wine Conventions; Cheese, Different Forms of Milk**, a biennial international cheese show (Bra, Cuneo, Italy); **Tasting Sessions**, a pleasurable tasting school with the most prestigious and rare specialities and wines.

Each convivium organizes social meetings, wine tastings, cooking courses, trips and visits of food and wine interest for its members. The convivia also promote programmes of international twinning to encourage the exchange and knowledge of different cultures and tastes.

An Ark to safeguard products and the planet of tastes
An important project aimed at **safeguarding** and **benefitting** small-scale agricultural and food production, which risks dying out. Thousands of different kinds of *charcuterie*, cheeses, animal breeds and plants are in danger of disappearing forever: the homologation of tastes, the excessive power of industrial companies, distribution difficulties and disinformation are the causes of a process which could lead to the loss of an irreplaceable heritage of traditional recipes, knowledge and tastes. The Ark is a scientific research and documentation programme which works towards relaunching businesses and outfits with important cultural and economic value.

The Fraternal Tables, activities related to food themes with a common cultural agenda

Slow   Italian Wines 1998

Slow features in-depth and often off-the-wall stories about food culture across the globe, with related lifestyle topics of a truly international scope, unlike anything you've seen before on the newsstand... 160 well-designed pages in full color, with exciting photography and articles by top authors, gourmets, wine experts, and food & travel writers worldwide. Just take your pick: English, deutsch or italiano...

For the first time in English, the most complete, reliable and influential guide to the best Italian wines. Published by Slow Food and Gambero Rosso, it is now in its eleventh edition. It describes the history and production of 1392 vineyards, describes and evaluates 8501 wines, awards 117 wines with "Tre Bicchieri" (Three Glasses): the élite of the great Italian wine-making tradition. Price £15.99 or $ 24.95

Registration Form

Slow Food is aimed at food and wine enthusiasts, those who do not want to lose the myriad of tastes in traditional foodstuffs from around the world, and those who share the snail's wise slowness. Annual membership includes:
- a personal membership card
- four issues of the quarterly magazine, *Slow*
- the right to attend all events organized by the Slow Food movement throughout the world
- a 20% discount on all Slow Food publications

If you have any questions, please feel free to contact us. We are only a FAX, phone call or e-mail away. Phone: ++39 172 419611 - FAX: ++39 172 421293 E-mail: international@slow-food.com

I would like to:
❑ start a convivium ❑ become a member ❑ subscribe to "Slow"

Full Name

(of company or restaurant or other)

Street Address   City

State/Prov./County   Country   Postal Code

Home Tel.   Day Tel.   Fax

Profession

I would prefer to receive Slow in: ❑ English   ❑ Italian   ❑ German

	Subscription fees to receive *Slow* only	membership fees to join *Slow Food*
U.K.	£26.00	£33.00
U.S.	$44.00	$60.00

Method of Payment

❑ Cash ❑ Eurocheque (in Italian lire) - no personal checks, please
❑ Credit Card: ❑ Visa ❑ AmEx ❑ Mastercard

|__|__|__|__| |__|__|__|__| |__|__|__|__| |__|__|__|__|

|__|__/__|__| X

Exp. Date   Signature

Cardholder   Total Amount

MANZANO (UD)

MANZANO (UD)

ABBAZIA DI ROSAZZO
VIA ABATE CORRADO, 55
FRAZ. ROSAZZO
33044 MANZANO (UD)
TEL. 0432/759693

BANDUT - COLUTTA
VIA ORSARIA, 32
33044 MANZANO (UD)
TEL. 0432/299208-501191

Under the stewardship of the Zamò family, the Abbazia di Rosazzo estate has confirmed its status as a first-rank winery. The '96 vintage is the last which they will make, the church authorities who own the land having rented it to other tenants. The Abbazia di Rosazzo brand will remain for another few years the exclusive property of Zamò, who will therefore be able to finish their stocks under the original label. Ronco dei Roseti '92 is a cabernet sauvignon-based red blend supplemented with cabernet franc, merlot and other local varieties. It is spicy on the nose, which has complex fruit nuanced with wild berries. The entry on the palate is soft, leading into a expansive, balanced mid-palate suffused with rich, concentrated red berry fruit and attractive tannins. The chardonnay, pinot bianco and tocai Ronco delle Acacie '94 won a well deserved Two Glasses. The bouquet is sweetish with lots of banana and yeast; the long, rich, full flavoured palate is a triumph of balance between acidity and fruit. The remarkable Tocai Friulano '96 has a nose of apple, honey, acacia blossom and hazelnuts. Soft and rounded on the palate, it has plenty of juicy fruit, consistency and good length. The Sauvignon '96 has an crisp, intense nose with typical chlorophyll and peach, good body on the palate and a lingering, zesty finish. The Ribolla Gialla is elegant and concentrated on the nose, following through nicely with fresh, tangy acidity on the palate and an intriguing finish of apples and whitecurrant. In contrast, the Chardonnay offers a moderately intense but very stylish nose and freshness in the mouth, where there is tons of fruit and an attractive hint of vanilla in the finish. Hats off to winemaker Franco Bernabei, with whose assistance the Zamò family continue to produce wines of excellence.

The Coluttas are a well-known family of pharmacists in Udine who divide their time between their chemist's shops in the city and their vineyards on the hill slopes of Buttrio, Manzano and Rosazzo. Last year, there were question marks against some of their wines, although the overall impression was not entirely negative. This year's production is much more convincing, and in fact the '96 vintage turned out to be a memorable one for the 70-hectare estate that Giorgio and Elisabetta Colutta run. The Pinot Grigio is a Two Glass wine with points to spare. The outstandingly intense, complex nose reveals a range of aromas that go from fruity to floral with overtones of pear and apple emerging above the rest. The acidity on the palate is balanced by the juicy structure of the fruit, and the finish is extremely pleasant. The Chardonnay has a nose strongly reminiscent of liquorice twists. The palate is balanced and fresh-tasting all the way through. The standard of the reds - both the varietals and the blended Selenard - is good. The grassy, moss-nuanced Cabernet gets a One Glass rating. It follows through well on the palate and has a well balanced, if slightly dull, finish. The Merlot got One Glass, too, for its vegetal notes over red berries on the nose and a palate where the fruit gets the upper hand; it has sound structure and a finish with a lot of charm. Mentions must also go to the Rosso Selenard '95, a refreshing wine with aromas of tea, vanilla and spices, and to the Refosco dal Peduncolo Rosso '96, which although a little too fresh on the nose has enough texture to sustain the characteristic spice of the variety. Another mention goes to the Bianco Nojâr '96, which is distinguished by marked acidity. The elderflower and crusty bread aromas in the nose are slightly unusual for chardonnay and ribolla, the two varieties used in the blend. There are also mentions for the Sauvignon and the Ribolla Gialla.

● Ronco dei Roseti '92	♟♟♟	4
○ COF Chardonnay '96	♟♟	4
○ COF Ribolla Gialla '96	♟♟	4
○ COF Sauvignon '96	♟♟	4
○ COF Tocai Friulano '96	♟♟	4
○ Ronco delle Acacie '94	♟♟	4
○ COF Picolit '93	♟	6
○ COF Pinot Grigio '96	♟	4
○ Ronco delle Acacie '93	♟♟♟	4
○ Ronco di Corte '87	♟♟♟	4
● Ronco dei Roseti '88	♟♟♟	5
● Ronco dei Roseti '90	♟♟♟	5

○ COF Pinot Grigio '96	♟♟	3
○ COF Chardonnay '96	♟	3
● COF Cabernet '96	♟	3
● COF Merlot '96	♟	3
● COF Refosco P. R. '96		3
● COF Rosso Selenard '95		4
○ COF Bianco Nojâr '96		4
○ COF Ribolla Gialla '96		4
○ COF Sauvignon '96		3

MANZANO (UD)

RONCHI DI MANZANO
VIA ORSARIA, 42
33044 MANZANO (UD)
TEL. 0432/740718

MANZANO (UD)

RONCO DELLE BETULLE
VIA A. COLONNA, 24
LOC. ROSAZZO
33044 MANZANO (UD)
TEL. 0432/740547

Ronchi di Manzano continues to consolidate its reputation as a top-quality producer not only of premium label crus but also of less expensive everyday wines. Congratulations, then, to Roberta Borghese who is the owner of the 45 hectares of vineyards located in some of the best locations of the Colli Orientali, at Manzano and in the new subzone of Rosazzo. Her golden Picolit '95 discloses aromas of mature fruit and yellow flowers, and remarkable balance in its off-dry palate. A rich symphony of soft yet never cloying flavours includes notes of honey, dried figs, and very ripe, sun-dried fruit. The Verduzzo Friulano '95 is equally golden in the glass. The nose has a very slightly more distinct note of wood with overtones of vanilla, milk, ripe melon, lavender and chamomile which are reflected on the palate, which is sweet, inviting, rich and well rounded with a long stewed apple finish. The Two Glass Merlot Ronc di Subule '95 is very young on the palate, with tannins very much in evidence under the red fruit and candied orange peel. The nose has sweet oak aromas, vanilla, liquorice, nutmeg and spices. All the other reds - the Refosco dal Peduncolo Rosso, the Cabernet Franc, the Merlot, the Pinot Nero and the Rosazzo Rosso - performed commendably. The Rosazzo Rosso, from a new vineyard, came very near to a higher score. On the nose there is sweet wood, red fruit, tar, liquorice, spices and mint, all echoed on the very impressive, full bodied and alcohol-rich palate. The bouquet of the Rosazzo Bianco reveals moss, tropical fruit and candied peel. Dry on the palate, it stays the course well through to a palate redolent of green peppers. Finally the more generously oaked Chardonnay Ronc di Rosazzo '96 also came out well at our tasting.

The Ronco delle Betulle estate is the realm over which the shy, very likeable Ivana Adami reigns. On the surface, she looks indecisive and full of reservations but when push comes to shove she makes sure her opinion on matters oenological is never disregarded. The cellar facilities are located around a skilfully restructured farmhouse on the terraced hill slopes that descend from the Abbazia di Rosazzo to Oleis. Visitors will not find any sophisticated machinery or space-age technology. What they will find is a down-to-earth policy of building on past achievements. The two most consistent performers are Tocai and Pinot Bianco. The Tocai is powerful and soft, with lingering fruit and an impeccably rounded palate while the Pinot Bianco offers a wealth of fruit and flowers and breadth of structure on the palate, something the variety tends to do with a certain regularity in Friuli. The Ribolla - floral and fruity with soft acidity - opens steadily after some initial signs of reduction. The Pinot Grigio behaves similarly, quickly presenting a dry, clean-tasting, balanced palate whose assurance and clarity make it ideal for serving with a wide range of dishes and cooking styles. The Cabernet Franc is less convincing, handicapped by a gamey, dusty nose. The fruit and the texture are not bad, but overall balance is missing.

O COF Picolit Ronc dei Scossai '95 ♈♈	5
O COF Verduzzo Friulano Ronc di Subule '95 ♈♈	4
● COF Merlot Ronc di Subule '95 ♈♈	4
● COF Pinot Nero '96 ♈	4
● COF Cabernet Franc '95 ♈	3
● COF Merlot '95 ♈	3
● COF Refosco P. R. '95 ♈	3
● COF Rosazzo Rosso '96 ♈	3
O COF Chardonnay Ronc di Rosazzo '96 ♈	4
O COF Rosazzo Bianco '96 ♈	3
O COF Pinot Grigio '95 ♈♈	3
● COF Merlot '94 ♈♈	3

O COF Pinot Bianco '96 ♈♈	3*
O COF Tocai Friulano '96 ♈♈	3*
O COF Pinot Grigio '96 ♈	3
O COF Ribolla Gialla '96 ♈	3
● COF Cabernet Franc '95	3
O COF Ribolla Gialla '95 ♈♈	3
O COF Tocai Friulano '95 ♈♈	3

MANZANO (UD)

MANZANO (UD)

TORRE ROSAZZA
LOC. POGGIOBELLO, 12
33044 MANZANO (UD)
TEL. 0432/750180

ZAMÒ & ZAMÒ
VIA ABATE CORRADO, 55
FRAZ. ROSAZZO
33044 MANZANO (UD)
TEL. 0432/759693

We have been able to observe a significant upturn in the quality at the Torre Rosazza estate which is managed by Piero Totis with the continuing assistance of Walter Filiputti. The property covers an area of about 80 hectares, producing just under 200,000 bottles a year. Their '95 vintage L'Altromerlot - the spectacular '94 will be released next year - confirms its potential greatness. The colour is intense and the nose has both delicacy and depth, releasing notes of bouquet garni and chocolate. This is followed up by an entry on the palate that is full bodied, although the tannins will need a little more time. The fruity Ribolla Gialla has lashings of elegance and hints of vanilla on the nose, carried through well on the clean, uncomplicated palate where the variety's typical acidity ensures lots of flavour and length. Torre Rosazza's Pinot Bianco is excellent. Complex and temptingly rich on the nose, it offers apples, pears and yellow fruit on the nose. The warm, lingering palate is attractively structured and the close-knit texture continuously proposes further nuances of flavour. Other wines worth a special mention include the refreshing Chardonnay, a wine with tropical fruit aromas, good acidity and satisfying length. Then there is a Sauvignon that flaunts aromatic herb, lemon tea and floral aromas and sufficient acidity to take the fatty edge off the palate. The acidity-rich Pinot Grigio has a solid basis of fruit while luscious apple dominates the aromas of the tangy Tocai Friulano. Notes of apple and peach tea enhance the elegance of the Verduzzo Friulano's pleasant wood, almond paste and ripe fruit, which are carried through in the moderate sweetness of the palate. The last wine is a Refosco dal Peduncolo Rosso, which reveals notes of spices and Morello cherries.

This year the Zamò family harvested the grapes of the Abbazia di Rosazzo estate for the last time, but acquired just a stone's throw away another superb property, which joins the existing holding at Villa Belvedere at Buttrio in the family portfolio. To mark the occasion the Zamòes have come up with a truly outstanding wine to which they have given the light-hearted name Vino di Là, which roughly translated means 'Do we have to go?' in Friulian. Obtained from pinot grigio, chardonnay, sauvignon and pinot bianco grapes, it entices the nose with delicate notes of fruit salad, with apple to the fore. The palate is complex and full bodied backed up by plenty of length. The Tocai Vigne Cinquant'anni is another memorable wine. The winemakers - with the exception of consultant Franco Bernabei - wanted to uproot the old vines but Pierluigi Zamò opposed the plan. Events have proved him right for this wine has a delicate, stylish nose of magnolia blossom and red delicious apples. The refreshing, balanced palate has a background note of wood and good texture, closing with a tangy finish. Once again, the Bianco TreVigne '95 white, a blend of tocai, chardonnay and sauvignon grapes, has come up trumps. Apples, pears and hazelnuts emerge in a complex chorus of aromas which follows through well on the palate, which has breadth, warmth, fullness and length. The basic Tocai Friulano is well worth Two Glasses for its moderately fruity nose and especially for its palate. The entry is understated, then the acidity emerges under cover of the fruit leading in to the rich, juicy texture of the finish. The Zamò & Zamò Merlot and Cabernet '95 also thoroughly deserve their Two Glass rating.

O	COF Pinot Bianco '96	🍷🍷	3*
O	COF Ribolla Gialla '96	🍷🍷	3*
●	COF Merlot L'Altromerlot '95	🍷🍷	4
●	COF Refosco P. R. '95	🍷	3
O	COF Chardonnay '96	🍷	3
O	COF Picolit '95	🍷	5
O	COF Pinot Grigio '96	🍷	3
O	COF Sauvignon '96	🍷	3
O	COF Tocai Friulano '96	🍷	3
O	COF Verduzzo Friulano '95	🍷	4
●	COF Merlot L'Altromerlot '90	🍷🍷	5
●	COF Merlot L'Altromerlot '91	🍷🍷	5
●	COF Merlot L'Altromerlot '93	🍷	5

O	COF Bianco TreVigne '95	🍷🍷	4
O	COF Bianco Vino di Là '96	🍷🍷	2*
O	COF Tocai Friulano '96	🍷🍷	3
O	COF Tocai Friulano Vigne Cinquant'anni '96	🍷🍷	4
●	COF Cabernet '95	🍷🍷	3
●	COF Merlot '95	🍷🍷	3
●	COF Refosco P. R. '95	🍷	3
O	COF Pinot Grigio '96	🍷	3
O	COF Tocai Friulano '96	🍷🍷	3
O	TreVigne '93	🍷🍷	4
O	TreVigne '94	🍷🍷	4

MARIANO DEL FRIULI (GO)   NIMIS (UD)

VIE DI ROMANS
LOC. VIE DI ROMANS, 1
34070 MARIANO DEL FRIULI (GO)
TEL. 0481/69600

DARIO COOS
VIA RAMANDOLO, 15
33045 NIMIS (UD)
TEL. 0432/790320

Rivers of ink have flowed to describe Gianfranco Gallo and recount the geological history of the alluvial plain of the Isonzo river, to say nothing of the Vie di Romans cellar that has become the physical symbol of Gallo's life work as a winemaker. And yet each year the Vie di Romans wines provide us with something new to write about. This year it is the Sauvignon that stands out above the rest. In the oak-conditioned version, it unleashes a stupendous breadth of aromas on the nose, ranging through plum, peach, red pepper, elderflower, mint and sage, all harmonizing over a "basso continuo" of sweet vanilla. The elegant, mouth-filling palate follows through deliciously with a hint of acidity that exalts its symphonic power. The Piere, in our opinion one of Italian winemaking's true legends, is a shade less impressive but is destined to improve with bottle age. The entry on the nose is soft and discreet, building up into a long, dry, complex bouquet with one or two fleeting uncertainties in the fine-grained grapefruit and peach texture. The two Chardonnays play second fiddle - on a Stradivarius - in this orchestra. The Vie di Romans is powerfully lactic, underpinned by ripe fruit and extract whereas the Campagnis Vieris is tangier and less demanding; it lacks the complexity of oak-ageing, but it is still interesting. Finally it would be wrong of us not to mention the Flors di Uis, made from malvasia, chardonnay and riesling. Releasing delicate aromas of apple and hawthorn on the nose, it carries through fluently and elegantly on the palate where delicate final aromas emerge.

Dario Coos was the first producer in Nimis to make new attempts to take Ramandolo upmarket. The wine is obtained from verduzzo grapes grown in the coldish microclimate of the area around the village of Ramandolo. Although white, the fruit has a thick, tannin-rich skin that gives the wine a fairly vegetal-dry palate. Dario's yields average 30 hectolitres per hectare and he generally harvests the grapes for his most straightforward wine, the Longhino, when they are super-ripe. The same fruit, left to raisin in trays for a few weeks and slowly fermented in small oak barrels, produces Coos' top wine. Other producers at Ramandolo - which boasts the first officially recognized village appellation in Friuli - are following Dario's lead, often with intriguing results. The '96 Longhino has an intense golden colour and clear notes of the variety's typical stewed apple and dry fruit. The sweet-yet-dry entry develops into a medium-bodied palate where the prominent tannins threaten to overpower the fruit in the finish. The superb '95 Ramandolo is the colour of lustrous old gold, and is broad, intense and elegant on the nose with notes of raisin, ripe fruit and stewed apple. The entry is very positive and the well rounded palate is rich and gently sweet. There are still evident tannins in the finish, but they soften with time.

O Isonzo Sauvignon Vieris '95	♀♀♀	4
O Isonzo Chardonnay Vie di Romans '95	♀♀	4
O Isonzo Sauvignon Piere '95	♀♀	4
O Isonzo Pinot Grigio Dessimis '95	♀	4
O Flors di Uis '95	♀	4
O Isonzo Chardonnay Ciampagnis Vieris '95	♀	4
O Chardonnay '86	♀♀♀	4
O Isonzo Chardonnay '91	♀♀♀	4
O Isonzo Piere Sauvignon '93	♀♀♀	4
O Isonzo Vieris Sauvignon '90	♀♀♀	4
O Isonzo Vieris Sauvignon '93	♀♀♀	4
O Isonzo Vieris Sauvignon '92	♀♀♀	4

O COF Ramandolo '95	♀♀	5
O COF Ramandolo Il Longhino '96	♀	4
O COF Ramandolo '94	♀♀	5
O COF Ramandolo Il Longhino '95	♀♀	4

PAVIA DI UDINE (UD)

F.LLI PIGHIN
V.LE GRADO, 1
FRAZ. RISANO
33050 PAVIA DI UDINE (UD)
TEL. 0432/675444

As usual, the wines produced by Pighin from their 30 hectares in the Collio DOC zone are superior, albeit only slightly, to those obtained from the 140-hectare estate in the Friuli Grave. Credit however must go to winemaker Paolo Valdesolo and the Pighin family for a range of wines of very satisfactory overall quality. The outstanding Tocai Friulano Collio '96 is a complex, elegant product with a nose in which pear gradually gives way to apple. The fleshy palate is balanced, full flavoured and closely textured, lingering agreeably. And the Collio Merlot '96 is every bit as good, its green notes hovering over a concentrated aroma of bramble and bilberry. The intensity of the nose is echoed by the full bodied palate, which has bags of structure. Another high-scoring Pighin wine is the Soreli '95, a white obtained from tocai, sauvignon and pinot bianco grapes from Capriva in the Collio DOC zone. The intensity of the fruit, especially apple, in the bouquet immediately grabs your attention as does the depth of aroma on the palate, together with a refreshingly tangy flavour and good length. The Baredo '91, a red blended from a number of varieties including cabernet sauvignon, merlot and refosco dal peduncolo rosso, is another winner. Stainless steel-fermented, it is then aged first in barriques, then large oak barrels and finally matured in the bottle. It has very ripe plum and tar on the nose and a complex, broad and tannin-rich palate. Of the other wines, we would single out the Tocai Vigna Casette '95, obtained from ungrafted root stock, whose attractive gooseberry aroma enlivens a seriously structured palate.

○	Collio Tocai Friulano '96	🍷🍷	3*
○	Soreli '95	🍷🍷	3*
●	Collio Merlot '96	🍷🍷	3
●	Baredo '91	🍷	4
●	Friuli Grave Merlot '96	🍷	2
○	Collio Pinot Grigio '96	🍷	3
○	Collio Sauvignon '96	🍷	3
○	Friuli Grave Tocai Friulano '96	🍷	3
○	Friuli Grave Tocai Friulano Vigna Casette '95	🍷	3
○	Friuli Grave Pinot Grigio '96		2
○	Collio Pinot Grigio '95	ΥΥ	3
○	Friuli Grave Tocai Friulano Vigna Casette '94	ΥΥ	3
●	Collio Cabernet '95	Υ	3

PINZANO AL TAGLIAMENTO (PN)

ALESSANDRO VICENTINI ORGNANI
VIA SOTTOPLOVIA, 2
FRAZ. VALERIANO
33090 PINZANO AL TAGLIAMENTO (PN)
TEL. 0432/950107

All winemakers, without exception, have to play the hand the vintage deals them. Some are lucky while others are less fortunate. Some are more expert, while others make up for inexperience with enthusiasm. Estates that have converted to premium wine production are less vulnerable to the weather; others still have work to do in this respect. Alessandro is one of the experts, but he has yet to complete the restructuring of the estate and this is reflected in his wines. The range is well up to standard, but wine lovers who have followed this producer know that there are still margins for improvement. His eminently reliable Sauvignon, which uses the R3 clone as well as other less aromatic bio-types, is delicately varietal on the nose, carrying through nicely onto a fresh, attractively textured palate with moderate length. The Chardonnay is obtained from twenty year-old, low-yielding vines. One quarter of the fruit ferments in 500-litre barrels. The final blend offers strong aromas of apple in the bouquet while the palate is slightly vegetal with a slight lack of balance. The Tocai offers faint notes of acacia blossom and honey before disclosing a palate that hovers elegantly between dryness and juicy fruit, alternating tangy notes with softer nuances. In contrast the Pinot has varietal aroma but lacks balance and length, is a shade dilute. Least convincing of all was the Cabernet, which is currently being replanted. The fruit and peat on the nose were spoiled by traces of undesirable, fermentation-derived odours.

○	Friuli Grave Chardonnay '96	🍷	2*
○	Friuli Grave Sauvignon '96	🍷	2*
○	Friuli Grave Tocai Friulano '96	🍷	2*
●	Friuli Grave Cabernet Sauvignon '96		2
○	Friuli Grave Pinot Grigio '96		2
●	Friuli Grave Merlot Braida Cjase '92	ΥΥ	3

POVOLETTO (UD)

TERESA RAIZ

LOC. MARSURE DI SOTTO
33040 POVOLETTO (UD)
TEL. 0432/679071

Teresa Raiz was the grandmother of Paolo and Giovanni Tosolini, the two brothers who run this winery. The in-house winemaker is the young Paolo Dolce, who is aided by the highly competent Piedmontese consultant Marco Monchiero. Production, which is based on both estate-grown and bought-in fruit, amounts to around 250,000 bottles a year. The flag-bearer red is Decano Rosso, a blend of merlot, cabernet franc and carbernet sauvignon. Predictably, the '95 vintage bears the scars of a difficult year but still comes within hailing distance of a Two Glass award. The nose releases all the toasty warmth of the wood, together with spices, tar, autumn leaves and liquorice. The entry on the palate pulls no punches, with robust tannins and a finish redolent of cherry and liquorice again. The other speciality is Ribolla Gialla, which this year gained good marks above all for the elegance of the nose, where flinty notes mingle with Morello cherry, both carried through well onto the palate. Ripe fruit then emerges in the finish. The stylish nose of the Pinot Grigio has a floral aromas, apple and pear. Hard acidity however tends to overwhelm the fruit on the palate, which is something of a disappointment. The Sauvignon opens with refreshing elderflower notes that carry through onto the palate. And finally the polished Tocai Friulano presents aromas of apple and pear, a fine entry on the palate and good, chewy fruit. The finish is fresh, if a little short.

○	COF Pinot Grigio '96	🍷	3
○	COF Ribolla Gialla '96	🍷	4
○	COF Sauvignon '96	🍷	3
○	COF Tocai Friulano '96	🍷	3
●	Decano Rosso '95	🍷	4
●	Decano Rosso '93	🍷🍷 (white)	4
●	Decano Rosso '94	🍷🍷 (white)	4

PRATA DI PORDENONE (PN)

VIGNETI LE MONDE

VIA GARIBALDI, 2
LOC. LE MONDE
33080 PRATA DI PORDENONE (PN)
TEL. 0434/626096-622087

Vigneti Le Monde can boast excellent winemaking credentials, not least the guarantee implicit in the name of the owner, Piergiovanni Pistoni. His 25 hectares of vineyard surround a lovely 18th-century group of farm buildings at the confluence of the Livenza and Meduna rivers. The soil is limestone-rich silt and clay. Density of planting varies from 2,300 to 3,200 vines per hectare. Yields of 60 to 90 quintals generate a total production of about 200,000 bottles a year, most of which is red wine, in accordance with a long-established estate tradition. Far and away the most interesting product is the Cabernet Franc. Deep ruby red in the glass, it reveals attractive but not over- intense varietal aromas enhanced by roses and bilberries. The palate is dry and sincere. Distinct notes of damson and cherry emerge from the Cabernet Sauvignon over a seamlessly smooth texture. The Querceto, a blend of the two previous varieties, is matured in 5-hectolitre Slavonian oak barrels. Garnet-ruby in the glass, it has clearly perceptible aromas of Peruvian bark, stewed fruit and dry leaves. The faintly vegetal palate has reasonable texture. The Pinot Nero, which Pistoni is intent on making one of the estate's leading wines, deserves a little introduction. Very successful in the past - the '91 and '93 were particularly good - this is a variety which has failed to recapture the élan of its earlier vintages. Recent editions have been well-made but unexciting. Whites worth mentioning include a refreshing Pinot Grigio with aromas of carob and flowers, a typical rough diamond of a Sauvignon that nonetheless has a fair bit of personality and a slightly dilute Tocai that lacks depth but still exhibits all classic varietal character.

●	Friuli Grave Cabernet Franc '96	🍷🍷	2*
●	Friuli Grave Cabernet Sauvignon '96	🍷	2
●	Querceto '93	🍷	4
●	Friuli Grave Pinot Nero '95		4
○	Friuli Grave Pinot Grigio '96		2
○	Friuli Grave Sauvignon '96		2
○	Friuli Grave Tocai Friulano '96		2
●	Friuli Grave Cabernet Sauvignon Ris. '92	🍷 (white)	4

PREMARIACCO (UD)

PREMARIACCO (UD)

DARIO E LUCIANO ERMACORA
VIA SOLZAREDO, 9
FRAZ. IPPLIS
33040 PREMARIACCO (UD)
TEL. 0432/716250

ROCCA BERNARDA
VIA ROCCA BERNARDA, 27
FRAZ. IPPLIS
33040 PREMARIACCO (UD)
TEL. 0432/716273

In the 1997 edition of the Guide, we registered our disappointment at this winery's performance, and looked forward to better things in the future. We have not had to wait long for improvements, for the brothers Dario - also president of the Consorzio Colli Orientali del Friuli - and Luciano have bounced right back with a range of seriously good wines this year. Considering their 20 years' experience with estate bottled wines, 14 hectares of excellently situated and maintained vineyards and a real passion for winemaking, this was predictable. We also understand that the brothers are working on two oak-conditioned blends of the kind to which the adjective "major" can appropriately be applied. To go back to this year's wines, it was satisfying to see that all those presented scored well. We particularly liked the Pinot Grigio '96, whose floral, appley nose followed through well on a palate with lingering aromas of apple and nice acidity. The varietal tomato leaf and elderflower nose of the Sauvignon '96 helped to win it Two Glasses. A stylish wine, it has good length and well balanced acidity. The Verduzzo Friulano and the Pinot Bianco both created a positive impression. The golden hue of the Verduzzo Friulano introduces moderate varietal character and just the right note of sweetness on the palate, where aromas of baked almonds and rennet emerge. The Pinot Bianco was rich and complex, revealing attractive banana nuances on the nose. Entry on the palate was promising but a surfeit of acidity makes the finish lean. Last of the whites is the Tocai Friulano, an uncomplicated, fruity wine that we judged worthy of a mention. No reds were submitted for tasting as they had only recently been bottled.

The marvellous castle that gives its name to the estate was built in 1567 but the cellars had already been constructed eight years previously. Brought back to prominence as the home of Picolit by count Gaetano Perusini, the winery passed on his death to the Sovereign Military Order of Malta. The 40 hectares planted to vine are supervised by an enthusiastic young manager, Mario Zuliani, who can count on the vast experience and insight of Piedmontese consultant, Marco Monchiero. And quality is definitely on an upward curve, if we look at the scores obtained this year. The Merlot Centis vintage '95, a poor year for reds in Friuli, confirms its status as the estate's outstanding wine. Well judged wood mingle with notes of cherry and bilberry on the nose and the palate is full flavoured, echoing the aromas of the nose. The slightly rough tannins will mellow after a year or two in the cellar. The golden-hued Picolit Riserva '94 also gained Two Glasses. Its concentrated raisin and dry fig aromas follow through superbly in a sweet but not cloying palate that is mouth-filling and soft at the same time. The Sauvignon '96 was another high scorer. Refreshing and varietal on the nose, it is warm, full bodied and well rounded in the mouth, with red pepper prominent in the finish. The up-front pear and apple nose of the Tocai Friulano is followed by a full flavoured plate with an attractive apple seeds finish. The Ribolla offers notes of ripe yellow fruit and the balanced acidity typical of the variety is nicely offset by luscious fruit. A mention also goes to the Chardonnay '96, an agreeable wine that had still to find a point of equilibrium when we sampled it.

O COF Pinot Grigio '96	🍷🍷	3*
O COF Sauvignon '96	🍷🍷	3*
O COF Pinot Bianco '96	🍷	3
O COF Verduzzo Friulano '96	🍷	3
O COF Tocai Friulano '96		3
O COF Pinot Bianco '95	🍷🍷	3

● COF Merlot Centis '95	🍷🍷	4
O COF Picolit Ris. '94	🍷🍷	6
O COF Ribolla '96	🍷	3
O COF Sauvignon '96	🍷	3
O COF Tocai Friulano '96	🍷	3
O COF Chardonnay '96		3
O COF Picolit Ris. '93	🍷🍷	6
● COF Merlot Centis '92	🍷🍷	4
● COF Merlot Centis '93	🍷🍷	4
● COF Merlot Centis '94	🍷🍷	4

PREMARIACCO (UD)

ROBERTO SCUBLA
VIA ROCCA BERNARDA, 22
FRAZ. IPPLIS
33040 PREMARIACCO (UD)
TEL. 0432/716258

We thought that Roberto Scubla's experimental phase was over but we were wrong. He maintains that he needs certain wines to satisfy the demands of particular clients. In future, he promises, he will concentrate on the mainstream estate wines, Sauvignon and Pinot Bianco, while still continuing to produce about 3,000 bottles each of what he calls his "small wines". The Pomédes, blended from tocai, pinot bianco and oak-fermented riesling, again impressed our tasters. The entry on the nose is broad, bright and rich in fruit and hedgerow aromas accompanied by a very stylish note of vanilla. The palate mirrors these aromas with nuances of banana emerging delightfully from the balanced, close-knit texture. Another limited production wine is the Graticcio, obtained from slowly air-dried verduzzo fruit. Amber in the glass, it is dense and sweet in the mouth. The milk and honey palate is nuanced with macaroon and the robust acidity counterbalances dry figs, sultanas and almond paste. Scubla's Pinot Bianco is luscious yet fresh-tasting, offering aromas of apples and pineapple over yeasty notes. The inviting palate is sustained by good alcohol and leads into an admirably unhurried finish. The Speziale is a cuvée of tocai, pinot bianco and sauvignon. Its vegetal nose is laced with hazelnuts and pears, which carry through onto the attractively acidity-rich, tangy palate. The Rosso Scuro is obtained from a blend of the two cabernet varieties with merlot, and aged in used oak barrels. It has a radiant, sunny personality, a nose redolent of warm red fruit and a persuasive palate marred only by slightly harsh tannins. The fresh-apple Tocai Sauvignonasse is a better wine than the Ancien version, which has undergone malolactic fermentation. Finally, the characteristically varietal Cabernet Sauvignon also won its spurs in the tasting.

PREMARIACCO (UD)

VIGNE DAL LEON
LOC. ROCCA BERNARDA, 38
33040 PREMARIACCO (UD)
TEL. 0432/716083-759693

Vigne dal Leon was the original estate of the Zamò family. In 1978 it was acquired by Tullio Zamò, a businessman and generous host whom a love of the countryside and fine wine has transformed into wine producer. The property's great wines are created in collaboration with consultant Franco Bernabei, whose team keep a watchful eye on the Zamò cellars. In recent years Barbara Maniacco, who married into the family, has decided to take up the most difficult challenge in Friuli - Pinot Nero. The quality and consistency of the results obtained so far justify her efforts. The '94 vintage has a concentrated, complex nose with notes of pepper and wild berries. Tannins come through strongly on the palate without masking the Morello cherry and vanilla. The '96 Sauvignon also has a distinctive nose over a background note of the variety's characteristic "cat's pee". The palate is full bodied and long, with nice acidity that shades off into bitter almond in the finish. One of Tullio's flag-bearer wines is the Malvasia Istriana. Yellow fruit triumphs over acacia blossom in the nose, the concentrated fruit carrying through onto the palate, and the zesty finish full of flavour. The '96 vintage Pinot Bianco - another of the cellar's heavyweights - strolled away with Two Glasses. The complex nose includes apple, pear and damson laced with oak, aromas picked up again on the intense, broad palate that has great structure and a spectacularly long, chewy finish. The Schioppettino '93 has typical notes of cherry and pepper, like the Tazzelenghe. A difficult wine at the best of times, Tazzelenghe was never really going to rate more than a mention in a poor year like '92.

○ COF Bianco Pomédes '96	�	4
○ COF Pinot Bianco '96	�	3
○ COF Verduzzo Friulano Graticcio '96	�	5
○ COF Bianco Speziale '96	�	3
○ COF Tocai Friulano Sauvignonasse '96	�	3
● COF Cabernet Sauvignon '95	�	3
● COF Rosso Scuro '95	�	4
○ COF Sauvignon '96		3
○ COF Tocai Friulano Ancien '96		3
○ COF Pinot Bianco '95	yy	3
○ COF Verduzzo Friulano Graticcio '95	yy	5

○ COF Malvasia Istriana '96	�	4
○ COF Pinot Bianco '96	�	4
○ COF Sauvignon '96	�	4
● COF Pinot Nero '94	�	4
● COF Schioppettino '93		4
● COF Tazzelenghe '92		4
● COF Pinot Nero '93	yy	4
● Rosso Vigne dal Leon '89	yy	5
● Rosso Vigne dal Leon '90	yy	5
○ COF Pinot Bianco '95	yy	4
○ Tullio Zamò '92	yy	4
○ Tullio Zamò '93	yy	4

PREPOTTO (UD)

LA VIARTE
VIA NOVACUZZO, 50
33040 PREPOTTO (UD)
TEL. 0432/759458

The La Viarte estate - the name means "springtime" in Friulian - comprises just over 20 hectares of vineyards surrounded by woods. The east-facing slopes of the property are remarkable for the ramrod-straight rows of vines in the beautifully kept vineyards. The care that the Ceschins devote to their estate is matched by the tidiness of their smoothly run cellar. Giulio Ceschin is turning out to be an increasingly valuable asset for his father Giuseppe, the professional oenologist who founded the family winery and established its excellent reputation, and mother Carla, a tirelessly courteous promoter of La Viarte wines. This year's range is up there in the top bracket, beginning with a stunning Ribolla Gialla that came within an ace of being awarded Three Glasses. Its floral aromas are elegant and complex, while the palate is extraordinarily rich and subtle. Yellow fruit and acidity are nicely balanced and the finish just won't let go. The Ceschins' exciting new sweet wine from the '94 vintage, Siùm ('dream'), is obtained from verduzzo friulano and picolit grapes air-dried in boxes and then crushed on Christmas Eve before spending 18 months in oak and six more ageing in the bottle before release. The clear amber colour introduces an elegant medley of almond paste and candied peel aromas that carries through attractively on the palate, which is sweet, substantial, broad and lingering. Two Glasses also go to the Pinot Bianco, delicately evocative of apples and mixed fruit as well as weighty in the mouth. The Tocai Friulano, with its herbal tea aromas and stylish, full bodied palate nuanced with almond aromas, also showed well, as did the Schioppettino, in which Morello cherry and brambles mingle in a soft, full texture sustained by excellent structure. Finally the Liende '95, already drinking very smoothly, is destined to improve with time.

PREPOTTO (UD)

LE DUE TERRE
VIA ROMA, 68/B
33040 PREPOTTO (UD)
TEL. 0432/713189

Remaining faithful to his chosen path, Flaviano Basilicata only presented two wines this year, the Sacrisassi Bianco and the Sacrisassi Rosso. According to Flaviano, the Picolit and the Pinot Nero from the '95 vintage were not worth vinifying separately so he used them in his blends. Le Due Terre, an estate of little more than four hectares, produces some very exciting cuvées indeed thanks to almost fanatical dedication in the vineyard; both the wines we sampled were right out of the top drawer. Sacrisassi Rosso was obtained by blending refosco, schioppettino and pinot nero harvested in the first week of October, then matured in French oak and 550-litre Slavonian oak casks for 14 months. Our panel's visit took place a few days after bottling so the assessment necessarily reflects less than ideal tasting conditions. The aromas recall green pepper, red fruit and nutmeg, which the full bodied palate echoes. There is good structure backed up by firm tannins and elegant body. The Sacrisassi Bianco '96 is a blend of tocai, ribolla gialla, sauvignon and picolit grapes harvested late, at the end of September, and then macerated on the skins for about a day before spending 12 months in oak. The resulting golden colour is crystal-clear, leading in to a highly distinctive nose of penetrating candied orange peel, honey, sweet tobacco and Mediterranean herbs. The palate is concentrated, perhaps more suitable for drinking on its own than with a meal, and full of elegance and long, complex flavour.

● COF Schioppettino '94	❦❦	4
○ COF Pinot Bianco '96	❦❦	4
○ COF Ribolla Gialla '96	❦❦	4
○ COF Tocai Friulano '96	❦❦	4
○ Siùm '94	❦❦	5
○ COF Bianco Liende '95	❦	4
○ COF Pinot Grigio '96	❦	4
○ COF Sauvignon '96	❦	4
● COF Tazzelenghe '93		4
○ COF Sauvignon '95	♀♀	4
○ Liende '94	♀♀	4

● Sacrisassi Rosso '95	❦❦	4
○ Sacrisassi Bianco '95	❦❦	4
○ Implicito '94	♀♀	5
● Sacrisassi Rosso '94	♀	4

PREPOTTO (UD)

CELESTINO PETRUSSA
VIA ALBANA, 49
33040 PREPOTTO (UD)
TEL. 0432/713192

For a number of years, Gianni and Paolo Petrussa's winery was relegated to the "Other Wineries" section, a consequence chiefly of the fact that we received from them wines that had spent only a few days in the bottle. This year, time was on their side so they have finally received a well-merited profile to themselves. In fact the brothers have been up-grading the quantity as well as the quality of their wines. Not content to vinify the grapes from their own five-hectare property, they now also buy in fruit from other producers whom they monitor constantly. Production has thus reached a total of 450 hectolitres, part of which goes into the 42,000 bottles that bear the Petrussa label. The gold-tinted Pensiero '95 is a sweet wine from late harvested, verduzzo friulano. The fruit, partially botrytis affected, was air-dried until well into December when it was crushed and the must put to ferment in small oak barrels until bottling in August '96. The resulting wine, neither sweet nor dry, is concentrated but still very elegant with keynote oak aromas and very good length. The Merlot Rosso Petrussa '94 almost gained Two Glasses. On the nose the tarry aromas and underlying Morello cherry, mint and hay are all sustained by well measured oak. Stewed damsons emerge on the palate together with red fruit. There is still a touch of greenish tannins, despite the roundness that comes from almost complete malolactic fermentation. The Tocai gets high marks particularly for its impact on the palate; there is weight, good breadth and pleasing acidity that makes for a very clean finish. The Merlot '96, matured in stainless steel, has good concentration and the Pinot Bianco and Cabernet are both worth an unqualified mention.

○	Pensiero '95	🍷🍷	4
○	COF Tocai Friulano '96	🍷	3
●	COF Merlot '96	🍷	3
●	COF Merlot Rosso Petrussa '94	🍷	4
●	COF Cabernet '96		3
○	COF Pinot Bianco '96		3

PREPOTTO (UD)

RONCHI DI CIALLA
FRAZ. CIALLA, 47
33040 PREPOTTO (UD)
TEL. 0432/731679

The Ronchi di Cialla winery is unique in a number of respects. The owners Dina and Paolo Rapuzzi, who have 14 hectares under vine, have always been pioneers of winemaking in Friuli. Their cellar was the first in the region to use small oak barrels and the first in Italy to use them for white wines. They work in close cooperation with the University of Udine, where their son Pierpaolo took his degree with a thesis on the beneficial effects of drinking wine and where their other son, Ivan, is still studying. Theirs is the only winery in the Cialla DOC subzone. All of the Ronchi di Cialla wines are obtained from native varieties and all are destined to age effortlessly in the cellar. The Picolit di Cialla '94 is a masterpiece. The gold and green highlights introduce an elegant nose of flowers and fruit, then an inviting, amabile-sweet palate that again has lots of style as well as notes of violets and apples. The Schioppettino di Cialla '93 is one of the finest wines made from this variety. It has a demure ruby colour and distinct notes of autumn leaves and red berries on the nose and on the palate, where Morello cherry emerges in a mixture of spices. Next to be sampled was the old gold Verduzzo di Cialla '94, which offers typical aromas of stewed apple, a good balance of sweetness with the characteristic varietal tannins and a very agreeable finish. The Ciallabianco '95, a blend of ribolla gialla, verduzzo friulano and picolit grapes, conjures up interesting aromas of ripe berries mingled with fresh fruit. The palate follows through well to present a delightful contrast between the distinctly dry flavour and notes of apples and very ripe figs. A new release this year is the Ciallarosso '94, a blend of schioppettino and refosco with an elegant bouquet of red fruit and spices.

○	COF Picolit di Cialla '94	🍷🍷	6
○	COF Ciallabianco '95	🍷	4
○	COF Verduzzo di Cialla '94	🍷	5
●	COF Schioppettino di Cialla '93	🍷	5
●	Ciallarosso '94	🍷	4
●	COF Refosco di Cialla '93		5
●	COF Refosco P. R. di Cialla '90	🍸🍸	5
●	COF Schioppettino di Cialla '90	🍸🍸	5
○	COF Verduzzo di Cialla '91	🍸🍸	5
●	COF Refosco P. R. di Cialla '91	🍸	5
●	COF Refosco P. R. di Cialla '92	🍸	5
●	COF Schioppettino di Cialla '91	🍸	5

RONCHI DEI LEGIONARI (GO)

S. CANZIAN D'ISONZO (GO)

TENUTA DI BLASIG
VIA ROMA, 63
34077 RONCHI DEI LEGIONARI (GO)
TEL. 0481/475480

LORENZON
VIA CA' DEL BOSCO, 6
LOC. PIERIS
34075 S. CANZIAN D'ISONZO (GO)
TEL. 0481/76445

The Blasig family settled 300 years ago at Ronchi, which was renamed Ronchi dei Legionari in honour of the patriotic exploits of the writer and aesthete, Gabriele D'Annunzio. The Blasigs were leading figures in the economic and political life of the area from the mid-19th century to the second decade of the 20th century. They linked their fortunes in the early 1960s to those of the Bortolotto-Sarcinelli family from Cervignano, whose interests included land, brickworks and other enterprises, by the marriage of the parents of the current owner, Elisabetta. After studying in Germany and the United States, Elisabetta Bortolotto-Sarcinelli decided to relaunch the family cellars at Ronchi, where previous restructuring work dated from as long ago as 1892. All the equipment was replaced except for the huge Slavonian oak barrels which were carefully conserved. Attention then concentrated on the estate's ten hectares of vines, which currently produce no more than 20,000 bottles a year, all sold under the Falconetto label. Silvio Spoladore is both cellarmaster and vineyard manager. His excellent Bianco is obtained from chardonnay grown outside the DOC zone. It has sweet notes of oak on the nose, together with an attractive mixture of tropical fruit, but it saves its best shot for the palate, where its balance, structure, complexity and length have the chance to shine. The Chardonnay Isonzo del Friuli is another fine wine. The nose has aromas of banana, tobacco and yeast, all present in the entry on the full palate, but the finish is rendered lean by over-assertive acidity. The Tocai Friulano is less ambivalent, maintaining the promise of the pale straw yellow colour in an intense, balanced nose where floral notes get the better of fruit. Robust structure underpins a satisfactory follow-through. In contrast, the palate of the Cabernet fails to live up to the attractive aromas of ripe fruit over nicely judged wood.

The Lorenzon estate embraces over 150 hectares planted to vine and is also active in farming fruit and other high value crops. The Feudi di Romans vineyards extend over 15 hectares in the part of the estate where Enzo Lorenzon has made his most significant investments in the countryside. Helped in the cellar by his son Davide and in marketing by Michela Sfiligoi, a young woman with a lot of flair and experience, Enzo has been able to provide concrete proof of the rising quality standards in the Isonzo DOC zone. The first thing you notice about the Lorenzon Cabernet Franc '96 are the concentrated aromas of ripe red fruit, mirrored on the palate and accompanied by the typical vegetal notes that the variety's admirers enthuse over. The '96 Tocai Friulano is every bit as valid as its predecessors. The delicate bouquet has floral nuances that enhance the prevailing notes of pear, there is plenty of body and texture on the palate and the finish lingers. On the nose, the Sauvignon recalls macerated flowers and kiwi while the palate is underpinned by distinct but appropriate acidity. Elegance and flowers sum up the Malvasia Istriana, a fresh-tasting wine that would go very well with fish. The Refosco dal Peduncolo Rosso reveals bilberry and moss on the nose, solid fruit on the palate and tannins that are perhaps a little too boisterous. The Alfiere Bianco, a blend of malvasia, tocai, pinot bianco and chardonnay, is an interesting wine with margins for improvement in the future. Finally, the Cabernet Sauvignon and the Pinot Grigio are decent bottles that have nothing to be ashamed of.

O Bianco	🍷🍷	2*
O Isonzo Friuli Chardonnay '96	🍷	2
O Isonzo Friuli Tocai Friulano '96	🍷	2
● Isonzo Friuli Cabernet '95		2

● Isonzo Friuli Cabernet Franc		
I Feudi di Romans '96	🍷	3
● Isonzo Friuli Refosco P. R.		
I Feudi di Romans '96	🍷	3
O Isonzo Friuli Malvasia Istriana		
I Feudi di Romans '96	🍷	3
O Isonzo Friuli Sauvignon		
I Feudi di Romans '96	🍷	3
O Isonzo Friuli Tocai Friulano		
I Feudi di Romans '96	🍷	3
O Isonzo Friuli Alfiere Bianco		
I Feudi di Romans '96		3

ASCEVI
VIA UCLANZI, 24
34070 S. FLORIANO DEL COLLIO (GO)
TEL. 0481/884140

BORGO LOTESSA
LOC. GIASBANA, 23
34070 S. FLORIANO DEL COLLIO (GO)
TEL. 0481/390302

The Ascevi holdings comprise two separate estates, under joint management, which produce similar ranges of varietals each with their own labels Both performed well in this year's tastings. Our panel did not exclude any of the Ascevi wines, nor indeed did tasters award any a mere mention, and the Luwa range, which we will consider first, came up with some high-scoring wines. The Luwa Sauvignon has elderflower and peachskin on the nose, leading into a lusciously rich, warm, broad palate. The Chardonnay hints at apple and pineapple, displaying lots of balance and elegance before signing off with a pleasantly long finish. While the Pinot Grigio is straightforward its uncomplicated, crisp flavours make it an ideal accompaniment for seafood. The Col Martin is a blend of sauvignon, tocai and pinot grigio fruit cold-macerated for 24 hours; on the nose it conjures up honey, spring flowers and new-mown grass and has good balance on the palate. Under the Ascevi label we find further examples of top quality winemaking. The Pinot Grigio is a textbook example of the varietal, revealing fragrances of pear and crusty bread. Long and refreshing on the palate, it takes its leave on a note of almonds. Vigna Verdana is obtained from sauvignon grapes with chardonnay and ribolla, matured in wood, on the lees for two months. The entry is fresh and dry, building up into a full flavoured palate with the sure balance that denotes class. The Ascevi Sauvignon is a more modest version of its sister. Its more marked acidity means that it is drinking now. Finally the Chardonnay, which has delicate but pleasant fruit and good balance.

Can Borgo Lotessa keep it up? A fair question, given the number of very successful wines the estate has produced this year. And those weren't the only surprises, for when we retasted the '95 Margravio Bianco blend of sauvignon, pinot grigio and chardonnay, it confirmed our impression that if the wine had been released a year later, it would have scored higher. Credit for these successes goes to the Fratepietro family, under the guidance of General Salvatore Fratepietro, a soldier from Apulia who retired to Friuli to look after his beloved vineyards. His son Roberto is a tall, likeable man who is turning out to be a proficient - and enthusiastic - winemaker. Gianni Crosato provides consultancy back-up in the cellar. This is the first year that the estate has bottled under its own label the wine obtained from its six hectares at Mossa, in the Friuli Isonzo DOC zone and it is well up to the standard of the bottles from the seven hectares in the Collio appellation. The Chardonnay '96 offers aromas of delicate confectioner's cream, rennet and hazelnut. It opens fresh and develops well on the palate, with plenty of texture. The Collio Pinot Bianco evokes pear, hay and yeast on the nose while the palate is balanced, refreshing and elegantly soft, with a lingering finish. Delicate, fresh and clean are the adjectives that best describe the bouquet of the Collio Sauvignon, which is equally well balanced in the mouth. Amongst the other, distinctly varietal, Borgo Lotessa wines, the Margravio Rosso caught the attention although this cuvée appears still in search of the right mix.

O	Collio Chardonnay Luwa '96	⏺⏺	3
O	Collio Pinot Grigio '96	⏺⏺	3
O	Collio Sauvignon Luwa '96	⏺⏺	3
O	Vigna Verdana	⏺⏺	4
O	Col Martin Luwa	⏺	4
O	Collio Chardonnay '96	⏺	3
O	Collio Pinot Grigio Luwa '96	⏺	3
O	Collio Sauvignon '96	⏺	3

O	Collio Chardonnay '96	⏺⏺	3
O	Collio Pinot Bianco '96	⏺⏺	3
O	Collio Pinot Grigio '96	⏺⏺	3
O	Collio Sauvignon '96	⏺⏺	3
O	Friuli Isonzo Pinot Bianco Le Grue '96	⏺⏺	3
O	Friuli Isonzo Pinot Grigio Le Grue '96	⏺	3
O	Friuli Isonzo Tocai Friulano Le Grue '96	⏺	3
O	Friuli Isonzo Sauvignon Le Grue '96		3
●	Il Margravio Rosso '95		4
O	Il Margravio Bianco '95	⏺	4

S. FLORIANO DEL COLLIO (GO) S. FLORIANO DEL COLLIO (GO)

BRDA
LOC. BUKUJE, 6
34070 S. FLORIANO DEL COLLIO (GO)
TEL. 0481/884192

CONTI FORMENTINI
VIA OSLAVIA, 5
34070 S. FLORIANO DEL COLLIO (GO)
TEL. 0481/884131

After gaining entry to the previous edition of the Guide, the Cooperativa da S. Floriano is present again this year thanks to products sold under the Vignaioli da S. Floriano label. The level of winemaking is generally workmanlike but there are also a number of highlights. Overall quality showed an encouraging improvement thanks also to a favourable vintage. Our tasting gave top marks to the copper-flecked Collio Pinot Grigio '96. Fruity and moderately complex on the nose, it follows through well on the full palate and reveals good length. The Ribolla Gialla '96 has aromas of yellow plum with refreshing nuances and is elegant on the palate, with good intensity but a disappointingly short finish. Next the intense, fruity Tocai Friulano '96 discloses ripe yellow and white berry fruit in the bouquet and fresh, rather green acidity on the palate. The last wine we sampled was the Collio Sauvignon '96. It offered faintly gamey notes on the slightly reduced nose, while the palate was straightforward but well balanced.

Since acquiring the Conti Formentini estate, the Gruppo Italiano Vini have shown admirable continuity in the production of premium wines. One of the best locations in the Collio DOC zone and a carefully monitored buying-in policy have enabled the winemaking staff, led by the Piedmontese oenologist, Marco Monchiero, to set their sights high. The cellar and the adjoining Museum of Wine opposite Castello Formentini alone make a visit worthwhile. Total output is currently just over 300,000 bottles a year but the aim is to exploit to the full the capacity of the winery, which is 4,000 hectolitres. The Pinot Grigio '96 is a very good wine. Its aromas of butter and vanilla mingle nicely on the nose with mixed fruit and the excellent follow-through on the palate is rounded off by a distinctly fruity finish. The Chardonnay Torre di Tramontana '96 just missed out on a higher score. The faint touch of wood blending with milk and crusty bread on the nose is again present on the palate, this time more emphatically, and the attractive acidity is accompanied by nuances of milky coffee under glycerine-rich fruit. The non-barriqued Chardonnay is simpler but still a very fine wine, mixing delicate notes of apple and alcohol on the nose. Agile and elusive on the palate, it takes its leave on a bitterish note. The Pinot Bianco is another tip-top product whose fresh aromas are mingled with cream and mirrored on the soft, yeasty palate. The finish features crusty bread and fruit. Finally the Cabernet Franc, although less complex, still proved worthy of a mention.

○ Collio Pinot Grigio Vignaioli da S. Floriano '96	🍷	3
○ Collio Ribolla Gialla Vignaioli da S. Floriano '96	🍷	3
○ Collio Tocai Friulano Vignaioli da S. Floriano '96	🍷	3
○ Collio Sauvignon Vignaioli da S. Floriano '96		3

○ Collio Pinot Grigio '96	🍷🍷	3*
○ Collio Chardonnay '96	🍷	3
○ Collio Chardonnay Torre di Tramontana '96	🍷	4
○ Collio Pinot Bianco '96	🍷	3
● Collio Cabernet Franc '96		3
● Collio Cabernet Franc '95	🍷🍷	3

S. FLORIANO DEL COLLIO (GO)

MUZIC
LOC. BIVIO, 4
34070 S. FLORIANO DEL COLLIO (GO)
TEL. 0481/884201

The story of the Muzic estate is typical of many small scale winemaking concerns in the region. Jolanda and Luigi Muzic started out as tenant farmers before acquiring a smallholding in 1962. For many years they sold their wine in bulk to nègociants, and their first, tentative attempts at bottling only began in 1990. A sound track record lead to their subsequent entry into the Guide. Today their son, Giovanni Muzic, personally manages the ten acres of Collio vineyards and the further two in the Isonzo DOC zone and in 1996 the cellar produced about 50,000 bottles. When we tasted the wines from the '95 vintage, we particularly liked the Ribolla Gialla, the Tocai Friulano and the Pinot Grigio. This year, we sampled the '95 Cabernet Sauvignon Collio, a complex, concentrated, oak-enhanced nose leading in to a broad, fruit-rich palate with slightly mouth-drying tannins, and the Cabernet Franc Isonzo, which has raspberry, bilberry and moss on the nose that carry through nicely onto the soft palate. The Collio Chardonnay '96 also performed well. The entry on the nose has notes of pear and apple, echoed on the fresh-tasting and moderately weighty palate. Other good whites that we sampled from the '96 vintage were all well worth a mention. The Ribolla Gialla is uncomplicated, while the Tocai Friulano, Sauvignon and Pinot Grigio have a little more character.

●	Collio Cabernet Sauvignon '95	🍷	3
●	Isonzo Cabernet Franc '95	🍷	3
○	Collio Chardonnay '96	🍷	3
○	Collio Pinot Grigio '96		3
○	Collio Ribolla Gialla '96		3
○	Collio Sauvignon '96		3
○	Collio Tocai Friulano '96		3

MATIJAZ TERCIC
VIA BUKUJE, 9
34070 S. FLORIANO DEL COLLIO (GO)
TEL. 0481/884193

In 1988, this estate went over to viticulture from livestock breeding, its primary business since the early 20th century. The vineyards - Guyot-trained and planted at 4-5,000 vines per hectare - extend over four hectares of steep, marl slopes at San Floriano. Annual output is now approaching 20,000 bottles. Matijaz and his father Zdenko began to bottle their Chardonnay and Pinot Grigio in '93 on the advice of Gianfranco Gallo. At the time, we tasted both wines, awarding One Glass to the Chardonnay and Two Glasses to its stablemate. The Tercic range has now grown to embrace six products: Chardonnay, Pinot Grigio, Sauvignon, Ribolla Gialla, Merlot and a white blend sold as Vino degli Orti. Our panel liked all four of the wines they tried, beginning with the Chardonnay '96. The nose offers beautifully balanced bread and apple, and the palate has warmth, freshness, weight and lasting balance. The Ribolla Gialla '96 reveals complex fruit and wisteria blossom on the nose, mirrored elegantly on a decently long palate. The garnet-highlighted ruby colour of the Merlot '95 heralds a nose of red fruit. The entry on the palate is low-key and there is good, clean balance, moderate intensity and a bitter note in the finish to be enjoyed. The Tercic Sauvignon discloses the characteristic varietal aroma of delicate tomato leaf and a refreshing entry on the palate, which is round and lingering. A slightly astringent note emerges to perk up the finish.

○	Collio Chardonnay '96	🍷🍷	3
○	Collio Ribolla Gialla '96	🍷🍷	3
○	Collio Sauvignon '96	🍷	3
●	Collio Merlot '95	🍷	3

S. FLORIANO DEL COLLIO (GO)   S. FLORIANO DEL COLLIO (GO)

FRANCO TERPIN
LOC. VALERISCE, 6/A
34070 S. FLORIANO DEL COLLIO (GO)
TEL. 0481/884215

VIGNA DEL LAURO
VIA CASTELLO, 5
34070 S. FLORIANO DEL COLLIO (GO)
TEL. 0481/60155

When we included Franco Terpin in the Guide after only his second year of own-label bottling we thought we were going out on a limb, but in hindsight, our expectations were not unreasonable. Franco comes from a long line of tenant farmers-turned-winemakers. The first plots were acquired by Franco's father Teodoro and he currently has about ten hectares under vine, although only part of the wine obtained is bottled under the Terpin label. Franco's Pinot Grigio had an enthusiastic reception at the Ljubljana trade fair and while it failed to set our panel's pulses racing it is still a very good wine. The nose has notes of apple and pear over a background aroma verging on the soapy and derived from partial malolactic fermentation. The fresh, elegant palate mirrors the bouquet with plenty of warmth and attractive length. Franco's Ribolla Gialla is another commendable wine. On the palate it evokes dust-sprinkled dry flowers and nice whitecurrant nuanced with apple and exalted by the characteristic ribolla gialla acidity, making it an ideal accompaniment for fish. The Chardonnay, too, is solidly varietal, revealing yeast, crusty bread and tropical fruit on the nose while the palate is tangy, soft and invitingly stylish. Finally the Sauvignon lacks balance and the bouquet hints at a certain maturity. The palate is a little too tangy for top marks but the remarkable finish seems to go on for ever.

More than once this year, hail ravaged the vineyards - known as the Vigne del Lauro after the superb laurels that surround them-that Fabio Coser rents from the countesses Tacco. This could be the reason why Fabio's varietal wines have not been up to their usual standard, with the exception of his marvellous Sauvignon. On the nose, it releases gamy aromas reminiscent of rue and red peppers. The entry in the mouth is soft and rich in alcohol, with a refreshing mid-palate that offers an ever-expanding medley of fruit and rounds off with an attractively long finish. The Collio Bianco, obtained from tocai friulano, ribolla gialla, malvasia istriana and pinot grigio, is even better. Its delicately oaked bouquet regales the nose with aromas of honey, banana and elderflower while the palate is soft and full, its elegantly rich flavour suggesting plums before giving way to the gloriously leisurely finish. The Tocai Friulano has a close-knit texture and plenty of freshness as well as a pear and apple seed aromas. In contrast, the Pinot Grigio is assertive on the nose and full flavoured on the palate, where the fruit and acidity balance each other nicely. The tannins and acidity in the Merlot '95 are in evidence to excess, but this can only be expected given the estate's bad luck with the weather. We await the next vintage, secure in the knowledge that Fabio's wines will surprise and delight us once again.

○ Collio Chardonnay '96	♈	3
○ Collio Pinot Grigio '96	♈	3
○ Collio Ribolla Gialla '96	♈	3
○ Collio Sauvignon '96		3

○ Collio Bianco '96	♈♈	3
○ Collio Sauvignon '96	♈♈	3
○ Collio Pinot Grigio '96	♈	3
○ Collio Tocai Friulano '96	♈	3
● Collio Merlot '95		3
● Collio Merlot '94	♈♈	3
○ Collio Bianco '95	♈♈	3
○ Collio Tocai Friulano '95	♈♈	3

S. GIORGIO DELLA RICHINVELDA (PN)   S. GIOVANNI AL NATISONE (UD)

DURANDI - MONTEFLOR
VIA CIASUTIS, 1/B
LOC. PROVESANO
33095 S. GIORGIO DELLA RICHINVELDA (PN)
TEL. 0427/96037

ALFIERI CANTARUTTI
VIA RONCHI, 9
33048 S. GIOVANNI AL NATISONE (UD)
TEL. 0432/756317

The 30 hectares of the Durandi-Monteflor estate near Spilimbergo are very representative of the subzone and produce absolutely typical wines. The gravel-rich terrain has a thin, lean layer of topsoil and yields headily perfumed wines that have marked varietal character. The two labels, Rojuzza and Durandi, account for a total of around 400,000 bottles each year. Lino Durandi, the driving force of the estate, looks after sales while Sig. Bianchini, the flamboyant winemaker, rules the roost in the cellar. The range of wines this year is as good as ever. The attractive Durandi Sauvignon is distinctly varietal with stylish aromas of elderflower and red pepper, which are mirrored well on the palate and lead into a very nice finish. The Rojuzza Traminer Aromatico is in the same high class. Pale gold in hue, it releases the variety's characteristic aromas of roses and citrus fruit, again present on the soft-textured palate. Next we tried the Durandi-label Pinot Grigio, a complex, well balanced wine with sweet fruit aromas. After that came the soft, full flavoured Durandi Refosco, mingling leather, fruit and wood on the nose. The well made Rojuzza Sauvignon, with its pleasant aromas of red pepper, sage and elderflower, and the Rojuzza Chardonnay, marked down by the panel for a lack of harmony between wood and fruit, just missed out on higher scores.

The Cantarutti estate is run by Antonella, daughter of Alfieri, the rather reclusive founder. She manages 24 hectares in the Colli Orientali del Friuli DOC zone and a further 16 in the Friuli Grave appellation. The consultant winemaker is Fabio Coser, a man with a proven track record in the production of white and red wines. This year, we retasted the Cantarutti Merlot Carato '93, which has improved considerably since last year to reveal new tasting pleasures. The youthful '94 version is full bodied and intense, with vibrant notes of autumn leaves. The nose is reminiscent of toasty oak and tar, leading into a palate that is still dominated by boisterous tannins and freshness. The panel will be fascinated to see how it develops. If we turn now to wines from the latest vintage, the Colli Orientali Pinot Grigio '96 is outstanding for its elegant mix of fruit and floral aromas, beautifully mirrored on the palate and rounded off by a marvellous finish. The Grave Pinot Grigio is an altogether less ambitious wine, rendered lean by its marked acidity, but still merits a mention. The COF Sauvignon '96 is an excellent bottle, with a bouquet of red pepper and elder leaves. The palate is warm, full bodied, deliciously rounded and backed up by great structure. The nose of the refreshing, stylish Ribolla Gialla is prevalently floral while apple emerges on the rich, fruity palate. Praise went to the COF Tocai Friulano in which tasters noted pear dominating a well balanced mixture of aromas on the nose and good follow through in the mouth. The very approachable Friuli Grave Chardonnay came close to matching the Tocai's score thanks to a characteristic yeast and crusty bread nose and lovely fresh fruit on the palate, where the moderate texture has you coming back for more.

○ Friuli Grave Pinot Grigio '96	♀	2*
○ Friuli Grave Sauvignon '96	♀	2*
○ Friuli Grave Traminer Aromatico Rojuzza '95	♀	2*
● Friuli Grave Refosco P. R. '95	♀	2*
● Friuli Grave Cabernet '95		2
● Friuli Grave Cabernet Sauvignon Rojuzza '95		2
● Friuli Grave Merlot '95		2
○ Friuli Grave Chardonnay '96		2
○ Friuli Grave Chardonnay Rojuzza '96		2
○ Friuli Grave Sauvignon Rojuzza '96		2

○ COF Pinot Grigio '96	♀♀	3*
○ COF Sauvignon '96	♀♀	3*
○ COF Ribolla Gialla '96	♀	3
○ COF Tocai Friulano '96	♀	3
● COF Merlot '94	♀	3
○ Friuli Grave Chardonnay '96		2
○ Friuli Grave Pinot Grigio '96		2
● COF Merlot Carato '93	♀	4

S. GIOVANNI AL NATISONE (UD)   S. GIOVANNI AL NATISONE (UD)

LIVON
VIA MONTAREZZA, 33
FRAZ. DOLEGNANO
33048 S. GIOVANNI AL NATISONE (UD)
TEL. 0432/757173-756231

RONCO DEL GNEMIZ
VIA RONCHI, 5
33048 S. GIOVANNI AL NATISONE (UD)
TEL. 0432/756238

"Lots of wines, lots of awards and one truly superlative product" is how we could sum up the Livon tasting this year. The estate's magnificent Sauvignon Valbuins '96 has a markedly varietal bouquet of red pepper, elderflower and aromatic herbs. Its combination of warmth and lovely acidity linger memorably in the mouth, leaving a very impressive sensation of aroma. The Chardonnay Braide Mate has an abundance of fruit and vanilla, good structure and overtones of buttermilk and honey. The stainless steel-vinified Tre Clas version has less weight and even though it is stylish and well made, it fails to excite. The standard label Pinot Bianco, however, was a revelation with its intensity and warmth. Soft and alcohol-rich, its flavours linger on the palate delightfully. The light, pleasant Pinot Grigio Braide Grande has elegant notes of pear on the nose and a fresh, dry palate but lacks something in balance. The light fruit of the Tocai Ronc di Zorz mingles with the confectioner's cream and mint which return on the full flavoured if unexciting palate. In our opinion, the Refosco Riul was the best of the reds. A dry, alcohol-rich wine with lots of chewy fruit, it released notes of pepper, cinnamon and cherry on the nose. The Merlot Tiare Marte has a pale ruby colour with faint highlights but makes up with a nose that offers pencil lead, ink, sweet fruit and mint. Dry and clean-tasting, it also has good length. The Verduzzo Casai Godia was the pick of the sweet wines. This elegant, well balanced version of a wine that is difficult to make outside Friuli has a pale gold colour and aromas of almonds and citron. The Picolit Cumins slowly but gradually reveals complex notes of dry flowers, lavender, pear and apple, and a very superior palate.

Serena Palazzolo did very much the right thing in delaying the release of all her wines. We compared the results of our retasting with notes from a year ago and every single product has improved - some of them quite spectacularly. It is no doubt the wise counsel of Francesco Serafini that has led to this progress at the Ronco del Gnemiz cellars. In fact the Chardonnay '95 very nearly won Three Glasses for we gave this wonderful product outstanding marks in a blind tasting. Its bouquet is an opulent mixture of vanilla, pineapple and ripe apricot, leading into a satisfyingly fat palate of tropical fruit and yeast subtly veiled by toasty oak. The sweet wines, the Verduzzo and the Picolit '94, are very impressive. Obtained from fruit partially air-dried on rush mats, they were both aged for six months in small oak barrels and 18 months in the bottle. The Verduzzo is the colour of old gold and reveals a rich nose where apricot and sultana aromas emerge. The palate has attractive complexity and perfectly judged wood leading up to a generous finish, again redolent of sultanas. The gold Picolit offers classy aromas of almond paste and very ripe fruit. The semi-sweet, full flavoured palate follows through well and there is a faint note of volatile acidity that mitigates the residual sugar. The aromas of the soft, weighty Rosso del Gnemiz '93 blend of merlot and cabernet mingle tar, coffee, liquorice and red fruit. Serena's elegant Tocai Friulano is velvet-smooth and beautifully oaked, disclosing acacia blossom and honey on the nose while the close-knit texture of the Sauvignon '96 has a bouquet of sage and elderflower and a delightful note of peach on the palate.

O Collio Sauvignon Valbuins '96	♈♈♈	4
O COF Picolit Cumins '94	♈♈	6
O COF Verduzzo Friulano Casali Godia '95	♈♈	4
O Collio Chardonnay Braide Mate '95	♈♈	5
O Collio Pinot Bianco '96	♈	3
● COF Refosco P. R. Riul '95	♈	4
● Collio Merlot Tiare Mate	♈	5
O Collio Chardonnay Tre Clas '96	♈	4
O Collio Pinot Grigio Braide Grande '96	♈	4
O Collio Tocai Friulano Ronc di Zorz '96	♈	4
O COF Verduzzo Friulano Casali Godia '94	♈♈♈	4

O COF Chardonnay '95	♈♈	4
O COF Picolit '94	♈♈	6
O COF Sauvignon '96	♈♈	4
O COF Tocai Friulano '96	♈♈	4
O COF Verduzzo Friulano '94	♈♈	4
● Rosso del Gnemiz '93	♈♈	5
● COF Schioppettino '93	♈	4
O Müller Thurgau '96	♈	4
O Chardonnay '87	♈♈♈	5
O Chardonnay '90	♈♈♈	5
O COF Chardonnay '91	♈♈♈	4
O Chardonnay '88	♈♈♈	5

S. LORENZO ISONTINO (GO)   S. LORENZO ISONTINO (GO)

LIS NERIS - PECORARI
VIA GAVINANA, 5
34070 S. LORENZO ISONTINO (GO)
TEL. 0481/80105-809592

PIERPAOLO PECORARI
VIA TOMMASEO, 36/C
34070 S. LORENZO ISONTINO (GO)
TEL. 0481/808775

The limestone gravel of the upper Isonzo subzone provides the "terroir" which Francesco Pecorari then interprets with the sure hand of a master craftsman. The end result is an increasing range of premium wines and some extremely high scores - for the St. Jurosa and Lis Neris in particular. Beginning with the Chardonnay cru, this is an elegant wine with a vanilla and jasmine bouquet that is echoed on the palate, where there is more depth and immediacy than in the basic varietal. The non-cru has a similar character to the St. Jurosa, but is lighter and nimbler, with aromas of apple and fruit salad. A comparison of the two Sauvignons also sees the selection coming out on top, its confectioner's cream, rose and elderflower and clean yet complex palate putting it a cut above the somewhat closed Picol which keeps its best aromas tucked well away. Both Pinot Grigios repay investigation. The Gris, field-selected and fermented in 500-litre casks, has length, depth, fruit and lots of class, while its richly alcoholic, smooth-tasting partner is vinified exclusively in stainless steel. The Lis Neris blend of 70 percent merlot and 30 percent cabernet sauvignon is macerated for two weeks in open vats - the cap being punched down frequently- and then spends 18 months in small oak barrels and at least a year in the bottle. This is a wine with attitude and a headily spicy nose nuanced with brambles. On the palate it is long, complex and mouth-fillingly delicious. The Verduzzo Tal Lûc, from grapes partially raisined for two months in an air-conditioned environment, is every bit as good as the previous vintage. The rich, concentrated nose offers variations on a theme of honey, almonds and orange blossom then gives way to a palate that has wonderful balance and after-aromas of apricot-jam croissants.

This estate's robust catalogue is organized into two sections: younger wines aged on the lees in stainless steel, and the special selections released two years after the harvest, which are fermented and aged in 500-litre casks and may also be distinguished by the place names on the label. There was a very encouraging series of scores this year after our panel had finished tasting, beginning with the Pratoscuro blend of steel-vinified müller thurgau and oak-fermented riesling. Tasters noted the fragrant, delicate bouquet that was perfectly mirrored on the palate both in its citrus aromas and in its intriguing elegance. A very fine Tocai - fresh, intense and full of both fruit and flowers - was matched and even surpassed by an equally convincing Pinot Bianco that had much in common but outscored its stablemate on elegance. The Sauvignon from the current vintage unveiled rich aromas of peach and mint, a full, soft buttery palate and lots of length. In contrast, the Kolàus selection had uncomfortably emphatic toasty and buttery notes that could not come to terms with the acidity. The beautifully balanced Soris can rely on well judged oak to sustain its aromas of mango and honey. Its elegance and sophisticated texture nicely complement the very drinkable standard version that is no mean performer, particularly on the palate. The basic Pinot Grigio has notes of hay, lots of freshness and good flavour while the Olivers selection can offer more intense colours, vanilla notes and a greater weight of alcohol, even though its oak-derived aromas are rather too assertive.

● Isonzo Rosso Lis Neris '94	🍷🍷	5	○ Isonzo Chardonnay Soris '95	🍷🍷	4
○ Isonzo Chardonnay St. Jurosa '95	🍷🍷	4	○ Isonzo Friuli Pinot Bianco '96	🍷🍷	3*
○ Isonzo Friuli Pinot Grigio '96	🍷🍷	4	○ Isonzo Friuli Sauvignon '96	🍷🍷	4
○ Isonzo Friuli Pinot Grigio Gris '95	🍷🍷	4	○ Isonzo Friuli Tocai Friulano '96	🍷🍷	3*
○ Isonzo Friuli Sauvignon Dom Picol '95	🍷🍷	4	○ Pratoscuro '95	🍷🍷	4
○ Tal Lûc '95	🍷🍷	5	○ Isonzo Friuli Chardonnay '96	🍷	4
○ Isonzo Friuli Chardonnay '96	🍷	4	○ Isonzo Friuli Pinot Grigio '96	🍷	4
○ Isonzo Friuli Sauvignon Picol '96		4	○ Isonzo Pinot Grigio Olivers '95	🍷	4
○ Isonzo Chardonnay St. Jurosa '94	🍷🍷	4	○ Isonzo Sauvignon Kolàus '95		4
○ Isonzo Pinot Grigio Gris '94	🍷🍷	4			
○ Tal Lûc '94	🍷🍷	5			
● Isonzo Rosso Lis Neris '93	🍷🍷	5			

SACILE (PN)

SAGRADO (GO)

VISTORTA
VIA VISTORTA, 87
33077 SACILE (PN)
TEL. 0434/71135

CASTELVECCHIO
VIA CASTELNUOVO, 2
34078 SAGRADO (GO)
TEL. 0481/99742

The splendid Vistorta estate is situated just outside the village of the same name, on the border that separates Friuli from the Veneto region. Is belongs to Brandino Brandolini d'Adda, whose family also has substantial winemaking investments in Bordeaux. And it is from that part of France that Brandino has acquired the know-how and entrepreneurial mentality which he applies to his 16 hectares of vineyards planted exclusively with merlot. He is proud to have as his consultant the oenologist, Georges Pauli, whose other clients include Château Gruaud-Larose. New clones - again from France - have recently been planted at a density of about 4,000 vines per hectare. The Vistorta property, only ten hectares of whose clay terrain are currently in production, was able to release 35,000 bottles of the '95 vintage. The low figure is a result of the rigorous selection carried out first in the vineyards and then in the cellar to ensure that only the very best fruit goes into estate-labelled bottles. Our panel tasted products from the '90 wines, the first Vistorta bottling, to the current vintage. All made a very favourable impression but it is the '95 vintage that marks a further major step forward in quality thanks to wider use of small oak barrels for malolactic fermentation and leisurely ageing (Brandino calculates "We're about halfway through our projected growth plans"). The Merlot '95 is a silky, mouth-filling wine. The wood has been judged to perfection and the wine has great cellar potential, even if it is already drinking wonderfully well. The attack on the nose is full of rich fruit in a bouquet with exceptional poise. We were delighted and look forward to coming back in five or ten years' time when it will have reached full maturity.

A difficult environmental for grape growing - high winds, thin, poor topsoil and karst terrain with very low water retention- have helped to make the Castelvecchio estate's fortune as well as being the source of many problems. It has been necessary to set up a full-scale drip-irrigation system and plant grass between the vines. The fruit is very healthy, despite minimal spraying against parasites. Yields are low so quality is high. The consultant winemaker is Gianni Bignucolo, whose vast experience ensures quality and consistency. The reds, as ever a strong suit at Castelvecchio, have spent two years in wood - first large casks, then smaller barrels; they are well-built and ready to drink on release. Two well earned Glasses go to the Cabernet Franc '93. Its complex aromas of wild berries, bramble and attractive oak are followed through by a fruity, full flavoured palate with moderate tannins. The Refosco '93 is another very enjoyable bottle with overtones of ripe red fruit and toasty oak. Cherry emerges distinctly on the palate to mingle with mellow refosco tannins. The Terrano '93 is obtained from a variety native to the Carso plateau. The prominent varietal tannins are immediately obvious on the palate against a background of fruit, including cherry and ripe plum. We like the Sauvignon '96 best of the Castelvecchio whites even though elegant aromas of green pepper, engaging acidity and freshness were let down by a rather lean finish. The well made, unpretentious Malvasia Istriana '96 with its characteristically floral aromas is straight out of the Castelvecchio tradition and, finally, we look forward to coming back to the Cabernet Sauvignon '93. At present, it is astringent and lacking in balance but it also has promising features, such as the complexity of the nose and its length on the palate. We'll keep you posted.

● Friuli Grave Merlot '95	♥♥	4

● Cabernet Franc '93	♥♥	3*
● Refosco P. R. '93	♥♥	3*
● Terrano '93	♥	3
○ Carso Malvasia Istriana '96	♥	3
○ Carso Sauvignon '96	♥	3
○ Carso Traminer Aromatico '96		3
● Carso Rosso Turmino '94		3
● Cabernet Sauvignon '93		3
● Terrano '95		3
● Cabernet Franc '92	♀	3
● Cabernet Sauvignon '92	♀	3

SPILIMBERGO (PN)

BORGO MAGREDO
VIA BASALDELLA, 5
LOC. TAURIANO
33097 SPILIMBERGO (PN)
TEL. 0427/51444

TORREANO (UD)

SANDRO & ANDREA IACUZZI
V.LE KENNEDY, 39/A
LOC. MONTINA
33040 TORREANO (UD)
TEL. 0432/715147

Borgo Magredo is one of the largest winemaking concerns in Friuli with 219 hectares under vine and an output of 700,000 bottles in '96. And year after year, it manages to maintain quality standards, thanks to careful clonal selection, high planting densities, an up-to-date cellar and a team of highly qualified experts including consultant winemaker Walter Filiputti, agronomist Oreste Mason and, this year, oenologist John Turato. Borgo Magredis sells under two labels, the standard range and a line of "Braide" wines, - named after the Friulian word for "field" or 'farmland' - which are partially or totally fermented in wood. This year, our tasters liked the Sauvignon '96 best. Its elegant mix of varietal aromas on the nose carries through well in the mouth, where there is good acidity and length. The thoroughly sound, deep ruby Cabernet Sauvignon Braida Vieri '95 hovers between fruit and wood on the nose then offers good fruit and attractive tannins on the lingering palate. The complexity of the Pinot Grigio '96's bouquet grabs your attention but slight over-acidity on the palate forced out panel to lower its score. There are fine varietal notes of grass and stewed fruit in the aromas of the Cabernet Franc, followed through well in the mouth, and the oak is very well judged. Like the Pinot Grigio, the Chardonnay Braida Longa suffers slightly from assertive acidity but the bouquet of pear drops, tropical fruit and vanilla is attractive. Over-enthusiastic oaking tends to mask the red pepper aromas of the Sauvignon Blanc Braida Curta while the Pinot Nero, Refosco dal Peduncolo Rosso, Chardonnay, Cabernet Sauvignon and Tocai Friulano are all well made varietal wines that impressed the panel enough to gain a mention.

The Iacuzzi brothers' estate is coming along nicely. It made its first appearance in the "Other Wineries" section of the Guide last year but this year gained a full profile thanks to a range of soundly made wines and a Two Glass flag-bearer in the Sauvignon '96. We also know that experiments are under way involving two oak-matured blends, one red and one white, that will be released in the near future. The property may be small (eight hectares producing 40,000 bottles) but the Iacuzzis are determined to go for quality. Their excellent Sauvignon '96 has stylish aromas of tomato leaf and elderflower echoed on the well balanced palate and accompanied by lovely fruit and perfectly calibrated acidity. The varietal Verduzzo Friulano '96 has characteristic golden highlights, fragrances of stewed apple, slightly astringent tannins and moderate sweetness. The Pinot Bianco reveals elegantly refreshing aromas of apple and a fruit-rich attack on the palate compromised by lean acidity that nevertheless recedes in the finish. The La Torca white is named after the local word for "witch" and is blended from carefully balanced percentages of müller thurgau and the Manzoni crossing. There are unusual fragrances of fresh fruit and pine needles on the nose with good acidity and fruit alternating on the palate. The pleasantly varietal Tocai Friulano also merits a mention. No reds were offered for tasting because of the brothers' decision to release a more mature product onto the market. Last but certainly not least; Iacuzzi wines are excellent value for money.

○ Friuli Grave Pinot Grigio '96	♀	2*
○ Friuli Grave Sauvignon '96	♀	2*
○ Friuli Grave Chardonnay Braida Longa '96	♀	3
● Friuli Grave Cabernet Franc '95	♀	2*
● Friuli Grave Cabernet Sauvignon Braida Vieri '95	♀	3
● Friuli Grave Cabernet Sauvignon '95		2
● Friuli Grave Pinot Nero '95		2
● Friuli Grave Refosco P. R. '95		2
○ Friuli Grave Sauvignon Blanc Braida Curta '96		3
○ Friuli Grave Chardonnay '96		2
○ Friuli Grave Tocai Friulano '96		2

○ COF Sauvignon '96	♀♀	3*
○ COF Pinot Bianco '96	♀	3
○ COF Verduzzo Friulano '96	♀	3
○ La Torca '96	♀	3
○ COF Tocai Friulano '96		2
● COF Merlot '94	♀	2

TORREANO (UD)

TORREANO (UD)

VALCHIARÒ
VIA LAURINI, 3
33040 TORREANO (UD)
TEL. 0432/712393

VOLPE PASINI
VIA CIVIDALE, 16
FRAZ. TOGLIANO
33040 TORREANO (UD)
TEL. 0432/715151

Last year, Valchiarò's many admirers were unhappy about its relegation to the "Other Wineries" section but it has bounced right back this year. The estate run by Lauro De Vincenti belongs to five friends who each look after their own vineyards as well as the odd plot they have rented. The area under vine comes to almost 15 hectares in total, producing 60,000 bottles a year at very competitive prices. Winemaking is supervised by consultant Giovanni Crosato. We particularly like the elegant fruit on the nose of the Pinot Grigio, which followed through with nice balance and notes of apple on the palate to round off with a soft, pleasing glycerine-rich finish. Pear, moderately ripe plum, nuances of petrol and dry flowers all came through on the nose of the Tocai Friulano to be mirrored in the mouth, where good acidity sustains the persistence of the flavours. The bouquet of the Pinot Bianco lacks balance but this is soon corrected on the palate of pear and green shoots, leading into an attractive finish. La Clupa, a blend of tocai friulano, sauvignon, pinot bianco and picolit, revealed the opposite tendency; its fresh, classy flower and fruit nose nuanced with beeswax was perfectly balanced but led into a palate from whose assertive acidity there emerged notes of pear, apple and honey. The Valchiarò reds, including a Refosco that might have scored higher but for its marked acidity, were less impressive than the whites.

Emilio Rotolo, originally from Calabria, is the new owner of the historic Volpe Pasini estate. He has revolutionized everything in the cellars and in the vineyards, totally reorganizing both administration and winemaking methods. A former doctor and estate agent, this affable southerner brought with him to North-east Italy his experience as a tourist operator. He invited Rosa Tomaselli on board to look after marketing and public relations as well as Flavio Zuliani, an experienced winemaker who has grabbed the opportunity to prove what he can do. All that remains for our panel is to congratulate the estate on the quality of its white wines for current drinking, and look forward to the promise of the reds and reserve-style whites which are still maturing. The outstanding Chardonnay Zuc di Volpe, partially aged in wood, has a memorably elegant nose with enticing notes of fruit and vanilla. The complex, fresh-tasting palate is redolent of toasty oak under tropical fruit and aromatic herbs. In contrast, the Tocai Friulano Zuc di Volpe is vinified and aged entirely in stainless-steel and offers a bouquet of herbs and spring flowers, with pear to the fore. These aromas are mirrored on the soft, rich, buttery palate that lingers nicely. All the elegance of the Pinot Bianco Zuc comes out in the bouquet of apples over notes of yeast and the delicately sustained follow-through on the palate. The Ribolla Gialla Zuc was only marginally inferior to the others in the range.

○ COF Pinot Grigio '96	▼▼ 3*
○ COF Pinot Bianco '96	▼ 3
○ COF Tocai Friulano '96	▼ 3
○ La Clupa '96	▼ 4
● COF Merlot '96	3
● COF Refosco P. R. '96	3
● El Clap '93	4

○ COF Chardonnay Zuc di Volpe '96	▼▼ 4
○ COF Pinot Bianco Zuc di Volpe '96	▼▼ 4
○ COF Tocai Friulano Zuc di Volpe '96	▼▼ 4
○ COF Ribolla Gialla Zuc di Volpe '96	▼ 4
○ COF Sauvignon Zuc di Volpe '96	▼ 4
○ COF Tocai Friulano Villa Volpe '96	▼ 3

OTHER WINERIES

The following producers obtained good scores in our tastings with one or more of their wines:

PROVINCE OF GORIZIA

Puiatti, Capriva del Friuli, tel. 0481/809922,
Collio Sauvignon '96,
Collio Chardonnay '96

Ronchi di Zegla, Cormons, tel. 0481/61155
Collio Tocai Friulano '96,
Collio Chardonnay '96

Villa Martina, Cormons, tel. 0481/60733,
Collio Pinot Grigio '96,
Collio Pinot Bianco '96

Crastin, Dolegna del Collio, tel. 0481/630310,
Collio Tocai Friulano '96,
Verduzzo '96

Roberto Ferreghini, Dolegna del Collio,
tel. 0481/60549,
COF Malvasia '96,
COF Sauvignon '96

Norina Pez, Dolegna del Collio tel. 0481/639951,
Collio Pinot Grigio '96,
Collio Tocai Friulano '96,
Collio Sauvignon '96

La Rajade, Dolegna del Collio, tel. 0481/639897,
Collio Ribolla Gialla '96,
Collio Pinot Bianco '96,
Collio Tocai Friulano '96

Colmello di Grotta, Farra d'Isonzo,
tel. 0481/888445,
Isonzo Friuli Pinot Grigio '96,
Isonzo Friuli Sauvignon '96

Attems Conte Douglas, Gorizia,
tel. 0481/390206,
Collio Merlot Ronco Arcivescovo '95,
Collio Cabernet Ronco Trebes '95

Redi Vazzoler, Mossa, tel. 0481/80519,
Collio Pinot Grigio '96, Collio Cabernet '93

Draga, S. Floriano del Collio, tel. 0481/884182,
Collio Pinot Grigio '96,
Collio Riesling '96

Marega, S. Floriano del Collio,
tel. 0481/884058,
Collio Chardonnay '96,
Holbar Rosso '93

PROVINCE OF PORDENONE

I Magredi, S. Giorgio della Richinvelda,
tel. 0427/94720,
Grave Chardonnay '96, Grave Pinot Grigio '96

PROVINCE OF UDINE

Forchir, Bicinicco, tel. 0427/96037,
Grave Sauvignon '96,
Grave Chardonnay '96,
Grave Tocai Friulano '96

Flavio Pontoni, Buttrio, tel. 0432/674352,
COF Cabernet '96,
COF Picolit '96

Benincasa,
Cividale del Friuli, tel. 0432/716419,
COF Chardonnay '95, Blanc dal Muini

Ronchi di Fornaz,
Cividale del Friuli, tel. 0432/701462,
COF Sauvignon '96, COF Pinot Grigio '96

Vignaioli Mitri,
Cividale del Friuli, tel. 0432/734066,
COF Sauvignon '96, COF Tocai Friulano '96

Nicola e Mauro Cencig,
Manzano, tel. 0432/740789,
COF Cabernet Franc '96, COF Pinot Grigio '96

Walter Filiputti, Manzano, tel. 0432/759429,
COF Ramandolo '94,
COF Ribolla Gialla '96

Oscar Filiputti,
Pavia di Udine, tel. 0432/676000,
Grave Tocai '96, Grave Cabernet Franc '96

Fantinel Vini, Pradamano, tel. 0432/670444,
Collio Pinot Bianco Vigneti S. Caterina '96,
Grave Refosco P.R. '95

Ronco del Castagneto,
Prepotto, tel. 0432/713072,
COF Ribolla Gialla '96, COF Pinot Bianco '96

Villa Chiopris,
S. Giovanni al Natisone, tel. 0432/757173,
Grave Pinot Grigio '96, Grave Chardonnay '96

Brojli-Franco Clementin,
Terzo di Aquileia, tel. 0431/32642,
Aquileia Refosco P. R. '96,
Aquileia Merlot '96

EMILIA ROMAGNA

Great success for Emilia Romagna! This year wines from two different estates have won the Guide's top accolade, the Three Glass award. For years we have been writing that the wines of Emilia Romagna had the potential to obtain remarkable results, and we were not mistaken. Our optimism was not based, as might reasonably be suspected, on regional chauvinism, nor on an uncritical devotion to certain indigenous grape varieties which, for better or worse, have governed the destiny of Emilia Romagna's wine production for many years. Our evaluation was prompted by the sweeping changes we observed in a great number of winemaking companies and above all by the fact that we saw the laws of quality guiding producers' decisions both in the vineyard and in the winery, and becoming an integral part of their philosophy. This is demonstrated by some bold and astute investments, research on grape varieties and clonal selection, and the arrival of highly-qualified oenological consultants. Apart from this desire to go forward and to succeed, another concept has begun to make headway among wine professionals in the region: from the commercial point of view, Emilia Romagna can no longer remain an inward looking island. In this context, a more modern approach to viticulture has encouraged growers to plant with renewed, and even greater enthusiasm, the so-called international varieties which, while not overshadowing the traditional grape types, have, in the space of a few short years, already given impressive results. Two estates in particular, both of relatively recent foundation, Tenuta la Palazza and Tenuta Bonzara, have achieved outstanding results with French varietals. These two small domains one from Romagna, the other from the Colli Bolognesi, stunned our tasting panel with a Chardonnay and a Merlot of top international quality. La Palazza's Tornese, tasted in the company of Italy's finest whites, emerged as one of the most exciting wines from anywhere in the country, while Tenuta Bonzara's Rocca di Bonacciara held its head up high amidst the nation's most highly quoted Merlots. But the success does not end there. The general desire to compete with better-known zones has meant that these days producers from all parts of the region are bringing out premium wines with impressive potential. In fact no fewer than six wines from Emilia Romagna took part in the final national tastings for the assignation of the Three Glass awards. Wineries such as La Zerbina, Castelluccio and the Vallania's Terre Rosse once again confirmed the excellent results obtained in past editions of the Guide, while other producers like Tre Monti, Podere del Nespoli, Casa Chiara, Bellei, La Tosa, La Stoppa and Il Poggiarello picked up numerous Two Glass awards. We are witnessing a period of great ferment. The winemaking revolution currently taking place calls for a concerted effort from the region as a whole, from public institutions and the private sector alike. And if it is to be successful it must avail itself of new forms of promotion and marketing and adopt an outlook in keeping with the modern international wine scene.

BERTINORO (FO) # BOMPORTO (MO)

VINI PREGIATI CELLI
V.LE CARDUCCI, 5
47032 BERTINORO (FO)
TEL. 0543/445183

FRANCESCO BELLEI
VIA PER MODENA, 80
41030 BOMPORTO (MO)
TEL. 059/818002

Constantly seeking to improve their products and services, Mauro Sirri and his partner Emanuele Casadei have just finished the construction of a new ageing cellar and a tasting facility. They have also introduced brand-new equipment in their winery and now, we are reliably informed, they are finally intending to purchase some vineyards of their own. Our blind tasting was perhaps a little hard on their wines, but we nevertheless renew our congratulations to these industrious producers, convinced as we are that their winery is making slow but steady progress. Leaving aside these considerations, let us look at the wines themselves, which are undoubtedly very interesting. The Poggio Ferlina '96 is a floral-scented and attractively fresh Trebbiano. The I Croppi '96 stands out from the rather sad assortment of Albanas made in this vintage; it displays sweet fresh fruit notes, with good alcohol and interesting fruit on the palate. The Le Grillaie '94 is also good, if not quite up to the standard of last year. This is a Sangiovese Riserva with a rustic nose, noticeable (but not intrusive) tannins, and broad, full-bodied flavours. The Sangiovese Superiore Le Grillaie '95 is lighter with higher acidity. The '95 Albana Passita Solara is a less blatantly sweet wine than in the past, but it also exhibits more oakiness and it too has higher acidity than usual. With its appealing resiny and honeyed scents, it only just missed out on a Two Glass rating.

Beppe Bellei's passion for sparkling wines is almost legendary. His many close contacts in France, his experience at Möet, his friendships with a large number of French winemakers; all of these factors have contributed over the years to the experience which manifests itself in his wines, wines which are able to compete on equal terms with the best that Italy has to offer. Bellei has had to invest notable amounts of time, energy and money in the production of premium sparkling wines in an area known primarily for fizzy reds, and definitely not for products made from pinot nero and chardonnnay. This year, true to his reputation as a meticulous winemaker, Beppe Bellei only presented one wine for us to taste, maintaining that the Extra Cuvée Brut '93 and the Extra Cuvée Brut Rose '93 were not yet ready to be assessed. We therefore tasted the Extra Cuvée Brut '94, which showed itself to be a wine of great breeding, with an elegant bead and fresh, floral aromas on a fragrant yeasty background On the palate it is rounded and displays good structure; and above all, it is absolutely delicious to drink. Finally, we have to confess that we found the Lambrusco di Sorbara slightly inferior to that of previous vintages. The nose is intense but not altogether clean. On the palate it shows rounded, savoury fruit.

○ Albana di Romagna Passita Solara '95	♀	4
○ Albana di Romagna Secca I Croppi '96	♀	1*
○ Trebbiano di Romagna Poggio Ferlina '96	♀	1
● Sangiovese di Romagna Le Grillaie Ris. '94	♀	3
● Sangiovese di Romagna Sup. Le Grillaie '95		1
○ Albana di Romagna Passita Solara '94	♀♀	4
● Sangiovese di Romagna Le Grillaie Ris. '93	♀♀	2

○ Spumante Extra Cuvée Brut '94	♀♀	4
● Lambrusco di Sorbara		3
○ Spumante Brut Cuvée Speciale '92	♀♀	5

BORGONOVO VAL TIDONE (PC) BRISIGHELLA (RA)

TENUTA PERNICE
LOC. PERNICE
FRAZ. CASTELNOVO VAL TIDONE
29010 BORGONOVO VAL TIDONE (PC)
TEL. 0523/860050

CASA CHIARA
VIA BACCAGNANO, 19
48013 BRISIGHELLA (RA)
TEL. 0546/85765

Maria Poggi Azzali, the company's founder, and her young partner Enrico Sgorbati now find themselves running a large and dynamic operation, with 75 hectares of vineyards located in the best areas of the Val Tidone. In the winery one finds all the equipment necessary for making quality wines, including stainless steel tanks, gentle membrane presses and the requisite plant for temperature-controlled fermentation. The wines are modern in style, with an emphasis on primary fruit aroma. The best of the still whites is the Collare Bianco, a blend of ortrugo and chardonnay, made with short, temperature controlled maceration. It is clean and round on the nose, with light fruity aromas, good balance and intensity on the palate and a fresh finish. Among the semi-sparkling wines, the Ortrugo leaves its mark, with a delicately aromatic bouquet which leads into a palate characterized by well-balanced acidity coupled with just the right amount of effervescence. The Sauvignon has an appealing exotic fruit bouquet and clean, attractively rounded fruit on the palate. The Marsanne, made exclusively from a grape variety known here as "uva sciampagna", provides a simple and charming curiosity. Among the reds, the Gutturnio Frizzante stands out for its fresh clean nose and savoury palate, with flavours of raspberries and spices. Last but decidedly not least, there is the Collare Rosso, a blend of Cabernet Sauvignon and Bonarda aged in oak casks of various sizes for about a year. It has rich, red berry fruit aromas; not particularly broad on the palate, but is well-balanced and attractive and it very nearly rated Two Glasses.

Franco di Natale and Francesca Guerrera's winery is not a flash in the pan. It appeared for the first time in our Guide last year with wines which were tangible proof of the owners' strong desire to make their mark in a zone which already boasts a number of well-established producers. Their relative lack of experience, the small scale of their operation and a certain precariousness of their winery facilities justify, to some degree, the minor problems we found in some samples, which were from the last three vintages. A slight, rustic tendency to excessive acidity particularly affected the white wines, but the other products, though somewhat short of elegance, display great richness of fruit and structure. Among these is the Sangiovese '95, with its aromas of ripe fruit and of violets and its full, satisfying palate. The '94 Sangiovese is less interesting and concentrated and it is not altogether clean on the nose. The best wines again come from non-autoctonous grape varieties. The Buldur, made from cabernet sauvignon, is fruity though a little too tannic in the '96 version, but the '95, in which the wood is better balanced by the substantial fruit, is full-bodied, round and rich. Tasting the different vintages of the Cionfolaio, a happy combination of merlot and small oak casks, also made us come down in favour of the '95. The '96 is lighter, but is graceful and attractive, whereas the '95 has an old-fashioned but rounded nose, and elegant, mouth-filling fruit on the palate.

○ Collare Bianco '96	♀	3
○ Colli Piacentini Ortrugo Frizzante '96	♀	2*
○ Colli Piacentini Sauvignon Frizzante '96	♀	2*
● Collare Rosso '95	♀	3
● Colli Piacentini Gutturnio Frizzante '96	♀	2
○ Marsanne '96		2*

● Buldur Cabernet Sauvignon '95	♀♀	3*
● Cionfolaio Merlot '95	♀♀	3*
● Buldur Cabernet Sauvignon '96	♀	4
● Cionfolaio Merlot '96	♀	4
● Sangiovese '95	♀	3
● Sangiovese '94		3
● Buldur Elevato in Legno '94	♀♀	4
● Cionfolaio Elevato in Legno '93	♀	4

CASTEL S. PIETRO (BO)

CASTELLO DI SERRAVALLE (BO)

UMBERTO CESARI
VIA STANZANO, 1120
FRAZ. GALLO BOLOGNESE
40024 CASTEL S. PIETRO (BO)
TEL. 051/941896-940234

VALLONA
VIA S. ANDREA, 203
LOC. FAGNANO
40050 CASTELLO DI SERRAVALLE (BO)
TEL. 051/6703058-6703066

This year we witnessed an authentic conversion in this producer who has always been considered one of the high priests of DOC wine production in Romagna. The best wines that we tasted in this year's sessions were not made from local grape varieties. We are always ready to judge wines on their merit, without preconceptions and therefore applaud the new and unsuspected resource revealed by a company which last year had shown some signs of fatigue. The Laurento '95, a decidedly well made Chardonnay came out top in our tastings: it has a full, elegant nose, with aromas of ripe fruit and on the palate it is rich and buttery, with caramel and tobacco notes. Another excellent wine is the Liano '94, a splendid combination of sangiovese and - surprise, surprise - cabernet sauvignon. We particularly liked the elegant and well-balanced fruit on the palate, with its dominant cherry and berry fruit flavours. The nose of the Sangiovese Riserva '94 is a bit rustic, but the wine does display its own individual character. The Malise '95, a successful blend of pignoleto and chardonnay, is almost grassy, but is fresh and appealing. The Trebbiano Parolino '96 and the Albana Secca Colle del Re '96 on the other hand are less interesting. The Albana di Romagna Passita Colle del Re '93, with its restrained sweetness and well-balanced soft fruit, is up to its usual standard.

The modernization of Maurizio Vallona's winery, one of the best-equipped in the Colli Bolognesi, has been completed: now everything is ready for the big improvement in quality which is widely expected from this producer. The estate vineyards, with their controlled, very low yields, are carefully groomed and enjoy a favourable south-westerly exposure. Small quantities mean top quality, and therefore generally successful results even in difficult vintages like the recent ones. A good example is the '95 Cabernet Sauvignon, perhaps the best red produced by this winery in the last few years. Aged for 18 months in small oak, it has a deep ruby colour and, on the nose, ripe fruit and bell pepper notes. On the palate the dominant sensations are those of soft, rich fruit, balanced by just the right amount of tannins. We also liked the whites we tasted, which have the unmistakable style of this producer, a style that emerges in the intense fruity nose, ripe flavours and weight on the palate. This is true of the Chardonnay and also of the interesting Sauvignon, which has intense, complex peach and elderflower aromas. On the palate, both wines display reasonable structure and elegance, and their well balanced acidity will help enable them to improve further with a little longer in the bottle. Finally, the '96 Pignoletto Frizzante is worthy of mention: it has a fine frothiness and just the right amount of softness on the palate.

● Liano '94	♟♟	3*
○ Laurento '95	♟♟	3*
○ Albana di Romagna Passita Colle del Re '93	♟	4
○ Malise '95	♟	3
● Sangiovese di Romagna Ris. '94	♟	3
○ Albana di Romagna Secca Colle del Re '96		2
○ Trebbiano di Romagna Vigna del Parolino '96		2
● Liano '93	♀	3
● Sangiovese di Romagna Ris. '93	♀	2

● Colli Bolognesi Cabernet Sauvignon '95	♟	3
○ Colli Bolognesi Chardonnay '96	♟	2
○ Colli Bolognesi Pignoletto '96	♟	2
○ Colli Bolognesi Sauvignon '96	♟	2
○ Colli Bolognesi Pignoletto Frizzante '96		2
○ Colli Bolognesi Chardonnay '95	♟♟	3
● Colli Bolognesi Cabernet Sauvignon '94	♀	3

CASTELVETRO (MO)

Vittorio Graziano
Via Ossi, 30
41014 Castelvetro (Mo)
tel. 059/799162

Vittorio Graziano, the eclectic and undisputed purist of Lambrusco Grasparossa, lives in perfect empathy with his vines. He takes all his decisions on which wines to produce as he strolls among his well-ordered rows of grasparossa and other local white varieties. When the conditions are favourable and the grapes are of sufficient quality to give a wine that is up to being bottled, he produces his Spargolino, which in lesser vintages, he sells in bulk instead. The Ruspantino, which he had produced two years running, was not considered good enough for bottling this year and will consequently be sold in demijohn. This extremely brave policy is not widely practised in this particular area where, indeed, wines are sourced from vineyards with, to say the least, decidedly generous yields. The Grasparossa '96 tasted this year is a wine with a handsome ruby-purple colour, and which is not terribly fizzy: on the nose one first finds floral notes and then those of red berry fruits; it has reasonable fruit on the palate, enlivened by fresh acidity and by just a hint of tannin. The finish is slightly reminiscent of bitter cherries, and is attractively savoury. The Spargolino, a semi-sparkling wine made by blending wines made from seven different grape varieties, is fermented in the bottle and degorged after two years. It has a pleasing, persistent mousse and its fragrant fresh aromas linger quite a long time on the nose On the palate, it is full, balanced and richly-structured.

○	Spargolino Frizzante	🍷	2
●	Lambrusco Grasparossa di Castelvetro '96	🍷	2*

CIVITELLA DI ROMAGNA (FO)

Poderi Dal Nespoli
Via Statale, 49/51
Loc. Nespoli
47010 Civitella di Romagna (FO)
tel. 0543/989637

To reach this winery, one needs to set aside a bit of time to negotiate the bends in the road which climbs up towards the Appennines, but the destination, a small village consisting of an old-fashioned manor house and elegant surrounding outbuildings, really is worth the effort. Here, the Ravaioli family fashions wines which, even though the cellars not equipped in any particularly sophisticated way, always succeed in obtaining impressively high scores. This year is no exception and the '94 version of the Borgo dei Guidi, an excellent blend of cabernet sauvignon and sangiovese, reveals itself to be a very fine wine indeed. The deliberately extended period of oak ageing has concentrated the bouquet, rendering it intense yet elegant. However, it is especially on the palate that this wine is amazing, with broad, evolving, rich fruit, reminiscent of spices, liquorice and wild berries, and a long, concentrated finish. This is certainly a bottle that will age well, despite a not particularly happy vintage. Il Nespoli '95 again displays the character of its best vintages: real ripeness on the nose, with suggestions of red berry fruit jam, and great finesse and balance on the palate. The late harvesting of the sangiovese grapes and vinification in traditional large casks contributes to the concentration of flavours. The Prugneto '95, a Sangiovese Superiore which does not demonstrate ideal balance but which does have an appealing old-fashioned flavour, also scored its usual high marks.

●	Borgo dei Guidi '94	🍷🍷	4
●	Il Nespoli '95	🍷🍷	3
●	Sangiovese di Romagna Sup. Vigna Il Prugneto '95	🍷	2
●	Borgo dei Guidi '93	🍷🍷 (white)	4
●	Il Nespoli '93	🍷 (white)	3
●	Sangiovese di Romagna Sup. Vigna Il Prugneto '94	🍷 (white)	2

FAENZA (RA)

LEONE CONTI
VIA POZZO, 1
TENUTA S. LUCIA
48018 FAENZA (RA)
TEL. 0546/25108-642149

FAENZA (RA)

TRERÉ
VIA CASALE, 19
48018 FAENZA (RA)
TEL. 0546/47034

Both we and our readers are well aware that the Guide's deadlines do not always coincide with the readiness of certain wines or with the bottling schedules of many producers. The samples tasted this year of Leone Conti's wines had only been bottled a short while beforehand and therefore suffered somewhat from the various minor problems which invariably follow bottling. In spite of this, they showed off the winemaking skills of this able grower from Romagna to great effect. The '96 Vignapozzo is perfectly true to type, and once again one of the best of the dry Albanas of the vintage. Under a slightly pungent nose one finds a wine of fine, elegant, yet attractively alcoholic style. The fresh, floral Chiaro di Luna of the same year, made from sauvignon, is also deserving of mention. The bouquet of the Non Ti Scordar di Me, a '94 Albana di Romagna Passita, is not absolutely clean; its palate, on the other hand, is much more attractive: long, round and full-bodied, with appealing ripe fruit and honey flavours. Pleasant surprises were provided by the Albana Dolce Vignacupa '96, which is particularly good on the palate, and by the Il Capanno '96, a sharp but very quaffable wine made from ciliegiolo, a traditional local grape variety.

Morena Trere lives in a beautiful house, surrounded by a huge number of brightly coloured peacocks, just outside Faenza. The small winery which is located next door to the home is a symbol of the skill and dedication with which all her wines are made. This year there emerge wines of an ever so slightly lower standard than that we had become accustomed to in the past, partly a result, no doubt, of particularly unfavourable vintages. Indeed, all of her products showed more marked acidity and less structure than usual. Nevertheless the wines of this able producer are still among the best to be found in the area: the Rebianco '96, for example, beat all competition in its class in our tastings. This wine is made from trebbiano with the addition of some chardonnay and it has a ripe, evolved nose and lots of flavour. It is not particularly varietal, but is very appealing indeed. The Albana Secca '96 Vigna della Compadrona has fresh fruit, just a hint of acidity and good body. The main features of the Albana Passita '94 are the warming, rich bouquet, and long, enticingly concentrated flavours of ripe fruit and honey. The Amarcord d'un Ross '94 is a Sangiovese Riserva, given greater backbone by a tiny percentage of cabernet sauvignon, which has spent some time in barriques. It is less rustic and more elegant than in previous vintages but unfortunately it is also less rich in structure. The fruity Sangiovese Superiore Vigna dello Sperone '96 is bright purple and on the palate reminds one of a good quality carbonic maceration wine.

○ Albana di Romagna Dolce Vignacupa '96	♀	3
○ Albana di Romagna Passita Non Ti Scordar di Me '94	♀	5
○ Albana di Romagna Secca Vignapozzo '96	♀	2*
○ Chiaro di Luna '96	♀	2
● Il Capanno '96	♀	2
○ Albana di Romagna Passita Non Ti Scordar di Me '93	♀♀	5
● Sangiovese di Romagna Ris. '93	♀♀	3

○ Albana di Romagna Passita '94	♀	4
○ Trebbiano di Romagna Rebianco '96	♀	2
● Sangiovese di Romagna Amarcord d'un Ross Ris. '94	♀	3
● Sangiovese di Romagna Sup. Vigna dello Sperone '96	♀	2
○ Albana di Romagna Secca Vigna della Compadrona '96		2
○ Albana di Romagna Passita '93	♀	4
● Sangiovese di Romagna Amarcord d'un Ross Ris. '93	♀	2

FAENZA (RA)

ZERBINA
VIA VICCHIO, 11
FRAZ. MARZENO
48010 FAENZA (RA)
TEL. 0546/40022

The night before our tasting of the wines of Romagna, Cristina Geminiani, the guiding spirit behind this estate, gave birth to her first child. Totally unaffected by the happy events taking place in her private life, Cristina did not disappoint our usual expections of her, and presented us with a series of excellently made wines. Let us begin with the Scacco Matto '93, which scored only marginally lower than in the previous vintage. Its flavour is full, with intriguing sweet notes ranging from almonds to honey, and unusually good length. The '93 version of the Marzieno, a red from sangiovese and cabernet sauvignon aged in oak, and only made in the best vintages, is also excellent; great depth of colour, broad bouquet and on the palate very long and round with liquorice and wild berry fruit. The Torre di Ceparano '95 is also very interesting. It is less robust than the Marzieno, but offers a very fine nose with scents of spices, vanilla and violets. On the palate it shows greater elegance and broad, well-integrated texture. The white Tergeno '95 also displays excellent balance. The Vicchio '96, made from chardonnay grapes, is warm and long, revealing nevertheless delightful, fresh floral aromas. The Ceregio '96 is a Sangiovese which, though it shows the typically high acidity of the vintage, still makes pleasant enough drinking.

○ Albana di Romagna Passita Scacco Matto '93	▼▼	5
○ Tergeno '95	▼▼	4
○ Vicchio '96	▼▼	2*
● Marzieno '93	▼▼	3*
● Sangiovese di Romagna Sup. Torre di Ceparano '95	▼▼	3*
● Sangiovese di Romagna Sup. Ceregio '96	▼	2
○ Albana di Romagna Passita Scacco Matto '92	▽▽	5
● Sangiovese di Romagna Pietramora Ris. '93	▽▽	3
● Sangiovese di Romagna Sup. Torre di Ceparano '94	▽▽	2

FORLÌ

DREI DONÀ TENUTA LA PALAZZA
VIA DEL TESORO, 23
MASSA DI VECCHIAZZANO
47100 FORLÌ
TEL. 0543/769371

The '93 vintage reds and the '95 chardonnay-based white have both been released and they certainly confirm our predictions about their potential. These wines represent the fruits of the labour of their enthusiastic producer, Claudio Drei Dona, a lawyer turned winemaker. Claudio has pulled out all the stops, transforming his 16 hectares of vines into an immaculate garden. He first fitted out his winery with state-of-the-art equipment so that he can rigourously control fermentaion temperatures and he then bought new oak casks of every size imaginable. Finally he entrusted supervision of the whole winemaking operation to the skills of one of Italy's top winemakers Franco Bernabei, whose precious advice he follows meticulously. The result is Il Tornese '95, the first white wine from Emilia Romagna to sail away with one of our Three Glass awards: it is a benchmark Chardonnay, one of the very best we tasted from anywhere in Italy this year. It has extremely intense aromas of citrus fruits, with a well-integrated vanilla note. On the palate, it is soft, rich and buttery. Among the reds, the Magnificat '93 again performed very well indeed. This cabernet sauvignon-based wine offers a broad and complex gamut of sensations: mint, chocolate, red berry fruits, soft, unobtrusive tannins, tarry fruit and notable length. The Pruno '93, a Sangiovese Superiore, is very enjoyable. Already pleasing on the nose and even more appealing on the palate, it is elegant and round, with greater structure than most wines of its class.

○ Il Tornese '95	▼▼▼	4
● Magnificat '93	▼▼	5
● Sangiovese di Romagna Pruno Ris. '93	▼▼	4
○ Il Tornese '94	▽▽	4
○ Il Tornese '93	▽▽	4
● Magnificat '92	▽▽	4
● Sangiovese di Romagna Pruno Ris. '92	▽▽	4
● Notturno '95	▽	3

FORMIGINE (MO)

BARBOLINI
VIA FIORI, 36
41041 FORMIGINE (MO)
TEL. 059/550154

At long last, from the '96 vintage onwards, all of Barbolini's wines are made and bottled at their own winery, which has been thoroughly renovated and equipped in the most up-to-date manner. The results are immediately apparent, and in our tastings four wines scored over 70 points out of 100. Of these, the Il Civolino is, in our opinion, the best wine. This semi-sparkling white, made from trebbiano scarsafoglia grapes, has very fine apple aromas, lovely soft fruit on the palate and fair length. Il Maglio, one of Emilia's best semi-sparkling reds, is always well made: ruby colour, with rich ripe fruit aroma, soft and pleasantly savoury on the palate. The Sorbara is also good. It is clean and fruity on the nose, with a typically acidulous but not at all aggressive flavour and reasonable aromatic length. The Rosa della Molina, made from lambrusco oliva, owes its deepish pink colour to brief skin-contact; vinous on the nose, with well-balanced acidity. Finally, we include the ruby-purple hued Grasparossa which does not have an especially intense nose, but shows good fruit and structure on the palate and discernible tannins on the finish.

○	Il Civolino '96	▼	2
⊙	Rosa della Molina '96	▼	2
●	Lambrusco di Modena Il Maglio '96	▼	2*
●	Lambrusco di Sorbara '96	▼	2
●	Lambrusco Grasparossa di Castelvetro '96		2

IMOLA (BO)

TRE MONTI
VIA LOLA, 3
40026 IMOLA (BO)
TEL. 0542/657122-657116

There is no question about it: this historic company has reassumed its rightful place in the regional hierarchy. In the world of wine, certain choices are often of crucial importance, such as investment in the vineyards, the selection of modern oenological equipment, or the purchasing and proper use of new wooden barrels. These are the kinds of decisions which have been taken by the dynamic Navacchia family, who are now joined on the estate by oenologist Donato Lanati, one of the wine world's keenest minds. The result from their new vineyards is the rather unusual Turico '96, made from cabernet sauvignon and aged in barrique. Even if it is still very young, this wine already displays good depth of colour and a very fine nose; on the palate it is full and very elegant, with soft tannins which enrich its structure without adversely affecting its softness. The Chardonnay Ciardo '96 is long and seductive on the palate; it spends some time in small oak barrels, from which it has drawn aromas of vanilla and almonds. It is a white whose appeal lies in its balance and drinkability, and is a worthy representative of the new quality-led philosophy of this winery. The more traditional wines from the '96 vintage also, however, display new-found cleanness and elegance: there are soft fruity notes in the Trebbiano, the Albana Secco is fresh, crisp and true-to-type and the Salcerella (a blend of albana and chardonnay) is well-crafted. Our comments are similar for the reds from the robust and tannic Sangiovese Riserva '94, to the richly-structured Boldo '95 (sangiovese and cabernet sauvignon) with its attractive toasty oak aromas and the Sangiovese Superiore '96 with its wild berry fruit. The Albana Passita '94 is also of a good standard.

○	Colli Imolesi Ciardo '96	▼▼	3*
●	Colli Imolesi Boldo '95	▼▼	3
●	Colli Imolesi Turico '96	▼▼	3*
○	Albana di Romagna Passita '94	▼	4
○	Albana di Romagna Secca '96	▼	2*
○	Colli Imolesi Salcerella '96	▼	3
○	Trebbiano di Romagna '96	▼	2
●	Sangiovese di Romagna Sup. '96	▼	2
●	Sangiovese di Romagna Ris. '94	▼	3
●	Boldo '92	▽▽	3
●	Sangiovese di Romagna Ris. '93	▽	3

LANGHIRANO (PR)

MODIGLIANA (FO)

ISIDORO LAMORETTI
STRADA DELLA NAVE, 6
LOC. CASATICO
43010 LANGHIRANO (PR)
TEL. 0521/863590

CASTELLUCCIO
VIA TRAMONTO, 15
47015 MODIGLIANA (FO)
TEL. 0546/942486

Isidoro Lamoretti has every right to be considered one of the fathers of the Colli di Parma DOC. Thanks to his outstanding vineyards overlooking the splendid castle of Torrechiara, and this gentleman producer's great passion for oenology, Lamoretti's wines have, for some years now, been among the top products in the zone. In this year's tasting, the '96 Malvasia Colli di Parma and the Moscato stood out clearly. The former wine, always one of the winery's standard-bearers, was one of the best Malvasias we tried. It has a brilliant straw-yellow colour, and it won us over with its beautifully clean, floral bouquet, and its freshness in the mouth. The Moscato (in effect partially-fermented grape must) shows Lamoretti's skills as a winemaker: it is a wine which succeeds perfectly in combining an easy-drinking style with very fine aromas, and is not at all cloying. Finally, we should like to bring an interesting new wine to your notice, a barrique-aged Cabernet Sauvignon from the Vigna Lunga vineyard. This plot consists of around two hectares, has a south-easterly exposure, and was planted with nebbiolo until 1990, when it was replanted with French varieties. The '95 is the first vintage to be released and due to not exactly favourable weather conditions during the harvest is possibly slightly dilute. It has a simple bouquet, in which the oak is not especially well-integrated. The potential of the cru however is evident and the '96, tasted from the cask, promises to be much more intense and deeply flavoured.

"Innovation through continuity" might be the motto of this estate which has, ever since the 1970s, continued to work with a difficult grape variety like sangiovese in a dynamic and creative manner. From wines whose "leitmotif" was their powerful personality and explosive concentration, Castelluccio has, more recently, gone on to make products which lay greater emphasis on elegance, soft fruit and balance. The desire however to produce wines that are out of the ordinary is common to both of these styles and, if we look carefully at the wines we can recognize features which are shared by both the older vintages and those of the present. The skills of winemaker Attilio Pagli have created minor masterpieces like the Ronco della Simia '93, a wine which displays great elegance, starting on the nose. On the palate, it has soft, round, almost sweet fruit and warming alcohol, as well as amazing length. The Ronco delle Ginestre has a more full-blown and less measured bouquet but, on the other hand, has an unsurpassable concentration of tannin and colour which takes us right back to the1980s. The '93 Ronco dei Ciliegi is more cutting, nervous and supple but also, surprisingly, more Barolo-like, in a style which also reveals a distant relationship with its forebears from the last decade. We also draw your attention to the following wines in the estate's assortment: Le More '94, is a more mature and evolved Sangiovese than usual which was sourced from various "Ronchi" vineyards in this not particularly happy vintage; the Lunaria '95 is a very well-balanced and attractive Sauvignon, with fruit which is just a little bit light.

O Colli di Parma Malvasia '96	♀	2*
O Moscato '96	♀	3
● Colli di Parma Rosso Vigna di Montefiore '95		2
● Vigna Lunga '95		3

● Ronco dei Ciliegi '93	♀♀	5
● Ronco della Simia '93	♀♀	5
● Ronco delle Ginestre '93	♀♀	5
● Le More '94	♀	3
O Lunaria '95	♀	3
● Ronco delle Ginestre '90	♀♀♀	5
● Ronco dei Ciliegi '92	♀♀	5
O Ronco del Re '93	♀♀	6
● Ronco della Simia '92	♀♀	5
● Ronco delle Ginestre '92	♀♀	5

MONTE S. PIETRO (BO)

MONTE S. PIETRO (BO)

TENUTA BONZARA
VIA S. CHIERLO, 37/A
40050 MONTE S. PIETRO (BO)
TEL. 051/6768324

SANTAROSA
VIA S. MARTINO, 82
40050 MONTE S. PIETRO (BO)
TEL. 051/969203

The Tenuta Bonzara winery at S. Chierlo, looks out over most of the 16 hectares of vineyards which stretch along the valley of the Lavino. In just a few short years, this estate has made some giant strides forward and its wines have rapidly shot to the attention of insiders. This year it has come up with some extraordinary results: the sure touch of a skilled winemaker such as Stefano Chioccioli has succeeded in turning the aspirations of the estate's dynamic owner, Professor Francesco Lambertini, into reality. We had absolutely no hesitation in awarding a Three Glass award to the amazing Merlot Rocca di Bonacciara '95, a wine which displays both exemplary structured with a long, rich finish. It is an outstanding Merlot and in comparative tastings unquestionably the equal of Italy's top wines made from this grape variety. The Lambertini estate confirms its vocation for red wines with the Bonzarone, of which two excellent vintages have been released this year: the '94 and more recently the '95. The former is made from a blend of 80 per cent cabernet sauvignon with merlot: it is rather vegetal on the nose, which also shows vanilla hints, but on the palate it is big and rounded, yet very elegant. The '95 Bonzarone deservedly scored a few points more. The '96 Merlot is a less serious wine, but certainly not a simple one. It has a very fruity nose, underscored by a distinct vein of alcohol; on the palate, the fruit is soft, but well-balanced by the acidity and tannins on the finish. The new dessert wine called U Pasa ("Semi-dried Grapes" in local dialect) is made from sauvignon. It displays good intensity on the nose, and reasonable concentration on the palate. Also worthy of mention are the agreeable varietals, Sauvignon, Pignoletto Frizzante and Pinot Bianco.

1996 represents an intermediary year for the estate run by Giovanna Della Valentina: the white wines, in fact, were bottled rather late, and this may well explain why, in our tastings, we came across a Pignoletto and a Pinot Bianco that were fairly unrepresentative of the usual standard of the Santarosa wines. Both wines, deep yellow-straw in colour, were very mature and evolved on the nose, with almost toasty hints; they displayed similar characteristics on the palate, along with a bit too much alcohol. On the whole, the structure of the two wines is excellent but they do lack the freshness and sheer enjoyable fruit on the palate that we have found in previous years. The '94 Cabernet Sauvignon, on the other hand, is excellent; its colour is dark and dense; there is ripe broad fruit on the nose, with vegetal and spicy tones; on the palate, it is rounded and soft, very elegant, and has a rich, silky finish. As we wait for the '94 Giò Rosso to be released, our tasting of the '93 and our appreciation of its development confirmed yet again the deft hand that the Santarosa estate seems to have enjoyed over the past few vintages as far as its red wines are concerned.

● Colli Bolognesi Merlot Rocca di Bonacciara '95	♟♟♟	4
● Bonzarone '94	♟♟	4
● Colli Bolognesi Cabernet Sauvignon Bonzarone '95	♟♟	4
● Colli Bolognesi Merlot '96	♟	3*
O Colli Bolognesi Pignoletto Frizzante '96	♟	3
O Colli Bolognesi Pinot Bianco Borgo di Qua '96	♟	3*
O Colli Bolognesi Sauvignon Sup. Le Carrate '96	♟	3
O U Pasa '95	♟	4
● Colli Bolognesi Merlot Rocca di Bonacciara '94	♟♟	4

● Colli Bolognesi Cabernet Sauvignon '94	♟♟	3*
O Colli Bolognesi Pignoletto '96		2
O Colli Bolognesi Pinot Bianco '96		2
● Giò Rosso '93	♟♟	3
● Colli Bolognesi Cabernet Sauvignon '93	♟	3

MONTEVEGLIO (BO)

OSPEDALETTO DI CORIANO (RN)

CANTINA DELL'ABBAZIA
VIA ABÈ, 33
40050 MONTEVEGLIO (BO)
TEL. 051/6702069

COOPERATIVA SAN PATRIGNANO
TERRE DEL CEDRO
VIA S. PATRIGNANO, 53
47040 OSPEDALETTO DI CORIANO (RN)
TEL. 0541/756436-362362

Gianni Morara takes the credit for having founded this estate, and his daughter Silvia for running it with style, professionalism and skill. Years of investment in the winery and, prior to that, in the vineyards, are bearing fruit and being reflected in the constantly improving quality of the wines. Thanks for this must also go to the estate's young oenologist, Giovanni Fraulini, who with his expert knowledge of the area, has done a great deal of research on the zone's traditional grapes, as well as certain other varieties which are completely new to the Colli Bolognesi. Going on to our tasting notes, the best wine we sampled was undoubtedly the Cabernet Sauvignon '95, with its attractive deep ruby colour, and mature vegetal aromas and vague suggestions of eucalyptus on the nose; its flavours echo the aromas perfectly, and it displays remarkable extract on the palate, as well as an appealing long finish sustained by firm but not exaggerated tannins. The Barbera is also good: it has an intense ruby colour with purplish highlights. It is perhaps still young and a little closed on the nose, but it does offer rich, soft fruit on the palate, with just the right amount of oak to take the edge off the wine's characteristic acidity. The Pignoletto Frizzante has a fine, persistent mousse and is initially soft in the mouth, but then evolves into a typical bitter-almondy finish. We also bring your attention to the still Pignoletto, with its very particular nose redolent of roasted nuts, its reasonable structure and medium length on the palate.

We are delighted that this unusual estate continues to warrant its place in our Guide. As it has followed the traditional way to success; that of planting new vineyards in the hills which surround the holiday resort like an amphitheatre, and swift up-dating of the equipment in the winery, a resulting high level of quality comes as no surprise. It is certainly true that here there is no lack of strong will or resources (both financial and cultural), but what is really surprising about this estate is its exciting "difference" within the context of Romagna's fast-changing panorama of wineries. The absence of wood in the winery gives their products particular aromas and flavours, rendering them more aromatic and elegant. The Zarricante '94 is a ruby-coloured Sangiovese Riserva, tinged with garnet; it has a remarkable and complex bouquet, rich fruit on the palate, and a long finish. The '95 Aulente is clean and pleasantly fruity. The Sangiovese di Romagna '96 is also appealing, though characterized by highish acidity (a common problem, sadly, of the region's wines in this difficult vintage). The estate's whites also follow attractively traditional lines: the '96 Trebbiano, fresh, well-balanced, and with alluring floral and peachy aromas, and the Brut, one of the few wines of this type produced in Romagna, yet remarkable for its cleanness and trueness to type as well as the evolved notes which suggest its capacity to age.

● Colli Bolognesi Cabernet Sauvignon '95	♟♟	3
● Colli Bolognesi Barbera '95	♟	4
○ Colli Bolognesi Pignoletto Frizzante	♟	2*
○ Colli Bolognesi Pignoletto '96		3
● Colli Bolognesi Barbera '94	♟	3
● Colli Bolognesi Cabernet Sauvignon '94	♟	3

● Sangiovese di Romagna Zarricante Ris. '94	♟♟	3
● Sangiovese di Romagna '96	♟	1
● Sangiovese di Romagna Sup. Aulente '95	♟	2
○ Trebbiano di Romagna '96	♟	1
○ Brut Terre del Cedro	♟	3
● Sangiovese di Romagna Sup. Aulente '94	♟	1
● Sangiovese di Romagna Zarricante Ris. '93	♟	2

OZZANO TARO (PR) PILASTRO (PR)

MONTE DELLE VIGNE
VIA COSTA, 27
43046 OZZANO TARO (PR)
TEL. 0521/809105

FORTE RIGONI
STRADA DELLA BUCA, 5
LOC. CALICELLA
43010 PILASTRO (PR)
TEL. 0521/637678

The Monte delle Vigne estate deserves a round of applause for having presented us with an interesting range of wines. Let us begin with the product that has, in the last few years, breached the "semi-sparkling only" rule for the wines of the zone: the Nabucco, a still wine made from barbera and merlot and aged in barrique. The '95 vintage, though certainly not memorable for its concentration or the richness of its aromas, scores well over 70 points out of 100 thanks to its excellent balance of tannins and acidity which allows the fruit to express itself fully. The 1996 Nabucco, tasted from the barriques, shows great promise (thanks also to a good vintage), revealing an intensity on the nose and rich extracts which are really out of the ordinary. We shall, however, talk about this wine in the next edition of our Guide. Andrea Ferrari, whilst confirming his vocation as a maker of soft, fruity reds, has also produced two delicious "frizzanti" wines: the '96 Lambrusco, with its sweet aromas and fleshy fruit on the palate, notably superior to many of its DOC "cousins" from around Modena, and the lively (and almost similarly pleasing) Barigazzo. As far as the whites are concerned, we note the excellent performance of the '96 Sauvignon Tenuta La Bottazza, perhaps the best Sauvignon tasted this year from around Parma. It offers an attractive expression of the variety's aromatic qualities, as well as good underlying cleanness of fruit, and freshness. Also worthy of mention are the Malvasia Tenuta la Bottazza and the Colli di Parma Rosso, from that same holding. The Malvasia Dolce '96 completes our listing of the wines of this estate; now that it has lost some of the rustic notes it had in previous vintages, it is particularly tempting.

Forte Rigoni, one of the longest-established producers in the Colli di Parma, boasts some excellent, well-sited vineyards. The holdings, planted mainly with sauvignon and malvasia, are in the commune of Langhirano (in the hamlet of Calicella) and at Arola, near the castle of Torrechiara. This estate's range of wines, which all bear the Colli di Parma DOC, impressed us this year; generally speaking, they were all up to the standard suggested by the potential of the vineyards. It is no accident that the Malvasia '96 was one of the best we tasted; pale straw in colour, it stands out for its floral, aromatic nose; on the palate it is elegant and reasonably long. We also tasted a still, barrique-matured white, which represents a really new style for the zone; it is a Colli di Parma Sauvignon which, even if it cannot boast great depth or complexity, is crisp and herbaceous on the nose, with attractive notes also deriving from the oak; on the palate it is fresh and long and is given added interest by the touch of richness which the barriques provide. This white, with its bold and singular style, proves that even within the Colli di Parma DOC there is room for producing wines which are modern and capable of finding a market even beyond the confines of the region. The range is completed by the bottle-fermented sparkling whites; the Malvasia '93 and the Sauvignon '94. These are two wines which, although they both have a good underlying style, display certain problems with the finesse of their bouquets and with their excessive acidity on the palate.

○ Colli di Parma Sauvignon		
Tenuta La Bottazza '96	♀	2*
○ Malvasia Dolce '96	♀	2
● Lambrusco '96	♀	2*
● Nabucco '95	♀	4
● Barigazzo Frizzante '96	♀	2
● Colli di Parma Rosso		
Tenuta La Bottazza '96		2
○ Colli di Parma Malvasia		
Tenuta La Bottazza '96		2
● Nabucco '93	♀♀	4

○ Colli di Parma Malvasia '96	♀	2*
○ Colli di Parma Sauvignon '96	♀	2

RIVERGARO (PC)

S. ILARIO D'ENZA (RE)

LA STOPPA
FRAZ. ANCARANO
29029 RIVERGARO (PC)
TEL. 0523/958159

MORO RINALDO RINALDINI
VIA PATRIOTI, 47
FRAZ. CALERNO
42040 S. ILARIO D'ENZA (RE)
TEL. 0522/679190

Situated in the Val Trebbiola, between the Val Trebbia and the Val Nure, at 250 metres above sea level, the La Stoppa estate comprises over 200 hectares, of which around 40 are planted to vines. Following their chosen path of concentrating mainly on the red wines, la Stoppa did not produce any whites this year. Let us begin, therefore, with the '95 Barbera, with its plums and sour cherries on the nose; it has an attractive entry on the palate, well-structured fruit, and evident tannins, all underpinned by fresh acidity. The red Macchiona, made from barbera and bonarda and partially aged in large barrels and casks remains one of the estate's signature wines; the '93 vintage is powerful on the nose, although the fruit and oak aromas are somewhat masked by the alcohol. On the front palate the fruit is nicely rounded, but the alcoholic note reemerges on the finish. Once again the Cabernet Sauvignon La Stoppa is up to its usually high standard, making it a veritable Grand Cru of the Colli Piacentini. This '95 is elegant, with sweet fruity aromas and spicy overtones; on the palate it shows well-balanced consistent fruit and fine tannins; its varietal notes form a well-integrated part of its fairly rich, deep structure. We also tasted the very successful first release of the Vigna del Volta '95, a dessert wine made from semi-dried malvasia di Candia grapes which, even at this "première" appearance, already showed that it is a fine wine. It has peach jam and apricots in syrup on the nose, echoed with well-balanced, intense fruit on the palate.

The path chosen by Rinaldo Rinaldini is certainly not the easiest; he has always preferred to give his wines a second fermentation in bottle, rather than make them sparkling by using practical and modern pressurized tanks. Most of the almost 200,000 bottles he produces, therefore, contain wines which have undergone the classic process of fermentation, "remuage" and disgorging. The chardonnay-based Spumante Brut is his best wine this year; its brilliant effervescence in the glass tempts one to go on and enjoy its fragrance of freshly-baked bread; on the palate, it is soft, rounded and has decent length of flavour. The youthful Pinot Frizzante's nose is decidedly herbaceous and vegetal; on the palate, it offers an unusual and attractive fruity flavour, with pleasant fresh notes. The Malvasia Secca, which is very difficult to vinify using a second fermentation in bottle, is, in this case, a great success. It has a rich, powerful nose, and on the palate, the bitter-almond flavours that are typical of the grape are only hinted at; the finish shows exemplary balance, cleanness and finesse. The Lambrusco Vecchio Moro, dedicated to Rinaldo's father, displays good structure, with ripe fruit of unusual substance on the palate. The Pjcol Ross, made by the "metodo classico" from the red-skinned variety of the same name, shows intensity on the nose and good structure, with soft fruit on the front palate and bitter cherry notes on the finish. Also worthy of mention are the Morone, made from lambrusco, and the Lambrusco Reggiano, which is not very fizzy but is pleasant and has a longish aftertaste.

○ Vigna del Volta '95	♟♟	4
● Colli Piacentini Cabernet Sauvignon Stoppa '95	♟♟	4
● Colli Piacentini Barbera '95	♟	3
● Macchiona '93	♟	4
○ Buca delle Canne '93	♟♟	5
● La Stoppa '91	♟♟	4
● Macchiona '91	♟♟	5

○ Malvasia Secca	♟	2
○ Colli di Scandiano e di Canossa Pinot Frizzante	♟	1
○ Spumante Metodo Classico Rinaldo Brut Chardonnay '94	♟	3
● Lambrusco dell'Emilia Vecchio Moro	♟	1
● Lambrusco Spumante Metodo Classico Pjcol Ross	♟	1*
● Lambrusco Reggiano		1
● Rosso Spumante Metodo Classico Morone		1

S. PROSPERO (MO)

UMBERTO CAVICCHIOLI
P.ZZA GRAMSCI, 9
41030 S. PROSPERO (MO)
TEL. 059/908828

This modern winery has, for some years now, stood as an example of how it is possible to reconcile producing large quantities of, on the whole, perfectly decent wines with the making of high quality products from the best vineyards. The grapes from the various sites and varieties are vinified separately, after careful research into their identification according to statistical and historical criteria. So for the first time this year we find a new Lambrusco di Modena, selected from four different sub-types of lambrusco, and made using the choicest grapes from the individual growing areas. It is a wine with a bright, appealing aspect, straightforward yet elegant in the modern idiom. Its fresh effervescence lifts its singular nose, which displays attractive vegetal and floral notes. On the palate it is pleasing, savoury and well-balanced. The Sorbara Vigna del Cristo, well made as always, has a handsome, brilliant ruby colour and an exemplary nose; on the palate, its lively acidity is nicely balanced by rounded, seductive fruit on the finish. This is the second year of production for the Grasparossa Col Sassoso, a wine whose quality has demonstrated Cavicchioli's wisdom in also investing in this denomination, which lies outside their normal sphere of operations. In fact, with this Col Sassoso, the estate finds itself right at the top of the quality tree for Grasparossa; the wine, with a characteristically light effervescence, has a fruity nose, and shows depth and softness on the palate, with just the right amount of tannin on the finish.

SCANDIANO (RE)

CASALI
VIA SCUOLE, 7
FRAZ. PRATISSOLO
42019 SCANDIANO (RE)
TEL. 0522/855441

Scandiano lies amidst the gentle foothills of the Reggian Appenines, where, according to age-old tradition, Lambrusco and Sauvignon have always been vinified in a fizzy style. This company, which is now 70 years old, has acquired a command of vinification techniques which allows them to offer a range of Charmat and Metodo Classico wines of appreciable quality. Topping the company's chart are the two wines made with a second fermentation in bottle. The Spumante Ca' Besina '92, disgorged in '96 and made from sauvignon, has a not particularly fine mousse, but it is persistent; its nose shows some maturity, with intense notes of vanilla and crusty bread. The carbon dioxide is fairly pronounced on the palate, but there is quite a lot of nice soft fruit on the finish. The Roggio del Pradello, a fully sparkling wine made from lambrusco grapes with an abundant, fine-beaded mousse, offers attractive ripe fruit aromas; the fruit on the palate is soft and well-structured. The Bosco del Fracasso, a blend, has an elegant and fruity bouquet, and is well balanced and appealing. The lambrusco-based Campo delle More is fruity and aromatic on the nose; it also displays long fruit flavours on the palate and hints of bitter cherries on the finish. The Borgo del Boiardo, a traditional white from the zone, is decently made: it makes a delicious and easy summer drink.

● Lambrusco di Modena '96	♀	2
● Lambrusco di Sorbara Vigna del Cristo '96	♀	2
● Lambrusco Grasparossa di Castelvetro Col Sassoso '96	♀	2

○ Acaia Malvasia dell'Emilia '96	♀	2
○ Spumante Metodo Classico Ca' Besina '92	♀	4
○ Colli di Scandiano e di Canossa Bianco Borgo del Boiardo '96	♀	1
● Lambrusco dell'Emilia Dolce Campo delle More	♀	1
● Lambrusco Roggio del Pradello	♀	3
● Lambrusco Reggiano Bosco del Fracasso '95	♀	2

TRAVO (PC)

VIGOLZONE (PC)

IL POGGIARELLO
FRAZ. SCRIVELLANO DI STATTO
29020 TRAVO (PC)
TEL. 0523/957241-571610

CONTE OTTO BARATTIERI
FRAZ. ALBAROLA
29020 VIGOLZONE (PC)
TEL. 0523/875111

Just a few years after its appearance on the market, Il Poggiarello has revealed itself to be an estate that is showing continuous growth and, as proof of the hard, serious work they have put in, Paolo and Stefano Perini offer a broadish range of ever more impressive wines. The whites are definitely continuing to improve; the '96 Ortrugo, fresh and well-balanced, displays harmonious aromas and similarly appealing fruit, which is well able to stand up to the oak, a bit dominant in the past. The Sauvignon Perticato II Quadri is even better; it has been aged for seven months in Nevers oak, where it also underwent a partial malolactic fermentation. Its nose is marked by the use of barriques; on the palate, the wine has a firm structure, and the grassy flavours of the sauvignon are well integrated with the oak. The Gutturino Riserva Vigna Valandrea '94 stands out among the reds, and is again one of the best examples of its type. It has an attractive sour cherry nose, with spicy notes too; in the mouth, it displays medium-weight and appealingly soft fruit. The Cabernet Sauvignon Perticato del Novarei '95, the most interesting of all their wines, has a really deep colour; its nose has vanilla and spice notes, with definite hints of green peppers; the palate is broad and ripe, but loses a few points because of a touch of herbaceousness - perhaps due to the youth of the vines, which limits its finesse a little. Missing from this edition of the Guide is the Pinot Nero '95 Perticato Le Giastre, which was not yet ready at the time of our tasting.

Count Barattieri's historic estate, situated in a vast park and surrounded by centuries-old trees, has, in recent years, tried to express to the full the great potential of its vineyards. In our tastings, the reds in particular have always shown well. Futhermore, this year, one wine has breached the Two Glass award wall; the '87 Vin Santo. This is a wine of very limited production, which has always been made according to tradition, but which has never been put on sale for reasons connected to the DOC regulations. Now the laws have finally changed and we are very happy to be able to tell you about it. It is made from semi-dried grapes and, after these have been pressed, it remains for nine years in barrel. Here, following an extremely long fermentation, it loses almost half of its volume. It has an amber colour, and a rich nose with hints of positive oxidation, candied fruits and tea leaves. These aromas are, remarkably, echoed on the palate, where the unctuous sweet fruit makes it very slightly cloying. Its long finish is excellent. Among the other wines, the Vignazza Alta '95 is good; this is an oak-aged Barbera from a vineyard planted in 1940. It has a rich, deep colour, with hints of strawberries and cherries on the nose; it is soft on the palate, its acidity being well balanced by the depth and mellowness of its fruit. The 1995 Barattieri Rosso '95, a Cabernet Sauvignon matured in wood, has a nice clean nose with hints of ripe red berry fruits, and is fleshy, savoury, but rather rustic on the palate. Il Poggio, made from semi-dried brachetto grapes, has an evolved nose with suggestions of cherry jam; on the palate, it is sweet and luscious, but with good underlying acidity.

● Colli Piacentini Cabernet Sauvignon Perticato del Novarei '95	♥♥	4
● Colli Piacentini Gutturnio Ris. Vigna Valandrea '94	♥	2*
○ Colli Piacentini Ortrugo Perticato del Gallo '96	♥	2*
○ Colli Piacentini Sauvignon Perticato II Quadri '96	♥	3
● Colli Piacentini Pinot Nero Perticato Le Giastre '94	♀	4

○ Colli Piacentini Vin Santo '87	♥♥	5
● Colli Piacentini Barbera Vignazza Alta '95	♥	3
● Colli Piacentini Cabernet Sauvignon Barattieri Rosso '95	♥	4
● Il Faggio	♥	4
● Colli Piacentini Gutturnio Frizzante '96		2
● Rosso Loghetto '96		2
● Colli Piacentini Cabernet Sauvignon Rosso Barattieri '93	♀	4
● Colli Piacentini Pinot Nero Vigneto Vignazzo '94	♀	4

VIGOLZONE (PC)

LA TOSA
LOC. LA TOSA
29020 VIGOLZONE (PC)
TEL. 0523/870727

ZIANO PIACENTINO (PC)

GAETANO LUSENTI E FIGLIA
CASE PICCIONI DI VICOBARONE
29010 ZIANO PIACENTINO (PC)
TEL. 0523/868479

La Tosa is an estate which has always conceived its development in terms of absolute quality. In this way it achieved its position of leadership in the Colli Piacentini, and is the reason why, even in not particularly good years, the Pizzamiglio brothers and their winemaker, Piero Ballario, continue to bring out a range of very good wines indeed. Let us begin with the La Tosa Bianco Frizzante '96, a blend of malvasia, trebbiano and ortrugo: this wine, with its fresh aromas of lemons and green apples, has a savoury, lively flavour, attractively underpinned by the acidity and carbon dioxide. The Sorriso di Cielo is once again charming: it is made from malvasia di Candia with yields limited to 28 hectolitres per hectare, and it partially aged and fermented in barriques. The '95 vintage has citrusy aromas which mingle with minerally notes, and fleshy, broad fruit on the palate, with just a hint of bitterness on the finish; it is undoubtedly a wine of remarkable style and personality. The '96 Sauvignon, though tasted prior to release, nevertheless displays a fine deep straw colour and varietal aromas of sage and lemon. It is fleshy and rich on the palate. It can be described as an "up front" sort of wine, however, lacking a bit of backbone it falls short of the Two Glass award. Going on to the reds; the new Vignamorello is not yet ready, but the Gutturnio does not quite come up to the mark, blemished as it is by a sulphury nose which masks what is no doubt very good fruit. All together better is the Luna Selvatica '94, with its handsome Bordeaux colour; the nose is still a little closed, but on the palate it is soft, concentrated, with good breadth and freshness, and with flavours of jam and ripe fruit.

The estate is located at Vicobarone di Ziano, the hub of winegrowing in the Valtidone. Gaetano Lusenti has, step by step, along with his daughter Lodovica, sought to overturn the estate's traditional role, geared as it was to selling its wine in bulk and to explore new avenues which are more gratifying, but also more difficult. The wines we tasted this year, though maintaining a good level of quality, seemed more anonymous, and did not reveal the personality and the special care which, in spite of their simple style, usually makes them stand out. Of the still wines, the Villante was not available this year, but we did taste the well-constructed and clean Pinot Nero La Picciona '94, as well as the Gutturnio '95. This wine has a deep colour, with hints of sour black cherries on the nose, good breadth of fruit on the palate, and with the alcohol dominating very slightly on the finish. The white Alba sulle Vigne, made from chardonnay and given a very brief spell in wood, shows elegant soft fruit, but is a little lacking in depth. Let us go on to the semi-sparkling wines; the whites are a bit below par compared to last year, with an Ortrugo which is less structured and is hampered by a surfeit of carbon dioxide. The Pinot Grigio does show reasonable finesse; it is fresh and clean on the palate, but nothing more. The most successful wine is definitely the Gutturnio Frizzante, it boasts a fine, deep colour with purplish highlights, and floral/spicy aromas; it shows fragrant fruit on the palate, with marked tannins and an attractive bitterish aftertaste. We should also like to remind you about the always charming Filtrato Dolce di Malvasia which, in spite of its deep yellow colour, is appealingly fresh and aromatic.

● Colli Piacentini Cabernet Sauvignon Luna Selvatica '94	♟♟	4
○ Colli Piacentini Malvasia Sorriso di Cielo '95	♟♟	4
○ Bianco La Tosa Frizzante '96	♟	2*
○ Colli Piacentini Sauvignon '96	♟	3
○ Colli Piacentini Malvasia Sorriso di Cielo '94	♟♟	4
● Cabernet Sauvignon Luna Selvatica '91	♟♟	4
● Colli Piacentini Cabernet Sauvignon Luna Selvatica '93	♟♟	4
● Cabernet Sauvignon Luna Selvatica '92	♟	4

● Colli Piacentini Gutturnio Frizzante '96	♟	2
● Colli Piacentini Gutturnio Sup. '95	♟	2
● Pinot Nero La Picciona '94	♟	4
○ Colli Piacentini Chardonnay Alba sulle Vigne '96	♟	3
○ Colli Piacentini Pinot Grigio '96		3
○ Filtrato Dolce di Malvasia '96		2
● Il Villante '93	♟♟	4

ZOLA PREDOSA (BO)

MARIA LETIZIA GAGGIOLI
VIGNETO BAGAZZANA
VIA RAIBOLINI, 55
40069 ZOLA PREDOSA (BO)
TEL. 051/753489-755137

This estate is situated in the hills immediately to the southwest of Bologna, with its modern winery at the centre of the property, surrounded by an amphitheatre of vines. It offers an excellent example to be followed as far as the cleanness and balance of its wines are concerned. Thanks to the attention to detail shown here, the white wines produced by Carlo Gaggioli in tandem with his daughter Letizia are generally ready for drinking right away and, usually age-worthy as well. The same goes for the reds which, sometimes, on first tasting, seem "merely" simple and appealing, but which then improve noticeably with a suitable period of bottle-ageing. The wines we tried this year are from a difficult vintage; the Pinot Bianco Crilò, the best example of this varietal from the zone, displays crisp, floral aromas. It has sufficient fruit, and the acidity sets off its relatively fragrant finish nicely. The Pignoletto Superiore, with its fine nose of fruit and confectionery notes, reveals precise fruit but a not particularly long finish. The Chardonnay Lavinio, with elegant aromas, very pleasant in the mouth and with good varietal characteristics, does not, however, quite live up to the promise of the nose. On the nose, the Cabernet Sauvignon offers sweet, ripe fruit and a fair amount of alcohol; its rounded fruit and subdued tannins make it immediately appealing. Il Francia Brut, the winery's most recent release, is a good Charmat sparkling wine made from pignoletto and chardonnay grapes; the nose is fruity, while on the palate it is fresh with a clean and long finish. The Pignoletto Frizzante and the Merlot, both decently made and quaffable wines, complete the estate's assortment.

○	Colli Bolognesi Chardonnay Lavinio '96	🍷	3
○	Colli Bolognesi Pinot Bianco Crilò '96	🍷	3
○	Il Francia Brut	🍷	3
●	Colli Bolognesi Cabernet Sauvignon '96	🍷	3
●	Colli Bolognesi Merlot '96		3
○	Colli Bolognesi Pignoletto Frizzante '96		3
○	Colli Bolognesi Pignoletto Superiore '96		3

ZOLA PREDOSA (BO)

VIGNETO DELLE TERRE ROSSE
VIA PREDOSA, 83
40069 ZOLA PREDOSA (BO)
TEL. 051/755845

In our tastings, we have never been let down by the wines from Terre Rosse; indeed, it has proved to be one of Italy's most consistently reliable estates. The Vallania family, strongly convinced as they are that stainless steel and glass are the only materials suitable for the storage and ageing of their wines, have again obtained excellent results and a very healthy sprinkling of high scores. The stunning Riesling Malago Vendemmia Tardiva '94, tops the list as usual; it offers broad, ripe fruit aromas on the nose and a long minerally finish; on the palate, it is soft, suitably alcoholic, elegant and well balanced. The interesting Chardonnay Cuvée '94, still slightly closed on the nose, though with the potential to show its full colours in time, is already rounded and harmonious on the palate. The "standard" Chardonnay and Riesling are also good, with our nod going to the Malago '96 with its intriguing bouquet and very typical varietal flavours. Among the reds, we draw your attention to the Enrico Vallania Cuvée '92, with its intense aromas of red berry fruits and jam; on the palate it shows rich extracts, is well balanced and displays an overriding elegance. The Rosso '93, less powerful than its "elder brother", is nevertheless a wine of considerable structure; it yields a fine bouquet and soft, long lasting fruit flavours in the mouth. Last, but also worthy of mention, is a slightly unusual Pinot Grigio, with correct varietal aroma and medium weight.

●	Colli Bolognesi Il Rosso di Enrico Vallania '93	🍷🍷	4
●	Colli Bolognesi Il Rosso di Enrico Vallania Cuvée '92	🍷🍷	5
○	Colli Bolognesi Riesling Malagò Vendemmia Tardiva '94	🍷🍷	4
○	Giovanni Vallania Chardonnay Cuvée '94	🍷🍷	4
○	Malagò Riesling '96	🍷🍷	3
○	Colli Bolognesi Chardonnay Giovanni Vallania '96	🍷	3
○	Colli Bolognesi Zola Predosa Pinot Grigio '96		3
●	Il Rosso di Enrico Vallania Cuvée '87	🍸🍸🍸	5

OTHER WINERIES

The following producers obtained good scores in our tastings with one or more of their wines:

PROVINCE OF DI BOLOGNA

Erioli,
Bazzano, tel. 051/830103,
Colli Bolognesi Cabernet Sauvignon '94

Giuseppe Beghelli,
Castello di Serravalle, tel. 051/6704786,
Colli Bolognesi Barbera '95

Isola,
Monte San Pietro, tel. 051/6768428,
Colli Bolognesi Pignoletto Superiore '96

Ca' Selvatica,
Monteveglio,
tel. 051/832506,
Colli Bolognesi Barbera Vigna delle More '94

Luigi Ognibene,
Monteveglio, tel. 051/830265,
Colli Bolognesi Pignoletto Frizzante '96

PROVINCE OF FORLÌ

Fattoria Paradiso,
Bertinoro, tel. 0543/445044,
Barbarossa '93,
Sangiovese di Romagna Ris. Vigna delle Lepri '93

Casetto dei Mandorli,
Predappio, tel. 0543/922361,
Sangiovese di Romagna Vigna del Generale '94

PROVINCE OF MODENA

Roberto Balugani,
Castelvetro, tel. 059/791546,
Lambrusco Grasparossa di Castelvetro '96

Manicardi,
Castelvetro, tel. 059/799000,
Lambrusco Grasparossa Castelvetro Ca' Fiore '96

Chiarli 1860,
Modena, tel. 059/310545,
Lambrusco di Modena
Tenuta Generale Cialdini '96

Maletti,
Soliera, tel. 059/563876,
Lambrusco di Sorbara Selezione '96

PROVINCE OF PARMA

Cantina Dall'Asta,
Parma, tel. 0521/484086,
Colli di Parma Malvasia '96

Vigneti Calzetti,
Sala Baganza, tel. 0521/830117,
Colli di Parma Malvasia '96

Ceci,
Torrile, tel. 0521/810134,
Colli di Parma Malvasia Le Terre dei Farnesi '96

PROVINCE OF PIACENZA

Cantina Valtidone,
Borgonovo Val Tidone, tel. 0523/862168,
Colli Piacentini Gutturnio Frizzante '96

Giulio Cardinali,
Castell'Arquato, tel. 0523/803502,
Montepascolo Dolce '96

Tenuta La Torretta,
Nebbiano, tel. 0523/998145,
Colli Piacentini Ortrugo Frizzante '96

Pusterla,
Vigolo Marchese, tel. 0523/896105,
Colli Piacentini Gutturnio Ris. '94

Villa Peirano,
Vigolzone, tel. 0523/875146,
Colli Piacentini Gutturnio Frizzante '96

PROVINCE OF RAVENNA

Cooperativa Brisighellese,
Brisighella, tel. 0546/81103,
Sangiovese di Romagna Sup. Brisigliè '93

La Berta,
Brisighella, tel. 0546/84998,
Sangiovese di Romagna Sup. '96,
Olmatello '94

PROVINCE OF REGGIO EMILIA

Giuseppe e Riccarda Caprari,
Reggio Emilia, tel. 0522/550220,
Lambrusco dell'Emilia La Foieta '96

Venturini Baldini,
Quattro Castella, tel. 0522/887080,
La Papessa Bianco '96

TUSCANY

The leading Three-Glass region this year was Tuscany, which achieved an all-time record score of 29 top wines, more than any other region has ever won. And only the draconian severity of our panels stopped the final total from being higher still. All this is par for the course, bearing in mind what the world's most authoritative critics have had to say about the wines of Tuscany and the spectacular success of Brunello di Montalcino, Chianti Classico and the Supertuscans with winelovers everywhere. Add to this that our tasters were sampling superior vintages this year in many parts of Tuscany and you have the explanation for the Three Glass ratings. We tasted the '95 vintage for Chianti Classico and many other premium IGT reds, the Riserva '93 for Vino Nobile di Montepulciano and the '94 and '95 wines from the Bolgheri zone. All of these are good quality vintages, with peaks of world-class quality. Obviously, selection was arduous. About 80 wines made it to the final round and at least 15 failed to win Three Glasses by the merest of whiskers. The zone that produced the finest results in absolute terms was Chianti Classico. Perhaps surprisingly, the star performers were not the DOCG wines, which only gained three top scores, but the Supertuscans. Thirteen of these reds, many of which are based on different "cépages" to that stipulated for Chianti Classico, won the coveted Three Glasses. Some, like Antinori's Solaia '94, the Cabreo Il Borgo '95 from Tenimenti Ruffino and the Felsina Fontalloro '93, confirmed an already exalted status. Others - the Brolio Casalferro '95, Vicchiomaggio's Ripa delle More '94 and the Rosso di Sera '95 from the Fattoria Poggiopiano - were newcomers to the top

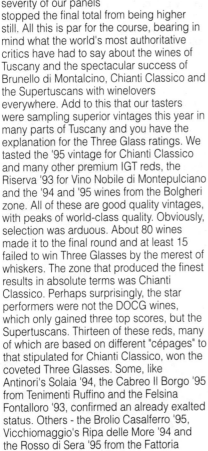

flight. Brunello di Montalcino, where the cellars are now releasing the wines of '92, did not have one of its best years. Indeed the vintage was so unexciting that many producers bottled nothing under their flag-bearer labels, which explains why estates such as Altesino and Pieve di Santa Restituta are missing from the Guide this year. In contrast alternative wines like Argiano's Solengo '95, the Frescobaldi/Mondavi Luce '94 and Excelsus from Castello Banfi, were generally good and for the first time a Rosso di Montalcino gained a Three Glass rating, an excellent result for Agostina Pieri's '95. Vino Nobile di Montepulciano had a good, albeit not exceptional, year. We were hoping for better things from the Riserva '93. Just one Three Glass award - to Il Macchione - is a disappointing result for a DOCG that has been improving steadily. There were great things from Bolgheri, however, where the Lupicaia and Giusto di Notri '95 and Masseto '94 took our breath away. Exciting wines also emerged from several apparently "minor" production zones which are coming on in leaps and bounds. Some of the rising stars we could mention in this context are Montellori, Fattoria di Manzano - which walked off with a Three Glass award for its superlative Syrah varietal, Podere Il Bosco '95 - and Tenuta di Ghizzano. Finally a special mention must go to the Maremma area in the province of Grosseto, the new frontier of premium-quality Tuscan wines. The Meleta and Le Pupille estates came very close to the highest accolade with excellent reds , and prospects look good for next year's tastings of the '96 vintage which are shaping up even better than their '94 and '95 counterparts.

BARBERINO VAL D'ELSA (FI)   BARBERINO VAL D'ELSA (FI)

CASA EMMA
FRAZ. CORTINE
LOC. SAN DONATO IN POGGIO
50021 BARBERINO VAL D'ELSA (FI)
TEL. 055/8072859

CASTELLO DELLA PANERETTA
STRADA DELLA PANERETTA, 37
50021 BARBERINO VAL D'ELSA (FI)
TEL. 055/8059003

Casa Emma has done it again. After the splendid Chianti Classico Riserva '93, this small Chianti estate has won another Three Glass award but for a different wine. This time the winner is a Supertuscan, one of the premium-quality "indicazione geografica" wines that do not comply with DOC regulations. The name on the label is Soloìo and it is a merlot cépage from '94. This splendid wine has heady, intense aromas of tobacco and violets over an enticing vanilla background. The palate follows through with equal conviction, its velvety tannins sustained by lots of body. All in all, a minor masterpiece. But the Casa Emma range this year, although limited, has more than one flag-bearer, for the Chianti Classico Riserva '94 is also worth investigating. It does not have the weight and concentration of the '93 but it is an attractive, soft wine whose fruit is well developed and while it may not be a wine to lay down, despite its excellent structure it is drinking beautifully now. Our tastings concluded with the Chianti Classico '95, a good product even though the tannins are a little rough and the nose rather closed. Only a slight misdemeanour, as it were, but we were hoping for a better wine. It was encouraging to see that Casa Emma is not just a one-hit wonder. The enthusiasm of the owner, Fiorella Bucalossi, and the expertise of winemaker Nicolò d'Afflitto evidently make a winning combination.

Every so often, we fall hopelessly in love with a wine from this lovely estate at Barberino Val d'Elsa. Not such a very hard thing to do since the picturesque vineyards, in some of the finest locations in the entire Chianti Classico DOC zone, from time to time produce genuine works of oenological art. And given that the consultant winemaker is the legendary Attilio Pagli, these love affairs can be particularly traumatic. This year, the exquisite Chianti Classico '95 stole our heart away. Soft yet weighty, it is a wine that keeps you coming back for more. It may not have the complexity of a great red for the cellar and there may be one or two faint, muzzy, vegetal notes on the nose if you really want to look for faults, but for sheer drinkability it is unbeatable. This is a bottle that gets drunk straight away once it is uncorked. In contrast the Chianti Classico Riserva '94 is less appealing. Already a little forward, it has a touch of phenolic bitterness in the finish. But the '94 vintage is notorious for the premature ageing, so it could be said that the wine is doing no more than running to type. Much the same thing could be said about the Terrine '94, obtained from sangiovese and canaiolo grapes, which we found to be even more over-evolved than the Chianti Classico Riserva.

● Soloìo '94	▼▼▼	5
● Chianti Classico Ris. '94	▼▼	4
● Chianti Classico '95	▼	3
● Chianti Classico Ris. '93	▽▽▽	4
● Chianti Classico '90	▽▽	3*
● Chianti Classico '93	▽▽	3
● Chianti Classico Ris. '90	▽▽	4
● Chianti Classico '91	▽	3*
● Chianti Classico '92	▽	3*
● Chianti Classico '94	▽	3

● Chianti Classico '95	▼▼	4
● Chianti Classico Ris. '94	▼	4
● Le Terrine '94		4
● Chianti Classico Ris. '90	▽▽	4*
● Chianti Classico Ris. '93	▽▽	4
● Chianti Classico '93	▽	3
● Chianti Classico '94	▽	3
● Le Terrine '90	▽	4
● Le Terrine '93	▽	5

BARBERINO VAL D'ELSA (FI)

BARBERINO VAL D'ELSA (FI)

ISOLE E OLENA
LOC. ISOLE, 1
50021 BARBERINO VAL D'ELSA (FI)
TEL. 055/8072763

LE FILIGARE
LOC. SAN DONATO IN POGGIO
VIA SICELLE
50020 BARBERINO VAL D'ELSA (FI)
TEL. 055/8072796

It would be nice if there were more people like Paolo De Marchi involved in winemaking in Italy. He's a true professional, knows more about viticulture than many university lecturers and makes his wine in a far from easy zone with outstanding results. He's also a quiet type who does not try to lay down the law but prefers to let his wines speak for themselves. Our panels have always liked De Marchi's products and have often awarded them Three Glasses. But for the last two years, we have been unable to give them top marks, largely because the vineyards at Isole and Olena are well up on the hill slopes and thus particularly exposed to the vagaries of the weather. It's a sad state of affairs for Paolo really ought to get Three Glasses simply for his approach to winemaking. The products we sampled this year were the Cepparello '94, the Cabernet Sauvignon '94 and the Chardonnay '95, the last two sold under the Collezione De Marchi label. The Cepparello, a monovarietal Sangiovese, is one of the most famous "Supertuscans" of them all. The aromas are slightly more open than they were in the '93 version and the palate is deliciously soft. Indeed the '94 is much more approachable than other vintages of this great red wine, which is generally more closed and intractable for a good few years. The Cabernet Sauvignon '94 is also interesting. Less concentrated than usual, it is nonetheless well balanced and very attractive. But the real stunner was the superbly made Chardonnay '95, perhaps the best white we have tasted in Tuscany this year. Delicately vanillaed on the nose with a firm, full flavour, it is not enormously complex but the more wines like this there are in our cellar, the better.

A few years ago Carlo Burchi, a Florentine gold and silversmith, purchased this lovely estate lying right on the route of the Via Francigena, Tuscany's main thoroughfare in the Middle Ages, between Barberino Val d'Elsa and Castellina in Chianti. Burchi completely restructured the villa and then turned his attention to the vineyards. But after a while, the difficulties and obstacles that face any newcomer to agriculture dampened his initial enthusiasm and he put the property up for sale. It was Giacomo Tachis, a famous oenologist whom Carlo met by chance, who persuaded him to change his mind and suggested he take on as consultant winemaker the youthful Vittorio Fiore. With Fiore's help, Burchi's estate got into gear and today it is one of the viticultural élite in the Chianti DOC zone. Le Filigare offered two wines for tasting this year, the Podere Le Rocce '94, obtained from sangiovese (65 percent) and cabernet sauvignon (35 percent) grapes, and the Chianti Classico Riserva, again from the '94 vintage. The Podere Le Rocce, as usual, is a magnificent wine, even though the less than satisfactory '94 vintage has left its mark. There are faintly vegetal aromas on the nose, where an unexpected note of asparagus emerges, while the palate is clean as a whistle but without the complexity we have enjoyed in the past. The Chianti Classico Riserva '94 is a stylish, attractive wine, beautifully made if perhaps a little mature on the nose.

● Cabernet Sauvignon '94	⧠⧠	5
● Cepparello '94	⧠⧠	5
○ Chardonnay '95	⧠⧠	5
● Cabernet Sauvignon '88	⧠⧠⧠	5
● Cabernet Sauvignon '90	⧠⧠⧠	6
● Cepparello '86	⧠⧠⧠	6
● Cepparello '88	⧠⧠⧠	6
● Cabernet Sauvignon '91	⧠⧠	5
● Cabernet Sauvignon '93	⧠⧠	5
● Cepparello '90	⧠⧠	5
● Cepparello '91	⧠⧠	5
● Cepparello '93	⧠⧠	5
● Chianti Classico '94	⧠⧠	4
○ Vin Santo '91	⧠⧠	5
○ Chardonnay '94	⧠	4

● Podere Le Rocce '94	⧠⧠	5
● Chianti Classico Ris. '94	⧠	4
● Podere Le Rocce '88	⧠⧠⧠	5
● Chianti Classico '88	⧠⧠	4
● Chianti Classico Ris. '85	⧠⧠	5
● Chianti Classico Ris. '87	⧠⧠	5
● Chianti Classico Ris. '88	⧠⧠	5
● Chianti Classico Ris. '90	⧠⧠	5
● Chianti Classico Ris. '91	⧠⧠	5
● Chianti Classico Ris. '93	⧠⧠	5
● Podere Le Rocce '87	⧠⧠	5
● Podere Le Rocce '90	⧠⧠	5
● Podere Le Rocce '91	⧠⧠	5
● Podere Le Rocce '93	⧠⧠	5

BARBERINO VAL D'ELSA (FI)   BARBERINO VAL D'ELSA (FI)

MONSANTO
VIA MONSANTO,8
50021 BARBERINO VAL D'ELSA (FI)
TEL. 055/8059000

MAJNONI GUICCIARDINI
VIA 2 GIUGNO, 8
FRAZ. VICO D'ELSA
50050 BARBERINO VAL D'ELSA (FI)
TEL. 055/8073002

The renaissance of modern Chianti began in the early 1970s when entrepreneurs and professionals from all over Italy and Europe started moving into the area. Properties changed hands. Estates were put to rights, vineyards were replanted and the largely neglected countryside came back to life again. But Fabrizio Bianchi, from Gallarate in Lombardy, was already established and had been making wine in Chianti for ten years before the boom, so to say that he anticipated developments is no more than the unadorned truth. It is also significant that the Chianti Classico DOC regulations have been changed to allow it to be made with 100 percent sangiovese fruit. Bianchi had been fighting for a decade to achieve just this. These are all things for which the sometimes cantankerous Fabrizio deserves credit, for his foresight and sound business acumen are undeniable. Today he continues to run the estate with the assistance of his daughter Laura, who manages to smooth her father's remaining rough edges with her patience and unfailing courtesy. This year, Monsanto presented wines from only moderately interesting vintages but the products themselves were still very successful. The Fabrizio Bianchi Rosso '93, obtained from sangiovese grapes, has nice fruit-rich aromas and a clean palate but lacks real complexity. Concentration is also the weak point of the Chianti Classico Il Poggio Riserva '93, a "minor" version of the cellar's flag-bearer. Finally the cabernet sauvignon-based Nemo '94 has good structure but again is a little too straightforward and uncomplicated. We were hoping for a rather more interesting wine.

The Colli Fiorentini is a zone that has inevitably developed an inferiority complex as a result of its contiguity to the prestigious Chianti Classico DOC and in adapting itself to a subordinate role has tended to fall into the trap of believing that it is unable to produce wines for ageing, as opposed to more immediately gulpable styles. If we were to make a - highly improbable - comparison with Bordeaux, we might say that the Colli Fiorentini area is the Entre-deux-Mers of the situation. Any producers who attempt to correct this tendency are therefore to be encouraged, something the Guide is only too happy to do by offering a showcase and a stimulus to promising winemakers in zones that are generally, and unfairly, thought to be "second-rank". It will be clear by now that Majnoni Guicciardini, a young grower-producer who presented us with an interesting range, albeit one that still has a long way to go, runs one of the estates that the Guide has taken under its wing. His Chianti Riserva came close to being awarded Two Glasses for its distinct notes of spices, vegetal aromas and fruit on the nose. The palate is consistent, soft and nicely balanced although the finish was closed with the slightly dry tannins we have noted on other occasions in wines from the '94 vintage. The Chardonnay Le Cantine is an attractively fresh-tasting wine with great balance on the palate and Guicciardini's base Chardonnay is also very well made, if not as convincing as the premium version.

● Chianti Classico		
Il Poggio Ris. '93	��	5
● Fabrizio Bianchi '93	♛♛	5
● Nemo '94	♛♛	5
● Chianti Classico		
Il Poggio Ris. '88	♛♛♛	5
● Chianti Classico		
Il Poggio Ris. '86	♛♛	5
● Chianti Classico		
Il Poggio Ris. '90	♛♛	5
● Nemo '85	♛♛	5
● Nemo '88	♛♛	5
● Nemo '90	♛♛	5
● Nemo '93	♛♛	5
● Tinscvil '88	♛♛	5

○ Chardonnay Le Cantine '96	♛	3
● Chianti Ris. '94	♛	3
○ Chardonnay '96		2

BOLGHERI (LI)

TENUTA BELVEDERE
LOC. BELVEDERE 140
57020 BOLGHERI (LI)
TEL. 0565/749735

BOLGHERI (LI)

LE MACCHIOLE
VIA BOLGHERESE
57020 BOLGHERI (LI)
TEL. 0565/763240

The first bottles of Vermentino from the vineyard planted a few years ago at Tenuta Belvedere are ready for drinking. In the next few years there will be many more available, given the considerable area planted in compliance with the Antinori marketing strategy. And planting vermentino instead of cabernet or merlot, both of which have enjoyed great success at Bolgheri, will have raised a few eyebrows. But even allowing for market-driven planting policies, it would be ridiculous to expect every square centimetre of cultivable soil at Bolgheri to produce big-hitting red wines. Tenuta Belvedere in any case already turns out a great red, Guado al Tasso, whose '94 vintage is well up to standard and absolutely typical of the wine's style. The fragrant aromas of Morello and black cherries over a rich, velvety body are the Guado al Tasso's distinguishing features. The '94 is also slightly unbalanced by fairly assertive vegetal flavours that have not quite been assimilated into the fruit and toasty oak. On the palate, however, there is no mistaking that soft, silky, seamless flavour. In many ways, this vintage comes closest to the legendary '90. There is a new look for that trusty old-timer, Scalabrone, reflecting a change of style. The '96 comes across as a very direct wine with lots of raspberry and strawberry fruit and a sweetish palate that is perhaps aimed at a younger market. The Vermentino is uncomplicated and crisp, its refreshing nose unveiling aromas of white and tropical fruit. Finally the Belvedere Rosso rounds up the Tenuta Belvedere's range of very approachable wines. A fruity, vegetal nose rich in alcohol leads into a lively, head-turning palate that has a faint hint of bitterness in the finish.

All in all, it is not hard to come to the conclusion that '94 was not the best of vintages in the Bolgheri area. The only producer who managed to maintain the standards of the previous years was probably Eugenio Campolmi, thanks to the love and attention he lavishes on his vines and cellar. This year he has even managed to come up with two excellent new wines. One is a Merlot, which he has called Messorio, and the other is a Syrah; both are monovarietal. The Merlot in particular exalts all the finest qualities of the variety with its remarkably luscious, opulent flavour. Unfortunately both of these wines are experimental and the quantities made are insufficient for us to be able to include them in the Guide. So while waiting for production to reach commercial levels, we sampled the Paleo '94, which once again confirmed its status as a top-flight red wine. Its fragrances are still a little closed but vegetal notes come through together with an earthy note of tobacco and pencil lead over a background of black berries. In the mouth, it is rich, sweet and mouth-filling. The Paleo Bianco is interesting, too. It is a masculine, vigorous wine where the smoky, piquant notes of the wood are still to the fore. The very reliable Le Contessine range showed well in our tastings. The Bianco is an agreeable wine, offering aromas of ripe yellow fruit and a balanced flavour while the Rosso is a stylish, easy-to-drink bottle with fruit and vegetal notes on the nose.

● Guado al Tasso '94	♟♟	6
○ Bolgheri Bianco Belvedere '96	♟	2
☉ Bolgheri Rosato Scalabrone '96	♟	3
● Bolgheri Rosso Belvedere '96	♟	2
● Guado al Tasso '90	♟♟♟	6
● Guado al Tasso '92	♟♟	4
● Guado al Tasso '93	♟♟	6
● Bolgheri Rosso Belvedere '95	♟	2
● Fattoria Belvedere '93	♟	1

○ Bolgheri Sauvignon Paleo '95	♟♟	4
● Bolgheri Sup. Paleo Rosso '94	♟♟	5
● Bolgheri Rosso Le Contessine '96	♟	3
○ Bolgheri Vermentino Le Contessine '96	♟	3
○ Paleo Bianco '93	♟♟	3
○ Paleo Bianco '94	♟♟	3*
● Paleo Rosso '91	♟♟	5
● Paleo Rosso '92	♟♟	2
● Paleo Rosso '93	♟♟	5
● Bolgheri Rosso Le Contessine '94	♟	2
● Bolgheri Rosso Le Contessine '95	♟	2*

BOLGHERI (LI)

Tenuta dell'Ornellaia
Via Bolgherese, 191
57020 Bolgheri (LI)
tel. 0565/762140-762141

As usual, the Tenuta dell'Ornellaia came up with a fine range of wines and we will start the list from the top. The Masseto has repeated last year's success and again wins a Three Glass award. In fact, this Merlot from Marchese Lodovico Antinori's estate has become one of the most sought-after wines in the entire Bolgheri subzone, not just because of its outstanding quality but also because despite an annual production of over 20,000 bottles it can still be hard to find on the domestic market. The wine's ruby hue glows warmly in the glass and is followed up by a complex, concentrated nose with notes of black berries, vanilla and a faint vegetal nuance. The attack on the palate is sweet and well rounded, unfolding in firm, orderly elegance enhanced by firm tannins and a deliciously lingering finish. The Ornellaia is also very good indeed. Its solid, fleshy structure is accompanied by complex aromas from which emerge ripe bramble, fruit preserves and a hint of capsicum. There were high marks, too, for the Poggio alle Gazze, which has more physical presence than its predecessors. The typical Sauvignon fragrances are spelled out rather than hinted at but the wealth of substance and flavour on the palate is thoroughly convincing. And to round off our visit, we tasted the Tenuta dell'Ornellaia second label, Le Volte, which is a well made, if somewhat predictable, red that can be enjoyed every day of the week.

BOLGHERI (LI)

Tenuta San Guido
Loc. Capanne, 27
57020 Bolgheri (LI)
tel. 0565/762003

Every year, the moment when we taste a wine like Sassicaia is of crucial importance in the compilation of this Guide both because the notes will inevitably become a benchmark against which other wines will be measured and because it provides significant clues as to how the vintage as a whole has gone. The weather in 1994 was relatively warm in Tuscany so the fruit ripened early but not always consistently. More specifically, on the basis of our tastings it that seems that in some cases the photosynthesis of sugars was out of step with the production of phenols. The wines obtained in 1994 tend to be soft-flavoured and very approachable but lack the stability ensured by sound tannins, and therefore show a tendency to evolve quickly. This trait is particularly notable in wines from warmer areas. The Sassicaia '94 reflects this general situation while at the same time making its own very personal statement. This is the first vintage to bear the name of the new Bolgheri Sassicaia DOC zone on the label. It is unlikely to make oenological history but it is a reassuring confirmation of the Tenuta San Guido "house style" and as such a lovely, supremely drinkable, wine. The attractively intense ruby colour introduces aromas that alternate fresh vegetal-through-to-cassis notes with more mature fragrances of tobacco and nuts. The entry on the palate is low-key but the flavour develops elegantly with textbook rigour: a hugely stylish wine conceived and executed with rare authority.

●	Masseto '94	♟♟♟	6
●	Ornellaia '94	♟♟	6
○	Poggio delle Gazze '96	♟♟	4
●	Le Volte '95	♟	3
●	Masseto '93	♟♟♟	6
●	Ornellaia '93	♟♟♟	6
●	Masseto '89	♟♟	6
●	Masseto '92	♟♟	6
●	Ornellaia '86	♟♟	6
●	Ornellaia '87	♟♟	6
●	Ornellaia '88	♟♟	6
●	Ornellaia '90	♟♟	6
●	Ornellaia '91	♟♟	6
●	Ornellaia '92	♟♟	6
○	Poggio delle Gazze '94	♟♟	6

●	Sassicaia '94	♟♟	6
●	Sassicaia '83	♟♟♟	6
●	Sassicaia '84	♟♟♟	6
●	Sassicaia '85	♟♟♟	6
●	Sassicaia '88	♟♟♟	6
●	Sassicaia '90	♟♟♟	6
●	Sassicaia '92	♟♟♟	6
●	Sassicaia '93	♟♟♟	6
●	Sassicaia '86	♟♟	6
●	Sassicaia '87	♟♟	6
●	Sassicaia '89	♟♟	6
●	Sassicaia '91	♟♟	6

BUCINE (AR)

BUCINE (AR)

FATTORIA DI AMBRA
LOC. AMBRA
52020 BUCINE (AR)
TEL. 055/996806

FATTORIA VILLA LA SELVA
MONTEBENICHI
52021 BUCINE (AR)
TEL. 055/998203-998200

Developments at Fattoria di Ambra continue apace, both in the vineyards and in the property's winemaking facilities. Several hectares have been replanted and there are going to be significant changes in the cellars in the next few months. But for now the owner, Vincenzo Zampi, a professor at the university of Florence, has only put forward two wines, his Chianti and his red table wine, for inclusion in this year's Guide. The other products are "not yet ready", in his opinion. And so we will have to wait until next year to try the Casamurli, the Vin Santo and the Percivalle, a new dessert wine from partially dried trebbiano and malvasia grapes. The Chianti Riserva La Bigattiera '95 has not undergone any substantial change of style with respect to the '93 version. The colour is intense and the complex citron fragrances are well developed. The palate is balanced but not fat, with a solid yet soft presence in the mouth. Given its relative youth, it is a distinctly mature wine but very drinkable nonetheless. In contrast, the '94 version of the Gavignano is obtained from a slightly different blend of grapes; this vintage has equal proportions of sangiovese and cabernet as opposed to the 65-35 mix of previous years. The resulting bright ruby wine is fresh-tasting and has medium body and a delicate, relatively unforthcoming nose leading into a lean, clean palate with loads of red fruit. It may not be a heavyweight (thank goodness!) but it is deliciously quaffable.

The quality of wines from Villa La Selva keeps improving with each passing year. Vittorio Fiore, the consultant winemaker, is a big name abroad as well as in Italy and he has high oenological ambitions for the estate. The owner, Sergio Carpini, backs him up to the hilt and the wines are first-rate, give or take the odd wobble due probably to the practical problems that any expanding grower-producer will experience. Yet again the Anna dei Fiori monovarietal oak-fermented Chardonnay white is not quite right. The yellow hue of the '95 looks tired, the nose is full but over-mature and the palate lacks pep. But this one false step aside, the rest of the range is very good indeed, starting with the Chianti Villa La Selva Riserva. The '93 version is sweet, soft and mature with delicious toasty oak. But the balance and complexity of even this excellent wine is surpassed by the two La Selva table wines, the Felciaia and the Selvamaggio. The Felciaia is a monovarietal Sangiovese fermented and matured in small oak barrels. The '94 vintage is deep ruby with a clean, intense, balmy nose and a sustained, well balanced palate that reveals silky tannins. The Selvamaggio, blended from 70 percent cabernet sauvignon and 30 percent sangiovese grapes, is equally impressive. The '93 has the characteristically vegetal aromas that signal the presence of cabernet fruit but without any excessively grassy notes. Satisfying on the palate, it has good extract and a long finish, where faint green nuances again come through. This pair of champions takes the field flanked by other fine supporting wines, such as the Vin Santo or the intensely sensual Fior di Luna, a dessert white from partially dried fruit that matures in small oak barrels for three full years.

● Chianti		
Vigna La Bigattiera Ris. '95	♀	3
● Gavignano '94	♀	3
○ Chardonnay '92		3
● Gavignano '93	♀♀	3
○ Chardonnay '93	♀	3
○ Chardonnay '94	♀	3

● Chianti Villa La Selva Ris. '93	♀♀	5
● Felciaia '94	♀♀	5
● Selvamaggio '93	♀♀	5
○ Vinsanto '93	♀	5
○ Anna dei Fiori '95		4
● Felciaia '93	♀♀	4
○ Fior di Luna Ris. '90	♀♀	6
● Selvamaggio '91	♀♀	5
● Selvamaggio '92	♀♀	5
● Selvamaggio Ris. '90	♀♀	6

CAPANNORI (LU)

TENUTA DI VALGIANO
FRAZ. VALGIANO
55010 CAPANNORI (LU)
TEL. 0583/402271

The wine bug has bitten the "Valgiano kids",
Laura and Moreno, hard and there is no
going back. They have just finished planting
one new vineyard, they are planning
another, and their vine stock already
includes sangiovese, syrah, merlot red
varieties as well as chardonnay and
traditional trebbiano whites. Saverio Petrilli is
making rapid progress in the cellar, where
he combines a desire to try out new
technology with the production of a solid,
dependable range. He is using lower
temperatures and shorter maceration to
enhance the fragrance of the Sangiovese
Rosso dei Palistorti and precisely the
opposite strategy to stabilize the phenols of
the Merlot Scasso dei Cesari, a skilfully
made Two Glass wine. It may lack depth but
its balance and elegance are eloquent
testimony to Saverio's expertise. The nose
alternates fruit, flowers and vegetal notes
with perfectly judged oak, while the palate
has good structure and concentration, with
bright, mellow tannins. The Rosso dei
Palistorti is an unexpectedly delicious drink,
obtained from a successful blend of
sangiovese and syrah in which the individual
varietal characters still manage to come
through. It is a fresh-tasting wine with a nose
of cherry, violets, vanilla and pepper which
follows through well on the attractive palate.
Crystal-clear flavours are the hallmark of the
moreish Giallo dei Muri, a trebbiano-based
white with a proportion of oak-fermented
chardonnay fruit. And for "dessert", there is
the Passito sulle Canne, a sublime
concentration of creamy sweetness.

CARMIGNANO (PO)

FATTORIA AMBRA
VIA LOMBARDA, 85
50042 CARMIGNANO (PO)
TEL. 055/486488-8719049

The Fattoria Ambra is one of the most firmly
established concerns in the Carmignano
area. Run by Beppe Rigoli, a man with his
sights set on quality, it can count on flexible
and effective winemaking. The blended reds
are vinified separately by variety
(sangiovese and canaiolo together, cabernet
sauvignon, merlot and syrah on their own)
and on the basis of vineyard selection
(Montalbiolo, Elzana and Santa Cristina a
Pilli). Sangiovese/canaiolo-based "Riserva"
wines are matured in oak casks that vary in
capacity from 3.5 to 7 hectolitres, producing
wines which have good structure and at the
same time are very approachable. The '96
vintage Barco Reale claimed a One Glass
rating for its youth, freshness and fruit as
well as its uncomplicated, enticing notes of
cherry. The Carmignano wines are
altogether more serious, beginning with the
Riserva Santa Cristina a Pilli '94. Deep and
rich in colour, it unveils clean fragrances of
Peruvian bark and pencil lead then a full
bodied, generous flavour complemented by
earthy tannins. Even better was the
Carmignano Riserva Le Vigne Alte, whose
'94 vintage won Two Glasses for its
wonderfully structured flavour. A very deep
red leads into a distinctly varietal cabernet
nose that has plenty of personality and nice
toasty notes of discreet oak. The palate has
good tannins and concentration, and the
overall impression it leaves is one of
balance. Finally, the '95 version of the new
Elzana cru promises to be at least as good.

● Scasso dei Cesari '95		♥♥	4
○ Colline Lucchesi Bianco			
Giallo dei Muri '96		♥	2
● Rosso delle Colline Lucchesi			
Rosso dei Palistorti '95		♥	2*
○ Colline Lucchesi Bianco			
Giallo dei Muri '95		♀	2*
● Scasso dei Cesari '94		♀	3*

● Carmignano			
Le Vigne Alte Ris. '94		♥♥	4
● Barco Reale '96		♥	3
● Carmignano			
Vigna S. Cristina a Pilli '94		♥	4
● Carmignano			
Le Vigne Alte Ris. '90		♀♀	4
● Carmignano			
Le Vigne Alte Ris. '93		♀	4
● Carmignano			
Vigna S. Cristina a Pilli '93		♀	3

CARMIGNANO (PO)

CARMIGNANO (PO)

FATTORIA DI ARTIMINO
LOC. ARTIMINO
50042 CARMIGNANO (PO)
TEL. 055/8792051

TENUTA CANTAGALLO
LOC. COMEANA
50040 CARMIGNANO (PO)
TEL. 0574/574323

The Fattoria di Artimino is one of the loveliest and most important winemaking estates in the whole of Tuscany. At the heart of this extensive property with its 80 hectares of vineyard, stands the magnificent Villa Medicea which enjoys a panoramic view over the countryside of Carmignano. Up-to-date equipment, installed in the last few years, immediately catches the eye in the cellar and although this combination of history and technology has produced uneven results in the recent past, the underlying standard has always been high. The lack of continuity is exemplified in the two flag-bearing wines, the Barco Reale and the Carmignano Riserva Medicea. The Barco Reale has fairly closed, super-ripe aromas and a very mature flavour that only just managed to gain a One Glass rating from an unconvinced tasting panel. But the Carmignano Riserva Medicea is the real kingpin in the Artimino set-up: the '93 vintage is a vastly superior wine to the Barco Reale, quite apart from the differences in their styles. Its ruby red is bright and lustrous while the nose is austere, clean and redolent of Peruvian bark and pencil lead. On the palate, there are loads of gutsy tannins in a structure of remarkable elegance. All in all, an outstanding wine with a lingering finish whose mature aromas are still accompanied by evident tannins.

The Tenuta Cantagallo is the most important of the three winemaking properties run by Enrico Pierazzuoli, a young, dynamic grower who is included in the Guide for the first time this year. His other estates are Le Farnete at Carmignano and the smaller Fattoria Matroneo at Greve in Chianti. The group sales offices and many of the winemaking facilities are at Tenuta Cantagallo in the Montalbano hills, an area whose image with consumers is a long way below its potential for producing premium wines. For example the Le Farnete Riserva '92 is a distinctly interesting product whose garnet hue discloses a certain maturity. The first surprises are in the aromas, which are satisfyingly intense, and the palate is even more convincing. Full, rich flavour is combined with a stylish "come-and-get-it" approachability and attractive balance. The Riserva '93 is not quite as good, but still rates highly. It is a similar wine with a more marked note of wood and perhaps a shade less style. The fleshy, well balanced Chianti Riserva is also very good and we were very pleasantly surprised by the Carleto, a monovarietal riesling-based wine vinified in stainless steel and new small barrels in equal proportions. Intense, and endowed with great depth and balance, it displays a superbly focused range of aromas on the nose. The Vin Santo was another very nice wine, revealing spicy and toasty notes on the nose together with nuts, while the vigorous palate had excellent length. And to round off the range, there are two unassuming but absolutely respectable cheaper wines, the Gioveto and the Chianti Montalbano.

●	Carmignano Ris. Medicea '93	ҬҬ	4
●	Barco Reale '95	Ҭ	2

○	Carleto '96	ҬҬ	4
●	Carmignano Ris. '92	ҬҬ	4
●	Carmignano Ris. '93	ҬҬ	4
●	Chianti Ris. '93	ҬҬ	3
○	Vin Santo Millarium '92	Ҭ	4
●	Chianti Montalbano '95		2
●	Gioveto '95		2

CARMIGNANO (PO)

CAPEZZANA
VIA CAPEZZANA, 100
LOC. SEANO
50042 CARMIGNANO (PO)
TEL. 055/8706005-8706091

There may well have been a disagreement over company strategy behind the decision by Filippo and Vittorio, the two sons of founder Ugo Contini Bonacossi, to split up the estate's vineyards. Vittorio now makes one of Capezzana's historic crus, the highly rated Villa di Trefiano, independent of the rest of the family-owned estate which maintains its decades-long tradition as one of the benchmark producers of the Carmignano zone. The more readily available wines aimed at the lower end of the market are decently made, but lack punch even in comparison with other similarly priced products. The '96 vintage of the Chianti Montalbano barely nods in the direction of elegance and personality, while the basic Carmignano - we tasted the '95 - offers veiled, rather closed aromas and a dry palate. But the panel found the Barco Reale '96 a much more interesting and enjoyable proposition. There were temptingly delicious aromas of strawberry and raspberry on the nose, carried through on the clean-tasting, consistent palate. And of course the real jewel in the Carmignano crown is the Ghiaie della Furba, one of Tuscany and Italy's longest-standing Bordeaux blends. The panel had no difficulty in awarding Two Glasses to the '95 vintage, which has a complex, quite balanced nose with ripe wild berries and a hint of vegetal aroma. Vigorous tannins provide the first impression on a palate that has structure and mouth-filling flavour and a long finish. Definitely a wine that can be tucked away in the cellar for a few years.

CARMIGNANO (PO)

IL POGGIOLO
VIA PISTOIESE, 76
50042 CARMIGNANO (PO)
TEL. 055/8711242

This year's tastings revealed an encouraging comeback by the wines of Carmignano to seriously good levels of quality, and as a consequence some of the estates which have made major contributions to winemaking in Tuscany have been readmitted to the Guide. Naturally, one such property is Il Poggiolo, owned by the noble Conti Cianchi Baldazzi family. The range is traditional, a common feature in Carmignano. (The fact that cabernet has always been authorised by the DOC has moderated the trend so evident in the rest of Tuscany towards the promotion of "Supertuscan" table wines). The panel was very pleased with both of this year's Il Poggiolo wines, awarding a prestigious Two Glasses to both. The garnet-ruby Carmignano reveals an interesting range of aromas from vegetal notes to fruit preserve, citron and tobacco, then a deliciously full flavour. It is a well balanced wine at the height of its powers, with elegance, length and personality of its own. All of these qualities can also be found in the Vin Santo, of which Il Poggiolo has always been rightly proud. The rich yellow-gold in the glass leads into a nose of nuts and candied peel laced with cinnamon and the juicy, sumptuously creamy flavour offers the palate a deliciously engrossing experience.

● Ghiaie della Furba '95	ŸŸ	5
● Barco Reale '96	Ÿ	3
● Carmignano '95	Ÿ	4
● Chianti Montalbano '96		2
● Ghiaie della Furba '94	ŸŸ	5
○ Vin Santo di Carmignano Ris. '89	ŸŸ	5
○ Vin Santo di Carmignano Ris. '90	ŸŸ	5
● Barco Reale '95	Ÿ	3*

● Carmignano '94	ŸŸ	4
○ Vinsanto '88	ŸŸ	5

CASTAGNETO CARDUCCI (LI) CASTAGNETO CARDUCCI (LI)

GRATTAMACCO
LOC. GRATTAMACCO
57022 CASTAGNETO CARDUCCI (LI)
TEL. 0565/763840

MICHELE SATTA
LOC. VIGNA AL CAVALIERE
57020 CASTAGNETO CARDUCCI (LI)
TEL. 0565/763894

This year the Podere Grattamacco seems to be asking itself where it is going. The Grattamacco Rosso '94 has two sides to its personality: on the one hand it has much more muscle than the estate's previous offerings but on the other it is also much less drinker-friendly. Of course this should come as no surprise. After all, you cannot program a wine as you can a computer. The panel was a little disappointed, but only because since the fabulous Three Glass '85, Grattamacco has produced seriously good Two Glass wines you could bank on year after year. The '94 will be popular with winelovers who like their reds beefy rather than elegant. The very deep ruby colour shades into garnet at the rim, which means that the wine is beginning to show its age. This was confirmed on the nose, where the panel picked out leather, jam, steak tartare and nuts. The palate was let down slightly by a lack of balance in the slightly hard finish, but still managed to convince thanks to its great concentration, a sure sign that the raw material was first quality. The main features of the Grattamacco Bianco were its aroma of ripe apricot and yellow flowers, typical of the local vermentino, and very respectable body.

The panel were finally able this year to record an unimpeachable performance by Michele Satta. Perhaps the progress made by Satta's latest wines did not really surprise us but it did, however, provide an opportunity for us to reward the unswerving commitment of a grower-producer who has always striven to combine quality with the search for a unique personal style. The Vigna del Cavaliere '95 is a minor masterpiece. The deep, bright red in the glass is barely tinged with garnet at the rim and the clean, up front aromas foreground flowers over a more restrained note of spices. The palate is elegant rather than muscular and has lots of nicely concentrated fruit. There is less personality but just as much pleasure in the Piastraia '95, obtained from an unusual blend of cabernet, merlot, syrah and sangiovese. Aromas of black berries rise up from an attractive deep red colour, accompanied by notes of pepper, vanilla and cloves. The sweet palate is captivatingly soft, delicious and balanced. The Vermentino Costa di Giulia '96 offers fragrant aromas of melon, apricot and broom flowers followed up by balanced, refreshing acidity. There was another pleasant surprise in the shape of the Bolgheri Bianco with its yellow flowers and honey aromas and attractively soft palate. And finally the lightweight and unpretentious - but deliciously well made - Diambra also deserves a mention.

O	Grattamacco Bianco '95	♟	3
●	Grattamacco Rosso '94	♟	5
●	Grattamacco Rosso '85	♟♟♟	5
●	Grattamacco Rosso '86	♟♟	5
●	Grattamacco Rosso '87	♟♟	5
●	Grattamacco Rosso '88	♟♟	5
●	Grattamacco Rosso '89	♟♟	5
●	Grattamacco Rosso '90	♟♟	5
●	Grattamacco Rosso '91	♟♟	5
●	Grattamacco Rosso '92	♟♟	4
●	Grattamacco Rosso '93	♟♟	5
O	Grattamacco Bianco '92	♟	3
O	Grattamacco Bianco '93	♟	3
O	Grattamacco Bianco '94	♟	3

●	Bolgheri Piastraia '95	♟♟	3*
●	Vigna al Cavaliere '95	♟♟	4
O	Bolgheri Bianco '96	♟	2*
O	Bolgheri Vermentino Costa di Giulia '96	♟	3
●	Bolgheri Diambra '96		2
●	Vigna al Cavaliere '90	♟♟	5
O	Costa di Giulia '95	♟	3
●	Diambra '93	♟	2
●	Diambra '94	♟	1
●	Piastraia '94	♟	3*
●	Vigna al Cavaliere '92	♟	4
●	Vigna al Cavaliere '93	♟	4
●	Vigna al Cavaliere '94	♟	4

CASTELLINA IN CHIANTI (SI) CASTELLINA IN CHIANTI (SI)

CASTELLARE DI CASTELLINA
LOC. CASTELLARE
53011 CASTELLINA IN CHIANTI (SI)
TEL. 0577/740490

CECCHI
LOC. CASINA DEI PONTI
53011 CASTELLINA IN CHIANTI (SI)
TEL. 0577/743024

All sorts of people who have a place in the country try to make wine but only a few manage to do so with any real success. Paolo Panerai, a financial journalist who today is the editor of Milano Finanza and Class magazine, is a member of this select band. For over 20 years, his passion has been winemaking, in which he has benefited from the assistance of Maurizio Castelli, one of the founding fathers of Italian oenology. This two-man team has always produced wine that is good, and on occasion stunning. Obviously, reds are their mainstay, and are mostly based on sangioveto grapes. The one we like best this year was the Chianti Classico '95, a moderately complex wine that is an instant candidate as a benchmark for the variety. At Castellina, in good years the Chianti Classico manages to combine superb body with an outstandingly sinewy texture. They are concentrated, instantly drinkable wines that are backed up by a sound acidity that also makes them reasonably cellerable. The '95 Castellare Chianti Classico marries these characteristics to intense fruit aromas and the resulting wine was one of the best of the type that we tasted this year. The '93 vintage brought with it a new Castellare product, the Vigna Il Poggiolo Chianti Classico, a red that has concentration and personality but which still needs time in the cellar to mellow out completely.

Luigi Cecchi is one of Tuscany's leading winemakers and for many years he has been a leading figure on the Chianti scene. His results in tastings have been remarkable in recent years, given that as a producer he is better known for his well made commercial range than for premium products. We are pleased to note this development as we believe that a high profile winery sooner or later has to try its hand at making fine wine. There were two Cecchi products that caught our eye this year. The Chianti Classico Messer Pietro di Teuzzo '95 is probably the finest vintage ever made of this particular wine. It has both power and concentration, and in fact the only criticism our panel had was that the tannins were a little too robust. There were no quibbles about the Two Glass rating, however. The Cabernet Sauvignon '94, matured in small oak barrels, was a pleasant surprise, grafting its own character onto the variety's well known tasting profile: in short, faint vegetal notes blending with vanilla over an excellently structured palate. Finally the monovarietal sangiovese Spargolo '94 turned out not to be up to its usual standard this year, proving that even for the Cecchi estate, some vintages are beyond redemption.

● Chianti Classico '95	▼▼	4
● Chianti Classico Vigna Il Poggiolo '93	▼	5
● Chianti Classico '90	▼▼	4
● Chianti Classico Ris. '90	▼▼	5
● I Sodi di San Niccolò '88	▼▼	6
● I Sodi di San Niccolò '90	▼▼	5
● I Sodi di San Niccolò '91	▼▼	5
● Chianti Classico '94	▼	3
● Chianti Classico Ris. '93	▼	4
● Coniale '91	▼	6

● Cabernet Sauvignon '94	▼▼	4
● Chianti Classico Messer Pietro di Teuzzo '95	▼▼	4
● Spargolo '94	▼	4
● Chianti Classico Messer Pietro di Teuzzo '88	▼▼	4
● Chianti Classico Messer Pietro di Teuzzo '93	▼▼	3*
● Spargolo '85	▼▼	5
● Spargolo '88	▼▼	5
● Spargolo '90	▼▼	4
● Spargolo '91	▼▼	4
● Chianti Classico '93	▼	2*
● Chianti Classico Messer Pietro di Teuzzo '94	▼	3

CASTELLINA IN CHIANTI (SI)

ROCCA DI CISPIANO
LOC. CISPIANO
53011 CASTELLINA IN CHIANTI (SI)
TEL. 0577/740961

CASTELLINA IN CHIANTI (SI)

CASTELLO DI FONTERUTOLI
VIA ROSSINI, 5
LOC. FONTERUTOLI
53011 CASTELLINA IN CHIANTI (SI)
TEL. 0577/740476

A few years ago Guido Busetto, a financial journalist from Milan, and his Japanese wife Nobuko Hashimoto made a major life-choice when they decided to go into winemaking in Chianti. And not just in any old corner of the DOC zone but in Cispiano, one of the finest subzones in the entire appellation and only a short distance from the renowned Conca d'Oro slopes at Castellina. Results so far have been mixed for a number of reasons, the main one being that winemaking at this level is simply not easy task. But this year the couple have availed themselves of the experience of consultant Stefano Porcinai and many of the problems have now been firmly consigned to the past. An estate like Rocca di Cispiano has vast potential for making really top quality wines and on this visit our panel tasted two, both of which gained excellent marks. The Rocca di Cispiano '94 is a sangiovese-based blend that was so good it was included in the magic circle of possible Three Glass wines for the final tastings. The aromas are perhaps a little mature but the ripe fruit and delicate nuances of vanilla are richly satisfying. In the mouth it is equally convincing. Softness easily has the better of the acidity and tannin content to reveal all the wine's depth and concentration. The Chianti Classico '95 was also very good indeed, its balm and spice fragrances underpinned by ripe red fruit. The palate has definite character and luscious concentration although let down slightly by a lack of length.

Castello di Fonterutoli has gained the distinction of two Three Glass awards for the second year running, a superb result that catapults Lapo Mazzei and his cellar right into the first rank of Chianti's winemaking élite. Much of the credit has to go to "ser" Lapo's clear strategic vision and his determination to involve his sons Filippo and Francesco in the business with far reaching decision-making powers, for this has initiated a process of renewal and regeneration that has few equals anywhere else in Tuscany. Mazzei's hiring of Carlo Ferrini as the estate consultant, one of the finest young winemakers in the region, did the rest. So the panel was once again delighted to be up against a range of stratospherically good wines, beginning with the deliciously fruity, uncomplicated Chianti Classico '95, an object lesson in how to make good Chianti Classico. The Chianti Classico Ser Lapo Riserva '94 is also good, despite being obtained from one of the least exciting of recent vintages. But the two real showpieces are the Concerto '94 and above all the Siepi '95, which is a masterpiece. The Concerto '94 was blended from sangiovese with a small proportion of cabernet sauvignon. Poor vintage or no poor vintage, this is a stunningly concentrated wine with class written all over it. The soft, mouth-filling palate reveals tannins of true distinction that hint at great things to come in the next five years for a wine that is drinking wonderfully now. The Siepi '95 is a heart-stopper of a wine that releases intense fragrances of red fruit and elegant oak-derived vanilla despite its obvious youth. The palate is elegant yet beefy and concentrated at the same time, the tannins are beautifully mellow and integrated into the palate which means - amazingly - that those who cannot wait to sample this wonderful bottle do not have to.

● Chianti Classico '95	♟♟	4
● Rocca di Cispiano '94	♟♟	5
● Chianti Classico Ris. '90	♟♟	4*
● Chianti Classico '90	♟	4
● Chianti Classico '91	♟	4

● Concerto '94	♟♟♟	5
● Siepi '95	♟♟♟	6
● Chianti Classico '95	♟♟	3*
● Chianti Classico Ser Lapo Ris. '94	♟♟	4
● Chianti Classico Ser Lapo Ris. '90	♟♟♟	5
● Concerto '86	♟♟♟	5
● Concerto '90	♟♟♟	5
● Concerto '93	♟♟♟	5
● Siepi '93	♟♟♟	5
● Siepi '94	♟♟♟	6
● Chianti Classico '94	♟♟	3*
● Chianti Classico Ser Lapo Ris. '93	♟♟	5
● Concerto '88	♟♟	5
● Concerto '91	♟♟	5

CASTELLINA IN CHIANTI (SI) CASTELLINA IN CHIANTI (SI)

GAGLIOLE
LOC. GAGLIOLE
53011 CASTELLINA IN CHIANTI (SI)
TEL. 0577/740369

PODERE LA BRANCAIA
LOC. BRANCAIA
53011 CASTELLINA IN CHIANTI (SI)
TEL. 0577/743084

Thomas Bär is Swiss. Like many of his countrymen, he fell in love with the charms of Chianti and its wines, deciding eventually to move there. And his choice of adopted home was inspired, for his vineyards at Gagliole enjoy a superb location. A committed supporter of organic viticulture, Bär aims to combine the potential of traditional varieties like sangiovese with a modern winemaking style entrusted to the skills of Luca d'Attoma. Production is limited to two labels only, one white table wine and one red. Gagliole Rosso is a sangiovese-based blend with a small proportion of cabernet sauvignon whose deep ruby colour and fragrances reveal rich fruit and attractive maturity, rounded off with hints of flowers and wood. The palate is clean-tasting and concentrated, sustained by solid tannins and a nicely judged note of acidity. The Gagliole Bianco also came out of our tasting with flying colours thanks to its good structure, even though the oak was a little too assertive and tended to mask the wine's aromas. Its blend contains a proportion of oak-fermented chardonnay but is based on a very interesting local sub-variety of trebbiano, which at Gagliole produces small, loose-packed berries.

"This is it". That was the spontaneous reaction of the entire panel on sampling the two wines presented by this small Castellina-based estate. The Brancaia '94, a blend of 90 percent sangiovese and 10 percent merlot, is a fantastic piece of winemaking. Although superbly concentrated, the palate offers mellow, noble tannins backing up an elegant body that exudes distinction. This is no slurp-and-chew, fruity little crowd-pleaser, this is a wine that conjures up stunningly complex fragrances of bramble and Morello cherry over a background of vanilla that is never intrusive. The Three Glass rating was never under discussion. But the La Brancaia Chianti Classico '95 also brought a smile to the tasters' lips. It has personality, sinew, clean, crisp aromas of red fruit and a very drinkable style - proof that the Podere La Brancaia has been investing heavily in the cellar and the vineyard, especially since it severed its links with the Castello di Fonterutoli estate. La Brancaia is now completely self-contained and the release of two wines like these marks the beginning of what looks like a brilliant future as an independent grower-producer.

● Gagliole Rosso '95	♟♟	5
○ Gagliole Bianco '96	♟	4

● Brancaia '94	♟♟♟	6
● Chianti Classico '95	♟♟	4
● Brancaia '88	♟♟	6
● Brancaia '90	♟♟	6
● Brancaia '91	♟♟	6
● Brancaia '93	♟♟	5

CASTELLINA IN CHIANTI (SI)   CASTELLINA IN CHIANTI (SI)

CASTELLO DI LILLIANO
LOC. LILLIANO
53011 CASTELLINA IN CHIANTI (SI)
TEL. 0577/743070

FATTORIA NITTARDI
LOC. NITTARDI
53011 CASTELLINA IN CHIANTI (SI)
TEL. 0577/740269

If we were to award a special prize to the best producer of traditional Chianti Classico wines then it would have to go to Castello di Lilliano, for this is an estate that has founded its considerable reputation on rigorous respect for the classic local style. And of course the winemaker is Giulio Gambelli, a man who for years has been creating great wines not only in Chianti but in Montalcino as well. Castello di Lilliano's owner is Principe Giulio Ruspoli, a nobleman who is a major player on the Tuscan winemaking scene and a man with very clear ideas about the style of his products. This year, he presented three wines and got the best results with what was apparently the least prestigious of the three, the cellar's basic Chianti Classico '95. The panel were pleased to note delightfully clean, intense fruit aromas, with notes of Morello cherry and Parma violets emerging in line with the best and most ancient traditions of Chianti Classico. The attack on the palate is positive and the body has lots of concentration, all adding up to make one of the vintage's most exciting Chianti Classico wines. The Chianti Classico Riserva '94 is another attractive wine which, although softer and more mature than the previous bottle, is smooth, mouth-filling and long. On a less positive note, the '94 Anagallis - the cellar's most innovative wine from almost 100 percent sangiovese fruit - is not as successful as in the past. Matured in small barrels, it has a nose that is perhaps over-oaked and its tannins have a roughish edge. Despite its undeniable concentration and flavour, it does lack balance.

Peter Femfert and the Fattoria di Nittardi have never come so close to Three Glasses. Their spectacularly good Chianti Classico '94 almost made it but for a slight lack of muscle power at the tape. The aromas are supremely elegant, mingling coffee and vanilla perfectly with Morello cherry-dominated fruit. The palate, however, is a little too long on tannins for a body whose richness did not quite last the course. But the makings are there and the ultimate goal will no doubt be reached at some time in the future for three even better vintages are due to be released shortly. One of them will no doubt enable Femfert and his redoubtable winemaker Carlo Ferrini to carry off our top prize before long. The promise of the '95 is clear from our tasting of the Chianti Classico Casanuova di Nittardi from the same vintage. It's a wine that has not got any -and never pretended to have - the complexity of the Riserva but it offers clean fragrances with faint notes of fruit and grass leading into a thoroughly persuasive palate that is all perkiness and drinkability. Not a bad start for a vintage that is certain to scale even greater heights with the heavyweight Riserva version.

● Chianti Classico '95	♟♟	3*	
● Chianti Classico Ris. '94	♟♟	4	
● Anagallis '94	♟	5	
● Chianti Classico E. Ruspoli Berlingieri Ris. '85	♟♟♟	6	
● Anagallis '88	♟♟	5	
● Anagallis '90	♟♟	5	
● Chianti Classico '88	♟♟	3*	
● Chianti Classico '90	♟♟	3*	
● Chianti Classico '94	♟♟	3*	
● Chianti Classico E. Ruspoli Berlingeri '88	♟♟	4	

● Chianti Classico Casanuova di Nittardi '95	♟♟	4
● Chianti Classico Ris. '94	♟♟	5
● Chianti Classico '91	♟♟	4
● Chianti Classico '93	♟♟	4
● Chianti Classico Ris. '88	♟♟	4
● Chianti Classico Ris. '90	♟♟	5
● Chianti Classico Ris. '93	♟♟	4
● Chianti Classico '90	♟	3
● Chianti Classico '92	♟	4
● Chianti Classico '94	♟	3

CASTELLINA IN CHIANTI (SI)   CASTELLINA IN CHIANTI (SI)

ROCCA DELLE MACÌE
LOC. MACÌE
53011 CASTELLINA IN CHIANTI (SI)
TEL. 0577/7321

SAN FABIANO CALCINAIA
LOC. CELLOLE
53011 CASTELLINA IN CHIANTI (SI)
TEL. 0577/979232

After several years in which we had to make a real effort to dig out any seriously valid wines, it looks as if Rocca delle Macìe has finally turned the corner. The somewhat over-mature style that their wines used to have is a thing of the past. Obviously the reds produced by this lovely and very big estate are not exactly the last word in fashion, but neither are they exhibits from an oenological museum, something they might have ended up as if there had not been any changes. The Ser Gioveto '94 is the estate's most representative wine and it has returned to its former glory thanks to a complex, nicely mature nose and great structure; it has soft, rich flavour and deliciously integrated tannins. The Chianti Classico Tenuta S. Alfonso '95 is another excellent bottle, which is much more concentrated and convincing than the '93 vintage we tasted last year. All the other wines we sampled are very good indeed, with a special mention going to the basic Chianti Classico '95, a very well made red that is wonderful value for money, and only a slight black mark against the sangiovese/cabernet sauvignon Roccato '94, which is too aggressive on the palate to repeat the Two Glass success of the '93 vintage. The Chianti Classico Fizzano Riserva '94, not one of the best vintages, is also a little too mature for comfort, but all in all the range presented was very satisfactory, particularly if we bear in mind how indifferent the '94 vintage was.

In Italian, the English term "winemaker" is often applied to consultant oenologists who work for more than one cellar. Usually, their clients are small-to-medium sized estates that cannot afford a full-time winemaker of their own. Naturally, the best and most fashionable are assiduously courted and hired or head-hunted in a way that has much in common with the world of football management. One of the most highly quoted such professionals at the moment is Carlo Ferrini, a young agronomist and oenologist who has attracted attention by producing a string of out-of-this-world reds. One of his most recent contracts came from Guidi Serio, owner of San Fabiano Calcinaia. We do not know whether the credit should go to Ferrini, or to the better-than-average vintages, or to sheer serendipity but the wines the panel tasted this year were furlongs clear of previous years' offerings. It would be all to easy to say that Ferrini has done it again, but that is exactly what it looks like. If we take for example the Cerviolo '95, a sangiovese-based red with 30 percent cabernet sauvignon, we are looking at a surprisingly good wine. The concentration and above all its whistle-clean execution took our breath away. It may not have won a full Three Glasses but it wo not be long before it does. The Chianti Classico '95 was also very good and actually made it into the top ten Chianti Classico wines from the vintage, which is a first for the San Fabiano Calcinaia winery.

● Chianti Classico		
Tenuta Sant'Alfonso '95	♟♟	3*
● Ser Gioveto '94	♟♟	5
● Chianti Classico '95	♟	3*
● Chianti Classico Fizzano Ris. '94	♟	5
● Chianti Classico Ris. '94	♟	4
● Roccato '94	♟	5
● Chianti Classico Fizzano Ris. '93	♟♟	5
● Chianti Classico Ris. '90	♟♟	4*
● Chianti Classico		
Tenuta di Sant'Alfonso '90	♟♟	4*
● Roccato '93	♟♟	5
● Ser Gioveto '85	♟♟	5
● Ser Gioveto '86	♟♟	5
● Ser Gioveto '88	♟♟	5

● Cerviolo Rosso '95	♟♟	4
● Chianti Classico '95	♟♟	3
● Cerviolo Rosso '91	♟♟	5
● Chianti Classico Cellole Ris. '90	♟♟	4
● Chianti Classico Cellole Ris. '93	♟♟	4
● Cerviolo Rosso '93	♟	4
● Cerviolo Rosso '94	♟	4
● Chianti Classico '91	♟	4

CASTELLINA IN CHIANTI (SI)   CASTELLINA MARITTIMA (PI)

VILLA CERNA
LOC. VILLA CERNA
53011 CASTELLINA IN CHIANTI (SI)
TEL. 0577/743024

TENUTA DEL TERRICCIO
VIA BAGNOLI
LOC. LE BADIE
56100 CASTELLINA MARITTIMA (PI)
TEL. 050/699709

Villa Cerna is a wonderfully picturesque estate that includes about 60 hectares of some of the finest winegrowing land at Castellina. It is also the property of the Cecchi family, an extremely well known dynasty of viticultural entrepreneurs. And Villa Cerna is the place where the Cecchis have decided to create a state-of-the-art cellar, in the setting of the fortified mediaeval hamlet that they are gradually restoring at the same time. The wines that have been coming out of Villa Cerna are the result of close attention to quality and this year the estate won its first Two Glass rating with a non-Riserva Chianti Classico, the '95. It is an excellently made red with a particularly clean, fruity nose. The palate is full and gratifyingly complex, underpinned by unassertive tannins and plenty of body. All in all, a highly successful Chianti Classico that means we can look forward with confidence to the Riserva version, which is due to be released next year.

The Terriccio estate is making progress at an astonishing rate. Such has been the speed of developments that things have sometimes happened without any real planning, but in the selection of his winemaking team Gian Annibale Rossi di Medelena has shown that he has a sure instinct. Graziana Grassini is working miracles with the whites and Carlo Ferrini is far beyond praise. Every single wine he presented this year in Tuscany was an event in itself. The Lupicaia is utterly fantastic. Deep, deep red - actually nearly black - in the glass, it somehow manages to be impenetrable yet lustrous at the same time. The stunningly rich aromas have intensity and depth that are hard to believe. Great bramble and cassis fruit fuses seamlessly into balmy notes of eucalyptus and mint, with a sprinkling of cocoa powder. Then the palate simply knocks you off your feet. The attack is juicy and amazingly concentrated, the tannins are awesomely textured while the finish is rich, elegant and superbly unhurried. This is a masterpiece of a wine. Inevitably, and completely unfairly, the Tassinaia tends to be overshadowed by such excellence. A great wine in its own right, the '95 Tassinaia is a blend of cabernet and merlot like the Lupicaia but with a proportion of sangiovese that helps to give it a distinct personality. A lovely wine. The Terriccio whites are worth investigation, beginning with the newcomer, Saluccio, blended from wood-fermented chardonnay and sauvignon. Our tasters were surprised to find rich aromas with a good follow-through on the deliciously rich palate. The Rondinaia performed well. It starts out with an uncomplicated nose but is much fuller and more satisfying in the mouth. Because it was slightly leaner, the monovarietal Con Vento scored a little lower but nonetheless reveals a textbook sauvignon bouquet.

● Chianti Classico '95	♥♥	3*
● Chianti Classico Ris. '91	♥♥	3
● Chianti Classico Ris. '93	♥♥	4
● Chianti Classico '94	♥	3
● Villa Cerna '93	♥	2

● Lupicaia '95	♥♥♥	6
○ Rondinaia '96	♥♥	4
○ Saluccio '96	♥♥	4
● Tassinaia '95	♥♥	5
○ Con Vento '96	♥	3
○ Montescudaio Bianco '96		1
● Lupicaia '93	♥♥♥	5
○ Con Vento '94	♥♥	3
● Lupicaia '94	♥♥	6
● Tassinaia '93	♥♥	4
● Tassinaia '94	♥♥	5
○ Con Vento '95	♥	3
● Lupicaia '91	♥	5*
○ Montescudaio Bianco '95	♥	1*
○ Rondinaia '95	♥	3

CASTELNUOVO BERARDENGA (SI)   CASTELNUOVO BERARDENGA (SI)

FATTORIA DELL'AIOLA
LOC. VAGLIAGLI
53010 CASTELNUOVO
BERARDENGA (SI)
TEL. 0577/322615

CASTELLO DI BOSSI
LOC. BOSSI IN CHIANTI
53010 CASTELNUOVO
BERARDENGA (SI)
TEL. 0577/359330

As you admire the hills near Vagliagli under a near-tropical sun, you could almost be persuaded that the sea was just a mile or two behind them. All you would find is Siena's Torre del Mangia since the city is just round the corner, yet the intense white light and sharp outlines of the region make it seem as if the sun is reflecting off the sea in this magical spot where vineyards dot the parched countryside and the olive groves appear to be growing in the desert. The soil here is richer in clay and the Crete Senesi are not far away, for we are right at the southern edge of the Chianti Classico DOC zone. It is here that Maria Grazia Malagodi runs the Fattori dell'Aiola, a 40-hectare estate on superb winemaking soil, a sort of cross between Chianti Classico and Montalcino. Sangiovese thrives in this environment, even though this year's wines are not quite all we had hoped for. They are good but the estate is capable of producing even better. We thought the most interesting of the batch was the Chianti Classico Riserva '94. A good entry on the nose with ripe fruit over acceptably clean oak aromas leads into a full flavoured palate where the tannins are understated, leaving the finish with an only faintly bitter note. The Chianti Classico '95 is both meaner as well as leaner while the mainly sangiovese-based Logaiolo '94 seemed to us to be past its best, despite plenty of underlying extract. Not a bad range of wines by any means but we expect even more from this superbly located estate.

The panel had a very pleasant surprise at Castello di Bossi. We had the estate marked down as one of the big suppliers of the anonymous Chianti Classico that is shuttled up and down Italy in tankers to mass market bottlers. Never had they come up against Bossi wines of the quality that was on offer this year. Evidently, there have been a few policy changes and the winemaker Andrea Mazzoni, one of the most professional oenologists around, has been given carte blanche in selecting the parcels to be bottled. And the moral of the story is that the Castello di Bossi makes its Guide debut with three own-label wines. The Corbaia '94, a blend of 75 percent sangiovese with 25 percent cabernet sauvignon, is an interesting wine in a very contemporary style that has plenty of flavour, despite the generally unexciting vintage. Much the same could be said about the '94 Chianti Classico Riserva, which our tasters put in the top ten of its category. Its aromas are intense and not over-mature, the flavour is rich and concentrated, with no harsh edges. The shortish finish knocked a few points off its overall score but this is definitely a wine to take seriously. Last, we tasted the Chianti Classico '95, a more relaxed bottle than the other two but still convincing and above all beautifully made. Producers with much more exalted reputations than Castello di Bossi would be more than happy to include wines like these in their ranges.

● Chianti Classico Ris. '94	♇♇	4
● Chianti Classico '95	♇	3
● Logaiolo '94	♇	5
● Chianti Classico Ris. '90	♇♇	5
● Chianti Classico '91	♇	4
● Chianti Classico '93	♇	3
● Chianti Classico '94	♇	3
● Chianti Classico Ris. '88	♇	5
● Logaiolo '91	♇	5
● Rosso del Senatore '90	♇	5

● Chianti Classico Ris. '94	♇♇	4
● Corbaia '94	♇♇	5
● Chianti Classico '95	♇	3*

CASTELNUOVO BERARDENGA (SI)   CASTELNUOVO BERARDENGA (SI)

FATTORIA DI DIEVOLE
LOC. DIEVOLE
53019 CASTELNUOVO
BERARDENGA (SI)
TEL. 0577/322613

★ FATTORIA DI FELSINA
STRADA CHIANTIGIANA, 484
53019 CASTELNUOVO
BERARDENGA (SI)
TEL. 0577/355117

Mario Schwemm is one of life's great characters. He manages to turn wine into a real show, for example with the incredible back labels which we mentioned in last year's Guide. This year, Mario has come up with his usual ample range of reds, all sangiovese-based with or without a small proportion of canaiolo. With the exception of the basic Chianti Classico, which is a '95, they are all '94-vintage wines. There are five of them. Some, like the Dieulele and the Novecento, are Chianti Classico selections; others are IGT, as is the case with the Broccato and the Rinascimento. Yet despite all the apparent similarities, no two wines are the same. Indeed so different are they that the panel was unsure of what Schwemm really wants to do and where he wants to go with his production. The Chianti Classico Novecento is a full flavoured, very concentrated wine that is well crafted and above all absolutely typical of this part of the Chianti. The Dieulele and the Chianti Classico Riserva struck us as being totally different - and much less plausible. Both were artless, lean products whose aromas, especially those of the Dieulele, were so lacking in complexity that we began to doubt they came from the same stable as the Novecento. The '94 version of the Broccato, another sangiovese-based red, was good, if not up to the standards of the '93. And finally the panel tasted the Chianti Classico '95, a very attractive wine that reveals notes of ripe fruit and splendid structure.

Since we do not have sufficient space in the Guide to list all the top wines from past editions, we have decided to assign a star to producers who have been awarded Three Glasses at least ten times. This year, the Fattoria di Felsina notched up its eleventh top rating, making it Tuscany's number one cellar. That eleventh Three Glass score went to the Fontalloro '93, the great monovarietal Sangiovese that has become the estate's flag-bearer. Yet again, it is a stunner of a wine with a complexity you would be hard pushed to find anywhere else in Tuscany or beyond. Many participants at blind tastings who have been brought up in the Piedmontese school, and who therefore tend to favour Nebbiolo over Sangiovese, will mistake Fontalloro for a wine from the North-west of Italy. It's a wine that rises above mere regional rivalries. For all its power, tannins and almost Piedmontese austerity, there is a faintly coquettish sweetness in the attack that gives it an entirely Tuscan allure. It blends sinew with grace, depth with elegance and personality with irresistible charm. Inevitably, after the Fontalloro the other excellent wines presented by general manager Giuseppe Mazzocolin and consultant winemaker Franco Bernabei seemed disappointing in comparison. The Chianti Classico Rancia Riserva '94 was softer than the '90 and '93 versions but also more predictable than its predecessors. The basic Chianti Classico '95 was one of the best of its vintage but given the very favourable year, we would have liked to see more concentration. The Maestro Raro '93, a Cabernet Sauvignon whose '91 vintage was a winner with our panel, has yet to be released. But whatever wines it presents, Felsina is, and will continue to be, one of the Guide's benchmark estates.

● Chianti Classico Novecento '94	♟♟	4
● Broccato '94	♟	4
● Chianti Classico '95	♟	3
● Rinascimento '94	♟	4
● Chianti Classico Dieulele '94		4
● Chianti Classico Ris. '94		4
● Chianti Classico Novecento '93	♟♟	4
● Chianti Classico Ris. '93	♟♟	4
● Broccato '93	♟	4
● Chianti Classico '93	♟	3
● Chianti Classico Dieulele '93	♟	4
● Rinascimento '93	♟	4

● Fontalloro '93	♟♟♟	6
● Chianti Classico '95	♟♟	3
● Chianti Classico Rancia Ris. '94	♟♟	5
● Chianti Classico Rancia Ris. '86	♟♟♟	5
● Chianti Classico Rancia Ris. '88	♟♟♟	5
● Chianti Classico Rancia Ris. '90	♟♟♟	5
● Chianti Classico Rancia Ris. '93	♟♟♟	5
● Chianti Classico Ris. '90	♟♟♟	4*
● Fontalloro '85	♟♟♟	5
● Fontalloro '86	♟♟♟	5
● Fontalloro '88	♟♟♟	5
● Fontalloro '90	♟♟♟	5
● Maestro Raro '91	♟♟♟	5

CASTELNUOVO BERARDENGA (SI)

FATTORIA DI PETROIO
VIA DI PETROIO, 43
LOC. QUERCEGROSSA
53010 CASTELNUOVO
BERARDENGA (SI)
TEL. 0577/328045

The Fattoria di Petroio is only a few kilometres from Siena at Quercegrosse, in the North-west corner of the commune of Castelnuovo Berardenga. It was here that a few years ago the well known neurologist and university professor, Gian Liuigi Lenzi, and his wife Pamela took over the family estate and started to make Chianti Classico with the help of oenologist Carlo Ferrini. They produced seriously good wine right from the first harvest and their Chianti Classico Riserva '90 very nearly won a third Glass. There were a few hiccups after that, when they presented a rather ordinary Riserva '93 and some '94 wines that were over-mature and a little rough and ready on the nose. But they're back on form again with a superbly made Chianti Classico '95 that brings out the best in a very fine vintage. The clean, fruity nose reveals the variety's distinctive Morello cherry and Parma violet aroma and, although there is the odd rough edge due to youthful acidity and tannins, the palate has good body and length. It may not be the world's most complex wine but it has all the makings of a thoroughly cellerable bottle to lay down for five or six years. A final comment does have to be made, though. In such a marvellous winemaking zone, the Fattoria di Petroio ought to be able to achieve better results and turn them out with greater consistency.

CASTELNUOVO BERARDENGA (SI)

SAN FELICE
LOC. SAN FELICE
53019 CASTELNUOVO
BERARDENGA (SI)
TEL. 0577/359087-359088

San Felice is a great wine producer that turns out a huge range of wines from its own grapes year after year. Sometimes they would be better advised to concentrate on their mainstays. A few years ago, we compared San Felice to a football team that has a good midfield but no attack. The strikers are there now but they need to be trained and fit before they take the field. This is one way of saying that the '94 Vigorello, a blend of sangiovese with a small proportion of cabernet sauvignon, did not quite live up to its reputation. The follow-through is uncertain and the already mature nose still has roughish, astringent edges. It gives the impression of having suffered in the small oak barrels. The Chianti Classico Poggio Rosso Riserva '94 is a much better wine. The vintage may have been a difficult one but this is a beautifully crafted product. Its complex nose has notes of pencil lead and red fruit, the flavour is full, potent and rich and the mellow tannins merge well into the structure. The Chianti Classico Il Grigio Riserva '94 has a lot in common with the preceding wine but is more dilute and has less polish, making it more of a lightweight. Finally the Chianti Classico '95 is the basic label in a vintage where most of the effort was concentrated on riserva wines which we will be tasting next year. Taking all things into consideration, the tasting went well, but we have every right to expect better things from an estate like San Felice. Above all, the powers-that-be are going to have to make their minds up about where the winery is going.

Wine	Rating	
● Chianti Classico '95	♟♟	3*
● Chianti Classico '90	♟♟	3*
● Chianti Classico '91	♟♟	3*
● Chianti Classico '93	♟♟	2*
● Chianti Classico Ris. '90	♟♟	4*
● Chianti Classico '94	♟	3*
● Chianti Classico Ris. '93	♟	4

Wine	Rating	
● Chianti Classico Poggio Rosso Ris. '94	♟♟	5
● Chianti Classico '95	♟	3
● Chianti Classico Il Grigio Ris. '94	♟	4
● Vigorello '94	♟	5
● Chianti Classico Poggio Rosso Ris. '90	♟♟♟	4
● Vigorello '88	♟♟♟	5
● Chianti Classico Campo del Civettino '90	♟♟	4
● Chianti Classico Il Grigio Ris. '90	♟♟	4
● Chianti Classico Poggio Rosso Ris. '93	♟♟	4
● Vigorello '90	♟♟	5
● Vigorello '93	♟♟	5

CASTIGLIONE DELLA PESCAIA (GR)   CHIANCIANO TERME (SI)

HARALD BREMER
PODERE SAN MICHELE
LOC. VETULONIA
58040 CASTIGLIONE
DELLA PESCAIA (GR)
TEL. 0564/939060

FATTORIA NUOVA SCOPETELLO
STRADA DELLA PIANA, 62
53042 CHIANCIANO TERME (SI)
TEL. 0578/30073

The number of non-Italians now making wine in Tuscany is so great that the phenomenon has become more of a tradition. Especially since some of them do it better than many of the locals. For decades, Harald Bremer has been importing and "blazing a trail" in Germany, as he puts it, for the great wines of Italy. Back in 1972, he bought eight hectares or so of vineyards on the hill slopes at Vetulonia, in the province of Grosseto. He and his son, Bodo, have been making wine here since the late 1970s but the Italian trade press has taken little interest as most of the wine is sold in Germany. Winemaking techniques are as state-of-the-art as you are likely to find anywhere, yields are kept low, at around 40 hectolitres per hectare, and fermentation is carried out in temperature-controlled stainless steel tanks. The cellar used to be stocked with barriques but today Harald prefers larger 500-litre casks, to which Bremer was introduced by the distinguished winemaker, Fausto Maculan. Our panel tasted two of the Bremer reds, both of which were excellent. It was the Vetluna Cabernet Sauvignon '94 that particularly impressed us. The outstandingly deep, inky hue ushers in a nose with fragrances ranging from bramble and raspberry to cassis, roasted coffee beans and cocoa powder. The palate is soft yet vigorously fruity and the mellow tannins are beautifully mature, making for an altogether very nice wine indeed. Its "little brother", the Monteregio di Massa Marittima Rosso Vetluna, is a blend of sangiovese, barbera and cabernet sauvignon. It's a leaner product than the previous wine with less punch on nose and palate, but it is still a well made and attractively fruity bottle.

The estate run by Luigi Frangiosa with the assistance of winemaker Paolo Vagaggini continues to go in the right direction. Its move up-market to premium quality is proceeding without a hitch, even though the final results will not be seen until the new plantings come on-stream. And with 85 hectares under vine, 14 of which dedicated to Vino Nobile, there is plenty of room for improvement. We sampled three wines. It was a disappointment to taste the Vino Nobile di Montepulciano Riserva '93 after the excellent performance of last year's non-Riserva version. The Riserva seemed to be ageing fast, almost as if it was feeling limp after its extended period of maturation. A second bottle confirmed the diagnosis. But the Vino Nobile di Montepulciano '94 was an altogether more serious contender, which earned its One Glass with marks to spare. The garnet ruby is moderately intense and leads into a broad, clean nose of flowers and red fruit with just a hint of oak-derived vanilla. Its texture on the palate may not be out of the ordinary but there is superb balance and the positive acidity is never intrusive. The '95 vintage Rosso di Montepulciano was one of the best in its class, offering a bright ruby hue and uncomplicated - but very clean and fruity - range of aromas.

● Vetluna '94	�♞	5
● Monteregio di Massa Marittima		
Rosso Vetluna '94	♞	3

● Rosso di Montepulciano '95	♞	2
● Vino Nobile di Montepulciano '94	♞	4
● Vino Nobile		
di Montepulciano Ris. '93		4
● Vino Nobile di Montepulciano '93	♞♞	4

CHIUSI (SI)

CORTONA (AR)

FICOMONTANINO
LOC. FICOMONTANINO
53043 CHIUSI (SI)
TEL. 0578/21180 - 06/5561283

FATTORIA DI MANZANO
VIA DI MANZANO, 15
LOC. CAMUCIA
52044 CORTONA (AR)
TEL. 0575/618667

One of the most exciting aspects of our annual tastings for the Guide is that we are able to investigate new or relatively unknown grower-producers that most winelovers never come to hear about. And the Ficomontanino estate, whose vineyards lie on the eastern edge of the province of Siena and whose offices are in Rome, is definitely one of those discoveries. Unsurprisingly, the names chosen for the range are Etruscan-inspired but the wines themselves are reassuringly contemporary in style. Pick of the bunch is the Tutulus, which has a beautiful deep ruby red accompanied by a broad but intense bouquet of plums, brambles and sweet vanilla nuanced with coffee. The attack on the palate shows lots of muscle even if the wine still needs time to mature and integrate the lovely notes of oak fully. There are also one or two hard edges in the finish that will mellow with time but this is a gutsy bottle with loads of personality. "Balanced", "clean-tasting" and "good structure" are the words that spring to mind on tasting the Lucumone, a Cabernet Sauvignon whose varietal grassy aromas are perhaps a little too much in evidence but which convinces thanks to a soft, well sustained follow through on the palate. The third wine we sampled was called, predictably given the estate's Etruscan theming, Porsenna and it turned out to be an equally predictable Sauvignon Blanc that exemplifies the house style in every detail. At present it has still to assimilate its oak aromas, which mask the varietal fruit with notes of toastiness and vanilla. The entry on the palate is sweet and, all in all, the flavour and balance in the mouth are good.

It was a foregone conclusion that the restructuring of cellars and vineyard carried out by the D'Alessandro brothers would bear fruit. For Massimo, an architect who holds a university chair in Rome, lavished all his professional skills, as well as his enthusiasm for winemaking, on the family property. The new vinification cellars that have been taking shape in recent months are being built to an innovative, rigorously conceived plan that Massimo drew up. Billions of lire, quite literally, have been spent on the vineyards and the results are there for all to see. Above all, the Fattoria di Manzano is now turning out wines of superb quality. The Three Glass award this year crowns a long series of increasingly appreciative reviews over the years and goes to the flag-bearer Podere Il Bosco wine. The '94 vintage was an eye-opener and the '95 version of this monovarietal Syrah is even better, showing even more marked personality. Its class, finesse and whistle-clean aromas on both the nose and palate are backed up by quite remarkable texture and structure. The red hue in the glass is intense and the nose features crisp fragrances of bilberry and ripe bramble subtly nuanced with white pepper. The palate is classy and clean-tasting, with soft fruit and loads of length. This thoroughbred of a wine has some very nicely turned out stablemates. The Podere Il Vescovo '96 is an uncomplicated, fruit-rich monovarietal Gamay and the Le Terrazze, a sauvignon-based blend, is refreshing and thirst-quenchingly drinkable. The only question mark on an otherwise impressive tasting sheet is next to the Podere Fontarca '96, a chardonnay and viognier blend that was off-target this year.

●	Chianti Colli Senesi Tutulus '95	♟♟	3
●	Lucumone '95	♟♟	5
●	Porsenna '96	♟	4

●	Podere Il Bosco '95	♟♟♟	5
○	Le Terrazze '96	♟	3
●	Podere Il Vescovo '96	♟	3
○	Podere Fontarca '96		4
○	Podere Fontarca '94	♟♟	4
●	Podere Il Bosco '94	♟♟	5
●	Vigna del Bosco '93	♟♟	4
○	Le Terrazze '94	♟	3
○	Le Terrazze '95	♟	3
○	Podere di Fontarca '93	♟	4
●	Podere Il Vescovo '95	♟	3
●	Rosso della Fattoria di Manzano '92	♟	2

FAUGLIA (PI)

FATTORIA DELL'UCCELLIERA
VIA PROVINCIALE LORENZANA
CUCIGLIANA, 1
56043 FAUGLIA (PI)
TEL. 050/662747

FIRENZE

MARCHESI ANTINORI
P.ZZA DEGLI ANTINORI, 3
50123 FIRENZE
TEL. 055/23595

This is the year in which the Fattoria dell'Uccelliera has begun to collect some of the rewards it deserves for the huge progress it has made in the recent past. The notes from our tastings fully confirm this view, for they reflect long-term strategic decisions that have put the emphasis on quality rather than happenstance or good weather. To give readers an idea, we might say that beyond any shadow of doubt the Castellaccio Rosso '95, a blend of sangiovese and cabernet, is the finest wine ever to emerge from the cellars at Fauglia. A seriously good wine that genuinely surprised members of our panel who did not know the estate. A marvellous inky-dark red in the glass, it offers deep, concentrated fragrances of coffee, brambles and plums on the nose and a soft palate as harmonious as a heavenly choir. It might not have quite the complexity and texture of a truly great red, but what a wine nonetheless! Its sister, the Castellaccio Bianco also performed extremely well. An oak-fermented Chardonnay, it scored well thanks to its lovely balance and elegance. The aromas of spring flowers, bananas, citrus fruits and spices are rounded off by a palate that has moderate, but very well balanced, depth and a perfectly judged notes of toasty oak. The estate Chianti, is a fairly intense ruby red wine with fragrances of red fruit, flowers, a vegetal note and a hint of wood. In the mouth, it shows decent texture and balance, and drinks very nicely. Finally the Rosato and the S. Torpé proved to be well made budget wines.

There is no argument about who is the "Lord of the wines" in Italy. It has to be Marchese Piero Antinori, one of the few top-flight négociants in the country who really understood that making premium wine was a fundamental, necessary condition, albeit not in itself sufficient, for market success. For it was Piero Antinori's marketing skills and ability to create a high-profile company image that made the difference between the Marchesi Antinori label and those of a host of other outstanding Tuscan cellars. Today the name Antinori is to the world of wine what Chanel or Armani are to fashion or Mercedes is to the car industry. It is a brand that guarantees image, quality and professionalism, which says just about all there is to say. Anyone who is remotely interested in wines cannot fail to fall under the Antinori spell and admire, as we do, the magician who cast it. Especially when you are sitting in front of a wine like the Solaia '94, one of the finest versions ever. A blend of cabernet sauvignon with a small proportion of sangiovese, Solaia releases complex, sophisticated fragrances of blackcurrant, Morello cherry and pencil lead. Full, soft and concentrated, the palate is astonishingly harmonious, the sweet, velvety tannins having mellowed to perfection. Awesome. The Chianti Classico Badia a Passignano Riserva '94 was almost as exciting; its mouth-filling, soft flavour is utterly convincing thanks to some serious support from the tannins. Then we tried the Tignanello '94, a rather uninspiring and distinctly mature wine this time, but still rich on the palate and very long. The catalogue continues, of course. A host of other wines also deserve a rating, but unfortunately our space is much more limited than the Antinori cellar.

O	Castellaccio Bianco '96	🍷🍷	4
●	Castellaccio Rosso '95	🍷🍷	4*
●	Chianti '95	🍷	2*
O	Bianco di S. Torpé Ficaia '96		2
☉	Rosaspina '96		2
●	Castellaccio Rosso '93	🍷🍷	4
O	Castellaccio Bianco '94	🍷	4
●	Castellaccio Rosso '92	🍷	4
●	Chianti '94	🍷	1*

●	Solaia '94	🍷🍷🍷	6
●	Chianti Classico		
	Badia a Passignano Ris. '94	🍷🍷	4*
●	Tignanello '94	🍷🍷	6
●	Solaia '86	🍷🍷🍷	6
●	Solaia '88	🍷🍷🍷	6
●	Solaia '90	🍷🍷🍷	6
●	Tignanello '83	🍷🍷🍷	6
●	Tignanello '85	🍷🍷🍷	6
●	Tignanello '93	🍷🍷🍷	6
●	Solaia '91	🍷🍷	6
●	Solaia '93	🍷🍷	6
●	Tignanello '88	🍷🍷	6
●	Tignanello '90	🍷🍷	6
●	Tignanello '91	🍷🍷	6

FIRENZE

FUCECCHIO (FI)

MARCHESI DE' FRESCOBALDI
VIA S. SPIRITO, 11
50125 FIRENZE
TEL. 055/27141

FATTORIA DI MONTELLORI
VIA PISTOIESE, 5
50054 FUCECCHIO (FI)
TEL. 0571/260641

There is little point in rehearsing for the umpteenth time the story of this ancient family and the crucially important role it has played in Tuscan viticulture. Frescobaldi is one of Italy's blue chip names, a member of that select group of grower-producers in a position to change the face of the market in premium wines. Their current overall level of quality is very encouraging, although improvements could be made right at the top of the range. This year the Frescobaldi flag-bearers lacked the strength and stamina to make it into the final round of tastings and missed out on the top awards. When the panel started with the Chianti Rufina Nipozzano Riserva '94, they were impressed by its performance despite an indifferent vintage. The light, uncomplicated fruit on the nose leads into a refreshingly drinkable palate with medium body. Good, but not really enough for a Riserva. The Montesodi '94, once a Chianti Rufina and today a mere "table wine", was altogether more convincing. It has balsamic aromas over a pleasantly fresh, fruity background with attractive oak which take you into a clean, rich palate underpinned by lively acidity. The Mormoreto '94 was another high scoring wine. A Cabernet that flaunts its typical aromas of blackcurrant and bramble, it reveals a palate with loads of beefy extract. The traditional Frescobaldi red, the Pomino '94 is a little green on the nose where the cabernet aromas come through unashamedly but the palate has more balance. Of the whites, a mention has to go to the standard Pomino '96, a nimble, alcohol-rich and fresh-tasting wine on the palate, and to the Pomino II Benefizio '95, which is strongly redolent of oak and has a well-sustained, if shortish, flavour.

The Fattoria di Montellori put up a good all-round show when the panel were visiting this year, albeit a touch below the outstanding levels of quality achieved for the Guide's last edition. However it is almost a racing certainty that the slight drop was due to the unspectacular nature of the '94 vintage, from which many of the wines the estate is now releasing come. The chardonnay-based Castelrapiti Bianco offers already mature fragrances of fruit before disclosing a soft, balanced palate with moderate structure. Its red stablemate, a blend of sangiovese and cabernet sauvignon, has even less pep and decidedly fuzzy aromas that are hard to pin down. But the Salamartano '94, a Bordeaux blend, is in a totally different league. It has much cleaner, fruity aromas and bags more life. Intense ruby red, it reveals a nicely defined, moderately deep nose nuanced with liquorice and pencil lead, and a full flavoured, masculine palate with deliciously mellow tannins. The '96 whites were less complex. The viognier-based Bonfiglio is clean, flowery and light. The Costa di Sant'Amato, a distinctly varietal Sauvignon reminiscent of sage and new-mown grass, has lovely balance in the mouth while the chardonnay-based Vigneto Le Rose had less focus on both nose and palate. And do not let us forget the Montellori Brut, which was as ever a well made and delightfully drinkable spumante.

● Montesodi '95	♙♙	6	
● Mormoreto '94	♙♙	6	
● Chianti Rufina			
Nipozzano Ris. '94	♙	4	
○ Pomino Bianco '96	♙	4	
○ Pomino II Benefizio '95	♙	5	
● Pomino Rosso '94	♙	4	
● Pomino Rosso '85	♙♙♙	5	

● Salamartano '94	♙♙	5	
○ Bonfiglio '96	♙	4	
○ Castelrapiti Bianco '94	♙	5	
● Castelrapiti Rosso '94	♙	5	
○ La Costa di Sant'Amato '96	♙	4	
○ Montellori Brut	♙	5	
○ Vigneto Le Rose '96		3	
○ Bonfiglio '94	♙♙	4	
● Castelrapiti Rosso '92	♙♙	5	
● Castelrapiti Rosso '93	♙♙	5	
● Salamartano '92	♙♙	5	
● Salamartano '93	♙♙	5	

GAIOLE IN CHIANTI (SI)

AGRICOLTORI
DEL CHIANTI GEOGRAFICO
VIA MULINACCIO, 10
53013 GAIOLE IN CHIANTI (SI)
TEL. 0577/749451-749489

The strategy adopted by this major Chianti co-operative cellar over the last few years has shown itself to be far-sighted and very effective. Winemaking has been entrusted to the capable hands of Vittorio Fiore, an oenologist with enormous experience who has boosted the quality of the entire range. Marketing policies have taken the consumer's point of view into account and prices have not gone through the roof. The upshot has been skyrocketing sales and an increasingly wide circle of admirers. And not just among consumers, for many professionals, including restaurateurs and merchants of the more exclusive variety, have included the co-operative's bottles in their wine lists and catalogues, often as a substitute for the products of over-optimistic producers who think that an arm and a leg is a small price to pay for the juice of the grape. And if we had to recommend a Chianti Classico to put on the table every day then the Geografico would be right up there at the top of the short list. It is very well made, with a delicately fruity nose and a balanced palate that has lots of length. The Chianti Classico Tenuta Montegiachi Riserva '94 is a much more serious proposition. The fragrances are complex, with notes of ripe fruit, and the rich palate is soft and mouth-filling. "Less convincing", however, was the panel's verdict on the Capitolare di Biturica I Vigneti del Geografico '94, which revealed vegetal and balsamic notes on the nose and a palate that lacked concentration. Better luck next time with that one.

GAIOLE IN CHIANTI (SI)

★ CASTELLO DI AMA
LOC. AMA
53010 GAIOLE IN CHIANTI (SI)
TEL. 0577/746031

For the Guide to award Three Glasses ten times means that our tasters hold the producer concerned and those who work there in very high esteem. Unfortunately, in the case of Castello di Ama, that esteem is not entirely reciprocal and the reason, it seems, is that Ama's Lorenza Sebasti and Marco Pallanti do not share our assessment of their wines. The couple are very much committed to their Chianti Classico and in particular the La Casuccia and Bellavista selections, but recently we have preferred the Vigna L'Apparita, a superb Merlot that Lorenza and Marco however believe is less representative of the estate. (Why then continue to make it, one might ask). The real issue is that neither Castello di Ama or any other producer can decree which wines get Three Glass ratings. Awards are based solely on the basis of the results of blind tastings, and it is only in this way that we can ensure the impartial evaluation that is in our own - and the producers' - best interests. Castello di Ama "retaliated" for this stance by denying us samples and so we have only been able to review two of their wines, those released before the Guide went to press. The better of the two, as we might have expected, was the '93 Vigna L'Apparita. It was very good indeed, but did not make Three Glass status, not through any motive of reprisal on the part of the tasters, but because the nose is still closed and the tobacco and redcurrant aromas were a little undefined. While intense on the palate, it lacked the complexity of the '92. Finally the '95 basic Chianti Classico earned One Glass, but only just.

● Chianti Classico		
Tenuta Montegiachi Ris. '94	♟♟	4*
● Chianti Classico '95	♟	2*
● I Vigneti del Geografico '94	♟	4
● Chianti Classico '90	♟♟	2*
● Chianti Classico		
Tenuta Montegiachi Ris. '87	♟♟	3*
● Chianti Classico		
Tenuta Montegiachi Ris. '88	♟♟	4*
● Chianti Classico		
Tenuta Montegiachi Ris. '90	♟♟	3*
● Chianti Classico		
Contessa di Radda '93	♟	3
● Chianti Classico		
Tenuta Montegiachi Ris. '93	♟	4

● Vigna l'Apparita Merlot '93	♟♟	6
● Chianti Classico '95	♟	4
● Chianti Cl. Bellavista '85	♟♟♟	6
● Chianti Cl. Bellavista '86	♟♟♟	6
● Chianti Cl. Bellavista '90	♟♟♟	5
● Chianti Cl. Bertinga '88	♟♟♟	6
● Chianti Cl. La Casuccia '88	♟♟♟	6
● Vigna l'Apparita Merlot '88	♟♟♟	6
● Vigna l'Apparita Merlot '90	♟♟♟	6
● Vigna l'Apparita Merlot '91	♟♟♟	6
● Vigna l'Apparita Merlot '92	♟♟♟	6
● Chianti Cl. Bellavista '91	♟♟	5
● Chianti Cl. Bellavista '93	♟♟	5
● Chianti Cl. La Casuccia '91	♟♟	5
● Chianti Cl. La Casuccia '93	♟♟	5

GAIOLE IN CHIANTI (SI)

BADIA A COLTIBUONO
LOC. BADIA A COLTIBUONO
53013 GAIOLE IN CHIANTI (SI)
TEL. 0577/749498

GAIOLE IN CHIANTI (SI)

CASTELLO DI BROLIO - RICASOLI
LOC. BROLIO
53013 GAIOLE IN CHIANTI (SI)
TEL. 0577/7301

The team at Badia di Coltibuono looks like a winner. Emanuela and Roberto Stucchi Prinetti have taken over the running of the estate while Maurizio Castelli continues to act as consultant winemaker. They have ambitious plans for the cellar involving the construction of an impressive new facility and in the vineyards, where experiments are already under way. The only thing missing now is a range of really good wines. Those currently on offer are well made, indeed some are very well made, but they tend to lack the concentration and texture we would like to see. Of course '94 was not the best of years but Badia di Coltibuono is not just any old estate. The prestige and history of this property are such that we hope to be able to report a significant improvement over the next few years. Meanwhile the Sangioveto, the most representative of the Badia di Coltibuono wines, notched up another Two Glass rating for its extremely decent '94 vintage. This is typical of the'94" vintage, a year in which the sugars developed well but phenols are lacking because the skins of the grapes were too thin. As a result the reds from the vintage, especially those made with sangiovese, tend to lack intensity of colour and have ripe fruit aromas that mature disturbingly quickly. Nevertheless, this Sangioveto has satisfying texture and attractive complexity. The Chianti Classico Riserva '94 is similar but much more dilute and straightforward. In contrast the Chianti Classico '95 is instantly approachable and very easy to drink, but no one could accuse it of being complex.

The Ricasoli family is to Chianti Classico what Dom Pérignon is to Champagne, so it was a mortifying experience to witness the systematic destruction of the reputation of the Castello di Brolio that went on from around 1970 until 1993. Truth to tell, it was not really the fault of the Ricasoli. Their family cellar and label had been sold off, leading to an unending succession of problems including an almost terminal decline in the quality of the products. Then the young Barone Francesco Ricasoli stepped in and, taking on a prodigious load of debt, bought out the company name and marketing rights. Francesco brought in Filippo Mazzei, a young executive and wine producer from Fonterutoli and top flight winemaker Carlo Ferrini. The Brolio foursome was then completed by the arrival of Maurizio Ghiori, a marketing wizard and former marketing director of Duca di Salaparuta. The results have gone far beyond any of the four's wildest dreams, for the wines became world-beaters overnight and a great vintage like the '95 was enough to reveal the potential of an estate which is also the birthplace of modern Chianti Classico. This year the panel were able to acknowledge the Casalferro '95 as the best monovarietal Sangiovese of its vintage, without doubt a great red, of unparalleled elegance. The aromas of red fruit over delicate hints of oak lead into a palate whose harmony is underpinned by wonderfully velvety tannins. The Casalferro '94 is only a shade less concentrated and mature, while the Chianti Classico Riserva '94 is a soft, mouth-filling wine. The extremely attractive Formulae '95 scored high for its fragrant nose and very drinkable style. It is also very competitively priced.

● Sangioveto '94	♟♟	5
● Chianti Classico '95	♟	3
● Chianti Classico Ris. '94	♟	4
● Chianti Classico '90	♟♟	4
● Chianti Classico '93	♟♟	3*
● Chianti Classico Ris. '85	♟♟	4
● Chianti Classico Ris. '88	♟♟	4
● Chianti Classico Ris. '90	♟♟	4
● Sangioveto '85	♟♟	5
● Sangioveto '86	♟♟	5
● Sangioveto '88	♟♟	5
● Sangioveto '90	♟♟	5
● Chianti Classico '94	♟	3
● Chianti Classico Ris. '93	♟	4

● Casalferro '95	♟♟♟	5
● Casalferro '94	♟♟	5
● Chianti Classico Castello di Brolio Ris. '94	♟♟	4
● Formulae '95	♟♟	3*
● Casalferro '93	♟♟	5
● Chianti Classico Brolio '93	♟♟	3*
● Chianti Classico Castello di Brolio Ris. '88	♟♟	5
● Chianti Classico Castello di Brolio Ris. '90	♟♟	4
● Chianti Classico Castello di Brolio Ris. '93	♟♟	4
● Chianti Classico Brolio '94	♟	3
● Chianti Ricasoli '95	♟	2*

GAIOLE IN CHIANTI (SI)

GAIOLE IN CHIANTI (SI)

CASTELLO DI CACCHIANO
LOC. CACCHIANO
FRAZ. MONTI IN CHIANTI
53010 GAIOLE IN CHIANTI (SI)
TEL. 0577/747018

S. M. LAMOLE & VILLA VISTARENNI
LOC. VISTARENNI
53013 GAIOLE IN CHIANTI (SI)
TEL. 0577/738186

Waiting for the spectacular Riserva wines and '95 selections still to be released, and with vivid memories of the stupendous Chianti Classico Millennio Riserva '90 we approached this year's tasting of the wines of the Castello di Cacchiano owned by the Ricasoli Firidolfi family. All the signs are that this great estate is about to launch itself to the very top of the oenological pyramid in Chianti. The conditions for making great wine are almost perfect in this corner of the region, and if we add the experience of Giulio Gambelli, one of the founding fathers of Tuscan winemaking, then things really begin to hum. Baronessa Elisabetta Ricasoli is a capable woman who knows her own mind and concentrates her talents on directing the production of one of the best Vin Santo di Toscana that you will find anywhere. The '91 vintage that we sampled this time round confirmed our previous impressions. Elisabetta's son, Giovanni, on the other hand is responsible for the Chianti Classico range. The '95 is a wine of great concentration and power. There is a slight lack of complexity, but this was only to be expected since the wine on show was the basic selection and not a Riserva. And if this is what the ordinary Chianti Classico can do, then the Millennio Riserva '95 is going to be utterly sensational. The RF Castello di Cacchiano '93, a monovarietal sangiovese, was also a very fine wine, if still just a shade assertive and tannin-rich. But all it needs is cellar time and, like all Cacchiano wines, character is one thing the RF Castello has in abundance.

The two estates of Lamole di Lamole and Villa Vistarenni have been amalgamated into a single company owned by the Marzotto group and things are now shaping up well. The arrival of new manager Alessandro Alì, formerly of Rocca di Castagnoli, has produced notable changes while the style of the new company's wines, particularly those from the Lamole di Lamole estate, continues in the best Chianti tradition. These historic vineyards are located fairly high up and the wines tend to reflect this. In '94, results in many other parts of the Chianti were disappointing but not at Lamole di Lamole. Like other properties located at relatively high altitudes of 400 to 500 metres above sea level, Lamole di Lamole did not suffer from the unusually serious summer drought that year, and in fact the Chianti Classico Lamole di Lamole '94 is actually better than the '93, revealing much more roundness and balance. The Chianti Classico Villa Vistarenni '95 from the company's second property is another very interesting wine. A fashionably meaty Chianti Classico from a vineyard at Gaiole with very different growing conditions, the Villa Vistarenni '95 is invitingly drinkable and all in all something of a surprise from a cellar that seemed to have lost its way. The Riserva wines were excluded from our tastings because they were obtained from grape harvests that predate the current ownership.

● Chianti Classico '95	♀♀	3*
● RF Castello di Cacchiano '93	♀♀	4
○ Vin Santo '91	♀♀	5
● Chianti Classico Millennio Ris. '90	♀♀♀	5
● Chianti Classico '88	♀♀	3*
● Chianti Classico '90	♀♀	3*
● Chianti Classico '93	♀♀	3*
● Chianti Classico Millennio Ris. '88	♀♀	5
● RF Castello di Cacchiano '88	♀♀	5
● RF Castello di Cacchiano '90	♀♀	5
● Chianti Classico '94	♀	3

● Chianti Classico Villa Vistarenni '95	♀♀	4
● Chianti Classico Lamole di Lamole '94	♀	4
● Chianti Classico '93	♀	3
● Chianti Classico Lamole di Lamole '93	♀	4
● Chianti Classico Lamole di Lamole Ris. '88	♀	4
● Chianti Classico Ris. '91	♀	4
● Chianti Classico Vigneto di Campolungo Ris. '88	♀	4
● Codirosso '93	♀	4

GAIOLE IN CHIANTI (SI)

PODERE IL PALAZZINO
LOC. MONTI IN CHIANTI
53010 GAIOLE IN CHIANTI (SI)
TEL. 0577/747008

Alessandro Sderci's day job is in a bank but he devotes most of his energy and enthusiasm to making wine. Some time ago, he decided to buck the trend that in the late 1980s saw many of the great Tuscan reds leave the DOC or DOCG fold for the greater freedom of "vino da tavola" classification. This ploy enabled many producers - and their winemakers - to enjoy greater flexibility in the selection of grape varieties, vinification techniques and ageing periods. Il Palazzino's premium-label wine, Grosso Sanese, a sangiovese-based red table wine with a long history, took the opposite route by re-classifying as a DOCG Chianti Classico in the early 1990s. The move has reinforced the already high prestige of the famous Tuscan appellation. The '94 vintage of the Chianti Classico Riserva Grosso Sanese is a clear, intense ruby red offering a delicately nuanced nose in which vanilla mingles with more mature notes. The soft palate is attractively sustained by impeccable tannins and the finish is deliciously long. It is drinking superbly now.

GAIOLE IN CHIANTI (SI)

RIECINE
LOC. RIECINE
53013 GAIOLE IN CHIANTI (SI)
TEL. 0577/749098

John Dunkley, the owner of this small but delightful estate, is one of those people who make the world of wine so fascinating. Wise and well-educated as well as being a charismatic maker of wine, he has become the focal point for a group of younger producers who look to him for advice and inspiration. For a number of years now, working with John has been a young winemaker by the name of Sean O'Callaghan, perhaps the only Scot to ply a similar trade. The consultant is Carlo Ferrini, and together they have produced some exceptional wines over the past few years. The reds are made for the cellar and although they may be unforthcoming when young, they have masses of character. The Chianti Classico Riserva and the La Gioia from the '94 vintage were very good. Both are obtained only from sangiovese fruit but whereas the Riserva is aged for two years in large oak casks, the La Gioia matures exclusively in small barrels. There are more similarities than differences between the two wines even if the denser, more concentrated La Gioia is a little more intractable and tannin-rich. The Chianti Classico Riserva may in comparison appear slightly dilute but it is nevertheless one of the finest wines of the vintage in its class. Finally, there was more fruit on the nose of the Chianti Classico '95 as well as firm concentration on the palate but this is still a young wine. It will blossom in the next five or six years.

● Chianti Classico Grosso Sanese Ris. '94	♟♟	5
● Chianti Classico Grosso Sanese Ris. '93	♟♟	5
● Chianti Classico '93	♟	4

● Chianti Classico '95	♟♟	4
● Chianti Classico Ris. '94	♟♟	5
● La Gioia '94	♟♟	5
● Chianti Classico Ris. '86	♟♟♟	5
● Chianti Classico Ris. '88	♟♟♟	6
● Chianti Classico '93	♟♟	4
● Chianti Classico '94	♟♟	4
● Chianti Classico Ris. '87	♟♟	5
● Chianti Classico Ris. '90	♟♟	6
● Chianti Classico Ris. '91	♟♟	5
● Chianti Classico Ris. '93	♟♟	5
● La Gioia '88	♟♟	6
● La Gioia '90	♟♟	6
● La Gioia '91	♟♟	5
● La Gioia '93	♟♟	5

GAIOLE IN CHIANTI (SI)

GAIOLE IN CHIANTI (SI)

ROCCA DI MONTEGROSSI
LOC. MONTI IN CHIANTI
53010 GAIOLE IN CHIANTI (SI)
TEL. 0577/747267

SAN GIUSTO A RENTENNANO
LOC. MONTI IN CHIANTI
53010 GAIOLE IN CHIANTI (SI)
TEL. 0577/747121

Marco Ricasoli is a young nobleman and estate owner whose surname gives him a lot to live up to. It is some time now since he split his property from the family estate of Castello di Cacchiano, to which the Rocca di Montegrossi vineyards used to belong. The cellars under the castle are still shared, as are the services of the winemaker, Giulio Gambelli but the 12 hectares under vine at Rocca di Montegrossi now form a separate property, managed by Marco himself and by Raffaello Biagi. It is a splendid estate whose new plantings at a density of 5,000 vines per hectare produce sangiovese fruit of the very highest quality. The Chianti Classico Vigneto S. Marcellino '93 was a real surprise. Its intensely balsamic, complex aromas lead into a very concentrated palate where the tannins are still to the fore but are also backed up by a body of outstanding depth. The Chianti Classico '95 is one of those wines you fall in love at first sip, with great aromas of intense fruit that keep you coming back for more. The Geremia '93 however was less successful. This sangiovese-based red, dedicated to the founder of the Ricasoli Firidolfi family and builder of Rocca di Montegrossi castle in 1172, is rather linear with not enough body to support the tannins. It's hard to say whether it will improve with bottle age. But the Vin Santo was once again magnificent. The '91 vintage we tasted fully deserves its reputation as the Rocca di Montegrossi flag-bearer.

The wines of San Giusto a Rentennano bear eloquent testimony to the vigorous yet cantankerous personality of the sangiovese grape on the Siena side of the Chianti appellation. This is a "terroir" where the classic Tuscan varietal can express the most intimate depths of its difficult nature. The hill slopes, the sun and the lean soil that makes growing anything but vines a difficult affair all contribute to the conditions that bring out the best in sangiovese, if of course the vineyard manager makes sure that yields per plant are kept low. The sangiovese wines that the Martini family make at Cigala have the power of Brunello, for example, but instead of the supple softness of Montalcino they are austere and firmly structured. The Percarlo '93 is a fine example of the genre. There is great style and personality in the nose with its hints of mineral, tobacco and leather leading into a palate with massive structure that has still some way to go before it mellows fully: a Two Glass wine if ever there was one. The '94 vintage was unable to provide the Percarlo with its customary presence but the relative lack of fullness and complexity did not detract significantly from the overall assessment, thanks to the wine's excellent balance. The Chianti '94, displayed good structure and quite a classy nose reminiscent of violets, tobacco and cherry jam.

● Chianti Classico '95	♉♉	3*
● Chianti Classico Vigneto S. Marcellino '93	♉♉	4
○ Vin Santo '91	♉♉	5
● Geremia '93	♉	5
● Chianti Classico '93	♉♉	3*
○ Vin Santo '88	♉♉	5
● Chianti Classico '94	♉	4

● Percarlo '93	♉♉	5
● Percarlo '94	♉♉	5
● Chianti Classico '94	♉	4
● Percarlo '88	♉♉♉	5
● Chianti Classico '92	♉♉	3*
● Chianti Classico Ris. '88	♉♉	5
● Percarlo '85	♉♉	5
● Percarlo '87	♉♉	5
● Percarlo '90	♉♉	5
● Percarlo '91	♉♉	5
● Percarlo '92	♉♉	5
○ Vin Santo '90	♉♉	6
● Chianti Classico '93	♉	3

GAIOLE IN CHIANTI (SI)

CASTELLO DI SAN POLO IN ROSSO
LOC. S. POLO IN ROSSO
53013 GAIOLE IN CHIANTI (SI)
TEL. 0577/746045-746070

FATTORIA VALTELLINA
LOC. CASTAGNOLI
53013 GAIOLE IN CHIANTI (SI)
TEL. 0577/731005

About halfway along the road from Radda to Lecchi, not far from the mediaeval village of Ama, stands the Castello di San Polo in Rosso, one of the loveliest estates in the northern part of Gaiole. Owned by Katrin Woeste Canessa, it is run under the supervision of Maurizio Castelli, one of Italy's finest oenologists. The pair have always managed to come up with exciting wines that often hovered just below the Three Glass mark and this year's three products are no exception. We thought the best was the Cetinaia '94, a monovarietal Sangiovese, a soft, mouth-filling red whose nose is perhaps a little more mature than it should be but which has plenty of depth and attractive notes of ripe red fruit and vanilla. The palate is light on concentration but as drinkable as they come. The '93 vintage of the same wine is a more straightforward, linear wine with tannins that are not quite backed up by the rest of the structure. It's still a very good red but it tends towards leanness and there are one or two rough edges. The same could be said of the slightly more dilute Chianti Classico Riserva '93, which nevertheless is absolutely typical of the "terroir". To sum up, once again the Castello di San Polo in Rosso has produced an interesting range of wines that will, however, need a few more years in the cellar before they are at their best.

Convivio, a barrique-aged red from 75 percent sangiovese and 25 percent cabernet sauvignon, is by now a classic of the Chianti scene. Its distinguishing feature is concentration without over-assertive astringency, characteristics that can be found in full measure in the '94 vintage. Its aromas are very intense and nuanced with toasty oak and ripe Morello cherries. The palate has huge presence and the tannins have been almost entirely absorbed by a very slightly excessive softness that prevented our panel from being able to give a Three Glass award. But that in no way compromises the standing of what is swiftly becoming one of Chianti's leading producers. Praise for this state of affairs goes to the dynamic young owner, Christoph Schneider, who bought the Fattoria Valtellina from Giorgio Regni a few years ago. And it is thanks to the arrival of people like the very un-Tuscan-sounding Schneider that the entire area has been able to enjoy the injection of fresh capital and ideas on which the "Chianti Renaissance" has been founded. Christoph is flanked in his efforts by the extremely experienced Vittorio Fiore, a winemaker who has had a very big hand in making the Fattoria Valtellina wines what they are today.

● Cetinaia '93	♟♟	5
● Cetinaia '94	♟♟	5
● Chianti Classico Ris. '93	♟	4
● Cetinaia '85	♟♟	5
● Cetinaia '86	♟♟	5
● Cetinaia '88	♟♟	5
● Cetinaia '90	♟♟	6
● Chianti Classico '91	♟♟	4
● Chianti Classico Ris. '86	♟♟	4
● Chianti Classico Ris. '90	♟♟	5
● Chianti Classico Ris. '91	♟♟	5
● Chianti Classico '93	♟	3

● Convivio '94	♟♟	5
● Convivio '91	♟♟♟	5
● Chianti Classico '90	♟♟	4
● Chianti Classico '91	♟♟	4
● Chianti Classico '93	♟♟	4
● Chianti Classico Ris. '90	♟♟	5
● Chianti Classico Ris. '93	♟♟	4
● Convivio '90	♟♟	5
● Convivio '93	♟♟	5
● Chianti Classico '88	♟	4
● Chianti Classico '94	♟	3
● Convivio '88	♟	5

GAMBASSI TERME (FI)   GHIZZANO (PI)

VILLA PILLO
VIA VOLTERRANA, 26
50050 GAMBASSI TERME (FI)
TEL. 0571/680212

TENUTA DI GHIZZANO
VIA DELLA CHIESA, 1
56030 GHIZZANO (PI)
TEL. 050/20596 - 0587/630096

The sheer size of the Villa Pillo estate is impressive with its 650 hectares of olive groves, arable land, woods and of course vineyards. The range of products has been expanding gradually and today includes seven labels, from the traditional Vin Santo to more innovative styles with an international appeal. This year's tastings provided encouraging, if rather uneven, results. Our main worry concerns one of the Villa Pillo reds, the Borgoforte, blended from sangiovese, cabernet and syrah. The aromas of the '95 are reduced and the palate is hard and closed. But this blip takes nothing away from the estate's other wines, which are generally excellent. The vibrant ruby Merlot is a stunner that effortlessly earned Two Glasses for its intense aromas of ripe fruit and toasty oak, and a full flavoured, sweet palate that is slightly undefined but exceptionally supple. The Vivaldaia, (cabernet franc with12 percent merlot) is also very attractive. It has a ruby red hue, a clean, fresh nose with notes of wild berries and an agile well balanced palate. The Syrah is also good drinking. There are technical faults on the nose but the palate has concentration, maturity and good flavour. The Villa Pillo white, a well made Chardonnay with a vaguely medicinal nose, medium body and a faintly bitter finish, is also interesting if a little pricey. Finally, a mention for the Vin Santo '91, which offers intense notes of walnuts and almonds and a shade too much sugar on the palate.

In a region like Tuscany, where there are so many great wines, it is not easy for the less well known names to grab the attention of the world's winelovers. But certainly one of the zones that has been sending out strong signals about its commitment and potential is the area referred to generically as the Colline Pisane, a part of the province of Pisa with the typically rolling landscape of the Tuscan countryside. The Tenuta di Ghizzano was the first estate in the area to go onto the offensive. They have been through the period of uncertainty that all growing businesses experience but they they have regained their initial impetus thanks to the creation of a solid winemaking team. The Venerosa '94 is ample proof that the estate is in a new positive phase. The original sangiovese/cabernet blend has been progressively beefed up with merlot to achieve a formula that now looks very convincing. The bright, intense ruby hue introduces a nose of black and red berries with hints of oak-derived toastiness. The palate unfolds with sure-footed elegance, firm tannins and good overall balance. A unanimous Two Glasses. The Chianti also left an excellent impression on the panel, and not for the first time. If only all second-label wines were as fresh, fruity, well balanced and well built as this!

● Merlot '95	🍷🍷	5
● Vivaldaia '95	🍷🍷	6
○ Chardonnay '96	🍷	5
● Syrah '95	🍷	5
○ Vinsanto '91	🍷	6
● Borgoforte '95		4
● Borgoforte '94	🍷	3
○ Chardonnay '95	🍷	3

● Veneroso '94	🍷🍷	4
● Chianti '96	🍷	2*
● Veneroso '85	🍷🍷	5
● Veneroso '86	🍷🍷	5
● Veneroso '88	🍷🍷	5
● Veneroso '90	🍷🍷	5
● Veneroso '91	🍷🍷	4
● Veneroso '93	🍷🍷	4
● Chianti '90	🍷	2*
● Chianti '92	🍷	2*
● Chianti '93	🍷	2*
● Chianti '94	🍷	2
● Chianti '95	🍷	1*

GREVE IN CHIANTI (FI)

CARPINETO
LOC. DUDDA
50020 GREVE IN CHIANTI (FI)
TEL. 055/8549062

It has not been the best of years for Carpineto, at least in comparison with the results that we have become used to in recent years, although the estate's standing as one of Chianti's most significant producers remains unchallenged. To be honest it would have been a miracle if they had managed to repeat last year's exploits; we look forward to better things in the future with the release of the Farnito and Chianti Classico Riserva from the very good '95 vintage. We will also take another look at the Farnito '94, which was not quite ready for our tasters this year. So things are looking pretty good. Obviously the 1998 Guide ratings are a bit lower than Carpineto is used to but the quality is there, starting with the Riserva '94. Typically for the vintage, it is maturing quickly, as the tertiary aromas and dryish tannins reveal. However it is a cut above most of '94s in its category. The concentrated aromas are laced with Morello cherries, leather and vanilla, the palate has creditable texture and above all nice style and length. The Chianti Classico '95 is a well constructed, close-textured wine that is handicapped slightly by a bitterish note in the tannins. Finally the Dogaiolo, a fresh-tasting, alcohol-rich glass redolent of cherries, a touch green but bright, youthful and very easy to make friends with.

● Chianti Classico Ris. '94	▼▼	4
● Chianti Classico '95	▼	3
● Dogaiolo '96	▼	3
● Chianti Classico Ris. '85	▽▽	4
● Chianti Classico Ris. '88	▽▽	4
● Chianti Classico Ris. '91	▽▽	4
● Chianti Classico Ris. '93	▽▽	4
● Dogaiolo '95	▽▽	3*
● Farnito Cabernet Sauvignon '90	▽▽	5
● Farnito Cabernet Sauvignon '91	▽▽	5
● Farnito Cabernet Sauvignon '93	▽▽	5
● Farnito Cabernet Sauvignon '89	▽▽	5
● Chianti Classico '90	▽	2*
● Chianti Classico '91	▽	3*
● Chianti Classico '93	▽	3

GREVE IN CHIANTI (FI)

CASTEL RUGGERO
LOC. ANTELLA
50011 GREVE IN CHIANTI (FI)
TEL. 055/6819237

Castel Ruggero is one of the rising stars in the North-east part of Greve in Chianti. The cellar is almost on the northern boundary of the DOCG zone while the vineyards lie a short distance to the south, where the microclimate can be significantly different to the rest of Greve in Chianti. This has meant, for example, that a generally disappointing year like '94 produced excellent results at Castel Ruggero, as the Chianti Classico '94 amply demonstrates. A series of separate tastings established it in the panel's opinion as one of the finest and most concentrated Chianti Classico Riserva wines of '94. Much of the credit has to go to the owner of the cellar, Nicolò d'Afflitto, a renowned and superbly skilful professional who never forgets the basics of winemaking. But everyone knows that a great wine cannot be made solely in the cellar, especially in the case of reds, where the raw material is crucial. The sangiovese grapes that went into this bottle must have had time to ripen fully, accumulating pigments and phenols - otherwise there is no explanation for the deep colour and the rich, lingering aromas of ripe red berries, or indeed the substantial body, intense flavour and delicious softness that is the hallmark of excellent concentration.

● Chianti Classico '94	▼▼	4
● Chianti Classico '90	▽▽	4
● Chianti Classico '93	▽▽	3*
● Chianti Classico Ris. '90	▽▽	4
● Chianti Classico Ris. '93	▽▽	4
● Chianti Classico '88	▽	4
● Chianti Classico '91	▽	4
● Chianti Classico '92	▽	4

GREVE IN CHIANTI (FI)

LA MADONNINA - TRIACCA
VICOLO ABATE, 1
LOC. STRADA IN CHIANTI
50027 GREVE IN CHIANTI (FI)
TEL. 055/858003

Make a note of the name of this estate, because you will be hearing about it again in the future. Any property with 400 hectares - 40 of which are olive groves and 100 under vine - has serious resources, especially when they translate into top quality wine. The La Madonnina-Triacca product range is laudably uncomplicated. Despite the scale of the estate's output, there are only three lines; Chianti Classico, Chianti Classico Riserva and a non-DOC cabernet-based wine. (Just think for a moment how many estates need eight labels for 20,000 bottles a year). But whatever the production strategy, it is the wine that counts. The Riserva '94 was comfortably one of the best of the vintage. It has a dark ruby colour and elegant, fairly complex nose with notes of Morello cherry, flowers and tobacco. The flavour is full, nicely balanced and satisfyingly long. Tasting notes for the Chianti '95 were also excellent. The nose is still closed, showing that it has concentration and lively, pure fruit. Its soft texture develops attractively on the palate, where there is plenty of length as well. Our final notes regard the Mandorlo, a cabernet-based red with a small proportion of sangiovese, which was not up to the standards of the two DOCG heavyweights. It is a pleasant, unassuming wine that releases fruit and slightly vegetal aromas on the nose, leading into a fragrant, balanced palate.

●	Chianti Classico '95	🍷🍷	3
●	Chianti Classico Ris. '94	🍷🍷	4
●	Il Mandorlo '94	🍷	4
●	Chianti Classico '94	🍸🍸	3*
●	Chianti Classico '93	🍸	3
●	Chianti Classico Ris. '91	🍸	4
●	Chianti Classico Ris. '93	🍸	4
●	Il Mandorlo '91	🍸	4
●	Il Mandorlo '93	🍸	4
●	Vino Nobile di Montepulciano '93	🍸	4

GREVE IN CHIANTI (FI)

LA TORRACCIA DI PRESURA
VIA DELLA MONTAGNOLA, 130
LOC. STRADA IN CHIANTI
50022 GREVE IN CHIANTI (FI)
TEL. 055/490563-489997

It was a good overall picture that emerged from our tastings at La Torraccia di Presura. All the samples presented came out extremely creditably, even though there were no high fliers. The list of wines is long, but the best of the bunch was the Chianti '94, a rich garnet-red in the glass, denoting a certain maturity, with a satisfying nose of bramble, plums, vanilla and liquorice. The high scores for the attractively mouth-filling palate took this wine very close to a Two Glass rating. The Riserva '91 was an intriguing customer for the panel. The nose is perhaps not as clean as it could be but the generous breadth of the rich palate ensured a favourable impression overall. We had been looking forward to tasting the Lucciolaio, a sangiovese-and-cabernet blend that turned out to have lots of gutsy character but was short on finesse and balance. It is a wine whose heavyweight alcohol content wants to do everything, overpowering the aromas, which were no more than grace notes of fruit preserve, and then slugging it out with the tannins on the palate. However it is still young: we will look at it again when some of that maladjusted muscle has mellowed. The Chianti '95 is lovely to look at. Its bright, intense ruby red proffers attractive black berry aromas that are still a little closed and the palate has not struck a balance yet either, for the tannins need more time. Anomalous aromas knocked marks of the score for the Riserva '93 but the palate had unexpectedly close-knit texture, hinting that a sojourn in the cellar could prove very rewarding.

●	Chianti Classico Il Tarocco '95	🍷	3
●	Chianti Classico Il Tarocco Ris. '91	🍷	4
●	Chianti Classico Il Tarocco Ris. '93	🍷	4
●	Lucciolaio '94	🍷	5
●	Chianti Classico Il Tarocco '92	🍸	3
●	Chianti Classico Il Tarocco '93	🍸	3
●	Chianti Classico Il Tarocco '94	🍸	3
●	Chianti Classico Il Tarocco Ris. '90	🍸	4

GREVE IN CHIANTI (FI)

GREVE IN CHIANTI (FI)

TENUTA MONTECALVI
VIA CITILLE, 8
50022 GREVE IN CHIANTI (FI)
TEL. 055/8544665

FATTORIA DI NOZZOLE
VIA DI NOZZOLE, 12
LOC. PASSO DEI PECORAI
50022 GREVE IN CHIANTI (FI)
TEL. 055/858018

Tastings this year have shown a marked improvement in wines from the part of the Chianti Classico that lies in the province of Florence. Some impressive newcomers have joined the area's established stars and one of the new arrivals is the Tenuta Moritecalvi, a smallish estate that turns out wine with lots of personality. The owner, Renzo Bolli comes from the Molise region and his wife Bernadette is Irish. They arrived in this enchanted corner of Greve in Chianti in 1989, firmly determined to make a serious wine of their own. They have been able to do so thanks to the assistance of Stefano Chioccioli, a highly competent wine professional who immediately began by getting the sangiovese- based vineyard into shape. The joint efforts of the Tenuta Montecalvi team are concentrated on the production of 15,000 bottles a year of a near-monovarietal red under their only Montecalvi label. We tasted the last two vintage to be released, the '93 and the '94. The '94 has a lovely, vibrantly intense, garnet ruby shade that introduces a nose that has yet to open fully but which offers rich fruit backed up by toasty oak and mineral notes. The flavour is concentrated albeit only moderately deep, revealing plenty of sturdy, mellow tannins. The '93 vintage has equally rounded but less intense aromas on the nose, where mature earthy notes and leather come through. The palate is nicely balanced and well structured.

If anyone needed concrete proof of the sea change that the Folonari family's business strategy has undergone, then the Fattoria di Nozzole can provide it. Here Folonari, who also own Ruffino, have a superb villa as their headquarters and an already modern cellar that will soon be joined by a new facility that looks as if it was designed by an adventurous science-fiction writer. The vineyards, too, are splendid, some having been replanted at a much greater density per hectare. And the results are stunning. In the past we have awarded Three Glasses to the '88, '90 and '93 vintages of the Pareto, a magnificent Cabernet Sauvignon and we could also add that the Pareto has outperformed big names from Bordeaux and California at our blind tastings - the '93 gaining better marks than even Opus One and Château Lafite for example. The Pareto '94 is not quite up to the same stratospheric standard. The vintage simply was not a good one and while still a very good wine, the Pareto '94 appeared to to be maturing slightly too quickly. The aromas are intense but mature and although the palate is sumptuous it is also soft and lacks the gutsy muscle of the '93. But the Chianti Classico La Forra Riserva '94 on the other hand more than upholds the great Chianti Classico tradition at Nozzole. The complex nose may appear a little developed at first but the distinctive palate has good breadth with just a hint of bitterness lurking in the background. The Le Bruniche '96, a monovarietal chardonnay only a very small proportion of which is oak-matured, turned out to be another lovely wine. The Chianti Classico '95 really caught the panel's attention and it looks like being the first of an excellent series of bottles from the vintage. Remarkable body and serious muscle put it in the top ten wines of its class.

● Montecalvi '94	♟♟	4
● Montecalvi '93	♟	4

● Chianti Classico '95	♟♟	3*
● Chianti Classico La Forra Ris. '94	♟♟	4
● Il Pareto '94	♟♟	6
○ Le Bruniche '96	♟♟	3*
● Chianti Classico La Forra Ris. '90	♟♟♟	5
● Il Pareto '88	♟♟♟	6
● Il Pareto '90	♟♟♟	5
● Il Pareto '93	♟♟♟	6
● Chianti Classico La Forra Ris. '88	♟♟	4
● Chianti Classico La Forra Ris. '93	♟♟	5
● Il Pareto '89	♟♟	6
○ Le Bruniche '95	♟	3

363

GREVE IN CHIANTI (FI)

PODERE POGGIO SCALETTE
LOC. RUFFOLI
50022 GREVE IN CHIANTI (FI)
TEL. 055/8549017

GREVE IN CHIANTI (FI)

CASTELLO DI QUERCETO
LOC. DUDDA
50020 GREVE IN CHIANTI (FI)
TEL. 055/8549064

If a wizard of Tuscan oenology and Chianti specialist like Vittorio Fiore has decided to make wine at Ruffoli, there has to be a good reason. Ruffoli is located near Mamole and behind Vignamaggio. It is not too high up so it avoids drought and not too low so frost is not a major problem either. The soil is some of the finest "galestro" marl that you could hope to find and the sangiovese vine is the undisputed lord of the manor, even in poorish years like '94. In fact the Carbonaione '94 can stand comparison with its predecessors even though it lacks the balance and concentration of the '93. The aromas are as intense and concentrated as ever but a little more mature and the tannins in the palate are literally smothered in a delicious softness that however probably means this is a wine to enjoy sooner rather than later. It is still a very good wine and absolutely typical of its vintage but will probably pale in comparison with the '95, which tasters who have been lucky enough to sample from the barrel have been enthusiastic about.

In September 1997, the François family proudly celebrated 100 years as owners of the Castello di Querceto. Theirs was the satisfaction of having exercised the stewardship of an important fragment of the history of Chianti with the passionate devotion that only a true winemaking family can feel. That dedication has ensured that the results at Castello di Querceto have always been good, and often excellent. This year's tastings went very well, even if the best of the wines was the one that in theory ought to have scored lowest: the basic Chianti Classico. The Cignale, a blend of cabernet sauvignon with a small percentage of merlot, had plenty of breadth on the palate and good overall balance but was rather too grassy on the nose. The Sangiovese La Corte had the classic garnet hue in the glass and aromas of leather and tobacco of evident bottle-ageing. The palate has style but lacks fruit and the tannins in the finish are slightly astringent. But the Chianti '94 was a very welcome surprise whose rich depth was evident to eye, nose and palate. The intense ruby colour leads into distinct notes of Morello cherry and violets, a close-textured mouth-filling palate and solid tannins in the finish.

● Il Carbonaione '94	♟♟	5
● Il Carbonaione '92	♟♟	5
● Il Carbonaione '93	♟♟	5

● Chianti Classico '94	♟♟	3
● Cignale '93	♟	5
● La Corte '93	♟	5
● Chianti Classico Il Picchio Ris. '88	♟♟	4
● Chianti Classico Il Picchio Ris. '90	♟♟	4
● Chianti Classico Ris. '90	♟♟	4
● Cignale '88	♟♟	5
● Cignale '89	♟♟	5
● Cignale '90	♟♟	5
● La Corte '88	♟♟	5
● La Corte '90	♟♟	5
● Querciolaia '88	♟♟	5
● Querciolaia '90	♟♟	5

GREVE IN CHIANTI (FI)

AGRICOLA QUERCIABELLA
VIA S. LUCIA A BARBIANO, 17
LOC. RUFFOLI
50022 GREVE IN CHIANTI (FI)
TEL. 055/853834-853307

The world of wine is full of individuals who have made their fortunes in other walks of life and then decided to go and settle - or perhaps live for a few months a year - in the country. On occasion, they apply the managerial skills which have brought them success in their field to the making of wine. One such highly successful entrepreneur is Giuseppe Castiglioni, known as "Pepito" to his friends, a man who keeps one eye on the bottom line while remaining very much aware that it takes experience and skill to make wine. The result is one of the most professionally run estates in Italy, but Castiglioni's business acumen has also been rewarded by the superb wines that come out of his cellar, for as well as being based in a lovely villa set in unbelievably beautiful countryside, the Fattoria Querciabella is a first-rank producer. Indeed the Chianti Classico '95, in the panel's opinion, is the finest of its vintage. The delicious nose of Parma Violets and Morello cherry is followed by a palate of such structure and concentration that it makes many Riserva-label wines look feeble by comparison. The man behind this miracle is winemaker Guido De Santi, under the benevolent supervision of Giacomo Tachis. In contrast the tannins of the Camartina '93 seemed to us to be over-austere, although the wine itself gained a good overall score. As always, the '95 vintage of the monovarietal Batàr Chardonnay was a complete success. Its vanilla notes are nicely understated and it has exceptional body.

GREVE IN CHIANTI (FI)

RISECCOLI
VIA CONVERTOIE, 9
50022 GREVE IN CHIANTI (FI)
TEL. 055/853598

Riseccoli is another of the Guide's new entries and if our tasting notes are anything to go by, the name is likely to feature regularly in the future. The Riseccoli estate has belonged to the Romanelli family for almost a century and includes about 12 hectares under vine scattered in the area between Greve and the Castello di Querceto. "Galestro" soils and the south-west facing vineyards are the two crucial environmental factors in the Riseccoli estate's success. The appointment of the experienced winemaker Giorgio Marone as consultant has also contributed to the reliable quality of the bottles that Ilaria Romanelli produces. It was the Saeculum that stood out at our tastings. This garnet red sangiovese and cabernet sauvignon blend has a well defined nose in which stylish flowery notes mingle with sweet hints of vanilla. The structure on the palate is solid, the density excellent and the tannins remarkably close-textured. The Riserva '94 is a moderately close-knit wine with good balance and its fair share of elegance. The aromas that emerge on the nose are Morello cherry and leather as well as vegetal notes and nuances of vanilla. In contrast, our tasters were expecting better things of the Chianti '95, which turned out to be over-mature and a bit of a lightweight. But two out of three is not a bad score, especially considering that Riseccoli is a newcomer to the Guide.

● Chianti Classico '95	♟♟♟	4
○ Batàr '95	♟♟	5
● Camartina '93	♟♟	5
● Camartina '88	♟♟♟	5
● Camartina '90	♟♟♟	5
○ Batàr '94	♟♟	5
○ Batard '92	♟♟	5
○ Batard '93	♟♟	5
● Camartina '87	♟♟	5
● Camartina '91	♟♟	5
● Chianti Classico '90	♟♟	4
● Chianti Classico '91	♟♟	4
● Chianti Classico Ris. '90	♟♟	5
● Chianti Classico Ris. '91	♟♟	4
● Chianti Classico Ris. '93	♟♟	4

● Saeculum '94	♟♟	5
● Chianti Classico '95	♟	3
● Chianti Classico Ris. '94	♟	4

GREVE IN CHIANTI (FI)

GREVE IN CHIANTI (FI)

CASTELLO DI VERRAZZANO
LOC. VERRAZZANO
50022 GREVE IN CHIANTI (FI)
TEL. 055/854243

CASTELLO DI VICCHIOMAGGIO
VIA VICCHIOMAGGIO, 4
50022 GREVE IN CHIANTI (FI)
TEL. 055/854079

It's been a less than wonderful year for Castello di Verrazzano as far as Guide assessments go, but only because the great wines, especially Sassello, either were not released or were not available in seriously good vintages. The point has to be made, since Luigi Cappellini's estate is one to keep an eye on and this young grower-producer is certain to make a stir with the '95, '96 and '97 wines from the Castello di Verrazzano. We are now beginning to see the fruits of the modern management techniques and long-term business plans that Cappellini and his winemaker, Marco Chellini, have adopted. The two wines they presented this year were thoroughly respectable, without setting any records. The Chianti Classico Riserva '94 was a little too unsophisticated on the nose, with rather uninteresting fruit, and suffered from a certain lack of depth on the palate. The Chianti Classico '95 is probably a better bottle, albeit from another category. Its fruit has good intensity and the palate is clean and pleasant, offering moderate concentration. Both are very well made wines but lack personality and they do not offer all that much to get your teeth into.

The Castello di Vicchiomaggio could not honestly be mistaken for a French Château: this is no genteel country house but a real castle with turrets and battlements, that you can also visit if you want to, and it is well worth it, because the wines are excellent. It was the Ripa delle More that stood out this year, a brilliant Sangiovese with superb overall balance. These are the tasting notes: intense ruby red in the glass shading into garnet at the rim; elegant fragrances of leather, liquorice and tobacco with exquisitely judged oak; and lovely full breadth of flavour with stunning depth and balance. This was a heart-stoppingly good red that cruised past the Three Glass score with points to spare. As luck would have it, the two Vicchiomaggio Riserva wines ended up next to each other at our tasting, thus underlining the interesting differences between the two wines. Both were good, but this time round we preferred the Riserva La Prima to the Petri. Their aromas are similar but in the Chianti La Prima the bramble and Morello cherry fruit emerges over the toasty oak that dominates the Petri. In the mouth, this difference comes out more clearly for there is a huge difference in the richness of texture: the La Prima has a softer, denser and much longer palate that easily earned it Two Glasses. The S. Jacopo was also a reasonably good wine, uncomplicated and fruity on the nose but a little uncertain on the palate. Finally the marks awarded to the Ripa delle Mandorle fell below the average for this year's Castello di Vicchiomaggio wines.

● Chianti Classico '95	▼	3
● Chianti Classico Ris. '94	▼	4
● Chianti Classico Ris. '90	▼▼▼	5
● Bottiglia Particolare '90	▼▼	5
● Chianti Classico '91	▼▼	3*
● Chianti Classico '94	▼▼	3*
● Chianti Classico Cinquecentenario Ris. '85	▼▼	5
● Chianti Classico Ris. '88	▼▼	4
● Sassello '90	▼▼	5
● Sassello '93	▼▼	5
● Bottiglia Particolare '88	▼	5
● Chianti Classico '93	▼	3
● Chianti Classico Ris. '91	▼	4
● Chianti Classico Ris. '93	▼	4

● Ripa delle More '94	▼▼▼	5
● Chianti Classico La Prima Ris. '94	▼▼	5
● Chianti Classico Petri Ris. '94	▼	4
● Chianti Classico San Jacopo '95	▼	3
● Ripa delle Mandorle '95		4
● Chianti Classico La Prima Ris. '86	▼▼	5
● Chianti Classico La Prima Ris. '88	▼▼	5
● Chianti Classico La Prima Ris. '90	▼▼	5
● Chianti Classico La Prima Ris. '93	▼▼	5
● Chianti Classico Petri Ris. '86	▼▼	5
● Chianti Classico Petri Ris. '90	▼▼	5
● Ripa delle More '90	▼▼	5
● Chianti Classico La Prima Ris. '91	▼	4
● Chianti Classico Petri Ris. '91	▼	5
● Ripa delle More '91	▼	5

GREVE IN CHIANTI (FI)

FATTORIA DI VIGNAMAGGIO
VIA DI PETRIOLO
50022 GREVE IN CHIANTI (FI)
TEL. 055/853007-853559

GREVE IN CHIANTI (FI)

VILLA CALCINAIA
VIA CITILLE, 84
50022 GREVE IN CHIANTI (FI)
TEL. 055/854008

An estate as large as the Fattoria di Vignamaggio always leads you to expect something special, and also to hope for that elusive, exceptional bottle which the potential of the property promises. This year we were able to note a reassuring compactness of quality in the range presented. The flag-bearer wines like the Gherardino were missing this year, but we hope to renew the acquaintance next year when the highly promising '95 is released. The Monna Lisa also has all the makings of a very fine wine, if the bottle we sampled this year is anything to go by. The intense ruby colour shades into garnet at the rim, the aromas have depth but perhaps not optimum balance for super-ripe notes prevail, alternating with hints of preserves and fresh red fruit. The palate is much denser, fuller and more mouth-filling. It was a courageous but debatable move to make a monovarietal Cabernet Franc in the Chianti. There is no question about the quality of the Vignamaggio '93, and it had no difficulty in earning Two Glasses thanks to its solid structure and dense, vigorous, concentrated palate. Yet while the nose also has depth and distinction, vegetal notes predominate with nuances of green pepper, grass and tomato leaves. The Chianti Classico '95 wines were also hovering around the Two Glass mark. The basic Chianti has all the hallmarks of the Monna Lisa, including the fruit nuances and hints of super-ripeness, whereas the Terre di Prenzano is closed on the nose at first. Here, too, there are super-ripe notes but they are amply offset by a rich, delicious palate.

It was a great pleasure for our panel to be able to re-admit Villa Calcinaia to the guide after a few years of rather unmemorable tastings, because this is one of the oldest and most traditional of the wineries in Greve. It has belonged to the noble Capponi family since 1524 but it should also be added that the Capponi themselves have been making wine since1435. It would have been a great disappointment if the current owner, Conte Sebastiano Capponi, had not managed to maintain the family's ancient and highly prestigious heritage. Fortunately events have shown that he has taken up the challenge and his Chianti Classico Riserva '93 easily won Two Glasses. It has intense, stylish aromas from which emerge notes of red fruit, vanilla and toasty oak, that indicate the arrival of new barriques in the cellar at Villa Calcinaia. The complex nose is complemented by a rich, structured palate that has elegance as well as muscle. All in all a lovely wine that delighted the panel. The Chianti Classico '95 was good but not exceptional, but also absolutely in line with our tasters' expectations. The nose offers notes of raspberry and bilberry and the palate is both interesting and enormously drinkable, which is precisely what you hope for from a good non-Riserva Chianti Classico. So Villa Calcinaia has made a creditable comeback. We look forward to even better things in the future.

● Chianti Classico Monna Lisa Ris. '94	♇♇	4
● Vignamaggio '93	♇♇	5
● Chianti Classico '95	♇	3
● Chianti Classico Terre di Prenzano '95	♇	4
● Chianti Classico Monna Lisa Ris. '88	♈♈	5
● Chianti Classico Monna Lisa Ris. '90	♈♈	4*
● Chianti Classico Monna Lisa Ris. '93	♈♈	4
● Gherardino '88	♈♈	5
● Gherardino '90	♈♈	5
● Gherardino '93	♈♈	5

● Chianti Classico Ris. '93	♇♇	4
● Chianti Classico '95	♇	3*
● Chianti Classico Ris. '90	♈♈	4*
● Chianti Classico Ris. '91	♈	4

GREVE IN CHIANTI (FI)

VITICCIO
VIA SAN CRESCI, 12/A
50022 GREVE IN CHIANTI (FI)
TEL. 055/854210

IMPRUNETA (FI)

PODERE LANCIOLA II
VIA IMPRUNETANA, 210
50023 IMPRUNETA (FI)
TEL. 055/208324-352011

For a number of years, the Fattoria Viticcio has been confirming its position as one of Greve's most interesting producers by releasing substantial quantities of wine while maintaining very good standards of quality. And on the subject of confirmation, it was the Monile which once again most impressed our tasters as the best wine in the Fattoria Viticcio range. Monile risks being better known for its unique - and now notorious - addition of a small proportion of nebbiolo to the cabernet-based cépage rather than for its excellence. The '94 may not be quite up to the standards of the superb '93 vintage but it is nonetheless a very attractive proposition. The rich ruby leads into an intense nose of vanilla, capsicum and ripe plums. The palate is soft, close-knit and admirably long, with vanilla after-aromas in the finish. Our tasting of the Chianti '95 was equally promising. The ruby hue is intense and there are deliciously mature aromas on the nose with notes of cherry preserve. The firmly assertive palate has lots of sinew and a good long finish in which the lovely tannins come through well. The sangiovese-based Prunaio scored 80 points thanks to a firm, long palate that dispelled any doubts the nose may have created with its marked notes of vanilla and coconut. Finally the Riserva '94 was a bit of a letdown - but you cannot win them all.

Podere Lanciola II is a producer with a very attractive headquarters and a huge range of wines to offer. In fact there are 12 labels altogether, from the Chianti Colli Fiorentini and Chianti Classico to "vins noveaux" and from easy drinking summer whites to a charmat-method spumante. The panel sampled the estate's most representative wines this year and found a good general level of quality that could, however, definitely be improved, especially if we bear in mind the in-house technical skills available both in the vineyard and in cellars where cold-maceration and barrique-ageing are long-established procedures. It was the reds that got the more flattering tasting notes. The Chianti Classico Le Masse di Greve Riserva '94 has a garnet-rimmed ruby hue and slightly vegetal nose of black berries and spices. It is fairly soft and close-knit on the palate but still greenish in the finish. The flag-bearer of the range is a blend of sangiovese grosso, cabernet sauvignon and cabernet franc called Terricci. The '94 vintage has style that is loftily austere rather than approachable. A very solemn red with vaguely medicinal aromas, it is unforthcoming on the nose but opens up in the mouth with a softer, but still weightier presence than one might have expected. Bitter notes return in the finish, though. The Chianti Colli Fiorentini Riserva '94 has great extract but the palate is out of synch with the nose, as well as being a little raw. To go on to the whites, the lightweight and nervy Chardonnay Terricci '94 failed to impress, but the Vin Santo '91 was decidedly better, offering a warm gold hue and lovely nuances of candied citrus peel, roasted hazelnut and vanilla on the nose. It is less rounded on the palate, and finishes with a slightly metallic note.

●	Chianti Classico '95	🍷🍷	4
●	Monile '94	🍷🍷	5
●	Prunaio '94	🍷🍷	5
●	Chianti Classico Ris. '94		4
●	Chianti Classico Ris. '90	🍷🍷	5
●	Chianti Classico Ris. '91	🍷🍷	4
●	Monile '91	🍷🍷	5
●	Monile '93	🍷🍷	5
●	Prunaio '90	🍷🍷	5
●	Prunaio '93	🍷🍷	5
●	Chianti Classico '93	🍷	3
●	Monile '90	🍷	5

●	Chianti Classico Le Masse di Greve Ris. '94	🍷	4
○	Terricci Vin Santo '91	🍷	5
●	Chianti Colli Fiorentini Ris. '94		3
●	Terricci '94		4
○	Terricci Chardonnay '96		4
○	Bianco della Lanciola '94	🍷	2*
●	Chianti Colli Fiorentini '94	🍷	2
●	Chianti Colli Fiorentini Ris. '93	🍷	3
●	Terricci '93	🍷	4
○	Terricci Chardonnay '95	🍷	4
○	Vin Santo '90	🍷	5

MAGLIANO IN TOSCANA (GR)　MANCIANO (GR)

LE PUPILLE
LOC. PERETA
58051 MAGLIANO IN TOSCANA (GR)
TEL. 0564/505129

LA STELLATA
VIA FORNACINA, 18
58014 MANCIANO (GR)
TEL. 0564/620190

The leaders in any field, those who write the agendas for change, may show the way forward with their own courageous decisions, or may on occasion be the enlightened executors of a mission begun by others. If the individual is a woman, then in a male-dominated society like ours people tend to be slightly surprised and clap a little louder. Here in the world of Maremma winemaking, the woman who embodies that ideal figure is Elisabetta Geppetti, a sort of Corinne Mentzelopoulos based at the Fattoria Le Pupille instead of Château Margaux. Getting it right and putting quality first are the two cornerstones of this young premium wine producer's business strategy, and quality is exactly what the panel found when they tasted this year's range. The '94 vintage of the classic Bordeaux blend Saffredi, a wine of depth and breeding, impressed with its concentration, rich, close-knit texture, silky tannins and noble character. Then the Morellino di Scansano Riserva '94 caught our attention with its lovely aromas of autumn leaves and tobacco as well as distinctly satisfying softness and length on the palate. And the rest of the line-up was just as good. There are two important pieces of news from the Fattoria Le Pupille. From this year the great Giacomo Tachis will no longer be Elisabetta's winemaker. His substitute, however, is Riccardo Cotarella, an oenologist who has earned a formidable reputation and is hardly likely to let standards slip. The other piece of news was the birth of Elisabetta's third child, Ettore, at the end of July. Goethe once said that to be young was to be drunk without wine but Elisabetta and her partner, Stefano, are perhaps thinking already of dedicating this year's vintage to Ettore, who will be three in the year 2000.

A Guide like this has to do more than just report the tasting sessions we have carried out during the year. All our contributors feel that there are other things to take into account in the selection of estates to include. Of course the quality of the wine is the deciding factor, but we also look at the role of producers in their local context. What they have accomplished over the years cannot in our opinion be ignored. It is for all the above reasons that we keep on writing about a number of very small producers who are nonetheless emblematic of a specific area or style. And that is certainly the case with La Stellata, the small estate owned and run by Manlio Giorni and Clara Divizia, without whose Lunaia for many years there would not have been a single premium white in the Pitigliano DOC zone. It was in '83 that the couple first demonstrated that the area could turn out serious wines from a blend of malvasia and trebbiano toscano. This delicious white has fruity aromas and a nice vein of acidity that brings to mind similar wines from Limoux in the Languedoc. The '96 vintage is even more drinkable than usual, perhaps to the detriment of the structure, but the panel still loved its light, uncomplicated nature and instantly accessible aromas. Bianco di Pitigliano Lunaia has a style you can rely on year after year.

● Morellino di Scansano Ris. '94	▼▼	4
● Saffredi '94	▼▼	5
● Morellino di Scansano '96	▼	2
○ Vin Santo di Caratello '91	▼	4
● Saffredi '90	▼▼▼	6
● Morellino di Scansano '95	▼▼	2
● Morellino di Scansano Ris. '89	▼▼	4
● Morellino di Scansano Ris. '90	▼▼	4
● Morellino di Scansano Ris. '91	▼▼	3
● Saffredi '87	▼▼	5
● Saffredi '88	▼▼	5
● Saffredi '89	▼▼	5
● Saffredi '91	▼▼	5
● Saffredi '93	▼▼	5
○ Vin Santo di Caratello '90	▼▼	4

○ Bianco di Pitigliano Lunaia '96	▼	3
○ Bianco di Pitigliano Lunaia '95	▼	2
● Lunaia Rosso '93	▼	2

MASSA MARITTIMA (GR)

MASSA VECCHIA
PODERE FORNACE
LOC. ROCCHE, 11
58024 MASSA MARITTIMA (GR)
TEL. 0566/915522

MASSA MARITTIMA (GR)

MORIS FARMS
LOC. CURANOVA
58020 MASSA MARITTIMA (GR)
TEL. 0566/919135

If and when the bookmaking giants from Britain invade the Italian market, then put a few lire on a boom in the Maremma. A winemaking boom, that is. Some of the biggest names in country's wine industry are investing heavily in the region and if the major league players are moving in, it is a fair indication that the profile of this corner of the region is about to rise. We had already noted a certain buzz of activity in the area but this year the excellent results achieved in tastings proved that something is going on. It is no longer fair to say that in Tuscany great wine is only made in Chianti or the area around Bolgheri. Investigate for yourselves. Those of our readers who have been following the Guide's Maremma notes carefully will have already noticed that we are fans of Massa Vecchia. We did not discover it very long ago but it earned its own Guide profile thanks especially to La Fonte di Pietrarsa, a cabernet sauvignon-based wine that is on our list of aspiring Supertuscans and earns its Two Glasses without fail each year. We sampled the '94 this time round. In the glass it is a bright, vibrant ruby tinged with faint garnet highlights. The nose is fleshy and redolent of blackcurrant and bramble but there are also notes of rosemary, moss and coffee underpinned by attractive oak. The attack on the palate is soft and very classy, with good weight and balance although the wood is still a little over-assertive. The '94 La Fonte di Pietrarsa is a lovely Cabernet just like the '93, which we took the opportunity to taste again. Sincere congratulations to Fabrizio and Patrizia Niccolaini, who do everything themselves. And do it well.

When we wrote about Moris Farms in the previous edition of the Guide, we mentioned the cypresses that stand guard around the 500 hectares belonging to one of the largest and most significant wine estates in the Maremma. Those trees have grown in the meantime but they also seem to acquired more authority, for their stature is symbolic of the increasing importance of Moris Farms on the Italian winemaking scene. The products we tasted this year were a convincing answer to the constructive criticism the panel put forward last time round. Hats off to the Morellino Riserva '94, which came within an ace of a Three Glass rating thanks to its deep, intense hue and the rich breadth of its aromas, where there were notes of bramble and fig jam. The palate was generous, powerful and concentrated, with soft tannins and excellent length and the follow-through from nose to palate speaks volumes about its pedigree. The Avvoltore '94 was another outstanding wine, offering plenty of depth in a nose of plums, printer's ink, cocoa and blackcurrant. There are vigorous tannins on the palate, where vegetal and leathery notes emerge, and the faintly bitterish finish has good length. Finally the Morellino '95 is a sound bottle revealing fruit and mint on the nose. It is eminently drinkable despite its marked acidity; congratulations all round to Adolfo Parentini and his skilful consultant winemaker, Attilio Pagli.

● La Fonte di Pietrarsa '94	♟♟	4
● La Fonte di Pietrarsa '92	♟♟	4
● La Fonte di Pietrarsa '93	♟♟	4
● Terziere '93	♟♟	4
● Le Veglie di Neri '90	♟	4

● Avvoltore '94	♟♟	5
● Morellino di Scansano Ris. '94	♟♟	4
● Morellino di Scansano '95	♟	2
● Avvoltore '93	♟	4
● Morellino di Scansano '94	♟	2
● Morellino di Scansano Ris. '93	♟	4

MERCATALE VALDARNO (AR)

FATTORIA PETROLO
LOC. GALATRONA
52020 MERCATALE VALDARNO (AR)
TEL. 055/9911322-992965

The Fattoria Petrolo is everybody's idea of a
vineyard in Tuscany. Its hill slopes are
covered mainly in galestro marl and lie at an
average of 300 metres above sea level. The
historic core of the property dates back to
Roman times and in the best Chianti
tradition, the main buildings are laid out to a
plan drawn up in the Middles Ages. The
production of wine and olive oil has been
going on here for hundreds of years. The
property is run by Lucia Sanjust, who is
helped by her son Luca and a young
agronomist, Claudio Palchetti. With the able
assistance of noted winemaker Giulio
Gambelli, Lucia has embarked on a
programme of ongoing improvement in
vineyard and cellar. The non-Riserva Chianti
from the Colli Aretini DOC zone is an
invitingly well made product while its Riserva
companion has more structure and weight
on the palate, together with more tannin, as
you would expect. But the most exciting
Petrolo products the panel tasted were two
red table wines, the Torrione and the
Galatrona. The Torrione is a monovarietal
Sangiovese whose '94 vintage has
impressive power and vigour. It has vibrant
colour and sensuously fruity, alcohol-rich
aromas that still have to open fully. On the
palate, massive structure mingles with
mature, earthy tannins. The merlot-based
Galatrona is similar in style to the Torrione,
but less triumphantly successful. The
powerful nose is a little closed and the
palate is dominated by tannins.
Nevertheless it is a solidly made wine that
will improve in the cellar as time mellows the
phenol content. The third and last Petrolo
wine that impressed the panel was the Vin
Santo '93, a classy number with a nut and
leather fragrance leading into a balanced
flavour that does not overdo the sweetness.

MONTAGNANA VAL DI PESA (FI)

LE CALVANE
50020 MONTAGNANA
VAL DI PESA (FI)
TEL. 0571/671073

The Le Calvane property extends over 26
hectares of farmland, 15 of which are under
vine. The clay and limestone soil supports
traditional vine varieties for the production of
Chianti and non-native types for wines made
in more contemporary styles. These include
chardonnay, sauvignon blanc, cabernet
sauvignon and traminer. The cellars have all
the most up-to-date equipment and the
technology available to control must
temperatures in particular strikes the visitor's
eye. La Calvane makes a wide range of
wines. There is a typical Chianti Colli
Fiorentini called Il Quercione, which has a
robust, full flavoured and very tannic style,
and an attractive Vin Santo Zipolo d'Oro.
This year we liked the unassuming but fresh-
tasting Collecimoli, whose '95 vintage is
evocatively aromatic. Then there was a
sangiovese and colorino-blend base red,
the Trecione, that scored well in the '94
vintage for texture and lively structure, even
though slightly aggressive tannins tended to
bring out the bucolic side of its nature. The
best wine was definitely the Borro del
Boscone '94, to which the panel had no
difficulty in awarding Two Glasses. A blend
of cabernet sauvignon and cabernet franc, it
is a limited production oak-matured red, only
3,500 bottles of which are available in the
vintage we sampled. The vibrant ruby red
has great depth and the aromas of ripe fruit
are also intense, albeit not yet fully open.
The flavour is mouth-filling and almost
meaty. It's a highly successful wine that you
will be able to leave in the cellar for a good
few years.

● Torrione '94	♟♟	5
○ Vinsanto '93	♟♟	5
● Galatrona '94	♟	6
● Chianti Titolato Ris. '90	♟♟	4
● Torrione '90	♟♟	5
● Chianti Ris. '91	♟	3
● Torrione '91	♟	4
● Torrione '93	♟	5

● Borro del Boscone '94	♟♟	4
○ Collecimoli '95	♟	3
● Trecione '94	♟	4
● Borro del Boscone '93	♟	4
● Chianti Colli Fiorentini Il Trecione '93	♟	3
● Chianti Colli Fiorentini Quercione '95	♟	2
● Trecione '92	♟	3

MONTALCINO (SI)

TENUTA DI ARGIANO
LOC. S. ANGELO IN COLLE, 54
53020 MONTALCINO (SI)
TEL. 0577/864037

The Tenuta di Argiano is one of the loveliest estates in the Montalcino area. The 20 hectares of brunello vineyards are as trim as an English garden, the cellar is modern and the consultant winemaker goes under the name of Giacomo Tachis. In addition for the last couple of years, Sebastiano Rosa, one of Italian oenology's young rising talents, has been designing the company's products. This year's offerings from the Tenuta di Argiano put up a very creditable show overall, particularly bearing in mind that '91 and '92 were anything but exceptional vintages in Montalcino. But our tastings of both the Riserva and the non-Riserva Brunello '92 revealed some pleasant surprises. Both are right at the top of their respective categories and are outstandingly well made. The Rosso di Montalcino '95 turned out to be a very sound wine, although the panel suspected that the best fruit from the harvest went into the Brunello, as is only right. Finally the Solengo '95, the new Argiano wine which is being released for the first time, is a truly awe-inspiring product that walked away with Three Glasses. Were the panel hasty? Might it have been better to wait a few years? We invite readers to try this wine and judge for themselves because we thought it was stupendously good. It is obtained from a blend of four varieties, cabernet sauvignon, merlot, sangiovese and syrah, in equal proportions. The ruby hue is unfathomably deep and introduces intense aromas nuanced with spice and vanilla that usher in supremely stylish notes of wild berries. The palate is full-bodied and stunningly potent. The high phenolic content is still very much in evidence, but there is no hint of aggression thanks to the moderating effect of mellow, blue-blooded tannins. Assigning the top award was our pleasure as well as our duty.

MONTALCINO (SI)

CASTELLO BANFI
CASTELLO DI POGGIO ALLE MURA
53024 MONTALCINO (SI)
TEL. 0577/840111

Ezio Rivella is one of the key figures in the world of Italian wine. Oenologist and managing director of Banfi, he is also President of the national DOC committee and is former chair of the Associazione Enotecnici Italiani and the Union International des Oenologues. But above all he is a charismatic leader and high-powered international business executive. Banfi is owned by the Mariani family, highly successful Italo-American wine entrepreneurs, but the estate is Rivella's creature. Its fame and success everywhere - and the nine Banfi wines that were awarded prizes at last year's Banco d'Assaggio in Torgiano are ample proof, if any were needed - bear cogent witness to Rivella's talents. A vast amount of water has flowed under the bridge since the early days when people at Montalcino still looked askance at the newly arrived "Americans". Today, all the wines released by the Banfi estate are beautifully made, whether they are premium products, middle of the range, or cheap and cheerful. Even in a poor vintage like '92, the Banfi Brunello was the best around and one of the few that offered genuine value for money. But the most interesting bottle this year is a minor masterpiece called Excelsus '93, which proves beyond doubt that Rivella is better at making wine than thinking up names for them. It's a classic Bordeaux blend red that has elegance written all over it. It's even better than the Summus '94, obtained from sangiovese, cabernet sauvignon and syrah fruit, which is an excellent red in its own right but lacks the sheer breeding that the Excelsus so effortlessly exudes. The remainder of the Castello Banfi range is about par for the course, although for the first time the merlot-based Mandrielle '94 outscored the Cabernet Sauvignon Tavernelle '94 in our tastings.

● Solengo '95	▼▼▼	6
● Brunello di Montalcino '92	▼▼	6
● Brunello di Montalcino Ris. '91	▼▼	6
● Rosso di Montalcino '95	▼	4
● Brunello di Montalcino Ris. '85	♀♀♀	5
● Brunello di Montalcino Ris. '88	♀♀♀	6
● Brunello di Montalcino '85	♀♀	5
● Brunello di Montalcino '87	♀♀	5
● Brunello di Montalcino '88	♀♀	5
● Brunello di Montalcino '90	♀♀	5
● Brunello di Montalcino '91	♀♀	5
● Brunello di Montalcino Ris. '90	♀♀	6
● Rosso di Montalcino '94	♀	3

● Excelsus '93	▼▼▼	6
● Brunello di Montalcino '94	▼▼	5
● Summus '94	▼▼	6
● Mandrielle Merlot '94	▼	4
● Rosso di Montalcino '95	▼	3*
● S. Antimo Centine '96	▼	3
● Tavernelle Cabernet '94	▼	5
● Brunello di Montalcino Poggio all'Oro '88	♀♀♀	6
● Brunello di Montalcino Poggio all'Oro Ris. '90	♀♀♀	6
● Brunello di Montalcino '90	♀♀	5
● Mandrielle Merlot '93	♀♀	4*
● Summus '90	♀♀	6
● Summus '93	♀♀	6

MONTALCINO (SI)

FATTORIA DEI BARBI E DEL CASATO
LOC. PODERNOVI
53024 MONTALCINO (SI)
TEL. 0577/848277

The Fattoria dei Barbi is one of Montalcino's most historic cellars, and also an estate that sets great store by its prestigious image and the distinctive style of its wine, neither of which owe anything to the passing fashions of the moment. The Colombini family maintain a close relationship with the land, and in the best tradition of Tuscan "fattorie" they do not restrict their activities to wine production, but are also justly famous for the salamis and cheeses that have been made here for hundreds of years. But of course since we are talking about Brunello, wine is of anything but secondary importance. The last two vintages of the Vigna del Fiore, the estate's top vineyard selection, have proved that this much envied "cru" really is a bit special. While the success of the '90 Vigna del Fiore could be ascribed to the wonderful vintage, this is not the case of the wine made in the following year, when conditions were much less favourable. But the outstanding quality of the vineyard produced a surprisingly good wine in that vintage, too. Obviously, the '91 does not have the superb structure of the great vintage that preceded it, but it maintains intact the subtle line that runs through all the wines obtained from this noble "terroir", offering breeding, elegance and glorious balance.

● Brunello di Montalcino Vigna del Fiore Ris. '91	▼▼	6
● Brunello di Montalcino Ris. '88	YY	6
● Brunello di Montalcino Vigna del Fiore Ris. '88	YY	6
● Brunello di Montalcino Vigna del Fiore Ris. '90	YY	6
● Brunello di Montalcino '89	Y	5
● Brunello di Montalcino '90	Y	4
● Brunello di Montalcino '91	Y	4
● Brunello di Montalcino Ris. '90	Y	6
● Rosso di Montalcino '94	Y	3

MONTALCINO (SI)

BIONDI SANTI SPA
VIA PANFILO DELL'OCA, 3
LOC. GREPPO
53024 MONTALCINO (SI)
TEL. 0577/847121

Iacopo Biondi Santi is the last scion of the dynasty that invented Brunello di Montalcino and one of the most astute marketing brains in Tuscan winemaking. He continues to be co-owner of Biondi Santi SpA, the company that distributes wines from the Il Greppo and Poggio Salvi estates as well as many other own-label products, for which he avails himself of the winemaking talents of consultant Vittorio Fiore. This year's range is one of the best there are in Montalcino; in fact the Schidione '93, obtained from 40 percent cabernet sauvignon, 40% sangiovese and 20 percent merlot fruit, very nearly won Three Glasses. It is a powerful, austere red that releases oak and wild berries on the nose and displays superb structure on the palate, where the occasional rough edges of the tannins are probably due to the nature of the '93 harvest. The Sassoalloro '94, which we came back to this year, is also interesting. A monovarietal Sangiovese, it comes from a less than wonderful vintage, as can be noted from the relative lack of complexity of the nose and a very drinkable approachability. We would also like to point out a very attractive Merlot from the Poggio Salvi range, the nicely made Lavischio '95, which is drinking beautifully straight from the cellar. And finally we come to the star of the show, the Brunello di Montalcino Il Greppo Riserva '90, the Brunello "par excellence". This is the finest of recent vintages even though the panel had doubts about the overall balance, which will need time. Nobody denies its cellarability or its exquisitely tradition style but its purchasers will have to be patient. It seems a shame to pay such a lot for a wine that only your grandchildren will be able to savour to the full.

● Brunello di Montalcino Il Greppo Ris. '90	▼▼	6
● Schidione '93	▼▼	6
● Lavischio di Poggio Salvi '95	▼	4
● Brunello di Montalcino '83	YYY	6
● Brunello di Montalcino '85	YY	6
● Brunello di Montalcino '88	YY	6
● Brunello di Montalcino '90	YY	6
● Brunello di Montalcino Ris. '85	YY	6
● Brunello di Montalcino Ris. '88	YY	6
● Sassoalloro '91	YY	5
● Sassoalloro '93	YY	4
● Sassoalloro '94	YY	4*
● Brunello di Montalcino Poggio Salvi Ris. '90	Y	6

MONTALCINO (SI)

CANALICCHIO DI SOPRA
DI FRANCO E ROSILDO PACENTI
53024 MONTALCINO (SI)
TEL. 0577/849277

This new entry to the Guide adds further lustre to the prestige of an area known locally as Canalicchi. The Pacenti family own a vineyard of about 4 hectares on the north-facing slopes of Montalcino, facing Buonconvento, a location that demands rigorous selection in the vineyard to obtain perfectly ripened bunches, especially in difficult years. The cellar offered our tasters two classic Montalcino wines, a Rosso '95 and a Brunello from '92, a vintage that was notoriously unexciting. Nevertheless the Brunello '92 gained its One Glass rating thanks to good body that nicely offsets the zone's characteristic acidity and beefy tannins that might have been a little sweeter. The garnet-tinged ruby colour heralds moderately long aromas with interesting notes of Morello cherry and walnut skin. The Montalcino '95 is very much along the same lines. Its ruby hue is firm right to the rim and the attractively intense nose has notes of vanilla, roasted coffee beans and cherry. It is still a little young on the palate, where the tannins tend to prevail.

MONTALCINO (SI)

CANALICCHIO DI SOPRA
DI PRIMO PACENTI
E PIERLUIGI RIPACCIOLI
LOC. CANALICCHIO DI SOPRA
53024 MONTALCINO (SI)
TEL. 0577/848316

Primo Pacenti again confirmed his reputation as a reliable producer of premium wines. This meticulous winemaker who owns four hectares of the cru Canalicchi is ably assisted by Paolo Vagaggini, a rising oenological star who knows Montalcino inside out. The team are getting excellent results with their Rosso di Montalcino and we will be interested to see how they handle Brunello in the future The Rosso di Montalcino '95 was one of the year's best. The Two Glass score came from keeping things simple. The wine has an intense ruby hue of formidable concentration which tell you that the body is going to be massive. The palate confirms this with a richly textured depth of flavour into which the tannins have merged seamlessly. Both the nose and after-aromas of eucalyptus-nuanced bramble and Morello cherry are intense and lingering, in demonstration of the winemaker's skill and finesse. The Brunello '92 is equally intriguing and gained Two Glasses, an outstanding result for the vintage. It has a nicely concentrated ruby hue tinged with garnet and the persistent tobacco and red berry preserve aromas which are very typical of the variety. The palate has reasonable body but it impresses above all for the technically impeccable execution: a perfectly balanced Brunello that has got just about everything right.

● Brunello di Montalcino '92	♙	5
● Rosso di Montalcino '95	♙	3

● Brunello di Montalcino '92	♙♙	5
● Rosso di Montalcino '95	♙♙	4
● Rosso di Montalcino		
Le Gode di Montosoli '94	♛♛	4
● Brunello di Montalcino '91	♛	5

MONTALCINO (SI)

MONTALCINO (SI)

CAPANNA DI CENCIONI
LOC. CAPANNA, 333
53024 MONTALCINO (SI)
TEL. 0577/848298

TENUTA CAPARZO
LOC. TORRENIERI
53028 MONTALCINO (SI)
TEL. 0577/848390-847166

It was a lower-key performance this year for the Capanna di Cencioni after they won a Three Glass rating last time for a magnificent Brunello Riserva. Despite all the efforts of Patrizio Cencioni, the power behind the estate for many years now, the Riserva '91 is only a shadow of the stunning '90. Its garnet ruby hue is intense and introduces equally intense aromas of sweet vanilla spices, but while it is pleasant enough on the palate, it lacks concentration and the tannins make the finish slightly astringent. Capanna di Cencioni have decided not to bottle the Brunello '92 as it was not considered up to the standards required. It is a decision that will cost the estate money but provides the consumer with a copper-bottomed guarantee that any wine sold under the estate label will be of premium quality. The Cencioni production is not restricted to Brunello but includes all the classic DOC wines of the Montalcino area. The nine-hectare estate also makes a Rosso di Montalcino, the '95 vintage of which was well worth a One Glass rating. It has a deep ruby hue and an attractive bouquet with a keynote of fresh cherries. The palate is uncomplicated but lingering and there are no histrionics from the tannins or acidity, which makes it very easy to drink. Finally, lovers of Moscadello will also find a very nice traditional version of that wine in the Capanna di Cencioni cellars.

Tenuta Carpazo did not release any estate-labelled Brunello di Montalcino '92. It was a difficult, and financially onerous, decision but one which also demonstrates the serious approach of an estate that has no intention of cutting any corners when it comes to quality. Our sincere congratulations on this policy. The general manager, Nuccio Turone, and consultant winemaker Vittorio Fiore, the man who has inspired the Tenuta Carpazo style, are both complete professionals who care as much about the company's image as they do about the quality of its products. The best wine from this year's releases was the Ca' di Pazzo '93, a blend of sangiovese and cabernet sauvignon in equal proportions. It is a wine with loads of class, offering vanilla fragrances on the nose laced with liquorice, violets and Morello cherry. The palate has good body with a wealth of rich extract - in fact the '93 is probably the best ever vintage of this particular wine. The two Rosso di Montalcino reds, the basic '95 and the La Caduta '94 vineyard selection, were less of a tasting event, as was only to be expected. It was the La Caduta that scored slightly higher in the end for its rich, concentrated texture. We should also make room to mention the white Le Grance '93, because we missed it last year. Obtained from chardonnay, sauvignon and gewürztraminer and oak-matured in small barrels, it revealed great complexity on the nose, where the aromas included yeast and white fruit notes of peaches and damsons over a faintly vanillaed background; the palate however, while elegant and nicely concentrated, is rather simpler.

●	Brunello di Montalcino Ris. '91	♟♟	6
●	Rosso di Montalcino '95	♟	4
●	Brunello di Montalcino Ris. '90	♟♟♟	6
●	Brunello di Montalcino '88	♟♟	5
●	Brunello di Montalcino Ris. '88	♟♟	6
●	Rosso di Montalcino '93	♟♟	2*
●	Brunello di Montalcino '91	♟	5
●	Brunello di Montalcino '90	♟	5
●	Rosso di Montalcino '94	♟	3

●	Ca' del Pazzo '93	♟♟	5
○	Le Grance '93	♟♟	3*
●	Rosso di Montalcino La Caduta '94	♟	4
●	Rosso di Montalcino '94		3
●	Brunello di Montalcino La Casa '88	♟♟♟	6
●	Brunello di Montalcino '88	♟♟	6
●	Brunello di Montalcino La Casa '85	♟♟	6
●	Brunello di Montalcino La Casa '86	♟♟	6
●	Brunello di Montalcino La Casa '91	♟♟	5
●	Brunello di Montalcino Ris. '88	♟♟	6
●	Brunello di Montalcino '90	♟	5
●	Brunello di Montalcino La Casa '91	♟	5
●	Brunello di Montalcino Ris. '90	♟	6

MONTALCINO (SI)

MONTALCINO (SI)

CASANOVA DI NERI
LOC. TORRENIERI
53028 MONTALCINO (SI)
TEL. 0577/834029

CASE BASSE
LOC. VILLA S. RESTITUTA
53024 MONTALCINO (SI)
TEL. 02/4697608-848567

The big news this year at Giacomo Neri's estate is the arrival of the renowned agronomist and oenologist, Carlo Ferrini, as consultant winemaker. Ferrini has been looking after the vineyard management of a number of properties in the Montalcino area, Barbi Colombini in particular, but never before has he tackled the challenge of making Brunello di Montalcino, a major test of any winemaker's ability. So the Neri-Ferrini team will be at work on Brunello starting with the '97 vintage, which looks like being a memorable one. The aim is to produce a wine that communicates the message of Brunello's rich heritage in an oenological "grammar" that will appeal to today's wine lovers. Those bottles will be released in the year 2001 and will probably become a benchmark for Brunello well into the next millennium. For the time being, we will have to make do with the two wines Giacomo Neri presented this year. As there was no Brunello di Montalcino '92, our tasters sampled an excellent, full bodied Rosso di Montalcino '95 and the Casanova di Neri Rosso '96, a very pleasant table wine with instantly appealing fruit aroma. Both stand out as the depressing harvests of '91 and '92 have taken their toll on this year's releases in Montalcino, and there are very few really interesting wines on show.

Recently, our tasters have crossed swords with Gianfranco Soldera over some of his vinification methods. They were particularly dissatisfied with the results he obtained from the stupendous fruit that went into, for example, the Brunello di Montalcino Riserva '90, where the panel detected excessive volatile acidity. Soldero has always upheld as marks of excellence features which we consider weaknesses or even inadmissible defects in a great red wine. The two points of view have no common ground. We simply see things differently. But even the panel had to acknowledge that Gianfranco's Brunello di Montalcino Riserva '91 had something that was reminiscent of the - in our opinion - great wines released by the estate some years ago. The '91 brought to mind the epoch-making '81 which, together with the '79, took Case Basse to the very top of the rankings in Montalcino at the time. It may have been the sumptuously rich red berry fruit on the nose, and its vanilla nuances. It may have been the use of newer, cleaner barrels than in the last few years. Or it may have been the full bodied concentration of the palate, so typical of all the wines from this estate. This Brunello may lack something in elegance but it is backed up to the hilt by a weight and texture that would be hard to match anywhere else. Soldera is not a man to lose any sleep over wine guides or panel ratings so he probably will not be impressed to know that he came very close to winning yet another Three Glass award. But we were happy to note that a great wine of the past is making a comeback.

● Rosso di Montalcino '95	🍷🍷	4
● Casanova di Neri Rosso '96	🍷	3
● Brunello di Montalcino Cerretalto Ris. '88	🍷🍷🍷	6
● Brunello di Montalcino '85	🍷🍷	5
● Brunello di Montalcino '88	🍷🍷	6
● Brunello di Montalcino '89	🍷🍷	6
● Brunello di Montalcino '90	🍷🍷	5
● Brunello di Montalcino '91	🍷🍷	6
● Brunello di Montalcino Cerretalto Ris. '90	🍷	6

● Brunello di Montalcino Ris. '91	🍷🍷	6
● Brunello di Montalcino '83	🍷🍷🍷	6
● Brunello di Montalcino '85	🍷🍷🍷	6
● Brunello di Montalcino Ris. '83	🍷🍷🍷	6
● Brunello di Montalcino '86	🍷🍷	6
● Brunello di Montalcino '87	🍷🍷	6
● Brunello di Montalcino '88	🍷🍷	6
● Brunello di Montalcino '90	🍷🍷	6
● Intistieti '85	🍷🍷	6
● Intistieti '87	🍷🍷	6
● Intistieti '88	🍷🍷	6
● Intistieti '91	🍷🍷	6

MONTALCINO (SI)

MONTALCINO (SI)

CASTELGIOCONDO
LOC. CASTELGIOCONDO
53024 MONTALCINO (SI)
TEL. 055/27141

CIACCI PICCOLOMINI D'ARAGONA
B.GO DI MEZZO, 62
LOC. CASTELNUOVO DELL'ABATE
53020 MONTALCINO (SI)
TEL. 0577/835616

To say the panel were expecting better things from the lovely Castelgiocondo estate owned by the Marchesi de' Frescobaldi would be the understatement of the decade. After the superb Brunello di Montalcino Riserva '90 we were privileged to taste on our last visit, this year's offerings were modest in comparison. Honour was saved thanks to the Lamaione '94, the best version of this merlot-based wine that Castelgiocondo has released so far. It has lovely depth of aroma on the nose, where the classic Merlot notes of tobacco and red berry come through splendidly. The palate is full flavoured and soft. The tannins are present but discreet, content to play an elegant second fiddle. The body is not what you would describe as massive but it does have plenty of length and great balance, making it a very decent wine indeed. In contrast we were much less keen on the Rosso di Montalcino Campo ai Sassi '95. Instead of bringing out the best in what after all was a very good vintage, it seemed dilute and rather lacking in structure. It was certainly no better than the '94 we had unkind words for on our last visit. But what the panel would really like to know is where the Brunello di Montalcino '92 went wrong. It is pale in colour, grassy on the nose and a featherweight on the palate. Clearly no one has been surreptitiously blending in other wines to perk up this '92 but that is no justification for such an undistinguished product. Given the great respect we have for Lamberto Frescobaldi and his winemaker, Nicolò d'Afflitto, we are as disappointed as anyone by this year's results and hope they were no more than the result of a momentary lapse of concentration. Fortunately, the '93 harvest was a good one in Montalcino, so next year the music should be different.

Under the guiding hand of Roberto Cipresso, the Ciacci Piccolomini D'Aragona estate continues to experiment with other varieties to plant alongside the traditional sangiovese. Already, plots of merlot and cabernet sauvignon are producing fruit. Cipresso's underlying strategy is to impose total quality, even if it hurts the balance sheet in the short term. For the second time running, there is no estate-label Brunello di Montalcino as neither the '91 and '92 harvest were held to be of sufficiently high quality. So while waiting for the '93 Brunello to be released, the panel sampled the Rosso di Montalcino '95 from the vineyard selection Vigna della Fonte. It turned out to be one of the best wines of the year in its class. Its intense ruby hue reveals purple highlights and although the nose is still a little austere we found good complexity in which oak-ageing aromas mingle nicely with varietal notes. The palate is youthful and concentrated; the tannins are still a little boisterous but they will mellow out with the passage of time. The Ateo '95 also impressed. It is obtained from a cépage of sangiovese and cabernet sauvignon aged in barrels of various sizes of both Slavonian and French oak. The name of the wine (which means "atheist" in Italian) alludes to the estate's scepticism about dogmatically making Brunello year in year out, regardless of the vintage. It was made for the first time in the very difficult 1989. Ateo has enjoyed considerable commercial success in its own right and instead of remaining a second-label alternative to Brunello, it is now a fixture in the estate catalogue. The '95 has a deep, purple-tinged ruby hue. On the nose it is a little over-mature, which detracts from the complexity, and the palate has a hint of astringency.

● Lamaione '94	🍷🍷	5
● Brunello di Montalcino '92		6
● Rosso di Montalcino Campo ai Sassi '95		3
● Brunello di Montalcino Ris. '88	🍷🍷🍷	6
● Brunello di Montalcino Ris. '90	🍷🍷🍷	6
● Brunello di Montalcino '89	🍷🍷	5
● Brunello di Montalcino '90	🍷🍷	5
● Brunello di Montalcino '91	🍷🍷	5
● Lamaione '91	🍷🍷	6
● Lamaione '92	🍷🍷	5

● Rosso di Montalcino Vigna della Fonte '95	🍷🍷	4
● Ateo '95	🍷	5
● Brunello di Montalcino Vigna di Pianrosso '88	🍷🍷🍷	6
● Brunello di Montalcino Vigna di Pianrosso '90	🍷🍷🍷	5
● Brunello di Montalcino '85	🍷🍷	5
● Brunello di Montalcino Ris. '88	🍷🍷	6
● Brunello di Montalcino '87	🍷	5
● Rosso di Montalcino Vigna della Fonte '94	🍷	4

MONTALCINO (SI)

TENUTA COL D'ORCIA
LOC. S. ANGELO IN COLLE
53020 MONTALCINO (SI)
TEL. 0577/808001

MONTALCINO (SI)

COLLEMATTONI
VIA DEL CAPANNINO
LOC. S. ANGELO IN COLLE
53024 MONTALCINO (SI)
TEL. 0577/864009

If we had been going to award a special prize for the best cellar in Montalcino this year, then we might very well have plumped for Tenuta Col d'Orcia, above all because of two excellent wines that demonstrate just how dependable this marvellous estate has become. But we should start by welcoming Tenuta Col d'Orcia back to the Three Glass club with a monumentally impressive Brunello di Montalcino Poggio al Vento Riserva '90. This wine has always shone like a beacon to lovers of great traditional-style Brunello, but the '90 is in a class of its own. The nose is more concentrated, with greater breadth and intensity and a range of aromas which takes you from ripe fruit to flowery notes and hints of cocoa and oak. The entry on the palate is even more positive than usual and the flavours are so full and lingering that they came out of a parallel tasting against Giovanni Conterno's legendary Barolo Monfortino Riserva '90 with flying colours. We urge you to try the test for yourselves if you have the time, passion and financial resources to invest in such a delightful entertainment. The cabernet sauvignon-based Olmaia '93 was also excellent; it has never performed as well before. The ruby hue is impenetrably intense, leading into aromas of ripe red fruit with hints of bramble and blackcurrant over a pleasantly toasty background. The palate is distinctive and full but suffers from a lack of complexity, which weighed against a second Three Glass award for the estate. It was close thing, though. In contrast the Brunello di Montalcino Riserva '91 was good but not great, even though is an impeccably made product. Its rough edges and only moderate concentration are the hallmarks of a vintage that failed to deliver the goods.

Collemattoni's Guide profile this year is a just reward for the dedication and skill of the Bucci family, who have owned this property and its 1.75 hectares of vineyard since 1984. The division of labour on the estate is clear-cut: Ado, who has many years' experience as a vine-grafter, manages the outdoors work while his son takes care of the cellar. Although Collemattoni has been making Brunello since 1988, Bucci preferred not to offer our panel any wines for tasting until they were absolutely sure of the quality. But there were no doubts about the Rosso di Montalcino '95, even if it is the cellar's first attempt at this style of wine. Collemattoni is not releasing any other wines this year because, to quote "'92 was not a Brunello year, in our opinion". Their Rosso, however, picked up an effortless Two Glasses for a vibrant ruby hue that keeps its depth right to the rim of the glass and a delicately complex nose where the mineral notes blend beautifully with oak-derived aromas, and the fruit ranges from redcurrant and bilberry through to the trademark Morello cherry. The entry on the palate is also attractive, and the tannins are backed up by fine-grained extract that bestows an air of elegance on this very interesting wine. And it should not be overlooked that a product of this quality, at the price Collemattoni ask, represents excellent value for money.

● Brunello di Montalcino Poggio al Vento Ris. '90	▼▼▼	6
● Olmaia '93	▼▼	5
● Brunello di Montalcino Ris. '91	▼	5
● Brunello di Montalcino Poggio al Vento Ris. '85	♈♈♈	6
● Brunello di Montalcino Poggio al Vento Ris. '88	♈♈♈	6
● Brunello di Montalcino '90	♈♈	5
○ Moscadello di Montalcino Vendemmia Tardiva Pascena '91	♈♈	5
● Olmaia '90	♈♈	6
● Olmaia '92	♈♈	6
● Brunello di Montalcino Ris. '88	♈	6
● Brunello di Montalcino Ris. '90	♈	6

● Rosso di Montalcino '95	▼▼	3

MONTALCINO (SI)

MONTALCINO (SI)

ANDREA COSTANTI
LOC. COLLE AL MATRICHESE
53024 MONTALCINO (SI)
TEL. 0577/848195

DUE PORTINE - GORELLI
VIA CIALDINI, 53
53024 MONTALCINO (SI)
TEL. 0577/848098

There are not many more reliable producers in Montalcino than Andrea Costanti, whose wines are always a benchmark for the evaluation of a vintage. Andrea, who is also President of the Consorzio del Brunello, runs his winery with a firm sense of direction. The estate has more than five hectares of vines in a particularly well-located spot in the higher, eastern part of the DOCG zone and the vineyards, as neatly kept as any garden, are renowned for the meticulous attention lavished on them. As you go up the road from Torrenieri towards Montalcino, Costanti's vines are the only ones with a rose bush at the end of each row. All this goes towards the production of elegant wines that earn respect without having to raise their voices. Once again, Andrea's denomination-label wines were well up to standard and only the IGT Vermiglio '93 failed to convince, gaining only a mention. The bottle we liked best was the '95 Rosso di Montalcino. Its intense ruby colour goes right to the rim of the glass and the nose has lovely oak-derived notes of vanilla, cinnamon and eucalyptus that mingle seamlessly with red fruit aromas of cherry and Morello cherry. Costanti's traditional softness is there on the palate with an elegance that Rosso di Montalcino only rarely achieves. This is the estate's best-ever Rosso. The Brunello '92 was a notch lower down the scale. Its slightly over-assertive tannins are its Achilles' heel, although the nose is attractive, with notes of Peruvian bark and spicy, balsamic aromas which just have the better of the fruit.

This tiny estate, which has barely one hectare of vineyard registered with the DOCG authorities, has managed to earn a profile of its own again this year. The man behind the constantly improving levels of quality (and quantity for the property has recently acquired new plots) is Giuseppe Gorelli. As well as being a highly competent grower, Giuseppe works at the Consorzio dei Vini di Montalcino and runs a wine shop where, of course, local products have pride of place. Best of the wines he presented this time round was his Brunello '92, which despite the poor vintage has plenty of personality and is up there with the best of them. The colour may not be perfect but the texture on the palate is deliciously close-knit, the tannins are delicate and complex, and the finish has good weight. On the nose there is an insistent, attractive, note of tobacco over a background of fruit. It is a well balanced wine that is very easy to like. The Rosso di Montalcino '95 was not quite as good. The colour is intense and firm but the nose is a little over-mature, although it does have plenty of depth and complexity. The palate is delicious, with a nice attack and fine grained but slightly intrusive tannins that detract a little from the finish. Overall, this was a very good performance from a meticulous producer of Montalcino wines.

●	Rosso di Montalcino '95	♈♈	4
●	Brunello di Montalcino '92	♈	6
●	Vermiglio '93		3
●	Brunello di Montalcino '88	♈♈♈	6
●	Brunello di Montalcino '83	♈♈	6
●	Brunello di Montalcino '85	♈♈	6
●	Brunello di Montalcino '86	♈♈	6
●	Brunello di Montalcino '87	♈♈	6
●	Brunello di Montalcino '89	♈♈	6
●	Brunello di Montalcino '90	♈♈	6
●	Brunello di Montalcino '91	♈♈	6
●	Brunello di Montalcino Ris. '88	♈♈	6
●	Brunello di Montalcino Ris. '90	♈♈	6

●	Brunello di Montalcino '92	♈♈	6
●	Rosso di Montalcino '95	♈	4

TENUTA FRIGGIALI

53024 MONTALCINO (SI)
TEL. 0577/849314-849454

Tenuta Friggiali can boast 29 hectares in the DOCG zone west of Montalcino so it has loads of potential, which still has to be realized to the full. The wines are very professionally made but tend to lack the character necessary to enter the top flight. There was not very much to choose between this year's range but the best was certainly the Pietrafocaia '93. Its intensely dark ruby hue introduces a slightly etheric nose in which the fruit is masked but nevertheless manages to emerge. The tannins on the palate are a little to the fore but they will probably mellow in the cellar. Of the two '95 Rosso di Montalcino products, we preferred the single vineyard Pietranera to the standard selection. The Pietranera has an admirably concentrated hue, moderately intense fruit on the nose and a palate where over-robust tannins penalize the finish. The basic '95 was less intense in colour, its paler ruby shading perceptibly into garnet. The nose was more mature but the palate was soft and comfortingly drinkable. The Brunello '92 also did well, earning its One Glass without difficulty. The bright garnet red has only moderate depth and hints of tobacco emerge on the nose to indicate that the wine is mature. On the palate, our tasters noted medium body, moderate balance and pleasant drinkability.

● Brunello di Montalcino '92	🍷	5
● Pietrafocaia '93	🍷	5
● Rosso di Montalcino '95	🍷	3
● Rosso di Montalcino Pietranera '95	🍷	4

MONTALCINO (SI)

EREDI FULIGNI

VIA S. SALONI, 33
53024 MONTALCINO (SI)
TEL. 0577/848039

The growth of the Eredi Fuligni estate and the constant improvement in its wines continue apace. While bottles from this property in the North-east of the Montalcino zone may sometimes lack the structure to win the very top accolades, they never fail to hit the spot when it comes to aroma. Roberto Guerrini, the owner's nephew and the one man who knows the estate inside out, laid down new vineyard quality standards a few years ago, drastically reducing yields and imposing more severe selection of the fruit. At the same time, he began experimenting with various types of oak barrels in the cellar. This year's releases not only show the effects of those changes, but also bring out the huge differences in the quality of the vintages presented. The '92 Brunello is a nicely made, honest-to-goodness bottle. It has clean aromas of cherry but lacks the complexity that is usually the hallmark of the estate. The palate reveals attractive acidity but the body is not up to the challenge, and the tannins are also a little on the boisterous side. In contrast, the Ginestreto '95 vineyard selection is very successful, and indeed is the best vintage of this wine we have tasted. This oak-matured Rosso di Montalcino easy clocked up Two Glasses on the panel's score sheets with its intense ruby hue and delicately complex nose of Morello cherry, spices, flowers and toast, although the latter was perhaps slightly too assertive. It had plenty of length, delicious fruit in the finish and solid tannins which will improve with a little bottle age.

● Rosso di Montalcino Ginestreto '95	🍷🍷	5
● Brunello di Montalcino '92	🍷	5
● Brunello di Montalcino '87	🍸🍸	6
● Brunello di Montalcino '88	🍸🍸	6
● Brunello di Montalcino '90	🍸🍸	5
● Brunello di Montalcino Ris. '88	🍸🍸	6
● Brunello di Montalcino Ris. '90	🍸🍸	6
● Brunello di Montalcino '91	🍸	5
● Rosso di Montalcino Ginestreto '93	🍸	3

MONTALCINO (SI)

Greppone Mazzi

Tenimenti Ruffino
Loc. Greppone
53024 Montalcino (SI)
tel. 055/8368307 - 0577/849215

Greppone Mazzi is part of the Tenimenti Ruffino holding. The winery manages more than seven hectares of vines near Montalcino beside the road that leads to Torrenieri. The recent renewal of the lease on these vineyards should allow the estate to make further progress and achieve production standards comparable to those reached by other Ruffino properties. The decision not to release a '92 Brunello should therefore be seen in a wider context, as part of a strategy aimed at quality over immediate financial returns. The Brunello Riserva '91 is being released now, in line with tradition, and it is distinctly superior to the non-Riserva wine from the same vintage. Nonetheless, it failed to achieve a Two Glass rating; despite its attractive garnet-ruby colour, the nose was distinctly mature with mineral notes, spice and toasty oak that prevailed over the fruit. The palate was much more interesting. The entry was memorable and evolved nicely with firm acidity. Overall the structure was convincing and the flavour was attractive, but we were really expecting more from Greppone Mazzi. Since it lies well up on the higher slopes of Montalcino, the estate probably suffered more than most from the unfavourable vintage.

• Brunello di Montalcino Ris. '91	🍷	6
• Brunello di Montalcino Ris. '90	YY	6
• Brunello di Montalcino '91	Y	6

MONTALCINO (SI)

Il Poggione

Loc. S. Angelo in Colle
53020 Montalcino (SI)
tel. 0577/864029

As always, Il Poggione has proved this year to provide a point of reference in the very heterogeneous environment of winemaking at Montalcino. Reliability is the estate's point of strength and its wines always live up to the label's high standards - especially when the vintage is nothing to write home about. The '92 Il Poggione Brunello di Montalcino for example is one of the best on the market. It may not have great complexity on the nose or palate but it is beautifully made and available at a price that represents good value for money. Not a bad deal, in the panel's opinion. There was also an excellent Rosso di Montalcino '95, an extremely well made wine that many another producers would have been proud to offer. In fact this wine, which its makers consider more a fall-back than a genuine own-label product, could well be a point of reference for those who are interested in serious Tuscan red wines. The credit for all this goes to a professional management team and the undisputed experience of Pierluigi Talenti, one of the zone's "éminences grises", who for many decades has been quietly steering this estate in the right direction.

• Brunello di Montalcino '92	🍷🍷	5
• Rosso di Montalcino '95	🍷🍷	4
• Brunello di Montalcino '89	🍷	5
• Brunello di Montalcino '88	YY	5
• Brunello di Montalcino '90	YY	4
• Brunello di Montalcino Ris. '88	YY	6
• Rosso di Montalcino '92	YY	3*
• Rosso di Montalcino '93	YY	3
• Brunello di Montalcino '91	Y	4
• Brunello di Montalcino Ris. '90	Y	6
• Rosso di Montalcino '94	Y	3

MONTALCINO (SI)

PODERE LA FORTUNA
LOC. PODERE LA FORTUNA
53024 MONTALCINO (SI)
TEL. 0577/848308

The story of this thriving label goes back to the early 1970s, when the renaissance of Brunello itself began. The cellars have been restructured and the barrel stock, of various sizes, is mainly new. Among the innovations there are a number of 500-litre tonneaux in which the Brunello '93 is ageing quietly (the owner prefers to call these "just a few experimental lots"). Modesty is the keynote at Podere La Fortuna, especially when the Brunello '92 is being discussed. They were reluctant to make it at all because of the poor vintage, but in the end the winemaker's insistence prevailed. Rightly so, for we think it is a good wine. Its moderately deep garnet ruby leads into fairly intense mature fruit on the nose and, although it has lots of body, the slightly rough tannins tend to compromise the length. But the real surprise this year from La Fortuna - and the wine that marks it out as a label to follow - is a sumptuous '95 Rosso di Montalcino. The nicely graded ruby colour is very attractive, and the nose is an explosion of aromas in which black cherries and redcurrant emerge amid intriguingly subtle notes of spice. The palate, too, is a delight. All in all, a wine with depth, texture and wonderful balance as well as outstanding length.

MONTALCINO (SI)

LA GERLA
LOC. CANALICCHIO
53024 MONTALCINO (SI)
TEL. 0577/848599

This estate owned by Sergio Rossi, an advertising executive from Milan, is located at Canalicchi and enjoys a superb view over the Siena countryside. It has makes a welcome return to the Guide this year, having suffered exclusion in the past because of the very limited number of profiles we are able to dedicate to Montalcino. Nevertheless, careful readers last year will have noted the La Gerla Brunello Riserva '90 in the "Other Wineries" section for Tuscany. The estate's problem is that the good results obtained with individual wines have not always been repeated across the range. This time round, things went differently. The Brunello di Montalcino Riserva '91 is an excellent wine, well worth Two Glasses. Its garnet-ruby is bright and intense in the glass and the nose burgeons into a complex bouquet with notes of ripe Morello cherry and bramble nuanced delicately by the oak, which has a hint of incense. On the palate, it is just as exciting and a credit to the winemaking which has brought out all the character of a very special "terroir". The finish is impressive, as well, and every bit as deep and long as you would expect from a true Brunello. It is an excellent all-round result from a year that was by no means favourable. The La Gerla Rosso di Montalcino '95 also impressed. A deep ruby in the glass, its nose is characterized by the grassy notes that dominate the fruit. Pleasantly drinkable, it lacks something in depth. Finally the oak-matured Birba '94, a monovarietal Sangiovese, was disappointing and failed to earn more than a mention.

● Rosso di Montalcino '95	♀♀	4
● Brunello di Montalcino '92	♀	5
● Brunello di Montalcino '83	♀♀	5
● Brunello di Montalcino '91	♀♀	5
● Brunello di Montalcino '85	♀	5
● Rosso di Montalcino '94	♀	3

● Brunello di Montalcino Ris. '91	♀♀	6
● Rosso di Montalcino '95	♀	4
● Birba '94		5
● Birba '90	♀♀	6
● Brunello di Montalcino Ris. '88	♀♀	6
● Brunello di Montalcino Ris. '90	♀♀	6
● Brunello di Montalcino '88	♀	6

La Togata

Via del Poggiolo, 222
53024 Montalcino (SI)
tel. 0577/847107 - 06/42871033

La Togata may be small but it is a meticulously industrious winery. The microscopic cellar has been very modestly extended and further plots have been acquired to increase production. In the meantime, La Togata continues to purchase grapes "on the vine" from outside suppliers; it is an expensive practice but the only way to guarantee the quality of the fruit. Another innovation at the estate is the addition of a Rosso di Montalcino to the range, the '95 being the first La Togata vintage of this DOC. An extremely interesting product, it was unfortunately produced in insufficient quantities to justify its inclusion here. The reliable estate Brunello came close to winning Two Glasses again for the '92 vintage. It underwent prolonged maceration and equally protracted sojourns in 25 and 30-hectolitre oak casks and it has a distinctly traditional personality. The intense aromas range from tobacco to bramble and are delightfully married to the barely perceptible wood. The palate has a nice overall feel, the positive entry developing pleasantly despite an intrusive note of acidity. The mellow tannins allow the finish, which mirrors the nose faithfully, to come through well. And finally, a note of congratulation to Carla and Danilo, the delightful couple who own the winery, on the arrival of a daughter, Azzurra.

● Brunello di Montalcino '92	🍷	5
● Brunello di Montalcino '90	🍷🍷	6
● Brunello di Montalcino '91	🍷🍷	6

MONTALCINO (SI)

Maurizio Lambardi

Podere Canalicchio di Sotto, 8
53024 Montalcino (SI)
tel. 0577/848476

The scene-stealer this year from Maurizio Lambardi's cellar was the Rosso di Montalcino '95, which put the Brunello, its nobler and better-known stablemate, completely in the shade. It has to be admitted that the '92 Brunello is a long way short of the standards reached in previous years, but in all likelihood this will turn out to be no more than a momentary stumble in the progress of an estate that is fast making a serious name for itself. The garnet colour of the Brunello weakens disappointingly at the rim. The aromas on the nose are over-mature, with fruit giving way to notes of tobacco. In the mouth, the flavour is lean and the tannins dominate a finish that lacks body. As we have been saying for years, the DOCG regulations impose a period of oak-maturing that poorer vintages simply cannot take. So, to go back to our initial comment, it was the Rosso di Montalcino '95 that impressed the panel and it is this wine which embodies everything that makes the estate special. The ruby hue is intense and enhanced by purple highlights while the nose has length and great depth of fruit, enhanced by a fascinating, faintly grassy undertone. The palate is full and the tannins, which will improve with bottle-ageing, are attractively sweet. And to conclude, the deeply satisfying finish rounds things off by recalling the fruit on the nose. A very comfortable Two Glasses.

● Rosso di Montalcino '95	🍷🍷	3
● Brunello di Montalcino '92	🍷	5
● Brunello di Montalcino '88	🍷🍷	5
● Brunello di Montalcino '90	🍷🍷	5
● Brunello di Montalcino '91	🍷🍷	5
● Rosso di Montalcino '90	🍷🍷	3*
● Rosso di Montalcino '91	🍷🍷	3*
● Rosso di Montalcino '92	🍷🍷	3
● Rosso di Montalcino '93	🍷🍷	2*

MONTALCINO (SI)

LISINI

FATTORIA DI S. ANGELO IN COLLE
53024 MONTALCINO (SI)
TEL. 0577/864040

Try asking any of the growers in the Montalcino zone where they would like their prize vineyard to be located. The answer is almost certain to be "Sesta". And it is on this particular hillside near the unmetalled road that leads from Sant'Angelo in Colle to Castelnuovo dell'Abbazia that the Lisini estate's nine hectares are situated. In addition to this natural asset, Lisini have the enormous advantage of being able to rely on the vast experience of consultant winemaker Franco Bernabei. The constant striving for quality above all else prompted Lisini not to release a Brunello '92 once it had become clear that the vintage would be poor. Financially, it was a brave decision but one that is indicative of Lisini's policy towards its clients. Admirers of this excellent label can however console themselves with the Brunello Ugolaia '91, a wine from an underrated vintage that gained a full Three Glasses. This vineyard selection, in only its second year of production, has quite stunning texture and elegance. The vibrant ruby hue and disarmingly gentle entry on the nose develop with the surefootedness of a thoroughbred. The majestic tannins on the palate are cloaked in velvet-textured glycerine and alcohol, giving softness and elegance to match the power. The finish is long and broad. A great wine and a splendid example of Brunello which will be talked about for years to come. The Rosso di Montalcino '95, too, plays its minor role well. Already drinking very pleasantly, it shows nice balance and while we might have liked to detect a little more complexity on the nose, it is nonetheless a very well made wine.

● Brunello di Montalcino Ugolaia '91	🍷🍷🍷 (black)	6
● Rosso di Montalcino '95	🍷 (black)	4
● Brunello di Montalcino '88	🍷🍷🍷	6
● Brunello di Montalcino '90	🍷🍷🍷	5
● Brunello di Montalcino '87	🍷🍷	5
● Brunello di Montalcino '89	🍷🍷	5
● Brunello di Montalcino '91	🍷🍷	5
● Brunello di Montalcino Ris. '85	🍷🍷	6
● Brunello di Montalcino Ris. '86	🍷🍷	6
● Brunello di Montalcino Ris. '88	🍷🍷	6
● Brunello di Montalcino Ugolaia '90	🍷🍷	6

MONTALCINO (SI)

LUCE

LOC. CASTELGIOCONDO
53024 MONTALCINO (SI)
TEL. 0577/848492

The big news from Montalcino is the foundation of Luce as a spin off of the Frescobaldi's Castelgiocondo property. For the time being, the new estate will continue to share the Castelgiocondo cellar and administration facilities but it deserves separate treatment, because it is half-owned by Robert Mondavi and his sons Michael and Tim. In short, the Luce estate is a joint venture involving Tuscany's biggest growers and the best known oenological entrepreneurs from the New World. They have bought vineyards and rented others, all in the Castelgiocondo area, to launch a highly ambitious project: to produce an Italian equivalent of Opus One, the superb red that the Mondavis make in the Napa Valley in collaboration with the Rothschilds. The name selected for this new wine, obtained from equal parts of sangiovese and merlot, is Luce. This year two vintages - the '93 and the '94 - were released simultaneously. In the '93, it is the sangiovese half of the blend that stands out and as a result the wine has a sinewy, rather unapproachable character, while the '94 is redolent of the tobacco and red berries that are the hallmark of merlot. It was the '94 that the panel preferred, thanks to a remarkable softness and concentration in the nose, very much in an international style but still unmistakably Tuscan. "Three Glasses" was the consensus of opinion from our tasters.

● Luce '94	🍷🍷🍷 (black)	6
● Luce '93	🍷🍷 (black)	6

MONTALCINO (SI)

MASTROJANNI
PODERI LORETO E S. PIO
LOC. CASTELNUOVO DELL'ABATE
53020 MONTALCINO (SI)
TEL. 0577/835681

For the last couple of years we have been singing the praises of Mastrojanni but this time round there was less excitement. This was mainly due to the cellar's very proper decision not to release a Brunello di Montalcino '92, given the poor quality of the vintage. It was a difficult choice to make and one which will cost the estate a considerable amount of revenue, so it should be noted with due respect. There were, however, two very good wines on offer this year to defend the Mastrojanni colours. The better of the two was the San Pio '93, a red table wine obtained from 75 percent sangiovese and 25 percent cabernet sauvignon. Its aromas of ripe red fruit and bramble jelly are perhaps slightly over-mature but the palate is mouth-filling, soft, lingering and decently textured. The other wine we tasted, the eminently drinkable Rosso di Montalcino '95, may not have outstanding structure but reveals attractive fruit and a laid-back style. On the subject of this wine however we would like to note that Mastrojanni, in common with many other grower-producers, decided to give priority to the '95 vintage Brunello rather than to their Rosso di Montalcino. In many cases, what could have been a truly great Rosso di Montalcino has turned out to be something of a disappointment.

MONTALCINO (SI)

SILVIO NARDI
LOC. CASALE DEL BOSCO
53024 MONTALCINO (SI)
TEL. 0577/808269

Since young Emilia Nardi has taken over the running of the family property, a lot of things have changed. First of the image of the label has rapidly improved. Silvio Nardi used to be well known for the moderate quality and excellent value for money of its Brunello and Rosso di Montalcino. A good deal of effort has been made in the vineyards with new plantings, and in the cellars, where barrel stock has been renewed and now the first, albeit uncertain, results can be seen in the products from the difficult '92 vintage, which are good enough to earn the cellar a profile of its own again. The deciding factor was a pleasant, very well made Brunello di Montalcino that outperforms many '92s from other, more famous producers. Our congratulations to the Nardi estate then. We look forward to even better things in future on the Brunello front. The Rosso di Montalcino '95 was also decent, even though it will not win any prizes for its structure. It does, however, reflect the genuine Rosso style and the ABC of good winemaking in general. Nevertheless, the panel were hoping for something a little more exciting from what was after all a very good vintage, that should have produced a more concentrated, full flavoured wine.

● San Pio '93	♟♟	5
● Rosso di Montalcino '95	♟	4
● Brunello di Montalcino '90	♟♟♟	6
● Brunello di Montalcino Ris. '88	♟♟♟	6
● Brunello di Montalcino Schiena d'Asino '90	♟♟♟	6
● Brunello di Montalcino '87	♟♟	5
● Brunello di Montalcino '88	♟♟	6
● Brunello di Montalcino '89	♟♟	5
● Brunello di Montalcino '91	♟♟	5
● Brunello di Montalcino Ris. '86	♟♟	6
● Brunello di Montalcino Ris. '90	♟♟	6
● San Pio '88	♟♟	5

● Brunello di Montalcino '92	♟	5
● Rosso di Montalcino '95	♟	3
● Brunello di Montalcino '90	♟♟	4
● Rosso di Montalcino '93	♟	2

MONTALCINO (SI)

MONTALCINO (SI)

SIRO PACENTI
LOC. PELAGRILLI, 1
53024 MONTALCINO (SI)
TEL. 0577/848662

AGOSTINA PIERI
VIA FABBRI, 2
53014 MONTALCINO (SI)
TEL. 0577/375785

You pick up signs of the dynamism that is the distinguishing characteristic of Giancarlo Pacenti, President of the Consorzio del Rosso di Montalcino, simply by walking round his cellars, where the traditional Slavonian oak casks are joined by innovative French barrels in a range of sizes. Pacenti's experiments extend beyond the barrel cellar to the vineyard; he has also been acquiring land and vineyards in some of the finest subzones of the entire Montalcino area, a forward-looking policy that is destined to bring interesting long term results. This year, the only wine presented was the Rosso di Montalcino '95 (the '92 vintage was regarded as too poor to make a Brunello, a view that one would have expected from a serious winemaker like Pacenti). His Rosso has a deep, even ruby hue and a nose with slightly medicinal aromas that limit its fruit and complexity. In contrast the palate is as complex as you could wish for and reveals the structure that was implicit in its colour. The soft alcohol and extracts are perfectly balanced by firm acidity and tannins to make this a deliciously drinkable Rosso. We hope that the slightly harsh initial notes on the nose will be eliminated in future versions of Pacenti wines so that the label can climb back to the top of the rankings, where it belongs.

After having won warm praise in the last edition of the Guide for its Rosso di Montalcino '94, which was one of the best from that vintage, Agostina Pieri has gone one better with this year's new release. The Agostina Pieri Rosso di Montalcino '95 literally wiped the floor with the stiff competition in its category to achieve a Three Glass award, the first ever given to a Rosso di Montalcino. The vibrant and almost impenetrable ruby hue is extraordinarily firm right to the rim of the glass, showing at once that this is a wine of superb concentration. The nose is stunning, its Morello cherry and bramble fruit mingling wonderfully with spicy notes of mint and eucalyptus. Great body emerges on the palate, which also offers deliciously rounded tannins which bode well for the longevity of a wine that changes all the rules about making Rosso di Montalcino. Agostina Pieri runs a modern cellar with no hang-ups about winemaking: casks of various sizes stand next to the barriques in which a percentage of both the Rosso di Montalcino and the Brunello age. Consultant winemaker Paolo Vagaggini's experience has enabled the winery to achieve Three Glass status in record time. We are going to have to wait until 1999 to sample the estate's first Brunello, when the '94 will be released but we sincerely hope that it will be of the same standard as this great Rosso di Montalcino. For then we really would be witnessing the birth of a new star.

● Rosso di Montalcino '95	♟♟	4
● Brunello di Montalcino '88	♟♟♟	6
● Brunello di Montalcino '89	♟♟	6
● Brunello di Montalcino '90	♟♟	5
● Brunello di Montalcino '91	♟♟	6
● Brunello di Montalcino Ris. '90	♟♟	6
● Rosso di Montalcino '88	♟♟	3
● Rosso di Montalcino '90	♟♟	4
● Rosso di Montalcino '92	♟♟	4
● Rosso di Montalcino '93	♟♟	4
● Rosso di Montalcino '94	♟	3

● Rosso di Montalcino '95	♟♟♟	4
● Rosso di Montalcino '94	♟♟	4

MONTALCINO (SI)

Poggio Antico

Loc. Poggio Antico
53024 Montalcino (SI)
tel. 0577/848044

There are certain characteristics of the Poggio Antico estate that mean it tends to suffer in poorer vintages, despite all the efforts of Paola Gloder's team in both cellar and vineyard. The relatively high altitude at which the vines grow enables them to produce powerful, elegant wines with matchless aromas in great vintages but the more modest '92 did not give the fruit any opportunity to ripen, thwarting all the best efforts of Massimo Albanese in the cellar. Soon the Madre vineyard, which is located lower down the hill slopes, will come on stream and Poggio Antico will therefore be able to manage difficult years with greater flexibility. Meticulous selection produced an intense garnet Brunello '92 with matching highlights and a nose reminiscent of mint and mushrooms. The body is insufficient to balance the acidity, but it is still a good clean wine that is typical of its vintage. The other wine the panel tasted was the Altero '92, a monovarietal Sangiovese that matured in oak for about two years before being racked into stainless steel vats until it was bottled. The ruby hue is satisfyingly deep and introduces a clean, delicate nose with characteristic sangiovese Morello cherry and tobacco aromas. On the palate, it has lovely balance that our tasters were unable to fault. Both wines scored comfortably over 70 points, which is not a bad result for such a difficult vintage. A final note for visitors to the area: the Poggio Antico winery is a superb setting from which to enjoy panoramic views of the Tuscan countryside before dining at the estate restaurant, without doubt the best in Montalcino.

● Altero '92	▼	6
● Brunello di Montalcino '92	▼	6
● Brunello di Montalcino '85	YYY	5
● Brunello di Montalcino '88	YYY	6
● Brunello di Montalcino Ris. '85	YYY	6
● Altero '85	YY	5
● Altero '90	YY	5
● Brunello di Montalcino '87	YY	6
● Brunello di Montalcino '89	YY	6
● Brunello di Montalcino '90	YY	5
● Brunello di Montalcino Ris. '88	YY	6
● Brunello di Montalcino '91	Y	5
● Brunello di Montalcino Ris. '90	Y	6

MONTALCINO (SI)

Poggio di Sotto di Piero Palmucci

Loc. Poggio di Sopra, 222
Fraz. Castelnuovo dell'Abate
53024 Montalcino (SI)
tel. 0577/835502

The story goes that when Piero Palmucci finally tasted his Brunello '91, he exclaimed, "At last! A Brunello!" Obviously it's not a phrase that went down very well with his producer colleagues but we think that Piero's exclamation was an expression of the emotion he felt at finally producing a vintage of this prestige DOCG after years of waiting. Poggio di Sotto comprises about 3.5 hectares in the area around Castelnuovo dell'Abate. The plots are scattered at altitudes ranging from 200 to 400 metres above sea level so the estate can take full advantage of the subzone's potential, no matter what the vagaries of the weather. Company policy favours slow ageing in oak, which is why the Rosso di Montalcino '94 was only released this year. It is a medium intense ruby tinged with garnet and reveals a nose of some austerity in which notes of crushed ripe fruit marry with oak-derived aromas and a faint hint of mushroom. It follows through attractively on the pleasant, well balanced palate. As there was no Brunello '92, we are including the panel's notes on the Brunello '91, the first Poggio di Sotto wine of this type. The results of the tasting were encouraging, for it revealed a deep garnet hue and very interesting length on the palate while the nose echoes the hints of mushroom that we had already noticed in the Rosso di Montalcino '94.

● Rosso di Montalcino '94	▼▼	4
● Brunello di Montalcino '91	▼	6

MONTALCINO (SI)

MONTALCINO (SI)

POGGIO SAN POLO
LOC. PODERE DI SAN POLO, 161
53024 MONTALCINO (SI)
TEL. 0577/835522

SALVIONI LA CERBAIOLA
P.ZZA CAVOUR, 19
53024 MONTALCINO (SI)
TEL. 0577/848499

The number of quality winemaking concerns in the zone around Castelnuovo dell'Abate continues to grow. The unique climatic conditions of the area, which is famous for the superb abbey of Sant'Antimo, enables producers to obtain excellent wines. Nicola Cucchelli runs one such estate and has confirmed his place in the Guide despite the absence of the '95 edition of the Rosso di Montalcino we liked so much on our last visit. The vintage was so good that a strategic decision was made to concentrate on the Brunello, especially since customers were clamouring for it. And this year we tried two Brunellos, the '92 and the Riserva '90 which we left out last time round because it had one or two - thankfully short-lived - problems on the nose. The Brunello '92 reveals the lack of stamina in the finish that characterizes the vintage but still earned a One Glass award for its attractive nose, where mature notes of leather emerged over bottled cherries. This year the Riserva '90 really impressed after its health-restoring sojourn in the bottle. The nose has lost the unsettling notes mentioned above and has blossomed into a clean, rich, lingering bouquet in which fruit preserves mingle effortlessly with oak-derived vanilla. The attack on the palate is a delight, developing nicely into a long finish with lots of depth. This is a very good Brunello. Unfortunately the cellar's San Polo Exe label wines, aimed at a large-scale market, are rather less exciting.

There is good news for admirers of the Salvioni La Cerbaiola cellar, whose wines have covered themselves in glory in past Guides, for the new Cerbaiola vineyard is about to go into production, which will enable Giulio e Mirella Salvioni to increase the number of bottles they release each year. Scrupulous vineyard management means that the cellar was able to offer us a Brunello this year, even if it does come from the notoriously poor '92 vintage, about which we have said enough already. The surprising thing about this wine is the concentration which makes it one of the best Brunellos from the vintage, and superior to the '91. This just goes to show how serious the cellar is and how good their winemaker, Attilio Pagli, is at obtaining silk purses from a sow's ear of a harvest. The Brunello '92 has a garnet hue of only moderate intensity, but that is typical of Cerbaiola. The nose is sumptuous, offering the characteristic aromas of tropical fruit that make this wine instantly recognizable in addition to the more traditional notes of tobacco and leather. The concentration on the palate is flanked by quite delicious tannins that enhance the finish and beautifully complement the nose. All in all this is a wine in which elegance prevails over power, but which nonetheless easily won a Two Glass rating from the panel. Finally we would like to repeat last year's comment: in difficult years, why not take advantage of the DOCG regulations and bottle a little sooner?

● Brunello di Montalcino Ris. '90	♗♗	6
● Brunello di Montalcino '92	♗	5
● Rubio '96		4
● Brunello di Montalcino '91	♗♗	5
● Rosso di Montalcino '94	♗♗	3

● Brunello di Montalcino '92	♗♗	6
● Brunello di Montalcino '85	♗♗♗	6
● Brunello di Montalcino '87	♗♗♗	6
● Brunello di Montalcino '88	♗♗♗	6
● Brunello di Montalcino '89	♗♗♗	6
● Brunello di Montalcino '90	♗♗♗	6
● Brunello di Montalcino '86	♗♗	6
● Brunello di Montalcino '91	♗♗	6

MONTALCINO (SI)

Talenti - Podere Pian di Conte

Loc. S. Angelo in Colle
53020 Montalcino (SI)
tel. 0577/864029

As well as being the driving force behind Il Poggione, Pierluigi Talenti has also for the past 20 years owned his own estate at Pian di Conte, a short distance from the mediaeval "borgo" of Sant'Angelo in Colle. The winery may not be huge, but in the past Talenti has presented our panels with well made products with the reliable quality which is the common feature of all the wines under his supervision. This year was no exception, despite the obvious handicap of the poor '92 vintage for the Brunello di Montalcino. We should say however that Talenti's own-label wines did not impress our tasters quite as much as the bottles he turns out for Il Poggione. There is not actually a great deal of difference as far as the Brunello di Montalcino is concerned, but it was enough to deprive Pian di Conte of the extra points that would have earned it a Two Glass rating. Where the panel did note a quality gap was in the Rosso di Montalcino '95. The Pian di Conte Rosso is invitingly drinkable but a little over-mature on the nose, and will probably have only a brief career in the cellar. A similar problem afflicts the Brunello di Montalcino '92, but given the vintage it is entirely understandable. Dominated by mature aromas on the nose, it makes a strong comeback on the palate thanks to a soft, pleasant texture that succeeds in dispelling your final reservations.

● Brunello di Montalcino '92	🍷	6
● Rosso di Montalcino '95	🍷	4
● Brunello di Montalcino '88	YYY	6
● Brunello di Montalcino '85	YY	5
● Brunello di Montalcino '86	YY	5
● Brunello di Montalcino '89	YY	5
● Brunello di Montalcino '90	YY	5
● Brunello di Montalcino Ris. '88	YY	6
● Brunello di Montalcino Ris. '90	YY	6
● Rosso di Montalcino '90	YY	3
● Brunello di Montalcino '91	Y	5
● Rosso di Montalcino '93	Y	3

MONTALCINO (SI)

Val di Suga

Loc. Val di Suga
53024 Montalcino (SI)
tel. 0577/848701

A gap seems to be opening up at Val di Suga between the flag-bearer wines and the rest of the range. Last year the cellar, which is owned by the Tenimenti Angelini, served up a brace of superbly made wines, one of which - the ravishingly stylish Brunello di Montalcino Vigna del Lago '90 - walked away with a Three Glass award. But this time panel tasters were asking themselves why the wines on offer performed so modestly. Naturally the vintages involved were part of the problem, but high profile grower-producers ought to be able to come up with a better basic level of quality. That is especially true of wines like Brunello di Montalcino, in both the Riserva and non-Riserva versions, because these wines are not exactly easy on the pocket. What we are saying is that a single One Glass award for three wines tasted is distinctly slim pickings. It was the Brunello di Montalcino Riserva '91 that rescued Val di Suga's honour. It's not a bad wine but it does not raise much excitement either. The nose lacks clarity and there are some initial signs of reduction, but the flavour is soft and the texture is good. Adequately mellow tannins contribute complexity. It was a much better wine than the Brunello di Montalcino '92, which had little to offer on the nose and was very short on the palate. The vintage is an alibi it is true, but Brunello is an expensive premium wine. Finally the Rosso di Montalcino '95 has no excuses. The harvest was excellent and for a '95 to be so over-mature seems to us to be a contradiction in terms. So we will have to wait and see what Val di Suga has done with the fruit from 1993, in the hope that the next batch of wines to be released will take us back to last year's heights.

● Brunello di Montalcino Ris. '91	🍷	6
● Brunello di Montalcino '92		5
● Rosso di Montalcino '95		4
● Brunello di Montalcino Vigna del Lago '90	YYY	6
● Brunello di Montalcino '87	YY	5
● Brunello di Montalcino '90	YY	5
● Brunello di Montalcino Ris. '88	YY	6
● Brunello di Montalcino Vigna del Lago '87	YY	6
● Brunello di Montalcino Vigna Spuntali '89	YY	6
● Brunello di Montalcino Vigna Spuntali '90	YY	6
● Brunello di Montalcino Ris. '90	Y	6

MONTECARLO (LU)

FATTORIA DEL BUONAMICO

VIA PROVINCIALE, 43
55015 MONTECARLO (LU)
TEL. 0583/22038

We are pleased to report that the Fattoria del Buonamico has made a very welcome habit of impressing our panel. This year's performance was as good as ever, especially when it came to the top of the range wines. The Fortino, obtained from cabernet and merlot grapes, is a wonderfully successful red that all our tasters liked very much. The intense aromas have character, the notes of oak mingling well with black berry and faintly vegetal nuances. The palate has a close-knit texture and lots of body, developing with great balance and breadth to pick up an effortless Two Glasses. That was also the assessment for the monovarietal pinot bianco Vasario, albeit with a slightly lower total score. The rich attack on the nose is immediately intriguing; the fruit blends nicely with spicy oak notes, and leads into a sweet, well rounded palate that derives balance from the underlying acidity. It may not have outstanding texture but the Vasario is a delightfully tidy bottle. These two wines were some way ahead of the rest of the Buonamico pack, all of which are nonetheless very decently made. For example the two whites, Montecarlo and Cercatoia, had weight and personality but were also distinctly mature. The Montecarlo Rosso was easy to drink with cheerful notes of flowers and red berries on the nose, although a little dilute. Overall, the tasting confirmed that Vasco Grassi is continuing along the right lines with the invaluable assistance of Vittorio Fiore and the ever more skilful Stefano Chioccioli.

●	Il Fortino Cabernet/Merlot '93	**YY**	5
○	Vasario '95	**YY**	4
○	Bianco di Cercatoia '95		3
○	Montecarlo Bianco '96		2
●	Montecarlo Rosso '96		2
●	Il Fortino Cabernet/Merlot '93	YY	4
●	Il Fortino Syrah '92	YY	5
●	Rosso di Cercatoia '90	YY	5
○	Vasario '91	YY	5
●	Il Fortino Cabernet/Merlot '90	Y	5
●	Il Fortino Cabernet/Merlot '92	Y	5
●	Il Fortino Syrah '90	Y	5
●	Montecarlo Rosso '93	Y	3
○	Vasario '92	Y	5
○	Vasario '93	Y	5

MONTECARLO (LU)

FUSO CARMIGNANI

VIA DELLA TINAIA, 7
LOC. CERCATOIA
55015 MONTECARLO (LU)
TEL. 0583/22381

If Duke Ellington had been able to sample the wine Gino Fuso has dedicated to him, he would probably have approved. For this year's For Duke is the best ever. Dark and intensely concentrated in the glass, it releases rich aromas of bramble, plum and pepper. The palate is magnificent, the immense structure and texture offering attractively chewy fruit and beefy tannins. For Duke came perilously close to the magic "90" score that would have earned it Three Glasses. The other Fuso Carmignani wines are much more down to earth but none of them are merely ordinary. They all have personality, but the one with most, in the panel's opinion, was the Pietrachiara, a trebbiano-based blend that contains a number of other white varieties from Fuso's estate. Its mineral notes on the nose are interesting and lead into a substantial, tangy palate featuring serious, mouth-cleaning acidity along the lines of some of the Rhône valley's Roussannes. The Sassonero has lots of style. The positive head-on attack on the palate carries through right to the end, so even the hints of reduction on the nose or the bitter note in the finish seem insignificant in comparison with the wine's undeniable virtues. In contrast, the house Vin Santo is as traditional as they come, its amber colour denoting the old-fashioned controlled oxidation style. The wide range of aromas go from candied peel to confectioner's cream over a curious background note of tobacco as sweet as the delicious palate.

●	For Duke '95	**YY**	5
○	Montecarlo Bianco Pietrachiara '96	**Y**	2*
●	Montecarlo Rosso Sassonero '96	**Y**	2*
○	Vinsanto Le Notti Rosse di Capo Diavolo '94	**Y**	4
●	For Duke '90	YY	5
●	For Duke '94	YY	5
●	For Duke '93	Y	4
○	Montecarlo Bianco Pietrachiara '95	Y	2*
●	Montecarlo Rosso '93	Y	3
●	Montecarlo Rosso '94	Y	3
●	Montecarlo Rosso Sassonero '95	Y	2*
○	Vinsanto Le Notti Rosse di Capo Diavolo '93	Y	5

MONTECARLO (LU)

MONTECATINI VAL DI CECINA (PI)

WANDANNA
VIA DON MINZONI, 38
55015 MONTECARLO (LU)
TEL. 0583/228989-22226

FATTORIA SORBAIANO
VIA PROVINCIALE TRE COMUNI
56040 MONTECATINI
VAL DI CECINA (PI)
TEL. 0588/30243

Wandanna has earned a Guide profile this year for the first time. Based in Montecarlo, the company turns out a fair number of products, perhaps too many, and not all of equal interest. The best of the bottles was Virente, an unusual cuvée of merlot, syrah and ciliegiolo. The attractive ruby hue is accompanied by a nose of lovely ripe fruit laced with spicy notes of pepper and cloves over warm toasty oak. The palate is firm and well balanced, the tannins round, and the finish clean. There are also two good wines, both white and red, under the Terre dei Cascinieri label. We preferred the white, obtained from a blend of chardonnay, sémillon, sauvignon and trebbiano that serves to remind you just how many varieties are grown around Lucca. The wine itself is pleasant and well made, its aromas of flowers, apples and pears mingling with vanilla and toastiness (part of the wine is oak-fermented). The flavour is refreshing, nicely balanced, rounded and decently long. The Terre dei Cascinieri red, from an equally unusual blend of syrah, ciliegiolo, cabernet and sangiovese, is not bad either. The vibrant ruby colour is followed up by aromas that lack a little focus but range from red berries through to vegetal notes by way of pepper and toasty oak. The palate has moderately good texture and develops well in the mouth. Finally the DOC Terre della Gioiosa red is a lightweight with an attractive nose. The rest of the range scored high enough to deserve a mention in the Guide.

The Fattoria Sorbaiano continues to defend its reputation in the world of wine despite being off the normal beaten track of Tuscan tourism. This time the panel was very taken with a white wine, the Lucestraia, which is odd in a zone best known for its reds. Lucestraia is a Montescudaio Bianco that actually owes very little to the DOC but a lot to good, universal white winemaking methods. The lovely golden hue is an invitation to savour a complex nose of citrus fruit, peaches, bananas, honey, lavender and oak-derived spices. The equally complex palate manages to be rich and refreshing at the same time and has a long, sweet finish. Buy it if you see it, because not many whites of this quality are so competitively priced. The Lucestraia was such a revelation that the Rosso delle Miniere took a something of a back seat. However it proved a well structured, attractively textured wine with lots of balance and a fine follow-through on the palate from a nose redolent of forest berries, toasty oak and a slightly overplayed vegetal note. The basic white from Fattoria Sorbaiano is one of the better products in its category. The moderately intense nose of spring flowers and fruit leads into an unexpectedly rich and full flavoured palate that the panel had no difficulty in awarding One Glass to. Finally the Montescudaio Rosso chipped in with an attractive nose and nicely textured palate, although the bitter note in the finish cost it one or two tasting points.

● Virente '94	♟♟	5
○ Montecarlo Bianco Terre dei Cascinieri '95	♟	3
● Montecarlo Rosso Terre dei Cascinieri '94	♟	3
● Montecarlo Rosso Terre della Gioiosa '96	♟	2
⊙ Cerasello '96		2
○ Montecarlo Bianco Terre della Gioiosa '96		2
○ Vermentino '96		2

○ Montescudaio Bianco Lucestraia '94	♟♟	3*
● Montescudaio Rosso delle Miniere '95	♟♟	4
○ Montescudaio Bianco '96	♟	2*
● Montescudaio Rosso '96		2
● Montescudaio Rosso delle Miniere '90	♖♖	4
● Montescudaio Rosso delle Miniere '92	♖♖	4
● Montescudaio Rosso delle Miniere '93	♖♖	4*
● Montescudaio Rosso delle Miniere '94	♖♖	4*

MONTEFOLLONICO (SI) MONTEMURLO (PO)

VITTORIO INNOCENTI
VIA LANDUCCI, 10/12
53040 MONTEFOLLONICO (SI)
TEL. 0577/669537

TENUTA DI BAGNOLO
DEI MARCHESI PANCRAZI
VIA MONTALESE, 168
50045 MONTEMURLO (PO)
TEL. 0574/652058

This small, very reliable, estate is located in the recently restored mediaeval village of Montefollonica. The cellar itself stands on the main street, next to the shop that sells its products direct to the public. Only about 60 percent of the estate's potential fruit production is actually vinified since in the vineyards bunches are rigorously thinned and the grapes selected with care. Visitors will note wood of various sizes in the cellar. Classic medium-sized barrels of Slavonian oak are used for ageing the Acerone while French barriques and larger casks are available for maturing Riserva versions of Vino Nobile di Montepulciano. The fermentation vats are not large, which means that the cap can easily be broken up and pushed under the surface of the fermenting must. The '93 Vino Nobile di Montepulciano Riserva has an intense, garnet-flecked hue and a nose in which fruit mingles with spices, vanilla in particular. It is a very drinkable wine, thanks to its remarkably inviting balance. But the cellar's flag-bearer is the Acerone, an oak-aged monovarietal sangiovese table wine. The wine we sampled was too young for us to come to any firm conclusions about its real worth. The nose, for example, has not had time to settle yet after bottling so we will be coming back next year to make a fuller assessment.

We wrote in our notes on the Tenuta di Bagnolo reds in last year's Guide that any attempt at comparison with the best Pinot Noirs from Burgundy would be inappropriate. And that, unfortunately, is the constraint that holds back all Italian Pinot Nero, not to mention most examples of the varietal made outside France. Notoriously, there is no more difficult grape for while cabernet, chardonnay or syrah may be capable of giving excellent results almost anywhere grapes can be grown, pinot noir refuses to co-operate. Even serious growers like Marchese Pancrazi struggle. The problem is not to produce a wine that photocopies a Pinot Noir from Burgundy but simply to make one with a recognizable identity of its own. The Tenuta di Bagnolo '95 Pinot Nero is a very good wine indeed, but once again hard to pin down to a type. The ruby hue is bright and the aromas intense but there are one or two off-key notes of cabbage stalks and wet pelts. The fruit, however, is very attractive on the nose and the palate while the solid, finely textured structure is excellent. All in all it is a wine that, despite reservations about style, remains one of the best Pinot Neros you will find anywhere in Italy.

● Vino Nobile di Montepulciano Ris. '93	▼	5
● Vino Nobile di Montepulciano Ris. '88	▼▼▼	4*
● Acerone '90	▼▼	4
● Vino Nobile di Montepulciano '93	▼▼	3
● Vino Nobile di Montepulciano Ris. '90	▼▼	5
○ Vin Santo '90	▼	5
● Vino Nobile di Montepulciano Ris. '91	▼	4

● Pinot Nero Vigna di Bagnolo '95	▼▼	5
● Pinot Nero Vigna di Bagnolo '94	▼▼	5
● Pinot Nero Villa di Bagnolo '89	▼▼	6
● Pinot Nero Villa di Bagnolo '91	▼▼	6
● Pinot Nero Villa di Bagnolo '92	▼▼	6
● Pinot Nero Villa di Bagnolo '93	▼▼	6
● Pinot Nero Villa di Bagnolo '90	▼	6

MONTEPULCIANO (SI)

AVIGNONESI
VIA DI GRACCIANO NEL CORSO, 91
53040 MONTEPULCIANO (SI)
TEL. 0578/757872-757873

Avignonesi is one of the select band of growers who have made Vino Nobile di Montepulciano a name familiar to winelovers everywhere. The estate is committed to experimenting with new varieties and new training systems (the "a raggiera" overhead system that greets visitors to the property is well known) and in the cellars of this dynamic producer the vast expanse of oak barrels takes your breath away. Lately, however, our impression has been that all this scrupulous effort has produced only modest results. Wines have been well made, even interesting, but nothing more. As a result, the Avignonesi management declined to present any wines for inclusion in the Guide this year. We did not consider this a very constructive decision, but we overcame the problem by purchasing the bottles ourselves for this evaluation. The best of our buys was the Merlot '93, which earned Two Glasses for its concentration on the palate. The nose, where green notes tended to predominate over the fruit, was less convincing. In contrast the '93 Riserva Vino Nobile di Montepulciano was not quite up to scratch. The garnet-tinged ruby colour precedes an interesting nose reminiscent of red berries and tobacco but the entry on the palate is a little weak, and it lacks the body to balance the tannins fully. The finish, which mirrors the nose well, is much better. A final note: the eagerly awaited Grandi Annate Riserva '93 is due to be released in 1998.

MONTEPULCIANO (SI)

PODERI BOSCARELLI
VIA DI MONTENERO, 28
LOC. CERVOGNANO
53040 MONTEPULCIANO (SI)
TEL. 0578/767277

Poderi Boscarelli is the estate that the enterprising Paola De Ferrari runs with the help of her children and consultant winemaker Maurizio Castelli, one of the best known and most capable oenologists in Italy. Work has only recently begun on restructuring the cellar, which had simply become too small even though every inch of space was exploited to the full. As usual, the Boscarelli wines we sampled this year scored high. The Vino Nobile di Montepulciano '94 is emblematic of the house style. The delicate aromas of crushed red berries so ripe they recall fruit preserve mingle with the spicier notes of oak-ageing. There is plenty of weight on the palate, although the tannins are a little too assertive, but this will be corrected with bottle-ageing. After the outstanding performance of the Vino Nobile di Montepulciano Riserva del Nocio '91, the '93 vintage also proved attractive, if not irresistible. It has a rich, intense nose, although the vegetal notes detract from the fruit and flower bouquet. But there is good length and the flavour is only marginally unbalanced by the tannins. On a less positive note, the Boscarelli '94 did not really come up to scratch, mainly because of a distinct lack of balance on the nose. However in the mouth, where there was structure and good length, it created a much better impression.

● Merlot '93	🍷🍷	6
○ Il Marzocco '95	🍷	3
● Vino Nobile		
di Montepulciano Ris. '93	🍷	5
● Grifi '90	🍷🍷	5
● Grifi '93	🍷🍷	5
● Merlot '90	🍷🍷	5
● Vino Nobile di Montepulciano		
Grandi Annate Ris. '90	🍷🍷	5
● Vino Nobile		
di Montepulciano Ris. '90	🍷🍷	5
○ Il Marzocco '94	🍷	3
○ Il Vignola '92	🍷	5
● Merlot '92	🍷	6
● Vino Nobile di Montepulciano '93	🍷	4

● Vino Nobile di Montepulciano '94	🍷🍷	4
● Vino Nobile di Montepulciano		
Ris. del Nocio '93	🍷🍷	5
● Boscarelli '94	🍷	5
● Vino Nobile		
di Montepulciano Ris. '88	🍷🍷🍷	5
● Vino Nobile di Montepulciano		
Ris. del Nocio '91	🍷🍷🍷	5
● Boscarelli '90	🍷🍷	6
● Vino Nobile di Montepulciano '92	🍷🍷	4
● Vino Nobile di Montepulciano '93	🍷🍷	4
● Vino Nobile		
di Montepulciano Ris. '90	🍷🍷	5
● Vino Nobile		
di Montepulciano Ris. '91	🍷🍷	4

MONTEPULCIANO (SI)

MONTEPULCIANO (SI)

CANNETO
VIA DEI CANNETI, 14
53045 MONTEPULCIANO (SI)
TEL. 0578/757737

FATTORIA LE CASALTE
VIA DEL TERMINE, 2
LOC. S. ALBINO
53045 MONTEPULCIANO (SI)
TEL. 0578/799138 - 06/9323090

Canneto has a number of interesting features that make it stand out on the sometimes very predictable winemaking scene at Montepulciano. Swiss-owned, it is a winery that has always given priority to Vino Nobile Riserva, a much sought after delight on the other side of the Alps. But it is a policy that means the estate is always exposed to the risk of poor vintages. So the technical staff at Canneto recently changed tack and came up with a Vino Nobile di Montepulciano '94, the first time the cellar has released a non-Riserva wine. It will be interesting to see how winelovers in Switzerland react to this major - and in our opinion very positive - change in strategy. The Canneto estate covers 56 hectares, 18 of which are under vine with nine new plots due to come on stream in the next few years. The modern cellar is, unsurprisingly, very well organized and the fact that the barrel stock was recently completely renewed hints at plans for further growth. The best of the wines proposed this year was in fact the Vino Nobile di Montepulciano '94. Its garnet ruby colour is moderately deep and the aromas are still rather closed but the fruit comes through on the nose together with an intriguing note of tobacco. On the palate, the tannins are fine but a little over-assertive, which gives the finish a faint hint of bitterness.

Guido Barioffi and his daughter Chiara are making good progress with their reorganization of Le Casalte. Until recently, the estate was mainly famous for the superb quality of its vineyards, which are among the finest in the entire Montepulciano area. Today, Barioffi are concentrating their attention on the cellar, where a new generation of Le Casalte wines is taking shape. Winemaker Roberto Cipresso, who is well known for his sure touch and gift of imparting both power and elegance to his products, has a range of new tools at his disposal. The cellars have been restructured, wooden fermentation vats installed, and small oak barrels and larger casks acquired for ageing. The effects of this revolution are beginning to make themselves felt and will continue to do so with an increasingly positive impact on quality over the next few years. The first wine the panel sampled this year was the Celius '96, a white obtained from chardonnay, malvasia and trebbiano, that regaled us with notes of warm toast and vanilla leading to a wax-smooth palate with hints of sweetness that may not have great body but certainly has plenty of charm. The Rosso di Montepulciano '95 is rather more austere, made in a style which accentuates the tannins rather than immediate drinkability. No Vino Nobile di Montepulciano was made from the poor '94 harvest and we will have to wait until April 1998 for the release of the '95, so Le Casalte could not show its top wine to the panel this year. Our tasters look forward to coming vintages, especially - as everyone will have guessed by now - the '97.

● Vino Nobile di Montepulciano '94	♀	4	
● Vino Nobile di Montepulciano Ris. '93		5	

○ Celius '96	♀	3	
● Rosso di Montepulciano '95	♀	3	
● Rosso di Montepulciano '93	♀♀	3	
○ Celius '95	♀	3	
● Vino Nobile di Montepulciano '93	♀	4	

MONTEPULCIANO (SI)

FATTORIA DEL CERRO
LOC. ACQUAVIVA
VIA GRAZIANELLA, 5
53040 MONTEPULCIANO (SI)
TEL. 0578/767722

Fattoria del Cerro is part of the Saiagricola group, whose wine interests also include La Poderina at Montalcino and Colpetrone in the Montefalco zone in Umbria. The Cerro holdings extend over 156 hectares of vineyards, which means that part of the vine stock can be replanted every year. The new plots are planted to patterns that are innovative for the local area but which elsewhere have become the norm: more vines per hectare and the introduction of selected clones, indicating that the estate is building a higher quality future. Away from the vineyards, the experience acquired by the Cerro winemakers has led to alterations in the cellar and the wines offered for tasting this year were of a very good standard. The Braviolo white was a revelation. A delicious monovarietal Trebbiano, it manages to side-step all the bitter flavours that usually characterize wines made from the variety. The chardonnay-based Cerro Bianco chalked up a One Glass rating for its fresh aromas of peach and banana, backed up by lively acidity on the palate. Moving over to the reds, the panel liked the Vino Nobile di Montepulciano Riserva '93 best. Its vibrant red hue is accompanied by notes of red berries and spices on the nose. Fruit is also to the fore on the palate and the interesting finish picks up the aromas on the nose very agreeably indeed. Then the Rosso di Montepulciano '96 really hit the spot; the structure and balance on the palate put it up there with the best in its category from the vintage. Finally, even though the Nobile '94 was very drinkable, it lacked the necessary complexity to get into the 80-90 points range.

MONTEPULCIANO (SI)

CONTUCCI
VIA DEL TEATRO, 1
53045 MONTEPULCIANO (SI)
TEL. 0578/757006

The wave of renovation we are witnessing at Montepulciano involves historic cellars like Conte Alamanno Contucci's as well as newer producers. This instantly likeable nobleman is renewing his entire barrel stock and throwing out the red and black chestnut casks that for centuries symbolized the Contucci estate and indeed Montepulciano itself. The venerable cellars located under the Contucci family castle are being cleared out to make way for oak in various sizes. In his capacity as President of the local producers' association, Contucci is conducting a particularly enlightened long-term policy that aims to marry the best traditional practices with the acquisitions of modern technology. The transition is apparent in the wines Contucci presented this year. The panel were able to observe the steady improvement in the range, particularly on examination of the nose of the wines. The better of the two Nobile '94s offered was the Pietrarossa vineyard selection thanks to the benevolent influence of new oak. The aromas of Morello cherry are more distinct and enhanced by the notes of spices. The palate is let down by the unimpressive vintage. The lack of concentration exposes a note of acidity, which fortunately is well within acceptable limits. The non-selection Nobile is a muted version of the Pietrarossa with rather less to offer on the nose. The Vin Santo is very nice, despite the poor year. It has elegance and attractive sweetness. While it may lack complexity, it is a pleasant wine with a lovely finish.

● Rosso di Montepulciano '96	🍷🍷	2*
● Vino Nobile di Montepulciano Ris. '93	🍷🍷	4*
○ Bravìolo	🍷	1*
○ Cerro Bianco '96	🍷	2
● Vino Nobile di Montepulciano '94	🍷	4
● Vino Nobile di Montepulciano Vigneto Antica Chiusina '93	🍷	5
● Vino Nobile di Montepulciano '90	🍷🍷🍷	4*
● Rosso di Montepulciano '93	🍷🍷	2
○ Thesis '93	🍷🍷	4
● Vino Nobile di Montepulciano '91	🍷🍷	4
● Vino Nobile di Montepulciano Ris. '90	🍷🍷	4

○ Vin Santo '91	🍷	5
● Vino Nobile di Montepulciano '94	🍷	4
● Vino Nobile di Montepulciano Pietra Rossa '94	🍷	4
● Rosso di Montepulciano '96		2
○ Vin Santo '86	🍷🍷	6
○ Vin Santo '90	🍷🍷	4
● Vino Nobile di Montepulciano '90	🍷🍷	4
● Vino Nobile di Montepulciano Pietra Rossa '90	🍷🍷	5
● Vino Nobile di Montepulciano Ris. '91	🍷🍷	4
○ Vin Santo '88	🍷	4
● Vino Nobile di Montepulciano '93	🍷	3

MONTEPULCIANO (SI)

MONTEPULCIANO (SI)

DEI
LOC. VILLA MARTIENA
53045 MONTEPULCIANO (SI)
TEL. 0578/716878

CAV. FANETTI TENUTA S. AGNESE
VIA CALAMANDREI, 29
53045 MONTEPULCIANO (SI)
TEL. 0578/757266

It was not very long ago that the dynamic Caterina Dei started producing wines under her own label, but the elegance of her products has already earned them a good reputation. Work finished recently on the new cellar, which alone is worth a visit to the 25 hectare property, whose consultant winemaker is Niccolò d'Afflitto. The estate has also been experimenting with alternative varieties to prugnolo gentile, the local name for the Tuscan sangiovese from which Vino Nobile di Montepulciano is partially or entirely obtained, and this has led to the creation of a new wine. This oak-matured blend of prugnolo gentile, cabernet sauvignon and syrah has been christened Santa Catharina. Its impenetrable hue reveals bluish highlights and the berry fruit on the nose is expertly nuanced with oak. The palate is less exciting, however, and it lacks the complexity that has become the estate's trademark. The Nobile '94 easily earned a One Glass rating for its bramble and wild flower aromas but the palate had insufficient texture to amalgamate the rough edges of the tannins. In contrast, the intriguing Riserva '93 vintage was almost a mirror image. The aromas are a little closed, even though the Parma Violets and fruit notes of Morello cherry, bramble and blackcurrant still come through nicely. But the entry on the palate is very positive, opening out with real elegance and a delicately judged balance of softness and sinew. Finally the Rosso di Montepulciano '96 offers a very pleasantly fruity style.

The name "Vino Nobile di Montepulciano" was formally created in 1925 on the Sant'Agnese estate and it was only after much argument - both in and out of court - that other producers were finally able to use it for their wines. That is why tradition reigns supreme at Sant'Agnese, to the point where white grapes are included in the blend for the estate's Vino Nobile. This total commitment to the label's unique heritage makes the Cavalier Fanetti wines seems dated at times but they are also extremely interesting. Cellar techniques and barrel stock for ageing continue to adhere to the dictates of past generations of winemakers so we find large casks, and fermentation is still in glass-lined cement vats. Outside, however, the story is very different. Sant'Agnese vineyard management techniques are right up to the minute and applied with an almost obsessive precision. Low yields and excellently located plots ensure that the raw material is first rate. The '94 Vino Nobile has a moderately pale ruby hue and flowery notes on the nose that are slightly masked by vegetal aromas. The entry on the palate is attractive even though the tannins are going to need more time to mellow fully. A decently made bottle from a noble tradition that earned its One Glass. The Nobile '93 was slightly better, although still scoring in the same range. The mature nose offers notes of leather and nougat, the palate has more weight than the '94, and the finish is stylish.

● Santa Catharina '94	▼▼	4
● Vino Nobile di Montepulciano Ris. '93	▼▼	4
● Rosso di Montepulciano '96	▼	3
● Vino Nobile di Montepulciano '94	▼	4
● Rosso di Montepulciano '93	▽▽	3*
● Rosso di Montepulciano '94	▽▽	2
● Vino Nobile di Montepulciano '90	▽▽	4
● Vino Nobile di Montepulciano '91	▽▽	4
● Vino Nobile di Montepulciano '93	▽▽	4
● Vino Nobile di Montepulciano Ris. '90	▽▽	4

● Vino Nobile di Montepulciano '94	▼	4
● Vino Nobile di Montepulciano Ris. '93	▼	4
○ Vin Santo '71	▽▽	5
○ Vin Santo '75	▽▽	6
● Vino Nobile di Montepulciano Ris. '88	▽▽	4
● Vino Nobile di Montepulciano Ris. '90	▽▽	4
● Aleatico '85	▽	4
● Vino Nobile di Montepulciano '93	▽	4
● Vino Nobile di Montepulciano Ris. '91	▽	4
● Vino Nobile di Montepulciano Vigna della Fonte '93	▽	4

MONTEPULCIANO (SI)

FASSATI
VIA DI GRACCIANELLO, 3/A
LOC. GRACCIANO
53040 MONTEPULCIANO (SI)
TEL. 0578/708708

Fassati has recently replaced its barrel stock, which was beginning to cramp the estate's style and ambitions, and Fazi Battaglia, the owners, have beefed up the winemaking resources by installing Franco Bernabei, who needs no introductions, as consultant. The results are there, for the wines we tasted this year reveal all the estate's potential as well as a laudable consistency. Every bottle presented won a very respectable Two Glasses. One of the best was the Rosso di Montepulciano '96 Selciaia. Deep ruby in the glass, it has good depth on the nose, where notes of very fresh red fruit emerge, and a close-knit texture on the palate. Our tasters sampled two versions of Fassati's Vino Nobile di Montepulciano, the Riserva '93 and the non-Riserva '94. The Riserva was the better wine, as was to be expected given the styles and vintages concerned. Its vibrant ruby hue was accompanied by complex, lingering aromas in which notes of coffee and toastiness tended to prevail over the fruit. The palate packed a punch but also revealed good balance, which will get even better when the somewhat intractable tannins have had time to mellow out in the cellar. The non-Riserva '94 was less memorable but in contrast is drinking beautifully right now. The nose stands out in particular for its aromas of bramble and cherry preserve as well as a distinctive note of flowers.

MONTEPULCIANO (SI)

PODERE IL MACCHIONE
VIA DI GRACCIANO
53045 MONTEPULCIANO (SI)
TEL. 0578/716493-758595

Last year's decision to vinify only the Riserva '93 cost Il Macchione its Guide profile because the panel literally did not have any wine to write about. It was worth the wait, though because the Vino Nobile di Montepulciano '93 was simply the best in its category. All our tasters awarded scores that shot it to the top end of the Three Glass range. No praise is too high for the work Robert Kengelbacher done on his 4 hectares in the Caggiole subzone. The unique nature of the "terroir" is brought out by severe selection of the fruit and expert use of new wood that enhances, without masking, the superb quality of the grapes. This Riserva has superb depth of colour and generous red berry aromas that marry magnificently with the spice of the wood. The stunning attack on the palate is matched by the wealth of extract and tannins whose breeding elegantly precludes any hint of astringency and the finish of this outstanding Vino Nobile is leisurely, broad and satisfying. The '94 non-Riserva is a less daunting bottle but still wins a One Glass award thanks to its delicious aromas of redcurrant and cherry. The poor '94 vintage shows through the cracks on the palate, where the tannins are uncomfortably prominent. There is also a bitter note in the finish. Il Macchione, however, is a serious producer, a fact underlined by the decision not to release a Riserva '94.

● Rosso di Montepulciano		
Selciaia '96	♟♟	3
● Vino Nobile di Montepulciano '94	♟♟	4
● Vino Nobile		
di Montepulciano Ris. '93	♟♟	5
● Vino Nobile di Montepulciano '90	♟♟	4
● Vino Nobile di Montepulciano '91	♟♟	4
● Vino Nobile di Montepulciano '93	♟♟	4
● Vino Nobile di Montepulciano		
Fonte al Vescovo Ris. '88	♟♟	5
● Vino Nobile di Montepulciano		
Podere Graccianello '90	♟♟	4
● Chianti '95	♟	2*
● Chianti Le Gaggiole '94	♟	2
● Rocca delle Querce Rosso '94	♟	2

● Vino Nobile di Montepulciano		
Le Caggiole Ris. '93	♟♟♟	5
● Vino Nobile		
di Montepulciano '94	♟	4

FATTORIA LA BRACCESCA

S.S. 326, 15
LOC. GRACCIANO DI MONTEPULCIANO
53040 MONTEPULCIANO (SI)
TEL. 0578/707058

La Braccesca has plots in three of the finest subzones of the Vino Nobile di Montepulciano appellation: Gracciano, Nottola and Cervognano. It is no hole-and-corner operation either, for the estate comprises 78 hectares under vine, 24 of which are included in the DOCG zone. The most recently renovated vineyards have been planted with clonal selections of prugnolo gentile, the variety at the heart of Vino Nobile di Montepulciano. Since 1990, the first year in which La Braccesca bottled under its own label, the estate has been supervised by Antinori, which looks after the vineyard management. The winemaking staff is led by the very experienced Renzo Cotarella, who has initiated a quality-driven production policy. The wines have lived up to his expectations. Significant investments have also been made in the cellar and the barrel stock continues to expand. For now, the range encompasses the classic Montepulciano styles, but new labels using imported grape varieties are in the pipeline. The Rosso di Montepulciano '96 is a pleasant bottle with clean, instantly attractive notes of cherry on the nose. The body is drinkable rather than substantial and the finish mirrors the aromas of the nose perfectly. It may not be monstrously complex but it was made by a professional hand. The Vino Nobile di Montepulciano '94 is rather different from its predecessor and much more representative of its "terroir". The ruby hue is good and deep while the range of aromas on the nose goes from red berries through to more mature notes, which combine attractively. The entry on the palate comes up to scratch but the texture necessary to balance the tannins is missing. The finish lingers but lacks depth so the final score did not take it past a One Glass rating.

● Rosso di Montepulciano '96	**Y**	2
● Vino Nobile di Montepulciano '94	**Y**	4
● Vino Nobile di Montepulciano '90	YY	4
● Vino Nobile di Montepulciano '93	YY	4
● Rosso di Montepulciano '93	Y	2
● Vino Nobile di Montepulciano '92	Y	4

LA CALONICA

LOC. VALIANO
53040 MONTEPULCIANO (SI)
TEL. 0578/724119

Ferdinando Cattani's estate basks in a particularly favourable microclimate thanks to the influence of the nearby Lake Trasimeno, which tempers the rigours of winter and ensures constant humidity in summer. The soils also have excellent potential, so we should be able to look forward to further improvement in the future. The 24 hectares are planted with local and internationally established varieties, including cabernet sauvignon, merlot, and - uniquely for the Montepulciano zone - riesling. Currently the cellar, where oak barrels and casks of various sizes are used, is being restructured. La Calonica's flag-bearer is the Girifalco, which is named after the Rocca di Cortona. It is an oak-matured monovarietal sangiovese obtained from carefully selected fruit. Since the '94 vintage was not considered of sufficiently high quality to be released under the Girifalco label, we sampled the '95. The ruby hue is deep and vibrant, introducing a nose of attractive complexity nuanced with tobacco and bottled cherries. The palate is moderately close-knit in texture, underpinned by good acidity that makes the wine very easy to drink. In contrast the Vino Nobile '93 was less enticing, especially on the nose where some of the aromas were anything but "noble" (a pungent argument for replacing the barrels at the earliest possible opportunity). It was still good enough to earn a One Glass rating, though, because it is very well balanced and as drinkable as they come.

● Girifalco '95	**YY**	5
● Vino Nobile di Montepulciano '93	**Y**	4
● Girifalco '93	YY	4
○ Bianco Vergine Valdichiana '95	Y	2
● Rosso di Montepulciano '95	Y	3
● Sangiovese '95	Y	2*
● Vino Nobile di Montepulciano '92	Y	3

MONTEPULCIANO (SI)

TENUTA LODOLA NUOVA
LOC. VALIANO
VIA LODOLA, 1
53023 MONTEPULCIANO (SI)
TEL. 0578/724032

Lodola Nuova has belonged to the Tenimenti Ruffino for some time now and is in the middle of a full-scale reorganization that involves both vineyard management and winemaking. New plots have been acquired in the excellent subzone of Gracciano, where experiments will be conducted with the new varieties that the revised Vino Nobile regulations allow to be used alongside the traditional prugnolo gentile. The elderly barrel stock is being completely replaced and new temperature-controlled stainless steel fermentation vats are already in operation. All this investment should enable Lodola Nuova to reach, in a very short time, the quality standards that are already taken for granted at other Tenimenti Ruffino estates. The potential is definitely there, even if for the time being the effects of reorganization are still being felt. Lodola Nuova wines are obviously well made but fail to capture the full character of their "terroir". The Vino Nobile di Montepulciano '94 presents an attractive, moderately intense ruby hue and aromas of tobacco that mingle with off-putting notes of very unaristocratic wood. However, the scores for the well balanced palate were a distinct improvement on those given to the nose. Finally, the Rosso di Montepulciano '96 proved less successful and only rates a mention.

MONTEPULCIANO (SI)

EREDI ANTONINO LOMBARDO
VIA UMBRIA, 59
LOC. MONTEPULCIANO STAZIONE
53040 MONTEPULCIANO (SI)
TEL. 0578/708321

Founded in the early 1970s by the father of the current owners, who started off with more than 20 hectares under vine, the Lombardo property has made a comeback into the Guide, earning a profile of its own again. The two Lombardo brothers have clearly defined roles around the estate: Francesco makes the wine and Gino manages the vineyards. Their new cellar was finished a few years ago, when the barrel stock was also replaced, and now Lombardo are turning their attention to new fermentation equipment. Improvement after all this effort is palpable, especially in the case of the Vino Nobile di Montepulciano. The humbler non-Riserva '94 version actually impressed our panel rather more than the Riserva '93, which was highly unusual given the respective merits of the two vintages. The '94 revealed clean aromas and nice intensity in a flower and fruit nose, backed up by fine structure and balance on the palate. The attractive tannins are well behaved and unobtrusive while the finish was good enough to take the overall score within an ace of Two Glasses. In contrast the Riserva '93 lacks depth on the nose, where faintly vegetal notes emerge to mask the fruit. The palate has moderately good body, plenty of style and a finish that may not have much breadth but is also thankfully free of the bitter notes that tend to mar the reds around Montepulciano. The Lombardo Rosso di Montepulciano '96 only scored enough for a mention but we were also pleased to note that it is excellent value for money.

● Vino Nobile di Montepulciano '94	▼	4
● Rosso di Montepulciano '96		2
● Vino Nobile di Montepulciano '93	▼▼	4

● Vino Nobile di Montepulciano '94	▼	4
● Vino Nobile di Montepulciano Ris. '93	▼	4
● Rosso di Montepulciano '96		2

MONTEPULCIANO (SI)

MONTEPULCIANO (SI)

NOTTOLA
LOC. BIVIO NOTTOLA
53045 MONTEPULCIANO (SI)
TEL. 0578/707060 - 0577/685240

PALAZZO VECCHIO
LOC. VALIANO DI MONTEPULCIANO
53040 MONTEPULCIANO (SI)
TEL. 0578/724226 - 02/48009704

Nottola is one of the most interesting Montepulciano estates. We believe that it is capable of making huge progress in the next few years. The area under vine has recently been extended to bring the total to about 13 hectares. When the current owners, the Giomarelli family, moved in eight years ago, they set about restructuring the cellars, which today are very well equipped. Experiments with wood of various types and sizes have been made, so now the visitor will see small barrels alongside larger traditional casks made of French oak. Chestnut wood has been banned as it is held to be incompatible with premium quality wine. The Vino Nobile di Montepulciano '94 is utterly typical of the Nottola house style. The ruby hue is deep but not impenetrable and the nose reveals aromas of red berries and bramble that need a few minutes' contact with the air to emerge. The palate follows through nicely, only slightly ruffled by the roughish tannins, to lead into a finish that is certainly pleasant, if lacking a little in breadth. We cannot report on the Vigna del Fattore vineyard selection, a barrique-aged Vino Nobile di Montepulciano, as it was still in the barrel when tastings were carried out.

The Palazzo Vecchio estate lies east of Valiano on the road that leads to Lake Trasimeno, where it owns 20 hectares of excellently located vineyard. The owners, Alessandro Zorzi and Marco Sbernadori, are in the process of reorganizing the property and replacing the antiquated equipment they found in the cellar when they took over. That Luca D'Attoma, a promising oenologist, has been taken on as winemaker shows how serious Zorzi and Sbernadori are about extracting the best from their potentially excellent property. Their new vineyards, which will come on stream with the '98 harvest, have been given the evocative names of Vigna del Bosco ("Vineyard of the Wood") and Vigna del Sole ("Vineyard of the Sun"). This time round they offered the panel a couple of very well made wines, particularly bearing in mind the transitional period the estate is going though. Their Vino Nobile di Montepulciano '94 is a garnet-tinged pale ruby, showing a certain maturity on the white fruit and leather nose. There is not much depth of extract but the palate's maturity and "drink-me" approachability won points. It may not be a wine to cellar but it is well worth enjoying a bottle now while you can. The Riserva '93 - from a much better vintage - was decidedly superior. It has the classic Nobile ruby-shading-into-garnet hue and slightly mature aromas of tobacco and leather emerge on a nose that still has plenty of fruit. Well balanced in the mouth, it concludes with a far from disagreeable finish.

● Vino Nobile		
di Montepulciano '94	♀	4
● Rosso di Montepulciano '93	♀	2*
● Vino Nobile		
di Montepulciano '93	♀	4
● Vino Nobile		
di Montepulciano Ris. '91	♀	4

● Vino Nobile		
di Montepulciano '94	♀	4
● Vino Nobile		
di Montepulciano Ris. '93	♀	4
● Vino Nobile		
di Montepulciano '91	♀♀	4
● Vino Nobile		
di Montepulciano '92	♀	4
● Vino Nobile		
di Montepulciano '93	♀	4
● Vino Nobile		
di Montepulciano Ris. '90	♀	4
● Vino Nobile		
di Montepulciano Ris. '92	♀	4

MONTEPULCIANO (SI)

POLIZIANO
VIA FONTAGO, 11
LOC. MONTEPULCIANO STAZIONE
53040 MONTEPULCIANO (SI)
TEL. 0578/738171

MONTEPULCIANO (SI)

MASSIMO ROMEO
VIA DI TOTONA, 29
LOC. NOTTOLA DI GRACCIANO
53045 MONTEPULCIANO (SI)
TEL. 0578/716997

Federico Carletti is well on the way to becoming one of Montepulciano's benchmark grower-producers. Year after year the improvement is palpable, thanks to impeccable management of the 120 hectares of vineyard under the watchful eye of Carlo Ferrini, an agronomist of proven worth. The best Poliziano Vino Nobile this time round was the Caggiole '94, a vineyard selection that belies its vintage, offering an interesting nose of sweet oak-derived spice over clean notes of cherry and violets, followed by a palate whose close-knit texture means good length and a distinctively elegant style. The Cabernet Sauvignon Le Stanze '95 delighted the panel with a rich, intriguing nose of infinite complexity as well as big, punchy extract and quite exceptional length. Three Glasses and no mistake. The Elegia '95 proved to be a truly wonderful drinking experience. A blend of barrique-matured sangiovese and cabernet with an impenetrably deep, purple-tinged ruby hue, Elegia unveils a generous breadth of lingering, fruit-rich aromas where Morello cherry and blackcurrant meld deliciously with the balsamic oak. The concentrated, fine-grained palate features delicate and perfectly integrated tannin. A perfect tasting is concluded by a satisfying finish that mirrors the nose delightfully. And a final word of praise for the Poliziano non-Riserva Vino Nobile di Montepulciano '94, which is as deliciously approachable a bottle as you are likely to find.

Massimo Romeo's estate is very small but it is also situated in one of the best subzones in Montepulciano, about 450 metres above sea level at Gracciano. Massimo's wines are instantly recognizable but their distinctive personality means that they are only at their best after a fair length of time in the cellar. That character emerges most strongly in the Lipitiresco, which we would recommend winelovers to drink after allowing it to age for a few months in the bottle. The range of wines we tasted demonstrated the Romeo estate's ability to cope with less than spectacular vintages. Their Rosso di Montepulciano '96 reveals a very deep ruby hue tinged with purple, notes of cherry on the nose and a palate that has you reaching for the bottle again. The Vin Santo bears the scars of the poor '89 harvest. Its deep golden yellow introduces a pleasant nose where nuts provide a keynote but the palate lacks weight, even though there is plenty of flavour. Moving over to the reds, we find a Vino Nobile '94 that only just failed to win a Two Glass rating. Its ruby hue shades off into garnet, leading into delicious notes of white fruit as well as the classic Nobile notes of Morello cherry. There is plenty of balance on the palate but not much depth. And finally the Lipitiresco lived up to its reputation as a full flavoured, laddishly muscular wine that really needs bottle age.

● Elegia '95	▼▼▼	5
● Le Stanze '95	▼▼▼	5
● Elegia '94	▼▼	5
● Vino Nobile di Montepulciano Le Caggiole Ris. '94	▼▼	4
● Vino Nobile di Montepulciano '94	▼	4
● Le Stanze '93	♀♀♀	5
● Vino Nobile di Montepulciano '90	♀♀♀	4*
● Vino Nobile di Montepulciano Vigna dell'Asinone '93	♀♀♀	5
● Vino Nobile di Montepulciano Vigna dell'Asinone Ris. '90	♀♀♀	5
● Vino Nobile di Montepulciano Vigna dell'Asinone Ris. '88	♀♀♀	5
● Rosso di Montepulciano '94	♀♀	2*

● Lipitiresco '94	▼	5
● Rosso di Montepulciano '96	▼	2
○ Vin Santo '89	▼	5
● Vino Nobile di Montepulciano '94	▼	5
● Lipitiresco '90	♀♀	4
○ Vin Santo '83	♀♀	6
○ Vin Santo '86	♀♀	5
● Vino Nobile di Montepulciano '91	♀♀	5
● Vino Nobile di Montepulciano Ris. '88	♀♀	5
● Lipitiresco '93	♀	4
● Vino Nobile di Montepulciano '93	♀	5
● Vino Nobile di Montepulciano Ris. '91	♀	4

MONTEPULCIANO (SI)

SALCHETO
VIA DI VILLA BIANCA, 15
53045 MONTEPULCIANO (SI)
TEL. 0578/799031

The tiny Salcheto property that Cecilia Naldoni and Fabrizio Piccin run with such loving attention makes a welcome return to the Guide after a couple of years' absence. In the meantime, the couple have added new plots bringing the total area under vine to around five hectares, while also considerably improving the quality of their barrel stock. These changes emerge clearly in their extremely interesting Vino Nobile di Montepulciano '94. The colour is deep and vibrant right to the rim of the glass and the notes of oak on the nose marry beautifully with the fruit. After an impressive attack, the palate loses a little steam by allowing a faint note of astringency to gain the upper hand. The nicely judged wood means that there are no bitter notes in the finish, which is very pleasant although we would have liked more breadth. We hope that Salcheto's inclusion in the Guide will be confirmed in future editions, particularly since we can now look forward to some very promising vintages indeed.

MONTEPULCIANO (SI)

TENUTA SANTAVENERE - TRIACCA
S. S. PER PIENZA, 39
53045 MONTEPULCIANO (SI)
TEL. 0578/757774

Santevere is owned by Triacca, a well known Valtellina-based producer that has decided to invest further in Tuscany. The original 12 hectares have grown to 30 and the estate's management team is now concentrating on the new cellar that is currently under construction. For the time being, vinification is carried out in the former farmhouse, but space is a problem and moving around in the barrel-stacked temporary cellars is a daunting task. The barrels themselves are a mixed lot and renewal is under way. Older casks stand alongside the new wood where recent vintages are maturing. The Vino Nobile di Montepulciano '94 that we sampled this year is very much a product of this transitional period, but impressive nonetheless. The ruby hue is deep and firm to the rim of the glass while the nose offers delicious notes of flowers, with violets emerging distinctly. The flavour reveals a professional winemaker's touch but although it avoids astringency it tends to lack depth and length in the finish. However it was still easily good enough for a One Glass rating, which is a good performance from a '94.

● Vino Nobile di Montepulciano		
Salcheto '94	�	4

● Vino Nobile		
di Montepulciano '94	�	4

MONTEPULCIANO (SI)

TERRE DI BINDELLA
VIA DELLE TRE BERTE, 10/A
LOC. ACQUAVIVA DI MONTEPULCIANO
53040 MONTEPULCIANO (SI)
TEL. 0578/767777

One of the finest estates in Montepulciano, Terre di Bindella again this year presented the panel with a lovely range of wines. These laudable results are achieved by a constant commitment to quality in the vineyard and modern cellar facilities which include a bottle store, a temperature-controlled bottling area and temperature-controlled fermentation vats. The return of winemaker Mazzamurro is a further guarantee for the future. Terre di Bindella also takes an active part in a promotional event every February at which the new wines released are presented to the public. There is no charge for admission and the show is a good opportunity for winelovers who rarely have the chance to taste so many Vino Nobile di Montepulcianos in one place. The Terre di Bindella Vallocaia '95 was still maturing in the barrel when we visited, so the panel turned its attention to the Vino Nobile di Montepulciano '94, with excellent results. The deep ruby hue shades into the classic shade known locally as "pigeon's blood". On the nose there are aromas of redcurrant and bramble fruit, slightly masked by the wood. The entry on the palate is promising but the tannins are a little too over-assertive for comfort, although the finish, which recalls the redcurrant and bramble of the nose, is lovely. This is an excellent wine and an object lesson in how professional vineyard management and low yields will always bring results.

MONTEPULCIANO (SI)

TENUTA TREROSE
VILLA BELVEDERE
FRAZ. VALIANO
53040 MONTEPULCIANO (SI)
TEL. 0578/724018

Lots of awards this year for the Trerose estate, which is owned by the Angelini pharmaceutical group. An increasingly important player on the Montepulciano winemaking scene, Trerose extends over fully 61 hectares of vineyard where the classic varieties of Montepulciano are joined by newcomers such as chardonnay, viognier, sauvignon, syrah and cabernet. Past experiments with a range of different types and sizes of wood have accumulated a very impressive barrel stock. The best of this year's wines, in the panel's opinion, was the Vino Nobile di Montepulciano Riserva '93, that came within the proverbial whisker of a Three Glass rating with an average score of 88. The attractive entry on the nose has distinct notes of bramble and Morello cherry subtly modulated by carefully judged wood-derived nuances. The palate displays great elegance and the delicious tannins are full integrated into the close-knit texture, while the finish is satisfyingly broad and leisurely. The Vino Nobile di Montepulciano Simposio '93 was almost as good. It has fine structure but the generously apportioned wood restricts the breadth of the aromas and there is a marked astringency on the palate. We also gave the Nobile '94 La Villa vineyard selection a good score. It is a very traditional red with flower and fruit aromas that lead into a stylish palate and a nice long finish. All the other Trerose wines easily racked up enough points for a One Glass rating, the most interesting being the delicious Flauto '95, an oak-fermented and matured sauvignon.

● Vino Nobile di Montepulciano '94	♥♥	4
● Vallocaia '90	♥♥	5
● Vallocaia '94	♥♥	5
● Vino Nobile di Montepulciano '90	♥♥	4
● Vino Nobile di Montepulciano '91	♥♥	4
● Vino Nobile di Montepulciano '92	♥♥	4
● Vino Nobile di Montepulciano Ris. '90	♥♥	5
● Vallocaia '93	♥	5
● Vino Nobile di Montepulciano '93	♥	4

● Vino Nobile di Montepulciano La Villa '94	♥♥	4
● Vino Nobile di Montepulciano Ris. '93	♥♥	4*
● Vino Nobile di Montepulciano Simposio '93	♥♥	5
○ Flauto	♥	4
● Vino Nobile di Montepulciano '94	♥	4
○ Liuto '94	♥♥	4
○ Salterio '94	♥♥	4
● Vino Nobile di Montepulciano '91	♥♥	4
● Vino Nobile di Montepulciano '93	♥♥	4
● Vino Nobile di Montepulciano La Villa '90	♥♥	5

MONTEPULCIANO (SI)

TENUTA VALDIPIATTA
VIA DELLA CIARLIANA, 25/A
53045 MONTEPULCIANO (SI)
TEL. 0578/757930

Valdipiatta has a marvellous cellar carved into the hill near the company offices, and the estate's original 13 hectares of vineyard yield wines that have brought the Valdipiatta label to the notice of winelovers everywhere. Recently two further hectares with high density planting were added to the estate and eight more have been rented in the Poggio della Sala subzone. On the winemaking side, the latest innovation at Valdipiatta is the partial modification of fermentation procedure, with the introduction of small wooden fermentation vats. We will have to wait for the '96 wines to be able to judge results, but in the meantime, the winery has released two excellent products: the Vino Nobile di Montepulciano '94 and the Nobile Riserva '93. The '94 has a very deep, even ruby colour and a nose of remarkable complexity. The weight on the palate nicely counterbalances the boisterous tannins, giving the finish attractive breadth. In contrast, the Riserva '93 offers more mature aromas where tobacco mingles with the fruit. Both components, however, take a back seat for oak tends to dominate. The tannins are sweet but just a little too assertive, hinting that this muscular wine will benefit from cellaring.

MONTEPULCIANO (SI)

VECCHIA CANTINA DI MONTEPULCIANO
VIA PROVINCIALE, 7
53045 MONTEPULCIANO (SI)
TEL. 0578/716092

This co-operative cellar has enormous potential thanks to the presence of members in the finest growing areas around Montepulciano. Recently, the winemaking staff, led by the oenologist Sig. Coltellini, has been selecting particularly interesting plots in the best vineyards to produce a distinctive premium range. These are sold under the Cantina del Redi label and mark a major step forward with respect to the past. The Nobile '94, for instance, is an excellent wine that easily crossed the Two Glass threshold at our tasting and actually turned out to be one of the best products in its category from the vintage. The ruby hue is deep and concentrated; the nose offers a broad range of clean fruit and flower aromas; the palate follows through elegantly, revealing sweet tannins and well integrated acidity. In contrast the Riserva '93 was less exciting. It is immediately evident that the nose lacks the elegance of the non-Riserva '94, with the vegetal aromas that intrude on the fruit, and a lack of concentration on the palate that exposes the acidity. On a more positive note, the Vin Santo '90 was a revelation. Its delicious nose offers apricot, walnutskin, dried fruit and candied peel while balance on the palate is ensured by the remarkable structure. Finally, the Rosso di Montepulciano '96 is a very pleasant, well made wine with lots of fruit.

● Vino Nobile di Montepulciano Ris. '93	♟♟	5
● Vino Nobile di Montepulciano Ris. '90	♟♟♟	5
● Vino Nobile di Montepulciano '90	♟♟	4
● Vino Nobile di Montepulciano '91	♟♟	4
● Vino Nobile di Montepulciano '93	♟♟	4
● Vino Nobile di Montepulciano '94	♟♟	4
● Vino Nobile di Montepulciano Ris. '91	♟♟	4
● Rosso di Montepulciano '93	♟	2
● Tre Fonti '93	♟	4
● Vino Nobile di Montepulciano '92	♟	4

○ Vin Santo Cantina del Redi '90	♟♟	5
● Vino Nobile di Montepulciano Cantine del Redi '94	♟♟	4
● Rosso di Montepulciano '96	♟	2
● Vino Nobile di Montepulciano Cantine del Redi Ris. '93	♟	4
● Vino Nobile di Montepulciano della Grotta Ris. '88	♟♟	4
● Vino Nobile di Montepulciano Ris. '90	♟♟	3*
● Vino Nobile di Montepulciano Vecchia Cantina Ris. '88	♟♟	3*
● Vino Nobile di Montepulciano '93	♟	4
● Vino Nobile di Montepulciano Cantine del Redi '93	♟	4

MONTEPULCIANO (SI)

VILLA S. ANNA
LOC. ABBADIA
53040 MONTEPULCIANO (SI)
TEL. 0578/708017

MONTESCUDAIO (PI)

POGGIO GAGLIARDO
LOC. POGGIO GAGLIARDO
56040 MONTESCUDAIO (PI)
TEL. 0586/630775

Villa Sant'Anna is a small-scale, top-quality winery where women rule the roost. The female members of the Fabroni family are passionate about wine, to the point where they are prepared to take major - and very expensive - decisions to raise their already high standards even further. Flanked by Sig. Mazzoni, their consultant winemaker, the Fabroni have adopted a policy of ongoing barrel turnover and have rented two more hectares of vineyard to boost production, since Villa Sant'Anna has difficulty in keeping up with demand. This year, the best wine we tasted was the Vino Nobile di Montepulciano '94. Its intense ruby shade is almost impenetrably deep, hinting at a palate of outstanding concentration, robust enough to counterbalance the traditional Villa Sant'Anna tannins. The Vin Santo '90, however, was not quite up to the usual standard. Its best feature is the nose, which offers dried fruit, almonds and apricot preserve. We would have liked to see a finish with a little more weight, which would not have jeopardized the elegance of this very stylish wine. The Villa Sant'Anna Chianti '95 was as good as ever. The bramble and Morello cherry-dominated aromas on the nose are in no hurry to fade and the palate is perfectly balanced and leads into a long, elegant finish.

Not for the first time, Poggio Gagliardo this year confirmed its status as a thoroughly reliable producer of well made wines right down the line. While this is genuine praise in any wine lover's terms, the estate did not really match either our expectations or the general trend to better quality that has manifested itself across the Montescudaio zone. In mitigation, it should be said that this is a property that, unlike nearly all of its peers, has not planted merlot and cabernet, the two varieties that have driven the zone's recent success. Once again, the Montescudaio Rosso Rovo was the best of the bunch and, although it failed to reach a Two Glass score, it is a good all-round red. The aromas have decent depth, revealing notes of ripe bramble, leather and cloves while the palate has good texture but is let down by a bitter note in the finish. The ever-dependable Linaglia is an object lesson in how a simple approach, properly interpreted, can mean sheer drinking pleasure. The fresh fruit and flower aromas are attractively mirrored in the palate, which is delightfully well balanced. The Vigna Lontana was also decent, its bright straw yellow leading into a nose distinctly redolent of oak-derived vanilla. The palate has good weight but still needs time to find a satisfactory equilibrium for its components. Both the pleasant, well made Montescudaio Bianco and the leanish, rather vegetal, Malemacchie came close to a One Glass rating.

●	Chianti Colli Senesi '95	🍷🍷	2
●	Vino Nobile di Montepulciano '94	🍷🍷	4
○	Vin Santo '90	🍷	5
●	Chianti '94	🍷🍷	2
●	Vino Nobile di Montepulciano '93	🍷🍷	4
●	Vigna Il Vallone '93	🍷	5

○	Montescudaio Bianco Linaglia '96	🍷	2*
○	Montescudaio Bianco Vigna Lontana '96	🍷	3
●	Montescudaio Rosso Rovo '95	🍷	4
●	Montescudaio Bianco '96		2
●	Montescudaio Rosso '96		2
●	Montescudaio Rosso Malemacchie '95		3
●	Montescudaio Rosso Malemacchie '92	🍷🍷	3*
●	Montescudaio Rosso Rovo '93	🍷🍷	4
●	Montescudaio Rosso Rovo '94	🍷🍷	4
○	Montescudaio Bianco Linaglia '95	🍷	2*
○	Montescudaio Bianco Vigna Lontana '95	🍷	3

MONTOPOLI VALDARNO (PI)

VARRAMISTA
VIA RICAVO, 31
LOC. VARRAMISTA
56020 MONTOPOLI VALDARNO (PI)
TEL. 0571/468121

The Varramista estate has what can only be described as a very distinguished owner - the Agnelli family. It is well worth pointing this out because the proprietors have declared that their overriding priority is to produce a truly great wine. Varramista has failed to feature in past editions of the Guide as its range was not yet considered to be of a sufficiently high standard to interest specialized wine journals. The estate's staff also tend to look down their noses at anyone who inquires about production techniques, almost as if they had better things to do with their time. It has to be said that Federico Staderini, the winemaker, is open and friendly as well as competent and it is thanks to his efforts that Varramista has turned out one particularly good red. It is obtained from about five hectares of vineyards that stand on sandy soil which is gravel-rich in parts. The wine is largely syrah-based but a range of other different red varieties will also go into the blend, depending on the fortunes of the vintage and vinification techniques are state-of-the-art. Part of the fruit ferments in stainless steel in the usual manner but a second parcel completes its alcoholic fermentation in oak. It then matures for over a year in small oak barrels, only some of which are new, and emerges as a wine of outstanding elegance. The '95 version has a deep red hue and aromas that recall peach - of all things - with nuances of white pepper and spices. The palate is clean-tasting and stylishly successful, maintaining a light touch through to the finish. Supple and sure-footed, it is much more approachable than many of the heavier Syrahs made elsewhere in Italy and abroad.

● Varramista '95	ΥΥ	5

ORBETELLO (GR)

RASCIONI CECCONELLO
FRAZ. FONTEBLANDA
LOC. POGGIO SUGHERINO
58010 ORBETELLO (GR)
TEL. 0564/885642

We have said it before and we will say it again: the Maremma is an area with superb growing potential. Even if only one in five of the zone's current rising stars actually make it to the top, the Maremma will be transformed in the coming decades into one of Italy's most important sources of premium wines. At this early stage, however, there are still relatively few good wineries. The top products are almost exclusively reds and nearly all are obtained from non-domestic varieties, cabernet sauvignon and merlot in particular. Rascioni Cecconello, with five hectares under vine and an outstanding consultant winemaker in the person of Attilio Pagli, is an exception to this rule for their two wines are obtained from those most Tuscan of grapes, sangiovese and ciliegiolo. Sangiovese goes into the very typical Poggio Capitana, matured in 20-hectolitre casks of Slavonian oak. The '93 vintage has a brilliant ruby hue, aromas of wild cherry, and a refreshingly bright palate with good, meaty extract. Surprisingly, ciliegiolo is the only variety in the Poggio Ciliegio. Most other producers use this grape only in small proportions for blending but the '94 vintage of the monovarietal Poggio Ciliegio was very well received. The oak-aged '95 has a deep cherry red hue ("ciliegio" is the Italian for "cherry tree") and deliciously intense aromas of spice-nuanced red fruit that have still to develop. The palate has gutsy acidity and tannins that will settle down with time. A wine for the cellar, where its present rumbustious energy will mellow into attractive elegance.

● Poggio Ciliegio '95	ΥΥ	4
● Poggio Capitana '93	Υ	4

PALAIA (PI)

PANZANO IN CHIANTI (FI)

SAN GERVASIO
LOC. SAN GERVASIO
56036 PALAIA (PI)
TEL. 0587/483360

CAROBBIO
VIA S. MARTINO A CECIONE, 26
50020 PANZANO IN CHIANTI (FI)
TEL. 055/852136

San Gervasio is not short of reminders of the past, such as the ancient watch tower that stands on the property, but it is a farm holiday complex with that looks to the future, thanks to the passionate commitment of Luca Tommasini, the man who has helped the estate to turn the corner. All the main points of a classic reconversion strategy have been put into operation: new vine stock has been planted and existing stock upgraded; the cellar has been restructured; and Luca D'Attoma, a top consultant winemaker, has been engaged. And results are already emerging for the Sirio blend of sangiovese with a small proportion of cabernet won a Two Glass score on its debut this year. A deep, vibrant ruby in the glass, it offers a good range of aromas with notes of ripe bramble, violets, pepper, earthy nuances and toasty oak. The attack on the palate is juicy and concentrated, the tannins are nicely textured and the finish has good length. The San Gervasio Marna is a blend of two thirds vermentino fruit with one third chardonnay which reveals intense aromas of apricots, pineapple and vanilla. The palate has plenty of balance and lays out its wares very attractively as it develops in the mouth. But Luca Tommasini's real pride and joy is the Ostro rosé. Vibrant in the glass and intense on the nose, it reveals rich notes of raspberry and strawberry. In the mouth it is refreshingly fruity and has unexpectedly good structure. Finally the nicely made if uncomplicated Chianti offers good fruit while the journeyman San Torpé also earned a mention.

In line with many other Chianti-based growers, Carobbio enjoyed a particularly good vintage in '95. We can therefore look forward to a very special tasting next year when the Riservas and vineyard selections are released. In fact this year it was the Chianti Classico '95 that best defended the colours of the estate and its traditional style of outstanding overall balance. It is a very well made wine with a deep ruby hue and moderately intense but exceptionally distinct aromas on the nose, where the fruit is underpinned by sweet oak-derived vanilla. The palate has complexity and structure, faithfully mirroring the aromas of the nose. The monovarietal Sangiovese Leone di Carobbio, although it seems something of a pussy cat next to the Chianti, the real "lion" of the range, is still a very serious wine. The ruby hue is impressively lustrous and the aromas probably reflect the vintage, for there is ripe fruit in the entry on the nose. Then come notes of jam and liquorice, nuanced with cocoa. The flavour is full, well rounded and lingering, notes of maturity again emerging. After these two "big cats", the cabernet-based Pietraforte was less exciting. Garnet ruby in hue, its nose is still dominated by oak-derived aromas. The palate has structure but lacks balance so there was only One Glass this time. But next year we will be back to taste that '95.

● A Sirio '95	🍷🍷	4
● Chianti Le Stoppie '96	🍷	2
○ Marna '96	🍷	3
⊙ Ostro '96	🍷	2*
○ S. Torpé Casina de' Venti '96		1

● Chianti Classico '95	🍷🍷	4
● Leone del Carobbio '94	🍷🍷	5
● Pietraforte del Carobbio '94	🍷	5
● Chianti Classico '88	🍷🍷	3
● Chianti Classico '90	🍷🍷	4
● Chianti Classico '93	🍷🍷	4
● Chianti Classico '94	🍷🍷	4
● Chianti Classico Ris. '88	🍷🍷	5
● Chianti Classico Ris. '90	🍷🍷	5
● Chianti Classico Ris. '93	🍷🍷	4
● Leone del Carobbio '93	🍷🍷	5
● Pietraforte del Carobbio '93	🍷🍷	5
● Chianti Classico '91	🍷	4
● Chianti Classico '92	🍷	3
● Chianti Classico Ris. '91	🍷	4

PANZANO IN CHIANTI (FI)

FATTORIA CASALOSTE
VIA MONTAGLIARI, 32
50020 PANZANO IN CHIANTI (FI)
TEL. 055/852725

Giovan Battista and Emilia d'Orsi's Fattoria Casaloste makes a triumphant entry into the Guide in this edition. The estate comprises almost seven hectares under vine, the fruit from which until a few years ago contributed to the success of neighbouring producers. Fattoria Casaloste may not be a large concern in relation to some of the other estates in Chianti but keep an eye out for it in the future, if our tasting was anything to go by. The Chianti '94 did well in the context of a disappointing vintage. The garnet ruby hue is attractive and despite the slightly closed nose, notes of ripe fruit still come through. On the palate there is moderately good body, nice balance and an attractive roundness. The vibrant ruby Riserva is an interesting wine. It has notes of black cherry and vanilla on the nose and a beguilingly sweet palate. It may lack weight but there are few other '94 Riservas that can come up with such rich aromas. In contrast, the Chianti '95 certainly has got plenty of structure. Its ruby hue is more lustrous than that of the Riserva '94 and the nose is slightly closed at first but, when it has had a little time to aerate, it then reveals the full depth of its fruit. The entry on the palate is also austere but there is lots of structure and rock solid tannins to back it up. It is a wine that can safely be left in the cellar for a few years and if the non-Riserva is this good, what is the '95 Riserva going to be like?

PANZANO IN CHIANTI (FI)

CASTELLO DEI RAMPOLLA
VIA CASE SPARSE, 22
50020 PANZANO IN CHIANTI (FI)
TEL. 055/852001

If there is one estate whose profile has given us real pleasure to write this year then it has to be Castello dei Rampolla. First of all because it it is indissolubly associated with the memory of Principe Alceo di Napoli, one of the greatest viticulturalists ever to have worked in Chianti Classico and, even more important, one of the finest individuals we have ever had the privilege to meet anywhere in the world of wine. Another reason is that this historic producer ran a very real risk of closing down completely after Principe Alceo's death. Thankfully, that period appears to be behind us now. The wines that have been coming out of the Castello dei Rampolla cellars recently are superb and the ones that are due to be released in the coming years promise to be even better. This success is all down to Alceo's son, Luca di Napoli, who has decided to devote his energies to the estate and to Giacomo Tachis, whose invaluable winemaking skills have always been on hand. The upshot is a version of the Sammarco, a cabernet sauvignon-based blend that includes a small proportion of sangiovese, that will go down in history. The '94 vintage has produced a wine this is quite awesomely good. The complex nose has just the faintest of vegetal notes over oceans of ripe red fruit. The soft, mouth-filling structure keeps the powerfully concentrated tannins nicely under control and the overall balance is sublime. A truly fine wine. In comparison the Chianti Classico Riserva '94 was less concentrated, obviously, but still very good indeed and our first tastings of next year's wine were an exciting foretaste of further delights in store. The forthcoming product is a mainly cabernet sauvignon and petit verdot-based blend of fruit from the '96 harvest and will be called La Vigna di Alceo. We would advise you book some straight away.

● Chianti Classico '95		♟♟	3
● Chianti Classico Ris. '94		♟♟	4
● Chianti Classico '94		♟	3

● Sammarco '94		♟♟♟	6
● Chianti Classico Ris. '94		♟♟	5
● Sammarco '85		♟♟♟	6
● Sammarco '86		♟♟♟	6
● Chianti Classico '88		♟♟	4
● Chianti Classico '91		♟♟	4
● Chianti Classico '92		♟♟	4
● Chianti Classico Ris. '85		♟♟	5
● Chianti Classico Ris. '86		♟♟	5
● Chianti Classico Ris. '88		♟♟	5
● Chianti Classico Ris. '90		♟♟	5
● Chianti Classico Ris. '93		♟♟	5
● Sammarco '88		♟♟	6
● Sammarco '93		♟♟	6

PANZANO IN CHIANTI (FI)

CENNATOIO
VIA DI S. LEOLINO, 35
50020 PANZANO IN CHIANTI (FI)
TEL. 055/852134

Year after year, the quality at Cennatoio continues to make excellent progress. It is even fair to say that improvement doesn't depend on the vagaries of the harvest for our tasting this year comprised four wines from the '94 vintage, a controversial year that generally yielded rather unexciting products. The panel was very pleased, especially by the Sangiovese wines, but then these by and large held their own around Panzano in '94. Indeed the Etrusco managed to make our tasters sit up and take notice with a virtuoso performance no one was expecting. The sheer abundance of the fruit was enough to overwhelm even wood as masterfully judged as the Etrusco's. The concentration is spectacular, the texture of the tannins deliciously close-knit, and the flavours unfold on the palate triumphantly. There were no objections to a Three Glass score. Next came the Cennatoio Riserva, one of the year's best Chianti Classico Riservas for the way it manages to embody the estate style of clean, if not very complex, aromas of bramble and black cherry and palate with good breadth and a sweetish entry. In contrast, the Cabernet Rosso Fiorentino was less intriguing. It is very well made and delightfully clean on the palate but its vegetal notes are frankly excessive. The bright, vibrant ruby of the Arciboldo '94 introduces a nose where faint vegetal nuances mingle with notes of super-ripe fruit and a solid palate with good structure. Much the same comments could be made about the Chianti '95, which is still a little closed on the nose but impresses on the palate. And at this point it only remains for us to extend our congratulations to winemaker Gabriella Tani.

PANZANO IN CHIANTI (FI)

TENUTA FONTODI
VIA S. LEOLINO, 87
50020 PANZANO IN CHIANTI (FI)
TEL. 055/852005

Giovanni Manetti is the young owner of Tenuta Fontodi and also one of the most far-sighted and intelligent grower-producers in the entire Chianti Classico zone. His estate is enchanting, not just because the villa where it is based is spectacularly beautiful but also because Manetti has consistently made quality the first priority in all areas of the business, from rootstock and planting patterns right through to the latest recruit to the sales staff. The cellar equipment is up-to-the-minute and the winemaker could only be Franco Bernabei, the oenologist who has won more Glasses than anyone else in the history of the Guide (the wineries for which Bernabei acts as consultant have totted up 36 Three Glass ratings). But Giovanni Manetti is also a respected producer and man whose common sense and commanding personality make others listen. As is quite often the case, his wine reflects its maker's character. They are well balanced, very pleasant, easy to understand and technically outstanding. In short, they are a professional's wines and the ones we sampled this year were very good indeed. The panel thought the pick of the range was the Chianti Classico Vigna del Sorbo Riserva '94, far and away the best Chianti Classico Riserva vineyard selection from its year. Aromas of red fruit, violets and pencil lead fuse to create a nose of rare finesse. The flavour has depth and richness yet is still delicate, thanks in part to elegant tannins without a trace of asperity. The Flaccianello della Pieve, also from the '94 vintage, scored only a few points less. It is not quite as soft on the palate, which is more "linear" and in which the tannins are perhaps too assertive. As we go down the scale, the Chianti Classico Riserva '94 had less complexity on the nose and was a touch more dilute on the palate. Finally the Chianti Classico '95 was a much simpler wine, but very well made and deliciously fruity.

● Etrusco '94	🍷🍷🍷	5
● Chianti Classico Ris. '94	🍷🍷	4
● Arcibaldo '94	🍷	5
● Chianti Classico '95	🍷	3
● Rosso Fiorentino '94	🍷	5
● Chianti Classico '93	🍷🍷	3*
● Chianti Classico Ris. '91	🍷🍷	4
● Chianti Classico Ris. '93	🍷🍷	4
● Etrusco '90	🍷🍷	5
● Etrusco '93	🍷🍷	5
● Mammolo '93	🍷🍷	6
● Rosso Fiorentino '93	🍷🍷	5
● Chianti Classico '92	🍷	3
● Chianti Classico '94	🍷	3
● Chianti Classico Ris. '90	🍷	5

● Chianti Classico Vigna del Sorbo Ris. '94	🍷🍷🍷	5
● Chianti Classico '95	🍷🍷	4
● Chianti Classico Ris. '94	🍷🍷	4
● Flaccianello della Pieve '94	🍷🍷	6
● Chianti Cl. Vigna del Sorbo Ris. '85	🍷🍷🍷	5
● Chianti Cl. Vigna del Sorbo Ris. '86	🍷🍷🍷	5
● Chianti Cl. Vigna del Sorbo Ris. '90	🍷🍷🍷	5
● Flaccianello della Pieve '88	🍷🍷🍷	6
● Flaccianello della Pieve '90	🍷🍷🍷	6
● Flaccianello della Pieve '91	🍷🍷🍷	5
● Flaccianello della Pieve '93	🍷🍷	5

PANZANO IN CHIANTI (FI)

PANZANO IN CHIANTI (FI)

La Doccia
Loc. Casole
50022 Panzano in Chianti (FI)
Tel. 055/8549049

La Massa
Via Case Sparse, 9
50020 Panzano in Chianti (FI)
Tel. 055/852701

It was another great performance this year from the small La Doccia estate at Panzano. Year after year, it seems to be able to trundle out wines of enviably reliable quality, despite the ups and downs of the harvest. There is only just over a hectare of vineyard at La Doccia but it is managed with scrupulous care to make sure the fruit ripens to the peak of maturity. The training system is the traditional Tuscan arched cane, still very popular in Chianti even though new vine stock in the zone tends to be cordon-trained and spur-pruned, a system which is both easier to work and gives less unpredictable results. Tradition is also the watchword in the cellar but small oak barrels have been introduced to age part of the wine. The annual output is less than 10,000 bottles, so we can already hear the complaints about reviewing such a small-scale operation. We are going to include despite such objections, in the knowledge that we have never been prejudiced against small wineries or indeed the large-scale "industrial" enterprises that the same purists also regard with suspicion. It is tasting that counts. And it has to be blind tasting so that producers large, medium and small are all playing on a level field. And it is at such tastings that Signora Cinuzzi Pancani's wines stand out above the rest. Her '94 has a dense, lustrous ruby hue and subtly layered aromas of black berries and cocoa that are still closed but run deep. The flavour is concentrated and close-knit without sacrificing elegance and has plenty of length in the finish.

Let us be honest about this. We just don't know where to find the right adjectives to describe this year's wines from La Massa without running the risk of sounding repetitive. After his magnificent exploits with the '94 wines, Giampaolo Motta has done it again for the '95s are even better. There are many reasons for this success and the credit has to be shared. The Panzano "terroir" is of course fantastic and Giampaolo knows exactly what it is he wants from it but there is also the oenological skill of winemaker Carlo Ferrini to take into account. Whatever the case, we have rarely had the chance to note such a satisfying sense of fullness in a sangiovese-based wine. The Giorgio Primo '95 is an almost unique example of a single-grape wine so sublime that it transcends the mere concept of "varietal". It has the rich complexity of a Cabernet, the concentrated elegance of a Syrah and the velvet-smooth opulence of a Merlot yet never relinquishes its absolutely unmistakable character, drawn from a marriage of grape and "terroir" that was made in heaven. The magnificent, typical aromas offer black cherry, violets and fresh spices and the palate has a subtle vein of acidity. Even the "ordinary" La Massa Chianti Classico is an outstanding good wine, albeit not on the same exalted level as the Giorgio Primo. The same basic characteristics are easily distinguishable: a remarkable combination of elegant drinkability and delicious concentration.

● Chianti Classico '94	♟♟	4
● Chianti Classico '90	♟♟	4*
● Chianti Classico '91	♟♟	4*
● Chianti Classico '92	♟♟	3*
● Chianti Classico '93	♟♟	3*

● Chianti Classico Giorgio Primo '95	♟♟♟	5
● Chianti Classico '95	♟♟	4*
● Chianti Classico Giorgio Primo '93	♟♟♟	4
● Chianti Classico Giorgio Primo '94	♟♟♟	5
● Chianti Classico '90	♟♟	4*
● Chianti Classico '92	♟♟	4*
● Chianti Classico '93	♟♟	3*
● Chianti Classico '94	♟♟	3*
● Chianti Classico Giorgio Primo '92	♟♟	4
● Chianti Classico Ris. '90	♟♟	5

PANZANO IN CHIANTI (FI)

PANZANO IN CHIANTI (FI)

PODERE LE CINCIOLE
VIA CASE SPARSE, 83
50020 PANZANO IN CHIANTI (FI)
TEL. 055/852636

VECCHIE TERRE DI MONTEFILI
VIA S. CRESCI, 45
50022 PANZANO IN CHIANTI (FI)
TEL. 055/853739

Not for the first time, tastings this year provided ample proof of Panzano's vocation as a "grand cru" and of Le Cinciole's standing as one of the producers who are best able to endow their wines with the true character of the Panzano "terroir". In addition, the '95 vintage in Chianti offered an opportunity, to those who were quick enough to grasp it, to make benchmark wines for the future: that is to say products that are not just well made, for there are no doubts about the local availability of the necessary skills, but wines with seriously good structure from vineyards that have been thoroughly upgraded. These general observation fit the specific case of Valeria Viganò and Luca Orsini very well. Their Chianti '95 is excellent and was awarded a high score by all the members of our panel. A brilliant, deep ruby hue introduces a rich, concentrated nose in which ripe fruit aromas are enhanced by elegantly floral aromas and a spicy background note. The attack of the mouth-fillingly fleshy palate is overwhelming, the tannins fine-grained and delicious. Although drinking well now, this Chianti will improve over the next few years. In contrast, the Riserva Valle del Pozzo gained a more modest score, thanks in part to the unexceptional '94 vintage. Nevertheless, it was not far off a Two Glass rating for it has style, good balance and a certain finesse. Unfortunately like many other wines from the same year, it has matured too quickly and tertiary aromas of leather and tobacco are already present, as well as a slight dryness in the finish.

Montefili is one of the most prestigious wineries in the entire Chianti Classico appellation and has no need of an introduction here. However, we do think we should point out here that the fame of the Montefili label depends entirely on the quality of its wines and certainly not on their market availability for the estate has less than ten hectares under vine and yields are deliberately kept very low. Obviously all this scrupulous attention makes itself felt in the final product and in fact Montefili wine will very rarely let you down. They certainly did not this year for all three bottles scored well over 80 points. The first to be tasted was the sangiovese and cabernet-based Bruno di Rocca '94 which we found more interesting than on other occasions. The vegetal notes were well under control, allowing the bramble and blackcurrant to emerge over oak-derived vanilla. The palate has concentration, balance and temptingly delicious tannins. Then the Chianti Classico '95 looked a winner straight away with its deep vibrant ruby hue. On the nose, there are hints of cherries, black cherries and violets while the palate of this lovely wine is deep, rich and delightfully evocative. We rounded the tasting off with the Anfiteatro '94, the monovarietal sangiovese-based Supertuscan that is Roccaldo Acuti's pride and joy. We loved it. The beautifully sustained palate has class, great balance and texture you won't forget in a hurry. The aromas are typical of a truly great wine. Delicate brush strokes of tobacco, pencil lead and wild berries shade into earthy nuances to paint a masterly portrait of red wine at its superb best.

● Chianti Classico '95	♉♉	3*
● Chianti Classico Ris.		
Valle del Pozzo '94	♉	4
● Chianti Classico '93	♉♉	3
● Chianti Classico '94	♉♉	3*

● Anfiteatro '94	♉♉♉	6
● Bruno di Rocca '94	♉♉	6
● Chianti Classico '95	♉♉	4
● Chianti Classico		
Anfiteatro Ris. '88	♉♉♉	5
● Chianti Classico Ris. '85	♉♉♉	6
● Anfiteatro '90	♉♉	6
● Anfiteatro '91	♉♉	6
● Anfiteatro '93	♉♉	6
● Bruno di Rocca '90	♉♉	5
● Bruno di Rocca '91	♉♉	6
● Bruno di Rocca '92	♉♉	5
● Bruno di Rocca '93	♉♉	6
● Chianti Classico '93	♉♉	4
● Chianti Classico '94	♉♉	4

PANZANO IN CHIANTI (FI) PELAGO (FI)

VILLA CAFAGGIO
VIA S. MARTINO IN CECIONE, 5
50020 PANZANO IN CHIANTI (FI)
TEL. 055/8549094

TRAVIGNOLI
VIA TRAVIGNOLI, 78
50060 PELAGO (FI)
TEL. 055/8311031

Villa Cafaggio has now established itself as one of the leading producer-growers in Chianti, which tells you that Stefano Farkas is not a man to sit back and let things happen. He knows very well that if you want to make premium quality wine, you have to start in the vineyard. For his new vine stock, he has abandoned the traditional Tuscan arched cane training system in favour of cordon-training and spur-pruning at a planting density of more than 5,000 vines per hectare, which means a yield of about one and a half kilograms per vine. But moving on to the nitty-gritty, we are happy to say that Villa Cafaggio came through the difficult '94 vintage with flying colours. The wines are every bit as good as could be expected from such modest raw material. In contrast the '95 has all the makings of a year to remember, if the Chianti Classico is anything to go by. It came out very well in comparison with the more prestigious estate labels from '94, showing enviable overall elegance with its very distinct aromas of flowers and red berries and excellent balance in the mouth. The Cortaccio '94 was good but only a shadow of the stunning '93. The colour is attractive and the nose is still closed but the palate has good balance and is deliciously well rounded. Our third wine was the San Martino '94. A garnet ruby in the glass, it has reasonably concentrated aromas with mature notes of leather. The palate is dominated by tannins but there is no doubting its character. Finally the over-mature Riserva '94 was well below the standard of its stablemates.

This year sees the Guide début of the historic Travignoli property in the Rufina subzone. For over two hundred years, it has belonged to the Busi family, who preside over an estate of more than 90 hectares, 55 of which are planted with almost exclusively sangiovese vine stock. The only significant exception is an eight-hectare plot of recently planted cordon-trained, spur-pruned, cabernet sauvignon. Annual production ranges from 200,000 to 250,000 bottles and is supervised from start to finish by Giovanni Busi, the owner's son. Our tasting revealed a good all round level of quality and a very pleasant surprise in this year's star, the Tegolaia '94. A blend of two-thirds sangiovese and one-third cabernet, the Tegolaia offers a deep garnet ruby hue and rich aromas from which black cherry, bramble jam, pencil lead, vegetal notes and toasty oak all emerge. The palate is not as muscular as some but it has good texture, its acidity well balanced by the tannins, and the final is elegantly long. The Rufina '96 is a very appealing little number with a bright, lustrous ruby hue that introduces interesting fruit on the nose, followed up by a palate with impressive structure and up-front tannins. Our last wine, the Chianti '95, was a bit of a lightweight, with rather vegetal aromas, although perfectly well made. One final note: a substantial part of Travignoli's output ends up abroad. Is it not about time a few more home-based distributors realized how good these wines are?

● Chianti Classico '95	♥♥	4
● Cortaccio '94	♥♥	6
● San Martino '94	♥♥	5
● Chianti Classico Ris. '94		5
● Cortaccio '93	♥♥♥	5
● Chianti Classico '91	♥♥	3
● Chianti Classico '93	♥♥	3*
● Chianti Classico Ris. '90	♥♥	5
● Chianti Classico Ris. '93	♥♥	5
● Cortaccio '90	♥♥	5
● San Martino '88	♥♥	5
● San Martino '90	♥♥	5
● San Martino '93	♥♥	5
● Solatio Basilica '88	♥♥	5
● Solatio Basilica '90	♥♥	5

● Tegolaia '94	♥♥	4
● Chianti Rufina '96	♥	2*
● Chianti Rufina '95		2

412

PIEVE AL BAGNORO (AR)   POGGIBONSI (SI)

VILLA CILNIA
LOC. MONTONCELLO
52040 PIEVE AL BAGNORO (AR)
TEL. 0575/365017

MELINI
LOC. GAGGIANO
53036 POGGIBONSI (SI)
TEL. 0577/989001

We welcome Villa Cilnia back to the Guide this year in the hope that re-admission is a good omen for the future. Newer readers might be unaware that until not so very long ago, Villa Cilnia rivalled Tuscany's most famous estates in prestige and was the leading winery in the Arezzo area. But let us get back to the present, where there are also good things to enjoy. The first of these is the Vocato, a blend of sangiovese and cabernet sauvignon fruit. Its vibrant ruby hue shades into garnet on the rim, the very persuasive nose reveals notes of maturity, the tertiary aromas from bottle-ageing enhanced by a solid, fruit-rich background. The palate is full bodied, round and elegantly textured, and the finish lingers. This excellent first impression was confirmed by the Riserva dei Colli Aretini, which came very close to a Two Glass score. The colour is a deep garnet and the aromas suggest red pepper, coffee and liquorice. The palate is soft, well balanced and endowed with an attractively racy structure. The simpler but refreshingly drinkable non-Riserva Chianti '95 revealed ripe cherry aromas and moderate weight on the palate, with only a note of hardness in the finish detracting from the overall impression. And the only white wine on the list, the Mecenate, also held its own. A blend of chardonnay and sauvignon fruit, it has an attractive yellow-gold hue and intense aromas even though the fruit tends to be masked by vanilla from the oak. The entry on the palate is sweetish, there is plenty of extract, and the fruit-rich finish is very pleasant indeed.

When you're talking about a winery like Melini, you tend to forget that its 100 or so hectares under vine make it one of the most extensive estates in the entire Chianti Classico zone. About half of that area comprises the marvellous La Selvanella vineyard in the Lucarelli subzone at Radda in Chianti, which lies right on the border with Panzano in one of Chianti Classico's most privileged locations. Once again, it was the Chianti Classico La Selvanella Riserva '93 that impressed our panel most, making it into the final round of tastings and very nearly winning the third Glass we have awarded so often in the past. It is made in a very traditional style and indeed is one of the wines that best embody what "classic" Classico should be like. The typical notes of violets, liquorice and oak are all there, with bottle-ageing aromas prevailing over primary. The palate has great structure but the tannins are rigidly austere and "linear", characteristics which fundamentalist devotees of old-style Chianti Classico insist on. Fruit and new wood on the nose are anathema to such purists. And that was not the only attractive Melini wine we found on our visit. The Chianti Classico Laborel Riserva '93, for example, scored almost as well as the La Selvanella. But the real surprise was the Vernaccia di San Gimignano Le Grillaie '96. It is the best-ever version of this wine and went right to the top of its category thanks to concentrated fruit aromas and a soft yet firm palate. And to round things off, there was a very nicely made and even more nicely priced Chianti Classico I Sassi '95.

● Vocato '93	♟♟	4
● Chianti Colli Aretini '95	♟	2
● Chianti Colli Aretini Ris. '93	♟	3
○ Mecenate '95	♟	4

● Chianti Cl. La Selvanella Ris. '93	♟♟	4*
● Chianti Classico Laborel Ris. '93	♟♟	3*
○ Vernaccia di S. Gimignano Le Grillaie '96	♟♟	3*
● Chianti Classico I Sassi '95	♟	2*
● Chianti Cl. La Selvanella Ris. '86	♟♟♟	4*
● Chianti Cl. La Selvanella Ris. '90	♟♟♟	4*
● Chianti Cl. La Selvanella Ris. '85	♟♟	4
● Chianti Cl. La Selvanella Ris. '87	♟♟	4
● Chianti Cl. La Selvanella Ris. '88	♟♟	4*
● Chianti Cl. La Selvanella Ris. '91	♟♟	5

PONTASSIEVE (FI)

PONTASSIEVE (FI)

TENUTA DI BOSSI
VIA DELLO STRACCHINO, 32
50065 PONTASSIEVE (FI)
TEL. 055/8317830

TENIMENTI RUFFINO
VIA ARETINA, 42/44
50065 PONTASSIEVE (FI)
TEL. 055/83605

Bonaccorso and Bernardo Gondi, as you might guess from their names, are aristocrats who belong to one of Tuscany's ancient noble houses. In Tuscany, aristocracy and viticulture have always gone hand in hand and the Tenuta di Bossi is a fine example of that time-honoured tradition. The estate extends over a total of 320 hectares, about 40 of which are olive groves and 16 under vine. As you would expect, a superb 16th-century villa stands in the middle of the grounds. The varieties grown are sangiovese, canaiolo, trebbiano, malvasia, colorino, cabernet sauvignon, chardonnay and sauvignon. Carlo Corino, who is in charge of winemaking, uses the fruit to make characterful wines with lots of breeding. The non-Riserva Chianti Rufina is usually a solidly built, tannin-rich wine with a tendency to be slightly unforthcoming. The '94 version has a medium-rich hue, an austere nose and a dry palate with good structure, the tannins emerging strongly in the finish. The estate's flag-bearer Riserva is the Villa di Bossi. The '93 is already showing signs of maturity on the nose, where rain-soaked earth and candied peel come through, and also on the palate with its notes of dried leaves and sweet, mature tannins. Not for the first time, the estate's best wine was the monovarietal Cabernet Sauvignon Mazzaferrata, which revealed a deep, lustrous colour in the glass and a nose of very distinct fruit and balm aromas, especially mint. The palate is one or two grassy notes and good, punchy extract, making for a well balanced and very drinkable wine. Finally the Bossi Vin Santo '93 was a magnificent way to round off our visit. Almost unfathomably deep, complex, creamy and lingeringly delicious, it added the final touch to an excellent range of wines that delivers exactly what it promises.

Back in the early 20th century, the Folonari family hitched its star to the Ruffino trademark. For the past few years, however, the company's traditional product lines have been joined by the Tenimenti label wines produced exclusively on Ruffino-owned estates. The standards are breath-takingly high for the range includes the two Cabreo wines, the La Pietra white and the Borgo red, the pinot noir-based Nero del Tondo and the Romitorio from the Santedame estate. There is also the Greppone Mazzi Brunello di Montalcino and the Lodola Nuova Vino Nobile di Montepulciano, both of which are dealt with in separate profiles. Here we shall restrict ourselves to the Tenimenti Ruffino wines made in the Chianti Classico zone and the first one out of the hat is a stunner. The Cabreo Il Borgo red was a Three Glass wine right from the word go. Obtained from sangiovese blended with a small proportion of cabernet sauvignon, it unveiled a delicious range of subtle aromas where elegant notes of bramble, raspberry and black cherry fruit mingle effortlessly over an impeccably discreet background note of vanilla. The palate is equally distinguished for the tannins are sweet and stylish, and the structure is awesome. The Romitorio di Santedame '95, a blend of prugnolo and colorino, is almost on the same level. Concentrated and utterly convincing, it has only one weak point: extract that is austere almost to the point of harshness. The Libaio '96, obtained from a chardonnay-based blend, was on top form but we were expecting more complexity and texture from the Cabreo La Pietra '95, obtained from chardonnay again but this time wood-matured. Finally the still closed Nero del Tondo '95 and the Riserva Ducale Oro '93 will have to wait for next year's tasting.

●	Mazzaferrata '93	🍷🍷	4
○	Vinsanto '93	🍷🍷	5
●	Chianti Rufina Ris. '94	🍷	4
●	Chianti Rufina Villa di Bossi Ris. '93	🍷	4
●	Chianti Rufina Ris. '90	🍷🍷	3*
●	Mazzaferrata '90	🍷🍷	4
●	Mazzaferrata '92	🍷🍷	3
○	Vinsanto Bernardo Gondi '88	🍷🍷	4
●	Chianti Rufina '93	🍷	2
●	Chianti Rufina Ris. '92	🍷	3

●	Cabreo Il Borgo '95	🍷🍷🍷	6
○	Cabreo La Pietra '95	🍷🍷	5
○	Libaio '96	🍷🍷	3*
●	Romitorio di Santedame '95	🍷🍷	5
●	Cabreo Il Borgo '85	🍷🍷🍷	6
●	Cabreo Il Borgo '93	🍷🍷🍷	5
●	Chianti Classico Ris. Ducale Oro '88	🍷🍷🍷	5
●	Chianti Classico Ris. Ducale Oro '90	🍷🍷🍷	5
●	Cabreo Il Borgo '88	🍷🍷	6
●	Cabreo Il Borgo '94	🍷🍷	5
○	Cabreo La Pietra '94	🍷🍷	5
●	Romitorio di Santedame '93	🍷🍷	4
●	Romitorio di Santedame '94	🍷🍷	4

PONTASSIEVE (FI)

FATTORIA SELVAPIANA
LOC. SELVAPIANA, 43
50065 PONTASSIEVE (FI)
TEL. 055/8369848

PORTOFERRAIO (LI)

ACQUABONA
LOC. ACQUABONA
57037 PORTOFERRAIO (LI)
TEL. 0565/933013

You could not call the Giuntini family newcomers to winemaking in Tuscany. Giuntinis were involved in viticulture in the early years of the 19th century and Selvapiana has been turning out some of the finest Chiantis in Rufina for decades. Their consultant winemaker, Franco Bernabei, needs no introduction. That heritage and human capital is what lies behind Fattoria Selvapiana's very traditional interpretation of Tuscan oenology. There are huge benefits deriving from adherence to these principles, first and foremost a very strong relationship with the "terroir". But on occasion it can be healthy to look at the past through more "modern" eyes and that is exactly what has been happening at the estate recently. The effects are most easily detected in the newest Selvapiana wine, the Chianti Rufina Fornace Riserva. The '94 has a satisfyingly deep ruby hue and fruity aromas veined with clean notes from the wood. The palate is solid, offering nice tannins as well as one or two grassy notes. It is a fine wine, and flanked by the equally attractive traditional Chianti Rufina Riserva from the same year. This is more mature both in colour and in aroma but is well made, if a little less exciting than its sister. However there can be no doubt about the structure or the refreshing acidity so typical of Selvapiana wines. The renowned third Selvapiana Riserva, the Bucerchiale, had not gone into the bottle when we visited so we will conclude our profile by mentioning another red, the Pomino Fattoria di Petrognano (from a property with the same name as the Colli Fiorentini producer). The '94 version has a fruit-rich nose laced with vegetal notes, a somewhat tousled entry on the palate that soon tidies itself up, and a finish that just gets better and better.

Acquabona has always been very punctilious about how its wines are made. They stand out from the run of the mill on Elba precisely because they are so clean-tasting and free of defects on the palate. This philosophy is obviously inspired by the expectations of the local market, which demands uncomplicated, reliable products, and takes into account the quality potential of the traditional varieties, such as sangiovese for reds and trebbiano - called "procanico" on Elba -, ansonica and vermentino for the whites. So unless the vintage is something out of the ordinary, there are few peaks on the horizon, just as there are very few troughs. Efforts to raise the levels of quality at Acquabona are concentrated on the Aleatico, which is indeed the only product that can match quality and typicity in a way that embodies the unique characteristics of the island's viticultural scene. However when we visited this time, the Aleatico was not ready for tasting and it left a palpable gap in the range. The wine we liked best was the Elba Bianco, a characteristically frank wine whose aromas were enhanced by notes of melon and acacia blossom and whose flavour was attractively well balanced. We had hoped for better things from the Rosso Riserva. The colour in the glass was pale and mature, like the nose, but which was more convincing in the mouth, where aromatic notes of cherry jam mingled with faint vegetal nuances. The Vermentino Acqua di Bona is nicely made but a little dull while the Rosso '96 is bit of a featherweight. Next year we will be back to taste the Aleatico '95, which should be a much more rewarding experience.

●	Chianti Rufina Fornace Ris. '94	▾▾	5
●	Chianti Rufina Ris. '94	▾	4
●	Pomino		
	Fattoria di Petrognano '94	▾	3
●	Chianti Rufina '88	♀♀	2*
●	Chianti Rufina '91	♀♀	3*
●	Chianti Rufina		
	Bucerchiale Ris. '88	♀♀	3*
●	Chianti Rufina		
	Bucerchiale Ris. '90	♀♀	5
●	Chianti Rufina Ris. '90	♀♀	5
●	Chianti Rufina		
	Bucerchiale Ris. '93	♀	4
●	Chianti Rufina Fornace Ris. '93	♀	5
●	Chianti Rufina Ris. '93	♀	4

○	Elba Bianco '96	▾	3
●	Elba Rosso Ris. '94	▾	4
○	Acqua di Bona '96		3
●	Elba Rosso '96		3
●	Aleatico di Portoferraio '91	♀♀	6
●	Aleatico di Portoferraio '94	♀♀	5
●	Aleatico di Portoferraio '92	♀	6
○	Ansonica '95	♀	2
○	Ansonica Passito '92	♀	5
●	Elba Rosso Ris. '94	♀	2

PORTOFERRAIO (LI)

TENUTA LA CHIUSA
LOC. MAGAZZINI 93
57037 PORTOFERRAIO (LI)
TEL. 0565/933046

The wines of the Tenuta La Chiusa made a convincing return to the guide this year. Aleatico, Elba Bianco and Elba Rosso were the three champions which enabled Signora Foresi's magnificent estate to get back into the Guide. What was especially encouraging was the fact that it was not the Aleatico, as is so often the case on Elba, that did the trick so much as the consistent performance of all three products. Which is not to say that the '95 Aleatico is not a very good wine indeed. The deep ruby hue ushers in a classic bouquet of spring flowers, Parma violets and black cherries. The palate is succulent, concentrated and full bodied; the only criticism is that the flavours tend to fall apart in the slightly bitter finish. The Elba Bianco was surprisingly good and a far cry from the usual pale Elban glass of unexciting or obviously oxidized white. This is a refreshing wine with lots of personality and an intense nose of peaches. The very attractive palate has excellent flavour and structure. Sincerity is the Elba Rosso's most endearing characteristic. A no-nonsense red that showers the nose and palate with fresh fruit, it has the odd rough edge but holds up well in the mouth. The yellow-gold Bianco Passito is well made and offers pleasant nutty aromas but is less persuasive on the palate. And the Aleatico '96 is not up to the standard of the '95 but, since La Chiusa seems to turn out its best Aleaticos in odd-numbered vintages, we will keep our fingers crossed for the '97.

● Aleatico dell'Elba '95	🍷	5
○ Elba Bianco '96	🍷	3
● Elba Rosso '96	🍷	3
● Aleatico dell'Elba '96		5
○ Bianco di Trebbiano '96		5
● Aleatico dell'Elba '92	YY	5
○ Anzonica '92	Y	4
○ Procanico '92	Y	4

RADDA IN CHIANTI (SI)

CASTELLO D'ALBOLA
LOC. PIAN D'ALBOLA, 31
53017 RADDA IN CHIANTI (SI)
TEL. 0577/738019

Castello d'Albola is one of the six Chianti Classico settings that come straight from Wonderland. The villa dominates the valley below and the view is quite simply unforgettable. Over the past few years, since the Zonin family acquired the property, the wines, too, have been finding a style and charm to match. There are about 130 hectares of vines, located relatively high up the hill slopes, so sangiovese, which doesn't always ripen fully at altitude, is not the only variety that is grown. In fact our tasters think that the estate's most successful wines are Le Fagge, one of the best oak-aged Chardonnays made anywhere in Tuscany, and the pinot nero-based Le Marangole. We tasted the '95 vintage of both, and had no difficulty in awarding Two Glasses in each case. The Le Fagge was as thoroughly convincing as ever, and the wood was quite outstandingly well judged, while the delicate, aristocratically typical Pinot Nero was a sheer delight to drink. When we moved on to the Chianti Classicos, however, we found that the non-Riserva '95 was slightly superior to the Riserva '94, which had only moderately good structure and was a little more mature. And we are going to have to wait until next year to see how good the Acciaiolo '95 is. It should also be noted that, starting from the '97 vintage, the Zonin - and therefore, obviously, the Castello d'Albola - winemaker is Franco Giacosa, one of Italy's best known and most highly skilled oenologists as well as the man who for over twenty years led the winemaking team at the Duca di Salaparuta estate.

○ Le Fagge Chardonnay '95	🍷🍷	4
● Le Marangole '95	🍷🍷	4
● Chianti Classico '95	🍷	3
● Chianti Classico Ris. '94	🍷	4
● Acciaiolo '88	YY	5
● Acciaiolo '93	YY	5
○ Le Fagge Chardonnay '91	YY	4*
○ Le Fagge Chardonnay '93	YY	4
● Acciaiolo '90	Y	4
● Chianti Classico '93	Y	2*
● Chianti Classico '94	Y	2*
● Chianti Classico Le Ellere '94	Y	3
● Chianti Classico Ris. '93	Y	4
○ Le Fagge Chardonnay '94	Y	5
● Le Marangole '94	Y	5

RADDA IN CHIANTI (SI)

CASTELLO DI VOLPAIA
P.ZZA DELLA CISTERNA, 1
LOC. VOLPAIA
53017 RADDA IN CHIANTI (SI)
TEL. 0577/738066

RADDA IN CHIANTI (SI)

FATTORIA DI MONTEVERTINE
LOC. MONTE VERTINE
53017 RADDA IN CHIANTI (SI)
TEL. 0577/738009

The two sangiovese-based wines from '94 presented by the Castello di Volpaia this time impressed at our tasting, further proof that the generally unexciting harvest that year produced much better results from vineyards on the higher slopes. Naturally winemaking skills also have to be taken into account and at La Volpaia, owners Giovanella Stianti and Carlo Mascheroni and consultant winemaker Maurizio Castelli have done an excellent job. The Coltassala '94, a red from sangiovese, was right on target. The aromas are elegant and intense, mingling notes of bramble and black cherry, while the palate is soft yet firm and concentrated. The '94 may not be a wine to lay down for any length of time but it is certainly drinking superbly now. The Chianti Classico Riserva '94 is a much more traditional product. It is a little dilute, a characteristic that derives from the vintage, but as always the texture is wonderfully concentrated and the balance is remarkable. There were less positive comments on our tasting notes for the other two wines we sampled. The '95 Chianti Classico was only moderately good for the structure is less than awesome and the palate lacks smoothness. Then the Balifico '94, a cabernet sauvignon-based blend with a small proportion of sangiovese, was a disappointment. There were vegetal and toasty notes on the nose and the structure again failed to impress. However in general terms, this range from one of the zone's classic properties is very sound.

Every time we go back to Montevertine, we have to reassure Sergio Manetti that we still respect him and even like him in the same way we would a rather grumpy favourite uncle. We have to go through all this particularly when, as was the case this year, none of Sergio's wines is awarded Three Glasses. It is not just Sergio's totally comprehensible disappointment that we dread. It is the way he takes our assessment as an arbitrary punishment or worse as a personal affront. So we would like to make it clear once and for all that if there is one man we esteem and admire for what he has meant and means to premium Italian wines then that man is Sergio Manetti. He is a beacon, and it was some of his wines that set the agenda that led to the rebirth of the great Tuscan reds. Last but not least, he has always behaved like a true gentleman. Having said all this, we also have to tell him that if his Le Pergole Torte '94 is not one of the world's classic wines, it is because of the vintage and its perhaps slightly super-ripe fruit with only moderately concentrated extract. It is not his fault and certainly not ours. Such things that happen in all the best families. No one wants to dispute Sergio's honesty or competence, and no one wants to question the winemaking skills of his consultant Giulio Gambelli. We are happy to wait for the '95, which promises to be legendary, and hope that it will repeat the success of the '88 and '90, a few bottles of which are tucked away in our cellars waiting for a suitable occasion and, of course, the right group of friends.

● Chianti Classico Ris. '94	♟♟	4
● Coltassala '94	♟♟	5
● Balifico '94	♟	5
● Chianti Classico '95	♟	3
● Balifico '86	♟♟	5
● Balifico '87	♟♟	5
● Balifico '88	♟♟	6
● Balifico '91	♟♟	5
● Chianti Classico Ris. '85	♟♟	5
● Chianti Classico Ris. '86	♟♟	5
● Chianti Classico Ris. '88	♟♟	5
● Chianti Classico Ris. '93	♟♟	4
● Coltassala '85	♟♟	5
● Coltassala '90	♟♟	6
● Coltassala '91	♟♟	5

● Le Pergole Torte '94	♟♟	6
● Le Pergole Torte '83	♟♟♟	6
● Le Pergole Torte '86	♟♟♟	6
● Le Pergole Torte '88	♟♟♟	6
● Le Pergole Torte '90	♟♟♟	6
● Le Pergole Torte '92	♟♟♟	6
● Monte Vertine Ris. '85	♟♟♟	5
● Il Novantuno '91	♟♟	6
● Il Sodaccio '90	♟♟	6
● Le Pergole Torte '85	♟♟	6
● Le Pergole Torte '93	♟♟	6
● Monte Vertine Ris. '90	♟♟	6
● Monte Vertine Ris. '91	♟♟	6
● Monte Vertine Ris. '92	♟♟	5

RADDA IN CHIANTI (SI)

RADDA IN CHIANTI (SI)

POGGERINO
VIA POGGERINO, 6
53017 RADDA IN CHIANTI (SI)
TEL. 0577/738232

PRUNETO
LOC. PRUNETO
53017 RADDA IN CHIANTI (SI)
TEL. 0577/738013

The small Poggerino estate comprises on 8 hectares at Radda in Chianti and is run with passion and professionalism by its blue-blooded owner, Piero Lanza. Lanza is a true viticulturalist, who personally looks after the vineyard and cellar management of his property, occasionally turning for advice to the renowned oenologist, Nicolò d'Afflitto, who is almost one of the family as well as a consultant at Poggerino. For several years, the team has been getting very encouraging feedback from Guide tastings, which goes to show just how seriously Piero Lanza takes his winemaking. Consistent results are not a matter of good luck and quality depends on precise management decisions in the vineyard, such as pruning back and keeping yields per plant low. Then you have got to keep your fingers crossed for the weather. This year the Poggerino cellar has produced a convincing overall performance. The Chianti Classico '95 is a great bottle, the fruit aromas are exceptionally delicate and free of any excessive oak-derived notes. The palate, too, has nice weight and lots of style, which comes out particularly in the fine texture of the tannins. The Chianti Classico Bugialla Riserva '94, which replaces the former non-DOCG Vigna di Bugialla vineyard selection, is obviously more mature on the nose and the vanilla aromas from the oak are more in evidence. The palate is soft and mouth-filling but less elegant than the non-Riserva and slightly less firm.

We have had better wines in the past from this small estate at Radda in Chianti. It is not clear whether this year's disappointment is the result of poor vinification or plain bad luck but there is no denying that both the Chianti Classico Riserva '93 and the Chianti Classico '94 were distinctly over-mature on the nose. The aromas were actually very similar; the notes of stewed fruit and preserve do not augur well for the wine's longevity. In contrast, both wines were much more persuasive on the palate, where the Riserva especially showed very good concentration and a quite pleasing softness of flavour. Naturally neither of these bottles is the product of an outstanding vintage but to release such mature wines a full year later than they would normally be available was not a very wise decision in our opinion. However it is not the end of the world. Owner Riccardo Lanza and consultant Giovanna Morganti are more than capable of serving up delights of a very different order. We look forward to returning next year, confident that Pruneto will be back on form.

● Chianti Classico '95	♟♟	3		● Chianti Classico '94	♟	3
● Chianti Classico				● Chianti Classico Ris. '93	♟	4
Bugialla Ris. '94	♟♟	4		● Chianti Classico Ris. '88	♟♟♟	4
● Chianti Classico Ris. '90	♟♟♟	5		● Chianti Classico '88	♟♟	3*
● Chianti Classico '90	♟♟	3*		● Chianti Classico '90	♟♟	4*
● Chianti Classico '91	♟♟	3*		● Chianti Classico '93	♟♟	3
● Chianti Classico '92	♟♟	4*		● Chianti Classico Ris. '90	♟♟	5
● Chianti Classico '93	♟♟	3*		● Chianti Classico Ris. '91	♟♟	4
● Chianti Classico '94	♟♟	3*		● Chianti Classico '91	♟	3*
● Chianti Classico Ris. '88	♟♟	4		● Chianti Classico Ris. '86	♟	4
● Vigna di Bugialla '88	♟♟	5				
● Vigna di Bugialla '90	♟♟	4				
● Vigna di Bugialla '91	♟♟	5				
● Vigna di Bugialla '93	♟♟	5				

RADDA IN CHIANTI (SI)

ROCCALBEGNA (GR)

FATTORIA TERRABIANCA
LOC. S. FEDELE A PATERNO
53017 RADDA IN CHIANTI (SI)
TEL. 0577/738544

VILLA PATRIZIA
LOC. VILLA PATRIZIA
FRAZ. CANA
58050 ROCCALBEGNA (GR)
TEL. 0564/982028

The splendid Terrabianca estate, owned by Roberto Guldener, only offered the panel two wines this time. One was the Chianti Classico Vigna della Croce Riserva '94 and the other the Chardonnay Piano della Cappella '95, a white matured in small oak barrels. The Vigna della Croce was not entirely convincing, in our opinion. The aromas are rather mature, there is evidence of reduction and the astringent tannins in the palate seemed to sit awkwardly with the rest of the structure. Perhaps we were allowed to taste it a little too soon for despite its excellent concentration, the balance is just not there yet. However the Piano della Cappella was a much more exciting proposition, indeed it is one of the best whites you will find anywhere in Tuscany. The complex aromas of fruit mingle with an especially delicately judged note of wood, which shows just how expertly oak-maturing was conducted. The palate was also very attractive: the structure is solid and the length exceptional. Taken all in all, though, this year's wines from Terrabianca were below par. Before we start reaching for the superlatives again, we're going to have to wait for the estate's flag-bearer Campaccio to be released. Now there is a wine that has often come close to winning a third Guide Glass.

Romeo Bruni and his children Maurizio, Patrizia and Tiziano are the owners of Villa Patrizia, which this year celebrates the thirtieth anniversary of its foundation. And "foundation" is the right word because some very solid groundwork has gone into this property, thanks to the wisdom of Romeo himself, who never tires of reminding you how important it is to be able to listen in this life. "Those who listen, learn" Bruni claims and it is difficult to disagree. But over the last thirty years, the Brunis have learned a lot from experience as well. Their range of wines is extensive and well worth investigating. There are ten hectares of vineyards at Villa Patrizia, lying at 380 metres above sea level, and the Brunis rent a further five. Annual output is around 80,000 bottles, 80 per cent of which is exported to Switzerland, Germany and the United Kingdom. Romeo and Maurizio, with the assistance of oenologist Luca D'Attoma, came up with a fine range of wines, especially the excellent Orto di Boccio '94, a blend of sangiovese, merlot and cabernet that came close to winning a second Glass. The ruby hue leads into a nose that is still closed but which reveals intriguing notes of fruit in syrup, cocoa and pencil lead. There is good body on the palate, which is young but full of promise for the future. The Morellino di Scansano '96 was another exciting, refreshing wine with nice texture on the palate and characteristic aromas of pepper. Other wines to note are the ciliegiolo and sangiovese-based Albatraia '94, the Sciamareti '96, a monovarietal Malvasia, the 100 per cent sangiovese Villa Patrizia Rosso and the Villa Patrizia Bianco, obtained from a vineyard of old trebbiano stock.

○	Piano della Cappella '95	🍷🍷	4
●	Chianti Cl.		
	Vigna della Croce Ris. '94	🍷	5
●	Campaccio '90	🍷🍷	5
●	Campaccio '91	🍷🍷	5
●	Campaccio '93	🍷🍷	5
●	Campaccio Sel. Speciale '93	🍷🍷	6
●	Chianti Cl.		
	Vigna della Croce Ris. '88	🍷🍷	4
●	Chianti Cl.		
	Vigna della Croce Ris. '90	🍷🍷	5
●	Chianti Cl.		
	Vigna della Croce Ris. '91	🍷🍷	4
●	Chianti Cl.		
	Vigna della Croce Ris. '93	🍷🍷	5

●	Albatraia '96	🍷	1*
●	Morellino di Scansano '96	🍷	2
●	Orto di Boccio '94	🍷	4
○	Sciamareti '96	🍷	2
○	Villa Patrizia Bianco '96		1
●	Villa Patrizia Rosso '95		3

ROCCATEDERIGHI (GR)

MELETA
LOC. MELETA
58028 ROCCATEDERIGHI (GR)
TEL. 0564/567155

RUFINA (FI)

FATTORIA DI BASCIANO
V.LE DUCA DELLA VITTORIA, 159
50068 RUFINA (FI)
TEL. 055/8397034

If your reviewer had to choose one red grape variety over the rest, the selection would not be easy for many vine types could reasonably claim to be unique. The same is probably true of all the other tasters around the globe. Should you acknowledge the austere perfection of cabernet sauvignon, surrender to the discreet charms of pinot noir, contemplate the magnificence of nebbiolo or allow yourself to be seduced by syrah? On second thoughts, why worry about it when merlot is always on hand to keep you company? It is a powerful yet delicate grape, versatile but full of character, and the perfect ally when you're entertaining. These were some of the thoughts that occurred to us when we were confronted with this year's new wine at Meleta, one of the Maremma's leading estates thanks to the efforts of Erica Suter and Franco Bernabei. The newcomer is a superb Merlot, which is up there with the very best from France and Italy. Its aromas are stylish and complement each other beautifully, the palate is soft and well balanced and the tannins are wonderfully mellow. There was no doubt about the Two Glass verdict. Next, the already famous Rosso della Rocca very nearly won a third Guide Glass. This blend of cabernet, merlot and sangiovese has a dark pigeon's blood hue and a lovely nose of citron and eucalyptus over a faint note of sweet wood. The palate of this formidable wine unfolds like a peacock's tail, rather in the manner of a Musigny, recalling redcurrant and wild cherry. Finally the Bianco della Rocca is also very nicely made, albeit lacking in complexity, while the Pietrello d'Oro, like all the other Meleta reds, is deliciously soft.

Here's yet another Tuscan new entry to the Guide: the Fattoria di Basciano, a well known name around Rufina since it belongs to the Masis, who can point to a long family tradition of making and selling wine. Paolo Masi is the man who supervises every stage of production, successfully combining a passion for winemaking with the demands of marketing. The wines we tasted all performed very well, with a consistency that was especially impressive. That reliability is probably the result of skilful blending in the cellar rather than a characteristic of the vineyard selections. Dependability is the watchword of the entire Fattoria di Basciano range, backed up by genuine value for money. The best of the wines we tried was the Il Corto '95, a red obtained from sangiovese fruit blended with ten per cent cabernet that came close to a second Glass. The ruby hue is deep and vibrant and the nose clean and intense, with fruit and vegetal notes merging nicely into oak-derived aromas. There is good concentration on the palate, where the delicious tannins take you into a very convincing finish. Then the I Pini '95 came close to matching its stablemate's score. This blend of equal proportions of sangiovese and cabernet has a palate very similar to, and perhaps even fuller than, the Il Corto but also reveals an over-assertive vegetal aroma of asparagus and red pepper. Truth to tell, there are green notes in all the Basciano wines, even the Rufina Riservas, both of which however have bewitching softness of structure. The rest of the wines in the range had moderate structure and no real complexity but were easily well enough made to be worth one Guide Glass.

● Merlot '94	♟♟	6
● Rosso della Rocca '94	♟♟	5
○ Bianco della Rocca '96	♟	4
● Pietrello d'Oro '95	♟	5
● Pietrello d'Oro '88	♟♟	4*
● Pietrello d'Oro '90	♟♟	4*
● Pietrello d'Oro '91	♟♟	4
● Rosso della Rocca '85	♟♟	5
● Rosso della Rocca '86	♟♟	5
● Rosso della Rocca '88	♟♟	5
● Rosso della Rocca '91	♟♟	5
● Rosso della Rocca '92	♟♟	4
● Rosso della Rocca '93	♟♟	4
● Pietrello d'Oro '93	♟	3
● Pietrello d'Oro '94	♟	4

● Chianti Rufina '95	♟	2
● Chianti Rufina Ris. '93	♟	2
● Chianti Rufina Ris. '94	♟	2
● I Pini '94	♟	3
● I Pini '95	♟	3
● Il Corto '94	♟	3
● Il Corto '95	♟	3

S. CASCIANO VAL DI PESA (FI)

CASTELLI DEL GREVEPESA
VIA GREVIGIANA, 34
LOC. MERCATALE VAL DI PESA
50024 S. CASCIANO VAL DI PESA (FI)
TEL. 055/821101-821196

Can a major co-operative cellar make high profile premium quality wines? It is a question to which the prestigious Castelli di Grevepesa winery provides a very clear answer with its huge range of enviably well made products. To cap it all, this year we were presented with a superb red obtained mainly from cabernet sauvignon, the Guado al Luco '93. Its balmy aromas mingle with elegant minty notes, leading into a firm, chewy palate that has great texture and length. Our congratulation to Grevepesa for this delightfully stylish bottle. As usual, the Chianti Classico Castelgreve wines, both the non-Riserva '95 and the Riserva '94, were very well made. The '95 is obviously the simpler and more dilute of the two although its raw material comes from a distinctly better vintage. The Riserva is soft and mouth-filling. We liked it better because of its complex aromas and robust balance on the palate. Our tasters left with the general impression that Castelli di Grevepesa is a cellar that is going places. Next year's releases could give us further proof in the shape of the Panzano, Lamole and Vigna Elisa vineyard selections, which have not yet been released.

S. CASCIANO VAL DI PESA (FI)

FATTORIA CORZANO E PATERNO
LOC. S. VITO
FRAZ. S. PANCRAZIO
50020 S. CASCIANO VAL DI PESA (FI)
TEL. 055/8248179-8249114

Neither Gelpke Wendelin, who owns the Fattoria Corzano e Paterno, nor Alioscha Goldsmith, the winemaker, have particularly Tuscan names but the wine they make is as traditional as any in the region. The property comprises eight hectares under vine, situated just outside the boundary of the Chianti Classico zone. That's why Corzano e Paterno Chianti is just "Chianti", even though it often matches its nobler neighbours for quality. The '94 vintage was not one of the best, however, and the Terre di Corzano Riserva only offered a slightly bitter, unripe impression on the palate and the nose, which also lacked clarity. There are problems for the Riserva '93 as well. The nose is rather muzzy and the unforthcoming palate is bitterish and closed. It was the non-Riserva Chianti that carried off all the prizes at our tasting, which is not surprising given the quality of the grapes. The '95 has a lovely ruby hue with lots of fruit on the nose and a palate that is refreshingly tart and very, very drinkable, if a little unsophisticated. However the Corzano red gets the lion's share of attention in the cellar. Obtained from equal proportions of cabernet sauvignon and sangiovese, it ages for 14 months in small oak barrels (70% new and 30% used for the second year). The '94 Corzano is very similar to its predecessor. Solidly built and very firm, it shuns virtuoso flights of fancy. The ruby hue is deep and vibrant, and the intense nose discloses medicinal nuances with notes of Peruvian bark. The muscular palate has concentration and generous fruit, with a distinctly bitter note in both mid-palate and finish.

● Guado al Luco '93	♟♟	5
● Chianti Classico Castelgreve '95	♟	2*
● Chianti Classico Castelgreve Ris. '94	♟	3
● Chianti Classico Castelgreve Ris. '88	♟♟	4
● Chianti Classico Clemente VII '88	♟♟	5
● Chianti Classico Grevepesa Ris. '90	♟♟	4
● Chianti Classico Montefiridolfi '90	♟♟	4
● Chianti Classico Vigna Elisa '90	♟♟	5
● Chianti Classico Clemente VII '94	♟	5
● Chianti Classico S. Angelo Vico l'Abate '90	♟	5

● Il Corzano '94	♟	5
● Chianti '95		3
● Chianti Ris. '93		3
● Chianti Terre di Corzano Ris. '94		5
● Chianti Terre di Corzano Ris. '90	♟♟	5
○ Vin Santo '90	♟♟	5
○ Aglaia '94	♟	3
○ Aglaia '95	♟	4
● Chianti Terre di Corzano '93	♟	3
Chianti Terre di Corzano '94	♟	3
● Il Corzano '90	♟	5
● Il Corzano '93	♟	5

S. CASCIANO VAL DI PESA (FI) S. CASCIANO VAL DI PESA (FI)

LA SALA
VIA SORRIPA, 34
50026 S. CASCIANO VAL DI PESA (FI)
TEL. 055/828111

FATTORIA LE CORTI - CORSINI
VIA S. PIERO DI SOTTO, 1
50026 S. CASCIANO VAL DI PESA (FI)
TEL. 055/820123

At La Sala we were lucky enough to taste to very well made wines that leave no doubt about where they come from. The panel were particularly struck by the "goût de terroir" that owner and guiding spirit Laura Baronti's commitment and sheer honest-to-goodness passion for wine continue to infuse into the cellar's products. The new consultant winemaker is Marco Chellini, an oenologist and agronomist with a very sensitive touch. Between them, Laura and Marco have created a lovely '94 version of the Campo all'Albero from a blend of sangiovese grapes with a small proportion of cabernet sauvignon. The intense, slightly balmy aromas herald a surprisingly drinkable wine for a product of such rich concentration. And their Chianti Classico '95 is another extremely attractive wine, and certainly much softer and more approachable than you might expect from the vintage. In both cases, as we said before, all the most characteristic features of the San Casciano "goût de terroir" are there to be enjoyed. These fine quality sangiovese reds are instantly accommodating and deliciously soft. And the same could be said about any of the wines that this small, highly professional cellar releases.

If you were to compile a list of the Chianti wineries that have been making interesting progress recently then you would have to include the estate of Principe Duccio Corsini, a man who is shrewd enough to avail himself of Carlo Ferrini's legendary winemaking talents. It is also true to say that even though quality levels have only been seriously good for a few years, Le Corti's 40 hectares of vineyard in the Chianti Classico zone and the winemaking skills currently available bode well for the future. This year all three wines presented did well. By far the best was the Chianti Classico Don Tommaso '95, a red matured in small oak barrels that had very stylish, intense aromas where oak-derived notes were perhaps a little too much in evidence. The palate is firm and deliciously textured, the tannins are delicate and there is plenty of body to sustain the other components. The Chianti Classico Cortevecchio Riserva '94 was more linear and less accessible. The palate not as fleshy as the Don Tommaso's and the wine is very much in the traditional Chianti mould. The Chianti Classico '95 was also good but could have been even better for it lacked concentration and the various aromas on the nose were less easily identifiable. Last but not least, it was encouraging to note that the '96 barrels the panel sampled were very promising indeed.

● Campo all'Albero '94	♟♟	4
● Chianti Classico '95	♟	3
● Campo all'Albero '93	♟	4
● Chianti Classico '90	♟	3*
● Chianti Classico '91	♟	3*
● Chianti Classico '93	♟	2*
● Chianti Classico Ris. '90	♟	4*
● Chianti Classico Ris. '93	♟	3*

● Chianti Classico Don Tommaso '95	♟♟	5
● Chianti Classico '95	♟	3
● Chianti Classico Cortevecchia Ris. '94	♟	4
● Chianti Classico '93	♟♟	3*
● Chianti Classico Don Tommaso '94	♟♟	4
● Chianti Classico Ris. '93	♟♟	4
● Chianti Classico '94	♟	2*

S. CASCIANO VAL DI PESA (FI)   S. CASCIANO VAL DI PESA (FI)

ANTICA FATTORIA MACHIAVELLI
LOC. S. ANDREA IN PERCUSSINA
50026 S. CASCIANO VAL DI PESA (FI)
TEL. 0577/989001

FATTORIA POGGIOPIANO
VIA DI PISIGNANO, 26/30
50026 S. CASCIANO VAL DI PESA (FI)
TEL. 055/8229629

This famous cellar, now part of the Gruppo Italiano Vini, is still in the middle of a major image and product rethink but compliments and even international awards are arriving thick and fast. Suffice it to say that this year, the Chianti Classico Vigna di Fontalle Riserva '94 won a gold medal at the International Wine Challenge held during Vinexpo at Bordeaux. International prizes don't come any more prestigious. On our visit, the Vigna di Fontalle did not produce quite the same tingling of the spine but it still reached the final round of tastings for it really is a beautifully crafted wine. It has intense aromas of fruit, where bramble and black cherry mingle against a delightful background note of vanilla. The palate is mouth-filling and velvet-smooth with a very modern style but it lacks a little in length, a characteristic of wines from the San Casciano subzone. They are as enticingly gluggable as you could wish but are often short on depth. For power and concentration, there was no comparison with the potent Ser Niccolò Solatio del Tani '93, a monovarietal Cabernet Sauvignon. Its aromas are intense, if somewhat lacking in complexity, but the palate has the texture of a world-beater. The Chianti Classico Conti Serristori was more dilute but there again it doesn't pretend to be on the same level of quality. This competitively priced bottle drinks like a budget version of the Vigna di Fontalle. The man who has put together this excellent range is cellar manager Nunzio Capurso, a professional with a gift for re-interpreting all that is best in the winemaking heritage of Chianti.

The Fattoria Poggiopiano is a new entry to the Guide this year and it has gone straight to the top with a Three Glass wine at its very first attempt. This is not something that happens often, partly because we are reluctant to encourage nine-day wonders. Every rule has its exception, though, and Fattoria Poggiopiano is the one in this case. There are a number of reasons for the estate's success but the driving force is the team that has created the cellar's products. Their names are Alessandro Bartoli, the owner, and Luca D'Attoma, a very promising young winemaker we have already mentioned elsewhere for D'Attoma works mainly in the provinces of Livorno and Pisa, supervising estates such as Tua Rita, Le Macchiole and Ghizzano. Alessandro and Luca have come up with two very interesting wines indeed, one of which in particular is a stunner. It is a Supertuscan with the evocative name of Rosso di Sera ("Red Sky at Night"), a blend of sangiovese with a modest proportion of colorino fruit from the '95 vintage. This whopper of a wine starts off with a bouquet of intense, splendidly rich fruit in which notes of black cherry are followed by blackcurrant and bramble over a delicious "basso continuo" of vanilla. But it is on the palate that Rosso di Sera's best qualities really emerge in gloriously soft concentration and an incredibly long finish. Mouth-filling tannins stud the silky texture like diamonds on velvet. Just this once, the adjective "outstanding" sounds like an understatement. The Poggiopiano Chianti Classico '95 was good, too, although rather more dilute and mature, especially on the nose. It is a very nice red, but not in the same class as that wonderful Rosso di Sera.

● Chianti Classico		
Vigna di Fontalle Ris. '94	♟♟	4
● Ser Niccolò Solatio del Tani '93	♟♟	5
● Chianti Classico		
Conti Serristori Ris. '94	♟	3*
● Ser Niccolò		
Solatio del Tani '88	♟♟♟	4*
● Chianti Classico		
Vigna di Fontalle Ris. '88	♟♟	4
● Chianti Classico		
Vigna di Fontalle Ris. '90	♟♟	5
● Chianti Classico		
Vigna di Fontalle Ris. '93	♟♟	4
● Ser Niccolò Solatio dei Tani '87	♟♟	5
● Ser Niccolò Solatio del Tani '93	♟♟	5

● Rosso di Sera '95	♟♟♟	5
● Chianti Classico '95	♟	3

S. CASCIANO VAL DI PESA (FI)   S. DONATO IN POGGIO (FI)

SOLATIONE
VIA CAMPOLI, 37
50024 S. CASCIANO VAL DI PESA (FI)
TEL. 055/821082

FERMIGNANO
50020 S. DONATO IN POGGIO (FI)
TEL. 055/8077253

Not long ago, the road that connects Mercatale to Panzano was unsurfaced but that never stopped it being the home of one of the highest concentrations of serious winemakers in the whole of Italy. Leaving Panzano, you pass La Massa, Villa Cafaggio, Carobbio and Vecchie Terre di Montefili while if you start from the Mercatale end, you will come to Solatione, a property owned by the Giachi family and best known for its extra-virgin olive oil. For quite a while now, the Solatione Chianti Classico has also been enjoying commercial success. At first, interest in the product was aroused above all by the effective marketing campaign organized by Selezione Fattorie, the company that has established its owner, Silvano Formigli, as a leading promoter of viticultural products. Recent releases, however, have shown that Solatione wines are capable of standing up for themselves. The Chianti Classico Riserva '93 in particular impressed our tasters. The nose is satisfying and the notes of new wood are well matched to the generous, concentrated fruit. In the mouth, it is fleshy and very powerful, with tannins that have mellowed nicely. In contrast, the Chianti Classico '94 is perhaps a little more straightforward but it is still one of the best in its class and we can only admire the way Solatione is narrowing the gap with its distinguished neighbours.

The Fermignano estate from San Donato in Poggio has made a near-triumphant entry into the Guide this year but let us take a look at the property first. It is owned by the Sestini family, who are well known locally for their decade-long experience in winemaking. The vineyards are lie in the Chianti Classico and Chianti Colli Senesi zones, in the territory of San Donato in Poggio and both of the wines we sampled were from Chianti Classico, a non-Riserva '95 and a Riserva '93. It was the '93 that had our tasters scribbling furiously for it is a wine with super concentration and huge fruit on the nose, where redcurrant, black cherry, bramble and tobacco mingle over an elegant note of vanilla. The flavour is close-knit and dense, enhanced by the lavish velvet softness that envelops the sweet tannins. This remarkable wine actually made it to the final round of tastings, missing out on Three Glasses only because it was a little too approachable to offer any real guarantees of cellarability. However, it is still a world-beater in anybody's book. The Chianti Classico '95 was very nice, too, but in as totally different category with its notes of ripe fruit and moderate concentration. Again, it is drinking very well now but don't expect the opulence on palate and nose offered by the Riserva '93.

● Chianti Classico '94	♥♥	4
● Chianti Classico Ris. '93	♥♥	5

● Chianti Classico Ris. '93	♥♥	4
● Chianti Classico '95	♥	3

S. GIMIGNANO (SI)

S. GIMIGNANO (SI)

BARONCINI
LOC. CASALE, 43
53037 S. GIMIGNANO (SI)
TEL. 0577/940600

CASA ALLE VACCHE
LOC. LUCIGNANO, 73/A
53037 S. GIMIGNANO (SI)
TEL. 0577/955103

Bruna and Stefano Baroncini turn out a million and a half bottles a year, which makes them the largest producers in the San Gimignano area. Over the past few years, they have been implementing a new strategy that has included the purchase of superb vineyards like Sovestro and Torre III and has permitted the Baroncini estate to become a modern grower-producer with a consistently excellent range. They've made the right move at the right time and again this year their best product is the Vernaccia di San Gimignano '95 Riserva Dometaia. The '93 and '94 versions were extremely successful and the '95 is a lovely wine, too. Straw yellow in the glass, it reveals aromas of spring flowers and pineapple shading off into an attractive note of vanilla. The palate is soft and refreshing, with nice length and a hint of almond. The Vernaccia '96 Poggio ai Cannicci earns respect for its light, refreshing bouquet and clean taste on the palate, even though it has no great length. The Baroncinis' red table wine, the Cortegiano '95, has the same virtues and the same defects as the '91 we awarded One Glass to last year. The aromas are alcohol-rich and moderately intense and the palate is attractive but the tannins are unruly and the wine lacks balance. However these are the characteristic problems of youth and should disappear in time.

We have said it before and we will say it again. Almost anybody can make a good wine if the vintage goes well but to achieve consistency takes talent. You have to prove that quality is the result of a deliberate winemaking policy. That's why we are happy to include the Casa alle Vacche cellar in the Guide again this year. Fernando and Lorenzo Ciappi have 13 hectares under vine in the Pancole subzone and are ably assisted by consultant oenologist Luigino Casagrande. Last year it was the reds that caught our fancy but this time we were impressed by the Vernaccias. A high One Glass score went to the Vernaccia di San Gimignano '96 Crocus. A vibrant straw yellow in hue, it offers moderately intense aromas of flowers. There is nice structure on the palate and good balance overall. The base Vernaccia '96 was also good, its pale straw yellow introducing delicate fruit and flower notes and a full flavoured palate. The '96 version of the Chianti Colli Senesi stood out for its fresh, alcohol-rich aromas of violets and bramble. It is a bit lean on the palate but well balanced and the tannins know their place. A Glass also went to the Chianti Colli Senesi '95 Cinabro for its heady notes of liquorice-nuanced tobacco. An unexpected note of rhubarb comes out on the warm, tannin-rich palate and the finish is only moderately long. Finally, a Guide mention must go to the Rosato '96, a typical San Gimignano rosé that accompanies the local cold meats superbly.

O	Vernaccia di S. Gimignano Dometaia Ris. '95	♥♥	3*
●	Cortegiano - Sovestro '95	♥	3
O	Vernaccia di S. Gimignano Poggio ai Cannici '96	♥	2
O	Baroncini Brut	♥	3
●	Chianti Colli Senesi. Vigna S. Domenico - Sovestro '96	♥	1
O	Vernaccia di S. Gimignano - Sovestro '96		2
O	Vernaccia di S. Gimignano Dometaia Ris. '93	♀♀	2*
O	Vernaccia di S. Gimignano Dometaia Ris. '94	♀♀	3
●	Cortegiano - Sovestro '91	♀	3

●	Chianti Colli Senesi '96	♥	1*
●	Chianti Colli Senesi Cinabro '95	♥	3
O	Vernaccia di S. Gimignano '96	♥	2
O	Vernaccia di S. Gimignano Crocus '96	♥	3
⊙	Rosato '96		2
●	Chianti Colli Senesi '95	♀	1*
●	Chianti Colli Senesi Cinabro '93	♀	3
O	Vernaccia di S. Gimignano Crocus '95	♀	3
O	Vernaccia di S. Gimignano I Macchioni '95	♀	2

S. GIMIGNANO (SI)

S. GIMIGNANO (SI)

VINCENZO CESANI
LOC. PANCOLE, 82/D
53037 S. GIMIGNANO (SI)
TEL. 0577/955084

FONTALEONI
LOC. S. MARIA, 39
53037 S. GIMIGNANO (SI)
TEL. 0577/950193

Thanks to his dedication and sheer hard work, Vincenzo Cesani is making admirable progress. Now that the cellar is in good shape, Cesani has turned his attention to the vineyards and, with the help of winemaker Luca D'Attoma, he has come up with a very tempting red table wine, the Luenzo '95. Obtained from late-harvested sangiovese and colorino fruit, it is vinified and aged in small oak barrels, then bottle-aged for several months. The Luenzo was still very young when we sampled it but that did not stop us awarding Two Glasses. Its ruby hue is deep and sombre, the aromas are headily intense, evoking a wealth of red berries, bramble and cherry. The warm, alcohol-rich palate has good balance despite the wine's relative youth and we look forward to coming back next year, when it ought to be drinking superbly. There was another good performance by the Vernaccia di San Gimignano Sanice '96, which achieved a One Glass score as it did last year. The straw yellow colour introduces moderately intense aromas of yellow flowers and ripe fruit. the palate is delicate yet sustained by good structure and balance, although the finish lacks length. Finally the crisp, clean-tasting Vernaccia '96 rounded our visit nicely with elusive aromas of delicate fruit and a refreshingly tangy palate.

Franco Troiani's Fontaleoni estate extends over 21 hectares of vineyards at Santa Maria, a tufa outcrop to the north of San Gimignano that overlooks the Valdelsa and Certaldo. We have been including Fontaleoni in the Guide for the last two years on the strength of the estate's excellent Vernaccias, which show that a forward-looking strategy rigorously applied will bring results. And our third tasting of the whites made by Troiani and his winemaker Paolo Caciornia was every bit as good as the others. The pale straw yellow Vernaccia '96 caught our fancy with its fairly intense notes of fresh-cut flowers and a balanced palate with nice structure that offers a hint of glycerine and the traditional Vernaccia after-aroma of almonds. The Vernaccia Vigna Casanuova '96 won a well-deserved Glass, even though it was not quite up to the standard of the highly impressive '95. It is pale yellow, with quite intense aromas of ripe fruit. The rounded palate lacks a little balance and shading off into a faint bitterish note with an almondy aftertaste.

● Luenzo '95		♟♟	4
○ Vernaccia di S. Gimignano '96		♟	2
○ Vernaccia di S. Gimignano Sanice '96		♟	4
○ Camperso '96			2
● Chianti Colli Senesi '95			2
● Chianti Colli Senesi '93		♟	2
● Chianti Colli Senesi '94		♟	2
○ Vernaccia di S. Gimignano '95		♟	2
○ Vernaccia di S. Gimignano Sanice '95		♟	3

○ Vernaccia di S. Gimignano '96		♟	2
○ Vernaccia di S. Gimignano Vigna Casanuova '96		♟	3
● Chianti Colli Senesi '96			1
○ Vernaccia di S. Gimignano Vigna Casanuova '95		♟♟	3
● Chianti Colli Senesi '95		♟	1
○ Vernaccia di S. Gimignano '95		♟	2

S. GIMIGNANO (SI)

S. GIMIGNANO (SI)

GUICCIARDINI STROZZI
FATTORIA DI CUSONA
53037 S. GIMIGNANO (SI)
TEL. 0577/950028

LA LASTRA
LOC. S. LUCIA
VIA D. GRADA, 9
53037 S. GIMIGNANO (SI)
TEL. 0577/941781

Roberto Guicciardini and Girolamo Strozzi's Fattoria di Cusona sprawls over more than 530 hectares and is one of our Guide regulars. This time round, the most interesting of the Guicciardini Strozzi wines was the '94 Millanni, specially created to celebrate the thousandth anniversary of the Cusona estate. Millanni is obtained from 80 per cent sangiovese and 20 per cent of a variety whose identity the makers refuse to reveal. The grapes were vinified separately and the wines blended later. After a carefully judged period of ageing in oak, Millanni spent about six months maturing in the bottle. The wine's ruby hue is impenetrably dark and leads into intense yet clearly identifiable aromas of red berries, autumn leaves and spices. There is lots of power on the palate which, with thanks in part to very attractive tannins, gained a Two Glass rating despite a certain lack of complexity. The Rosso da Tavola Sodole '95 also turned out to be a thoroughly drinkable red table wine, if not quite as good as the '93. Its bright ruby hue is flecked with purple highlights and the heavily oak-laced aromas are elegant and delicate. The palate has lots of structure, good alcohol and tannins that are still green but very refined. The '96 Vernaccia di San Gimignano Perlato is very pale golden yellow in the glass, releasing intense notes of ripe fruit with vegetal nuances. "Substantial" is the word for the fat, soft body to which a pleasant note of acidity lends balance before the classic Vernaccia almondy finish. And "traditional" is the adjective for the Vernaccia Riserva '95, a clear golden yellow wine with a nose of ripe fruit and vanilla. The entry on the palate is bitter-sweet but leads into a weighty, characterful flavour and a gain that typical hint of bitter almonds in the finish.

This is the second year running that La Lastra, a small estate owned by Renato Spanu and Nadia Betti which releases about 30,000 bottles a year, has been one of the most interesting producers in the San Gimignano area. Located at Ghermona, near Santa Lucia, its name derives from the "lastra", or huge slab, of cavernous limestone that lies under the vineyard from which Rovaio is obtained. It means that there is only a shallow layer of soil for the plants to grow in and yields are very low at around 30 quintals per hectare. Last year, we only awarded 78 points to the Rovaio '95 red table wine because we were tasting it too soon. This time, the panel were able to appreciate its true worth, and awarded Two Glasses. Food for thought, there, on the subject of when to release San Gimignano reds. We knew all about the Rovaio but it was the Vernaccia Riserva '95, made with the contribution of consultant Enrico Paternoster, that provided us with a pleasant surprise. A monovarietal Vernaccia, half vinified in oak and half in stainless steel, its straw yellow hue introduces faint but very elegant aromas that mingle spring flowers, sage and broom. The beautifully balanced palate is full flavoured but very drinkable, the wood making a nice contribution to the balance. Next the crisp Vernaccia '96 disclosed understated notes of ripe fruit and a soft, delicious palate. And finally the Chianti Colli Senesi '96 was as clean on nose and palate as the Vernaccia. Its alcohol-rich aromas exude generous warmth while the soft palate proffers demurely docile tannins.

●	994 Millanni '94	♟♟	6
●	Sodole '95	♟	5
○	Vernaccia di S. Gimignano Perlato '96	♟	4
○	Vernaccia di S. Gimignano Ris. '95	♟	4
●	Chianti Colli Senesi Titolato '96		3
○	Vernaccia di S. Gimignano Titolato Strozzi '96		3
●	Sodole '91	♟♟	4
●	Sodole '93	♟♟	5
○	Vernaccia di S. Gimignano Perlato '94	♟♟	3
○	Vernaccia di S. Gimignano S. Biagio '95	♟	3

○	Vernaccia di S. Gimignano Ris. '95	♟♟	4
●	Chianti Colli Senesi '96	♟	3
○	Vernaccia di S. Gimignano '96	♟	3
●	Chianti Colli Senesi '95	♟	3
●	Rovaio '95	♟	4
○	Vernaccia di S. Gimignano '95	♟	3

S. GIMIGNANO (SI)

S. GIMIGNANO (SI)

TENUTA LE CALCINAIE
LOC. MONTEOLIVETO, 3
53037 S. GIMIGNANO (SI)
TEL. 0577/943007

MORMORAIA
LOC. S. ANDREA
53037 S. GIMIGNANO (SI)
TEL. 0577/943096

Tenuta Le Calcinaie comprises about six hectares under vine at Affittacci, near Monteoliveto, and has been producing wine since 1994 with the assistance of consultant winemaker Andrea Mazzoni. It is the enthusiasm of owner Simone Santini, together with the declared intention of making premium wines from low yield fruit, that drives this small estate and when work in cellar and vineyard is finally complete, we are sure that Santini will get the outstanding results he deserves. For the time being, his red table wine, Teodoro, earned a very encouraging score for the '95 version, confirming the promise of the '94. It is a blend of sangiovese and merlot, with small percentages of cabernet and malvasia nera, and matures in the oak for 12 months. The colour in the glass is a deep ruby that leads into a good nose of broad bramble and new wood aromas. There is breadth on the palate, too, and the sweet, beefy tannins are accompanied by a distinct grassy note. The palate is reasonably well balanced and tannic, if a little unsophisticated, but it is a lovely example of Chianti from San Gimignano. The pale straw yellow Vernaccia '96 has moderately intense aromas of ripe fruit, a soft palate with a marked note of acidity and the typical almondy aftertaste of the variety.

For many years, Giuseppe Passoni and Francesca Zagon nursed the dream that one day they would be able to settle in Tuscany and make wine. In 1990, they decided to take the plunge and began to restructure La Mormoraia, taking on Franco Bernabei as their consultant winemaker. The estate now comprises 90 hectares in total, 15 of which are under vine. Giuseppe and Francesca have a very simple philosophy: not to make too many wines and to make all of them well. The first wine they released - with some trepidation - was their Vernaccia '95 and this year the three products they presented to the panel were proof that the Mormoraia winemaking philosophy is the right one. We particularly liked the Ostrea '95 white table wine. Obtained from vernaccia and chardonnay grapes, it is vinified without the skins and matured for 6 to 9 months in small oak barrels. Its pale golden yellow is tinged with green and offers a delicately elegant nose where mint and sage emerge. The palate is well made and nicely balanced, the wood being neither over-assertive nor understated and the aromatic finish satisfyingly long. We gave it Two Glasses straight away. The sangiovese and cabernet-based Neitea '95 red table wine also broke the 80-point barrier. Matured in oak for at least a year, its purple-tinged ruby accompanies a headily alcohol-rich nose with aromas of red fruit and tobacco. The broad palate has beefy tannins and a faintly note of acidity in the finish. Finally we sampled the interesting Vernaccia '96, which was mature on both nose and palate and proffered rich flavour veined with a pleasant toastiness.

● Chianti Colli Senesi Geminiano '95	♟	4
● Teodoro '95	♟	4
○ Vernaccia di S. Gimignano '96	♟	3
○ Vernaccia di S. Gimignano Vigna ai Sassi '96	♟	3
● Chianti Colli Senesi Geminiano '94	♀	3
● Teodoro '94	♀	4
○ Vernaccia di S. Gimignano '95	♀	3

● Neitea '95	♟♟	4
○ Ostrea '95	♟♟	4
○ Vernaccia di San Gimignano '96	♟	3
○ Vernaccia di San Gimignano '95	♟	3

S. GIMIGNANO (SI)

PALAGETTO
VIA MONTEOLIVETO, 46
53037 S. GIMIGNANO (SI)
TEL. 0577/942098-943090

S. GIMIGNANO (SI)

GIOVANNI PANIZZI
LOC. RACCIANO - S. MARGHERITA
53037 S. GIMIGNANO (SI)
TEL. 02/90938796 - 0577/941576

"I'm going to do a Riserva version of the Vernaccia and then I'll set about making a serious red." It is nice when people keep their promises. We noted what owner Simone Niccolai said in the 1994 edition of the Guide and only a few years later we can affirm without fear of contradiction that Palagetto has got both its Vernaccia Riserva and a very good red wine. The Vernaccia Riserva '94 was reasonably successful but the '95 version is an excellent wine that came close to a Two Glass score. Made exclusively from vernaccia fruit and vinified without the skins, with soft-crushing and temperature-controlled fermentation, it spent six months ageing in the bottle. The straw yellow in the glass heralds moderately intense aromas of ripe fruit and almonds. There is good structure on the palate and an attractive aroma of toasty oak. The Sottobosco '95 red table wine also came within a whisker of an 80-point total. Obtained from sangiovese fruit blended with a proportion of cabernet, it spent a year maturing in oak. The vibrant, bright ruby hue leads into lingering aromas of spices, bramble and vanilla. The palate has good length, too, as well as mellow tannins and well judged wood. Then the Vernaccia '96 Santa Chiara managed to keep up the excellent Palagetto standard despite a far from favourable vintage. Faint notes of fresh-cut flowers and citrus come forth in the bouquet and the palate is pure Vernaccia, with a faint bitterish note emerging in the after-aroma. Finally the Chianti Colli Senesi '96 turned out to be an unpretentious and thoroughly typical example of the genre.

It is been some time since Giovanni Panizzi's Riserva last had a bad year. Indeed, recent versions have been up there hovering on the verge of our Three Glass rating and sooner or later he is going to get a top award. The estate's policy is very straightforward: low yields, a modern cellar, an accomplished winemaker in the person of Salvatore Maule and a determination to make premium wines. The '93 and '94 versions of Panizzi's Riserva were excellent and the '95 is just as good. The yellow hue glows brilliantly in the glass and the delicate, stylish aromas are laced with beautifully judged liquorice-nuanced vanilla. It is full bodied, well structured and elegant on the palate, which reveals outstanding length. This is a wine made in the modern idiom for an international market that still manages to keep in touch with its roots. The dark ruby Chianti Colli Senesi '95 is almost as intriguing, with its fresh, clean aromas of red berries and vanilla. The palate is warm and soft, the tannins mellow, and the balance just right. Panizzi's non-Riserva Vernaccia is, as always, irresistibly seductive. The aromas are suggested rather than stated but the palate is deliciously drinkable. The Ceraso table wine, from sangiovese and canaiolo vinified with very brief skin contact, lies halfway between a rosé and a light red. There is substantial alcohol in the very approachable '96 version, a "drink-me" wine redolent of red berries, strawberries and blackcurrant.

● Chianti Colli Senesi '95	♥	3
● Sottobosco '95	♥	4
○ Vernaccia di S. Gimignano '96	♥	3
○ Vernaccia		
di S. Gimignano Ris. '95	♥	4
○ Vernaccia di S. Gimignano		
Vigna Santa Chiara '96	♥	3
● Chianti Colli Senesi '95	♀	1
● Palagetto Rosso	♀	2
● Sottobosco	♀	3
○ Vernaccia di S. Gimignano '95	♀	1
○ Vernaccia di S. Gimignano		
Vigna Santa Chiara '94	♀	2*
○ Vernaccia di S. Gimignano		
Vigna Santa Chiara '95	♀	1

○ Vernaccia		
di S. Gimignano Ris. '95	♥♥	5
● Ceraso '96	♥	3
● Chianti Colli Senesi '95	♥	3
○ Vernaccia di S. Gimignano '96	♥	4
○ Vernaccia		
di S. Gimignano Ris. '91	♀♀	5
○ Vernaccia		
di S. Gimignano Ris. '92	♀♀	5
○ Vernaccia		
di S. Gimignano Ris. '93	♀♀	5
○ Vernaccia		
di S. Gimignano Ris. '94	♀♀	5
● Ceraso '95	♀	3
○ Vernaccia di S. Gimignano '95	♀	4

S. GIMIGNANO (SI)

FATTORIA PARADISO
LOC. STRADA, 21
53037 S. GIMIGNANO (SI)
TEL. 0577/941500

We have never doubted the potential of Graziella Cappelli and Vasco Cetti's Fattoria Paradiso. The location of the 17-hectare estate is ideal for viticulture and they've been turning out good wines for a number of years, establishing a track record of consistent quality that had been missing in the past. The Chardonnay '95 and the Vernaccia di San Gimignano Biscondola '95 are the proof of that particular pudding. The hand of winemaker Paolo Caciornia is not hard to detect for chardonnay from the San Gimignano area has immediately recognizable characteristics, giving wines with faint, subtle aromas and lots of structure. The Paradiso Chardonnay is no exception but it stands out from the crowd thanks to its head-turning elegance. The Vernaccia di San Gimignano Biscondola '95, a selection of the estate's best vernaccia grapes aged in oak for eight months, is another very fine wine. Its stylish ripe fruit and vanilla aromas are followed by a well balanced palate backed up by nicely judged oak and an attractive note of acidity. The panel also thought the Eurus '96 white table wine was well worth a Guide Glass. A curious blend of 50 per cent trebbiano with chardonnay, vernaccia, grechetto, malvasia and san colombano fruit, it is a pale straw yellow in the glass, from which emerge notes of sage and mint. The palate is unsophisticated but has good weight. Moving on to Paradiso's two beefy reds, the Saxa Calida '94 and the Paterno '95, the panel found them to be well worth investigation. Indeed, we think the Paterno still has some way to go. Finally we should mention the refreshing, light Vernaccia di San Gimignano '96 and the Paradiso Brut, the best sparkling Vernaccia to be found in the San Gimignano area.

○	Chardonnay '95	▼▼	4
○	Vernaccia di S. Gimignano Biscondola '95	▼▼	4
●	Chianti Colli Senesi '96	▼	2
○	Eurus '96	▼	3
●	Paterno '94	▼	4
●	Saxa Calida '94	▼	4
○	Vernaccia Brut	▼	3
○	Vernaccia di S. Gimignano '96	▼	3
⊙	Rosa del Paradiso '96		3
○	Vinsanto '91		4
○	Vernaccia di S. Gimignano Biscondola '93	▽▽	3
●	Chianti Colli Senesi '95	▽	2
●	Saxa Calida '93	▽	4

S. GIMIGNANO (SI)

FATTORIA PONTE A RONDOLINO
LOC. PONTE A RONDOLINO
53037 S. GIMIGNANO (SI)
TEL. 0577/940143

Ponte a Rondolino, owned by Enrico Teruzzi and Carmen Puthod, is a big producer in a number of different senses. The 74 hectares of vineyards, the million or so bottles sold each year, forward-looking management policies that often turn out to be ahead of their time, the state-of-the-art cellar, the quality of the wine and even the aesthetic appeal of the bottles all put Ponte a Rondolino firmly in the top flight. The Vernaccia di San Gimignano Terre di Tufi '95 is every bit as good as the two preceding vintages and easily passed the 80-point mark to earn Two Glasses. As many as 200,000 bottles were made of the Terre di Tufi '96, a bright straw yellow wine with elegant aromas of ripe fruit and vanilla. The palate is warm and full, its nice balance complemented by a long, typically almondy finish. The Carmen '95 white table wine was obtained from an unusual cépage of trebbiano, vermentino, vernaccia di San Gimignano and sangiovese vinified without the skins. Although it won its Guide Glass, the '95 did not really reach the heights of previous versions. The straw yellow is so pale it shades into notepaper white but the aromas of fruit and vanilla are reasonably intense. The palate is moderately full and a pleasant note of vanilla provides contrast. The delicate bouquet of the Vernaccia '96 offers delicious fruit aromas and there is plenty of flavour in a palate that plays on the contrasting delights of glycerine and acidity. We also gave the pale ruby Peperino '95 a Glass for its heady aromas of strawberry and red fruit. The palate may not be very complex but it is a well made wine that drinks beautifully.

○	Carmen '95	▼▼	4
○	Vernaccia di S. Gimignano Terre di Tufi '95	▼▼	5
●	Peperino '95	▼	3
○	Vernaccia di S. Gimignano '96	▼	3
○	Carmen '94	▽▽	4
○	Vernaccia di S. Gimignano Terre di Tufi '92	▽▽	5
○	Vernaccia di S. Gimignano Terre di Tufi '93	▽▽	4
○	Vernaccia di S. Gimignano Terre di Tufi '94	▽▽	4
●	Peperino '94	▽	3
○	Vernaccia di S. Gimignano '94	▽	2*
○	Vernaccia di S. Gimignano '95	▽	3

S. GIMIGNANO (SI)

S. GIMIGNANO (SI)

FATTORIA S. QUIRICO
LOC. PANCOLE, 39
53037 S. GIMIGNANO (SI)
TEL. 0577/955007

FATTORIA S. DONATO
LOC. S. DONATO, 6
53037 S. GIMIGNANO (SI)
TEL. 0577/941616

The Fattoria San Quirico has made a welcome return to the Guide after a year in "Purgatory". The estate has not been wasting its time, either, for although it has stayed faithful to the clean, traditional style and classic Vernaccia aromas that have always been the hallmark of San Quirico, this year the panel found evidence of progress. The potential is certainly there. San Quirico's 25 hectares lie in the Pancole subzone, one of the best in the area, their winemaker is the accomplished Luigino Casagrande, and Andrea Vecchione, the owner, has style as well as enthusiasm. Our tasters first sampled the Vernaccia Riserva I Campi Santi, whose '95 version came close to a second Glass. The colour is straw yellow and the elegant sage-nuanced aromas mingle splendidly with the wood. The palate has medium body and a finish with satisfying length. All in all a nice wine that with a touch more concentration would have been superlative. The refreshing Vernaccia '96 also impressed with a fine bouquet in a vintage that generally yielded wines which are anything but aroma-rich. Its pale straw yellow introduces mint-laced floral notes and a well constructed palate with a faint note of glycerine. Finally the dark ruby Chianti Colli Senesi '95 revealed intriguing aromas of red berries and tobacco, good structure and an astringent palate that signs off with a slightly bitterish flourish.

One of the great satisfactions of our tasting safaris is the joy of discovering new cellars but we are even more delighted when one of our discoveries performs well the second time round. And the Fattoria San Donato has done it again this year. Umberto Fenzi's winery lies on the main road to Volterra in the middle of the village of San Donato and it is here that, with the assistance of winemaker Paolo Salvi, Fenzi has created for the second time - and from a fairly unexciting harvest - a Vernaccia Selezione that came within an ace of earning Two Glasses. The '96 San Donato Vernaccia Selezione is pale yellow with attractive aromas of ripe fruit on the nose. The palate has a solid, rather glycerine-rich, structure redolent of fruit salad and vanilla. But there is more: after a series of brave tries that failed to light any fires, this year Fenzi and Salvi have produced a fine Vernaccia Riserva. The '95 vintage was above average for Vernaccia Riservas and San Donato's is better than most, in fact almost a Two Glass product. Its bright straw yellow hue leads into a stylishly delicate bouquet where aromatic notes of mint and jasmine mingle with vanilla. There is good depth on the palate, which is not short of length either and will need a little more time to find an ideal balance. The refreshing, well balanced Chianti Colli Senesi '96 and the Vernaccia '96 are both very professional products.

●	Chianti Colli Senesi '95	♟	3
○	Vernaccia di S. Gimignano '96	♟	2
○	Vernaccia di S. Gimignano I Campi Santi Ris. '95	♟	3
○	Vernaccia di S. Gimignano I Campi Santi Ris. '92	♟♟	4
○	Vernaccia di S. Gimignano '94	♟	2*
○	Vernaccia di S. Gimignano I Campi Santi Ris. '93	♟	3

●	Chianti Colli Senesi '96	♟	2
○	Vernaccia di S. Gimignano '96	♟	3
○	Vernaccia di S. Gimignano Ris. '95	♟	4
○	Vernaccia di S. Gimignano Selezione '96	♟	4
●	Chianti Colli Senesi '95	♟	2
○	Poggio alle Corti '95	♟	1
○	Vernaccia di S. Gimignano Selezione '95	♟	4
○	Vinsanto	♟	5

S. GIMIGNANO (SI)

SIGNANO
VIA DI S. MATTEO, 101
53037 S. GIMIGNANO (SI)
TEL. 0577/940164

S. GIMIGNANO (SI)

F.LLI VAGNONI
LOC. PANCOLE
53037 S. GIMIGNANO (SI)
TEL. 0577/955077

When it comes to consistent quality, you have got to hand it to Manrico Biagini's winery. Thanks to its excellent location, Signano always seems to be able to obtain very attractive wines from the 23 hectares under vine. Recently extensions were made to the Poggiarelli vineyard, which will go into full production in a few years' time. Again, it was the Vernaccia Selezione that turned out to be the best of the range. The straw yellow '95 has deliciously intense aromas that are enhanced rather than masked by generous oak. The full, fat palate is longish, with the characteristic Vernaccia almondy after-aroma. A shade more complexity and it would have won Two Glasses. The '96 Poggiarelli Vernaccia vineyard selection, named after a vineyard that backs on to the mediaeval walls of San Gimignano, also performed well. Its pale straw yellow reveals aromas of flowers and fruit, especially pineapple. The palate is soft, refreshing and leads nicely into a rewarding finish. For the third time, the Chianti Colli Senesi '95 Poggiarelli proved its worth. The deep ruby hue is tinged with purple highlights and the intense, alcohol-rich aromas reveal notes of vanilla. There is good structure and length on the palate but the tannins need to mellow further. Last on our list was the Vernaccia Riserva '95, a tolerably good version that brings out all the typical characteristics of the variety.

The Vagnonis arrived in San Gimignano from the Marche region in 1953. Forty years later, they have every right to be considered owners of one of the best properties in the area. This year's results - and you need go no further than the Vernaccia Mocali for confirmation - come from a superbly equipped cellar, meticulous vineyard management, low yields and the clean-tasting, modern style with which winemaker Salvatore Maule has imbued the Vagnoni wines. And that Vernaccia Mocali '96 really is something special. It is obtained from the rigorously selected fruit of the I Mocali and Il Mulino vineyards, fermented in small barrels of French oak. In the glass it is a brilliant straw yellow and the nose has an elegant, delicate bouquet of ripe fruit and vanilla, delightfully nuanced with honey. The palate is full, round and well structured, with a length, balance and sheer presence in the mouth that took the panel by surprise. The cabernet and sangiovese-based I Sodi Lunghi '95 red table wine was also interesting. Ruby in the glass, with fairly intense aromas of red berries and vanilla, it offers just the right note of tannins on the palate but it will take a little time for them to mellow. And of course the Vagnoni Vernaccia '96 is, as usual, a very drinkable wine in the traditional style with the characteristic varietal note of bitter almonds in the finish.

● Chianti Colli Senesi Poggiarelli '95	♟	4
○ Vernaccia di S. Gimignano Poggiarelli '96	♟	3
○ Vernaccia di S. Gimignano Ris. '95	♟	3
○ Vernaccia di S. Gimignano Selezione '95	♟	4
○ Signano Brut		3
○ Vernaccia di S. Gimignano '96		2
● Chianti Colli Senesi Poggiarelli '93	♟	2
● Chianti Colli Senesi Poggiarelli '94	♟	3
● Chianti Colli Senesi Signano '94	♟	1*
○ Vernaccia di S. Gimignano Poggiarelli '95	♟	3
○ Vernaccia di S. Gimignano Selezione '94	♟	4

○ Vernaccia di S. Gimignano Mocali '96	♟♟	4
● I Sodi Lunghi '95	♟	4
○ Vernaccia di S. Gimignano '96	♟	2
● Chianti Colli Senesi '96		2
⊙ Rosato '96		2
○ Vernaccia di S. Gimignano Mocali '94	♟♟	3
○ Vernaccia di S. Gimignano Mocali '95	♟♟	4
● Chianti Colli Senesi '95	♟	2
● I Sodi Lunghi '94	♟	4
○ Vernaccia di S. Gimignano '95	♟	2

SCANSANO (GR)

SCANSANO (GR)

ERIK BANTI
LOC. FOSSO DEI MULINI
58054 SCANSANO (GR)
TEL. 0564/508006

CANTINA COOPERATIVA
MORELLINO DI SCANSANO
LOC. SARAGIOLO
58054 SCANSANO (GR)
TEL. 0564/507288

With each passing year, we realize just how much the character of certain people who are involved in the world of Italian wine counts in the long run. A particular way of looking at life is the natural precursor of a distinctive philosophy of winemaking. And you could not find a better example than Erik Banti. His roots run deep and are anything but ordinary. His personality is marked by restlessness and a love of travel. So it is no surprise to find that his wines are the epitome of freedom and imagination, with all the virtues and, occasionally, defects those qualities will inevitably entail. If in the past we have detected here a certain maturity in a bottle, there a less than perfect use of oak, we were probably paying the price that had to be paid to get to know Erik's indisputably passionate approach to winemaking. However last year it was obvious that the wood in Banti's wines was getting sweeter and this year we have proof. The Aquilaia '95, obtained from morellino and alicante grapes, has a moderately intense ruby hue and good depth on the nose, where oak-derived aromas still hog centre stage. The entry on the palate is toasty by the fruit is remarkably sweet and the tannins are deliciously textured. It is a young wine but one that is both powerful and nicely balanced. The Ciabatta also caught the panel's attention with a luscious nose reminiscent of red berry preserve. Perhaps a little over-mature, it reveals good balance in the mouth although it could have done with some more body.

"Unity is strength", so the saying goes, but after tasting the wines of the Morellino di Scansano co-operative cellar, panel members were forced to admit that strength united with intelligence can work wonders. Co-operative cellars are not generally renowned for the quality of their products, with one or two noteworthy exceptions, mainly in Alto Adige. At Scansano, however, quality is very much on the agenda. The grapes of the numerous co-operative members are now being transformed into wines that are more than simply well made. And that's where the intelligence of Attilio Pagli, a truly outstanding winemaker, comes in. Thanks to Pagli, and to production managers Santino Ceccarelli and Benedetto Grechi, the 500,000 bottles that Morellino di Scansano turns out now include some very fine wines indeed. We will start with the Roggiano '96, a wine with attractive cherry and pepper aromas on the nose and a soft palate whose firm acidity in no way compromises its attractive drinkability. The Morellino Riserva '94 has a clean, tobacco-laced nose and is remarkably well balanced in the mouth but the jewel in the Morellino di Scansano crown is the Vigna Benefizio '96, which offers amazingly good value for money. Rarely have Two Glasses cost so little. The concentration of bottled fruit aromas on the nose is followed up by the close-knit texture of the entry on the palate. It is a lovely wine which has got fruit, delicious softness and even a nice long finish.

● Aquilaia '95	▼▼	4
● Ciabatta '94	▼	4
● Aquilaia '90	▼▼	4*
● Aquilaia '94	▼▼	4
● Ciabatta '90	▼▼	5
● Morellino di Scansano '94	▼▼	2*

● Morellino di Scansano		
Vigna Benefizio '96	▼▼	2*
● Morellino di Scansano Ris. '94	▼	3
● Morellino di Scansano		
Roggiano '96	▼	2

SINALUNGA (SI)

SINALUNGA (SI)

CASTELLO DI FARNETELLA
FRAZ. FARNETELLA
RACCORDO AUTOSTRADALE
SIENA-BETTOLLE, KM 37
53040 SINALUNGA (SI)
TEL. 0577/663520

TENUTA FARNETA
LOC. FARNETA, 161
53048 SINALUNGA (SI)
TEL. 0577/631025

The guardian spirits of Castello di Farnetella are two of the most illustrious names in Tuscan winemaking: Giuseppe Mazzocolin and Franco Bernabei, the team that brought fame and fortune to the Fattoria di Felsina in Chianti Classico. Since the two properties share their owner and oenologist, they have many things in common. Obviously Farnetella wines do not aspire to the structure and ageing potential of the powerful Felsina products nor are they anywhere near as complex. As the French . would say, it is a question of "terroir". What Farnetella wines do have is personality. The Chianti Colli Senesi is the cornerstone of the range. As such, it has no pretensions to complexity, offering up its charms with guileless spontaneity. The Nero di Nubi monovarietal Pinot Nero is rather more of a sophisticate, and for some years has been striving for an ever more subtle style. We tasted the '93 this time as the '94 had not been released when we visited. The red in the glass suggests maturity, and the nose discloses candied peel and flowers. Well developed notes of fruit emerge on the delicate, elegant palate. But it was the superbly drinkable Farnetella Sauvignon that provided the day's major surprise. Its brilliant straw yellow introduces a fresh, bright, whistle-clean nose with the classic Sauvignon aromas of sage and cat's pee. The palate follows through nicely, if without any great weight, but the balance is a sheer delight. In fact it may not be so very long before the wines of Farnetella are competing on an equal footing with those of Felsina and some of the other "aristocrats" from Chianti Classico.

Not for the first time, the Tenuta Farneta offers a valid range of wines that does not quite hang together. As we pointed out in the last edition of the Guide, on this estate some excellent bottles rub shoulders with much less successful products and the contradictory messages this sends out do nothing for the good name of the label. The wines to leave aside are the distinctly watery '96 Chianti and the unmemorable Bonagrazia rosé. Thankfully the two best Farneta reds, the Bongoverno and the Bentivoglio, are still there to defend the house colours. The Bongoverno is a monovarietal Sangiovese, and the '93 version is superbly put together. The intense ruby hue takes you on to a nose of ripe but not sweet fruit laced with attractive notes of oak. The slightly mature palate is clean and full bodied, with just the right notes of tannin. Like the Bongoverno, the Bentivoglio is obtained from 100 per cent sangiovese fruit and is inferior to its "big brother" only in terms of concentration and, of course, price. The two wines have much in common. Both aim for a refreshingly drinkable style, rather than going for body and structure. And we can recommend them, with the caveat that while the Bentivoglio is great value for money, the Bongoverno is somewhat optimistically priced.

○ Sauvignon '95	🍷🍷	4
○ Sauvignon '91	🍷🍷	4
● Nero di Nubi '93	🍷	5
○ Sauvignon '92	🍷	4
○ Sauvignon '93	🍷	4
○ Sauvignon '94	🍷	4

● Selezione di Bongoverno Vigneto Casai '93	🍷🍷	6
● Bentivoglio '94	🍷	2*
● Bentivoglio '91	🍷🍷	4
● Selezione di Bongoverno Vigneto Casai '85	🍷🍷	5
● Selezione di Bongoverno Vigneto Casai '86	🍷🍷	5
● Selezione di Bongoverno Vigneto Casai '88	🍷🍷	5
● Selezione di Bongoverno Vigneto Casai '90	🍷🍷	6
● Selezione di Bongoverno Vigneto Casai '91	🍷🍷	5

SOIANA (PI)

ELYANE & BRUNO MOOS
VIA PIER CAPPONI, 98
56030 SOIANA (PI)
TEL. 0587/654180

After a "fallow" year when their wines were not ready for tasting, Bruno and Elyane Moos are back in the Guide. It is not so much a triumphal return as confirmation of the hard work the couple have done in the past. The panel may not have been overwhelmed by this year's offerings but the Canadian couple deserve respect for the distinctive personality of their wines, which are instantly recognizable and untouched by the whims of fashion. The Moos cellar takes a back seat for it is the quality of the harvest that counts, not winemaking mumbo-jumbo. We thought the best wine on offer was the Elige, a monovarietal Merlot with a moderately intense garnet colour and clean vegetal and black berry aromas. In the mouth, there was nice balance and goodish texture. The Soianello, obtained from a prevalently sangiovese blend of fruit, was almost as delicious. Its vibrantly intense ruby hue announces fruit-rich aromas enhanced by piquant notes of spice, which are mirrored in the mouth by a palate with satisfyingly rugged structure. Finally we included the Fontestina, not only for its intrinsic merit, but also to provide a point of reference by which to judge the magnificent '90 vintage. The '93 has a moderately intense garnet ruby hue and a slightly closed but elegant nose where bottle-ageing aromas of leather, tobacco and jam peep through. The attack on the palate is dominated by alcohol but it then settles down and the finish is very assured.

●	Elige '94	🍷	4
●	Fontestina '93	🍷	4
●	Soianello '96	🍷	2*
●	Soianello '93	🍸	3*
●	Soianello '94	🍸	2
○	Soiano '94	🍸	2
○	Vio '94	🍸	2

SOVICILLE (SI)

POGGIO SALVI
LOC. POGGIO SALVI, 221
53018 SOVICILLE (SI)
TEL. 0577/349045-45237

The six hectares under vine of the Poggio Salvi estate belong to one of the largest winemaking concerns in Chianti Classico, the Agricola San Felice. Leonardo Bellaccini is in charge of operations in the cellar and the vineyard here, too, and in any case all Poggio Salvi wines are bottled, labelled and packed at San Felice. So we can expect the quality level to be good and winemaking standards to be high. The Chianti Colli Senesi is a chorus girl rather than a prima donna: refreshing lively, moderately tannic and as typical of the genre as they come. The other two Poggio Salvi wines are more interesting. The Refola, a sauvignon and trebbiano-based white, is a very nice '96. The straw yellow hue is crystal clear and the aromas are clean, fruity and nicely expressive of the varieties. The uncomplicated but very well made palate is rich in delicious fruit. The Vigna del Bosco red was even better, and came close to a Two Glass score. The '94 vintage gave lots of substantial extract, although the nose lacks a little clarity. The full flavoured palate is soft, rich and backed up by compact tannins. A wine made for lovers of the style which should be drinking perfectly in a couple of years' time.

○	Refola '96	🍷	3
●	Vigna del Bosco '94	🍷	4
○	Refola '93	🍸	3
○	Refola '95	🍸	3
●	Vigna del Bosco '93	🍸	4

SUVERETO (LI)

LORELLA AMBROSINI
LOC. TABARO, 95
57028 SUVERETO (LI)
TEL. 0565/829301

SUVERETO (LI)

GUALDO DEL RE
LOC. NOTRI, 77
57028 SUVERETO (LI)
TEL. 0565/829888-829361

The results of this year's tastings at the Lorella Ambrosini estate were highly significant, especially for the Riflesso Antico, which stood out as a premium wine of real breeding. It should be said straight away that we are not talking about one of the usual Cabernets or Merlots but about a monovarietal Montepulciano d'Abruzzo, which just goes to show the potential to be found in the native varieties of central and southern Italy. Riflesso Antico is an intense ruby, shading into garnet at the rim. The nose is powerfully concentrated, the notes of black fruit and spice still swaddled in toasty wood aromas. There is plenty of weight behind the flavours in the mouth and robust tannins emerge as the palate develops. For the time being, only limited quantities of the wine are available so demand outstrips supply but the vines planted a few years ago should improve the situation in the near future, both for customers and for the estate's coffers. The Riflesso Antico is a bit of a loner at the moment, partly because the 100% vermentino Armonia has not yet been released and partly because the Subertum, a blend of sangiovese and merlot, has matured in too much of a hurry, which is probably a consequence of the '94 vintage. Its moderately intense garnet in the glass introduces initially reduced aromas that open on vegetal notes mingling with steak tartare and leather. The palate is much more persuasive: the entry is sweetish, there is nice body and above all it has lovely balance. Finally, there is not much to say about the two Val di Cornia wines. The harvest was poor and they're both below their usual standard.

As usual, Nico and Teresa Rossi welcomed us with a wide range of wines and the overall quality was very encouraging. We are still waiting, though, for the major leap forward we feel is just round the corner. The Gualdo del Re Riserva is emblematic in this respect. Every year, it promises to deliver the goods but then for one reason or another falls just short of the mark. The '94 has a lustrous, deep hue but is let down by one or two notes of reduction on the nose. In contrast, the flavour reveals a wonderfully fruity texture and delightfully firm tannins. Cautiously, we scored it just below 80 points but we would not be at all surprised if it made the big time after a certain period of bottle-ageing. Like the Gualdo del Re Riserva, the Federico Primo is rather more convincing on the palate than the nose. A blend of cabernet, merlot and sangiovese, it discloses gamy, vegetal and fruit preserve notes as well as a faint hints of reduction while the palate is not as meaty as its stablemate's. Nonetheless, there is attractive thrust sustained by good balance. Once again, it was the Pinot Bianco, with its ripe peach and apricot aromas and well rounded palate, that proved to be the most dependable bottle in the range. We were a little disappointed by the Vigna Valentina, however. The '96 just was not as good as the previous year's version. And to round off there were the two Val di Cornia wines: the refreshing, nicely balanced, Bianco earned its One Glass while the well made but leanish Rosso hovered just below.

● Riflesso Antico '94	♔♔	4
● Subertum '94	♔	4
○ Val di Cornia Tabarò Bianco '96		2
● Val di Cornia Tabarò Rosso '96		2
● Riflesso Antico '92	♀	3
● Riflesso Antico '93	♀	4
● Val di Cornia Ambrosini Rosso '93	♀	2
○ Val di Cornia Armonia Bianco '95	♀	2*
○ Val di Cornia Tabarò Bianco '95	♀	1*
● Val di Cornia Tabarò Rosso '94	♀	1

● Federico Primo '94	♔	4
○ Pinot Bianco '96	♔	3
○ Val di Cornia Bianco '96	♔	2
● Val di Cornia Gualdo del Re '94	♔	4
● Val di Cornia Rosso '96		2
○ Vigna Valentina '96		3
● Federico Primo '93	♔♔	4
○ Vigna Valentina '95	♔♔	2*
○ Pinot Bianco '95	♀	2*
● Val di Cornia Gualdo del Re '92	♀	4
● Val di Cornia Gualdo del Re '93	♀	4
● Val di Cornia Rosso '94	♀	1*

SUVERETO (LI)

SUVERETO (LI)

MONTEPELOSO
LOC. MONTEPELOSO, 82
57028 SUVERETO (LI)
TEL. 0565/828180

TUA RITA
LOC. NOTRI 81
57028 SUVERETO (LI)
TEL. 0565/829237

The winery owned by husband and wife team Willi Doeni and Doris Neukom confirmed last year's excellent first impression. Indeed we really ought to admit that the Nardo '94 has matured magnificently and is probably worth more than the prudent One Glass we awarded in the last Guide after tasting the product just after it went into the bottle. The '95 sangiovese also revealed traits that are characteristic of this corner of Suvereto: robust and a little unruly early on, it has acquired a much more compact, well balanced personality at subsequent tastings. A glance at the glass, where a vibrant, bright ruby delights the eye, will tell you that this is a wine with serious structure, complemented by vigorous acidity. "Territory" is also the keynote on the nose, where leather, tobacco and autumn leaves mingle with earthy notes. After an introduction like that, the palate could only be powerful. Anyone who had doubts about the potential of sangiovese at Suvereto will have to revise their opinion after tasting a no-nonsense "terroir" wine like this. And while we were waiting for the Nardo '95, which - wisely - will not be released until next year, we sampled the cellar's other products: a very pleasant Rosato with moderate texture and a Bianco that was well made but nothing more.

There is no easy way to guarantee a Three Glass rating in the Guide. Only one wine in a hundred makes it that far. So to win Three Glasses two years in succession, as Virgilio Bisti and the Tua Rita cellar have done, is an exceptional achievement, particularly if we bear in mind all the variables and imponderables that can influence the harvest and the final quality of the wine. The '95 Giusto di Notri does not have quite the massive impact on the palate that the previous version so triumphantly revealed. It is powerful all right but the long suits this time are style and elegance. The lustrous, concentrated hue in the glass is a fitting prelude to an austere yet deep, rich nose of tobacco, pencil lead and black berries. Then the attack on the palate is broad and mouth-filling, and the mid-palate solid and well balanced. Just a couple of points lower down the scale comes the 100 per cent merlot Redigaffi. It may not have the voluptuous opulence of the stunning '94 but the palate has weight and vigour to spare. Next we sampled the Sileno, a cépage of chardonnay, riesling and traminer that greets you with aromas of citrus fruit, banana and vanilla, which are mirrored satisfyingly on the palate. Then the sangiovese-based Perlato almost broke the 80-point barrier. Its nose has yet to open and is still very redolent of toasty oak but underneath there are typical earthy and red berry notes. These lead into a thoroughly persuasive palate that unfolds to reveal softness, good concentration and commendable length. The long list of Tua Rita wines is brought to a close by another two whites, both very well made: the Val di Cornia is the more refreshing and the Perlato the more substantial.

● Val di Cornia Rosso		
Montepeloso '95	♟♟	4
⊙ Val di Cornia Rosato '96	♟	2
○ Val di Cornia Bianco '96		2
● Nardo '94	♟	4
● Val di Cornia Rosso		
Montepeloso '94	♟	3

● Giusto di Notri '95	♟♟♟	5
● Redigaffi '95	♟♟	6
○ Sileno '96	♟♟	3*
○ Perlato del Bosco Bianco '96	♟	3
● Perlato del Bosco Rosso '95	♟	4
○ Val di Cornia Bianco '96	♟	2
● Giusto di Notri '94	♟♟♟	5
● Giusto di Notri '92	♟♟	5
● Giusto di Notri '93	♟♟	5
○ Sileno '95	♟♟	3*
○ Perlato del Bosco Bianco '95	♟	2*
● Perlato del Bosco Rosso '92	♟	2
● Perlato del Bosco Rosso '93	♟	2
● Perlato del Bosco Rosso '94	♟	3
○ Val di Cornia Bianco '95	♟	1*

TAVARNELLE VAL DI PESA (FI)   TERRICCIOLA (PI)

POGGIO AL SOLE
LOC. BADIA A PASSIGNANO
50020 TAVARNELLE VAL DI PESA (FI)
TEL. 055/8071504

BADIA DI MORRONA
LOC. LA BADIA
56030 TERRICCIOLA (PI)
TEL. 0587/658505

It was a tasting to remember this year at Poggio al Sole, where Giovanni and Caterina Davaz presented five wines, all of them very successful, so we will get straight on with our report. There was no doubt about the best of the bunch - the very impressive Chianti Casasilia '94. Its bright, deep ruby hue already augurs well, introducing an elegant, interestingly complex nose where richly concentrated ripe wild berries are married to hints of cocoa. Then the broad, muscular palate develops deliciously, unveiling all its compact texture, to win Two Glasses with points to spare. The Casasilia '93, which is very similar in colour, was also very good. The aromas are penetratingly intense, hinting at bramble jelly and stylish oak. The entry on the palate is full flavoured and very positive, then close-knit tannins emerge in a balanced overall structure. The '94 Seraselva has all the distinguishing features of a Poggio al Sole wine: a dense, dark ruby hue and great depth on the nose, where black cherries mingle with new-mown grass and toasty oak. The palate still needs time to find a length for the entry is irresistibly soft but the finish is dominated by tannins that will need time to mellow. And the prospects for the wines of '95 look rosy if the non-Riserva Chianti Classico is as good as this. It has great texture, power and structure while under the still closed aromas very nice fruit is beginning to emerge. We will close our notes with the Riserva, whose garnet-tinged hue reveals greater maturity. The attractive flowery aromas are laced with distinct notes contributed by the delicious wood, which is also present in the palate. It is a soft, very supple wine that regrettably lacks something of the fruit-rich texture displayed by the rest of the range.

Badia di Morrona's collection of "Glassware" is getting bigger every year. The average standard of the range is good but two wines stand out from the crowd: the N'Antia and the Vigna Alta. The first, a blend of sangiovese and cabernet sauvignon, is hardly a newcomer because previous versions have enjoyed excellent reviews in past Guides but this time N'Antia was even better than we thought it would be. The dark, intense ruby hue accompanies equally penetrating aromas where oak-derived notes of vanilla and cocoa dominate the underlying fruit. The entry on the palate is full, soft and low-key, developing steadily through the mid-palate to a long finish where oak again provides the theme. In contrast, the Vigna Alta is being released for the first time. Obtained from old, very low-yield, vines of sangiovese, supplemented with a little canaiolo fruit, Vigna Alta makes a thumping impression with its sheer structure and profusion of riches. The garnet ruby hue is enticingly intense, offering mature aromas of leather, steak tartare, tobacco and liquorice, enhanced by spicy notes of pepper and cloves. The entry on the palate is decidedly sweet but very powerful while the meaty flavour has good breadth and lingers attractively. Definitely a wine with attitude. The Chianti Riserva, which came close to winning a second Glass, has lots to recommend it, starting with an intense garnet hue and a medley of aromas that includes leather, jam, citron and vanilla. The palate is lively and very stylish, with just a hint of bitter almonds in the finish. Next the La Suvera chardonnay-based white offered a fairly elegant, clean nose with notes of honey and toastiness. There is nice balance on the reasonably full bodied palate and the aromas of the nose are mirrored satisfyingly in the mouth. Finally, a little below the level of the rest of the range, are the uncomplicated but very drinkable Chianti and the S. Torpé.

● Chianti Classico '95	ΨΨ	3*
● Chianti Classico Casasilia '93	ΨΨ	5
● Chianti Classico Casasilia '94	ΨΨ	5
● Seraselva '94	ΨΨ	5
● Chianti Classico Ris. '94	Ψ	4
● Chianti Classico Ris. '91	ΨΨ	4
● Chianti Classico '93	Ψ	3
● Chianti Classico '94	Ψ	3

● N'Antia '94	ΨΨ	5
● Vigna Alta '94	ΨΨ	5
● Chianti Ris. '93	Ψ	3
● Chianti Sodi del Paretaio '96	Ψ	2
○ La Suvera '96	Ψ	3
○ S. Torpè Felciaio '96	Ψ	2
○ La Suvera '94	ΨΨ	2
● N'Antia '93	ΨΨ	4
● N'Antia '91	ΨΨ	3*
● Chianti '95	Ψ	1*
● Chianti Sodi del Paretaio '94	Ψ	2
○ La Suvera '95	Ψ	2
● N'Antia '92	Ψ	3
○ Vin Santo '88	Ψ	4

OTHER WINERIES

The following producers obtained good scores in our tastings with one or more of their wines:

PROVINCE OF FIRENZE

Savignola Paolina,
Greve in Chianti, tel. 055/853139,
Chianti Classico Ris. '94

Vignano,
Marcialla, tel. 0571/660041,
Rosso N. 13 '94

Fattoria di Petrognano,
Montelupo Fiorentino, tel. 0571/542001,
Pomino Rosso '94

Il Vescovino,
Panzano in Chianti, tel. 055/852512,
Chianti Classico Vigna Piccola '95

La Marcellina,
Panzano in Chianti, tel. 055/852126,
Chianti Classico '95

Le Fonti,
Panzano in Chianti, tel. 055/852194,
Fontissimo '94

Fattoria Sant'Andrea,
Panzano in Chianti, tel. 055/8549090,
Chianti Classico Panzanello '95

Podere La Cappella,
S. Donato in Poggio,
tel. 055/8072727,
Chianti Classico Ris. '94 Querciolo

PROVINCE OF GROSSETO

C. S. Cooperativa di Capalbio,
Capalbio,
tel. 0564/890253,
Ansonica Costa dell'Argentario '96

Motta,
Grosseto, tel. 0564/405105,
Sirio '95,
Morellino di Scansano '96,
Morellino di Scansano Ris. '94

San Giuseppe-Mantellassi,
Magliano in Toscana,
tel. 0564/592037,
Querciolaia '94,
Morellino di Scansano Ris. '94

Serraiola,
Monterotondo Marittimo,
tel. 0566/910026,
Lentisco '96

La Parrina,
Orbetello, tel. 0564/862636,
La Parrina Ris. '93

Santa Lucia,
Orbetello, tel. 0564/885474,
Ansonica Costa dell'Argentario '96

I Botri,
Scansano, tel. 0564/507921,
Bianco di Pitigliano '96,
Morellino di Scansano Ris. '93

La Carletta,
Scansano, tel. 0564/585045,
Morellino di Scansano '96

Macereto,
Scansano, tel. 0564/507219,
Morellino di Scansano Ris. '93 Publio

PROVINCE OF LIVORNO

Graziani,
Campiglia Marittima,
tel. 0565/843043,
Di Ciocco '96

Jacopo Banti,
Campiglia Marittima,
tel. 0565/838802,
Il Peccato Barrique '95

Volpaiole,
Campiglia Marittima, tel. 0565/843194,
Val di Cornia Rosso '95

Cipriana,
Castagneto, tel. 0565/877153,
Cabernet San Martino '95

Rosa Gasser Bagnoli,
Castagneto Carducci, tel. 0565/775272,
Bolgheri Bianco '96

Cecilia,
Isola d'Elba, tel. 0565/977322,
Ansonica '96

Tenuta Il Vignale,
Piombino, tel. 0565/20847,
Mosaico Ris. '94

Podere S. Michele,
San Vincenzo,
tel. 0565/701393,
Allodio '95

Falcone,
Suvereto, tel. 0565/829294,
Boccalupo '95

La Bulichella,
Suvereto, tel. 0565/829892,
Tuscanio '95

Villa Monte Rico,
Suvereto,
tel. 0565/829550,
Villa Monte Rico '91

PROVINCE OF LUCCA

Camiliano,
Lucca, tel. 0583/490420,
Sauvignon '96

Le Murelle,
Lucca, tel. 0583/394497,
Chardonnay '96

Fattoria del Teso,
Montecarlo, tel. 0583/286288,
Stella del Teso '96

Mazzini,
Montecarlo, tel. 0583/22010,
Montecarlo Rosso '95,
La Salita '96

Montechiari,
Montecarlo, tel. 0583/22189,
Cabernet '94

Vigna del Greppo,
Montecarlo, tel. 0583/22593,
Sauvignon '96

PROVINCE OF SIENA

Concadoro,
Castellina in Chianti, tel. 0577/741285,
Chianti Classico '95

Rodano,
Castellina in Chianti,
tel. 0577/743107,
Chianti Classico '95,
Chianti Classico Viacosta Ris. '93,
Monna Claudia '90

Borgo Scopeto,
Castelnuovo Berardenga,
tel. 0577/356827,
Chianti Classico '94

Podere San Luigi,
Colle Val d'Elsa, tel. 0577/959724,
San Luigi Vigna Casanuova '93

Rietine,
Gaiole in Chianti, tel. 0577/731110,
Chianti Classico '95

Rocca di Castagnoli,
Gaiole in Chianti, tel. 0577/731004,
Chianti Classico Poggio a' Frati Ris. '94

San Martino,
Gaiole in Chianti,
tel. 0577/749517,
Chianti Classico '95,
Chianti Classico Ris. '93

Campogiovanni,
Montalcino, tel. 0577/864001,
Brunello di Montalcino '92

Cerbaiona,
Montalcino, tel. 0577/849314,
Cerbaiona '94

Tenuta Collosorbo,
Montalcino, tel. 0577/835534,
Rosso di Montalcino Vigna di Capraia '95

Corte Pavone,
Montalcino, tel. 0577/848110,
Brunello di Montalcino '91,
Brunello di Montalcino Ris. '90

La Fuga,
Montalcino, tel. 0577/866039,
Brunello di Montalcino Ris. '91,
Rosso di Montalcino '95

La Poderina,
Montalcino, tel. 0577/835737,
Brunello di Montalcino '92

Le Macioche,
Montalcino,
tel. 0577/847024-849168,
Brunello di Montalcino '92

Marchesato degli Aleramici,
Montalcino, tel. 010/396634,
Brunello di Montalcino '92

Mocali,
Montalcino, tel. 0577/849485,
Brunello di Montalcino Ris. '91

Il Poggiolo,
Montalcino, tel. 0577/864057,
Brunello di Montalcino Il Beato '92

Tenuta Valdicava,
Montalcino, tel. 0577/848261,
Rosso di Montalcino '95

Verbena,
Montalcino, tel. 0577/848432,
Brunello di Montalcino '92

Casale,
Montepulciano, tel. 0578/738257,
Vino Nobile di Montepulciano '94,
Vino Nobile di Montepulciano Ris. '93

Ercolani,
Montepulciano, tel. 0578/758711,
Vino Nobile di Montepulciano '94

Ormanni,
Poggibonsi, tel. 0577/937212,
Chianti Classico '95

Podere Capaccia,
Radda in Chianti,
tel. 0577/738385,
Chianti Classico '94,
Querciagrande '94

Vignavecchia,
Radda in Chianti, tel. 0577/738090,
Chianti Classico '95,
Chianti Classico Ris. '93

Castello di Modanella,
Rapolano Terme,
tel. 0577/704604,
Le Voliere Cabernet Sauvignon '94

Casa alla Madonna,
San Gimignano,
tel. 0577/944881,
Agresto '95

Casa Rossa,
San Gimignano,
tel. 0577/941140,
Vernaccia di San Gimignano Melandre '96

Casale Falchini,
San Gimignano, tel. 0577/941305,
Campora '93,
Vernaccia di San Gimignano
Vigna a Solatio Ris. '95

Il Lebbio,
San Gimignano, tel. 0577/944725,
I Grottoni '96

La Rampa di Fugnano,
San Gimignano,
tel. 0577/941655,
Vernaccia di San Gimignano Privato '95,
Vernaccia di San Gimignano Ballata '96

Montenidoli,
San Gimignano,
tel. 0577/941565,
Vernaccia di S. Gimignano Fiore '96

Fattoria di Pancole,
San Gimignano, tel. 0577/955078,
Chianti Colli Senesi '96

Pietrafitta,
San Gimignano,
tel. 0577/943200,
Vernaccia Ris. '95 Vigna la Costa

Pietraserena,
San Gimignano,
tel. 0577/940083,
Chianti Colli Senesi '96

MARCHE

The wines of the Marche have again achieved flattering results, evidence of the established trend towards quality. We start this review with the estates which won Three Glass awards for their wines this year. First of all our congratulations go to Elvio Alessandro's Boccadigabbia winery, which for the third year running has scored a bull's-eye with its Cabernet Sauvignon Akronte, now rightly considered one of Italy's top reds. The success of the '94 Akronte is even more praiseworthy because it follows the outstanding '93 vintage. We would also like to stress the excellent placings of at least three other reds: Umani Ronchi's Pélago '94, a very convincing blend making its first appearance this year, the Sassi Neri '95 from Le Terrazze and Enzo Mecella's Rubelliano '94. The last two wines, both Rosso Conero, reveal the potential of this flourishing DOC and the enormous technical progress made by the estates behind them. Still in the province of Ancona, we congratulate the producers of Verdicchio dei Castelli di Jesi on the production of first class versions of the region's leading white. Three Glass awards in this category go to Sartarelli, for the second year running, to Garofoli and San Michele. Sartarelli's superb Contrada Balciana '95 selection is even more stunning than the previous vintage, displaying an even greater poise as well as enormous power. Garofoli's Podium '95 confirms the status of the Castelli di Jesi DOC and that of the estate in question, which produces Verdicchio in a number of styles. Among these, the Serra Fiorese '94, a Verdicchio aged in French oak, got only slightly lower marks than the prize winning Podium. In fact the whole of the Garofoli range is excellent, both whites and reds, and the estate is one of the authentic leaders in the Marche. The great attributes of Verdicchio, freshness combined with complexity, are wonderfully balanced in Vallerosa Bonci's San Michele cru. It amply merits a Three Glass award which also takes into account the reliability and steady progress made over the years by this estate. Flanking these protagonists of the renaissance of Verdicchio, we wish to record the names of others like La Monacesca or Bucci, to cite just two of many, who are boosting the reputation of Castelli di Jesi and Matelica. Finally we would like to express our appreciation of the progress made in the southern part of the Marche, although this part of the region has still to realise its full potential. For top quality Rosso Piceno (in particular the Superiore version) and Falerio dei Colli Ascolani, Cocci Grifoni and Velenosi are the estates which lead the way. There is also movement in the north of the region, with the emergence of new wines and the confirmation of old favourites in the revised DOCs of the province of Pesaro.

ANCONA

ANCONA

LUCA E BEATRICE LANARI
VIA POZZO, 142
FRAZ. VARANO
60100 ANCONA
TEL. 071/2861343

MARCHETTI
VIA DI PONTELUNGO, 166
60100 ANCONA
TEL. 071/897386

This estate has only been in the Guide for a few years and despite various difficulties, such as no Rosso Conero from the '95 vintage because the grapes were not good enough, is steadily on the rise. Luca Lanari, with his sister Beatrice who is in charge of administration and sales, runs this small winery situated within the area of the Parco del Conero. There are now eight hectares of vineyard: this extension of the area planted to vine should guarantee sufficient quantities and at the same time offer a wider choice of clones and the possibility to control yields for the red wine selections, of which the Fibbio '94 was a splendid example. The '96 vintage, a rather difficult one in the Marche, was on the whole reasonably good for the Lanaris, thanks to a great deal of hard work during harvesting and vinification. The Casino is back, a wine which takes its name from the random blending of whatever grapes happened to be in the vineyard, in this case malvasia and moscato. It is pale yellow, with aromas of moscato and a citrusy fragrance, and with freshness and the right amount of body. It is easy drinking with a long, dry finish. The Angiolo is a correctly made trebbiano, with all the limitations of this grape vinified as a monovarietal, plus those of an indifferent year: straw-yellow, aromas lacking intensity, clean on the palate but meagre. The Rosso Conero '96 is an intense garnet colour with purple tints and a vivid aroma of cherries. It has freshness, good concentration and a clean, well defined finish. Finally, confirming the excellent impression recorded in last year's Guide, the '94 vintage of the Fibbio selection is in perfect form.

Longevity has always been a characteristic of the wines of this estate from Ancona, a veteran producer of Rosso Conero. We still remember the first labels to appear in the wine shops towards the end of the sixties, when the DOC was first granted to this wine made from montepulciano and sangiovese grapes. It has maintained a recognisable style for its long lived wines, which are much appreciated abroad. In these last few years Marchetti's Rosso Conero wines have been vinified with an extra touch of modernity, which in no way upsets the style of the estate, but is an advantage in terms of smoothness, technical accuracy and easy drinking. The Villa Bonomi Riserva is an example of the right balance between the modern and the traditional: the wine has further developed thanks to its generous body, but has also preserved an appreciable softness. The '94 vintage of the recently released Rosso Conero Riserva is also a compelling wine: on the nose it has well assimilated boisé aroma and also evokes plum and morello cherries, which are repeated on the firm, well made palate. The normal Rosso Conero of the latest vintage is a direct wine, with a verve typical of young wines from this DOC. The two '96 Verdicchio wines are an agreeable surprise, the estate being traditionally committed to reds. Both the Villa Bonomi selection and the basic vintage gained One Glass ratings for their marked varietal character, good body and balance on the palate.

○ Casino '96	♀	2
● Rosso Conero '96	♀	2
○ L'Angiolo '96		1
● Rosso Conero Fibbio '94	♀♀	4

● Rosso Conero '96	♀	1*
● Rosso Conero Ris. Villa Bonomi '94	♀	3
○ Verdicchio dei Castelli di Jesi '96	♀	1
○ Verdicchio dei Castelli di Jesi Cl. Villa Bonomi '96	♀	3
● Rosso Conero Ris. Villa Bonomi '91	♀	4

ANCONA

ASCOLI PICENO

ALESSANDRO MORODER
FRAZ. MONTACUTO, 112
60029 ANCONA
TEL. 071/898232

ERCOLE VELENOSI
VIA DEI BIANCOSPINI, 11
63100 ASCOLI PICENO
TEL. 0736/341218

This year the main developments on this estate in Montacuto regard not so much the cellar as the floor above it, where Alessandro and Serenella Moroder have done up an attractive area destined for rural tourism as well as for tastings. The modernisation of the cellar has been completed, and the cooperage renewed with Allier oak barrels of varying capacity and others of Slavonian oak, suitable for ageing montepulciano. The estate's consultant oenologist is Franco Bernabei and their agronomist Mario Ghergo. At the moment the Dorico '93, the Rosso Conero selection which was awarded our Three Glasses last year, as were the previous vintages of '88 and '90, is still being sold. During the year we tasted the Dorico '93 to assess its evolution. We appreciated its excellent structure and above all its elegance; violet and plum gradually developing on the nose while in the mouth it is broad, smooth and concentrated. The basic version of Rosso Conero, the1995 vintage released this year, again proves enjoyable, combining youthful grapiness with soft, easy drinking. Also highly drinkable is the '96 vintage of Rosa di Montacuto, obtained from montepulciano grapes and small percentages of aglianico, tocai rosso and aleatico. To finish with, there is a real novelty. From the same grapes used for making the Candiano - trebbiano and, in smaller amounts, malvasia and moscato - the Moroders in1996 started to vinify a dessert wine, obtained from late harvested grapes; an interesting and successful cépage and convincing final result.

The admirable wines of this Ascoli Piceno estate are again witness to a pursuit of quality which is by now constant and justifiably ambitious. With the help of technician Romeo Taraborelli, the winery is working towards a well defined objective: experimentation with wines derived from non-native varieties and improvement in the quality of the local DOCs, Rosso Piceno Superiore and Falerio dei Colli Ascolani. Two special selections of these wines are made, respectively the Roggio del Filare and the Vigna Solaria. The Brecciarolo line includes all the reds, plus a rosé. Last year the estate's best wine was the Rosso Piceno Superiore '93 Roggio del Filare, a few points ahead of the Rosso Piceno Brecciarolo; with the '94 vintage, presented this year, it was the opposite way round. When we tasted them, the Brecciarolo, with its excellent fruity fragrance and concentration, was definitely ahead of the Roggio del Filare which displayed too much wood and lack of harmony on the palate. The Falerio Vigna Solaria '96 is another very successful wine: elegant and broad on the nose, it is rich, fragrant and soft on the palate, with a good capacity for ageing. The Barricato di Villa Angela '95, a Chardonnay whose wood ageing has now been gauged to perfection, displays a wide array of citrus fruit and toasty flavours. For an unfavourable year, the normal version of the Brecciarolo Falerio is correct and worthy of mention, together with the Linagre, the Floreo and the '96 Rosato. Finally, the sparkling wine made with traditional bottle fermentation gained a well deserved One Glass rating.

O	L'Oro di Moroder	♟	4
⊙	Rosa di Montacuto '96	♟	2
●	Rosso Conero '95	♟	2
●	Rosso Conero Dorico '90	♟♟♟	4
●	Rosso Conero Dorico '93	♟♟♟	4
●	Rosso Conero Dorico '92	♟♟	4

O	Falerio dei Colli Ascolani Vigna Solaria '96	♟♟	3
O	Il Barricato di Villa Angela '95	♟♟	4
●	Rosso Piceno Superiore Il Brecciarolo '94	♟♟	2*
●	Rosso Piceno Superiore Roggio del Filare '94	♟	4
O	Falerio dei Colli Ascolani Il Brecciarolo '96	♟	1*
O	Velenosi Brut Metodo Classico	♟	4
O	Villa Angela Chardonnay '96	♟	3
O	Floreo di Villa Angela '96		2
O	Linagre Sauvignon di Villa Angela '96		3
⊙	Rosato Il Brecciarolo '96		1

BARBARA (AN)

SANTA BARBARA
BORGO MAZZINI, 35
60010 BARBARA (AN)
TEL. 071/9674249

The overall impression of Stefano Antonucci's winery remains positive. In a year like '96, when it rained during the ripening and harvesting of the grapes, he still did an excellent job, steadily pursuing quality with praiseworthy determination. The basic version of the Verdicchio di Jesi is agreeable, fresh and long. The Pignocco is fresh but not aggressive, satisfying on the nose and enjoyable drinking. Le Vaglie, a Verdicchio made from a vineyard selection, has a better nose, richer texture and a pleasantly bitter finish, but it is somewhat lacking compared to previous vintages. The Selezione Stefano Antonucci, again a Castello di Jesi Classico, vintage '94, which has spent time in small oak barrels, has a good array of delicate aromas: hints of vanilla, floral and fruity, the structure is good and the flavour has a certain complexity. Going on to the reds, the Pignocco Rosso is a blend of montepulciano, lacrima di Morro d'Alba, moscato rosso, and cabernet sauvignon in percentages varying from year to year. The result is a freshly scented wine which is enjoyable easy drinking. The Rosso delle Marche Stefano Antonucci '93, a wine from a Bordeaux-style cépage aged in barriques, has the clean, varietal aroma of ripe cabernet, and an excellent soft structure with good concentration of fruit. It is a wine with balance and a long, broad finish, definitely for keeping. The San Bartolo '95, from montepulciano and cabernet, has a limited range of aromas and mediocre structure, but overall balance makes it on the whole an enjoyable wine. The Moscatell, made from moscato, is a pleasant dessert wine.

CASTEL DI LAMA (AP)

TENUTA DE ANGELIS
VIA S. FRANCESCO, 10
63030 CASTEL DI LAMA (AP)
TEL. 0736/87429

The '96 harvest was not an easy one in this area due to heavy rainfall at the crucial moments, and the effects were felt more or less everywhere, mainly by the whites. The two produced by the De Angelis estate located in a hills near Offida deserve to be recorded if nothing else because of their flawless vinification. We refer to the Prato Grande, from a blend of chardonnay and sauvignon, and to the Falerio dei Colli Ascolani, a local white DOC obtained from trebbiano, verdicchio, passerina and other varieties. The latest vintage of the Rosso Piceno Superiore, in terms of rating in the Guide, is a different matter. This is the most important wine, not only of the estate, but of whole the area. The '94 vintage, now on the market, is a robust wine, and thanks to a successful period of ageing in wooden casks of various origins and dimensions, has softness with a profusion of aromas. Production norms for this DOC are shortly going to be revised: for twenty years they have prescribed the same blend as for the larger Rosso Piceno appellation, at least 60 percent sangiovese supported by montepulciano, but all producers now tend to manoeuvre the percentages in favour of the latter variety. Results are generally better, with higher alcohol and more importance given to length and methods of ageing. The last wine presented this year by the De Angelis estate, which has the collaboration of oenologist Roberto Potentini, is the Rosso Piceno '96, an undemanding, drinkable wine.

● Rosso delle Marche Stefano Antonucci '93	♙♙	4
○ Verdicchio dei Castelli di Jesi Cl. Sel. Stefano Antonucci '94	♙♙	4
○ Moscatell '96	♙	3
○ Verdicchio dei Castelli di Jesi Cl. Le Vaglie '96	♙	3
○ Verdicchio dei Castelli di Jesi Pignocco '96	♙	2
● San Bartolo '95	♙	3
● Pignocco Rosso '96		3
○ Verdicchio Castelli Jesi Cl. '96		1
● Pignocco Rosso '95	♟♟	3
● Rosso delle Marche Stefano Antonucci '92	♟♟	4

● Rosso Piceno Superiore '94	♙♙	2*
○ Falerio dei Colli Ascolani '96		1
○ Prato Grande '96		1
● Rosso Piceno '96		1

CASTELPLANIO (AN)

CINGOLI (MC)

FAZI BATTAGLIA
VIA ROMA, 117
60032 CASTELPLANIO (AN)
TEL. 0731/813444

LUCANGELI AYMERICH DI LACONI
LOC. TAVIGNANO
62011 CINGOLI (MC)
TEL. 0733/617303

This historic estate from Castelplanio, founded in1949 at Cupramontana, continues in its role as the international market leader of Verdicchio. Today the Fazi Battaglia vineyards cover about 340 hectares, in twelve different areas. They are vertically trained, with the Sylvoz and the arched cane systems, and density of planting varies according to the characteristics of the vineyard from 1,800 to 2,500 vines per hectare. The technical team consists of oenologist Dino Porfiri, agronomists Mario Ghergo and Antonio Verdolini and winemaker Franco Bernabei who joined them as a consultant a few years ago. The Titulus, one of the four Verdicchio dei Castelli di Jesi wines produced, is certainly the best known. Perhaps this is due to the bottle designed in1954 and inspired by Etruscan amphorae, supposedly known in English speaking countries as the "sex bottle" because of its curves. Or it could be that few Italian whites produced in such vast quantities maintain such a constant level of quality. The '96 vintage of the basic Verdicchio, which is the Titulus, is a fresh and reliable wine, of marked varietal character both in its herbal aromas and in its tangy flavour with a slightly bitter finish. The Le Moie '96 has more texture: it is freshly perfumed and balanced on the palate, with a long finish. The San Sisto '94, fermented and aged in small oak casks, is excellent: modern in conception but with a slight risk of the wood overpowering its fragrance. The sparkling version, again from verdicchio grapes, is as enjoyable as always. Especially successful, to end with, is the Rosso Conero '96.

This is an emerging estate from the Castelli di Jesi, located in the historic production area defined by the DOC as the "Classico" zone. The property consists of 230 hectares on the first hills facing Jesi, at an average altitude of 250 metres, and has recently restructured its vineyards: 16 hectares were planted in 1992, all verdicchio, with the Guyot training system, and two hectares of red grapes, not yet in production, have just been added. Well positioned vineyards facing south yield the grapes for the two selections of Verdicchio, Misco and Vigneti di Tavignano, of which 20,000 bottles are produced. We tasted the last two vintages, which are also the first released by the estate, of the first of these two wines. The '95 vintage is still good, as a Verdicchio of structure and character should be, but perhaps lacking length on the palate. The latest vintage has greater impact, with promise of further development; broad on the nose with delicate hints of citrus fruit which are repeated in the mouth, it is a soft wine with a clean, admirable finish, especially when bearing in mind that the general standard of the1996 vintage is not very high. Although a different style of wine, the Vigneti di Tavignano '96 is just as good: it is more varietal in aroma, with a nose of lime flowers and chlorophyll, and is fresh, vigorous and long. These are impressive wines, to which the estate, run with enthusiasm by Giancarlo Soverchia, will in the future add a late harvest of undoubted interest.

○ Verdicchio dei Castelli di Jesi Cl. Le Moie '96	🍷🍷	2*
○ Verdicchio dei Castelli di Jesi Cl. San Sisto '94	🍷🍷	4
○ Verdicchio dei Castelli di Jesi Cl. Titulus '96	🍷	1
○ Verdicchio dei Castelli di Jesi Fazi Battaglia Brut	🍷	3
● Rosso Conero '96	🍷	2
○ Verdicchio dei Castelli di Jesi Cl. Le Moie '95	🍷🍷	3
○ Verdicchio dei Castelli di Jesi Cl. San Sisto '93	🍷🍷	4

○ Verdicchio dei Castelli di Jesi Cl. Misco '96	🍷🍷	3
○ Verdicchio dei Castelli di Jesi Cl. Vigneti di Tavignano '96	🍷🍷	1*
○ Verdicchio dei Castelli di Jesi Cl. Misco '95	🍷	3

CIVITANOVA MARCHE (MC) CIVITANOVA MARCHE (MC)

BOCCADIGABBIA
VIA DELL'ARGANO, 3
62012 CIVITANOVA MARCHE (MC)
TEL. 0733/70728

LA MONACESCA
VIA D'ANNUNZIO, 1
62012 CIVITANOVA MARCHE (MC)
TEL. 0733/812602

Elvio Alessandri's estate is not in France but in the Marche. There is however a specific historical explanation for the French varieties grown here, chardonnay, pinot nero and grigio and cabernet sauvignon: the farm was part of the property of Eugenio Beauharnais, viceroy of Italy. As for the wines, produced with the collaboration of Giovanni Basso and Fabrizio Ciufoli, the masterpiece is the Akronte '94 which for the third year running has won the Three Glass award. Made from 100 per cent cabernet sauvignon, it is dark ruby in colour with garnet tints. The characteristic varietal aroma is softened by hints of vanilla and when it opens out, spicy tobacco overtones become perceptible. In the mouth, the tannic component is powerful but not astringent and there is great concentration and flavour; with time it will gain in balance and softness and it has great ageing potential. Moving on to the other wines, the Rosso Piceno '95 again proves enjoyable, also the Garbi '96; this is a basic commercial line but it continues to offer good aroma and amazingly fresh, easy drinking. The Montalperti '95, a Chardonnay matured in small oak barrels, is a deep straw-yellow colour with toasted aromas which perhaps slightly overpower the varietal character of the grape. In the mouth it is creamy and concentrated with good structure, but still has to acquire balance. The Aldonis, again from chardonnay, is a pleasant straw-yellow, and evokes yellow plums and citrus on the nose: in the mouth it is fleshy and soft with a long, satisfying finish. The pinot grigio Castelletta '96 did not seem as good as previous vintages. A final mention for two wines Colli Maceratesi wines from the Villamagna estate which has appeared in the Guide in the past and has recently been bought by Elvio Alessandri, the Rosso Piceno DOC '94 and the Bianco dei Colli Maceratesi '96.

For years we have considered La Monacesca, founded by Casimiro Cifola and managed with enthusiasm and determination by his son Aldo, one of the most coherent producers of the Marche in its strict adherence to quality and its approach to estate management. The vineyards are at an average altitude of 450 metres above sea level; the crop is carefully selected and the time for harvesting accurately chosen. For a few years Aldo has had the valuable technical support of oenologist Roberto Cipresso; for the future, besides the "monotheistic" range of splendid whites, they are planning a red, for which they both have high hopes. It should revive the old tradition of Matelica as a red wine production area which goes back to the first half of the century, before the success of Verdicchio di Matelica. This DOC, incidentally, was the first to be granted in the region, and celebrated its thirtieth year in 1997. To come to the wines tasted this year, the Mirum '95 did not repeat last year's achievement, but is extremely attractive, with its refined aristocratic nose evocative of aniseed and white flowers; on the palate it is soft and ready for drinking, with a good alcoholic component and the right degree of freshness. Considering the vintage, the cru La Monacesca '96 is laudable: here too the fresh, well expressed aroma of aniseed is supported by a correct balance of alcohol and acid, with room for development. The basic version of the Verdicchio di Matelica, '96 vintage, is enjoyable and correct as usual.

●	Akronte '94	♓♓♓	5
○	Aldonis Chardonnay '96	♓♓	3
○	La Castelletta Pinot Grigio '96	♓	3
○	Montalperti Chardonnay '95	♓	4
○	Colli Maceratesi Villamagna '96	♓	2
○	Garbì '96	♓	2
●	Rosso Piceno '95	♓	3
●	Rosso Piceno Villamagna '94	♓	3
●	Akronte '93	♓♓♓	5
●	Akronte '92	♓♓♓	5
●	Girone '93	♓♓	4
●	Rosso Piceno Saltapicchio '93	♓♓	2

○	Mirum '95	♓♓	4
○	Verdicchio di Matelica La Monacesca '96	♓♓	3
○	Verdicchio di Matelica '96	♓	3
○	Mirum '94	♓♓♓	4
○	Mirus '91	♓♓♓	4
○	Verdicchio di Matelica La Monacesca '94	♓♓♓	3
○	Mirus '93	♓♓	4

CUPRAMONTANA (AN)

CUPRAMONTANA (AN)

VALLEROSA BONCI
VIA TORRE, 17
60034 CUPRAMONTANA (AN)
TEL. 0731/789129

COLONNARA VITICULTORI
IN CUPRAMONTANA
VIA MANDRIOLE, 6
60034 CUPRAMONTANA (AN)
TEL. 0731/780273

The recent opening of a handsome room for tastings next to the main buildings of the estate and the vinification cellar, which includes a collection of rural exhibits, has a special meaning for the Bonci family: they are known for their love for the land, spontaneous sense of hospitality and strong desire to improve the quality of their production. The estate is situated in the heart of the DOC Classico zone and has 50 hectares of land, of which 35 are planted to vines. Two of the vineyards are given over to viticultural experiments under the guidance of oenologist Sergio Paolucci, in collaboration with the Arboreal Institute of Milan university. The vineyards, located at an average altitude of 450 metres, are in particularly suitable zones: San Michele, Colonnara, Torre, Carpaneto, Alvareto, Pietrone. This year the estate's two crus, San Michele and Le Case, were found so exceptional by the tasting commission that the former achieved the Guide's maximum award. Three highly merited Glasses for the Verdicchio San Michele, a white with great texture and firm structure: brilliant yellow in colour, it is intensely perfumed with unusual aromatic nuances, delicate and summery. On the palate it is balanced, round and creamy, with a long, sweet finish. The other cru, which has slightly less impact, has a similar structure and range of aromas. The basic Verdicchio, of praiseworthy flawlessness, is made with grapes from the Carpaneto and Torre vineyard, while the Bonci Brut Metodo Classico, a sparkling wine combining elegance with marked varietal character, comes from the Alvareto and Pietrone vineyards.

The fame of the Colonnara cooperative is mainly due to the selection of Verdicchio dei Castelli di Jesi named Cuprese, its flag bearer wine. Few white wines from the Marche - they can be counted on one hand - possess the staying power and ageing potential of this wine, which succeeds in combining freshness and varietal character with a mature complexity. Established in 1959, Colonnara now has about 200 member-growers; Independent as regards vinification, it makes use of the services of an agronomist and an associated company, Cupravit, for the management of the vineyards. 1996, although not a particularly favourable year in central Italy, confirms the characteristics which make Cuprese a wine of such outstanding interest: green, herbal nose with a softer fragrance which will become better defined with time. Previous vintages, when re-tasted, confirmed a most interesting evolution, which reveals all the potential of a grape beginning to receive due attention from consumers. The Colonnara Metodo Classico, again a Verdicchio but this time the sparkling version, is one of the best of the Marche in terms of personality and texture. Good results were achieved by the Tornamagno '94, a red from sangiovese grosso, sangiovese montanino and montepulciano and aged in small French oak casks; it has quite good berry fruit on the nose and is broad and soft on the palate.

O Verdicchio dei Castelli di Jesi		
Cl. Sup. San Michele '96	♟♟♟	3
O Verdicchio dei Castelli di Jesi		
Cl. Sup. Le Case '96	♟♟	3
O Spumante Brut Bonci		
Metodo Classico	♟	4
O Verdicchio dei Castelli di Jesi		
Cl. '96	♟	2
O Verdicchio dei Castelli di Jesi		
Cl. Sup. San Michele '95	♟♟	3
O Verdicchio dei Castelli di Jesi		
Cl. Sup. Le Case '95	♟♟	3

O Verdicchio dei Castelli di Jesi		
Cl. Cuprese '96	♟♟	2*
O Colonnara Brut Metodo Classico	♟	4
● Tornamagno '94	♟	3
O Verdicchio dei Castelli di Jesi		
Cl. Sup. Romitello		
delle Mandriole '95	♟♟	4
O Verdicchio dei Castelli di Jesi		
Cl. Cuprese '95	♟♟	2

FABRIANO (AN)

FANO (PS)

ENZO MECELLA
VIA DANTE, 112
60044 FABRIANO (AN)
TEL. 0732/21680

CLAUDIO MORELLI
V.LE ROMAGNA, 47/B
61032 FANO (PS)
TEL. 0721/823352

Enzo Macella has done very well this year, presenting a range of wines of genuinely high quality. The first and most important is the Rosso Conero '94 Rubelliano. It has a very concentrated appearance. Dark red with purplish tints, on the nose it displays nicely blended aromas of camphor, vanilla and soft red fruit, especially redcurrants; on the palate it is already soft, rounded and long, with an aftertaste of coffee. The Lavi, the other selection of Rosso Conero '94 is less demanding but still enjoyable. It has characteristic aromas of plum and soft red fruit, good concentration again discernible in the colour and on the nose and palate. The '94 version of the Antico di Casa Fosca, the best produced to date, is another outstanding wine from the Fabriano estate. We can remember the first vintages of this lovely wine, which in the early eighties caused an outcry and was branded as an affront to tradition in local circles. However we believed then in Mecella's ability as an experimenter (he now has the reputation of a pioneer) and a master in the use of wood. The Antico, with its complex nose recalling almonds, hazelnuts and mint and its broad, soft palate, is a wine which should be tried. The Casa Fosca '95 is also very good: aniseed and herbs dominate on the nose, while the palate displays good structure and balanced acidity in the finish. The Rosso Piceno Malvano is a convincing wine: ruby-coloured with hints of fruit and vanilla and pleasantly drinkable. The Rosa Gentile '96 is as inviting as always. It is a rosé with a delicate onion-skin shade of pink, flowery, plummy nose and delightfully fresh palate.

For the last few years Claudio Morelli's estate has been steadily acquiring a reputation as one of the best and most reliable producers of the Pesaro area. Négociants since the 1930's, the Morelli family later started to produce their wine. Now, under Claudio's management, they own some vineyards and rent others at Roncosambaccio well-known to experts for their good position and favourable mesoclimates; Roncosambaccio has always been one of the most sought-after zones in the Pesaro hills. It is with the Bianchello del Metauro selection La Vigna delle Terrazze '96 that Morelli achieves his best results this year. Although it lacks some body, the Bianchello can be considered a model of its type: well-defined, clean, and long with a pleasantly bitter finish. The Borgo Torre '96, the other selection of Bianchello made by the estate, is also successful: its aromas, floral and fruity, are well expressed and on the palate it is firm, with good bite. The San Cesareo, another Bianchello, is a pale straw-yellow with greenish tints, delicate aroma and a certain tartness in the mouth. The Sangiovese Vigna delle Terrazze '96 is an agreeably fruity, easy drinking varietal while the other red, the very well made Sant'Andrea in Villis, is more demanding: it has attractive soft fruit and flowers on the nose and good balance on the palate.

● Rosso Conero Rubelliano '94	▼▼	4
○ Verdicchio di Matelica Antico di Casa Fosca '94	▼▼	3
○ Verdicchio di Matelica Casa Fosca '95	▼	3
☉ Rosa Gentile '96	▼	2
● Rosso Conero I Lavi '94	▼	2
● Rosso Piceno Colle Malvano '94	▼	3
● Braccano '93	▼▼	4
● Rosso Conero Rubelliano '93	▼▼	4

○ Bianchello del Metauro La Vigna delle Terrazze '96	▼▼	2*
○ Bianchello del Metauro Borgo Torre '96	▼	2
● Colli Pesaresi Sangiovese La Vigna delle Terrazze '96	▼	2
● Sant'Andrea in Villis '93	▼	3
○ Bianchello del Metauro San Cesareo '96		2
● Colli Pesaresi Sangiovese La Vigna delle Terrazze '95	▽	2
● Suffragium '93	▽	3

JESI (AN)

LORETO (AN)

BRUNORI
V.LE DELLA VITTORIA, 103
60035 JESI (AN)
TEL. 0731/207213

GIOACCHINO GAROFOLI
VIA ARNO, 9
LOC. VILLA MUSONE
60025 LORETO (AN)
TEL. 071/7820163

Year after year the Brunori brothers turn out consistent and highly representative examples of the wines from the Classico zone which in the past comprised the old Contado di Jesi. The Jesi address is the Brunori business office which has a wine shop next to it. The actual estate is located at an altitude of about 200 metres above sea level in the commune of San Paolo di Jesi, at San Nicolò, the village which gives its name to the well-known selection of Verdicchio dei Castelli di Jesi. The vineyard, which faces south/south-west, has yields between 80 and 90 quintals of grapes per hectare. The Brunori family, first the founder Mario, then his son Giorgio who now in his turn works with his son Carlo, have always made their wines with 12-18 hours of skin contact; fermentation takes place in containers of 20-25 hectolitres and the wine undergoes sterile filtration and completely automatic bottling. Although the vintage was not an easy one for this wine, the San Nicolò presented by the Brunoris has good substance and will probably improve with bottle age. At the moment of tasting it was still at an early stage. The normal version of the Verdicchio dei Castelli di Jesi is a correct wine, with crisp acidity. Finally a mention for the Lacrima di Morro d'Alba which is straightforward, easy drinking.

Among the recently released Verdicchio wines, the Macrina '96 was slightly penalised by the unsatisfactory vintage: it has a delicate nose of acacia and is clean and smooth on the palate but lacks concentration. The Verdicchio dei Castelli di Jesi Podium '95 is an entirely different story: the best from the estate so far and unquestionably one of the best of its type in recent years. It has pronounced, long-lasting flowery aromas with elegant nuances of hazelnut and green apples; on the palate it is concentrated, smooth and intense but with soft and elegant structure and a hint of almonds on the finish. It fully deserves the Three Glasses, but there was also very high praise for the Serra Fiorese '94, a barrique-aged Verdicchio which is fruity and floral on the nose with slight vanilla overtones. The Komaros '96 is a rosé with an onion skin shade of pink and nice but rather short aromas of cooked fruit; it is fresh on the palate but lacking in structure. The Rosso Piceno Colle Ambro '95 is a strong ruby in colour with garnet tints and vinous nose, while in the mouth it is soft and tannic without being harsh. The Rosso Conero Vigna Piancarda '95 is a vivid, clear ruby and is soft and elegant on the palate. The Rosso Conero Riserva Grosso Agontano '94 is a thick, dark, ruby wine, still unsettled on the nose and austere on the palate with tannins still unintegrated. The Rosso Conero Riserva Grosso Agontano '93, released almost a year ago, is a wine with great class: the colour is dark and intense with vivid purplish tints, the nose is evocative of cherries, plum and sweet pepper, and on the palate it is powerful but soft and elegant. Lastly, there is the Ross, an excellent red from late harvested montepulciano and sagrantino grapes.

○ Verdicchio dei Castelli di Jesi Cl. San Nicolò '96	♟♟	2*
○ Verdicchio dei Castelli di Jesi Cl. '96	♟	2
● Lacrima di Morro d'Alba '96		2

○ Verdicchio dei Castelli di Jesi Cl. Sup. Podium '95	♟♟♟	3
○ Verdicchio dei Castelli di Jesi Cl. Ris. Serra Fiorese '94	♟♟	4
● Ross '94	♟♟	4
● Rosso Conero Ris. Grosso Agontano '93	♟♟	4
● Rosso Conero Ris. Grosso Agontano '94	♟♟	4
● Rosso Conero Vigna Piancarda '95	♟	2
○ Verdicchio dei Castelli di Jesi Cl. Sup. Macrina '96	♟	2
☉ Komaros '96		2
● Rosso Piceno Colle Ambro '95		2

MAIOLATI SPONTINI (AN) MATELICA (MC)

LA VITE
VIA VIVAIO
FRAZ. MONTE SCHIAVO
60030 MAIOLATI SPONTINI (AN)
TEL. 0731/700385-700297

CANTINA SOCIALE BELISARIO
DI MATELICA E CERRETO D'ESI
VIA MERLONI, 12
62024 MATELICA (MC)
TEL. 0737/787247

This Monte Schiavo winery last year underwent a change of ownership and from being a cooperative became a privately owned estate. The entire concern was bought up by Pieralisi, the major share holder in the cooperative, and its name was changed from Monte Schiavo to La Vite. At the moment the cellar is being extended and renovated in view of the ambitious plans of the new owners. The range of wines, sourced from over 100 hectares of vineyard owned by the estate, for the present remains unchanged. The various Verdicchio cru selections stand out: Bando di S. Settimio, Coste del Molino, Palio di S. Floriano, Colle del Sole, all reflect the different locations of their vineyards of origin and expressing differences in winemaking style. They also show the technical innovations of oenologist Pierluigi Lorenzetti. The best of the production this year is the Verdicchio Palio di S. Floriano '96, a soft, fresh, minerally white. The Bando di S. Settimio '95, matured in French oak and released about a year after the harvest, has a ripeness on the nose only partially repeated in the mouth. The Coste del Molino '96, is fresh but also weighty, like the Coste del Sole, and has an inviting fruitiness. It is a very reliable bottle. The basic Verdicchio is correct but has been affected by the poor vintage. The new Rosso Piceno Superiore Sassaiolo should be mentioned, as well as the Lacrima and the Rosso Conero, but the real novelty in reds will be a blend of cabernet and montepulciano which at the moment is still ageing.

Among the most interesting of Belisario's wines this year are those confirming the staying power of the Verdicchio di Matelica, starting with the second release of the Cinque Annate al Duemila, vintage '95. This project consists of a series of five wines which will mark the vintages up till the year 2000. The '95 wine, with a label specially designed by a local artist, is a cuvée of Matelica with well-developed aromas, fruity and flowery, and soft on the palate. The top wine this year is however the Cambrugiano '95, which for the first time joins the Riserva category as specified by the norms of the revised DOC. The wine has good alcohol which does not however compromise the freshness or the overall balance. The '94 vintage of the Cambrugiano is almost as good and displays an excellent capacity for bottle age. The Verdicchio del Cerro '96, which in the past has also shown its ability to combine freshness and good staying power, maintains to perfection the characteristics of a young but well-structured wine. The Belisario '95, perhaps a little shorter on the palate, is still smooth and elegant, and the basic Verdicchio vintage '96 is correctly made. The new DOC of the Marche, Esino, deserves to be mentioned: the white has fragrance and spontaneity. A final note for two experimental "passito" wines, obtained respectively from verdicchio and vernaccia di Cerreto: the second, the Serrae Rubrae, is the more convincing of the two.

● Rosso Conero '96	♀	2
● Rosso Piceno Sup. Sassaiolo '95	♀	2
○ Verdicchio dei Castelli di Jesi Cl. Bando di S. Settimio '95	♀	3
○ Verdicchio dei Castelli di Jesi Cl. Colle del Sole '96	♀	2
○ Verdicchio dei Castelli di Jesi Cl. Coste del Molino '96	♀	2
○ Verdicchio dei Castelli di Jesi Cl. Palio di S. Floriano '96	♀	2
● Lacrima di Morro d'Alba '96		1
○ Verdicchio dei Castelli di Jesi '96		1

○ Verdicchio di Matelica Belisario '95	♀♀	2*
○ Verdicchio di Matelica Cinque Annate al Duemila '95	♀♀	3
○ Verdicchio di Matelica Ris. Cambrugiano '95	♀♀	3
○ Verdicchio di Matelica Del Cerro '96	♀	2
○ Verdicchio di Matelica Ris. Cambrugiano '94	♀	3
○ Carpe Diem		4
○ Esino Bianco Ferrante '96		1
● Serrae Rubrae '94		4
○ Verdicchio di Matelica '96		2

MATELICA (MC)

CASTIGLIONI - F.LLI BISCI
VIA FOGLIANO, 120
62024 MATELICA (MC)
TEL. 0737/787490

MONTECAROTTO (AN)

TERRE CORTESI MONCARO
VIA PIANDOLE, 7/A
60036 MONTECAROTTO (AN)
TEL. 0731/89245

One of the few leader estates of the small Verdicchio di Matelica DOC returns with its specialities: two whites with structure and marked personality.The property of the Bisci brothers comprises about 105 hectares, of which 25 are specialized vineyard, gradually planted since the 1970s. The vineyard, divided exactly between the provinces of Ancona and Macerata, in the communes of Matelica and Cerreto d'Esi, is situated on low hills at an altitude of 250 to 350 metres and faces south. The two versions of Verdicchio presented this year by the Bisci brothers, the Vigneto Fogliano '94 selection and the basic '95 vintage, are derived entirely from verdicchio with no other varieties such as trebbiano or malvasia. They bear witness to the merit of the estate and the DOC with their positive varietal character, uncommon display of staying power and vigorous impact. Particularly interesting is the Vigneto Fogliano selection with its deep, brilliant yellow colour and intense array on the nose of lime blossom, chlorophyll and ripe fruit; on the palate it is well-defined, broad and fulfilling. The '95 vintage standard version is again strongly representative and intense in aroma, but it is less complete on the palate and lacks elegance in the finish.

Moncaro has been making constant progress over the last few years, both in its selections, for example the single vineyard Vigna Novali, and in its large-scale production. Established in 1964 and situated in the DOC zone of Verdicchio dei Castelli di Jesi, the cooperative now has over 700 member growers. Since 1980, 30 hectares have been cultivated strictly organically, but all the members make use of technical assistance and monitoring of atmospheric conditions in order to limit the impact on the environment of vineyard management. The Verdicchio '95 Tordiruta Biologico, an organic wine reviewed by us last year and re-tasted this year to check its stability, is a commendable product of the small winemaking sector which supports a drastic reduction in the use of agrochemicals in farming. We were likewise impressed by the development of the Verde di Ca' Ruptae, a Verdicchio with elegance and balance. Moving on, the second and most recent release of the Vigna Novali, the '95 vintage, is now on the market. It has outstanding depth and texture, with a touch of elegance which makes it one of the best wines in its category. The basic Verdicchio is up to its usual standards of correctness, while the second Verdicchio selection, Le Vele '96, is of great interest. It is in its second year of production and for the moment is destined for the overseas market; the aromas are intense and appealing and it is full but fresh on the palate. The Barocco, a blend of montepulciano, sangiovese, cabernet and ciliegiolo, shows promise: it is dense and mouth-filling, soft and long on the palate. The Rosso Conero Riserva '93 has the characteristic plummy, alcoholic nose, but is slightly meagre on the palate.

O Verdicchio di Matelica Vigneto Fogliano '94	YY	3
O Verdicchio di Matelica '95	Y	2

O Verdicchio dei Castelli di Jesi Cl. Vigna Novali '95	YY	3
● Barocco '94	Y	3
● Rosso Conero Ris. Tordiruta '93	Y	2
O Verdicchio dei Castelli di Jesi Cl. Le Vele '96	Y	3
O Esino Bianco '96		1
O Verdicchio dei Castelli di Jesi Cl. '96		2
O Verdicchio dei Castelli di Jesi Cl. Tordiruta Biologico '95	Y	3
O Verdicchio dei Castelli di Jesi Cl. Verde di Ca' Ruptae '95	Y	3

MORRO D'ALBA (AN)

STEFANO MANCINELLI
VIA ROMA, 62
60030 MORRO D'ALBA (AN)
TEL. 0731/63021

NUMANA (AN)

CONTE LEOPARDI DITTAJUTI
VIA MARINA II, 26
60026 NUMANA (AN)
TEL. 071/7390116-7391479

Stefano Mancinelli is the leading producer of Lacrima di Morro, both in quantity, which in any case is low since the entire DOC covers little more than 20 hectares, and in quality, which he aims for by vinifying the variety on its own, although production regulations allow the addition of 15% of other grapes, red or white. The support of Roberto Potentini in the cellar has helped produce a highly representative range of wines with a degree of elegance not easy to achieve in a vintage like '96 which was beset by bad weather. The two versions of Verdicchio, the basic and the cru, have good varietal character even though they unfortunately lack structure and concentration. The Lacrima, also affected by the poor vintage, has sufficient aroma but the overall lack of extract is noticeable in both the colour and the palate. The best wine in the cellar in our opinion was the Lacrima '95 selection Sensazioni di Frutto, made by combining carbonic maceration with traditional tank fermentation. Being a '95 it has better structure and more intense concentration of colour and aroma, and a much richer palate. It has distinct appeal, and could be a model for the future for this wine which still has to establish its identity. The San Michele is again in production, a Rosso Piceno fermented with lacrima skins: it is attractive on the nose but is elusive on the palate.

Count Piervittorio Leopardi's estate has again reached good levels of quality with the '96 vintage, demonstrating the excellent judgement of Romeo Taraborelli in the cellar. Among this year's wines, the Vigna d'Oro '96, from trebbiano and a smaller percentage of sauvignon, has a nose lacking in finesse, with conspicuous aromas of under ripe fruit. In the mouth, although there is a certain fragrance, it lacks elegance; but as it is the cellar's basic wine too much cannot be expected. The Bianco del Coppo has a nose of honey with none of the grassiness which might be expected from a sauvignon, and a rather short finish. It is very fresh on the palate, with zingy acidity but not much concentration. The Calcare '96 has typical sauvignon aromas, with pronounced, persistent herbal overtones and hints of sage; in the mouth it is creamy and concentrated with good soft structure and an elegant, clean finish. The Villa Marina '95 is a sauvignon aged in barriques, of a deep, almost golden yellow colour. Toasty, vanilla aromas predominate over the varietal fruit, while on the palate it is creamy, fresh and fairly long, but still needs to achieve balance. The Rosso Conero '94 Vigna del Coppo is a good, clear ruby with garnet tints; the nose is spicy, toasty, almost resinous and on the palate it is concentrated and elegant.The Rosso Conero '93 Pigmento is broad on the nose with an herbaceous note which masks the fruit of the montepulciano grape. On the palate the tannins blend fairly smoothly.

● Lacrima di Morro d'Alba Sensazioni di Frutto '95	♀♀	3
● Lacrima di Morro d'Alba S. Maria del Fiore '96	♀	2
○ Verdicchio dei Castelli di Jesi Cl. S. Maria del Fiore '96	♀	2
○ Verdicchio dei Castelli di Jesi Cl. '96		2
● Lacrima di Morro d'Alba '96		1
● Rosso Piceno San Michele '96		1
● Lacrima di Morro d'Alba S. Maria del Fiore '95	♀♀	3
● Lacrima di Morro d'Alba '95	♀	2

○ Calcare Sauvignon '96	♀♀	3
● Rosso Conero Pigmento '93	♀♀	4
● Rosso Conero Vigneti del Coppo '94	♀	3
○ Villa Marina Sauvignon '95	♀	4
○ Bianco del Coppo Sauvignon '96		2
○ Vigna d'Oro '96		2
○ Calcare Sauvignon '95	♀♀	3
● Rosso Conero Vigneti del Coppo '93	♀♀	3

NUMANA (AN)

OFFIDA (AP)

FATTORIA LE TERRAZZE
VIA MUSONE, 4
60026 NUMANA (AN)
TEL. 071/7390352

VILLA PIGNA
C.DA CIAFONE, 63
63035 OFFIDA (AP)
TEL. 0736/87525

Good producers know how to cope with difficult harvests. In the Conero area the last two years were almost impossible so Antonio and Giorgina Terni can feel satisfied with what they have achieved with their Rosso. This DOC is rapidly gaining ground, showing that montepulciano is one of Italy's great varieties, no longer a blending grape but a truly noble variety with its own personality. The team formed by oenologist Attilio Pagli and Leonardo Valente - a lecturer from Milan university who has been giving advice on farm management for the last few years, has produced results. The Rosso Conero '95, one of the best young examples of this wine that we can remember, is a dark ruby colour with purple tints and warm aromas of morello cherries typical of the grape; on the palate it is soft, balanced and mouth-filling, fresh and drinkable. The Rosso Conero '94 Sassi Neri, a dense, dark ruby, is full of aroma, with fruit, spiciness and toasty flavours. In the mouth it is warm and concentrated but with softness, balance and a well judged tannin component. The Sassi Neri '95 vintage is a real gem, one of the best examples of Rosso Conero of recent years: the colour is a dark, intense purplish ruby, it is richly perfumed with hints of vanilla, red fruit and spices. On the palate it is smooth, balanced and wonderfully soft, with a long, clean finish. The Chardonnay '96, more appealing than in previous vintages, displays well-defined aromas and fragrance, but although there is a good bite of acidity, it lacks substance on the palate and the finish is insignificant.

Of the estates operating in the small DOC zone of Rosso Piceno Superiore, the Rozzi family's Villa Pigna undoubtedly has the greatest production capacity with over 300 hectares of vineyard and a cellar of proportions to match. Production is not restricted to the local DOCs Falerio dei Colli Ascolani and Rosso Piceno Superiore, but also includes Montepulciano and Trebbiano from the nearby Abruzzi, Verdicchio dei Castelli di Jesi and some vino da tavola from non-DOC varieties. Among the wines we tasted from Villa Pigna's wide range, the Rozzano '94 came out top. Reviewed by us in the last edition of the Guide, many attractive features have emerged in the interim, strengthening the good impression we had of it. The same goes for the Rosso Piceno Superiore '92, characterized by abundant spicy, tobacco aromas, concentrated palate and the right amount of tannin. The Rozzano '95, from montepulciano grapes, aged in small French oak casks, is slightly inferior to the previous vintage in terms of richness of extract and balance. The Rosso Piceno '96, taking into account the poor vintage, is correctly made. The Falerio dei Colli Ascolani '96 is also penalised by the difficult year: vinous on the nose with notes of acacia, but lacking in intensity and acidulous. Both the sparkling Riserva Extra Brut and the Cabernasco '95 up to their usual standard.

● Rosso Conero '95	♟♟	2
● Rosso Conero Sassi Neri '94	♟♟	4
● Rosso Conero Sassi Neri '95	♟♟	4
○ Chardonnay '96	♟	2
● Rosso Conero Sassi Neri '93	♟♟	4

● Cabernasco '95	♟	2
● Rozzano '95	♟	3
○ Spumante Riserva Extra Brut	♟	3
○ Falerio dei Colli Ascolani '96		1
● Rosso Piceno '96		1
● Rosso Piceno Superiore '92	♟♟	2
● Rozzano '94	♟♟	4

OSIMO (AN)

Umani Ronchi
S.S. 16, Km. 310+400,74
60027 Osimo (AN)
tel. 071/7108019

This historic estate from Osimo has gained considerable ground in these last two or three years, achieving flattering results at an international level. The Bernetti family is planning a major extension to the Osimo cellar, which has always been used mainly for the reds, while the Verdicchio wines are made at the Castelbellino cellar and the Bianchello at Piagge. The technical staff, consisting of oenologist Tombelli with Piersanti and Modi in charge of the vineyards, now has the collaboration of Giacomo Tachis who supervises the whole production and has contributed in particular to the creation of a new, important red called Pélago. This wine impresses with its dense texture, its almost silky consistence and its coherence of aromas and flavour. On the nose there is concentrated plummy fruit and liquorice; it has lots of body but at the same time is soft, persuasive and delightful in the mouth. The Rosso Conero '94, with elegant varietal character, harmony of aroma and soft palate, is also technically flawless. The Rosso Conero '96, slightly astringent but pleasantly drinkable, has an appropriate youthful grapey aroma, with hints of cherries. The Jorio '95, a 100 per cent montepulciano, is still purplish in colour and dense, with plummy aromas and overtones of mint; in the mouth it is soft and not very long-lasting. The two selections of Verdicchio dei Castelli di Jesi '96, Casal di Serra and Villa Bianchi are among the best in their category. The first is more opulent, but the second too, although fresher, has plenty of substance. Finally the Tajano, from sauvignon grapes, is an enjoyable wine.

●	Pélago '94	▼▼	5
●	Rosso Conero Cùmaro '94	▼▼	4
○	Verdicchio dei Castelli di Jesi Casal di Serra '96	▼▼	3
○	Verdicchio dei Castelli di Jesi Cl. Villa Bianchi '96	▼▼	2*
●	Montepulciano d'Abruzzo Jorio '95	▼	3
●	Rosso Conero '96	▼	2
●	Rosso Conero San Lorenzo '95	▼	3
○	Tajano '96	▼	3
○	Bianchello del Metauro '96		1
○	Maximo '93	▽▽	4
●	Rosso Conero Cùmaro '93	▽▽	4
○	Le Busche '95	▽	4

OSTRA VETERE (AN)

F.lli Bucci
Via Cona, 30
Fraz. Pongelli
60010 Ostra Vetere (AN)
tel. 071/964179 - 02/6554470

Anyone who does not know this estate at Ostra Vetere might be amazed to go through the series of Verdicchio vintages, from '96 back to '88 reviewed here. Anyone familiar with this producer, on the other hand, knowing that Ampelio Bucci is never in a hurry to release his incredibly long-lasting wines, with their wonderful depth and personality, might find it amazing that the '96 vintage is already on the market. The estate has 20 hectares of vineyard, 15 of which are planted to verdicchio and five to red grapes, mainly sangiovese and montepulciano. The production of Verdicchio derives from five vineyards all differing in their position and altitude (200-350 metres) whose grapes are vinified separately and then assembled to form a blend. Starting with the most recently released wine, the '96 normal vintage, the nose is obviously still green and restrained, but on the palate it already reveals buttery, almondy flavours which are also evident in the other two Verdicchio vintages tasted this year, the '94 and the '95: these wines both combine elegance and harmony of aroma with a firm structure. Bucci's style stands out in the Villa Bucci selections: the '94 vintage, the latest release, is perhaps slightly lacking compared to others, but has an acidity to guarantee its further evolution with time. The other three vintages still available, with special reference to the '88 which is complex and harmonious, are simply excellent. The Rosso Piceno deserves the last mention; this wine reflects what could be called the French style of the estate and, disregarding convention, can even be appreciated slightly cooled, with fish courses.

○	Verdicchio dei Castelli di Jesi Cl. '94	▼▼	3
○	Verdicchio dei Castelli di Jesi Cl. '95	▼▼	3
○	Verdicchio dei Castelli di Jesi Cl. '96	▼▼	3
○	Verdicchio dei Castelli di Jesi Cl. Villa Bucci '94	▼▼	4
●	Rosso Piceno Tenuta Pongelli '94	▼	3
○	Verdicchio dei Castelli di Jesi Cl. Villa Bucci '88	▽▽	6
○	Verdicchio dei Castelli di Jesi Cl. Villa Bucci '90	▽▽	5
○	Verdicchio dei Castelli di Jesi Cl. Villa Bucci '92	▽▽	4

PESARO

MANCINI

Strada dei Colli, 35
61100 Pesaro
tel. 0721/51828

This estate, making its first appearance in the Guide, operates in the Pesaro hills, on the whole one of the backwaters of winemaking in the Marche. A couple of years ago the production norms were revised and new DOCs recognised: the Sangiovese dei Colli Pesaresi DOC of 1972 was replaced by the Colli Pesaresi DOC, of which there are two types, Rosso (or Sangiovese) and Bianco. There is also the possibility to label wines separately from the subzones Roncaglia and Focara, respectively white and red. The Fattoria Mancini, whose cellars are currently being renovated, produces the complete DOC range. It grows sangiovese, montepulciano, the native albanella and some sauvignon, but the speciality is pinot nero, which has been in these vineyards since the time of Luigi Mancini, great-grandfather to the present owners. It is cultivated on seven different sites in the hills, on steep slopes fairly near the sea, and therefore in favourable conditions, and is vinified as a monovarietal, also in the case of the white Roncaglia. The Pinot Nero '95 is its best wine. It has good concentrated colour, clean, gamey aromas with delicate spicy overtones and a touch of toastiness on the palate. It definitely deserves its One Glass award. The Roncagli '96 is also enjoyable and original: it is a white with good depth and staying power, again pleasantly toasty on the palate. Although correct, the Colli Pesaresi Bianco has less character. The young, fruity Sangiovese '96 and the mature Focara '91, from sangiovese grapes with some pinot nero, are both agreeable.

● Colli Pesaresi Rosso Focara '91	🍷	1*
● Colli Pesaresi Sangiovese '96	🍷	1*
● Pinot Nero '95	🍷	1*
○ Colli Pesaresi Bianco Roncaglia '96	🍷	1*
○ Colli Pesaresi Bianco '96		1

POGGIO S. MARCELLO (AN)

SARTARELLI

Via Coste del Mulino, 26
60030 Poggio S. Marcello (AN)
tel. 0731/89732-89571

We have been interested in this estate for years because it is unfailingly one of the best producers of Verdicchio. For some years now, whatever the weather conditions, production has been of high quality. This is due to the position of the vineyards in the particularly favourable locality of Coste del Mulino, the will-power of Patrizio Chiacchierini and his wife Donatella Sartarelli and the valuable collaboration of oenologist Giancarlo Soverchia. The estate's wines are full of personality, well-built, concentrated (as high in dry extract as a good red) and long-lasting. The Verdicchio dei Castelli di Jesi '96, the basic wine of the cellar, has an intense, fresh, typical nose, good structure tasty acidity and good concentration. The cru Tralivio '96 is a typical, pale straw-yellow Verdicchio, broad on the nose, with aromas of fresh fruit. On the palate it has vigour and freshness due to good but not excessive acidity. But the superlative wine of the estate is, once again, the Contrada Balciana, a late harvest Verdicchio dei Castelli di Jesi. The '95 is a good deep yellow with greenish tints, the aromatic impact is intense but full of nuances, among which ripe apples, honey, and a sweet spiciness are noticeable. In the mouth the powerful alcohol is agreeably smooth and round, the structure is elegant with an almondy finish typical of the variety. It is a superb expression, probably the greatest we can remember, of this type of wine and it will triumph far beyond its native region.

○ Verdicchio dei Castelli di Jesi Cl. Sup. C.da Balciana '95	🍷🍷🍷	4
○ Verdicchio dei Castelli di Jesi Cl. Sup. Tralivio '96	🍷🍷	3
○ Verdicchio dei Castelli di Jesi Cl. '96	🍷	1*
○ Verdicchio dei Castelli di Jesi Cl. Sup. C.da Balciana '94	🍷🍷🍷 (outline)	4
○ Verdicchio dei Castelli di Jesi Cl. Sup. Tralivio '95	🍷🍷 (outline)	3

RIPATRANSONE (AP)

SPINETOLI (AP)

COCCI GRIFONI
C.DA MESSIERI, 11
FRAZ. S. SAVINO
63030 RIPATRANSONE (AP)
TEL. 0735/90143

SALADINI PILASTRI
VIA SALADINI, 5
63030 SPINETOLI (AP)
TEL. 0736/899534

Guido Cocci Grifoni can be considered the grower who wrote the history of the Piceno with his wines: we still remember the first vintage of his Rosso Piceno Superiore, the '69, which was in a way a milestone for the area and continues to be an important point of reference. Returning to this year's wines, the Rosso Piceno Superiore '94 has a good, strong colour, with wild berries on the nose and plenty of body on the palate. The Rosso Piceno Superiore Vigna Messieri '95, a top class wine, different in style from previous vintages, is high in alcohol, mouth-filling, with a softness on the palate recalling the bouquet of soft red fruit. The Rosso Piceno '96 is grapy and highly drinkable with spicy notes on the nose. Moving on to the whites, the Falerio dei Colli Ascolani '96 reflects the problems of this year's harvest : its floral aromas are light and it is short on the palate with awkward acidity. The Vigneti S. Basso selection, with more body, is yellow with greenish tints, flowery and fruity aromas, good structure and length on the palate and an almondy fragrance on the finish. The Podere Colle Vecchio '96, another attractive white from the native variety pecorino, of which Cocci Grifoni has been a keen promoter, has aromas of tropical fruit discernible also on the palate and capable of further unfolding with bottle age. The first version of the Podere Colle Vecchio, the '95 vintage aged in barriques, was not entirely satisfactory: the wood masks the aromas and fragrance of the wine. A final mention for the Passerina Brut, an original and enjoyable Italian-style sparkler which has been made with success for the last few years.

The Rosso Piceno DOC zone, which covers a considerable part of the provinces of Ascoli Piceno, Macerata and Ancona and is the largest in the Marche, and in particular the smaller Rosso Piceno Superiore zone, is in a state of turmoil. Heated discussions are taking place over the proposed revision of production norms, with many favouring a substantial increase of the percentage of montepulciano and less sangiovese. It is an issue which undoubtedly concerns Saladini Pilastri, an estate whose origins go back to the early 1970s, the period of the first local DOCs, and which in the last few years has embarked on a programme to up-grade the quality of its production. At the moment the most inspiring achievement is the Rosso Piceno Vigna Piediprato. This wine has great appeal, with its deep colour, fragrant aromas of cherry and plum and smooth, concentrated elegance. It is the joint effort of a recently-formed collaboration between Domenico d'Angelo, a keen and highly competent oenologist, and winemaker Roberto Cipresso. Near misses for Two Glass awards among the wines tasted are the Pregio del Conte Rosso, a soft and complex blend of aglianico and montepulciano and the Bianco made from falanghina and fiano, which is not quite balanced but needs only slight correction. The Falerio dei Colli Ascolani, although hampered by the difficult vintage, is correct and fresh.

O Podere Colle Vecchio '96	♀♀	3*
● Rosso Piceno Superiore Vigna Messieri '95	♀♀	3*
● Rosso Piceno Superiore '94	♀	2
O Falerio dei Colli Ascolani Vigneti S. Basso '96	♀	2
O Passerina Brut '96	♀	3
O Falerio dei Colli Ascolani '96		1
O Podere Colle Vecchio Barrique '95		3
● Rosso Piceno '96		1

● Rosso Piceno Vigna Piediprato '95	♀♀	3*
● Pregio del Conte Rosso '93	♀	2
O Falerio dei Colli Ascolani '96		1
O Pregio del Conte Bianco '95		2

STAFFOLO (AN)

STAFFOLO (AN)

CORONCINO
C.DA CORONCINO, 7
60039 STAFFOLO (AN)
TEL. 0731/779494

ZACCAGNINI
VIA SALMÀGINA, 9/10
60039 STAFFOLO (AN)
TEL. 0731/779892

The distinguishing mark of the Coroncino estate has always been quality, obtained through reduced yields, grape selection and irreproachable methods of vinification. Lucio and Fiorella Canestrari have always worked in this way and their dogged pursuit of quality has resulted in products of an invariably high level. The wines are elegant, soft and powerful and admirably preserve their varietal character. Le Lame '96, a blend of trebbiano and verdicchio, is a pale straw-yellow wine with good impact on the nose, clean and intense. It is soft on the palate with an elegant finish. The Verdicchio Bacco, the estate's standard line, is straightforward and representative both in its straw-yellow colour with green tints and in its aromas, herbaceous rather than floral, which are in harmony with its freshness. The Coroncino '96 has unexpected structure and concentration for such an unfavourable vintage; the aromas are a little slow to open out, but overall the wine is soft, tangy, well-balanced and clean and elegant in the finish. The estate's top wine, the Gaiospino was still ageing when the Guide was completed; we will review the '96 next year.

The fairly short history of this Staffolo estate makes it a witness to the new era of Verdicchio dei Castelli di Jesi, which began about 15 years ago. The Zaccagnini brothers were among the first to really aim for top quality, which found realisation in their Salmàgina. This wine is named after the village where the estate is located at about 450 metres above sea level. It was one of the very first successful Verdicchio crus to be presented. The '96 vintage of this wine, which is best a year after the harvest, has again achieved our Two Glasses award thanks to its well expressed varietal aromas and to its structure. It is not particularly powerful but it is very well balanced. The basic Verdicchio comes as a pleasant surprise, although perhaps not so unexpected bearing in mind that the grapes come from new plantings based on careful clonal selection. It has fresh, herbal, highly typical aromas and unusual complexity on the palate. The Verdicchio '94 Pier delle Vigne was rather unsatisfactory but we trust that this year's experience will be salutary and serve for the next vintage; when re-tasted in July after a two-months gap the wine showed signs of deterioration with strong oak aromas from the barriques masking its fragrance. The two sparkling wines, the Zaccagnini Brut and the Zaccagnini Metodo Tradizionale, have developed favourably. Going on to the reds, a mention is deserved for the correctly made Rosso Conero '94 and the Vigna Vescovi, from an original blend of montepulciano, cabernet sauvignon and pinot nero; a red with herbal and vanilla overtones which is soft on the palate and easy to drink.

O	Verdicchio dei Castelli di Jesi Cl. Il Coroncino '96	▼▼	3
O	Le Lame '96	▼	2
O	Verdicchio dei Castelli di Jesi Cl. Bacco '96	▼	2

O	Verdicchio dei Castelli di Jesi Cl. '96	▼▼	2
O	Verdicchio dei Castelli di Jesi Cl. Salmàgina '96	▼▼	3
O	Verdicchio dei Castelli di Jesi Cl. Pier delle Vigne '94	▼	4
O	Verdicchio dei Castelli di Jesi Spumante	▼	3
●	Vigna Vescovi '93	▼	3
O	Zaccagnini Brut	▼	2
O	Zaccagnini Metodo Tradizionale	▼	4
●	Rosso Conero '94		2
O	Verdicchio dei Castelli di Jesi Cl. Ris. Cesolano '92	♀	4

OTHER WINERIES

The following producers obtained good scores in our tastings with one or more of their wines:

PROVINCE OF ANCONA

Antonio Canestrari,
Apiro, tel. 0733/611315,
Verdicchio dei Castelli di Jesi Cl. Lapiro '96

Poggio Montali,
Monteroberto, tel. 0731/702825,
Verdicchio Castelli di Jesi '96

Maurizio Marconi,
S. Marcello, tel. 0731/267374,
Verdicchio dei Castelli di Jesi Cl.
La Grotta '96

Amato Ceci,
S. Paolo di Jesi, tel. 0731/779052,
Verdicchio dei Castelli di Jesi Cl. Sup.
Vignamato '96

Angelo Accadia,
Serra S. Quirico, tel. 0731/85172,
Verdicchio dei Castelli di Jesi Cantori '95

Medoro Cimarelli,
Staffolo, tel. 0731/779307,
Verdicchio dei Castelli di Jesi Cl.
Frà Moriale '96

Armando Finocchi,
Staffolo, tel. 0731/779534,
Verdicchio dei Castelli di Jesi Cl. '96

Franco e Giuseppe Finocchi,
Staffolo, tel. 0731/779573,
Verdicchio dei Castelli di Jesi Cl. '96

Esther Hauser,
Staffolo, tel. 0731/770203,
Cupo Rosso '94

La Staffa,
Staffolo, tel. 0731/779430,
Verdicchio dei Castelli di Jesi Cl.
La Rincrocca '96

Schiavoni,
Staffolo, tel. 0731/779757,
Verdicchio di Jesi Cl. Poggio sulla Cupa '96

PROVINCE OF ASCOLI PICENO

Rio Maggio,
Montegranaro, tel. 0734/889587,
Sauvignon Telusiano '96

Aurora,
Offida, tel. 0736/810007,
Rosso Piceno Superiore '95

San Giovanni,
Offida, tel. 0736/889032,
Falerio dei Colli Ascolani Leo Guelfus '96

La Cantina dei Colli Ripani,
Ripatransone, tel. 0735/9505,
Rosso Leo Ripanus '96

Le Caniette,
Ripatransone, tel. 0735/9200,
Rosso Piceno Ris. Morellone '94

Filippo Veccia,
Ripatransone, tel. 0735/9496,
Rosso Piceno Fontursio '95

Romolo e Remo Dezi,
Servigliano, tel. 0734/750408,
Rosso Piceno Regina del Bosco '93

PROVINCE OF MACERATA

Saputi,
Colmurano, tel. 0733/508137,
Colli Maceratesi Bianco '96

Fattoria dei Cavalieri,
Matelica, tel. 0737/84024,
Verdicchio di Matelica Podere Fornacione '96

Gino Gagliardi,
Matelica, tel. 0737/85611,
Verdicchio di Matelica Maccagnano '95

San Biagio,
Matelica, tel. 0737/83997,
Bragnolo Rosso '95

Alberto Quacquarini,
Serrapetrona, tel. 0733/908180,
Vernaccia di Serrapetrona '96

Lanfranco Quacquarini,
Serrapetrona, tel. 0733/908103,
Vernaccia di Serrapetrona '96

Massimo Serboni,
Serrapetrona, tel. 0733/904088,
Vernaccia di Serrapetrona '96

PROVINCE OF PESARO

Valentino Fiorini,
Barchi, tel. 0721/97151,
Bianchello del Metauro Tenuta Campioli '96

Anzilotti Solazzi, Saltara,
tel. 0721/895491,
Bianchello del Metauro '96

Cà Vagnarello,
Urbino, tel. 0722/349193,
Parnaso Rosso '96

UMBRIA

Even international commentators are now giving Umbria's wines and producers the recognition they deserve. For at least a couple of years now, the wines of this region have appeared with ever-greater frequency in the ratings of specialized magazines and guides, often earning dizzyingly high scores. It is all a great change from the isolationist image which, in many cases, went with being an Umbrian producer until just a few years ago. The impetus for this change, according to some, came from Antinori's pioneering work. With the avant-garde wines produced at Castello della Sala in the '70s, the famous Florentine company created a model estate, a sort of laboratory where their oenologists could experiment using the most advanced vineyard and winery techniques. This activity, it should be remembered, brought into being wines like the Cervaro della Sala and the Muffato, which, for a decade now, have been numbered among the classic wines of Italy. Obviously, an example of this scope and importance, as well as the success on international markets of a major producer such as Giorgio Lungarotti have, in the long run, made many growers in the region question some of their long-held convictions. As the younger generations have started to work in, and take over, various wineries in the region, so an awareness of Umbria's potential and a desire to improve have taken root. These are young people of the calibre of Marco Caprai in Montefalco and Giovanni Dubini in Orvieto, both prize-winners this year for their stunning red wines, who have had the courage to take the quality path and follow it all the way. Theirs is a well deserved success, won through total dedication to their estates. Fortunately, there are now a number of enterprises coming into being in Umbria which are following suit. These are either old companies which have decided to modernize completely, or small recently-formed estates with go-ahead ideas. Nor are the cooperatives out of place in this scenario: at the Cantina dei Colli Amerini or Co.Vi.O. in Orvieto, for example, the wind of change is blowing, and these wineries today offer a huge range of products of faultless style at very keen prices indeed. From the Colli Perugini to Orvieto, passing through Montefalco the oenological map of this little Italian Burgundy is being redrawn. Some traditional firms have not fully taken on board the extent of change required, and continue to offer the same wines as they have always done, made in the same way and with the same taste profiles which made them popular some twenty years or so ago. It is a real shame. These hills and these grapes have it in themselves to give, as they are now demonstrating, some of the best wines in the world.

AMELIA (TR)

BASCHI (TR)

CANTINA SOCIALE DEI COLLI AMERINI
LOC. FORNOLE
05020 AMELIA (TR)
TEL. 0744/989721

BARBERANI - VALLESANTA
LOC. CERRETO
05023 BASCHI (TR)
TEL. 0744/950113

The wines we tasted this year literally seduced us, from the power of the Torraccio to the elegance of the Carbio, not forgetting the pleasantly surprising Moscato Donna Olimpia. The other wines which earned One Glass all lived up to their previous performances. The most interesting of the new wines is the Sangiovese Torraccio '95, a still youthful red, with good depth and a definite oaky tone on the nose, as well as a satisfying balance between fruit and tannin on the palate. It thoroughly deserves its Two Glass status. The '95 Carbio is excellent again this year: it is a well-structured red which improves its balance between power and elegance in every vintage. It has well-integrated oak and reasonable complexity. The other wines from this winery - which offers a huge range - are certainly also worthy of note and are always excellent value for money. Among the whites, we very much enjoyed the Malvasia La Corte '96, which very nearly scored Two Glasses: it has improved markedly on previous editions and is now, in our opinion, a very attractive wine, with good personality and a very fair price. Grechetto has always been one of the region's most popular whites, and the '96 Vignolo is an outstanding example. It is fresh, full-flavoured and fruity, and we preferred it to the version fermented in wood. Going on to the Chardonnays, we note the extremely well-made '96: it is a fresh, straightforward wine, but really expresses varietal aromas to the full. It fully deserves its Glass. The oak-fermented Chardonnay Rocca Nerina is more ambitious, and very nearly scored Two Glasses. The Moscato Donna Olimpia '96 is very well made indeed, and all of this winery's other wines (too many to mention!) are extremely reliable.

Barberani has, for some years now, been steering a steady course. The general quality of the wines is excellent (thanks also to the skill of the oenologist, Maurizio Castelli), and they all lie within the local winemaking tradition. But, as everyone knows, traditions cannot stand still, or decline will surely follow. The major improvements carried out in the last few years in both the vineyards and the winery have, therefore, been invaluable. This year, Barberani again offers a reliable range but, it should be stressed, not yet the outstanding wines which would place the company among Italy's absolute élite. Also, the wines shown scored slightly lower than in last year's edition of our Guide. It may be that this can be put down to the adverse effects of a far from favourable growing season. The top wine is the Orvieto Classico Calcaia '95, a white wine with a handsome golden yellow colour and rich, broad and complex ripe fruit aromas. On the palate it is warming and well-structured, though elegant in flavour: it well deserves its Two Glasses. The rest of the range is less exciting. The Grechetto '96 is light, with attenuated fruit, and a little bitter. The Orvieto Classico Castagnolo has clean, pleasant aromas and flavours, but insubstantial fruit; the Sauvignon Pomaio is fairly similar: pleasant enough, but thin. The estate also presented two vintages of Foresco, a well-structured red made from sangiovese and cabernet. Between the '94 and the '95 we slightly preferred the earlier vintage, with its marginally more successful balance of wild berry fruit and oaky tones. The Orvieto Classico Amabile Pulicchio '96 was not exactly convincing, with a slightly bitter note on the finish.

●	Colli Am. Rosso Sup. Carbio '95	♟♟	3*
●	Colli Am. Sangiovese Torraccio '95	♟♟	3*
○	Colli Am. Bianco Terre Arnolfe '96	♟	2*
○	Colli Am. Chardonnay '96	♟	2*
○	Colli Am. Chardonnay Rocca Nerina '96	♟	3*
○	Colli Am. Grechetto Vignolo '96	♟	2*
○	Colli Am. Malvasia La Corte '96	♟	2*
○	Colli Am. Moscato Donna Olimpia '96	♟	2
●	Colli Am. Rosso Terre Arnolfe '96	♟	2*
○	Orvieto Classico '96	♟	2
●	Colli Am. Rosso Sup. Carbio '94	♟♟	3*

○	Orvieto Classico Calcaia '95	♟♟	5
●	Foresco '94	♟	4
●	Foresco '95	♟	4
○	Grechetto '96	♟	3
○	Orvieto Classico Castagnolo '96	♟	3
○	Pomaio '96	♟	3
○	Orvieto Classico Amabile Pulicchio '96		3
●	Foresco '93	♟♟	4
○	Orvieto Classico Calcaia '92	♟♟	5
○	Orvieto Classico Calcaia '93	♟♟	5
○	Orvieto Classico Calcaia '94	♟♟	5

CITTÀ DELLA PIEVE (PG)

VILLA PO' DEL VENTO
VIA PO' DEL VENTO, 8
06062 CITTÀ DELLA PIEVE (PG)
TEL. 0578/299950

Francesco Anichini, oenologist and graduate agronomist, founded this estate at the end of the 1970s. Villa Po' Del Vento now produces just over a thousand hectolitres of wine a year, almost all of which is sold in bottle. Anichini himself only owns a few hectares of vineyards, the rest of the grapes being supplied by a small group of growers whose production he oversees. Francesco makes a Colli del Trasimeno Bianco from trebbiano and grechetto which, in the '96 vintage, is fresh, light, pleasantly fruity, and above all quaffable. The estate also has a '96 Pinot Bianco, which offers fruity scents and a balsamic tone on the nose and which, on the palate, shows fresh acidity as well as delicate fruit. The '96 Riesling has a pale straw colour, and is lightly aromatic, with mineral and balsamic hints. On the palate it has highish acidity, and was still young and slightly out of kilter when our tastings were held. The range is completed by a good Colli del Trasimeno Rosso, a decently-made wine. It is not perfectly clean on the nose but on the palate, however, it displays fine tannins, reasonable fruit and a certain length.

○	Colli del Trasimeno Bianco '96	🍷	2
●	Colli del Trasimeno Rosso '94	🍷	2
○	Pinot Bianco '96	🍷	2*
○	Riesling '96		2

CORCIANO (PG)

PIEVE DEL VESCOVO
LOC. PIEVE DEL VESCOVO
VIA LUCCIAIO
06073 CORCIANO (PG)
TEL. 075/6978874

The Pieve del Vescovo estate is undoubtedly the top producer in the Colli del Trasimeno area. At its helm is Iolanda Tinarelli, who avails herself of technical assistance from Riccardo Cotarella, the oenologist most in demand in Central and Southern Italy. Once again this year, the estate's best wine is the Lucciaio '95, a Colli del Trasimeno Rosso aged in barrique for about a year. It has a deep, opaque ruby colour, and on the nose shows rich wild berry fruit, as well as elegant oak. On the palate it is broad and elegant, round and very concentrated, with berry fruit flavours and extremely fine, soft tannins. It is a shade or two better than the '94 vintage, which is well-made and appealing but in a more straightforward manner. We also found the Etesiaco '96, a special selection of Colli del Trasimeno Bianco, of interest. It has a straw-yellow colour, a rich nose with fruity notes (apples in particular), and shows good intensity and freshness on the palate, characteristics which enable it to earn its One Glass rating with considerable ease. The ruby-purple hued Colli del Trasimeno Rosso '96 is also decent. Fragrant and with rich red berry fruit notes on the nose, it is fresh and crisp on the palate, with medium structure. The Colli del Trasimeno Bianco '96 is only worthy of a listing. It has a straw-yellow colour with greenish highlights, and is fruity and fragrant on the nose; medium-bodied on the palate, but nevertheless pleasantly refreshing.

●	Colli del Trasimeno Rosso Lucciaio '95	🍷🍷	3*
○	Colli del Trasimeno Bianco Etesiaco '96	🍷	3
●	Colli del Trasimeno Rosso '96	🍷	2*
○	Colli del Trasimeno Bianco '96		2
●	Colli del Trasimeno Rosso Lucciaio '94	🍸🍸	3*
○	Colli del Trasimeno Bianco Etesiaco '95	🍸	3
●	Colli del Trasimeno Rosso '95	🍸	2*
●	Colli del Trasimeno Rosso Lucciaio '93	🍸	2*

FICULLE (TR)

CASTELLO DELLA SALA
LOC. SALA
05016 FICULLE (TR)
TEL. 0763/86051

Renzo Cotarella has done it again: his '95 Cervaro has earned the Three Glass accolade for the umpteenth time and confirms this wine's extraordinary reliability - in the eight vintages between '88 and '95, it has won our top award seven times - while at the same time reflecting the character of the vintage from which it comes. We have, therefore, tasted fat, opulent Cervaros like the '88 and the '90, and fresher, more lively wines such as the '89 and the '93: whatever the style, it is always a great wine. The 1995 version is still a little backward. It is already clearly a fine wine but we shall have to wait a few months yet for it to show at its best. It is very elegant, and though it does not display the power of a year like 1994, in our blind tastings it nevertheless laid claim to a deserved place among Italy's finest Chardonnays of the vintage. It has a complex, intense nose, with the vanilla notes in perfect harmony with the fruit and the elegant spicy hints. On the palate one is aware of its youthfulness, but also of its great richness. It shows elegant spicy tones, buttery flavours, a very slightly vegetal touch, and an extremely long and satisfying finish. It probably will not impress you with its power, but the key features are subtlety and balance: just wait for it to mature! The Muffato '95 is very good, too, demonstrating remarkable concentration and length on the nose, with definite fresh exotic fruit aromas(particularly pineapple and grapefruit) to the fore. On the palate it echoes the complexity of the nose and, on the finish, offers suggestions of honey, vanilla and candied citrus peel. There are Two Glasses for the admirably concentrated and typically varietal Pinot Nero '94, even if it is still a bit closed. The '96 Chardonnay and Sauvignon are well made and charming, confirming again (if it were still necessary) the wisdom of the programme which the Antinoris have been running at Castello della Sala since the '70s.

○	Cervaro della Sala '95	🍷🍷🍷	5
○	Muffato della Sala '95	🍷🍷	5
●	Pinot Nero '94	🍷🍷	5
○	Chardonnay della Sala '96	🍷	3*
○	Orvieto Classico '96	🍷	3
○	Sauvignon della Sala '96	🍷	3*
○	Cervaro della Sala '89	YYY	5
○	Cervaro della Sala '90	YYY	5
○	Cervaro della Sala '92	YYY	5
○	Cervaro della Sala '93	YYY	5
○	Cervaro della Sala '94	YYY	5
○	Muffato della Sala '93	YYY	5
○	Muffato della Sala '94	YY	5
●	Pinot Nero '92	YY	5

GUALDO CATTANEO (PG)

COLPETRONE
VIA DELLA COLLINA, 4
LOC. MADONNUCCIA
06035 GUALDO CATTANEO (PG)
TEL. 0578/767722

The Colpetrone estate in Montefalco returns to the Guide. Situated in the commune of Gualdo Cattaneo in the Province of Perugia, this domain, which comprises 18 hectares of vineyards, is the property of Saiagricola, which also owns the Fattoria del Cerro in Montepulciano and La Poderina in Montalcino. Colpetrone had already impressed us last year with the quality of its wines. These continue to improve and, with the very accomplished winemaker Lorenzo Landi at its helm, this year the winery scored well with the local Sagrantino and Rosso di Montefalco, wines which have become two of Central Italy's most highly-appreciated reds. The '93 Sagrantino di Montefalco confirms once again its success of last year, easily meriting our One Glass award. It is an opaque ruby red with garnet reflections, and has a broad nose with attractive suggestions of undergrowth and well-integrated oak. It has good structure and is warming on the palate, with well-expressed varietal character; the tannins are relatively soft, and the wine has good length in the mouth. The Rosso di Montefalco '93, a blend of sangiovese, sagrantino and other grapes, has a ruby red colour with garnet highlights. On the nose it displays wild berry fruit scents of reasonable ripeness, as well as appealing oaky tones. Of medium body and reasonable elegance, it shows just the right amount of tannin on the palate. To sum up, Colpetrone's overall performance is a reassuringly impressive one, and the wines also offer good value for money.

●	Rosso di Montefalco '93	🍷	3
●	Sagrantino di Montefalco '93	🍷	4

MONTEFALCO (PG)

ANTONELLI
LOC. S. MARCO, 59
06036 MONTEFALCO (PG)
TEL. 0742/379158

Antonelli is a winery to watch. Located in the hamlet of San Marco in the commune of Montefalco, and owned by Filippo Antonelli, this interesting estate boasts some 15 hectares of vineyards, out of a total estate area of around 140 hectares. Once again this year the winery shows its worth, particularly as far as the red wines are concerned. They are all of interest, including the well-made Rosso di Montefalco '94. An opaque ruby red in colour, it opens up on the nose, with attractive hints of undergrowth and spices; on the palate it has good body, and is warming, appropriately alcoholic, and rich in tannins. The standard-bearer of the estate, however, is undoubtedly the Sagrantino di Montefalco '93: garnet in colour, on the nose it has scents of undergrowth and of oak. It shows reasonable finesse on the palate, too, with its soft, round fruit and well balanced alcohol and tannins. The Sagrantino di Montefalco '94, however, seemed to us to be considerably more intense and concentrated, revealing greater structure and character. It is a handsome deep,dark red with garnet highlights, and has a rich nose with red berry fruit notes and a sweet oakiness. On the palate it is full and warming, with soft, elegant tannins: a fine, typical Sagrantino, which in this vintage has no difficulty in claiming Two Glass status. Less interesting this year are the white wines made from Grechetto. We merely list the Colli Martani Grechetto '96, a pale straw-yellow in colour, with good fruit on the nose, but sharp and not very well balanced on the palate.

MONTEFALCO (PG)

ARNALDO CAPRAI - VAL DI MAGGIO
LOC. TORRE
06036 MONTEFALCO (PG)
TEL. 0742/378802-378523

In last year's Guide, we were amazed by this estate's top wine, the Sagrantino di Montefalco 25 Anni, which walked away with one of our Three Glass awards. Many people were surprised at Caprai Val di Maggio's performance, and even more went off in search of the few bottles of this nectar still available. The secret of this success? Large-scale investment in both the vineyards and winery, careful research into new clones of sagrantino, and state-of-the-art vinification techniques. The people behind this ascent to the summit of Italian winemaking are Marco Caprai, able and astute proprietor of the estate, and Attilio Pagli, young, upwardly mobile oenologist. This year, too, they presented a powerful Sagrantino di Montefalco 25 Anni. This time it is from the '94 vintage but again the wine earns Three Glasses with ease, reconfirming the enormous potential of this grape variety and of the Montefalco area as a whole. An opaque, intense and concentrated red in colour, it has a broad, rich nose, with ripe red berry fruit, silky alcoholic nuances and noble, spicy tones. On the palate it is fat, broad, and extremely long. The standard Sagrantino '94 is excellent, too, and also very concentrated. The Rosso di Montefalco Riserva '94 and the Rosso di Montefalco of the same year complete the red assortment: the former has good concentration, the latter is more quaffably fruity. Among the whites, the Grecante Vigna Belvedere '95 is noteworthy: it has a deep straw-yellow colour, rather intense aromas and fairly complex flavours. The Montefalco Bianco '96 is also good: straw-yellow in hue, fruity and clean on the nose; fresh acidity yet good depth on the palate. Lastly, the Grecante, a Grechetto dei Colli Martani '96, is decent and true-to-type.

●	Sagrantino di Montefalco '94	ŶŶ	4*
●	Rosso di Montefalco '94	Ŷ	3
●	Sagrantino di Montefalco '93	Ŷ	4
O	Colli Martani Grechetto '96		2
O	Colli Martani Grechetto '95	Ŷ	2*
O	Colli Martani Grechetto Vigna Tonda '95	Ŷ	3
●	Rosso di Montefalco '93	Ŷ	2*
●	Sagrantino di Montefalco '92	Ŷ	3*
●	Sagrantino di Montefalco Passito '93	Ŷ	4

●	Sagrantino di Montefalco 25 Anni '94	ŶŶŶ	6
●	Rosso di Montefalco Ris. '94	ŶŶ	5
●	Sagrantino di Montefalco '94	ŶŶ	6
O	Grecante Vigna Belvedere '95	Ŷ	4
O	Montefalco Bianco '96	Ŷ	3
●	Rosso di Montefalco '94	Ŷ	3
O	Colli Martani Grechetto Grecante '96		3
●	Sagrantino di Montefalco 25 Anni '93	ŶŶŶ	5
●	Cabernet Sauvignon dell'Umbria '94	ŶŶ	3*
●	Rosso di Montefalco Ris. '93	ŶŶ	3*
●	Sagrantino di Montefalco '93	ŶŶ	4

MONTEFALCO (PG)

GIULIANO RUGGERI
VIA MONTEPENNINO, 5
06036 MONTEFALCO (PG)
TEL. 0742/379294

Giuliano Ruggeri is a small grower who, without a shadow of a doubt, produces the very best Sagrantino di Montefalco Passito. In Montefalco, some people claim that this is the true style of Sagrantino, since the sagrantino grape was traditionally dried in order to obtain a sweet wine, while the dry red is a diabolical modern invention. The method for making this "passito" is fairly complex and indeed, it is not easy to achieve perfect balance between the tannins, the fruit and the alcohol in this type of wine. It is hard to conceive of a sweet version of a fine red wine, but Ruggeri's Sagrantino Passito '93 gives us a good idea of what such a product should be like: it is rich, intense, concentrated and elegant. It is decidedly sweet, but he skilfully avoids either cloying stickiness or unbalanced tannins. The Rosso di Montefalco '95, on the other hand, seemed to us well made, if slightly lighter than in previous vintages. It again earns our One Glass rating, even if Ruggeri had accustomed us to a more intense and well balanced Rosso.

● Sagrantino di Montefalco Passito '93	🍷🍷	5
● Rosso di Montefalco '95	🍷	3
● Sagrantino di Montefalco Passito '92	♀♀	5
● Rosso di Montefalco '94	♀	3

ORVIETO (TR)

BIGI
LOC. PONTE GIULIO, 3
05018 ORVIETO (TR)
TEL. 0763/316224-316391

For years the name Bigi was synonymous in the consumer's mind with the wines of Orvieto: wines which amongst other things were offered at very reasonable prices indeed. Bigi, founded in 1880 and today owned by the Gruppo Italiano Vini, continues to specialize in the production of white wines, all characterized by a carefully-made, modern style. From the Ponte Giulio winery at Orvieto come something like five million bottles a year, destined partly for the Italian market, but especially for export. The company buys in part of its grapes but also controls, directly or indirectly, about 200 hectares of vineyards,. At the helm is a winemaker of proven ability, Francesco Bardi, assisted by Massimo Panattoni. Their most interesting wine in our tastings was, once again, the Orvieto Classico Torricella, with its richly fruity bouquet and dry, fresh, soft and full flavour: it is one of the best examples of this DOC, and remains a wine of real interest, just as it was some ten years or so ago when the revolution in winemaking in this part of Umbria had yet to get under way. The Grechetto dell'Umbria is an enjoyable, fresh and quaffable vino da tavola of medium body. Aside from the above wines, we find an extremely well made and well typed Orvieto Classico, as well as the Marrano, a barrique-fermented Grechetto. This is a wine with reasonable structure and certain pretensions too, but for some years now we have been perplexed by the fact that it tends to be already rather over-mature at the time of its release.

○ Grechetto dell'Umbria '96	🍷	2
○ Marrano '95	🍷	3
○ Orvieto Classico Vigneto Torricella '96	🍷	2*
○ Orvieto Classico '96		2
○ Marrano '93	♀♀	4
○ Marrano '94	♀♀	4

ORVIETO (TR)

CO.VI.O.
LOC. CARDETO, 18
FRAZ. SFERRACAVALLO
05019 ORVIETO (TR)
TEL. 0763/343189-341286

With over 400 supplier-members, 1200 hectares under vines, state-of-the-art technology and the potential to produce around a million hectolitres, the Cooperativa Vitivinicola di Orvieto is the largest winery in the Orvieto zone. Guided by the famous oenologist Riccardo Cotarella, Co.Vi.O. has demonstrated once again this year its particular attention to relaunching the wines of the area. In their wide and carefully-selected assortment, the range of Orvieto stands out in particular. The Orvieto Classico Cardeto '96 has an attractive pale straw-yellow colour; its nose is pleasingly fruity, and it is dry and balanced on the palate. The Orvieto Classico Febeo '96 again lived up to our expectations: straw-yellow in hue, it offers fruity and quite complex aromas on the nose, whilst its flavours are fresh and well-balanced, with an almondy finish. A new wine this year, and an absolute revelation as well, is the Orvieto Jazz '96. This wine was specially made to celebrate the Winter '97 edition of Umbria Jazz, and is the product of very careful selection in the vineyard and advanced technology in the winery. It has a pale straw colour, a broad yet elegant and well-balanced bouquet, and good fruit and length on the palate. The Matile Rosa '96 is also unexceptionable: it has an attractive onion-skin colour, fragrant aromas and youthful, fresh flavours. Co.Vi.O's reds also display a certain personality. The Fantasie del Cardeto '94 is excellent: it is an opaque ruby red and has quite intense aromas, with scents of red berry fruit and of oak. On the palate it is broad and alcoholic, with rich spicy tones and complex mushroomy notes. The '96 Cardeto Rosso is again an interesting wine: it is refreshing and fruity on the nose, and soft and fragrant in the mouth.

●	Cardeto Rosso '96	🍷	1*
●	Fantasie del Cardeto '94	🍷	3*
⊙	Matile Rosa '96	🍷	1*
○	Orvieto Classico Cardeto '96	🍷	1*
○	Orvieto Classico Febeo '96	🍷	2*
○	Orvieto Classico Jazz '96	🍷	1*
⊙	Matile Rosa '95	🍸	1*
○	Orvieto Classico Cardeto '95	🍸	2*
○	Orvieto Classico Febeo '95	🍸	2*

ORVIETO (TR)

DECUGNANO DEI BARBI
LOC. FOSSATELLO, 50
05019 ORVIETO (TR)
TEL. 0763/308255

Decugnano dei Barbi is one of Orvieto's oldest and most illustrious winemaking companies. Owned by Claudio and Marina Barbi, it is now considered by many (including ourselves) to be one of the zone's most consistent and quality-conscious producers. The Barbi family, who also avail themselves of the collaboration of director Alessandro Lattuada, have again come out with an excellent range. This year we noticed a marked improvement in quality, starting with the very well made Metodo Classico Millesimato '92, based on a blend of chardonnay, verdello and procanico. Straw-yellow in colour, it has a fragrant, delicate bouquet, with yeasty notes. On the palate it is rounded and elegant. The various selections of Orvieto yet again all showed very well: the faultless Classico Barbi '96 easily earns a One Glass rating, as does the Orvieto Classico Decugnano dei Barbi '96, which reveals good intensity on the nose and good body on the palate. The barrique-fermented Orvieto Classico "IL" '96 is more complex. It has a fine straw-yellow colour and a concentrated nose, with rich ripe fruit notes and delicate spicy aromas. On the palate it is savoury, elegant and well structured. The reds include the decent Lago di Corbara '94, the fruity Rosso '95 and, most impressive of all, the '94 "IL". This wine has a ruby colour, is fruity and quite broad on the nose, with rich red berry fruit notes and a sweet spiciness. Finally, the Orvieto Classico Pourriture Noble '94 is straw-yellow with golden highlights, and is rich and fairly complex on the nose, with marked exotic fruit tones; it also displays medium structure and good length.

●	"IL" '94	🍷🍷	5
○	Orvieto Classico "IL" '96	🍷🍷	4
○	Decugnano dei Barbi Brut '92	🍷	5
●	Decugnano dei Barbi Rosso '95	🍷	3
○	Orvieto Classico Barbi '96	🍷	2*
○	Orvieto Classico Decugnano dei Barbi '96	🍷	3
○	Orvieto Classico Pourriture Noble '94	🍷	5
●	Lago di Corbara '94		3
●	"IL" '93	🍸🍸	5
●	Decugnano dei Barbi Rosso '94	🍸🍸	3*
○	Orvieto Classico "IL" '95	🍸🍸	4
●	Lago di Corbara '93	🍸	3

ORVIETO (TR)

LA CARRAIA
LOC. TORDIMONTE, 56
05018 ORVIETO (TR)
TEL. 0763/64013

ORVIETO (TR)

TENUTA LE VELETTE
LOC. LE VELETTE
05018 ORVIETO (TR)
TEL. 0763/29090

For years now La Carraia has been producing a pretty good Orvieto, which we have always tasted with pleasure. This was probably not really enough to warrant the winery having its own entry in the Guide, so we were waiting for the Poggio Calvelli selection to come up trumps before giving La Carraia its own full listing. This year, however, the estate - yet another of Riccardo Cotarella's protégés - has produced a Merlot which qualifies it right away for inclusion here. The wine is called Fobiano and is from the '95 vintage: it is made from merlot (90 per cent) and cabernet sauvignon, and has been aged for about a year in wood: dark ruby-purple colour; broad, rather alcoholic nose with rich spicy, vanilla and red berry fruit notes; round fruit evolves well on the palate which has fine, soft tannins. It is an intense, full-bodied and harmonious wine which will definitely improve yet further with a few years' ageing. This wine confirms the astute intuition of winemakers like Cotarella who see merlot as a variety which is particularly suited to the climate and soils of the region, which can undoubtedly yield excellent reds as well as round, supple whites. We should also like to bring to your attention the winery's two Orvietos, in particular the Poggio Calvelli '96 which is a fruity wine of considerable potential.

Well done, Tenuta le Velette! Founded in 1965 and run by Corrado and Cecilia Bottai, this company, which owns 95 hectares of land, confirmed the quality of its wines yet again this year. Thanks to the deft touch of Gabriella Tani, who looks after the winemaking, and thanks also to careful vineyard husbandry, this winery succeeds in giving a really distinctive style to its products. The Orvieto Classico '96 is absolutely faultless and true-to-type. It has a pale straw-yellow colour, a rich, intensely fruity nose, and broad flavours with ripe fruit notes and a subtle spiciness. The Orvieto Classico Amabile '96 is also interesting: straw-yellow in colour; fruity nose and rounded palate, which is sweet but not at all cloying. The Orvieto Classico Velico '96, with its delicate, fruit bouquet, is also well made. On the palate, it displays good balance, freshness and intensity. However, among the estate's whites it is the oak-conditioned sauvignon Traluce '96 which stands out, and indeed it merits one of our Two Glass awards. This wine has a straw-yellow colour and intense varietal aromas on the nose and fleshy fruit on the palate complemented by rich yet well-integrated vanilla flavours. The Calanco '94 - a blend of sangiovese and cabernet sauvignon - is also very good: it has a dark, deep red colour, and an intense warming nose. On the palate, it is soft and well balanced, if somewhat lacking in backbone.

●	Fobiano '95	🍷🍷	4
○	Orvieto Classico		
	Poggio Calvelli '96	🍷	3
○	Orvieto Classico '96		2

○	Traluce '96	🍷🍷	3*
●	Calanco '94	🍷	4
○	Orvieto Classico Amabile '96	🍷	2*
○	Orvieto Classico Secco '96	🍷	2*
○	Orvieto Classico Velico '96	🍷	3
●	Calanco '91	🍷🍷	4
●	Calanco '92	🍷	4
●	Calanco '93	🍷	4
☉	Monaldesco '95	🍷	1*
○	Orvieto Classico Amabile '95	🍷	2
○	Orvieto Classico Secco '95	🍷	2*
●	Rosso di Spicca '94	🍷	1

ORVIETO (TR)

PALAZZONE
LOC. ROCCA RIPESENA, 68
05019 ORVIETO (TR)
TEL. 0763/344166

The Palazzone estate has been owned by the Dubini family since the 1970s and, with its roughly 22 hectares of specialized vineyards, it has now become one of Italy's most highly regarded domaines. The men behind this rise to the highest realms of Italian winemaking are Giovanni Dubini, eclectic personality and impassioned viticulturist, and Riccardo Cotarella, the internationally renowned oenologist and consultant. Il Palazzone merits awards for all of its wines, but the Three Glass accolade goes to the great Armaleo '95. Made exclusively from cabernet sauvignon, it has an opaque ruby colour and rich, intense and persistent wild berry fruit aromas on the nose. On the palate, it is warming and complex, with marked red berry fruit flavours and well-integrated oak. L'Ultima Spiaggia '96, their Viognier, also displays excellent substance. It has a deepish straw-yellow colour and an intense bouquet, with rich, ripe fruit and sweet spicy notes. On the palate it is warming, well-structured and with rich vanilla hints on the finish. The Rubbio '96 is good too, with its lively nose and easy drinking style, as are the two whites, the Terre di Vineate '96 and the Campo del Guardiano '95, both of which earn a One Glass rating. Last, but certainly not least, the Muffa Nobile '96 was definitely the best sweet wine produced from botrytis-affected grapes in Umbria this year. Made from sauvignon and gewürztraminer, it has a deep golden-yellow colour, with intense amber highlights. The bouquet is broad and very complex, with ripe exotic fruit, citrus peel and sweet spicy notes. On the palate it is powerful and oily, with an extremely long, elegant and balanced finish.

●	Armaleo '95	🍷🍷🍷	4
O	L'Ultima Spiaggia '96	🍷🍷	3
O	Muffa Nobile '96	🍷🍷	4
O	Campo del Guardiano '95	🍷	3
●	Rubbio '96	🍷	2*
O	Terre di Vineate '96	🍷	2
●	Armaleo '92	ΥΥ	5
●	Armaleo '94	ΥΥ	4
O	L'Ultima Spiaggia '95	ΥΥ	4
O	Muffa Nobile '95	ΥΥ	5
O	Orvieto Classico Terre Vineate '94	ΥΥ	2*
O	Orvieto Classico Terre Vineate '95	Υ	2
O	Orvieto Classico Vendemmia Tardiva '93	Υ	4

ORVIETO (TR)

TENUTA DI SALVIANO
LOC. PRODO
05019 ORVIETO (TR)
TEL. 0763/308322

Last year we wrote of this estate's first successful appearance on the market, and now it is our pleasant duty to confirm that success. The Salviano winery, owned by Nerina Incisa della Rocchetta Corsini, is managed by Sebastiano Rosa, who is also responsible for the Tenuta di Argiano in Montalcino. With around 50 hectares under vine and a total of 2,000 hectares of land, Salviano lies on both sides of the Tiber between Todi and Orvieto, and along the shores of Lake Corbara. The wines continue to improve. The Orvieto Classico '96 has a brilliant straw-yellow colour and displays good richness and intensity on the nose, with subtle fruity aromas and floral notes. These are characteristics which we also find on the palate, where the fruit is full bodied, rich and very well balanced: it is a very well made wine. Another wine which again shows its class is the Vin Santo (no vintage stated), obtained from partly dried and botrytis affected trebbiano and malvasia toscana grapes. The bunches are laid out on reed mats until December, and then vinified; the wine then undergoes about three years' ageing in small casks. This year the Vin Santo again earns our Two Glass award: it has a deep amber colour, and a bouquet rich with floral, candied fruit and honeyed notes. On the palate it has fat, aromatic fruit, and a delicate, measured spiciness on the finish. On the other hand, the Lago di Corbara Rosso Turlo '96, made from sangiovese and cabernet sauvignon, seemed to us slightly below par: it was not particularly elegant or well balanced, either on the nose or on the palate.

O	Orvieto Classico Salviano '96	🍷🍷	3*
O	Vin Santo	🍷🍷	5
●	Lago di Corbara Rosso Turlò '96		3
O	Orvieto Classico Salviano '95	ΥΥ	2*
●	Lago di Corbara Rosso '95	Υ	2
O	Vin Santo	Υ	4

PENNA IN TEVERINA (TR)   SPELLO (PG)

RIO GRANDE
LOC. MONTECCHIE
05028 PENNA IN TEVERINA (TR)
TEL. 0744/993374

F.LLI SPORTOLETTI
VIA LOMBARDIA, 1
06038 SPELLO (PG)
TEL. 0742/651461

The Rio Grande estate, hidden away among the Umbrian hills which sweep down towards the River Tiber, a stone's throw away from the border with Lazio, has been under the ownership of the Pastore family for the past ten years or so. With 12 hectares of vineyards lying in the commune of Penna in Teverina, it has established itself as one of the rising domaines in the Orvieto area. Francesco Pastore is yet another producer who benefits from the valuable advice and assistance given by oenologist Riccardo Cotarella, who has placed the estate and its wines on a very sound footing in the last few years. In our tastings this year, the wines lived up to their previous performances. The top wine is the Casa Pastore Rosso '95, made from cabernet sauvignon (80 per cent) and merlot, which matures for about a year in French oak barrels. It has an opaque ruby colour, and is broad and intense on the nose, where it shows elegant wild berry fruit notes as well as sweetish oaky tones. On the palate it is fine and concentrated, with elegance and good round fruit. The Colle delle Montecchie '96, a wine named after a vineyard site owned by the estate, is again of interest this year. Made from chardonnay with a small percentage of grechetto, it has a pale straw-yellow colour and on the nose it has suggestions of apples, pears and peaches. On the palate, it is savoury and rather elegant. We should also like to mention how favourably the Campo Antico '95, the white wine made from sauvignon and pinot grigio which we referred to in last year's Guide, has evolved.

We welcome the Sportoletti estate back to the Guide. Lying in the hills between Spello and Assisi, it is owned by brothers Remo and Ernesto Sportoletti, who have been bottling their wines since 1979. With 20 hectares under vine and a total production of around 200,000 bottles, this is perhaps the most interesting wine company in the Assisi area (which will have its own DOC from the '97 vintage). The wines we tasted this year were excellent. Their best wine is the Villa Fidelia Bianco '95, made from chardonnay and grechetto, and fermented in French oak. It has a deepish straw-yellow colour and an intense and complex bouquet, with elegant oaky notes well integrated with the fruit. Its flavour is broad and long, with rich ripe fruit and a very crisp, clean style. The Villa Fidelia Rosso '94 is also of interest: made from a blend of pinot nero and merlot, it has a dark red colour and an intense bouquet with suggestions of undergrowth, as well as herbaceous notes. It also shows good intensity and structure on the palate, with tannins slightly evident on the finish. The Bianco di Assisi '96 is also good. It has a straw-yellow colour, is fruity and rich on the nose, and is fresh and rather elegant in the mouth. The Rosso di Assisi '96 is also flawless. The handsome cherry-red colour is very attractive and is followed by a fresh nose rich with the fragrant red berry fruit and savoury, quite broad fruit on the palate. We also draw your attention to the Grechetto dell' Umbria '96, which is concentrated and fruity on the nose, and has a crisp quaffable style on the palate.

● Casa Pastore Rosso '95	🍷🍷	4
○ Chardonnay Colle delle Montecchie '96	🍷	3
○ Chardonnay Colle delle Montecchie '95	🍷🍷	3
● Casa Pastore Rosso '93	🍷	3
● Casa Pastore Rosso '94	🍷	4
○ Campo Antico '95		2

○ Villa Fidelia Bianco '95	🍷🍷	4
○ Bianco di Assisi '96	🍷	1*
● Rosso di Assisi '96	🍷	1*
● Villa Fidelia Rosso '94	🍷	4
○ Grechetto dell'Umbria '96		1

STRONCONE (TR)

TORGIANO (PG)

LA PALAZZOLA
LOC. VASCIGLIANO
05039 STRONCONE (TR)
TEL. 0744/607735 - 272357

CANTINE LUNGAROTTI
VIA MARIO ANGELONI, 16
06089 TORGIANO (PG)
TEL. 075/9880348

Last year we described this company and its guiding spirit, Stefano Grilli, as now being an established force, and no longer a surprise. Well, this year, Stefano Grilli has succeeded in surprising us once again, because he has come up with a number of new wines. There is nothing particularly odd about the Merlot '95, but what do you say to a Riesling Brut made with a second fermentation in bottle? It has a handsome straw-colour, a fine bead and intense, fruity aromas, with elegant toasty and yeasty notes. On the palate it has good structure and soft fruit, and is complex and long: characteristics that are really very rarely found in sparkling wines from Central or Southern Italy. An outstanding '95 Merlot makes its debut this year. It has an extremely opaque ruby colour and is still very young, with a nose that is still rather closed, but which shows excellent potential for development. Its weight and substance on the palate are extraordinary: this is an intense, rich, concentrated, yet elegant and long wine, with a long life ahead of it. The Rubino '95 is also a great success. Powerful and concentrated it confirms yet again what a good vintage this was for the winery. The Pinot Nero '95 is satisfactory. The bouquet is good but it loses a few points because the sheer power and concentration of the fruit in this vintage makes it slightly unbalanced, even if its richness is attractive in itself. Finally, we draw your attention to the Vendemmia Tardiva '94, a sweet wine made from botrytized grapes with a very bright golden yellow colour, with rich aromas of honey and exotic fruits and elegant pastry-like nuances. It is not yet perfectly balanced on the palate and it perhaps lacks a touch of richness, but it is well made and is also eminently enjoyable.

The general standard of the new vintages of the Lungarotti wines is high, but they continue to lack that extra spark of quality which this historic Umbrian estate undoubtedly has the potential to give them. We are definitely impressed with the dependable level of quality of the larger volume wines but a little perplexed about Giorgio Lungarotti's premium products, and the Rubesco Vigna Monticchio, his most prestigious wine, in particular. The '87, released this year, seemed below par to us compared to previous editions of this wine. It is probably just a question of the vintage itself, but it seems tired, its colour tending decidedly towards garnet, and the mature aromas on the nose making no concessions to fruit. On the palate, the wine shows richness and roundedness on entry, but then lacks depth. Is ten years that bit too old? The Lungarotti whites, on the other hand, are showing well. The Torre de Giano '96, in particular, is very well made, fresh and appealing, and the extremely enjoyable Chardonnay '96 is of a similar style. The Chardonnay Vigna I Palazzi '95 scored fairly high, too, with its typically varietal nose and full bodied fruit on the palate. The '96 Castel Grifone rosé makes a good substitute for a red during the summer, and the Rubesco '94, Lungarotti's top-selling wine, also deserves a mention: it is a clean, well balanced red.

● Merlot '95		♟♟	4
○ Riesling Brut '94 M. Cl.		♟♟	4
● Rubino '95		♟♟	4
○ La Palazzola Vendemmia			
Tardiva '94		♟	5
● Pinot Nero '95		♟	4
○ La Palazzola Vendemmia			
Tardiva '93		♟♟	5
● Rubino '93		♟♟	3*
● Rubino '94		♟♟	4

⊙ Castel Grifone '96		♟	3
○ Chardonnay di Miralduolo '96		♟	3
○ Chardonnay I Palazzi '95		♟	4
○ Torgiano Bianco			
Torre di Giano '96		♟	3
● Torgiano Rosso			
Vigna Monticchio Ris. '87		♟	5
● Torgiano Rosso Rubesco '94			3
● Torgiano Rosso			
Vigna Monticchio Ris. '78		♟♟♟	6
● Il Vessillo '93		♟♟	4
● San Giorgio '86		♟♟	5
● Torgiano Rosso			
Vigna Monticchio Ris. '86		♟♟	5

OTHER WINERIES

The following producers obtained good scores in our tastings with one or more of their wines:

PROVINCE OF PERUGIA

Tili,
Assisi, tel. 075/8064370,
Grechetto dell'Umbria '95,
Rosso dell'Umbria Marilù '90,
Muffa Reale '94

F.lli Adanti, Bevagna, tel. 0742/360295,
Rosso di Montefalco '94,
Sagrantino di Montefalco Passito '93

Rocca di Fabbri,
Montefalco, tel. 0742/399379,
Sagrantino di Montefalco '93

Goretti,
Perugia,
tel. 075/607316,
Chardonnay dell'Umbria '96,
Grechetto dell'Umbria '96,
Colli Perugini Rosso Arringatore '94

PROVINCE OF TERNI

Poggio del Lupo,
Allerona Scalo,
tel. 0763/68850,
Orvieto Secco '96

VI.CO.R.,
Castel Viscardo,
tel. 0763/66064,
Orvieto Classico Roio '96,
Orvieto Classico Salceto '96

LAZIO

A year of great variability in Lazio: the 1996 vintage will be remembered in this region as one of great expectations and equally great disappointments. Heavy rains during the most delicate period of the growing season allowed mould and mildew to develop in a vast area of the Castelli Romani. Very few producers were able to combat this disaster effectively. In the north of the region, too - with just a few exceptions - we noted a drop in the quality of the wines presented. It was as if (and this was particularly true of the whites) a sort of heaviness had wafted over the wines, damping down the typical fragrance of their aromas. It was a year that the likeable Trappolini from Castiglione in Teverina would prefer to forget, whereas their near-neighbours at the Mottura estate make their début with a good '96 Orvieto and the impressive Muffo, a sweet wine made from botrytis affected grapes. We withhold judgment, for the first time, on the Conte Vaselli estate of Castiglione in Teverina, where the wines are suffering due to internal problems at the winery. The Orvieto Torre Sant'Andrea is not up to its usual level and the Santa Giulia red seems to have vanished without trace. We expected more exciting wines from Castel De Paolis, a company that in previous years we had commended for the high overall standard of their entire range. Casale Marchese's star also burns a little less brightly: the Frascati they are offering is a bit below par. Is the overall picture rather depressing, then? Certainly not. In our detailed assessment of Lazio's wine producers, we nevertheless managed to come up with some exciting bottles. First of all, we are delighted to award Three Glasses once again to a truly great Montiano '95 from the Falesco estate. Riccardo Cotarella, guiding spirit of this small but dynamic winery, as from this year, has also set his seal on the wines of Colle Picchioni. This has allowed Paola di Mauro to breathe a big sigh of relief: she returns to the spotlight with a sensational Marino Etichetta Oro '96. The wines of the Cantina di Cerveteri are very good once again this year. There is also important news from the centre of the region. On particularly excellent form is Casale del Giglio, which has succeed in producing an incredible range of outstanding wines. Several of these have not yet been released, but we feel confident in betting on their success. The considerable leap forward taken by the giant Fontana Candida winery is worthy of note: they wowed us with a very well made Frascati Santa Teresa and with the again-improved Terre dei Grifi range. Villa Simone with its single-vineyard Filonardi and Vigna dei Preti bottlings confirms its quality status, even if its wines were slightly penalized by a far from exciting year. Checco Papi's Le Quinte estate impressed us again this year with a delicious Virtù Romane. And what more can one say about the impeccable Count Zandotti and his enticing Frascati? This year, too, we present a numerous group of "Other Wineries" for whom, alas, there is not room for a full listing. We strongly recommend you to take note of them, however, because there are some real oenological pearls to be found among their wines.

ANAGNI (FR)

COLACICCHI
LOC. ROMAGNANO
03012 ANAGNI (FR)
TEL. 06/4469661

No Torre Ercolana this year. The Trimani family has not yet presented the latest version of the legendary red from Anagni: the new vintage, the '91, will only be released next year. For the time being, we shall just have to make do with the Bianco Romagnano '96, made from malvasia puntinata, passerina and romanesco grapes, partially vinified on the skins. This wine is acquiring greater personality year after year, and the '96 is one of the best versions to be made so far. It has firm structure and ripe fruit in abundance, underpinned by good fixed acidity and length. We were also conscious of a marked improvement in the second label of the Torre Ercolana, the Romagnano Rosso. The '95 is much improved both as far as structure and bouquet are concerned. The nuances provided by the cabernet combine with the herbaceousness of the merlot to yield a very well balanced wine indeed. We know that the inspired Marco Trimani has plans for new acquisitions in the Anagni area: watch this space!

○ Romagnano Bianco '96	🍷	4
● Romagnano Rosso '95	🍷	4
○ Romagnano Bianco '93	🍷🍷	3
○ Romagnano Bianco '94	🍷🍷	4
● Torre Ercolana '88	🍷🍷	6
● Torre Ercolana '90	🍷🍷	5
● Romagnano Rosso '91	🍷	4
● Romagnano Rosso '93	🍷	4

ARICCIA (RM)

FONTANA DI PAPA
CANTINA SOCIALE COLLI ALBANI
LOC. FONTANA DI PAPA
VIA NETTUNENSE KM 10,800
00040 ARICCIA (RM)
TEL. 06/9340071

Immersed in the veritable sea of vineyards that stretch down from Ariccia and Albano towards Cecchina, right to the border with the territory of Campoleone in the Province of Latina, this large, modern cooperative remains one of the cardinal points in the panorama of wine production in the Casteli Romani. It produces vast quantities of decently-made wines that at least allow the zone's many growers not to have to give up their most traditional activity, thereby conserving the countryside and safeguarding the area from the ravages of property speculators who would love to see the area covered in estates of small detached houses. Once again this year, the wines offered are never less than decent, and also represent excellent value for money. The best of the range is again the Calathus, a red made from cesanese, merlot and montepulciano, this time from the '95 vintage. It is certainly not a heavyweight, but it is eminently quaffable and has an attractively elegant, fruity aroma. Also worthy of attention is the Colli Albani Vigneto Poggio del Cardinale '96, a local white with fresh aromas of white peaches and Golden Delicious apples. Both of these wines are part of the range called Antico Ducato dell'Ariccia. Finally, the sweet white Meditatio '95, made from gently-dried malvasia puntinata grapes, is elegant and well balanced and bursting with honeyed, ripe fruit and vanilla tones: it is one of the best dessert wines we tasted this year from Lazio.

○ Meditatio '95	🍷🍷	4
● Calathus '95	🍷	2*
○ Colli Albani Vigneto Poggio del Cardinale '96	🍷	2*
● Calathus '94	🍷	2*
○ Colli Albani Vigneto Poggio del Cardinale '95	🍷	2*

BOLSENA (VT)

BORGO MONTELLO (LT)

ITALO MAZZIOTTI
L.GO MAZZIOTTI, 5
01023 BOLSENA (VT)
TEL. 0761/799049

CASALE DEL GIGLIO
STRADA CISTERNA-NETTUNO, KM 13
04010 BORGO MONTELLO (LT)
TEL. 06/5742529

The Mazziotti company of Bolsena is one of the historic producers of Est Est Est. The estate was founded in 1900 by Gerardo Mazziotti, the man responsible for the renaissance of this wine whose fame and popularity date back to the Middle Ages. Of the 100 hectares of land owned by the domain, 24 are planted to vines, surrounded by woodland, on volcanic soils on the eastern shore of Lake Bolsena. The traditional grape varieties prosper in this outstanding microclimate with its excellent southwesterly exposure. Here we find procanico, malvasia and rossetto, trained on a double guyot system with low yields per hectare. Flaminia Mazziotti and her husband Alessandro Laurenzi have entrusted oenologist Gaspare Buscemi with the winemaking and he has come up with a white wine of firm structure and fairly traditional style. The wine has a golden straw colour and a reasonably intense, clean bouquet, in which one finds the gently aromatic notes of malvasia, the scent of hay and a delicate suggestion of fresh almonds. On the palate, the wine is bone dry, with good acidity, rich fruitiness and reasonable body. In the best vintages Flaminia Mazziotti, who believes strongly in the ageing capacity of her wines, produces a special selection called Canuleio, which matures for a few months in barrique. The '92 currently available has a handsome deepish golden colour, gentle aromas of ripe fruit and vanilla, and displays full bodied, well balanced structure on the palate.

Working with great dedication but without any fuss, the very able Paolo Tiefenthaler has succeeded in producing a collection of authentic oenological gems. Our well deserved applause also goes to Antonio Santarelli, the owner of this beautiful estate which comprises over 150 hectares, who astutely managed to find the right man for the job. Among the vast range of wines produced here this year, we particularly enjoyed the extremely attractive Satrico '96, a white wine made from chardonnay and trebbiano with very elegant fruity aromas. The Chardonnay '96 has also improved: here one finds a wealth of fruit sensations combined with an appealing freshness. Even the '96 Albiola rosé, made from sangiovese and gamay, is delicious: it offers a pleasing fragrance reminiscent of red berry fruits, underpinned by mouth-watering fresh acidity. Tiefenthaler is probably more at ease making red wines, because again this year it was with these that we were particularly impressed. The Shiraz once again stands out. The '96 vintage, which was not an especially favourable one for the whites, did not have any adverse effects whatsoever on the taste profile of this red - indeed, quite the opposite. Its rich bouquet displays the grape variety's typical spicy notes combined with plump red berry fruit aromas. The structure of the fruit, mellowed by six months' ageing in barrique, is rounded and velvety, with good but soft underlying tannins. Value for money is, as always, outstanding. The Mater Matuta '94, made from the unusual blend of syrah with petit verdot, had already impressed us when tasting for last year's edition of the Guide. The '95, although still not ready, promises great things: we shall come back to it in due course.

○	Est Est Est di Montefiascone '96	♊	2
○	Est Est Est di Montefiascone Canuleio '92	♊	3

⊙	Albiola '96	♊	2
○	Chardonnay '96	♊	2
○	Satrico '96	♊	2
●	Shiraz '96	♊	2*
○	Chardonnay Antinoo '95	♊♊	3
○	Chardonnay '94	♊	2
●	Madreselva '93	♊	1
●	Madreselva '95	♊	2
●	Mater Matuta '94	♊	3
○	Satrico '94	♊	1
●	Shiraz '95	♊	2*

CERVETERI (RM)

CANTINA COOPERATIVA DI CERVETERI
VIA AURELIA KM 42,700
00052 CERVETERI (RM)
TEL. 06/9905697-9903707

CIVITELLA D'AGLIANO (VT)

TENUTA MOTTURA
LOC. RIO CHIARO, 1
01020 CIVITELLA D'AGLIANO (VT)
TEL. 0761/914501

It may be a result of the Cotarella treatment (we are talking about Riccardo here, the oenologist who for the past few years has been this cooperative's Director), but this year the Cantina di Cerveteri really impressed us with the quality of the wines they presented. In '96 the winery produced 105,000 hectolitres of wine overall, of which around 40,000 were selected for bottling. We especially bring your attention to the excellence of the reds. The Cerveteri Rosso Fontana Morella '96, made from montepulciano and sangiovese, has very finely nuanced aromas, which are fresh but also display a soft, almost vinous vein. It is an easy-drinking, but not banal, wine, and also offers incredible value for money. We also found a marked improvement in the Cerveteri Rosso Vigna Grande '95, made from a complex blend of sangiovese, montepulciano and merlot, and aged for around 10 months in oak barrels. On the nose, raspberry mingles with very concentrated red berry fruit, along with floral and oaky hints. On the palate, the wine - which apart from anything else is very clean - lacks a little bit of backbone. This is probably due to its excessively soft fruit, but it nevertheless remains a charmingly rounded wine with good richness of extract. We found the Cerveteri Bianco Fontana Morella '96, made from malvasia and trebbiano, to be not at all bad either: it has fresh, delicate aromas, and a very fine, elegant finish. On the other hand, the Cerveteri Bianco Vigna Grande '96 seemed to us to be slightly below par: it does indeed offer well-structured fruit and very pleasant, fresh acidity, but also less precise and positive aromas than usual.

Father and daughter Sergio and Francesca Mottura are the driving force behind this large, handsome estate which lies almost on the border with Umbria. Now that they can also count on the skilled technical assistance of Marco Monchiero, their wines will certainly perform even better. They have 60 hectares under vine, planted with grape varieties such as grechetto, procanico, rupeccio and verdello. The wines which these grapes go into all display common underlying features: a certain maturity in their aroma and flavours and the ever-present almondy note given by the grechetto. According to Monchiero these are typical traits without which the wines would risk losing their personality. Be that as it may, when compared with all the region's other whites in a blind tasting, the Mottura wines come out at a slight disadvantage. From the '96 vintage, for example, we liked best by far the standard Orvieto, which has good structure and fruit, and is clean and quaffable. At the time of our tastings, neither the Orvieto Vigna Tragugnano '96 nor that year's Grechetto Poggio della Costa had been released. Experimentation continues with the barrique-aged Grechetto, encouraged as the Motturas are by the words of praise from Burgundian "négociant" Louis Latour, who has also provided some of his barrels for its maturation. The '95, however, reveals an excessive oakiness which overwhelms the varietal aromas, and also displays signs of oxidation which prevent it from earning our One Glass recognition. We found the Muffo '94, a dessert wine made from late-picked grapes, interesting: it has intense fig and apricot aromas, and is sweet and soft on the palate.

● Cerveteri Rosso Vigna Grande '95	ⓎⓎ	3*
○ Cerveteri Bianco Vigna Grande '96	Ⓨ	1*
● Cerveteri Rosso Fontana Morella '96	Ⓨ	1*
○ Cerveteri Bianco Fontana Morella '96		1
○ Cerveteri Bianco Vigna Grande '94	Ⓨ	1*
○ Cerveteri Bianco Vigna Grande '95	Ⓨ	1*
● Cerveteri Rosso Vigna Grande '94	Ⓨ	2
● Cerveteri Rosso Vigna Grande '94	Ⓨ	1*

○ Muffo '94	Ⓨ	4
○ Orvieto Secco '96	Ⓨ	2
○ Grechetto Latour '95		4
○ Grechetto Poggio della Costa '94	ⓎⓎ	3
○ Grechetto Poggio della Costa '95	ⓎⓎ	3
○ Grechetto Latour '94	Ⓨ	4
○ Orvieto Vigna Tragugnano '94	Ⓨ	1
○ Orvieto Vigna Tragugnano '95	Ⓨ	2
● Rosso di Civitella Magone '93	Ⓨ	3
● Rosso di Civitella Magone '94	Ⓨ	4

FRASCATI (RM)

Casale Marchese

Via di Vermicino, 34
00044 Frascati (RM)
tel. 06/9408932

This vintage represents something of an intermediary year for the wines of Salvatore Carletti. The vagaries of the climate also made themselves felt at this beautiful estate situated on a sun-drenched slope just outside the built-up area of Frascati. The wines produced in '96 display much lighter aromas than those of the previous vintage. It would seem that not even the new winemaker, Sandro Facca, was able to do much to counteract the inclemency of the weather. The '96 Frascati, for example, though maintaining its habitual elegance, does not seem to display that peachy fragrance and those delicate exotic tones that have always been part and parcel of its particular style. On the other hand, it does offer good crisp acidity, balanced by delicate soft fruit. The same goes for the Cortesia '96, made from ancient local grape varieties of the region. Its gentle sweetness is slightly dimmed by a general sensation of heaviness, and its aromatic length is also rather shorter than usual. Carletti presented for the first time this year the '96 Rosso di Casale Marchese, made from a fairly complex blend of grape varieties. On first tasting, it appears to be of some interest, though still not entirely in perfect balance. We shall try it again. In the context of a region whose wines were certainly not on top form, this year Casale Marcheses's products again put up an honourable showing.

○	Frascati Superiore '96	🍷	2
○	Cortesia di Casale Marchese '96		3
●	Rosso di Casale Marchese '96		2
○	Cortesia di Casale Marchese '94	YY	2
○	Cortesia di Casale Marchese '95	YY	3
○	Frascati Superiore '94	YY	1*
○	Frascati Superiore '95	YY	2*

GROTTAFERRATA (RM)

Castel De Paolis

Via Val De Paolis, 41
00046 Grottaferrata (RM)
tel. 06/9413648

The same wines, but with two different souls: that is the impression we gleaned from the numerous tastings of the wines of Castel De Paolis which we carried out throughout the course of the year. The great enthusiasm we experienced in tasting the wines presented in last year's edition of our Guide gave way, this year, to a certain amount of perplexity. The hard work put in by Giulio and Adriana Santarelli is constant and relentless. But how can such splendid vineyards, combined with some of the world's finest grape varieties and the skill of winemakers of the highest calibre, produce wines as weak as these? This observation arises from the fact that the estate's top wines, the Frascati Superiore '96 and the Selve Vecchie '95, both display a common characteristic: they are big wines, both on the nose and palate, and have intense, mouth-filling fruit, but they both lack appropriate structure and, as a consequence, length. All in all, then, they are short of freshness and the crisp acidity which would give them grip. The red Quattro Mori '95 has neither the concentration nor the depth of last year's wine, and merely retains its One Glass rating. A Two Glass score was achieved, however, by the special selection of Frascati, the Vigna Adriana '96, which showed better balance and good length. The wines in the basic Campo Vecchio range were decidedly more interesting. The Frascati Superiore '96 is very well made and displays a good balance of its various components. The Campo Vecchio Rosso '95, a blend of syrah, montepulciano, sangiovese and cesanese, offers an intense spectrum of positive and fairly elegant fruit, spice and jam aromas. The Cannellino '96, made from a blend of ancient grape varieties, continues to improve, and this year earns our Two Glass accolade.

○	Frascati Superiore Cannellino '96	🍷🍷	4
○	Frascati Superiore Vigna Adriana '96	🍷🍷	4
●	Campo Vecchio Rosso '95	🍷	3
○	Frascati Superiore '96	🍷	4
○	Frascati Superiore Campo Vecchio '96	🍷	3
●	Quattro Mori '95	🍷	5
○	Frascati Superiore Vigna Adriana '94	YY	4
○	Frascati Superiore Vigna Adriana '95	YY	4
○	Muffa Nobile '94	YY	4
●	Quattro Mori '93	YY	4
●	Quattro Mori '94	YY	4

MARINO (RM)

PAOLA DI MAURO - COLLE PICCHIONI
VIA COLLE PICCHIONE DI MARINO, 46
00040 MARINO (RM)
TEL. 06/93546329

MARINO (RM)

GOTTO D'ORO
VIA DEL DIVINO AMORE, 115
LOC. FRATTOCCHIE
00040 MARINO (RM)
TEL. 06/930222-93547037

Those who are not fond of Paola di Mauro have always maintained that her abundant energy and her irrepressibly friendly nature often masked the limits of her good, though not exceptional, wines. We (apart from the fact that we have sometimes found the wines to be exceptional indeed) uphold that if it had not been for Paola di Mauro, the wines of Lazio would have had a much more difficult time establishing a quality image. However, in the last few years, we too have had some doubts about the standard of her wines, not least because the improvements she had made between '88 and '93 seemed to have come to a halt. What was needed was a breath of fresh air, something or someone who would join up with Paola and her son Armando to give new impetus to the wines of Colle Picchioni. And, as if by magic, one of the best oenologists on the current Italian wine scene, Riccardo Cotarella, has come to their aid. The first effects were already apparent in the wines presented last year. Now, the release of the Marino Oro '96 places a definitive seal on the marked change of direction taken by this small but famous winery. It is a wine which is technically perfect: it is perfumed and soft, quaffable and elegant. It is a minor masterpiece which more than easily wins our Two Glass accolade, and indeed takes its place at the top of the quality tree among Central Italy's white wines. Besides this white, which really stands out in the winery's range, we also tasted an excellent '96 version of the Marino Etichetta Verde and a '93 Vigna del Vassallo, the cabernet/merlot blend, which augurs well for new developments in the future, with considerably more skilled use of small new oak barrels.

When this large cooperative winery was founded at the end of the 1940s, few would have laid bets on its making quality wines and achieving commercial success. The Italian wine sector as we now know it was barely in its infancy and in the Castelli Romani the unbottled house wine in the local taverns flowed plentifully. A couple of decades later an extremely modern winery was built, and the company brand name was definitively launched: a brand that, shortly afterwards, would become known halfway around the globe thanks to a very efficient distribution network. Marino Gotto d'Oro, just as we know it today, had been born. It was a wine which no longer had an orange hue, but was pale straw; with delicately fruity rather than rustic or vinegary aromas; and with a light, well-balanced flavour. In short, it had become a modern wine which went on to win over hosts of consumers, slowly replacing the now-unmarketable house wines of yore, which often did not remain drinkable for even six months after the vintage. The '96 version of Marino Superiore, too, substantially reproduces those characteristics which, over the years, have made it one of the most famous whites of the region. For some years now, the Marino cooperative has also bottled a Frascati Superiore, the '96 vintage of which seemed to us just a shade more delicate than its better-known stable mate, but on the whole fairly similar in style. The most recent release from the winery is the Malvasia del Lazio '96, a decent, fairly aromatic white, which is still however a little too rustic.

○ Marino Colle Picchioni Oro '96	♟♟	4
● Vigna del Vassallo '93	♟♟	5
○ Marino Etichetta Verde '96	♟	3
● Vigna del Vassallo '85	♟♟♟	5
● Vigna del Vassallo '88	♟♟♟	5
○ Le Vignole '92	♟♟	4
○ Le Vignole '93	♟♟	3
○ Marino Colle Picchioni Oro '95	♟♟	3
● Vigna del Vassallo '89	♟♟	5
● Vigna del Vassallo '90	♟♟	4
● Vigna del Vassallo '92	♟♟	4
● Colle Picchioni Rosso '93	♟	3
○ Marino Colle Picchioni Oro '94	♟	3
○ Marino Etichetta Verde '95	♟	2*

○ Frascati Superiore '96	♟	2*
○ Marino Superiore '96	♟	2*
○ Malvasia del Lazio '96		2

MONTECOMPATRI (RM)

MONTEFIASCONE (VT)

LE QUINTE
VIA DELLE MARMORELLE, 71
00040 MONTECOMPATRI (RM)
TEL. 06/9438756

FALESCO
S.S. CASSIA NORD, KM 94,500
01027 MONTEFIASCONE (VT)
TEL. 0761/827032

Is the Montecompatri DOC really capable of producing wines of high quality? If this has indeed come about, after years of neglect and anonymous wines, the merit belongs exclusively to Francesco Papi and to his impressive Le Quinte estate, situated on the border between the communes of Montecompatri and Colonna. Year after year his wines have made further inroads into public attention. Standing out above the others in the range is the delicious Montecompatri Superiore Virtù Romane which, in the '96 version, displays considerable general finesse and more restrained exotic aromas, scents which are typical of its particular style. It is a wine whose fruit in this vintage shows great roundness and softness, even perhaps to a slightly exaggerated degree. However, it again demonstrates that it is one of the most interesting wines to come out of Lazio in the last few years, and it also represents outstanding value for money. The Casale dei Papi '96 is also very pleasant: it offers the same features as the major label, but in a more subdued style. It has a deliciously crisp and delicate citrus vein. There is a new wine this year, the Rasa di Marmorata '95, a red made from cesanese, montepulciano and other local varieties. Its structure is quite good, but we believe its aromatic progression from nose to palate could still be improved. There is another new wine which we actually found more interesting: the Dulcis Vitis '96. Made from local grape varieties, this wine, a sort of alternative to Cannellino, is notable for its gentle, and decidedly uncloying sweetness, and its soft, silky fruit.

What a great Montiano '95! This really is an outstanding Merlot: its greatness lies in its breadth, in its elegant succession of aromas in which spices give way to jam, then to coffee, then to vanilla. It also has extraordinary length on the palate, where the fruit is concentrated and mouth-filling: it is rich and satisfying, yet without being overblown. The success of the wine is in proportion to Riccardo Cotarella's competence and confidence in his own skills and raw materials. A wine like this certainly deserves our highest accolade. And what about the others? Last year we had the impression that the Falesco estate had already expressed its full potential. How wrong we were! Just try the '96 Grechetto. A brief period in oak combined with rich, fleshy fruit make it a very skillfully-composed wine indeed. The slight bitter-almondy notes typical of the variety are diluted by the vanilla of the oak, but without being overwhelmed altogether. The wine has extraordinary aromatic length, as well as an extremely keen price. The Poggio dei Gelsi '96 also shows a marked improvement. Perhaps it does not have much to do with the Est Est Est available on the market nowadays, but it does have a great deal in common with Italy's finest whites. It is elegantly fruity, with peach and Golden Delicious apple notes, and is underpinned by an excellent vein of acidity which makes it very refreshing; it also has a long, gentle finish. The Vitiano '95 is made from cabernet sauvignon grapes grown in Umbria, but vinified and aged at Montefiascone. In size and structure it is not far behind the Montiano. Finally, the '95 Vendemmia Tardiva, made from the same grapes as the Est Est Est, but picked late, is also very interesting. It is a wine with a broad spectrum of aromas and it is sweet and round, with rich honey and apricot jam notes.

○ Montecompatri Colonna Superiore Virtù Romane '96	🍷🍷	2*
○ Dulcis Vitis '96	🍷	3
○ Montecompatri Colonna Superiore Casale dei Papi '96	🍷	1
● Rasa di Marmorata '95		2
○ Montecompatri Colonna Superiore Virtù Romane '94	♀♀	2*
○ Montecompatri Colonna Superiore Virtù Romane '95	♀♀	2
○ Montecompatri Colonna Superiore Casale dei Papi '94	♀	1*
○ Montecompatri Colonna Superiore Casale dei Papi '95	♀	1

● Montiano '95	🍷🍷🍷	5
○ Est Est Est di Montefiascone Poggio dei Gelsi '96	🍷🍷	3
○ Est Est Est di Montefiascone Vendemmia Tardiva '95	🍷🍷	4
○ Grechetto '96	🍷🍷	3*
● Vitiano '96	🍷🍷	3*
○ Est Est Est di Montefiascone Falesco '96	🍷	1
● Montiano '94	♀♀♀	4
○ Est Est Est di Montefiascone Poggio dei Gelsi '94	♀♀	1*
○ Est Est Est di Montefiascone Poggio dei Gelsi '95	♀♀	3

MONTEPORZIO CATONE (RM)

Fontana Candida
Via Fontana Candida, 11
00040 Monteporzio Catone (RM)
tel. 06/9420066

Are you looking for one of the best '96 whites from Lazio? Then you will find it at Fontana Candida. The name? Frascati Superiore Santa Teresa. We were struck, in this wine, by the harmonious combination of the silky elegance of its fruity, nuanced bouquet with its measured, velvety and gentle fruit on the palate. Francesco Bardi, the company's winemaker, has transformed a long-held dream into brilliant reality. The grape varieties are those which have always been grown in the Santa Teresa vineyard, but carefully selected, mixed and vinified so as to bring out the very best of their aromas and flavours. For this level of quality, it is a bargain. The new Terre dei Grifi range, too, named after an old noble family of the area, displays the modern style of the Frascatis produced by Fontana Candida. The Frascati Superiore Terre dei Grifi '96 impresses with the breadth of its aromas and its general sensations of freshness. The Malvasia del Lazio Terre dei Grifi '96 has a warm straw-yellow colour; though more gentle and understated than the Frascati, it is tightly-knit and flavourful and reveals some unexpected nuances of aroma, among them banana and sage. We should also like to remind our readers of these products' excellent value for money. Finally, the winery's top-selling wine, the Frascati Superiore Fontana Candida '96, is more than just satisfactory, and is consistently reliable.

○ Frascati Superiore Santa Teresa '96	🍷🍷	2*
○ Malvasia del Lazio '96	🍷🍷	2*
○ Frascati Superiore '96	🍷	1
○ Frascati Superiore Terre dei Grifi '96	🍷	2
○ Frascati Superiore Santa Teresa '94	YY	2*
○ Frascati Superiore Santa Teresa '95	YY	2
○ Frascati Superiore Terre dei Grifi '95	YY	2*
○ Malvasia del Lazio '95	YY	2

MONTEPORZIO CATONE (RM)

Villa Simone
Via Frascati Colonna, 29
00040 Monteporzio Catone (RM)
tel. 06/3213210-9449717

The Vigna dei Preti is the name of a vineyard which Piero Costantini has rented from a monastery just outside Frascati, and which, together with Filonardi and the Villa Simone complex, constitutes the 30 hectares of vines from which he picks the grapes for his wines. In this vineyard he selects the fruit for the Frascati of the same name, which is always characterized by a general lightness of style. In the '96 version the Vigna dei Preti displays an interesting nose, with reasonably intense aroma, and fruit which, though still on the delicate side, is slightly fleshier. Villa Simone's star wine, the Filonardi (which comes from a vineyard that used to belong to Sergio Zavoli), suffered the effects of a rather less than exciting year, and is a bit below par compared to the '95. The Frascati Villa Simone '96, made from malvasia puntinata, bellone and trebbiano, also seems a little subdued to us in this vintage. It has an attractive, well-balanced bouquet, in which we find fruity aromas of tart apples and bananas, but displays rather unsubstantial fruit on the palate. The Cannellino '95, though unbalanced on the nose, is rich and balanced on the palate, with hints of honey and peaches.

○ Frascati Superiore Cannellino '95	🍷	5
○ Frascati Superiore Vigna dei Preti '96	🍷	2
○ Frascati Superiore Vigneto Filonardi '96	🍷	3
○ Frascati Superiore Villa Simone '96	🍷	2
○ Frascati Superiore Cannellino '92	YY	5
○ Frascati Superiore Vigna dei Preti '94	YY	2
○ Frascati Superiore Vigna dei Preti '95	YY	2
○ Frascati Superiore Vigneto Filonardi '94	YY	3

PIGLIO (FR)

Massimi Berucci

Via Prenestina, km 42
03010 Piglio (FR)
tel. 0775/501303-68307004

If in '95 we were rather disappointed by the unkind whims of the weather, '96 only partly made up for the previous year's poor showing. From tastings of cask samples, we got the impression that the '96 Cesanese Casal Cervino will not be up to the standard of the '93 and '94 this year either. Though displaying more positive fruit and structure and a more impressive colour than the '95, it cannot show the class and complexity of the two preceding vintages. All the same, the unflappable Manfredi Berucci seems to be optimistic about the way the wine will finally turn out. We shall see. Anyway, we did try two good wines from this small winery. The first is a pleasant '95 Rosato, made from cesanese; it has good, tightly-knit fruit, with aromas of sour cherries and raspberries, and pretty good length. The other interesting wine is the unusual Berucci Bianco, also made from the cesanese variety. Manfredi has had the unconventional idea of coming out now with the '94 vintage, and on the whole it is rather appealing. It is a wine with good, lively structure, which is round and quaffable on the palate, and which has a gentle, though not simple, bouquet. A mere 3,500 bottles of it were made, but, in our opinion, there is the potential there for its production to grow and quality to improve over the next few years. We have already mentioned the Passerina '95 in last year's Guide, so we therefore look forward with optimism to the release of the wines which are still maturing in the cellar.

⊙	Berucci Rosato '95	**Y**	1
○	Berucci Bianco '94		1
●	Cesanese del Piglio Casal Cervino '94	YY	2
○	Berucci Bianco '94	Y	1
●	Cesanese del Piglio Casal Cervino '95	Y	2
○	Passerina del Frusinate '94	Y	1
○	Passerina del Frusinate '95	Y	1

ROMA

Conte Zandotti

Via Vigne di Colle Mattia, 8
00132 Roma
tel. 06/20609000

Count Enrico Zandotti has made a number of changes. The changes we glimpsed at this winery last year have resulted in the arrival of young and able winemaker Marco Ciarla, who has produced a very well made Frascati Superiore '96. The grapes - of the classic malvasia puntinata, trebbiano and bellone varieties - come, as always, exclusively from the estate's own 30 hectares of vineyards. Now that pasteurization has finally been abandoned, the wine's bouquet can express its real fresh, fruit aromas. Both the body and fruit on the palate also seem to us to have improved. In spite of the far from exciting vintage, this wine managed to score very well indeed, coming close to a Two Glass rating. From the same, but late-harvested, grape varieties as Frascati comes the fragrant Frascati Cannellino '96, whose delicately sweet tones make it highly attractive. It is soft and silky, with harmonious aromas and flavours of ripe fruit and honey. Enrico Zandotti also has a new wine up his sleeve which will not be released until next year. We have had a sneak preview of it, and we can assure you that it is a real stunner.

○	Frascati Cannellino '96	**YY**	3
○	Frascati Superiore '96	**Y**	2
○	Frascati Cannellino '95	YY	3
○	Frascati Superiore '94	YY	1*
○	Frascati Superiore '95	YY	2
○	Frascati Cannellino '94	Y	2

OTHER WINERIES

The following producers obtained good scores in our tastings with one or more of their wines:

PROVINCE OF FROSINONE

Antonello Coletti Conti,
Anagni, tel. 0775/728610,
Cesanese del Piglio Hærnicus '94

Giuseppe Iucci,
Cassino, tel. 0776/311883,
Merlot di Atina Tenuta La Creta '95

La Selva,
Paliano, tel. 0775/533125,
Cesanese del Piglio '95,
Passerina del Frusinate '96

PROVINCE OF LATINA

Pouchain,
Ponza, tel. 06/30365644,
Vino di Bianca '96

PROVINCE OF ROMA

Casale Mattia,
Frascati, tel 06/9426017,
Frascati Superiore '96

Casale Vallechiesa,
Frascati, tel. 06/95460086,
Frascati Superiore '96

Cantina San Marco,
Frascati, tel. 06/9422689,
Frascati Superiore Selezione '96

L'Olivella,
Frascati, tel. 06/9424527,
Frascati Superiore Racemo '96

Tenuta di Pietra Porzia,
Frascati, tel. 06/9464392,
Frascati Superiore '96

Baldassarri,
Genzano, tel. 06/9396106,
Colli Lanuvini '96

Cantina Sociale La Selva,
Genzano, tel. 06/9396085,
Colli Lanuvini Fontanatorta '96

CO.PRO.VI,
Velletri, tel. 06/9587444,
Velletri Bianco Villa Ginnetti '96,
Torreto Rosso '95

Cesare Loreti,
Zagarolo, tel. 06/9575956,
Zagarolo Superiore '96

PROVINCE OF VITERBO

Trappolini,
Castiglione in Teverina, tel. 0761/948381,
Grechetto dell'Umbria Brecceto '96

Cantina Oleificio Sociale,
Gradoli, tel. 0761/456087,
Aleatico di Gradoli Liquoroso

Vittorio Puri,
Montefiascone, tel. 0761/799190,
Est Est Est di Montefiascone Villa Puri '96

ABRUZZO AND MOLISE

There is lots of news from Abruzzo, including the approval this year of the new Controguerra DOC. His Majesty Montepulciano d'Abruzzo however remains the front page story: it is still this wine which is leading the recovery of Abruzzo's viticulture. Apart from Edoardo Valentini, who will release his '92 Montepulciano in December, new wines come from many other more or less famous wineries, demonstrating that there is a wide pool of quality-led producers and that the region is not dominated by just a few large companies. Today, alongside the success reaped at Loreto Aprutino and in certain zones around Teramo, we find continual experimentation throughout the region, which covers everything from the use of barriques to the rediscovery of indigenous grape varieties. Close behind Valentini comes Gianni Masciarelli, one of the few this year to offer an outstanding Trebbiano d'Abruzzo and who deserves applause for his bold efforts in creating modern-style wines. And there is no shortage of others who are attempting to follow this courageous path. Among them, with variations on a theme, and justified ambitions, there is the Illuminati family, for whom, however, the traditional Zanna is still their real forte. Then there is Cataldi Madonna, which is definitely on the way up to the top of the regional tree by virtue of the high quality of its entire range. Cantina Tollo, the cooperative which has convinced the other large producers to combine quantity with quality, is another major figure. And let us not forget Montori and Nicodemi, who are still very dependable but whose wines performed slightly below par compared to recent years. This is also, to some extent, the case of Lepore, the young and promising estate in the Province of Teramo, which is currently going through a - we trust, brief - identity crisis: Zaccagnini, thankfully, appears to have come out of his. Emerging producers reveal different aspects of the modernisation of wine growing in Abruzzo: Marramiero makes his début with a good number of wines in the innovative styles proposed by others; Orlandi Contucci Ponno is the only estate to have obtained appreciable results with international varieties (particularly with the Sauvignon Ghiaiolo); another recently-founded estate, La Valentina, has staked its reputation on wines of a traditional stamp, but of good technical quality and with a high degree of varietal character. Others are striving for recognition, and it will not be long before we are talking about them too. It is a pity that this wind of change has not yet blown over Molise. But even as soon as next year there may be a valid competitor for the famous, and so far unchallenged, Di Majo Norante winery. This producer may not be up to its usual standard but nevertheless succeeded in this year's tastings in once again charming us with some well-structured whites.

BOLOGNANO (PE)

CICCIO ZACCAGNINI
C.DA POZZO
65020 BOLOGNANO (PE)
TEL. 085/8880195

A warm welcome back to the Guide for Marcello Zaccagnini, one of Abruzzo's best-known producers. Last year he showed signs of improvement, and this year, celebrating his purchase of new vineyards, he reconfirms the progress made. We are still not at an outstanding level of excellence, but the favourable impression we received from tasting the wines in the standard range was mirrored by the higher-quality reds. An example is the Capisco '93, which comes close to claiming a Two Glass award: made from cabernet franc, and matured first in large oak barrels and then, more briefly, in barriques, it is a red with ripe floral and bilberry aromas, and substantial tannins as well, but which is a little too short on the palate. Close behind is the Montepulciano Riserva of the same year, which is perhaps more concentrated and lively in colour and in the mouth (with just the right amount of tannins), but which loses points on the nose because of its over-ripe fruit aromas. The Cerasuolo, his traditional forte, is also in good form: it is also made from montepulciano grapes, and displays bright colour, some depth, and great quaffability. Of the whites, neither the Ibisco nor the Trebbiano Castello di Salle seemed as good as the wines just mentioned, and in fact the "basic" Bianco di Ciccio scored higher.

CAMPOMARINO (CB)

DI MAJO NORANTE
C.DA RAMITELLO, 4
86042 CAMPOMARINO (CB)
TEL. 0875/57208

Di Majo Norante is, for now at any rate, the only producer in Molise worthy of note, and deserves praise for rediscovering and protecting traditional old grape varieties, as well as for its experimentation with DOC wines and new blends alike. We liked, in their different ways, the Falanghina and the Greco: the former offers attractive aromas of broom and has good acidity and structure on the palate, as well as a slightly bitter-almondy finish. The Greco, which has a brighter straw colour is elegant, with broad, rich fruit on the nose, and would score more highly on the palate if it were not for a slight lack of balance. The Fiano (diluted aromas and excessively savoury flavour) and the Moli Bianco are not really up to scratch, whereas the Biblos '95, a new blend of falanghina and greco, is very impressive. It has a brilliant appearance, good acidity, round, fleshy fruit and excellent balance: a really impressive début. The Ramitello Bianco, too, made from falanghina and fiano, deserves its One Glass rating. It has a lively colour and displays aromas of flowers and hazelnuts on the nose, and is refreshing and fruity on the palate. The disappointing notes came from the reds. The Ramitello, though it displays good aromas redolent of plums and liquorice, has a rather unbalanced finish; the Moli Rosso and the Prugnolo reveal very little bouquet at all. The Aglianico seemed to have been made from over-ripe grapes - we do not know whether deliberately or not - with not especially happy results. Finally, our One Glass award goes to the Apianae, a Moscato which is pleasant, aromatic (oranges, honey) and refreshing in the mouth.

●	Capsico Rosso '93	♟	3
☉	Montepulciano d'Abruzzo Cerasuolo '96	♟	2
●	Montepulciano d'Abruzzo Ris. '93	♟	3
○	Bianco di Ciccio '96		2
○	Ibisco Bianco '96		3
●	Montepulciano d'Abruzzo '95		2
☉	Myosotis Rosé '96		3
○	Trebbiano d'Abruzzo Castello di Salle '96		2

○	Biblos '95	♟♟	3
○	Apianae '94	♟	4
○	Falanghina '96	♟	3
○	Greco '96	♟	3
○	Ramitello Bianco '96	♟	2*
●	Aglianico '95		3
○	Molì Bianco '96		1
●	Molì Rosso '95		1
●	Prugnolo '95		2
●	Ramitello Rosso '95		2
○	Apianae '93	♟♟	4
○	Greco '95	♟	3
○	Ramitello Bianco '95	♟	2*
●	Ramitello Rosso '93	♟	2

CONTROGUERRA (TE)

ILLUMINATI
C.DA S. BIAGIO
64010 CONTROGUERRA (TE)
TEL. 0861/808008

CONTROGUERRA (TE)

CAMILLO MONTORI
PIANE TRONTO, 23
64010 CONTROGUERRA (TE)
TEL. 0861/809900

Last year we heralded the début of a new red from Illuminati, a company which combines commercial dynamism with a fairly large range of high quality wines. On its first release, however, the Lumen'93 - made from montepulciano and cabernet sauvignon grapes - was slightly disappointing. It is intensely coloured and full and dry (perhaps a bit too dry) on the palate; but its rather unsatisfactory nose prevents it from gaining a Two Glass rating, even though it did come quite close. This award however was obtained, as usual, by the Zanna, which impresses with its depth of colour and its refined aromas of ripe red berry fruits, as well as the structure and power accompanied by soft, fleshy fruit. The Riparosso, the other Montepulciano d'Abruzzo, is up to its usual standard; the Nico (made from the same grapes, but late-harvested) was just a little below par. But Illuminati were back on form with the Cerasuolo Campirosa, with its excellent colour and fruity aromas. It is youthful and fresh, with a typical, slightly bitter cherry note on the finish. The whites were not entirely faultless as the following wines suggest: the Ciafre '95 (a more successful blend on other occasions); the Daniele '94 (barrique-aged trebbiano with traces of oxidation); the basic Costalupo Trebbiano (lacking in bouquet). On the other hand, the new Controguerra DOC made a good first appearance in the shape of the Cenalba, made exclusively from chardonnay (of which 10 per cent has spent some time in barrique). This wine represents excellent value for money. A brilliant straw-yellow in colour, with scents of bananas and flowers, it is well balanced and well structured. The range is completed by the Loré, a sweet wine made from botrytis-affected grapes, which we found very pleasant both on the nose and palate.

What is happening to good old Camillo Montori? After years and years of progress and hard work in order to spread the word about - and improve - the good name of Abruzzo (among other things, Montori may be considered the father of the new Controguerra DOC), it seems that recently he has taken a pause for reflection. We have no doubt it will only be a brief one. Meanwhile, this year he has renovated his winery premises and his ageing cellar but of the wines which he presented for tasting, the only one to shine was the Montepulciano Fonte Cupa '94 (which rather saved the entire range from anonymity). It has a deep ruby red colour, full, rich, intense aromas and fruit on the palate which succeeds in combining complexity and softness. This is a wine of a quality which is not all that common, neither in this region nor in the rest of Italy. As for the other wines, we found the white Leneo d'Oro and the Fauno of some interest. The Trebbiano Fonte Cupa (never so off-form in recent years) did not even score as highly as the standard Trebbiano; and in fact the basic range is generally correct and true-to-type. The Cerasuolo in this line is particularly enjoyable: it was the only wine to come near scoring One Glass.

● Montepulciano d'Abruzzo		
Zanna Vecchio '93	ΥΥ	4*
○ Cenalba '96	Υ	2
○ Loré '94	Υ	4
● Lumen '93	Υ	5
⊙ Montepulciano d'Abruzzo		
Cerasuolo Campirosa '96	Υ	2*
● Montepulciano d'Abruzzo		
Riparosso '96	Υ	2
○ Brut Metodo Classico '91		4
○ Ciafrè '95		2
○ Daniele '94		3
● Nicò '93		5
● Montepulciano d'Abruzzo		
Zanna Vecchio '91	ΥΥ	3*

● Montepulciano d'Abruzzo		
Fontecupa '94	ΥΥ	4*
○ Fauno '96		2
○ Leneo d'Oro '95		3
● Montepulciano d'Abruzzo '95		2
⊙ Montepulciano d'Abruzzo		
Cerasuolo '96		2
⊙ Montepulciano d'Abruzzo		
Cerasuolo Fontecupa '96		3
○ Trebbiano d'Abruzzo '96		2
○ Trebbiano d'Abruzzo		
Fontecupa '96		3
● Leneo Moro '94	ΥΥ	4
● Montepulciano d'Abruzzo		
Fontecupa '93	ΥΥ	3*

LORETO APRUTINO (PE)

EDOARDO VALENTINI
VIA DEL BAIO, 2
65014 LORETO APRUTINO (PE)
TEL. 085/8291138

Sometimes the symbolic value of a wine goes far beyond its mere tasting profile and reminds us that, like it or not, we are dealing with something that is at the very basis of Mediterranean civilization. The wines produced by Edoardo Valentini manage to encapsulate this concept, and are masterly ambassadors for the "terroir" and the ecosystem from which they hail. Valentini is not only a grower of extraordinary sensibility, he is also a cultured and determined man with a profound knowledge of his vineyards, and one who employs winemaking techniques that not only respect his raw material, the grapes, but also the environment in which he works. This year he presented us with three wines for tasting. The Montepulciano d'Abruzzo Cerasuolo '95 - the best vintage ever - displays fresh fruit aromas and a structure worthy of a fine red. The Trebbiano d'Abruzzo '93 shows perhaps a little less roundness and body compared to the previous year's wine. It comes from what was a very early harvest, and offers a bouquet that is a tiny bit less complex and with more emphasis on straightforward fruit than on those deriving from the evolution of primary aromas from the grapes themselves. Many people will like it more than the '92, but to us it seems a little bit more simple. Really outstanding, though, is the Montepulciano d'Abruzzo '92, yet another masterpiece, with less alcohol but greater balance than the legendary '90 vintage. It has a bouquet in which one can find intense aromas of sour cherries, as well as fruit on the palate of rare finesse, with tannins that have never been so elegant. These outstanding characteristics remove any possible doubt about the '92 vintage which elsewhere - but certainly not in this area - was not a very good one. And so the legend of one of the world's great "vignerons" continues.

● Montepulciano d'Abruzzo '92	▼▼▼	6
⊙ Montepulciano d'Abruzzo Cerasuolo '95	▼▼	5
○ Trebbiano d'Abruzzo '93	▼▼	5
● Montepulciano d'Abruzzo '77	▽▽▽	6
● Montepulciano d'Abruzzo '85	▽▽▽	6
● Montepulciano d'Abruzzo '88	▽▽▽	6
● Montepulciano d'Abruzzo '90	▽▽▽	5
○ Trebbiano d'Abruzzo '88	▽▽▽	5
○ Trebbiano d'Abruzzo '92	▽▽▽	6
● Montepulciano d'Abruzzo '87	▽▽	6
○ Trebbiano d'Abruzzo '85	▽▽	5
○ Trebbiano d'Abruzzo '87	▽▽	5
○ Trebbiano d'Abruzzo '90	▽▽	6

NOTARESCO (TE)

BRUNO NICODEMI
C.DA VENIGLIO, 8
64024 NOTARESCO (TE)
TEL. 085/895493-895135

We had hoped for a definitive consecration for this winery, but instead we have to register something of a false step, probably partly due to the sad and premature death of owner Bruno Nicodemi. It was he, many years ago, who breathed new life into the company by acquiring its present splendid 28 hectares of vineyards and by building its very well equipped winery. And it was he, too, who skilfully ran what is today one of the few utterly dependable wineries in the region, which for example has always made a basic range at virtually the same level as its premium wines. Last year we noted a certain leaning towards the whites, but this year we were more favourably struck by the Montepulciano d'Abruzzo Colli Venia '95, a red which offers excellent value for money and earns a One Glass award thanks to its pleasant, clean, if light aromas, and to an overall balance which softens the initial impression of rusticity. Even more impressive was its elder brother, the Bacco Riserva '93: this hyper-ripe wine has a dense, dark red colour and explodes on the nose and palate with fruit reminiscent of cherry jam, and with huge power and concentration. Among the rest of the wines produced, we pick out the Trebbiano d'Abruzzo Bacco '96, which is a white that displays an attractive, measured style both on the nose and palate.

● Montepulciano d'Abruzzo Bacco '93	▼▼	4
● Montepulciano d'Abruzzo Colli Venia '95	▼	2*
○ Trebbiano d'Abruzzo Bacco '96	▼	3
⊙ Montepulciano d'Abruzzo Cerasuolo Colli Venia '96		2
○ Trebbiano d'Abruzzo Colli Venia '96		2
● Montepulciano d'Abruzzo Bacco '91	▽	3
● Montepulciano d'Abruzzo Bacco Masseria De Luca '90	▽	4
● Montepulciano d'Abruzzo Colli Venia '94	▽	2

OFENA (AQ)

TENUTA CATALDI MADONNA
LOC. PIANA, 1
67025 OFENA (AQ)
TEL. 0862/954252-4911680

ROSCIANO (PE)

MARRAMIERO
C.DA S.ANDREA,1
65010 ROSCIANO (PE)
TEL. 085/8505766

We have always believed in the capabilities of this winery, the standard-bearer of the Province of Aquila, even after some wines that, for a couple of years, did not live up to the winery's potential. After last year's return to the Guide, we have witnessed yet further improvement, despite the death of the much-lamented Antonio (Toni) Cataldi Madonna. His son Luigi, who had always been his right-hand man in the running of the estate, this year has brought out a full range of successfully made wines. We begin with the excellent Montepulciano d'Abruzzo Toni '91, a satisfyingly fleshy and mouth-filling red, with aromas of ripe fruit, fine tannins and remarkable overall balance. Three wine in the standard line also showed well. They are the Montepulciano d'Abruzzo (deep red, with purple highlights; a satisfying bouquet of cherries and bilberries; a slightly unbalanced finish); the Cerasuolo version, which offers great value for money, (typical "cerasuolo" colour; aromas of flowers and red berry fruits; easy, quaffable style and an almondy aftertaste); the Trebbiano d'Abruzzo, the most complete of the three, with good acidity and aromas of fresh fruit, good balance and a lightly vegetal tone. An interesting novelty, which we also reward with One Glass, comes from the first 2,000 bottles of Pecorino (made from an indigenous, low yielding variety reintroduced seven years ago) which is characterized by high natural acidity, and which displays aromas and flavours which are reminiscent at first of lemons, and then of aniseed. The Cabernet Sauvignon again loses points because of its not very distinct aromas and its modest breadth.

It was the first appearance of this producer in our "blind" tastings, and this is now the first full entry in our Guide, for an estate which has nothing new about it apart from its image and approach. For some years now the Marramieros have been severe in their vineyard management, and they have also refurbished their winery, where they make widespread (if sometimes exaggerated) use of new barriques under the direction of winemaker Romeo Taraborrelli. They have only been bottling for two years, but have already come up with several noteworthy wines. The Montepulciano Inferi '93 makes a reputation for itself with its breadth and character: it is a red with rich, concentrated colour and aromas. On the nose one finds elegant and long red berry fruit notes; on the palate it reveals notable substance, and is soft and round, with hints of liquorice and tobacco. A well-deserved One Glass rating is earned by the Trebbiano d'Abruzzo Altare '95 (fine colour and intriguing vanilla aromas, but excessive use of oak) which is a great deal better than last year's version (slightly bitter and a bit too evolved). A similar award goes to the Trebbiano Anima '95, made from grapes of the same variety, grown in the same vineyard, but matured in stainless steel: it is superior to the '96 thanks to its satisfyingly well-knit and positive nose, as well as quite good length on the palate. On the other hand, the Chardonnay Punta di Colle and two of the three wines in the standard Dama range (the Montepulciano and the Trebbiano) do not seem particularly well focussed. The Dama Cerasuolo, however, does have a pleasing profile: it has just the right amount of colour; it is vinous on the nose, with notes of red berry fruit, and full and well made on the palate.

● Montepulciano d'Abruzzo Tonì '91	🍷🍷	4*
● Montepulciano d'Abruzzo '95	🍷	2
☉ Montepulciano d'Abruzzo Cerasuolo '96	🍷	2*
O Pecorino '96	🍷	3
O Trebbiano d'Abruzzo '96	🍷	2*
● Cabernet Sauvignon '93		3
O Sauvignon '96		3
☉ Montepulciano d'Abruzzo Cerasuolo '95	🍷	2*
● Montepulciano d'Abruzzo Rubino '94	🍷	2
● Montepulciano d'Abruzzo Tonì '90	🍷	3
O Trebbiano d'Abruzzo '95	🍷	2

● Montepulciano d'Abruzzo Inferi '93	🍷🍷	4
☉ Montepulciano d'Abruzzo Cerasuolo '96	🍷	2*
O Trebbiano d'Abruzzo Altare '95	🍷	3
O Trebbiano d'Abruzzo Anima '95	🍷	3
O Chardonnay Punta di Colle '96		3
● Montepulciano d'Abruzzo Dama '95		2
O Trebbiano d'Abruzzo Anima '96		3
O Trebbiano d'Abruzzo Dama '96		2

ROSETO DEGLI ABRUZZI (TE)

Orlandi Contucci Ponno

C.da Voltarrosto
Via Piana degli Ulivi, 1
64026 Roseto degli Abruzzi (TE)
tel. 085/8931206

Abruzzo offers us another company which, though founded almost thirty years ago, has only recently decided to bottle its own wines on a regular basis. The credit for this goes to Marina Orlandi Contucci, who has wanted to give a more business-like stamp to the estate started up by her father. After planting a large number of international grape varieties, and after a careful selection of those typical to the zone, this winery at Roseto degli Abruzzo (for which oenologist Donato Lanati acts as external consultant) now offers a good range of wines. If they have a weakness it is that perhaps they are still looking for their own precise style and character. This is not the case, however, among the whites, of the Sauvignon Ghiaiolo, which hits the spot with its colour and clean varietal character of its aromas; it has just the right amount of acidity, as well as good overall balance. In the Chardonnay Roccesco and the Pinot Adrio, on the other hand, even though their aromas have nice fruit, we also find anomalous vegetal notes. The Trebbiano Colle della Corte and the Cerasuolo, made from montepulciano vermiglio grapes, are reasonable, but both show room for improvement; though they are substantially well-made, there is a jarring greenness in the background. Standing out among the reds are the satisfactory Cabernet Sauvignon Colle Funaro (deep inky red with herbaceous and red berry fruit aromas, but perhaps not sufficiently rich and full) and the Montepulciano d'Abruzzo La Regia Specula, which is correct and straightforward. On the nose it reminds us (once again!) of its international stablemate, but with lesser depth.

●	Cabernet Sauvignon Colle Funaro '94	🍷	3
○	Chardonnay Roccesco '96	🍷	2
●	Montepulciano d'Abruzzo La Regia Specula '95	🍷	2
○	Pinot Adrio '96	🍷	2
○	Sauvignon Ghiaiolo '96	🍷	3*
⊙	Montepulciano d'Abruzzo Cerasuolo Vermiglio '96		2
○	Trebbiano d'Abruzzo Colle della Corte '96		2

S. MARTINO SULLA MARRUCINA (CH)

Masciarelli

Via Gamberale, 1
66010 S. Martino
sulla Marrucina (CH)
tel. 0871/85241

Gianni Masciarelli is the most entrepreneurial character on the Abruzzo wine scene. This intelligent and hard-headed "vigneron" has made rapid progress and, together with his wife Marina Cvetic, has prepared a range of wines which embody what has been termed "the modern Italian style" - a style of which they are, in a sense, the pioneer exponents in Abruzzo. The production consists of Montepulciano, Trebbiano d'Abruzzo and Cabernet Sauvignon, all aged in barrique (there is also a Chardonnay, not shown this year). The first of these wines, the excellent red Villa Gemma '92, goes beyond previous vintages in terms of complexity and concentration: apart from its opaque colour it offers a deep, yet elegant nose with liquorice and spice notes. On the palate, it is full-bodied, with firm tannins and a long, decidedly tarry finish. The Trebbiano Marina Cvetic '95 has an attractive and bright deep yellow colour, as well as rich aromas (flowers; candied fruit; a strong oaky toastiness). On the palate it has clean fruit with good acidity and overall balance. The Cabernet Sauvignon (again with the Marina Cvetic label) is full, and perfectly typed in its colour and black berry fruit aromas; it also has mildly vegetal notes, which are, however, pretty much dominated on the palate by the tannins and quite heavy use of oak. Less significant are the Trebbiano, the Cerasuolo Villa Gemma and the standard range, with the exception of the well made and well balanced Montepulciano d'Abruzzo.

●	Montepulciano d'Abruzzo Villa Gemma '92	🍷🍷🍷	4*
●	Cabernet Sauvignon Marina Cvetic '92	🍷🍷	4*
○	Trebbiano d'Abruzzo Marina Cvetic '95	🍷🍷	4*
●	Montepulciano d'Abruzzo '95	🍷	1*
○	Bianco Villa Gemma '96		3
⊙	Montepulciano d'Abruzzo Cerasuolo Villa Gemma '96		3
⊙	Rosato Masciarelli '96		1
○	Trebbiano d'Abruzzo '95		1
●	Montepulciano d'Abruzzo Villa Gemma '91	🍸🍸	3*
●	Montepulciano d'Abruzzo '94	🍸	2*

SPOLTORE (PE)

TOLLO (CH)

FATTORIA LA VALENTINA
VIA COLLE CESI,10
65010 SPOLTORE (PE)
TEL. 085/4478158

CANTINA TOLLO
V.LE GARIBALDI
66010 TOLLO (CH)
TEL. 0871/961726

Fattoria La Valentina is the third and last new entry from the region in this year's Guide. Once again this is a recently created winery (founded in 1990), run by a young entrepreneur, Sabatino Di Properzio. The Fattoria, which avails itself of the advice of consultant winemaker, Anselmo Paternoster, besides offering the classic range of Montepulciano, Cerasuolo and Trebbiano d'Abruzzo, all of which represent very good value for money, also produces a small selection of "vini da tavola" which were not available for us to taste. Of the wines we tasted blind, the Montepulciano d'Abruzzo '95 stood out, and was indeed superior to the Riserva '92: probably a sign of the continuous improvement of the winery. The former is ruby red with purple highlights, and with precise aromas of red berry fruits; it is full and well balanced, even if not particularly long. The latter, though showing excellent concentration and attractive scents of ripe cherries on the nose, seemed none too clean on the palate. Skipping over the Cerasuolo, which has a typical colour but which also displays excessive acidity and a rather bitter aftertaste, the basic Trebbiano d'Abruzzo (with light aromas and modest structure on the palate) and the Trebbiano Vigneto Spilla, the winery's most recently-released product, are both worthy of mention. In this last wine a percentage of sauvignon is added to the trebbiano. The wine has short maceration on the skins and also spends a brief period in barrique, with the aim of tempering the bouquet (pleasantly reminiscent of broom) and accentuating the flavour, which has nice acidity and good overall balance.

Cantina Tollo has shown the way, and now many of the cooperatives in the region are following its example of combining quantity with quality. Here one finds a high-calibre staff of oenologists headed up by the able Goffredo Agostini, state-of-the-art equipment and experimental fervour. Cantina Tollo produces wines which, in blind tastings, may not have the élan of the stars of the oenological firmament, but which do surprise us with a correctness and cleanness of execution which we have not often found, even in the wines of those who work with smaller (indeed far smaller) yields per hectare. Not to mention their value for money (only the Cagiòlo is over 10,000 lira a bottle). Let us start with the good Montepulciano d'Abruzzo Cerasuolo Valle d'Oro, one of the very few this year to respect in full the character of this wine: rich cherry colour; a fresh floral aroma; dry, soft and well-balanced, with a lightly bitter finish on the palate. From the same Valle d'Oro line (all at just over 4,000 lira) the Montepulciano (even if it does lose points for some residual carbon dioxide and for vaguely herbaceous aromas) and the Montepulciano Colle Secco Rubino both earn One Glass. The latter wine does not have a particularly clean nose but gains marks for its full, rustic but not unbalanced flavour. The Montepulciano Cagiòlo was the highest-scoring wine in the range. As usual it demonstrates the typical vigour of this wine, coupled with the right amount of concentration, and displays its elegance in its spicy aromas and in the full fruit on the palate. Among the whites, the Trebbiano d'Abruzzo Colle Secco is correct and true-to-type.

●	Montepulciano d'Abruzzo '95	🍷	2*
●	Montepulciano d'Abruzzo Ris. '92	🍷	2
○	Trebbiano d'Abruzzo Vigneto Spilla '96	🍷	2*
◉	Montepulciano d'Abruzzo Cerasuolo '96		2
○	Trebbiano d'Abruzzo '96		2

●	Montepulciano d'Abruzzo Cagiòlo '93	🍷	2*
◉	Montepulciano d'Abruzzo Cerasuolo Valle d'Oro '96	🍷	1*
●	Montepulciano d'Abruzzo Colle Secco Rubino '94	🍷	2*
●	Montepulciano d'Abruzzo Valle d'Oro '95	🍷	1*
◉	Montepulciano d'Abruzzo Cerasuolo Rocca Ventosa '96		1
●	Montepulciano d'Abruzzo Colle Secco '94		2
○	Trebbiano d'Abruzzo Colle Secco '96		2

OTHER WINERIES

The following producers obtained good scores in our tastings with one or more of their wines:.

PROVINCE OF CHIETI

Pasetti,
Francavilla a Mare, tel. 085/61875,
Testarossa '93

Santoleri,
Guardiagrele, tel. 0871/82250,
Montepulciano d'Abruzzo
Crognaleto Ris. '90,
Montepulciano d'Abruzzo
Crognaleto Ris. '94

Tenuta di Valletta,
Ripa Teatina, tel. 0871/390152,
Montepulciano Cenacolo
della Mezzanotte '94,
Laus Deo '94

PROVINCE OF PESCARA

Filomusi Guelfi,
Popoli, tel. 085/98353,
Le Scuderie del Cielo '96,
Montepulciano d'Abruzzo '95

Bosco,
Nocciano, tel. 085/847345,
Montepulciano d'Abruzzo '95,
Montepulciano d'Abruzzo Ris. '92

PROVINCE OF TERAMO

Barone Cornacchia,
Torano Nuovo,
tel. 0861/887412,
Poggio Varano '95

Lepore,
Colonnella,
tel. 0861/70860,
Montepulciano d'Abruzzo
Luigi Lepore Ris. '92

Costa del Monte,
Mosciano S. Angelo,
tel. 085/8071804,
Rosso della Cattedrale,
Moscatello '94

Pepe,
Torano Nuovo,
tel. 0861/856493,
Montepulciano d'Abruzzo Ris. '85,
Montepulciano d'Abruzzo Ris. '93

CAMPANIA

We have been repeating for some years now our comments on the positive developments in winemaking in Campania. This year we go further: we believe that Campania is currently Italy's fastest growing wine region. After decades of inactivity, an impressive number of producers have now made a firm commitment to premium wine production, and this is recognised in the Guide by an increase in the number of winery profiles, although it was not possible to include all the estates who might deserve a place. We are also confident for the future, since in many cases leadership is in the hands of a younger generation which seems to have rediscovered viticulture as career (and as a viable business activity!). By now the inclusion of highly qualified professionals such as agronomists and oenologists on the staff of wine estates is a widespread phenomenon. And the expansion of the quality wine sector is not limited to the production side; there is active consumer interest in local wines, an interest stimulated by both the restaurant and the specialist retail trade. Another aspect of recent developments is the way in which estates previously bound to local tradition almost to the point of stagnation have adopted modern approaches, with outstanding results. Examples in this category include D'Ambra of Ischia, Villa Matilde in Massico, Feudi di San Gregorio in Irpinia and many other of the top wineries in the region. Behind these successes, apart from the human factor, lies a wide range of excellent local varieties and soils and climate which made Campania one of the most important sources of wine production in the ancient world. For the second consecutive year however, it is not a local varietal which emerged as the region's top wine, but a red based on cabernet and merlot, with a 10 percent presence of aglianico, called Montevetrano. Hard on the heels of this great wine, and just below Three Glass award level however there are a number of wines from indigenous varieties; the Taurasi from Feudi di San Gregorio, Villa Matilde's Falerno Rosso, and the recent Fontana Galardi's Terra di Lavoro. The potential of the southern regions is becoming one of the key themes in modern Italian wine. We are only sorry that space does not allow us to give a place in this Guide to many other producers. We have had to be selective and have tended to give preference to new, emerging wineries in the belief that a healthy turn over reflects the vitality and the continuing evolution of this region and its wines.

ATRIPALDA (AV)

Antonio, Carlo e Pietro Mastroberardino
Via Manfredi, 75/81
83042 Atripalda (AV)
tel. 0825/626123

This year the products of this well-known winery from Atripalda are again correct and well balanced, as would be expected from a top estate like Mastroberardino, which has always been one of the leaders in local winemaking. And certainly it would take more than just a difficult vintage to dent the prestige of such a celebrated name. Among the wines tasted this year, the Taurasi '93 stands out in the rankings; intense, complex fruit and hints of spices on the nose; soft and elegant structure, harmonious and concentrated on the palate. In the Fiano di Avellino selections the special character of the grape and the estate's style are well expressed, and tastings of previous vintages confirm the qualities that emerge with time in these wines. The vintages still commercially available ('95, '94, '93, and '92) demonstrate not only the longevity of the wine but also the amount of hard work put into its production and promotion by the Mastroberardino family. The two Vesuvio wines, the Bianco and Rosso versions of the Lacryma Christi, were enjoyable and are also excellent value for money, as is the Lacrimarosa, a typical pale rosé which easily scored a One Glass rating. The Fiano Radici '96 is not quite up to last year's standards. We were used to thinking of it as an automatic Two Glass wine, but although it is a pleasant drink with soft vanilla on the nose, it seemed slightly past it and had rather high unassimilated acidity on the palate.

●	Taurasi Radici '93	TT	4
○	Fiano di Avellino Radici '96	T	4
⊙	Lacrimarosa '96	T	3
○	Lacryma Christi Bianco '96	T	3
●	Lacryma Christi Rosso '96	T	3
●	Aglianico d'Irpinia Avellanio '96		3
○	Falanghina Sireum '96		3
○	Greco di Tufo Novaserra '96		3
●	Taurasi Radici '90	YYY	4
○	Fiano di Avellino Radici '95	YY	4
○	Fiano di Avellino Vignadora '95	YY	4
●	Lacryma Christi Rosso '95	Y	3
●	Mastro Rosso '95	Y	2
●	Taurasi '91	Y	4

CASTELLABATE (SA)

San Giovanni
Loc. Punta Tresino
84071 Castellabate (SA)
tel. 089/224896

The San Giovanni estate is situated in one of the most charming, unspoilt areas of the Parco Nazionale del Cilento, at Punta Tresino in the commune of Castellabate. It belongs to the Corrado and Cammarano families who have succeeded in saving vineyards that otherwise would have been abandoned. The area planted with vines, which now covers four hectares, consists of a single terrace overlooking the sea which yields the equivalent of 15,000 bottles a year, although there are plans for its extension. The only wine presented by San Giovanni this year was a Fiano made from the grape of the same name with the addition of about 15 per cent greco and trebbiano. It made an excellent impression. It is not yet entitled to the Cilento appellation because it was made and bottled outside the DOC zone; due to restrictions on planning permission the owners have not yet managed to complete the construction of a cellar. The project are going ahead and a new winery facility should be ready for the '98 vintage. Returning to the wine, it has a rich concentration of ripe fruit aromas, with nuances of apple and vanilla. These flavours are again detectable on the palate which has plenty of body and good acidity. It is a wine which gives us a glimpse of the great potential in Cilento, and it is also very good value for money.

○	Fiano '96	TT	3*

CELLOLE (CE)

FURORE (SA)

VILLA MATILDE
S.S. DOMITIANA, KM. 4,700
81030 CELLOLE (CE)
TEL. 0823/932088-932134

CUOMO
VIA G.B. LAMA, 14
84010 FURORE (SA)
TEL. 089/830348 - 0336/610544

Villa Matilde is responsible for the rediscovery of Falerno, an important red wine which was sadly neglected up till a few years ago. The origins of this wine are as ancient as they are noble, and its re-establishment was the fervent ambition of Francesco Paolo Avallone, father of the actual owners, an ambition which in our opinion his sons have amply realised. The wines reflect the philosophy of the producer; elegant and sensitively made, they never disappoint. This year the production included a new release, a Falerno Rosso of exceptional power. Based on aglianico and piedirosso grapes, it is the first wine made by the top new consultant, Riccardo Cotarella and it demonstrates how well these two varieties work together. Although powerful it also has great elegance, with red berries and chocolate on the nose and a dense, concentrated beautifully textured palate. This is not the only news on the winemaking front: the Falerno Vigna Caracci, a single vineyard selection from 100 per cent falanghina grapes, this year has been aged in wood, which has lent complexity to this already excellent wine. The traditional Falerno Bianco is enjoyable, easy drinking, fresh, fruity and balanced. Also good quality is the Terre Cerase, a white obtained from aglianico vinified off the skins, and the Vigna Camarato, a traditional 100 per cent aglianico with elegant tannins, made only in the best years.

Cuomo is the result of the takeover by Andrea Ferraioli of the rival Gran Furor Divina Costiera winery, whose label is still used by the new company. The wines are remarkably consistent. Growers Andrea and his wife Marisa Cuomo immediately understood the need to meet the growing demand for quality. Their efforts to recover specialized vineyards and equip themselves with modern vinification facilities have been admirable. This is a winemaking zone of great potential but limited scale production due to the extremely difficult location of the vineyards literally quarried from the rocky cliff face. The two sub zones of this recent Costa d'Amalfi DOC are Ravello and Furore. The wines are made from bianca zita and bianca tenera, which are the local names for biancolella and falanghina. This year the Ravello got slightly higher marks in the tasting, with its pleasant flowery nose and fresh, grassy flavours. The Furore is a little thinner and lighter than last year's vintage, but it preserves all the wine's typical features. The reds too showed well, and are evidence of good winemaking: the Furore, from piedirosso and aglianico, reveals well defined, alcoholic aromas of red berries, with hints of vanilla as yet undeveloped. The aromas will unfold with bottle age.

● Falerno del Massico Rosso '96	♟♟	3
○ Falerno del Massico Vigna Caracci Bianco '96	♟♟	4
○ Falanghina '96	♟	1*
○ Falerno del Massico Bianco '96	♟	3
○ Terre Cerase '96	♟	3
● Vigna Camarato '90	♟	4
○ Eleusi Vendemmia Tardiva '95	♀	4
○ Falerno del Massico Bianco '95	♀	3
○ Falerno del Massico Campostellato '93	♀	4
● Falerno del Massico Rosso '93	♀	3
○ Falerno del Massico Vigna Caracci Bianco '95	♀	4
○ Pietre Bianche '95	♀	3

○ Costa d'Amalfi Furore Bianco '96	♟	3
● Costa d'Amalfi Furore Rosso '96	♟	3
○ Costa d'Amalfi Ravello '96	♟	3
○ Costa d'Amalfi Furore Bianco '95	♟♟	3*
● Costa d'Amalfi Furore Rosso '95	♀	3
○ Costa d'Amalfi Ravello '95	♀	3

GROTTOLELLA (AV)

GUARDIA SANFRAMONDI (BN)

MARIANNA
VIA FILANDE, 6
83030 GROTTOLELLA (AV)
TEL. 0825/627252

DE LUCIA
C.DA STARZE
82034 GUARDIA SANFRAMONDI (BN)
TEL. 0824/817705

The young producers from this winery in Irpinia, which only started to operate in 1995 but is already in the Guide, communicate an authentic passion for wine. Their premises are in what used to be an old winery, recently restored to its original purpose. The prime mover behind the revival is Ciriaco Coscia. His wines all have good balance and show personality, the most successful being the Fiano di Avellino '96, which has deservedly gained a Two Glass award for its clean, fruit aromas with honeyed, balsamic overtones, and its softness on the palate. This is followed by the Greco di Tufo. The colour here, with its pale greenish tints, is slightly lacking in intensity, but on the nose the wine is fresh and fruity with a hint of flowers. Altogether it is a pleasant, correctly made white. The two Irpinia IGT wines, the Bianco and the Rosso, have well-defined flavours. The first is made from fiano, coda di volpe and greco grapes, and the second from aglianico, piedirosso and sciascinoso. They are both original and enjoyable, although the Rosso, which is aged in chestnut casks for twelve months, is slightly superior. It is agreeable drinking with good aroma and good wood integration. Another wine worth a mention, the Ghirlandaio, made from fiano grapes and aged for a short time into oak barriques, is well made and should improve with future vintages.

The De Lucia cousins Enrico, Cosimo and Enrico (again) are young and enthusiastic producers, with a constant desire to improve. They are a good example of the trend towards quality in Campania which is leading to better expression of the region's winemaking potential. Their wines are also all excellent value for money. The Coda di Volpe, although correct and pleasant enough, did not seem as good as last year's which almost won a Two Glass award, but still deserves to be mentioned. The estate makes an interesting, quite rich Solopaca Bianco with fruit, honey and almonds on the nose and very gentle acidity. Also attractive are the Aglianico del Sannio Beneventano and the Solopaca Rosso. The first is a brilliant ruby colour with fresh red berries on the nose and good structure; the second is pleasant, easy drinking with a youthful zest which will soften with ageing. The other wines in the range, the Solopaca Falanghina and the Greco del Sannio Beneventano, are sound and well made. The Falanghina has intense flavours of honey and dried fruit and a good, smooth palate; the Greco has lots of fresh fruit and nutty aromas, while on the palate it is fresh, soft and long.

○ Fiano d'Avellino '96	🍷🍷	4
○ Greco di Tufo '96	🍷	3
● Irpinia Rosso Plinio il Giovane '95	🍷	3
○ Fiano d'Avellino '95		4
○ Fiano d'Avellino Ghirlandaio '95		4
○ Greco di Tufo '95		3
○ Irpinia Bianco '96		3

● Aglianico del Sannio Beneventano '96	🍷	3
○ Greco del Sannio Beneventano '96	🍷	3
○ Solopaca Bianco '96	🍷	2*
○ Solopaca Falanghina '96	🍷	3
● Solopaca Rosso '96	🍷	2*
○ Coda di Volpe del Sannio Beneventano '96		3
○ Coda di Volpe del Sannio Beneventano '95	🍷	3
○ Greco del Sannio Beneventano '95	🍷	3
○ Solopaca Bianco Vigna Pezzalonga '95	🍷	2*
○ Solopaca Falanghina '95	🍷	2*
● Solopaca Rosso '95	🍷	2*

LAPIO (AV)

CLELIA ROMANO
FRAZ. ARIANIELLO
83030 LAPIO (AV)
TEL. 0825/982191-982184

Clelia Romano's Fiano comes from Lapio, one of the best areas for this variety, from a vineyard which for years has yielded rich and concentrated grapes, so it was easy to foresee its success even the first time we tasted it last year. This year's tastings, although the wine is still very young and shows lack of balance, provided confirmation of its quality. And in fact returning to it subsequently we have already found greater softness and balance. Wines like these are undoubtedly at their best with a certain amount of bottle age and it is a pity to drink them too soon, before they can show their best. Cellar practices at the winery are good but could be improved. Pneumatic presses and modern bottling plants have not yet appeared here, but the important thing is that temperature control and overall hygiene are optimal, even if the traditional press will not be easily replaced. For the moment success is sweet and a more progressive approach to vinification can wait. The wine is a brilliant straw yellow with greenish tints, and ripe fruit and pear on the nose; in the mouth it is richly textured, fairly acid and high in extract. There is pronounced dried fruit on the aftertaste and a delicate toastiness.

MANOCALZATI (AV)

VEGA - D'ANTICHE TERRE
C.DA LO PIANO
S.S. 7 BIS
83030 MANOCALZATI (AV)
TEL. 0825/675358

Thanks to increased application and old fashioned hard work, this Irpinia estate has managed within the space of a few years to establish a reputation for quality which is confirmed by this year's tastings. It is a family-run estate: Gaetano Ciccarella and Carmine Cornacchia, profiting from their past experience, are in charge of production while the rest of the family deals with the commercial side. Another important member of the partnership is Saverio Landoli, who is in charge of vineyard management. There are currently 35 hectares in production, yields are limited and methods are applied to restrict as far as possible the use of agrochemicals, with consequent advantages for total quality. The most surprising wine was the Fiano di Avellino which has fresh, fruity-vegetal aromas, and is soft on the palate with a slight flavour of bitter almonds and hazelnuts; a smooth, finely structured, white. The other wines are all good quality and all fully worth a mention, starting with the Greco di Tufo, with its delicate fruit and scents of honey, good balance of flavours in the mouth and slightly bitter finish. The red, made from aglianico grapes, is also appealing. It has intense, fresh aromas of soft fruit which reappear on the plate together with supple tannins. The Irpinia Bianco is just as agreeable, with its light, flowery-herbal nose and dry, well flavoured palate. We must wait until next year to try the first vintage of the Taurasi, which is currently maturing in the new barrel cellar in Manocalzati.

O Fiano di Avellino '96	ΨΨ	3*
O Fiano di Avellino '95	ΨΨ	4

O Fiano di Avellino '96	ΨΨ	4
● Coriliano '96	Ψ	2
O Eliseo di Serra '96	Ψ	3
O Greco di Tufo '96	Ψ	3
O Eliseo di Serra '95	Ψ	3
O Fiano di Avellino '95	Ψ	4
O Greco di Tufo '95	Ψ	3

MONTEFREDANE (AV)

VADIAPERTI
C.DA VADIAPERTI
FRAZ. ARCELLA
83030 MONTEFREDANE (AV)
TEL. 0825/36263-607270

Antonio Troisi's efforts to bring out the true character of Irpinia's wines are thoroughly praiseworthy. Aware of the ageing potential of Fiano di Avellino and Greco di Tufo, he has for some time been experimenting with long periods of maturation for white wines, investing considerable sums in this project. We are sure that the results of this policy will not be long in coming; for some years now older vintages of the professor's Greco and Fiano have been sought after by wine lovers and dealers. At the tasting this year the great charm of these first-rate whites, which are still commercially available, was fully appreciated. This year's wines are also of excellent quality, beginning with the Fiano di Avellino, which as always reveals personality and elegance. The new release from the '96 vintage is a magnificent 100 per cent Coda di Volpe. The Fiano is highly individual, powerful and well-textured, with its intense nutty, honeyed and biscuity flavours; it has great freshness and, of course, longevity. The Coda di Volpe has great appeal both on the nose which is intense and flowery with delicious fruity scents and hints of vanilla, and on the palate, where it displays excellent structure and balance. It is an elegant wine and easily wins a Two Glass award. The Greco di Tufo this year is not at the level of past vintages. It reveals its usual good structure but it is a little over mature. We confirm our assesment of the previous vintages, which on retasting prove to have gained in elegance and complexity.

MONTEFUSCO (AV)

VIGNADORA
VIA SERRA
83030 MONTEFUSCO (AV)
TEL. 0825/968215-963022

Vignadora, which belongs to the Mastroberardino brothers Paolo and Lucio and their sister Daniela, has reached its third vintage, confirming all expectations with wines of excellent quality. This estate has only been established for a few years but can draw on a store of experience at the highest levels of winemaking in Campania. With over 120 hectares of land in the various traditional DOC zones of Campania, it is a winery from which we expect great things. Vineyard management follows modern methods such as increased density planting, up to around 3,000 vines per hectare, and vertical training systems on the double Guyot model. The wines tasted this year can already be appreciated for their elegance. The Fiano di Avellino and the Greco di Tufo Loggia della Serra we found excellent. The first has intense, plum and apricot flavours with hints of sage, and softness on the palate. The Greco di Tufo Loggia della Serra displays marked personality. It is obtained from the vineyards of Montefusco, of ancient vinegrowing fame, at an altitude of 600 metres; fresh, fruity and slightly floral on the nose, and smooth, creamy and long on the palate. The Fiano di Avellino Vignadora almost achieved a Two Glass rating with its delightful aroma. The basic Greco di Tufo, the Vignadangelo, Aglianico and Falanghina are all sound wines which complete a most interesting range. We look forward to the future vintages of Taurasi.

O Coda di Volpe '96		♥♥	3*
O Fiano di Avellino '96		♥♥	4
O Greco di Tufo '96		♥	3
O Greco di Tufo Federico II '95		♥	4
O Fiano di Avellino Arechi '95			4
O Fiano di Avellino '93		♥♥	5
O Fiano di Avellino '94		♥♥	4
O Fiano di Avellino '95		♥♥	4
O Greco di Tufo			
Vigna del Principato '94		♥♥	4
O Greco di Tufo '95		♥	3

O Fiano di Avellino '96		♥♥	4
O Greco di Tufo			
Loggia della Serra '96		♥♥	3
O Fiano di Avellino Vignadora '96		♥	4
O Greco di Tufo '96		♥	3
⊙ Irpinia Rosato '96		♥	3
O Greco di Tufo Vignadangelo '96			3
O Fiano di Avellino '95		♥♥	4
O Fiano di Avellino Vignadora '95		♥	4
O Greco di Tufo '95		♥	3
O Greco di Tufo			
Loggia della Serra '95		♥	3
O Greco di Tufo Vignadangelo '95		♥	3

PANZA D'ISCHIA (NA)

D'Ambra Vini d'Ischia
Via Mario D'Ambra, SS 270
80070 Panza d'Ischia (NA)
tel. 081/907210-907246

D'Ambra of Ischia is firmly established as one of the most representative producers on the regional winemaking scene. This is above all due to consistent quality and the ability to harness the potential of the viticulture on Ischia. Winegrowing is still full of life on the island, with around 4,000 people working the beautiful vineyards which have earned Ischia the name "isola verde". At the tastings this year the Biancolella Tenuta Frassitelli again stood out. With its fresh and balanced aromas, delicate herbal overtones, its richness of extract, soft palate and pronounced length it is one of the best whites of the region. The Forastera, from the grape of the same name, is also very attractive, with complex, fruity aromas harmonising with the smooth and well balanced palate. The Biancolella Vigne di Piellero has lots of fruit and flowery nuances on the nose, good structure, softness and very appealing flavours. Another excellent '96 white, the Forastera Vigna Cimentorosso, has soft, mature fruit and a pronounced but enjoyable acidity which should develop interestingly with age. The basic Biancolella is also a captivating wine with its clean scents and freshness on the palate, and the Verdolino, with its rich tropical fruit, is delightful. Both the basic version and the Montecorvo cru of the Per'e Palummo seemed slightly below par compared to previous years.

○	Biancolella Tenuta Frassitelli '96	🍷🍷	4
○	Biancolella Vigne di Piellero '96	🍷🍷	3
○	Ischia Forastera '96	🍷🍷	2*
○	Forastera Vigna Cimentorosso '96	🍷	3
○	Ischia Biancolella '96	🍷	2*
●	Per'e Palummo Tenuta Montecorvo '96	🍷	4
○	Verdolino '96	🍷	2*
●	Ischia Per'e Palummo '96		3
○	Biancolella Tenuta Frassitelli '95	🍸🍸	4
●	Per'e Palummo Tenuta Montecorvo '94	🍸🍸	4
○	Kalimera Brut dell'Isola d'Ischia	🍸	4

PONTE (BN)

Ocone
Via del Monte
82030 Ponte (BN)
tel. 0824/874040-874328

The Ocone family has been producing fine wines in the Sannio area since the beginning of the century. Domenico Ocone, who is the estate's top man, has within the last few years carried out extensive alterations to the cellar, with is now complete with the most up-to-date equipment. Surrounding it, in an excellent position at the foot of Monte Taburno, are the estate's ten hectares of vineyard which provide the local varieties from which the wines are produced. Domenico's declared objective is to bring out the potential of his native soil and its grapes. At our tastings this year the best wine was the Aglianico del Taburno '94. This is a good dark ruby colour with purplish tints and its aromas of soft red fruit are fresh and intense with herbal overtones and hints of vanilla. On the palate it comes over as an exemplary southern red: it is mouth-filling, well structured and soft, with a good acid bite and plenty of tannin, but at the same time very finely textured. It is a wine for long ageing and gives us an indication of what Campania's reds could be like in the future. The rest of the wines, in our opinion, do not do justice to the estate's potential. The '96 vintages of the Greco and the Falanghina are pleasant and correct but unexciting. Since the validity of the raw material is beyond question, perhaps it is the timing and the methods of harvesting or the subsequent vinification which need looking at. After tasting the Piedirosso, the Falanghina cru Vigna del Monaco and the Coda di Volpe, this seems to be a high priority.

●	Taburno Aglianico '94	🍷🍷	4
○	Falanghina del Taburno '96	🍷	3
○	Greco del Taburno '96	🍷	3
○	Coda di Volpe del Taburno '96		3
○	Falanghina del Taburno Vigna del Monaco '96		4
●	Piedirosso del Taburno '96		3
●	Aglianico del Sannio Vigna Pezza la Corte '91	🍸🍸	4
●	Aglianico del Sannio Vigna Pezza la Corte '93	🍸🍸	4

QUARTO (NA)

S. AGATA DEI GOTI (BN)

CANTINE GROTTA DEL SOLE
VIA SPINELLI
80010 QUARTO (NA)
TEL. 081/8769470

MUSTILLI
VIA DEI FIORI, 20
82019 S. AGATA DEI GOTI (BN)
TEL. 0823/717433

The Martusciello family has been involved in winemaking for over a century. Since 1989 it has taken on the difficult task of promoting the winegrowing potential of the Campi Flagrei zone, where it has established an ultra-modern winery. The new cellar came into operation in 1992, its first priority being the important recovery of two grape varieties grown in the area since ancient times: falanghina and piedirosso. The credit for this piece of viticultural archeology is mainly due to Gennaro Martusciello, a sensitive and meticulous oenologist. Two other traditional Neapolitan wines are to be found among those produced by the Cantina Grotta del Sole, Lettere and Gragnano, from two small towns in the Lattari hills. These are followed by two classics, the Lacryma Christi del Vesuvio and the Asprinio, which come from traditional vineyards at Agro Aversano. The cellar turns out about 700,000 bottles and has ultra-modern equipment for sparkling wine-making. The wines tasted are all of consistently high standard, correct and well balanced. The Falanghina dei Campi Flegrei was typically fruity and the Asprinio di Aversa had pleasant acidity and floral aromas. Finally the two sparkling wines: the Asprinio di Aversa Brut, fresh and fragrant, and the Metodo Classico Millesimato, with its yeasty aromas of toasted bread are further evidence of what is all in all an extremely promising start.

In the last edition we noticed a slight drop in the quality of the wines of this well-know estate, which can claim amongst other things to have promoted the commercial revival of the falanghina grape, grown in the region since Roman times. Vintages variations are one thing, but independent of the year the richness of aroma, the sound structure and the technical perfection once displayed by Mustilli's wines are becoming less and less discernible. Only three wines this year scored over 70 points: the Piedirosso '95, the Aglianico Conte Artus '94 and the Greco di Primicerio'96. The first is a dark ruby colour, with intense aromas of soft fruit, vanilla and toast. Structure is good on the palate, and although it still needs to open out it promises well. The Conte Artus, from aglianico and piedirosso, lacks this texture and has pronounced grassy aromas, but it is still clean, enjoyable drinking. The whites, with the exception of the correctly made Greco di Primicerio, all show some fault, either over-filtration further impoverishing wines that are already light in structure, or imperfection of aroma, with off-odours due to refermentation or lack of barrel hygiene (as noticed in the Greco). We advise a serious review of cellar procedures in general. It would be a pity if an estate like this were to be left behind in the modernisation taking place in the best cellars of the region.

O	Asprinio d'Aversa '96	♟	3	O	S. Agata dei Goti Greco di Primicerio '96	♟	4
O	Asprinio d'Aversa Brut	♟	3	●	S. Agata dei Goti Piedirosso '95	♟	3
O	Campi Flegrei Falanghina '96	♟	3	●	S. Agata dei Goti Rosso Conte Artus '95	♟	4
O	Grotta del Sole Extra Brut '91	♟	4	O	S. Agata dei Goti Falanghina '96		3
●	Gragnano '96		3	O	S. Agata dei Goti Greco '96		3
O	Greco di Tufo '96		3	●	Vigna Cesco di Nece '91	♟♟	3
●	Lacryma Christi Rosso '95		3	O	Greco di S. Agata dei Goti '95	♟	2
●	Lettere '96		3	O	Greco di S. Agata dei Goti Vigna Fontanella '95	♟	3
O	Talea Bianco '96		2				

S. CIPRIANO PICENTINO (SA)   SALZA IRPINA (AV)

MONTEVETRANO
VIA MONTEVETRANO
84099 S. CIPRIANO PICENTINO (SA)
TEL. 089/882285

DI MEO
C.DA COCCOVONI, 1
83050 SALZA IRPINA (AV)
TEL. 0825/981419

Silvia Imparato, after getting off to a flying start and surviving the flood of demands following the success of her superb wines, has again achieved an outstanding quality with another delectable Montevetrano, vintage '95. We remember everybody being stunned by the '93 and many foreseeing as a result of tasting it new horizons for a zone hitherto unknown for winegrowing. The 3,000 or so bottles of that unforgettable red have increased to 6,500, and the numbers will rise again when the new vineyards are in production. The blend is the same: 60 per cent cabernet sauvignon, 30 per cent merlot and 10 per cent aglianico. Montevetrano is one of the top creations, and one of the first in chronological order, of the celebrated Umbrian oenologist Riccardo Cotarella, who has succeeded in producing a wine with even greater finesse and elegance than in the previous vintages. Dark ruby in colour, it has intense aromas of cherries and blackberries, with vanilla and tobacco overtones; the palate has spiciness with good structure, elegant tannins and wonderful length. A year later, another success meriting the Three Glass award. Above all we have the satisfaction of seeing the great potential of the South finally expressed.

The Di Meo brothers run their recently established estate with enthusiasm, but not without difficulties. Their wines are always of a good standard, as past tastings have shown, but they are finding it hard to achieve the decisive quality leap which in our opinion they are capable of. The Taurasi, released for the first time this year, earned good marks at the tasting and scored over 70 points, with its ruby colour, and aromas of cherry and oak on the nose, with slight herbal tones. On the palate it has length and freshness with good fruit, and fine, balanced tannins. The Greco di Tufo is enjoyably fruity, with fresh notes of pear, aromatic herbs and spices; it is delicate in the mouth with a slight bitterish note on the finish, typical of this wine. The Fiano di Avellino when tasted in May lacked harmony but its positive evolution after some months scored it a few more points. It is a traditionally made wine with ripe fruit on the nose and typical nutty, toasty aromas in marked evidence on the palate. An original red is the Vigna Olmo '94 which has ripe cherry on the nose, and on the palate is warm, tannic, soft and balanced.

● Montevetrano '95	♟♟♟	5
● Montevetrano '93	♟♟♟	5
● Montevetrano '94	♟♟	5

○ Greco di Tufo '96	♟	3
● Taurasi '93	♟	5
● Vigna Olmo Rosso '94	♟	2
○ Fiano di Avellino '96		4
○ Vigna Olmo Bianco '96		3
○ Fiano di Avellino '95	♟	4
○ Greco di Tufo '95	♟	3
○ Greco di Tufo Vigna Vittoria '95	♟	3
● Vigna Olmo Rosso '92	♟	4

SESSA AURUNCA (CE)

FONTANA GALARDI
VIA PROV.LE
FRAZ. SAN CARLO
81030 SESSA AURUNCA (CE)
TEL. 06/4741190 - 0823/708034

Fontana Galardi is one of the most interesting new entries of the Guide. It is a magnificent property which used to be part of a large landed estate. Some of the inheritors, with a passion for wine in common, decided to join forces and some years ago, where there used to be woods and a hazel grove, they planted the first vineyards. It is 500 metres up on the south-east slope of the volcano of Roccamonfina, where the view stretches over the gulf of Gaeta. Roberto and Maria Luisa Selvaggi, Arturo and Dora Celentano, together with Francesco Catello and convinced of the potential of this "terroir", employed the services of consultant oenologist Riccardo Cotarella. The result was the Terra di Lavoro, a top quality and proudly southern red from aglianico grapes supplemented by piedirosso and just a little merlot. The wine is called after the former name for this area, roughly corresponding to the present province of Caserta, during the reign of the Two Sicilies. For the moment just three hectares of vineyard are in production, but these will increase to about 12 in the next two to three years. The '94 is a good dark ruby in colour, with intense, captivating aromas of ripe berries, elegantly assimilated with the spicy notes of new wood, while on the palate it is powerful and concentrated with refined tannins. In short, an important first appearance underpinned by barrel tastings of the excellent '95 and '96 vintages. It only remains to wait.

SORBO SERPICO (AV)

FEUDI DI SAN GREGORIO
LOC. CERZA GROSSA
83050 SORBO SERPICO (AV)
TEL. 0825/986266-986230

The estate of Feudi di San Gregorio is one of the cornerstones of the oenological revival in Campania. Founded with the aid of government grants for private enterprise in the south, it has managed in a short space of time to achieve significant results, giving prime importance to the use of the most up-to-date technology. All this is due to the Ercolino brothers: Enzo, the estate's leading force, Mario, oenologist, and Luciano, in charge of the business side. This year both the reds and the whites scored high marks in our tastings. The Taurasi '93 is rich and elegant, traditional but also with modern character, revealing once more the potential of the grape and terroir of Irpinia. This potential shows up again in one of the novelties of this edition, the Serpico '95, a wonderfully textured red from aglianico, piedirosso and a small amount of sangiovese, matured in oak barriques. These wines are flanked by the estate's classic range of whites which now includes a series of new labels. Alongside the Fiano '96, one of the best of this year, are the excellent Pietracalda and Pian delle Vigne which at their first release both score Two Glass ratings. The basic Greco di Tufo was unexciting this year, but the Camigliano cru wins Two Glasses and so does the Campanaro, an unusually full-bodied blend of fiano and greco. In 1998 the release of another Greco cru, the Cutizzi, is expected, as well as a Taurasi Piano di Montevergine and a dessert wine the Privilegio, from botrytis affected fiano grapes.

● Terra di Lavoro '94	♟♟	5

○ Campanaro '96	♟♟	5
○ Fiano di Avellino '96	♟♟	4
○ Fiano di Avellino Pian delle Vigne '96	♟♟	4
○ Fiano di Avellino Pietracalda '96	♟♟	4
○ Greco di Tufo Camigliano '96	♟♟	4
● Serpico '95	♟♟	6
○ Falanghina '96	♟	3*
○ Greco di Tufo '96	♟	3
● Rubrato '96	♟	2
● Taurasi '93	♟	4
○ Albente '96		2
○ Fiano di Avellino '95	♟♟	4
● Taurasi '91	♟♟	4
● Taurasi '92	♟♟	4

TAURASI (AV)

TRAMONTI (SA)

ANTONIO CAGGIANO
C.DA SALA
84030 TAURASI (AV)
TEL. 0827/74043

GIUSEPPE APICELLA
VIA CASTELLO S. MARIA, 1
FRAZ. CAPITIGNANO
84010 TRAMONTI (SA)
TEL. 089/876075

Along with the increasing successes of the newly modernised Irpinia estates, it is a pleasure to present a producer from the wonderful area of Taurasi. This estate was founded a few years ago thanks to the will power and dedication of Antonio Caggiano, a very unusual person who loves a tough challenge. For the moment the wines he produces are vini da tavola, but 1998 should see the release of a Taurasi DOCG '94 which we are looking forward to with interest, after tasting the most recent vintages. The Saledomini, a 100 per cent aglianico, is aged in new French oak barriques; the Taurì is made from a blend of 80 per cent aglianico, 15 per cent piedirosso and 5 per cent fiano; and as can be guessed from the name, the Fiagrè is a blend of 70 per cent fiano and the rest greco. The former wine has intense aromas of soft fruit, while on the palate it has good texture and is soft and long-lasting. The Fiagrè is fresh and fruity on the nose, with pronounced apricot jam aromas and spicy overtones; it is soft, balanced and long on the palate. Both wines earn their Two Glasses, although the complex and interesting Taurì was the biggest surprise. The separate vinification of the grapes and barrique ageing lend a fruity, elegant structure to the wine, which is long and vigorous on the palate. The estate is a worthy newcomer to the Guide. We must hope that the eagerly-awaited Taurasi will be worthy of the estate.

This small estate is a new entry this year. It is located in lush green hills with vineyards a few kilometres from the sea at Maiori. Giuseppe Apicella, the owner, is helped to run the estate by all his family. He is an artisan winegrower who little by little has succeeded in creating a highly individual wine. In spite of difficulties, over the last few years he has made radical alterations to his small, old-fashioned cellar in order to fit it out with all the modern vinification equipment and give a proper reception to his frequent visitors. The wine which impressed us most, as a faithful expression of the terroir, is the Costa d'Amalfi Tramonti Rosso, made from aglianico (called tintore here) and piedirosso. It is freshly scented with agreeable notes of tobacco and soft fruit. On the palate it is densely-textured, fragrant, with fruity aromas and elegant tannins. From the Santa Marina vineyard, with its modern, vertically trained vines, Apicella produces his Costa d'Amalfi Tramonti Bianco. Made from biancolella and falanghina plus some local varieties, it is straw coloured with golden tints, with berries and aromatic herbs on the nose; on the palate it is tasty, correctly made and good easy drinking. The Rosé, made from piedirosso, completes this entry.

O Fiagrè '96	▼▼	3
● Taurì '95	▼▼	3*
● Saledomini '95	▼	5

● Costa d'Amalfi Tramonti Rosso '95	▼▼	2*
⊙ Costa d'Amalfi Rosato '96		2
O Costa d'Amalfi Tramonti Bianco Vigna Santa Maria '96		2

VENTICANO (AV)

GIOVANNI STRUZZIERO
VIA L. CADORNA, 214/216
83030 VENTICANO (AV)
TEL. 0825/965065

After a few years' absence Struzziero has returned to the Guide. Founded in 1928, this is one of Irpinia's historic estates. Among the wines for tasting this year the Taurasi Campo Ceraso '92 stood out with its dark ruby colour, and intense aromas of ripe berries. On the palate it has concentrated fruit, hints of tobacco and soft tannins. The Greco di Tufo Villa Giulia '96 also seemed exceptionally good, a pale, brilliant straw yellow with golden tints. It is broad on the nose with fruity, citrusy flavours and hints of spiciness and orange flowers. On the palate it is fresh, round and fruity with length and good structure. The Fiano di Avellino of the same year maintains a good enough level to score One Glass; the nose is broad and grassy and the structure satisfactory but it is slightly lacking in balance and length. Even if the other wines do not achieve more than an honourable mention, they are enjoyable and correctly made, and this goes particularly for the basic Greco di Tufo and the Falanghina del Sannio Beneventano. The sparkling Greco di Tufo Metodo Classico scored just under 70 points. It is pleasant to drink and rare, few other producers in Irpinia attempting this style of wine. The estate also presented a Taurasi Riserva '89 which we mention for its good structure, rich extract and unusual complexity, with spicy, chocolatey aromas and hints of tobacco. This red has already reached its peak, but drunk now can be very satisfying.

VITULAZIO (CE)

VILLA SAN MICHELE
VIA APPIA, KM. 198
81050 VITULAZIO (CE)
TEL. 0823/963775

Villa San Michele is on the Appian Way a few kilometres from Capua, in a particularly attractive area facing towards Mount Vesuvius. This is the estate's first appearance in the Guide for its interesting and reliable wines, the result of good vineyard management and sound vinification. Renovation has recently been carried out both in the old villa, the estate's administrative centre, and in the vineyards, under the guidance of the Arboreal Institute of Naples university. Campania's classic varieties are grown here: greco, falanghina, piedirosso, and aglianico, all vinified as monovarietals. Villa San Michele's sparkling wines have a long standing tradition and the ones we tasted this year, the Don Carlos Brut and the Don Carlos Demi-Sec, both made by the Metodo Classico, are attractive and elegant. The Brut is vinified from pinot bianco, greco and chardonnay; it has yeasty aromas on the nose, and good structure and freshness on the palate. The second wine is a blend of pinot bianco and chardonnay and is softer and rounder with a very appealing fruit. The vineyards are on soils of volcanic origin, marls mixed with clay, yielding grapes with a high concentration. This is reflected in the wine we found most impressive this year, the Greco Terre del Volturno. This IGT stands out for its fruit aroma and its abundant flowery overtones on the nose and palate, which is soft and fresh with the slight bitterish finish typical of the grape. We also liked the Falanghina Terre del Volturno with its elegant, balanced fruit.

O	Greco di Tufo Villa Giulia '96	🍷🍷	3	O	Greco Terre del Volturno '96	🍷🍷	3
●	Taurasi Campoceraso '92	🍷🍷	4	O	Don Carlos Brut	🍷	4
O	Fiano di Avellino '96	🍷	4	O	Don Carlos Demi-Sec	🍷	4
O	Falanghina '96		2	O	Falanghina		
O	Greco di Tufo '96		3		Terre del Volturno '96	🍷	2*
O	Greco di Tufo Spumante M. Cl.		5	●	Aglianico Terre del Volturno '95		2
●	Taurasi '89		5	●	Piedirosso		
					Terre del Volturno '96		2

OTHER WINERIES

The following producers obtained good scores in our tastings with one or more of their wines:

PROVINCE OF AVELLINO

Nicola Romano,
Lapio, tel. 0825/982189,
Fiano di Avellino '96

Mollettieri,
Montemarano, tel. 0827/63722,
Taurasi '93

Montesole,
Montemileto, tel. 0825/963972,
Fiano di Avellino '96,
Greco di Tufo '96

Casa dell'Orco,
Pratola Serra, tel. 0825/967038,
Greco di Tufo '96,
Fiano di Avellino '96

Azienda Agricola Giulia,
Principato Ultra, tel. 0825/961219,
Greco di Tufo '96,
Fiano di Avellino '96

Cantina dei Monaci,
Santa Paolina, tel. 0825/964350,
Greco di Tufo '96

PROVINCE OF BENEVENTO

Antica Masseria Venditti,
Castelvenere, tel. 0824/940306,
Solopaca Bianco Vigna Bacalàt '96,
Solopaca Bianco Vigna Foresta '96

Fattoria Torre Gaia,
Dugenta, tel. 0824/9781172,
Bianco Dugenta '96,
Asprinio di Aversa '96

Cantina del Taburno,
Foglianise, tel. 0824/871338,
Taburno Greco '96

Cantina S. di Solopaca,
Solopaca, tel. 0824/97792,
Solopaca Aglianico '93

PROVINCE OF CASERTA

Moio,
Mondragone, tel. 0823/978017,
Falerno del Massico Rosso '94

Cantine Caputo,
Teverola, tel. 081/5033955,
Asprinio d'Aversa '96,
Lacryma Christi Bianco'96,
Lacryma Christi Rosso '95,
Aglianico Terre al Volturno '95

Cicala, Teverola,
tel. 081/8118103,
Asprinio di Aversa '96,
Falanghina del Sannio Beneventano '96,
Aglianico d'Irpinia San Sabino '95

PROVINCE OF NAPOLI

Sorrentino,
Boscotrecase, tel. 081/8584194,
Fior di Ginestra '95,
Lacryma Christi Bianco '96

Caprense,
Capri, tel. 081/8376835,
Capri Rosso Solaro '95,
Capri Bianco Bordo '96

PROVINCE OF SALERNO

De Conciliis,
Prignano Cilento, tel. 0974/831090,
Vigna Perella '96,
Donna Luna '96

Episcopio,
Ravello, tel. 089/857244,
Costa d'Amalfi Ravello Bianco '96,
Costa d'Amalfi Ravello Rosso '95

Sammarco,
Ravello, tel. 089/872774,
Costa d'Amalfi Ravello Bianco '96,
Costa d'Amalfi Ravello Rosso
Selva delle Monache '95

Lia Giannella,
San Marco di Castellabate, tel. 0974/966345,
Kratos '96

BASILICATA

Unlike neighbouring Campania, this region has not witnessed a great deal of change in recent years. The production remain essentially red and is almost all bottled as Aglianico del Vulture, the region's only DOC. The names to be mentioned are therefore well-known, the historic ones of the local wine industry: D'Angelo, Sasso, Marino and Paternoster among independent producers and the cooperatives of Rionero in Vulture, Barile and Venosa. These wineries vinify almost all of Basilicata's wines, which they generally offer in the dry version, which may occasionally be fizzy and, more rarely, as a sparkling wine, which may be more or less sweet. From the point of view of quality, the potential for these wines is enormous: aglianico has always been recognized as one of the great Southern Italian varieties, which is capable of making powerful and long-lived reds. The wines of D'Angelo and Paternoster show the quest for a more modern style and are the result of experimentation with new wood and longer maturation and ageing periods. There are also interesting new wines from the Cooperative wineries. The Barile producers' Consorzio and the Cantina della Riforma Fondiaria di Venosa offer attractive and persuasive wines at the basic level, products which are also notable for their excellent price/quality ratio. And, considering the rather unhappy weather conditions experienced during the '94 growing season, the wines we tasted indicate that Basilicata could be capable of great things. If the basic Aglianico del Vulture from these wineries is so good, what is one to say, then, about special selections such as the Carato Venusio and the Carpe Diem? These are wines with strong varietal character which underline the huge potential of the region. We are sure Basilicata will enjoy proper recognition in the not too distant future, but much depends on the successful application of the research and hard work that is currently going on in the region. The quality-led approach followed by the independent producers' is exemplified by Paternoster. Last year they did not present their freshly-bottled Aglianico '94, but this year this delicious wine drew approval for its style, complexity and balance. It is an excellent representative of the overall standard of quality which Basilicata may well be capable of. Paternoster's Don Anselmo and D'Angelo's Canneto have now become international ambassadors for this small but increasingly significant wine growing region. They are, we must repeat, the results of the hard work and dedication of two independent producers. But we are also convinced that they are the major expressions of a general trend, which encapsulates the dynamism and best efforts of this region.

BARILE (PZ)

Consorzio Viticoltori Associati del Vulture

S.S. 93
85022 Barile (PZ)
tel. 0972/770386

The Consorzio dei Viticoltori Associati del Vulture in Barile returns to the Guide after some years' absence. It is a group which consists of five cooperative wineries, covering a vast area that includes some fifteen communes in Basilicata. The hilly production zones are of volcanic origin. The consortium's principal winery is equipped with modern winemaking plant capable of yielding 80,000 hectolitres of wine a year, a volume which makes the Consorzio a giant among Aglianico del Vulture producers. Carpe Diem is a special selection of Aglianico that highly-skilled oenologist Sergio Paternoster makes from his suppliers' best vineyards. Aged in oak barrels, the wine has an opaque ruby colour, while the nose has frank red berry fruit aromas, with notes of chocolate and balsamic herbs. On the palate, it is round, tannic and has excellent aromatic length. Also good is the Aglianico del Vulture '94: an attractive and well-structured wine, with hints of ripe red berry fruits, warming on the palate thanks to its great alcoholic strength. It is a mature and complex wine, which fully deserves its One Glass rating. Another interesting wine in the range is the sparkling Ellenico, again made from aglianico grapes, which is gently medium-sweet as local tradition dictates. A traditional and appealing sparkling Moscato completes the range of this large winery group.

●	Aglianico del Vulture Carpe Diem '93	▼▼	3*
●	Aglianico del Vulture '94	▼	2*
●	Aglianico Spumante Ellenico '96		2
○	Moscato Spumante '96		2

BARILE (PZ)

Paternoster

Via Nazionale, 23
85022 Barile (PZ)
tel. 0972/770224-770658

The unusual name of the place where this winery is located, Barile (which means "barrel" in Italian), is in itself a charming invitation for a wine lover to visit an area which has, for centuries, been devoted to viticulture and winemaking. The Paternoster family has been vinifying aglianico grapes since the 1920s, and with each new harvest presents reds which more than live up to our expectations. The third generation is even more geared towards quality than ever, as is demonstrated by even the winery's most simple and straightforward wines. The range of products includes, first of all, the standard Aglianico del Vulture, which in the '94 version has a fresh and vegetal nose, with distinct forest fruit notes; on the palate, it has good acidity and fine, elegant tannins. This is a complex and soft wine with good potential for improving with bottle-age. The more prestigious special selection, the famous Don Anselmo, in the '92 vintage has soft, attractive character, but is perhaps a bit over-mature. The Barigliott is another red from aglianico grapes; its '96 vintage shows particular liveliness and freshness. Testifying to the versatility of this grape variety, there is also the Antico, a sparkling Aglianico which is straightforward but has good fruit and flavour. Another traditional grape variety to be found in the panorama of Vulture wines is moscato, which is beginning to show notable potential on these volcanic soils. The Clivus, a low-pressure sparkling moscato with attractive, balanced flavour, is a good demonstration of this.

●	Aglianico del Vulture '94	▼▼	3*
●	Aglianico del Vulture Ris. Don Anselmo '92	▼	5
●	Barigliott '96	▼	2
●	L'Antico Spumante Aglianico '96		2
○	Clivus Moscato della Basilicata '96		2
○	Moscato Spumante '96		2
●	Aglianico del Vulture Ris. Don Anselmo '88	▽▽	5
●	Aglianico del Vulture '93	▽	3
●	Barigliott '95	▽	2*
●	L'Antico Spumante Aglianico '95	▽	2

D'ANGELO
VIA PROVINCIALE, 8
85028 RIONERO IN VULTURE (PZ)
TEL. 0972/721517

MARTINO
VIA LUIGI LA VISTA, 2/A
85028 RIONERO IN VULTURE (PZ)
TEL. 0972/721422

Lucio and Donato D'Angelo continue to represent a dependable benchmark for the quality which it is possible to achieve in Basilicata with a monovarietal product like Aglianico del Vulture. Their reds always live up to our expectations, and represent an increasingly interesting combination of tradition and innovation. The D'Angelo wines in this year's tastings all scored well, but it is definitely the Canneto, with its austere character, which deserves, as always, our Two Glass award. The production zone is in the commune of Rionero in Vulture, the yield per hectare is very low and the grapes are picked late. On the nose the wine is quite mature, with distinct scents of cherries under spirit and chocolate, while on the palate it is soft, velvety and warming, and also fairly long. This year the Aglianico del Vulture '94 is also very enjoyable: it has sweet, mature aromas, soft, elegant fruit, and a rich aromatic structure. The grapes come from vineyards in the communes of Rionero in Vulture, Ginestra, Barile and Rapolla, and it is aged for over two years before being released. The Vigna dei Pini, is a blend of chardonnay (40 per cent), pinot bianco (40 per cent) and incrocio manzoni (20 per cent), from the company's own vineyards situated at 550 metres above sea level, planted with a density of 5,000 vines per hectare. This attractive white is the only digression D'Angelo permit themselves from aglianico.

Modernizing and seeking to keep up to date does not merely involve finding more attractive packaging for one's wines. It means hard work on one's vines, on clonal selection, and on improving one's winery equipment. We say this because we have the impression that, for some years now, the wines of this historic Aglianico producer, in spite of their stylish labelling, have not fully expressed the potential of their grapes and their "terroir". Among the wines we tried this year, we found the Aglianico del Vulture '95 agreeable and typical. It is, on the whole, a satisfying and well-made red. We have some reservations, on the other hand, about all of the other many products in the winery's wide range. These include the Aglianico Rosé, the fizzy Aglianico Carolin, and the sparkling version of Aglianico del Vulture DOC. Apart from the above products, in a bid the courage of which we recognize, Armando Martino has diversified his selection by offering a white blend from the '95 vintage called Vulcanello, a '96 Chardonnay and a traditional Moscato Spumante. These are all wines which could be interesting, but which for the moment do not rate more than an honourable mention.

● Canneto '94	▼▼	5	
● Aglianico del Vulture '94	▼	3	
● Aglianico del Vulture Ris. Vigna Caselle '91		4	
○ Vigna dei Pini '96		3	
● Aglianico del Vulture '90	♼♼	3	
● Canneto '90	♼♼	5	
● Canneto '91	♼♼	5	
● Canneto '93	♼♼	4	
● Aglianico del Vulture Ris. Vigna Caselle '91	♼	3	
○ Vigna dei Pini '95	♼	3	

● Aglianico del Vulture '95	▼	3*	
● Aglianico del Vulture Spumante		4	
● Carolin '96		2	
○ Chardonnay della Basilicata '96		3	
○ Moscato Spumante		3	
☉ Rosato Donna Livia '96		2	
○ Vulcanello '95		2	
● Aglianico del Vulture '90	♼	2	
● Aglianico del Vulture '93	♼	2*	

RIONERO IN VULTURE (PZ)

SASSO
VIA ROMA, 209
85028 RIONERO IN VULTURE (PZ)
TEL. 0972/721022

Aglianico del Vulture, one of the undiscovered classics of Italian wine, finds one of its greatest allies in Francesco Sasso. His winery at Rionero in Vulture produces some unforgettable reds, which need several years before they are able to express themselves to the full, and in fact rival the very finest of Italian wines. The definition of Aglianico as the "Barolo of the South" contains a great truth, but it is also an implicit underestimation of this great wine, (Barolo has never been defined as the "Aglianico of the North"). But let us examine the wines which Sasso presented to us this year. There were no recent vintages of the Il Brigante and Federico II selections. We are, therefore, still with the '90 Il Brigante and the '93 Federico II, but tasting both wines again confirms the positive judgments we have made over the course of the last few years. We tried the '94 vintage of the standard Aglianico del Vulture, called Il Viola, which has a violet label. It is a good quality red, particularly as it comes from an only average harvest. It offers a deep garnet colour and a rich bouquet with, at first, a light note of reduction. This disappears a few minutes after drawing the cork, giving way to scents of violets and cherries bottled in alcohol. It has a reasonable concentration of polyphenols, well supported by mouth-filling and well-balanced fruit.

●	Aglianico del Vulture '94	🍷	3
●	Aglianico del Vulture Brigante '90	🍷🍷	5
●	Aglianico del Vulture '92	🍷	2*
●	Aglianico del Vulture Brigante '93	🍷	3
●	Aglianico del Vulture Federico II '93	🍷	3
●	Aglianico del Vulture Il Viola '93	🍷	2
●	Eleano '92	🍷	3
●	Eleano '93	🍷	3

VENOSA (PZ)

CANTINA RIFORMA
FONDIARIA DI VENOSA
CONTRADA VIGNALI SAN FELICE
85029 VENOSA (PZ)
TEL. 0972/35891

This is the first listing in the Guide for this cooperative. Founded in 1957 at the behest of the former Ente di Riforma di Puglia, Lucania e Molise, it now vinifies something like six million kilos of grapes, produced by over 500 grower-members. The principal wines produced are Aglianico del Vulture and the Carato Venusio. From this year's tastings, the basic version excited us with its very appealing character. The '94 is a red with a lovely, complex and harmonious bouquet of black berries and violets, cherries and tobacco. On the palate, it is soft and warming, with elegant tannins: considering its decidedly reasonable price, it is undoubtedly a very interesting wine indeed. The cooperative's oenologist, Sergio Paternoster, has, through scrupulous efforts both in the vineyard and in the winery, succeeded in bringing out all of this wine's most attractive aspects. Another interesting product is the Aglianico del Vulture Carato Venusio, a red created to mark the 25th anniversary of the cooperative. Aged in small wooden casks, it was a little too mature and slight, though remaining reasonably appealing. To sum up, this winery turned out some very good wines this year, thereby confirming the substantial progress made by Basilicata's two cooperatives, which between them are responsible for the vast majority of the Aglianico del Vulture produced each year.

●	Aglianico del Vulture '94	🍷🍷	3
●	Aglianico del Vulture Carato Venusio '94		3
⊙	Rosato Boreano		2

PUGLIA

There has been such a marked improvement generally in the wines of Puglia that if we had not been limited to 20 estate profiles in this edition, many others would have been included. What Puglia is lacking however is a Three Glass wine, a wine of the year. Cosimo Taurino has twice won the award in previous editions of the Guide and this year a couple of wines came very close to the crucial ninety points, but in the end just missed out. Having come so close however is already quite an achievement for a region which, although traditionally committed to viticulture, has always been looked down on as a poor relation by the rest of Italy. This is a region which has always been there to make for up the deficiencies in structure and colour of celebrated wines in the rest of the country. But things have begun to change since the days of bulk shipments of wine to the north. Although bottled wines represent little more than two per cent of Puglia's average output of about 10 million hectolitres, they have earned their place, and a good reputation, on many overseas markets. A steady stream of experts and opinion leaders continue to arrive in Italy and make their way to Puglia in search of attractive wines at bargain prices. In recent years the southern regions of the world have become increasingly the focal point of international winemaking: California, Australia, South Africa, Spain and Portugal, in the same way as Puglia, Sicily and Sardinia, are lands where the grapes ripen differently under a hotter, more friendly sun. With the perfectly ripe crop which can be grown in these latitudes it is easier to make premium wines, and there is a great future for the native varieties and the best wine growing areas of Puglia. So far few producers have succeeded in getting a real process of transformation underway, but this year's entries show that Puglia and its wines are beginning to make a move. Tuscany used to be considered the southernmost frontier of quality winemaking beyond which hardly anybody bothered to venture. This is no longer the case, thanks to wines like Salice Salentino, Brindisi Rosso and the excellent whites and rosés to be found in Puglia. Experts of the New World have realised the potential of warm climate winemaking and we are confident that Puglia's wine producers will not be far behind.

ALEZIO (LE)

ROSA DEL GOLFO
VIA GARIBALDI, 56
73011 ALEZIO (LE)
TEL. 0833/281045

The Rosa del Golfo '96 is an excellent wine, full bodied and cheerful. It is the best rosé produced in the area which is traditionally the home of this type of wine (those who think of rosé as a non-wine should visit the area to test their prejudice). It is pale pink with coral tints, the bouquet is intense and fruity with reminiscences of red berries, the palate is soft, elegant and balanced with a long fruity finish. A wine for all occasions: all through the meal, with Italian-style starters, pasta, fish-stew, grilled fish, white meats and medium mature cheese. Equally good is the Bolina, a modern-style wine which at the tasting emerged round and balanced with inviting scents of peach and melon. It is mouth-filling, balanced and elegant on the palate, with biscuity nuances. It is a pity that at least one of Mino Calò's two reds is not ready. The most recent is the Portulano from the '93 vintage, while the last Quarantale was the excellent '88. If he is planning a surprise, from a grower like Calò it will be worth waiting for. Few people have given greater impetus to winemaking in Puglia, leading by example through the difficult period in the past when no-one had any praise to spare for the very few good wines that were being produced in Puglia.

ANDRIA (BA)

RIVERA
S.S. 98, KM 19,800
C.DA RIVERA
70031 ANDRIA (BA)
TEL. 0883/541310

We never had any doubt about Il Falcone emerging as one of Puglia's great red wines; for one thing it is only made in very good years, such as '94. This vintage gave a wine that is created that is at the top of the regional production, with a structure which lends it great ageing capacity. It is garnet coloured with orange tints and the bouquet is rich with good tertiary aromas. In the mouth it is dry and full bodied with attractive ripe fruit reminiscent of cherries, and well balanced tannins. All Rivera wines are of good quality, and several this year, like the Bianca di Svevia, the Preludio (in a new style of bottle this year), the Rupicolo di Rivera and the Aglianico '95 came close to a Two Glass rating. Some wines are vinified as monovarietals, with the name of the grape indicated on the label as permitted by the DOC. This is the case of the Aglianico, Pinot Bianco, Chardonnay and Sauvignon presented in the Terre al Monte line. The reds of the Castel del Monte Classico range derive from blends of nero di Troia and montepulciano; the Bianca di Svevia is from pampanuto and bombino bianco grapes, while the rosé is from100 per cent bombino nero fermented at controlled temperatures: all easily scored over 70 points in our tastings.

○ Bolina '96	🍷🍷	3
⊙ Rosato del Salento		
Rosa del Golfo '96	🍷🍷	3
○ Bolina '95	🍷🍷	2*
⊙ Rosato del Salento		
Rosa del Golfo '95	🍷🍷	2*
● Rosso del Salento		
Portulano '93	🍷🍷	2*

● Castel del Monte Rosso		
Il Falcone Ris. '94	🍷🍷	3
⊙ Castel del Monte Aglianico		
Rosato Terre al Monte '96	🍷	2
● Castel del Monte Aglianico		
Terre al Monte '95	🍷	3
○ Castel del Monte		
Bianca di Svevia '96	🍷	2*
○ Castel del Monte Preludio n. 1 '96	🍷	3
⊙ Castel del Monte Rosé		
di Rivera '96	🍷	2*
● Castel del Monte		
Rupicolo di Rivera '95	🍷	2*
○ Castel del Monte Sauvignon		
Terre al Monte '96	🍷	2

CELLINO SAN MARCO (BR)   COPERTINO (LE)

LIBRA
C.DA BOSCO
72020 CELLINO SAN MARCO (BR)
TEL. 0831/619211

CANTINA SOCIALE DI COPERTINO
VIA MARTIRI DEL RISORGIMENTO, 6
73043 COPERTINO (LE)
TEL. 0832/947031

Al Bano and Romina Power have been producing wine for almost 20 years at Cellino San Marco, where they own a large estate specializing in viticulture. Here they grow negroamaro, malvasia nera, primitivo, sauvignon and chardonnay, part of which they vinify themselves. After the first releases of the Don Carmelo line, named after Al Bano's father, these popular singers had the bright idea of naming their wines after their most successful hits, hence the red Nostalgia, the rosé Mediterraneo and the white Felicità came into being. The choice of names is certainly open to debate, but at the tastings the wines scored good marks. The Nostalgia, a blend of negroamaro and primitivo, is a good ruby colour with slight orange tints, an intense grapey aroma with spicy notes, and a warm, dry, pleasantly tannic flavour. The Mediterraneo, from the same grape-mix, is a brilliant pink in colour with fruity aromas. It is dry, intensely flavoured and balanced on the palate. Sauvignon is the principal variety in the white blend Felicità which presents a pale straw yellow with all the varietal character of the grape on the nose, and is dry, slightly acid and balanced on the palate.

Cigliano was the first rosé to be bottled in Puglia, towards the end of the thirties, by the region's oldest cooperative winery. With the '96 vintage and the introduction of the IGT category, Severino Garofano, who is in charge of winemaking, and the managing director Mario Petitto have retrieved the old name for this wine, although it is not made every year in order not to deprive the red wine of resources. So after sixty years the Rosato Cigliano has returned, made as then from 100 per cent negroamaro. It is salmon-pink in colour with coral tints, the aromas are fruity, delicate and inviting, and on the palate it is full and balanced with flavours of ripe berries. It can be drunk all through the meal, although some prefer it with soup and grilled fish. But the masterpiece of Garofano, who by now has the leadership of this important cellar, is the Copertino, an impressive red which once bottled never lets its supporters down. The performance of the Riserva '94 is on a level with that of previous vintages: it is a good ruby colour, with elegant aromas and excellent body; warm and mouth-filling. Finally the Chardonnay, the Cigliano of recent years, which has always been one of the best international varietals in the region. It is straw yellow, fresh with delicate fruit on the nose, lively and enjoyable on the palate.

⊙ Salento Rosato Mediterraneo '96	🍷	3
● Salento Rosso Nostalgia '94	🍷	3
○ Salento Bianco Felicità '96		3

● Copertino Ris. '94	🍷🍷	2*
○ Chardonnay del Salento Cigliano '96	🍷	2*
⊙ Rosato del Salento Cigliano '96	🍷	2*
● Copertino '94	🍷🍷	2*
● Copertino Ris. '91	🍷🍷	2*
○ Chardonnay del Salento Cigliano '95	🍷	2*

COPERTINO (LE)

MASSERIA MONACI
TENUTA MONACI
73043 COPERTINO (LE)
TEL. 0832/947512

After a years absence, the Masseria Monaci estate makes an impressive return to the Guide. The property, part of what used to be a large landed estate belonging to Baron Bacile di Castiglione, now includes 30 hectares of vineyard, almost al planted to negroamaro and chardonnay. From the point of view of quality it is already established as one of the best cellars in Puglia, but continues to improve almost daily - perhaps because Severino Garofano, the oenologist in charge, has a free hand in crafting new wines of top quality. Besides the Copertino, the production includes Salento IGT wines such as Simposia, Santa Brigida and Le Vicarie. The two reds, Copertino and Simposia, both merit a Two Glass rating. Made from different varieties, 100 per cent negroamaro for the Copertino and a blend of negroamaro, malvasia nera and montepulciano for the Simposia, they both have velvety texture and lots of body. On the palate they are dry and balanced with enjoyable toasty scents and a hint of tobacco. The rosé Santa Brigida is fresh and fragrant with inviting fruity aromas which make it a wine to drink all through the meal. Le Vicarie, which almost scored Two Glasses, is 95 per cent chardonnay with a small amount of sauvignon and other minor local varieties. It is a delicate wine with pronounced tropical fruit on the nose, and is excellent with fish, especially shell fish.

CORATO (BA)

SANTA LUCIA
STRADA COMUNALE SAN VITTORE, 1
70033 CORATO (BA)
TEL. 080/8721168

We are still hoping that this attractive estate, with its small but well-equipped cellar, will produce a really impressive Riserva Castel del Monte for us to try. We know that an interesting wine is being kept in their oak barrels, but neither Giuseppe Perrone Capano nor his son Roberto, and certainly not their oenologist Luigi Cantatore, are willing to let us have a taste in advance. So in this entry we have only been able to include our valuation of the wines already released, the three from the Castel del Monte range and the Quarati, made from chardonnay. They are modern style wines, but they maintain good varietal character. The Castel del Monte Rosso, a blend of 30 per cent nero di Troia plus sangiovese and montepulciano, is a fine ruby red with ripe fruit on the nose and full, dry and slightly tannic flavours on the palate. The Rosato, made from bombino nero is correctly made and enjoyable to drink all through the meal, while the simple, fresh Bianco, a blend of bombino bianco and pampanuto is a classic aperitif or a wine for seafood starters.

● Copertino Rosso Eloquenzia '94	▼▼	2*
● Simposia Rosso '94	▼▼	3
○ Le Vicarie '96	▼	2*
⊙ Santa Brigida Rosato '96	▼	2*

○ Castel del Monte Bianco '96	▼	2*
⊙ Castel del Monte Rosato '96	▼	2*
● Castel del Monte Rosso '96	▼	2*
○ Quarati '96	▼	2*
○ Castel del Monte Bianco '95	♀	2*
⊙ Castel del Monte Rosato '95	♀	2*
● Castel del Monte Rosso '95	♀	2*

CORATO (BA)

TORREVENTO
LOC. CASTEL DEL MONTE
S.S. 170, KM 29
70033 CORATO (BA)
TEL. 080/8980973

GRAVINA IN PUGLIA (BA)

BOTROMAGNO
VIA F.LLI CERVI, 12
70024 GRAVINA IN PUGLIA (BA)
TEL. 080/2365865

Last year we reported in the Guide that Gaetano and Francesco Liantonio with their winemaker Lino Carparelli had stored away what little red wine they had been able to make in the '94 vintage in order to guarantee a reasonable quantity of Vigna Pedale. An intelligent decision, because their Castel del Monte Riserva, which in the few years since its first release has gained a place among the best wines in Puglia, has done well at our tastings. It has the structure, tannins, balance and rich bouquet of a top wine. The red, rosé and white versions of the Castel del Monte '96 are all good quality. The Rosso, from nero di Troia and aglianico grapes goes very well with grilled red meat. The Rosato is made from bombino nero, this being a classic variety for wines of fresh, easy drinking. The Bianco derives from a blend of pampanuto, bombino bianco and chardonnay. It is a fresh, fruity, tangy wine which can be drunk as an aperitif and to go with raw seafood. Finally the Moscato di Trani dolce naturale, produced with grapes from the Moscato Reale Producers' Cooperative, is an interesting dessert wine which has been brought back to the attention of enthusiasts by the efforts of Torrevento. One last remark: the new cellar started operating with the '97 harvest, so great things can be expected for the future.

The '96 vintage again confirms the Gravina Botromagno made from local varieties greco di tufo, malvasia bianca and bianco d'Alessano, as one of the best whites of Puglia. It is an attractive straw yellow colour with greenish tints, and a flowery bouquet with ripe fruit. On the palate it is dry, elegant, and balanced with good grip. It is a wine which thoroughly deserves the Two Glass rating, and is especially delicious with raw seafood and fish courses. A novelty which has had great success with the British public, seeing that 9,000 bottles of the 15,000 produced were sold in Great Britain, should be recorded here: it is a dessert wine called Gravesano. Its production is a return to the old tradition of a fine sweet wines for drinking on feast-days and special occasions. To make it, the best malvasia and moscato grapes are laid out to dry on racks before they are crushed, and the wine fermented and aged. The Gravesano at the tasting displayed the structure of a good wine for ageing and the lusciousness of southern dessert wines. The Silvium, a rosé from montepulciano and sangiovese grapes selected from the vineyards of La Murgia near Bari, is also of good quality. The '96 is a brilliant vermilion colour with fruity aromas, a dry, full flavour and good overall balance, making it a wine to go with pasta and all meat dishes. The Pier delle Vigne '93 vintage, still in the maturation stage, is a red from aglianico and montepulciano grapes aged in small French oak casks.

● Castel del Monte Rosso		
Vigna Pedale Ris. '94	♛♛	2*
O Castel del Monte Bianco '96	♛	1*
⊙ Castel del Monte Rosato '96	♛	1*
● Castel del Monte Rosso '96	♛	1*
O Moscato di Trani '94	♛	3
⊙ Castel del Monte Rosato '95	♛♛	1*
O Castel del Monte Bianco '95	♛	1*
● Rosso delle Murge		
Torre del Falco '95	♛	1*

O Gravina '96	♛♛	2*
O Gravesano '92	♛	4
⊙ Silvium Rosato '96	♛	1*
O Gravina '95	♛♛	2*
O Gravina '93	♛	2*
O Gravina '94	♛	1*
● Pier delle Vigne '92	♛	2*

GUAGNANO (LE)

COSIMO TAURINO
S.S. 605 SALICE-SANDONACI
73010 GUAGNANO (LE)
TEL. 0832/706490

LECCE

AGRICOLE VALLONE
VIA XXV LUGLIO, 7
73100 LECCE
TEL. 0832/308041

Without Patriglione and Notarpanaro, the post-1990 vintages not yet being ready, Cosimo Taurino relinquishes the title of regional record holder in our tastings. Only two wines were available for inclusion in the Guide this year, the Salice Salentino '94 vintage and the rosé Scaloti, which is entitled to the Salento IGT label as from the '96 harvest. Both these products are slightly inferior to those we were used to from Taurino. The Salice Salentino, which we have always highly commended and often preferred to the Notarpanaro, and sometimes (if only for the excellent value it represents) even to the great Patriglione, was a little too mature at the tasting. On the palate it does not display the traditional richness of the great vintages of the past. However it is still one of Puglia's most attractive wines, thanks to the reliability of the Taurino cellar which incidentally in the last few months has been undergoing various forms of modernisation. Neither does the Scaloti reach the exciting level of the '95 which we found comparable to a Rosé de Provence. The colour is a little faded and so is the traditional Salento fruitiness; on the palate it tends to fizzle out. The two Chardonnays, the barrique-aged version and the Stria, were not yet ready when we wrote this entry. We will have to wait for the return of Patriglione and Notarpanaro to see Taurino's wines restored to their past splendour.

With the exception perhaps of the Graticciaia, Vallone's whole range is wonderful value for money. We defy anyone to find bottles on sale which at the same retail prices can compete with the Vigna Flaminio and Salice Salentino from Vallone. Luckily there are still wine growers who wish to make a reasonable margin on their wines and not just lots of fast money. Their most expensive wine, the Graticciaia, has often nearly won the Three Glass award. It is made from negroamaro and malvasia nera harvested in the oldest, bush-trained vineyard on the Flaminio estate. The grapes are then left to dry on racks for a few weeks before being vinified. The '92 is a really splendid vintage: garnet in colour with orange hues, on the nose and palate it is intense, warm and fruity with hints of tobacco and it has an attractive bitterish aftertaste. The Brindisi and the Salice are from the same grape-mix as the Graticciaia: both have a rich, inviting bouquet and good grip on the palate with a dry, slightly tannic flavour.

●	Salice Salentino Ris. '94	🍷🍷	3*	●	Brindisi Rosso		
◉	Rosato del Salento Scaloti '96	🍷	3		Vigna Flaminio '94	🍷🍷	1*
●	Brindisi Rosso Patriglione '85	🍷🍷🍷	5	●	Graticciaia '92	🍷🍷	5
●	Brindisi Rosso Patriglione '88	🍷🍷🍷	5	●	Salice Salentino Rosso '94	🍷🍷	2*
◉	Rosato del Salento Scaloti '95	🍷🍷	2	◉	Brindisi Rosato		
●	Rosso del Salento				Vigna Flaminio '96	🍷	1*
	Notarpanaro '88	🍷🍷	3*	○	Sauvignon del Salento		
●	Rosso del Salento				Corte Valesio '96	🍷	1*
	Notarpanaro '90	🍷🍷	3*	●	Salice Salentino Rosso '93	🍷🍷	2*
●	Salice Salentino Ris. '93	🍷🍷	2*	●	Brindisi Rosso		
●	Brindisi Rosso Patriglione '90	🍷	5		Vigna Flaminio '93	🍷	2*
○	Chardonnay del Salento '95	🍷	3				

LEVERANO (LE)

CONTI ZECCA
VIA CESAREA
73045 LEVERANO (LE)
TEL. 0832/925613

Last year we reported in the Guide that the Zecca brothers seemed uninterested in DOC wines, since almost their entire production, hundreds of thousands of bottles of Donna Marzia, was labelled as VDT. We still cannot make out if there has been a change of heart, but it is clear that this prominent Salento cellar is obtaining its best results with DOC wines. During the various tastings prior to writing these entries, the wine which scored the highest marks was the DOC Salice Salentino Cantalupi '93. This achieved the same scores as the first Salice produced by Zecca, the '92 Cantalupi, although the later vintage is more modern and fresher with delicious fruity, jammy aromas and toasty overtones. Good results too from the Leverano DOC Vigna del Saraceno which missed the high score of the previous vintage by a hair's breadth, and from the rosé which is one of the best of the '96 vintage in Salento. The whites are a little thin, as are the two Salice DOCs, but they are correctly made, fruity, fresh and ready drinking, in some cases up to a year after the harvest. One last thing: all the wines in Zecca's range are excellent value for money.

LOCOROTONDO (BA)

CANTINA SOCIALE COOPERATIVA
DI LOCOROTONDO
VIA MADONNA DELLA CATENA, 99
70010 LOCOROTONDO (BA)
TEL. 080/9311644

The Tallinajo, a Locorotondo cru made from verdeca, bianco d'Alessano and fiano grapes, is a wine of definitely modern conception. Among the whites tasted this year, it is one of Puglia's best, with a good aroma of ripe fruit and hints of apple, and a fresh, dry flavour. Its only weakness is a rather short finish; a pity in otherwise such an attractive wine, which a little extra body would have rounded off. The rosé Case Bianche from pinot nero grapes partially vinified off the skins is a very decent drink: pale pink in colour, with delicate aromas and a dry, elegant palate just right for grilled fish and pasta. The Roccia Bianca should also be mentioned, a white made from verdeca, bianco d' Alessano and chardonnay which when tasted revealed an intense fruity bouquet with a hint of walnuts and a fresh, dry flavour. It is ideal for drinking with starters, seafood and all kinds of fish. The classic wine of this big cooperative winery deserves also to be recorded: the Locorotondo specially created for the restaurant trade.

● Salice Salentino Rosso Cantalupi '93	🍷🍷	1*
⊙ Leverano Rosato Vigna del Saraceno '96	🍷	1*
● Leverano Rosso Vigna del Saraceno '95	🍷	1*
⊙ Rosato del Salento Donna Marzia '96	🍷	1*
● Rosso del Salento Donna Marzia '95	🍷	1*
○ Bianco del Salento Donna Marzia '96		1*
○ Salice Salentino Bianco Cantalupi '96		1*

○ Locorotondo in Tallinajo '96	🍷	2
⊙ Case Bianche Rosato '96		2
○ Locorotondo '96		1
○ Valle d'Itria Roccia '96		1

LOCOROTONDO (BA)

CARDONE
VIA MARTIRI DELLA LIBERTÀ, 28
70010 LOCOROTONDO (BA)
TEL. 080/9311624

After light-heartedly beginning with a few thousand bottles of Locorotondo, Franco Cardone's production was soon over the 100,000 mark. This shows that Locorotondo is a wine which still has a sizeable market, and Cardone is fully aware of its commercial potential. The Locorotondo '96 which we tasted is a pale straw yellow, fresh, delicate and long on the nose with biscuity, almondy overtones and a dry, balanced palate. Cardone has another interesting wine, the Placeo, a 100 per cent Chardonnay which he makes with soft pressing and temperature controlled fermentation. The '96 vintage is pale yellow, broad, intense and fruity on the nose and full, dry and soft on the palate with excellent balance. Like the Locorotondo, it is sold in elegant, champagne-style bottles and is excellent with starters, risotto, white meat and all kinds of sea fish. The Primaio is a red from primitivo grapes selected from old vineyards with gobelet training and harvested late in mid-October. The '95 is broad, fragrant and intense in aroma, while in the mouth it is smooth and balanced with good structure.

O Chardonnay di Puglia Placeo '96	🍷	2
O Locorotondo '96	🍷	2
● Primaio Rosso '95	🍷	2
O Chardonnay di Puglia Placeo '95	🍸	2
O Locorotondo '94	🍸	2
O Locorotondo '95	🍸	2

MANDURIA (TA)

FELLINE
VIA N. DONADIO, 20
74024 MANDURIA (TA)
TEL. 099/9711660

This progressive wine which makes its first appearance in the Guide this year is from one of Puglia's classic varieties, primitivo, and is the result of a joint effort on the part of Antonio Perrucci, local wine grower, and noted oenologist Roberto Cipresso. Perrucci has a vineyard of 20 hectares of which five are planted to primitivo, and he has to decided to try to make the most of the potential of a cultivar whose presumed descendent (zinfandel) is one of the premium varieties of California. He has achieved this objective by careful attention to vineyard management and correct, modern vinification. The '96 vintage is his first and it is impressive: a well-balanced wine of international appeal, intense ruby red; rich in aromas of soft fruit and vanilla with inky overtones; on the palate clean and warm with outstanding structure and balance. The research which resulted in this Primitivo di Manduria began a few years back and included the purchase of several different types and sizes of oak in the form of barriques, barrels and casks in order to assess this wine's reaction to ageing. The tradition of barrel ageing is not a long-standing one in the region and it was therefore considered the most delicate stage of the winemaking process. The result is spectacular: Puglia's most classic wine harmonises perfectly with small wood. Without losing its varietal character it has the international style that Puglia's wines need if they are to secure their place on overseas markets.

● Primitivo di Manduria '96	🍷🍷	3*

MANDURIA (TA)

S. PIETRO VERNOTICO (BR)

PERVINI
VIA SANTO STASI PRIMO
C.DA ACUTI
74024 MANDURIA (TA)
TEL. 099/9711660

SANTA BARBARA
VIA M. INFANZIA, 23
72027 S. PIETRO VERNOTICO (BR)
TEL. 0831/652749

The Pervini estate is the creation of Gregorio, Fabrizio and Alessia Perrucci, whose father Costantino Perrucci is the biggest exporter of wines from Puglia. These three are making swift headway and have a clear idea of what they want to do: bring out the potential of the primitivo grape which, if properly handled, can give exceptional results. In addition to this, they have not stayed wrapped up in their own concerns but have been active in promoting a producers' consortium for Primitivo. The Primitivo from the Pervini estate is definitely one of the most attractive wines of this type on the market. When tasted it displayed all the character of the grape, which is selected from old vineyards with gobelet training: it is a deep red with purplish tints; very intense grapey aromas; balanced on the palate with plenty of body and a pleasant fruity flavour. Pervini's range includes the Bizantino line of IGT Salento wines which consists of a red, a rosé and a good chardonnay. There is also a cheaper line, Galante, and a naturally fizzy wine called Marea.

We were very favourably impressed last year by the reds of the '93 harvest from this cooperative, and for this year's edition were confident that it would come up with one or more wines meriting Two Glass ratings. We regret that this has not been the case, and we were rather disappointed by what we considered the top wine made by Pietro Giorgiani, Santa Barbara's president and oenologist, the Barbaglio blend of negroamaro and primitivo. This red which should have been be a winner, but in fact the Barbaglio '94 has turned out to be inferior to the '93 vintage. It is still an attractive wine however and will certainly keep its appeal for drinkers of Salento reds. It has also been the means of drawing attention to the primitivo grape, a variety which when handled properly is an undoubted asset in the creation of fine wines for ageing. The Brindisi and the Squinzano of the '94 vintage are both good wines, more or less of the same quality as those of the previous harvest. The first is from a blend of negroamaro and malvasia nera, while the second is based on the same varieties with the addition of primitivo. They are both ruby in colour with garnet tints, broad on the nose with a delicate nuance of almonds, and warm, full bodied and balanced on the palate. The range of production also includes two DOC rosés, Squinzano and Brindisi, and the white, red and rosé versions of the Salento IGT.

○ Chardonnay del Salento Bizantino '96	2
● Primitivo di Manduria '93	2*
⊙ Rosato del Salento Bizantino '96	1*
● Rosso del Salento Bizantino '93	2*
● Primitivo di Manduria '92	1
● Primitivo di Manduria '94	2
● Rosso del Salento Bizantino '94	2

● Brindisi '94	2*
● Rosso del Salento Barbaglio '94	2*
● Squinzano '94	2*
⊙ Squinzano Rosato '96	2
● Brindisi '93	1*
● Rosso del Salento Barbaglio '93	2*
● Squinzano '93	1*

S. SEVERO (FG)

GIOVANNI D'ALFONSO DEL SORDO
C.DA SANT'ANTONINO
S.S. 89, KM 5
71016 S. SEVERO (FG)
TEL. 0882/321444

Gianfelice D'Alfonso del Sordo, having got back his place in the Guide, is not prepared to lose it again. The wines he submitted to the tasting commission were of good quality, both the San Severo DOCs and the IGT wines such as the Bombino Bianco and the Riserva Casteldrione, and all of them well worth their retail price. The Catapanus Bombino Bianco is the best of the range. It is straw yellow with greenish tints, fruity with pronounced scents of apple and pear on the nose, and fresh, dry and well-flavoured on the palate, with an agreeable bitterish finish. Next comes the Casteldrione '92, a red from a blend of montepulciano, sangiovese and uva di Troia which underwent a period of ageing in oak. It is an intense garnet-ruby colour, broad on the nose with good tertiary aromas, dry, warm and full bodied on the palate. The San Severo DOCs are all of encouraging quality. The Rosso and the Rosato derive from 100 per cent montepulciano, and the Bianco from a blend of bombino bianco, malvasia and verdeca. D'Alfonso del Sordo only vinifies grapes from his own vineyards, which are considered among the best of the area round Foggia.

SALICE SALENTINO (LE)

LEONE DE CASTRIS
VIA SENATORE DE CASTRIS, 50
73015 SALICE SALENTINO (LE)
TEL. 0832/731112

Year after year the Five Roses and the Salice Salentino Riserva are the best wines produced by Leone de Castris. The Salice '94 is well structured and fresh, powerful on the nose with a pleasant inky note, and balanced, fruity and inviting on the palate with a toasty, jammy flavour. Also stylish is the company's leading wine, the Five Roses. The '96 vintage is a pale vermilion pink, intense, grapey and fruity on the nose, and fresh, full, smooth and dry on the palate with an agreeable bitterish streak. As usual it is excellent for drinking all through the meal, and especially suitable for fish stew and tripe dishes. The Primitivo del Tarantino was unexpectedly good, doing full justice to this wonderful variety, which we would like to see put to better use because we are sure that it can yield excellent wines, and at very good prices too. With regard to the other wines, Leone Castris has a very wide range and we have sometimes had difficulty in sorting it out. Amongst the Salice DOCs, good marks were obtained by the Imago '96 Chardonnay, the Rosso Maiana vintage '95, and the historic Negrino, an aleatico of the '92 vintage. Finally there should be a mention of IGT wines like the Messapia, a good white varietal based on verdeca, which is fresh and dry with an enjoyable bite of acidity.

●	Casteldrione Riserva '92	♀	2*
○	Catapanus Bombino Bianco '96	♀	1*
⊙	San Severo Rosato '96	♀	1*
●	San Severo Rosso '95	♀	1*
○	San Severo Bianco '96		1
○	Bombino '95	♀	1*
●	Contrada del Santo '92	♀	3

●	Salice Salentino Rosso Ris. '94	♀♀	3
●	Primitivo del Salento La Rena '96	♀	3
⊙	Rosato del Salento Five Roses '96	♀	4
●	Salice Salentino Negrino '92	♀	4
●	Salice Salentino Rosso Maiana '95	♀	2*
○	Verdeca del Salento Messapia '96	♀	3
●	Salice Salentino Rosso Donna Lisa Ris. '92	♀♀	4
⊙	Rosato del Salento Five Roses '95	♀	3
○	Salice Salentino Bianco Imago '95	♀	2
●	Salice Salentino Rosso Maiana '94	♀	2*
○	Sauvignon del Salento Vigna Case Alte '95	♀	2

SANDONACI (BR)

TUGLIE (LE)

FRANCESCO CANDIDO
VIA A. DIAZ, 46
72025 SANDONACI (BR)
TEL. 0831/635674

MICHELE CALÒ & FIGLI
VIA MASSERIA VECCHIA, 1
73058 TUGLIE (LE)
TEL. 0833/596242

Giacomo and Sandro Candido confirm their status as Puglia's top wine growers. We can say this with confidence since at the tastings of the whole of the region's production the wines created by Severino Garofano for the Candido estate always outstripped the rest, consistently gaining the highest marks. At the top of the list there is the Duca D'Aragona, which is a more or less permanent high scorer. The '91 vintage, a barrique-aged blend of negroamaro, malvasia nera and montepulciano is in our opinion a more complete wine than the '90. It is more modern in style with its intense bouquet and characteristically clean aromas, and its delectable palate in which inviting spicy, toasty notes mingle with tobacco. As far as the other wines are concerned, Candido's other two superior reds, the Cappello di Prete '94 and the Salice Salentino Riserva '93, are very good. They are both from a more or less identical blend of negroamaro and malvasia nera, the grapes being selected from different vineyards, and offer well structured, enjoyable drinking. The Vignavinera is a 100 per cent sauvignon and is excellent and the underrated Aleatico di Puglia has all the requisites to be compared with the best port wines. Another successful effort is the Paule Calle, made from a blend of malvasia and chardonnay grapes left to dry and fermented in new barriques: it is perhaps Puglia's best dessert wine with its coppery yellow colour, complex fruit and flowery bouquet.

Michele Calò seems to manage better with reds than with whites, and it was in fact his Alezio Rosso vintage '95 which scored the highest marks at the tasting, achieving the Two Glass rating which has become a yearly fixture. This wine is a deep ruby colour, with ripe soft fruit on the nose, chocolatey overtones and good body and structure on the palate. The Rosato and the Bianco are slightly thinner than usual but are technically correct and of a good standard. Calò's latest release, the Stella Tulliae, attractively labelled in Californian style, is an interesting wine. Obtained from 100 per cent white moscato grapes from the Stella vineyard which lies close to the cellar, it is broad, elegant and balanced on the nose, dry and well-flavoured but with a slightly elusive aromatic note which means that the wine seems to lack a sense of completeness. However it goes well with shell fish and all kinds of seafood. The impressive Vigna Spano, which has twice been a candidate for the maximum award of our Guide, will not be ready for some time yet as the '96 vintage is still maturing.

● Aleatico di Puglia '89	♙♙	3
● Cappello di Prete '94	♙♙	3*
● Duca d'Aragona '91	♙♙	5
○ Paule Calle '94	♙♙	5
● Salice Salentino Rosso Ris. '93	♙♙	2*
○ Vignavinera Bianco '96	♙♙	2*
○ Salice Salentino Bianco '96	♙	2*
☉ Salice Salentino Rosato Le Pozzelle '96	♙	2*
● Aleatico di Puglia '87	♟♟	3*
● Cappello di Prete '93	♟♟	2*
○ Paule Calle '95	♟♟	3
● Salice Salentino Rosso Ris. '92	♟♟	1*
☉ Salice Salentino Rosato Le Pozzelle '95	♟	1*

● Alezio Rosso Mjere '95	♙♙	3
☉ Alezio Rosato Mjere '96	♙	3
○ Mjere Bianco '96	♙	3
○ Stella Tulliae Bianco '96	♙	3
☉ Alezio Rosato Mjere '95	♟♟	2*
● Alezio Rosso Mjere '90	♟♟	3*
● Alezio Rosso Mjere '94	♟♟	2*
○ Bianco del Salento Mjere '95	♟♟	2*
● Alezio Rosso Mjere '92	♟	3*

OTHER WINERIES

The following producers obtained good scores in our tastings with one or more of their wines:

PROVINCE OF BARI

I Pastini,
Corato, tel. 080/8980973,
Locorotondo '96,
Murgia Rosso '96,
Negramaro del tarantino '96

Coppi, Turi, tel. 080/8915049,
Gioia del Colle Primitivo '93 Siniscalco,
Gioia del Colle Primitivo Ris. '91 Vanitoso,
Turello Chardonnay '96

PROVINCE OF FOGGIA

Antica Enotria,
Cerignola, tel. 0885/424688,
Daunia Aglianico '95,
Daunia Montepulciano '96,
Daunia Sangiovese '96,
Daunia Garganega '96

D'Aprarì,
San Severo, tel. 0882/333927,
Metodo Classico Brut,
Metodo Classico Pas Dosé,
Metodo Classico Brut Rosé,
Metodo Classico Gran Cuvée '91

PROVINCE OF LECCE

Coppola,
Gallipoli, tel. 0833/274447,
Alezio Rosato Li Cuti '96,
Alezio Rosso Li Cuti '94,
Doxi Vecchio Rosso '91

Cantina Sociale Cooperativa Vecchia Torre,
Leverano,
tel. 0832/925053,
Leverano Bianco '96,
Leverano Rosso '95,
Leverano Rosato '96

PROVINCE OF TARANTO

Soloperto,
Manduria, tel. 099/9794286,
Primitivo di Manduria '94,
Primitivo di Manduria Ceppo Nuovo '92,
Primitivo di Manduria Ceppo Vecchio '92

Cantina ed Oleificio Sociale di Sava,
Sava, tel. 099/8726139,
Primitivo di Manduria '92,
Primitivo di Manduria Terra di Miele '89

Vinicola Savese,
Sava, tel. 099/8726232,
Primitivo di Manduria '96

CALABRIA

The results which emerged from our tastings of Calabrian wines this year were contradictory and, frankly, sometimes a little disappointing. Quality was rather a long way from that of the wines which impressed us in the past to the point of bringing a coveted Three Glass award to the Cirò Marina area. Not just in Calabria, but all over the South, these accolades have always been fairly thin on the ground. It is true that such thoroughbreds as Gravello, Duca Sanfelice, Ronco dei Quattroventi, Vigna Mortilla and Valeo, were absent from this series of tastings. However, we were also left perplexed by the latest vintages of wines which we had in the past designated as valid examples of the renewal of viticulture in a region which is often trapped in the most conservative form of tradition. Instead, we found ourselves confronted by (at least temporary) stagnation. This disappoints us above all as we have always stressed what a rich heritage Calabria possesses in terms of natural resources; the sunshine, climate and geophysical factors which facilitate a healthy winemaking industry. We would like to think that it is only a momentary hiccup and that it has been poor vintages that have forced a few winemakers to bottle products that are not up to the standard of previous years. Next year's tastings will serve to clarify the situation. There should then be samples available from Librandi of their more important wines, as well as new products from Odoardi, while Francesco Siciliani will present the wines made in his brand new winery which came into operation with the '97 harvest. In the meantime, there has been a change in the listings: two wineries which have been present since the first editions are no longer in the Guide: Caparra & Siciliani (we had already given some indication of a fall off last year) and Ippolito. The Cantina Enotria and Dattilo, both of which produce interesting and well-made wines, now make their début this year.

CIRÒ (KR)

FATTORIA SAN FRANCESCO
CASALE SAN FRANCESCO
88071 CIRÒ (KR)
TEL. 0962/32228

The effort involved in setting up his own winery perhaps distracted Francesco Siciliani from paying the necessary attention to the wines made at Caparra & Siciliani on behalf of Fattoria San Francesco. Thus his various Cirò wines and also his Donna Madda riserva were of slightly lower quality than we had become used to in the past. Now, with a new winery fitted out with the most modern equipment available, we are certain that he will be back on track for the next edition of the Guide. We really do hope so, because the ten year's hard work which brought Cirò back into the public eye when no one else was willing to say a good word about Calabria's flagship wine cannot be thrown down the drain. We can therefore consider this a period of transition, in which winemaking operations will be transferred from the winery of a third party to Francesco's own vinification plant. Our One Glass award was only won by the '94 Donna Madda this year. It is undoubtedly good, but its structure, body and balance are inferior to those of the wines of previous years. It is ruby red in colour, with garnet reflections; its aroma is persistent, fruity and alcoholic, with hints of marasca cherries; on the palate, it is already mature, and it shows good aromatic length. The Rosso Classico, on the other hand, earns its listing more for its good fruit and hints of spice on the nose than for its colour, which is almost that of a rosé. The Rosato and the Bianco are also merely deserving of an honourable mention.

●	Cirò Rosso Classico Sup. Donna Madda '94	🍷	3
○	Cirò Bianco '96		2
⊙	Cirò Rosato '96		2
●	Cirò Rosso Classico '95		2
●	Cirò Rosso Classico Ronco dei Quattro Venti '92	YY	4
●	Cirò Rosso Classico Sup. '91	YY	3*
●	Cirò Rosso Classico Sup. Donna Madda '92	YY	3
●	Cirò Rosso Classico Sup. Donna Madda '93	YY	3
●	Cirò Rosso Classico '94	Y	2

CIRÒ MARINA (KR)

ENOTRIA
S.S. 106
88072 CIRÒ MARINA (KR)
TEL. 0962/371181

Thanks to the perseverance of Gaetano Cianciaruso and to the good results achieved by the company's oenologists, Cantine Enotria makes its début in our Guide. This large, modern winery was created around 30 years ago by 23 winegrowers, who today own around 200 hectares of gaglioppo and greco bianco vines, bush-trained in the traditional manner. Indeed all of their production methods for Cirò hark back to tradition, from the harvest itself to the preparation of the wine for sale. The grower-members of Cantine Enotria are convinced of the need to continue producing Cirò according to the dictates of the past, without allowing themselves to be swayed by innovation in the form of the introduction of grape varieties held to be more in tune with international tastes. The wines, however, are of a good standard. In our tastings, the Cirò Classico Superiore Riserva '91 and the Classico from the '95 vintage both earned One Glass awards. The former is a robust wine with a fairly deep ruby colour, which displays the intense, vinous aromas typical of the gaglioppo grape; on the palate, it is warming, velvety and has good body. It is a red to serve with roasts, braised meats and game. A little more modest is the Rosso '95, which is a simpler wine with less imposing structure. The range is completed by the Rosato (from 100 per cent gaglioppo) and the Bianco (made from 100 per cent greco bianco), both DOC wines.

●	Cirò Rosso Classico '95	🍷	2
●	Cirò Rosso Classico Superiore Ris. '91	🍷	3
○	Cirò Bianco '96		2

CIRÒ MARINA (KR)

LIBRANDI
S.S. 106
C.DA S. GENNARO
88072 CIRÒ MARINA (KR)
TEL. 0962/31518-31519

In the absence of their two star wines, Gravello and Duca Sanfelice, the Librandi brothers' entry in this edition of the Guide is somewhat scaled down. Also, the Cirò Classico '95 performed a little less well than in previous years, when we had held it up as an example of how one could modernize and make appealing a wine which for decades had been conditioned by uncritical adherence to tradition. It remains, however, the best Cirò from the '95 harvest, with a warming, dry flavour and reasonable overall balance. Also good is the Bianco, obtained from 100 per cent greco bianco, which displays good general balance, freshness, and appealing fruity aromas. On the other hand, we were a bit disappointed by the Critone and by the Terre Lontane rosé. In the Critone we did not find the elegance, harmony and distinctive personality which in past years allowed it to earn a Two Glass rating. The same can be said for the Terre Lontane, a blend of gaglioppo and cabernet franc which, we are very sorry to say, did not score more than an honourable mention. We are sure that Librandi will be able to get back on track right away next year, especially with the Duca Sanfelice '93, which is now maturing in bottle and, if it is ready, with the Gravello '93, which should be up to the same standard it has shown in those years when it won our Three Glass award.

○	Cirò Bianco '96	🍷	1*
●	Cirò Rosso Classico '95	🍷	1*
○	Critone '96	🍷	2
⊙	Cirò Rosato '96		1
⊙	Terre Lontane '96		2
●	Gravello '90	YYY	4
●	Cirò Rosso Duca Sanfelice Ris. '90	YY	2*
●	Cirò Rosso Duca Sanfelice Ris. '91	YY	3*
●	Gravello '91	YY	4

COSENZA

GIOVANBATTISTA ODOARDI
V.LE DELLA REPUBBLICA, 143
87100 COSENZA
TEL. 0984/29961

No Savuto this year, after the good performance put up by the Vigna Mortilla from the '93 vintage. Therefore, as far as the reds are concerned, Giambattista Odoardi's flag is held - though not very high to tell the truth - by the Scavigna '95. (Odoardi sadly passed away in February '97, but had already handed over the running of the company to his son Gregorio some years earlier). The whites, on the other hand, continue to improve, in particular the single-vineyard Scavignas from the Pian della Corte site, 6 hectares at 500 metres above sea level, overlooking the Tyrrhenian Sea. The vineyard was replanted in 1988 with low, cane-pruned chardonnay, pinot bianco and riesling italico, which today make up the blend of the Pian della Corte, both in the white and blue label versions. These are two whites which have been fermented and aged in Allier barriques, and which have a similar taste profile. Their colour is a fairly deep straw; the attractively strong aromas are of dried fruit, vanilla and hazelnuts and the flavours are savoury, well balanced, elegant and nicely textured. However, we are sure a more judicious use of wood would have meant higher marks. The Scavigna Bianco and Rosato are also interesting. The former (from trebbiano toscano, prosecco, malvasia and chardonnay) is of straw colour with greenish highlights; it has fresh, fruity aromas and is dry on the palate. The blend of grapes used in the Rosato is, on the other hand, a mixture of tradition and innovation: gaglioppo, nerello cappuccio, sangiovese and cabernet sauvignon. the result is a bright pink, fresh and flavourful wine.

○	Scavigna '96	🍷	2*
○	Scavigna Pian della Corte '96	🍷	3
○	Scavigna Pian della Corte etichetta blu '96	🍷	4
⊙	Scavigna Rosato '96		2
●	Scavigna Rosso '95		2
●	Savuto Sup. Vigna Mortilla '93	YY	4
○	Valeo '95	YY	5
●	Savuto '95	Y	2*

LAMEZIA TERME (CZ)

CANTINE LENTO
VIA DEL PROGRESSO, 1
88041 LAMEZIA TERME (CZ)
TEL. 0968/28028

The reds were Lento's most interesting wines this year, and therefore, obviously, received the highest scores. The Lamezia Riserva '92, to begin with, shows all the character of Calabria's red grape varieties: gaglioppo, greco nero and nerello cappuccio. After a brief spell in barrique and some bottle ageing, it shows a handsome, deep ruby red colour, which signals a wine of good body which is rich, dry and has attractive vinous aromas. Around 7,000 bottles were produced, most of which are destined for overseas markets. The fine Lamezia '95, on the other hand, combines an intense vinous bouquet with a good, highly quaffable style. Among the whites, the Villa Caracciolo, made from a blend of greco bianco and malvasia, is of interest. It displays a fruity aroma, with hints of very ripe exotic fruit, while on the palate it is pleasantly crisp, dry and balanced. When we tasted the whites from Calabria we were somewhat perplexed by the - really very pronounced - aromatic vein of the Lamezia Greco, 13,000 bottles of which were produced from the '96 harvest. This is a pity, because it is actually a nice wine, with a pale straw colour, fruity aromas and good overall balance. The Lamezia Rosato and the Bianco, Rosso and Rosato (IGT Valdamato) with the Lieò label complete Lento's range.

STRONGOLI MARINA (KR)

DATTILO
C.DA DATTILO
88078 STRONGOLI MARINA (KR)
TEL. 0962/865613

The Dattilo estate, where Roberto Ceraudo grows his grapes using organic methods, is the second Calabrian winery this year to make its début in our Guide. This is thanks to the Amineo Rosso '95, a red made primarily from gaglioppo (over 80 per cent) to which a small percentage of aglianico and cabernet sauvignon is added. From our tastings of the Amineo wines - this is the name chosen by Ceraudo for his range - the absence of modern vinification equipment is rather evident, however. Ceraudo's fruit is good because he has devoted attention to his vineyards, but the wines display a certain lack of harmony and their flavours are a bit rustic. The Amineo Rosso and the Rosato are, however, quite interesting wines: the former has a not particularly deep ruby colour but broad aromas typical of the Calabrian red varieties such as gaglioppo and full flavour, with distinct hints of ripe cherries. The Rosato also has fairly marked aromas of red berry fruits, and on the palate the wine is refreshing, delicate and attractive. Completing the Dattilo range are two really rather modest whites: the Donnamaria, made from chardonnay grapes, and the Donnasusi, made from greco.

● Lamezia Rosso Ris. '92	▼	3
○ Lamezia Bianco '96		2
○ Lamezia Greco '96		2
● Lamezia Rosso '95		2
○ Valdamato Villa Caracciolo '96		2
● Lamezia Rosso Ris. '84	♟♟	4
● Lamezia Rosso Ris. '91	♟♟	3
● Lamezia Rosso '91	♟	3*
● Lamezia Rosso '92	♟	1
● Lamezia Rosso Ris. '90	♟	2*

● Amineo Rosso '95	▼	2*
⊙ Amineo Rosato '96		2

SICILY

The vineyards of the South are beginning to come into their own. Large conglomerates, such as Zonin and Marzotto, are considering investing in vineyards in Sicily (or have already done so) and there is now a widespread conviction that the future of Italian wines will be in this region. There are those, like the famous oenologist Giacomo Tachis, who predict a great future, particularly for the reds of the island and for the grape varieties such as nero d'Avola, a sort of Sicilian version of syrah, which has already demonstrated its potential in wines like Corvo's Duca Enrico and the Rosso del Conte of Tasca d'Almerita. Sicily could, therefore, be one of the major players on the Italian wine scene in the coming years. It will, in all probability, be the new frontier for Italian high quality wines, after years in which its production was debased and considered to be primarily suitable for blending wines or for making concentrated musts. But it is no use crying over spilt milk (or wine), and the thing to do straight away is to erase from our memory the names and even the faces of those who, for years, have ruined the name of Sicilian wines. The situation is finally changing: a great deal of boring and anonymous wine does still exist, but more and more wineries, both large and small, are beginning to produce better wines. New, more modern and quality-oriented vineyards are springing up everywhere. These are just the first steps, it is true, but they are signs of a definite trend and of the producers' desire not to return to the bad old days. In light of the above, the fact that in our Guide this year only one Sicilian wine, the Tasca d'Almeritas' '95 Chardonnay, was awarded the Three Glass accolade is merely a matter of chance. At the same time, the wineries with full listings in the Guide have gone from 16 to 20, and some larger companies, like Rapitala and Settesoli, have returned in triumph. Then there are two real revelations, Planeta and Cos, names that are, as yet, not particularly well-known to the wine loving public or, indeed, to people in the trade, but whose ranges show that they can hold their own with the very best in the region. Finally, a number of wineries have confirmed their quality: Tasca d'Almerita above all. Then come Corvo and Donnafugata, dependable as always, and also the former Tenuta di Castiglione estate, which this year is renamed after its owner, Benanti. We conclude with two small domaines which we believe will have a great future: Palari, near Messina, and D'Ancona on Pantelleria, both of which are real gems. As regards Pantelleria, we have to relate that there is a sort of all-out war going on at the moment between certain producers, just at a time when their Moscato Passito was beginning to be widely appreciated. Whatever the rights and wrongs of the issues, it would be hard to find a clearer example in the world of wine of producers shooting themselves in the foot.

ACATE (RG)

CASTELBUONO (PA)

CANTINA VALLE DELL'ACATE
C.DA BIDINI
97011 ACATE (RG)
TEL. 0932/874166

ABBAZIA SANTA ANASTASIA
C.DA SANTA ANASTASIA
90013 CASTELBUONO (PA)
TEL. 0921/671959

Gaetana Jacono, general manager of this large winery, is one of the most important women on the Sicilian wine scene. Thanks to her efforts, the Valle dell'Acate brand is becoming one of the most reliable and widely-found labels from the island. This is also due to the huge area under vine on which the company can depend - over 150 hectares. Ample resources gives the winery room for manoeuvre in choosing the level of quality of a given wine, by being more or less rigorous in its grape selection. Once again this year, we were not disappointed with the wines which this company presented. The best of the range is the company's most representative wine, the Cerasuolo di Vittoria '95. It is a fruity and easy red which well represents the typical characteristics of this DOC, one of the most southern in Italy. Similar, but even more forward, is another varietal the Frappato '96. We would particularly like to emphasize how well made both these wines are. Two versions of the Bidis white, from the '95 and the '96 vintage, complete the range. The former, obviously, is more mature, whereas the latter is more fruity and also less oaky. All of the above wines represent incredibly good value for money.

One of the rising stars of the Sicilian wine scene is to be found in the foothills of the Madonie highlands. It is situated on the border between the province of Palermo and that of Messina, not far from Cefalu and from Castelbuono, and its vineyards look out over the coast below, and the islands of Alicudi and Filicudi in the distance. The estate is owned by Franco Lena, a construction entrepreneur, and his wife Paola Moriconi, an architect. It takes its name from the Abbey of Santa Anastasia, founded in the 12th century by the Norman Count Ruggero d'Altavilla in the area that was formerly a Byzantine possession with the rather exotic name of Ypsigro. They have been producing quality wine for only a short time, but have done so unfailingly since they have been able to avail themselves of the masterly advice of Giacomo Tachis, the greatest of all Italian oenologists. One wine in particular greatly impressed us. It is the Passomaggio '95, a red made from nero d'Avola and merlot grapes, in whose finely fruity aromas one finds marked scents of tobacco and vanilla, and which is rich and full on the palate, with a barely perceptible, delicate acidity that underpins the fruit and makes it deliciously easy to drink. On the other hand, the Santa Anastasia Rosso '95 is made from nero d'Avola and pericone grapes: it is less concentrated than the Passomaggio, but it is certainly attractive and very well made. Less interesting, at the moment, are the two whites, the Santa Anastasia and the Zurrica, both of which are from the '96 vintage - not a great year for Sicilian wines.

O Bidis '95	♀	2*
O Bidis '96	♀	2*
● Cerasuolo di Vittoria '95	♀	2*
● Cerasuolo di Vittoria Frappato '96	♀	2*
O Bidis '94	♀	2*
● Cerasuolo di Vittoria '94	♀	2*
● Cerasuolo di Vittoria Frappato '95	♀	2*

● Passomaggio '95	♀♀	4
● Santa Anastasia Rosso '95	♀	3
O Santa Anastasia Bianco '96		3
O Zurrica '96		3

CASTELDACCIA (PA)

CATANIA

DUCA DI SALAPARUTA - VINI CORVO
VIA NAZIONALE, S.S. 113
90014 CASTELDACCIA (PA)
TEL. 091/945111

BARONE SCAMMACCA DEL MURGO
P.ZZA SCAMMACCA, 1
95131 CATANIA
TEL. 095/7130090

In the life of a winery there are certain periods which are particularly eventful and newsworthy. This most representative of Sicilian wineries is going through just such a phase. We will try to bring you up to date. To begin with, a new President, Sergio Vizzini - a noted Palermo figure and university professor - has been nominated. Enzo Toia, who has been a member of the staff for many years, has taken over as Commercial Director from Maurizio Ghiori. Also, at the end of October, Franco Giacosa, the oenologist, left the post of Technical Direction in order to move to the court of Gianni Zonin in Gambellara. Gaetano Zangara, on the other hand, remains in his role as Managing Director, thereby guaranteeing continuity of company policy. In short, there is enough material here to fill a whole book. On the production front, however, everything continues as before. Quality is reliable as ever, and again this year the Corvo wines, with their splendid new labels, have done very well in our tastings. Unfortunately, the Duca Enrico '93, the release of which is scheduled for the early part of '98, was not yet ready for judging for this edition of the Guide. We did taste, however, the best version ever of the Bianco di Valguarnera from the '94 vintage: this white made from inzolia grapes is characterized by a deliciously fruity bouquet and by a full and satisfying flavour. The Terre d'Agala '94, a red from nero d'Avola and frappato, is excellent, as is the Corvo Rosso '95. The Colomba Platino and the Glicine '96 are very correct (the former a little thinner than usual) as is the Corvo Bianco, also from the '96 vintage, the standard-bearer of the winery.

As careful observers and passionate supporters of Etna's winemaking scene, we cannot but hold in high regard what the Scammacca family is achieving on their estate. Their main efforts have had to do with the strictly viticultural aspects of production, with wide ranging experimentation, also on vines which are not traditional to the area. All this is overseen by Michele Scammacca, a young agronomist who graduated from the University of Brussels. The results of his efforts are beginning to be really interesting and we are certainly not being clairvoyants in predicting that, in the next few years, this winery will be one of the leaders in the rebirth of Sicilian wine: an event which it is now common for a great many people in the industry to forecast. The estate's best wine this year is the Tenuta San Michele '94, a red made from cabernet sauvignon, which, though displaying slightly evolved aromas, shows a tannic structure worthy of a great Bordeaux. It is certainly still a little severe and edgy, but in time it should soften considerably. Very enjoyable, but thinner than last year's version, is the Etna Bianco '96, which offers aromas dominated by hints of exotic fruit, pineapple in particular. The Etna Rosso '95, on the other hand, is light and a bit dilute: frankly we expected just a little more from this wine.

○	Bianca di Valguarnera '94	𝟏𝟏	4
●	Terre d'Agala '94	𝟏𝟏	3
○	Corvo Bianco '96	𝟏	2*
○	Corvo Colomba Platino '96	𝟏	3
○	Corvo Glicine '96	𝟏	2*
●	Corvo Rosso '95	𝟏	2*
●	Duca Enrico '84	𝟏𝟏𝟏	6
●	Duca Enrico '85	𝟏𝟏𝟏	6
●	Duca Enrico '86	𝟏𝟏𝟏	6
●	Duca Enrico '87	𝟏𝟏𝟏	6
●	Duca Enrico '88	𝟏𝟏𝟏	6
●	Duca Enrico '90	𝟏𝟏𝟏	5
●	Duca Enrico '92	𝟏𝟏𝟏	5
○	Bianca di Valguarnera '94	𝟏𝟏	4
○	Corvo Colomba Platino '95	𝟏𝟏	3

●	Tenuta San Michele '94	𝟏𝟏	4
○	Etna Bianco '96	𝟏	2*
●	Etna Rosso '95		3
○	Etna Bianco '95	𝟏𝟏	2*
●	Tenuta San Michele '92	𝟏𝟏	4
●	Etna Rosso '93	𝟏	3
●	Etna Rosso '94	𝟏	3
●	Tenuta San Michele '93	𝟏	4

LICATA (AG)

BARONE LA LUMIA
FRAZ. POZZILLO
92027 LICATA (AG)
TEL. 0922/891709

Each wine producing zone has an estate which flies the flag of tradition. In the Montalcino zone there is Biondi Santi, in the Langhe, there is Rinaldi and Mascarello, in Trentino there is Barone de Cles. In Sicily there is Barone La Lumia. His are wines of times past, perhaps a bit old-fashioned in style, but certainly they have charm and personality enough to stand out from the crowd in blind tastings. They come from vineyards situated in the Licata zone, not far from Agrigento, a viticultural area that is still little known but one which may well offer big surprises in the future. The top wine is a complex and fairly heavy red made from nero d'Avola grapes, the Signorio Rosso, now on the market in the '93 vintage. It has a ruby colour with deep garnet highlights and a bouquet in which one finds hints of ripe fruit and jam. On the palate it is still slightly edgy, with aggressive acidity and tannin and a very faintly bitter aftertaste. All in all it is a traditional wine, which does not make any allowance for the application of modern winemaking techniques either during maceration or wood ageing. Slightly less interesting is the white version of Signorio from the '95 vintage. This wine is already mature, with evolved aromas and with a flavour in which the acidity is still a little bit separate from the general structure of the wine. On the other hand, it is excellent value for money.

○	Signorio Bianco '95	🍷	2
●	Signorio Rosso '93	🍷	3

MARSALA (TP)

MARCO DE BARTOLI
C.DA FORNARA, 292
91025 MARSALA (TP)
TEL. 0923/962093

We are delighted to welcome Marco De Bartoli and his wines back to the Guide proper, after a year in Sicily's "Other Wineries" section. De Bartoli is a key person in Sicilian wine production, who, in around twenty years of activity, has succeeded in recreating the image of zones such as Marsala and the island of Pantelleria which seemed to be destined for a slow but inexorable decline. Over a period of time he has created wines such as Vecchio Samperi, the Moscato di Pantelleria Bukkuram and the Vigna La Miccia which had the great merit to act as a stimulus for other producers, sometimes to the extent of real provocation. For example, there was the famous controversy which De Baroli stirred up with his criticisms of the DOC regulations for Marsala, going so far as to renounce that denomination for his Vecchio Samperi, which is in effect a Marsala Vergine though it does not use the DOC label. The Vecchio Samperi, indeed, is still his standard-bearer, with its complex aromas in which on finds notes of cocoa and dried fruits in alcohol. Until some years ago he produced several different types, with different periods of ageing. On the market at present there is just one version, which seems very much like the 10 year-old wine of yore. We actually preferred the Vigna La Miccia, less pale than in the past and fairly concentrated both on the nose and palate. Good, but lacking the complexity which has made it a real star in the past, is the Moscato di Pantelleria Bukkuram, another classic of the winery. Our general feeling is that the wines have gained in correctness of execution, but display a bit less character - a situation which disappoints us just a little.

○	Vigna La Miccia	🍷🍷	4
○	Moscato di Pantelleria Bukkuram	🍷	4
○	Vecchio Samperi	🍷	4

MARSALA (TP)

TENUTA DI DONNAFUGATA
VIA SEBASTIANO LIPARI, 18
91025 MARSALA (TP)
TEL. 0923/999555

For the second year running this splendid estate owned by the Rallo family places itself among Sicily's winemaking élite. We are talking here about an upward spiral which, in our opinion, will carry the wines of Donnafugata still higher in the next edition of the Guide, as the modern vineyards which have been planted from 1992 onwards come into production. This year, meanwhile, we tasted the best vintage yet of the Chiarandà del Merlo, the '95. This is a white made from chardonnay and aged in small casks, which this time around appears to us to be less dominated by vanilla notes and much finer and more satisfying on the palate, with more fleshy fruit and fewer hints of toasted wood on the finish. The Tancredi '94, a red made from nero d'Avola and cabernet sauvignon grapes, is very interesting, even if it is a bit more severe and astringent than the '93 version, and also simpler on the nose. Even more delicious than it has ever been in the past, the Contessa Entellina Vigna di Gabri '96 displays fruity tones with light vanilla on the nose, and soft, full flavours, without any hint of harshness, but with really surprising concentration. It seemed to us to be better than either the light and quaffable Chardonnay La Fuga '96 or the Lighea '96. The range is suitably rounded off by the Rosso di Donnafugata '95, which is straightforward and simple, yet very well-made.

MARSALA (TP)

VINICOLA ITALIANA FLORIO
VIA VINCENZO FLORIO, 1
91025 MARSALA (TP)
TEL. 0923/781111

There are few wineries left which can effectively uphold the image and quality of Marsala, one of the most famous of Italy's wines around the world. Without a doubt, this is a product that deserves the DOCG recognition which it has not been granted so far. Among Marsala producers, the most representative is Florio, a large and ancient winery which has, for many years now, been owned by Cinzano. The name Florio is synonymous with high-quality Marsala, which may be compared with the world's great fortified white wines, in their dry, semi-dry and sweet styles: from Fino and Amontillado Sherry to White Port, from venerable old Madeira to Pineau de Charentes. The above considerations seemed to us particularly appropriate during a vertical tasting we carried out of the Marsala Vergine Baglio Florio, perhaps the most representative product of the winery, which finished with the last vintage to be released, the '86. This great Marsala has a yellow-topaz colour with amber reflections; well expressed, ethereal and tightly-knit aromas, with distinct vanilla notes that emphasize scents of raisins, honey and roasted hazelnuts. On the palate, it is dry but not harsh; it is warming, savoury and lively, with very good body and balance, and suggestions of liquorice root and bitter almonds on the long, aristocratic finish. The Marsala Vergine is excellent, with a robust body (44.05 grams of total extract) underpinned by notably crisp acidity (a PH of 3.20). It is a wine which, as it is today, just misses out on a Three Glass award, but which is still very young and therefore difficult to judge. If, in fact, one wanted to go back a few years, one could find a Baglio Florio '79 which is today in dazzling shape and is indeed considerably more impressive than when it made its first appearance.

O Chiarandà del Merlo '95	🍷🍷	4
O Contessa Entellina Vigna di Gabri '96	🍷🍷	3
● Tancredi '94	🍷🍷	4
O Contessa Entellina Chardonnay La Fuga '96	🍷	4
● Il Rosso '95	🍷	3
O Lighea '96	🍷	3
O Chiarandà del Merlo '93	🍷🍷	4
O Chiarandà del Merlo '94	🍷🍷	4
O Contessa Entellina Chardonnay La Fuga '94	🍷🍷	4
O Opera Unica	🍷🍷	5
● Tancredi '93	🍷🍷	4

O Marsala Vergine Baglio Florio '86	🍷🍷	5
O Marsala Superiore Targa Ris. '88	🍷🍷	4
O Marsala Vergine Baglio Florio '85	🍷🍷	5
O Marsala Vergine Terre Arse '86	🍷🍷	4
O Marsala Superiore Vecchioflorio	🍷	3
O Morsi di Luce '92	🍷	4

MARSALA (TP)

MENFI (AG)

CARLO PELLEGRINO
VIA DEL FANTE, 39
91025 MARSALA (TP)
TEL. 0923/951177

SETTESOLI
S.S. 115
92013 MENFI (AG)
TEL. 0925/75255

The Pellegrino winery is noted primarily for being one of the best producers of Marsala. It makes several types, but the best known is undoubtedly the Marsala Superiore, which has always proved consistent and reliable over the years. But the part of Pellegrino's range which has become increasingly more significant in recent times is the ever-wider selection of table wines under the Duca di Castelmonte label. From all of these, we have chosen the four which seemed to us to be the most interesting. Among the whites, we suggest the Fiorile Bianco '96 and the Cent'Are '96. Both are light and well made, but the former, which is based on the variety grecanico, is slightly more satisfying and concentrated. For the reds, on the other hand, we recommend the Fiorile Rosso '95 and the Etna Rosso Ulysse '94; the former being softer and more immediate and the latter still showing slightly edgy acidity, a characteristic which is nevertheless normal in a youthful 3 year-old red from this area. All this leads us to consider what the future may hold for this winery which, besides its traditional production of Marsala, will also have an increasingly wide and impressive range of non-fortified wines: their decision to diversify the range find us in perfect agreement.

Though we recognize the improvements in quality already seen in the wines made by this large cooperative, we are convinced that it still has a considerable way to go before it realizes its full potential. With such a modern winery, the undoubted technical bravura of its oenologists and the profound knowledge of the island's wine and its vineyards of the president Diego Planeta, this company should surely be able to achieve much more substantial results than those we saw this year. Our feeling is that the main concern is still to produce basic wines of acceptable commercial standard, rather than work decisively towards top-quality selections. But let us deal with this year's wines, which, as we said, seemed to us to be an improvement on the past. The most interesting product was the Bonera '94, the winery's top red, which is made from nero d'Avola, sangiovese and cabernet sauvignon. It has intense aromas of ripe red berry fruit and a soft, appealing flavour without excessively harsh acids or tannins; the'94 is one of the best versions ever of this classic Sicilian red. Staying with the reds, we should like point out the Soltero Rosso '95 (made from nero d'Avola and nerello mascalese) and the Settesoli Rosso '95 (made from nero d'Avola, pignatello and sangiovese), two rather similar well made, mid-weight wines. Among the whites, the Porto Palo '96 and the Feudo dei Fiori '96 merit our One Glass award. Both are light and delicately fruity; the former is made from a blend of inzolia and catarratto, and the latter from inzolia and chardonnay.

● Etna Rosso Ulysse '94	♛	3
○ Fiorile Bianco '96	♛	2*
● Fiorile Rosso '95	♛	2*
○ Marsala Superiore	♛	3
○ Cent'Are '96		2
○ Marsala Vergine Vintage '62	♛♛	5
○ Alcamo Duca di Castelmonte '95	♛	2*
○ Marsala Superiore	♛	4
○ Moscato di Pantelleria '94	♛	3
○ Moscato Passito di Pantelleria '94	♛	4

● Bonera '94	♛♛	3*
○ Feudo dei Fiori '96	♛	2*
○ Porto Palo '96	♛	1*
● Settesoli Rosso '95	♛	1*
● Soltero Rosso '95	♛	2*
○ Settesoli Bianco '96		1
○ Soltero Bianco '96		1

MESSINA

PALERMO

PALARI
LOC. S. STEFANO BRIGA
98123 MESSINA
TEL. 090/694281

RAPITALÀ ADELKAM
VIA SEGESTA, 9
90141 PALERMO
TEL. 091/332088

When we listed this tiny winery in our Guide for the first time, we knew it was something of a special case. The passion of its owner, the architect Salvatore Geraci, who makes wines as a hobby, had infected both us and the famous Piedmontese oenologist Donato Lanati, who agreed to act as a consultant for the winery even though it is over 1500 kilometres from his home. After the tastings which we conducted this year, we can happily assert that we were confronted with wines of excellent quality, among the best from Sicily and from Southern Italy in general. The Faro Palari '95, re-tasted after a year in bottle, achieved a score very near the 90-point mark and demonstrated really impressive keeping ability. As things stand at the moment, it is one of the top three or four Sicilian reds. But the real surprise was the company's second wine, the Rosso del Soprano '95, from nerello mascalese, nerello cappuccio and nocera grapes. Even though Geraci chooses to pass it off as an altogether lesser wine, it is in reality a red with very refined, ripe fruity aromas, and a rich, soft flavour. It is, in fact, a small masterpiece, but above all it is a wine that well expresses its "terroir" and microclimate.

For some years now this famous winery has not appeared in our Guide. We do not wish to labour the question as to whether this was due to the severity or carelessness of our tasting panel, or if the wines were simply not of a sufficiently high standard. Suffice to say that today we are delighted finally to be able to comment on a quality range of wines from such an important and well known producer. And we would like to go further and offer our compliments for a wine that we especially liked: the Alcamo Rapitalà Grand Cru '95. This is a splendid Mediterranean white which has intense aromas of ripe fruit and is soft and mouth-filling on the palate, but which above all is long and shows good concentration. It is without question one of the best whites from the region and a benchmark for style and quality over the coming years. The two basic Rapitalà wines also scored better than in the past. The Alcamo Rapitalà '96 is a well made white, which is perhaps not very rich in aromas, but let us remember that there was rain during the '96 harvest; it was definitely not a memorable vintage. The Rapitalà Rosso '95 is very correctly made; it is fruity on the nose with hints of ripe cherries, and has a delicate acid vein on the palate which points up the wine's far from exceptional body, but does make it very pleasant and quaffable. Count Hugues de La Gatinais, the French nobleman who owns the winery, will surely forgive us if we seek a comparison with certain Beaujolais Villages wines with which he is certainly familiar, and which have a profile not so very different from that of this red.

● Rosso del Soprano '95	ΨΨ	3*		○ Alcamo Rapitalà		
● Faro Palari '95	ΨΨ	5		Grand Cru '95	ΨΨ	4
				○ Alcamo Rapitalà '96	Ψ	3
				● Rapitalà Rosso '95	Ψ	3

PALERMO

PALERMO

SPADAFORA
VIA A. DE GASPERI, 58
90146 PALERMO
TEL. 091/514952

CANTINE TORREVECCHIA
VIA L. ARIOSTO, 10/A
90144 PALERMO
TEL. 091/342208

The Spadafora winery achieves its best scores yet in this year's Guide, a demonstration of how important experimentation in the vineyard is in order to improve quality. This winery is, in fact, one of the most avant garde in the field of viticultural research. It is no coincidence that it also houses the Experimental Winery of the Regional Institute for Vines and Wine. The most representative wine in the range is, without doubt, the Don Pietro Rosso, whose '95 vintage has now been released. This is made from a blend of nero d'Avola, cabernet sauvignon and merlot, and is aged in stainless steel, without any contact with wood. It displays very positive and clean aromas, with fruity hints and very light vegetal notes. On the palate, the round fruit dominates the acids and tannins, conferring fullness and a plump softness to the wine. All the whites from the '96 vintage are decent, with the basic Alcamo and the Don Pietro Bianco, made from inzolia and müller thurgau grapes, actually better than the Alcamo Vigna Virzi, which is a tiny bit thinner and more neutral than in the past. We wish to emphasize the really excellent value for money shown by all of these wines - one of the strong suits of this winery.

One can briefly sum up our judgment of the Torrevecchia winery by saying that the good impression this winery made last year has been substantially confirmed. This is a modern winery, with very large vineyard holdings situated mainly between Gela and Vittoria, in south-eastern Sicily. It is run by Daniela and Giuseppe Favuzza, while the commercial director is Santi Buzzotta, one of the island's most brilliant marketing men. The best wine is again the Casale dei Biscari (a red made from nero d'Avola), this time from the '94 vintage. It is a wine of slightly more evolved and mature aromas than we found in the '93 vintage presented in the last edition. However, it still has the same softness and good concentration of flavour which make it one of the most interesting reds from the island. The '94 Cerasuolo di Vittoria also again performs well, and displays straightforward but extremely clean and typical varietal aromas, which are fruity and somewhat estery. The flavour follows suit with a very pleasant, easy drinking style, making this a not very complex, but a technically extremely well made wine. The fresher and more immediate Pietra di Zoe '96 (based on frappato) is an interesting red with delicately fruity aromas and a light, pleasing flavour. The Bianco d'Alcamo '96, on the other hand, is not quite as good as we expected; its bouquet is overly mature and it is neutral in flavour.

● Don Pietro Rosso '95	ΨΨ	3*
○ Alcamo '96	Ψ	1*
○ Alcamo Vigna Virzì '96	Ψ	2*
○ Don Pietro Bianco '96	Ψ	2*
○ Alcamo Vigna Virzì '95	Ψ	1*
● Don Pietro Rosso '94	Ψ	2
● Vigna Virzì Rosso '95	Ψ	2*

● Casale dei Biscari '94	ΨΨ	3*
● Pietra di Zoe '96	Ψ	2*
○ Bianco d'Alcamo '96		2
● Casale dei Biscari '93	ΨΨ	3*
○ Bianco d'Alcamo '95	Ψ	2*
● Cerasuolo di Vittoria '94	Ψ	2*
○ Inzolia '95	Ψ	2*

PANTELLERIA (TP)

SALVATORE MURANA
C.DA KHAMMA, 276
91017 PANTELLERIA (TP)
TEL. 0923/915231

There are very few producers for whom we reserve the honour of a full listing featuring only "empty" Glasses. This occurs when, in the course of the year, no wines are released by a winery which, however, we consider so important that we cannot leave it out of the Guide. Thus we continue to include the listing for Salvatore Murana and, in the grid at the bottom of the page, we list the wines tasted for our previous editions, and therefore with all the Glasses empty. But what happened to Murana and his small winery in Pantelleria is worth telling you about. The problem is an example of the in-fighting which is typical among the producers of Moscato di Pantelleria. The purists, in fact, maintain that the grapes used for the wine should be exclusively sun-dried. Those who use other drying techniques, which, amongst other things, are authorized under the present European Union rules, have been treated as criminals and subjected to a series of measures which have bordered on persecution. This means that Murana's wines will be released late due to a series of bureaucratic delays and requests for analyses which are, to say the least, abnormal. This is a problem which seriously damages the image of a producer who is, without any doubt, the finest interpreter of the wines of Pantelleria. But above all it is a matter which will, in all probability, turn out to be a storm in a teacup (or at least we hope so). With this entry in the Guide we wish to demonstrate our support for one of the best "vignerons" in Italy who, in our opinion, has been unjustly involved in an ugly story which probably has its origin in some personal squabble rather than any real intent to safeguard the interests of consumers.

PANTELLERIA (TP)

D'ANCONA
C.DA CIMILIA
PANTELLERIA (TP)
TEL. 0923/918350

If you really wish to understand what making hand-crafted wines are, you should go and seek out Giacomo and Solidea D'Ancona. If the "mad angels" - as Veronelli once described the growers of the island of Pantelleria - still indeed exist, these two are certainly part of their band. In their tiny winery they produce little more than 9,000 bottles of Moscato Passito, made with sun-dried grapes, nurtured with incredible care. They actually stay up all night when rain threatens so that they can immediately cover the grapes before the first drops fall. The results are absolutely amazing over the entire range they offer. There are four wines all based on the zibibbo grape, which can be divided into two subgroups. Two are dry and aromatic, the Bianco Sciuvaki and the Scirocco, both of which we tried in the '96 vintage. The former is an aromatic white with clean aromas and good body. The latter is a splendid wine, with an intensely aromatic bouquet which is almost reminiscent of Gewürztraminer, and has a notable structure. It is, in short, a great white to serve with foie gras. But the two wines which literally made the members of our tasting panel jump up out of their seats, were the two versions of Moscato Passito di Pantelleria. The normal version is concentrated and aromatic, and delicately sweet: in a word, delicious. At its price it is a gift. The Solidea '93 is much more evolved and dense, and is intensely sweet: it must one of Italy's very finest dessert wines and it came extremely close to being awarded our Three Glass rating. We are certain that this tiny winery will produce some real oenological pearls in the very near future.

	Wine		
O	Moscato Passito di Pantelleria Martingana '93	♟♟♟	6
O	Moscato di Pantelleria Mueggen '93	♟♟	5
O	Moscato di Pantelleria Mueggen '94	♟♟	5
O	Moscato Passito di Pantelleria Khamma '92	♟♟	5
O	Moscato Passito di Pantelleria Khamma '93	♟♟	5
O	Moscato Passito di Pantelleria Martingana '90	♟♟	6
O	Moscato Passito di Pantelleria Martingana '92	♟♟	6

	Wine		
O	Moscato Passito di Pantelleria	♟♟	3
O	Moscato Passito di Pantelleria Solidea '93	♟♟	4
O	Scirocco '96	♟♟	2*
O	Bianco Sciuvaki '96	♟	2*

SAMBUCA DI SICILIA (AG)　　VALLELUNGA PRATAMENO (CL)

PLANETA
LOC. ULMO E MAROCCOLI
92017 SAMBUCA DI SICILIA (AG)
TEL. 0925/80009

TASCA D'ALMERITA
C.DA REGALEALI
93010 VALLELUNGA PRATAMENO (CL)
TEL. 0921/544002

Do you want a new name that will shape the future of Sicilian wines? Well, here it is: this is without doubt the winery of the future for the island and beyond. It is owned by the Planeta family, a very well-known surname in Sicilian wine, and was created just three years ago: already however half the world is talking about their wines. In our opinion, perhaps they are doing so with excessive enthusiasm, given that the wines are certainly very interesting but that they also have a great deal of room to improve. The technical direction is entrusted to Carlo Corino, an oenologist of great experience both in Italy and abroad. But let us go on to the wines, which all share a style that emphasizes softness and roundedness, rather logical qualities to strive for given the character of the soil and climate in the area from which they come. We begin with the two most prestigious reds, the Merlot and the Cabernet Sauvignon, both from the '95 vintage, and both splendid. We slightly prefer the former, which seems to us to display the fundamental character of its variety to a greater degree, with lactic tones and very strong hints of tobacco. The wines are more similar on the palate, which is dominated by plump, rich and very concentrated fruit. The Chardonnay '95 is interesting, but its perhaps faintly too toasty nose and a slightly bitter finish made us only guess at what the potential for this grape variety here might be. The two La Segreta wines are both excellent. The Bianco '96 (made from grecanico, catarratto and chardonnay) is aromatic and soft on the palate, and the Rosso '95 (made from nero d'Avola and merlot) displays just a hint of bitter-cherry fruit on the finish. The Alastro '95, a white from grecanico and catarratto, dominated by notes of ripe fruit on the nose but rather neutral on the palate, was less impressive.

And so we come to the company which this year stands at the very top of the Sicilian ratings. This is nothing new, but never before have we noted such a wide gap between the splendid winery belonging to the noble Tasca d'Almerita family and the other - still excellent - producers on the island. Indeed, the region's only Three Glass award went to a Chardonnay from the vineyards of this estate, located right in the centre of Sicily. The Tasca d'Almerita's Chardonnay '95 is a very forceful wine, rich and voluptuous on the nose, with notes of peanut butter and of ripe fruit, barely tinged with light hints of vanilla. On the palate it is full, opulent, fat and incredibly long, and is enlivened by a light vein of acidity which sustains its very notable structure. It is among the best Italian Chardonnays in this edition of the Guide. The Cabernet Sauvignon '94 is interesting, but certainly without the richness of the '92 version; it is concentrated and full, but with the usual slightly bitter finish, a symptom perhaps of a certain over-ripeness of the grapes. Good news, on the other hand, comes from the Rosso del Conte '94, perhaps the best that we have ever tasted, which is concentrated and shows real conviction. There is elegant ripe fruit on the nose, as well as body which is finally rich and complex, with the tannins completely dominated by soft, fleshy fruit. Very good, besides, is the Regaleali Rosso '95, which makes us predict great things for the more important reds from this vintage which will be released next year. The three whites, on the other hand (the Regaleali and the Villa Tasca, both from the '96 vintage, and the Nozze d'Oro '95) performed slightly below par, but within a range of this quality level this can hardly be construed as a criticism.

●	Cabernet Sauvignon '95	🍷🍷	5
○	Chardonnay '95	🍷🍷	5
○	La Segreta Bianco '96	🍷🍷	3
●	La Segreta Rosso '95	🍷🍷	3
●	Merlot '95	🍷🍷	5
○	Alastro '95	🍷	4

○	Chardonnay '95	🍷🍷🍷	6
●	Cabernet Sauvignon '94	🍷🍷	6
●	Regaleali Rosso '95	🍷🍷	3*
●	Rosso del Conte '94	🍷🍷	4
○	Nozze d'Oro '95	🍷	3
○	Regaleali Bianco '96	🍷	2*
⊙	Regaleali Rosato '96	🍷	2*
○	Villa Tasca '96	🍷	2*
●	Cabernet Sauvignon '89	🍷🍷🍷	6
●	Cabernet Sauvignon '90	🍷🍷🍷	6
●	Cabernet Sauvignon '92	🍷🍷🍷	4
○	Chardonnay '90	🍷🍷🍷	5
○	Chardonnay '92	🍷🍷🍷	6
○	Chardonnay '94	🍷🍷🍷	5
○	Chardonnay '93	🍷🍷🍷	5

VIAGRANDE (CT)

BENANTI
VIA GARIBALDI, 475
95029 VIAGRANDE (CT)
TEL. 095/7893533

VITTORIA (RG)

COS
P.ZZA DEL POPOLO, 34
97019 VITTORIA (RG)
TEL. 0932/864042

The wine growing area which stretches around Etna and whose DOC is named after the volcano, is one of the most interesting on the island. It boasts vineyards situated at notably high altitudes, indigenous grape varieties of particular worth, such as the white carricante and the red nerello mascalese, as well as producers who practise the most modern winemaking techniques: all these factors contribute to producing wines of great personality and character. The best example of this is the wines presented by the Benanti winery, formerly known as Tenuta di Castiglione. It is a series of very high quality wines, with some of absolute excellence. In our opinion the best of all seems to be the Etna Rosso Rovittello '94, which is aged in small casks. It has a very deep ruby colour and aromas in which the fruity tones blend very well with vanilla notes which are a result of wood contact. These features of great elegance are echoed in the flavour, in which particularly soft tannins are evident; the wine has a very solid general structure, and is well balanced. The Etna Bianco Superiore Pietramarina '94 is good, but a fraction less convincing than last year's version; it is more mature than the '93 and lacks those minerally hints we so appreciated last year. We found the Etna Bianco Bianco di Caselle '95 more satisfying, and this clearly augurs well for a fine version of Pietramarina from the same year. More or less on the same level as the '93, on the other hand, is the Etna Rosso Rosso di Verzella '94, which is appealingly fruity, and a little bit softer and more forward than in previous vintages.

We cannot but ask ourselves where Sicilian wine might be if only there were more producers with the skills of Giusto Occhipinti, the owner of Cos: in other words, with the ability of this serious and capable man who has, over the years, demonstrated the enormous potential of the Cerasuolo di Vittoria DOC located in south-eastern Sicily. And along the same lines, one cannot help remembering what an oenologist of the calibre of the great Giacomo Tachis has been saying for a number of years now: that the future of top-quality Italian wine lies increasingly with the south, where the sun shines and the sky is almost always blue. And Occhipinti's wines taste of sunshine and blue skies; they have the warmth and the softness of ripe grapes, and we like them a lot. This year, he only just missed out on a Three Glass award. In fact, his Cerasuolo di Vittoria Sciri '95 got through to our final round, but also the Le Vigne di Cos Bianco and Rosso, both from the '95 vintage, and the Cerasuolo Di Vittoria Vigna di Bastonaca '95 showed very well in our tastings. The Le Vigne di Cos range consists of two very modern and innovative products: the Rosso is made from cabernet sauvignon and the Bianco from chardonnay, and both are aged in small casks. The last wine we bring to your attention is the basic Cerasuolo di Vittoria '95: it is a wine with a very fair price which scored only a couple of points lower than its more prestigious stablemates.

● Etna Rosso Rovittello '94	♥♥ 5	● Cerasuolo di Vittoria '95	♥♥ 3*
○ Etna Bianco Bianco di Caselle '95	♥ 3	● Cerasuolo di Vittoria Sciri '95	♥♥ 4
○ Etna Bianco Superiore Pietramarina '94	♥ 4	● Cerasuolo di Vittoria Vigna di Bastonaca '95	♥♥ 4
● Etna Rosso Rosso di Verzella '94	♥ 3	○ Le Vigne di Cos Bianco '95	♥♥ 4
○ Etna Bianco Superiore Pietramarina '93	♥♥ 4	● Le Vigne di Cos Rosso '95	♥♥ 4
● Etna Rosso Rovittello '93	♥♥ 5	● Cerasuolo di Vittoria '94	♥♥ 3
○ Etna Bianco Superiore Pietramarina '92	♥ 4	● Le Vigne di Cos Rosso '93	♥♥ 4
● Etna Rosso Rosso di Verzella '93	♥ 3	● Le Vigne di Cos Rosso '94	♥♥ 4
● Etna Rosso Rosso di Verzella '92	♥ 2*	● Cerasuolo di Vittoria '93	♥ 3
		○ Le Vigne di Cos Bianco '95	♥ 4
		● Le Vigne di Cos Rosso '92	♥ 4
		○ Ramingallo '94	♥ 3
		○ Ramingallo '95	♥ 3

OTHER WINERIES

The following producers obtained good scores in our tastings with one or more of their wines:

PROVINCE OF AGRIGENTO

Milazzo,
Campobello di Licata, tel. 0922/878207,
Maria Costanza Bianco '96,
Maria Costanza Rosso '92

PROVINCE OF CATANIA

Antica Tenuta del Nanfro,
Catania, tel. 095/514825,
Iago '96,
Cerasuolo di Vittoria '96

Barone di Villagrande,
Milo, tel. 095/7082175,
Etna Bianco Superiore '96,
Etna Rosso '95

PROVINCE OF MESSINA

Hauner,
Lingua di Salina, tel. 090/9843141,
Malvasia delle Lipari Naturale '95,
Malvasia delle Lipari Passita '95

Caravaglio,
Malfa Salina, tel. 090/9844368,
Salina Bianco '95

Colosi, Messina, tel. 090/53852,
Malvasia delle Lipari Naturale '95,
Malvasia delle Lipari Passita '95

PROVINCE OF PALERMO

Mid,
Palermo,
tel. 091/6396237,
Inzolia '96,
Ligorio Bianco '96

Vesco,
Palermo,
tel. 091/204702,
Alcamo Carta d'Oro '96,
Vesco '96

Terre di Ginestra,
San Cipirello,
tel. 091/8576767,
Terre di Ginestra '96,
Pelavet '95

PROVINCE OF RAGUSA

Avide,
Comiso,
tel. 0932/967456,
Barocco '93,
Cerasuolo di Vittoria Etichetta Nera '95,
Dalle Terre di Herea '96

PROVINCE OF SIRACUSA

Cooperativa Interprovinciale Elorina,
Rosolini,
tel. 0931/857068,
Eloro Rosso Villa Dorata '96,
Eloro Rosso Pachino '95

SARDINIA

The whole of Sardinia will remember the 1996 harvest for the dramatic drop in the volume of wine made. In the Province of Nuoro, in particular, the production of some wineries was down by as much as 95 per cent. The failure of the fruit to set and rainstorms during the critical period of the vintage had a deleterious effect on much of the harvest. Few wineries succeeded in saving their crop and obtaining healthy and perfectly ripe grapes. Red wines accounted for the lion's share of the around 180 wines we tasted, and we want to stress once again that the majority of them were not DOC wines. But the big news in this edition of the Guide is that Sardinia has increased the number of its wines to win our Three Glass accolade. This is an unequivocal sign of the continued improvement shown by the region's winemaking. For the third year running we have awarded our Three Glasses to the Argiolas estate's Turriga and for the second time the Marchese di Villamarina from Sella & Mosca has also received this coveted award. These wines are joined by the Terre Brune from the Cantina Sociale di Santadi which earns our top award for the first time. But there are also many reds which rated Two Glasses. The addition of cabernet sauvignon, merlot, sangiovese, montepulciano and small percentages of indigenous grape varieties to cannonau and carignano, the region's main red grape varieties, has given a new direction to Sardinia's winemaking. There are now many Sardinian winegrowers who are also concentrating on new grape varieties in order to produce wines of international flavour. This is undoubtedly a positive step, though if it were to be exaggerated it would present the risk of compromising, in a brief period of time, the identity of many traditional wines and zones. We should not forget however that the closure of many of the island's cooperative wineries can be attributed to either vineyards being abandoned or to the low standards of winemaking. Of the whites which we tasted, the best seemed to be those from the Gallura district, particularly the Vermentinos, which this year carry the DOCG designation, the first assigned to a Sardinian wine. Many of these scored over 80 points in our tastings, ratings such as these augur very well for the future. The rosés, which were vinified to exalt their aromas and bring out their freshness, were also good and the sweet wines were excellent. Many of these easily won Two Glass awards, with the Argiolas estate's Angialis at the top of its category, thanks to one of the most seductive versions of recent years. The majority of these wines are made from malvasia, girò, nasco and moscato. Meanwhile the production zone for Vernaccia di Oristano, one of Italy's most interesting wines, did not, unfortunately, show signs of recovery. The product range of the island is completed by some really interesting brut and demi-sec sparkling wines. The quality level of Sardinian wines has, undoubtedly, improved. Perhaps it is no accident that this has coincided with a fall in production and the shut down of several cooperative wineries. If this trend is confirmed over the next few years, Sardinia can be proud of having embarked on the road to quality, in the long run the only one which pays.

ALGHERO (SS)

Tenute Sella & Mosca
Loc. I Piani
07041 Alghero (SS)
tel. 079/997700

In last year's edition we suggested that we would have a pleasant surprise with the new vintage of the Marchese di Villamarina red. The '92 beat the 90-point margin, and was again awarded our Three Glass accolade. This confirms the commitment of a winery which is at the very top of the Italian oenological tree, and which is always striving for even better results, with high-quality products that are destined not only for the domestic market, but for the international one as well. This '92 has an intense and complex bouquet, in which one finds vanilla scents along with notes of toasted wood, dried roses and red berry fruits. On the palate it is full, soft and broad with elegant structure. It is a concentrated and long-lived wine, which has not yet reached its full maturity. Among the other reds we found the Tanca Farrà '92 (a blend of cannonau and cabernet sauvignon) very good. It has evolved an ethereal bouquet, and on the palate it displays full, interesting fruit: we awarded it Two Glasses. The Cannonau di Sardegna Riserva '93 is also very interesting. It has intense and lightly balsamic aromas; on the palate, it is warming and well balanced. The vintage Anghelu Ruju is produced only in particularly good years. The '87 has aromas of vanilla and red berry fruits; it is mouth-filling, sweet, rich and long and well deserved its Two Glass award, which we also gave to the other dessert wine, the Monteluce (made from nasco grapes), which is delicately sweet and very long on the palate. Among the '96 whites, the Vermentino di Sardegna La Cala and the Sauvignon Le Arenarie stand out: two wines that are clean and appealing in style, and richly fresh and aromatic.

●	Marchese di Villamarina '92	▼▼▼	6
○	Alghero Le Arenarie '96	▼▼	3
●	Anghelu Ruju Ris. '87	▼▼	4
○	Monteluce	▼▼	4
●	Tanca Farrà '92	▼▼	3
○	Vermentino di Sardegna La Cala '96	▼▼	2
⊙	Alghero Oleandro '96	▼	2
○	Alghero Torbato Terre Bianche '96	▼	3
●	Cannonau di Sardegna Ris. '93	▼	3
●	Marchese di Villamarina Rosso '90	▽▽▽	5
○	Alghero Le Arenarie '95	▽▽	3
●	Tanca Farrà '89	▽▽	3
●	Tanca Farrà '90	▽▽	3

ARZACHENA (SS)

Tenute Capichera
Loc. Capichera
07021 Arzachena (SS)
tel. 0789/80612

The Ragnedda brothers, Vermentino specialists, have diversified their production. Vermentino still remains the basis of their range, but is vinified in different ways to obtain three different styles. For some years Capichera has been synonymous - mainly due to its traditional Vermentino di Gallura - with extremely high quality whites. After this came the Vigna 'Ngena, which literally translated means "the others' vineyard", and the special selection (which used to be labelled as Riserva) but which, from this vintage, is to be called "Vendemmia Tardiva". The name ("late harvest") is somewhat reminiscent of the wines produced in Northern European vineyards or some white dessert wines from Central Italy which are inspired by French models. But here, on the other hand, we are dealing with a wine which is inspired, rather than by the dessert wines of the North, by those made in the past by the farmers of the upper Gallura district, for which the extremely ripe grapes were picked in October. We have no hesitation in awarding Two Glasses to the Vermentino di Gallura Vendemmia Tardiva '96 for its rich personality, which is apparent even on the nose, where one finds a blend of ripe pear and exotic fruit aromas. It is a full bodied white, which is soft and round, warming and substantial on the palate. We found some of these sensations again, if to a less intense degree, in the other Vermentino, the Vigna 'Ngena '96, which is a little thinner on the palate. The standard Vermentino di Gallura '96 is not up to the level of former vintages but it is well-made, attractive on the nose and well balanced on the palate.

○	Vermentino di Gallura Vendemmia Tardiva '96	▼▼	5
○	Vermentino di Gallura Capichera '96	▼	5
○	Vermentino di Gallura Vigna 'Ngena '96	▼	4
○	Capichera '95	▽▽	5

CABRAS (OR)

ATTILIO CONTINI
VIA GENOVA, 48/50
09072 CABRAS (OR)
TEL. 0783/290806

Established almost a century ago, this winery has long been recognized and appreciated for its fine Vernaccia di Oristano. The chronic crisis in whose grip this wine has lived for many years has forced many wineries to broaden and diversify their product base. The Continis were among the first to reverse this trend: a brave choice and one filled with uncertainty but which, in the end, proved to be correct. The estate's principal wine, the Vernaccia di Oristano, is backed up by two interesting whites: Karmis and Arethusa. The former is made from 100 per cent vernaccia grapes and is vinified at controlled temperatures. It has ripe and a slightly almondy fragrance which is typical of young Vernaccia; there is notable body and structure, but on the palate it is very soft, attractive and appealingly drinkable. The Arethusa (made from a blend of vernaccia and nuragus) seemed to us not to be quite so good. Its nose is characterized by notes of vanilla and ripe fruit; fresh, soft and quite full on the palate. The rosé Nieddera is also very good: clean and delicate on the nose, if not very intense. On the palate, it is fruity and better balanced than in previous years. Less interesting is the Vermentino di Sardegna, which along with the Cannonau di Sardegna, completes the range of wines which were available for tasting. Among the Vernaccias, the '88 has a deep golden colour, a sweet ethereal aroma characterized by hints of nuts - particularly almonds - and by the lightly oxidized tones which are typical of this wine. On the palate, however, it did not seem particularly full, although its length is quite good. A re-tasting of the Antico Gregori (made from vernaccia grapes), evaluated in previous editions of the Guide, confirmed its excellence.

○ Karmis '96	🍷🍷	2
○ Vernaccia di Oristano '88	🍷🍷	3
○ Arethusa '96	🍷	3
⊙ Nieddera Rosato '96	🍷	1
○ Antico Gregori	♀♀	6
○ Elibaria '94	♀	3
○ Karmis '94	♀	2

CARDEDU (NU)

ALESSANDRO LOI & FIGLI
S.S. ORIENTALE SARDA, KM. 124,200
08040 CARDEDU (NU)
TEL. 070/657259

This winery has returned to the Guide after three eventful years. The most important change has been the restructuring of the vineyards, with the extension of the area under vine, which has gone from 17 to 50 hectares. The Lois also envisage renting other selected vineyards in the most suitable sites in the Ogliastra zone. The predominant grape variety in their wines is cannonau backed up by other varieties such as cabernet sauvignon and cabernet franc, sangiovese and merlot. The winery has also been totally renovated, though maintaining its original look with wooden beams and granite in full view. The ageing cellar is particularly atmospheric, with its large Slavonian oak barrels and small barriques. The total capacity of the winery is around 20,000 hectolitres. Among the immediate projects of the Loi siblings (Anna Giulia, Sergio, Gianluigi, Alessandro and Renato) is a programme, from the next harvest onwards, to bring out the best in the cannonau, which will be vinified both on its own and blended with other varieties. For this edition of the Guide we tried the entire range of their Cannonaus, which, however, seemed to us a little too evolved, both on the nose and on the palate. The wines from recent vintages have maintained, on the other hand, a good, deep ruby colour; they have richly fruity aromas, in which raspberry and cherry notes dominate. On the palate, particularly in the specially selected Cardedo '95, one finds a certain depth, good structure and highish alcohol, which are all typical characteristics of Cannonau. In short, this is a wine which gives us an indication of what the Loi's future wines may be like.

● Cannonau di Sardegna Cardedo '95	🍷	3
● Cannonau di Sardegna Montiferru '93		3

DOLIANOVA (CA)

CANTINA SOCIALE DOLIANOVA
LOC. SANT'ESU
S.S. 387, KM. 17,150
09041 DOLIANOVA (CA)
TEL. 070/740643

DORGALI (NU)

CANTINA SOCIALE DI DORGALI
VIA PIEMONTE, 11
08022 DORGALI (NU)
TEL. 0784/96143

This winery, too, has notably reduced its production in the last few years, but not, however, to the detriment of its quality. This year we were pleasantly surprised by the wines which were presented to us for tasting. The highest score went to the white Dolicante, a blend of nasco, vermentino, nuragus and clairette - the percentages vary from year to year. The '96 has a very complex nose in which one finds vegetal and vanilla notes. On the palate, it displays a rich gamut of flavours with particularly strong aromatic notes of sage and ripe fruit; the structure is notable and it has good length. The Vermentino di Sardegna '96 is interesting, with a bouquet which is reminiscent of ripe peaches and melons; it is well balanced, savoury and fresh on the palate. More straightforward but equally attractive is the Nuragus di Cagliari '96. We were not excited by the chardonnay-based Capidiana '96: it has good aroma but it is short in the mouth. We also awarded One Glass to the rosé Sibiola '96 for its attractive aroma, even if this was not really carried through on the palate. Among the reds the Falconaro, made from a complex blend of cannonau, monica, barbera, carignano and pascale, stands out. The Monica di Sardegna '96 is also good and in fact it was among the best we tasted this year. It has fresh, slightly herbaceous aromas and is well balanced on the palate. The Cannonau di Sardegna, on the other hand, was a little under par, unbalanced by lowish acidity and subdued aroma. The sparkling wines, Caralis Brut and Scaleri Demi-sec, are very good and both earn One Glass, a rating which we have rarely awarded to Sardinian sparkling wines.

This year witnessed something of a lull for the cooperative winery of Dorgali. The disastrous vintage decimated the harvest throughout the entire Province, sparing only a very few zones. For some years now, however, this winery has not depended exclusively on small suppliers for its grapes, having planted quite a lot of hectares of vineyard, all at a single site. This has allowed the Cantina to produce healthier grapes of more even quality, and also to stop the continual division of properties, a factor that has led inexorably to the impoverishment of the viticultural resources of many parts of Sardinia. The production area consists of around 700 hectares, comprising the Cantina's own vineyards and those of its members, and is spread around the choicest sites of the Baronia. The main variety is still cannonau, even if other indigenous grapes are being cultivated and new experimental vineyards are being planted with international vines. In its continued quest to keep up with the times, the Cantina has built some new premises, including a large conference room and a wine shop with a tasting bar. The best wine from Dorgali tasted this year was the red Filieri '95. It has a deep ruby colour and fairly broad aromas with vegetal notes, where in particular one finds hints of green pepper; on the palate, the wine is refreshing, soft and long. It is a young wine which needs no additional ageing. We also wish to bring to your attention the Cannonau di Sardegna '95 and, in particular, the Filieri Rosato '96, a fresh and appealing wine on the palate, even if it is a little unexpressive on the nose.

O Dolicante '96	♥♥	3
O Caralis Brut	♥	3
● Falconaro	♥	3
● Monica di Sardegna '96	♥	2
O Nuragus di Cagliari '96	♥	2
O Scaleri Demi-sec	♥	3
☉ Sibiola Rosato '96	♥	2
O Vermentino di Sardegna '96	♥	2
O Capidiana Chardonnay '96		4

● Filieri Rosso '96	♥	2
● Cannonau di Sardegna '95		3
☉ Filieri Rosato '96		2
● Cannonau di Sardegna '94	♀	3
● Cannonau di Sardegna Filieri '95	♀	2

JERZU (NU)

CANTINA SOCIALE DI JERZU
VIA UMBERTO I, 1
08044 JERZU (NU)
TEL. 0782/70028

The Cantina Sociale di Jerzu appears intermittently in our Guide. In the '96 edition, we wrote about a series of good quality wines, while the following year, its results were less successful. This year we have re-tasted the '93 Cannonau di Sardegna, which has not aged gracefully, and the '95 in both the red and rosé versions. They are both very good, especially the red, which has very intense and fairly persistent aromas, which are reminiscent of dried wild flowers and ripe forest fruits. On the palate, it displays a certain freshness and vinosity which are well balanced by the acidity and soft tannins. The rosé is less structured and is clean on the nose and palate, but without any marked aromatic character. At the risk of repeating ourselves, though, - and we have been doing so for years - we continue to believe that this winery could produce much higher quality wines, thanks to its vast vineyard holdings: its notable potential has not yet been fully exploited. In spite of the fact that, at least on paper, the conditions for a major increase in quality exist our expectations remained unfulfilled. Perhaps those at the top of the Cantina Sociale di Jerzu lack the conviction to smarten up the old-fashioned image of Cannonau: a difficult task, certainly, but one that is feasible (and moreover imperative).

● Cannonau di Sardegna '95	🍷	3
⊙ Cannonau di Sardegna Rosato '96		2

MAGOMADAS (NU)

GIANVITTORIO NAITANA
VIA ROMA, 2
08010 MAGOMADAS (NU)
TEL. 0785/35333

We are happy to bring this small "vigneron" to your attention because he is the only producer engaged in seeking to produce a quality Malvasia from the Planargia area (which also includes the production zone for Malvasia di Bosa) in its most traditional Amabile version. The DOC norms for this wine have many lacunae, the most obvious being that of omitting the "amabile" version, which is the only one really appreciated by true wine lovers. The estate uses the wine name Planargia followed by that of the vineyard, such as Murapiscados, which is a cru of outstanding quality (the production norms do not allow an indication of grape variety). Naitana's property includes several small vineyards which are scattered around the area, in prime positions with regard to climate, soil and slope. Some were planted recently and will go into production in the next few years, thus guaranteeing some few thousand more bottles. In '96 a mere 4,000 were produced: yields are kept very low, on average around 28 hectolitres per hectare. In the Planargia area, the '96 vintage was characterized by weather which damaged grapes in the majority of the vineyards. Naitana wisely took preventative measures, obtaining healthy grapes, even if they were not very high in sugar, with fairly balanced acidity. The wine has a handsome straw-colour and an intense and fruity bouquet with nuances of peach and apricot, and it has rich, soft fruit which makes it elegant and velvety, well balanced and long.

○ Planargia Murapiscados '96	🍷🍷	4

MARRUBIU (OR)

MONTI (SS)

CANTINA SOCIALE MARRUBIU
S.S. 126, KM 117,600
09094 MARRUBIU (OR)
TEL. 0783/859213

CANTINA SOCIALE DEL VERMENTINO
VIA S. PAOLO, 1
07020 MONTI (SS)
TEL. 0789/44012

Even if the area under vine in the Province of Oristano has notably declined, this winery continues to do well because it has known how to chart a sensible course. Now that there are only two cooperatives, it will be easier, by reorganizing production, to improve quality and diversify the choice of wines. This year the winery celebrates its first forty years of activity, and after tasting its wines, we can say that it is in good shape. Its growth has been gradual with unavoidable hiccups due more to climatic factors than to less-than-careful management. From the commercial point of view, the winery has decided to aim at a fairly large slice of the market, offering, apart from bottled wines, wine in demijohns, and setting up sales outlets for jug wines all over the region. We have pleasant memories of this winery's rich and full bodied red wines and in fact in our most recent tastings these seemed to us the most interesting products. We appreciated in particular the intensity and fragrance of the Arborea Sangiovese Rosato '96. It has a rich, almost balsamic bouquet, with dominant hints of eucalyptus and sage, which are also echoed on the palate. In the Campidano di Terralba '95, the aromas are more herbaceous and its full bodied flavour reveals the firmness of its structure. The Arborea Sangiovese and the Monica di Sardegna '96 are pleasant but not quite up to earning One Glass. The whites from the Isola group of wineries, absorbed by the Marrubiu cooperative a few years ago, are a bit disappointing.

The ups and downs of this winery continue. Last year it brought home just a One Glass rating for its Abbaia and its Funtanaliras, but this year things went much better. Should credit go to the skill of the oenologist or to the favourable vintage? This year saw the return to Two Glass standard of the Vermentino di Gallura Superiore Aghiloja '96, a wine which we have always considered to be one of the most representative of this area. Its colour is deep straw-yellow and its aroma is rich, alcoholic and floral with a slight almondy tone; on the palate, it is soft, concentrated, round and powerful. Also this year, an abundant One Glass score goes to the Vermentino di Gallura Funtanaliras, which favourably impressed us with its '96 vintage. Fresh and fruity on the nose, it is dry and soft, but with attractive acidity on the palate. Scoring only very lower is the Vermentino di Gallura S' Eleme of the same year, in which one appreciates the floral hints, both on the nose and on the palate, which create a pleasant freshness and harmony. One Glass also goes to the red Abbaia, made from a judicious blend of local varieties. It has pleasant, light yet fruity aromas, and on the palate it is soft with a long, lingering finish. The company's new wine, called Aldiola, is a Vermentino made from semi-dried grapes. It has a fine yellow-gold colour and aromas of ripe fruit. The flavour is sweet but not cloying and the finish a little thin and of medium length: it deserves its One Glass rating. Below par this year were the rosé Thaora and the white Balari.

⊙	Arborea Sangiovese Rosato '96	🍷	2
●	Campidano di Terralba		
	Madrigal '95	🍷	2
●	Arborea Sangiovese '96		2
●	Monica di Sardegna '96		2
●	Arborea Sangiovese '95	🍷	2
●	Campidano di Terralba '94	🍷	2

O	Vermentino di Gallura		
	Aghiloja '96	🍷🍷	2*
●	Abbaia '96	🍷	1*
O	Aldiola '94	🍷	3
O	Vermentino di Gallura		
	Funtanaliras '96	🍷	3
O	Vermentino di Gallura		
	S'Eleme '96	🍷	1*
⊙	Thaora Rosato '96		1
O	Vermentino di Gallura		
	Funtanaliras '95	🍷	2
O	Vermentino di Gallura		
	S'Eleme '95	🍷	1*

NUORO

OLBIA (SS)

GIUSEPPE GABBAS
VIA TRIESTE, 65
08100 NUORO
TEL. 0784/31351

PIERO MANCINI
LOC. CALA SACCAIA
08026 OLBIA (SS)
TEL. 0789/50717

Among the small and emerging independent producers on the island, Giuseppe Gabbas is the one to achieve the greatest success with the '96 vintage. His vineyards are situated in the Locoe Valley, between Oliena and Orgosolo, and have a special mesoclimate which enjoys a considerable difference between day and night temperatures. In addition to this fundamental factor, there is also the great attention paid by Giuseppe, who is an agronomist, to the care of his vineyards. On his 12 hectares, the most widely planted grape variety is cannonau, followed by sangiovese, montepulciano, cabernet sauvignon, merlot and some indigenous varieties, such as pascale di Cagliari and bovale. All, in different percentages, go into the making of the winery's reds, Lillovè and Dule. The former is a Cannonau di Sardegna, made with the addition of a small percentage of local varieties. We consider this wine to be the Cannonau of the new generation; it is a wine that will surely leave its mark on Sardinian winemaking, particularly in the Nuoro area. It has the body and structure of a Cannonau, but has been softened by the other grape varieties which give the wine better balance. The Dule is made from a blend of 60 per cent cannonau with other recently introduced varieties. The wine was vinified at the Centro Enologico Sardo at Villasor. Its long maceration and brief time in wood have definitely contributed to its soft and round character, giving it an opaque ruby colour and a fresh fragrance which few Sardinian reds can boast. It is a wine of great concentration of flavour, with a long finish, distinguished by notes of ripe red berry fruits.

Piero Mancini's sons, Alessandro and Antonio, are taking an ever more active role in the running of the winery, and generally things are proceeding well. The estate's founder has done the right thing in giving more space to the younger generation. A relatively young company like his needs to be run with dynamism and, when age starts to become a factor, the best solution is usually to hand over the reins. Piero's youthful and pugnacious spirit, however, has always served as a great stimulus to his sons. Only three wines from this estate were presented to us for tasting this year: the Mancinis, too, must have had a few problems at harvest time. The highest score went to the red Saccaia, made from cabernet sauvignon and barbera. The vintage is not shown on the label, but the wine is notably different from that tasted last year which only earned an honourable mention. We were surprised by the richness of its aromas, which were reminiscent of cherries, blackberries and cherries in alcohol; on the palate one tastes highish acidity, typical of not excessively tannic young reds. It just missed out on a Two Glass rating. The Vermentino di Gallura '96 also showed an improvement over last year. It has delicately fruity and long aromas; on the palate one is aware of reasonable body and it is pleasantly quaffable. We also mention the Chardonnay, although this year it did not particularly excite us. It is a perfectly well made wine, with clean aromas, but is a little thin and evanescent on the palate.

● Cannonau di Sardegna			
Lillovè '96		♟♟	3
● Dule '96		♟♟	4
● Dule '94		♟♟	2
● Dule '95		♟♟	2*
● Cannonau di Sardegna			
Lillovè '95		♟	2

● Saccaia		♟	2
○ Vermentino di Gallura			
Cuccaione '96		♟	2
○ Chardonnay			
dei Colli del Limbara '96			2
● Saccaia '94		♟♟	2
○ Chardonnay			
dei Colli del Limbara '95		♟	2
○ Pinot Chardonnay			
Spumante Brut '95		♟	3

PIRRI (CA)

GIGI PICCIAU
VIA ITALIA, 196
09100 PIRRI (CA)
TEL. 070/560224

Some years ago Gigi Picciau, President of the Sardinian winemakers' association, told us that his dream was to rediscover the ancient grape varieties which had once been cultivated around Cagliari. His diligent work, together with his great abilities as an agronomist and oenologist, are now bearing fruit - he already produces the rare Semidano and Nasco, as well as the typical Malvasia - but today one also needs to pay attention to market forces. The winery's range has therefore broadened to include Vermentino, Cannonau, and even Pinot. In our recent tastings, a Nasco di Cagliari '94 stood out. It is a full, fat and velvety wine with complex aromas in which one finds musky tones which are characteristic of this varietal when grape yields are kept low. Also good is the Malvasia di Cagliar which has a bright yellow-gold colour, and sage and apricot aromas; on the palate, it is soft and warming, and has good length. We gave both wines a well-deserved One Glass rating. Less successful is the Sardegna Semidano '96. This white has very light aromatic and vegetal notes, but is fresh on the palate with a medium-long finish. The Vermentino di Sardegna '96 also received a One Glass award. Its aromas are delicate but well-defined and persistent; on the palate, it is fresh, soft and long.

○	Malvasia di Cagliari '94	🍷	4
○	Nasco di Cagliari '94	🍷	4
○	Vermentino di Sardegna '96	🍷	2
○	Sardegna Semidano '96		2
○	Malvasia di Cagliari '93	🍷🍷	3
●	Cannonau di Sardegna '94	🍷	2*
○	Pinot Primato '95	🍷	2
○	Sardegna Semidano '95	🍷	2
○	Vermentino di Sardegna '95	🍷	2

S. ANTIOCO (CA)

CANTINA SOCIALE DI S. ANTIOCO
VIA RINASCITA, 46
09017 S. ANTIOCO (CA)
TEL. 0781/83055

This year the Cantina Sociale di S. Antioco appears for the first time in the Guide. This winery, which is in one of the hottest parts of the region, was founded in 1949 and for many years it produced red wines of good alcoholic strength, which were often destined for blending with wines from other parts of Italy and even other countries. Only a small part of the production used to be bottled, for local consumption. The majority of the vineyards in this area are planted with carignano and monica grapes, which are used to produce two different lines, one of DOC wines and the other IGTs. The former category includes the Carignano del Sulcis '95, a medium-bodied and well balanced wine with herby-floral hints on the nose, and the full bodied Monica di Sardegna '95, in which one finds a note of roasted coffee on the nose, and good body and freshness on the palate. Both earn One Glass awards. We were also impressed by the Sardus Pater red. It is rich, with broad fruity aromas and good body, and well deserves its One Glass rating. We were not fully convinced on the other hand by the Vermentino di Sardegna '96, which has light and not very persistent aromas, and whose flavour is marred by too much acidity, or by the white Sardus Pater with its overly pale colour, decidedly citric aromas and lack of flavour and depth on the palate. In general then, a positive début, but the quality of this company's wines does not yet do justice to the potential of this zone and its grapes.

●	Carignano del Sulcis Rosso '95	🍷	1*
●	Monica di Sardegna '95	🍷	1*
●	Sardus Pater Rosso	🍷	1*

S. MARIA LA PALMA (SS)   SANTADI (CA)

CANTINA SOCIALE
S. MARIA LA PALMA
07040 S. MARIA LA PALMA (SS)
TEL. 079/999008

CANTINA SOCIALE DI SANTADI
VIA SU PRANU, 12
09010 SANTADI (CA)
TEL. 0781/950012-950127

There are not any great changes to relate this year at S. Maria La Palma. We note with pleasure the commercial success of the Vigne del Mare range, even if the label emphasizes the brand and style (white, rosé, red) rather than the Alghero DOC from which the wine comes. We have always been impressed by the work of the winemaker at this winery, who has contributed greatly to its growth, and we are sure that he will offer us yet more quality wines in the future. Those from the Vigne del Mare range are particularly good and offer extremely keen value for money. Especially worth tasting is the Rosso '95, with its attractive fragrance on the nose, in which one finds fruit aromas and balsamic, eucalyptus notes. On the palate, it is clean and well balanced, even if it does not have powerful structure. The rosé version also showed well and was among the best of the vintage. It has a bright, deep pink colour with clean, fruity aromas which are echoed on the palate, along with an attractively long finish. The other wine which was awarded One Glass is the Vermentino di Sardegna '96 Aragosta. Its delicate, lightly aromatic bouquet has floral and slightly appley notes; on the palate, it is savoury, refreshing and well balanced. The Cannonau di Sardegna Le Bombarde '95 (a wine which has shown much better in the past), the Vermentino di Sardegna I Papiri 96 and the Alghero Rosato Cantavigna '96 are all rather disappointing.

For years, this winery has been hoping for a Three Glass rating for its Terre Brune. More than once it has come very near, but has lacked that little something extra to make it truly excellent. We are confident in our assessments, both in the past when it did not quite make the grade and this year, when the '93 Terre Brune finally wins our top award. The great '93 vintage of this wine has intense, rich aromas of red berry fruits and vanilla, with notes of chocolate and balsam. On the palate, it is powerful, elegant and particularly soft, thanks to a structure of perfect harmony. The finish is long, fruity and seductive. Also very interesting is the Araja '95, made from a blend of sangiovese and carignano. This has intense aromas of oak and ripe red berry fruits which are echoed on the well balanced palate: it fully deserves its Two Glass rating. The same score goes to the Carignano del Sulcis Riserva Rocca Rubia '93, another well structured and attractive red. The two whites are also very good: the Cala Silente (made from vermentino, nuragus and pinot bianco) and the Villa di Chiesa (the most recent addition to the range. This latter wine is made from vermentino (60 per cent) and chardonnay, and is fermented in barrique where it matures for an additional five months before it is bottled. The aromas still have a strong vanilla tone, while on the palate, it is fresh, richly fruity and mouth-filling, with notable length. Among the other wines we would like to mention are the very high quality Carignano del Sulcis Baie Rosse '94, the Villa Solais Bianco, the Carignano del Sulcis '95 and the Monica di Sardegna: all well made and attractive. We will soon see the debut of some new wines, created, as in the case of Terre Brune, from the union of excellent grapes with the talent of the great oenologist Giacomo Tachis.

	Wine		Glasses	Score
☉	Alghero Rosato Vigne del Mare '96	♈	1*
●	Alghero Rosso Vigne del Mare '95	♈	1*
○	Vermentino di Sardegna Aragosta '96	♈	1*
○	Alghero Bianco Vigne del Mare '96		1
☉	Alghero Rosato Cantavigna '96		1
●	Cannonnau di Sardegna Le Bombarde '95		2
○	Vermentino di Sardegna I Papiri '96		2
●	Le Bombarde '93	♈♈	1*
○	Alghero Bianco Vigne del Mare '95	♈	1*
○	Vermentino di Sardegna Aragosta '95	♈	1*

	Wine		Glasses	Score
●	Terre Brune '93	♈♈♈	6
●	Araja '95	♈♈	3*
○	Cala Silente '96	♈♈	3
●	Carignano del Sulcis Rocca Rubia Ris. '93	♈♈	4
○	Villa di Chiesa '96	♈♈	4
●	Carignano del Sulcis '94	♈	2
●	Carignano del Sulcis Baie Rosse '94	♈	4
●	Monica di Sardegna '95	♈	2*
○	Villa Solais '96		2
●	Carignano del Sulcis Rocca Rubia '91	♈♈	3
●	Terre Brune '91	♈♈	4
●	Terre Brune '92	♈♈	4

544

SENORBÌ (CA)

CANTINA SOCIALE DELLA TREXENTA
V.LE PIEMONTE, 28
09040 SENORBÌ (CA)
TEL. 070/9808863

SERDIANA (CA)

ANTONIO ARGIOLAS
VIA ROMA, 56/58
09040 SERDIANA (CA)
TEL. 070/740606

It was not a great year for this winery either. The weather undoubtedly had an effect on the quality of the wines which were presented to us for tasting. It is a shame, because in recent years this cooperative has done well, offering interesting wines, especially among traditional styles. For this edition, the best result was garnered by the Monica di Sardegna '96, which earns a One Glass rating. It is fresh and well balanced, with reasonable structure and fine tannins, a very unusual feature in a traditional Monica. We also liked the Vermentino di Sardegna '96 which has winning aromas and an easy-drinking style, while the other Vermentino, the Tanca Sa Contissa, is interesting on the nose but short on the palate. The Nuragus di Cagliari '96 also seemed a little lacklustre: its aromas were tired and it was lacking in intensity. The Cannonau di Sardegna '94 La Venere also rated One Glass. It is a pleasant, if somewhat unremarkable and atypical, example of Cannonau. Even though it is not particularly young, it displays fresh, grassy aromas; on the palate, it is clean and lightly tannic, with a medium long finish, making it a classic wine to serve throughout a meal.

This winery again emerges as one of the most interesting in Sardinia and, for that matter, the rest of Italy. For the third year running we award the Three Glasses to its Turriga, the most significant of the reds produced by Franco and Pepetto Argiolas, with the advice of their consultant, Giacomo Tachis. The '92 has broad and intense aromas in which one finds scents of red berry fruits along with nuances of chocolate, vanilla and a touch of tar. It displays power and great elegance on the palate, which is full-bodied, long and softly tannic. It is a wine which can still continue to mature for a decade or so. Once again the Angialis '94 (made from semi-dried malvasia and nasco grapes) almost received the Three Glass award too. It has intense aromas of vanilla and apricot jam and on the palate there is breadth and elegance which makes it probably the most interesting sweet wine of the region. Confirming the high standards of last year are the Cannonau di Sardegna Costera '95, which earns Two Glasses, and the fruity, full and attractively aromatic Argiolas, which is always among the most modern and attractive whites of the island. The Vermentino di Sardegna Costamolino '96 just misses out on Two Glasses with its very floral aromas fresh palate. Also enjoyable are the Nuragus di Cagliari S'Elegas '96, which has an elegant nose in which one finds hints of dried hay and blossom. The Monica di Sardegna Perdera '95 appeared clean and soft both on the nose and on the palate, and we also found the Serralori rosé '96 interesting.

● Cannonau di Sardegna La Venere '94	♥	2
● Monica di Sardegna '96	♥	1*
○ Vermentino di Sardegna '96	♥	1*
● Monica di Sardegna '93	♀	1*
● Monica di Sardegna '94	♀	1*
● Segolai Rosso '95	♀	1*
○ Simieri Moscato Liquoroso	♀	4
● Tanca Su Conti '93	♀	5
○ Vermentino di Sardegna '95	♀	1*

● Turriga '92	♥♥♥	5
○ Angialis '94	♥♥	4
○ Argiolas '96	♥♥	3
● Cannonau di Sardegna Costera '95	♥♥	3
● Monica di Sardegna Perdera '95	♥	2
○ Nuragus di Cagliari S'Elegas '96	♥	2
○ Vermentino di Sardegna Costamolino '96	♥	2
⊙ Serralori Rosato '96		2
● Turriga '90	♥♥♥	4
● Turriga '91	♥♥♥	5
○ Angialis '92	♥♥	4
○ Argiolas '95	♥♥	3*

TEMPIO PAUSANIA (SS)　　USINI (SS)

CANTINA SOCIALE GALLURA
VIA VAL DI COSSU, 9
07029 TEMPIO PAUSANIA (SS)
TEL. 079/631241

GIOVANNI CHERCHI
VIA OSSI, 18
07049 USINI (SS)
TEL. 079/380273

The wines of this large cooperative continue to improve. It is among the most active wineries in the region and is probably the one which best succeeds in combining a medium-to-high quality with excellent value for money. The new wine presented this year is the Canayli '96, a Vermentino di Gallura Superiore, which is made from a special selection of grapes. Its aromas are fresh, intense and persistent, with nuances of green peppers and tropical fruit; on the palate, it is full, soft and well-balanced. Among the other '96 Vermentinos, we drawn your attention to the Mavriana, with its fruity and slightly exotic bouquet, and the Piras, which is the richer of the two, although slightly less concentrated than the '95. Nevertheless it is a lovely wine, with intense and long tropical fruit aromas and full yet elegant character on palate. We also enjoyed the red Dolmen '94 made from nebbiolo. It has a rich bouquet in which the hints of vanilla from the wood blend well with chocolate notes. On the palate it is full bodied, with soft but noticeable tannins: it well deserves its Two Glass rating. We believe that the Karana '96, also made from nebbiolo, is one of the best wines of the region as far as value for money is concerned. It has fruity and appealing aromas of ripe blackberries while on the palate it is clean, fresh and well-balanced. The rosé Campos '96 with its delicate aroma and immediately appealing flavour receives a One Glass rating, as does the Moscato di Tempio Spumante '96: its fruity aromas give way to an attractive flavour of perfectly ripe moscato grapes which make the wine refreshing, fine and elegant.

Every year Giovanni Cherchi surprises us. Perhaps it is because he is still searching for the right formula which will make his wines, which were at one time held in high regard, more consistently reliable. In spite of his ups and downs, we are convinced that the right conditions exist to make fine wines at Usini. Of course, vintages are not all the same but we really cannot explain the variable quality of the wines produced here. To his already well-known Vermentino di Sardegnas, among which the Tuvaoes stands out, he has added the Billia, which is an IGT Vermentino. This is supposed to be, in theory at least, one of the basic, commercial wines of the range, but to our surprise, we found it the best of the wines we tasted. With a score in the high 70s, it came very close to earning a Two Glass rating. It is fresh and fruity both on the nose and on the palate, where it displays good length, attractive style and fine aromatic balance. Also earning a One Glass rating was the Vermentino di Sardegna Tuvaoes '96. On the nose, this fresh and well made white has slightly vegetal notes - in particular tomato leaves - but is not particularly rich or concentrated. On the palate it is a little dilute compared to the wine we have tasted in the past. The Vermentino di Sardegna just misses out on a One Glass award: it is very similar to the Tuvaoes, but has less immediate appeal. For this winery, it was not a great year for the reds either. The Cannonau was not produced, while the Cagnulari was slightly out of balance, with a little too much acidity and a rather thin texture. Finally, just before closing the Guide, we tasted the pleasant Luzzana '96 which has a good ruby colour and a rich nose with scents of wild red berry fruits; on the palate it is fresh with attractively fragrant fruit.

● Dolmen '94	🍷🍷	4
○ Vermentino di Gallura Canayli '96	🍷🍷	2*
⊙ Campos Rosato del Limbara '96	🍷	1*
● Karana Nebbiolo dei Colli del Limbara '96	🍷	1*
○ Moscato di Tempio Pausania Spumante '96	🍷	4
○ Vermentino di Gallura Mavriana '96	🍷	1*
○ Vermentino di Gallura Piras '96	🍷	1*
● Nebbiolo di Sardegna Karana '94	🍷🍷	1*
○ Vermentino di Gallura Piras '95	🍷🍷	2
● Dolmen '93	🍷	4
● Karana Nebbiolo dei Colli del Limbara '95	🍷	1*

○ Billia	🍷	1*
● Luzzana '96	🍷	4
○ Vermentino di Sardegna Tuvaoes '96	🍷	4
○ Vermentino di Sardegna '96		2
● Cagnulari di Sardegna '94	🍷	2
● Luzzana '93	🍷	4
● Luzzana '94	🍷	4
○ Vermentino di Sardegna '94	🍷	2

OTHER WINERIES

The following producers obtained good scores in our tastings with one or more of their wines:

PROVINCE OF CAGLIARI

Villa di Quartu,
Quartu S. Elena, tel. 070/826997,
Malvasia di Cagliari,
Moscato di Cagliari Gutta'e Axina

Meloni,
Selargius, tel. 070/852822,
Cannonau di Sardegna Selvatico,
Cannonau di Sardegna Le Ghiaie,
Vermentino di Sardegna Astice '96,
Moscato Spumante '96

PROVINCE OF NUORO

Cantina Sociale di Flussio,
Flussio, tel. 0785/34886,
Malvasia di Bosa '92

Cantina Sociale di Sorgono,
Sorgono,
tel. 0784/60113,
Rosso del Mandrolisai

Zarelli-Sanna,
Magomadas, tel. 0785/35311,
Malvasia della Planargia Spumante

F.lli Porcu,
Modolo, tel. 0785/35420,
Malvasia di Bosa '93

Perdarubia,
Nuoro, tel. 0784/32832,
Cannonau di Sardegna '92,
Cannonau di Sardegna '94

PROVINCE OF ORISTANO

Cantina Sociale Il Nuraghe,
Mogoro, tel. 0783/990196,
Capodolce '95

Cantina Sociale della Vernaccia,
Oristano,
tel. 0783/33155,
Vernaccia Ris. '87

PROVINCE OF SASSARI

F.lli Tamponi,
Calangianus,
tel. 079/660945,
Brut Metodo Classico,
Moscato Spumante '96

Soletta,
Florinas,
tel. 079/43816,
Vermentino di Sardegna Prestizu '96

INDEX OF WINES

567

INDEX OF PRODUCERS

Santa Barbara	444	Sturm, Oscar	277
Santa Barbara	515	Suavia	243
Santa Lucia	438	Subida di Monte	278
Santa Lucia	510	Talenti - Podere Pian di Conte	388
Santa Margherita	256	Tamponi, F.lli	546
Santa Sofia	239	Tanorè	250
Santarosa	320	Tasca d'Almerita	532
Santavenere - Triacca, Tenuta	401	Taurino, Cosimo	512
Santi	219	Tedeschi, F.lli	240
Santoleri, Nicola	488	Tenuta degli Angeli	167
Saputi	458	Tenuta dei Fiori	39
Saracco, Paolo	54	Tenuta La Tenaglia	114
Sartarelli	455	Tenuta La Volta	36
Sasso	506	Teracrea, Tenuta	256
Satta, Michele	339	Tercic, Matijaz	302
Savese, Vinicola	518	Terenzuola, Podere	131
Savignola Paolina	438	Teresa Raiz	294
Scagliola	38	Terpin, Franco	303
Scammacca del Murgo, Barone	525	Terrabianca, Fattoria	418
Scarpa	101	Terre Bianche	130
Scarzello & Figli, Giorgio	35	Terre Cortesi Moncaro	451
Scavino, Paolo	51	Terre da Vino	95
Schiavoni	458	Terre del Barolo	52
Schiopetto, Mario	264	Terre di Bindella	402
Schmid - Oberrautner, Anton	210	Terre di Ginestra	534
Schwanburg, Castello	205	Terre Rosse, Cascina delle	130
Scrimaglio, Franco e Mario	101	Terriccio, Tenuta del	345
Scubla, Roberto	296	Thurnhof	193
Scuropasso, Cantine	168	Tiefenbrunner	200
Sebaste	35	Tili, Pietro	470
Sebaste, Mauro	23	Tollo, Cantina	487
Sebastiani, Cantina	186	Tommasi, F.lli	240
Seghesio, F.lli	92	Toròs, Franco	278
Sella & Mosca, Tenute	536	Torre Gaia	501
Sella	124	Torre Rosazza	291
Selvapiana, Fattoria	414	Torrevecchia, Cantine	530
Serafini & Vidotto	232	Torrevento	511
Serboni, Massimo	458	Torti, Pietro	168
Serraiola	438	Trabucchi	219
Sertoli Salis, Conti	165	Trappolini	480
Settesoli	528	Travaglini, Giancarlo	64
Settimo, Aurelio	78	Travaglino	168
Signano	431	Travignoli	411
Simoncelli, Armando	181	Tre Monti	318
Solatione	423	Treré	316
Soletta, Tenute	546	Trerose, Tenuta	402
Soloperto	518	Trevisani	154
Sölva & Sohn - Paterbichl, Peter	210	Triacca	166
Sorbaiano, Fattoria	390	Trinchero, Renato	20
Sorrentino	501	Tua Rita	436
Sottimano	99	Uberti	154
Spadafora	530	Uccelliera, Fattoria dell'	351
Spagnoli, Andrea	136	Umani Ronchi	454
Spagnolli	186	Vadiaperti, Azienda Agricola	494
Spagnolli, Enrico	186	Vagnoni, F.lli	431
Specogna, Leonardo	280	Vajra, Aldo	36
Speri, F.lli	239	Val di Suga	388
Spertino, Luigi	83	Valchiarò	309
Spezia, Stefano	167	Valdicava, Tenuta	440
Sportoletti, F.lli	468	Valdipiatta, Tenuta	403
Srednik, Giovanni	277	Valditerra, Laura	103
Stocker, Sebastian	210	Valdo Spumanti	256
Stra e Figlio, Giovanni	124	Valentini, Edoardo	484
Stroblhof	210	Valgiano, Tenuta di	336
Struzziero, Giovanni	500	Vallarom	170